THE U.S. INTELLIGENCE COMMUNITY

SEVENTH EDITION

THE U.S. INTELLIGENCE COMMUNITY

JEFFREY T. RICHELSON

WESTVIEW PRESS

A Member of the Perseus Books Group

Westview Press was founded in 1975 in Boulder, Colorado, by notable publisher and intellectual Fred Praeger. Westview Press continues to publish scholarly titles and high-quality undergraduate-and graduate-level textbooks in core social science disciplines. With books developed, written, and edited with the needs of serious nonfiction readers, professors, and students in mind, Westview Press honors its long history of publishing books that matter.

Westview Press books are available at special discounts for bulk purchases in the United States by corporations, institutions, and other organizations. For more information, please contact the Special Markets Department at the Perseus Books Group, 2300 Chestnut Street, Suite 200, Philadelphia, PA 19103, or call (800) 810-4145, ext. 5000, or e-mail special.markets@perseusbooks.com.

Library of Congress Cataloging-in-Publication Data

Richelson, Jeffrey.
  The U.S. intelligence community / Jeffrey T Richelson. -- Seventh edition.
    pages cm
  Includes bibliographical references and index.
  ISBN 978-0-8133-4918-3 (paperback) -- ISBN 978-0-8133-4919-0 (e-book) 1. Intelligence service--United States. I. Title.
  JK468.I6R53 2015
  327.1273--dc23
                                        2015005759

10 9 8 7 6 5 4 3 2 1

CONTENTS

LIST OF ILLUSTRATIONS

TABLES

FIGURES

PHOTOS

PREFACE

As with past editions, this book is titled *The U.S. Intelligence Community*, although it might be more properly titled *The U.S. Intelligence Community Plus.* The home page of the Office of the Director of National Intelligence (ODNI) describes the Intelligence Community as "a coalition of 17 agencies and organizations, including the ODNI, within the Executive Branch that work both independently and collaboratively to gather and analyze the intelligence necessary to conduct foreign relations and national security activities." Such a description is highly misleading because a number of organizations that are counted as single entities—including the Defense Intelligence Agency, the 25th Air Force, and the ODNI itself—contain within them a number of entities that are, in reality, distinct organizations. In addition, there exist numerous intelligence organizations and activities that take place outside the designated Intelligence Community organizations. Thus, the U.S. Intelligence Community represents a subset of what might be referred to as the "Federal Intelligence Enterprise."

Although not all of the federal intelligence organizations and activities outside the Intelligence Community are discussed in this work, a good number are—as they have been in earlier editions. To omit them would create a misleading impression as to the nature of U.S. intelligence organization and activities. Organizations thus discussed include the intelligence components of the Unified Commands, while entities that are not part of the Intelligence Community manage a number of the strategic measurement and signature intelligence (MASINT) and space surveillance activities described.

This edition involves a number of changes in terms of organization and titles. I have reversed the order of the chapters on departmental civilian intelligence organizations and Unified Command intelligence organizations, reflecting the fact that the latter are not officially part of the Intelligence Community. I have titled Chapter 7 "Geospatial Intelligence Collection, Processing, Exploitation, and Dissemination," although the key part still involves imagery intelligence. Chapter 8 has become "Signals Intelligence and Cyber Collection," and its content reflects the fact that, in addition to intercepting data in motion, a crucial part of the National Security Agency's mission is to acquire "data at rest," a term used initially to describe the extraction of information residing in computers around the world. Parts of the chapter also reflect the significant disclosures due to Edward Snowden. In addition, the title of Chapter 12, "Open Sources, Site Exploitation, and Foreign Materiel Acquisition," reflects my decision to move discussions of emplaced sensors into the chapters covering the relevant disciplines.

The content of the book, of course, reflects both its basic structure and the developments since the sixth edition went to press in the spring of 2011. These most prominently include the raid that resulted in the demise of Osama bin Laden, the administration's release of a white paper concerning targeted killings, and the disclosures concerning U.S. and allied signals intelligence activities that have appeared in (or on the websites of) the *Intercept, Guardian, Washington Post, New York Times, Der Spiegel*, and elsewhere. For the first nineteen chapters I have tried to maintain a neutral approach in the discussion of U.S. intelligence activities—particularly as I find annoying books whose authors' would claim to be objective but whose constant, one-sided editorializing suggests that they are not.

The final chapter contains my discussion of five issues—the extent of U.S. intelligence operations around the world, the covert (and not so covert) fight against terrorist organizations, domestic surveillance by the FBI and NSA, congressional oversight, and secrecy and leaks—as well as some observations on the extent to which Intelligence Community performance with regard to transparency and civil liberties reflects not so much the unique circumstances of the intelligence world but problems in bureaucratic behavior at all levels of government.

The information in this book comes from a variety of sources: interviews; official documents, many obtained under the Freedom of Information Act (FOIA); books written by former intelligence officers, journalists, and academics; websites; trade and technical publications; and newspapers and magazines. The public literature on intelligence is vast, and I have done my best to sort the wheat from the chaff. I have also sought to incorporate the most recent information available at each stage of the production process to minimize the inevitable discrepancies between the situation described and the situation at the time of publication. In addition, I have identified sources to the maximum extent possible, while protecting the identities of those individuals who wish to remain anonymous.

A number of institutions and individuals were instrumental in providing material for this book. There are the FOIA and public affairs offices and officers who responded to my requests (although some deserve to be noted for their obstruction, which I will do in Chapter 20). In addition, a number of individuals and websites have made it easy to obtain a large number of relevant and valuable documents and articles with little effort—specifically, Matthew Aid (http://www.matthewaid.com), Steve Aftergood (http://fas.org/blogs/secrecy), John Young (http://www.cryptome.org), and those responsible for the Public Intelligence (http://www.publicintelligence.net) and Government Attic (http://www.governmentattic.org) sites.

In addition, those who provided assistance have included Matthew Aid, William Burr, Ted Molczan, and Robert Windrem, and they have my thanks. I would also like to thank the National Security Archive for its support in a variety of ways. Finally, thanks are due to Ada Fung, Krista Anderson, Carolyn Sobczak, Jennifer Kelland Fagan, and others at Westview who turned my manuscript into a book.

1

INTELLIGENCE

The U.S. government contains a substantial number of officials and organizations that require intelligence (domestic or foreign) to fulfill their responsibilities, whether those responsibilities involve making policy or implementing it. Intelligence can be defined as "the product resulting from the collection, processing, integration, evaluation, analysis, and interpretation of available information concerning foreign nations, hostile or potentially hostile forces or elements, or areas of actual or potential operations."[1] Those individuals and institutions that deal with national security issues have the most prominent need for such intelligence. Hence, the President and his National Security Advisor, the Vice President, the National Security Council and its staff, the Departments of State, Defense, Homeland Security, Treasury, and Justice, the Joint Chiefs of Staff (JCS) and their Joint Staff, the military services, and the general and admirals who head the nation's unified commands are the most obvious consumers of foreign and domestic intelligence.

Today, those individuals and institutions face a multitude of concerns, including the capabilities, activities, financing, and plans of al-Qaeda and its offshoots, the Islamic State in Iraq and Syria (ISIS), Hezbollah, and other terrorist groups; the threat from cyber operations (including computer network attacks and exploitation); weapons of mass destruction (WMD) programs and associated personnel in Iran, North Korea, and a number of other nations; Russian and Chinese foreign policies and military activities; internal turmoil in a number of Middle Eastern nations; and developments involving India, Pakistan, and Latin America. Other concerns involve the threat of domestic terrorism, returning jihadists, and threats to the power grid.[2]

A number of events in the new millennium have illustrated the potential value of good intelligence to U.S. officials, as well as the consequences of poor or limited intelligence: the attacks of September 11, 2001, and subsequent failed and successful terrorist attacks, the operations that resulted in the death of Osama bin Laden and failure to capture al-Shabaab personnel, the failure of U.S. forces to find WMD stockpiles in Iraq after the 2003 invasion and the insurgency that followed, the difficulties in trying to halt the North Korean and Iranian nuclear weapons programs, Iranian and North Korean missile launches, Russia's seizure of the Crimea, Syria's pursuit of nuclear weapons and the regime's actions (including the use of chemical weapons) to retain power, and the inability to rescue American journalists held by ISIS.[3]

In addition, other policymakers have a need for intelligence, even if dealing with less pressing concerns. Those with responsibilities in the areas of international economics, trade and technology transfer, energy, the environment, and public health may require foreign intelligence. The actions of foreign governments and groups can influence both the security of foreign energy resources and the stability of the dollar.

The Environmental Protection Agency (EPA) may require intelligence on environmental accidents, foreign government compliance with international environmental obligations, and the status of environmentally sensitive areas. With respect to compliance, the EPA has been interested in the disposal of nuclear wastes, illegal ocean dumping, and the smuggling of animals and animal products. The National Aeronautics and Space Administration (NASA) is concerned with foreign technology developments and foreign space programs, as well as space debris that might threaten its spacecraft—debris that might result from an antisatellite test monitored by the Intelligence Community. The Department of Agriculture has been concerned with foreign government compliance with negotiated agricultural agreements, the development of global trading blocks, agricultural production and supply, and the food requirements of countries with chronic food deficits.[4]

INTELLIGENCE ACTIVITIES

Intelligence activities fall into four categories: collection, analysis, counterintelligence, and covert action. Collection—defined as the purposeful acquisition of any information that an analyst, consumer, or operator might desire—can involve any of several overlapping forms: open source collection, human source collection and interrogation, and technical collection. Open source collection includes the acquisition of material in the public or semipublic domains. Targets of open source collection include radio and television broadcasts, newspapers, magazines, technical and scholarly journals or papers, books, unclassified government reports or other documents, open activities that defense attachés or foreign service officers can monitor, and the various components of the Internet (including social media).

Human intelligence (HUMINT), concerning military, political, or economic matters, may be obtained from recruiting a foreign national to secretly provide information (or, as has often been the case, accepting an offer to provide such information). Human source collection may also involve a straightforward interview with a willing (or semiwilling) source or the interrogation of a hostile detainee. And it may be conducted in person or in cyberspace.

Technical collection comes in a number of different forms. Geospatial collection involves the use of several different sensors (electro-optical, infrared, radar) to produce images and maps. Much of signals intelligence (SIGINT) collection has relied on the placement of antenna systems on platforms as diverse as submarines and satellites to intercept communications, foreign instrumentation signals (including missile telemetry), and radar emissions. In addition, cyber collection through computer network exploitation (accomplished either remotely or by direct access) can yield data stored in foreign computer systems. Audio surveillance or emplaced sensors can also gather signals. Measurement and signature intelligence collection represents, in effect, "all other" technical collection activities, including nonimaging infrared, seismic detection, and acoustic collection. Such collection activities may be conducted remotely, from miles to tens of thousands of miles away, or using sensors covertly installed quite near a target.[5]

Analysis involves the integration and evaluation of collected information—that is, employing raw intelligence to produce finished intelligence. The finished intelligence product might be a simple statement of facts, an evaluation of the capabilities of another nation's military forces, a projection of the likely course of political events in a foreign country, or an analysis of the capabilities and objectives of a terrorist group.

Counterintelligence encompasses all information acquisition and all activity designed to assess foreign intelligence and security services (including those of terrorist groups) and neutralize hostile services. These activities involve human, technical, and open source collection, as well as analysis of information concerning the structure and operations of foreign services. Such collection and analysis, with respect to the technical collection activities of foreign services, can guide denial and deception operations. Counterintelligence may also involve the direct penetration and disruption of hostile intelligence organizations and their activities.

Traditionally, covert action included any operation designed to influence foreign governments, persons, or events in support of the sponsoring government's foreign policy objectives, while keeping the sponsoring government's support of the operation secret. Today, terrorist organizations are an even more important target for covert action operations; as a result there may at times be no need or ability to hide the sponsorship of certain activities—for example, the support of Northern Alliance forces seeking to overthrow the Taliban or the post-9/11 use of armed drones to kill al-Qaeda personnel. There are several distinct types of covert action: black propaganda (which purports to emanate from a source other than the true one); gray propaganda (in which the true sponsorship is not acknowledged); paramilitary or political actions designed to overthrow, undermine, or support a regime; paramilitary or political actions designed to counteract a regime's attempts to procure or develop advanced weaponry; support (aid, arms, training) of individuals or organizations (government components, opposition forces and political parties, and labor unions); economic operations; deception; and targeted killings.

THE INTELLIGENCE CYCLE

The concept of the "intelligence cycle" puts the collection and analysis activities conducted by various intelligence units into perspective—that is, it relates those activities to the requirements of the government officials who use the intelligence produced. The intelligence cycle is the theoretical sequence in which information is requested, acquired, transformed into finished intelligence, and disseminated to policymakers or implementers. The cycle consists of six steps: planning and direction, collection, processing and exploitation, analysis and production, dissemination, and evaluation.[6]

The planning and direction component involves the management of the entire intelligence effort, from the identification of the need for data to the final delivery of an intelligence product to a consumer. Requests for intelligence, based on the needs of the president, the Departments of State, Defense, Homeland Security, or Treasury, or other consumers, may initiate the process. Collection, as indicated above, involves the gathering, by a variety of means, of raw data from which finished intelligence is produced. The next step, processing and exploitation, concerns conversion of the vast amount of information flowing into the system into a form suitable for the production of finished intelligence. This may involve the interpretation and measurement of images and signals, including identification of a nuclear reactor in an image, determination of the accuracy of a missile, or estimation of the yield of a nuclear detonation. It may also involve language translation, decryption, subject matter sorting, or data reduction. The analysis and production element entails the conversion of basic information into finished intelligence and includes the integration, evaluation, and analysis of all available data and the preparation of various intelligence products. Because the "raw intelligence" collected is often fragmentary and at times contradictory, specialists are needed to give it meaning and significance. Dissemination involves the distribution of the finished intelligence to its consumers: the policymakers and operators whose needs triggered the process. The final step includes evaluation by and feedback from consumers who receive the product.

Like any model, the outline of the intelligence cycle simplifies reality. Certain requirements become standing requirements. Thus, the Intelligence Community need not be reminded to collect information on al-Qaeda or Hezbollah activities, nuclear proliferation, Chinese or Russian nuclear forces, or developments in the Middle East. And policymakers do not specify, except in rare cases, particular items of information to be collected (which may also serve to permit them to deny that they approved specific techniques or targets). The collectors take responsibility for determining how to obtain the information necessary to satisfy the standing or consumer-initiated requirements. In addition, the collection agencies have certain internal needs to acquire information to support their continued operations—information related to counterintelligence and security and information that will be useful in potential future operations. It should be noted that decision makers, particularly in the midst of a crisis, may require only processed intelligence. Thus, in the midst of the Cuban missile crisis, the most important intelligence was purely factual reporting concerning Soviet activities in Cuba and on the high seas.

VARIETIES OF FINISHED INTELLIGENCE

Just as one can distinguish different types of intelligence activities, one can also identify the different types of intelligence they produce. The varieties of intelligence include political, military, scientific and technical, financial, economic, sociological, and medical/biometric. Political intelligence encompasses both foreign and domestic politics. Clearly, the foreign policies of other nations have an impact on the United States and might involve a number of issues: support or opposition to U.S. initiatives in dealing with Iran, North Korea, or Syria, other nations' political and economic relations with those countries, attitudes and policies concerning the Middle East, support of terrorist groups, and perceptions of U.S. leadership and policies. In addition, terrorist groups and nongovernmental organizations have policies that guide their actions with regard to the United States and its allies.

The domestic politics of other nations—whether friendly, neutral, or hostile—are also of significant concern to the United States. The resolution of domestic conflicts—whether by coup, civil war, or election—can affect the orientation of that nation in the world, the regional balance of power, the accessibility of resources critical to the United States, or the continued presence of U.S. military or intelligence facilities. In addition, terrorist organizations also have their own internal, sometimes quite deadly, politics, with outcomes of potentially vital importance to the United States. One aspect of intelligence on domestic politics is leadership intelligence, focusing on the personalities, histories, powers, position, and preferences (policy and personal) of key officials.

Military intelligence has a variety of uses. To determine its own military requirements—whether nuclear, conventional, or special operations—the United States must have a good grasp of the capabilities and vulnerabilities of both friends and potential adversaries. The government also requires military intelligence to assess the need and impact of any military aid the United States might be asked to provide. Furthermore, it needs military intelligence to assess the balance of power between pairs of nations (e.g., India-Pakistan, North Korea–South Korea) whose interactions can affect U.S. interests. And, as with foreign and domestic political intelligence, one subset of military intelligence is military leadership intelligence, including biographic reports as well as reports on the ups and downs of military officials.[7]

Scientific and technical intelligence includes both civilian- and military-related scientific and technical developments. A nation's ability to employ modern agricultural methods or efficiently extract energy resources may affect its stability. In many cases, technological developments in the civilian sector have military applications. Examples include information and computer technology, biotechnology, mirrors and optical systems, and lasers. Hence, intelligence concerning a nation's progress or ability to absorb foreign-produced technology in those areas is relevant to its potential military capability.

One aspect of scientific and technical capabilities, atomic energy intelligence, has been of constant concern for more than seventy years. In addition to the obvious need to determine whether various foreign nations are developing nuclear weapons, there has been a perceived need to acquire secret intelligence in support of decision making concerning applications for nuclear-technology-related exports. In 1947 the first Director of Central Intelligence noted that the United States "cannot rely on information submitted by a licensee" and that it was necessary for the United States to "determine actual use, [to] endeavor to discover secondary diversions."[8] A nation's scientific and technical expertise relevant to the production of biological or chemical weapons—the "poor man's atomic bomb"—has also been of concern to U.S. intelligence. In addition, the potential of terrorist organizations to make use of such weapons of mass destruction is a major concern to those charged with protecting the U.S. homeland and overseas possessions and facilities.[9]

Financial intelligence focuses on both the individuals and the institutions involved in the transfer of funds for the financing of organizations, activities, or facilities of interest, including terrorist groups, weapons-related technology sales, and the construction of nuclear facilities, as well as the data or communications involved in funds transfers. Such intelligence forms the basis for U.S. designations of individuals or institutions involved in activities that result in sanctions. It can serve as a deterrent or a means to prevent or disrupt terrorist activities.[10] Figure 1.1 shows the results of one product of the financial intelligence effort.

Economic intelligence is also of great importance. One component includes the strengths and vulnerabilities of national economies. Knowledge of the strengths aids

FIGURE 1.1 The Execution of Imam Khomeini's Order (EIKO) International Financial Network

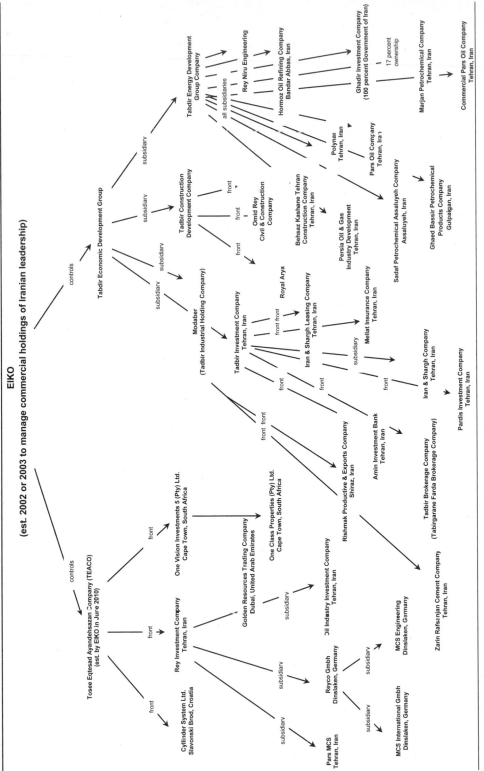

Source: U.S. Department of the Treasury.

in understanding a nation's capacity for conflict, whereas knowledge of the vulnerabilities may be key in assessing threats to stability as well as the likelihood that economic sanctions will induce a change in policy. Another component is the availability and pricing of key resources, from oil to an assortment of metals and minerals. In addition, economic intelligence looks at regional and other economic organizations, national fiscal and monetary policy, and international payments mechanisms. It also concerns topics such as sanctions busting, money laundering, bribery and corruption, and economic espionage.[11]

Sociological intelligence involves group relations within a nation. Relations between groups, be they ethnic, religious, or political groups, can significantly impact a nation's stability as well as its foreign policy—as demonstrated in the last two decades by events in Iraq, Syria, Yugoslavia, Africa, and Russia.

Medical intelligence can involve both the conditions of single individuals and threats to large groups. Determining the medical and psychological condition of foreign leaders and other key foreign officials has been a responsibility of the Central Intelligence Agency (CIA) since the early days of the Cold War. In addition, the CIA and other intelligence organizations have been concerned with medical hazards (from diseases to poisonous snakes) to U.S. military personnel in foreign environments as well as with the spread of disease in foreign nations. Biometric/identity intelligence includes DNA samples, which can be used to uniquely identify individuals (whether dead or alive).[12]

TARGETS

The U.S. Intelligence Community has an impressive array of intelligence targets to monitor. These fall into three, sometimes overlapping, categories:
- Transnational targets
- Regional targets
- National targets

Transnational targets extend across regions and may require nontraditional approaches with respect to the collection and analysis of relevant intelligence, as well as to the organization of the intelligence effort. Among the most prominent transnational targets are international terrorist or criminal groups, organizations and activities that could result in WMD proliferation, and illicit arms or narcotics trafficking. Targets also include international organizations including the United Nations and, at least potentially, nongovernment organizations hostile to the United States and the West.[13]

Although individual governments undertake attempts to develop nuclear weapons, Iraq, Iran, Pakistan, and Libya not only made use of indigenous capabilities in their efforts but also relied on a significant international supplier network and the assistance of foreign governments. This contrasts sharply with the largely indigenous manner in which the Soviet Union and China developed their nuclear arsenals. Likewise, Syria's accumulation of chemical weapons depended on foreign assistance along with indigenous effort.[14]

Terrorist groups, whether located in the Middle East, Africa, or Asia, have killed, maimed, and destroyed property around the world—in New York and Washington,

D.C., in Madrid and London, in Africa and Indonesia. Furthermore, such groups, unlike states, can relocate when a host government deems their presence too burdensome at a particular location or they become the target of retaliation. Likewise, the tentacles of South American and Asian drug cartels, as well as of the Russian Mafia, extend far beyond the borders of their home territories.[15]

Other transnational concerns include developments in cyber capabilities, the state of the environment (including the impact of toxic waste dumping in the oceans), uncontrolled refugee migrations, population growth, communications technology, the spread of diseases such as HIV/AIDS, Ebola, or the avian flu, and international economic activity.[16]

The concept of regional targets recognizes that developments in a particular area of the world may stem not only from individual governments' choices but also from the interaction between governments. Clearly, a war in the Middle East, in Southwest Asia, or on the Korean Peninsula would represent the most violent of such regional targets. Regional targets, which increase the chance of war, include border clashes, arms races, and cross-national movements of weapons and troops. Thus, the criteria for U.S. arms-transfer policy have included taking into account "consistency with U.S. regional stability interests, especially when considering transfers involving power projection capability or introduction of a system which may foster increased tension or contribute to an arms race."[17]

Regional activity of interest to the U.S. Intelligence Community may extend beyond governmental activities. The Asian financial crisis of 1997 concerned U.S. officials, for it had the potential to affect internal political developments, the foreign trade activities of a number of nations, and, ultimately, the U.S. economy. The same could be said of the 2008–2009 financial crisis.

National targets, the most traditional type, include all nations whose policies may have a significant impact on the United States, from the friendliest to the most hostile, although the type of information required and the means employed to acquire it vary considerably. China is a major national target, given its impact on international trade and finance, its arms trade, its potential to help or hinder in alleviating problems with Iran, Syria, and North Korea, its cyber activities, its growing military space operations, its air and naval operations in the Pacific, its nuclear relations with Pakistan and other nations, and the ongoing transformation of the People's Liberation Army "from a mass army designed for protracted wars of attrition on its territory to one capable of fighting and winning short-duration conflicts along its periphery against high-tech adversaries."[18] Other significant national targets include, for a variety of reasons, Iran, Syria, North Korea, Yemen, and Pakistan. Items of interest are Iran's and North Korea's nuclear and missile programs, Iranian support for terrorist groups, the Syrian government's adherence to its pledge to turn over its stock of chemical weapons, the internal conflicts within and foreign policies of Iran and North Korea, terrorist activity in Yemen and the consequences of the fall of Yemen's government for U.S. counterterrorism efforts, and the stability of Pakistan's government as well as the security of its nuclear weapons.[19]

Even after the collapse of the Soviet Union and the end of the Cold War, Russia remained a significant nation of concern to U.S. national security officials, and that concern has undoubtedly increased in recent years. Topics of interest to U.S. officials regarding Russia include Vladimir Putin's health and behavior, the personalities and views of key Russians, the prospects for Russian democracy, the state of the economy, organized crime and corruption, the security of Russian nuclear weapons, the state of Russia's armed forces, the status of its strategic weapons programs, its arms sales and technology-transfer activities, its policies toward Iran, Syria, North Korea, China, and other entities, its activities in Ukraine, and its intelligence activities targeting the United States.[20]

Director of National Intelligence James R. Clapper Jr. noted some examples of topics of concern to the U.S. Intelligence Community in 2015—undoubtedly a small subset of the full range—in a statement to the Senate Armed Services Committee. The global issues he discussed included the global cyber threat, unauthorized disclosures and foreign intelligence threats, terrorism, weapons of mass destruction proliferation, space and counterspace, transnational organized crime, economics and national resources, and human security.[21] Clapper also identified threats in the Middle East and North Africa, South Asia, Sub-Saharan Africa, East Asia, Russia and Eurasia, Latin America and the Caribbean, and Europe.[22]

THE UTILITY OF INTELLIGENCE

The utility of intelligence activity, here narrowly construed to mean collection and analysis, depends on the extent to which it aids national, departmental, and military decision makers and those who implement their policies and decisions. Two questions arise in this regard: In what ways does intelligence aid those individuals, and what attributes make intelligence useful?

With respect to the first question, intelligence can be useful to national decision makers in five distinct areas: policymaking, planning, managing conflict situations (ranging from negotiations to war), warning, and monitoring treaty compliance. In their policymaking roles, national decision makers set the basic outlines of foreign, defense, and international economic policy and decide specific actions with regard to key issues. The Rockefeller Commission's 1975 report summed up the need for intelligence: "Intelligence is information gathered for policymakers which illuminates the range of choices available to them and enables them to exercise judgment. Good intelligence will not necessarily lead to wise policy choices. But without sound intelligence, national policy decisions and actions cannot effectively respond to actual conditions and reflect the best national interests or adequately protect . . . national security."[23]

In addition to its value in policymaking and guiding decisions about alternative courses of action, intelligence is vital to planning decisions. Some planning decisions may concern the development and deployment of new weapons systems. One Air Force regulation noted, "Timely, accurate, and detailed intelligence is a vital element in establishing requirements and for planning and initiating RDT&E (Research, Development, Test, and Evaluation) efforts and continues to impact these efforts throughout the development and system life cycle." A more recent Navy instruction states, "Intelligence is key to understanding the potential current and future threat posed by foreign weapon and Information Technology (IT) system capabilities, and must be integral to U.S. system development and acquisition decisions."[24]

One incident illustrating the role of intelligence in weapons development occurred in 1968, when the U.S. Navy monitored a member of the oldest class of Soviet nuclear submarines traveling faster than thirty-four miles per hour, with apparent power to spare. That speed exceeded previous CIA estimates for the submarine and led the agency to order a full-scale revision of speed estimates for Soviet submarines. The revised estimates also provoked one of the largest programs in the history of the U.S. Navy—the production of the SSN 688-class attack submarine.[25]

At the same time, intelligence can help save substantial sums of money by avoiding unnecessary research and development and deployment programs. Several of the CIA's human assets, including Peter Popov, Adolf G. Tolkachev, and Dmitri Polyakov, provided information that saved the United States billions of dollars in research and development costs. Two former CIA officers wrote that Tolkachev "provided details on Soviet military weaponry long before it was deployed, and thus long before information on the systems could be picked up by technical collection. It sometimes changed the direction of our own research and development and, by so doing, saved the U.S. government billions of dollars."[26] In addition, The first successful U.S. photographic reconnaissance satellite system, code-named CORONA, produced information that eliminated fears of a missile gap and thus permitted the United States to cap its deployment of strategic missiles at a lower level than otherwise would have been possible. The successor program, HEXAGON, was instrumental in facilitating arms control agreements with the Soviet Union that would limit U.S. expenses on strategic weapons systems.[27]

Another set of planning decisions involves the development of war plans. In the months between the Iraqi invasion of Kuwait (August 1990) and the beginning of Operation DESERT STORM (January 1991), the United States collected a massive quantity of intelligence about Iraqi nuclear, chemical, and biological weapons programs, electrical power networks, ballistic missiles, air defense systems, ground forces, and air forces. The data collected allowed the development and implementation of a war plan based on the most up-to-date information possible. Likewise, planning for the attacks on Serbian targets in 1999 required gathering and evaluating information on air defense forces. Preparations for the invasion of Afghanistan in 2001 and Iraq in 2003, as well as the mission into Pakistan in May 2011, required significant intelligence collection and analysis efforts.[28]

Other decisions aided by intelligence include the suspension or resumption of foreign aid, the employment of trade sanctions and embargoes, and attempts to block the transfer of commodities related to nuclear or ballistic missile proliferation. Intelligence can inform decision makers of the likely effects of such actions, including the reactions of nations targeted by decisions. Thus, the Carter administration went ahead with the planned sale of planes to Saudi Arabia in part as a result of intelligence indicating that if the United States backed out of the deal, the Saudis would simply buy French planes.[29]

Several actions taken to inhibit Iran's pursuit of a nuclear weapons capability have followed acquisition of related intelligence. In 1992 the United States, based on intelligence indicating a "suspicious procurement pattern" by Iran, acted to forestall the sale of equipment that the Iranians could use to begin manufacturing nuclear weapons. Argentina halted certain sales to Iran after the United States expressed concern that the equipment in question would allow Iran to convert natural uranium into precursor forms of highly enriched uranium. Similarly, the United States successfully lobbied the People's Republic of China to halt the sale of a large nuclear reactor that would have included a supply of enriched fuel and permitted Iran to conduct research related to the nuclear fuel cycle.[30]

In January 1998, intercepted communications between a senior Iranian official and mid-level counterparts in Beijing indicated that Iran was negotiating to purchase "a lifelong supply" of a chemical it could use to transform naturally occurring uranium into the highly enriched form required for nuclear weapons. Senior Chinese officials informed White House aides that the contract had been suspended and was under review. During the spring of 2000, U.S. intelligence agencies uncovered plans for the D. V. Efremov Institute in St. Petersburg to provide Iran with a laser facility that could be used for uranium enrichment. Once U.S. officials became aware of the proposed transaction, they urged Russian officials to cancel it because, in the words of one official, there was "no question that the turn-key facility was intended for" Iran's nuclear weapons program. During preparations for the September 2000 meeting between U.S. President Bill Clinton and President Vladimir Putin of Russia, the subject was raised again. Russian officials informed White House aides that the contract had been suspended and was under review.[31]

Intelligence is also useful in a variety of conflict situations, most prominently combat. Indeed, with the issuance of Presidential Decision Directive 35, "Intelligence Requirements," the Clinton administration designated "support to military operations," including combat operations as well as planning and exercise activities, the first priority of U.S. intelligence. Regardless of how well developed a war plan is, combat forces require intelligence on the movements and actions of enemy forces and on the impact of air and other attacks against enemy facilities and troops. Thus, even after months of extensive collection prior to Operation DESERT STORM, the United States still needed to conduct an intense intelligence collection campaign during the conflict. Similarly, the prolonged combat operations in Iraq and Afghanistan required an extensive use of intelligence resources.

Intelligence is also of value in nonmilitary conflict situations, including any in which nations have at least partially conflicting interests, such as arms control negotiations, trade negotiations, or international conferences. Intelligence can indicate how far the United States can push other parties and the extent to which it must modify its own position. In 1969 the United States intercepted Japanese communications concerning negotiations between Washington, D.C., and Tokyo regarding the reversion of Okinawa to Japanese control. It has also relied on communications intelligence during the negotiations that led to the first Strategic Arms Limitation Treaty and during the 2003 UN debate over Iraq.[32]

Intelligence can also provide warning of upcoming hostile or unfavorable military, terrorist, or other actions against the United States or an ally. Sufficient advance notice allows defenses to be prepared, responses to be considered and implemented, and pre-emptive diplomatic or military action taken to forestall or negate the action. In 1980, on the basis of human intelligence, President Jimmy Carter warned Soviet general secretary Leonid Brezhnev of the consequences of invading Poland. In March 1991, on the basis of communications intelligence indicating Iraq's intention to use chemical weapons against rebel forces, the United States warned the Iraqis that it would not tolerate such an action. Intelligence has been credited with short-circuiting the plot, hatched in Yemen, to destroy two U.S. freight aircraft in flight over the United States in 2010.[33]

Intelligence is also necessary to assess whether other nations are in compliance with various international obligations. The United States wishes to know, for example, if Russia or China is complying with arms control agreements currently in force. Intelligence is also vital in detecting violations of agreements and treaties limiting nuclear proliferation and testing. In 1993 the United States was reportedly concerned with China's apparent violation of its pledge not to sell M-11 missiles to Pakistan. In 2014 intelligence on Russian testing of a new ground-launched cruise missile led to the conclusion that Moscow was "in violation of its obligations under the intermediate-range nuclear forces (INF) treaty."[34]

For maximum utility the intelligence must not only address relevant subjects but also possess the attributes of quality and timeliness. Unless intelligence assessments on a subject marshal all relevant information, the quality of the finished product may suffer. As Professor Hugh Trevor-Roper observed, "Secret intelligence is the continuation of open intelligence by other means. So long as governments conceal a part of their activities, other governments, if they wish to base their policy on full and correct information, must seek to penetrate the veil. This inevitably entails varying methods. But, however the means may vary, the end must still be the same. It is to complement the results of what for convenience we may call 'public' intelligence: that is, the intelligence derived from the rational study of public or at least available sources. Intelligence is, in fact, indivisible."[35]

In addition to resting on all relevant information, the assessment process must be objective. As former secretary of state Henry Kissinger told the U.S. Senate in 1973, "Anyone concerned with national policy must have a profound interest in making sure that intelligence guides, and does not follow, national policy."[36] Furthermore, intelligence much reach decision makers in good time for them to act decisively—either by warning a foreign government before it commits irrevocably to a particular course of diplomatic or military action or by ordering actions to undermine or negate such actions.

THE INTELLIGENCE COMMUNITY

Almost forty years ago a National Security Council study noted, "U.S. intelligence is unique in the world for its state of the art, the scope of its activities, and the extraordinary range and variety of [its] organizations and activities."[37] Its activities include the collection of information using reconnaissance satellites, aircraft, ships, ground stations, emplaced sensors, computer network exploitation, and undersea surveillance, along with traditional overt and clandestine human sources. It also acquires and exploits open sources, foreign materiel, as well as videos and documents. In addition, its personnel process and analyze the information collected using the most advanced computers and a variety of specially developed techniques for extracting a maximum of information from the data. The 2016 National Intelligence Program and Military Intelligence Program budget requests envisioned the expenditure of $53.9 and $17.9

billion, respectively, to fund the activities of the more than 100,000 members of the U.S. Intelligence Community.[38]

That community officially consists of seventeen organizations: the Office of the Director of National Intelligence; the Central Intelligence Agency; the National Security Agency; the National Reconnaissance Office; the National Geospatial-Intelligence Agency; the Defense Intelligence Agency; the Bureau of Intelligence and Research of the State Department; the intelligence elements of the five military services; the Federal Bureau of Investigation; and intelligence components of the Drug Enforcement Administration, the Department of Energy, the Department of the Treasury, and the Department of Homeland Security. Those intelligence elements can be grouped into four categories:

- National intelligence organizations
- Department of Defense intelligence
- Military service intelligence organizations
- Civilian departmental intelligence organizations

A fifth group of intelligence organizations plays a significant role in the production of intelligence: the intelligence components of the unified commands.

Notes

1. Department of Defense, Joint Publication 1-02, *Department of Defense Dictionary of Military and Associated Terms*, March 14, 2013, 141.

2. Ellen Barry, "Al-Qaeda Open Branch on Indian Subcontinent," *New York Times*, September 5, 2014, A13; Mark Mazzetti, "A Terror Cell That Avoided the Spotlight," *New York Times*, September 25, 2014, A1, A12; Michael Madden, "Meet Kim Jong Un's New Nuclear Warriors," www.foreignpolicy.com, September 22, 2014, http://foreignpolicy.com/2014/09/22/meet-kim-jong-uns-new-nuclear-warriors; "Major Military Drills Underway Against Simulated Enemy in Seas of Okhostsk and Japan," *Siberian Times*, September 15, 2014, http://siberiantimes.com/other/others/news/major-military-drills-underway-against-simulated-enemy-in-seas-of-okhotsk-and-japan; Rebecca Smith, "Nation's Power Grid Vulnerable to Sabotage," *Wall Street Journal*, March 13, 2014, A1, A6; Bill Sweetman, "Russian Renaissance," *AW&ST*, November 11–18, 2013, 48–50; Office of the Director of National Intelligence, *The National Intelligence Strategy of the United States*, 2014, 4.

3. Ken Dilanian, "A Big Surprise for the Spies?," *Los Angeles Times*, March 5, 2014, 6; Nicholas Kulish and Eric Schmitt, "'Imperfect Intelligence' Said to Hinder U.S. Raid on Militant in Somalia," *New York Times*, October 9, 2013, A10; Office of the Press Secretary, White House "U.S. Government Assessment of the Syrian Government's Use of Chemical Weapons on August 21, 2013," August 30, 2013, http://www.whitehouse.gov/the-press-office/2013/08/30/government-assessment-syrian-government-s-use-chemical-weapons-august-21; Adam Entous, Siobhan Gorman, and Jaeyeon Woo, "Portrait of New Leader Takes Shape," *Wall Street Journal*, December 20, 2011, A14.

4. Environmental Protection Agency, "EPA NSR-29 Intelligence Requirements," May 14, 1992; National Aeronautics and Space Administration, "NSR-29 Intelligence Requirements," January 17, 1992; "Space Surveillance Network NASA Support Requirements Matrix," attachment to Daniel S. Goldin, Administrator, NASA, to General Howell M. Estes III, August 27, 1997; Department of Agriculture, "NSR-29 Intelligence Requirements," January 15, 1992.

5. For a discussion of the diverse elements of technical collection, see Robert M. Clark, *The Technical Collection of Intelligence* (Washington, DC: CQ Press, 2011).

6. Office of the Director of National Intelligence, *U.S. National Intelligence: An Overview 2013*, April 9, 2013, http://www.dni.gov/index.php/newsroom/reports-and-publications/193 -reports-publications-2013/835-u-s-national-intelligence-an-overview-2013-sponsored-by-the -intelligence-community-information-sharing-executive, 5–6.

7. See, for example, Choe Sang-Hun, "North Korean Leader Tightens Grip with Removal of His Top General," *New York Times*, October 11, 2013, A4; Jeremy Page, "China Party Fills Top Military Posts," *Washington Post*, November 5, 2012, A11.

8. Sidney Souers, "Atomic Energy Intelligence," Record Group (RG) 218 (Joint Chiefs of Staff), July 1, 1947, National Archives and Records Administration, College Park, Maryland.

9. See, for example, CIA, *Chemical and Biological Weapons: The Poor Man's Atomic Bomb*, December 1988; CIA, *The Chemical and Biological Weapons Threat*, March 1996. With regard to recent concerns, see Eric Schmitt and Thom Shanker, "Qaeda Trying to Harness Toxin for Bombs, U.S. Officials Fear," *New York Times*, August 13, 2011, A1, A3.

10. Department of the Treasury, TG-838, "Treasury Designates al-Qai'da Finance Section Leader," August 24, 2010; Peter Fritsch, "Small Bank in Germany Tied to Iran Nuclear Effort," *Wall Street Journal*, July 19, 2010, A1, A14; Chico Harlan, "U.S. Official Outlines Plan Targeting Firms, Banks That Help Fund North Korea," www.washingtonpost.com, August 3, 2010, http://www.washingtonpost.com/wp-dyn/content/article/2010/08/02/AR2010080201697.html; Greg Miller, "Syrian Money Transfers Tracked," *Washington Post*, March 6, 2012, A1, A11; Helene Cooper, "Treasury Dept., Citing Six People as Operatives, Accuses Iran of Aiding Al Qaeda," *New York Times*, July 29, 2011, A4; Matthew Levitt, "Leveraging Financial Intelligence to Combat Transnational Threats," *Georgetown Journal of International Affairs* 12, no. 1 (Winter/Spring 2011): 34–43; Yochi Dreazen, "Inside the Treasury Department's War on Iran," www.foreignpolicy .com, November 6, 2013, http://foreignpolicy.com/2013/11/06/inside-the-treasury-departments -war-on-iran; Joby Warrick, "Islamic Charity Officials Gave Millions to al-Qaeda, U.S. Says," www.washingtonpost.com, December 22, 2013, http://www.washingtonpost.com/world/national -security/islamic-charity-officials-gave-millions-to-al-qaeda-us-says/2013/12/22/e0c53ad6-69b8 -11e3-a0b9-249bbb34602c_story.html; W. J. Hennigan and Brian Bennett, "Targeting Militants' Cash," *Los Angeles Times*, September 28, 2014, A1, A4.

11. U.S. Congress, Senate Select Committee on Intelligence, *Current and Projected Threats to the United States and Its Interests Abroad* (Washington, DC: U.S. Government Printing Office, 1997), 92; Department of the Treasury, "Treasury Targets Columbian Money Laundering Network Tied to FARC," May 6, 2010.

12. Mark Landler and Choe Sang-Hun, "In Kim's Death, an Extensive Intelligence Failure," *New York Times*, December 20, 2011, A1, A12; "Spies Track Physical Illnesses of Foreign Leaders," www.voanews.com, September 20, 2011, http://www.voanews.com/content/spies-track-physical -illnesses-of-foreign-leaders-130222673/171599.html; Alyce M. Gladi, Leslie R. Pyenson, Jon Morris, and Francis X. Brickfield, "Impact of Coronary Heart Diseases on World Leaders," *Annals of Internal Medicine* 134, no. 4 (February 20, 2001): 287–290; U.S. Interests Section Havana, Subject: Cuba: How Believable Is a Fidel Castro Comeback?, www.nytimes.com, March 16, 2007, http://www.nytimes.com/interactive/2010/11/28/world/20101128-cables-viewer.html #report/cuba-07HAVANA258; David E. Sanger, "Militant in Beheading Videos Has Been Identified, F.B.I. Chief Says," *New York Times*, September 26, 2014, A11.

13. Canadian Security Intelligence Service (CSIS), *The Future of al-Qaeda: The Results of a Foresight Project* (Ottawa: CSIS, 2013); U.S. Congress, *Al Qaeda in Yemen and Somalia: A Ticking Time Bomb* (Washington, DC: U.S. Government Printing Office, 2010); Ernest Sternberg, "Purifying the World: What the New Radical Ideology Stands For," *Orbis* 54, no. 1 (Winter 2010): 61–86.

14. See David Albright, *Peddling Peril: How the Secret Nuclear Trade Arms America's Enemies* (New York: Free Press, 2010); Gordon Corera, *Shopping for Bombs: Nuclear Proliferation, Global Insecurity and the Rise of the A. Q. Khan Network* (New York: Oxford University Press,

2006); David E. Sanger, Andrew Lehren, and Rich Gladstone, "With the World Watching, Syria Amassed Nerve Gas," *New York Times*, September 8, 2013, 1, 9; Gunther Latsch, Fidelius Schmid, and Klaus Wiegrefe, "Did German Companies Aid Syrian Chemical Weapons?" *Spiegel Online*, January 23, 2015, http://www.spiegel.de/international/germany/german-companies-suspected-of -aiding-syrian-chemical-weapons-program-a-1014722.html.

15. Barack Obama, White House, *National Strategy for Counterterrorism*, June 29, 2011, http://www.whitehouse.gov/blog/2011/06/29/national-strategy-counterterrorism; U.S. Congress, House Committee on International Relations, *The Threat from Russian Organized Crime* (Washington, DC: U.S. Government Printing Office, 1996); June S. Beittel, Congressional Research Service, *Mexico's Drug Trafficking Organizations: Source and Scope of the Violence*, April 15, 2013, https://www.fas.org/sgp/crs/row/R41576.pdf.

16. Richard Smith, "The Intelligence Community and the Environment: Capabilities and Future Missions," *Environmental Change and Security Project Report* 2 (Spring 1996): 103–108; National Geospatial-Intelligence Agency, Press Release 2015-01, "NGA, Digital Globe Human Geography Data and Satellite Imagery and International Ebola Response," January 7, 2015, https://www1.nga.mil/MediaRoom/PressReleases/Pages/2015-01.aspx.

17. Office of the Press Secretary, White House, "Criteria for Decisionmaking on U.S. Arms Exports," Washington, D.C., February 17, 1995, 1.

18. Office of the Secretary of Defense, *Annual Report to Congress: Military Power of the People's Republic of China 2008*, Department of Defense, 2009, http://www.defense.gov/pubs/pdfs/ China_Military_Report_08.pdf, 1; Ken Dilanian, "Quick Strides by China's Military," *Los Angeles Times*, January 7, 2011, A1, A22; Keith Bradsher, "China Said to Bolster Missile Capabilities," *New York Times*, August 25, 2012, A5; Edward Wong and Nicola Clark, "China's Arms Industry Makes Global Trends," *New York Times*, October 21, 2013, A1, A3; Saeed Shah, "China-Pakistan Reactor Deal Spurs Concern," *Wall Street Journal*, October 16, 2013, A11; Jane Perlez and Martin Fackler, "China Patrols Air Zone over Disputed Islands," *New York Times*, November 29, 2013, A17; Bill Gertz, "China Conducts Second Flight Test of New Long-Range Missile," *Washington Free Beacon*, December 17, 2013; Office of the Secretary of Defense, *Annual Report to Congress: Military and Security Developments Involving the People's Republic of China 2013*, 2013, http://www .defense.gov/pubs/2013_china_report_final.pdf; Shirley A. Kan, Congressional Research Service, *China and Proliferation of Weapons of Mass Destruction and Missiles: Policy Issues*, January 5, 2015, http://fas.org/sgp/crs/nuke/RL31555.pdf.

19. U.S. Congress, Senate Select Committee on Intelligence, Report 113–71, *Report of the Select Committee on Intelligence, United States Senate, Covering the Period January 5, 2011 to January 3, 2013*, 2013, https://www.fas.org/irp/congress/2013_rpt/srpt113-7.pdf, 9; David E. Sanger, "Intelligence on North Korea, and Its New Leader, Remains Elusive," *New York Times*, May 7, 2013, A6; Entous, Gorman, and Woo, "Portrait of New Leader Takes Shape"; Adam Entous, Julian E. Barnes, and Nour Malas, "Elite Syrian Unit Scatters Chemical Arms Stockpile," *Wall Street Journal*, September 13, 2013, A1, A7; Robert F. Worth, "Yemen Emerges as Base for Qaeda Attacks," *New York Times*, October 30, 2010, A6; Rick Gladstone, "Launching Site in Iran Raises Missile Worries," *New York Times*, August 9, 2013, A5; Office of the Secretary of Defense, *Annual Report to Congress: Military and Security Developments Involving the Democratic People's Republic of Korea 2013*, 2013, http://www.defense.gov/pubs/North_Korea_Military_Power_Report_2013-2014 .pdf; Ken E. Gausse, *North Korean Leadership Dynamics and Decision-Making Under Kim Jong-un: A Second Year Assessment*, Center for Naval Analyses, March 2014, https://www.cna.org/sites/ default/files/news/FlipBooks/NKorea_Year2_web/flipviewerxpress.html.

20. Andrew E. Kramer, "Russia Sending Missile Systems to Shield Syria," *New York Times*, June 16, 2012, A1, A8; Daniel Michaels, "Russia's New Air Power Turns Heads," *Wall Street Journal*, June 21, 2013, B8; "Russia Fields More Topol-M ICBMs," *Global Security Newswire*, December 21, 2010, http://www.nti.org/gsn/article/russia-fields-more-topol-m-icbms; David M. Herszenhorn, "Prosecutor Urges Six-Year Term for Russian Opposition Leader," *New York Times*,

July 6, 2013, A4; Jim Nichol, Congressional Research Service, *Russian, Political, Economic, and Security Issues and U.S. Interests*, September 13, 2013, https://www.fas.org/sgp/crs/row/RL33407.pdf; Maxim Pyadushkin, "Russian Resurgence," *AW&ST*, December 16, 2013, 32; Bill Gertz, "Russia Tests Multi-Warhead ICBM," www.freebeacon.com, April 14, 2014, http://freebeacon.com/national-security/russia-tests-multi-warhead-icbm; Trude Pettersen, "Russia Builds Huge Nuclear Missile Depot in Severomorsk," www.barentsobserver.com, December 13, 2013, http://barents observer.com/cn/security/2013/12/russia-builds-huge-nuclear-missile-depot-severomorsk-13-12; Reid Standish, "Where in the World Is Vladimir Vladimirovich Putin? Not Giving Birth," www .foreignpolicy.com, March 13, 2015, http://foreignpolicy.com/2015/03/13/where-in-the-world-is -vladimir-vladimirovich-putin-not-giving-birth.

21. James R. Clapper, Director of National Intelligence, *Worldwide Threat Assessment of the US Intelligence Community*, Statement for the Record before the House Permanent Select Committee on Intelligence, February 26, 2015, http://www.dni.gov/files/documents/Intelligence%20Reports /2014%20WWTA%20%20SFR_SSCI_29_Jan.pdf, ii.

22. Ibid., ii–iii.

23. Commission on CIA Activities Within the United States, *Report to the President* (Washington, DC: U.S. Government Printing Office, 1975), 6.

24. Headquarters, U.S. Air Force, Assistant Chief of Staff, Intelligence, I INOI 80-1, "The Intelligence Role in Research, Development, Test and Evaluation (RDT&E)," January 18, 1985, Internet Archive, https://archive.org/stream/CIADocuments/CIA-303_djvu.txt; Chief of Naval Operations, OPNAV Instruction 3811.1E, "Subject: Threat Support to the Defense Acquisition System," January 4, 2012, 1.

25. Patrick Tyler, "The Rise and Fall of the SSN 688," *Washington Post*, September 21, 1986, A1, A18.

26. Jeffrey T. Richelson, *A Century of Spies: Intelligence in the Twentieth Century* (New York: Oxford University Press, 1995), 257–258, 269, 272, 395; David Wise, *Nightmover: How Aldrich Ames Sold the CIA to the KGB for $4.6 Million* (New York: HarperCollins, 1995), 59–66, 105–106, 124, 271, 327; Barry G. Royden, "Tolkachev, a Worthy Successor to Penkovsky," *Studies in Intelligence* 47, no. 3 (2003): 5–33; Sandra Grimes and Jeanne Vertefeuille, *Circle of Treason: A CIA Account of Traitor Aldrich Ames and the Men He Betrayed* (Annapolis, MD: Naval Institute Press, 2012), 76.

27. Dwayne A. Day, John Lodgson, and Brian Latell, eds., *Eye in the Sky: The Story of the CORONA Spy Satellites* (Washington, DC: Smithsonian Institution Press, 1998); Curtis Peebles, *The CORONA Project* (Annapolis, MD: Naval Institute Press, 1997); Frederic C. E. Oder, [deleted], and Paul E. Worthman, *The HEXAGON Story* (Washington, DC: National Reconnaissance Office, December 1992), 93, 136, 138, 174.

28. DCI Interagency Balkan Task Force, *Bosnian Serb Air Defense Forces*, June 12, 1995; Craig Whitlock and Barton Gellman, "To Hunt Osama bin Laden, Satellites Watched over Abbottabad, Pakistan, and Navy SEALs," www.washingtonpost.com, August 29, 2013, http://www .washingtonpost.com/world/national-security/to-hunt-osama-bin-laden-satellites-watched-over -abbottabad-pakistan-and-navy-seals/2013/08/29/8d32c1d6-10d5-11e3-b4cb-fd7ce041d814_ story.html.

29. Zbigniew Brzezinski, *Power and Principle: Memoirs of the National Security Adviser, 1977–1981* (New York: Farrar, Straus & Giroux, 1983), 248.

30. Steve Coll, "U.S. Halted Nuclear Bid by Iran," *Washington Post*, November 17, 1992, A1, A30.

31. Barton Gellman and John Pomfret, "U.S. Action Stymied China Sale to Iran," *Washington Post*, March 13, 1998, A1, A20; Walter Pincus, "Russia: Laser Deal with Iran Blocked," *Washington Post*, September 20, 2000, A25.

32. Seymour Hersh, *The Price of Power: Kissinger in the Nixon White House* (New York: Summit, 1983), 103.

33. Benjamin Weiser, "A Question of Loyalty," *Washington Post Magazine*, December 13, 1992, 9ff.; Benjamin Weiser, *A Secret Life: The Polish Officer, His Covert Mission, and the Price He Paid to Save His Country* (New York: Public Affairs, 2004); Patrick E. Tyler, "U.S. Said to Plan Bombing of Iraqis if They Gas Rebels," *New York Times*, March 10, 1991, 1, 15; Mark Mazzetti, Robert F. Worth, and Eric Liptor, "Quick Response to Intelligence Foiled Bombers," *New York Times*, November 1, 2010, A1, A6.

34. Ann Devroy and R. Jeffrey Smith, "U.S. Evidence Suggests China Breaks Arms Pact," *Washington Post*, May 18, 1993, A9; Douglas Jehl, "China Breaking Missile Pledge, U.S. Aides Say," *New York Times*, May 6, 1993, A1, A6; John M. Goshko, "U.S. Warns China of Sanctions of Missile Exports to Pakistan," *Washington Post*, July 26, 1993, A10; "Psst . . . Want to Buy a Missile?," *Newsweek*, September 6, 1993, 28; R. Jeffrey Smith, "Ukraine Begins to Dismantle Nuclear Missiles Aimed at U.S.," *Washington Post*, July 28, 1993, A13; Department of State, *Adherence to and Compliance with Arms Control, Nonproliferation, and Disarmament Agreements Commitments*, July 2014, http://www.state.gov/documents/organization/230108.pdf, 8.

35. Hugh Trevor-Roper, *The Philby Affair: Espionage, Treason and Secret Services* (London: Kimber, 1968), 66.

36. U.S. Congress, Senate Committee on Foreign Relations, *Nomination of Henry A. Kissinger* (Washington, DC: U.S. Government Printing Office, 1973). For evidence that Kissinger did not always follow his own advice, see Hersh, *The Price of Power*, 529–560.

37. National Security Council, *Report on Presidential Review Memorandum/NSC 11: Intelligence Structure and Mission*, 1977, 1.

38. Office of the Director of National Intelligence, ODNI News Release No. 1, "DNI Releases Requested Budget Figure for FY 2016 Appropriations," February 2, 2015; Department of Defense, Release No. NR-034-15, "DOD Releases Military Intelligence Program Base Request for Fiscal Year 2016," February 2, 2015, http://www.defense.gov/releases/release.aspx?releaseid=17128.

2

NATIONAL INTELLIGENCE ORGANIZATIONS

Of the seventeen organizations that officially constitute the U.S. Intelligence Community (IC), four are national collection and/or analysis organizations: the Central Intelligence Agency (CIA), the National Security Agency (NSA), the National Reconnaissance Office (NRO), and the National Geospatial-Intelligence Agency (NGA). Collectively, these organizations' proposed budgets accounted for almost $41 billion in the fiscal year 2013 budget request (the most recent year for which budget request data are available for individual agencies). Two additional national organizations, while not among the seventeen officially listed, are the Special Collection Service (a joint CIA-NSA operation whose budget comes out of the CIA and NSA budgets) and the still-classified National Underwater Reconnaissance Office (NURO). Collectively, they account for virtually all of the National Intelligence Program budget and over 50,000 Intelligence Community employees.

CENTRAL INTELLIGENCE AGENCY

World War II resulted in the creation of the Office of Strategic Services (OSS), America's first central intelligence organization. Its functions included espionage, covert action (ranging from propaganda to sabotage), counterintelligence (CI), and intelligence analysis. The OSS represented a revolution in U.S. intelligence not only because of the varied functions performed by a single national agency but also because of the breadth of its intelligence interests and its use of scholars to produce finished intelligence.[1] In the aftermath of World War II, President Harry S. Truman ordered the OSS disbanded; it officially closed down on October 1, 1945. Its secret intelligence and counterintelligence branches were transferred to the War Department to form the Strategic Services Unit, while the Research and Analysis Branch was moved into the State Department.[2]

At virtually the same time that he ordered closure of the OSS, Truman authorized studies of the intelligence apparatus required by the United States in the postwar world. The result was the creation of the National Intelligence Authority (NIA) and its operational element, the Central Intelligence Group (CIG). Initially responsible for coordinating and synthesizing the reports produced by the military service intelligence agencies and the Federal Bureau of Investigation (FBI), the CIG was soon tasked with clandestine intelligence collection.[3]

The National Security Act of 1947, as part of a general consideration of national security needs, established the Central Intelligence Agency as an independent agency within the Executive Office of the President. The CIA replaced the CIG, and the NIA was eliminated. According to the act, the CIA was to have five functions:

1. To advise the National Security Council [NSC] in matters concerning such intelligence activities of the government departments and agencies as relate to national security.
2. To make recommendations to the National Security Council for the coordination of such intelligence activities of the departments and agencies of the government as related to national security.
3. To correlate and evaluate the intelligence relating to national security and to provide for the appropriate dissemination of such intelligence within the government, using, where appropriate, existing agencies and facilities.
4. To perform for the benefit of existing intelligence agencies such additional services of common concern as the National Security Council determines can be more effectively accomplished centrally.
5. To perform other such functions and duties related to intelligence affecting national security that the National Security Council may from time to time direct.[4]

The provisions of the act left considerable scope for interpretation. Thus, the fifth and final provision has been cited as authorization for covert action operations. In fact, the provision was intended only to authorize espionage.[5] The ultimate legal basis for covert action is presidential direction and congressional approval of funds for such programs.

Whatever the intentions of Congress in 1947, the CIA developed in accord with a maximalist interpretation of the act. Thus, the CIA became the primary U.S. government intelligence agency for intelligence analysis, clandestine human intelligence collection, and covert action. It also came to play a major role in the development of reconnaissance and other technical collection systems employed for gathering imagery, signals, and measurement and signature intelligence.

President Ronald Reagan's Executive Order 12333, still partially in effect, permits the CIA to secretly collect "significant" foreign intelligence within the United States if the collection effort does not target the domestic activities of U.S. citizens and corporations. The order also gives the CIA authority to conduct, within the United States, "special activities" or covert actions approved by the president, that are not intended to influence U.S. political processes, public opinion, or the media.[6]

The CIA's founding legislation established the position of Director of Central Intelligence (DCI), responsible for managing the activities of the entire Intelligence Community as well as running the CIA. The Intelligence Reform and Terrorism Prevention Act of 2004 eliminated the DCI position and established the position of Director of National Intelligence (DNI) to oversee and guide the activities of the Intelligence Community. The individual heading the CIA became the Director, Central Intelligence Agency (D/CIA).[7]

Headquartered in Langley, Virginia, just south of Washington, D.C., the CIA has a number of other offices scattered around the Washington, D.C., area, particularly in northern Virginia. In 1991 the CIA had approximately 20,000 employees, but

PHOTO 2.1   CIA headquarters, Langley, Virginia. *Photo credit:* CIA.

post–Cold War reductions in the 1990s and the transfer of the CIA's imagery analysts to the National Imagery and Mapping Agency (NIMA) probably reduced that number to about 16,000. In the aftermath of 9/11, the CIA expanded; by September 2011, its approximate personnel strength passed the 21,000 mark. Its requested budget for the 2013 fiscal year was $14.7 billion, approximately a fivefold increase from its 1994 budget ($3.1 billion).[8]

As Figure 2.1 indicates, in addition to the offices and staff elements that report to the CIA's director, deputy director and deputy executive directors, there were, as of March 2015, four major directorates. Two, the National Clandestine Service (NCS) and the Directorate of Science and Technology (DS&T), were fully or partially involved in intelligence collection; another, the Directorate of Intelligence (DI), was responsible for intelligence analysis; the fourth, the Directorate of Support, was responsible for a variety of support functions.

The NCS, formerly the Directorate of Operations and before that the Directorate of Plans, was responsible for clandestine collection and covert action. Established in 2005, it also absorbed the clandestine collectors of the Defense HUMINT Service (DHS), created in the mid-1990s to consolidate service human intelligence (HUMINT) activities. The NCS was headed by a director appointed to manage human intelligence and covert action operations of the CIA and to "coordinate, deconflict, and assess HUMINT operations through the IC." The NCS director had two deputies, one responsible for the daily activities of the NCS divisions and centers of the CIA and another who focused on human intelligence activities across the Intelligence Community.

FIGURE 2.1   Organization of the Central Intelligence Agency

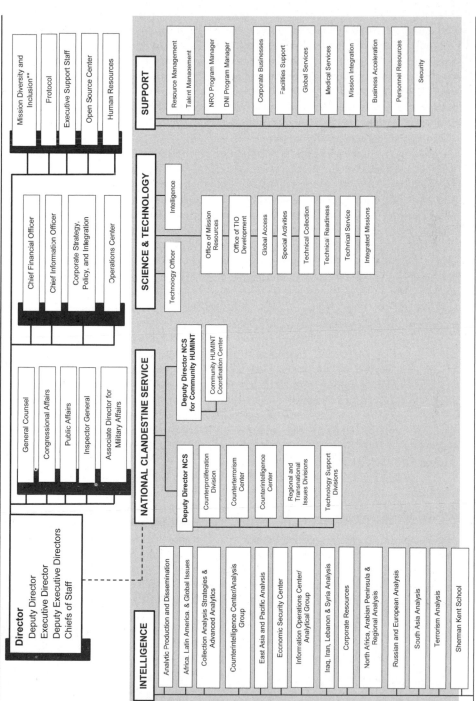

Source: CIA.

The latter, the Deputy Director of the NCS for Community HUMINT, supervised the Community HUMINT Coordination Center, the National HUMINT Requirements Tasking Center, and a center devoted to HUMINT standards and practices.[9]

Figure 2.1 shows the structure of the NCS as presented in the unclassified 2015 CIA organizational chart. It indicates the existence of a number of "Technology Support Divisions" that probably augment the work of the DS&T's Office of Technical Service (OTS). These divisions, in turn, probably trace their origin to Deputy Director of Operations Thomas Twetten's creation, in the early 1980s, of a rival technology group with the operations division.[10]

The other components of the NCS comprised seven regional divisions, one division with a worldwide mission, and five centers. The National Resources Division (NRD), established by the 1991 merger of the Foreign Resources Division (FRD) and the National Collection Division, operated in the United States. The NRD had offices in about thirty U.S. cities. In 2005 it was reported that NRD headquarters would be relocated to Denver, Colorado, "for operational reasons."[11]

The two divisions that merged to form the NRD became its branches. The FRD was created in 1963 as the Domestic Operations Division and assigned responsibility for "clandestine operational activities of the Clandestine Services conducted within the United States against foreign targets." Today, the Foreign Resources Branch (FRB) is responsible for locating foreign nationals of special interest residing in the United States and recruiting them to serve as CIA assets when they return home (or to some other foreign location). To identify such individuals the FRD has relationships with scores of individuals in U.S. academic institutions, including faculty. These individuals do not attempt to recruit students but assist by providing background information and occasionally brokering introductions.[12] According to one report, a key element of FRB operations (which constituted nearly 30 percent of the NRD's activities) is the recruitment, while they are in the United States, of foreign scientists, engineers, and corporate officials to provide telecommunications intelligence or assist the U.S. Intelligence Community in acquiring such intelligence. The program involved is, or was, designated MXSCOPE, according to the report.[13]

The National Collection Branch (NCB), which before being known as the National Collection Division had been designated the Domestic Collection Division and the Domestic Contact Service, collected intelligence from U.S. residents who had traveled abroad, including scientists, technologists, economists, and energy experts returning from foreign locations of interest. Among those interviewed were academics; in 1982 the Domestic Collection Division was in touch with approximately nine hundred individuals on 290 campuses in the United States.[14] The chief of the NRD (and probably the NCB and FRB chiefs) could approve the use of employees or invitees of an organization within the United States to collect significant foreign intelligence at fairs, workshops, symposia, and similar types of commercial or professional meetings open to those individuals in their overt roles but closed to the general public. After 9/11 the division received additional funding, and some offices closed in the 1990s were reopened, bringing the total number of NRD offices to about thirty.[15]

The regional divisions, covering the rest of the world, were the Central Eurasian, Latin American, European, East Asian, Near East, and African divisions. Such divisions formed the core of the CIA's clandestine collection operations since the agency's creation, directing the activities of the various CIA stations whose officers are responsible for recruiting and/or running sources as well as conducting covert action operations.[16]

One division had worldwide responsibilities. The Special Activities Division (SA) handled paramilitary activities, such as those directed against the Sandinista government in Nicaragua and the Soviet intervention in Afghanistan during the 1980s, as well as those in support of the U.S. efforts directed against al-Qaeda, at unseating the Taliban in Afghanistan, and at deposing Saddam Hussein. One component of the division was the Global Response Staff (GRS), whose members "scrve[d] as armed guards for the agency's spies" and in some cases provided security for personnel from other agencies, "including National Security Agency teams deploying sensors or eavesdropping equipment in conflict zones." GRS personnel might also assess the security of potential meeting sites and even make first contact to ensure that case officers were not walking into a trap. SA's heritage included a number of earlier incarnations, including the International Activities Division, the Paramilitary, Insurgency, Narcotics Staff, the Special Activities Staff, and the Military and Special Programs Division.[17]

Two of the five NCS centers, the Counterterrorism Center (CTC) and the Counterintelligence Center (CIC), were established as "DCI Centers" during the tenures of William J. Casey (1981–1987) and William Webster (1987–1991), respectively. The objective was to give heightened status to the counterterrorism and counterintelligence missions as well as to bring together representatives of different Intelligence Community components, including analysts, involved in those missions. In 1997 a Terrorism Warning Group was established within the CTC with the mission of alerting civilian and military leaders to specific terrorist threats. As early as 1996, the CTC established a special unit with about twenty-five staff members, designated Alec Station, to track Osama bin Laden and his top aides. That unit was closed in late 2005. The CTC itself grew from about 300 to more than 1,100 analysts and operators after the terrorist attacks of September 11, 2001.[18]

A June 2005 CIA Office of the Inspector General (OIG) report was critical of the CTC's performance prior to the 9/11 attacks: "Agency officers from the top down worked hard against the al-Qa'ida and Usama Bin Ladin (UBL) targets," but "they did not always work effectively and cooperatively." There were, according to that report, "failures to implement and manage important processes, to follow through with operations, and to properly share and analyze critical data." Those judgments were in sharp contrast to an OIG report published (within classified channels) only a month before the attacks. The executive highlights section of that report began, "The DCI Counterterrorist Center (CTC) is a well-managed component that successfully carries out the Agency's counterterrorist responsibilities to collect and analyze intelligence on international terrorism and to undermine the capabilities of terrorist groups." Nearly a decade later, leading up to May 2, 2011, CTC analysts "found a courier trail that led them to bin Laden's compound in Abbottabad."*[19] In 2013 the CTC was described as the "hub of America's targeted killing operations in Pakistan, Yemen, and

---

*The Counterterrorist Center was renamed the Counterterrorism Center in 2005. See Mark Mazzetti, *The Way of the Knife: The CIA, a Secret Army, and a War at the Ends of the Earth* (New York: Penguin Press, 2013), 162n.

other places where presidents might choose to wage war in the future." The center's Pakistan-Afghanistan Department directed operations in Pakistan and Afghanistan. The expansion of counterterrorist operations in Yemen and Somalia led to the creation of a department to manage counterterrorist operations in those nations.[20]

The CIC consolidated the Counterintelligence Staff, the Foreign Intelligence Capabilities Unit (established in 1983 to look for attempts by foreign intelligence agencies to influence the perceptions of U.S. intelligence), elements of the administration directorate's Office of Security, and other Intelligence Community elements. The director of the CIC was given the status of Associate Deputy Director for Operations for Counterintelligence. The center "analyzes the capabilities, intentions, and activities of foreign intelligence services."*[21]

Creation of the Counterproliferation Center (CPC) was announced in August 2010. One key element of the CPC is the former NCS Counterproliferation Division (CPD) established in the mid-1990s in recognition of the transnational character of the proliferation of weapons of mass destruction. The CPD was intended to facilitate the CIA's collection of information regarding or neutralization of proliferation activities involving multiple regions of the world—such as those involving A. Q. Khan—without having to operate through several divisions. In addition to the CPD, the CPC, headed by an undercover NCS officer with deputies for operations and analysis, included elements from the DI's Weapons Intelligence, Nonproliferation, and Arms Control Center (WINPAC).[22]

The Information Operations Center (IOC), established in the very late 1990s, absorbed some of the functions of the DS&T's Clandestine Information Technology Office, established in 1996. The office was officially described as responsible for addressing "collection capabilities within emerging information technologies," which at the time included the Internet. A fifth center within NCS was the National Resettlement Operations Center, previously known as the Defector Resettlement Center, established to remedy CIA deficiencies in handling defectors, such as those who played a role in the redefection of Vitaly Yurchenko.[23] The complete organization chart of the NCS probably looks like the one shown in Figure 2.2.

The Directorate of Science and Technology, with over 5,000 employees, was created in 1962 as the Deputy Directorate of Research and assumed responsibility for the CIA's efforts in developing and/or operating technical collection systems, particularly the U-2 and OXCART (A-12) spy planes as well as the CORONA reconnaissance satellite. It became the Deputy Directorate of Science and Technology in 1963 and the Directorate of Science and Technology in 1965.[24]

The DS&T has undergone several reorganizations and has gained and lost responsibilities over the years. In 1963 the DS&T assumed control of the Office of Scientific Intelligence, which had been in the Directorate of Intelligence. In 1976 all science and technical analysis functions reverted to the DI. In 1996 the National Photographic Interpretation Center (NPIC), transferred to the DS&T in 1973, was merged into the

---

*Whether the centers could truly be considered interagency centers was a matter of perspective. See Douglas E. Garthoff, *Directors of Central Intelligence as Leaders of the U.S. Intelligence Community, 1946–2005* (Washington, D.C.: Center for the Study of Intelligence, 2005), 188–189.

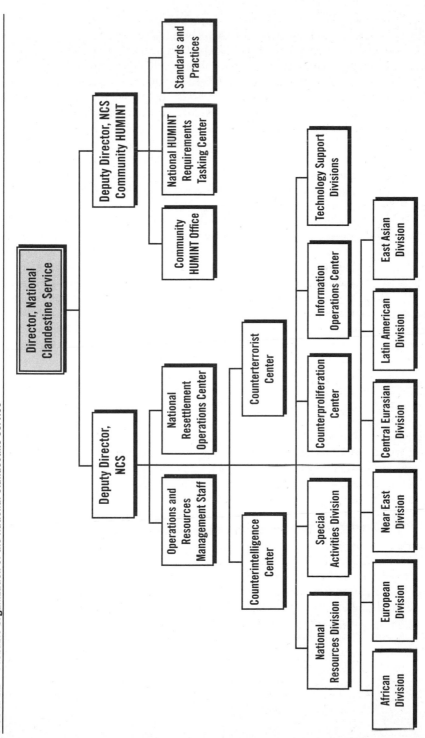

FIGURE 2.2 Probable Organization of the National Clandestine Service

newly created National Imagery and Mapping Agency. In 2005 the responsibility for open source collection, including the activities of the Foreign Broadcast Information Service (FBIS), was transferred from the DS&T to the Office of the Director of National Intelligence, although it is administered by the Director of the CIA.[25]

The post-9/11 impacts on the directorate have included a greater overseas presence, estimated as a 150 percent increase by October 2008. There has also been a greater emphasis on close-access collection relative to that obtained by remote sensors. In addition, "there was a big explosion after 9/11 in the need for tracking and locating technology," the Deputy Director for Science and Technology stated in 2008.[26] Figure 2.1 indicates that a number of DS&T components have been disestablished in the last few years, including the Office of Development and Engineering (OD&E), the Office of Special Communications Programs, and the Office of Systems Engineering and Analysis.

The OD&E could trace it origins directly to the Special Projects Staff established in 1963 to manage CIA reconnaissance satellite efforts, which became the Office of Special Projects in 1965 and the OD&E in 1973. It was involved in the development of major technical collection systems, such as the KH-11 imaging satellite. The office "provide[d] total systems development for major systems—from requirements definition through design engineering, and testing and evaluation, to implementation, operation and even support logistics and maintenance." Prior to the reorganization of the NRO in 1992, the office constituted the NRO's Program B; subsequent to the reorganization it was responsible for providing CIA personnel to work at the reconnaissance office.[27]

The now defunct Office of Special Communications Programs, established in 2003, served as an advocate for programs in the CIA and the wider national security community that were used to provide for the continuous worldwide transfer of data in support of intelligence activities outside the United States. The Office of Systems Engineering and Analysis had been established in 2002 to provide a more independent CIA capability in the field of reconnaissance satellite development in response to concerns that the NRO had become less imaginative and innovative.[28]

The early 2015 version of the DS&T, as shown in Figure 2.1, included eight offices: Mission Resources, Technical Intelligence Officer (TIO) Development, Global Access, Special Activities, Technical Collection, Technical Readiness, Technical Service, and Integrated Missions. The Office of TIO Development is the career development organization for the DS&T (since the term "technical intelligence officer" applies to all DS&T officers). Subsets of the TIO category include operations tradecraft, technical research, technical development, and technical analysis.[29]

A declassified CIA description characterized the Office of Global Access, established in 2003, as responding to "[deleted] requirements combining operations, analysis, and engineering to attack the most difficult technical collection challenges worldwide." The description also stated, somewhat repetitively, that the office "integrate[s] analysis, technology, and tradecraft to attack the most difficult targets, and to provide worldwide collection capability." Also established in 2003, the Office of Special Activities (OSA) provided technical, engineering, research, and analytical expertise for tactical and strategic operations. Both were created out of already existing directorate components.[30]

The Office of SIGINT Operations (OSO) and the Office of Special Projects were merged to form the Office of Technical Collection (OTC). The OSO "develop[ed], operat[ed] and maintain[ed] sophisticated equipment required to perform collection and analysis tasks." OTC personnel provided the CIA contribution to the Special Collection Service (SCS; see below). OSO and its predecessor, the Office of Electronic Intelligence (OEL), were involved in the construction of signals intelligence (SIGINT) facilities operated by China and Norway, in those nations' training of personnel, and in the maintenance of equipment at the sites. The Office of Special Projects, in its last incarnation, was involved in the development and operation of support of systems, including emplaced sensor systems, that collected measurement and signature intelligence (MASINT), SIGINT, and nuclear intelligence. According to a CIA document, the office "develop[ed] collection systems tailored to specific targets." One component of the OTC was the Clandestine MASINT Operations Coordination Center, which likely monitors the output of emplaced MASINT sensors. OTC has also worked with the U.S. Marshals Service to develop technology that can be carried on aircraft and trick cell phones into providing their unique registration information.[31]

The Office of Technical Readiness (OTR), also created in 2003 out of an already existing directorate component, provided support to DS&T technical personnel and facilities overseas, including the construction, operation, and maintenance of directorate facilities. According to its Intellipedia entry, "OTR manages all the elements entailed in field operations." In addition, it worked on the concealment of CIA devices and capabilities as an aid to tradecraft.[32]

The Office of Technical Service was the Technical Services Division of the Directorate of Operations before being transferred to the DS&T in 1973. OTS services included devising secret writing methods, bugging equipment, hidden cameras, coding and decoding devices, enhancing videos and images, and providing chemical imaging. Prior to the April 1980 mission to rescue U.S. hostages in Iran, OTS devised battery-powered landing lights that could be emplaced easily and switched on remotely from the air. After the September 1988 explosion of Pan Am Flight 103 over Lockerbie, Scotland, the OTS matched the timing device to be used in the planned Libyan terrorist operation with a part of the timing device that survived the explosion. In the early 1990s, the service implanted a beacon in a walking stick provided to Osman Ato, an arms importer and financial supporter of Somali warlord General Mohammed Farah Aidid. The beacon allowed Delta Force personnel to capture Ato as he drove through Mogadishu. In 1993 OTS developed a locating system that provided "continuous near-real-time global geolocation information for targets of special interest," the director of OTS reported. In late 2001, a six-member ordnance team from the OTS arrived in Kandahar, Afghanistan, to help dismantle explosive devices encountered by the first CIA teams deployed to the country after 9/11. The team discovered a 2,500-pound improvised explosive device (IED) and disarmed it shortly before it was to explode.[33]

The Office of Integrated Missions, established in March 2009, absorbed elements of the Office of Systems Engineering and Analysis, the In-Q-Tel Interface Center, and one other agency entity. According to a DS&T announcement, over the previous five years, those offices had "delivered new solutions to the toughest problems the Intelligence Community faces, improved the efficiency of our mission infrastructure backbone and provide access to leading edge commercial technologies."[34] The In-Q-Tel Interface Center served as a liaison between individuals and organizations inside and outside the intelligence agency. The CIA created In-Q-Tel in late 1999 as an in-house nonprofit venture capital firm and appropriated $28.5 million in agency funds for its support. By 2012 it had funded more than 180 companies and had 87 in its current portfolio, a third of which were located in Silicon Valley.[35]

One project funded by In-Q-Tel involved a commercial search engine, named NetOwl, that relied on natural-language processing in place of key words to locate information. In-Q-Tel funding was also vital in developing the Presidential Intelligence Briefing System, used to produce the *President's Daily Brief*. Rather than having intelligence sort through hundreds of cables, the system placed the cables in a Lotus Notes database, performed a variety of search and analysis functions, and then placed the brief on a notebook computer. A third project involved enhancing a piece of software called Triangle Boy, which allowed users to examine websites anonymously.[36]

More recent In-Q-Tel projects involved support to Sonitus Medical, which was developing a tiny, wireless, two-way communications device that is covertly placed in an individual's mouth, as well as to Infinite Z, which makes holographic simulations. Fluidigm and Silver Tail Systems, also recent recipients of In-Q-Tel funding, make microchips that analyze genetic samples and detect suspicious activity on government websites, respectively. Additional recent recipients of In-Q-Tel supported have included Lens Vector, which produces technology for miniature cameras, 3VR, which produces video surveillance equipment that can analyze faces, license plates, and other images, and NetBase, which provides semantic-search capabilities that can read online posts in English, Spanish, French, German, and Portuguese. In 2012, then CIA director David Petraeus reported, "Among the analytic projects underway with In-Q-Tel startups is one that enables collection and analysis of worldwide social media feeds, along with projects that use either cloud computing or other methods to explore and analyze Big Data."[37]

The DS&T also participated in the activities of the NCS Information Operations Center.[38] The Directorate of Intelligence underwent extensive reorganization in the post–Cold War years, including between 2009 and 2013. The 1996 reorganization, the directorate's first major one since 1981, reduced the number of directorate offices from nine to six. After 2009, a number of directorate components were eliminated (with their functions absorbed by other entities), while some new offices were established and others were renamed to reflect a change in the scope of their responsibilities. Disestablished components included the Crime and Narcotics Center (CNC) and the Office of Transnational Issues (OTI). The CNC was staffed by analysts from the CIA, FBI, NSA, and the Defense, State, Treasury departments, who produced finished intelligence on narcotics trafficking and international organized crime. The CNC was established in 1989 as the DCI Counternarcotics Center; its name was changed in 1994 to reflect its additional role in gathering international organized crime intelligence.[39]

The Office of Transnational Issues examined developments in international energy, trade, and finance, as well as topics such as refugee flows, food security, and border tensions. OTI analysts also focused on money laundering, illicit finance, corruption, and sanctions violations. Other office analysts analyzed foreign denial and deception efforts as well as attempts to manipulate U.S. perceptions. Within OTI was the

Medical and Psychological Analysis Center, which produced assessments on global health issues (such as disease outbreaks) and the health of foreign leaders.[40]

As indicated in Figure 2.1, as of early 2015 six directorate offices focused on specific geographic regions. Only one of the geographic offices that existed in 2009, the Office of Russian and European Analysis, remained unchanged. The other geographic offices were Africa, Latin America, & Global Issues (which assumed the responsibilities previously assigned to OTI); East Asia and Pacific Analysis; Iraq, Iran, Lebanon, & Syria Analysis; North Africa, Arabian Peninsula, & Regional Analysis; and South Asia Analysis.

Other key elements of the directorate were the Counterintelligence Center Analysis Group, the Information Operations Center Analytical Group, the Economic Security Center (ESC), the Office of Terrorism Analysis, and the Weapons Intelligence, Nonproliferation, and Arms Control Center. The directorate also houses the Analysis Group of the NCS Counterterrorism Center. The Counterintelligence Center's Analysis Group focused on two specific types of counterintelligence threats. One type is transnational threats, including the counterintelligence component of terrorism or the threats posed to the U.S. government, intelligence operations, and U.S. government information systems by emerging or changing technologies. The second type pertains to the threat posed by foreign intelligence services. The Information Operations Center's Analytical Group evaluated foreign threats, from both state and non-state organizations to U.S. computer systems, particularly those that support critical infrastructures.[41]

The Economic Security Center, a recent addition to the Directorate of Intelligence's analytical components, was established during David Petraeus's brief tenure (September 2011–November 2012) as CIA director. The CIA did not release any information on the center's function, but it would appear to have been responsible, inter alia, for examining the potential impact of economic and resource issues on the probability of conflict and instability. In that vein, the ESC reportedly absorbed the duties assigned to the joint DS&T-DI Center for Climate Change and National Security, disestablished in 2012, whose mission included examining the impact of desertification, rising sea levels, population shifts, and increased competition for natural resources.[42]

The Office of Terrorism Analysis was the analytic component of the NCS Counterterrorism Center. Its analysts tracked terrorists and states that sponsor terrorism and assessed terrorists' vulnerabilities, analyzing their ideologies, goals, capabilities, associates, and locations. The analysts also examined worldwide terrorist threat information and look for patterns that would allow them to warn of planned terrorist activity. In addition, they sought to identify emerging and nontraditional terrorist groups and possible collusion among terrorist groups. Finally, the office was involved in "identifying, disrupting, and preventing international financial transactions that support terrorist networks and operations."[43]

The core of the Weapons Intelligence, Nonproliferation, and Arms Control Center was established in September 1991 as the DCI Nonproliferation Center (NPC) after disclosures about Iraq's ability to produce nuclear and other weapons of mass destruction indicated that the Intelligence Community had underestimated both the diversity and progress of the program. By 1999, the NPC consisted of about two hundred intelligence analysts and clandestine operators, about a quarter to a third of whom had come from agencies other than the CIA. The center monitored the worldwide development and acquisition of production technology, designs, components, and entire military systems in the area of nuclear, chemical, and biological weapons, as well as advanced conventional weapons.[44]

NPC also developed strategic plans to help guide the U.S. government's response to the proliferation problem and provided support to collection and law enforcement organizations. It also worked on collection platform development and produced a "gaps" study that identified deficiencies in proliferation-related collection activities. Furthermore, the NPC was authorized to review the Intelligence Community's performance on proliferation activities and to make relevant budget recommendations.[45]

WINPAC was created in March 2001 from the merger of the NPC, the DCI's Arms Control Intelligence Staff, and the OTI's Weapons Intelligence Staff. It is responsible for (1) "studying the development of the entire spectrum of threats, from weapons of mass destruction . . . to advanced conventional weapons like lasers, advanced explosives, and armor, as well as all types of missiles," and (2) providing intelligence support to U.S. nonproliferation, threat reduction, and arms control efforts.[46]

Additional Directorate of Intelligence components included the Offices of Analytic Production and Dissemination, Corporate Resources, and Collection Analysis and Strategies, as well as the Sherman Kent School for Intelligence Analysis. The Office of Collection Analysis and Strategies assists DI analysts in making use of collection systems and provided guidance for the development of future systems. Specifically, its functions include informing the president and other senior policymakers about U.S. collection capabilities and intelligence-gathering issues, running special collection efforts, evaluating the use and value of current collection capabilities, guiding the development of future collection programs, and providing twenty-four-hour collection support to the CIA's Operations Center.[47]

The offices under the Directorate of Support consisted of the Offices for Corporate Business, Facilities Support (previously Global Infrastructure), Global Services, Medical Services, Mission Integration, Business Acceleration (the new office), Personnel Resources, and Security. Of these components, the oldest was the Office of Medical Services, which has been responsible for medical examinations and immunizations for employees and dependents traveling overseas, health education, emergency health care, and psychiatric services. It also helped develop the Psychological Assessment Program to determine which individuals are best suited for the agency and is involved in psychiatric and medical intelligence production.[48]

The Office of Security had been split into separate components responsible for personnel security and physical security, but these were then reunited, giving the office responsibility for clearing personnel, investigating possible security breaches, and ensuring the security of CIA facilities. The other offices in the directorate provide a variety of functions essential to CIA operations, including provision of facilities for communications between CIA headquarters and overseas personnel, logistics, maintenance of facilities, disbursement of funds for CIA operations, determination of personnel requirements, and training and education. The directorate operated the CIA's training facilities, including the Armed Forces Experimental Training Facility at Camp Peary, Virginia, and the Harvey Point Defense Testing Activity in Hertford, North Carolina. A CIA arms depot, presumably the responsibility of the Directorate of

Support and designated the "Midwest Depot," appears to be located at the U.S. Army Camp Stanley Storage Activity in San Antonio, Texas.[49]

In early March 2015, CIA director John Brennan announced a major reorganization of the agency that would involve the renaming of several major components, the establishment of ten hybrid mission centers, and the creation of a new directorate. Specifically, the Directorate of Intelligence would become the Directorate of Analysis, while the National Clandestine Service would revert to its previous name—the Directorate of Operations. Further, both would serve largely as recruiting and training organizations. Responsibility for both analytical and operational (including liaison) activities would be shifted to the ten centers (managed by assistant directors), seven of which would be regional and three functional. The new Directorate of Digital Innovation will focus on exploiting advances in computer technology and communications.[50]

In addition to the seven regional centers, the functional centers will include expanded versions of at least two already in existence—the Counterproliferation Center and the Counterterrorism Center—and possibly, a third, the Counterintelligence Center. The Digital Innovation Directorate will absorb the Open Source Center as well as the Information Operations Center from NCS. It will also seek to assist the CIA in employing digital means of persuading targets to provide secret information. In addition, the directorate will assist CIA officers in evading detection overseas due to the use of phones, computers, or ATM cards.[51]

In explaining the creation of the centers, Brennan observed, "There was . . . great esprit de corps in those directorates, but also at times, those directorates were a bit siloed, and were stovepiped." He also observed that critical data about threats could still fall into gaps between different divisions. With regard to creation of the Directorate of Digital Innovation, he noted that "the digital world touches every aspect of our business" and that the CIA had been slow to rise to the challenge of digital espionage.[52]

The announcement left a number of questions unanswered, not just because of classification issues but because Brennan indicated that the reorganization was a work in progress that would take several months to accomplish. Questions involved how it would impact the organizational structure of the Support and Science & Technology directorates (which retained their names), what would happen to organizations within the NCS that don't fit neatly into a geographic structure (e.g., the Special Activities Division, the National Resettlement Operations Center), whether the National Resources Division would be part of a geographic center, and whether the Counterintelligence Center would become the third mission center.

NATIONAL SECURITY AGENCY

The predecessor of the National Security Agency, the Armed Forces Security Agency (AFSA), was established within the Department of Defense (DOD) under the command the Joint Chiefs of Staff on May 20, 1949. In theory, the AFSA was to direct the communications intelligence activities of the military service SIGINT units (at the time consisting of the Army Security Agency, Naval Security Group, and Air Force Security Service). In practice, the AFSA had little power since its functions were defined in terms of activities not performed by the service units.[53]

On October 24, 1952, President Harry S. Truman sent a top secret, eight-page (now declassified) memorandum titled "Communications Intelligence Activities" to the Secretaries of State and Defense; the memorandum abolished the AFSA and transferred its personnel to the newly created National Security Agency, established that day by draft National Security Council Intelligence Directive No. 9. (The draft was formally approved in December.)[54]

The NSA had its origins in a December 10, 1951, memo sent from Walter Bedell Smith to National Security Council executive secretary James B. Lay, stating that "control over, and coordination of, the collection and processing of Communications Intelligence had proved ineffective" and recommending a survey of communications intelligence activities. The resulting report, completed within six months, identified the need for a much greater degree of coordination and direction at the national level. As the change in the security agency's name indicated, the NSA's role was to extend beyond the armed forces; hence, the NSA is considered to be "within but not part of DOD."[55]

Although the agency was created in 1952 and the fact of its existence was never classified, the *U.S. Government Organization Manual* did not note it as a "separately organized agency within the Department of Defense" that "performs highly specialized technical and coordinating functions relating to national security" until 1957. But the NSA's existence was a matter of public knowledge from at least early 1954, when Washington, D.C., newspapers ran several stories concerning the construction of its new headquarters at Fort George G. Meade, Maryland. In late 1954 the NSA was again in the news when one of its employees was caught taking secret documents home.[56]

The charter for NSA is a National Security Council Intelligence Directive (NSCID). The current version, NSCID No. 6, "Signals Intelligence," which has not been updated since January 17, 1972, directs the NSA to produce SIGINT "in accordance with the objectives, requirements, and priorities established by the Director of Central Intelligence Board." The directive also authorizes the Director of NSA (DIRNSA) "to issue direct to any operating elements engaged in SIGINT operations such instructions and assignments as are required" and states that "all instructions issued by the Director under the authority provided in this paragraph shall be mandatory, subject only to appeal to the Secretary of Defense."[57]

NSCID No. 6 defines SIGINT activities as consisting of communications intelligence (COMINT) and electronic intelligence (ELINT). The directive states, "COMINT activities shall be construed to mean those activities which produce COMINT by interception and processing of foreign communications. . . . Interception comprises range estimation, transmitter operator identification, signal analysis, traffic analysis, cryptanalysis, decryption, study of plain text, the fusion of those processes, and the reporting of results. COMINT and COMINT activities as defined herein shall not include (a) any intercept and processing of unencrypted written communications, press and propaganda broadcasts, or (b) censorship."[58]

When established, the NSA did not have authority over ELINT operations, which remained the responsibility of the military services, but this authority was assigned to the agency in 1958. NSCID No. 6 defines ELINT as "the collection (observation and recording) and the processing for subsequent intelligence purposes, of information derived from foreign noncommunications, electro-magnetic radiation emanating from

PHOTO 2.2   NSA headquarters, Fort George G. Meade, Maryland. *Photo credit:* NSA.

other than atomic detonation or radioactive sources. ELINT is the technical and intelligence product of ELINT activities."[59] From its inception, ELINT was primarily associated with the interception of emanations from radar systems. Telemetry intelligence (TELINT), the interception and exploitation of signals from foreign missile tests, was originally a branch of ELINT but became a separate "INT" in 1971. Subsequently, it became part of a new third component of SIGINT, foreign instrumentation signals intelligence (FISINT), which included telemetry, missile and satellite command signals, beacons, and computer-based data.

The SIGINT responsibilities of NSA and its director are specified by a 2010 DOD directive, "The National Security Service and Central Security Service." It specifies that NSA will

- Collect (including through clandestine means), process, analyze, produce, and disseminate SIGINT information and data for foreign intelligence and counterintelligence purposes to support national and departmental missions. . . .
- Provide SIGINT support for the conduct of military operations, pursuant to tasking, priorities, and standards of timeliness assigned by the Secretary of Defense.
- Establish and operate an effective, unified organization for SIGINT activities, including executing any SIGINT-related functions the Secretary of Defense so directs.
- Develop rules, regulations, and standards governing the classification and declassification of SIGINT. . . .
- Exercise SIGINT operational control and establish policies and procedures for departments and agencies to follow when appropriately performing SIGINT activities.[60]

Computer network exploitation, an adjunct to the traditional SIGINT mission (whether involving remote collection or close access via technical surveillance), has been defined as "enabling operations and intelligence collection to gather data from target or adversary automated systems or networks." Such exploitation can be intended to produce information in support of intelligence collection or as a prelude to computer network attack, an activity delegated to the NSA in March 1997 by the Secretary of Defense.[61]

The NSA has another major mission, originally known as communications security (COMSEC), which became information security in the 1980s and is currently known as information assurance (IA). In its IA role, NSA creates, reviews, and authorizes the communications procedures of a variety of government agencies, including the State and Defense departments, the CIA, and the FBI. This role includes development of secure data and voice transmission links on satellite systems, including those for defense communications satellites. Likewise, for sensitive communications, FBI agents have used a special scrambler phone requiring a different code from the NSA each day. The agency's IA responsibilities also include securing communications security for strategic weapons systems so as to prevent unauthorized intrusion, interference, and jamming. In addition, NSA is responsible for developing the codes by which the president must identify himself in order to authorize the release of nuclear weapons. As part of its IA mission, NSA is also responsible for protecting national security data banks and computers from unauthorized access by individuals or governments.[62]

NSA headquarters at Fort George G. Meade houses from 20,000 to 24,000 employees in three buildings. The NSA's requested budget for the 2013 fiscal year was $10.8 billion. This figure does not take into account funding for the military service cryptologic elements that conduct eavesdropping operations on behalf of NSA, just as the personnel figure does not include the personnel in those units.[63]

In addition to directing the agency's activities, the NSA director is responsible for supervising the SIGINT activities of the Service Cryptologic Elements (SCEs), which consists of the Navy Fleet Cyber Command, Marine Corps support battalions, components of the Army Intelligence and Security Command, components of the 25th Air Force, and the Coast Guard Deputy Assistant Commander for Intelligence. In this role, the director serves as the head of the Central Security Service (CSS). The CSS function of the NSA, with the DIRNSA serving simultaneously as CSS chief, was established in 1971 "to provide a unified, more economical and more effective structure for executing cryptologic and related operations presently conducted under the Military Departments." There is, however, no separate CSS staff.[64]

As shown in Figure 2.3, NSA consists of five directorates (Signals Intelligence, Information Assurance, Research, Technology, and Foreign Affairs) and other components, but the two that perform its fundamental functions are the Directorates of Signals Intelligence and Information Assurance (IAD). The Signals Intelligence Directorate (formerly the Directorate of Operations), whose organization chart is shown in Figure 2.4, contains three directorates that highlight the three key elements of the directorate's mission: collecting SIGINT (Directorate for Data Acquisition), analyzing data and producing reports (Directorate for Analysis and Production), and providing those reports to the appropriate individuals in NSA or in other government agencies (Directorate for Customer Relationships).

FIGURE 2.3   Organization of the National Security Agency

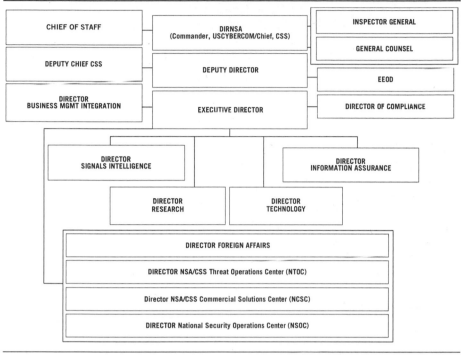

Source: NSA.

FIGURE 2.4   Organization of the NSA Signals Intelligence Directorate

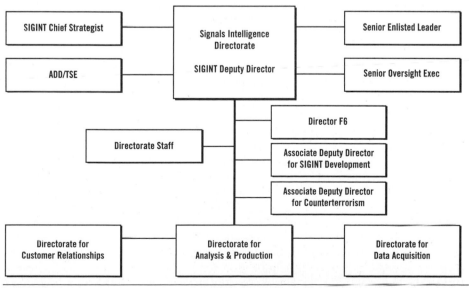

Source: NSA.

Among the key offices of the Directorate for Data Acquisition are the Office of Tailored Access Operations, which engages in computer network exploitation; Global Access Operations, which operates a variety of remote collection operations, including satellites and satellite communications intercept stations; and Special Source Operations, which handles relations with corporate entities, including Internet service providers and telecommunications companies. Within the Directorate for Analysis and Production are a number of regional and transnational "product lines," including South Asia, Russia, counterterrorism, foreign counterintelligence, combating proliferation, and arms control.[65]

Another product line is the one for weapons and space, and a key element in that product line is the Defense Special Missile and Aerospace Center (DEFSMAC), established as the Defense Special Missile and Astronautics Center (then referred to as Defense/SMAC) via a secret April 27, 1964, DOD directive. Its current charter is Department of Defense Instruction S-5100.43 of September 24, 2008, which reflects the replacement of "Astronautics" with "Aerospace," a change made in 2002. DEFSMAC was reported to have a staff of more than 230 in 2001.[66]

According to a history of DEFSMAC, its mission is "to accomplish 24 hour surveillance of foreign missile and space activities; alert and exercise technical control of DOD intelligence collection systems directed against foreign missile and space events; provide technical support, including tip-off, to all DOD missile and space intelligence collection activities to enable mission accomplishment; and perform all source current analysis and reporting of all detected foreign missile and space events based on initial site reporting of all detected foreign missile and space events received up to 72 hours after the event."[67] According to a former NSA deputy director, "DEFSMAC is a combination of [Defense Intelligence Agency (DIA)] with its military components and the NSA. It has all the inputs from all the assets and is a warning activity. They probably have a better 'feel' for any worldwide threat to this country from missiles, aircraft or overt military activities, better and more timely, at instant fingertip availability than any group in the United States. So DEFSMAC is an input to NSA, but it also [is] an input to DIA and the CIA and the White House Situation Room and everybody else."[68] DEFSMAC receives data related to space and missile launches by Iran, North Korea, Russia, China, and other nations. In turn it notifies those who task or operate collection assets—from satellites to aircraft to ground stations—that a launch is imminent so that they can prepare to monitor the event and obtain the maximum intelligence available.[69]

The mission of the Information Assurance Directorate "involves detecting, reporting, and responding to cyber threats; making encryption codes to securely pass information between systems; and embedding IA measures directly into the emerging Global Information Grid. It includes building secure audio and video communications equipment, making tamper protection products, and providing trusted microelectronic solutions." In addition, its work "entails testing the security of customers' systems, providing OPSEC [operations security] assistance, and evaluating commercial software and hardware against nationally set standards, to better meet our nation's IA needs."[70] Figure 2.5 shows the IAD's organization chart.

Two key centers outside the Signals Intelligence and Information Assurance directorates are the National Security Operations Center (NSOC) and the NSA/CSS Threat Operations Center (NTOC). The NSOC, formerly the National SIGINT Operations

FIGURE 2.5   Organization of the Information Assurance Directorate

Information Assurance Directorate				Chief of Staff (I0)
Trusted Engineering Solutions (I2)	Information Assurance Operations (I3)	Fusion, Analysis, and Mitigations (I4)		Engagement (IE)
Architecture (I21)	Cryptographic Assurance Operations (I31)	Analytics (I41)		Strategic Mission Integration (IC)
Engineering (I22)	Operations Technology Development (I32)	Analysis & Data Fusion (I42)		Oversight & Compliance (IV)
Fielded Solutions (I23)	Remote and Deployed Operations (I33)	Mitigations (I43)		Mission Managers
				IAD Corporate Information Manager

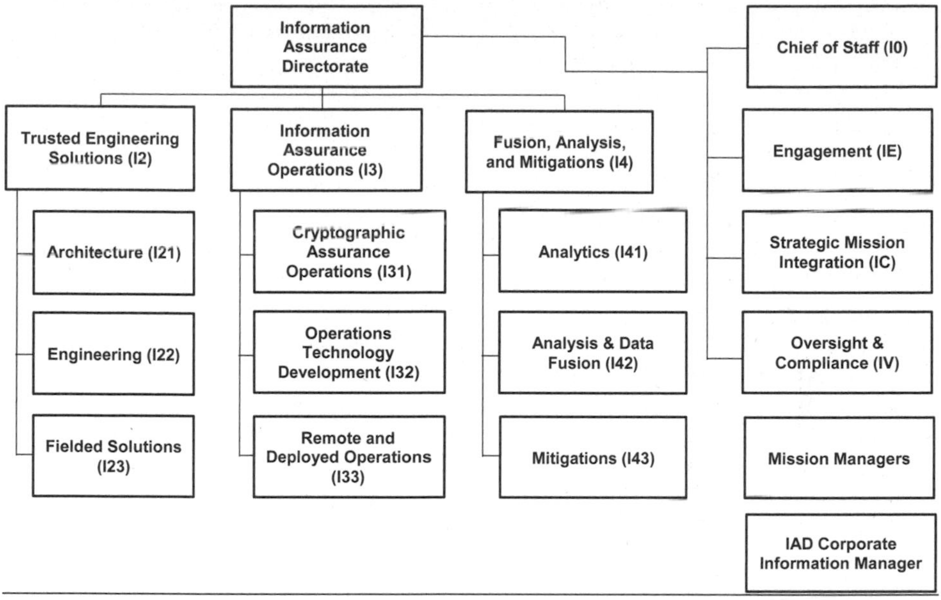

Source: NSA.

Center, was responsible for overseeing and directing the SIGINT coverage of any crisis event. It operated around the clock and was in instantaneous touch with every major NSA facility in the world. In the event a facility intercepted signals it deemed significant, the facility personnel filed a Critical Intelligence Communications (CRITIC) report with NSOC, which could immediately pass the message on to DIRNSA. If NSOC authorities felt that the event lacked sufficient importance, they could revoke the report's CRITIC status. As a result of the increased emphasis on information warfare, the National SIGINT Operations Center was rechristened the National Security Operations Center, which continues to perform the previous missions but now operates the Information Protect Cell and includes the Defensive Information Operations Staff.[71] The NTOC, staffed by representatives of both the Signals Intelligence and Information Assurance directorates, attempts to identify cyber threats posed by foreign nations or terrorist groups to NSA, DOD, and military service computer systems.

Among its collection facilities in the United States (discussed in Chapter 8), the NSA has a major facility located at Camp Williams, Utah, near Bluffdale. Known as the Utah Data Center or the Intelligence Community Cybersecurity Initiative Data Center, it serves as a repository for very large amounts of data gathered from domestic NSA stations, overseas listening posts, and satellite systems.[72]

SPECIAL COLLECTION SERVICE

The Special Collection Service is not one of the seventeen organizations listed as constituting the U.S. Intelligence Community since it is a joint operation of the CIA and NSA (which designates the service as "F6"). But it does have its own three-hundred-acre headquarters complex outside Beltsville, Maryland, and a worldwide presence (discussed in Chapter 8). While the existence of the SCS is not classified, all details of its mission are, and the sign at its headquarters reads "Communications Security Support Group."[73]

At the beginning of 1976, the CIA had two entities involved in SIGINT operations: the Office of Electronic Intelligence in the Directorate of Science and Technology and Division D in the Directorate of Operations. The latter organization, originally established to serve as the funnel for COMINT into the CIA, had expanded its mission to include operations against foreign cipher personnel and embassy-based intercept operations, primarily as a means of supporting the CIA's case officers and their clandestine collection activities. Then, in February 1977, OEL and Division D were merged to form the Office of SIGINT Operations.[74]

By that time the staff director of the House Armed Services Committee, Charlie Snodgrass—who seemed, according to NSA historian Thomas Johnson, "to harbor a visceral distrust of the CIA"—had launched a study focusing on U.S. SIGINT activities. He concluded that there was too much duplication, not enough coordination, and a lack of clear lines of authority. It had been the CIA's practice to ignore the edicts issued by NSA's director, who was ostensibly the national manager for SIGINT. The study and congressional pressure forced the CIA to acknowledge the NSA as the national SIGINT authority. A memorandum of agreement—or "Peace Treaty," according to Johnson—between the two covered liaison, overhead collection, and a number of other subjects. The CIA also agreed to merge their embassy intercept operations with those of NSA (whose operations had aimed at supporting national and military decision makers).[75]

Details of the merger were worked out between the Director of NSA and the head of the CIA OSO. They agreed that a CIA official would initially head the joint enterprise, to be called the Special Collection Service, serving a two-year term. The SCS's deputy director would be selected from NSA, and an NSA official would become director after the CIA official completed his term. The director's job would continue to alternate between CIA and NSA officials, with the deputy director succeeding the director.[76]

A leaked document from 2002 described the SCS effort as involving "covert SIGINT collection abroad from official U.S. Government establishments, typically U.S. embassies and consulates" and stated, "NSA partners with the CIA in the SCS construct in which NSA employees under diplomatic cover conduct SIGINT collection."* The same document also reported, "Special Collection Sites provide considerable perishable intelligence on leadership communications largely facilitated by the site presence within a national capital."[77]

By the end of 1983, a Special Collection Element (SCE) would be present in about a third of U.S. embassies abroad. In 1988 there were SCEs at eighty-eight sites; by

---

*By mid-1994, individuals from the military services were being seconded to work for the SCS after cover problems had been overcome. Four Air Intelligence Agency (AIA) candidates were selected to participate in the program, designated SENSOR SILVER. (See Joyce M. Hons, Juan R. Jimenez, Gabriel G. Marshall, and Jimmy D. Ford, *History of the Air Intelligence Agency, 1 January–31 December 1994,* Volume 1 (San Antonio, TX: AIA, December 1995), 1:39.

FIGURE 2.6   Organization of the Special Collection Service

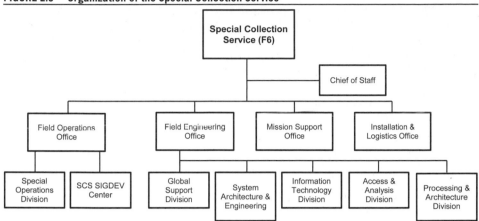

Source: NSA, SCS, Pacific STGDEV Conference, March 2011.

2002, the number had shrunk to sixty-five, a change explained by the fact that "SCS has always opened and closed sites based on productivity." The teams, which might consist of only two or three people, produced excellent intelligence, particularly if the embassy was located on high ground or near the foreign or defense ministries or other key offices in the capital. In 2010 there were ninety-six SCS sites in five categories: staffed locations (seventy-four), unmanned remote (fourteen), dormant (three), active survey (three), and technical support activity (two).[78]

According to several accounts, SCS personnel are also involved in placing antennas in nondescript locations as well as undertaking "black-bag jobs" since "sometimes . . . it's easier to simply break into a building and install a hidden microphone, whereupon intelligence can be gathered and voices recorded before encryption ever takes place."[79] Figure 2.6 shows the SCS organization chart.

NATIONAL RECONNAISSANCE OFFICE

In its May 2, 1946, report, *Preliminary Design for an Experimental World-Circling Spaceship*, the Douglas Aircraft Corporation examined the potential value of satellites for scientific and military purposes, including "observation." Almost nine years later, on March 16, 1955, the U.S. Air Force issued General Operational Requirement No. 80, officially establishing a requirement for an advanced reconnaissance satellite. Over the next five years, the U.S. reconnaissance satellite program evolved in a variety of ways. The Air Force program was first designated the Advanced Reconnaissance System, then SENTRY, and finally SAMOS.[80]

Concern about the amount of time it would take to achieve the SAMOS program's primary objective—development of a satellite that could return its imagery electronically—led to President Dwight D. Eisenhower's approval, in early February 1958, of a CIA program. Designated CORONA, it aimed to develop a satellite that would return imagery in a canister. By June 1960, continued problems with SAMOS led Eisenhower to order a review of the program. The review culminated in an August 25, 1960, meeting in which Eisenhower accepted a recommendation for streamlined management for the SAMOS program. The new arrangement would establish a direct line of authority from the Secretary of the Air Force to the SAMOS project director, eliminating intervening levels of bureaucracy, including the Air Staff.[81]

On August 31, Secretary of the Air Force Dudley C. Sharp ordered creation of an Office of Missile and Satellite Systems within his own office to assist the secretary "in discharging his responsibility for the direction, supervision and control of the Samos project." That same day, Sharp also directed the formation of a SAMOS project office at the California headquarters of the Air Force Ballistic Missile Division as a field extension of the Office of the Secretary of the Air Force. The order stated, "The Director is responsible to and will report directly to the Secretary of the Air Force."[82]

Those orders established a new structure for the Air Force program but did not affect the management arrangements for the CIA's CORONA program. However, a number of events and individuals would lead to the creation of a national reconnaissance organization. Among them were James Killian and Edwin Land, two key presidential scientific advisors. Looking at the successful U.S. Air Force–CIA partnerships that had existed with respect to the U-2, OXCART, and CORONA programs, they pushed for permanent, institutionalized collaboration between the two organizations.[83]

Subsequent to John F. Kennedy's assumption of the presidency, Under Secretary of the Air Force Joseph Charyk drafted a proposal, at Killian and Land's request, for the establishment of a national coordinating agency for satellite reconnaissance. Sometime after mid-July, Secretary of Defense Robert McNamara asked Charyk to draft the specific documents that would put the proposal into effect. A key change between the original and final drafts was the expansion of the office's responsibility from satellite reconnaissance to overhead reconnaissance of denied areas, thus including in its set of responsibilities both satellites and selected manned and unmanned aerial systems.[84]

On September 6, 1961, an agreement signed by the acting DCI, General Charles Pearre Cabell, and Deputy Secretary of Defense Roswell Gilpatric established the National Reconnaissance Office as a joint CIA–U.S. Air Force operation. In 1962 the U.S. Navy's space reconnaissance effort, the GRAB electronic intelligence satellite, became part of the NRO framework. In keeping with the "matrix" nature of the organization, the essence of the NRO structure for the next thirty years included an NRO director (and eventually deputy director), an NRO staff (headed by an Air Force brigadier general who reported to the director), and three programs: Program A (Air Force Office of Special Projects in El Segundo); Program B (the CIA's U-2, OXCART, and satellite efforts); and Program C (Navy, originally headquartered in Washington). In early 1963, a second Air Force element, Program D, was established, initially encompassing what was then designated the R-12 (and subsequently became the SR-71, the Air Force version of the OXCART). Program D also assumed responsibility for the TAGBOARD/D-21 reconnaissance drone and a nonreconnaissance project, the interceptor version of the R-12. Program D continued as a component of the NRO until responsibility for the SR-71 was turned over to the Strategic Air Command in 1969; it was formally dissolved in 1970 or 1971.[85]

In 1992, after thirty years as an organization whose existence was classified the "fact of" the NRO's existence was declassified. DCI Robert Gates announced

PHOTO 2.3   NRO headquarters, Chantilly, Virginia. *Photo credit:* NRO.

reorganization plans before a joint public hearing of the Senate and House intelligence oversight committees. He stated that there would be "a far-reaching internal restructuring of the Intelligence Community organization responsible for designing, building, and operating our overhead reconnaissance assets."[86]

That restructuring involved replacing the alphabetic program offices with three major directorates—the Imagery Intelligence (IMINT), SIGINT, and Communication Systems Acquisition and Operations directorates—each responsible for both acquiring and supervising contract research and development as well as for purchasing and operating the relevant spacecraft and ground stations.[87]

The NRO headquarters are located in a four-tower structure in Chantilly, Virginia, near Dulles International Airport. Government personnel working for the NRO are drawn largely from the Air Force, CIA, NSA, and Navy. In 1997 the 2,753 NRO government employees consisted of 1,456 from the Air Force (53 percent), 649 from the CIA (24 percent), 412 from the NSA (15 percent), 214 from the Navy (8 percent), and 22 from other agencies such as the DIA and Army (<1 percent). In March 2006, the Government Accountability Office estimated that Air Force personnel made up approximately 57 percent of NRO employees. With the disestablishment of the Office of Development and Engineering, CIA personnel assigned to the NRO would be tied to specific DS&T mission areas. Today, NRO government employees total about 2,800, although NRO contractors account for many thousand more, either working at NRO headquarters or with NRO projects at contractor sites. Its fiscal year 2013 budget request was $10.3 billion.[88]

Just as the NRO operated for decades with its Program A-B-C structure, it also operated for decades under two charter documents: a 1964 DOD directive and a 1965 agreement between the Director of Central Intelligence and the Secretary of Defense. In 2009 Congress, via the Intelligence Authorization Act for Fiscal Year 2010, mandated that the Director of National Intelligence and Secretary of Defense produce a new charter for the NRO, updating the 1965 DCI-DOD agreement.[89]

On September 21, 2010, DNI James R. Clapper Jr. and Secretary of Defense Robert Gates signed a memorandum of agreement concerning the NRO, specifying that the NRO was responsible for "research and development, acquisition, launch, deployment, and operation of overhead systems and related data processing facilities to collect intelligence." The agreement also specified that the NRO director had three broad sets of responsibilities: to manage and operate NRO programs, to act as principal advisor to the Secretary of Defense and DNI on overhead reconnaissance, and to share responsibility for "leading and managing the national security space sector." The agreement also specified that the NRO director should establish and chair an Overhead Reconnaissance Advisory Group (ORAG) to serve as a principal advisor to the director on overhead reconnaissance.[90]

A more detailed DOD directive issued in June 2011 serves as the current charter for the NRO. It repeats the mission statement in the agreement and goes on to discuss organization and management, responsibilities and functions with regard to operations (including support for the military, Intelligence Community, security, and counterintelligence), creation of the ORAG, acquisition, and relationships, among other topics.[91] A key element of the directive is its definition of "overhead reconnaissance," a term that traditionally included both space and aerial reconnaissance overflights of denied areas, reflecting the NRO's involvement in developing and operating both space and aerial systems (both manned and unmanned). However, the directive defines overhead reconnaissance as "activities carried out by space-based capabilities whose principal purpose is conducting and/or enabling intelligence collection," implying that the NRO will have no role in developing aerial reconnaissance systems. The definition also specifies that overhead reconnaissance includes "associated R&D, acquisition, test and evaluation, and system operations performed on or by satellites, communications, and facilities for data processing as well as command and control of spacecraft and payloads."[92] In addition, the directive specifies that the NRO director should identify a Special Communications focal point to represent NRO interests to the DOD Special Communications Enterprise Office, a reflection of the NRO's role in data exfiltration—receiving and relaying through its satellites data acquired by emplaced sensor systems.[93]

The current structure, shown in Figure 2.7, represents a significant expansion in the number of directorates, which in turn reflects a significant change in the organization's approach to carrying out its mission. The three directorates established in 1992 and 1993 continued the cradle-to-grave approach in which a single NRO component conceived, developed, constructed, and operated satellites. Over the subsequent two plus decades, the NRO has distributed those functions over a number of directorates.

The IMINT Systems Acquisition and Operations Directorate and the SIGINT Systems Acquisition and Operations Directorate have become the Imagery Intelligence Systems Acquisition Directorate and the Signals Intelligence Systems Acquisition Directorate, indicating that they are now responsible only for the acquisition part of the space reconnaissance effort. Responsibility for operating the orbiting spacecraft

FIGURE 2.7   Organization of the National Reconnaissance Office

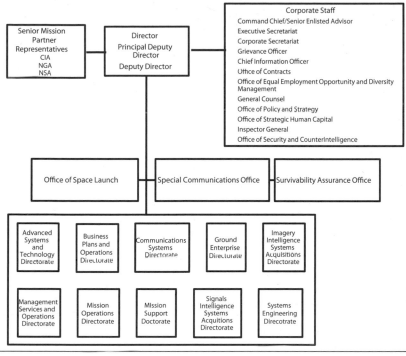

Source: NRO.

belongs to the Mission Operations Directorate, while handling the ground stations and processing the data they receive is the job of the Ground Enterprise Directorate. Creation of the Mission Operations Directorate reflected the desire to give customers a single point of contact for space intelligence data, regardless of the collection system that obtained it. Creation of the Ground Enterprise Directorate reflected the expectation that it would result in greater attention to the ground component of NRO operations.[94]

Three additional key NRO directorates are those for Advanced Systems & Technology (AS&TD), Systems Engineering (SED), and Mission Support (MSD). The Advanced Systems & Technology Directorate was established in 1997, as recommended by a review group, by upgrading and expanding the functions of the Office of Systems Applications, established to investigate the feasibility of small satellites for reconnaissance. The directorate's mission is to investigate and conduct research and development for systems that would differ significantly from those currently in operation.[95]

On October 15, 2006, the Office of the Deputy Director for Systems Engineering was replaced by a fifth directorate, the Directorate for Systems Integration and Engineering, created to establish standards for systems engineering, to develop and coordinate with other NRO directorates a high-level NRO architectural description, and to "review all major trade-offs analyses [and] architectural alternatives . . . prior to their presentation outside the NRO."[96] Today, it is known as the Systems Engineering Directorate.

The origin of the Mission Support Directorate goes back to April 1990 when the position of Deputy Director for Military Support (DDMS) was established to facilitate the provision of NRO support to military commanders. In late 1996 the position of Deputy Director for National Support (DDNS) was established to balance the DDMS position. According to the DDNS mission statement, the new official was to "maintain close coordination with senior officials in all national-level departments and agencies who can represent their respective current and future space-based reconnaissance needs." The position was created in response to a frequently expressed concern about the extent of focus on supporting military operations. In 2006 the two positions were merged into the single DDMS position. Subsequently, the deputy director position was eliminated and the functions placed in a directorate.[97]

Among the offices constituting the NRO Corporate Staff is the Office of Security and Counterintelligence. In June 1992, the NRO established a Counterintelligence Staff to "increase the awareness of foreign intelligence threats to NRO programs, facilities and personnel, . . . communicating that information to NRO CI activities." Its primary functions included research and analysis; coordination within the NRO, the CI community, and investigative agencies; and operations support. In March 2006, the director of the NRO announced that the Counterintelligence Staff would be realigned within the Office of the Director of Security, whose position would become Director of NRO Security and Counterintelligence. The Director of Security and Counterintelligence reports to the Principal Deputy Director.[98]

NATIONAL GEOSPATIAL-INTELLIGENCE AGENCY

In his April 1992 testimony before the House and Senate intelligence committees, DCI Robert Gates noted that the Imagery Task Force he had established upon becoming DCI had recommended the creation of a National Imagery Agency (NIA), which would absorb the CIA's National Photographic Interpretation Center as well as the Defense Mapping Agency (DMA).[99]

The task force's vision for an NIA was not as broad as that recommended by some in congressional hearings and written into proposed legislation by both the House and Senate intelligence committees. The broader vision would have created an NIA responsible for virtually the entire range of imagery functions, decisions on spacecraft and aircraft capabilities, research and development to support those decisions, tasking, collection operations, and analysis.[100] During his testimony Gates rejected the recommendations of both his task force and the congressional committees, in part because Chairman of the Joint Chiefs of Staff Colin Powell wanted to maintain DOD control of the Defense Mapping Agency. However, Gates and Secretary of Defense Richard Cheney agreed to a less dramatic fix, and a month later the Central Imagery Office (CIO) was established within the Department of Defense. The intent was to address some of the same concerns that had led to suggestions for the establishment of an NIA, including congressional frustration with a lack of coherent imagery management, imagery collection, and dissemination problems that surfaced during the Persian Gulf War, budgetary constraints, and changing requirements for the support of military operations. Thus, the CIO was established on May 6, 1992, chartered by both Department of Defense Directive 5105.26 and Director of Central Intelligence Directive 2/9 as a DOD combat support agency.[101]

In contrast to the proposed alternative national imagery agencies, the CIO was not designed to absorb existing agencies or to take on their collection and analysis functions. Rather, its mission included tasking of national imagery systems (assuming that mission in place of the DCI Committee on Imagery Requirements and Exploitation) to ensure responsive imagery support for the Department of Defense, combatant commanders, the CIA, and other agencies and advising and evaluating the performance of imagery components. Pursuant to the provision of imagery support, the CIO was assigned the role of systems development—specifically, establishing imagery architectures and standards for interoperability of imagery dissemination systems and supporting and conducting research and development.[102]

Establishing the CIO delayed but did not prevent creation of a national imagery and mapping agency. In April 1995, DCI-designate John Deutch told the Senate Select Committee on Intelligence that, if confirmed, he would "move immediately to consolidate the management of all imagery collection, analysis, and distribution," arguing that "both effectiveness and economy can be improved by managing in a manner similar to the National Security Agency's organization for signals intelligence."[103] After his confirmation, Deutch established a National Imagery Agency Steering Group, which in turn chartered an NIA Task Force. The task force produced eleven different options for an NIA, ranging from a strengthened CIO to a highly centralized NIA, with program, budget, and management authority for all aspects of imagery. In late November 1995, Deutch and Secretary of Defense William J. Perry sent a joint letter to congressional leaders and relevant committees about their plan to establish a National Imagery and Mapping Agency as a combat support agency within the Department of Defense on October 1, 1996. Their letter noted that the proposed agency would consolidate the DMA, CIO, NPIC, DIA's imagery exploitation element, and portions of the Defense Airborne Reconnaissance Office and NRO involved in imagery exploitation and dissemination.[104]

The planned agency would leave the acquisition and operation of space systems and their ground stations to the NRO and the service intelligence organizations' imagery exploitation activities in their hands. According to the letter, the task force recommended the proposed consolidation for three basic reasons:

1. A single, streamlined and focused agency could best serve the imagery and mapping needs of a growing and diverse customer base across government;
2. The current disposition of imagery and mapping responsibilities does not allow one agency to exploit the tremendous potential of enhanced collection systems, digital processing technology and the prospective expansion in commercial imagery;
3. The revolution in information technology makes possible a symbiosis of imagery intelligence and mapping which can best be realized through more central management.[105]

Former intelligence (particularly CIA) officials and many within Congress questioned the wisdom of the plan. The primary concern was that, as a result of the transfer of NPIC personnel from the CIA to the DOD, imagery support for national policy-makers would suffer in order to support the requirements of military commanders. However, although the opposition was unable to block the creation of the new agency, the Senate Select Committee on Intelligence did persuade the Senate Armed Services Committee to amend the legislation creating the NIMA to stipulate that the DCI would retain tasking authority over national imagery systems and that the Secretary of Defense needed to obtain the DCI's concurrence before appointing the NIMA director or else note the DCI's lack of concurrence to the president. In addition, the Senate Armed Services Committee agreed to the modification of the National Security Act to state explicitly NIMA's responsibility to provide intelligence for national policymakers.*[106]

NIMA came into being as projected on October 1, 1996, incorporating all the elements mentioned in the late-November statement as well as the Office of Imagery Analysis of the CIA's Directorate of Intelligence and the Defense Dissemination Program Office. It would also eventually absorb some activities of the CIA's Office of Development and Engineering. The consolidation thus created an agency with around 9,000 personnel—about 2,000 imagery interpreters and about 7,000 individuals from the Defense Mapping Agency.[107]

Like the CIO, NIMA was chartered by both a DOD directive—5105.60 of October 11, 1996, "National Imagery and Mapping Agency (NIMA)"—and a DCI directive. To emphasize the fact that the organization "merges imagery, maps, charts and environmental data to produce . . . 'geospatial intelligence' [GEOINT]—the exploitation and analysis of imagery and geospatial information to describe, assess, and virtually depict physical features and geographically referenced activities of the earth," Director James Clapper sought to change NIMA's name to the National Geospatial-Intelligence Agency (NGA), an alteration authorized by the 2004 National Defense Authorization Bill, which took effect when President George W. Bush signed the legislation on November 24, 2003.[108]

Because of the geographical distance between the agencies absorbed by NGA, significant portions of the agency were not at first colocated but could be found at the Washington Navy Yard (NPIC's location); in Washington, D.C. (various offices of DIA); in Bethesda, Maryland (DMA headquarters and hydrographic production); in St. Louis, Missouri (DMA aerospace production); and at Fort Belvoir, Virginia (the main ground station for the NRO's electro-optical satellites). NGA began moving into new headquarters at Fort Belvoir in January 2011. When established, NIMA had about 9,000 employees, but there were plans to reduce that number to 7,500. Today, there are 16,000 NGA employees who largely work either at the Fort Belvoir or St. Louis facilities. The agency's 2013 fiscal year budget request was $4.8 billion.[109]

The current charter for NGA is a July 29, 2009, DOD directive that specifies NGA's mission, organization, and management, as well as the responsibilities and functions of the NGA director. It outlines the director's forty-two responsibilities with regard to the production of GEOINT, GEOINT architecture and standards, GEOINT systems,

---

*There was also some concern about the proposed merger from DMA officials, who feared that their formal inclusion in the Intelligence Community might have a negative impact on their relationships with foreign nations that provided mapping information.

GEOINT training and education, GEOINT functional management and program management, and GEOINT international engagement. Those responsibilities include the requirements to
- Provide responsive GEOINT products, support, services, and information
- Manage GEOINT planning, collection, operations, analysis, production, and dissemination
- Establish and/or consolidate DOD geospatial data collection requirements and, as appropriate, task or coordinate collection with the DOD components to collect and provide these data
- Monitor and evaluate the performance of the DOD components having GEOINT planning, programming, tasking, collection, processing, production, exploitation, dissemination, and retention functions in meeting national and military GEOINT requirements and, to the extent authorized by the DNI, monitor the performance of other U.S. government departments having GEOINT functions
- Serve as the DOD lead for GEOINT standards and prescribe, mandate, and enforce standards and architectures related to GEOINT and GEOINT tasking, collection, processing, exploitation, and international geospatial information
- Establish end-to-end and system architectures related to GEOINT in compliance with National and Defense Information Infrastructure guidance and standards
- Develop, acquire, and field GEOINT-related systems
- Serve as the program manager for the National Geospatial-Intelligence Program within the National Intelligence Program
- Establish and maintain international GEOINT agreements and arrangements with foreign governments and international organizations.[110]

The NGA's organizational structure comprises the five directorates shown in Figure 2.8. The Analysis Directorate is home to imagery interpreters focused on particular nations and regions as well as on specific topics such as warning, global navigation, and counterproliferation. They "provide geospatial intelligence and services to policymakers, military decision makers, and tailored support to civilian federal agencies and international organizations."[111] The key function of the Source Operations & Management Directorate is carried out by its Source Operations Group. The group is responsible, like the CIO's Central Imagery Tasking Office and the Committee on Imagery Requirements and Exploitation in earlier years, for the tasking of U.S. imagery satellites: sorting through requests for imagery coverage of targets from government, military, and civilian organizations, determining which satellites to employ against specific targets, and selecting the altitude and angle from which to obtain imagery.[112]

Beyond being renamed and reorganized since its 1996 establishment, the agency has also evolved in a number of ways. The development of high-resolution commercial imagery satellites has made it possible for the NGA to procure significant quantities of imagery through commercial channels that in the past could be obtained only from the NRO's classified systems. As a result, NGA has become a significant factor in the financial health of commercial imagery firms.[113] The terrorist attacks of 9/11 led to NGA's assuming a homeland security role through the provision of detailed

FIGURE 2.8 Organization of the National Geospatial-Intelligence Agency

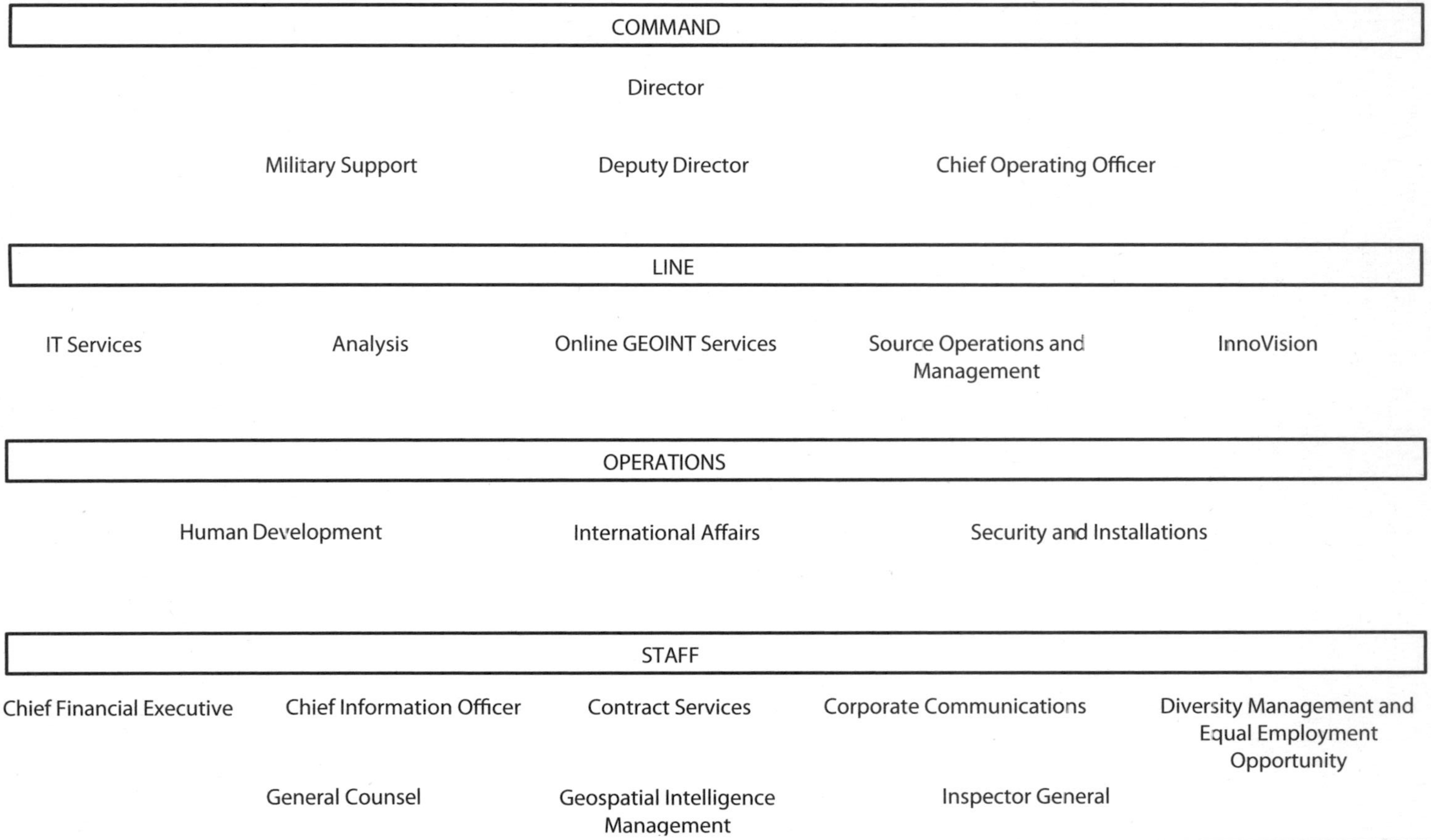

COMMAND

Director

Military Support

Deputy Director

Chief Operating Officer

LINE

IT Services

Analysis

Online GEOINT Services

Source Operations and Management

InnoVision

OPERATIONS

Human Development

International Affairs

Security and Installations

STAFF

Chief Financial Executive

Chief Information Officer

Contract Services

Corporate Communications

Diversity Management and Equal Employment Opportunity

General Counsel

Geospatial Intelligence Management

Inspector General

Source: NGA.

maps and imagery to federal, state, and local agencies, including the Department of Homeland Security, Secret Service, involved in securing facilities and protecting domestic activities, such as those designated as National Special Security Events (e.g., Super Bowls, presidential inaugurations, Major League Baseball All-Star Games, and Olympic Games in the United States). NGA products have also been employed in disaster-relief operations in the United States and abroad, including operations dealing with the devastation of Hurricane Katrina in the southeastern United States, the 2004 Asian tsunami, the 2006 earthquake in Pakistan, the 2010 oil spill in the Gulf of Mexico, and the series of tornadoes that hit the U.S. Midwest and South in 2014. In the latter case NGA provided damage assessments of close to 2,000 structures across fifty locations throughout Arkansas, Mississippi, Oklahoma, Alabama, and Kansas. The assessments included evaluation of damage to key infrastructure, roads, and communication networks. Furthermore, in addition to providing products NGA has deployed personnel within the United States and abroad to provide on-site assistance to support such security and disaster-relief operations, as well as military operations. Beginning in the spring of 2014, NGA began providing support to U.S. and other organizations involved in analyzing or combating the Ebola outbreak in Africa. NGA provided maps that showed the location of treatment facilities and others that illustrated the impact of the terrain on the spread of the disease.[114]

In 2006, legislation added ground-based photography, including still photographs and full-motion video, to NGA's overhead imagery products (from satellites and aircraft) in NGA's library. One objective was to provide information to soldiers about what facilities looked like from their perspective on the ground rather than just aerial views. In a 2010 assessment, the Senate Select Committee on Intelligence concluded that such "products should be better incorporated into NGA data holdings."[115]

NATIONAL UNDERWATER RECONNAISSANCE OFFICE

In 1969, as a result of an agreement between the CIA and U.S. Navy, an underwater counterpart to the NRO, the National Underwater Reconnaissance Office (NURO), was established, with Secretary of the Navy John Warner as its first director. The office served as a means of managing the conduct of submarine intelligence missions and the exploitation of their product. Those missions involved the recovery of sunken submarines (the Soviet K-129), taping of underwater Soviet communications cables (the IVY BELLS program), ocean floor mapping (under a program designated DESKTOP), and imagery and SIGINT collection from submarines (a program at one time designated the Special Navy Control Program). Some of the covert U.S. submarine operations were allegedly conducted in the territorial waters of non–Soviet bloc nations, sometimes with consent, including Sweden, to test the nation's defenses. The existence of the NURO was classified at its inception and remains so today.[116]

Notes

1. See R. Harris Smith, *OSS: The Secret History of America's First Central Intelligence Agency* (Berkeley: University of California Press, 1981); Bradley Smith, *The Shadow Warriors: O.S.S. and the Origins of the C.I.A.* (New York: Basic Books, 1983); Joseph E. Persico, *Roosevelt's Secret War:*

FDR and World War II Espionage (New York: Random House, 2001); Douglas Waller, *Wild Bill Donovan: The Spymaster Who Created the OSS and Modern American Espionage* (New York: Free Press, 2011).

2. Harry S. Truman, "Executive Order 9621: Termination of the Office of Strategic Services and Disposition of Its Functions," September 20, 1945, in *Emergence of the Intelligence Establishment*, ed. C. Thomas Thorne Jr. and David S. Patterson (Washington, DC: U.S. Government Printing Office, 1996), 44–46.

3. Thomas F. Troy, *Donovan and the CIA: A History of the Establishment of the Central Intelligence Agency* (Frederick, MD: University Publications of America, 1981), 325–349.

4. U.S. Congress, House Permanent Select Committee on Intelligence, *Compilation of Intelligence Laws and Executive Orders* (Washington, DC: U.S. Government Printing Office, 1983), 7; Michael Warner and Kevin C. Ruffner, "The Founding of the Office of Special Operations," *Studies in Intelligence* 44, no. 2 (Summer 2000).

5. Lawrence Houston, "Memorandum for the Director, Subject: CIA Authority to Perform Propaganda and Commando Type Functions," September 25, 1947.

6. Ronald Reagan, "Executive Order 12333: United States Intelligence Activities," December 4, 1981, *Federal Register* 46, no. 235 (December 8, 1981): 59941–59954, at 59950.

7. On the transition from DCI to DNI, see Jeffrey T. Richelson, ed. National Security Archive Electronic Briefing Book 144, *From Director of Central Intelligence to Director of National Intelligence*, August 12, 2005, http://www2.gwu.edu/~nsarchiv/NSAEBB/NSAEBB144.

8. Ronald Kessler, *Inside the CIA: Revealing the Secrets of the World's Most Powerful Spy Agency* (New York: Pocket Books, 1992), xxvii, 114; Walter Pincus, "CIA Struggles to Find Identity in a New World," *Washington Post*, May 9, 1994, A1, A9; Greg Miller and Julie Tate, "Since Sept. 11 CIA's Focus Has Taken Lethal Turn," *Washington Post*, September 2, 2011, A1, A6; Office of the Director of National Intelligence, *FY 2013 Congressional Budget Justification*, Vol. 1: *National Intelligence Program Summary*, 2012, 133–134; U.S. Congress, House Committee on Appropriations, *Department of Defense Appropriations for 1995*, pt. 3 (Washington, DC: U.S. Government Printing Office, 1994), 784.

9. CIA, "DNI and D/CIA Announce Establishment of the National Clandestine Service," October 13, 2005, https://www.cia.gov/news-information/press-releases-statements/press-release-archive-2005/pr10132005.html; CIA, Fact Sheet, "Creation of the National HUMINT Manager," October 13, 2005; CIA, "Transcript of Interview of Major General Michael E. Ennis, USMC, Deputy Director of the National Clandestine Service for Community HUMINT, by WTOP Radio J. J. Green, February 28, 2007," March 7, 2007, https://www.cia.gov/news-information/press-releases-statements/press-release-archive-2007/february-28-2007.html; Jose A. Rodriguez Jr., with Bill Harlow, *Hard Measures: How Aggressive CIA Actions After 9/11 Saved American Lives* (New York: Threshold, 2012), 146–148; Matthew M. Aid, *Intel Wars: The Secret History of the Fight Against Terror* (New York: Bloomsbury, 2012), 231.

10. Jeffrey T. Richelson, *The Wizards of Langley: Inside the CIA's Directorate of Science and Technology* (Boulder, CO: Westview, 2001), 223–224, 224n.

11. Kessler, *Inside the CIA*, 18; David Wise, *Nightmover: How Aldrich Ames Sold the CIA to the KGB for $4.6 Million* (New York: HarperCollins, 1995), 77n; Robert Dreyfuss, "Left Out in the Cold," *Mother Jones* (January–February 1998): 52–84; Vernon Loeb, "Gathering Intelligence Nuggets One by One," *Washington Post*, April 19, 1999, A17; Massimo Calabresi, "When the CIA Calls," *Time*, June 6, 2001, http://www.time.com; Dana Priest, "CIA Plans to Shift Work to Denver," *Washington Post*, May 6, 2005, A21.

12. David Wise, *The American Police State* (New York: Vintage, 1976), 188; U.S. Congress, Senate Select Committee to Study Governmental Operations with Respect to Intelligence Activities, *Final Report, Book I: Foreign and Military Intelligence* (Washington, DC: U.S. Government Printing Office, 1976), 439; Ralph E. Cook, "The CIA and Academe," *Studies in Intelligence* (Winter 1983): 33–42, at 38–39; Kessler, *Inside the CIA*, 18.

13. Dreyfuss, "Left Out in the Cold."

14. U.S. Congress, Senate Select Committee to Study Government Operations with Respect to Intelligence Activities, *Final Report, Book I: Foreign and Military Intelligence*, 439; Cook, "The CIA and Academe," 38; Wise, *The American Police State*, 189.

15. CIA, *Appendices to Guidance for CIA Activities Within the United States and Outside the United States*, November 30, 1982, 30; Dana Priest, "CIA Is Expanding Domestic Operations," *Washington Post*, October 23, 2002, A2.

16. "The CIA's Darkest Secrets," *U.S. News & World Report*, July 4, 1994, 34–37; Duane R. Clarridge, *A Spy for All Seasons: My Life in the CIA* (New York: Scribner, 1997), 8, 49, 180, 193; Walter Pincus, "Justice Asked to Investigate Leaks by Ex-CIA Officials," *Washington Post*, July 19, 1997, A16.

17. Robert Parry, "CIA Manual Producers Say They're Scapegoats," *Washington Post*, November 15, 1984, A28; "Aides Disciplined by CIA Are Irked," *New York Times*, November 15, 1984, A1, A8; Clarridge, *A Spy for All Seasons*, 190; Barton Gellman, "Broad Effort Launched After '98 Attacks," *Washington Post*, December 19, 2001, A1, A26; Bob Woodward, "Secret CIA Units Playing a Central Combat Role," *Washington Post*, November 18, 2001, A1, A16; Andrew Koch, "Covert Warriors," *Jane's Defence Weekly*, March 29, 2003, 22–27; Gary Bernsten and Ralph Pezzullo, *Jawbreaker: The Attack on bin Laden and Al Qaeda: A Personal Account by the CIA's Key Field Commander* (New York: Crown, 2005), 82–83, 191, 211, 236, 268, 275–276; Greg Miller and Julie Tate, "CIA's Global Response Staff Emerging from Shadows After Incidents in Libya and Pakistan," www .washingtonpost.com, December 26, 2012; Mark Mazzetti, *The Way of the Knife: The CIA, a Secret Army, and a War at the Ends of the Earth* (New York: Penguin Press, 2013), 258; private information.

18. Loch Johnson, "Smart Intelligence," *Foreign Policy* 89 (Winter 1992): 53–69; Clarridge, *A Spy for All Seasons*, 322–329; Robert Suro, "2 Terrorist Groups Set Up U.S. Cells, Senate Panel Is Told," *Washington Post*, May 14, 1997, A4; Vernon Loeb, "Where the CIA Wages Its New World War," *Washington Post*, September 9, 1998, A17; James Risen, "C.I.A. Unit on bin Laden Is Understaffed, a Senior Official Tells Lawmakers," *New York Times*, September 15, 2004, A18; Mark Mazzetti, "CIA Closes Unit Focused on Capture of bin Laden," *New York Times*, July 4, 2006, A4; "DCI Counterterrorist Center," www.cia.gov/terrorism.ctc.html (accessed October 5, 2001); Douglas Waller, "At the Crossroads of Terror," *Time*, June 30, 2002, http://www.time.com; Miller and Tate, "Since September 11"; Henry A. Crumpton, *The Art of Intelligence: Lessons from a Life in the CIA's Clandestine Service* (New York: Penguin Press, 2012), 121–167.

19. Office of Inspector General, CIA, *Report on CIA Accountability with Respect to the 9/11 Attacks*, June 2005, http://www.fas.org/irp/cia/product/oig-911.pdf, v; Office of Inspector General, CIA, *Inspection Report of the DCI Counterterrorist Center Directorate of Operations*, August 2001, iii; Greg Miller, "The CIA's Enigmatic al-Qaeda Hunter," *Washington Post*, March 25, 2013, A1, A16. Also see Paul Pillar, *Intelligence and Foreign Policy: Iraq, 9/11, and Misguided Reform* (New York: Columbia, 2011), 287–291; National Commission on Terrorist Attacks upon the United States, "Interview—Winston Wiley," November 25, 2003 (available at www.cryptome.org).

20. Miller and Tate, "CIA Shifts Focus to Killing Targets," www.washingtonpost.com, September 1, 2011, http://www.washingtonpost.com/world/national-security/cia-shifts-focus-to -killing-targets/2011/08/30/gIQA7MZGvJ_story.html.

21. Johnson, "Smart Intelligence"; David Wise, *Molehunt: The Search for Traitors That Shattered the CIA* (New York: Random House, 1992), 298–299; Angelo Codevilla, *Informing Statecraft: Intelligence for a New Century* (New York: Free Press, 1992), 155; CIA, "Spotlight on CIA's Centers," June 26, 2014, https://www.cia.gov/news-information/featured-story-archive/2014 -featured-story-archive/spotlight-on-cias-centers.html.

22. George Tenet, with Bill Harlow, *At the Center of the Storm: My Years at the CIA* (New York: HarperCollins, 2007), 283, 453; CIA, "CIA Launches New Counterproliferation Center," August 18, 2010, https://www.cia.gov/news-information/press-releases-statements/press-release-2010 /cia-launches-new-counterproliferation-center.html. For more on the CPD, see Valerie Plame Wilson, *Fair Game: How a Top CIA Agent Was Betrayed by Her Own Government* (New York: Simon & Schuster, 2008), 60–62, 352–354 (afterword by Laura Rozen).

23. CIA, "Restructuring in the DS&T," June 1996; Jeffrey T. Richelson, "CIA's Science and Technology Gurus Get New Look, Roles," *Defense Week*, August 19, 1996, 6; "The CIA's Darkest Secrets"; Barry G. Royden, "CIA and National HUMINT: Preparing for the 21st Century," *Defense Intelligence Journal* 6, no. 1 (Spring 1997): 15–22. On the CIA's handling of Yurchenko, see Ronald Kessler, *Escape from the CIA: How the CIA Won and Lost the Most Important KGB Spy Ever to Defect to the U.S.* (New York: Pocket Books, 1991).

24. Richelson, *The Wizards of Langley*, 39–73.

25. Ibid., 72–73, 195–196, 271–276; CIA, "DNI and D/CIA Announce Establishment of DNI Open Source Center," November 8, 2005, http://www.cia.gov.

26. Peter Eisler, "Post 9/11 CIA Has Shifted Its Emphasis for Foreign Ops," www.abcnews.com, October 27, 2008, http://abcnews.go.com/Technology/story?id=6116942.

27. Richelson, *The Wizards of Langley*, 114, 121, 165–172; Directorate of Science and Technology, *Central Intelligence Agency* (Washington, DC: CIA, n.d.), unpaginated.

28. Private information; Central Intelligence Agency, "DS&T Realignment Overview," n.d.

29. CIA, "Careers & Internships—Science, Engineering & Technology Positions," March 26, 2013, https://www.cia.gov/careers/opportunities/science-technology.

30. CIA, "Office of Global Access," n.d.; private information.

31. *Office of SIGINT Operations* (Washington, DC: CIA, n.d.), unpaginated; Desmond Ball, *A Suitable Piece of Real Estate: American Installations in Australia* (Sydney: Hale & Iremonger, 1980), 73; CIA document fragment, released under the Freedom of Information Act; Kessler, *Inside the CIA*, 168; Devlin Barnett, "CIA Aided Program to Spy on U.S. Phones," *Wall Street Journal*, March 11, 2015, A1, A10.

32. CIA, "Office of Technical Readiness" (Intellipedia entry), n.d.; private information.

33. Directorate of Science and Technology, *Central Intelligence Agency*; Thomas Powers, *The Man Who Kept the Secrets: Richard Helms and the CIA* (New York: Knopf, 1979), 340n38; U.S. Congress, Senate Select Committee to Study Governmental Operations with Respect to Intelligence Activities, *Final Report, Book IV: Supplementary Detailed Staff Reports on Foreign and Military Intelligence* (Washington, DC: U.S. Government Printing Office, 1976), 101; William Colby, with Peter Forbath, *Honorable Men: My Life in the CIA* (New York: Simon & Schuster, 1978), 336; Robert Gates, *From the Shadows: The Ultimate Insider's Story of Five Presidents and How They Won the Cold War* (New York: Simon & Schuster, 1996), 154; Ronald Kessler, *The CIA at War: Inside the Secret Campaign Against Terror* (New York: St. Martin's Press, 2003), 137; Vernon Loeb, "After-Action Report," *Washington Post Magazine*, February 27, 2000, 7ff.; CIA, *Devotion to Duty: Responding to the Terrorist Attacks of September 11, 2001*, 2010, https://www.cia.gov/library/publications/additional-publications/devotion-to-duty/15601-pub-FINAL-web.pdf, 37–39; Staff Writer, CRS, National Photographic Interpretation Center, "Senior Officials Team Up to Highlight Accomplishments," *NPIC Update*, April 1994, 2, 11.

34. Directorate of Science and Technology, "DS&T Organizational Changes," February 23, 2009.

35. Gary H. Anthes, "Cloak & Dagger IT," www.computerworld.com (accessed February 6, 2001); Rick E. Yannuzzi, "In-Q-Tel: A New Partnership Between the CIA and the Private Sector," *Defense Intelligence Journal* 9, no. 1 (Winter 2000); Daniel G. Dupont "The Company's Company," *Scientific American* (August 2001): 26–27; Anne Laurent, "Raising the Ante," *Government Executive* (June 2002): 34–44; Steve Johnson, "Spy Agency Fund Targets Bay Area Technology," www.mercurynews.com, June 12, 2012, http://www.mercurynews.com/ci_20826233/spy-agency-fund-targets-bay-area-technology-cia-nsa-surveillance-clandestine.

36. Anthes, "Cloak & Dagger IT"; Neil King Jr., "Small Start-Up Helps the CIA to Mask Its Moves on the Web," *Wall Street Journal*, February 12, 2001, B1, B6; "Battery Startup Gains CIA Funding," www.eetimes.com, November 13, 2006, http://www.eetimes.com/document.asp?doc_id=1164333.

37. Johnson, "Spy Agency Fund Targets Bay Area Technology"; David H. Petraeus, "CIA's Directorate of Science & Technology, In-Q-Tel and the Private Sector," *Intelligencer* 19, no. 2 (Summer/Fall 2012): 7–10; Debra Werner, "How the CIA Grows Tech," www.defensenews.com, June 17, 2013, http://mobile.defensenews.com/article/306170026. An in-depth examination of In-Q-Tel is Michael E. Belko, *Government Venture Capital: A Case Study of the In-Q-Tel Model* (Wright-Patterson Air Force Base, OH: Air Force Institute of Technology, 2004).

38. Directorate of Science and Technology, Organization Chart, 2012.

39. Robin Wright and Ronald J. Ostrow, "Webster Unites Rival Agencies to Fight Drugs," *Los Angeles Times*, August 24, 1989, 1, 27; Michael Isikoff, "CIA Creates Narcotics Unit to Help in Drug Fight," *Washington Post*, May 28, 1989, A12; CIA, *A Consumer's Guide to Intelligence*, 1993, 18; CIA, "The DCI Crime and Narcotics Center (CNC)," www.cia.gov (accessed June 1, 2006).

40. "The Office of Transnational Issues (OTI)," www.cia.gov (accessed June 1, 2006); Jonathan D. Clemente, "CIA's Medical and Psychological Analysis Center (MPAC) and the Health of Foreign Leaders," *International Journal of Intelligence and Counterintelligence* 19, no. 3 (Fall 2006): 385–427; Jonathan D. Clemente, "In Sickness and in Health," *Bulletin of the Atomic Scientists* (March–April 2007): 38–44, 66.

41. CIA, "The Information Operation Center Analysis Group (IOC/AG)," January 23, 2013, https://www.cia.gov/offices-of-cia/intelligence-analysis/organization-1/ioc-ag.html; CIA, "The Counterintelligence Center Analysis Group," January 23, 2013, https://www.cia.gov/offices-of -cia/intelligence-analysis/organization-1/cic-ag.html.

42. "Former CIA Director Gen. David Petraeus to Speak at Duke," *Duke Today*, August 22, 2013, http://m.today.duke.edu/2013/08/petreaus; Liz Klimas, "C.I.A. Puts an End to 'Unnecessary, Wasteful and Totally Out of Place' Climate Change Unit," www.theblaze.com, November 21, 2012, http://www.theblaze.com/stories/2012/11/21/c-i-a-puts-an-end-to-unnecessary-wasteful -and-totally-out-of-place-climate-change-unit; CIA, "CIA Opens Center on Climate Change and National Security," September 25, 2009, https://www.cia.gov/news-information/press-releases -statements/center-on-climate-change-and-national-security.html.

43. CIA, "The Office of Terrorism Analysis," January 23, 2013, https://www.cia.gov/offices -of-cia/intelligence-analysis/organization-1/ota.html; Rowan Scarborough, "CIA Exercise Reveals Consequences of Defeat," www.washingtontimes.com, December 21, 2006, http://www .washingtontimes.com/news/2006/dec/21/20061221-122441-5208r.

44. "Bush Approved Covert Action by CIA to Halt Spread of Arms," *Los Angeles Times*, June 21, 1992, A20; Bill Gertz, "CIA Creates Center to Monitor Arms," *Washington Times*, December 3, 1991, A5; "Intelligence Will Be Key in Proliferation Battle," *Defense Week*, December 9, 1991, 3; Johnson, "Smart Intelligence"; Barbara Starr, "Woolsey Tackles Proliferation as the Problem Gets Worse," *Jane's Defence Weekly*, November 13, 1993, 23; CIA, *A Consumer's Guide to Intelligence*, 1995, 18.

45. U.S. Congress, House Permanent Select Committee on Intelligence, *Intelligence Authorization for Fiscal Year 1998*, pt. 1, Report 105-135 (Washington, DC: U.S. Government Printing Office, 1997), 25.

46. Vernon Loeb, "CIA Is Stepping Up Attempts to Monitor Spread of Weapons," *Washington Post*, March 21, 2001, A15; Douglas F. Garthoff, *Directors of Central Intelligence as Leaders of the U.S. Intelligence Community, 1946–2005* (Washington, DC: Center for the Study of Intelligence, 2005), 189; CIA, "The CIA Weapons, Intelligence, Nonproliferation, and Arms Control Center," January 23, 2013.

47. CIA, "The Office of Collection Strategies and Analysis (CSAA)," March 18, 2013, https://www.cia.gov/offices-of-cia/intelligence-analysis/organization-1/csaa.html.

48. Victor Marchetti and John Marks, *The CIA and the Cult of Intelligence* (New York: Knopf, 1974), 73–74; Commission on CIA Activities in the United States, *Report to the President* (Washington, DC: U.S. Government Printing Office, 1975), 91; Directorate of Administration, *Central*

Intelligence Agency (Washington, DC: CIA, n.d.), unpaginated; David Atlee Phillips, *Careers in Secret Operations: How to Be a Federal Intelligence Officer* (Frederick, MD: University Publications of America, 1984), 27.

49. Marchetti and Marks, *The CIA and the Cult of Intelligence*, 73–74; Jeffrey Lenorovitz, "CIA Satellite Data Link Study Revealed," *AW&ST*, May 2, 1997, 25–26; Arnaud de Borchgrave, "Space-Age Spies," *Newsweek*, March 6, 1978, 37; Commission on CIA Activities in the United States, *Report to the President*, 91–92; Directorate of Administration, *Central Intelligence Agency*; R. James Woolsey, "National Security and the Future Direction of the Central Intelligence Agency," Address to the Center for Strategic and International Studies, Washington, D.C., July 18, 1994; John Hudson, "Satellite Images of the CIA's Secret bin Laden Training Facility," www.thewire.com, October 9, 2012, http://www.thewire.com/global/2012/10/satellite-images-capture-cias-secret-bin-laden-training-facility/57771; Charlie Savage, "Arms Cache Most Likely Kept in Texas by the C.I.A.," *New York Times*, May 5, 2014, A14; Allen Thomson, *The U.S. Army Camp Stanley Storage Activity and the CIA Midwest Depot*, April 29, 2014, http://www.fas.org/irp/eprint/midwest.pdf.

50. Greg Miller, "CIA Plans Major Reorganization and a Focus on Digital Espionage," www.washingtonpost.com, March 6, 2015, http://www.washingtonpost.com/world/national-security/cia-plans-major-reorganization-and-a-focus-on-digital-espionage/2015/03/06/87e94a1e-c2aa-11e4-9ec2-b418f57a4a99_story.html; CIA, "Unclassified Version of March 6, 2015 Message to the Workforce from CIA Director John Brennan: Our Agency's Blueprint for the Future," March 6, 2015, https://www.cia.gov/news-information/press-releases-statements/2015-press-releases-statements/message-to-workforce-agencys-blueprint-for-the-future.html.

51. Miller, "CIA Plans Major Reorganization and a Focus on Digital Espionage"; Sean D. Naylor, "From Cyberspace to Africa, the CIA Looks to Fights of the Future," www.foreignpolicy.com, March 6, 2015, http://foreignpolicy.com/2015/03/06/from-cyberspace-to-africa-the-cia-looks-to-fights-of-the-future; Brian Bennet, "CIA Is Creating Digital Spying Division," *Los Angeles Times*, March 7, 2015, A1, A8.

52. Bennett, "CIA Is Creating Digital Spying Division."

53. *Report to the Secretary of State and the Secretary of Defense by a Special Committee Appointed Pursuant to Letter of 28 December 1951 to Survey Communications Intelligence Activities of the Government*, June 13, 1952, 47–48; National Cryptologic School (NCS), *On Watch: Profiles from the National Security Agency's Past 40 Years* (Fort Meade, MD: NCS, 1986), 17.

54. Harry S. Truman, "Memorandum for the Secretary of State and the Secretary of Defense, Subject: Communications Intelligence Activities," October 24, 1952; Center for Cryptologic History, *The Origins of NSA* (Fort Meade, MD: National Security Agency, n.d.), 4.

55. Walter Bedell Smith, "Proposed Survey of Communications Intelligence Activities," December 10, 1951; *Report to the Secretary of State and the Secretary of Defense by a Special Committee*, 118; U.S. Congress, Senate Select Committee to Study Governmental Operations with Respect to Intelligence Activities, *Final Report, Book III: Foreign Policy and Military Intelligence* (Washington, DC: U.S. Government Printing Office, 1976), 736; National Security Agency (NSA)/Central Security Service, *NSA/CSS Manual 22-1* (Fort Meade, MD: NSA, 1986), 1.

56. *United States Government Organization Manual* (Washington, DC: U.S. Government Printing Office, 1957), 137; "Washington Firm Will Install Ft. Meade Utilities," *Washington Post*, January 7, 1954, 7; "U.S. Security Aide Accused of Taking Secret Documents," *New York Times*, October 10, 1954, 1, 33.

57. NSCID No. 6, "Signals Intelligence," February 17, 1972; Department of Justice, *Report on CIA-Related Electronic Surveillance Activities* (Washington, DC: Department of Justice, 1976), 77–78; National Security Agency, "Oversight of Signals Intelligence Activities," January 8, 2007, http://www.aclu.org.

58. NSCID No. 6, "Signals Intelligence."

59. Ibid.

60. Department of Defense Directive 5100.20, "The National Security Agency and the Central Security Service," January 26, 2010, 3–4.

61. Department of Defense Directive O-3600.1, Subject: Information Operations, August 14, 2006; William B. Black Jr., "Thinking Out Loud About Cyberspace," *Cryptolog* (Spring 1997): 1–4.

62. U.S. Congress, Senate Select Committee to Study Governmental Activities with Respect to Intelligence Activities, *Final Report, Book I,* 354; U.S. Congress, House Committee on Appropriations, *Department of Defense Appropriations for 1983*, pt. 3 (Washington, DC: U.S. Government Printing Office, 1981), 824–829; Leslie Maitland, "FBI Says New York Is a 'Hub' of Spying in U.S.," *New York Times*, November 14, 1981, 12; Patrick E. Tyler and Bob Woodward, "FBI Held War Code of Reagan," *Washington Post*, December 13, 1981, 1, 27; Committee on National Security Systems, CNSSI No. 1200, *National Information Assurance for Space Systems Used to Support National Security Missions*, Cryptome, May 7, 2014, http://cryptome.org/2014/08/cnssi-1200-space.pdf.

63. Office of the Director of National Intelligence, *FY 2013 Congressional Budget Justification*, Vol. 1: *National Intelligence Program Summary*, 2012, 133.

64. James Bamford, *The Puzzle Palace: A Report on NSA, America's Most Secret Agency* (Boston: Houghton Mifflin, 1982), 157; Melvin Laird, *National Security Strategy of Realistic Deterrence: Secretary of Defense Melvin Laird's Annual Defense Department Report, FY 1973* (Washington, DC: U.S. Government Printing Office, 1977), 135; "Central Security Service Insignia," National Security Agency, November 21, 2012, https://www.nsa.gov/about/central_security_service/css_insignia.shtml (accessed December 8, 2012).

65. "NSA's Organizational Designations," *Top Level Telecommunications*, January 10, 2014, http://electrospaces.blogspot.gr/2014/01/nsas-organizational-designations.html; Matthew Aid, "Organizational Structure of the National Security Agency," MatthewAid.com, August 15, 2013, http://www.matthewaid.com/post/58339598875/organizational-structure-of-the-national-security; "Inside TAO: Documents Reveal Top NSA Hacking Unit," *Spiegel Online*, December 29, 2013, http://www.spiegel.de/international/world/the-nsa-uses-powerful-toolbox-in-effort-to-spy-on-global-networks-a-940969.html; Matthew M. Aid, "The NSA's New Code Breakers," www.foreignpolicy.com, October 15, 2013, http://foreignpolicy.com/2013/10/15/the-nsas-new-code-breakers.

66. Department of Defense Instruction S-5100.43, "Defense Special Missile and Astronautics Center (DEFSMAC)," April 27, 1964; Richard L. Bernard, Center for Cryptologic History, *A Brief 50-Year (1960–2010) History of the Defense Special Missile and Aerospace Center (DEFSMAC)*, 2011; Department of Defense, "Defense Special Missile and Astronautics Center: Organization, Mission, and Concept of Operations," September 27, 1982, 1; National Security Agency, "FOIA J9347-98," June 15, 1998; James Bamford, *Body of Secrets: Anatomy of the Ultra-Secret National Security Agency, from the Cold War Through the Dawn of a New Century* (New York: Doubleday, 2001), 503; Department of Defense Instruction S-5100.43, "Defense Special Missile and Aerospace Center (DEFSMAC)," September 24, 2008. Also see Jeffrey T. Richelson, ed., National Security Archive Electronic Briefing Book 489, *DEFSMAC: NSA's Missile and Space Launch Reporting Center*, October 21, 2014, http://nsarchive.gwu.edu/nukevault/ebb489.

67. [Deleted], DEFSMAC, *DEFSMAC-A Community Asset* (1964–1989), n.d., 2.

68. Raymond Tate, "Worldwide C3I and Telecommunications," Harvard University Center for Information Policy Resources Seminar on C3I, 1980, 30.

69. Bamford, *Body of Secrets*, 503–504.

70. National Security Agency, "Information Assurance," September 11, 2014, https://www.nsa.gov/ia; *JASON Global Grid Study* (Arlington, VA: MITRE Corporation, 1992).

71. Seymour Hersh, *"The Target Is Destroyed": What Really Happened to Flight 007 and What America Knew About It* (New York: Random House, 1986), 52–53, 67–69; "NSOC Opens New Information Protect Cell (IPC)," *NSA Newsletter*, July 1997, 7.

72. "Utah Data Center," Wikipedia, http://en.wikipedia.org/wiki/Utah_Data_ Center (accessed May 16, 2014); James Bamford, "The NSA Is Building the Country's Biggest Spy Center (Watch What You Say)," www.wired.com, March 15, 2012, http://www.wired.com /2012/03/ff_nsadatacenter/all.

73. Tom Bowman and Scott Shane, "Espionage from the Front Lines," *Baltimore Sun*, December 8, 1995, 1A, 20A–21A; D. B. Grady, "Inside the Secret World of America's Top Eavesdropping Spies," www.theweek.com, April 12, 2012, http://theweek.com/articles/476482/inside-secret -world-americas-eavesdropping-spies.

74. Interview with Roy Burks, North Potomac, Maryland, May 10, 1999; interview with Robert Singel, Great Falls, Virginia, February 25, 1999.

75. Interview with Robert Phillips, Rosslyn, Virginia, June 4, 1999; Burks interview; Bob Woodward, *VEIL: The Secret Wars of the CIA, 1981–1987* (New York: Simon & Schuster, 1987), 313; Thomas R. Johnson, *American Cryptology During the Cold War, 1945–1989, Book III: Retrenchment and Reform, 1972–1980* (Fort George G. Meade, MD: National Security Agency, 1998), 229, 231.

76. Burks interview; Phillips interview.

77. Philip Wilan, "NSA Spies on Italians from Roof of US Embassy in Rome, Magazine Reports," www.pcworld.com, December 6, 2013, http://www.pcworld.com/article/2070480/nsa -spies-on-italians-from-roof-of-us-embassy-in-rome-magazine-reports.html.

78. Woodward, *VEIL*, 314; National Security Agency, "vPCS to Deploy to 80 SCS Sites," August 13, 2010.

79. Grady, "Inside the Secret World."

80. Douglas Aircraft Corporation, *Preliminary Design for an Experimental World-Circling Spaceship* (Santa Monica, CA: Douglas Aircraft Corporation, 1946); Robert L. Perry, *Origins of the USAF Space Program, 1945–1946* (Washington, DC: Air Force Systems Command, June 1962), 42–43; Jeffrey T. Richelson, *America's Secret Eyes in Space: The U.S. KEYHOLE Spy Satellite Program* (New York: Harper & Row, 1990), 31–64.

81. Jeffrey T. Richelson, "Undercover in Outer Space: The Creation and Evolution of the NRO, 1960–1963," *International Journal of Intelligence and Counterintelligence* 13, no. 3 (Fall 2000): 301–344.

82. Carl Berger, *The Air Force in Space: Fiscal Year 1961* (Washington, DC: Air Force Historical Liaison Office, 1966), 41–42; Secretary of the Air Force Order 115.1, "Organization and Functions of the Office of Missile and Satellite Systems," August 31, 1960; Secretary of the Air Force Order 116.1, "The Director of the SAMOS Project," August 31, 1960.

83. Richard M. Bissell Jr. to Allen W. Dulles, August 8, 1961; Donald Welzenbach, "Science and Technology: Birth of a Directorate," *Studies in Intelligence* 30, no. 2 (Summer 1986): 13–26; Albert Wheelon, "CORONA: A Triumph of American Technology," in *Eye in the Sky: The Story of the CORONA Spy Satellites*, ed. Dwayne Day, John S. Logsdon, and Brian Latell (Washington, DC: Smithsonian Institution Press, 1998), 29–47.

84. Richelson, "Undercover in Outer Space."

85. Frederic C. E. Oder, James C. Fitzpatrick, and Paul E. Worthman, *The CORONA Story* (Washington, DC: NRO, 1987), 69; Richelson, "Undercover in Outer Space."

86. U.S. Congress, Senate Select Committee on Intelligence, *S. 2198 and S. 421 to Reorganize the United States Intelligence Community* (Washington, DC: U.S. Government Printing Office, 1993), 18.

87. Jeffrey T. Richelson, "Restructuring the NRO: From the Cold Wars' End to the 21st Century," *International Journal of Intelligence and Counterintelligence* 15, no. 4 (Winter 2002–2003): 496–535.

88. Commission on Roles and Capabilities of the United States Intelligence Community, *Preparing for the 21st Century: An Appraisal of U.S. Intelligence* (Washington, DC: U.S. Government Printing Office, 1996), 132; "NRO Organization," Briefing Slide for Presentation of Frank

Strickland, NRO, to National Military Intelligence Association, November 19, 1997; Government Accountability Office, "Defense Space Activities: Management Actions Are Needed to Better Identify, Track, and Train Air Force Space Personnel," September 21, 2006, http://www.gao .gov/products/GAO-06-908, 9; Glenn A. Gaffney, "Changes to DS&T Support to NRO," December 3, 2010; Office of the Director of National Intelligence, *FY 2013 Congressional Budget Justification*, Vol. 1: *National Intelligence Program Summary*, 2012, 133–134.

89. Department of Defense Directive TS-5015.23, Subject: National Reconnaissance Office, March 27, 1964; Cyrus Vance, Deputy Secretary of Defense, and W. F. Raborn, Director of Central Intelligence, "Agreement for Reorganization of the National Reconnaissance Program," August 13, 1965; U.S. Congress, House of Representatives, Report 14-186, *Intelligence Authorization Act for Fiscal Year 2010*, June 26, 2009, 36.

90. James R. Clapper Jr., Director of National Intelligence, and Robert M. Gates, Secretary of Defense (signatories), "Memorandum of Agreement between the Secretary of Defense and the Director of National Intelligence concerning the National Reconnaissance Office," September 21, 2010.

91. Department of Directive 5105.23, Subject: National Reconnaissance Office (NRO), June 28, 2011.

92. Ibid., 20.

93. Ibid., 8.

94. National Reconnaissance Office, "Transforming the NRO Enterprise," April 2008, http://www.nro.gov.

95. Admiral David Jeremiah et al., *Report to the Director, National Reconnaissance Office: Defining the Future of the NRO for the 21st Century, Executive Summary*, August 26, 1996, https://www .fas.org/irp/nro/jeremiah.htm, 24; Richelson, "Restructuring the NRO," 523, 530.

96. National Reconnaissance Office, Director's Note 2006-03, "National Reconnaissance Office Enterprise System Engineering," January 26, 2006.

97. National Reconnaissance Office, "Deputy Director for National Support (DDNS)," n.d.

98. National Reconnaissance Office, "Mission Statement, NRO," June 14, 1996; National Reconnaissance Office, Director's Note 2006-07, "Organizational Announcement," March 17, 2006.

99. Robert M. Gates, DCI, *Statement on Change in CIA and the Intelligence Community*, April 1, 1992, 28; Imagery Blue Ribbon Task Force, *Restructuring the Imagery Community: Recommendations of the Blue Ribbon Task Force*, 1992, 14.

100. H.R. 4165, "National Security Act of 1992," 1992; S. 2198, "Intelligence Reorganization Act of 1992," 1992.

101. Garthoff, *Directors of Central Intelligence as Leaders*, 209; Department of Defense Directive 5105.26, "Central Imagery Office," May 6, 1992; Central Imagery Office, Briefing Slides (16M7906/2/HC), "CIO," 2–3; Director of Central Intelligence Directive 2/9, "Management of National Imagery Intelligence," June 1, 1992.

102. Central Imagery Office, Briefing Slides (16M7906/2/HC), "CIO," 2.

103. Statement of John Deutch Before Senate Select Committee on Intelligence, April 26, 1995, 8–9.

104. "DCI Plans a National Imagery Agency," *Communiqué* (August 1995): 1, 8; CIA, "National Imagery and Mapping Agency Proposed to Congress," November 28, 1995, https://www.cia .gov/news-information/press-releases-statements/press-release-archive-1995/pr112895.html; "Creating the National Imagery and Mapping Agency," *Studies in Intelligence* 42, no. 1 (Spring 1998).

105. CIA, "National Imagery and Mapping Agency Proposed to Congress."

106. U.S. Congress, Senate Select Committee on Intelligence, *Special Report of the Senate Select Committee on Intelligence, January 4, 1995 to October 3, 1996* (Washington, DC: U.S. Government Printing Office, 1997), 7–8.

107. National Imagery and Mapping Agency, "National Imagery and Mapping Agency Established," Department of Defense, October 1, 1996, http://www.defense.gov/Releases/Release.aspx

?ReleaseID=1055; William S. Cohen and George J. Tenet, "Memorandum of Agreement Between the Secretary of Defense and the Director of Central Intelligence on the National Imagery and Mapping Agency," October 16, 1998.

108. National Geospatial-Intelligence Agency, "NGA History," https://www.nga.mil/About/History/Pages/default.aspx(accessed July 14, 2006); James R. Clapper Jr., *NGA Today*, n.d.

109. Clapper, *NGA Today*, 5; Missy Frederick, "Murrett Striving for Right Balance at NGA," *Space News*, November 20, 2006, http://spacenews.com/murrett-striving-right-balance-nga, 12; Marjorie Censer, "Letitia A. Long Becomes First Female Director of NGA," www.washingtonpost.com, August 10, 2010, http://www.washingtonpost.com/wp-dyn/content/article/2010/08/09/AR2010080905771.html; "NGA Staff Begin Moving into Massive New Headquarters," *Space News*, January 24, 2011, http://spacenews.com/nga-staff-begin-moving-massive-new-headquarters, 9; Office of the Director of National Intelligence, *FY 2013 Congressional Budget Justification*, Vol. 1: *National Intelligence Program Summary*, 133; Nicholas J. C. Pistor, "Government Intelligence Agency Plans New Facility in St. Louis Area, Could Leave City," *St. Louis Post-Dispatch*, June 4, 2014, http://www.stltoday.com/news/local/metro/government-intelligence-agency-plans-new-facility-in-st-louis-area/article_5722180d-1835-53f3-9315-3571e2be610d.html.

110. DoD Directive 5105.60, "National Geospatial Intelligence Agency (NGA)," July 29, 2009, 1–7. The NGA director's responsibilities are also noted in DOD Instruction 3115.15, "Geospatial Intelligence (GEOINT)," December 6, 2011.

111. "The National Geospatial Intelligence Agency (NGA): Major Organizations," www.nga.mil (accessed July 17, 2006); NGA, "How We Are Organized," www.nga.mil (accessed March 4, 2010).

112. Richelson, *America's Secret Eyes in Space*, 252–256. On the directorate's other functions, see Gene Reich, "Source Directorate Expands," *Pathfinder* (May–June 2006): 9–10; NGA, "How We Are Organized."

113. Rick Akers, "Next View Will Provide the Vision and Solutions for New U.S. Policy on Commercial Imagery," *Pathfinder* (July–August 2003): 8–9; Frank Morring Jr., "NIMA Sets Big Jump in Commercial Imagery Buy," *AW&ST*, September 9, 2002, 30–31.

114. Robert Wall, "Homeland Security Demands Strain NIMA's Resources," *AW&ST*, February 3, 2003, 37; Warren Ferster, "NGA Embraces Disaster Relief Role, Collaboration," *Space News*, November 7, 2005, 17; Katherine S. Whitaker, "NGA Supports Gulf of Mexico Spill Remediation Efforts," *Pathfinder* (July–August 2010): 12–13; Sara Fiske, "Evolution of the NGA Deployer Program—Providing GEOINT Forward," *Pathfinder* (September–October 2011): 15–17; Moyan W., "Expeditionary Operations Directorate Contributes to GEOINT Evolution," *Pathfinder* (January–February 2011): 14; NGA, "NGA History," n.d.; Al Schulte, "Integrated Intel Focus of NGA-Hosted Workshop," *Pathfinder* (Fall 2013): 22; NGA, "NGA Responds to FEMA's Call for Assistance in Tornado Aftermath," May 7, 2014, https://www1.nga.mil/MediaRoom/LeadingStories/Pages/NGARespondstoFEMA'sCAllforAssistanceinTornadoAftermath.aspx; Paul Frommet, "NGA Supports Ebola Crisis," *Pathfinder* (Fall 2014): 20–24.

115. Missy Frederick, "Bill Allows NGA to Provide Ground-Based Photography," *Space News*, June 19, 2006, 11; Walter Pincus, "Senators Seek Better Defense Imagery," *Washington Post*, June 6, 2006, A13; U.S. Congress, Senate Select Committee on Intelligence, *Intelligence Authorization Act for Fiscal Year 2010*, Report 111-223, July 19, 2010, 60–61.

116. Sherry Sontag and Christopher Drew, with Annette Lawrence Drew, *Blind Man's Bluff: The Untold Story of American Submarine Espionage* (New York: Public Affairs, 1998), 83; Norman Polmar and Michael White, *Project AZORIAN: The CIA and the Raising of the K-129* (Annapolis, MD: Naval Institute Press, 2007), 58–59. In response to a September 2013 Freedom of Information Act request, the CIA refused to confirm or deny the existence of the office.

3

DEFENSE DEPARTMENT INTELLIGENCE: THE DEFENSE INTELLIGENCE AGENCY

In addition to the national intelligence organizations within the Department of Defense (DOD), discussed in Chapter 2, the department has its own agency, the Defense Intelligence Agency (DIA), which operates in support of the Secretary of Defense, Joint Chiefs of Staff (JCS), and military commanders and participates in the production of national intelligence. DIA contains within it organizations for the collection of human intelligence (HUMINT), for technical collection, and for intelligence production.

HISTORY AND CURRENT CHARTER

The Defense Intelligence Agency was one manifestation of the trend toward centralization that began with the Dwight D. Eisenhower administration, which saw a need in the late 1950s for consolidation of the military services' general (that is, all nonsignals, nonoverhead, nonorganic) intelligence activities. That belief was, according to one analyst, a by-product of the missile gap controversy of the time: "Faced with the disparate estimates of Soviet missile strength from each of the armed services which translated into what have been called self-serving budget requests for weapons of defense, the United States Intelligence Board created a Joint Study Group in 1959 to study the intelligence producing agencies."[1]

The Joint Study Group, chaired by Lyman Kirkpatrick of the Central Intelligence Agency (CIA), concluded that there was considerable overlap and duplication in defense intelligence activities, resulting in a maldistribution of resources. As a consequence the "overall direction and management of DOD's total intelligence effort becomes a very difficult if not impossible task. Indeed, the fragmentation of efforts creates 'barriers' to the free and complete interchange of intelligence information among the several components of the Department of Defense." The study group recommended that the Secretary of Defense "bring the military intelligence organization within the Department of Defense into full consonance with the concept of the Defense Reorganization Act of 1958."[2]

How to do this was a subject of controversy. The study group's report noted a suggestion that a single intelligence service be established for the entire Defense Department, reporting directly to the Secretary of Defense. The group concluded, however, that "on balance it would be unwise to attempt such an integration of intelligence activities so long as there are military services having specialized skills and knowledge."[3]

Despite the group's conclusions, in a February 8, 1961, memorandum to the Joint Chiefs of Staff, Secretary of Defense Robert McNamara observed, "It appears that the most effective means to accomplish the recommendation of the Joint Study Group would be the establishment of a Defense Intelligence Agency which may include the existing National Security Agency [NSA], the intelligence and counterintelligence functions now handled by the military departments, and the responsibilities of the Office of the Assistant Secretary, Special Operations."[4] McNamara requested that the JCS provide, within thirty days, a defense intelligence agency concept, a draft DOD directive establishing such an agency, and an implementation schedule. He also provided some preliminary guidelines for developing a plan that included complete integration of all defense intelligence requirements and elimination of duplication in intelligence collection and production. On February 9, the Joint Staff suggested that the JCS direct the staff to develop a concept of the DIA consistent with McNamara's memo and placing the new agency under the control of the JCS.[5]

On March 2, 1961, the Joint Chiefs sent McNamara their recommendations, including an organizational concept for the establishment of a Military Intelligence Agency under the JCS. On April 3, McNamara requested advice on several basic issues concerning the proposed agency, including its placement under the JCS and its specific functions. Ten days later, the JCS approved a Joint Staff draft memorandum for the Secretary of Defense. The memo justified placing the new agency under the JCS on the grounds that the DOD Reorganization Act of 1958 specifically assigned the Joint Chiefs responsibility for strategic planning and operational direction of the armed forces, and the fulfillment of such responsibilities required control of appropriate intelligence assets. In contrast, placing the agency in the Office of the Secretary of Defense would "concentrate military intelligence assets at a level above, and isolated from, the organization charged with strategic planning and operational direction of the armed forces."[6]

The Joint Staff memo also suggested placing the NSA under the authority of the JCS. In addition, it argued that total integration of all military intelligence activities might not be a sound concept. It recommended charging the agency director with closely monitoring any intelligence activities left with the services and authorizing the director to eliminate duplication, review all service intelligence programs and budgets, and assign priorities to military intelligence collection requirements.[7]

The agency that resulted was a compromise, although it came close to the JCS's vision. On July 5, 1961, McNamara decided to establish a DIA reporting to the Secretary of Defense through the JCS. On August 1, he did so through DOD Directive 5105.21 and made the DIA responsible for (1) organization, direction, management, and control over all DOD intelligence resources assigned to or included within the DIA; (2) review and coordination of those DOD intelligence functions retained by or assigned to the military departments; (3) supervision over the execution of all approved plans, programs, policies, and procedures for intelligence functions not assigned to the DIA; (4) exercise of maximum economy and efficiency in allocation and management of DOD intelligence resources; (5) response to priority requests by the United States Intelligence Board; and (6) fulfillment of the intelligence requirements of major DOD components. As a consequence of DIA's creation, the Joint Staff Director for Intelligence (J2) was abolished, as was the Office of Special Operations, the small intelligence arm of the Secretary of Defense.[8]

On December 16, 1976, the Secretary of Defense issued a new charter for the DIA (i.e., a new version of 5105.21), limiting the JCS's operational control over the DIA to (1) obtaining the intelligence support required to perform the Joint Chiefs' statutory function and assigned responsibilities, and (2) ensuring the availability of adequate, timely, and reliable intelligence support to the unified and specified commands. In all other matters, the Director of the DIA would report to the Secretary of Defense through the Assistant Secretary of Defense for Intelligence. The DIA's mission was also stated more concisely as being "to satisfy, or to ensure the satisfaction of, the foreign intelligence requirements of the Secretary of Defense, the Joint Chiefs of Staff, DOD components and other authorized recipients, and to provide the military intelligence contribution to national intelligence."[9]

About five months later, on May 19, 1977, the Secretary of Defense signed a new version of DIA's charter that slightly altered the agency's organization and administration. Under the revised charter, the director would report to the Secretary of Defense and the Chairman of the JCS. In addition, the Director of the DIA would be under the operational control of the JCS for purposes of (1) obtaining intelligence support required to perform the statutory and assigned responsibilities of the JCS, and (2) ensuring adequate, timely, and reliable intelligence support for the unified and specified commands. Staff supervision of the DIA would be exercised by the Assistant Secretary of Defense (ASD) for Command, Control, Communications, and Intelligence (C3I) with respect to resources and by the ASD for International Security Affairs with respect to policy.[10]

In February 1990, the ASD (C3I) established a steering group of senior officers in DOD intelligence organizations to review the readiness of the defense intelligence system in the face of the changing international security environment. The effort, which would be labeled "Defense Intelligence in the 1990s," was intended to identify the potential risks and opportunities expected to emerge in the 1990s. In June 1990, the group prepared a fairly brief TOP SECRET/CODEWORD draft interim executive summary of issues raised by the participants in the effort and appended a list of "issues," suggesting alternative ways of addressing individual topics.[11]

The draft summary was intended as a forerunner of the final review. However, because of a shift in thinking at the senior level of the DOD, no final review study was completed, although the results of the study were presented to the Secretary of Defense, Deputy Secretary of Defense, and other senior defense officials between September and December 1990. On December 14, 1990, Under Secretary of Defense Donald J. Atwood issued a memorandum titled "Strengthening Defense Intelligence Functions," which noted that senior-level DOD officials had reviewed the department's intelligence activities and requested detailed plans to achieve a variety of objectives, including strengthening "the role and performance of the Defense Intelligence Agency in the intelligence requirements, production, and management processes."[12]

The memo resulted in the March 15, 1991, ASD (C3I) *Plan for Restructuring Defense Intelligence.* With respect to the DIA, the plan called for
- Strengthening the role of DIA as a combat support agency
- Improving the quality of the DIA product by streamlining and reconfiguring DIA to improve its estimative capability with emphasis on quality analysis and reporting strategically important intelligence
- Strengthening DIA's management of intelligence production and analysis
- Assigning DIA responsibility for performing and overseeing basic encyclopedic data production
- Establishing within DIA a capability to validate threat information to ensure an independent intelligence input to the acquisition process
- Establishing within DIA a Policy Issues Office to improve support to the Office of the Secretary of Defense.[13]

Much of the effort to implement these and other aspects of the plan took place during the administration of Lieutenant General James R. Clapper Jr., who became DIA director in November 1991. Nearly six years after the March 1991 plan was laid out, a new DIA directive reflecting many of the DIA's new responsibilities was finally issued. The directive itself was produced only after several years of effort reflected partially in organizational changes. DOD Directive 5105.21, "Defense Intelligence Agency," of February 18, 1997, replaced the 1977 directive, which had been modified only slightly in 1978. That directive was ultimately replaced by the March 18, 2008, version of 5105.21.[14]

The new directive or charter specified twelve categories of responsibilities or functions, with over seventy specific responsibilities and functions for the DIA director. The director's responsibilities and functions include
- All-source intelligence analysis: providing all-source intelligence to joint task force and combatant commanders, as well as to defense planners and national security policymakers
- Human intelligence: centrally managing the DOD-wide HUMINT enterprise as well as conducting DIA HUMINT collection activities worldwide
- Joint Staff intelligence: operating the Joint Staff Intelligence Directorate (J2) to respond to the direct intelligence support requirements of the Chairman of the JCS and the Secretary of Defense
- Technical collection: conducting integrated planning, coordination, and execution of DOD measurement and signature intelligence (MASINT) and designated technical collection management activities
- Counterintelligence (CI) and security: performing assigned CI functions as well as Sensitive Compartmented Information (SCI) policy implementation, security clearance adjudication, and facility accreditation
- International engagement: entering into military and military-related intelligence agreements and arrangements with foreign governments and other entities
- Resource management: developing and managing the DIA Military Intelligence Program resources and capabilities, the General Defense Intelligence Program

PHOTO 3.1   DIA center, Bolling AFB, Washington, D.C. *Photo credit:* DOD.

(GDIP), and the DIA portion of the Foreign Counterintelligence Program (FCIP) as an element of the National Intelligence Program.*[15]

OVERVIEW

DIA Headquarters (formerly the Defense Intelligence Analysis Center) is located at the Joint Base Anacostia-Bolling in Washington, D.C. The DIA also occupies a twin-tower building in Reston, Virginia, and operates a Joint-Use Intelligence Facility near Charlottesville, Virginia, managed by the DIA Field Support Activity–Rivanna Station. The activity's chief serves "as the focal point for DIA interactions with the National Ground Intelligence Center (NGIC), the University of Virginia, and the greater Charlottesville community." About eight hundred DIA employees work at the facility. The DIA employs approximately 17,000 people, a significant majority of whom are civilians. Thousands of the agency's personnel are located around the world in over 142 countries and 240 locations. Included are personnel deployed to combat areas (including Afghanistan and Iraq), to the headquarters of combat commands, and at defense attaché offices. Its fiscal year 2013 budget request was for $3.15 billion ($739 million of which was to cover overseas contingency operations).[16]

The DIA underwent several extensive reorganizations during the 1960s and 1970s; occasional changes made to DIA's organizational structure in subsequent years were not as sweeping as the earlier changes. From 1991 to 1993, however, the DIA underwent two extensive reorganizations designed to improve performance, deal with mandated personnel and budget reductions, adapt to changing international realities, and better coordinate military intelligence activities, as intended by the March 1991 *Plan for Restructuring Defense Intelligence.* The primary result of the latter was the creation of three DIA centers: the National Military Intelligence Collection Center, the

---

*The intelligence authorization act for 2014 and 2015 directed the merger of the FCIP into the GDIP. See U.S. Congress, House Permanent Select Committee on Intelligence, Report 113–463, *Intelligence Authorization Act for Fiscal Years 2014 and 2015*, May 27, 2014, 7.

FIGURE 3.1 Organization of the Defense Intelligence Agency

COMMAND ELEMENT

DIRECTOR

DEPUTY DIRECTOR

J2 Directorate for Intelligence

Joint Functional Component Command—
Intelligence, Surveillance, and Reconnaissance

STAFF ELEMENTS

Chief Financial Officer	General Counsel	Inspector General	Senior Enlisted Advisor	Equal Opportunity	National Intelligence University
Strategic Planning, Policy, and Performance Management		Senior Executive Management		Office of Corporate Communications

PRINCIPAL DIRECTORS

Principal Deputy Director Intelligence Integration

Principal Deputy Director Mission Services

DIRECTORATES

Directorate for Analysis

Directorate for Operations

Directorate for Science and Technology

REGIONAL CENTERS

Americas Center

Asia/Pacific Center

Defense Combating Terrorism Center

Europe/Eurasia Center

Middle East/Africa Center

Source: DIA.

National Military Intelligence Production Center, and the National Military Intelligence Systems Center. These centers were renamed after Clapper, who had established them, retired as DIA director.

In February 2003, DIA Director Lowell Jacoby approved yet another significant reorganization, which created the Director's Special Staff and seven primary operating elements: directorates for HUMINT, MASINT and technical collection, analysis, information management, external relations, intelligence support for the Joint Staff, and administration. Subsequent organizational changes included the creation of a human intelligence and counterintelligence center and the Defense Intelligence Operations Coordination Center.[17]

After assuming the director's job in July 2012, Lieutenant General Michael Flynn, who had become known for his critique of U.S. intelligence efforts in Afghanistan, instituted some significant changes in DIA, including the renaming of some directorates and the creation of a series of centers (as shown in Figure 3.1).

DIRECTORATE FOR OPERATIONS

The extent of DIA's involvement in human intelligence collection has varied over the years and involved both defense attaché collection and clandestine collection. In 1965 DIA became responsible for operating the set of military attachés that had been under the supervision of the military services. The Defense Attaché System involves the deployment of openly acknowledged attachés in embassies around the world, although their activities may extend beyond open contacts with foreign military officers (which, inter alia, allows them to provide information relevant to the production of biographic profiles of those officers), observation and photographing of parades and military exercises to which they are invited, and collection of open source or gray literature of interest to U.S. government intelligence analysts.*[18]

DIA's involvement in clandestine collection operations appeared to reach new heights with the creation of the Defense HUMINT Service (DHS) in the mid-1990s. During the early years of the Ronald Reagan administration, Deputy Under Secretary of Defense Richard Stillwell launched a number of initiatives to establish new organizations concerning intelligence and deception. One effort was code-named MONARCH EAGLE and envisioned, in response to military service dissatisfaction with CIA HUMINT collection priorities, creation of a DOD HUMINT agency. Congress vetoed the project, however, on the grounds that it would overlap with CIA HUMINT collection efforts and make control of sensitive operations more difficult.[19]

In December 1992, DOD Directive 5200.37, "Centralized Management of DoD Human Intelligence (HUMINT) Operations," centralized HUMINT decision making under a DOD HUMINT manager, established the concept of HUMINT support elements at combatant command, and required consolidation of HUMINT support services. In June 1993, in response to discussions with Director of Central Intelligence (DCI) James Woolsey during the annual Joint Review of Intelligence Programs, Deputy Secretary of Defense William J. Perry requested that the ASD (C3I) develop

---

*Various attaché collection activities are discussed in Chapter 11.

a plan to consolidate the separate HUMINT components of the Defense Department into a single organization.[20]

Perry approved the *Plan for the Consolidation of Defense HUMINT* in a November 2, 1993, memorandum. It specified that the ASD (C3I) should effect the consolidation of the service HUMINT operations in fiscal year 1997 to establish a Defense HUMINT Service. The plan also called for the Director of DIA to activate the DHS as a provisional organization, "using existing DOD GDIP HUMINT resources and structures within FY 1994," and "to establish a headquarters structure . . . followed by support, clandestine, and overt elements in accordance with [a] time-phased schedule."[21]

Thus, the DIA director was responsible for consolidating the DIA's small clandestine human intelligence activities with those of the Army, Navy, and Air Force. The most significant contribution in forming DHS came from the Army, specifically the Army Intelligence and Security Command's Foreign Intelligence Activity. The Army had maintained a significant clandestine HUMINT effort throughout the Cold War. Not surprisingly, significant opposition to creation of the DHS emanated from Army intelligence officials.[22]

In 1966 the Navy established an organization, first known as the Naval Field Operations Support Group and then as Task Force 157, to conduct clandestine and overt collection operations. That organization was disestablished in 1977. At the same time, Task Force 168 was tasked with overt collection. The Navy contribution to DHS came from the turnover of many of 168's assets, which the Office of Naval Intelligence had absorbed in 1993, as well as the contingent of clandestine case officers (intended to reach a maximum of one hundred) that the Navy began recruiting around 1993.[23]

The Air Force contribution to the DHS came from the transfer of personnel from the former Air Force Intelligence Command's 696th Intelligence Group. The group, which conducted clandestine collection activities and debriefed defectors, was previously known as the Air Force Special Activities Center, the 7612th Air Intelligence Group, and the 1127th Field Activities Group. The 1127th was described as "an oddball unit, a composite of special intelligence groups, who 'conducted worldwide operations to collect intelligence from human sources.' The men of the 1127th were con artists. Their job was to get people to talk—Russian defectors, North Vietnamese soldiers taken prisoner."[24]

By October 1995, when the DHS was declared to have achieved its initial operating capability, it had "over 2000 personnel in over 100 locations, including Washington, D.C." It was declared fully operational in September 1996. In the late 1990s, key components of the DHS's collection operation outside the Washington, D.C., area were the HUMINT Support Elements (HSE) located at the headquarters of the commanders in chief of the Atlantic, Southern, Pacific, European, and Central Commands and at the headquarters of the subunified commands in order to "improve support to the warfighters." The HSEs helped "commands develop and process HUMINT collection requirements and facilitate planning and coordination of DOD HUMINT support to operational commands." The HSEs also "develop[ed] exercise scenarios and Command contingency plans to ensure HUMINT support [was] planned, practiced, and available for deployment."[25]

Other DHS elements overseas included a large number of operating bases. The largest of the bases outside the United States at the turn of the century was Operations

Base Stuttgart with fifteen separate operating locations. It served as "the primary resource for DIA personnel deploying in support of Operation Joint Endeavor." The 2003 reorganization of DIA created a separate Directorate of Human Intelligence out of the HUMINT activities that had been contained in the Directorate for Intelligence Operations.[26]

Subsequent to that reorganization, a Strategic Support Branch was established within DHS. Similar to the service's HSEs, the branch's Strategic Support Teams (SSTs), originally known as HUMINT Augmentation Teams, were deployed into the field to support the intelligence requirements of HSEs in the field. SSTs engaged in a variety of collection missions in conjunction with members of U.S. Special Forces units, including prisoner interrogation, recruitment of foreign assets, and direct intelligence collection.[27]

Subsequent to the creation of the National Clandestine Service, the Defense HUMINT Service component of the DIA Directorate of Human Intelligence was disestablished, with much of its personnel and operations transferred to the NCS. Then, in July 2008, the Directorate of Human Intelligence, responsible for centrally directing and managing DIA HUMINT personnel, was merged into a larger DIA entity, the Defense Counterintelligence and Human Intelligence Center, when the latter was established via a memorandum from the Deputy Secretary of Defense. That memorandum simultaneously disestablished the Pentagon's controversial Counterintelligence Field Activity (CIFA) and transferred its non–law enforcement functions to DIA, resulting in the creation of a Directorate for Counterintelligence. A DOD instruction superseded the deputy secretary's memo and served as the center's charter.[28]

Along with the changes in DIA HUMINT following the dissolution of the DHS, there was also a resurgence of military service HUMINT. The Army Intelligence and Security Command established the Army Operations Activity, while the Office of Naval Intelligence established a HUMINT capability, which it subsequently transferred to the Naval Criminal Investigative Service. A Navy HUMINT capability was also developed in the Navy Expeditionary Combat Command. The Air Force established a small HUMINT unit, Detachment 6 at Wright-Patterson Air Force Base (AFB) in Ohio, which targeted secret Russian and Chinese aircraft programs; it became the Global Activities Squadron in June 2010. In addition, there was significant expansion of human intelligence within the U.S. Special Operations Command, particularly in relation to the special mission units of the Joint Special Operations Command.*

On April 20, 2012, Secretary of Defense Chuck Hagel signed a classified memorandum titled "Establishment of the Defense Clandestine Service [DCS]," reflecting the decision to establish a DOD counterpart to the NCS. Creation of the DCS followed the completion of a 2011 study by the Office of the Director of National Intelligence that the Defense Department's HUMINT efforts needed a more strategic focus, beyond the tactical targets of Iraq and Afghanistan, to include Iran, China, terrorism, and weapons of mass destruction. It also found the Pentagon sometimes negligent in promoting those serving as case officers.[29] The directive specified, "The DCS shall

---

*These efforts are discussed in Chapters 4 and 6.

be the primary DoD element authorized to conduct clandestine human intelligence (HUMINT) operations in response to high priority national-level intelligence requirements, as identified by the [Under Secretary of Defense (Intelligence)]." It also stated, "DCS shall operate worldwide, to including high [counterintelligence] threat and politically sensitive environments."[30]

The new service's personnel would include current DIA case officers then working out of American embassies under the supervision of the NCS; some assignments would also be shifted from military service and Special Forces intelligence units, including HUMINT personnel from Delta Force. Due to the creation of the DCS, the total number of DOD case officers was expected to grow "from several hundred to several more hundred"—from 300 to 600 according to one estimate and from 500 to 1,000 according to another.[31]

Subsequent to the announcement, the DCS faced resistance from Congress and various congressional oversight committees, based in part on DOD's past experience as a manager of clandestine collection operations. In June 2012, the National Defense Authorization Act for fiscal year 2013 contained a provision that prohibited DOD's devoting an increased number of personnel to the clandestine collection mission, called for a investigation into the costs involved, and asked the USD (I) to provide the congressional defense and intelligence committees with a report by February 1, 2013, that explained where case officers would be deployed and the schedule for deployments, certified that planned locations were feasible, and outlined the objectives established for each service, the U.S. Special Operations Command, and DIA for improving career management for case officers.[32]

The hurdle for DOD to clear was lowered substantially in the 2014 fiscal year authorization act. The act banned use of 50 percent of any funds authorized for the DCS until the Secretary of Defense had certified to several congressional committees that the DCS was designed "primarily to fulfill priorities of the Department of Defense that are unique to the Department of Defense or otherwise unmet; and provide unique capabilities to the intelligence community" and the secretary had "designed metrics" to ensure that the DCS would be employed to fulfill unique DOD or unmet requirements. The service was also supported in congressional testimony by Director of National Intelligence (DNI) James R. Clapper Jr.[33]

DIRECTORATE FOR SCIENCE AND TECHNOLOGY

In 2013 DIA Director Lieutenant General Michael Flynn created a Directorate for Science and Technology from the Directorate for MASINT and Technical Collection, established in 2003 via the merger of the Central MASINT Office (CMO) and the Defense Collection Group, both of which had been located in DIA's Directorate of Intelligence Operations. The DIA director's 2003 message to agency personnel stated that the directorate's primary mission would be "providing DoD and the larger Intelligence Community [IC] with invigorated MASINT and the DoD with expert collection management and specialized collection."[34]

Established in 1993, the Central MASINT Office had about forty employees in 1999. It was described as a "joint combat support directorate, [which] serves a dual role as the Director of Central Intelligence's Executive Agent for MASINT and as the

DoD MASINT Manager." Hence, its responsibilities were enumerated in both DCI Directive (DCID) 2/11 of December 1992 and a DOD directive.[35]

Subsequently, the DIA's MASINT and technical collection responsibilities were specified in the March 18, 2008, DOD directive concerning DIA. This directive specified that DIA and thus the Directorate for MASINT and Technical Collection were to

- Manage and implement Secretary of Defense and DNI plans and policies on designated technical collection matters
- Develop and implement standards, architectures, and procedures providing for integrated MASINT capabilities
- Develop, coordinate, and advocate defense intelligence positions on technical collection needs, capabilities, and strategies; collection management applications; and future collection systems and architectures
- Conduct research, development, testing, and evaluation activities to enhance technical collection
- Define and present consolidated DOD positions on technical intelligence collection issues to the USD (I) and Chairman of the Joint Chiefs of Staff; chair and operate a board or panel to support these processes
- Execute the tasking of DOD MASINT collection platforms to meet national-level collection requirements, with the exception of those activities assigned to the National Geospatial-Intelligence Agency, and conduct end-to-end oversight of tasked collection, processing, exploitation, reporting, and customer satisfaction
- Provide MASINT services of common concern for the IC on behalf of, and as assigned by, the DNI in coordination with the USD (I)
- Plan, enable, and conduct MASINT and technical intelligence collection training and operations in support of military operations, counterterrorism, counterinsurgency operations, and Homeland Defense
- Employ air-, ground-, and sea-based systems for close-access collection and persistent surveillance capabilities in support of the COCOMs
- Lead the DOD Special Communications Enterprise Office and manage the National Signatures Program
- Manage and implement technical identity management and biometrics plans and policies consistent with DOD, interagency, and international information-sharing activities.[36]

The CMO produced or participated in the production of documents such as the *U.S. Spectral Plan*, the *CMO MASINT Plan*, and *MASINT 2010: Planning the U.S. MASINT System for the 21st Century.*[37]

As a result of the reorganization of the directorate, the CMO became its MASINT Group, one element of which was the MASINT Operations Coordination Center (MOCC), formed in October 2000. The center serves as an around-the-clock unit that "provides continuous access to MASINT products, visibility of MASINT activities and the ability to optimally task sensors in time-sensitive situations to a diverse list of customers." The MOCC produces a Daily MASINT Summary that "provides critical intelligence to senior leadership and analysts alike," including current information on MASINT collections and the status of MASINT resources.[38]

The Collection Management Group (known as the Defense Collection Group prior to the 2003 reorganization) supported military forces and policymakers through placing intelligence requirements on collection agencies and resources, monitoring collection responses, and evaluating collection efforts in terms of reliability, efficiency, and cost. It also operated the twenty-four-hour Defense Collection Coordination Center (DCCC). During the Persian Gulf War, the DCCC acted as the executive agent for all national imagery in support of Desert Storm operations. All overhead imagery supporting the war effort was planned and developed at the coordination center. Other elements of the directorate included the Collection Operations Group, the Science and Technology Group, the National Signatures Program, and the Overhead Non-Imaging Infrared Group.[39]

One component established as part of the Directorate for Science and Technology is the Office of Development and Engineering. Its South Division has worked with the Air Force Technical Applications Center, responsible for the operation of nuclear detonation detection sensors.[40]

DIRECTORATE FOR ANALYSIS

The Directorate for Analysis was created by merging the Directorate for Analysis and Production with most of the elements of the Directorate for Policy Support. One focus of the directorate has been information warfare, and it has produced studies on computer and cybernetic warfare, electronic warfare, psychological operations, deceptions, and physical destruction of information systems. Support to joint warfare operations has been another focus, with the directorate providing all-source intelligence, including intelligence to U.S. Special Forces, with regard to the operational environment, physical vulnerability, geospatial analysis, denial and deception, and POW/MIA affairs.[41]

The directorate has also devoted considerable attention to counterterrorism analysis, producing terrorism assessments and studies for the Defense Department intelligence community. It has produced and maintained the DOD terrorism database, which contains more than 200,000 finished intelligence products on terrorist threats, groups, incidents, facilities, and personalities. It also reviews the terrorist threat to hundreds of Defense Department exercises and deployment operations annually and has been responsible for terrorism-related indications and warning and crisis support, as well as staffing the National Military Command Center Support Division Terrorism Desk. In addition, the directorate produces the daily *Defense Intelligence Terrorism Summary*, which "serves as the primary source of terrorism-related analysis and threat information for senior policymakers as well as commanders, security officers, and planners."[42]

Narcotics trafficking has also been a component of the directorate's analytical effort, and it has produced the *Interagency Assessment of Cocaine Movement*. It also deployed five all-source analysts to assist the Colombian government in counterdrug operations. Working with the FBI on Project DOMINANT CHRONICLE, the office translated and exploited over 160,000 documents. The directorate also has provided intelligence support to counternarcotics operations in Southeast and Southwest Asia.[43]

A major responsibility of the directorate is the production of various intelligence concerning foreign military forces, including the numbers, locations, and capabilities of current ground, naval, and air weapons systems; weapons research and development (R&D) efforts; command, control, and communications systems and facilities; and military doctrines, military exercises, and biographical sketches of foreign military leaders.

Other directorate personnel work for three centers located in Alabama, Maryland, and Virginia, respectively: the Missile and Space Intelligence Center (MSIC), the National Center for Medical Intelligence (NCMI), and the Underground Facility Analysis Center (UFAC).

In its 1991 report, *Intelligence Authorization Act, Fiscal Year 1992*, the House Permanent Select Committee on Intelligence strongly recommended that the "Armed Forces Medical Intelligence Center [and] the [Army] Missile and Space Intelligence Center . . . be transferred in their entirety to DIA and become designated Field Production Activities of DIA." By early 1992 the DIA had developed a plan for transfer of the centers to its control, and the transfer orders were issued.[44]

The Missile and Space Intelligence Center, located at Redstone Arsenal, near Huntsville, Alabama, has several hundred employees. In June 1956, the Special Security Office of the Army Ballistic Missile Agency was established to procure missile and space intelligence data for the agency's commander. To analyze the data, a Technical Intelligence Division (TID) was established. After all Army activities at Redstone Arsenal were consolidated into the Army Ordnance Missile Command (AOMC) in March 1958, the fifty-person TID was redesignated the Office of the Assistant Chief of Staff for Missile Intelligence (OACSMI). The AOMC was absorbed in 1962 by the Army Missile Command. The OACSMI was redesignated the Directorate of Missile Intelligence and in September 1970 became the Missile Intelligence Agency, which, on August 1, 1985, was redesignated the U.S. Army Missile and Space Intelligence Center with the mission to "produce worldwide scientific and technical intelligence (S&TI) on surface-to-air missiles, ballistic missile defense systems (both strategic and tactical), antitank guided missiles, antisatellite missiles, directed energy weapons, and relevant space programs/systems and command, control, communications, and computers."[45]

The center produces finished intelligence on the characteristics, performance, and operations of surface-to-air missiles, antitank guided missiles, ground-based antisatellite systems and short-range ballistic missiles. Its personnel evaluate the effectiveness of a weapon, how it works, its vulnerabilities, and how it can be neutralized. Surface-to-air missiles of concern to MSIC include both those fired by a single individual from the shoulder and longer-range air defense systems that can attack targets at a distance of hundreds of miles. The center also works with services that design air survivability equipment. In addition, it devotes significant attention to ground-based weapons that employ missiles or directed energy to attack satellites. Short-range ballistic missiles that can hit targets from tens to up to six hundred miles away represent another important focus of the center's research.[46]

In 1982 the Army's Medical Intelligence and Information Agency (MIIA), which provided medical intelligence for the entire defense community, was transformed into the Armed Forces Medical Intelligence Center (AFMIC). AFMIC's formation may have stemmed from dissatisfaction with the MIIA's performance. In 1981, discussions between Defense Audit Service personnel and the director of the General Defense Intelligence Program Staff indicated Intelligence Community concern about lack of adequate medical intelligence in Southwest Asian and Third World countries, "where casualties from unusual diseases and environmental conditions could occur."[47]

Medical intelligence is particularly vital in planning combat operations, particularly in areas significantly different from the United States in terms of environment and prevalence of disease. One aspect of AFMIC's activities involved producing general medical intelligence on health and sanitation, epidemiology, environmental factors, and military and civilian medical care capabilities, as in AFMIC's *Medical Capabilities Study: Democratic People's Republic of Korea*, *Asia: Health Impacts from Indonesian Earthquake and Tsunami*, and *Poisonous Snakes of Europe*. A second aspect of its work involved the production of medical, scientific, and technical intelligence concerning all basic and applied biomedical phenomena of military importance, including biological, chemical, psychological, and biophysical information. The AFMIC report titled *Medical Effects of Non-ionizing Electromagnetic Radiation—LASER* represents one example of that effort. AFMIC was also responsible for assessing foreign biomedical R&D and its impact on the physiological effectiveness of medical forces, as well as assessing the exploitation of foreign medical materiel obtained under the DOD Foreign Materiel Exploitation Program.[48]

More recent AFMIC activities, beginning in the fall of 2005, included production of nine articles for the *President's Daily Brief* and a weekly situation report for operational forces and policymakers that assessed the risk from avian flu. In addition, AFMIC analysts supported the Northern Command's Joint Task Force–Katrina as well as Joint Task Force–Burma, established after Cyclone Nargis hit Burma in May 2008. Center analysts also evaluated the threat from chlorine-enhanced improvised explosive devices in Iraq and the military implications of human performance modification.[49]

In January 2008, the Director of DIA requested that AFMIC be renamed the National Center for Medical Intelligence, since "AFMIC is, de facto, a national intelligence center." The memo noted, "AFMIC is the primary producer of medical intelligence for the U.S. government and provides finished, all-source medical intelligence on infectious disease risks, military and civilian medical systems, environmental health risks, medical science and technology, and, in partnership with domestic agencies, health protection." The DIA director also noted that such an action would be consistent with departmental actions establishing the National Air and Space Intelligence Center, National Media Exploitation Center (NMEC), and National Ground Intelligence Center.[50]

A 2009 DOD directive on NCMI described it as "the DOD lead activity for the production of medical intelligence" and stated, "It will prepare and coordinate integrated, all-source intelligence for the Department of Defense and other government and international organizations on foreign health and other medical issues to protect U.S. interests worldwide." The new name and the directive's language reflected the increased responsibility assigned to the center, specifically its homeland health protection mission. The additional responsibility dated back to 2006, when the Secretary of Defense instructed NCMI to include assessment of foreign human health threats to the homeland and began expanding its contacts with other agencies.[51]

About 150 people work in the four divisions of NCMI, headquartered at Fort Detrick, Maryland. The Infectious Disease Division's mission "is to understand the risk of every type of [endemic] infectious disease in every country," including avian flu, West Nile virus, anthrax, Ebola, and plague. As with other divisions, it produces, in addition to alerts and threat forecasts, a baseline product, in its case the Baseline Infectious Disease Risk Assessment. The Environmental Health Division monitors and assesses the risks from industrial chemicals, materials, and facilities around the world and produces the Environmental Health Risk Assessment. It also produces radiological hazard areas models. Some facilities are monitored on a twenty-four-hour basis. The Global Health Systems Division's responsibilities include understanding the medical capabilities of every nation, as well as the quality of its blood supply. Its baseline product is its Medical Capabilities Assessment. The Science and Technology Division is responsible for understanding each nation's medical defense capabilities against chemical, radiological, and nuclear weapons. NCMI/AFMIC products produced by its divisions include *Infectious Disease Risk Assessment: Afghanistan* (2005), *Baseline Infectious Disease Risk Assessment: Haiti* (2009), *Worldwide: New 2009-H1N1 Influenza Virus Poses Potential Threat to U.S. Forces* (2009), and *Haiti: Health Risks and Health System Impacts Associated with Large-Scale Earthquake* (2010).[52]

The Underground Facility Analysis Center, established in 1997 and located in Herndon, Virginia, is dedicated to "detecting, identifying, characterizing and assessing for defeat adversarial underground facilities or Hardened and Deeply Buried Targets." Such targets include command and control facilities, personnel relocation centers, weapons factories, and aircraft and submarine berthing sites. UFAC seeks to provide intelligence and related data to national policymakers, weapons developers, and military forces concerned about the nature of underground facilities or means to destroy them.[53]

While UFAC is located in the DIA Directorate for Analysis, the center is an interagency effort, sponsored by the Director of National Intelligence (and before that the Director of Central Intelligence). Agencies with personnel working at the center include the CIA, DIA (particularly from the Directorate for Science and Technology), the Defense Threat Reduction Agency, the NSA, the U.S. Geological Survey, and the U.S. Strategic Command Joint Intelligence Operations Center. In addition, personnel from the Air Force Technical Applications Center probably work there. When established, it had a staff of 20, but by 2009 that number had grown to 240.[54]

REGIONAL CENTERS

DIA Director Flynn's reorganization led to the establishment of five centers to support military forces: the Americas Center, Asia/Pacific Center, Europe/Eurasia Center, Middle East/Africa Center, and Defense Combating Terrorism Center. The centers, Flynn stated, have three key qualities: (1) fusing analysis and collection (which, based on experience from Iraq, Afghanistan, and elsewhere, is the most successful model for intelligence production and support), (2) flexibility, with team members no longer having to contend with organizational boundaries, and (3) integration, with each center having interagency embeds from across the Intelligence Community and close relationships with combatant commands and service intelligence centers. In September 2013, the Middle East/Africa Center was responsible for DIA assessments of the crisis in Syria in close coordination with the Central Command, Joint Staff, Office of the Secretary of Defense, Office of the Director of National Intelligence, and White House.[55]

The Defense Combating Terrorism Center is the result of the evolution of DIA's counterterrorist analytical effort. After the attack on the USS *Cole* in October 2000, DIA's counterterrorism office was transformed into the Joint Terrorism Analysis Center (JTAC); after the September 11, 2001, attacks, JTAC's mission was expanded, and it became the Joint Intelligence Task Force–Combating Terrorism (JITF-CT). In late September 2001, Secretary of Defense Donald Rumsfeld passed on to DCI George J. Tenet a proposal from DIA Director Admiral Thomas Wilson to establish an enhanced version of the task force. Wilson's presentation advertised the task force as supporting an aggressive, unified national counterterrorism campaign that would provide warning for force protection and homeland security and establish a single focused effort. Its mission would be to "generate actionable intelligence to drive planning and operations by exposing and exploiting terrorist vulnerabilities." The proposal depicted the task force as operating a fusion center receiving intelligence from the U.S. Intelligence Community, law enforcement, and individual allies and coalitions. The task force, Wilson suggested, should be located at DIA's Bolling AFB headquarters and have a personnel contingent of seven hundred people.[56]

Wilson's proposal was approved, and in 2012 the JITF-CT became the Defense Combating Terrorism Center. It consolidates national-level all-source terrorism-related intelligence and serves as the senior Defense Department representative within the Intelligence Community for threat warning, proposing and coordinating warnings to Defense Department organizations and combatant commands. Its analysts produce daily assessments of possible terrorist threats to Defense Department personnel and facilities. The task force also provides analytical support to interrogations, debriefings, HUMINT collection, and law enforcement, including to operations seeking to disrupt terrorist travel. Its exploitation branch has produced guidelines for personnel involved in interrogations and debriefing activities.[57]

DIRECTORATE FOR INTELLIGENCE

The Directorate for Intelligence (J2) serves as the Joint Chiefs of Staff intelligence directorate. It assesses, coordinates, produces, and integrates all-source current indications and warning intelligence for the Secretary of Defense, the Chairman of the JCS, and other DOD officials. It also produces a Morning Summary, daily Defense Intelligence Notices, and intelligence appraisals, as well as contributing to the *Worldwide Intelligence Review*.[58]

The J2 and the JCS Plans Directorate (J3) together operate the National Joint Operations and Intelligence Center (NJOIC), which "monitors the global situation on a continual basis and provides the [Chairman of the JCS] and [Secretary of Defense] a DoD planning and crisis response capability." The intelligence component of the NJOIC maintains an alert center that consists of the deputy director for intelligence, regional desks for the combatant commands, and representatives from each service intelligence component, the service SIGINT agencies, and the CIA. Customers include the president, Secretary of Defense, combatant commanders, deployed forces, the military services, and others.[59]

NATIONAL MEDIA EXPLOITATION CENTER

DCI George J. Tenet established the National Media Exploitation Center, located in Vienna, Virginia, in October 2002, with DIA becoming responsible for managing the center in January 2003. In 2005 DIA Director Lieutenant General Michael Maples placed the Directorate for Human Intelligence Document Exploitation and Translation Services Element, the Joint Document Exploitation Centers, and the Combined Media Processing Center–Qatar under NMEC's organization and management, thus combining both headquarters and field elements in one organization. In October 2008, NMEC became an independent center/directorate reporting directly to the DIA command element. As of 2013, it had over seven hundred personnel and a budget of over $100 million.[60]

As its name indicates, the center is responsible for extracting intelligence from both paper documents as well as electronic and visual media, particularly in support of military commanders and forces (such as the Joint Improvised Explosive Device Defeat Organization), but also in support of the Intelligence Community, law enforcement, and the Department of Homeland Security. In November 2005, NMEC received 1.2 terabytes of data for exploitation. By June 2008, the monthly average exceeded 25 terabytes. The NMEC reporting element produces more than 1,000 intelligence information reports per year, while the center's collection management element oversees the response to homeland security and Intelligence Community requirements.[61]

Notes

1. U.S. Congress, Senate Select Committee to Study Governmental Operations with Respect to Intelligence Activities, *Final Report, Book I: Foreign and Military Intelligence* (Washington, DC: U.S. Government Printing Office, 1976), 325; U.S. Congress, Senate Select Committee to Study Governmental Operations with Respect to Intelligence Activities, *Final Report, Book VI: Supplementary Reports on Intelligence Activities* (Washington, DC: U.S. Government Printing Office, 1976), 266. Official histories of DIA include DIA History Office, *Defense Intelligence Agency, 35 Years: A Brief History* (Washington, DC: Defense Intelligence Agency, 1996); DIA Office of Historical Research, *A History of the Defense Intelligence Agency* (Washington, DC: DIA, Office of Historical Research, 2007).

2. Secretary of Defense Robert McNamara, Memorandum for the President, Subject: The Establishment of a Defense Intelligence Agency, July 6, 1961, Declassified Document Reference System, 1986-000085; Joint Study Group, *The Joint Study Group Report on Foreign Intelligence Activities of the United States Government*, December 15, 1960, 31.

3. Joint Study Group, *The Joint Study Group Report on Foreign Intelligence Activities of the United States Government*, 23.

4. Robert McNamara, Memorandum for the Chairman, Joint Chiefs of Staff, Subject: Establishment of a Defense Intelligence Agency, February 8, 1961, National Archives and Records Administration (NARA), Record Group (RG) 218, CCS 2010 (Collection of Intelligence), 1960 Box, December 20, 1960 Folder, 1127.

5. Ibid., 1129; Joint Staff, DJSM-156-61, Memorandum for General Lemnitizer et al., Subject: Establishment of a Defense Intelligence Agency, February 8, 1961, NARA, RG 218, CCS 2010 (Collection of Intelligence), 1960 Box, December 20, 1960 Folder.

6. JCS 2031/166, Joint Chiefs of Staff Decision on JCS 2031/166, Memorandum by the Director, Joint Staff on Establishment of a Defense Intelligence Agency, April 13, 1961; JCS 2031/166,

"Memorandum by the Director, Joint Staff for the Joint Chiefs of Staff on Establishment of a Defense Intelligence Agency," April 7, 1961, with Enclosure ("Revised Draft Memorandum [April 12, 1961] for the Secretary of Defense, Subject: Establishment of a Defense Intelligence Agency [DIA]"), both in NARA, RG 218, CCS 2010 (Collection of Intelligence), 1960 Box, December 20, 1960 Folder.

7. "Revised Draft Memorandum for the Secretary of Defense, Subject: Establishment of a Defense Intelligence Agency (DIA)."

8. Historical Division, Joint Secretariat, JCS, *Development of the Defense Agencies*, November 3, 1978, B-1.

9. Ibid., B-2, citing Department of Defense Directive 5105.21, "Defense Intelligence Agency," December 16, 1976.

10. Historical Division, Joint Secretariat, JCS, *Development of the Defense Agencies*, B-2 to B-3.

11. William K. O'Donnell, Memorandum for W. M. MacDonald, Director, Freedom of Information and Security Review OASD (PA), Subject: Freedom of Information of Act (FOIA) Appeal—Jeffrey T. Richelson, July 31, 1991.

12. Ibid.; Assistant Secretary of Defense (Command, Control, Communications, and Intelligence), *Plan for Restructuring Defense Intelligence*, March 15, 1991, 1; Donald J. Atwood, Memorandum for Secretaries of the Military Departments et al., Subject: Strengthening Defense Intelligence Functions, December 14, 1990.

13. Assistant Secretary of Defense (Command, Control, Communications, and Intelligence), *Plan for Restructuring Defense Intelligence*, 3.

14. Department of Defense Directive 5105.21, "Defense Intelligence Agency," March 18, 2008.

15. Ibid.

16. Vernon Loeb, "Intelligence Priorities Set for Modern Battlefield," *Washington Post*, September 14, 2000, A33; Defense Intelligence Agency, DIA Release 10-04-02, "Phillip Roberts Selected to Head DIA Activity at Rivanna Station," April 22, 2010; DIA Public Affairs, "DIA Dedicates Facility to an American Patriot," May 2, 2014, http://www.dia.mil/News/Articles/tabid/3092/Article/8830/dia-dedicates-facility-to-an-american-patriot.aspx; Lieutenant General Ronald L. Burgess Jr., "The Defense Intelligence Agency: National Intelligence and Military Intelligence Are Indivisible," *Intelligencer* 18, no. 3 (Summer/Fall 2011): 11–16; "Locations," www.dia.mil (accessed January 16, 2014); Sarah Krouse, "Defense Intelligence Agency Signs Massive Reston Lease with Boston Properties," *Washington Business Journal*, September 20, 2010, http://www.bizjournals.com/washington/stories/2010/09/13/daily39.html; "Inside the Looking Glass, Watching the World with the Defense Intelligence Agency," *Washington's Top News*, October 21, 2013, http://wtop.com/j-j-green-national/2013/10/inside-the-looking-glass-watching-the-world-with-the-defense-intelligence-agency; "Inside the Looking Glass: The Staggering Pace of Change," *Washington's Top News*, October 24, 2013, http://wtop.com/j-j-green-national/2013/10/inside-the-looking-glass-the-staggering-pace-of-change; Office of the Director of National Intelligence, *National Intelligence Program, FY 2013 Congressional Budget Justification*, vol. 1, February 2012, 135, 137.

17. Vice Admiral Lowell E. Jacoby, Memorandum Subject: Agency Restructuring, February 11, 2003.

18. DIA Historical Research Office, *A History of the Defense Intelligence Agency*, 25.

19. Raymond Bonner, "Secret Pentagon Intelligence Unit Is Disclosed," *New York Times*, May 11, 1983, A13; Robert C. Toth, "U.S. Spying: Partnership Re-emerges," *Los Angeles Times*, November 14, 1983, 1, 12; Robert M. Lisch, *Implementing the DHS: View from the Leadership* (Washington, DC: Joint Military Intelligence College, 1995), 9; Margaret H. Livingstone, "Directorate for Intelligence Operations Renews Its Focus on the Fifth Thrust," *Communiqué* (June–July 2001): 12–14; "Professional Profiles: David L. Church," *Communiqué* (March–April 2008): 39–40.

20. Office of the Assistant Secretary of Defense (Command, Control, Communications, and Intelligence), *Plan for the Consolidation of Defense HUMINT*, 1993, 1. For an account of

the formation of the Defense HUMINT Service, see Jeffrey T. Richelson, "From MONARCH EAGLE to MODERN AGE: The Consolidation of U.S. Defense HUMINT," *International Journal of Intelligence and Counterintelligence* 10, no. 2 (Summer 1997): 131–164.

21. William J. Perry, Memorandum for Secretaries of the Military Departments et al., Subject: Consolidation of Defense HUMINT, November 2, 1993; Office of the Assistant Secretary of Defense (Command, Control, Communications, and Intelligence), *Plan for the Consolidation of Defense HUMINT*, 7.

22. Richelson, "From MONARCH EAGLE to MODERN AGE"; private information.

23. Jeffrey T. Richelson, "Task Force 157: The U.S. Navy's Secret Intelligence Service," *Intelligence and National Security* 11, no. 1 (January 1996): 106–145; Office of Naval Intelligence, "ONI-65 Mission Statement," n.d.

24. Benjamin Schemmer, *The Raid* (New York: Harper & Row, 1975), 26–27.

25. Nick Eftimiades, "DHS Stands Up," *Communiqué* (October 1995): 1, 10; Barbara Starr, "Military Network Now Handles DOD HUMINT," *Jane's Defence Weekly*, March 11, 1995, 13; Les Aspin, *Secretary of Defense Annual Report to the President and the Congress* (Washington, DC: U.S. Government Printing Office, 1995), 240; Howard E. Locke, "HUMINT Support Element Synchronizes Full-Spectrum Intelligence," *Communiqué* (July–August 2006): 24–25; David W. Becker, *Coming in from the Cold . . . War: Defense HUMINT Services Support to Military Operations Other Than War* (Fort Leavenworth, KS: Army Command and Control Staff College, 2000), 19.

26. Starr, "Military Network Now Handles DOD HUMINT"; Aspin, *Secretary of Defense Annual Report to the President and the Congress*, 240; "Director Visits DHS Element," *Communiqué* (September 1996): 35.

27. Barton Gellman, "Secret Unit Expands Rumsfeld's Domain," www.washingtonpost.com, January 23, 2005; Josh White and Barton Gellman, "Defense Espionage Unit to Work with CIA," www.washingtonpost.com, January 25, 2005, A3; Barton Gellman, "Controversial Pentagon Espionage Unit Loses Its Leader," *Washington Post*, February 13, 2005, A8; "DOD Background Briefing on Strategic Support Teams," January 24, 2005, http://www.defense.gov/Transcripts/Transcript.aspx?TranscriptID=1667; Vice Admiral Lowell E. Jacoby, "Subject: Message to the Workforce—DH Strategic Support Teams," January 27, 2005.

28. Gordon England, Subject: Directive-Type Memorandum (DTM) 08-032—Establishment of the Defense Counterintelligence and Human Intelligence Center (DCHC), July 22, 2008; Office of the Assistant Secretary of Defense (Public Affairs), Release No. 651-08, "DoD Activates Defense Counterintelligence and Human Intelligence Center," August 4, 2008; "Defense Counterintelligence and Human Intelligence Center Established," *Communiqué* (March 2009): 2–3; DOD Instruction O-5100.93, "Defense Counterintelligence (CI) and Human Intelligence Center," August 13, 2010; "CI & HUMINT—Partners in the HUMAN DOMAIN," *Communiqué* (November–December 2008): 19–22. On CIFA's history, see Michael J. Woods and William King, "An Assessment of the Evolution and Oversight of Defense Counterintelligence Activities," *Journal of National Security Law & Policy* 3, no. 1 (2009): 169–219; Jeffrey T. Richelson, ed., National Security Archive Electronic Briefing Book No. 230, *The Pentagon's Counterspies*, September 17, 2007, http://www2.gwu.edu/~nsarchiv/NSAEBB/NSAEBB230.

29. Greg Miller, "Pentagon Establishes Defense Clandestine Service, New Espionage Unit," www.washingtonpost.com, April 23, 2012, http://www.washingtonpost.com/world/national-security/pentagon-creates-new-espionage-unit/2012/04/23/gIQA9R7DcT_story.html; Kimberly Dozier, Associated Press, "Pentagon Spies Get New Service, Stepped Up Mission," NBC News, April 23, 2012, http://usnews.nbcnews.com/_news/2012/04/23/11353781-pentagon-spies-get-new-service-stepped-up-mission; Eric Schmitt, "Defense Department Plans New Intelligence Gathering Service," *New York Times*, April 24, 2012, A5; Adam Entous, "Pentagon Creates New Spy Service in Revamp," *Wall Street Journal*, April 24, 2012, A5.

30. Leon Panetta, Memorandum, Subject: Establishment of the Defense Clandestine Service, April 20, 2012.

31. Miller, "Pentagon Establishes Defense Clandestine Service, New Espionage Unit"; Schmitt, "Defense Department Plans New Intelligence Gathering Service"; Tyrone C. Marshall Jr., "New Defense Service Enhances Intelligence Capabilities," April 24, 2012, http://www.defense.gov/news/newsarticle.aspx?id=116064; Matthew Aid, "Another Pentagon Spy Unit Is Born," MatthewAid.com, April 24, 2012, http://www.matthewaid.com/post/21707899457/another-pentagon-spy-unit-is-born; Greg Miller, "DIA Sending Hundreds More Spies Overseas," www.washingtonpost.com, December 1, 2012, http://www.washingtonpost.com/world/national-security/dia-to-send-hundreds-more-spies-overseas/2012/12/01/97463e4e-399b-11e2-b01f-5f55b193f58f_story.html; Marc Ambinder, "What You Need to Know About the Pentagon's New Spy Service," *Week*, December 2, 2012, http://theweek.com/articles/469885/need-know-about-pentagons-new-spy-service.

32. U.S. Congress, Senate Committee on Armed Services, *National Defense Authorization Act for Fiscal Year 2013*, Report 112-173 (Washington, DC: U.S. Government Printing Office, 2012), 126; Greg Miller, "Senate Moves to Block Pentagon Plans to Increase Number of Spies Overseas," www.washingtonpost.com, December 10, 2012; John T. Bennett, "On Capitol Hill, Skepticism about Proposed DIA Expansion," www.defensenews.com, December 18, 2012, http://archive.defensenews.com/article/20121218/C4ISR01/312180008/On-Capitol-Hill-Skepticism-About-Proposed-DIA-Expansion.

33. John T. Bennett, "House Republicans Signal Support for Cadre of Military Spies," www.defensenews.com, May 21, 2013, http://archive.defensenews.com/article/20130521/DEFREG02/305210021/House-Republicans-Signal-Support-Cadre-Military-Spies; Ken Dilanian, "Congress Wary of Pentagon's New Spy Service," *Los Angeles Times*, December 24, 2013, A11; John T. Bennett, "Analysis: Defense Clandestine Service Is Here to Stay," www.defensenews.com, February 12, 2014, http://archive.defensenews.com/article/20140212/DEFREG02/302120039/Analysis-Defense-Clandestine-Service-Here-Stay; U.S. Congress, House Armed Services Committee, *Markup, National Defense Authorization Act*, December 10, 2013, 386.

34. Jacoby, Memorandum, Subject: Agency Restructuring; Amber Corrin, "DIA Director, Deputy to Step Down," www.defensenews.com, April 30, 2014, http://archive.defensenews.com/article/20140430/DEFREG02/304300045/DIA-Director-Deputy-Step-Down.

35. Defense Intelligence Agency, "Mission Description" (Central MASINT Office), n.d.; Central MASINT Office, "Script for CMO Brief to the 8th Annual Defense Intelligence Status Symposium," November 1996, 1.

36. Department of Defense Directive 5105.21, "Defense Intelligence Agency."

37. Central MASINT Office, "Script for CMO Brief to the 8th Annual Defense Intelligence Status Symposium," 1–2.

38. Mike Elliot, "MASINT's 24/7 Watch," *Communiqué* (February 2004): 12.

39. William B. Huntington, "DIA's Collection Group," *Communiqué* (November–December 1996): 18; Laura F. Sifuentes, "Attention! DT-101 Is Here!," *Communiqué* (July–August 2005): 9.

40. "DIA/ST/ODE3 Support Services, Solicitation Number: HHM402-14-R-0029," Federal Business Opportunities, January 29, 2014, https://www.fbo.gov/index?s=opportunity&mode=form&id=ab50fa1203d0ac309f199a50b9ebbf11&tab=core&tabmode=list&=; "Meet Mark Mueller, Chief Engineer at Defense Intelligence Agency," DIA Alumni, http://www.diaalumni.org/whatsnewatdia.html (accessed May 28, 2014); Jacob Goodwin, "DIA Wants Support Services from a Small Biz for Its RDT&E and O&M Activities at Patrick AFB," *Intelligence Community News*, February 14, 2014, http://intelligencecommunitynews.com/2014/02/14/dia-wants-support-services-from-a-small-business-for-its-rdte-and-om-activities-at-patrick-afb.

41. Defense Intelligence Agency, *Vector 21: A Strategic Plan for the Defense Intelligence Agency*, 1996, 13; John Y. Yurchenko, "On Guard Against Information Warfare," *Communiqué* (April–May 1997): 37; "Joint Warfare Support Office Gets New Chief," *Communiqué* (May 2003): 10.

42. Major Chip Cutler and Jeff Rote, "Terrorism: Threat and Response," *Communiqué* (March 1997): 15–17; "Interview with the Director for Intelligence, J2," *Communiqué* (May–June 2006): 21–23.

43. Rex Mills, "Office of Counterdrug Analysis," *Communiqué* (June–July 1997): 17; Tony M. Tomlinson, "The Circle of Life: The Evolution of Counterdrug Analysis," *Communiqué* (May–June 2006): 4–6.

44. U.S. Congress, House Permanent Select Committee on Intelligence, *Intelligence Authorization Act, Fiscal Year 1992*, pt. 1, Report 102-65 (Washington, DC: U.S. Government Printing Office, 1991), 8; Letter, John W. Shannon, Acting Secretary of the Army, to Lieutenant General James R. Clapper Jr., Director, Defense Intelligence Agency, February 4, 1992; Defense Intelligence Agency, *Plan for the Transfer of the Armed Forces Medical Intelligence Center to Defense Intelligence Agency*, n.d.

45. *Organization, Mission and Functions: U.S. Army Missile and Space Intelligence Center, Redstone Arsenal, Alabama* (Redstone Arsenal, AL: Army Missile and Space Intelligence Center, n.d.), 4–6; Missile and Space Intelligence Center, "Missile and Space Intelligence Center (MSIC)," 1996.

46. Cheryl Pellerin, "Missile, Space Intelligence Center Saves Warfighter Lives," Armed Forces Press Service, March 8, 2013, http://www.defense.gov/news/newsarticle.aspx?id=119474.

47. Defense Audit Service, *Semiannual Audit Plan, First Half, Fiscal Year 1982*, 1981, 32. On the evolution of post–World War II medical intelligence, see Jonathan D. Clemente, "The Fate of an Orphan: The Hawley Board and the Debates over the Post-War Organization of Medical Intelligence," *Intelligence and National Security* 20, no. 2 (June 2005): 264–287.

48. Armed Forces Intelligence Center, *Organization and Functions of the Armed Forces Medical Intelligence Center* (Fort Detrick, MD: AFMIC, April 1986), vi; Defense Audit Service, *Semiannual Audit Plan, First Half, Fiscal Year 1982*, 1981, 32; Defense Intelligence Agency, *Poisonous Snakes of Europe*, September 1986; Department of Defense Directive 6420.1, "Armed Forces Medical Intelligence Center," October 9, 2004; Lynn A. McNamee, "AFMIC Responds to Tsunami Disaster," *Communiqué* (January 2005): 10–11.

49. "AFMIC Transitions to a National Center," *Communiqué* (March 2009): 10.

50. Michael D. Maples, Lieutenant General, USA, Director, Defense Intelligence Agency, "For: Under Secretary of Defense (Personnel and Readiness), Subject: Establishment of the National Center for Medical Intelligence," January 9, 2008.

51. DOD, "National Center for Medical Intelligence," DOD Instruction 6420.1, March 20, 2009; "AFMIC Transitions to a National Center."

52. Damien K., "Medical Intelligence Relies on Teamwork," *Pathfinder* (March–April 2010): 10–11; "Center for Medical Intelligence Expanding," Boston.com, July 2, 2008; Anthony L. Kimery, "National Medical Intelligence Capabilities Expanded," *Homeland Security Today*, July 7, 2008, http://www.hstoday.us/briefings/daily-news-analysis/single-article/national-medical -intelligence-capabilities-expanded/6a61b96f5f832deb8897af48af19f49d.html; Jonathan Bor, "Fort Detrick Unit to Track Diseases that Affect U.S.," *Baltimore Sun*, July 7, 2008, http://articles .baltimoresun.com/2008-07-03/news/0807020192_1_medical-intelligence-fort-detrick-defense -intelligence-agency; Defense Intelligence Agency, "U.S. Dedicates National Center for Medical Intelligence: Pentagon Facility Expands into National Mission," July 2, 2008; Cheryl Pellerin, Armed Forces Press Service, "Medical Intelligence Center Monitors Health Threats," October 10, 2012, http://www.defense.gov/news/newsarticle.aspx?id=118163; Defense Intelligence Agency, *Infectious Disease Risk Assessment: Afghanistan*, August 2005; Defense Intelligence Agency, *Baseline Infectious Disease Risk Assessment: Haiti*, 2009; Defense Intelligence Agency, *Haiti: Health Risks and Health System Impacts Associated with Large-Scale Earthquake*, January 13, 2010; Defense Intelligence Agency, *Worldwide: New 2009-H1N1 Influenza Virus Poses Potential Threat to U.S. Forces*, May 1, 2009.

53. Major Mark Esterbrook, "'Unearthing' the Truth in Defense of Our Nation," *Pathfinder* (January–February 2005): 19–21; Jeffrey T. Richelson, ed., National Security Archive Electronic Briefing Book No. 439, *Underground Facilities: Intelligence and Targeting Issues*, September 23, 2013, http://www2.gwu.edu/~nsarchiv/NSAEBB/NSAEBB439.

54. Esterbrook, "'Unearthing' the Truth in Defense of Our Nation"; Scott Robertson, "Collaboration Is Cornerstone of UFAC," *Pathfinder* (May–June 2007): 21–22; "UFAC Digs Deep to

Find Covert Facilities," *Communiqué* (May–June 2010): 29; "Tunnel Vision," www.defensenews
.com, August 1, 2009, http://archive.defensenews.com/article/20090801/C4ISR02/908010316/
Tunnel-vision. The Air Force Technical Applications Center, in response to a Freedom of Information Act request for a copy of any memorandum of agreement between Air Force Technical
Applications Center and Underground Facility Analysis Center, refused to confirm or deny the
existence of such an agreement. However, the DIA, in response to a similar request, while deny-
ing the request, stated, "A search of DIA's system of records located one document responsive to
your request." Alesia Y. Williams, Chief, Freedom of Information Act Staff, Defense Intelligence
Agency, to Jeffrey Richelson, July 8, 2010.

55. Cheryl Pellerin, Armed Forces Press Service, "Intelligence Agency Director Discusses
Roadmap for Future," September 16, 2013, http://www.defense.gov/news/newsarticle.aspx?id
=120797; Greg Miller and Adam Goldman, "Head of Pentagon Intelligence Agency Forced Out,
Officials Say," www.washingtonpost.com, April 30, 2014, http://www.washingtonpost.com/world
/national-security/head-of-pentagon-intelligence-agency-forced-out-officials-say/2014/04/30/
ec15a366-d09d-11e3-9e25-188ebe1fa93b_story.html.

56. Donald Rumsfeld to George Tenet, "Subject: JITF-CT," September 26, 2001, with att:
Briefing slides: JITF-CT: Supporting a Unified National CT Campaign.

57. Lieutenant General Ronald L. Burgess Jr., "History of Defense Intelligence Agency," *Intelligencer* 19, no. 2 (Summer/Fall 2012): 49–53; David Eisenberg, "Multitude of Data Bases Com-
plicates Information Sharing," Center for Defense Information, October 29, 2002, http://www.cdi
.org/terrorism/infosharing-pr.cgm; JITF-CT, Exploitation Branch, *Guidelines for Personnel Supporting Interrogations and Debriefing Activities*, August 2004; National Counterterrorism Center, *National Strategy to Combat Terrorist Travel*, May 2, 2006, 10; "David Cattler," LinkedIn,
https://www.linkedin.com/pub/david-cattler/5/226/417 (accessed May 24, 2014).

58. "Interview with the Director for Intelligence, J2."

59. Joint Chiefs of Staff, Joint Publication 2-0, *Joint Intelligence*, October 22, 2013, III-7.

60. "NMEC Matures Under LTG Maples," *Communiqué* (March 2009): 11; "SAIC Gets
Big Intelligence Contract," MattewAid.com, May 25, 2012, http://www.matthewaid.com/post
/23727755270/saic-gets-big-intelligence-contract; Defense Intelligence Agency, "Biography: Roy
L. Apseloff," February 2013.

61. "NMEC Matures Under LTG Maples"; Roy I. Apseloff, "National Media Exploitation
Center—WAY AHEAD," *Communiqué* (May–June 2009): 29–31; Roy I. Apseloff, "NMEC
Strives for 'Legendary' CUSTOMER SERVICE," *Communiqué* (November–December 2008):
32–33.

4

MILITARY SERVICE INTELLIGENCE ORGANIZATIONS

In January 1961, during the final weeks of his presidency, Dwight D. Eisenhower bemoaned the fact that the U.S. military still operated three major independent intelligence services, those of the Army, Navy, and Air Force. In this regard, he remarked, he would be leaving his successor "a legacy of ashes."[1] And despite the successor administration's creation of the Defense Intelligence Agency (DIA), the United States has continued to devote substantial funds and personnel to the operation of military service intelligence organizations.

The continued major role of U.S. service intelligence organizations, in contrast to the evolution of military intelligence in other Western nations, is partly a function of bureaucratic politics, partly a function of law (Title 10), and partly the result of the structure and requirements of the U.S. military. A military force with large service components (responsible for research, development, and acquisition) and major combatant commands distributed around the globe may be better served in terms of intelligence support by organizations that are not too detached from the service components and commands.

Throughout the 1960s, 1970s, and 1980s, each of the major services maintained not only separate intelligence services but intelligence communities of their own—distinct, often geographically separated intelligence organizations directed by the service's intelligence chief. Then, in 1991, a significant process of disestablishment and/or consolidation of formerly separate intelligence organizations began in each of the major services. The factors producing the changes included budget and personnel cuts taking place in the aftermath of the Cold War and pressure exerted by congressional oversight committees. In a 1990 report, the Senate Select Committee on Intelligence observed,

> While new requirements and the increasing cost of collection systems have driven a share of the increase in intelligence, the cost of maintaining large numbers of intelligence organizations internal to the Department of Defense [DOD] has also contributed. Every echelon from the Office of the Secretary of Defense, to the Service Departments, to the CINCs [commanders in chief of the unified commands] and below have their own organic intelligence arms. For each organization, we need

separate buildings, separate administration, separate security, separate communications and separate support services.

Over the years, numerous individuals and reports . . . have criticized the Defense Department for significant duplication of effort; insufficient integration and sharing of information; uneven security measures and regulations; pursuit of parochial service, CINC, [and] other interests rather than joint intelligence interests; and gaps in intelligence support and coverage, despite the number of intelligence organizations.[2]

As a result of the report, the committee, along with the Senate Armed Services Committee, directed the Secretary of Defense to review all of the Defense Department's intelligence activities and "to the maximum degree possible, consolidate or begin consolidating all disparate or redundant functions, programs, and entities." The following year, on March 15, the Assistant Secretary of Defense (ASD) for Command, Control, Communications, and Intelligence (C3I) issued his *Plan for Restructuring Defense Intelligence*, which instructed each military service to "consolidate all existing intelligence commands, agencies, and elements into a single intelligence command within each Service."[3] Although that objective was never completely met, each of the major services instituted significant consolidations of their intelligence activities.

ARMY INTELLIGENCE ORGANIZATIONS

U.S. Army intelligence collection and production operations are the ultimate responsibility of the Deputy Chief of Staff, G-2. Those operations are carried out by the U.S. Army Intelligence and Security Command (INSCOM), which conducts collection operations, and the National Ground Intelligence Center (NGIC), which produces scientific and technical, as well as general, military intelligence. NGIC is formally subordinate to INSCOM.

The Deputy Chief of Staff, G-2, determines Army intelligence policy, supervises the activities of INSCOM, NGIC, and other Army intelligence activities, and represents Army intelligence in military and national intelligence fora. The Office of the Deputy Chief of Staff consists of six directorates (Foreign Liaison, Plans & Integration; Counterintelligence, Human Intelligence, Security and Disclosure; Resource Integration; Intelligence Community Information Management; Foreign Intelligence), two offices (the Army Management Services and Intelligence Personnel Management offices), and two groups (the Command Group and the Initiatives Group).[4] Figure 4.1 shows the organizational structure of the office.

The Foreign Intelligence Directorate is responsible for estimative support to the Army, the DOD, and the national intelligence community; current intelligence support to the Army Operations Center; and threat support to acquisition programs. The Counterintelligence, Human Intelligence, Security and Disclosure directorates are responsible for policy formulation, planning, programming, oversight, and representation for counterintelligence, human intelligence (HUMINT), and security countermeasures. The Army Foreign Liaison Directorate oversees foreign visits to Department of Army headquarters, supports foreign military attachés in Washington, and provides "foreign protocol support" to the Army leadership.[5] Liaison directorate personnel probably also provide biographic information to military leadership intelligence analysts about the attachés with whom they interact.

FIGURE 4.1   Organization of the Deputy Chief of Staff, G-2

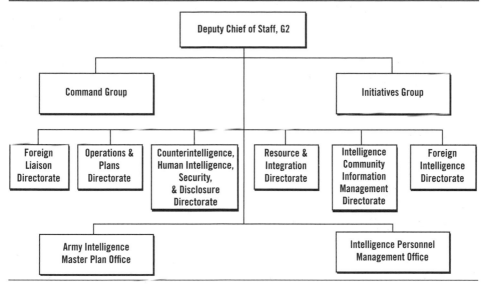

Source: U.S. Army.

On January 1, 1977, the U.S. Army Security Agency was redesignated as the U.S. Army Intelligence and Security Command, eventually absorbing the U.S. Army Intelligence Agency, the Forces Command Intelligence Group, the Intelligence Threat Analysis Detachment, and the Imagery Interpretation Center. The latter three organizations had been field-operating activities of the Assistant Chief of Staff for Intelligence.* In addition, INSCOM assumed command of several overseas intelligence groups: the 66th Military Intelligence Group in Germany, the 470th Military Intelligence Group in Panama, and the 500th Military Intelligence Group in Japan.[6] INSCOM's commanding general is therefore responsible both to the Army's Chief of Intelligence and the Chief of the Central Security Service (i.e., the Director of the National Security Agency [NSA]). INSCOM personnel staff signals intelligence (SIGINT) collection facilities at numerous overseas bases. In addition, INSCOM conducts measurement and signature intelligence (MASINT) and imagery collection operations, as well as offensive counterintelligence. In 1992 it was assigned responsibility for supervising the intelligence production activities of the Foreign Science and Technology Center and the Intelligence Threat Analysis Center. The two organizations were subsequently merged to form the NGIC. INSCOM, headquartered at Fort Belvoir, Virginia, had 17,000 assigned personnel in 2013 and probably had a budget of approximately $2 billion.[7]

Within INSCOM are a number of different Assistant Chiefs of Staff (ACSs). There are ACSs for Personnel (G1), Security (G2), Operations (G3), Logistics (G4),

---

*A new version of the Army Intelligence Agency was subsequently established and absorbed by INSCOM in 1991. See INSCOM History Office, "The INSCOM Story," www.inscom .army.mil/organization/History.aspx (accessed November 18, 2013.)

Information Management (CIO/G6), and Resource Management. The G2X element of the security component is responsible for coordinating and overseeing the Army's counterintelligence and HUMINT activities. Its components include the Army Counterintelligence Coordinating Authority and the Army HUMINT Operations Center. INSCOM's Assistant Chief of Staff for Operations is responsible for managing the command's human, technical, cyber, and open source collection activities as well as production.[8]

INSCOM's key activities are conducted not at headquarters but by the units deployed in the United States and overseas. As shown in Figure 4.2, the units fall into five basic groups: SIGINT units; aerial intelligence, surveillance, and reconnaissance (AISR) units; functional units; counterintelligence/human intelligence (CI/HUMINT) groups; and theater military intelligence brigades (MIBs). One SIGINT unit is the 704th Military Intelligence Brigade at Fort George G. Meade, Maryland, deployed in support of NSA, with subordinate components at Fort Meade and Buckley Air Force Base (AFB), Colorado. Additional elements are assigned to support a variety of Army and joint commands, which include the U.S. Central Command, the Army Special Operations Command, and the Army Forces Command. The brigade's 741st MI Battalion provides personnel for "information superiority" operations within the National Security Agency and other U.S. agencies. The 742nd MI Battalion contributes analysis and reporting via the Army Technical Control and Analysis Battalion. And the 743rd MI Battalion at Buckley, the ground station for a number of satellites, "provides personnel for exercises and in support of technical commanders."[9] The 706th MI Group, another SIGINT unit, located at Fort Gordon, Georgia, is host to NSA/CSS Georgia and "provides personnel, intelligence assets and technical support to conduct signals intelligence operations within . . . NSA/CSS Georgia . . . and worldwide." A third SIGINT unit, the 780th MIB, located at Fort Meade, "conducts signals intelligence, computer network operations, and enables Dynamic Computer Network Defense operations of Army and Defense networks." INSCOM's other SIGINT elements are at the Misawa Security Operations Center at Misawa Air Base (AB) in Japan and the European Cryptologic Center in Darmstadt, Germany.[10]

INSCOM's two Aerial Exploitation Batallions—the 206th and 306th—are headquartered at Fort Hood, Texas, but are employed in the combat theater. Task Force ODIN-A (Observe, Detect, Identify, Neutralize–Afghanistan) has operated from Bagram AB in Afghanistan, employing King Air 300 manned aircraft and MQ-12 Sky Warrior unmanned aerial vehicles. ODIN-I has conducted similar missions over Iraq. The Army also provides aircrew members who serve aboard Joint Surveillance Target Attack Radar System (JSTARS) aircraft in support of "surveillance and targeting operations of Army land component and joint or combined task force commanders worldwide." The ground-based element of JSTARS is the Army and Marine Corps Common Ground Station.[11]

INSCOM's CI/HUMINT units are, respectively, the 902nd MI Group and the Army Operations Group (AOG). Located at Fort George G. Meade, the 902nd provides direct and general counterintelligence support to Army activities and major commands. It also provides support to other military department counterintelligence and intelligence elements, unified commands, defense agencies, and national agency

FIGURE 4.2   Organization of U.S. Army Intelligences and Security Command

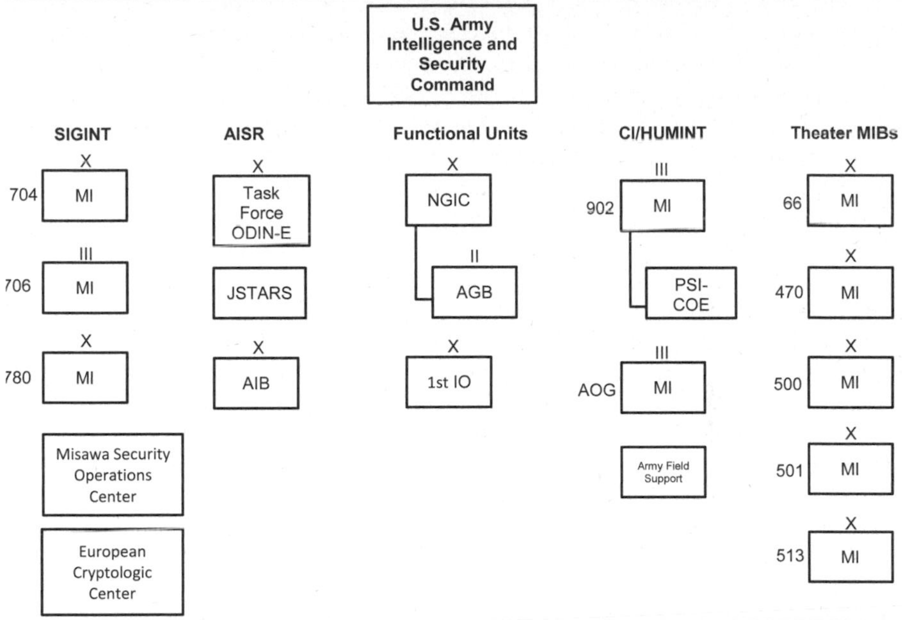

SIGINT	AISR	Functional Units	CI/HUMINT	Theater MIBs

U.S. Army Intelligence and Security Command

704 MI (X)
706 MI (III)
780 MI (X)
Misawa Security Operations Center
European Cryptologic Center

Task Force ODIN-E (X)
JSTARS
AIB (X)

NGIC (X)
AGB (II)
1st IO (X)

902 MI (III)
PSI-COE
AOG MI (III)
Army Field Support

66 MI (X)
470 MI (X)
500 MI (X)
501 MI (X)
513 MI (X)

Source: INSCOM.

counterintelligence and security activities and organizations. Its 308th MI Battalion "conducts counterintelligence investigations, operations, collection and analysis to detect, exploit and neutralize the foreign intelligence entities, international terrorism and insider threats to the U.S. Army Forces, technologies, information and infrastructure." The 310th MI Battalion "conducts proactive technical counterintelligence operations and support, counterespionage investigations . . . and analysis and production." The group's Army Counterintelligence Center "assesses foreign intelligence entities, terrorist and cyber threats" intended to permit the protection of "Army forces, facilities, information and technologies."[12]

The Army Operations Group, formerly the Army Operational Activity, was established in March 2003 on a provisional basis and is located at Fort Meade. AOG conducts operations "in all HUMINT disciplines and supports commanders from the tactical to strategic and Army levels, including units involved in combat operations in Iraq, Afghanistan and worldwide." Its creation and expansion reflect the regrowth of service HUMINT, which was to have been restricted to low-level overt HUMINT following the creation of the Defense HUMINT Service.[13]

INSCOM's theater intelligence brigades, as shown in Figure 4.2, are the 66th, 470th, 500th, 501st, and 513th MI brigades, with responsibilities that include HUMINT, SIGINT, and aerial reconnaissance. The 66th MIB, headquartered in Wiesbaden, Germany, with over 1,100 personnel in 2010, provides intelligence support to the European Command. Its personnel have supported Operations ENDURING FREEDOM, ODYSSEY DAWN, UNIFIED PROTECTOR, and IRAQI

FREEDOM, provided humanitarian assistance in the nation of Georgia, and conducted counterterrorist activities. The 470th MIB, also with over 1,100 personnel, headquartered at Fort Sam Houston, Texas, supports the Central, Northern, and Southern commands. Its 204th MI Battalion conducts airborne SIGINT operations in support of the Southern Command, while its 314th MI Battalion at Lackland AFB, Texas, provides SIGINT support to deployed U.S. forces. Its Operations Battalion provides counterintelligence support to contingency operations.[14]

The 500th MIB, headquartered at Schofield Barracks, Hawaii, with almost 1,300 personnel, supports U.S. Pacific Command operations. Its 15th MI Battalion (aerial exploitation), based at Fort Hood, Texas, has provided support to operations in Iraq and Afghanistan and forms part of the Army's AISR fleet, gathering both aerial imagery and signals intelligence. The brigade's 205th MI Battalion, at Fort Shafter, Hawaii, is responsible for all-source analysis; it deployed to Iraq in 2005. The 301st MI Battalion, headquartered in Phoenix, Arizona, provides "multi-discipline intelligence support" to U.S. Army Pacific and Pacific Command." The 441st MI Battalion (Provisional), located at Camp Zama, Japan, conducts counterintelligence and human intelligence operations throughout the Pacific area of responsibility. The brigade's 715th MI Battalion, also at Schofield Barracks, conducts SIGINT operations under the operational control of the National Security Agency.[15]

The 501st MI Brigade at Seoul, South Korea, with over 1,300 personnel, provides support to U.S. Forces Korea. It conducts imagery, SIGINT, MASINT, and HUMINT activities. Its 3rd MI Battalion, located at U.S. Army Garrison Humphreys, in Pyongtaek, Korea, operates both RC-12 Guardrail and RC-7 Airborne Reconnaissance Low aircraft. The 532nd Battalion processes, analyzes, produces, and disseminates intelligence. The 719th MI Battalion, which operates Field Station Korea at U.S. Army Garrison Humphreys, also collects signals intelligence from three sites along the Demilitarized Zone.[16]

The 513th MIB, headquartered at Fort Gordon, Georgia, has provided support to a variety of military operations since Operation DESERT SHIELD, including Operations ENDURING FREEDOM and IRAQI FREEDOM. Its 202nd MI Battalion provides counterintelligence and human intelligence services throughout the Central Command's area of responsibility. The 224th MI Battalion, located at Hunter Army Airfield, conducts both aerial signals intelligence and imagery intelligence operations. The brigade's 297th MI Battalion provides intelligence support to the Coalition Forces Land Component Command headquarters in the Central Command area of responsibility.[17]

The two functional INSCOM units are the 1st Information Operations (1st IO) Command (Land), at Fort Belvoir, and the National Ground Intelligence Center. While under the administrative control of INSCOM, the command's operations are directed by the U.S. Army Cyber Command. One INSCOM publication described the command as "a key component in the operationalization of cyberspace and the evolution and integration of IO and cyber."[18]

NGIC, located in Charlottesville, Virginia, produces analytical work on foreign ground forces. Established in 1962 as the Foreign Science and Technology Center, it consolidated the intelligence offices of the individual Army technical services, among

PHOTO 4.1   NGIC headquarters, Charlottesville, Virginia. NGIC was formed in 1995 with the merger of the Army Foreign Service and Technology Center (FSTC) and the Army Intelligence Threat Analysis Center. *Photo credit:* FSTC.

them the Signal, Ordnance, Quartermaster, Engineering, and Chemical services. Redesignated as NGIC in 1994, it absorbed the Intelligence Threat and Analysis Center in 1995.[19] NGIC functions include

- Developing and maintaining a database of ground forces intelligence
- Producing ground intelligence in support of the research, development, and acquisition programs of the Department of the Army, U.S. Marine Corps, warfighting commanders, Army force modernization community, DIA, DOD, and national policymakers
- Discovering science and technology (S&T) threats to the security of U.S. ground forces
- Forecasting foreign military trends and developments through study of worldwide S&T and general military intelligence accomplishments
- Identifying significant foreign improvements that may be incorporated into U.S. weapon and equipment systems
- Pinpointing deficiencies in foreign developments to assist in evolving U.S. countermeasures for exploitation
- Managing the U.S. Army program for the acquisition and exploitation of foreign materiel
- Providing support to the U.S. Army S&T intelligence collection effort.[20]

NGIC's specific focuses include close combat, fire support, air combat, maneuver support, battlefield reconnaissance, battlefield electronics, chemical warfare, biotechnology, advanced military applications, military technologies, acquisitions strategies, emerging technologies, signatures, imagery exploitation, biometrics, improvised explosive devices, and foreign materiel exploitation.[21]

NGIC has approximately nine hundred employees, over three-quarters of whom are located at the Charlottesville headquarters, with the remainder at NGIC facilities at Maryland's Fort Meade and Aberdeen Proving Ground.[22]

NAVY INTELLIGENCE ORGANIZATIONS

Of all the military services, the U.S. Navy experienced the most dramatic changes in its intelligence structure in the early 1990s. On September 30, 1991, it had seven distinct intelligence organizations: the Office of Naval Intelligence (ONI), the Naval Intelligence Command (NIC), Task Force 168, the Naval Technical Intelligence Center (NTIC), the Navy Operational Intelligence Center (NOIC), the Naval Intelligence Activity, and the Naval Security Group Command (NSGC). On January 1, 1993, it had two: ONI and NSGC. In December 2005, the NSGC was disestablished and its SIGINT responsibilities transferred to a command with broader responsibilities.

ONI represented the apex of the naval intelligence community and was responsible for management, direction, and some intelligence production. The second-echelon Naval Intelligence Command performed a variety of management functions; the remaining organizations, with the exception of the Naval Security Group Command, were third-echelon commands and reported to NIC. Task Force 168 engaged in overt human source collection and provided support to fleet technical collection operations. The Naval Technical Intelligence Center was the Navy's scientific and technical intelligence organization, focused primarily on the Soviet navy. The Navy Operational Intelligence Center monitored naval movements, relying heavily on signals intelligence acquired by national and Navy collection systems. The Naval Intelligence Activity was responsible for providing automatic data processing support to naval intelligence organizations. As noted above, NSGC performed the SIGINT collection mission.

On October 1, 1991, Task Force 168, NOIC, and NTIC were disestablished as separate organizations, and their functions and personnel were assigned to a newly created Naval Maritime Intelligence Center (NAVMIC). Under the new arrangement the analytical functions previously performed by NTIC and NOIC were integrated into NAVMIC's Intelligence Directorate. The consolidation was designed to achieve several objectives, including satisfying congressional and Secretary of Defense instructions to consolidate and reorganize the service intelligence structures and adjusting "to current and anticipated future changes in the threat to maritime forces and to an expected redefinition of requirements levied upon naval intelligence." On January 1, 1993, an even more drastic consolidation took place. The Naval Intelligence Command, Naval Maritime Intelligence Center, and Naval Intelligence Activity were all disestablished; the Office of Naval Intelligence (ONI) absorbed their functions and most of their personnel.[23]

PHOTO 4.2   NMIC, Suitland, Maryland. The NMIC houses the ONI (which absorbed the NTIC, Task Force 168, and the NOIC in 1993), along with U.S. Coast Guard and Marine Corps intelligence organizations. *Photo credit*: ONI.

Although plans had been in place in the fall of 1991 to merge the NSGC with the Naval Intelligence Command, no such merger took place.[24] Thus, unlike the Army and Air Force, the Navy did not merge its Service Cryptologic Element with one or more of its major intelligence components. However, the Navy consolidation represented the most complete consolidation among the services. All other intelligence functions were assigned to the new ONI with no subordinate commands, and all activities were consolidated in a single location, the National Maritime Intelligence Center complex at Suitland, Maryland, which also houses the personnel from the Marine Corps Intelligence Activity, Coast Guard Intelligence Coordination Center, and Naval Information Warfare Activity.[25]

In February 2013 joint testimony before House Committee on Armed Services, the Under Secretary of Defense for Intelligence (USD [I]), and Director of the DIA identified naval intelligence as consisting of three organizations: ONI, the Fleet Intelligence Office, and the Naval Criminal Investigative Service (NCIS).[26]

Today, ONI has over 3,000 employees worldwide, made up of civilian, military, reservist, and contractor personnel. Its customers include "fleet commanders, operators and analysts, warfighters, the Navy acquisition community, national Intelligence Community organizations, law enforcement agencies, and foreign and coalition partners."[27] ONI produces analysis concerning:

- Worldwide scientific and technical developments
- Military research, development, testing, and evaluation
- Military production and proliferation
- Military systems characteristics and performance
- Foreign naval forces leadership, organization, strategy, doctrine, tactics, techniques, procedures, and readiness
- Identification and tracking of merchant shipping.[28]

FIGURE 4.3   Organization of the Office of Naval Intelligence
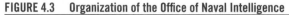

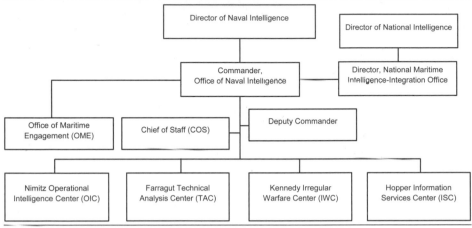

Source: ONI.

In February 2009, ONI was reorganized into four centers, a number of offices, and one directorate, as indicated in Figure 4.3. Its Hopper Information Services Center "provides mission-related information technology and services to the . . . ONI . . . its subordinate Commands, and the fleet, and Joint Forces"; the Kennedy Irregular Warfare Center provides intelligence support with regard to irregular warfare to the Department of Defense, Naval Special Warfare, and Naval Expeditionary Combat Command.[29]

ONI's two main intelligence analysis units are the Nimitz Operational Intelligence Center (NOIC) and the Farragut Technical Analysis Center (FTAC). NOIC's Fleet Support Department contains geographically oriented groups as well as a Global Maritime Watch (with its own regional desks), which together "provide current and [long-] term analysis of foreign naval and maritime operations and capabilities to the fleet, DoD, national intelligence agencies, U.S. law enforcement organizations, and other U.S. government agencies and partners." The center's Naval Warfare Department contains four components: SABER (Surface Analysis Branch for Evaluation and Reporting), SPEAR (Strike Projection Evaluation and Anti–Air Warfare Research Division), SWORD (Submarine Warfare Operations Research Division), and SPECTRUM (Speciality Products for Electronic Warfare and C5ISR/Cyber Threats Related to USN Maritime). As their names indicate, SABER, SPEAR, and SWORD provide analyses of foreign surface, air, and submarine capabilities, tactics, and operations. The SPECTRUM unit produces all-source intelligence analyses of "foreign non-kinetic threats to naval forces and assesses vulnerabilities of foreign maritime-related command, control, communications, computers, combat systems, intelligence, surveillance, reconnaissance (C5ISR) systems and networks to support U.S. Navy operations."[30]

NOIC's Transnational Threat Department produces maritime counterproliferation, counternarcotics, and civil maritime analysis. Its work includes analysis of maritime strategic trade, infrastructure, environments, and cargo. It is also responsible for maintaining national databases on merchant shipping. The center's Fleet Imagery Support Team provides naval commanders with imagery analysts. Composed of a

FIGURE 4.4 Organization of the Farragut Technical Analysis Center

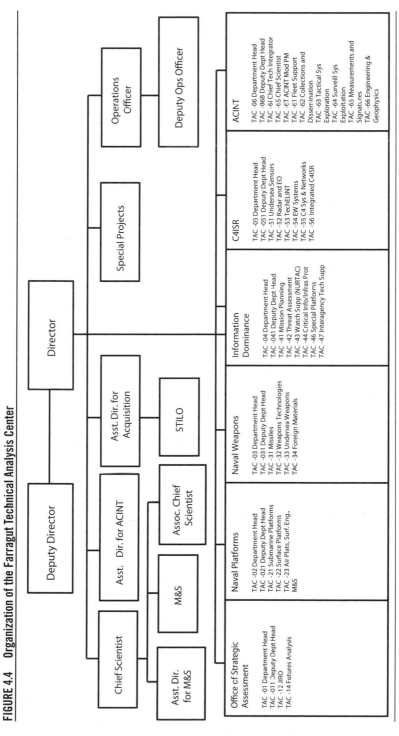

Source: ONI.

Direct Support Element (Afloat) and a Tactical Reachback Element (Shore), it operates a twenty-four-hour watch center and is responsible for indications and warnings via exploitation of imagery obtained from government and civilian systems.[31]

The technical analysis center is responsible for producing analysis of foreign navies, platforms, and weapons; strategic assessments of foreign future capabilities; analysis of naval platform capabilities, signatures, performance assessments and projections; geophysical signature measurements, modeling, and projections; analysis of acoustic and nonacoustic sensor capabilities; technical electronic intelligence analysis; command, control, communications, computers, intelligence, surveillance, and reconnaissance (C4ISR) assessments; foreign materiel exploitation; foreign weapon system and engineering assessments, modeling, and projections; critical information and infrastructure protection threat assessments; and acoustic intelligence.[32]

As shown in Figure 4.4, key components of FTAC are its Office of Strategic Assessments and its Naval Platforms, Naval Weapons, Information Dominance, C4ISR, and Acoustic Intelligence departments. The Office of Strategic Assessments is responsible for "projecting the future environment in which the U.S. Navy will operate, and characterize foreign efforts that could put U.S. naval forces at risk." The Naval Platforms Department is responsible for the study of all surface ships, submarines, aircraft, unmanned aerial vehicles, and merchant ships. The Naval Weapons Department includes a Foreign Materiel Laboratory and studies torpedoes, mines, naval guns, cruise and ballistic missiles, surface-to-air missiles, and directed energy weapons.[33]

The C4ISR Department analyses foreign sensors and communications systems, including radar and electro-optical sensors, undersea sensors, electronic warfare systems, C4 systems and networks, and intelligence, surveillance, and reconnaissance systems. The Information Dominance Department is responsible for identifying, analyzing, and warning of cyber threats to the Navy, both on land and on sea, including cyber threats to Navy acquisition programs. The department's efforts involve both defensive and offensive elements. As its name indicates, the Acoustic Intelligence (ACINT) Department is responsible for the analysis of acoustic intelligence, such as that collected by the Navy's Sound Surveillance System (discussed in Chapter 9).[34]

The ONI Collections Office and its Technical Collection, Requirements Management, Foreign Materiel, and Knowledge Center components are "responsible for articulating and implementing all-source intelligence collection strategies to satisfy . . . gaps in information as identified by Naval Intelligence Analysts."[35] The Fleet Collection Office was formerly a component of the NOIC and is now a separate office, reporting to ONI. It was established in 2009 to improve the tradecraft of afloat operational intelligence officers and intelligence specialists with respect to imagery interpretation.[36]

The Naval Criminal Investigative Service headquarters are located in Quantico, Virginia, with regional offices in the United States and a number of field offices around the world, specifically in Naples, Italy (Europe & Africa Field Office), Juffair, Bahrain (Middle East Field Office), Singapore (Singapore Field Office), and Yokosuka, Japan (Far East Field Office).[37] Figure 4.5 shows its headquarters organization chart.

The NCIS website describes the service as "the federal law enforcement agency charged with conducting investigations of felony-level offenses affecting the Navy and Marine Corps" and performing "investigations and operations aimed at identifying and neutralizing foreign intelligence, international terrorist, and cyber threats to the

FIGURE 4.5   Organization of the Naval Criminal Investigative Service

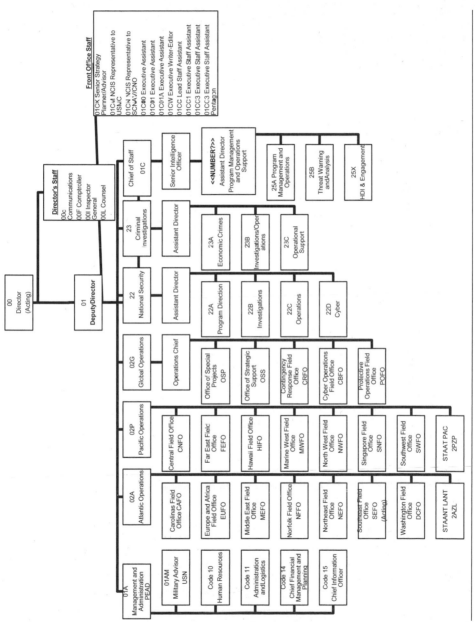

Department of the Navy." The Directorate of Intelligence and Information Sharing analyses and disseminates information concerning terrorist, foreign intelligence, and other threats relevant to NCIS or Navy/Marine operations.[38]

The website does not mention that since 2009, the NCIS's foreign operations have included serving as the Navy's HUMINT collection service. The transfer of ONI's HUMINT Department (from its Collection Office) to NCIS, approved in January 2009, was predicated on the premise that it would be advantageous to place the Navy's counterintelligence and HUMINT activities in the same organization.[39]

From the early days of the Cold War until late 2005, the Navy's signals intelligence collection operations were conducted by the Naval Security Group Command, a descendant of the Communications Security Group (OP-20-G) within the Office of Naval Communications, which was established in March 1935. After World War II it was renamed the Communications Supplementary Activities, and in 1950 it became the Naval Security Group. In 1968 it was redesignated the Naval Security Group Command.[40]

For over two decades the NSGC was responsible for signals intelligence and communications security. As a result, NSGC personnel staffed land-based high-frequency direction-finding collection sites, installed and operated SIGINT and communications security (COMSEC) equipment on ships and submarines, manned the downlinks for the Navy's ocean surveillance satellite systems, and conducted COMSEC monitoring operations. On September 30, 2005, the Navy's disestablished the NSGC and merged all its information operations capabilities under one authority, with NSGC becoming the Information Operations Directorate (IOD) of the Naval Network Warfare Command (NETWARCOM).[41]

Today, the Navy's service cryptologic operations are subordinate to the Navy Information Dominance Force. A 2012 presentation identified the cyber command's Navy Information Operations Command (NIOC) units conducting SIGINT operations, some of which were subsequently disestablished. NIOCs that were designated as Service Cryptologic Components were those located at Menwith Hill Station (CTG 1000.1), Georgia (CTG 1000.5), Hawaii (CTG 1000.7), Texas (CTG 1000.4), Maryland (CTG 1000.6), and Colorado (CTG 1000.8). In addition Navy Information Operations Detachments include those at Alice Springs, Australia (TG 1000.10), and Seoul, South Korea.[42]

In late September 2014, the Chief of Naval Operations ordered creation of a new naval intelligence organization—the Naval Intelligence Activity (NIA). The activity's mission is "to oversee and manage intelligence and intelligence-related activities, ensure the naval intelligence enterprise meets Navy, Department of Defense, and National Intelligence requirements." As a result, NIA oversees the activities of ONI and other naval intelligence activities and has administrative control of ONI's centers, although ONI's director directs their day-to-day operations.[43]

AIR FORCE INTELLIGENCE ORGANIZATIONS

The three primary Air Force intelligence entities are the Office of the Deputy Chief of Staff (DCS), Intelligence, Surveillance, and Reconnaissance (ISR), the 25th Air Force, and the National Air and Space Intelligence Center (NASIC). In addition,

FIGURE 4.6   Organization of the Deputy Chief of Staff for Intelligence, Surveillance, and Reconnaissance

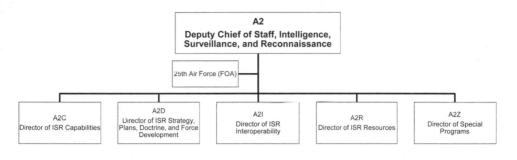

Source: USAF, as of December 2013.

the functions of the Air Force Office of Special Investigations (AFOSI) include counterintelligence.[44]

In early 1997, the Air Force disbanded the Office of the Assistant Chief of Staff, Intelligence, and assigned its tasks to the Directorate of Intelligence, Surveillance, and Reconnaissance within the Office of the Deputy Chief of Staff for Air and Space Operations. In 2005 the Air Force reestablished the position, which was subsequently upgraded to Deputy Chief of Staff, Intelligence, then later retitled Deputy Chief of Staff of the Air Force for Intelligence, Surveillance, and Reconnaissance.[45]

As supervisor of all matters pertaining to Air Force intelligence, surveillance, and reconnaissance capabilities and activities, the Deputy Chief of Staff has responsibility for "a 30,000 person enterprise." As Figure 4.6 shows, subordinate to the deputy chief in 2013 were five directorates and two field-operating agencies. The Directorate of ISR Capabilities monitors the performance and effectiveness of operational ISR assets and directs the implementation of plans and procedures to improve the collection, processing, exploitation, and dissemination of ISR data. The Director of ISR Strategy, Plans, Doctrine, and Force Development develops Air Force ISR strategy plans in support of national security and military strategy.[46] The ISR resources directorate represents the Air Force with regard to policy, manpower, funding, and requirements issues on Intelligence Community and Defense Department committees and boards. The Special Programs directorate is responsible for the "management, oversight, and integration of operational, research and development and limited access programs within the intelligence community."[47]

The AFIAA and the 25th Air Force were the ultimate products of a 1971 directive issued by the Secretary of the Air Force mandating reassignment of Air Staff operating and support functions to other organizations. In response to the directive, the Air Force Intelligence Service (AFIS) was established on June 27, 1972. In 1988 AFIS's status was upgraded, and it became the Air Force Intelligence Agency (AFIA). On October 1, 1991, as part of a reorganization of Air Force intelligence activities, it became the Air Force Intelligence Support Agency (AFISA).[48]

The AFISA was deactivated on October 1, 1993, and activated as a field-operating agency (AFIAA) on February 1, 2001. Headquartered at Joint Base Anacostia-Bolling,

Washington, D.C., it had 124 employees. AFIAA's mission was to "provide intelligence, special security services, and imagery products" as well as to analyze foreign air and air defense tactics. It was also concerned with "foreign civil aviation–related entities associated with illicit activities or posing a threat to the United States." AFIAA was inactivated in October 2014.[49]

A second part of the 1991 reorganization involved the establishment of the Air Force Intelligence Command (AFIC), merging the Electronic Security Command,* the Foreign Technology Division (FTD) of the Air Force Systems Command, the Air Force Special Activities Center, and other elements of the AFIA. The result was the creation of an Air Force equivalent of INSCOM that combined SIGINT operations with intelligence production and HUMINT functions in the same organization. And like INSCOM, AFIC had a center located a significant distance from headquarters that had its own identity and produced S&T intelligence.[50] In addition to fulfilling the ASD (C3I)'s mandate to consolidate and satisfying congressional oversight committees, AFIC was intended to provide "enhanced intelligence support to theater commanders in the conduct of their warfighting responsibilities" by establishing a "single focal point across intelligence disciplines to satisfy intelligence requirements to support operations." The new command was also intended to improve Air Force support to national agencies.[51]

On October 1, 1993, yet another reorganization occurred. Under the new plan, mandated by the June 15, 1993, HQ USAF Program Action Directive 93-8, "Restructuring Air Force Intelligence," and detailed in Air Force Programming Plan 93-01, "Establishment of the Air Force Field Operating Agency," AFIC became the Air Intelligence Agency (AIA). Nontactical HUMINT operations were transferred to the Defense HUMINT Service. In addition, an internal restructuring of the remaining AFIC elements was undertaken. On February 1, 2001, AIA was "realigned under the Air Combat Command as a primary subordinate unit."[52]

In August 1997, AIA had over 16,000 military and civilian employees distributed among ninety-five locations, including Kelly Air Force Base, Texas. By early 2006, the numbers had been reduced to 12,000 and seventy. Then, on June 15, 2007, AIA became the Air Force Intelligence, Surveillance, and Reconnaissance Agency. Beyond the title, the new agency and the AIA differed in two ways. AFISRA was to be transformed from a SIGINT-centric agency into one with greater emphasis on geospatial intelligence, imagery, HUMINT, and MASINT. In addition, rather than being subordinate to the Air Combat Command, like the AIA, the new agency reported to the Deputy Chief of Staff of the Air Force for Intelligence, Surveillance, and Reconnaissance. As of May 2014, AFISRA had 16,511 personnel working at approximately seventy-five locations worldwide.[53]

---

*The Electronic Security Command was established informally as the Air Force Security Group, consisting of eleven officers and some enlisted clerical personnel on loan from the Army Security Agency in May 1948, and then formally on July 1, 1948. In October 1948 it became the Air Force Security Service. See Gabriel Marshall, "FOA Becomes Fact," *Spokesman* (November 1993): 8; Electronic Security Command, *Electronic Security Command: Master of the Electronic Battlefield*, n.d., 1.

On October 1, 2014, the AFISRA was disestablished and transformed into an "ISR Command"—an action that had been proposed in 2006. The newly created 25th Air Force, with its headquarters also at Joint Base San Antonio–Lackland, absorbed the AFISRA's intelligence collection wings (the 480th ISRW and 70th ISRW), as well as two aerial reconnaissance units from the Air Combat Command, which became the 25th Air Force's parent command. Also transferred to the 25th were the Air Force Technical Applications Center (from AFISRA) and the Air Force Targeting Center, with plans to convert it into a targeting and analysis wing.[54] Figure 4.7 shows the organization of the 25th Air Force, as of October 1, 2014.

The 480th, with over 5,000 personnel and headquartered at Joint Base Langley-Eustis, Virginia, has subordinate groups at Fort Gordon, Georgia (480th); Langley-Eustis (497th); Beale Air Force Base, California (548th); Joint Base Pearl Harbor–Hickam, Hawaii (692nd); Ramstein Air Base, Germany (693rd); and Osan Air Base, South Korea (694th). The wing is responsible for the "collection, processing, exploitation, and dissemination of ISR data" from a variety of overhead assets, including U-2, RQ-4 Global Hawk, MQ-1 Predator, MQ-9 Reaper, MC-12 Liberty, and other aircraft.[55]

The 70th ISRW, whose headquarters are at Fort Meade, Maryland, has subordinate ISR groups at Misawa, Japan (373rd); Joint Base San Antonio–Lackland (543rd); Peterson AFB, Colorado (544th); and Fort Meade (the 659th and 707th). The 70th ISRW, the Air Force's Cryptologic Wing, conducts "worldwide, real-time SIGINT and information assurance missions." Its 373rd ISR Group, with units at Misawa and Joint Base Elmendorf-Richardson, Alaska, provide "time-critical combat intelligence to U.S. theater battle commanders, unified and specified commands, as well as national and Department of Defense leadership. Subordinate to the 659th at Fort Meade are several Intelligence Squadrons (the 5th, 37th, and 41st) that represent the Air Force's initial Cyber Mission Force and serve as part of the U.S. Cyber Command Cyber Mission Force.[56]

The 70th wing's 544th ISR Group manages units that engage in SIGINT collection, including SIGINT collection targeted on foreign space operations. Its key components are the 586th Intelligence Squadron at Buckley AFB, which has a detachment at Alice Springs, Australia—both the sites of ground stations for U.S. SIGINT satellites. The group's 18th Intelligence Squadron at Wright-Patterson AFB, Ohio, has detachments at Osan Air Base and Feltwell, United Kingdom.[57]

The wing's 543rd ISR Group, headquartered at Joint Base San Antonio–Lackland, provides personnel for national SIGINT operations as well as SIGINT support to the Department of Homeland Security. The 707th ISR Group has more than 1,900 personnel, conducts national SIGINT operations, and has customers that include the Office of the President, Secretary of Defense, and combatant commanders. The group "serves as the lead for the Global Air Analysis SIGINT Mission which analyzes and reports high-interest aerial activity" and conducts computer network operations.[58]

One of the aerial reconnaissance units transferred to the 25th Air Force is the 9th Reconnaissance Wing, with headquarters at Beale AFB. It operates U-2, RQ-4, and MC-12 aircraft and has 4,500 personnel—divided among groups at Beale, Grand Forks, North Dakota, and multiple overseas locations. The 55th Wing, with

FIGURE 4.7 Organization of the 25th Air Force

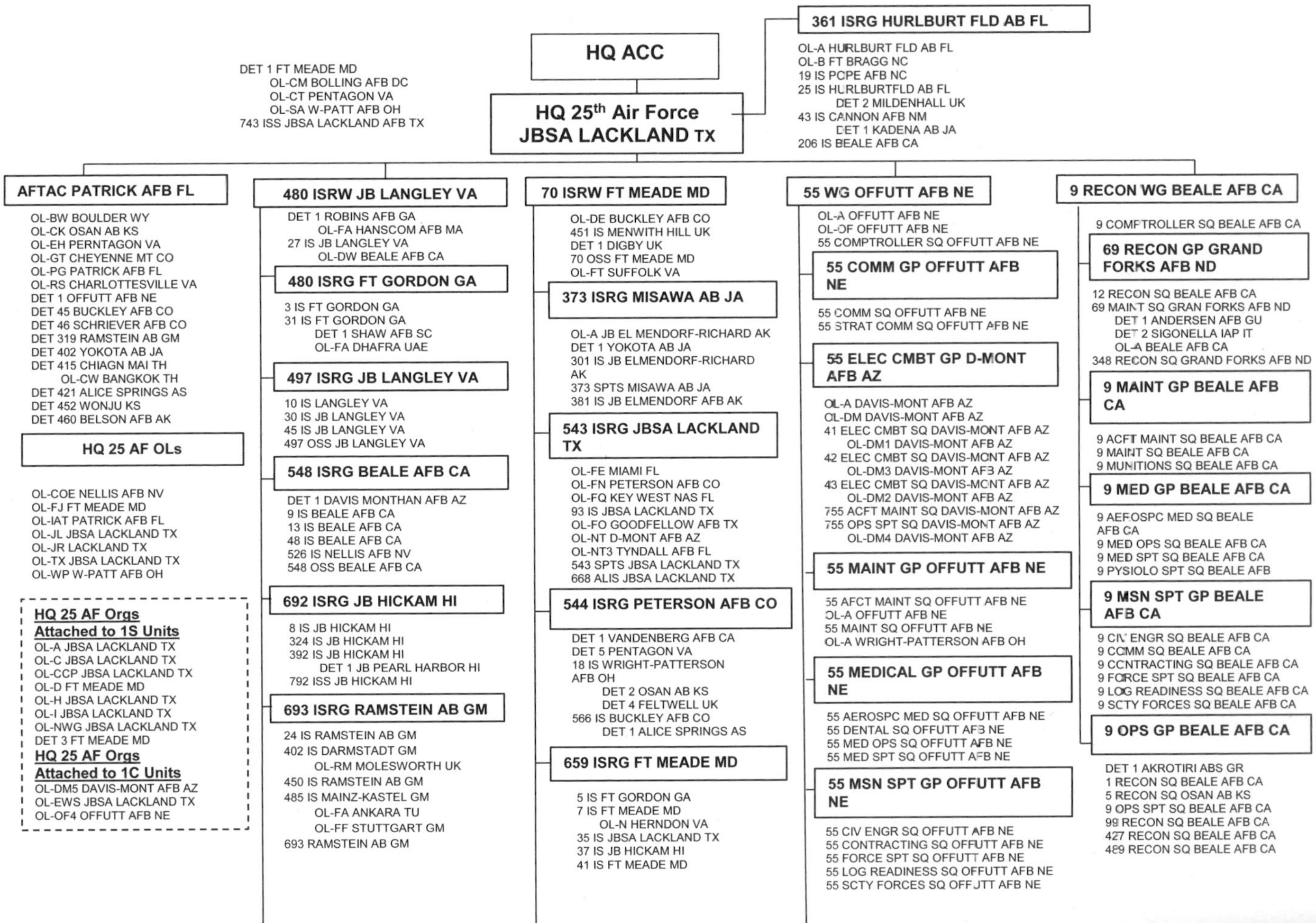

HQ ACC

HQ 25th Air Force JBSA LACKLAND TX

DET 1 FT MEADE MD
OL-CM BOLLING AFB DC
OL-CT PENTAGON VA
OL-SA W-PATT AFB OH
743 ISS JBSA LACKLAND AFB TX

361 ISRG HURLBURT FLD AB FL
OL-A HURLBURT FLD AB FL
OL-B FT BRAGG NC
19 IS POPE AFB NC
25 IS HLRLBURTFLD AB FL
DET 2 MILDENHALL UK
43 IS CANNON AFB NM
CET 1 KADENA AB JA
206 IS BEALE AFB CA

9 RECON WG BEALE AFB CA
9 COMPTROLLER SQ BEALE AFB CA

69 RECON GP GRAND FORKS AFB ND
12 RECON SQ BEALE AFB CA
69 MAINT SQ GRAN FORKS AFB ND
DET 1 ANDERSEN AFB GU
DET 2 SIGONELLA IAP IT
OL-A BEALE AFB CA
348 RECON SQ GRAND FORKS AFB ND

9 MAINT GP BEALE AFB CA
9 ACFT MAINT SQ BEALE AFB CA
9 MART SQ BEALE AFB CA
9 MUNITIONS SQ BEALE AFB CA

9 MED GP BEALE AFB CA
9 AEF-OSPC MED SQ BEALE AFB CA
9 MED OPS SQ BEALE AFB CA
9 MED SPT SQ BEALE AFB CA
9 PYSIOLO SPT SQ BEALE AFB CA

9 MSN SPT GP BEALE AFB CA
9 CIV ENGR SQ BEALE AFB CA
9 COMM SQ BEALE AFB CA
9 CCONTRACTING SQ BEALE AFB CA
9 FORCE SPT SQ BEALE AFB CA
9 LOG READINESS SQ BEALE AFB CA
9 SCTY FORCES SQ BEALE AFB CA

9 OPS GP BEALE AFB CA
DET 1 AKROTIRI ABS GR
1 RECON SQ BEALE AFB CA
5 RECON SQ OSAN AB KS
9 OPS SPT SQ BEALE AFB CA
99 RECON SQ BEALE AFB CA
427 RECON SQ BEALE AFB CA
489 RECON SQ BEALE AFB CA

55 WG OFFUTT AFB NE
OL-A OFFUTT AFB NE
OL-OF OFFUTT AFB NE
55 COMPTROLLER SQ OFFUTT AFB NE

55 COMM GP OFFUTT AFB NE
55 COMM SQ OFFUTT AFB NE
55 STRAT COMM SQ OFFUTT AFB NE

55 ELEC CMBT GP D-MONT AFB AZ
OL-A DAVIS-MONT AFB AZ
OL-DM DAVIS-MONT AFB AZ
41 ELEC CMBT SQ DAVIS-MONT AFB AZ
42 ELEC CMBT SQ DAVIS-MONT AFB AZ
43 ELEC CMBT SQ DAVIS-MCNT AFB AZ
OL-DM1 DAVIS-MONT AFB AZ
OL-DM2 DAVIS-MONT AFB AZ
OL-DM3 DAVIS-MONT AFB AZ
OL-DM4 DAVIS-MONT AFB AZ

55 MAINT GP OFFUTT AFB NE
55 AFCT MAINT SQ OFFUTT AFB NE
OL-A OFFUTT AFB NE
55 MAINT SQ OFFUTT AFB NE
OL-A WRIGHT-PATTERSON AFB OH

55 MEDICAL GP OFFUTT AFB NE
55 AEROSPC MED SQ OFFUTT AFB NE
55 DENTAL SQ OFFUTT AF3 NE
55 MED OPS SQ OFFUTT AFB NE
55 MED SPT SQ OFFUTT A-B NE

55 MSN SPT GP OFFUTT AFB NE
55 CIV ENGR SQ OFFUTT AFB NE
55 CONTRACTING SQ OFFUTT AFB NE
55 FORCE SPT SQ OFFUTT AFB NE
55 LOG READINESS SQ OFFUTT AFB NE
55 SCTY FORCES SQ OFFJTT AFB NE

70 ISRW FT MEADE MD
OL-DE BUCKLEY AFB CO
451 IS MENWITH HILL UK
DET 1 DIGBY UK
70 OSS FT MEADE MD
OL-FT SUFFOLK VA

373 ISRG MISAWA AB JA
OL-A JB EL MENDORF-RICHARD AK
DET 1 YOKOTA AB JA
301 IS JB ELMENDORF-RICHARD AK
373 SPTS MISAWA AB JA
381 IS JB ELMENDORF AFB AK

543 ISRG JBSA LACKLAND TX
OL-FE MIAMI FL
OL-FN PETERSON AFB CO
OL-FQ KEY WEST NAS FL
93 IS JBSA LACKLAND TX
OL-FO GOODFELLOW AFB TX
OL-NT D-MONT AFB AZ
OL-NT3 TYNDALL AFB FL
543 SPTS JBSA LACKLAND TX
668 ALIS JBSA LACKLAND TX

544 ISRG PETERSON AFB CO
DET 1 VANDENBERG AFB CA
DET 5 PENTAGON VA
18 IS WRIGHT-PATTERSON AFB OH
DET 2 OSAN AB KS
DET 4 FELTWELL UK
566 IS JBSA LACKLAND TX
DET 1 ALICE SPRINGS AS

659 ISRG FT MEADE MD
5 IS FT GORDON GA
7 IS FT MEADE MD
35 IS JBSA LACKLAND TX
37 IS JB HICKAM HI
41 IS FT MEADE MD

480 ISRW JB LANGLEY VA
DET 1 ROBINS AFB GA
OL-FA HANSCOM AFB MA
27 IS JB LANGLEY VA
OL-DW BEALE AFB CA

480 ISRG FT GORDON GA
3 IS FT GORDON GA
31 IS FT GORDON GA
DET 1 SHAW AFB SC
OL-FA DHAFRA UAE

497 ISRG JB LANGLEY VA
10 IS LANGLEY VA
30 IS JB LANGLEY VA
45 IS JB LANGLEY VA
497 OSS JB LANGLEY VA

548 ISRG BEALE AFB CA
DET 1 DAVIS MONTHAN AFB AZ
9 IS BEALE AFB CA
13 IS BEALE AFB CA
48 IS BEALE AFB CA
526 IS NELLIS AFB NV
548 OSS BEALE AFB CA

692 ISRG JB HICKAM HI
8 IS JB HICKAM HI
324 IS JB HICKAM HI
392 IS JB HICKAM HI
DET 1 JB PEARL HARBOR HI
792 ISS JB HICKAM HI

693 ISRG RAMSTEIN AB GM
24 IS RAMSTEIN AB GM
402 IS DARMSTADT GM
OL-RM MOLESWORTH UK
450 IS RAMSTEIN AB GM
485 IS MAINZ-KASTEL GM
OL-N HERNDON VA
OL-FF STUTTGART GM
693 RAMSTEIN AB GM

AFTAC PATRICK AFB FL
OL-BW BOULDER WY
OL-CK OSAN AB KS
OL-EH PERNTAGON VA
OL-GT CHEYENNE MT CO
OL-PG PATRICK AFB FL
OL-RS CHARLOTTESVILLE VA
DET 1 OFFUTT AFB NE
DET 45 BUCKLEY AFB CO
DET 46 SCHRIEVER AFB CO
DET 319 RAMSTEIN AB GM
DET 402 YOKOTA AB JA
DET 415 CHIAGN MAI TH
OL-CW BANGKOK TH
DET 421 ALICE SPRINGS AS
DET 452 WONJU KS
DET 460 BELSON AFB AK

HQ 25 AF OLs
OL-COE NELLIS AFB NV
OL-FJ FT MEADE MD
OL-IAT PATRICK AFB FL
OL-JL JBSA LACKLAND TX
OL-JR LACKLAND TX
OL-TX JBSA LACKLAND TX
OL-WP W-PATT AFB OH

HQ 25 AF Orgs Attached to 1S Units
OL-A JBSA LACKLAND TX
OL-C JBSA LACKLAND TX
OL-CCP JBSA LACKLAND TX
OL-D FT MEADE MD
OL-H JBSA LACKLAND TX
OL-I JBSA LACKLAND TX
OL-TX JBSA LACKLAND TX
OL-NWG JBSA LACKLAND TX
DET 3 FT MEADE MD

HQ 25 AF Orgs Attached to 1C Units
OL-DM5 DAVIS-MONT AFB AZ
OL-EWS JBSA LACKLAND TX
OL-F4 OFFUTT AFB NE

694 ISRG OSAN AB KS

6 IS OSAN AB KS
303 IS OSAN AB KS
DET 1 YONG SAN KS
694 ISS OSAN AB KS

707 ISRG FT MEADE MD

22 IS FT MEADE MD
 OL-AM SCOTT AFB
 OL-BA AL UDEID QA
 OL-DX ROSECRANS MO
 OL-FD PENTAGON VA
 OL-FP SCOTT AFB IL
 OL-FS OFFUTT AFB NE
 OL-ND FT BELVOIR VA
 OL-NT2 BARKSDALE AFB LA
 OL-NT4 QUANTICO VA
 OL-QB MACDILL AFB FL
29 IS FT MEADE MD
32 IS FT MEADE MD
34 IS FT MEADE MD
94 IS FT MEADE MD
707 CS FT MEADE MD
707 FSS FT MEADE MD

55 PERATIONS GP OFFUTT AFB NE

1 ABN CMD CONTROL SQ OFFUTT AFB NE
38 RECON SQ OFFUTT AFB NE
 OL-AS1 OFFUTT AFB NE
45 RECON SQ OFFUTT AFB NE
55 ISS OFFUTT AFB NE
 OL-CS1 OFFUTT AFB NE
55 ODD OFFUTT AFB NE
82 RECON SQ KADENA ABS JA
95 RECON SQ MILDENHALL ABS UK
 DET 1 SOUDA BAY GR
97 IS OFFUTT AFB NE
 OL-OF1 OFFUTT AFB NE
338 CMBT TNG SQ OFFUTT AFB NE
 OL-OF3 OFFUTT AFB NE
343 RECON SQ OFFUTT AFB NE
 OL-AS2 OFFUTT AFB NE
390 IS KADENA ABS JA
488 IS MILDENHALL ABS UK
 OL-RS SOUDA BAY GR

HQ 25 AF–Gaines Arc Units

AFRC
16 IS FT MEADE, MC*
28 IS HURLBURT FLD FL*
36 IS BEALE AFB CA*
50 IS BEALE AFB CA*
63 IS JB LANGLEY VA*
64 IS W-PATT AFB OH*
71 IS W-PATT AFB OH*
718 IS JB LANGLEY VA*

MA ANG
102 IG OTIS ANGB MA
101 IS OTIS ANGB MA
102 ISS OTIS ANGB MA
102 OSS OTIS ANGB MA

AL ANG
117 IS BIRMINGHAM AL

AR ANG
123 IS LITTLE ROCK AR

OH ANG
124 IS SPRINGFIELD OH
125 IS SPRINGFIELD OH
126 IS SPRINGFIELD OH
127 SPRINGFIELD OH
178 ISRG SPRINGFIELD OH

GA ANG
139 IS FT GORDON GA*

NV ANG
152 IS RENO NV

IN ANG
181 IG TERRE HAUTE IN
137 IS TERRE HAUTE IN
181 ISS TERRE HAUTE IN
191 OSS TERRE HAUTE IN

KS ANG
184 IG MCCONNELL AFB KS
161 IS MCCONNELL AFB KS
184 ISS MCCONNELL AFB KS
184 OSS MCCONNELL AFB KS

KY ANG
223 IF _OUISVILLE KY

VA ANG
192 IS JB HICKAM HI*

WA ANG
256 IS FAIRCHILD AFB WA

CA ANG
234 IS BEALE AFB CA*
222 ISS BEALE AFB CA*
222 OSS BEALE AFB CA*

*Classic Associate Units
NOTE: ARC units are gained by HQ 25 AF Agency upon mobilization

Source: AFISRA.

headquarters at Offutt AFB, Nebraska, is the second—and is responsible for both reconnaissance and electronic attack missions. It operates the family of RC-135 aircraft employed on SIGINT and/or MASINT missions (discussed in Chapters 8 and 9).[59]

In February 2015, the 363rd ISR Wing, with headquarters at Joint Base Langley-Eustis, was added to the 25th Air Force with the mission of "providing integrated cross-domain targeting and analysis, and producing tailored integrated analytical and targeting products for the operational and tactical-level warfighters." It absorbed the Air Force Targeting Center, which had conducted a targeting and effects study for the Central Command's Air Force component, produced terminal area models for attack planning for the stealthy Joint Air-to-Surface Standoff Missile and the conventional air-launched cruise missile, and created training and target materials. Two intelligence squadrons from the Air Force Warfare Center at Nellis AFB, Nevada, and the 361st ISR Group at Hurlburt Field, Florida, were also assigned to the new wing. Its targeting responsibilities include air defenses, counterspace, counter-ISR, theater ballistic missile/cruise missile threats, and air threats.[60]

The Air Force Technical Applications Center (AFTAC) was originally an independent organization and then an "AIA-supported" organization; now it is a subordinate unit of the 25th Air Force. First established in 1948 as the Special Weapons Squadron and subsequently known as the Air Force Office of Atomic Energy, Section 1 (AFOAT-1), AFTAC received its present name in July 1959. Until the 1970s it mission was classified, and it was described in sanitized congressional hearings only as "Project CLEAR SKY."[61]

With about eight hundred personnel (who count against the total of 25th Air Force personnel) and headquartered at Patrick AFB, Florida, AFTAC operates the Atomic Energy Detection System (AEDS), a worldwide system that employs space-based, aerial, ground, and hydroacoustic sensors to detect indications of nuclear detonations and accidents, collect information relevant to discriminating between earthquakes and nuclear detonations, and identify signs of nuclear weapons research and development and production. AFTAC's operations and the analysis, by AFTAC and other organizations, of the data collected are relevant to the monitoring of a variety of treaties: the Limited Test Ban Treaty (which prohibits atmospheric tests), the Threshold Test Ban Treaty (which prohibits underground tests with a yield of over 150 kilotons), the Comprehensive Test Ban Treaty (which prohibits all tests), the Non-Proliferation Treaty, the Peaceful Nuclear Explosions Treaty, the Intermediate-Range Nuclear Forces Treaty, and the Strategic Arms Reduction Treaty. AFTAC was also responsible for tracking debris from the 1986 Chernobyl disaster. In addition, today's operations are particularly directed at collecting data on the nuclear activities of Iran, North Korea, Pakistan, and India. Furthermore, AFTAC collection and analysis activities are directed at monitoring chemical and biological warfare programs, both for intelligence and treaty verification purposes.[62]

AFTAC worldwide operations are managed through its headquarters organization components, shown in Figure 4.8, and carried out by its detachments and operating locations, which are discussed in Chapter 9.

AFTAC's Directorate of Operations is responsible for planning, coordinating, operating, and reporting the product of U.S. Atomic Energy Detection System data collection efforts, which employ "underwater, subsurface, surface, sea-based, airborne, and [space-based sensors]." The Directorate of Materials Technology is responsible for laboratory analysis, evaluation, and reporting of the various materials obtained from collection systems. It also provides forensic support to civilian authorities for nuclear smuggling and counterterrorism investigations as well as looking for evidence of nuclear accidents. The Directorate of Nuclear Treaty Monitoring plans, manages, and coordinates research and development and sustainment for all seismic, hydroacoustic, and infrasonic systems of the AEDS and National Data Center employed in monitoring nuclear test ban treaties. The Directorate of Atmospheric and Space Systems, inter alia, "identifies, develops, and maintains techniques and procedures for the processing and analysis of nuclear, optical, and electromagnetic radiation from nuclear explosions and other sources of interest."[63]

Reports produced by AFTAC include a Daily AEDS Activity Bulletin, which routinely summarizes all events AFTAC reporting through alert and special event process and all routinely reported events, as well as the Monthly AEDS Monitoring Report, the AFTAC Monthly Success Stories Report, a Large Earthquake Notification Report, and Alert and Special Event Reports, which are generated "when an event is sufficiently suspicious."[64]

One component of the AFISRA that did not move to the 25th Air Force is the National Air and Space Intelligence Center at Wright-Patterson AFB, Ohio. An analytical agency, it became the responsibility of the Deputy Chief of Staff for Intelligence, Surveillance, and Reconnaissance.[65] NASIC is, in one sense, the latest version of what began in 1917 as the Foreign Data Section of the Airplane Engineering Department, which shortly after its creation was transferred from Washington, D.C., to Dayton, Ohio. Its subsequent redesignations included the Technical Data Section (1927), the Technical Data Laboratory (1942), and T-2 (Intelligence) of the Air Technical Service Command (1945). In 1947 all nonintelligence functions were removed from T-2, and it became the Air Materiel Command Intelligence Department. In 1951 the department became the Air Technical Intelligence Center and, in 1961, the Foreign Technology Division of the Air Force Systems Command.[66]

The FTD's intelligence activities were directed at avoiding technological surprise, advancing U.S. technology by use of foreign technology, identifying weaknesses in foreign weapons systems, and using certain design traits of foreign weapons systems as indicators of strategic intent. Under the October 1, 1991, restructuring of Air Force intelligence, the FTD was removed from control of the Air Force Systems Command, renamed the Foreign Technology Center, and placed under the AFIC. In 1992 it became the Foreign Aerospace Science and Technology Center (FASTC).[67]

As part of the restructuring that produced the AIA, the National Air Intelligence Center (NAIC) was established on October 1, 1993, with the organizational (but not geographic) consolidation of FASTC with the 480th Intelligence Group, which was subsequently moved out of the center and subordinated to the Air Intelligence Agency. On February 15, 2003, it became the National Air and Space Intelligence Center, reflecting its role in the production of intelligence concerning foreign space systems.[68] NASIC remains headquartered at Wright-Patterson AFB, Ohio, and has about 3,000 military and civilian employees and a budget of more than $330 million. Approximately 250 personnel are stationed at five overseas locations. As shown in Figure 4.9, NASIC analytical work is the responsibility of four groups: Air & Cyberspace

FIGURE 4.8 Organization of Air Force Technical Applications Center

COMMAND SECTION
Commander
Vice Commander
Chief Scientist
Technical Advisor
STNFO Program Mgr.
Executive Officer

Knowledge Operations Management
Superintendent
Commander's Action Group

Continuous Process Improvement
Director of Staff
Multimedia
Command Historian
Human Resources
Inspector General
Public Affairs Office
Occupational Health & Safety
Distributed Missions Operations

COMMANDER'S SUPPORT STAFF
Squadron Section Commander
First Sergeant
Training Office

SECURITY OFFICE
Chief Security Officer
Security Office Assistant
Computers & Comsec

Info, Industrial & Classification Division
Information Security Branch
Industrial Security Branch
Classification Branch
Operations Security Division

(Directorate of Logistics & Systems CNT'D)
Information Support Flight
Cyber Transport Flight

Cyber Operations Support Flight
Cyber Operations Flight
Logistics Support Division

Acquisition Support Branch
Documentation Branch
Supply & Transportation Branch
Warehouse Branch
Maintenance Division

Geophysical Equip Maintenance Branch
Materials Collection Branch
Systems Control Branch
Systems Control 24/7
Plans and Resources Division

Enterprise Arch & Engineering Branch
Plans & Implementation Branch

DIRECOTRATE OF ATMOSPHERE AND SPACE
Director
Deputy Director
Superintendent

Knowledge Operations Management
Research & Development Division

Nudet R&D Branch
Development Branch
Adv. Concepts & Experimentation Branch

(Directorate of Materials Technology CNT'D)
Verification Sciences Division

Airborne Systems Branch
Ground-Based Systems Branch
Laboratory

DIRECTORATE OF NUCLEAR TREATY MONITORING
Director
Deputy Director
Superintendent

Knowledge Operations Management
Data Systems Engineering Division

Configuration Management Branch
Data Quality Branch
Engineering Branch
Geophysics Division

Evaluation Branch
NDC Branch
Research Branch

DIRECTORATE OF PLANS AND PROGRAMS
Director
Deputy Director
Superintendent
Financial Management & Program Division
Construction Division
Interior Design
Mil Con

Personnel Security Division
Physical Security Division
FOIA Privacy Act Division

DIRECTORATE OF OPERATIONS
Director
Deputy Director
Directorate Technical Advisor
Superintendent

Security
Knowledge Operations Management
Current Operations Division

Intelligence Branch
Operations Analysis Branch
Operations Training Eval Branch
Radar Division

Treaty Operations Division

Airborne Ops Branch
Ground Ops Branch

DIRECTORATE OF LOGISTICS &
SYSTEMS
Director
Technical Advisor
Superintendent
Knowledge Operations Management

Standardization and Evaluation Officer
Cyber Division

Directed Energy (DEW) Branch
Field Test Branch
Special Mission Support Branch
Operations Division

Ops Assessment Branch
Standardization & Training Branch
Systems Division

Programs Branch
Systems & Programs Branch

DIRECTORATE OF MATERIALS
TECHNOLOGY
Director
Deputy Director of Operations
Deputy Director of Technology

Superintendent
Knowledge Operations Management
Atmospheric Science Division

Meteorology Branch
Nuclear Sciences Division

Collection Support Branch
Nuclear Assessments Branch
Technology Support Branch
Technical Applications Support Branch
Resources & Acquisition Division

Budget Branch
Sciences Support Division

Materials Support Branch
Laboratory Management Branch
Research Division

International Affairs Office

Manpower Capabilities & Presentations Div.
Presentation Division

Programming Office Phone Plans,
Exercises, & Rqmts Div., Com

Agreements Branch
Exercise Branch
Plans Branch
Requirements & Future Concepts Branch
Capabilities & Assessments

OL-TC TECHNOLOGY COORDINATION
OFFICE
Director
Deputy Director
Superintendent
Science Division
Engineering Division
Acquisition Division
Test Division

Source: AFTAC.

Intelligence, Geospatial & Signatures Intelligence, and Space, Missiles, & Forces Intelligence, and Global Exploitation Intelligence.[69]

The Air & Cyberspace Intelligence Group "produces integrated intelligence defining present and future air and defense systems" in support of military operations, force planning, and policymaking. A squadron from the group located at Lackland AFB, Texas, "provides critical foreign network intelligence." The Geospatial & Signatures Intelligence Group analyzes data produced by a variety of technical collections systems, including imagery satellites (geospatial) and geosynchronous infrared systems such as the Defense Support Program and Space-Based Infrared System (persistent infrared). The Space, Missiles & Forces Intelligence Group produces approximately 90 percent of the nation's assessments and estimates concerning foreign space, counterspace, and ballistic missile all-source scientific and technical intelligence.[70]

The Global Exploitation Intelligence Group consists of three analytical units—the Information Exploitation Squadron, the Foreign Materiel Squadron (which analyses foreign aerospace systems or system components that the United States has acquired or obtained access to) and the Signals Analysis Squadron. Also subordinate to the group is the Global Activities Squadron, which has detachments at Colorado Springs, Colorado (Det. 1), Joint Base Pearl Harbor–Hickam (Det. 2), Ramstein Air Base, Germany (Det. 3), and Joint Base Anacostia-Bolling, Washington, D.C. (Det. 4), as well as an operating location at Scott AFB, Illinois (OL-GS). In contrast to the other squadrons, the Global Activities Squadron and its detachments are responsible for human intelligence collection. The squadron was established as a result of the successive upgrading of OL-Dayton and Detachment 6. The targets of the squadron are the aerospace programs of China, Russia, and other potential U.S. adversaries.[71]

The Air Force Office of Special Investigations, established on August 1, 1948, in response to a congressional suggestion to consolidate Air Force investigative activities, is the Air Force counterpart of the NCIS. Headquartered at Quantico, Virginia, it has eight field investigative regions across the world, with 144 units in the continental United States and 63 overseas. As of May 2014, it had over 2,348 active-duty, reserve, and civilian personnel. Its mission is "to identify, exploit, and neutralize criminal, terrorist, and intelligence threats to the Air Force, Department of Defense and U.S. Government."[72]

AFOSI's Office of Special Projects, whose motto is "Secretum Conservo Populi" (protecting the people's secrets), has nine detachments and four operating locations (including at Las Vegas, Nevada, and a variety of Air Force bases); it is responsible for "performing program, inspection, investigative and counterintelligence functions for all Air Force Special Access Programs." AFOSI's production includes studies of foreign intelligence service organizations and operations. In 2012 it produced more than 7,000 intelligence reports.[73]

MARINE CORPS INTELLIGENCE ORGANIZATIONS

Management of Marine Corps intelligence activities is the responsibility of the Corps' Director of Intelligence, who heads the Intelligence Department, established by the Commandant of the Marine Corps in April 2000 to enhance Marine Corps intelligence capabilities. The director represents the Marine Corps within the national

FIGURE 4.9   Organization of the National Air and Space Intelligence Center

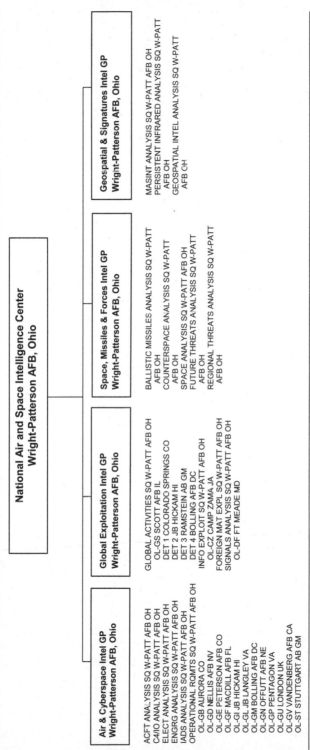

Source: AFISRA.

FIGURE 4.10 Organization of the Marine Corps Intelligence Department

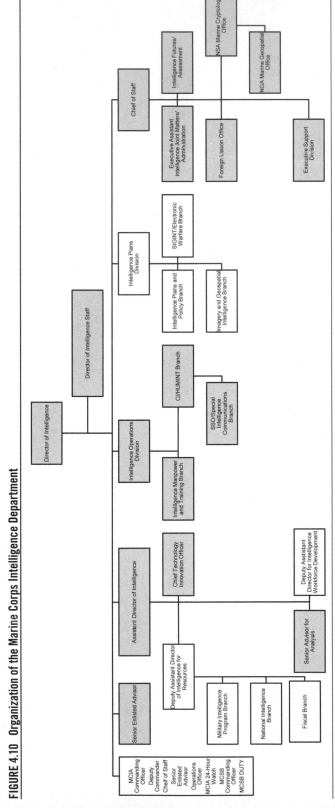

Source: U.S. Marine Corps.

Intelligence Community and manages the Intelligence Department's collection and analysis activities. As indicated in Figure 4.10, the department includes an Intelligence Plans Division, whose branches are responsible for oversight of intelligence requirements and capabilities; planning, development, and integration; and imagery/geospatial and signals intelligence operations. The department's Intelligence Operations Division includes a component that focuses on counterintelligence and HUMINT.[74]

Also subordinate to the director of intelligence is the Marine Corps Intelligence Activity (MCIA), whose organization is shown as part of Figure 4.11. Located at the National Maritime Intelligence Center complex at Suitland, Maryland, and the Marine Corps facility at Quantico, Virginia, MCIA was originally created as the Marine Corps Intelligence Center as the result of a 1987 study on Marine Corps intelligence requirements. On January 1, 1993, the center was redesignated as the MCIA, and in mid-1995 it had a staff of eighty-two analysts. Its overall workforce in early 1997 was 130 and had grown to 250 by 2002, when a further restructuring of Marine Corps intelligence quadrupled it size to more than 1,000 marines, civilians, and contractors.[75]

The MCIA Office of Production and Analysis Company's functions include the following:

- Providing tailored intelligence analysis and estimates to the Commandant of the Marine Corps in his role as Marine Corps member of the Joint Chiefs of Staff
- Producing tailored general military intelligence and science and technical intelligence
- Providing support to the Marine Corps Combat Development Command
- Serving as the Service Threat Validator for threats, assessments, and estimates used in service concepts, plans, and scenarios
- Providing tailored mid- and long-range threat analysis, assessments, and estimates supporting the development of expeditionary, naval, joint, and combined concepts, plans, and doctrines
- Preparing threat portions of Marine Corps plans, including the Marine Corps Long-Range Plan.[76]

The CI/HUMINT Support Company was established to provide administrative control of marines serving in defense HUMINT activities and in positions funded by the Foreign Counterintelligence Program. The Marine Corps Support Battalion, headquartered at Fort Meade, Maryland, provided for Marine Corps participation in signals intelligence activities, with lettered companies assigned to NIOC field sites throughout the world. Those companies are A (Denver, Colorado), B (Fort Meade, Maryland), D (Fort Gordon, Georgia), G (Menwith Hill Station, United Kingdom), H (Medina, San Antonio, Texas), I (Kunia, Hawaii), and L (Suitland, Maryland).[77]

COAST GUARD INTELLIGENCE ORGANIZATIONS

The U.S. Coast Guard, the nation's fifth military service, was placed within the Department of Transportation after that department was established in October 1966; then, on December 28, 2001, it became a component of the Department of Homeland Security (DHS). Three Coast Guard missions are classified as homeland security missions. The first involves conducting harbor patrols, vulnerability assessments,

FIGURE 4.11 Organization of Marine Corps Intelligence Activity

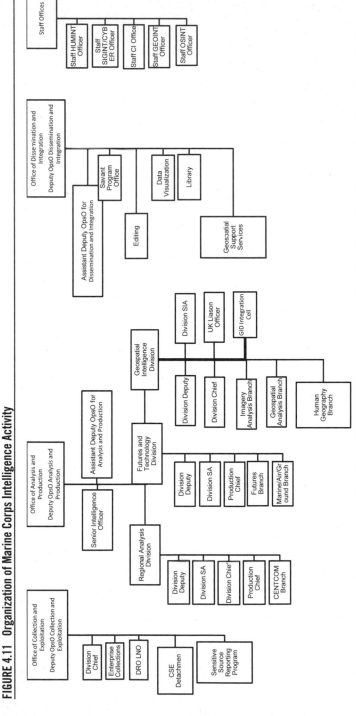

Source: U.S. Marine Corps.

intelligence gathering and analysis, and other activities "to prevent terrorist attacks and minimize the damage from attacks that occur." Additional homeland security missions include defense readiness (which includes deploying cutters and other boats in and around harbors to protect Department of Defense force mobilization operations) and migrant interdiction using cutters and aircraft. Non-homeland-security missions include drug interdiction, aids to navigation, search and rescue, enforcement of fishing laws, marine safety, ice operations, and marine environmental protection.[78]

On the same day that the Coast Guard became an element of DHS, Coast Guard intelligence (which traces its origins to the appointment of a Coast Guard Chief Intelligence Officer in 1915) became a member of the U.S. Intelligence Community when George W. Bush signed an amendment to the 1947 National Security Act. From 2002 to 2004, the number of active-duty Coast Guard personnel working on intelligence matters increased from 194 to 437; by August 2005 it stood at 800.[79]

The Coast Guard's intelligence components are the responsibility of the Assistant Commandant for Intelligence and Criminal Investigations, who reports to the Coast Guard Commandant. The Assistant Commandant determines which Coast Guard intelligence organizations constitute the service's National Intelligence Element, in contrast to those that constitute the service's Law Enforcement Intelligence Element. Coast Guard intelligence elements include the Coast Guard Investigative Service, the Coast Guard Counterintelligence Service (CGCIS), the Coast Guard Cryptologic Group, the Coast Guard Intelligence Coordination Center (CGICC), the Atlantic and Pacific Area Intelligence Divisions, and the Maritime Intelligence Fusion Centers (MIFCs).[80]

The CGCIS is responsible for protecting the "operations, personnel, systems, facilities and information [of the Coast Guard] from Foreign Intelligence and Security Services," from the intelligence efforts of terrorist organizations, drug trafficking elements, and other organized crime groups, and from insider threats. It prepares foreign intelligence threat and awareness briefings on foreign intelligence, terrorist, and other threats. The Coast Guard Cryptographic Group provides personnel to conduct signals intelligence operations.[81]

The Coast Guard Intelligence Coordination Center, whose organization chart is shown as Figure 4.12, is located at the National Maritime Intelligence Center. It is the Coast Guard's strategic-level intelligence analysis and production center, generating intelligence derived from human and technical sources to support Coast Guard operations. It is also responsible for ensuring "the adequacy of Coast Guard intelligence support to other government agencies." It validates requests from Coast Guard elements for tasking of national collection systems, such as reconnaissance satellites, and inserts validated requirements into the national collection systems' requirements and tasking processes. It is also the Coast Guard representative on interagency assessments as well as the designated center for the exploitation of imagery to support maritime interdiction, detection, and monitoring operations.[82]

The CGICC's COASTWATCH program, conducted in cooperation with the Office of Naval Intelligence and the U.S. Customs and Border Protection (CBP), "identifies vessels of interest that may raise national security concerns regarding the people or cargo aboard, business practices, or crew or ownership associations. Its Automated

FIGURE 4.12   Organization of the Coast Guard Intelligence Coordination Center

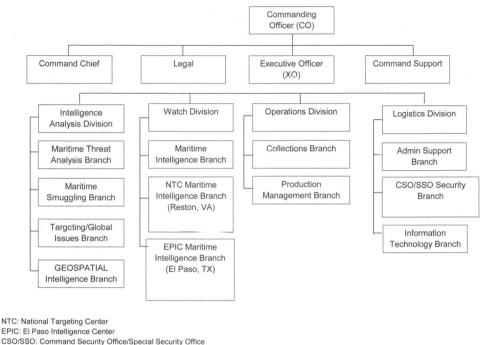

NTC: National Targeting Center
EPIC: El Paso Intelligence Center
CSO/SSO: Command Security Office/Special Security Office

Source: U.S. Coast Guard.

Targeting System–Passenger allows for real-time database checks and can provide information to the FBI, CBP, and National Counterterrorism Center."[83]

In 1999 the CGICC produced, along with the Office of Naval Intelligence, *Threats and Challenges to Maritime Security 2020.* In December 2005, the center's Intelligence Analysis Division produced an analysis of the proposed transfer of port operations from the London-based Peninsular & Oriental Steam Navigation Company to the Dubai-based DP World. The report stated, "There are many intelligence gaps, concerning the potential for DPW or P&O assets to support terrorist operations that preclude an overall threat assessment of the potential merger." More recently, the coordination center produced an unclassified report titled *Yemen: Internal Situation Report for October 2009.*[84]

Beginning in September 2003, the Coast Guard established two facilities, the Maritime Intelligence Fusion Center, Atlantic, at Dam Neck, Virginia, and the Pacific Area Maritime Intelligence Fusion Center at Alameda, California, to provide around-the-clock monitoring of maritime traffic and developments. The centers monitor areas of interest, track events, follow vessels of interest, produce analysis, and evaluate trends. In the Atlantic center's watch office, Coast Guard members survey individual computers while a large monitor displays tracking maps, station locators, radar, and several other news networks. The Atlantic center produces daily intelligence briefings and teleconferences for each of the five Coast Guard districts in the Atlantic region. The centers' reporting is also sent to the DHS Office of Intelligence & Analysis and to national intelligence agencies and is posted on the classified Interlink computer network.[85]

Notes

1. Nicholas Dujmovic, "Elegy of Slashes," *Studies in Intelligence* 51, no. 3 (September 2007): 33–43; Marion W. Boggs, Memorandum, Subject: Discussion at the 473rd Meeting of the National Security Council, Thursday, January 5, 1961, January 5, 1961; Ann Whitman File, Eisenhower Papers, 1953-61, Dwight D. Eisenhower Library.

2. U.S. Congress, Senate Select Committee on Intelligence, Report 101–358, *Authorizing Appropriations for Fiscal Year 1991 for the Intelligence Activities of the U.S. Government, the Intelligence Community Staff, the Central Intelligence Agency Retirement and Disability Systems, and for Other Purposes* (Washington, DC: U.S. Government Printing Office, 1990), 4–5.

3. Ibid.; Assistant Secretary of Defense (Command, Control, Communications, and Intelligence), *Plan for Restructuring Defense Intelligence*, March 15, 1991, 7.

4. "G-2 Staff Organizational Chart," www.dami.army.pentagon.mil/MainOrgChart.aspx (accessed March 15, 2015); "Operations and Plans Directorate (DAMI-OP)," www.dami.army .pentagon.mil/DAMI op.aspx (accessed March 15, 2015); "Intelligence Forces Directorate (G-2 (7)) (DAMI-IF)," www.dami.army.pentagon.mil/DAMI-IF.aspx (accessed December 11, 2010).

5. "Foreign Intelligence Directorate (DAMI-FI)," www.dami.army.pentagon.mil/DAMI-FI .aspx (accessed December 27, 2014); "Army G-2X Counterintelligence, Human Intelligence, Security and Disclosure Directorate (DAMI-CD)," www.dami.army.pentagon.mil/DAMI-CD.aspx; "Army Foreign Liaison Directorate (DAMI-FL)," www.damil.army.pentagon.mil/DAMI-FL.aspx (accessed December 27, 2014).

6. U.S. Army, "Memorandum to Correspondents," n.d.; James L. Gilbert, "In '77, Command Created New Identity," *INSCOM Journal* (Summer 2002): 14–16; INSCOM History Office, "The INSCOM Story," www.inscom.army.mil/organization/HIstory.aspx (accessed November 18, 2013).

7. Letter, Paul D. Sutton, U.S. Army Intelligence and Security Command, to Jeffrey Richelson, November 20, 1992; INSCOM Permanent Order 41-1, "United States Army and Intelligence Security Command, Intelligence Production Management Activity (Provisional), Falls Church, Virginia, 22041," April 9, 1992; INSCOM Permanent Order 41-2, "United States Army Foreign Science and Technology Center (WOKPAA), Charlottesville, Virginia, 22901, United States Intelligence and Threat Analysis Center (W3YDAA), Washington, D.C. 20370," April 9, 1992; Brigadier General Robert L. Walter Jr., Overview Briefing for National Defense Industrial Association (NDIA), *US Army Intelligence and Security Command (INSCOM)*, April 3, 2013.

8. U.S. Army Intelligence and Security Command, "Command & Staff Phone Numbers," www.inscom.army.mil/Organization/Phone.aspx (accessed October 23, 2013); U.S. Army Intelligence and Security Command, INSCOM Regulation 10-2, *Organizations and Functions: United States Army Intelligence and Security Command (INSCOM)*, February 10, 2011, 3–4, 41, 53, 63, 64, 72, 101, 117, 131, 143.

9. Walter, Overview Briefing for National Defense Industrial Association (NDIA), *US Army Intelligence and Security Command (INSCOM)*; "704th Military Intelligence Brigade," *INSCOM Journal*, Almanac 2009, 21; U.S. Army Intelligence and Security Command, "704th Military Intelligence Brigade," https://www.inscom.army.mil/msc/704mib.aspx (accessed March 16, 2015).

10. U.S. Army Intelligence and Security Command, "Major Subordinate Commands," www .inscom.army.mil/MSC (accessed October 23, 2013); Walter, Overview Briefing for National Defense Industrial Association (NDIA), *US Army Intelligence and Security Command (INSCOM)*; U.S.

Army Intelligence and Security Command, "706th Military Intelligence Group," https://www.inscom.army.mil/MSC/706MIG.aspx (accessed March 16, 2015); U.S. Army Intelligence and Security Command, http://www.inscom.army.mil (accessed March 16, 2015).

11. "Task Force Observe, Detect, Identify, and Neutralize— Afghanistan Enhanced (Task Force ODIN-A)," http://www.globalsecurity.org/military/agency/army/tf-odin-e.htm (accessed March 15, 2015); "Task Force ODIN Afghanistan," *Afghan War News*, http://www.afghanwarnews.info/units/taskforceodinafghanistan.htm (accessed June 3, 2014); U.S. Army Intelligence and Security Command, "Major Subordinate Commands"; "JSTARS," *INSCOM Journal*, Almanac 2011, 23.

12. "902 MI Group," *INSCOM Journal*, Almanac 2009, 13; Walter, Overview Briefing for National Defense Industrial Association (NDIA), *US Army Intelligence and Security Command (INSCOM)*; U.S. Army Intelligence and Security Command, "902nd Military Intelligence Group," www.inscom.army.mil/MSC/902MIG.aspx (accessed March 15, 2015).

13. "AOA," *INSCOM Journal*, Almanac 2009, 27; "AOG," *INSCOM Journal*, Almanac 2011, 24; U.S. Army Intelligence and Security Command, "Army Operations Group," www.inscom.army.mil/MSC/AOG.aspx (accessed October 23, 2013).

14. Walter, Overview Briefing for National Defense Industrial Association (NDIA), *US Army Intelligence and Security Command (INSCOM)*; "66th MI Brigade," *INSCOM Journal*, Almanac 2011, 13, 14; U.S. Army Intelligence and Security Command, "Welcome to the 66th MI Brigade Public Web Site," 66th Military Intelligence Brigade, June 24, 2011, https://www.inscom.army.mil/MSC/66MIB; U.S. Army Intelligence and Security Command, "Quick Facts," 66th Military Intelligence Brigade, http://www.inscom.army.mil/MSC/66MIB/index.html (accessed June 3, 2014); U.S. Army Intelligence and Security Command, "66th Military Intelligence Brigade," www.inscom.army.mil (accessed March 15, 2015).

15. Walter, Overview Briefing for National Defense Industrial Association (NDIA), *US Army Intelligence and Security Command (INSCOM)*; "500th MI Brigade," *INSCOM Journal*, Almanac 2011, 15; U.S. Army Intelligence and Security Command, "500th MI Brigade," https://www.inscom.army.mil/msc/500mib/index.html (accessed October 23, 2013).

16. Walter, Overview Briefing for National Defense Industrial Association (NDIA), *US Army Intelligence and Security Command (INSCOM)*; "501st MI Brigade," *INSCOM Journal*, Almanac 2011, 16; U.S. Army and Intelligence Security Command, "501st Military Intelligence Brigade," www.inscom.army.mil/MSC/501MIB.aspx (accessed March 15, 2015).

17. Walter, Overview Briefing for National Defense Industrial Association (NDIA), *US Army Intelligence and Security Command (INSCOM)*; "513th MI Brigade," *INSCOM Journal*, Almanac 2011, 17; U.S. Army Intelligence and Security Command, "513th Military Intelligence Brigade," www.inscom.army.mil/MSC/513MIB.aspx (accessed March 15, 2015).

18. Walter, Overview Briefing for National Defense Industrial Association (NDIA), *US Army Intelligence and Security Command (INSCOM)*; "1st IO (Land)," *INSCOM Journal*, Almanac 2011, 22; U.S. Army Intelligence and Security Command, "1st Information Operations Command (Land)," www.inscom.army.mil/MSC/001Ioe.aspx (accessed March 16, 2015).

19. Foreign Science and Technology Center, *U.S. Army Foreign Science and Technology Center Unit History, FY 63–77*, n.d., 3; Paul E. Menoher, "INSCOM Thrives Despite Changes," *INSCOM Journal*, September 1994, 1; National Ground Intelligence Center, "Lineage of the NGIC," n.d.

20. National Ground Intelligence Center, " . . . About the National Ground Intelligence Center," 1998; "NGIC," *INSCOM Journal*, Almanac 2011, 21.

21. National Ground Intelligence Center, " . . . About the National Ground Intelligence Center"; "NGIC," *INSCOM Journal*, Almanac 2011, 21.

22. "Army Intelligence Site Lifts Secrecy Veil," *Washington Post*, January 5, 1997, A10; Walter Pincus, "Intelligence Center, Contractor MZM on Cozy Terms," *Washington Post*, July 7, 2005, A7.

23. R. M. Walsh, Assistant Vice Chief of Naval Operations, "Memorandum for the Secretary of the Navy, Subject: Disestablishment and Establishment of Certain Naval Intelligence Command Shore Activities," July 31, 1991; OPNAV Notice 5450, "Subject: Disestablishment and

Establishment of Commander, Naval Intelligence Command Shore Activities, and Modification of Detachments," September 13, 1991; Naval Intelligence Command, *Organization, Mission, and Key Personnel: Naval Intelligence Command, HQ, Naval Maritime Intelligence Center, Naval Intelligence Activity*, October 1991, 59–80; "Fact and Justification Sheet: COMNAVINTCOM Claimancy Reorganization," attachment to R. M. Walsh, Assistant Vice Chief of Naval Operations, "Memorandum for the Secretary of the Navy"; "Memorandum for the Secretary of the Navy, Subject: Disestablishment of Three Shore Activities and Establishment of One Consolidated Shore Command," December 1, 1992; Office of Naval Intelligence, *Consolidating the Naval Intelligence Command, Naval Maritime Intelligence Center, Naval, Intelligence Activity*, January 7, 1993.

24. Major Herbert M. Strauss, Office of the Assistant Secretary of Defense (Command, Control, Communications, and Intelligence), *Status Report: Strengthening Defense Intelligence*, 1991, 4.

25. Maryland Department of Business & Economic Development, "Maryland, Federal Facilities Profile: National Maritime Intelligence Center (NMIC)," June 2009.

26. Dr. Michael G. Vickers and Lieutenant General Michael T. Flynn, "Statement for the Record Before the House Armed Services Committee Subcommittee on Intelligence, Emerging Threats and Capabilities," February 27, 2013, 6.

27. Office of Naval Intelligence, "Office of Naval Intelligence Fact Sheet," www.oni.navy.mil (accessed March 15, 2015).

28. Ibid.

29. Chief of Naval Operations, OPNAV Notice 5400, Subject: Establishment of Nimitz Operational Intelligence Center, Washington, D.C., Farragut Technical Analysis Center, Washington, D.C., Kennedy Irregular Warfare Center, Washington, D.C., and Hopper Information Services Center, Washington, D.C.," January 14, 2009; Office of Naval Intelligence, "Hopper Information Services Center Fact Sheet," January 16, 2014, http://www.oni.navy.mil/commands/Hopper .html (accessed June 5, 2014); Office of Naval Intelligence, "Kennedy Irregular Warfare Center Fact Sheet," September 24, 2013, http://www.oni.navy.mil/commands/Kennedy.html (accessed June 5, 2014).

30. Office of Naval Intelligence, "Nimitz Operational Intelligence Center Fact Sheet," http://www.oni.navy.mil/commands/Nimitz.html (accessed March 15, 2015).

31. Ibid.

32. Office of Naval Intelligence, "Farragut Technical Analysis Center Fact Sheet," September 24, 2013, http://www.oni.navy.mil/commands/Farragut.html (accessed June 5, 2014).

33. Office of Naval Intelligence, *Transforming for the 21st Century*, January 2009, 21.

34. Ibid., 23, 24.

35. Ibid., 6, 27.

36. Office of Naval Intelligence, "Nimitz Operational Intelligence Center Fact Sheet."

37. Naval Criminal Investigative Service, "NCIS Office Locations," http://www.ncis.navy.mil /AboutNCIS/Locations/Pages/default.aspx (accessed June 5, 2014).

38. Naval Criminal Investigative Service, "About NCIS," http://www.ncis.navy.mil/ AboutNCIS/Pages/default.aspx (accessed June 5, 2014); Naval Criminal Investigative Service, "Intelligence and Information Sharing," http://www.ncis.navy.mil/MissionSupport/Pages/ IntelligencyInformationSharing.aspx (accessed June 5, 2014).

39. Office of Naval Intelligence, *Transforming for the 21st Century*, January 2009, 6, 27; Letter, Jeana D. Watson, to Jeffrey Richelson, November 19, 2009; Deputy Commander, Office of Naval Intelligence, "To: All ONI-36 Employees, Subject: Civilian ONI-36 Employees Notice of ONI-36 Transfer of Function and Request for Decision to Exercise Transfer Rights," January 22, 2009.

40. HQNSGINST 5450.2G CH-1, *Headquarters, Naval Security Group Command Organization Manual*, August 17, 1995, I-1 to I-2.

41. Ibid.; Joseph Grunder, "Naval Security Group Aligns with NETWARCOM," America's Navy, October 5, 2005, http://www.navy.mil/submit/display.asp?story_id=20444; "IOD— Information Operations Directorate," http://ekm.netwarcom.navy.mil, August 1, 2006.

42. Dr. Starnes Walker, Technical Director/CTO Fleet Cyber Command, Presentation to the Armed Forces Communications Electronics Association, *U.S. Fleet Cyber Command/U.S. Tenth Fleet,* 2012; Office of the Chief of Naval Operations, OPNAV Notice 5400, "Subject: Disestablish Navy Information Operations Detachment, Jacksonville, FL," August 16, 2012; Office of the Chief of Naval Operations, OPNAV Notice 5400, "Subject: Disestablish Navy Information Operations Detachment, Yakima, WA," January 25, 2013; Office of the Chief of Naval Operations, OPNAV Notice 5400, Subject: Disestablish Navy Information Operations Command, Sugar Grove, WV, April 22, 2013; Office of Naval Operations, OPNAV Notice 5400, "Subject: Disestablishment of Navy Information Operations Command, Misawa, JA and Realignment of Navy Information Operations Command Detachment, Seoul, Kor," September 5, 2014.

43. Chief of Naval Operations, OPNAV Notice 5400, Subj: Establishment of Naval Intelligence Activity, Washington DC as New Echelon Two and Realignment of Office of Naval Intelligence to Echelon Three, September 29, 2014; Chief of Naval Operations, OPNAV Notice 5400, Subj: Realignment of Administrative Command of Office of Naval Intelligence Subordinate Activities, September 29, 2014.

44. Chairman, Joint Chiefs of Staff, Joint Publication 2-01, *Joint and National Intelligence Support to Military Operations,* January 5, 2012, II-17; Air Combat Command Public Affairs, "Air Combat Command to Host New ISR Numbered Air Force," July 14, 2014, http://www.acc.af.mil/news/story.asp?id=123417589.

45. Jeffrey Richelson, "A New Look for Air Force Intelligence," *Defense Week,* March 31, 1997, 6; Office of the Director of National Intelligence, *An Overview of the United States Intelligence Community,* 2007, 22.

46. U.S. Air Force, "Lieutenant General Robert P. 'Bob' Otto," July 2013, http://www.af.mil/AboutUs/Biographies/Display/tabid/225/Article/108133/lieutenant-general-robert-p-bob-otto.aspx; Headquarters, U.S. Air Force, HAF Mission Directive 1-33, "Deputy Chief of Staff of the Air Force Intelligence, Surveillance & Reconnaissance," September 4, 2009.

47. Ibid.

48. "Air Force Intelligence Service" *Air Force Magazine* (May 1982): 126.

49. "Air Force Intelligence Analysis Agency," *Air Force Magazine* (May 2015): 56; U.S. Air Force, "Air Force Intelligence Analysis Agency," Fact Sheet, http://www.afhra.af.mil (accessed December 4, 2013); DOD Instruction 3115.14, "Civil Aviation Intelligence," July 29, 2011; Carlo Munoz, "Air Force Tackles New Intel Mission," *Breaking Defense,* August 9, 2011, http://breakingdefense.com/2011/08/air-force-tackles-new-intel-mission.

50. Department of the Air Force, "Air Force Creates New Intelligence Command," June 6, 1991.

51. Ibid.

52. Headquarters, U.S. Air Force, "Basic Plan to HQ USAF Program Action Directive (PAD) 93-8, Restructuring Air Force Intelligence," June 15, 1993; Headquarters, Air Force Intelligence Command, HQ AFIC Programming Plan 93-01, "Establishment of the Air Force Intelligence Field Operating Agency," August 17, 1993; "Air Intelligence Agency," www.af.mil/factsheets (accessed February 12, 2006).

53. U.S. Air Force, Office of Public Affairs, "Air Intelligence Agency," Fact Sheet 95-10, September 1995; "About the Agency," *Air Intelligence Agency Almanac* (August 1997): 12–13; "Air Intelligence Agency," www.af.mil/factsheets (accessed February 12, 2006); Theresa Shannon, "AFISR Agency," *Spokesman* (July 2007): 4; "Air Force Aligns Intelligence Agency Under Intelligence Directorate," *Spokesman* (June 2007): 4; "Personnel Strength by Commands, FOAs, and DRUs," *Air Force Magazine* (May 2014): 29; "Air Intelligence Agency to Become Air Force ISR Agency," *Air Force Print News Today,* May 15, 2007, http://www.af.mil; U.S. Air Force, Fact Sheet, "Air Force ISR Agency," http://www.afisr.af.mil (accessed June 6, 2014).

54. Air Combat Command, "Air Combat Command to Host New ISR Number Air Force; [author name deleted], *History of the Air Force Intelligence, Surveillance, and Reconnaissance Agency 1 January—31 December 2012* (San Antonio, TX: Air Force Intelligence, Surveillance, and Reconnaissance Agency History Office, 2014), 23.

55. U.S. Air Force, Fact Sheet, "480th Intelligence, Surveillance and Reconnaissance Wing," Twenty-Fifth Air Force, February 13, 2014, http://www.25af.af.mil; Marge McGlinn, "Cohee Takes Command of 480th ISR Group," Air Force Intelligence, Surveillance, and Reconnaissance Agency, July 15, 2014, http://www.25af.af.mil/news/story.asp?id=123417801.

56. U.S. Air Force, Fact Sheet, "70th Intelligence, Surveillance and Reconnaissance Wing," Twenty-Fifth Air Force, November 20, 2014, http://www.25af.af.mil/library/factsheets/factsheet .asp?id=14145 (accessed November 20, 2014); Samuel Daub, "659th Stands-Up Air Force's Newest Cyber Squadron," *Air Force Print News Today*, October 8, 2014, http://www.25af.af.mil/news /story.asp?id=123427628.

57. U.S. Air Force, "70th Intelligence, Surveillance and Reconnaissance Wing.

58. Ibid.; Aram Roston, "Interview: Col. Michael L. Downs, Commander, 707th ISR Group," www.defensenews.com, April 9, 2013, http://mobile.defensenews.com/article/304090013.

59. U.S. Air Force, Fact Sheet, "9th Reconnaissance Wing," Beale Air Force Base, February 3, 2014, http://www.beale.af.mil/library/factsheets/factsheet.asp?id=3942 (accessed October 3, 2014); U.S. Air Force, Fact Sheet, "55th Wing," March 15, 2011, http://www.offutt.af.mil/library /factsheets (accessed Mach 15, 2015).

60. Air Combat Command Public Affairs, "New ISR Wing Joints AF with Unique Mission," *Air Force Print News Today*, Twenty-Firth Air Force, February 19, 2015, http://www.25af.af.mil /news/story_print.asp?id=123439614; U.S. Air Force, Fact Sheet, "Air Force Targeting Center," January 15, 2010, http://www.afhra.af.mil/factsheets/factsheet.asp?id=16203; Lt. Col. Matt Johnson, 361S/CC, "Air Force Targeting Center, Precision Strike Annual Review," February 23, 2011, http://www.dtic.mil.

61. U.S. Congress, Senate Committee on Appropriations, *Department of Defense Appropriations, FY 1973*, pt. 4 (Washington, DC: U.S. Government Printing Office, 1972), 364–365; "Air Force Technical Applications Center," *Air Force Magazine* (May 2006): 123–124; Mary Welch, "AFTAC Celebrates 50 Years of Long Range Detection," *AFTAC Monitor* (October 1997): 8–32; Science Applications International Corp., *Fifty Year Commemorative History of Long Range Detection: The Creation, Development, and Operation of the United States Atomic Energy Detection System* (Patrick Air Force Base, FL: Air Force Technical Applications Center, 1997), 4–5.

62. "Air Force Technical Applications Center," *Air Force Magazine* (May 1997): 126; Air Force Technical Applications Center, Center Instruction 38-101, *Organization and Functions Chartbook*, February 12, 2012, 4; U.S. Air Force, Fact Sheet, "Air Force Technical Applications Center," November 7, 2014, http://www.25af.af.mil/library/factsheets/factsheet.asp?id=10309.

63. "Air Force Technical Applications Center, Staff Directory," October 1, 2013; Air Force Technical Applications Center, Center Instruction 38-101, *Organization and Functions Chartbook*, 12, 18–22, 25.

64. Air Force Technical Applications Center, Center Instruction 10-102, *USAEDS Event Processing and Reporting Procedures*, February 26, 2007, 41.

65. Marc V. Schanz, "Introducing the 25th Air Force," www.airforcemag.com, July 15, 2014, http://www.airforcemag.com/DRArchive/Pages/2014/July%202014/July%2015%202014/ Introducing%20the%2025th%20Air%20Force.aspx.

66. Wright-Patterson Air Force Base, "Unit Designations and Assignments," www.wpafb.af .mil/naic/history7.html (accessed February 12, 2006); *FTD 1917–1967* (Dayton, OH: FTD, 1967), 8, 10, 12, 22, 26; Colonel Robert B. Kalisch, "Air Technical Intelligence," *Air University Review* 12 (July–August 1971): 2–11, at 7, 9; "National Air Intelligence Center," *Air Intelligence Agency Almanac*, 1997, 14–15; National Air and Space Intelligence Center, "National Air and Space Intelligence Center," n.d.

67. Kalisch, "Air Technical Intelligence"; Bruce Ashcroft, "National Air Intelligence Center Emerges from FASTC, 480th IG," *Spokesman* (November 1993): 12; Robert Young, "National Air Intelligence Center," *Spokesman* (September 1996): 4–5.

68. "Unit Designations and Assignments"; "National Air Intelligence Center Emerges from FASTC, 480th IG"; U.S. Air Force, Office of Public Affairs, Fact Sheet 95-10, "Air Intelligence Agency."

69. Barrie Barber, "New Commander Named for Intelligence Center," *Dayton Daily News*, March 26, 2014, http://www.daytondailynews.com/news/news/nasic-names-new-commander/nfLf4 (accessed March 26, 2014); U.S. Air Force, Fact Sheet, "National Air and Space Intelligence Center," October 2012, http://www.25af.af.mil/library/factsheets/factsheet_print.asp?fsID=20004.

70. U.S. Air Force, Fact Sheet, "National Air and Intelligence Center," June 23, 2008; U.S. Air Force, "National Air and Space Intelligence Center."

71. "Air Force Intelligence, Surveillance, and Reconnaissance Agency Organizational Chart," October 2013; [author name deleted], *History of the Air Force Intelligence, Surveillance, and Reconnaissance Agency*, vol. 1: *Narrative and Appendices* (San Antonio, TX: Air Force Intelligence, Surveillance, and Reconnaissance Agency, 2014), 93–94, 190–191; Jeffrey T. Richelson, "The Grounded Spies," *Air Force Magazine* (December 2014): 64–67.

72. U.S. Air Force, Fact Sheet, "Air Force Office of Special Investigations," May 9, 2011, http://www.osi.af.mil/library/factsheets/factsheet.asp?id=4848; Secretary of the Air Force, Air Force Mission Directive 39, "Air Force Office of Special Investigations," July 6, 2011; "Personnel Strength by Commands, FOAs, and DRUs."

73. Air Force Office of Special Investigations, *2013 OSI Fact Book*, 2013, 16, 30. On AFOSI history, see Christine E. Williamson, "The Air Force Office of Special Investigation: Postured for the Future," *Air & Space Power Journal* (Summer 2005): 23–28.

74. Marines Corps, "Headquarters, United States Marine Corps—Intelligence Department," http://www.hqmc.marines.mil/intelligence/UnitHome.aspx.

75. Neil Munro, "Center Will Spearhead Marines' Data Analysis," *Defense News*, January 20, 1992, 12; "Director Visits MCIA," *Communiqué* (January–February 1997): 30; Robert W. Livingston, "Marine Corps Intelligence Activity—Excellence in Expeditionary Intelligence," *American Intelligence Journal* 17, nos. 1–2 (1996): 29–33; Commandant of the Marine Corps (CMC), "Subject: Reorganization of the Marine Corps Intelligence Activity (MCIA)," July 31, 2002.

76. "MCIA Mission," n.d., provided by the Marine Corps in response to a Freedom of Information Act request.

77. "Marine Corps Intelligence," *Military Intelligence* (July–September 1983): 121ff.; CMC, Subject: Reorganization of the Marine Corps Intelligence Activity (MCIA); Marine Corps, *Marine Corps 2005–2015 ISR Roadmap Version 1.1*, October 2, 2006, 46; Marine Corps, "Marine Cryptologic Support Battalion," http://www.hqmc.marines.mil/intelligence/Units/MarineCryptologicSupportBattalion.aspx (accessed April 17, 2014).

78. Government Accountability Office, GAO-10-411T, "Statement of Stephen L. Caldwell, Coast Guard: Observations of the Requested Fiscal Year 2011 Budget, Past Performance, and Current Challenges," February 25, 2010, 26–27.

79. U.S. Coast Guard, "Missions," http://www.uscg.mil/top/missions (accessed August 11, 2006); Intelligence.gov, "US Coast Guard Intelligence," www.intelligence.gov/1-members_coastguard.shtml (accessed August 11, 2006). An examination of how the Coast Guard's intelligence element became a member of the Intelligence Community can be found in Kevin E. Wirth, *The Coast Guard Intelligence Programs Enters the Intelligence Community: A Case Study of Congressional Influence on Intelligence Community Evolution* (Washington, DC: National Defense Intelligence College, 2007). Also see U.S. Coast Guard, *Intelligence*, Coast Guard Publication 2-0, May 2010.

80. U.S. Coast Guard, *Intelligence*, 13.

81. Ibid., 20.

82. Ibid.; Office of National Drug Control Policy, *General Counterdrug Intelligence Plan*, February 2000, A-14.

83. Admiral Robert J. Papp, Commandant, U.S. Coast Guard, Testimony Before the Subcommittee on Border & Maritime Security, House Committee on Homeland Security, "Securing the Nation's Ports and Maritime Border—a Review of the Coast Guard Post 9/11 Homeland

Security Missions," June 14, 2011, http://www.gpo.gov/fdsys/pkg/CHRG-112hhrg72241/pdf/ CHRG-112hhrg72241.pdf.

84. Commander Jim Howe, *The Fifth Side of the Pentagon: Moving the Coast Guard to the Department of Defense* (Quantico, VA: Marine Corps War College, 2002), 29; Liz Sidoti, "Paper: Coast Guard Has Port Co. Intel Gaps," February 27, 2006, http://www.comcast.net; Carl Hulse and David E. Sanger, "Coast Guard Had Concerns About Ports Deal," *New York Times*, February 28, 2006, A15; Coast Guard Intelligence Coordination Center, *Yemen: Internal Situation Report for October 2009*, October 22, 2009.

85. Patricia Kime, "Maritime 'Fusion' Centers Expand Coast Guard Intelligence Capabilities," *Sea Power* 47, no. 5 (May 2004): 16; Admiral Thomas H. Collins, "Transportation Security," Statement Before the Senate Committee on Commerce, Science, and Transportation, September 9, 2003; Sue A. Lackey, "More Clout," Military.com, August 2005, http://www.military.com/ NewContent/0,13190,NL_USCG_081605,00.html.

5

CIVILIAN DEPARTMENTAL INTELLIGENCE ORGANIZATIONS

The bulk of U.S. intelligence resources, whether in terms of personnel or dollars, lies in the hands of the Defense Department, the military services, and the national intelligence organizations, including the civilian CIA. However, components of the Departments of State, Energy, Treasury, Homeland Security, and Justice (the Federal Bureau of Investigation [FBI] and the Drug Enforcement Administration [DEA]) carry out intelligence and/or counterintelligence activities. The focus of those activities includes terrorist groups, proliferation, foreign policies, military forces, economic affairs, and narcotics trafficking. In addition to supporting departmental activities, they also contribute to the national intelligence effort.

DEPARTMENT OF STATE INTELLIGENCE

With the dissolution of the Office of Strategic Services after World War II, its research and analysis functions were transferred to the State Department and an Interim Research and Intelligence Service. Two subsequent name changes followed until the service became the Bureau of Intelligence and Research (INR) in 1957. INR's fiscal year 2013 budget request was for 363 personnel and $72.65 million.[1]

The bureau does not engage in clandestine collection, although it receives reports through normal diplomatic channels, conducts open source collection, and receives intelligence gathered through human and technical methods by other agencies. It does perform several functions concerning operational matters, serving as a liaison between the Department of State and the Intelligence Community (IC) to ensure that the actions of other intelligence agencies are consistent with U.S. foreign policy.[2]

In terms of production, INR, as its director stated in 2009, has "as a State Department bureau and element of the IC . . . two masters." One master is the Director of National Intelligence (DNI), since INR is involved in interagency intelligence production efforts, such as National Intelligence Estimates. It also "serves . . . as a bridge between the worlds of diplomacy and intelligence." Its second master is the Secretary of State and the rest of the State Department, for which INR prepares a variety of intelligence products. The Secretary of State's Morning Summary informs the secretary or his or her principal deputies of current events and current intelligence. INR also prepares a variety of regional and functional summaries as well as single-subject reports. Its analytical reach has been described as ranging "from pirates in Somalia and North Korean missile launches, to narco-violence in Mexico, new cyber threats, and infectious diseases."[3]

The Director of INR is simultaneously the Assistant Secretary of State for Intelligence and Research. As shown in Figure 5.1, the assistant secretary is assisted by the Principal Deputy Assistant Secretary, the Deputy Assistant Secretary for Analysis, and the Deputy Assistant Secretary for Intelligence Policy and Coordination. The Principal Deputy Assistant Secretary supervises the INR Watch, the Office of Opinion Research, the Office of Outreach, and the Office of the Executive Director.[4] INR Watch serves as the around-the-clock State Department center for "monitoring, evaluating, alerting, and briefing time-sensitive intelligence to the Department and bureau principals" and is the primary liaison to other Intelligence Community operations centers. The Office of Opinion Research has a number of functions, including managing surveys of foreign public and elite opinion on major issues and remaining current with worldwide public opinion research of interest to U.S. foreign policy decision makers. The Office of Outreach "organizes and funds analytic exchanges with outside experts to inform the thinking of U.S. government policymakers and intelligence analysts."[5]

The Deputy Assistant Secretary for Analysis supervises analysis offices for Africa, East Asia and the Pacific, Europe, Western Hemisphere Affairs, the Near East and South Asia, Russia and Eurasia, and Europe. These offices produce analyses of developments that are, or will be, of concern to policymakers. The offices are also responsible for preparing regional and other special summaries and for contributing to Intelligence Community estimates. An analyst for the Office of Analysis for Europe might be asked to examine the domestic situation in Germany or the likely outcome of an upcoming French election. An East Asia and Pacific analyst might be concerned with the role of the Chinese People's Liberation Army in domestic politics.[6]

The Deputy Assistant Secretary for Analysis is also responsible for supervising the Office of Economic Analysis, the Office of the Geographer and Global Issues, the Office of Analysis for Strategic, Proliferation, and Military Issues, and the Office of Analysis for Terrorism, Narcotics, and Crime. In addition, the Director of Analytic Effectiveness reports to the Deputy Assistant Secretary.[7] The Office of Economic Analysis produces assessments of international economic issues, including economic growth and development, economic security, trade, energy, and terrorist financing. The Office of the Geographer and Global Issues focuses, inter alia, on humanitarian crises and multilateral interventions, human rights and war crimes, natural resource and energy issues, and the activities of the United Nations and other international organizations. The Office of Analysis for Strategic, Proliferation, and Military Issues produces analyses concerning proliferation of weapons of mass destruction, international transfers of advanced conventional weapons, arms control agreements, and military conflicts and balances in areas of interest to State Department customers. The Office of Analysis for Terrorism, Narcotics, and Crime produces assessments on those subjects, including the structure and operations of drug cartels and their impact on U.S. security and diplomatic efforts.[8]

FIGURE 5.1   Organization of the Bureau of Intelligence and Research, Department of State

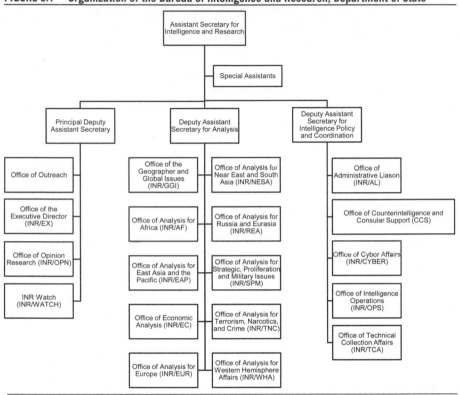

Source: Department of State, *Foreign Affairs Manual.*

The Deputy Assistant Secretary for Intelligence Policy and Coordination supervises five offices: Administrative Liaison, Counterintelligence and Consular Support, Cyber Affairs, Intelligence Operations, and Technical Collection Affairs. The Office of Counterintelligence and Consular Support is INR's principal contact with the FBI, supports State Department participation on the National Counterintelligence Policy Board, and supports State Department activities involving the issuing or revoking of visas to individuals believed to be a threat to U.S. national security. The Office of Cyber Affairs focuses on cyber-related intelligence policy and analyzes the implications for U.S. foreign policy of foreign cyber activities as well as foreign responses to U.S. cyber policy and activities. The Office of Intelligence Operations is responsible for coordinating the department's review of sensitive CIA and military intelligence operations and programs, acting as liaison with the CIA and DIA, and coordinating the collection and analysis of biographic information on foreign leaders.[9]

The Office of Technical Collection Affairs coordinates with the State Department and other federal agencies on U.S. technical collection programs and policies and relations with foreign technical collection agencies; it provides support to INR analysts and department policymakers on tasking technical collection systems and represents

State on interagency bodies concerned with future imagery, signals intelligence (SIGINT), and measurement and signature intelligence (MASINT) architectures. In 1992 the director of a predecessor office of the technical collection component advised the National Reconnaissance Office (NRO) on how to handle the forthcoming declassification of its existence.[10]

DEPARTMENT OF ENERGY INTELLIGENCE

The intelligence role of the Department of Energy (DOE) can be traced to July 1946, when the National Intelligence Authority decided that the Atomic Energy Commission (AEC) had an appropriate foreign intelligence role and authorized AEC representation on the Intelligence Advisory Board. On December 12, 1947, National Security Council Intelligence Directive No. 1, "Duties and Responsibilities," affirmed the AEC's intelligence role.[11]

The Energy Reorganization Act of 1974 transferred the AEC's intelligence operations to the Energy Research and Development Administration, and the Department of Energy Act of 1977 transferred them to the newly created Department of Energy. In April 1990, the Energy Department consolidated its intelligence functions by establishing an Office of Intelligence, bringing under one roof the Offices of Foreign Intelligence, Threat Assessment, and Counterintelligence. A 1994 reorganization resulted in the redesignation of the office as the Office of Energy Intelligence (OEI) within the Office of Nonproliferation and National Security, with the Office of Threat Assessment moved outside the new intelligence unit.[12]

A 1998 reorganization in response to concerns about the effectiveness of Energy Department security and Presidential Directive 61 of February 11, 1998, "U.S. Department of Energy Counterintelligence Program," split the OEI into two offices: the Office of Intelligence and the Office of Counterintelligence. At the end of 2005, according to one Energy Department document, "DOE's intelligence components were a highly fractured assortment of organizations: one focusing on foreign intelligence analysis, another on counterintelligence operations at NNSA [National Nuclear Security Administration] facilities and organizations, and a third responsible for counterintelligence at non-NNSA portions of DOE as well as counterintelligence policy for the entire Department." As a result, in the spring of 2006, the intelligence and counterintelligence offices were renamed directorates and resubordinated to a joint office, the Office of Intelligence and Counterintelligence. By 2013, in addition to the Intelligence and Counterintelligence directorates, a third major component had been added to the office: the Cyber Directorate. In 2012 the office had 199 federal employees.[13] Figure 5.2 shows the organization chart of the Office of Intelligence and Counterintelligence.

Topics addressed by the Office of Intelligence include foreign nuclear weapons programs. It produces studies and reports for intelligence, military planning, diplomatic, and treaty-monitoring purposes. During Operations DESERT SHIELD and DESERT STORM, it provided the Joint Chiefs of Staff and Defense Intelligence Agency with assessments of the Iraqi nuclear weapons program and its capabilities. It has also been concerned with issues such as the command, control, and security of tactical and strategic nuclear weapons in Russia and other former Soviet states,

122

FIGURE 5.2 Organization of the Office of Intelligence and Counterintelligence, Department of Energy

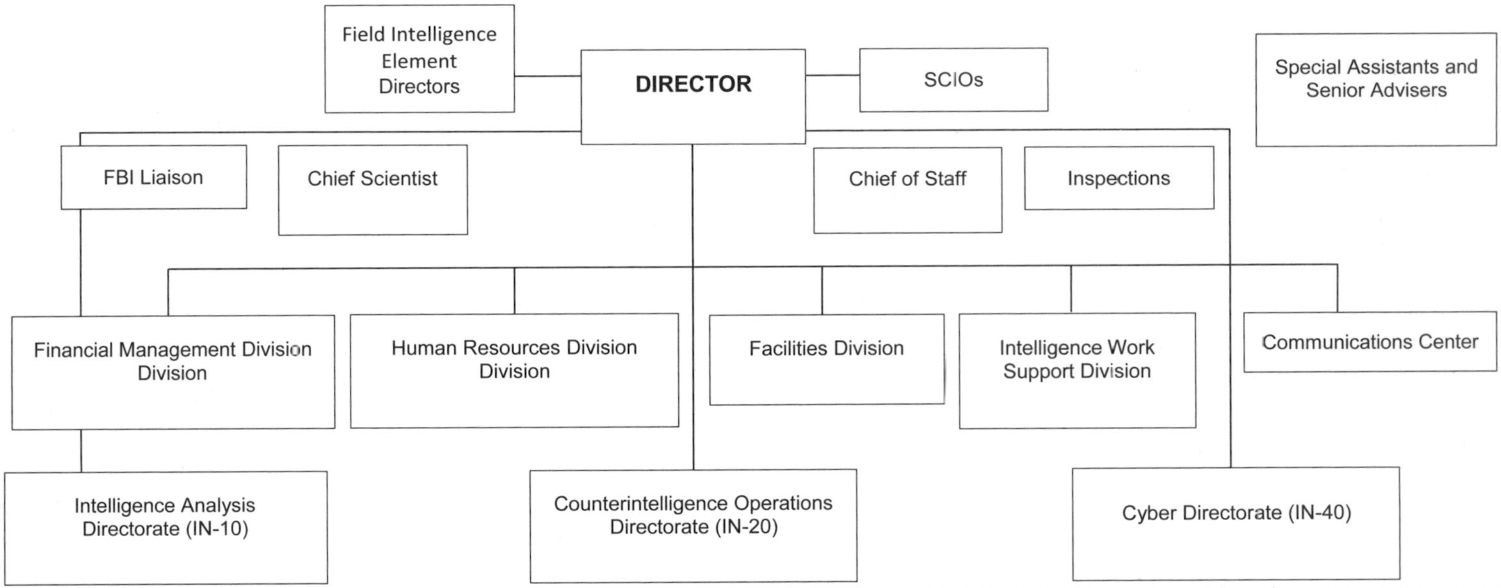

Source: DOE.

the dismantlement of nuclear weapons in the former Soviet Union, the disposition of the nuclear materials removed from those weapons, and the proliferation potential (through a "brain drain") of the former Soviet republics.[14]

The Office of Intelligence has also addressed energy security. It has focused on international developments that could affect the overall U.S. energy posture and the Strategic Petroleum Reserve. Special studies conducted by the office examined the prospects for disruption of energy supplies due to worldwide political, economic, and social instabilities. In addition, the office analyzed overall energy balances within Russia and other nations, focusing on total energy needs that might influence supply and demand. It also examined energy technologies that may have dual uses (civil and military) in support of foreign availability studies related to the Energy Department's Militarily Critical Technologies List.[15]

Counterterrorism responsibilities of the Office of Intelligence include monitoring and analyzing developments related to terrorist groups to obtain or produce nuclear or radiation dispersal devices, including scientific publications, the security at Russian and other nuclear installations, and attempts to acquire fissile material. Other matters examined by the office include developments in science and technology that affect the ability of nations or groups to produce nuclear weapons.

The Office of Counterintelligence conducts counterintelligence risk assessments, including assessments of the Energy Department's susceptibility to economic espionage. The DOE's counterintelligence products have included *Statistical Analysis of Foreign Visits to DOE Facilities* (September 1993) and *Information Brokers* (August 1994). Counterintelligence newsletters and bulletins cover such topics as "Targeting of DOE Travelers."[16]

A geographically separated, subordinate unit of the office is the Nevada Intelligence Center (NVIC). It represents the Energy Department with respect to intelligence and intelligence-related activities at the Nevada Test Site (NTS), where nuclear tests and related experiments have been conducted, and with respect to DOE-sponsored activities at the Tonopah Test Range (TTR). Specific functions include intelligence oversight, intelligence collection management (coordinating Intelligence Community activities related to the NTS and the TTR), foreign intelligence (providing research and analysis sources for National Nuclear Security Administration/Nevada Site Office [NNSA/NSO] customers), support for the counterintelligence element of the office, and management of the NNSA/NSO Sensitive Compartmented Information Facility.[17]

The NVIC is one of thirteen Field Intelligence Elements (FIEs). The remaining FIEs are located at national laboratories and other DOE facilities and report to the Office of Intelligence and Counterintelligence. Lawrence Livermore National Laboratory's intelligence program is the responsibility of the Z Program of the Global Security Principal Directorate. The Z Program was established in 1965 as the Special Projects Division through an agreement with the CIA and what was then the Lawrence Radiation Laboratory to analyze the Soviet nuclear weapons program and, shortly thereafter, the Chinese program. In the mid-1970s, Z Division (as it was then known) began analyzing the nuclear proliferation activities of smaller nations and later focused on the "control and accountability of nuclear weapons, materials, and technology in Russia." In 2008 Z Division was renamed Z Program as part of an organizational realignment.[18] By that time, it had added chemical and biological weapons proliferation, as well as information operations, to its list of research subjects. Thus, in May 2006 it advertised for a biomedical scientist "with a background in virology, microbiology, immunology, epidemiology, agricultural biological or other areas of science and medicine relevant to Biological Weapons issues." At least one member of Z Program has been assigned to work at the National Biodefense Analysis and Countermeasures Center at Fort Detrick, Maryland.[19]

As shown in Figure 5.3, the Z Program consists of four major components: Collection Systems Innovation, International Assessments, Information Operations and Analytics, and Counterproliferation and Operational Intelligence Support. The International Assessments component provides nuclear intelligence with respect to

- National capability assessments of potential proliferation countries
- Analyses of state-of-the-art fuel cycle technologies, such as enrichment and reprocessing, that proliferants could use to acquire fissile material
- Assessments of worldwide availability of related but nonnuclear weapons technology, such as safety arming, firing, and fusing systems
- Assessments of the activities and behavior of nuclear supplier states and international organizations involved in nuclear commerce, safeguards, and physical security.[20]

The Information Operations and Analytics component focuses on foreign cyber threats. In June 2002, the director of the Lawrence Livermore Laboratory claimed that Z Division has "one of the strongest capabilities in the country for analysis and research related to foreign nuclear weapons and other weapons of mass destruction, including early-state foreign technology development and acquisition, patterns of cooperation, and foreign cyber threats."[21]

Other national laboratories or Department of Energy organizations that operate FIEs are the Argonne National Laboratory, the Idaho National Laboratory, the Kansas City Plant, the Oak Ridge National Laboratory, the Pantex Plant, the Pacific Northwest National Laboratory, the Remote Sensing Laboratory, the Savannah River National Laboratory, and the Special Technologies Laboratory. The FIE at Los Alamos is the Threat Identification & Response division of the laboratory's Global Security Principal Directorate and is responsible for "assessing, monitoring, and countering the capabilities of proliferant nations."[22]

The Oak Ridge National Laboratory also operates a Global Security Directorate, which contains the Oak Ridge FIE, an Oak Ridge counterintelligence unit, and an international security and analysis component. The Deputy Director for International Security and Analysis Programs administers "a special DOE headquarters field element with responsibility for highly sensitive global security work." Similarly, at Pacific Northwest Laboratory there is an FIE under the on-site supervision of the laboratory's National Security Directorate.[23]

DEPARTMENT OF THE TREASURY INTELLIGENCE

The Department of the Treasury's intelligence apparatus has also undergone radical changes since 9/11, particularly with regard to intelligence concerning terrorist activities. Prior to September 11, Treasury had been "a minor institutional player in the

FIGURE 5.3   Organization of the Z Program, Lawrence Livermore National Laboratory

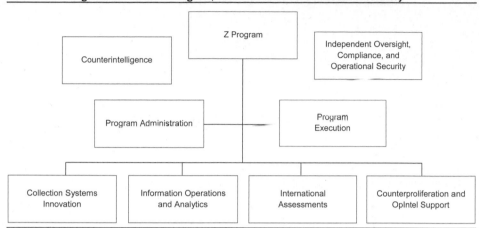

Source: Lawrence Livermore National Laboratory.

world of terrorism," according to a former assistant secretary for terrorist financing and financial crimes.[24]

On September 10, 2001, the Treasury's intelligence organization was the Office of Intelligence Support (OIS), headed by the Special Assistant to the Secretary for National Security, who reported to the secretary and deputy secretary. Established in 1977, the OIS succeeded the Office of National Security, created in 1961. The office began representing the Treasury within the Intelligence Community as a result of a 1971 presidential memorandum and became a member of the National Foreign Intelligence Board in 1972.[25]

The office overtly collected foreign economic, financial, and monetary data in cooperation with the Department of State. Its three primary functions were providing intelligence related to U.S. economic policy to the Secretary of the Treasury and other Treasury officials, representing the Treasury on Intelligence Community committees and maintaining liaison with other elements of the Intelligence Community, and reviewing all proposed support relationships between the Intelligence Community and any Treasury office or bureau. As part of its participation on Intelligence Community committees and its liaison role, the OIS developed intelligence requirements for the Treasury Department and disseminated them to the relevant intelligence agencies.[26]

Today, the Treasury Department's senior intelligence official is the Under Secretary of the Treasury for Terrorism and Financial Intelligence, who heads the Office of Terrorism and Financial Intelligence (OTFI), created in 2004 by the Consolidated Appropriations Act of 2005. The OTFI, according to the Treasury Department, "marshals the department's intelligence and enforcement with the twin aims of safeguarding the financial system against illicit use and combating rogue nations, terrorist facilitators, weapons of mass destruction (WMD) proliferators, money launderers, drug kingpins, and other national security threats."[27]

As shown in Figure 5.4, two assistant secretaries report to the under secretary. One heads the Office of Intelligence & Analysis (OIA), established even before OTFI in

FIGURE 5.4   Organization of the Office of Terrorism and Financial Intelligence, Department of the Treasury

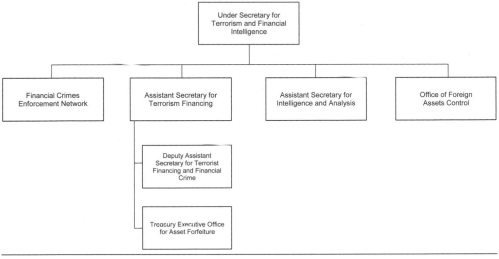

Source: DOT.

2004 by the Intelligence Authorization Act for Fiscal Year 2004 to replace the OIS. OIA, rather than OTFI, is designated as a formal member of the U.S. Intelligence Community and represents the Treasury Department on Intelligence Community boards and committees. In 2010 the DNI designated the Assistant Secretary for Intelligence and Analysis as the National Intelligence Manager for Threat Finance.[28] The 2004 Intelligence Authorization Act mandated that OIA would be responsible for the receipt, analysis, collation, and dissemination of foreign intelligence and foreign counterintelligence information related to the operation and responsibilities of the Department of the Treasury. Specifically, OIA's mission is to provide "analysis and intelligence production on financial and other support networks for terrorist groups, proliferators, and key national security threats," as well as intelligence support on economic, political, and security issues. It is also responsible for coordinating intelligence analysis within the Treasury Department.[29]

As shown in Figure 5.5, there are three deputies to the Assistant Secretary for Intelligence and Analysis: those for Intelligence Community Integration, Analysis and Production, and Security. The Analysis and Production organization contains offices that cover illicit finance, economics and finance, counterproliferation and strategic analysis, Afghanistan/Pakistan, Middle East/Europe/Africa, and sanctions support and analysis.

OIA outputs include current intelligence (including "readbooks" for senior Treasury officials), network and systemic intelligence (which includes mapping of network structures and funding mechanisms, identification of vulnerabilities, and assessment of the impact of Treasury Department actions directed against key nodes and actors), and risk and threat assessments (identification and evaluation of external entities that might threaten Treasury Department people, facilities, and systems). OIA is also

FIGURE 5.5 Organization of the Office of Intelligence and Analysis, Department of the Treasury

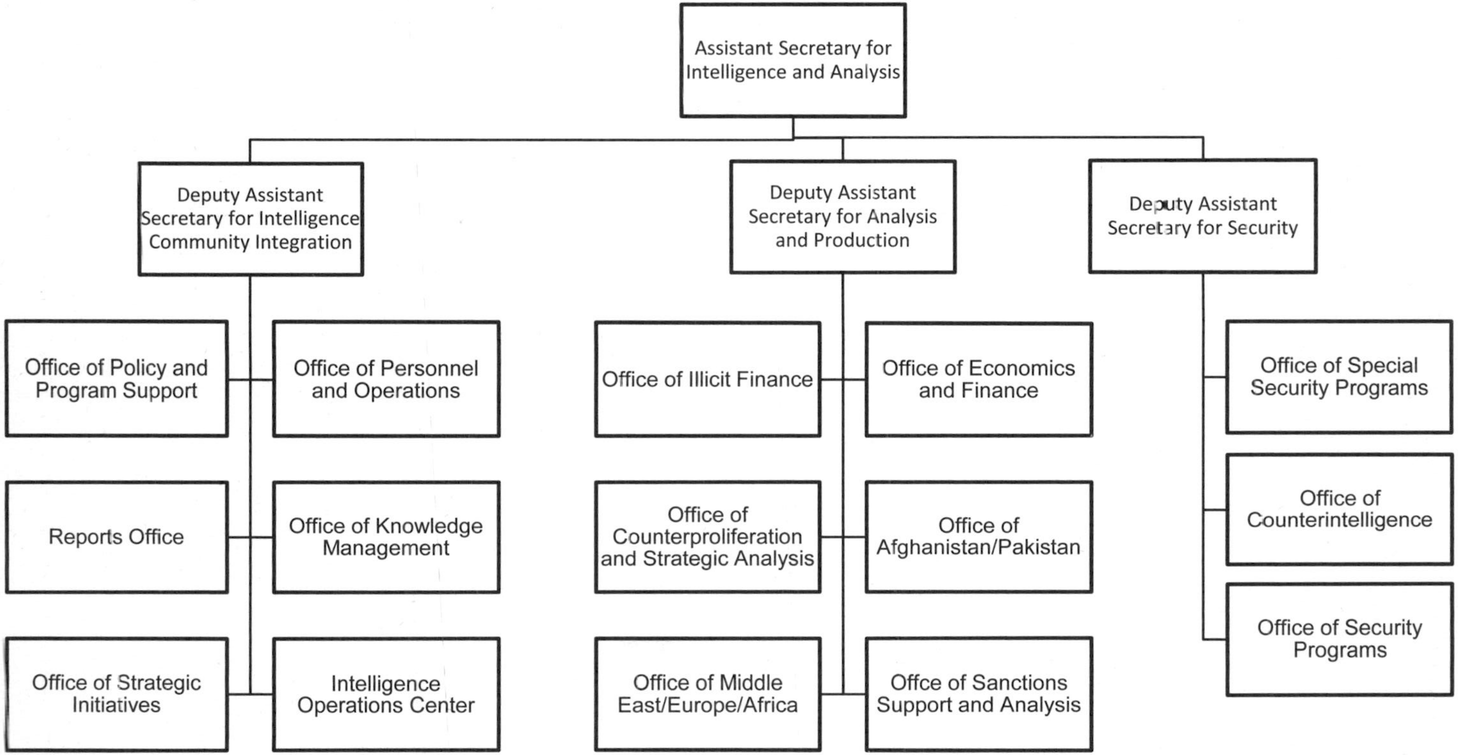

Source: DOT.

responsible for establishing "policies and procedures that guide the Treasury Intelligence Information Reports program and declassifying and sharing information in support of efforts to inform foreign governments of assorted threats."[30]

According to OIA's 2012 *Strategic Direction: Fiscal Years 2012–2015*, OIA's intelligence support is intended to enable its customers to
- Make informed decisions and build strategies in response to international financial and national security issues
- Anticipate illicit finance and systemic risks to global financial stability
- Mitigate illicit finance and systemic vulnerabilities in the global financial system
- Mitigate national security risks by exploiting the financial, commercial, or logistical vulnerabilities of bad actors
- Identify security risks and vulnerabilities of the Treasury
- Mitigate security risks to the department.[31]

The Assistant Secretary for Terrorism Financing supervises the Office of Terrorist Financing and Financial Crime as well as the Executive Office for Asset Forfeiture. Two other offices, the Office of Foreign Assets Control (OFAC) and the Financial Crimes Enforcement Network (FINCEN), report to the under secretary and OTFI. FINCEN, created in April 1990, is, according to its strategic plan, the "nation's financial intelligence unit," responsible for "managing, analyzing, safeguarding, and appropriately sharing financial transaction information collected under the Bank Secrecy Act."[32]

In the aftermath of the September 11 terrorist attacks, the Treasury Department developed the Terrorist Finance Tracking Program "to identify, track, and pursue suspected foreign terrorists . . . and their financial supporters." As part of the program, the Office of Foreign Assets Control has issued subpoenas to financial institutions to provide records on international financial transactions. One of these institutions is the Belgian-based Society for Worldwide Interbank Financial Telecommunications (SWIFT), which has offices in the United States and operates an international messaging system used to transmit bank transaction information.[33] Figure 5.6 shows "Ten Facts About TFI" produced by the Treasury Department.

DEPARTMENT OF HOMELAND SECURITY INTELLIGENCE

In January 2003, the Department of Homeland Security (DHS) was established, as mandated by the Homeland Security Act of 2002, and assumed management responsibility for twenty-two different agencies. Agencies placed under the DHS included the U.S. Customs Service and U.S. Secret Service (from the Department of the Treasury), part of the Immigration and Naturalization Service (from the Department of Justice), part of the Animal and Plant Health Inspection Service (from the Department of Agriculture), the U.S. Coast Guard and Transportation Security Administration (from the Department of Transportation), and the Federal Emergency Management Agency.[34]

The initial structure of the DHS included a Directorate for Information Analysis and Infrastructure Protection, which was "to fuse and analyze intelligence and other information pertaining to threats to the homeland from multiple sources." Those sources included members of the Intelligence Community, such as the CIA

FIGURE 5.6   Ten Facts About Terrorism and Financial Intelligence (TFI)

1. Office of Foreign Assets Control (OFAC), the Office of Terrorist Financing and Financial Crimes (TFFC), the Financial Crimes Enforcement Network (FinCEN), and the Treasury Executive Office of Asset Forfeiture (TEOAF).

2. OFAC enforces financial and economic sanctions programs against countries of concern and groups of individuals involved in illicit activity, such as terrorists and narcotics traffickers.

3. There are currently 5,928 names on OFAC's Specially Designated Nationals List. In 2001, the list was around 2,000 names.

4. TFFC develops policies and implements strategies to strengthen the integrity of the financial system and safeguard it from terrorist financing, money laundering, drug trafficking, organized crime, and proliferation finance.

5. Since 2004, there have been over 160 mutual evaluations conducted by the FATF global network. As part of this assessment process, virtually all of these countries have enacted legislation to strengthen their AML/CFT regimes.

6. OIA is the only intelligence office in the world based in a finance ministry.

7. Since the Foreign Narcotics Kingpin Designation Act was passed, more than 1,500 drug traffickers and money launderers have had their access to the U.S. financial system cut off.

8. FinCEN is the Financial Intelligence Unit of the United States and engages with law enforcement on investigative efforts while fostering interagency and global cooperation against domestic and international financial crimes.

9. TEOAF uses assets forfeited by ringleaders of financial fraud, such as Ponzi schemes or credit card hackers, to pay back financial victims. In FY2013, TEOAF remitted over $76 million of forfeited funds to financial victims. TEOAF uses its funding to help law enforcement stay on the cutting edge of financial investigations.

10. TFI's unprecedented sanctions on Iran have led the way in demonstrating the power and efficacy of our financial measures.

Nearly every national security threat has an important financial component. Effectively mitigating these threats requires creative thinking about how to leverage, pressure, and often exploit our adversaries' financial vulnerabilities. That is where TFI comes in.

Source: DOT.

and National Security Agency (NSA), and other elements of the government, such as the Customs Service and Department of Transportation. The directorate was to use that information to "identify and assess current and future threats to the homeland, map those threats against . . . current vulnerabilities, issue timely warnings, and immediately take or effect appropriate preventive and protective action." The directorate would also be responsible for evaluating the vulnerabilities of the nation's critical infrastructure, including food and water systems, emergency services, transportation, energy, and national monuments.[35]

A reorganization resulted in the creation of the position of Assistant Secretary of Homeland Security for Intelligence and Analysis, heading the Office of Intelligence & Analysis. Subsequently, the position was upgraded, such that the Office of Intelligence & Analysis is now headed by the Under Secretary of Homeland Security for Intelligence and Analysis. In addition to being responsible for the office, the under secretary is also charged with "coordinating and enhancing integration" among the numerous additional intelligence organizations of DHS components, including the Secret Service, Customs and Border Protection, Immigration and Customs Enforcement, as well as the Transportation Security Administration.[36]

In September 2009, the Acting Under Secretary for Intelligence and Analysis identified four areas that, in collaboration with other agencies, would be the focus of his office's analytical effort: analysis of weapons of mass destruction (in coordination with the FBI), violent radicalization (in collaboration with the National Counterterrorism Center [NCTC]), domestic terrorism (in collaboration with the FBI and other law enforcement organizations), and health security (in collaboration with the Office of Health Affairs and several other organizations).[37]

In 2010 the under secretary stated, "Our analysts—in partnership with the NCTC and FBI—address threats to the homeland from both international and domestic terrorist groups and actors, and also analyze terrorist tactics, techniques, and procedures to inform the development of protective measures at home." She also observed, "I&A has primary responsibility with the IC to analyze, evaluate and disseminate analysis on threats to homeland critical infrastructure." Office border and security analysts, she added, "focus not only on terrorist threats to the U.S. on or at our borders, but also address trends regarding travel, asylum and refugee issues and rising violence and instability affecting the Southwest Border," with those analysts supporting efforts "to identify, track, deter and prevent terrorists from traveling to the United States." With regard to cyber issues, office analysts "provide a national intelligence analytical framework in support of key cyber-security customers."[38]

As shown in Figure 5.7, subordinate to the under secretary are the Principal Deputy Under Secretary for Intelligence and Analysis and three deputy under secretaries responsible for the office's thirteen divisions. The Office of Intelligence & Analysis's fiscal year 2013 budget request was for 885 personnel and $284,332,000 in funds.[39]

The Deputy Under Secretary for Plans, Policy, and Performance Management supervises the Program Performance Management Division, the Strategy, Plans & Policy Division, and the Information Sharing & Intelligence Enterprise Management. The Deputy Under Secretary for Enterprise & Mission Support (formerly Operations) is responsible for supervising five divisions: Knowledge Management; Mission

FIGURE 5.7   Organization of the Office of Intelligence & Analysis, Department of Homeland Security

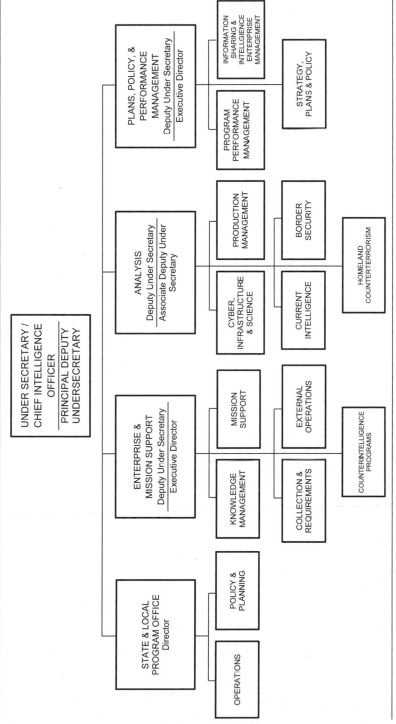

Source: DHS.

Support; Collection & Requirements; External Operations; and Counter-Intelligence Programs.[40]

The Collection & Requirements Division vets requests for intelligence collection to be carried out by agencies such as NRO, NSA, and CIA and presents those requests to Intelligence Community organizations that task collection systems. A DHS report on intelligence and information requirements from January to July 2005 organized the requests into six broad categories: homeland security; indications of acquisition of, movement of (by land, sea, or air), or experimentation with explosive materials, accelerants, and components for the construction of improvised explosive devices (IEDs); terrorism; terrorist groups and individuals; support for terrorism; and cyber threats to U.S. infrastructure. Specification of subcategories and explanations consumed ten single-spaced pages. The Counterintelligence Program was established in January 2007 "to detect and deter the growing threat posed by foreign intelligence services, terrorists, and foreign criminal enterprises."[41]

One particular aspect of the Collection & Requirements Division's activity is operating the Interagency Remote Sensing Coordination Cell, whose membership includes, but is not limited to, the Federal Emergency Management Agency, Customs and Border Protection, the Army Corps of Engineers, Civil Air Patrol, the U.S. Geological Survey, the Department of Agriculture, the Northern Command, and the National Reconnaissance Office. Its responsibilities include coordinating, synchronizing, and tracking remote sensing data acquisition activities and capabilities; ensuring that "information needs of first responders, state emergency managers, and [the] Federal [government] are established and addressed," and improving "the governance of Federal remote sensing operations."[42]

The Office of Intelligence & Analysis's analytical effort is managed by the Deputy Under Secretary for Analysis and carried out by five divisions: Cyber Infrastructure & Science, Production Management, Current Intelligence, Border Security, and Homeland Counterterrorism. Also reporting directly to the Principal Deputy Under Secretary is the Director of the State & Local Program Office, which supports information sharing between state, local, tribal, and federal law enforcement partners, including seventy-two fusion centers, and coordinates support from all elements of the DHS.[43]

In the fall of 2005, Richard Ben-Veniste, a member of the 9/11 Commission, told a joint hearing of subcommittees of the House Committee on Homeland Security and the House Permanent Select Committee on Intelligence that "nearly all now agree that [Intelligence and Analysis] has not fulfilled [its] mandate" to be the primary intelligence shop within DHS. Among the problems was that DHS did not have a centralized, integrated database of its own intelligence. In an attempt to remedy the situation, senior Intelligence Community official Charles Allen, who had served as National Intelligence Officer for Warning and Assistant Director of Central Intelligence for Collection, was appointed as the department's chief intelligence officer. Allen subsequently established a Homeland Security Intelligence Council (HSIC), consisting of the heads of the intelligence elements within the department. A more recent (September 2014) complaint has been that "an exodus of top-level officials from the Department of Homeland Security is undercutting the agency's ability to stay ahead of a range of emerging threats, including potential terrorist strikes and cyberattacks."[44]

PHOTO 5.1   FBI headquarters, Washington, D.C. *Photo credit:* FBI.

FEDERAL BUREAU OF INVESTIGATION

The FBI's responsibilities lie predominantly in the areas of criminal law enforcement, domestic counterterrorism, and domestic counterintelligence, although the bureau maintains an extensive overseas presence and its activities at times enter the areas of foreign intelligence and foreign counterintelligence.

The FBI's internal structure was significantly affected by the events of September 11, 2001. In a May 20, 2002, message to the FBI workforce, Director Robert Mueller identified the FBI's ten top priorities. The top three were "protect the United States from terrorist attacks," "protect the United States against foreign intelligence operations and espionage," and "protect the United States against cyber-attacks and high technology crimes." In his memo, Mueller stated that the bureau's goal with regard to terrorism would be prevention, which meant "less focus on traditional law enforcement operations and much more on intelligence and analysis."[45]

The investigation that followed the terrorist attacks found that FBI headquarters had not followed up on warnings from the Minneapolis and Phoenix field offices that might have uncovered the 9/11 plot. Even prior to the attacks, there had existed long-standing concerns about the effectiveness of an organization whose culture was far more rooted in law enforcement and the prompt arrest of criminals than in the patient monitoring of spies and terrorists. In the wake of 9/11 there were calls not only for reorganization of the FBI's national security efforts but for the creation of an entirely new agency for counterterrorism and counterintelligence along the lines of the British Security Service, the Australian Security Intelligence Organization, or the Canadian Security Intelligence Service.[46]

The National Commission on Terrorist Attacks upon the United States, concerned that creating a new domestic intelligence agency would divert the attention of officials responsible for counterterrorism efforts at a time when the threat remained high, recommended a less radical alternative. Instead, the commission suggested, "A specialized and integrated national security workforce should be established at the FBI consisting of agents, analysts, linguists, and surveillance specialists who are recruited, trained, rewarded, and retained to ensure the development of an institutional culture imbued with a deep expertise in intelligence and national security."[47]

In March 2005, the Commission on the Intelligence Capabilities of the United States Regarding Weapons of Mass Destruction recommended the creation of a new National Security Service within the FBI under a single executive assistant director to ensure that the FBI's intelligence elements were responsive to the Director of National Intelligence and "to capitalize on the FBI's progress." The commission also recommended that the new service include the FBI's counterterrorism and counterintelligence divisions and its Directorate of Intelligence. That directorate had been established, in the aftermath of 9/11, as the Office of Intelligence with the mission of implementing FBI intelligence strategies and supervising FBI intelligence collection and sharing as well as analyst recruitment and training. Subsequently, the Intelligence Reform and Terrorist Prevention Act of 2004 directed that the Office of Intelligence become the Directorate of Intelligence and assigned its director responsibility for the "supervision of all national intelligence program projects and activities in the Bureau."[48]

On June 29, 2005, in a memorandum to several officials with national security responsibilities, including the Attorney General, President George W. Bush ordered the creation of such a service, one that would "combine the missions, capabilities, and resources of the counterterrorism, counterintelligence, and intelligence elements of the FBI." The memo also drew from the language of *The 9/11 Commission Report*, directing the Attorney General to "establish programs to build an FBI National Security Service workforce."[49]

In response, on September 12, 2005, the FBI officially established a National Security Branch (NSB), headed by an executive assistant director responsible for the counterterrorism and counterintelligence divisions as well as the Directorate of Intelligence. The directorate, which is responsible for all FBI intelligence functions, operates from FBI headquarters, and each field division operates through Field Intelligence Groups (FIGs), of which there were fifty-six in March 2014. In January 2009, the directorate added a Geospatial Intelligence Unit. On July 26, 2006, a Weapons of Mass Destruction Directorate was added to the NSB and would, according to FBI director Robert Mueller, "study the consequences of a WMD attack, increase our level of preparedness, and coordinate the Government's response in the event of a WMD attack." In 2007 the bureau reorganized the Counterterrorism Division by merging its two international terrorism units—the one for al-Qaeda and the one for more established groups such as Hezbollah—and began to funnel raw intelligence and threat information through desk officers who were experts on specific world regions and terrorist groups.

In July 2011, the FBI established a Counterproliferation Center, which is responsible for all bureau investigations concerning counterproliferation, including attempts to acquire information and technologies that "would enhance a foreign government's ability to create, use, share, or sell weapons of mass destruction . . . , missile delivery systems, and/or space or advanced conventional weapons or components." In 2013 congressional testimony, Director Muller stated that the "center combines the operational activities of the Counterintelligence Division, the subject matter expertise of the WMD Directorate, and the analytical capabilities of the Directorate of Intelligence."[50]

The methods available to the NSB in gathering domestic intelligence in pursuit of its mission include, in addition to human sources, surveillance of the Internet and voice communications intercepts (via its Data Intercept Technology Unit), surveillance helicopters (which were used to photograph construction of the new Chinese embassy in Washington, D.C.), and drones. In July 2013, a letter from the FBI to Senator Rand Paul noted, "Since late 2006, the FBI has conducted surveillance using UAVs in eight criminal cases and two national security cases." In the past, the FBI's foreign-intelligence-related activities have also included wiretapping as well as break-ins directed against foreign embassies in Washington as part of the Surreptitious Entry Program. FBI agents regularly monitored the phones in the offices of all Communist governments represented in Washington. The phones in offices of non-Communist governments were also tapped, especially when those nations were engaged in negotiations with the United States or when significant developments were taking place in those countries. At one point, the FBI tapped the phones of an ally's trade mission in San Francisco. In addition, the FBI has conducted break-ins at foreign embassies to obtain cryptanalytic material and other foreign intelligence. Both types of operations reportedly continue.[51]

Figure 5.8 shows the current organizational structure of the NSB. In addition to the two divisions, one directorate, and one center, there is a Terrorist Screening Center and a High-Value Detainee Interrogation Group (HVDIG). The center's mission is to consolidate the federal government's approach to terrorist screening and create a single comprehensive watch list of known or suspected terrorists. It is also responsible for ensuring that local, state, and federal screeners "have ready access to information and expertise." The HVDIG is an interagency entity housed within the NSB and staffed with members from assorted Intelligence Community organizations. Its mission is "to gather and apply the nation's best resources to collect intelligence from key terror suspects in order to prevent terrorist attacks against the United States and its allies." The National Security Council issued the group's charter, "Charter for Operations of Interagency High-Value Detainee Interrogation Group," on April 19, 2010.[52]

In 1939 President Franklin D. Roosevelt gave the FBI responsibility for the collection of intelligence in the Western Hemisphere and the bureau created a Special Intelligence Service (SIS) for this function. The SIS had approximately 360 agents, mostly in Mexico, Argentina, and Brazil. Despite J. Edgar Hoover's proposal, shortly after World War II, that the SIS's mandate be extended to the rest of the world, the bureau was stripped of its foreign intelligence role, which was assumed by the Strategic Services Unit, then the Central Intelligence Group and the CIA.[53]

The bureau did maintain representatives as legal attachés (LEGATs) in ten embassies as of 1970. They functioned officially as liaisons with national police forces on

FIGURE 5.8 Organization of the National Security Branch, Federal Bureau of Investigation

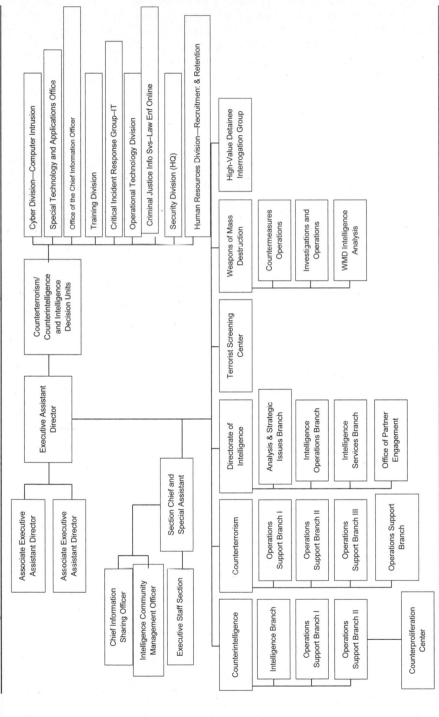

Source: FBI.

matters of common concern and dealt with Americans who found themselves in legal trouble. In 1970 the bureau doubled the number of embassies with FBI representation and instructed agents to collect foreign intelligence, with particularly interesting intelligence identified as HILEV (High Level) by overseas agents. Some material was distributed to senior officials, including Henry Kissinger, outside normal channels. In the aftermath of J. Edgar Hoover's death in 1972 and revelations concerning FBI activities, the program was terminated, and FBI representation abroad was reduced to fifteen embassies.[54]

At least two instances of FBI attempts to engage in foreign clandestine collection have come to light. During the investigation of the murder of former Chilean defense minister Orlando Letelier, the FBI operated an undercover agent in Chile. The agent told the FBI that the right-wing Partia Libertad had contracted with Chilean narcotics traffickers to murder Letelier. The FBI agent, however, turned out to be a DEA informant terminated and blacklisted years earlier for deception and moral turpitude. A more successful operation involved the FBI placement of a young woman informant in one of the first groups of U.S. leftists to visit China in the 1970s.[55]

The FBI does maintain a substantial presence overseas in the form of legal attachés. The program has been expanding from the twenty-three offices and seventy agents overseas of the mid-1990s. In 1996 there were plans to add another twenty-three offices and fifty-nine agents over the next four years. By mid-1998, new offices had been opened in Tel Aviv, Cairo, Riyadh, Buenos Aires, Pretoria, Tallinn, Warsaw, and Kiev, with others in planning or under consideration. The expansion was intended to permit closer liaison with foreign counterpart organizations with respect to investigating international terrorism, narcotics trafficking, and organized crime.[56]

In March 2004, the FBI maintained LEGAT offices in forty-six countries, staffed by about 119 special agents and 75 support personnel. In October 2007, it had sixty fully operational LEGAT offices and fifteen suboffices, with 165 agents and 103 support personnel. As of August 2010 the program, under the purview of the bureau's Office of International Operations and LEGATs, involved sixty offices. The investigative priorities of these offices "mirror those of the FBI as a whole," according to a Department of Justice audit. Tier One for the bureau and the attaché offices includes "foreign intelligence, terrorist, and criminal activities that directly threaten the national or economic security of the United States."[57] Table 5.1 lists of the locations of the offices and their areas of responsibility.

Even when those offices were not authorized to collect foreign intelligence, the FBI has been involved in domestic activities that generate foreign intelligence. Executive Order 12333 allows the FBI to "conduct within the United States, when requested by the officials of the intelligence community designated by the President, activities undertaken to collect foreign intelligence or support foreign intelligence collection requirements of other agencies within the intelligence community."[58]

In September 1980, the Joint Staff briefed two FBI officials on intelligence requirements in support of a possible second attempt to rescue U.S. hostages in Iran. One of the officials was the Deputy Assistant Director for Intelligence, who was responsible for coordinating the use of non-U.S. persons in the United States for intelligence purposes. The Joint Staff asked the FBI officials for their assistance in developing information relevant to the rescue mission, instructing them to "seek any potential

TABLE 5.1   Main Legal Attaché Offices and Areas of Responsibility

Location	Area of Responsibility
Abu Dhabi, UAE	Oman, United Arab Emirates
Amman, Jordan	Jordan, Lebanon, Syria
Baghdad, Iraq	Iraq
Doha, Qatar	Qatar
Islamabad, Pakistan	Pakistan
Kabul, Afghanistan	Afghanistan
Riydah, Saudi Arabia	Bahrain, Kuwait, and Saudi Arabia
Sanaa, Yemen	Djibouti, Eritrea, Ethiopia, Yemen
Tel Aviv, Israel	Israel, Palestinian National Authority
Berlin, Germany	Germany
Bern, Switzerland	Liechtenstein, Switzerland
Brussels, Belgium	Belgium, Luxembourg, The Netherlands, US Mission to European Union, US Mission to NATO and Europol
Copenhagen, Denmark	Denmark, Finland, Greenland, Iceland, Norway, Sweden
London, England	United Kingdom, Republic of Ireland, Channel Islands
Madrid, Spain	Andorra, Gibraltar, Portugal, Spain
Paris, France	France, Monaco
Rome Italy	Italy, Malta
Vienna, Austria	Austria, Hungary, Slovenia
Astana, Kazakhstan	Kazakhstan, Kyrgyzstan, Tajikistan, Turkmenistan, Uzbekistan
Ankara, Turkey	Turkey
Athens, Greece	Greece, Cyprus
Bucharest, Romania	Hungary, Moldova, Romania
Kyiv, Ukraine	Belarus, Ukraine
Moscow, Russia	Russia
Prague, Czech Republic	Czech Republic, Slovakia
Sarajevo, Bosnia-Herzegovina	Bosnia-Herzegovina, Croatia, Serbia, Montenegro, Kosovo
Sofia, Bulgaria	Albania, Bulgaria, Macedonia
Tallinn, Estonia	Estonia, Latvia, Lithuania
Tbilisi, Georgia	Armenia, Azerbaijan, Georgia
Warsaw, Poland	Poland
Bangkok, Thailand	Burma, Laos, Thailand
Beijing, China	Mongolia, People's Republic of China
Canberra, Australia	Australia, New Zealand, and South Pacific islands

TABLE 5.1 *(continued)*

Location	Area of Responsibility
Hong Kong, China	Hong Kong, Macau, Taiwan
Jakarta, Indonesia	Indonesia, Timor Leste (East Timor)
Kuala Lumpur, Malaysia	Malaysia
Manila, Philippines	Philippines
New Delhi, India	India
Phnom Penh, Cambodia	Cambodia, Vietnam
Seoul, South Korea	Republic of Korea
Singapore, Singapore	Brunei, Diego Garcia, Singapore
Tokyo, Japan	Japan
Cairo, Egypt	Egypt, Libya, Sudan
Dakar, Sengal	Burkino Faso, Cape Verde, Central African Republic, Cote D'Ivoire, Democratic Republic of Congo, Gabon, Gambia, Guinea, Guinea Bissau, Republic of Congo, Senegal
Freetown, Sierra Leone	Liberia, Sierra Leone
Lagos, Nigeria	Benin, Cameroon, Equatorial Guinea, Ghana, Nigeria, Sao Tomé and Principe, Togo
Nairobi, Kenya	Burundi, Kenya, Rwanda, Somalia, Tanzania, Uganda
Pretoria, South Africa	Botswana, Angola, Comoros, Lesotho, Madagascar, Malawi, Mayotte, Mauritius, Mozambique, Namibia, Reunion Islands, Seychelles, South Africa, Swaziland, Zambia, Zimbabwe
Rabat, Morocco	Chad, Mali, Mauritania, Morocco/Western Sahara, Niger, Tunisia
Bogota, Colombia	Colombia, Ecuador
Brasilia, Brazil	Brazil
Bridgetown, Barbados	Caribbean Islands
Buenos Aires, Argentina	Argentina, Paraguay, Uruguay
Caracas, Venezuela	French Guiana, Guyana, Suriname, Trinidad, Tobago, Venezuela
Mexico City, Mexico	Mexico
Ottawa, Canada	Canada
Panama City, Panama	Panama, Costa Rica, Nicaragua
Santiago, Chile	Bolivia, Chile, Peru
Santo Domingo, Dominican Republic	Dominican Republic, Haiti, Jamaica
San Salvador, El Salvador	Belize, El Salvador, Guatemala, Honduras

information relevant to the rescue mission" and "any potential Iranian leads that they may spot for exploitation in the conduct of their programs"[59]

In 2003, in the wake of the U.S. invasion of Iraq, the FBI launched Operation DARKENING CLOUDS, which involved interviewing Iraqi natives living in the United States, an effort that led to the collection of information on more than 130,000 people and certainly some foreign intelligence information. By 2011, with the United States involved in military operations directed against the government of Muammar Qadhafi, FBI agents were questioning Libyans living in the United States in an attempt to identify Libyan-supported spies or terrorists and gather information that might aid allied military operations.[60]

DRUG ENFORCEMENT ADMINISTRATION INTELLIGENCE

The Drug Enforcement Administration, which like the FBI is a component of the Department of Justice, operates in the United States and abroad. It has nearly 5,000 special agents, a budget of $2.02 billion, 86 foreign offices in 67 countries, and over 680 intelligence analysts distributed around the world. DEA intelligence operations are the responsibility of the Chief of Intelligence, who heads the DEA Intelligence Division.[61] The division is responsible for

- Collecting and producing intelligence in support of the administrator and other federal, state, and local agencies
- Establishing and maintaining close working relationships with all agencies that produce or use narcotics intelligence
- Increasing efficiency in the reporting, analysis, storage, retrieval, and exchange of such information and undertaking a continuing review of the narcotics intelligence effort to identify and correct deficiencies.[62]

Intelligence of interest to DEA falls into three categories: tactical, investigative, and strategic. The first is "evaluated information on which immediate enforcement action—arrests, seizures, and interdictions can be based." Investigative intelligence "provides analytical support to investigations and prosecutions to dismantle criminal organizations and gain resources." Strategic intelligence "focuses on the current picture of drug trafficking from cultivation to distribution" for use in management decision making, resource allocation, and policy planning.[63]

As shown in Figure 5.9, the DEA Intelligence Division consists of one section, three offices, and two centers: the Strategic Intelligence Section; the Office of Intelligence Warning, Plans & Programs; the Office of Special Intelligence; the Office of National Security Intelligence (ONSI); the El Paso Intelligence Center (EPIC); and the Fusion Center. The Office of National Security Intelligence was established in early 2006 as a result of the DEA leadership's desire to have the DEA "rejoin" the Intelligence Community, an idea proposed by individuals in Congress, the Intelligence Community, academia, and the executive branch. Except for a brief time between the executive orders signed by Presidents Jimmy Carter and Ronald Reagan, DEA intelligence was not formally considered part of the Intelligence Community. With the signing of Executive Order 12333 by President Reagan in 1981, DEA remained on the law enforcement side of the imaginary wall between intelligence and law enforcement. A

FIGURE 5.9   Organization of the Drug Enforcement Administration Intelligence Division

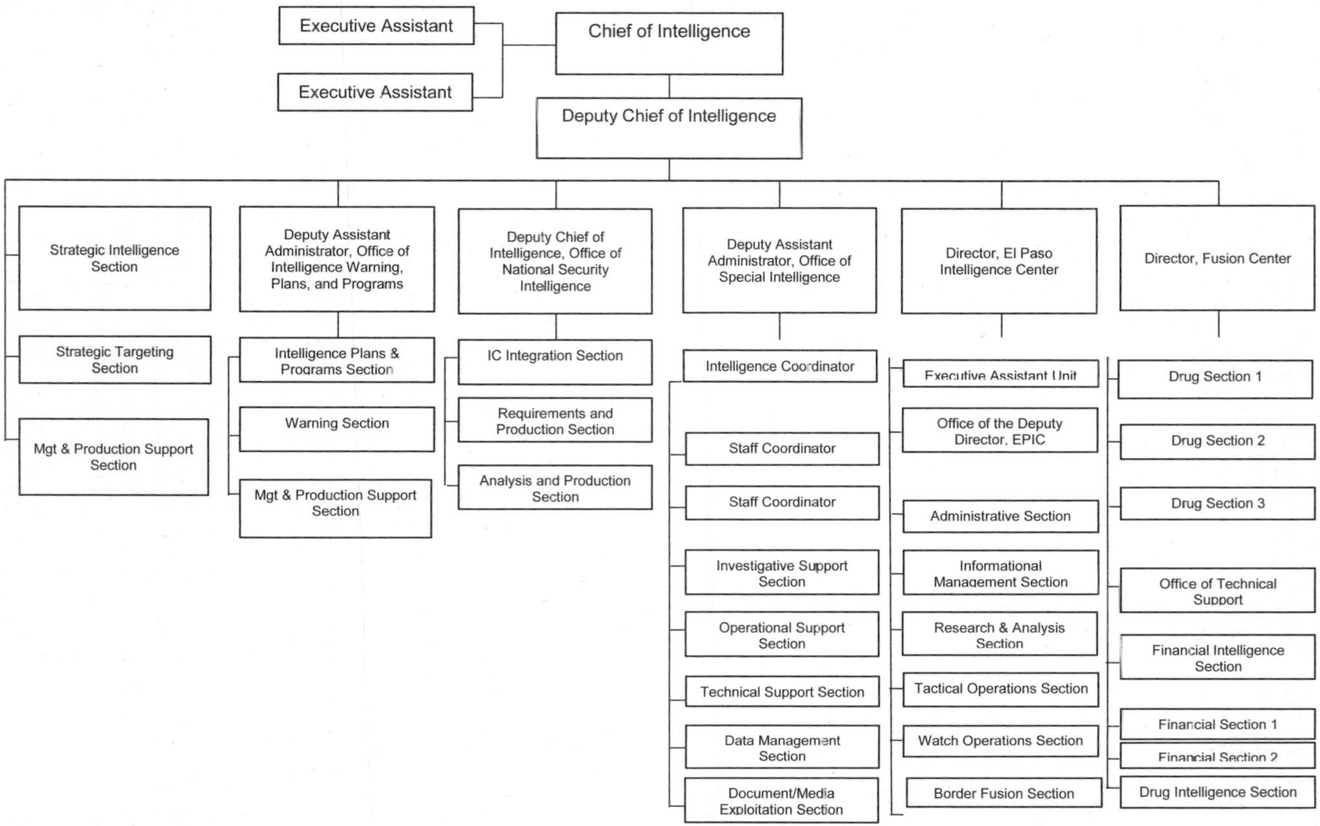

Source: DEA.

February 2006 memorandum signed by the DNI and the Attorney General designated ONSI as a member of the Intelligence Community.*[64]

ONSI is responsible for providing drug-related information relevant to Intelligence Community requirements. The office is responsible for establishing and maintaining a centralized tasking system of requests and analyzing national security information obtained in the course of the DEA's drug enforcement activities. ONSI also manages requests from the Intelligence Community for information either held by DEA or obtained for the community through existing DEA assets operating pursuant to the DEA's law enforcement missions.[65]

The relationship between the DEA and the Intelligence Community and the rationale for establishing the ONSI have been explained as follows:

> The DEA and the IC have a history of partnering for purposes of identifying and disrupting illegal drug trafficking. This partnership has been successful in facilitating the exchange of vital information and the leveraging of expertise. [ONSI's] membership in the Community helps optimize the overall U.S. government counternarcotics interdiction and security effort and furthers creative collaboration between the many organizations involved in countering the threats from narcotics trafficking, human smuggling/trafficking, immigration crimes, and global terrorism.
>
> It is at the nexus of these transnational threats that some of the most serious threats to national security exist. Having DEA as a member of the IC permits greater exploitation of its intelligence capabilities against . . . international targets.[66]

In its 2010 congressional budget submission, the DEA requested $758,000 in support of Special Field Intelligence Programs (SFIPs) to respond to national foreign intelligence priorities, explaining that "part of DEA's Office of National Security Intelligence . . . mission is to proactively provide reports of foreign intelligence value to the Intelligence Community." The submission further stated that the SFIPs are intended, inter alia, to
- Identify emerging drug trafficking organizations and their modus operandi.
- Determine relationships of the drug trade or drug trafficking organizations with terrorists or other insurgent groups to include human smuggling organizations.
- Identify all aspects of money laundering, including bulk cash movement and the use of drug proceeds.
- Determine if illicit drugs are financing terrorist or insurgent activities.

---

*About two and half years prior to the signing of that memorandum, the Acting DEA Assistant Administrator for Intelligence led a briefing to the National Commission on Terrorist Attacks upon the United States, explaining that "DEA does not want to be part of the IC" and giving a number of reasons for this view, including DEA's desire not to receive requirements tasking and the fear that such status would interfere with DEA's foreign relationships and result in DEA's being overseen by congressional intelligence oversight committees. The commission was also told that "'foreign intelligence' is not a known term at DEA." See "Briefing by the Drug Enforcement Administration (DEA)," October 16, 2003, http://cryptome.org/nara/dea/dea-03-1016.pdf.

- Develop Cooperating Individuals (CIs) to satisfy requirements levied on DEA field offices to collection information as required by DEA Headquarters.[67]

In the 2007 fiscal year the DEA's Rome office initiated an African Frontier Special Field Intelligence Program intended to address "a variety of significant intelligence gaps across the African continent," and "DEA personnel in Europe and Africa participated in broad-based intelligence collection efforts focused on cocaine, heroin, and precursor chemical trafficking organizations operating in Africa, as well as on groups involved in narco-terrorism and international money laundering activities."[68]

The Strategic Intelligence Section produces strategic intelligence assessments, studies, reports, and estimates based on both foreign and domestic sources. It assesses the drug situation in Europe, Asia, Africa, and Latin America, including drug production capability and activity, transportation systems, makeup of trafficking groups, effectiveness of traffic interdiction, and local political attitudes regarding drug trafficking.[69]

The Office of Special Intelligence is responsible for planning, organizing, coordinating, and implementing the DEA's investigative intelligence programs. The cocaine and heroin investigative units of the office's Investigative Intelligence Section are responsible for identifying major traffickers and organizations engaged in cultivation, production, transportation, and distribution as well as in the laundering of drug proceeds.[70]

The El Paso Intelligence Center was established in 1974 as the result of a Department of Justice study, *A Secure Border: An Analysis of Issues Affecting the Department of Justice*, which focused on drug and border enforcement strategies and programs and proposed the creation of a regional intelligence center to be staffed by representatives of the Immigration and Naturalization Service, the U.S Customs Service, and the DEA. Today, EPIC still concentrates primarily on drug movement and immigration violations, although its geographic area of responsibility has expanded to include all of the Western Hemisphere "where drug and alien movements are directed toward the United States." EPIC coordinates a staff of more than three hundred analysts, agents, and support personnel across fifteen federal agencies, the Texas Department of Public Safety, the Texas Air National Guard, the El Paso County Sheriff's Office, and the police forces of two railroads.[71] According to the DEA, "with the increased use of aircraft, seagoing vessels, and global networks to facilitate drug trafficking, EPIC's focus broadened and became international in scope"; as a result, EPIC "supports law enforcement efforts conducted by foreign counterparts throughout the world" and has memoranda of understanding with Canada, Australia, and the Netherlands.[72]

A 2010 assessment based on leaked diplomatic cables posted by WikiLeaks states that the DEA "has been transformed into a global intelligence organization with a reach that extends far beyond narcotics, and an eavesdropping operation so expansive it has to fend off foreign politicians who want to use it against their political enemies." The DEA's eavesdropping unit, the Office of Investigative Technology, is located not in the Intelligence Division but in its Operational Support Division.[73]

A second unit, located outside the Intelligence Division, with a significant intelligence role is the Special Operations Division (SOD), a component of DEA's Operations Division. The SOD was created in 1994 and has grown from several dozen employees to several hundred. A 2004 review of the DEA reported that the SOD was viewed in the Intelligence Community "as one of the components that is the most

forward-looking in terms of sharing and coordinating Intelligence data with others."
One unidentified member of the community reported that SOD-provided "leads" were
vital to its operations.[74] More recently, it was revealed that SOD was providing leads
in the other direction—from the Intelligence Community, particularly the National
Security Agency, to aid in criminal investigations. But those leads were employed in
"parallel construction," recreating an investigative trail to obscure the original source
of the information. The division's original targets were Latin American drug cartels
and expanded to include narcoterrorists, organized crime, and gangs.[75]

Notes

1. U.S. Congress, Senate Select Committee to Study Governmental Activities with Respect to
Intelligence Activities, *Final Report, Book VI: Supplementary Reports on Intelligence Activities* (Washington, DC: U.S. Government Printing Office, 1976), 271–276; Department of State, "DC&P—
Bureau of Intelligence and Research," www.state.documents.gov/documents/organizations/123571
.pdf (accessed August 11, 2010); Senate Select Committee on Intelligence, *Statement of Daniel
Bennett Smith, Nominee for Assistant Secretary of State for Intelligence and Research*, December 17,
2013, 1–2; Office of the Director of National Intelligence, *FY 2013 Congressional Budget Justification*, Vol. 1: *National Intelligence Program Summary*, February 2012, 133–134.

2. U.S. Congress, House Committee on Foreign Affairs, *The Role of Intelligence in the Foreign Policy Process* (Washington, DC: U.S. Government Printing Office, 1980), 57; "State INR and Its Role
in the Intelligence Community" (summary of presentation by Dr. Thomas Fingar, MIT Security
Studies Seminar, April 6, 2005), http://web.mit.edu/ssp/seminars/wed_archives05spring/fingar.htm.

3. *INR* (Washington, DC: U.S. Government Printing Office, n.d.), 2, 4; Philip S. Goldberg,
"Prehearing Questions for Ambassador Philip S. Goldberg upon His Nomination to Be Assistant Secretary, Bureau of Intelligence & Research, Department of State," 2009, http://fas.org/irp
/congress/2009_hr/120109goldberg-resp.pdf, 3; "DC&P—Bureau of Intelligence and Research";
U.S. Senate, Select Committee on Intelligence, *Prehearing Questions for Ambassador Daniel B.
Smith, upon His Nomination to Be Assistant Secretary, Bureau of Intelligence & Research, Department of State*, n.d. (but 2013), answer to question 11. For a brief discussion of INR performance,
see Douglas Jehl, "The Reach of War: Intelligence; Tiny Agency's Iraq Analysis Is Better Than
Big Rivals'," www.nytimes.com, July 10, 2004, http://www.nytimes.com/2004/07/19/world/reach
-war-intelligence-tiny-agency-s-iraq-analysis-better-than-big-rivals.html.

4. Department of State, *Foreign Affairs Manual*, vol. 8, June 2013, 1 FAM 431, 3; Department
of State, "Telephone Directory," http://www.state.gov/m/a/gps/directory, OD-35 to OD-36 (accessed June 11, 2014).

5. Department of State, *Foreign Affairs Manual*, vol. 8, 1 FAM 431, 5–6.

6. Ibid., 6–7.

7. Ibid., 6.

8. Ibid., 7–9.

9. Ibid., 9–11.

10. Ibid., 12; Jeffrey T. Richelson, "Out of the Black: The Disclosure and Declassification of
the National Reconnaissance Office," *International Journal of Intelligence and Counterintelligence*
11, no. 1 (Spring 1998): 1–25.

11. Statement by Robert W. Daniel Jr., Director, Office of Intelligence, Department of Energy,
in U.S. Congress, House Committee on Appropriations, *Energy and Water Development Appropriations for 1992*, pt. 6 (Washington, DC: U.S. Government Printing Office, 1991), 819–836, at 820.

12. Ibid.; "Watkins Reorganizes DOE's Intelligence Work," *Washington Post*, April 18, 1990,
A25; U.S. Congress, Senate Committee on Armed Services, *Department of Defense Authorization for Appropriations for Fiscal Years 1992 and 1993*, pt. 1 (Washington, DC: U.S. Government

Printing Office, 1991), 657; Department of Energy, *National Telephone Directory* (Washington, DC: U.S. Government Printing Office, 1994), 46.

13. "Secretary Pena Strengthens DOE Intelligence Programs" *DOE News*, February 10, 1998; Department of Energy, Organization Chart, "Office of Intelligence and Counterintelligence," July 28, 2006; Alfred Cumming, Congressional Research Service, *Intelligence Reform at the Department of Energy: Policy Issues and Organizational Alternatives*, September 25, 2009, http://fas.org/sgp/crs /intel/RL33355.pdf, 2; President's Foreign Intelligence Advisory Board, *Science at Its Best/Security at Its Worst*, June 1999; John A. Russack, Director, Office of Intelligence, to Hon. Laurence H. Silberman, n.d., w/ enclosure: Question for the Record, Commission on Intelligence Capabilities of the United States Regarding Weapons of Mass Destruction; Department of Energy, *Telephone Directory*, June 2013, http://www.energy.gov, 15; Department of Energy, *U.S. Department of Energy Corporate Overview, 2012*, Section 6, November 27, 2012, 33; Department of Energy, *United States Department of Energy Transition, Important Issues*, Book 2, 2008, Intelligence: Foreign Intelligence/Counterintelligence Consolidation Section.

14. U.S. Congress, Senate Committee on Armed Services, *Department of Defense Authorization for Fiscal Years, 1992 and 1993*, pt. 1 (Washington, DC: U.S. Government Printing Office, 1991), 657; Daniel, *Energy and Water Development Appropriations for 1992*, pt. 6, 823; Statement of Robert W. Daniel Jr., Director, Office of Intelligence, Department of Energy, in U.S. Congress, House Committee on Appropriations, *Energy and Water Development Appropriations for 1993*, pt. 6 (Washington, DC: U.S. Government Printing Office, 1992), 2081.

15. Daniel, in U.S. Congress, House Committee on Appropriations, *Energy and Water Development Appropriations for 1992*, pt. 6, 823; Daniel, in U.S. Congress, House Committee on Appropriations, *Energy and Water Development Appropriations for 1993*, pt. 6, 2195.

16. U.S. Congress, House Committee on Appropriations, *Energy and Water Development Hearings for 1997*, pt. 4 (Washington, DC: U.S. Government Printing Office, 1996), 441; Department of Energy, Office of Intelligence, Office of Counterintelligence, *Statistical Analysis of Foreign Visits to DOE Facilities,* September 1993; Department of Energy, Office of Intelligence, Office of Counterintelligence, *Information Brokers*, August 1994; Department of Energy, Office of Counterintelligence, OCI Bulletin Number 93-007, "Targeting of DOE Travelers," 1993.

17. "Nevada Intelligence Center Awarded for Training Program," *Site Lines* 120 (October 2006): 1–2; Department of Energy, *National Nuclear Security Administration, Functions, Responsibilities, and Authorities Manual*, February 3, 2004, II-16 to II-17; Frederick T. Martin, "To: ICAHST Council Members, Subject: Feedback from 14 April 2009 ICAHST Meeting," April 15, 2009; "Intelligence Research Specialist," SimplyHired, April 29, 2014, http://www.simplyhired .com/k-intelligence-research-specialist-jobs.html.

18. "Lawrence Livermore National Laboratory," June 9, 2014, http://www.llnl.gov; W. F. Raborn, Director of Central Intelligence, and Glenn T. Seaborg, Chairman, Atomic Energy Commission, "Memorandum of Understanding Between the Atomic Energy Commission and the Central Intelligence Agency Concerning Work to Be Performed at the Lawrence Radiation Laboratory," August 3, 1965; Stephen Wampler, "NAI Realigns to Changing Security Environment," *LLNL Newsline*, March 31, 2006, 2; Lauren de Vore, "Doesburg Realigns Global Security to Enhance Efficiency," https://newsline.llnl.gov, February 22, 2008, https://www.llnl.gov/news/ doesburg-realigns-global-security-enhance-efficiency; "Z Program," Lawrence Livermore National Laboratory, https://www-gs.llnl.gov/zprogram.html (accessed March 24, 2010).

19. "Jobs at LLNL," Lawrence Livermore National Laboratory, http://jobs.llnl.gov (accessed May 23, 2006).

20. U.S. Congress, House Committee on Armed Services, *Department of Energy National Security and Military Applications of Nuclear Energy Authorization Act of 1984* (Washington, DC: U.S. Government Printing Office, 1983), 394.

21. Michael R. Anastasio, "Establishment of the Department of Homeland Security," Statement Before the U.S. Senate Energy and Natural Resources Committee, July 10, 2002, 8.

22. "Field Intelligence Elements," August 13, 2014, Department of Energy response to Freedom of Information Act request; Los Alamos National Laboratory, "Organization Chart," http://www.lanl.gov/about/leadership-governance/organization-chart.php (accessed June 16, 2014); Los Alamos National Laboratory, "Intelligence Analysis, Integration, and Exploitation," www.lanl.gov (accessed August 23, 2013); John E. McLaughlin, Deputy Director of Central Intelligence, letter to Kyle E. McSlarrow, Deputy Secretary of Energy, December 3, 2004.

23. Oak Ridge National Laboratory, "About ORNL: Organization," http://www.ornl.gov/ornl/about-ornl/organization (accessed June 18, 2014); Oak Ridge National Laboratory, "Global Security: Organization," http://web.ornl.gov/adm/directorates/gsd/organization.shtml (accessed June 18, 2014); Oak Ridge National Laboratory, "National Security," http://www.ornl.gov/science-discovery/national-security (accessed June 18, 2014); "John O'Neil," http://presidential search.fsu.edu (accessed June 19, 2014); Pacific Northwest Laboratory, National Security Directorate, "About Us: Organization," http://www.pnnl.gov/nationalsecurity/about (accessed June 18, 2014).

24. Juan C. Zagarte, *Treasury's War: The Unleashing of a New Era of Financial Warfare* (New York: Public Affairs, 2013), 46.

25. Office of the Director of Central Intelligence, "Treasury Department—Office of Intelligence Support," n.d.; Office of Intelligence and Analysis, Department of the Treasury, *Strategic Direction: Fiscal Years 2012–2015*, 2012, 2.

26. Ronald Reagan, "Executive Order 12333: United States Intelligence Activities, December 4, 1981," *Federal Register* 46, no. 235 (December 8, 1981): 59941–59954, at 59946; "Foreign Intelligence—It's More Than the CIA," *U.S. News and World Report*, May 1, 1981, 35–37; Department of the Treasury Order 100-3, "Functions of the Executive Secretariat," January 13, 1987, 2; Department of the Treasury, "Office of Intelligence Support," 1997.

27. Department of the Treasury, "Terrorism and Financial Intelligence," www.treasury.gov/about (accessed June 19, 2014); Department of the Treasury, "Under Secretary for Terrorism and Financial Intelligence Stuart Levey, Testimony Before the Senate Committee on Finance," April 1, 2008, http://www.treasury.gov/press-center/press-releases/Pages/hp898.aspx; Office of Intelligence and Analysis, Department of the Treasury, *Strategic Direction*, 2; Associated Press, "US Treasury Sanctions Kuwait for Iraq, Syria," August 6, 2014; W. J. Hennigan and Brian Bennett, "Targeting Militants' Cash," *Los Angeles Times*, September 28, 2014, A1, A14. On the creation of the office, see Zagarte, *Treasury's War*, 201–216.

28. "Office of Intelligence and Analysis, U.S. Department of the Treasury," www.intelligence.gov/1-members.treasury.shtml (accessed February 12, 2006); U.S. Congress, Senate Select Committee on Intelligence, *Nomination of Janice B. Gardner to Be Assistant Secretary of the Treasury for Intelligence and Analysis* (Washington, DC: U.S. Government Printing Office, 2006), 1; Office of the Director of National Intelligence, *An Overview of the United States Intelligence Community*, 2007, 13; Office of Intelligence and Analysis, Department of the Treasury, *Strategic Direction*, 2; John W. Snow, Secretary of the Treasury, "Treasury Order 105-18, Subject: Agreements and Arrangements with Intelligence Community Agencies," December 17, 2004.

29. Intelligence.gov, "Office of Intelligence Analysis, U.S. Department of the Treasury"; U.S. Congress, Senate Select Committee on Intelligence, *Nomination of Janice B. Gardner to Be Assistant Secretary of the Treasury for Intelligence and Analysis*, 4.

30. Office of Intelligence and Analysis, Department of the Treasury, *Strategic Direction*, 2.

31. Ibid., 12.

32. U.S. Congress, Senate Select Committee on Intelligence, *Nomination of Janice B. Gardner to Be Assistant Secretary of the Treasury for Intelligence and Analysis*, 13; Financial Crimes Enforcement Network, *Strategic Plan FY 2006–2008: Safeguarding the Financial System from the Abuse of Financial Crime*, February 2005, http://www.fincen.gov/news_room/rp/files/strategic_plan_2006.pdf, 3.

33. Department of the Treasury, "Terrorist Finance Tracking Program Fact Sheet," June 23, 2006, http://www.treasury.gov; Barton Gellman, Paul Blustein, and Dafna Linzer, "Bank Records Secretly Tapped," www.washingtonpost.com, June 23, 2006. Also see Erich Lichtblau and James Risen, "Bank Data Sifted in Secret by U.S. to Block Terror," *New York Times*, June 23, 2006, A1, A10; Glenn R. Simpson, "Treasury Tracks Financial Data in Secret Program," *Wall Street Journal*, June 23, 2006, A1, A2; Josh Meyer and Greg Miller, "U.S. Secretly Tracks Global Bank Data," *Los Angeles Times*, June 23, 2006, A1, A18–A19; Greg Miller, "Officials Defend Bank Data Tracking," *Los Angeles Times*, June 24, 2006, A1, A12; Karen DeYoung, "Officials Defend Financial Searches," www.washingtonpost.com, June 24, 2006; Jennifer K. Elsea and M. Maureen Murphy, Congressional Research Service, *Treasury's Terrorist Finance Program's Access to Information Held by the Society for the Worldwide Interbank Financial Telecommunications (SWIFT)*, July 7, 2006, http://www.fas.org/sgp/crs/natsec/RS22469.pdf; National Commission on Terrorist Attacks upon the United States, *Monograph on Terrorist Financing*, 2004, http://govinfo.library.unt.edu/911/staff_statements/911_TerrFin_Monograph.pdf; Kim Murphy, "Keeping an Eye on Bank Data," *Los Angeles Times*, August 24, 2006, A6; Martin Rudner, "Using Financial Intelligence Against the Funding of Terrorism," *International Journal of Intelligence and Counterintelligence* 19, no. 1 (Spring 2006): 32–58; Thomas Winston, "Intelligence Challenges in Tracking Terrorist Internet Fund Transfer Activities," *International Journal of Intelligence and Counterintelligence* 20, no. 2 (Summer 2007): 327–343; Leonard H. Schrank and Juan C. Zarate, "Data Mining, Without Big Brother," *New York Times*, July 3, 2013, A23; Zarate, *Treasury's War*, 201–216.

34. Department of Homeland Security, *Securing Our Homeland: U.S. Department of Homeland Security Strategic Plan*, 2004, 6; "History: Who Will Become Part of the Department?," www.dhs.gov (accessed August 9, 2006); "Department of Homeland Security Organization Chart," November 7, 2005. For a recent critique of the department, see Michael Coleman, "Mission Creep: Homeland Security a 'Runaway Train,'" www.abqjournal.com, April 27, 2014, http://www.abqjournal.com/390438/news/homeland-security-a-runaway-train.html; Michael Coleman, "New DHS Head Says Agency Needs Change," www.abqjournal.com, May 4, 2014, http://www.abqjournal.com/394239/news/dhs-head-agency-needs-change.html (accessed May 7, 2014); John Hudson, "Who Needs the Department of the Homeland Security Anyway?," www.foreignpolicy.com, February 26, 2015, http://foreignpolicy.com/2015/02/26/who-needs-the-department-of-homeland-security-anyway; Senator Tom Coburn, Senate Committee on Homeland Security and Governmental Affairs, *A Review of the Department of Homeland Security's Missions and Performance*, January 2015.

35. President George W. Bush, White House, *The Department of Homeland Security*, 2002, 3, 14–15.

36. U.S. Congress, Senate Select Committee on Intelligence, *Additional Prehearing Questions for Mr. Francis X. Taylor upon His Nomination to Be the Under Secretary for Intelligence and Analysis of the Department of Homeland Security*, February 25, 2014, http://www.intelligence.senate.gov/140225/taylorprehearing.pdf, 16. On the scope of DHS intelligence activities, see Mark A. Randol, Congressional Research Service, *The Department of Homeland Security Intelligence Enterprise: Operational Overview and Oversight Challenges for Congress*, March 19, 2010, http://fas.org/sgp/crs/homesec/R40602.pdf; Michael W. Studeman, "Strengthening the Shield: U.S. Homeland Security Intelligence," *International Journal of Intelligence and Counterintelligence* 20, no. 2 (Spring, 2007): 195–216; Harold M. Greenberg, "Is the Department of Homeland Security an Intelligence Agency?," *Intelligence and National Security* 24, no. 2 (April 2009): 216–235; Government Accountability Office, GAO-14-397, *DHS Intelligence Analysis: Additional Actions Needed to Address Analytic Priorities and Workforce Challenges*, June 2014; U.S. Congress, House Committee on Homeland Security, *The DHS Intelligence Enterprise: Past, Present, and Future* (Washington, DC: U.S. Government Printing Office, 2012), 2.

37. *Statement of Bart R. Johnson, Acting Under Secretary of Intelligence and Analysis, Before the Subcommittee on Intelligence, Information Sharing, and Terrorism Risk Assessment, Committee on Homeland Security, U.S. House of Representatives,* September 24, 2009, 8.

38. Department of Homeland Security, *Testimony of Under Secretary Caryn Wagner Before the House Subcommittee on Homeland Security on the President's Fiscal Year 2011 Budget Request for the Department's Office of Intelligence Analysis,* March 4, 2010, http://www.dhs.gov/news/2010/03/04 /under-secretary-wagners-testimony-presidents-fy-2011-budget-request-departments.

39. Office of the Director of National Intelligence, *FY 2013 Congressional Budget Justification,* vol. 1, *National Intelligence Program Summary,* 133–134.

40. Department of Homeland Security, "Office of Intelligence & Analysis, Organization Chart," June 7, 2011, http://www.dhs.gov/xlibrary/assets/org-chart-ianda.pdf (accessed June 23, 2014).

41. Department of Homeland Security, "Preserve, Protect, Secure," March 2006, 8; Office of Intelligence and Analysis, Department of Homeland Security, *Priority Intelligence/Information Requirements, January 2005–July 2005,* January 7, 2005; William Arkin, "The Department of Homeland Security's Unlimited Priorities," *Early Warning Blog,* July 13, 2006, http://www .washingtonpost.com; "Prepared Statement of Charles E. Allen, U.S. Congress, House Committee on Homeland Security," in *A Report Card on Homeland Security Information Sharing* (Washington, DC: U.S. Government Printing Office, 2009), 49–57, at 56.

42. Office of Intelligence and Analysis, *Interagency Remote Sensing Coordination Cell,* July 15, 2011; Department of Homeland Security, *Homeland Security Geospatial Concept of Operations (GeoCONOPS), Version 4.0, Draft,* June 2012, Appendix D.

43. Department of Homeland Security, "Office of Intelligence & Analysis, Organization Chart"; U.S. Congress, Senate Select Committee on Intelligence, *Prehearing Questions for Caryn Wagner upon Nomination to Be Under Secretary for Intelligence and Analysis, Department of Homeland Security,* March 2010, 18.

44. Richard Ben-Veniste, "Intelligence and Information Analysis Within the Department of Homeland Security," Statement Before the Subcommittee on Intelligence, Information Sharing, and Terrorism Risk Assessment, House Committee on Homeland Security and the Subcommittee on Terrorism, Human Intelligence, Analysis, and Counterintelligence, House Permanent Select Committee on Intelligence, October 19, 2005; "Share the Wealth," *AW&ST,* October 24, 2005, 23; "Allen Leaves CIA to Lead Homeland Security Intelligence Shakeup," www.bloomberg.com, March 15, 2006, http://www.bloomberg.com/apps/news?pid=newsarchive&sid=aSgw7_IMnvJw; "Allen: Chief Intelligence Officer," www.washingtonpost.com, January 11, 2006; Jeff Stein, "Allen's Wrench at Work on Homeland Security," November 23, 2005, http://www.cq.com; Robert Block, "Homeland Security Attracts More Scrutiny," *Wall Street Journal,* February 5, 2007, A7; Eric Lipton, "CIA Veteran Races Time to Rescue Fledgling Agency," *New York Times,* February 10, 2007, A16; Office of the Director of National Intelligence, *An Overview of the United States Intelligence Community,* 2007, 11. On developments with regard to the HSIC, see U.S. Congress, House Committee on Homeland Security, *The DHS Intelligence Enterprise,* 2; Jerry Markon, Ellen Nakashima, and Alice Crites, "Top-Level Turnover Makes It Harder for DHS to Stay on Top of Evolving Threats," www.washingtonpost.com, September 21, 2014.

45. Robert S. Mueller, III, Director, "Message from the Director," May 20, 2002.

46. National Commission on Terrorist Attacks upon the United States, *The 9/11 Commission Report: Final Report of the National Commission on Terrorist Attacks upon the United States* (New York: W. W. Norton, 2004); Richard A. Posner, *Uncertain Shield: The U.S. Intelligence System in the Throes of Reform* (Lanham, MD: Rowman & Littlefield, 2006), 87–140.

47. National Commission on Terrorist Attacks upon the United States, *The 9/11 Commission Report,* 424–426.

48. Commission on the Intelligence Capabilities of the United States Regarding Weapons of Mass Destruction, *Report to the President* (Washington, DC: U.S. Government Printing Office,

2005), 495; FBI, "FBI Creates Structure to Support Intelligence Mission," April 3, 2003; Alfred Cumming and Todd Masse, Congressional Research Service, *Intelligence Reform Implementation at the Federal Bureau of Investigation: Issues and Options for Congress*, August 16, 2005, http://fas .org/sgp/crs/intel/RL33033.pdf, 10.

49. President George W. Bush, "Memorandum for the Vice President, Secretary of State, Secretary of Defense, Attorney General, Secretary of Homeland Security, Director of OMB, Director of National Intelligence, Assistant to the President for National Security Affairs, Assistant to the President for Homeland Security and Counterterrorism, Subject: Strengthening the Ability of the Department of Justice to Meet Challenges to the Security of the Nation," June 29, 2005.

50. FBI, *The National Security Branch of the Federal Bureau of Investigation*, n.d.; FBI, "FBI National Security Branch" (Organization Chart), January 9, 2006; FBI, National Security Branch Overview, n.d., http://www.fbi.gov/hq/nsb/whitepaper.htm, 7–8 (accessed December 13, 2006); Office of the Director of National Intelligence, *An Overview of the United States Intelligence Community*, 15–16; Roy Clark, "FBI Cultivates GEOINT Capability," *Pathfinder* (November– December 2010): 20–21; FBI, "FBI Announces Restructuring," July 26, 2006, http://www.fbi .gov/news/pressrel/press-releases/fbi-announces-restructuring; Dan Eggen, "New FBI Division to Probe Weapons Terrorists May Use," www.washingtonpost.com, July 27, 2006, http://www .washingtonpost.com/wp-dyn/content/article/2006/07/26/AR2006072601629.html; John Solomon, "FBI Reorganizes Effort to Uncover Terrorist Groups' Global Ties," www.washingtonpost .com, September 26, 2007, http://www.washingtonpost.com/wp-dyn/content/article/2007/09 /25/AR2007092502291.html; FBI, Integrating Intelligence and Operations to Protect America, n.d., http://www.fbi.gov (accessed August 17, 2010); FBI, "FBI Counterproliferation Center," http://www.fbi.gov/about-us/nsb/fbi-counterproliferation-center (accessed June 25, 2014); Robert S. Mueller III, "Oversight of the Federal Bureau of Investigation," Statement Before the Senate Committee on the Judiciary, June 19, 2013; FBI, *FY 2015 Authorization and Budget Request to Congress*, March 2014, I-17.

51. Declan McCullagh, "FBI Quietly Forms Secretive Net-Surveillance Unit," CNET, May 22, 2012, http://www.cnet.com/news/fbi-quietly-forms-secretive-net-surveillance-unit; Richard A. Serrano and Brian Bennett, "FBI Uses Spy Drones in U.S.," *Los Angeles Times*, June 20, 2013, A16; Letter, Stephen D. Kelly, Assistant Director, Office of Congressional Affairs, to Honorable Rand Paul, July 19, 2013; Jennifer Valentino-DeVries and Danny Yadron, "FBI Taps Hacker Tactics to Spy on Suspects," *Wall Street Journal*, August 2, 2013, A5; Shane Harris, "Meet the Spies Doing the NSA's Dirty Work," www.foreignpolicy.com, November 21, 2013, http://foreignpolicy .com/2013/11/21/meet-the-spies-doing-the-nsas-dirty-work; Matthew Aid, "Spy Copters, Lasers, Break-In Teams," www.foreignpolicy.com, November 19, 2013, http://foreignpolicy.com/2013/11 /19/spy-copters-lasers-and-break-in-teams; Victor Marchetti and John Marks, *The CIA and the Cult of Intelligence* (New York: Knopf, 1974), 204; "Mole Tunnels Under a Soviet Consulate," *Newsweek*, August 15, 1983, 21; Douglas Watson, "Huston Says NSA Urged Break-Ins," *Washington Post*, March 3, 1975, 1, 6; "Declaration of [Deleted]," *In Re Directives to Yahoo Inc., Pursuant to Section 105B of the Foreign Intelligence Surveillance Act, Docket Number: 105B(g) 07–01*, January 16, 2008, available at www.dni.gov.

52. FBI, "National Security Branch," http://www.fbi.gov/about-us/nsb; Barack Obama, "Executive Order 13491—Ensuring Lawful Interrogations," White House, January 22, 2009, http://www.whitehouse.gov/the_press_office/EnsuringLawfulInterrogations; Anne E. Kornblut, "New Unit to Question Key Terror Suspects," August 24, 2009, http://www.washingtonpost.com; DoD Directive 3115.13, "DoD Support to High-Value Detainee Interrogation Group," December 9, 2010, 3.

53. G. Gregg Webb, "The FBI and Foreign Intelligence: New Insights into J. Edgar Hoover's Role," *Studies in Intelligence* 48, no. 1 (Spring 2004): 45–58; Sanford J. Ungar, *The FBI* (Boston: Little, Brown, 1976), 225–226, 242.

54. Ungar, *The FBI*, 225–226, 242.

55. Ibid., 240–241; Taylor Branch and Eugene M. Proper, *Labyrinth* (New York: Viking, 1992), 231, 350, 358.

56. R. Jeffrey Smith and Thomas W. Lippman, "FBI Plans to Expand Overseas," *Washington Post*, August 20, 1996, A1, A14; telephone conversation with Michael Kortan, FBI, March 27, 1998; Alan G. Ringgold, "The FBI's Legal Attaché Program," *Investigator*, June 1997, 1. On FBI legal attachés in earlier years, see "FBI Legal Attachés—Then and Now," *Intelligencer* 19, no. 3 (Winter/Spring 2013): 35–37.

57. Todd Masse and William Krouse, Congressional Research Service, *The FBI: Past, Present, and Future*, October 2, 2003, http://fas.org/irp/crs/RL32095.pdf, 46; Office of the Inspector General, Department of Justice, *Federal Bureau of Investigation Legal Attaché Program*, March 2004, i, iii; Thomas V. Fuentes, Assistant Director, Office of International Operations, FBI, "Statement Before the Subcommittee on Border, Maritime, and Global Counterterrorism, House Homeland Security Committee," October 4, 2007, 1.

58. Ronald Reagan, "Executive Order 12333: United States Intelligence Activities," Section 1.14, Provision C, 59949.

59. JCS Joint Staff, "Memorandum for the Record, Subject: Briefing of FBI Representatives," September 25, 1980.

60. Devlin Barrett, "FBI Questioning Libyans," *Wall Street Journal*, April 5, 2011, A3.

61. Drug Enforcement Administration, "DEA History," www.justice.gov/dea/about/history.shtml (accessed June 27, 2014); Drug Enforcement Administration, "Foreign Office Locations," http://www.dea.gov/about/foreignoffices.shtml (accessed June 27, 2014); Drug Enforcement Administration, "Intelligence Topics at DEA: El Paso Intelligence Center/National Drug Pointer Index," www.justice.gov/dea/ops/intel.shtml (accessed June 27, 2014); Drug Enforcement Administration, "Drug Enforcement Administration Organization Chart," www.justice.gov/dea/about/orgchart-new.jpg (accessed December 15, 2013).

62. Drug Enforcement Administration, "Intelligence Topics at DEA."

63. Ibid.

64. "Intelligence Division Organization Chart," June 5, 2013; Barry A. Zulauf, "The DEA and the IC: Back to the Future," *Naval Intelligence Professionals Quarterly* (Summer 2006): 24–26; Office of the Director of National Intelligence, ODNI News Release No. 6-06, "Drug Enforcement Administration Element Becomes 16th Intelligence Community Member," February 17, 2006, http://fas.org/irp/news/2006/02/odni021706.html; John D. Negroponte, "To My Intelligence Community Colleagues," February 7, 2006, https://www.fas.org/irp/dni/dni020706.pdf; John Negroponte and Alberto Gonzalez (signatories), "Joint Designation of an Element of the Drug Enforcement Administration Intelligence Division as a Member of the Intelligence Community," February 6, 2006.

65. "Drug Enforcement Administration: Office of National Security Intelligence," www.intelligence.gov/1-members-dea.shtml (accessed August 11, 2006).

66. Ibid.

67. Drug Enforcement Administration, *FY 2010 Performance Budget, Drug Enforcement Administration, U.S Department of Justice, Congressional Budget Submission*, Department of Justice, http://www.justice.gov/sites/default/files/jmd/legacy/2014/01/21/fy10-dea.pdf (accessed December 12, 2010).

68. Drug Enforcement Administration, "DEA History in Depth: 2003–2008," http://www.dea.gov/about/history/2003-2008.pdf, 189 (accessed June 27, 2014).

69. "Memorandum from Thomas A. Constantine, Administrator, to Paul V. Daly, Assistant Administrator, Intelligence Division, Subject: Reorganization of the Intelligence Division," June 7, 1996, 18–19, 21–23.

70. Ibid., 3–7.

71. Drug Enforcement Administration, "El Paso Intelligence Center," www.dea.gov/progams/epic.html (accessed February 21, 2006); Drug Enforcement Administration, "Intelligence Topics at DEA."

72. Drug Enforcement Administration, "Intelligence Topics at DEA." For a review of EPIC's performance, see Office of the Inspector General, *Review of the Drug Enforcement Administration's El Paso Intelligence Center*, June 2010.

73. Drug Enforcement Administration, "DEA Organizational Chart, May 2011," http://www .dea.gov/about/orgchart.jpg (accessed April 23, 2013). Several Office of Investigative Technology briefings, including "Emerging Communications" (April 8, 2010) and "Diminishing Electronic Surveillance Capabilities in the Communications Age" (August 10, 2010), can be found on the website of the Electronic Frontier Foundation.

74. Science Applications International Corporation and ICF Incorporated, *DEA Intelligence Program Top-Down Review*, 2004, 61; John Shiffman and Kristina Cooke, Reuters, "Exclusive: U.S. Directs Agents to Cover Up Program Used to Investigate Americans," June 27, 2014, http://www.reuters.com/article/2013/08/05/us-dea-sod-idUSBRE97409R20130805.

75. Scott Shane and Colin Moynihan, "Drug Agents Use Vast Phone Trove Eclipsing N.S.A.'s," *New York Times*, September 2, 2013, A1, A10; Shiffman and Cooke, "Exclusive"; Karen McVeigh, "US Drug Agency Surveillance Unit to Be Investigated by Department of Justice," www.theguardian.com, August 6, 2013, http://www.theguardian.com/world/2013/aug/06/justice -department-surveillance-dea.

6

UNIFIED COMMAND INTELLIGENCE ORGANIZATIONS

In addition to the intelligence functions performed by organizations reporting to the headquarters of the Department of Defense (DOD) and military services, a substantial intelligence capability is maintained within the unified military commands. The missions, responsibilities, force structures, and geographic areas of responsibility of those commands are detailed in the Unified Command Plan (UCP), drawn up by the Joint Chiefs of Staff (JCS) and approved by the president. The most recent version of the UCP was the subject of two presidential memoranda: the first, signed on April 6, 2011, approved the initial version; the second, signed on September 12, 2011, approved a number of changes to the plan.[1]

Like other parts of the national security establishment, the terrorist attacks of September 11, 2001, had a significant impact on the UCP. Within a month of the terrorist attacks, it was reported that consideration was being given to creation of a new "Americas Command" for defense of the Western Hemisphere as well as to expanding the powers of the U.S. Special Operations Command (USSOCOM) so that it could carry out operations rather than simply provide forces to regional commanders. In addition, "the most radical and controversial change" contemplated would have moved away from the structure that divided the world among four regional commanders.[2]

The commanders, each formerly known as a Commander in Chief (CINC), of those regional commands were responsible for directing the conduct of military operations in their area of responsibility, employing the military forces in the component commands assigned to them.* Technically, the chain of command runs from the president to the Secretary of Defense and then to the commander of each of the unified commands, bypassing the Joint Chiefs of Staff, although the JCS chairman may exercise oversight if desired by the secretary.[3]

Although the regional commands survived, since early 2002 two commands have been created; another was transformed, one was abolished outright, and another was abolished and absorbed by another command. By the time the 2008 UCP was

---

*A component command of a unified command is generally a service command. For example, the Pacific Fleet is a component command of the Pacific Command.

issued, the U.S. Space Command (SPACECOM) had been abolished, and its key component command, the Air Force Space Command, had been assigned to the U.S. Strategic Command (STRATCOM). The changes approved by 2011 presidential memoranda included realigning responsibilities for the Arctic, codifying the disestablishment of the U.S. Joint Forces Command, expanding the Strategic Command's responsibility for combating weapons of mass destruction (WMD), and transferring the Joint Warfare Analysis Center's missions from the Joint Forces Command to the Strategic Command. More radical proposals, including merging of some of the geographic commands and replacing the commands with joint task forces, were not adopted.[4]

Thus, there are six regional commands: Africa Command (AFRICOM), Central Command (CENTCOM), European Command (EUCOM), Northern Command (NORTHCOM), Pacific Command (PACOM), and Southern Command (SOUTHCOM). Figure 6.1 shows the geographic areas of responsibility of the relevant unified commands. Three commands have worldwide responsibilities: the U.S. Special Operations Command, the U.S. Strategic Command, and the U.S. Transportation Command (TRANSCOM).

The intelligence responsibilities of the unified commands have included intelligence analysis for both the command and higher authorities, as well as supervision of national reconnaissance and other sensitive collection operations conducted within the command's theater. Until 1991, intelligence analytical functions were often distributed across several unified and component command organizations. However, in *Plan for Restructuring Defense Intelligence*, the Assistant Secretary of Defense for Command, Control, Communications, and Intelligence specifically required consolidation of the analysis centers of the Atlantic, Pacific, and European commands and their components into joint intelligence centers under the control of the unified command's commander in chief. That other commands would be expected to follow this lead was clear. It was believed that such action "would not only yield resource savings through elimination of duplicative efforts but . . . strengthen support to the CINC and components through improved efficiency." The Joint Chiefs of Staff's National Military Strategy described the joint intelligence center as "the principal element for ensuring effective intelligence to combat commanders in chief and theater forces."[5]

The formation of the joint intelligence centers resulted in the disestablishment of the Fleet Intelligence Center, Pacific (FICPAC), the European Defense Analysis Center, and the Fleet Intelligence Center, Europe and Atlantic. Their responsibilities and personnel were assigned to the new joint intelligence organizations. In Hawaii, five major intelligence organizations under the Pacific Command or its component commands, including FICPAC, were combined into the Joint Intelligence Center, Pacific (JICPAC).[6]

The plan allowed for retention of intelligence staffs in the form of J2/intelligence directorates at both the unified and component command levels in order to "support planning for and conduct of current military operations and to provide focused intelligence requirements statements."[7] In November 1997, approximately 4,000 individuals worked in the various joint intelligence centers; a 10 percent reduction in personnel announced at that time was probably reversed in recent years. On April 3, 2006, Secretary of Defense Donald Rumsfeld issued a directive to establish a Joint Intelligence

FIGURE 6.1   Map of the Unified Command Plan

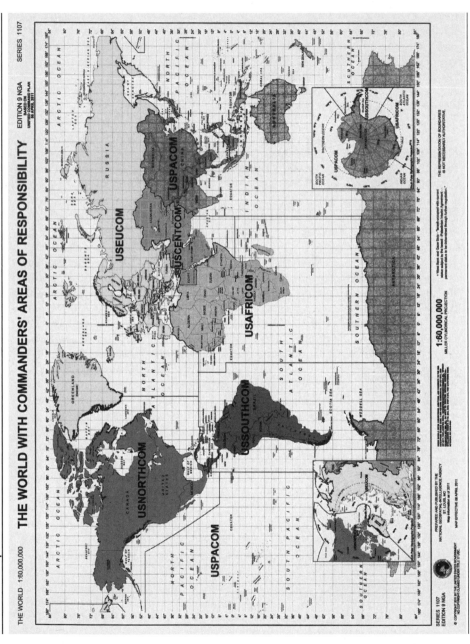

Source: DOD.

Operations Center at the Defense Intelligence Agency (DIA), as well as at each unified command, in order to provide better intelligence support to combatant commanders.[8]

In October 2007, the process of converting employees of the unified commands' intelligence directorates (including joint intelligence centers) into employees of DIA began as a consequence of the Joint Intelligence Centers/Joint Analysis Center Military Intelligence Program Implementation Study (JMIS). Even before the process was complete, over 4,000 personnel and $2 billion in funds had been transferred to DIA.[9]

AFRICA COMMAND

On February 6, 2007, President George W. Bush announced plans to establish a Unified Combatant Command with responsibility for the African continent (except for Egypt, which remains the responsibility of the Central Command). The new Africa Command, according to a Congressional Research Service study, "evolved in part out of concerns about DOD's division of responsibilities for Africa among three geographic commands, which reportedly posed coordination challenges." In addition, the wars in Iraq and Afghanistan reportedly overstretched the demands on the European and Central commands.[10]

AFRICOM began as a subunified command on October 1, 2007, under the European Command and became a fully operational command on October 1, 2008. According to its mission statement, "in concert with interagency and international partners, [the command] responds to crisis, and deters and defeats transnational threats in order to advance U.S. national interests and promote regional security, stability, and prosperity." In March 2014 testimony before the Senate Armed Services Committee, the AFRICOM commander identified the command's "immediate priorities" as countering violent extremism and enhancing stability in East Africa, countering violent extremism and enhancing stability in North and West Africa, protecting U.S. personnel and facilities, enhancing stability in the Gulf of Guinea, and countering the Lord's Resistance Army.[11]

AFRICOM headquarters are located at Kelly Barracks in Stuttgart, Germany, since, because EUCOM was previously responsible for most of the nations now in AFRICOM's area of responsibility, most of the personnel working on Africa issues were located in Stuttgart, and because African leaders were not receptive to establishing command headquarters in Africa. About 2,000 personnel are assigned to the command, including servicemen, federal civilian employees, and contractor personnel, about 1,500 of whom work at headquarters. Its programs are coordinated through Offices of Security Cooperation and Defense Attaché Offices in approximately thirty-eight nations. There are also command liaison officers in residence at the headquarters of the African Union in Ethiopia, the headquarters of the Economic Community of West African States in Nigeria, and the Kofi Annan International Peacekeeping and Training Centre in Ghana.[12]

AFRICOM's subordinate commands include U.S. Army Africa, with headquarters at Vicenza, Italy, and U.S. Naval Forces Africa, located in Naples, Italy. The naval component's primary mission is to improve the maritime security capability and capacity of African partners. Two additional service components are U.S. Air Forces Africa and U.S. Marine Corps Forces Africa, located in Stuttgart. The final two component commands are the Combined Joint Task Force–Horn of Africa, with about 2,000 personnel, headquartered at Camp Lemonnier, Djibouti, and U.S. Special Operations Command Africa, located in Stuttgart.[13]

Among the AFRICOM's headquarters components is its Intelligence and Knowledge Development Directorate (J2), whose organization chart is shown in Figure 6.2. Headquartered at Stuttgart, it has detachments at Molesworth, United Kingdom, Tampa, Florida, and Washington, D.C. The directorate "executes intelligence operations; and manages intelligence collection, analysis, production, dissemination, and knowledge development for HQ Africa Command, its components and designated partners." There are 200 personnel assigned to J2 in Stuttgart and 253 at Molesworth, where the European Command's joint intelligence center is located (until it is located to Royal Air Force [RAF] Croughton, where building of a joint intelligence center is scheduled to begin in 2016).[14] The Tampa detachment apparently works in concert with the U.S. Special Operations Command intelligence center.

CENTRAL COMMAND

The U.S. Central Command was formed on January 1, 1983, as a successor of the Rapid Deployment Force. Headquartered at MacDill Air Force Base (AFB) in Tampa, it assumed responsibility for the nations of the Middle East and the Persian Gulf area, Northeast Africa, and Southwest Asia. With the demise of the Soviet Union it also became responsible for Turkmenistan, Uzbekistan, Kyrgyzstan, Tajikistan, and Kazakhstan. Its area of responsibility also includes Afghanistan, Bahrain, Egypt, Iran, Iraq, Jordan, Kuwait, Lebanon, Oman, Pakistan, Qatar, Saudi Arabia, Syria, United Arab Emirates, and Yemen.[15]

In 2014 CENTCOM's commander identified for Congress the command's top ten priorities. The top five were (1) transitioning from Operation ENDURING FREEDOM and support to a "regionally integrated, secure, stable and developing" Afghanistan, (2) preventing the proliferation of weapons of mass destruction, (3) countering malign Iranian influence, (4) managing and containing the potential consequences of the Syrian civil war and other "fault line" confrontations across the Middle East, and (5) defeating al-Qaeda.[16]

In addition to its headquarters directorates, CENTCOM has four subordinate service component commands (U.S. Air Forces Central Command, U.S. Army Central, U.S. Naval Forces Central Command, and U.S. Marine Forces Central Command), as well as three other subordinate entities (Security Assistance Offices, U.S. Special Operations Command Central, and the Combined Air and Space Operations Center). The Army and Air Force component commands are headquartered at Shaw AFB, Sumter, South Carolina; the Navy component is at the Naval Support Activity, Bahrain; and the Marine and Special Operations Command elements are located at MacDill. There are also command and component facilities in Kuwait and Qatar. Personnel totals for various CENTCOM elements are 2,140 for headquarters, 3,268 for the service component commands, and 589 for the other subordinate entities.[17]

Of the personnel at headquarters, as of June 2014, 1,169 worked for CENTCOM's intelligence organizations: the Intelligence Directorate and the subordinate Joint Intelligence Center, Central (JICCENT). The Intelligence Directorate "provides threat

FIGURE 6.2 Organization of the Africa Command J-2

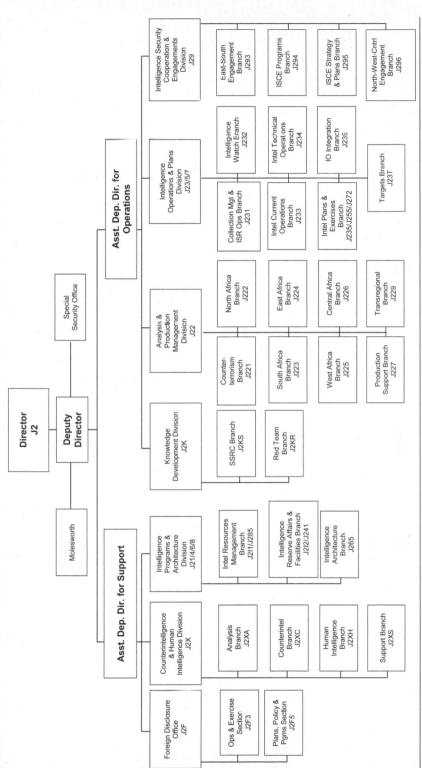

Source: AFRICOM.

warning, targeting intelligence, and assessments" to the CENTCOM commander, component commands, U.S. embassy country teams, and the president and Secretary of Defense through "the conduct of all-source collection, analysis, fusion, targeting, production, and dissemination." As the directorate's organization chart, shown in Figure 6.3, indicates, its main components include five divisions—Intelligence, Surveillance, and Reconnaissance (ISR); Operations; Plans; Resources & Requirements; and Counterintelligence and Security (X)—which focus largely on collection issues. According to CENTCOM's commanding general, the directorate maintains a "close working relationship" with the Office of the Director of National Intelligence.[18]

As Figure 6.4, indicates, analytical intelligence support for the command comes from the JICCENT, whose mission is to provide all-source intelligence and warning, operational intelligence, and assessments to the CENTCOM commander to meet wartime and peacetime needs, provide mission-oriented intelligence support to component commanders, and produce and disseminate finished intelligence. Its primary components are the Analysis & Production Department (with South & Central Asia, Iran, Near East, Regional, and Nonstate Threats divisions) and the Targeting & Geospatial Readiness Department (with a Joint Targeting Element, Geospatial Intelligence, and Order of Battle divisions).[19]

EUROPEAN COMMAND

The European Command was responsible for a geographic area that included fifty-one countries. As noted above, the creation of AFRICOM eliminated the EUCOM's responsibility for the nations of the African continent. In the aftermath of the Soviet Union's collapse, EUCOM assumed responsibility for Georgia, Armenia, and Azerbaijan. It is also responsible for Israel.[20]

Headquartered in Stuttgart, EUCOM is one of two forward deployed geographical combat commands; it has five component commands with over 94,000 personnel (over 73,000 military and over 20,000 civilian): U.S. Naval Forces Europe and Africa (Naval Support Activity, Naples), U.S. Army Europe and Africa (Wiesbaden, Germany), U.S. Air Forces Europe and Africa (Ramstein AB, Germany), U.S. Marine Forces Europe and Africa (Stuttgart), and U.S. Special Operations Command Europe and Africa. The command also has twenty-one bases or sites in the theater.[21]

EUCOM's J2 manages the Joint Intelligence Operations Center–Europe (JIOCEUR), which "focuses on the commander's priorities to provide advanced warning, situation understanding, relevant predictive estimates, and strategic content for its strategy of 'active security' and lines of operation," according to a EUCOM fact sheet, which also states that the J2 "balances the requirements of theater strategic decision makers and operational commanders." As its organization chart, shown in Figure 6.5, indicates, the center's key components include its Plans, Operations, and Human Intelligence (HUMINT) and Counterintelligence (CI) divisions.[22]

The command's analytical intelligence production is the responsibility of the Joint Analysis Center (JAC), located at Molesworth (until its relocation to RAF Broughton) and subordinate to the J2. The functions of the JAC include
- Theater-wide, all-source analyses and assessments
- Collection management

FIGURE 6.3 Organization of the Central Command Intelligence Directorate

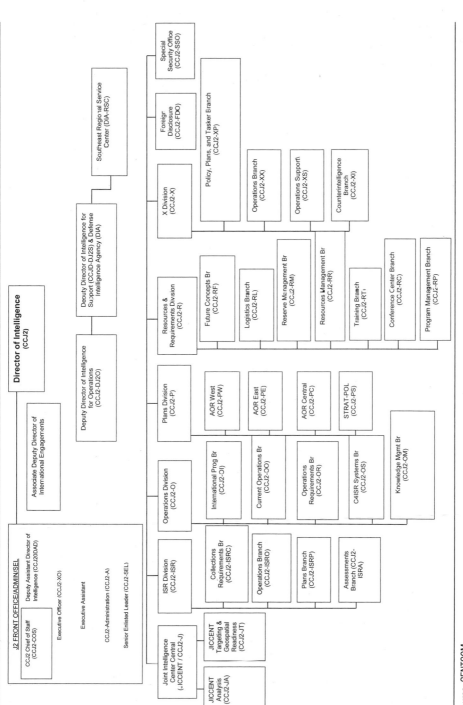

Source: CENTCOM.

FIGURE 6.4   Organization of the Central Command Joint Intelligence Center

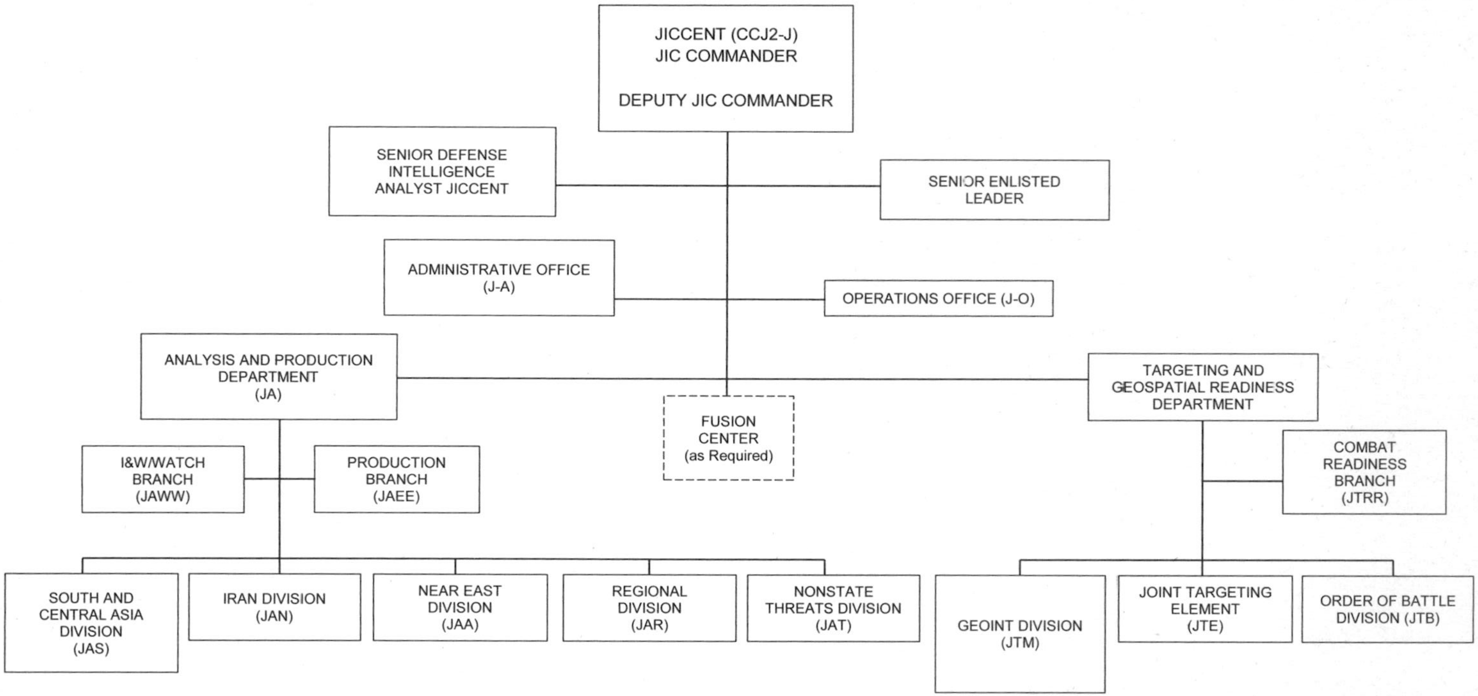

JICCENT (CCJ2-J)
JIC COMMANDER

DEPUTY JIC COMMANDER

SENIOR ENLISTED LEADER

SENIOR DEFENSE INTELLIGENCE ANALYST JICCENT

OPERATIONS OFFICE (J-O)

ADMINISTRATIVE OFFICE (J-A)

FUSION CENTER (as Required)

TARGETING AND GEOSPATIAL READINESS DEPARTMENT

COMBAT READINESS BRANCH (JTRR)

ORDER OF BATTLE DIVISION (JTB)

JOINT TARGETING ELEMENT (JTE)

GEOINT DIVISION (JTM)

ANALYSIS AND PRODUCTION DEPARTMENT (JA)

PRODUCTION BRANCH (JAEE)

I&W/WATCH BRANCH (JAWW)

NONSTATE THREATS DIVISION (JAT)

REGIONAL DIVISION (JAR)

NEAR EAST DIVISION (JAA)

IRAN DIVISION (JAN)

SOUTH AND CENTRAL ASIA DIVISION (JAS)

Source: CENTCOM.

FIGURE 6.5 Organization of the European Command Joint Intelligence Operations Center

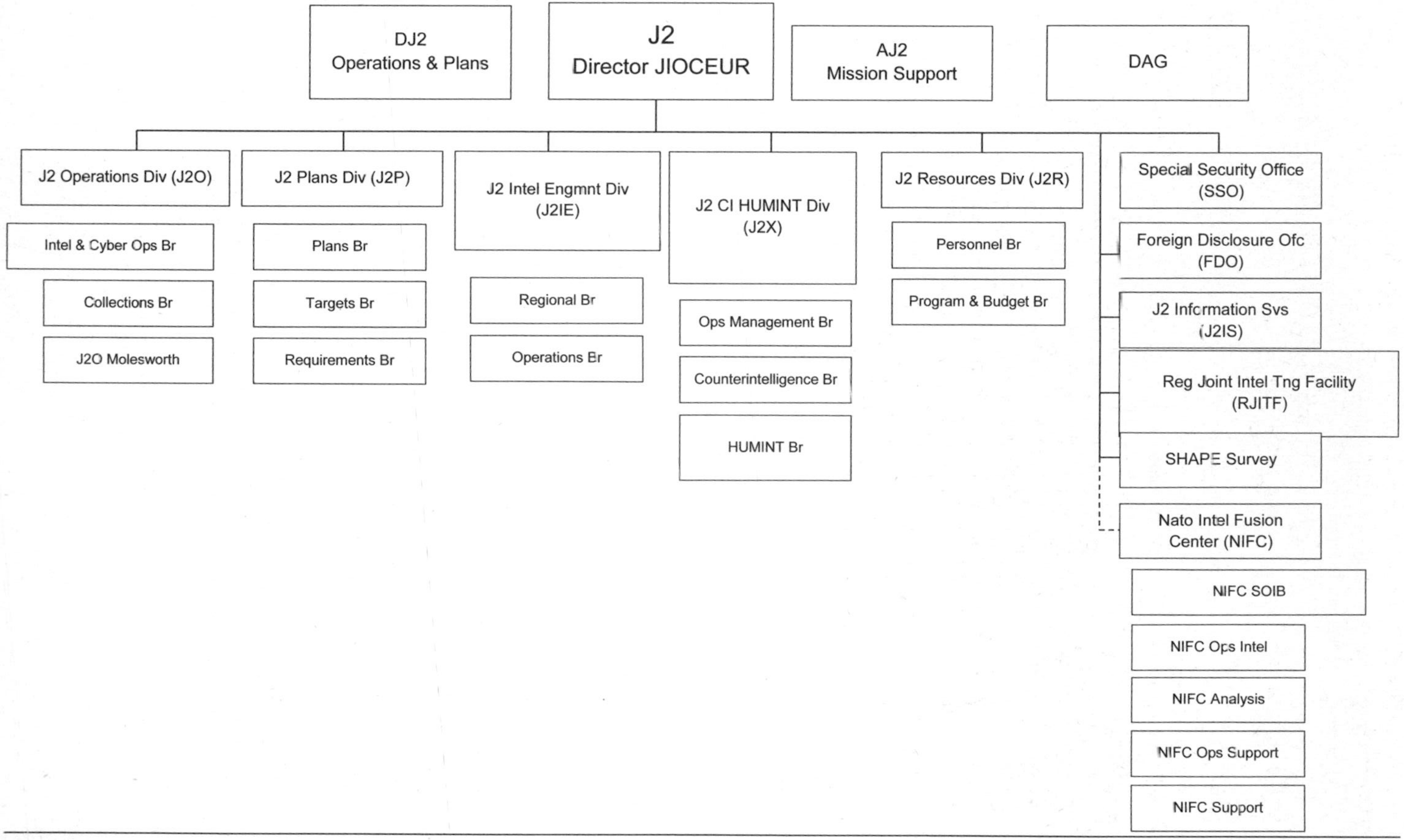

J2
Director JIOCEUR

DAG

DJ2
Operations & Plans

AJ2
Mission Support

J2 Operations Div (J2O)

J2 Plans Div (J2P)

J2 Intel Engmnt Div (J2IE)

J2 CI HUMINT Div (J2X)

J2 Resources Div (J2R)

Intel & Cyber Ops Br

Plans Br

Regional Br

Ops Management Br

Personnel Br

Collections Br

Targets Br

Operations Br

Counterintelligence Br

Program & Budget Br

J2O Molesworth

Requirements Br

HUMINT Br

Special Security Office (SSO)

Foreign Disclosure Ofc (FDO)

J2 Information Svs (J2IS)

Reg Joint Intel Tng Facility (RJITF)

SHAPE Survey

Nato Intel Fusion Center (NIFC)

NIFC SOIB

NIFC Ops Intel

NIFC Analysis

NIFC Ops Support

NIFC Support

Source: EUCOM.

- Multisource processing, exploitation, and dissemination
- Indications and warning (I&W) support
- Target intelligence support
- Support to NATO multinational forces and U.S. joint task forces
- Distribution of intelligence products.[23]

The JAC's products include theater current intelligence summaries; theater regional assessments; electronic, air, defensive missile, and ground orders of battle; topical reports; indications and warning reports; counterterrorism, counterintelligence, and counternarcotics event reports; and exercise analyses and support.[24]

In March 2005, EUCOM commander General James L. Jones told a congressional committee that JAC "has provided support for peacekeeping operations in the Balkans, U.S. policymakers in the Caucasus, and supported crises response and counterterrorism operations in Africa." In addition, Jones stated that the JAC "supports the GWOT [Global War on Terrorism] with counter-terrorism analysis and has almost a quarter of its analysts temporarily deployed to Iraq and Afghanistan."[25]

The JAC contains two primary directorates: Support and Intelligence. As shown in Figure 6.6, the later directorate has five divisions: Counterterrorism (IDX), Europe/Levant (IDE), Eurasia (IDR), Geospatial Intelligence (IDG), and Operational Awareness (IDO).[26]

NORTHERN COMMAND

The most dramatic change in the unified command structure that resulted from the terrorist attacks of September 11, 2001, was the creation of the Northern Command, an idea favored by the nation's top military officials that emerged not long after the attacks. Before the command could be established, a number of issues needed to be resolved, including whether the command would control its own forces or rely on forces supplied by other military commands and the legal restrictions on the use of military forces for law enforcement purposes. Such a command had been proposed during the Bill Clinton administration, but the idea was dropped after protests from civil libertarians and, reportedly, right-wing militia groups.[27]

On April 17, 2002, the Department of Defense announced the creation of the U.S. Northern Command to bring together in a single military command the homeland defense and civil support missions being performed by other military organizations. The command, which is colocated with the headquarters of the Northern Aerospace Defense Command (NORAD) at Peterson AFB in Colorado, reached initial operational capability on October 1, 2002.*[28]

The U.S Northern Command has two primary missions:

- Conducting operations to detect, prevent, and defeat threats and all aggression aimed at the United States, its territories, and interests within its assigned area

---

*Beyond colocation, the commands also share many organizational components. See NORTHCOM, "HQ NORAD and USNORTHCOM Organizations and Functions," NORTHCOM and USNORTHCOM Mission Directive 1, September 16, 2013, http://www.northcom.mil/Portals/28/Documents/HQ%20N-NC%20Orgs%20and%20Functions%20(NNCMD1).pdf.

FIGURE 6.6   Organization of the European Command Joint Analysis Center

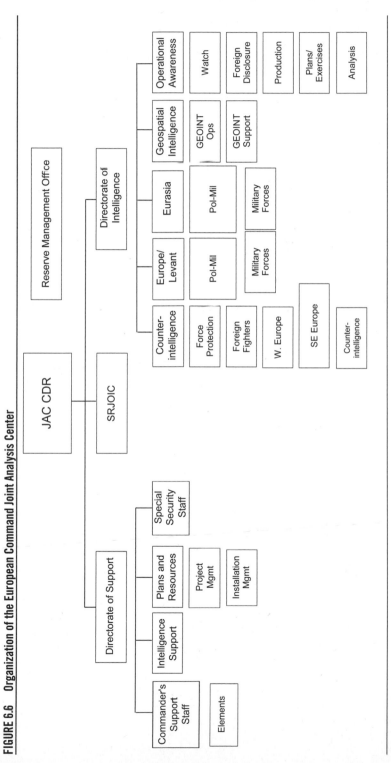

Source: EUCOM.

of responsibility, which includes the air, land, and sea approaches to the continental United States, Alaska, and the surrounding water out to approximately five hundred nautical miles, as well as the Gulf of Mexico, Puerto Rico, and the U.S. Virgin Islands
- Providing defense support of civil authorities, including consequence management, at the direction of the President or Secretary of Defense.[29]

In carrying out its missions NORTHCOM "conducts maritime operations to deter terrorist operations and prevent attacks on the United States and its allies." With regard to land operations, the command "postures and positions forces to deter and prevent attacks." During the 2004 election period, NORTHCOM provided assistance for border security, conducted airport vulnerability assessments, and deployed forces, at the request of the Department of Homeland Security, trained in radiological detection.[30]

In addition to its headquarters directorates, NORTHCOM includes four service military component commands: the U.S. Fleet Forces Command (Norfolk, Virginia), the U.S. Marines Forces Northern Command, Air Forces Northern (Tyndall AFB, Florida), and U.S. Army North (Fort Sam Houston, Texas). A Special Operations Command North was provisionally established in 2013.[31]

In addition, four joint task forces are subordinate to the command. Joint Task Force Alaska, at Elmendorf AFB, Alaska, is responsible for coordinating with other government agencies to "deter, detect, prevent and detect threats within the Alaska Joint Operations Area." Joint Task Force North, based at Briggs Army Airfield at Fort Bliss, Texas, is "tasked to support . . . federal law enforcement agencies in the interdiction of suspected transnational threats within and along the approaches to the continental United States." Fort McNair, Washington, D.C., is the headquarters for Joint Force Headquarters National Capital Region, which "is responsible for land-based homeland defense, defense support of civil authorities . . . and incident management in the National Capital Region." The fourth task force, Joint Task Force Civil Support, headquartered at Fort Eustis, Virginia, "plans and integrates DOD support to the Primary Agency for domestic chemical, biological, radiological, nuclear, or high-yield explosive (CBRNE) consequence management operations."[32]

The NORTHCOM Intelligence Directorate (J2) is simultaneously the Joint Intelligence Operations Center–North. Its mission is to "plan, integrate, direct, synchronize and manage on a continuous basis intelligence operations for NORAD and USNORTHCOM, integrating Department of Defense (DOD) and National Intelligence capabilities and enabling joint intelligence preparation of the battle space." As shown in Figure 6.7, it comprises five divisions: Terrorism Analysis & Warning, Strategic Threats, Intelligence Operations, Mexico, and Mission Support. Three of those divisions are responsible for intelligence production, while the Intelligence Operations Division is responsible for planning, coordinating, and executing NORTHCOM counterintelligence and HUMINT operations.[33]

Subordinate to the Intelligence Operations Directorate is the NORTHCOM Joint Reconnaissance Center, which serves as the functional point of contact for ISR (including sensitive reconnaissance operations) and incident awareness and assessment coordination, planning, and execution.[34]

FIGURE 6.7   Organization of the Northern Command Intelligence Directorate

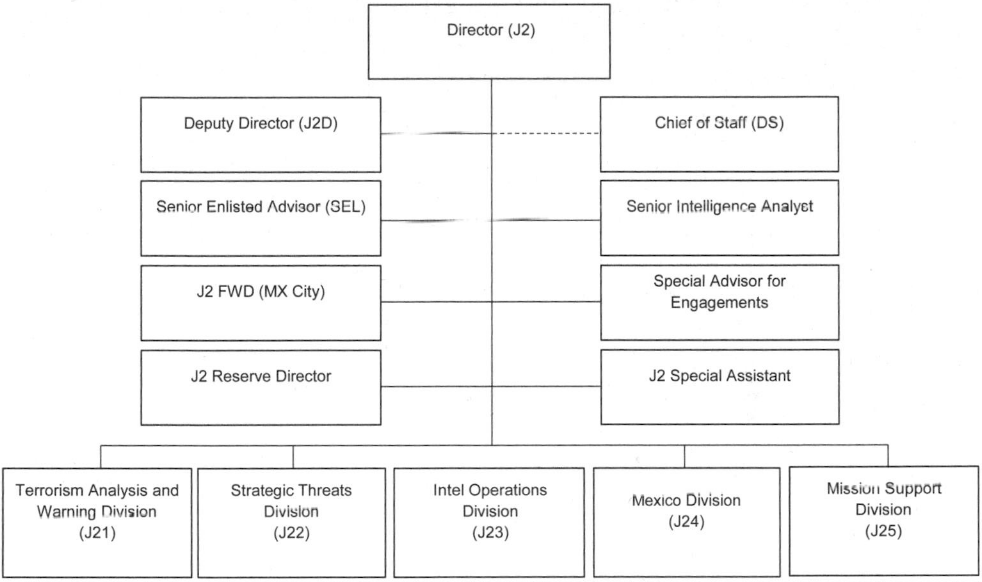

```
                          ┌─────────────────────┐
                          │    Director (J2)     │
                          └─────────────────────┘

┌─────────────────────────┐             ┌─────────────────────────┐
│  Deputy Director (J2D)   │ - - - - - - │   Chief of Staff (DS)    │
└─────────────────────────┘             └─────────────────────────┘

┌─────────────────────────┐             ┌─────────────────────────┐
│ Senior Enlisted Advisor  │             │ Senior Intelligence      │
│        (SEL)             │             │      Analyst             │
└─────────────────────────┘             └─────────────────────────┘

┌─────────────────────────┐             ┌─────────────────────────┐
│    J2 FWD (MX City)      │             │  Special Advisor for     │
│                          │             │     Engagements          │
└─────────────────────────┘             └─────────────────────────┘

┌─────────────────────────┐             ┌─────────────────────────┐
│   J2 Reserve Director    │             │  J2 Special Assistant    │
└─────────────────────────┘             └─────────────────────────┘
```

Terrorism Analysis and Warning Division (J21)	Strategic Threats Division (J22)	Intel Operations Division (J23)	Mexico Division (J24)	Mission Support Division (J25)

Source: NORTHCOM.

PACIFIC COMMAND

The Pacific Command, the oldest and largest of the unified commands, was established on January 1, 1947, and is headquartered at Camp H. M. Smith, Hawaii. Its geographic area of responsibility includes the Indian and Pacific Oceans, Japan, China, Mongolia, North and South Korea, the countries of Southeast Asia, the southern Asian landmass to the western border of India, Australia, New Zealand, Hawaii, and Guam.[35] PACOM has both subordinate unified commands and subordinate component commands. The unified commands include U.S. Forces Japan, U.S. Forces Korea Alaskan Command, and the Special Operations Command Pacific. The component commands are U.S. Marine Forces Pacific, U.S. Pacific Fleet, U.S. Army Pacific, and U.S. Pacific Air Forces.[36]

As noted above, PACOM was one of three commands specifically directed to establish a joint intelligence center. On July 3, 1991, the JICPAC was commissioned. It absorbed the Intelligence Center, Pacific (IPAC), the 548th Reconnaissance Technical Group, Task Force 168's Forward Area Support Team, Pacific (PACFAST), the Fleet Intelligence Center, Pacific (FICPAC), and the Fleet Ocean Surveillance Information Center (FOSIC), creating a single organization with more than 1,200 personnel.[37] Those organizations had been responsible for intelligence analysis concerning the nations within PACOM's areas of responsibility (IPAC), imagery interpretation (the 548th), technical support to fleet collection operations (PACFAST), intelligence on foreign naval capabilities and issues (FICPAC), and the monitoring of maritime movements (FOSIC).

In addition to producing port directories, target materials in support of conventional and special operations actions, and battle damage assessments, JICPAC employed multispectral imagery in support of amphibious and special operations and analyzed target systems. The center was also responsible for indications and warning, operational intelligence concerning maritime movements, first-phase imagery analysis, and production of current intelligence products. In addition, it produced political and military analysis, general military intelligence, and order of battle products for the Russian Far East, both Koreas, China, Taiwan, Japan, Mongolia, Macau, and Hong Kong. The South Asia Department performed similar tasks for more than twenty nations, from Indonesia, Vietnam, and India to Bhutan, the Comoros, and Réunion.[38] The center also produced intelligence on air defense systems throughout the North and South Asia regions, conducted penetration and attrition analysis, and provided current intelligence support. Components of JICPAC also produced counterterrorism and counterintelligence products, including force protection analytical products, counterintelligence and counterterrorism support to operations, and assessments of the terrorist threat to U.S. interests.[39]

As part of the transformation to joint intelligence operations centers, the JICPAC was replaced by the PACOM Joint Intelligence Operations Center (JIOC), whose commander reports to the PACOM Intelligence Directorate (J2), as reflected in Figure 6.8. The JIOC's mission has been to

- Conduct intelligence operations (defined as comprehensive, end-to-end unilateral, bilateral, and combined intelligence actions and functions, such as planning, analysis, production, dissemination, exploitation, collection)
- Develop and carry out strategic concepts (defined as activities focused on the creation and preservation of capabilities and long-range plans for the intelligence enterprise)
- Direct intelligence activities of all defense intelligence components within the Pacific theater so that they are aligned with the PACOM commander's priorities.[40]

As Figure 6.8 shows, the center's has three key directorates: Mission Support, Operations, and Strategic Outcomes. The Operations Directorate is responsible for intelligence analysis (the China, Northeast Asia, Southeast Asia, and South Asia divisions), as well as for intelligence collection (the Operations Division) and counterintelligence (the J2X Division).

SOUTHERN COMMAND

The U.S. Southern Command has been responsible for U.S. military activities in Central and South America since 1946, when it was established as the Caribbean Command. As a result of a 1995 review of the unified command structure, SOUTHCOM took over the U.S. Atlantic Command's responsibility for the Gulf of Mexico, the Caribbean Sea and the nations and territories within it, and adjoining waters around Central and South America. With its creation, NORTHCOM was assigned responsibility for Mexico and parts of the Caribbean. Today, without responsibility for Cuba, SOUTHCOM's area of responsibility encompasses thirty-one countries

FIGURE 6.8   Organization of the Pacific Command Intelligence Directorate/Joint Intelligence Operations Center

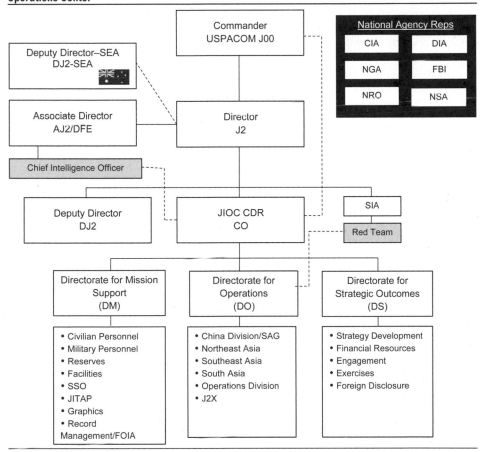

Source: PACOM.

and fifteen areas of special responsibility, which are distributed across the landmass of Latin America south of Mexico, in the waters adjacent to Central and South America, and in the Caribbean, the Gulf of Mexico, and a portion of the Atlantic Ocean.[41]

SOUTHCOM's component commands include U.S. Army South (Fort Sam Houston, Texas), the Twelfth Air Force (Davis-Monthan AFB, Arizona), U.S. Naval Forces Southern Command (Mayport Naval Base, Florida), and U.S. Marine Corps Forces South (Miami, Florida). Its fifth component command is U.S. Special Operations Command South at Homestead Air Reserve Base near Miami, Florida. Three task forces also operate under its command: Joint Task Force Bravo (Soto Cano Air Base, Honduras), Joint Task Force Guantánamo (U.S. Naval Station Guantánamo Bay, Cuba), and Joint Interagency Task Force South (Key West, Florida). Their functions include, respectively, operating an all-weather day/night air-transport-capable air base, conducting detention and interrogation operations, and conducting counterdrug operations.[42]

In 2008, as part of a reorganization, the SOUTHCOM Security and Intelligence Directorate was established; it has since been replaced by the J2 Intelligence, Surveillance, and Reconnaissance Directorate, whose organizational structure is shown in Figure 6.9. Its mission is to "execute all-source, multi-discipline intelligence operations, fully synchronized and integrated with theater, component, national, interagency and partner nation organizations." It is also to "fully inform and enhance senior leader decision-making and enable theater and regional campaign plans and operations to shape the environment and conduct ISR operations in support of the US-SOUTHCOM Commander's Priorities." In 2014 SOUTHCOM's commander identified those priorities as being "continuing humane and dignified detention operations" at Guantánamo, countering transnational organized crime, building partner capacity, and contingency planning.[43] SOUTHCOM intelligence activities to address those priorities include providing analytical support the Treasury Department's Counter-Threat Finance Branch, working with the Joint Improvised Explosive Device Defeat Organization to defeat improvised explosive devices used by the Revolutionary Armed Forces of Columbia (FARC) and other terrorist groups, supporting special operations directed against narcotics cartels and terrorist groups, and analyzing political developments in countries within the command's area of responsibility.[44]

U.S. SPECIAL OPERATIONS COMMAND

On April 16, 1987, pursuant to Public Law 99-661 of November 1986, Secretary of Defense Caspar Weinberger established the U.S. Special Operations Command, on instructions from President Ronald Reagan, to supervise the activities of the military services special operations units, which became component commands of the USSOCOM. Today, those service component commands include the Army Special Operations Command (Fort Bragg, North Carolina), the Naval Special Warfare Command (Naval Base Coronado, California), the Air Force Special Operations Command (Hurlburt Field, Florida), and the Marines Special Operations Command (Camp Lejeune, North Carolina). Also subordinate to USSOCOM is the Fort Bragg–based Joint Special Operations Command (JSOC). USSOCOM is headquartered at Mac-Dill AFB, Florida.*[45]

In addition to the component commands are the subunified commands, whose personnel draw from the service component commands and are under the authority of the unified combatant commanders, including Special Operations Command South (Homestead AFB, Florida), Special Operations Command Africa (Stuttgart, Germany), Special Operations Command Europe (Stuttgart), Special Operations Command Central (MacDill AFB, Florida), Special Operations Command Pacific (Camp Smith, Hawaii), Special Operations Command Korea (Yongsang, Korea), and Special Operations Command U.S. Northern Command (Peterson AFB, Colorado).[46]

---

*Each of the commands has numerous components that may be located at a number of sites. See Andrew Feickert, Congressional Research Service, *U.S. Special Operations Forces (SOF): Background and Issues for Congress*, May 8, 2014, http://fas.org/sgp/crs/natsec/RS21048.pdf, 3–6.

FIGURE 6.9   Organization of the Southern Command Intelligence, Surveillance, and Reconnaissance Directorate

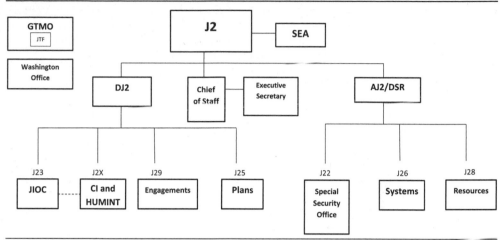

Source: SOUTHCOM.

In 1997 USSOCOM had a budget of approximately $3 billion and 47,000 personnel: 30,000 on active duty, 14,000 reservists and National Guard members, and 3,000 civilians. In 2007 the command budget was approximately $8 million, and its personnel numbered around 53,000. As of 2014, approximately 2,500 individuals worked at USSOCOM headquarters, while the command's strength was 66,000, with plans to expand to 69,700. Its budget had reached $10.5 billion by early 2012. Acknowledged strengths for the individual commands are 29,000 for the Army, 8,800 for the Navy, 18,000 for the Air Force, and 3,000 for the Marines. That leaves approximately 4,700 as JSOC's personnel number. As of March 2013, special operations forces, included Special Operations Liaison Officers in key U.S. embassies, were deployed in seventy-five countries on a daily basis. In 2015, USSOCOM received $10 billion in funding.[47]

Originally, ten missions were specified for USSOCOM: direct action, strategic reconnaissance, unconventional warfare, foreign internal defense, civil affairs, psychological operations, counterterrorism, humanitarian assistance, theater search and rescue, and other activities as specified by the president or Secretary of Defense. Table 6.1 provides a description of those original activities. In May 1995, at the direction of the president and Secretary of Defense, counterproliferation was added to the list. The most recent U.S. Special Operations Command fact book listed seventeen different command activities: civil affairs, counterinsurgency, counterterrorism, countering weapons of mass destruction, direct action, foreign internal defense, hostage rescue and recovery, interdiction and offensive counter-WMD, military information support, preparation of the environment, security force assistance, Special Operations Force (SOF) Combat Support, SOF Service Combat Support, special reconnaissance, stability, support to major combat operations, and unconventional warfare.[48]

In the aftermath of 9/11, counterterrorism became the primary mission of U.S. special operations forces, particularly the special mission units of JSOC. The 2008

TABLE 6.1   Description of Activities Assigned to U.S. Special Operations Command

Activity	Description
Direct Action	Short-duration strikes and other small-scale offensive actions undertaken to seize, destroy, capture, recover, or inflict damage on designated personnel or materials.
Strategic Reconnaissance	Reconnaissance and surveillance actions conducted to obtain or verify, by visual observation or other collection methods, information concerning the capabilities, intentions, and activities of an actual or potential enemy or to secure data concerning the meteorological, hydrographic, or geographic characteristics of a particular area.
Unconventional Warfare	A broad spectrum of military and paramilitary operations, normally of long duration, predominately conducted by indigenous or surrogate forces that are organized, trained, equipped, supported, and directed in varying degrees by an external source.
Foreign Internal Defense	Participation by civilian and military agencies of a government in any of the action programs taken by another government to free and protect its society from subversion, lawlessness, and insurgency.
Civil Affairs	Operations that establish, maintain, influence, or exploit relations between military forces, government and nongovernment civilian organizations and authorities, and the civilian populace in friendly, neutral, or hostile areas of operations in order to facilitate military operations and consolidate and achieve U.S. national objectives.
Psychological Operations	Planned operations to convey selected information and indicators to foreign audiences to influence their emotions, motives, objective reasoning, and ultimately the behavior of foreign governments, organizations, groups, and individuals.
Counterterrorism	Offensive measures taken to prevent, deter, and respond to terrorism.
Humanitarian Assistance	Programs conducted to relieve or reduce the results of natural or man-made disasters or other endemic conditions such as hunger pain, disease, hunger, or deprivation that might present a serious threat to life or loss of property. This assistance supplements or complements the efforts of host national civil authorities or agencies that may have the primary responsibility for providing this assistance.
Theater Search and Rescue	Actions performed to recover distressed personnel during wartime or contingency operations.
Other Activities	Specified by the President or the Secretary of Defense.

Unified Command Plan specified that the USSOCOM "leads, plans, synchronizes, and as directed, executes global operations against terrorist networks." Ad hoc numbered task forces have searched for al-Qaeda in Afghanistan and Pakistan, searched for Iraqi weapons of mass destruction, and pursued Abu Musab al-Zarqawi and Saddam Hussein in Iraq; a Naval Special Warfare unit conducted the raid that led to the killing of Osama bin Laden. In addition to those that spent years in countries such as Colombia and the Philippines, teams were operating in Yemen and other Middle Eastern nations, Africa, and Central Asia, with plans for increased use in Somalia, where a special operations forces attack in 2009 resulted in the death of the alleged head of al-Qaeda's East Africa branch.[49]

Intelligence production responsibilities for USSOCOM are located in the Intelligence Directorate (J2), with about 470 personnel, and the USSOCOM Joint Intelligence Center, a subordinate element of the directorate. The Intelligence Directorate's mission is to provide all-source intelligence "to support the Global War on Terrorism." The joint intelligence center mission has been described as providing "intelligence to the [Commander, USSOCOM], Center for Special Operations (CSO), SOCOM Staff, Component Commands, and Subordinate Units; advocate[ing] for SOF intelligence requirements; interfac[ing] with national/theater intelligence agencies; and [monitoring/integrating] enhanced intelligence capabilities to support SOF."[50]

Figures 6.10 and 6.11 show the 2010 organization charts for the Intelligence Directorate and Joint Intelligence Center Special Operations Command (JICSOC). The boxes that begin "SOC" in the chart for JICSOC illustrate a key fact about deployed USSOCOM elements: they operate under control of theater command (e.g., the CENTCOM or EUCOM commander) and not the USSOCOM commander. Also appearing on the JICSOC chart are boxes for the Global Mission Support Center and the Strategic Analysis Division. The latter focuses on producing an assessment of the strategic environment in which operations take place rather than on threats from terrorist organizations or WMD suppliers.[51]

Significant intelligence activities, including HUMINT and clandestine signals intelligence (SIGINT), are conducted by JSOC and by some elements of its components, which consist of 1st Special Forces Operational Detachment Delta (Delta Force, also known as the Combat Applications Group and the Army Compartmented Element), the Naval Special Warfare Development Group (formerly SEAL Team Six), the 75th Ranger Regiment, the 160th Special Operations Aviation Regiment, the 24th Special Tactics Squadron, and probably the Mission Support Activity (formerly the Intelligence Support Activity [ISA] and the U.S. Army Security Coordination Detachment).[52]

One JSOC intelligence unit, the Joint Intelligence Brigade (JIB) located at Fort Bragg, has hundreds of analysts and evaluates intelligence in support of the command's special missions units (e.g., Delta Force). Another JSOC intelligence component, the Intelligence Crisis Action Center located in Rosslyn, Virginia, was reported to have fifty employees and report to JSOC's Directorate of Intelligence and Security, whose director serves as JSOC's chief intelligence officer.[53] In addition to the JSOC headquarters intelligence capability, Delta Force has an Operational Support Troop responsible for preceding Delta into a country and gathering relevant intelligence.

FIGURE 6.10   Organization of the U.S. Special Operations Command Intelligence Directorate, 2010

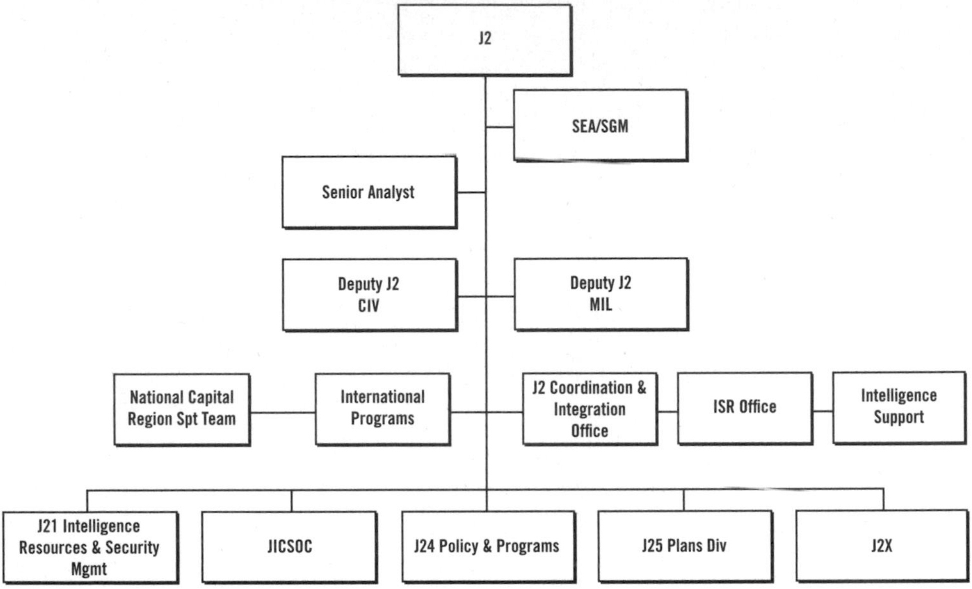

Source: USSOCOM.

A special unit, known for many years as the Intelligence Support Activity, was first established as the Foreign Operating Group in 1980 in response to the Iran hostage crisis; it conducts clandestine HUMINT and SIGINT collection and other operations in support of special operations forces, particularly JSOC units. Since its creation, ISA, which has also been designated changing code names—among the most recent being CENTRA SPIKE and GREY FOX—has engaged in at least nine different types of activities: (1) intelligence collection, (2) pathfinder missions, (3) foreign leadership protection, (4) security and intelligence assessment, (5) prestrike reconnaissance, (6) operational support, (7) training of foreign personnel, (8) hostage rescue, and (9) acquisition of foreign weapon systems. GREY FOX personnel, as part of Task Force 20, were among those pursuing Saddam Hussein. Apparently the most recent designation for the unit is the Mission Support Activity, although it is also known as Task Force Orange. Its headquarters is at Fort Belvoir, Virginia.[54]

In August 2005, the Chief of Naval Operations approved creation of two units to provide intelligence in support of Navy special warfare operations: Naval Special Warfare Group One Support Activity (Naval Base Coronado, California) and Naval Special Warfare Group Two Support Activity (Naval Amphibious Base Little Creek, Virginia). The Group One support activity was created to provide intelligence support to Naval Special Warfare Group One and its SEAL teams: Teams One, Three, Five, and Seven. The Group Two support activity was created to provide similar support to Naval Special Warfare Group Two and its SEAL teams: Teams Two, Four, Eight, and Ten. The activities were reported to be capable of conducting HUMINT, SIGINT, and measurement and signature intelligence (MASINT) operations.[55]

FIGURE 6.11   Organization of the Joint Intelligence Center, Special Operations Command, 2010

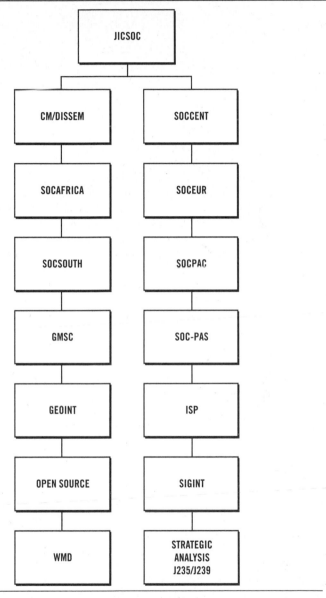

Source: DOD.

In early 2011, the two support activities were realigned under a newly created special warfare group, Naval Special Warfare Group Ten, along with the Naval Special Warfare Mission Support Center. The two activities were renamed Naval Special Warfare Support Activity One and Naval Special Warfare Support Activity Two to "remove their attachment to a specific NSW Group."[56]

STRATEGIC COMMAND

On September 27, 1991, President George H. W. Bush announced plans to disestablish the Strategic Air Command (SAC) and create two new commands to take over its functions. Operation of SAC aircraft would be assigned to the Air Combat Command (ACC), and nuclear targeting planning would be assigned to the new U.S Strategic Command. Like SAC, STRATCOM is located at Offutt AFB in Omaha, Nebraska.[57]

In late June 2002, Secretary of Defense Donald Rumsfeld announced his intention to transform the Strategic Command by having it absorb another unified command, the U.S. Space Command, established in 1985 to provide overall direction to U.S. military (other than reconnaissance) space activities. Previous Unified Command Plan reviews had considered that action as both commands had global missions that supported regional commanders. The merger took effect, as scheduled, on October 1, 2002.[58] A Defense Department press release explained, "The missions of SPACE-COM [the command of military space operations, information operations, computer network operations, and space campaign planning] and STRATCOM [command and control of nuclear forces] have evolved to the point where merging the two into a single entity will eliminate redundancies in the command structure and streamline the decisionmaking process."[59]

Today's STRATCOM is responsible for strategic deterrence, global strike, and operation of DOD's Global Information Grid. It also provides strategic warning; integrated missile defense; global command, control, and communications; measures to combat weapons of mass destruction; and intelligence, surveillance, and reconnaissance.[60]

Subordinate to STRATCOM are numerous service component commands, functional commands, and task forces. Service component commands include the Air Force Global Strike Command, U.S. Army Forces Strategic Command, Fleet Forces Command, Marine Corps Forces Strategic Command, and Air Force Space Command. Functional commands include the U.S. Cyber Command, Joint Forces Combatant Command (JFCC)–Global Strike, JFCC-Space, JFCC–Integrated Missile Defense, JFCC–Intelligence, Surveillance, and Reconnaissance, USSTRATCOM Center for Combating Weapons of Mass Destruction, Standing Joint Force Headquarters for Elimination, and the Joint Warfare Analysis Center. Among its subordinate task forces are those responsible for airborne communications, submarine operations, strategic bomber and reconnaissance aircraft, intercontinental ballistic missiles, and aerial refueling.[61]

STRATCOM's senior intelligence officer, the J2 Director of Intelligence, is simultaneously head of the STRATCOM Joint Intelligence Operations Center (STRATJIOC), whose organizational chart is shown in Figure 6.12. As the chart indicates, subordinate to the center's Director of Operations are the Operations, Strategic Relocatable Target (SRT), and Regional divisions. The first is responsible for current intelligence, ISR, collection and requirements, and operation of a watch office. The SRT Division is responsible for providing intelligence on those targets, in different regions, that might be the subject of U.S. strike planning. Other intelligence analysis is produced by the Regional

FIGURE 6.12 Organization of Strategic Command Joint Intelligence Operations Center

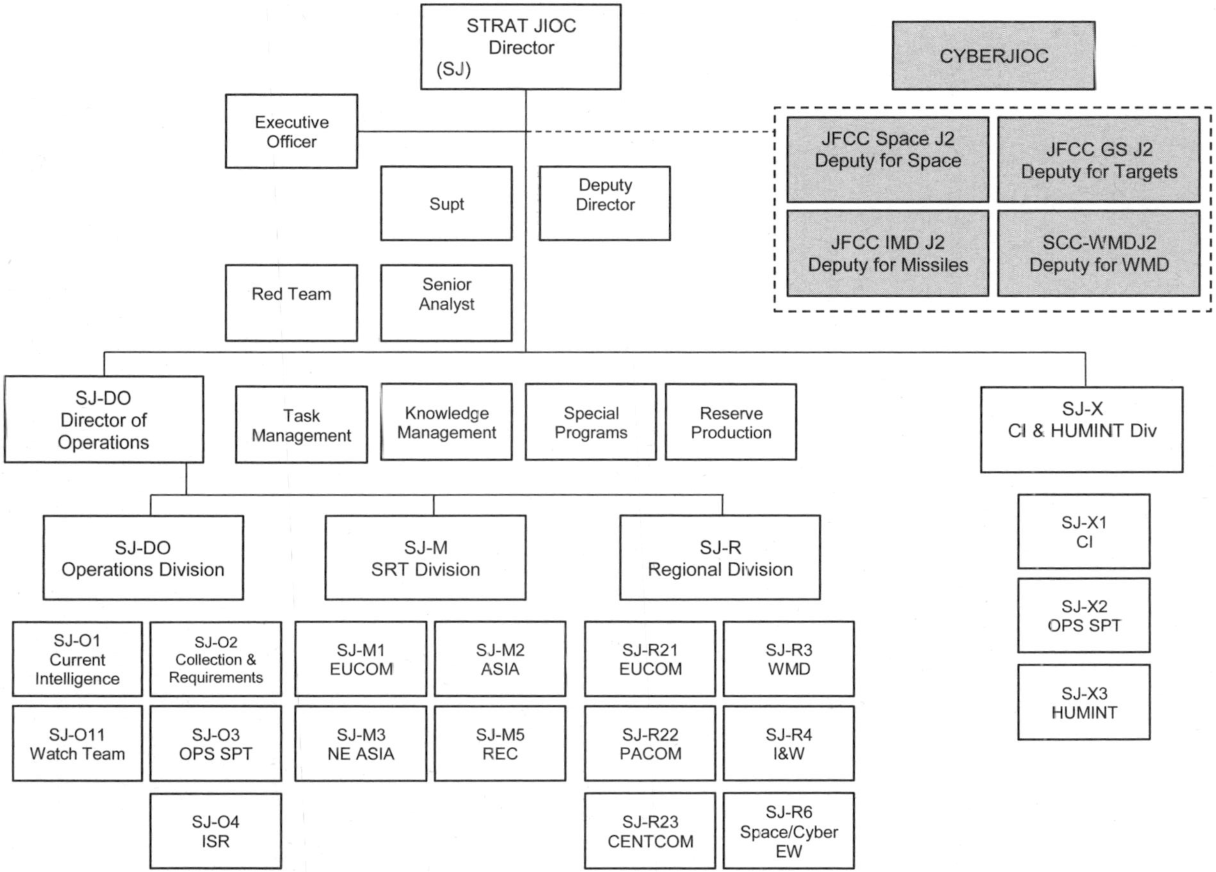

Source: STRATCOM.

Division, which also produces intelligence on WMD and space/cyber issues. Reporting directly to the STRATJIOC director is the CI & HUMINT Division, responsible for tasking and deconflicting operations relevant to STRATCOM.

TRANSPORTATION COMMAND

On February 28, 1986, the Blue Ribbon Commission on Defense Management, appointed by President Ronald Reagan, recommended the creation of a single unified command to integrate global air, land, and sea transportation for the military. On April 1, Reagan signed National Security Decision Directive 219, "Implementation of the Recommendations of the President's Commission on Defense Management," which directed the Secretary of Defense to "take those steps necessary to establish a single Unified Command to provide global air, land and sea transportation," once legislation prohibiting such a command was repealed.[62]

Later in 1986, the Department of Defense Reorganization Act ordered the Secretary of Defense to consider creation of a Unified Transportation Command (UTC) and repealed the law that blocked such action. On October 1, 1987, the U.S. Transportation Command, as the UTC had been renamed, was activated at Scott AFB, Illinois, with a staff of fifty. On February 14, 1992, the Secretary of Defense gave enhanced responsibility to the TRANSCOM, charging it with providing "air, land, and sea transportation for the Department of Defense, both in time of peace and time of war." TRANSCOM's component commands include the Army's Surface Deployment and Distribution Command, the Navy's Military Sealift Command, and the Air Force Air Mobility Command. Also subordinate to TRANSCOM is the Joint Enabling Capabilities Command.[63]

The Transportation Command's Intelligence Directorate (J2) is simultaneously the TRANSCOM Joint Intelligence Operations Center (JIOC-TRANS). As indicated in Figure 6.13, it has four major divisions: Intelligence Operations, Plans & Programs, Current Intelligence, and Counterintelligence and Human Intelligence.[64]

The Intelligence Operations Division "conducts all-source, multi-discipline intelligence analysis and production" in support of TRANSCOM's commander and the command's components. Its products include "Joint Special Reports, focused analysis, stoplight planning graphics, GEOPORT [a product concerning commercial seaports that relies on imagery and other data], and commercial seaport infrastructure information." The Plans & Programs Division is responsible for JIOC-TRANS planning, programming, and budgeting of intelligence resources within the Military Intelligence Program; it also compiles and submits the JIOC-TRANS annual Intelligence Program Objective Memorandum.[65]

The Current Intelligence Division is responsible for current intelligence and indications and warning, providing "transportation operators and planners actionable, all-source current intelligence, I&W, threat identification, situational awareness, and force protection information 24/7 in support of global [TRANSCOM] operations." The functions of the Counterintelligence/Human Intelligence Division include deconflicting all CI/HUMINT operations and activities in support of TRANSCOM operations, coordinating tasking of CI/HUMINT organizations in the command's area of interest, and ensuring that "CI/HUMINT requirements are articulated in the development of USTRANSCOM's Intelligence Architecture Plans."[66]

FIGURE 6.13   Organization of the Transportation Command Intelligence Directorate

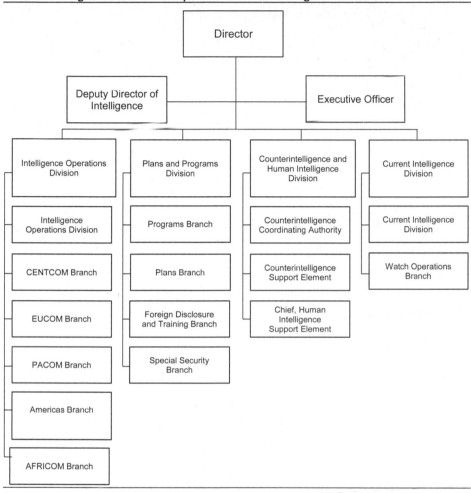

Source: USTRANSCOM, Pamphlet 38-1, United States Transportation Command Office and Phone Directory, September 5, 2013.

The Directorate of Intelligence chairs the TRANSCOM Quarterly Threat Working Group, which "analyzes and assesses the full spectrum of threats to worldwide [Transportation Command] operations to ensure protection of its personnel and assets." It then disseminates assessments, reports, or other products.[67]

Notes

1. General Accounting Office, GAO/NSIAD-97-41-BR, *Unified Command Plan: Atlantic and Southern Command Participation in 1995 Review,* December 1996, 9; Andrew Feickert, Congressional Research Service, *The Unified Command Plan and Combatant Commands: Background and Issues for Congress,* January 3, 2013, http://fas.org/sgp/crs/natsec/R42077.pdf, 1, 9; Barack Obama, The White House, "Presidential Memorandum—Unified Command Plan 2011," April 6,

2011, http://www.whitehouse.gov/the-press-office/2011/04/06/presidential-memorandum-unified-command-plan-2011.

2. Thomas E. Ricks, "Military Overhaul Considered," *Washington Post*, October 11, 2001, A1, A18.

3. Eric Schmitt, "Pentagon Revamping Command Structure," *New York Times*, April 17, 2002, A19. Feickert, *The Unified Command Plan and Combatant Commands*, 11. For an account of the power and status of the CINCs when they were so designated and a discussion of the decision by Secretary of Defense Donald Rumsfeld to eliminate the designation, see Dana Priest, "A Four-Star Foreign Policy?," *Washington Post*, September 28, 2000, A1, A18–A19; Vernon Loeb, "One 'Chief' Commands: Others Are Out of CINC," *Washington Post*, October 29, 2002, A19.

4. Feickert, *The Unified Command Plan and Combatant Commands*, 8–9, 63; Nathan Freier, "The 2011 Unified Command Plan—a Missed Opportunity?," Center for Strategic & International Affairs, May 24, 2011, http://csis.org/print/30520; Edward J. Drea, Ronald H. Cole, Walter S. Poole, James F. Schnabel, Robert J. Watson, and Willard J. Webb, *History of the Unified Command Plan, 1946–2012* (Washington, DC: Joint History Office, Office of the Chairman of the Joint Chiefs of Staff, 2013), 103–109.

5. Assistant Secretary of Defense (Command, Control, Communications, and Intelligence), *Plan for Restructuring Defense Intelligence*, March 15, 1991, 4; "Joint Intelligence Center JICPAC-USPACOM," February 23, 2006. For the history of earlier joint intelligence centers, see James D. Marchio, "The Evolution and Relevance of Joint Intelligence Centers," *Studies in Intelligence* 49, no. 1 (Spring 2005), https://www.cia.gov/library/center-for-the-study-of-intelligence/csi-publications/csi-studies/studies/vol49no1/html_files/the_evolution_6.html.

6. Arthur D. Baker III, "Farewell to the FICs," *Naval Intelligence Professionals Quarterly* (Winter 1992): 7–9; Captain J. R. Reddig, "The Creation of JICPAC," *Naval Intelligence Professionals Quarterly* (Fall 2001): 18–21.

7. Assistant Secretary of Defense (Command, Control, Communications, and Intelligence), *Plan for Restructuring Defense Intelligence*, 4; William S. Cohen, *Defense Initiative Reform Report* (Washington, DC: U.S. Government Printing Office, November 1997), 76.

8. "DOD to Set Up Joint Intelligence Operations Centers Worldwide," Intelligence Summit, April 18, 2006, http://intelligence-summit.blogspot.gr/2006/04/dod-to-set-up-joint-intelligence.html.

9. "JMIS and the Enterprise: A Retrospective Look," *Communiqué* (March 2009): 6–7.

10. George W. Bush, *Unified Command Plan*, White House, December 17, 2008; Lauren Ploch, Congressional Research Service, *Africa Command: U.S. Strategic Interests and the Role of the U.S. Military in Africa*, April 3, 2010, http://fas.org/sgp/crs/natsec/RL34003.pdf, 1–2. Also see David E. Brown, *AFRICOM at 5 Years: The Maturation of a New Combat Command* (Carlisle Barracks, PA: Strategic Studies Institute and U.S. Army War College Press, 2013); Carmel Davis, "AFRICOM's Relationship to Oil, Terrorism, and China," *Orbis* (Winter 2009): 122–136.

11. Ploch, *Africa Command*, 1; U.S. Africa Command, "About the Command," http://www.africom.mil/about-the-command (accessed July 4, 2014); "Statement of General David M. Rodriguez, USA, Commander, United States Africa Command Before the Senate Armed Services Committee Posture Hearing," March 6, 2014, 8–15, http://www.africom.mil/newsroom/document/23013/u-s-africa-commands-formal-report-to-the-u-s-senate-armed-services-committee.

12. Ploch, *Africa Command*, 10, 12n3; Craig Whitlock, "Pentagon Hunting for a Home for Africom," www.washingtonpost.com, November 27, 2010, http://www.washingtonpost.com/wp-dyn/content/article/2010/11/26/AR2010112604889.html; Government Accountability Office, GAO-13-646, *Defense Headquarters: DOD Needs to Reassess Options for Permanent Location of U.S. Africa Command*, September 2013, 4–6.

13. U.S. Africa Command, "About the Command."

14. U.S. Africa Command, "J2—Intelligence and Knowledge Development," http://www.africom.mil/about-the-command/directorates-and-staff/j2-intelligence-and-knowledge-development

(accessed December 14, 2013); Government Accountability Office, GAO-13-646, *Defense Head-quarters*, 24.

15. U.S. Congress, House Committee on Armed Services, *Hearings on HR 1816* (Washington, DC: U.S. Government Printing Office, 1983), 955; U.S. Central Command, "About U.S. Central Command (CENTCOM)," http://www.centcom.mil/en/about-centcom-en (accessed December 14, 2013). Also see Thomas E. Ricks, "A War That's Commanded at a Distance," *Washington Post*, December 27, 2001, A1, A4; Bush, *Unified Command Plan*, December 17, 2008.

16. "Statement of General Lloyd J. Austin III, Commander, U.S. Central Command Before the Senate Armed Services Committee on the Posture of U.S. Central Command," March 6, 2014, 7–8.

17. Government Accountability Office, GAO-14 440, *Defense Headquarters: Guidance Needed to Transition U.S. Central Command's Costs to the Base Budget*, June 2014, 8, 41.

18. Ibid., 41; U.S. Central Command, "J2 Mission: Intelligence Director's Mission Statement," n.d.; U.S. Central Command, "Intelligence Directorate (Organization Chart)," December 23, 2013; "Statement of General Lloyd J. Austin III, Commander, U.S. Central Command Before the Senate Armed Services Committee on the Posture of U.S. Central Command," 37.

19. U.S. Central Command, "Joint Intelligence Center Central (JICCENT)," January 10, 2013; U.S. Central Command, "The CENTCOM Perspective: CENTCOM/SOCOM Joint Intelligence Support Concept," 1992; Richard Lardner, "Behind CENTCOM's Closed Doors," March 15, 2004, http://www.tampatrib.com.

20. "501st Combat Support Wing," http://www.501csw.usafe.af.mil (accessed April 1, 2010); U.S. Congress, House Committee on National Security, *Hearings on National Defense Authorization Act for Fiscal Year 1997–H.R. 3230 and Oversight of Previously Authorized Programs, Authorization and Oversight* (Washington, DC: U.S. Government Printing Office, 1997), 734; United States European Command, ED 40-1, "Intelligence Mission and Responsibilities," May 24, 1996; Bush, *Unified Command Plan*, 10.

21. U.S. European Command, "Fact Sheet: EUCOM by the Numbers," n.d., http://www.eucom.mil/doc/24344/by-the-numbers.pdf (accessed July 5, 2014); U.S. European Command, "Fact Sheet: U.S. European Command," n.d., http://www.eucom.mil/doc/22822/u-s-european-command.pdf (accessed July 5, 2014).

22. U.S. European Command, "J2-Intelligence," http://www.eucom.mil/organization/command-structure/j2-intelligence (accessed July 5, 2014); U.S. European Command, "JIOCEUR Organization Chart," February 19, 2014.

23. U.S. European Command, "USEUCOM Plan for Theater Intelligence," July 1, 1991, 2–3.

24. Ibid., 2–4.

25. General James L. Jones, U.S. Marine Corps, Commander, U.S. European Command, "Statement Before the Senate Armed Services Committee," March 1, 2005, 10–11, http://www.eucom.mil.

26. U.S. European Command, "JAC Organization Chart," February 19, 2014; e-mail, EUCOM Stuttgart ECJ1 to Jeffrey Richelson, Subject: RE: FOIA Request 14-F-30, February 20, 2014.

27. Yochi J. Dreazen and David S. Cloud, "Pentagon, White House Consider New Command Against U.S. Attacks," *Wall Street Journal*, November 21, 2001, A8; Bradley Graham, "Military Favors a Homeland Command," *Washington Post*, November 23, 2001, A1, A6.

28. "U.S. Northern Command: A History," www.northcom.mil (accessed February 23, 2006); Department of Defense, News Release 188-02, "Unified Command Plan," April 17, 2002, http://www.defense.gov/Releases/Release.aspx?ReleaseID=3309; Jim Garamone, Armed Forces Press Service, "Unified Command Plan Changes Transparent, But Important," May 22, 2002, http://www.defense.gov/news/newsarticle.aspx?id=44026.

29. "U.S. Northern Command," www.northcom.mil (accessed February 23, 2006). Other responsibilities are listed in Bush, *Unified Command Plan*, 12–14. Also see "Statement of General

Charles H. Jacoby, United States Army Commander United States Northern Command and North American Aerospace Defense Command Before the House Armed Services Committee," February 26, 2014.

30. "Statement of Lieutenant General Joseph R. Inge, USA, Deputy Commander, United States Northern Command Before the Senate Armed Services Committee Subcommittee on Emerging Threats and Capabilities," March 10, 2006, 2.

31. Ibid., 3–4; Bradley Graham, "War Plans Drafted to Counter Terror Attacks in U.S.," *Washington Post*, August 8, 2005, A1, A7; the fact sheets for the task forces, all dated May 16, 2013, are available at www.northcom.mil/Newsroom/FactSheets.

32. The fact sheets for the task forces, all dated May 16, 2013, are available at www.northcom.mil/Newsroom/FactSheets.

33. North American Aerospace Defense Command and U.S. Northern Command, NORAD and USNORTHCOM Publication 1-01, *Battle Staff Standard Operating Procedures*, March 11, 2011, E-1; U.S. Northern Command, NNCMAN38-153, *NORTHCOM Organization and Functions Manual*, August 1, 2007, ch. 5, 1.

34. North American Aerospace Defense Command and U.S. Northern Command, NORAD and USNORTHCOM Publication 1-01, *Battle Staff Standard Operating Procedures*, E-2.

35. U.S. Pacific Command, "USPACOM History," http://www.pacom.mil/AboutUSPACOM /History.aspx (accessed July 6, 2014); Bush, *Unified Command Plan*, 16.

36. U.S. Pacific Command, "Organization Chart," http://www.pacom.mil/Organization/ OrganizationChart.aspx (accessed July 6, 2014).

37. Letter, K. Kibota, Chief, Administrative Support Division, Joint Secretariat, U.S, Pacific Command, to Jeffrey Richelson, October 8, 1991; "The New Boy on the Block," *Naval Intelligence Professionals Quarterly* (Spring 1992): 2; "West Coast Intelligence Consolidations," *Naval Intelligence Bulletin* (Fall/Winter 1990): 22–23.

38. Joint Intelligence Center, Pacific, *JICPAC Quick Reference Office and Function Guide*, June 1996, 11–15.

39. Ibid., 15–16.

40. U.S. Pacific Command, "PACOM JIOC Mission," n.d.

41. General Accounting Office, *Unified Command Plan*, 9–10; Garamone, "Unified Command Plan Changes Transparent, But Important"; U.S. Southern Command, "Area of Responsibility," http://www.southcom.mil/aboutus/Pages/Area-of-Responsibility.aspx (accessed July 10, 2014).

42. U.S. Southern Command, *Command Strategy 2018: Partnership for the Americas*, n.d., 16–17.

43. General Accounting Office, GAO-10-801, *U.S. Southern Command Demonstrates Interagency Collaboration, but Its Haiti Disaster Response Revealed Challenges Conducting a Large Military Operation*, July 2010, 21; U.S. Southern Command, "Directorate of Security and Intelligence," www.southcom.mil (accessed March 8, 2010); U.S. Southern Command, "J2 Intelligence Surveillance, and Reconnaissance Directorate," www.southcom.mil (accessed December 14, 2013); *Posture Statement of General John F. Kelly, United States Marine Corps, Commander, United States Southern Command Before the 113th Congress, House Armed Services Committee*, February 26, 2014, 2.

44. *Posture Statement of General John F. Kelly, United States Marine Corps, Commander, United States Southern Command Before the 113th Congress, House Armed Services Committee*, 18; Aram Roston, "Update: SOUTHCOM ISR Helped Kill 32 'Narco-Terrorists,'" www.defensenews.com, May 30, 2013, http://archive.defensenews.com/article/20130530/C4ISR01/305300009/Update -SOUTHCOM-ISR-Helped-Kill-32-Narco-Terrorists-; Marc V. Schanz, "SOUTHCOM's Concerns," *Air Force Magazine*, August 2011, 46–49; "Going Dark: SOUTHCOM, Where Modern ISR Was Born, Is Hoping for Assets," www.defensenews.com, May 13, 2013, http://archive .defensenews.com/article/20130514/C4ISR/305140017/Going-Dark-SOUTHCOM-Where -Modern-ISR-Born-Hoping-Assets; U.S.Southern Command, "US Military Helping Colombia

Fight IED Threat," June 30, 2014, http://www.southcom.mil/newsroom/Pages/US-military-helping-Colombia-deal-with-IED-threat.aspx.

45. Ronald Reagan, Memorandum for the Honorable Caspar W. Weinberger, Secretary of Defense, Subject: Establishment of Combatant Commands, April 13, 1987; Caspar Weinberger, Memorandum for the President, Subject: Establishment of the U.S. Special Operations Command, April 16, 1987; General Accounting Office, GAO/NSIAD-97-85, *Special Operations Forces: Opportunities to Preclude Overuse and Misuse*, May 1997, 1; Andrew Feickert, *U.S. Special Operations Forces (SOF): Background and Issues for Congress*, March 28, 2011, 2–5; Government Accountability Office, GAO-14-439, *Defense Headquarters: DOD Needs to Evaluate Its Approach for Managing Resources Devoted to the Functional Combatant Commands*, June 2014, 44. On the origin of the Marines Special Operations Command, see Donald Rumsfeld, To: Gen. Doug Brown, Subject: Marines Special Operations Command, February 7, 2005, http://library.rumsfeld.com/doclib/sp/3268/2005-02-07%20To%20Gen%20Doug%20Brown%20re%20Marines%20Special%20Operations%20Command.pdf; Donald Rumsfeld, To Gen. Pete Pace, Gen. Mike Hagee, Gen. Doug Brown, Subject: Marine Special Operations Command (MARSOC), November 4, 2005, http://www.rumsfeld.com.

46. Government Accountability Office, GAO-14-439, *Defense Headquarters*, 2; U.S. Special Operations Command, *United States Special Operations Fact Book 2014*, 2014, 35–41.

47. U.S. Special Operations Command, *United States Special Operations Fact Book 2014*, 12, 18, 22, 26, 31; General Accounting Office, GAO/NSIAD-97-85, *Special Operations Forces*, 2; Ann Scott Tyson, "New Plans Foresee Fighting Terrorism Beyond War Zones," www.washingtonpost .com, April 23, 2006, http://www.washingtonpost.com/wp-dyn/content/article/2006/04/22/AR2006042201124.html; Michael D. Lumpkin, Assistant Secretary of Defense Special Operations and Low Intensity Conflict, *Statement Before the 113th Congress, Senate Armed Services Committee, Emerging Threats and Capabilities Subcommittee*, March 11, 2014, 4; Admiral William H. McRaven, Commander, U.S. Special Operations Command, *Posture Statement Before the 113th Congress Senate Armed Services Committee*, March 5, 2013, 3, 6; Eric Schmitt, Mark Mazzetti, and Thom Shanker, "Admiral Pushing for Freer Hand with Commandos," *New York Times*, February 13, 2012, A1, A6; Marcus Weinberger, "Peeling the Onion Back on the Pentagon's Special Operations Budget," www.defenseone.com (accessed January 27, 2015).

48. U.S. Special Operations Command, *Fact Book 2014*, 14.

49. Thom Shanker, "Study Is Said to Find Overlap in U.S. Counterterror Effort," *New York Times*, March 18, 2006, A5; Dana Priest and Thomas E. Ricks, "U.S. Units Attacking Al Qaeda in Pakistan," *Washington Post*, April 25, 2002, A1, A8; Rowan Scarborough, "Elite U.S. Unit Keeps Heat on Terrorists," *Washington Post*, July 12, 2002, A1, A10; William M. Arkin, "Zarqawi's Death and Task Force 145," *Early Warning Blog*, June 9, 2006, http://www.washingtonpost .com; Barton Gellman, "Covert Unit Hunted for Iraqi Arms," *Washington Post*, June 13, 2003, A8, A14–A15; Karen DeYoung and Greg Jaffe, "U.S. 'Secret War' Expands Globally as Special Operations Forces Take Larger Role," www.washingtonpost.com, June 4, 2010, http://www .washingtonpost.com/wp-dyn/content/article/2010/06/03/AR2010060304965.html; Ken Dilanian and David S. Cloud, "A Deepening Role for the U.S. in Yemen," *Los Angeles Times*, May 17, 2012, A1, A6; Eric Schmitt, "Elite U.S. Troops Helping Africans Combat Terror," *New York Times*, May 27, 2014, A1, A8; Mark Owen with Kevin Maurer, *No Easy Day: The Autobiography of a Navy SEAL: The Firsthand Account of the Mission That Killed Osama bin Laden* (New York: Dutton, 2012).

50. "J2 Mission" (briefing slide provided by USSOCOM in response to Freedom of Information Act request); "J23 (JIC) Mission," n.d., provided in response to Freedom of Information Act request; Government Accountability Office, GAO-14-439, *Defense Headquarters*, 49.

51. Kathy L. Weyenberg, "Strategic APPRECIATION: Focus for SOCOM Intelligence Support," *Communiqué* (May–June 2009): 16–17.

52. See Andrew Feickert and Thomas K. Livingston, *U.S. Special Operations Forces (SOF): Background and Issues for Congress*, March 28, 2011, 5; Marc Ambinder, "Delta Force Gets a Name Change," www.theatlantic.com, October 12, 2010, http://www.theatlantic.com/politics/archive/2010/10/delta-force-gets-a-name-change/64310 (accessed December 4, 2012).

53. Marc Ambinder and D. B. Grady, *Deep State: Inside the Government Secrecy Industry* (New York: Wiley, 2013), 144–145.

54. See Jeffrey T. Richelson, "Truth Conquers All Chains; the U.S. Army Intelligence Support Activity, 1981–1989," *International Journal of Intelligence and Counterintelligence* 12, no. 2 (Summer 1999): 168–200; Peter Beaumont, "'Grey Fox' Closes In on Prize Scalp: Saddam," www.theguardian.com, June 22, 2003, http://www.theguardian.com/world/2003/jun/22/iraq3; Michael Smith, *The Killer Elite: The Inside Story of America's Most Secret Special Operations Team* (London: Weidenfeld & Nicolson, 2006), 254–256; Ambinder and Grady, *Deep State*, 153–154; Sean D. Naylor, "Clandestine Somalia Missions Yield AQ targets," www.armytimes.com, March 29, 2013, http://archive.armytimes.com/article/20111114/NEWS/111140317/Clandestine-Somalia-missions-yield-AQ-targets.

55. Chief of Naval Operations, OPNAV Notice 3111, Subject: Establishment of Naval Special Warfare Group One Support Activity (NAVSPECWARGRU ONE SPT ACT) and Naval Special Warfare Group Two Support Activity (NAVSPECWARGRU TWO SPT ACT), August 24, 2005; "2 New Intel Units Will Support SEALs," March 5, 2007, http://navyseals.com/nsw/2-new-intel-units-will-support-seals.

56. Chief of Naval Operations, OPNAV Notice 5400, Subject: Realign Naval Special Warfare Mission Support Center, Coronado, Ca., Naval Special Warfare Group One Support Activity and Naval Special Warfare Group Two Support Activity and Rename the Support Activities, January 11, 2011; Chief of Naval Operations, OPNAV Notice 5400, Subject: Establishment of Naval Special Warfare Group Ten, February 16, 2011; U.S. Special Operations Command, *United States Special Operations Fact Book 2014*, 23; National Security Agency/Central Security Service, Press Release, "NSA/CSS Adds Two Heroes to Its Cryptologic Memorial Wall," May 27, 2014.

57. "Intelligence Community Notes," *Defense Intelligence Journal* 1 (1992): 105–112.

58. Department of Defense, Release No. 331-02, "DOD Announces Merger of U.S. Space and Strategic Commands," June 26, 2002, http://www.defense.gov/Releases/Release.aspx?ReleaseID=3396; William B. Scott, "'Stratcom' to Be All-New Command," *AW&ST*, July 29, 2002, 48; Sonja Chambers, "Strategic, Space Commands Merge," Department of Defense, October 1, 2002, http://www.defense.gov/news/newsarticle.aspx?id=42665; William B. Scott, "'New' Strategic Command Could Assume Broader Roles," *AW&ST*, October 14, 2002, 63; Bush, *Unified Command Plan*, 27.

59. Department of Defense, Release No. 331-02, "DOD Announces Merger of U.S. Space and Strategic Commands."

60. U.S. Strategic Command, "History—U.S. Strategic Command," http://www.stratcom.mil/history (accessed July 12, 2014). For a ten-year history of the command, see HQ USSTRATCOM/CSH, *History of the United States Strategic Command, June 1, 1992–October 1, 2002*, January 2004, http://www.stratcom.mil/files/History.pdf.

61. For details on the history, locations, and functions of the subordinate elements, see U.S. Strategic Command, "Service Components—U.S. Strategic Command," www.stratcom.mil/service_components; "Functional Components—U.S. Strategic Command," www.stratcom.mil/functional_components; and "Task Forces—U.S. Strategic Command," www.stratcom.mil/task_forces (accessed July 12, 2014).

62. U.S. Transportation Command, *United States Transportation Command: 10 Years of Excellence, 1987–1997*, n.d., 9; Ronald Reagan, National Security Decision Directive 219, "Implementation of the Recommendations of the President's Commission on Defense Management," April 1, 1986.

63. U.S. Transportation Command, *United States Transportation Command*, 9–10; "A Brief History of TRANSCOM," www.transcom.mil/about/briefHistory.cfm (accessed July 12, 2014); James W. Canan, "Can TRANSCOM Deliver?," *Air Force Magazine* (October 1987): 40–46; U.S. Transportation Command, "About TRANSCOM: Component Commands," http://www.transcom.mil/about/cocom.cfm (accessed July 12, 2014).

64. U.S. Transportation Command, "Command Organization: Intelligence," www.transcom.mil/about/org/tcj2.

65. USTRANSCOM Pamphlet 38-1, Volume 6, *Intelligence Directorate (TCJ2)/Joint Intelligence Operations Center (JIOC-TRANS) Organization and Functions*, May 12, 2011, 3, 8.

66. Ibid., 9–10, 12.

67. USTRANSCOM Instruction 31-35, "Threat Working Group," December 7, 2012.

7

GEOSPATIAL INTELLIGENCE COLLECTION, PROCESSING, EXPLOITATION, AND DISSEMINATION

During the Civil War, the United States attempted to employ balloons as a means of obtaining an overhead view of Confederate troop deployments, although little intelligence of value was obtained. In January 1911, the San Diego waterfront became the first target of cameras carried aboard an airplane. That same year the U.S. Army Signal Corps added aerial photography to the curriculum at its flight training school. From 1913 to 1915, the U.S. Army flew visual and photographic reconnaissance missions in the Philippines and along the Mexican border. During World War II the United States made extensive use of airplane photography using remodeled aircraft. The remodeled B-24, known as the F-7, carried six cameras internally, all triggered via remote control by an operator.[1]

After the war, with the emergence of a hostile relationship with the Soviet Union, the United States began conducting photographic missions along the Soviet periphery, but the aircraft cameras could capture images of territory within only a few miles of the flight path. On some missions, aircraft actually flew into Soviet airspace, but those missions could not provide coverage of the vast Soviet interior. As a result, in the early 1950s the United States began seriously exploring more advanced methods for obtaining images of targets across the Soviet Union. The result was the development, production, and employment of a variety of aircraft and spacecraft that permitted the U.S. Intelligence Community to closely monitor developments in the Soviet Union and other nations through overhead imagery.[2]

In the years since the United States began operating such systems, their capabilities have improved in numerous ways. Satellites now have longer lifetimes, produce more detailed images, and transmit their imagery almost instantaneously (i.e., in "near-real-time"). Aircraft are also able to relay their imagery as soon as it has been obtained, and unmanned aerial vehicles are capable of loitering for substantial periods and providing full-motion video of the events being monitored.

FIGURE 7.1   The Electromagnetic Spectrum

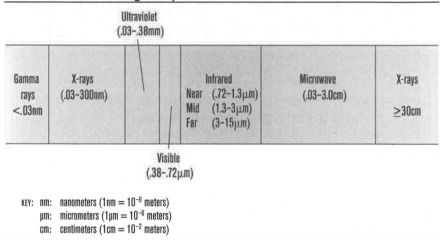

KEY: nm: nanometers (1nm = 10^{-9} meters)
      µm: micrometers (1µm = 10^{-6} meters)
      cm: centimeters (1cm = 10^{-2} meters)

Source: Created from James B. Campbell, *Introduction to Remote Sensing* [New York: Guilford,1987], 24.

In addition, the capabilities of spacecraft and aircraft evolved from being limited to black-and-white visible-light photography to producing images using different parts of the electromagnetic spectrum (see Figure 7.1). As a result, imagery can often be obtained in circumstances (darkness, cloud cover) where standard visible-light photography is not feasible. In addition, employment of different portions of the electromagnetic spectrum, individually or simultaneously, has expanded the information that can be produced concerning a target. Photographic equipment can be film based or electro-optical. A conventional camera captures a scene on film by recording the varying light levels reflected from all of the separate objects in the scene. In contrast, an electro-optical camera converts the varying light levels into electrical signals. A numerical value is assigned to each of the signals, which are called picture elements, or pixels. The process transforms a picture, or analog image, into a digital image that can be transmitted electronically to distant points. The signal can then be reconstructed from the digital to the analog format. The analog signal can be displayed on a video screen or transformed into a photograph.[3]

In addition to the visible-light portion of the electromagnetic spectrum, the near-infrared portion, which is invisible to the human eye, can be employed to produce images. Near-infrared imagery, like visible-light imagery, depends on objects reflecting solar radiation rather than on their emission of radiation. As a result, such imagery can be produced only in daylight and in the absence of substantial cloud cover.[4]

Thermal infrared imagery, obtained from the mid- and far-infrared portions of the electromagnetic spectrum, provides imagery purely by detecting the heat emitted by objects. Thus, a thermal infrared system can detect buried structures, such as missile silos or underground construction, as a result of the heat they generate. Since thermal infrared imagery does not require visible light, it can be obtained under conditions of darkness if the sky is free of cloud cover.[5]

Imagery can be obtained during day or night in the presence of cloud cover by employing an imaging radar (an acronym for radio detection and ranging). Radar imagery is produced by bouncing radio waves off an area or an object and using the reflected returns to produce an image of the target. Since radio waves are not attenuated by the water vapor in the atmosphere, they are able to penetrate cloud cover.*[6]

The imagery obtained from collection systems is employed to produce imagery intelligence, which has been defined as "the technical, geographic, and intelligence information derived through the interpretation or analysis of imagery and collateral materials." Geospatial intelligence is something more and has been defined as "a likeness of any natural or manmade feature or related object or activity *and the positional data acquired at the same time [as] the likeness of the representation*" (emphasis added).[7]

COLLECTION

The images needed to produce geospatial intelligence or imagery can be obtained by a variety of collection systems, including space systems (both government and commercial) and aerial systems (both manned and unmanned).

Space Systems

Space systems are the most important means employed by the U.S. Intelligence Community for producing imagery due to the volume they can produce, the access they provide to even the most denied territories, and their revisit capabilities. Three key operators of the current constellation of imagery spacecraft employed in support of U.S. national security users are the National Reconnaissance Office (NRO), commercial firms, and the Operationally Responsive Space (ORS) Office.

At one time, the only spacecraft producing significant imagery intelligence (for the United States) were those operated by the NRO. A variety of such spacecraft have been employed since the first successful photographic reconnaissance spacecraft was launched in August 1960. Some, such as the KH-8 (KEYHOLE-8), took highly detailed pictures of specific targets. In contrast, the KH-9 produced images of broader areas, allowing imagery interpreters to examine a large area and select targets for closer inspection. In addition, many of the KH-9 spacecraft also carried a mapping camera. In December 1976, the KH-8 and KH-9 systems were joined by the KH-11,† which became the sole type of intelligence imaging satellite operated by the United States between October 18, 1984, when the last KH-9 mission concluded, and December 2, 1988.[8]

---

*Two additional forms of imagery—multispectral and hyperspectral—are, because of the information that can be extracted from them, considered components of MASINT and are discussed in Chapter 9.

†The KH designation with respect to satellites actually referred to the satellite's optical system, although it is often used to designate the satellite program itself; NRO satellite programs have also been designated by code names: GAMBIT in the case of both the KH-7 and the KH-8 and HEXAGON in the case of the KH-9. The use of KH designations was terminated in 1987 because of repeated press disclosures of those designations. See R. Cargill Hall, *The Air Force and the National Security Space Program, 1946–1988* (Maxwell AFB, AL: U.S. Air Force Historical Research Center, 1988), 55n.

The KH-11 represented a quantum leap in imagery capabilities because, in contrast to the KH-8 and KH-9, it could return its imagery in near-real-time. That is, rather than recording images on film, with film canisters being deorbited after full exposure of a reel of film, the KH-11 was an electro-optical system. First employing light-sensitive diodes and then charge-coupled devices, the KH-11s optical system converted images into electronic signals that were transmitted to elliptically orbiting relay satellites and on to a ground station for near-instantaneous transformation back into images.[9]

The origins of the KH-11, known by the code name KENNEN at the time of its first launch and from 1982 as CRYSTAL, reach back to the early days of the U.S. satellite reconnaissance program. Intelligence and defense officials had always recognized that it would be desirable, particularly for indications and warning purposes, to have imagery data returned in near-real-time. Not until the late 1960s, however, did technological developments make such a system a realistic possibility.[10]

In 1969 a study conducted by the Director of Central Intelligence's Committee on Imagery Requirements and Exploitation (COMIREX) examined the potential utility of a near-real-time system. It looked at how such data could have been used during the Cuban missile crisis, the Six-Day War, and the Soviet invasion of Czechoslovakia. The ultimate result was a presidential decision to authorize development of the near-real-time system proposed by the Central Intelligence Agency (CIA).[11]

On December 19, 1976, the first KH-11, known by the numerical designation 5501,* was launched from Vandenberg Air Force Base (AFB) into an orbit of 164 × 329 miles. Another four of the first-generation KH-11s were subsequently orbited successfully, the last on November 17, 1982. The satellites were about sixty-four feet long and weighed about 30,000 pounds. They flew lengthwise, with the axis of the optical system parallel to the Earth. Primarily because they employed an optical system that did not rely on a finite supply of film, KH-11 lifetimes far exceeded those of its film-return predecessors, growing from approximately twenty-five months for the first satellite to between thirty-two and thirty-eight months for the first generation's remaining four.[12]

The inclination of the satellites, approximately 97 degrees, meant that they flew in a sun-synchronous orbit, so that the sun angle was the same each time the satellite was over a target. In the front was a downward-looking mirror that could be flipped from side to side, allowing moment-to-moment adjustment of the area under observation. Several benefits resulted from that capability. One was that the menu of targets included areas not only under the spacecraft but also to the side and for hundreds of miles in front. In addition to expanding the Intelligence Community's ability to monitor a given target, the mirror complicated foreign denial and deception activities. It also permitted the production of stereoscopic images and, when combined with the longer lifetimes, allowed a doubling of the "target deck" from 20,000 to 40,000 entries.[13]

In late 1978, President Jimmy Carter approved an improved version of the KH-11, known, at least at first, as Improved KENNEN. The first of the three "IK" satellites, launched in December 1984, was the first to carry charge-coupled devices in place of light-sensing diodes. The last of the three was orbited on October 26, 1987, and remained operational for more than seven years.[14]

---

*The designation consists of two components. The "55" portion of the designation indicated that the satellite was a KH-11, while the "01" portion indicated it was the first KH-11 mission.

Today, several descendants of the original KENNEN program are in orbit. One probably comes from the series of four satellites launched between November 1988 and December 1996. The second of these satellites, known as Improved Metric CRYSTAL, was the first to carry a thermal infrared imagery system, code-named DRAGON, permitting nighttime imagery. The satellites also carry the Improved CRYSTAL Metric System, which places the necessary markings on return imagery to permit full geolocation for mapping purposes. The third and fourth, which also carried the DRAGON system along with their electro-optical imaging system, were launched on December 5, 1995, and December 20, 1996—the latter into an orbit of 155 × 620 miles with an inclination of 97.9 degrees. All were launched from Vandenberg AFB, employing Titan IV boosters. In November 2008, the satellite launched in 1995 was deorbited, but the 1996 satellite remains in orbit with a 97.5-degree inclination in an orbit of 149 × 417 miles.[15]

Press accounts and congressional testimony have referred to the latest generation of descendants, the Enhanced CRYSTAL System (ECS), as the Enhanced Imaging System, or "8X," due to its reputed ability to capture in an image eight times as much territory (800 to 1,000 square miles) as the previous generation of KENNEN descendants could. This enhanced capability was developed after the 1991 Persian Gulf War, when the U.S. inability to simultaneously monitor significant parts of the battlefield posed significant problems. According to a Defense Intelligence Agency (DIA) official, only the enemy's "large static defense strategy allowed us to track his numbers and disposition with acceptable accuracy." The lack of broad, synoptic, or near-simultaneous coverage made it difficult to fix the table of organization of some Iraqi units, led to an overestimate of Iraqi troop numbers, and contributed to the problems NATO countries confronted in trying to completely eliminate the mobile Scuds.[16]

ECS-1 and ECS-2 were launched on October 5, 2001, and October 19, 2005, respectively—the latter into an initial orbit of 109 × 632 miles, although it was reported that the perigee would be raised to 171 miles. In addition to carrying the DRAGON infrared system along with the electro-optical system, the satellites are capable of longer dwell time over targets and faster data transmission. A third ECS was under construction in 2006, using spare parts, due to delays in the Future Imagery Architecture (FIA) program. It was launched from Vandenberg AFB into a polar orbit on a Delta IV Heavy launch vehicle on January 20, 2011. The first of a successor series, the Evolved Enhanced CRYSTAL System, was apparently launched from Vandenberg on January 20, 2011, followed by a second on August 28, 2013, in near identical orbits of 163 × 607 and 167 × 593 miles at inclinations of 97 degrees.[17]

The second major component of the U.S. space imaging constellation comprises satellites developed and deployed under a program first known as INDIGO, then as LACROSSE, and finally as ONYX, with the latter change occurring before first launch. Rather than employing an electro-optical system, these satellites carry an imaging radar. The first two deployed were known by numerical designations 3101 and 3102, respectively. These satellites closed a major gap in U.S. capabilities by allowing the U.S. Intelligence Community to obtain imagery even when targets were covered by clouds. Mission 3101 was launched on December 2, 1988, from the space shuttle orbiter Atlantis; 3102 was orbited on March 8, 1991, from Vandenberg AFB on a Titan IV. The satellites operated in orbits of approximately four hundred miles and at inclinations of 57 and 68 degrees, respectively. Satellite 3101 was deorbited in early 1997, and a replacement was successfully launched into orbit from Vandenberg on October 24 of that year. The fourth and fifth ONYX satellites were launched on August 17, 2000, and August 21, 2005.[18]

The fourth ONYX satellite was estimated to weight about 30,000 pounds and was launched from Vandenberg, whereas the fifth was launched from Cape Canaveral Air Force Station in Florida. That satellite was placed in a 57-degree, 445-mile circular orbit, and it was expected to be operational until at least 2012. The ONYX satellite launched in October 1997 may have had greater resolution than its predecessors. It was reported to have a resolution of two to three feet, an improvement from the three to five feet of the first ONYX, which was reportedly sufficient to allow discrimination of bomb craters six to ten feet in diameter.[19]

The primary purpose envisioned for the satellite was monitoring Soviet and Warsaw Pact armor, defeating both cloud cover and Soviet denial and deception measures. But the ONYX satellites proved very useful in a broad range of missions, such as providing imagery for bomb-damage assessments of Navy Tomahawk missile attacks on Iraqi air defense installations in September 1996, monitoring Iraqi weapons storage sites, and tracking Iraqi troop movements, such as the dispersal of the Republican Guard when threatened with U.S. attack in early 1998. The satellites may also have been used to determine whether submarines operating underwater could be located and tracked via radar imagery. More recently, they may have been employed in attempts to track vehicles in the mountainous terrain of Afghanistan and Pakistan, to detect attempts at camouflage, and to identify efforts at underground construction.[20]

A new generation of radar imagery satellites, designated TOPAZ (recycling a code name used for a long-defunct aerial reconnaissance program), had its inaugural launch on September 21, 2010, followed by a second launch on April 3, 2012. Both satellites launched from Vandenberg AFB and entered near-circular orbits of over 620 miles. Another three satellites will make up the first block, although some performance improvements are being delayed until the second block of satellites.*[21]

In the past several years, U.S. imagery satellites have been used to monitor a large number of activities and facilities around the world. As indicated in Table 7.1, they have imaged various targets in Russia; nuclear facilities in Iran, Iraq, Algeria, and North Korea; two Libyan chemical warfare facilities during early stages of construction; Israeli–South African missile development activities; Israeli West Bank settlement

---

*A third component of the U.S. imagery constellation may be now defunct. On February 28, 1990, the Space Shuttle Atlantis from Cape Canaveral and on May 22, 1999, a Titan IVB rocket from Vandenberg each placed a satellite code-named MISTY into orbit. The satellites carried both electro-optical and DRAGON thermal infrared imagery sensors. In addition to being operated in unusual orbits for imagery satellites (with 63-degree inclinations and perigees of 434 and 494 miles, respectively), they were equipped with stealth technology to reduce the chance of detection by foreign space surveillance systems. A plan to purchase a third MISTY satellite, whose cost was estimated at $10.5 billion, was cancelled in 2007 by Director of National Intelligence John McConnell. See Jeffrey T. Richelson, "A Satellite in the Shadows," *Bulletin of the Atomic Scientists* (May–June 2005): 26–33; Mark Mazzetti, "Spy Director Ends Program on Satellites," *New York Times*, June 22, 2007, A16.

PHOTO 7.1   LACROSSE/ONYX radar imagery satellite under construction. *Photo credit:* NRO.

construction; and drug production facilities.[22] The targets and uses of satellite imagery can be further illustrated by some additional details:

- In late May 1992, imagery satellites were used to monitor activity at Israel's Ramat David air base in anticipation of a possible Israeli airstrike on Hezbollah facilities. Satellites then monitored the aftermath of the Israeli strike of May 31 on the Hezbollah Janta Camp in Lebanon.[23]
- In 1996 a satellite image obtained over central China showed one of five Chinese B-6D bombers converted into air-refueling tankers. According to DIA, the tankers allow Chinese planes to fly well into the South China Sea.[24]
- Satellite photos of a military complex of China's Nanchang Aircraft Company showed that equipment sold to China in 1994 for civilian purposes had been diverted to military use.[25]
- In late 1995, U.S. imagery satellites detected "a flurry of activity at [India's] Pokaran test site in the Rajasthan desert, "causing concern that India was planning to test a nuclear device."[26]
- In 1995 the Bill Clinton administration showed satellite images to foreign leaders to demonstrate that Iraq had been rebuilding factories that could produce chemical weapons or missiles and armored vehicles.[27]
- In July 1996, satellite photographs showed that North Korea was adding more powerful, longer-range artillery along the Demilitarized Zone (DMZ) separating the two Koreas.[28]
- Satellite photographs showed that the layout of a plant in the suburbs of Rawalpindi, Pakistan, was similar to a M-11 rocket facility in Hubei province in central China.[29]

- In 1996 and 1997 U.S. imagery satellites monitored Russian construction of a huge underground military complex inside Yamantau mountain in the Urals as well as a second underground facility at the same location.[30]
- In February 1998, it was reported that satellite photographs showed Iraqi forces—both Republican Guard and regular Army units—throughout the country were increasing their war-fighting readiness within garrisons.[31]
- In October 1999, U.S. spy satellites imaged construction at a People's Liberation Army missile base at Yanang, about 275 miles from Taiwan.[32]
- In May 1999, NRO satellites imaged elements of the main offensive strike force of the Indian army loading tanks, artillery, and other heavy equipment onto flatbed railcars.[33]
- In early 2001, U.S. spy satellites imaged a trainload of Chinese short-range CSS-7 ballistic missiles outside a factory in Yuanan.[34]
- In May 2002, it was reported that U.S. imaging satellites had detected that Iranian military forces had moved additional air defense missiles to the vicinity of the Bushehr nuclear reactor.[35]
- In July 2002, NRO satellites detected activity at an Iraqi factory near Taji associated with Iraq's biological weapons program.[36]
- It was reported in January 2003 that American satellites had spotted trucks at the Yongbyon nuclear facility in North Korea that appeared to be moving 8,000 nuclear fuel rods out of storage.[37]
- In April 2005, NRO satellites detected the digging of a tunnel, similar to the one used by Pakistan in its 1998 nuclear tests, in the northern Kilju region of North Korea, which was considered a possible nuclear test site.[38]
- In August 2006, a U.S. reconnaissance satellite detected the loading of crates, believed to be of C-802 antiship missiles, onto a Iranian transport aircraft near Tehran.[39]
- In January 2010, NRO satellites spotted wisps of steam emanating from the cooling towers of a new Pakistani nuclear reactor.[40]
- In October 2010, a U.S. spy satellite was reported to have detected "continual movements of personnel and vehicles at North Korea's main nuclear test site."[41]
- In February 2012, it was reported that the United States was "using satellites and other surveillance equipment to monitor suspected chemical and biological weapons storage sites in Syria."[42]
- In April 2012, it was reported that a U.S. spy satellite had detected that North Korea was digging a new underground tunnel at the site of previous nuclear tests.[43]
- In January 2013, it was reported that U.S. intelligence, apparently via satellite reconnaissance, had detected the movement of KN-08 mobile missiles in North Korea.[44]
- In May 2014, it was reported that a U.S. spy satellite had detected signs of an "imminent" test at the North Korean nuclear test site, including imagery of a tarpaulin covering one of the tunnels at the site.[45]

Of course, U.S. imaging satellites were used extensively against targets before and during military conflicts in the Balkans, Afghanistan, and Iraq. Poststrike images

TABLE 7.1   Targets of U.S. Imagery Satellites, 1990–2014

Country	Target	Year
Afghanistan	Garmabak Ghar terrorist training camp	2001
	Qandahar surface-to-air missile site	2001
	Herat Airfield	2001
Algeria	Nuclear reactor	1991
Bosnia	Air-dropped air bundles	1993
China	M-11 canisters	1995
	Fighter/refueling aircraft	1995/1996
	Nuclear test preparations	1996
	Aircraft/missile plants	1996
	IRBM complexes	1996
Croatia	Aircraft/arms shipment	1994
Cuba	Russian Lourdes SIGINT facility	1990
	Russian freighter	1992
India	Pokaran nuclear test site	1995/1998
	Missile movements	1997
Iran	Bushehr nuclear facility	2002
	Loading activity at airport	2010
Iraq	Compliance evasion activities	1991
	Attack on Shiite dissidents	1991
	Work on chemical and biological weapons facilities	1992
	Scud bunkers	1992
	Presidential palaces	1994
	Reconstruction operations	1995
	Al Furat manufacturing facility	1998
	Abu Ghurayb presidential grounds	1999
	MEK headquarters complex	2000
	Basrah petroleum facility	2000
	Biological-weapons-related facility, Taji	2002
	Amiryah Serum and Vaccine Institute	2002
	Special Security Offices, Baghdad	2003
Israel	West Bank settlements	1992
	Patriot missile batteries	1992
	Ramat David/Tel Nof air bases	1992

Country	Target	Year
Kenya	Port of Mombasa	2009
Laos	Military/narcotics convoy	1991
Lebanon	Hezbollah Janta Camp	1992
Libya	Rabat chemical weapons facility	1990/1991
	Tarhuna chemical weapons facility	1996/1997
North Korea	Ballistic missiles	1990/1991
	Nuclear facility	1991
	Tunnel construction	1991
	Nuclear waste storage facility	1992
	Taepo-Dong IRBM mock-ups	1994
	Artillery deployments/DMZ<	1995
	Nodong mobile launchers	1996/1997
	Yongbyon nuclear facility	2003
	Kilju nuclear test tunnel	2005
	Nuclear test site	2010/2012
	KN-08 mobile missile	2013
Pakistan	M-11 canisters/Sargodha Air Base	1994
	M-11 production plant	1997
	Chagai Hills nuclear test site	1998
	Nuclear reactor	2010
Russia	Military exercise	1992
	Train carrying SA-12 canisters	1996
	Urals underground military complex	1996
	Second Urals underground military complex	1997
	Novaya Zemlya nuclear test site	1997
Rwanda	Refugee movements	1995
Serbia	Nis Airfield	1999
	Pristina Army Garrison	1999
	Belgrad Internal Security Institute	1999
	Leskovac Army Barracks & Ammo Depot	1999
Syria	Biological and chemical weapons storage sites	2012
United States	Murrah Federal Building, Oklahoma City	1996
Yugoslavia	Vinca Institute of Nuclear Science	1999

obtained during the conflict in the Balkans included Army garrisons, a radar facility, an explosive storage facility, a petroleum products storage facility, a communications site, a surface-to-air missile site, security headquarters, a repair base, and a highway bridge. Among the targets imaged in Iraq were presidential palaces; VIP facilities; WMD sites; military sites such as military headquarters; command, control, and communications sites; security and intelligence facilities; and civilian sites such as mosques and petroleum refineries.[46]

In the late 1990s, the next generation of NRO electro-optical and radar imagery satellites was to be the Future Imagery Architecture. However, due to delays in the FIA schedule and escalating costs, Director of National Intelligence John Negroponte cancelled the electro-optical portion of FIA and awarded Lockheed Martin a contract to build ECS-3, while leaving the TOPAZ program with Boeing. In April 2009, President Barack Obama agreed to a plan for the next generation of electro-optical satellites that could include both procurement of satellites by the NRO (the Evolved Enhanced CRYSTAL System) and increased use of commercial imagery. A February 2012 budget document called for expenditures of over $1.2 billion in the 2012 and 2013 fiscal years.[47]

In addition to NRO imagery systems, systems have been developed or are under development by military organizations to provide tactical imagery support to military forces. The Pentagon's Operationally Responsive Space Office built the ORS-1 satellite, carrying a U-2 SENIOR YEAR Electro-optical Reconnaissance System (SYERS) camera adapted for space operations, to provide imagery to the Central Command (CENTCOM). It was launched on June 30, 2011, from Wallops Island, Virginia, into a 40-degree inclined orbit approximately 250 miles above the Earth. In early January 2012, it achieved full operational capability. Once in orbit it focused heavily on Afghanistan and Iraq and in 2013 provided CENTCOM with images when a CH-53 helicopter crashed in a remote location. ORS-1 is expected to continue providing imagery until December 2016.[48]

The United States has also obtained significant quantities of imagery from commercial imagery systems. In past years, the only such systems were very low-resolution systems such as LANDSAT (Land Remote Sensing Satellite System) (which did have the virtue of a multispectral imagery capability) and France's SPOT (Satellite pour l'Observation de la Terre) satellites with resolutions of about thirty-three feet for black-and-white imagery. The most recent version of LANDSAT can produce multispectral imagery with a resolution of about sixteen feet, while SPOT satellites have a resolution of thirty-three feet. Both were used for a variety of purposes in the 1991 Persian Gulf War, including identifying disturbances in the terrain (indicating possible passage of Iraqi forces) and detecting wet areas that might slow down an advance.[49]

For over a decade, fueled by government interest, relaxed restrictions on the resolution of commercial satellites, and technological capability, commercial firms have been launching satellites with resolutions that can produce imagery of significant intelligence value. Digital Globe's Quickbird satellite, launched in October 2001, operates in a sun-synchronous 280-mile orbit (which will gradually descend to 186-miles at the end of its operational life) and produces black-and-white images with a maximum twenty-three-inch resolution. Its Worldview-1 satellite, launched in September 2007, provides black-and-white imagery with a 19.5-inch resolution at nadir and operates at

PHOTO 7.2   U.S. satellite photograph of Shifa Pharmaceutical Plant, Sudan. This degraded photo was released after the August 1998 U.S. attack on the plant in retaliation for attacks on two U.S. embassies in Africa. *Photo credit:* DOD.

308 miles. The company's Worldview-2 satellite, launched in October 2009, operates in a 477-mile orbit and produces black-and-white images with a resolution of eighteen inches at nadir. Worldview-2 is able to cover over 10,000 square kilometers in a single pass and has a rapid retargeting capability. Worldview-3, launched in August 2014, operating at approximately 383 miles, can produce imagery with resolution of under twelve inches as a result of its operating in a lower orbit than Worldview-2.[50]

Digital Globe also operates three other satellites that produce imagery of intelligence value, which it inherited from its merger with GeoEye (originally Space Imaging). Ikonos, launched in September 1999, orbits at 423 miles and returns images with about 2.7-foot resolution that can be downlinked directly to more than a dozen ground stations. GeoEye-1, launched in September 6, 2008, orbits at the same altitude as Ikonos, returns panchromatic images with sixteen-inch resolution, and can collect up to 700,000 square kilometers in day. Due to the merger with Digital Globe, the launch of GeoEye-2, with an expected resolution of thirteen inches, was postponed from late 2012 to 2016.[51]

Such satellites both augment U.S. intelligence capabilities and provide imagery that can be shared or publically released without constraint, such as images of the conflict in Syria, the Russian move into Ukraine, Iranian construction of deep-water frigates, patterns of life in Monrovia, Liberia, during the Ebola crisis, or postblast destruction at an Iranian air base.[52]

The National Geospatial-Intelligence Agency is also augmenting the product from NRO radar imaging satellites with the product of foreign commercial radar imagery satellites. In December 2009, the agency awarded three contracts for commercial synthetic radar imagery data products and downlink services. The satellites involved in providing the imagery are the Italian COSMO-SkyMed satellites (three of which were launched between June 2007 and October 2008), Canada's RADARSAT-2 (launched in December 2007), and the German TerraSAR-X (with an accuracy of 0.1 meter or better). The Southern Command has also obtained radar imagery from Israel's TecSAR satellite to obtain additional intelligence on narcotics activities in South America.[53]

A different type of space system that could well be employed for reconnaissance is the Air Force Rapid Capabilities Office's unmanned X-37B space plane, which is about one-fourth the size of a space shuttle, with a height of 9.5 feet, a length of 29.4 feet, and a wingspan of 14.9 feet. Through 2014 there were three X-37B missions. The first launch of Orbital Test Vehicle-1 (OTV-1) took place on April 22, 2010, using an Atlas V rocket. It landed at Vandenberg AFB, on December 3, 224 days later. The second mission, of OTV-2, launched on March 5, 2011, and concluded with a landing at Vandenberg on June 16, 2012, after 469 days in orbit. While in orbit it operated at about 206 miles above the Earth with a 42.79-degree inclination that resulted in the spaceplane making a large number of passes over Middle Eastern territory. The third mission, also launched via an Atlas rocket and ending at Vandenberg, employed a refurbished OTV-1 vehicle. Launched on December 11, 2012, it returned to Earth on October 17, 2014, after 675 days in orbit. All details of the mission, claimed to be experimental, were classified, but the vehicles can carry a payload of hundreds of pounds, and experts have raised the possibility of their having carried imagery or other intelligence collection sensors.[54]

Manned Aerial Systems

The United States also employs a variety of manned aerial systems to gather imagery. Such systems can supplement the coverage of satellites, provide a quick reaction capability, and produce imagery that can be distributed more widely than classified satellite imagery. In addition, aircraft can fly a route that focuses on a particular region or track, thus monitoring troops' movements or refugee flows without interruption—in contrast to satellite coverage, which is limited by a combination of satellite orbits and the rotation of the Earth.

The most important aerial system for many years has been the U-2, which the CIA and Lockheed began developing in 1954. It became operational in 1956 and started overflying the Soviet Union that July. U-2 aircraft returned significant imagery of airfields, missile testing and training facilities, nuclear weapons storage sites, submarine production sites, and atomic facilities. Overflights of the Soviet Union ended after a U-2 was shot down on May 1, 1960, in the vicinity of Sverdlovsk.[55]

Despite the end of U-2 operations over the Soviet Union, the aircraft was employed against a variety of targets, either for overflights or on peripheral missions outside a nation's borders. In the 1980s, U-2s regularly took pictures of military construction and arms depots in Nicaragua in order to document the buildup of forces there. During Operations DESERT SHIELD and DESERT STORM, U-2s flew more than eight hundred missions over the Persian Gulf region, enabling U.S. personnel to track Iraqi troop and armor buildups, assess bomb damage, survey Iraq for nuclear, chemical, and biological sites, and monitor a massive Persian Gulf oil spill. On two occasions, U-2s provided warning of incoming Scud missiles. In 2009 U-2s flew more than three hundred missions over Iraq and almost six hundred flights over Afghanistan. In January 2010, a U-2 collected wide-area images of the damage from the earthquake in Haiti.[56]

Today, there are twenty-seven U-2s, including five two-seat trainers and two ER-2s operated by the National Aeronautics and Space Administration (NASA). In 1992 all U-2s were designated as U-2Rs—both the planes originally produced under the TR-1 designation and the U-2Rs that began flying in 1967. Upgrades to the airframe, sensors, and engines have resulted in the redesignation of all the aircraft as U-2S. They have a wingspan of 105 feet and are 16 feet high and 63 feet long. Their standard speed is over 410 miles, their range is over 7,000 miles, and they can fly at an altitude above 70,000 miles.[57]

The plane can carry three imagery sensors, although not all at once. One of those sensors is the five-hundred-pound SENIOR YEAR Electro-optical Reconnaissance System, which has evolved from a two-band visible/infrared system into a multispectral one. The latest version of the system, the SYERS-2C, can collect data in ten bands: six visible, two shortwave infrared, and two mid-wave infrared. Planes equipped with the SYERS also have an ability to provide precise geolocation of targets. Their ability to collect in both visible and infrared bands has proven useful in detecting improvised explosive devices. A SYERS can collect approximately sixty images per hour.[58]

A SYERS-equipped U-2 contributed to the 2010 operation that resulted in the seizure of Marijah in central Helmand province, which had been in the hands of the Taliban. The U-2 detected approximately 150 suspected bombs implanted in roads and at helicopter landing sites in the vicinity.[59]

The second imagery sensor, of which nine have been procured, is the Advanced Synthetic Aperture Radar System IIA (ASARS-IIA), an all-weather, day-night, stand-off imaging system designed to detect, locate, classify, and, in some cases, identify ground targets. ASARS was designed to collect and process radar imagery in near-real-time at a ten-foot resolution. The ASARS-IIA also has an enhanced ground moving target indicator (GMTI) mode. Ground station operators can select from eight synthetic aperture radar and two GMTI options. ASARS can also detect disturbed ground in areas where mines or explosive devices have been planted.[60]

The third imagery sensor available for placement on a U-2S is the Optical Bar Camera (OBC), a thirty-inch, focal-length panoramic camera capable of providing black-and-white images with less than five-inch resolution. Up to 10,500 feet of film can be carried on a single mission, and that mission can image about 100,000 square miles. The film from an OBC mission can be processed in the field via the Deployable Shelter System–Film.*[61]

All U-2s are directed by the 9th Reconnaissance Wing at Beale AFB in California, which since October 2014 has been part of the 25th Air Force. Overseas units

---

*At least one U-2 has been employed to carry the Spectral Infrared Remote Imagery Transition Testbed (SPIRITT) as an experiment. See "Conversation: Sharp Intelligence, Tight Budget," *Aerospace America* (February 2015): 24–26.

include Detachment 1 (aka the 1st Expeditionary Reconnaissance Squadron [ERS] and Operation OLIVE HARVEST) at Royal Air Force (RAF) Akrotiri on Cyprus; Detachment 4 (aka the 99th ERS of the 380th Air Expeditionary Wing) at Al Dharfa Air Base in the United Arab Emirates (UAE); and the 5th Reconnaissance Squadron at Osan, South Korea, from which planes have flown over Afghanistan and other parts of the Middle East.[62]

Missions flown from RAF Akrotiri include those that focus on the Middle East, treaty-monitoring flights, and flights over Lebanon to monitor Hezbollah activities. During Operation IRAQI FREEDOM, fifteen U-2s flew from Akrotiri, as well as Al Dharfa in the UAE and Al Kharj in Saudi Arabia, and completed 169 missions. During the last fourteen days of major combat operations, at least one U-2 was always airborne, searching for Scud mobile missiles in western Iraq. On April 5, 2003, four days before U.S. forces consolidated control in Baghdad, a U-2, flying from the UAE, spotted thirty Iraqi artillery pieces as well as three tanks north of the city. An analyst alerted the operations center, which directed planes to attack the target, which, in turn, they did within ten minutes. U-2s on Middle Eastern and Southwest Asian missions have detected soil disturbances in Afghanistan suggesting the presence of roadside bombs, tracked Syrian movement of chemical weapons, and flown along the Iranian border.[63]

The three U-2s based at Osan, as well as those that may fly from Kadena Air Base in Japan, focus on North Korea and the Chinese border, although not necessarily without encountering Chinese fighter planes, as they did in June 2011 while flying down the Taiwan Strait. The 5th Reconnaissance Squadron was the first U-2 unit to receive U-2Ss equipped with moving target indicators to ease the task of monitoring the movement of missiles and heavy mortars in and out of North Korean mountain caves. A U-2 mission from Osan was also employed to image the portions of Japan damaged by an earthquake and tsunami that struck in March 2011.[64]

In 2011, U-2s flew 215 sorties in support of Operation NEW DAWN (which had replaced Operation IRAQI FREEDOM as the name for U.S. military operations in Iraq) and 839 missions in support of Operation ENDURING FREEDOM (U.S. military operations in Afghanistan). In 2012, U-2s flew 377 missions in support of the Pacific Command and 1,522 sorties in support of ENDURING FREEDOM, the Central Command, and Operation COPPER DUNE (U.S. operations directed against al-Qaeda in the Arabian Peninsula in Yemen).[65]

In 2014, as a result of budget restrictions, the Air Force announced the latest in a series of plans to retire the U-2. The head of the Air Combat Command told reporters, "I have no choice but to sacrifice the U-2," although he noted that the U-2's replacement (the Global Hawk) would not meet 90 percent of the U-2's capability for eight years. The plan called for retirement of the entire fleet during the 2016 fiscal year, although that plan ran into congressional objections, and the U-2 program received a reprieve, with funding for the 2016–2018 fiscal years restored.[66]

With the collapse of the Soviet Union, the Navy's P-3C Orion aircraft, originally employed and equipped to detect and monitor Soviet submarines, has been used on overland imagery missions. There are presently about eighty-five P-3Cs in the Navy's inventory, based at twelve VP squadrons, whose locations are listed in Table 7.2. The P-3C, according to one account, had "become a crucial photographic reconnaissance

TABLE 7.2   Location of P-3C VP Squadrons

Squadron	Location
VP-1	NAS Whidbey Island, Washington
VP-4	Marine Corps Base, Hawaii
VP-8	Jacksonville, Florida
VP-9	Marine Corps Base, Hawaii
VP-10	NAS Jacksonville, Florida
VP-26	NAS Jacksonville, Florida
VP-30	NAS Jacksonville, Florida
VP-40	NAS Whidbey Island, Washington
VP-46	NAS Whidbey Island, Washington
VP-47	Marine Corps Base, Hawaii
VP-62	NAS Jacksonville, Florida
VP-69	NAS Whidbey Island, Washington

Source: Adapted from "Patrol Squadrons," www.gonavy.jp/NavalSqn06.html.

tool for operations to monitor peacekeeping in Bosnia and to track the new crisis in Albania." During a fourteen-month period in 1996 and 1997, P-3Cs were employed in 324 missions and examined 2,425 targets. P-3C crews attempted to detect leaders of the Taliban and al-Qaeda who attempted to escape the 2001 attacks on Afghan targets by fleeing to Pakistan or Iran. The planes also monitored coastal freighters used by smugglers that might have been carrying escaping leaders to Lebanon, Syria, Somalia, or Yemen. In 2013, P-3C operations were also conducted over Yemen. Flying over the Philippines, the planes supported the campaign against the Abu Sayyaf group. They have also flown over Baghdad, Basra, and Fallujah.[67]

P-3Cs have carried standard cameras under the base of the plane as well as an infrared camera (the Infrared Detection System) and synthetic aperture radar. But P-3Cs are also capable of providing full-motion video, which is sometimes used to monitor activity fifty nautical miles ahead of a convoy. In 2007 it was reported that the video often showed insurgents digging holes to emplace improvised explosive devices. A smaller set of P-3Cs, designated EAGLE ARCHER, carry the Littoral Surveillance Radar System, which has proven useful in hunting insurgents in Iraq and Afghanistan. The radar can track vehicles as well as smaller objects, presumably including people.[68]

The Navy is currently in the process of replacing the P-3C with the P-8A Poseidon Multi-mission Maritime Aircraft. Its sensors include, in addition to an active/passive acoustic sensor system, an electro-optical/infrared sensor, an inverse synthetic aperture/synthetic aperture radar, and a magnetic anomaly detector. The plane is 129.5 feet long and 42 feet high, has a wingspan of 117 feet, and can fly at 490 knots. It has a ceiling of 41,000 feet and a 1,200 nautical mile range with four hours on station. It carries a crew of nine. Production of 109 P-8As is planned through 2019. Initial

PHOTO 7.3   P-8A Poseidon aircraft. *Photo credit:* Copyright © Boeing.

deployment of the thirty-seven extant aircraft has resulted in creation of three P-8A-only VP squadrons—VP-5, VP-16, and VP-45—all at Naval Air Station (NAS) Jacksonville. P-8As, along with P-3Cs, are also deployed at VP-30, also located at NAS Jacksonville. In December 2013, six P-8As from VP-16 arrived at Kadena Air Base, Okinawa, to perform patrol and reconnaissance operations for the 7th Fleet. In 2014 a P-8A was employed in the hunt for Malaysian Airlines Flight MH370, flying from Kuala Lumpur. As did a U-2, a P-8A confronted a Chinese J-11 fighter, this time in August 2014.[69]

Another component of the U.S. manned aerial reconnaissance fleet is the MC-12W Liberty plane, a medium-to-low-altitude, twin-engine turboprop aircraft. It is a military version of the Hawker Beechcraft Super King Air 350 and the Super King 350 Extended Range (ER). Its primary mission is to provide intelligence, surveillance, and reconnaissance (ISR) support directly to ground forces. The operational system includes the aircraft with sensors along with a ground exploitation cell.[70]

With a wingspan of almost fifty-eight feet, the MC-12W is over forty-six feet long and just over fourteen feet high, with a ceiling of 35,000 feet. Depending on whether the modified plane is a 350 or 350 ER, it has a range of 1,500 or 2,400 nautical miles, respectively. The plane carries an electro-optical infrared sensor and "other sensors as the mission requires." It is capable of providing full-motion video.[71]

By June 2012, the Air Force MC-12W fleet contained forty-two planes. In June 2009, the first MC-12W to fly a combat sortie did so from Joint Base Balad in Iraq, home of the 362nd Expeditionary Reconnaissance Squadron. Six months later, MC-12Ws began to arrive in Afghanistan. Eventually, there were four MC-12W units: the 362nd ERS at Balad; the 489th ERS at Beale AFB, California; the 4th ERS at Bagram Air Base, Afghanistan; and the 361st ERS at Kandahar Airfield. By October 2011 the 4th ERS had flown more than 10,000 sorties, logged 50,000 flight hours, and, according to an Air Force press release, supported ground operations that led to the capture or elimination of over 4,000 targets. The 361st, established in May 2010, flew 115,000 combat hours and scanned over 8,000 miles. In September 2014 it flew its last mission and was deactivated, leaving the 4th ERS to cover targets in

Afghanistan. Then, on October 1, 2014, the 4th ERS flew its final MC-12W mission in Afghanistan. In February 2015, it was reported that the Air National Guard was establishing a new MC-12 operations unit at Will Rogers Air National Guard Base, Oklahoma, before the end of the year—with MC-12s "divested by the Air Combat Command and acquired via US Special Operations Command."[72]

The Army is developing a Liberty-type reconnaissance plane, the Enhanced Medium Altitude Reconnaissance and Surveillance System (EMARSS), that will carry an electro-optical sensor. Like some of the MC-12Ws, the planes are based on Beechcraft King Air 350 ER twin turboprop aircraft.[73]

Unmanned Aerial Vehicles

Unmanned aerial vehicles (UAVs), commonly known as drones, have taken on an increasing importance in U.S. strategic and tactical reconnaissance.* In February 1994, the CIA deployed a UAV unit to an Albanian base on the northern Adriatic coast to operate two specially modified General Atomics (GNAT) 750 UAVs. A primary mission of the unmanned reconnaissance craft was the monitoring of Serbian artillery emplacement in Bosnia.[74]

Today, there are several UAV programs in operations. The GNAT 750-45, better known as the Predator, is an advanced version of the UAVs flown over Bosnia by the CIA in 1994. The original version of the Predator, the RQ-1, had an approximate range of 450 miles and a maximum altitude of 25,000 feet. It carried electro-optical and infrared imagery systems as well as synthetic aperture radar. In the aftermath of 9/11, the Air Force armed Predators with Hellfire missiles—an effort first code-named NIGHT FIST and then POSITIVE PILOT—so as to eliminate the delay between detecting and attempting to destroy a target. Since the armed version of the Predator is a multimission aircraft, its designation was changed to MQ-1 in 2002.[75]

Prior to its transformation to the MQ-1, the Predator performed a variety of intelligence collection missions from Eastern Europe. Three of the vehicles were deployed to Gjader, Albania, from July to November 1995. Another three were deployed to Taszar, Hungary, in 1996. During the late summer and early fall of 1996, the Predators based at Taszar monitored mass grave sites near Sarajevo. In September 1996, the UAVs also monitored election activities in Bosnia, and in October they monitored the deployment of peacekeeping forces. Imagery could be simultaneously transmitted to ground commanders in Europe and to officials in the United States, employing Joint Broadcast Satellites. In October 1998, Predators were designated for surveillance duty over Kosovo.[76]

---

*In earlier decades the U.S. relied on a variety of UAVs, operated by the air force or CIA, to conduct reconnaissance over denied territory or in war zones. One exceptionally expensive and sensitive program, designated QUARTZ, was cancelled in 1991. See Thomas P. Ehrhard, *Air Force UAVs: The Secret History* (Portland, ME: Mitchell Institute, 2010); Jeffrey T. Richelson, *The Wizards of Langley: Inside the CIA's Directorate of Science and Technology* (Boulder, CO: Westview, 2001), 129, 148–149, 176, 225; Amy Butler and Bill Sweetman, "Family Business," *AW&ST*, December 9, 2013, 22–23.

†The use of armed UAVs as part of CIA/Joint Special Operations Command covert action and paramilitary operations is discussed in Chapter 8.

The active force consists of 130 MQ-1Bs. With a wingspan of fifty-five feet and a length of twenty-seven feet, they can cruise at eighty-one miles per hour and reach a maximum altitude of 25,000 feet (although a normal mission altitude is 15,000 feet above ground level). With a maximum payload, the MQ-1B can fly for sixteen hours. The current version "is a medium-altitude, long-endurance" vehicle with an endurance of twenty-two hours. It carries the Multi-spectral Targeting System (MTS)–A, which integrates an infrared sensor, a color/monochrome daylight TV camera, an image-intensified TV camera, a laser designator, and a laser illuminator into a single sensor package. The full-motion video from each video sensor can be viewed as individual video streams or fused together. Squadrons operating the Predators are the 15th and 17th Reconnaissance Squadrons at Creech AFB, Nevada.[77]

The Predators, under Air Force as well as CIA control, have flown from a variety of bases and gathered intelligence on assorted targets. Flights from Kandahar and detachments outside Jalalabad and at Shindand Air Base supported U.S. military operations in Afghanistan. They were used to obtain high-resolution images of Libyan government troops digging into civilian neighborhoods to avoid NATO air attacks. Subsequent to November 2011, Predators flew from Incirlik Air Base, Turkey, in an operation designated NOMAD SHADOW. The vehicles would fly for twelve hours over Iraq and transmit imagery to the Turkish armed forces to provide support for their operations directed against the Kurdistan Worker's Party (PKK). In 2012, MQ-1s were used to fly 7,797 sorties in support of ENDURING FREEDOM, 238 in support of NOMAD SHADOW, and 1,119 in support of the African Command and JUKEBOX LOTUS (the U.S. response to the September 2012 attack on U.S. personnel in Benghazi). In early 2013, U.S. troops would deploy to Niamey and then Djibouti (Camp Lemonnier) and Niger to set up a base for unarmed Predators that would be employed to assist France in its battles with militants in Mali. In May 2014, the United States deployed a Predator unit to Chad to help search for three hundred schoolgirls kidnaped by the Boko Haram group. Predators have also flown from bases in Ethiopia, the Seychelles, and Pakistan.[78]

The more advanced Global Hawks are continuing missions in unarmed intelligence collection and reconnaissance. The initial version of the RQ-4A was retired in 2011. The more capable RQ-4B comes in three varieties: Block 20, Block 30, and Block 40. Block 20 vehicles are equipped with an enhanced electro-optical intelligence payload, Block 30s have imagery and signals intelligence payloads, and Block 40 aircraft have an advanced radar surveillance capability. Two Block 40 aircraft were deployed in September 2013. As of March 2014, the Air Force had purchased forty-five Global Hawks.[79]

The RQ-4Bs currently in operation are operated by the 12th Reconnaissance Squadron at Beale AFB, subordinate to the 9th Reconnaissance Wing. The RQ-4B, 47 feet long with a wingspan of 130 feet and a cruising speed of 357 miles per hour, can carry up to 3,000 pounds of payload and has a range of 8,700 nautical miles. The Global Hawks are able to stay on station for twenty-four hours (if flown to maximum radius) at an altitude of 60,000 feet. In that time, they can obtain 1,900 two-kilometer-square images covering an area of 40,000 nautical square miles. Data can be transmitted to ground stations below or to satellites for relay to the United States or other locations.[80]

Three Global Hawk test platforms were pressed into service after the terrorist attacks of 9/11. By December 2002, Global Hawk vehicles, flying from a base in Al Dharfa in the UAE, had flown more than fifty missions and provided 15,000 images in support of U.S. and Allied operations in Afghanistan (Operation ENDURING FREEDOM). In Operation IRAQI FREEDOM, in March and April 2003, a Global Hawk provided continuous, real-time images of Republican Guard tanks, troops, and artillery to the Combined Air Operations Center at Prince Sultan Air Base, Saudi Arabia. In addition, the UAVs' radar allowed the detection of Iraqi movements through some large sandstorms. By late February 2006, Global Hawks had performed more than 260 missions over Iraq and Afghanistan, totaling more than 5,400 hours.[81]

From late 2001 until at least 2006, Global Hawk missions were flown from the Royal Australian Air Force Base at Edinburgh in South Australia, apparently against targets in Afghanistan. Additional Global Hawk missions, flown from Guam along the North Korean coast, have photographed targets inside the country. Other Global Hawk missions have been flown from Sigonella Air Base in Sicily to monitor targets in North Africa and the Middle East. In 2011, RQ-4s flew 61 sorties in support of Operation NEW DAWN and 365 missions in support of Operation ENDURING FREEDOM. In September 2013, Japan agreed to host two to three Global Hawks, whose primary mission would be to fly in the vicinity of North Korea gathering intelligence. The following May, the first of two vehicles, previously based at Andersen AFB in Guam, arrived at Misawa Air Base—it would be easier to fly from there between May and October, when frequent typhoons limit flights from Guam. In mid-October the two vehicles at Misawa returned to Guam. In May 2014, at least one Global Hawk was employed in the search for the schoolgirls kidnaped by Boko Haram. A Global Hawk has been employed to collect intelligence in support of airstrikes targeting Islamic State in Iraq and Syria (ISIS) forces.[82]

In anticipation of the U-2s retirement in 2019, a number of upgrades to the Global Hawk have been identified, including a weather radar and a universal payload adapter that will allow Global Hawks to carry a broader array of electro-optical and infrared sensors as well as the U-2's Optical Bar Camera.[83]

The MQ-9 Reaper is also a "medium-altitude, long-endurance" craft that can fly for fourteen hours at altitudes in the 25,000–30,000 foot range. It has a wingspan of sixty-six feet, is thirty-six feet long, and can cruise at around 230 miles per hour. It carries the MTS-B, which has essentially the same capabilities as the MTS-A system carried by the Predator. As with the Predator, full-motion video from the sensors can be viewed separately or fused together. The Reapers are operated by the 17th Reconnaissance Squadron as well as the 42nd Attack Squadron, both at Creech AFB, Nevada, and by the 9th Attack Squadron at Holloman AFB, New Mexico. The inventory in August 2010 was 104, and as of October 2014, the Air Force intended to cap procurement at 346, with procurement extending through 2019. Each Reaper system consists of four aircraft, a ground control station, a satellite communications terminal, and operations personnel to support around-the-clock operations.[84]

Installation of an upgraded sensor pod, Gorgon Stare, was scheduled to begin on MQ-9s in spring 2010. A December 30, 2010, draft report by the 53rd Wing of the Air Combat Command stated that the surveillance system was "not operationally effective" and had "significant limitations that degrade its operational utility," including

PHOTO 7.4 Global Hawk unmanned aerial vehicle. *Photo credit:* DOD.

an inability to monitor people on the ground in real-time and delays in transmitting real-time images to the ground. The Air Force asserted in late January 2011 that some of the problems had already been resolved. In July 2014, it was reported that the Air Force had declared an upgraded version the Gorgon Stare system ready for operations. The upgraded system was reported to provide a fourfold increase in area coverage while doubling resolution. The system consists of nine cameras that produce city-size images taken twice per second as well as images of specific targets. The "sensor is a synoptic, wide-area motion imagery system, capable of watching its full field-of-view, which has a 2.4 mile diameter."[85]

MQ-9s have been flying missions in "overseas contingency operations" since 2007. In 2011, MQ-9s flew 2,227 sorties in support of Operation ENDURING FREEDOM, and in 2012 they flew a combined 1,889 missions in support of Operations ENDURING FREEDOM and COPPER DUNE and the Central Command. In July 2013, two Reapers based at Niamey, Niger, were streaming live video to American analysts working with French military officers to support the French efforts directed at jihadists in northern Mali.[86]

The RQ-170 Sentinel, whose unofficial nickname is Wraith, is a tailless flying wing that became known in the trade press as the "Beast of Kandahar" after it was spotted in Afghanistan in 2009. Apparently part of a program designated DESERT PROWLER, it is a low-observable UAV operated by two units: the Air Combat Command's 432nd Wing and 30th Reconnaissance Squadron (relocated from Tonopah Test Range, Nevada) at Creech AFB, Nevada. The fleet apparently consists of twenty to thirty vehicles with a wingspan of forty-five feet and a length of over seventeen feet. The vehicles were initially capable of carrying an electro-optical and infrared imagery package. In 2009 the RQ-170s were equipped with full-motion video. Their operational altitude is 50,000 feet.[87]

The RQ-170s have been operated on behalf of the Air Force and CIA. They were detected flying over Iraq during the period before the 2003 invasion of Iraq. RQ-170

Sentinels appeared in Afghanistan as early as 2007. They also deployed to South Korea in 2009. In 2010 the drones flew from Al Dharfa, apparently flying over Iran. In May 2011, when U.S. forces conducted Operation NEPTUNE SPEAR and raided Osama bin Laden's Pakistan compound, a RQ-170 was overhead, providing imagery of the raid—after having provided full-motion video of the compound, allowing it to be modeled for intelligence analysts and mission planners.[88]

In late 2011, a CIA RQ-170 crashed in Iran, where it was apparently attempting to monitor Iranian nuclear facilities and searching for tunnels and underground facilities that might be connected to the Iranian nuclear program. Despite claims from Iran that it had brought the plane down, U.S. officials asserted that the crash was due to mechanical failure. After considering a plan to conduct a covert mission to recover or destroy the RQ-170, U.S. officials decided to take no action, believing Iran could not reverse engineer the vehicle. Subsequently Iran claimed to have recovered the drone's data. An RQ-170 was used in support of an October 18, 2012, test of a Massive Ordnance Penetrator, designed to destroy buried and hardened facilities.[89]

Another UAV to emerge from the black world is the stealthy RQ-180, which is scheduled to begin operations in 2015, with apparent emphasis on surveillance of targets in denied or contested areas, such as Iran and North Korea. Its wingspan apparently exceeds 130 feet. The vehicle is envisioned as useful not only for intelligence collection but for support to special military and CIA missions—and possibly fighter and bombers operations.[90]

A number of other imagery UAVs of varying sizes and capabilities are in operation or development. Another version of the Predator, the MQ-1C Gray Eagle has been developed for the Army; it will be able to carry electro-optical/infrared and synthetic aperture radar/GMTI payloads. In February 2013, the Army Chief of Staff approved fielding 152 MQ-1Cs, with the vehicles being distributed to ten Army divisions, two special operations units, and two Army Intelligence and Security Command aerial exploitation battalions. In November 2013, the 160th Special Operations Aviation Regiment received twelve Gray Eagles. Meanwhile the Navy's MQ-4C Triton UAV, a variant of the Global Hawk, is in development and expected to operate from five land-based sites around the world as part of the Navy's family of maritime patrol and reconnaissance systems. Its initial sensors are to provide 360-degree electro-optical/infrared coverage, with a signals intelligence capability to be added in future years. April 2014 plans called for procurement of sixty-six aircraft through 2028, with the first aircraft to be procured in the 2016 fiscal year.[91]

PROCESSING AND EXPLOITATION

As noted above, imagery can be obtained by relying on single portions of the electromagnetic spectrum (visible light, infrared, radio) or by combining a number of bands into a single image (multispectral, hyperspectral, or ultraspectral). However, after being obtained, the imagery requires processing and exploitation to convert it to intelligence data.

Computers can be employed to improve the quantity and quality of the information extracted. Obviously, digital electro-optical imagery arrives in form that facilitates such operations, but even analog imagery obtained by a conventional camera can be converted into digital signals. In any case, a computer disassembles a picture into millions of electronic pulses and then uses mathematical formulas to manipulate the color, contrast, and intensity of each spot. Each image can be reassembled in various ways to highlight special features and objects hidden in the original image.[92]

Computer processing allows interpreters to

- Build multicolored single images out of several pictures taken in different bands of the spectrum, making the patterns more obvious
- Restore the shapes of objects by adjusting for the angle of view and lens distortion
- Change the amount of contrast between objects and backgrounds
- Sharpen out-of-focus images
- Restore ground details largely obscured by clouds
- Conduct electronic optical subtraction, which subtracts earlier pictures later ones, making unchanged objects in a scene disappear, while new objects, such as missile silos under construction, remain
- Enhance shadows
- Suppress glint.[93]

Computer processing plays a crucial role in easing the burden of photogrammetrists and imagery interpreters. Photogrammetrists are responsible for determining the size and dimensions of objects from overhead photographs, using, along with other data, the shadows cast by the objects. Imagery interpreters provide information about the nature of the objects in the photographs, based on information as to what type of crates carry MiG-29s, for instance, or what an intermediate-range ballistic missile (IRBM) site or fiber-optics factory looks like from 150 miles in space. Such information is provided in interpretation keys such as those listed in Table 7.3. Thus, an interpreter might see an image with excavations, mine headframes, derricks, piles of waste, conveyor belts, bulldozers, and power shovels but just a few buildings. The key would suggest that this is a mine. Special kinds of equipment, the tone or color of the waste and ore piles, and local geology could further indicate that this is a uranium mine.[94]

The ultimate utility of any electro-optical, infrared, or radar imaging system is a function of several factors, the most prominent being spatial resolution, a simple measure of which is the minimum size at which an object is measurable and detectable by interpreters. The "higher" the resolution, the greater the detail that can be extracted from an image. It should also be noted that resolution is a product of several factors, including the sensors, atmospheric conditions, and orbital parameters. The degree of resolution required depends on the specificity of the intelligence desired.[95]

Digital satellite imagery can also be employed for purposes beyond intelligence on a target facility or activity. Such data, when combined with elevation data, can be used to produce a three-dimensional image of the landscape of an area of interest, be it Iraq or Nigeria. The capability, first developed at the Jet Propulsion Laboratory, can be used to familiarize individuals, from national leaders to special forces to clandestine intelligence personnel, with a particular geographical area or facility.

In the spring of 1994, the CIA acquired an additional capability. Once a three-dimensional view of an area has been created, an individual can use a joystick to wander around the area as well as inside the three-dimensional buildings. Such an orientation experience is particularly useful to inspectors, intelligence officers, and

TABLE 7.3   Joint Imagery Interpretation Keys

World Tanks and Self-Propelled Artillery	Major Surface Combatants
World Towed Artillery	Minor Surface Combatants
General Transportation Equipment	Mine Warfare Types
World Tactical Vehicles	Amphibious Warfare Types
Combat Engineer Equipment	Naval Auxiliaries
World Mobile Gap and River Crossing Equipment	Intelligence Research Vehicles
Coke, Iron, and Steel Industries	Shipborne Electronics
Chemical Industries	Shipborne Weapons
World Electronics	Airfield Installation
World Missiles and Rockets	Petroleum Industries
Military Aircraft of the World	Atomic Energy Facilities
Submarines	

Source: Defense Intelligence Agency Regulation 0-2, " Index of DIA Administrative Publications," December 10, 1982, 35–36.

Special Forces personnel, who benefit from the experience of being able to preview a building or area before actually entering it.

Five different interpretation tasks have been differentiated. Detection involves locating a class of units or objects or an activity of interest. General identification involves determining a general target type, and precise identification involves discrimination within the target type of known types. Description involves specifying the size-dimension, configuration-layout, components-construction, and number of units. Technical intelligence involves determining the specific characteristics and performance capabilities of weapons and equipment.[96] Table 7.4 gives estimates of the resolution required for interpretation tasks.

Factors other than resolution that are considered significant in evaluating the utility of an imaging system include coverage speed, readout speed, analysis speed, reliability, and enhancement capability. Coverage speed is the area that can be surveyed in a given amount of time; readout speed is the speed with which the information is processed into a form that is meaningful to imagery interpreters, and reliability is the fraction of time in which the system produces useful data. Enhancement capability refers to whether the initial images can be enhanced to draw out more useful data.

The incorporation of metadata, such as geographic coordinates, with photos was tested using a Predator. Such metadata, which would not appear on the image but could be read by computer, could be employed to "generate a moving digital terrain map with a graphic overlay, shown on a separate screen."[97]

In 2009 it was reported that the CIA was investing in technology intended to allow satellite and aerial imagery to be merged with maps so that thousands of data sources could be mined for information about points of interest in the images. The expectation was that when the project was completed, CIA personnel would be able to click on a building or other facility shown in the video, and various information would pop up, including the identity of the tenants and their phone numbers, company records, links

TABLE 7.4   Resolution Required for Different Levels of Interpretation

Target	Detection	General Identification	Precise Identification	Description	Technical Intelligence
Bridge	20 ft.	15 ft.	5 ft.	3 ft.	1 ft.
Communications radar/radio	10 ft./10 ft.	3 ft./5 ft.	1 ft./1 ft.	6 in./6 in.	1.5 in./6 in.
Supply dump	5 ft.	2 ft.	1 ft.	1 in.	1 in.
Troop units (bivouac, road)	20 ft.	7 ft.	4 ft.	1 ft.	3 in.
Airfield facilities	20 ft.	15 ft.	10 ft.	1 ft.	6 in.
Rockets and artillery	3 ft.	2 ft.	6 in.	2 in.	.4 in.
Aircraft	15 ft.	5 ft.	3 ft.	6 in.	1 in.
Command and control HQ	10 ft.	5 ft.	3 ft.	6 in.	1 in.
Missile sites (SSM/SAM)	10 ft.	5 ft.	2 ft.	1 ft.	3 in.
Surface ships	25 ft.	15 ft.	2 ft.	1 ft.	3 in.
Nuclear weapons components	8 ft.	5 ft.	1 ft.	1 in.	.4 in.
Vehicles	5 ft.	2 ft.	1 ft.	2 in.	1 in.
Land minefields	30 ft.	20 ft.	3 ft.	1 in.	—
Ports and harbors	100 ft.	50 ft.	20 ft.	10 ft.	1 ft.
Coasts and landing beaches	100 ft.	15 ft.	10 ft.	5 ft.	3 in.
Railroad yards and shops	100 ft.	50 ft.	20 ft.	5 ft.	2 ft.
Roads	30 ft.	20 ft.	6 in.	2 ft.	6 in.
Urban area	200 ft.	100 ft.	10 ft.	10 ft.	1 ft.
Terrain	—	300 ft.	15 ft.	5 ft.	6 in.
Surfaced submarines	100 ft.	20 ft.	5 ft.	3 ft.	1 in.

Sources: Adapted from U.S. Congress, Senate Committee on Commerce, Science, and Transportation, *NASA Authorization for Fiscal Year 1978*, Part 3 (Washington, D.C.: U.S. GPO, 1977), 1642–1643; Bhupendra Jasani, ed., *Outer Space: A New Dimension in the Arms Race* (Cambridge, MA: Oelgeschlager, Hunn & Hain, 1982), 47.

to company and organization websites, news reports concerning tenants or incidents at the location, and property records.[98]

The availability of full-motion video from UAVs has led to research and development work on systems that can more efficiently transmit and exploit that imagery. As of June 2010, the military's archive contained 400,000 hours of video gathered by Predator UAVs, although the archive was of little utility because analysts had no means of searching for information. In 2015 it was reported that the Air Force Intelligence,

Surveillance, and Reconnaissance Agency had been collecting about 1,600 hours of video each day, while over seven terabytes of data had been streaming through the Distributed Common Ground System daily. In 2010 the Air Force and other reconnaissance experts were working with experts from the television industry to adapt the methods used in NFL and other sports broadcasts to quickly find and show replays as well as to annotate the images.[99]

Other agencies have funded other work in the area. In September 2008, Kitware, a small software company, along with nineteen partners, won the initial phase of a Defense Advanced Research Projects Agency (DARPA) contract to create the capability to monitor live video feeds as well as search large volumes of archived videos for activities of interest. In August 2009, the Defense Information Systems Agency, on behalf of the (now defunct) Joint Forces Command and the National Security Agency, launched an initiative designated VALIANT ANGEL, which involved hiring Lockheed Martin and Harris Broadcasting "to deliver a military version of Harris software that manages and displays videos for sportscasters and newscasters." The objective is to give intelligence users the ability to retrieve videos through the use of keywords, location, or time.[100]

Another effort to enhance the utility of imagery data has been conducted at Lawrence Livermore National Laboratory. The prototype system compresses raw wide-area video from manned and unmanned reconnaissance aircraft by a factor of 1,000, which improves the ability to quickly transmit the data. The system, designated Persistics, compresses irrelevant data, including nonmoving background images, jitter, and atmospheric aberrations. In addition, the system's algorithms permit surveillance systems "to 'stare' at key people, vehicles, locations, [for a] day at a time while automatically searching . . . for anomalies or preselected targets."[101]

DISSEMINATION

At one time, when imagery was obtained solely by film-based cameras, there was a simple dissemination sequence. Imagery was returned from satellites in capsules or on aircraft when they returned from a mission. The film was transported to the relevant national, departmental, service, or command imagery interpreters. The imagery interpretation reports produced, as well as the reports incorporating the imagery-derived intelligence, were then disseminated to the appropriate organizations and individuals. For a significant part of the history of the satellite reconnaissance program, this was a highly restricted set of individuals, in part because film-return systems were not terribly useful in the heat of battle, with long delays between the imaging of a target and the intelligence reaching military commanders.

The advent of real-time digital imagery dramatically increased the potential value of the imagery obtained from national systems for military commanders and combatants, as the technology made it possible to provide military commanders with a very current view of enemy forces and movements. Even before the first KH-11 was placed into orbit in December 1976, the Intelligence Community had begun studying how the system might be used to support forces in the field. In January 1976, one of a series of Tactical-National Intelligence Interface Studies, *Report on the Pilot Study on National Intelligence Support to Field Commanders*, was completed well in advance of the first KH-11 launch.[102]

The dissemination sequence for digital imagery begins with the downlinking of the raw imagery from a spacecraft or aircraft to a ground station. In some cases, the downlink may be direct; in others, the process may require a relay because the ground station is not in the line of sight of the satellite. For the various versions of the CRYSTAL and MISTY satellites, the primary ground station has been the Aerospace Data Facility–East at Fort Belvoir, Virginia, about twenty miles south of Washington, D.C. It is a large, windowless, two-story concrete building first known as the Defense Communications Electronics Evaluation Test Activity and also as Area 58. Although the Fort Belvoir site was initially the only downlink for the KH-11, additional sites were subsequently added, apparently in Hawaii and Europe.[103]

The signals arriving at the Mission Ground Site are relayed from more than one type of relay satellite, all of which receive the electronic signals from an imagery satellite and forward them to a ground station. At first only one version of the Air Force's Satellite Data System (SDS) satellites was employed—those in a highly elliptical orbit. The initial SDS spacecraft was launched into an orbit of 240 × 24,000 miles inclined at 63 degrees in June 1976. Additional launches followed in August 1976 and August 1978 and in the 1980s and 1990s—all into highly elliptical orbit. Furthermore, the geosynchronous Defense Satellite Communications System satellites may have been used to relay advanced KH-11 data.[104]

Because SDS satellites had a number of additional, non-NRO related functions— including relay communications between the central hub of the Air Force Satellite Control Facility and its ground stations around the world, as well as hosting nuclear detonation detectors—they were originally operated by the Air Force. But after several of the satellites were out of position when needed to relay KH-11 imagery, the CIA component of the NRO (Program B) assumed responsibility in 1983. Eventually, the relay satellite program was designated QUASAR (which remains its name), and it has come to involve satellites in both highly elliptical and geosynchronous orbits.[105]

Since 1998, apparently seven QUASAR satellites have been placed into orbit. Two spacecraft, launched on January 21, 1998, and on August 31, 2004, respectively, went into highly elliptical orbits and up to five—including the ones launched on March 11, 2011, June 20, 2012, and May 22, 2014—were placed into geosynchronous orbit.[106] All were acknowledged to be NRO spacecraft and relied on one version or another of the Atlas booster to get them into orbit.

In contrast, the signals from the ONYX and TOPAZ radar imagery satellites are relayed via NASA's Tracking and Data Relay Satellite System, of which there are six in geosynchronous orbit. Three of these are available at any time; the others provide backup in the event of the failure of operational spacecraft. The signals are transmitted to the Aerospace Data Facility–Southwest at White Sands, New Mexico.[107]

The U-2, Global Hawk, Predator, and Reaper systems can all downlink their data to the Air Force Distributed Common Ground System (DCGS), operated by the 25th Air Force's 480th ISR Wing Operations Center. Composed of twenty separate but networked sites, the DCGS is the successor to the Deployable Ground Station–1, which began operations in July 1994. In addition to the Air Force system, there is the Distributed Common Ground System–Army, which receives data from Army-operated aerial surveillance assets.[108]

A variety of systems can also relay or disseminate imagery to forces on the ground, at sea, or in the air. The Global Broadcast System (GBS), which employs the Navy's

PHOTO 7.5   Aerospace Data Facility–East, Fort Belvoir, Virginia, the U.S. receiving station for KH-11 and advanced KH-11 imagery. *Photo credit:* Robert Windrem.

Ultra High Frequency Follow-On (UFO) spacecraft, provides a near-global capability to forward NRO imagery to a wider spectrum of users than in the past. NRO helped set up a "GBS Phase 1" demonstration, which involved the transmission of imagery and other data to U.S. forces in Bosnia. The first GBS Phase 2 satellite (UFO F8), in what would become a three-satellite constellation, was launched in March 1998. Imagery can be uplinked to the satellites from ground stations in Hawaii, Virginia, and Europe. Among those receiving data via GBS terminals were U.S. forces participating in Operation ENDURING FREEDOM in Afghanistan.[109]

U.S. forces operating at sea have also benefited from improved dissemination capabilities developed over the past several decades. By the early 1990s, the Fleet Imagery Support Terminals on U.S. aircraft carriers, which could transmit imagery from shore locations and from ship to shore and ship to ship, could also receive data directly from space systems. In 2001 newly developed (by NRO) Rapid Targeting System data receivers were in place on key Navy ships and in forward-deployed ground command centers in Afghanistan. In 2002, in an experiment designated RADIANT ETHER, a system for the receipt of national intelligence data was tested on the USS *Theodore Roosevelt*.[110]

Throughout the 1990s, a number of systems that would allow the transmission of imagery (and signals intelligence) directly to aircraft cockpits were tested. Under a program designated TALON SWORD, tests conducted in April 1993 used intelligence data to directly cue missiles fired at simulated enemy radars by F-16 and EA-6B aircraft. Another phase of TALON SWORD involved transmitting satellite intelligence into F-15E cockpits for targeting enemy positions with smart bombs. Another program, TALON LANCE, was directed at equipping aircraft with a computer package that would allow high-speed processing of space intelligence data. TALON LANCE–equipped aircraft would be able to locate and identify an enemy on the ground or in the air. The aircraft crew could then decide whether to attack or avoid contact long before the aircraft's normal onboard sensors could detect the enemy. TALON SHOOTER encompassed a number of programs, including Project STRIKE, to provide threat, target, and weather information to the cockpit "to make space a reality for operational aircraft." In July 1995, the program was tested on B-1B and F-15E aircraft.[111]

Notes

1. William E. Burrows, *Deep Black: Space Espionage and National Security* (New York: Random House, 1986), 32; Jeffrey T. Richelson, *American Espionage and the Soviet Target* (New York: William Morrow, 1987), 16; Robert E. Dupré, "Guide to Imagery Intelligence," *Intelligencer* (Winter/Spring 2011): 61–64.

2. Richelson, *American Espionage and the Soviet Target*, 16; Donald E. Welzenbach, "From the U-2 to Corona and Those Who Searched for Invisibility," in *CORONA: Between the Sun and the Earth—the First NRO Reconnaissance Eye in Space*, ed. Robert A. McDonald (Baltimore, MD: American Society for Photogrammetry and Remote Sensing, 1997), 135–140.

3. Farouk el-Baz, "EO Imaging Will Replace Film in Reconnaissance," *Defense Systems Review* (October 1983): 48–52.

4. Richard D. Hudson Jr. and Jacqueline W. Hudson, "The Military Applications of Remote Sensing by Infrared," *Proceedings of the IEEE* 63, no. 1 (1975): 104–128; James B. Campbell, *Introduction to Remote Sensing* (New York: Guilford, 1987), 26.

5. Hudson and Hudson, "The Military Applications of Remote Sensing by Infrared"; Bruce G. Blair and Garry D. Brewer, "Verifying SALT," in *Verification and SALT: The Challenge of Strategic Deception*, ed. William Potter (Boulder, CO: Westview, 1980), 7–48; Campbell, *Introduction to Remote Sensing*, 26.

6. Homer Jensen, L. C. Graham, Leonard J. Porcello, and Emmet N. Leith, "Side-Looking Airborne Radar," *Scientific American* (October 1977): 84–95.

7. Joint Staff, Joint Publication 2-03, *Geospatial Intelligence Support to Joint Operations*, vii.

8. The KH-10, which was the camera system for the Manned Orbiting Laboratory (MOL), never became operational, since the MOL program was canceled before the first flight. For a history of the KEYHOLE program, see Jeffrey T. Richelson, *America's Secret Eyes in Space: The U.S. KEYHOLE Spy Satellite Program* (New York: Harper & Row, 1990); Jeffrey T. Richelson, *The Wizards of Langley: Inside the CIA's Directorate of Science and Technology* (Boulder, CO: Westview, 2001).

9. Richelson, *America's Secret Eyes in Space*, 128–131.

10. Ibid.

11. Ibid., 126; private information. The CIA's Imagery Analysis Service did its own study of the impact, completed in December 1969—*Impact of a Near Real Time Collection System on CIA's Imagery Analysis Needs*—the declassified portion of which can be found in the CREST database at the National Archives and Records Administration in College Park, Maryland.

12. Richelson, *America's Secret Eyes in Space*, 362; confidential interview.

13. R. Cargill-Hall, *The Air Force and the National Security Space Program, 1946–1988* (Maxwel Air Force Base, FL: U.S. Air Force Historical Research Center, 1988), 171.

14. Richard A. Stubbing, "Improving the Output of Intelligence," in *National Insecurity: U.S. Intelligence After the Cold War*, ed. Craig Eisendrath (Philadelphia: Temple University Press, 2000), 172–189, at 177–178; confidential interview.

15. Richelson, *America's Secret Eyes in Space*, 362; Craig Covault, "Advanced KH-11 Broadens U.S. Recon Capability," *AW&ST,* January 6, 1997, 24; Craig Covault, "Fade to Black," *AW&ST,* May 15, 2006, 24–26; e-mail from Ted Molczan, September 10, 2010; confidential interviews; Heavens Above, "USA-129—Satellite Information," http://www.heavens-above.com/satinfo.aspx?SatID=24680&Session=kebgffhbcgpclmheldnljfce (accessed October 23, 2014).

16. R. Jeffrey Smith, "Senators, CIA Fight over $1 Billion," *Washington Post*, July 16, 1993, A4; David A. Fulghum, "Key Military Officials Criticize Intelligence Handling in Gulf War," *AW&ST*, June 24, 1991, 83; Roger Guillemette, "Titan 4B to Launch Classified Payload from California," wn.com, September 29, 2001, http://article.wn.com/view/2001/09/30/Titan_4B_to _Launch_Classified_Payload_from_California. Also see Robert D. Vickers Jr., "Desert Storm and the BDA Controversy," *Studies in Intelligence*.

17. "New Recon Satellite Poised for Liftoff," *AW&ST*, August 7, 2000, 66; Craig Covault, "Titan, Adieu," *AW&ST*, October 24, 2005, 28–29; National Reconnaissance Office, Release #02-11, "NRO Satellite Successfully Launched Aboard Delta IV Heavy," January 20, 2011; Justin Ray, "Delta 4-Heavy's Hush-Hush Payload Found and Identified," www.spaceflightnow.com, January 23, 2011, http://spaceflightnow.com/delta/d352; Heavens Above, "USA 224—Satellite Information," http://www.heavens-above.com/satinfo.aspx?satid=37348&lat=0&lng=0&loc =Unspecified&alt=0&tz=UCT (accessed October 23, 2014); Heavens Above, "USA 245— Satellite Information," http://www.heavens-above.com/satinfo.aspx?satid=39232&lat=0&lng =0&loc=Unspecified&alt=0&tz=UCT&cul=en (October 23, 2014); interview.

18. Bob Woodward, *VEIL: The Secret Wars of the CIA, 1981–1987* (New York: Simon & Schuster, 1987), 221; private information; "Space Reconnaissance Dwindles," *AW&ST*, October 6, 1980, 18–20; "Navy Will Develop All Weather Ocean Monitor Satellite," *AW&ST*, August 28, 1978, 50; Craig Covault, "USAF, NASA Discuss Shuttle Use for Satellite Maintenance," *AW&ST*, December 17, 1984, 14–16; "Washington Roundup," *AW&ST*, June 4, 1979, 11; Robert C. Toth, "Anaheim Firm May Have Sought Spy Satellite Data," *Los Angeles Times*, October 10, 1982, 1, 32; Bill Gertz, "New Spy Satellite, Needed to Monitor Treaty, Sits on Ground," *Washington Times*, October 20, 1987, A5; Bill Gertz, "Senate Panel Asks for Radar Funds," *Washington Times*, April 5, 1988, A4; Craig Covault, "'Atlantis' Radar Satellite Payload Opens New Reconnaissance Era," *AW&ST*, December 12, 1988, 26–28; Vincent Kiernan, "Satellite Buffs Conclude That Titan Carried Lacrosse," *Space News*, April 8–14, 1991, 22; Philip S. Clark, "Satellite Digest," *Spaceflight* 40, no. 1 (January 1998): 35–36; "World News Roundup," *AW&ST*, August 21, 2000, 24; National Reconnaissance Office, "Reconnaissance Office Satellite Successfully Launched," October 23, 1997; Craig Covault, "Secret Mission Surge," *AW&ST*, May 9, 2005, 24–25.

19. David Fulghum and Craig Covault, "U.S. Set to Launch Upgraded Lacrosse," *AW&ST*, September 20, 1996, 34; Covault, "Secret Mission Surge"; Gertz, "New Spy Satellite, Needed to Monitor Treaty, Sits on Ground."

20. Gertz, "New Spy Satellite, Needed to Monitor Treaty, Sits on Ground"; Covault, "'Atlantis' Radar Satellite Payload Opens New Reconnaissance Era"; "Radar Satellite Assesses Raids," *AW&ST*, September 16, 1996, 26; David Fulghum and Craig Covault, "U.S. Set to Launch Upgraded Lacrosse," *AW&ST*, September 23, 1996, 34; William Claiborne, "Taiwan-Born Scientist Passed Defense Data," *Washington Post*, December 12, 1997, A23; Craig Covault, "Secret Relay, NRO Spacecraft Revealed," *AW&ST*, March 23, 1998, 26–28.

21. Office of the Director of National Intelligence, *National Intelligence Program Summary, FY 2013 Congressional Budget Justification*, February 2012, 2, 167; "USA 215—Satellite Information," http://www.heavens-above.com/satinfo.aspx?lat=50.217&lng=15.833&loc=Hradec+Kralove&alt =223&tz=CET&satid=37162 (accessed October 23, 2014); "USA 238–Satellite Information," http://www.heavens-above.com/satinfo.aspx?lat=38.9833333333&lng=-75.9333333333&loc =Tuckahoe+State+Park&alt=0&tz=EST&satid=38758 (accessed October 23, 2014).

22. Craig Covault, "Recon Satellites Lead Allied Intelligence Effort," *AW&ST*, February 4, 1991, 25–26; Bill Gertz, "S. Africa to Test Ballistic Missile," *Washington Times*, May 3, 1991, A3; Bill Gertz, "Laotian Military Smuggling Drugs," *Washington Times*, April 25, 1991, A11; Bill Gertz, "Soviets Testing Rail-Mobile Rocket," *Washington Times*, April 12, 1991, A5; Bill Gertz, "China Helps Algeria Develop Nuclear Weapons," *Washington Times*, April 11, 1991, A3; David E. Sanger, "Furor in Seoul over North Korea's Atomic Plant," *New York Times*, April 16, 1991, A3; Bill Gertz, "Satellites Spot Poison Bomb Plant in Libya," *Washington Post*, March 5, 1991, 3; "International," *Military Space*, January 27, 1992, 6; Covault, "Secret Mission Surge."

23. Boerfink MHE to 26 TW et al., Subject: TFC Southern Region Disum (SORD) NR 146-92, May 26, 1992, 3–4; Boerfink MHE to 26 IW et al., Subject: TFC Southern Region Disum (SORD) NR 211–92, July 30, 1992.

24. Bill Gertz, "Beijing Creates Military Monster," *Washington Times*, April 10, 1997, A1, A10.

25. Jeff Gerth, "Officials Say China Illegally Sent U.S. Equipment to Military Plans," *New York Times*, April 23, 1997, A1, A9.

26. Tim Weiner, "U.S. Suspects India Prepares for Nuclear Test," *New York Times*, December 15, 1995, A6.

27. Elaine Sciolino, "U.S. Says It's Won Votes to Maintain Sanctions on Iraq," *New York Times*, March 5, 1995, 1, 9.

28. Bill Gertz, "N. Korea Masses Artillery at Border," *Washington Times*, July 25, 1996, A1, A9.

29. Douglas Waller, "The Secret Missile Deal," *Time*, June 30, 1997, 58.

30. Michael R. Gordon, "Despite Cold War's End Russia Keeps Building a Secret Complex," *New York Times*, April 16, 1996, A1, A6; Bill Gertz, "Moscow Builds Bunkers Against Nuclear Attack," *Washington Times*, April 1, 1997, A1, A16; Bill Gertz, "Russian Nuke Shelters Don't Concern Pentagon," *Washington Times*, April 2, 1997, A6.

31. Bill Gertz, "Hidden Iraqi Scuds Threaten Israeli, Gulf Countries," *Washington Times*, February 11, 1998, A1, A12.

32. Bill Gertz, "China Points More Missiles at Taiwan," *Washington Times*, November 22, 1999, A1, A9.

33. John Lancaster, "Kashmir Crisis Was Defused on Brink of War," *Washington Post*, July 26, 1999, A1, A15.

34. Bill Gertz and Rowan Scarborough, "Inside the Ring," *Washington Times*, April 6, 2001, A7.

35. Bill Gertz and Rowan Scarborough, "Inside the Ring," *Washington Times*, May 10, 2002, A10.

36. Bill Gertz, "Iraqis 'Moving Stuff' at Germ Plant," *Washington Times*, August 14, 2002, A1, A18.

37. David E. Sanger and Eric Schmitt, "Satellites Said to See Activity at North Korean Nuclear Site," *New York Times*, January 31, 2003, A1, A10.

38. David E. Sanger and William J. Broad, "U.S. Cites Signs of Korean Steps to Nuclear Test," *New York Times*, May 6, 2005, A1, A6.

39. John Diamond, "Trained Eye Can See Right Through Box of Weapons," www.usatoday.com, August 17, 2006, http://usatoday30.usatoday.com/news/world/2006-08-17-missiles-iran_x.htm.

40. David E. Sanger and William J. Broad, "Agenda on Nuclear Talks Leaves Out a New Threat," *New York Times*, April 12, 2010, A1, A8.

41. Hyung-Jim Kim, "S. Korea Denies N. Korea Is Preparing Nuclear Test," www.utsandiego.com, October 21, 2010, http://www.utsandiego.com/news/2010/oct/21/skorea-denies-nkorea-is-preparing-nuclear-test.

42. Adam Entous and Jay Solomon, "U.S. Steps Up Watch of Syria Chemical Weapons," *Wall Street Journal*, February 15, 2012, A9.

43. Jung-Yoon Choi, "North Korea May Be Setting Up Nuclear Test," *Los Angeles Times*, April 10, 2012, A3.

44. Thom Shanker and David E. Sanger, "Movement of Missiles by North Korea Worries U.S.," *New York Times*, January 18, 2013, A3.

45. "U.S. Satellite Sees Signs of 'Imminent' North Korea Nuclear Test: Report," *Global Security Newswire*, May 7, 2014, http://www.nti.org/gsn/article/military-satellite-reportedly-detects-signs-imminent-north-korea-nuclear-test.

46. See Jeffrey T. Richelson ed., National Security Archive Electronic Briefing Book No. 13, *U.S. Satellite Imagery, 1960–1999*, http://www2.gwu.edu/~nsarchiv/NSAEBB/NSAEBB13;

Jeffrey T. Richelson, ed., National Security Archive Electronic Briefing Book No. 88, *Eyes on Saddam*, April 30, 2003, http://www2.gwu.edu/~nsarchiv/NSAEBB/NSAEBB88.

47. Jeremy Singer, "Air Force Satellite Program Faces Delay, Higher Cost," *Space News*, July 8, 2002, 8; Annie Marie Squeo, "Officials Say Space Program Facing Delays Are 'in Trouble,'" *Wall Street Journal*, December 4, 2002, A1, A3; Joseph C. Anselmo and Amy Butler, "Beyond Repair?," *AW&ST*, September 5, 2005, 23–24; Douglas Jehl, "Boeing Lags in Building Spy Satellites," *New York Times*, December 4, 2005, C1, C8; Office of the Director of National Intelligence, ODNI News Release No. 12-09, "DNI Blair Announces Plan for the Next Generation of Electro-optical Satellites," April 7, 2009; Office of the Director of National Intelligence, *National Intelligence Program Summary, FY 2013 Congressional Budget Justification*, 167.

48. Stephen Clark, "Tactical Spy Satellite Streaks into Space on Minotaur Rocket," www.spaceflightnow.com, June 30, 2011, http://www.spaceflightnow.com/minotaur/ors1; Scott Pratter, "ORS-1, Ground System Gain Final Ops Acceptance," February 2, 2012, http://www.schriever.af.mil/news/story.asp?id=123288487; Mike Gruss, "UTC Wins Support Contract for ORS-1 as Satellite Nears End of Life," *Space News*, October 13, 2014, 7.

49. Campbell, *Introduction to Remote Sensing*, 137–138, 149–153; Headquarters, U.S. Space Command, *Command History, January 1990–December 1991*, 83–84, 307, 309–310; "Spot-4 Images Released," *AW&ST*, April 13, 1998, 75.

50. Data sheets for "Quickbird"; "Worldview-1"; "Worldview-2," "Worldview-3," all accessed from https://www.digitalglobe.com/about-us/content-collection; William Graham, "ULA Atlas V Launches Worldview-3 Satellite Out of Vandenberg," www.nasaspaceflight.com, August 13, 2014, http://www.nasaspaceflight.com/2014/08/ula-atlas-v-worldview-3-launch; Chuck Herring, "At the Tipping Point: How Digital Globe's Latest Satellite Launch Is Breaking Down Barriers," *Imaging Notes* 25, no. 1 (Winter 2010): 24–28.

51. Digital Globe data sheets: "Ikonos," "GeoEye-1," both accessed from https://www.digitalglobe.com/about-us/content-collection; Digital Globe, "Overview," www.digitalglobe.com/about-us/content-collection (accessed October 21, 2014); Justin Ray, "One Commercial Earth-Imager Deferred in Favor of Another," www.spaceflightnow.com, February 4, 2013, http://www.spaceflightnow.com/news/n1302/04geoeye2/#.VOOV80K3jwM; Peter B. de Selding, "Digital Globe Raising Geoeye-1's Orbit to Keep Up with Demand," *Space News*, August 26, 2013, 5.

52. Andrew E. Kramer, "U.S. Says Images Show Russian Armaments Near Embattled Ukraine Town," www.nytimes.com, February 14, 2015, http://www.nytimes.com/2015/02/15/world/europe/us-says-images-show-russian-armaments-near-embattled-ukraine-town.html; Stephen Clark, "Satellites Spot Syrian Violence from Space," www.spaceflightnow.com, February 11, 2012, http://www.spaceflightnow.com/news/n1202/11syria; William J. Broad, "Images Show Devastation at Iran Base after Blast," *New York Times*, November 30, 2011, A6; Chris Biggers, "Iran's Moudge Class Assembly at Bander Abbas," www.bellingcat.com, December 4, 2014, https://www.bellingcat.com/news/mena/2014/12/04/irans-moudge-class-assembly-at-bander-abbas; Amy Butler, "Widening the Aperture," *AW&ST*, February 2–15, 2015, 64–65.

53. Thomas A. "NGA Employs Emerging Commercial Space Radars," *Pathfinder* (September–October 2010): 8–9; Amy Butler, "New Image," *AW&ST*, April 12, 2010, 50–51.

54. Tariq Malik, "X-37B Wraps Up 7-Month Mission Shrouded in Secrecy," *Space News*, December 6, 2010, 17; William J. Broad, "Surveillance Is Suspected as Main Role of Spacecraft," *New York Times*, May 23, 2010, 1, 18; Stephen Clark, "Inspections Have Begun on Air Force Space Plane," www.spaceflight.com, December 12, 2010, http://www.spaceflightnow.com/news/n1012/12x37review; Stephen Clark, "Air Force's Second Robotic Space Shuttle Circling Earth," www.spaceflightnow.com, March 5, 2011, http://www.spaceflightnow.com/atlas/av026; Guy Norris, "Down and Back," *AW&ST*, June 25, 2012, 37; Justin Ray, "Air Force's Mini Space Shuttle Prepares for Landing," www.spaceflightnow.com, May 30, 2012; http://www.spaceflightnow.com/atlas/av026/preland; Stephen Clark, "X-37B Space Plane Scheduled to Return to Earth Soon," www.spaceflightnow.com, October 13, 2014, http://www.spaceflightnow.com/atlas/av034

/141013prelanding/#.VOOXUUK3jwM; Stephen Clark, "U.S. Military's X-37B Space Plane Lands in California," www.spaceflightnow.com, October 17, 2014, http://www.spaceflightnow .com/atlas/av034/141017landing/#.VOOXdEK3jwM; "USAF's X-37B Minishuttle Returns to Space on Atlas 5," *Space News*, March 14, 2011, 8; Elizabeth Howell, "X-37B Space Plane Returns: 5 Theories About Its Secret Mission," Live Science, October 17, 2014, http://www.livescience .com/48338-x37b-space-plane-conspiracy-theories.html. Also see Michael Listner, "The X-37B Program: An American Exercise in the Art of War?," *Space Review*, January 5, 2015, http://www .thespacereview.com/article/2670/1.

55. Chris Pocock, *Dragon Lady: The History of the U-2 Spyplane* (Shrewsbury, UK: Airlife, 1989), 18–32.

56. Ibid., 90–106, 146–163; Howard Silber, "SAC U-2s Provided Nicaraguan Pictures," *Omaha World Herald*, March 10, 1982, 2; Frank Oliveri, "The U-2 Comes in from the Cold," *Air Force Magazine*, September 1994, 45–50; Christopher Drew, "U-2 Spy Plane Evades the Day of Retirement," *New York Times*, March 22, 2010, A1, A6; Amy Butler, "Devil in the Details," *AW&ST*, July 12, 2010, 26–27.

57. U.S. Air Force, "U-2S/TU-2S," Fact Sheet, May 25, 2005, http://www.af.mil/AboutUs /FactSheets/Display/tabid/224/Article/104560/u-2stu-2s.aspx; "Military Aircraft Update," *AW&ST*, November 11–18, 2013, 88.

58. Amy Butler, "More, More, More," *AW&ST*, June 16, 2008, 26–27; Amy Butler and David A. Fulghum, "Dragon Lady in Korea," *AW&ST*, September 1, 2008, 50–51; Chris Pocock, *Dragon Lady Today: The Continuing Story of the U-2 Spyplane* (CreateSpace, 2014), 27–28.

59. Pocock, *Dragon Lady Today*, 28.

60. Michael A. Dornheim, "U-2 Runs at Frenzied Pace in New World Order," *AW&ST*, April 29, 1996, 55–56; Coy F. Cross, *The Dragon Lady Meets the Challenge: The U-2 in Desert Storm* (Beale Air Force Base, CA: 9th Reconnaissance Wing, 1995), 15; Chris Pocock, "U-2: The Second Generation," *World Airpower Journal* 28 (Spring 1997): 50–99; Chris Pocock, *50 Years of the U-2: The Complete Illustrated History of the "Dragon Lady"* (Arglen, PA: Schiffer Military History, 2005), 325; Pocock, *Dragon Lady Today*, 25–26.

61. Dave Majumdar, "High Altitude, High Stakes," *C4ISR Journal* (September 9): 2010, http://www.c4isrjournal.com; Pocock, *Dragon Lady Today*, 30–31.

62. U.S. Air Force, "U-2S/TU-2S"; David A. Fulghum, "Searching for Clues," *AW&ST*, September 1, 2008, 51–52; Ross Tweten, "U-2 Squadron Continues to Fly High," *Air Force Print News Today*, March 12, 2008, http://www.af.mil/News/ArticleDisplay/tabid/223/Article/124133 /u-2-squadron-continues-to-fly-high.aspx; Pocock, *50 Years of the U-2*, 327, 329; Kevin Whitelaw, "No Rest for a Cold Warrior," *U.S. News*, September 20, 2007, http://www.usnews.com/news /national/articles/2007/09/20/no-rest-for-a-cold-warrior; U.S. Air Force, "5th Reconnaissance Squadron," Fact Sheet, Beale Air Force Base, http://www.beale.af.mil/library/factsheets/factsheet _print.asp?fsID=3978 (accessed October 4, 2014); U.S. Air Force, Fact Sheet, "380th Air Expeditionary Wing," April 2013, http://www.380aew.af.centaf.mil; Pocock, *Dragon Lady Today*, 59, 61–62.

63. Richard Sisk, "Global Hawk Trails U-2 Despite Retirement Plans," *DoD Buzz*, February 27, 2014, http://www.dodbuzz.com/2014/02/27/global-hawk-trails-u-2-despite-retirement-plans; "News Breaks," *AW&ST*, November 21, 1994, 23; "More Eyes"; Eric Schmitt, "6,300 Miles from Iraq, Experts Guide Raids," *New York Times*, June 24, 2003, A13; Pocock, *50 Years of the U-2*, 330–331.

64. Amy Butler, "Going Global," *AW&ST*, March 12, 2007, 60–61; Eric Talmadge, Associated Press, "Famed Cold War-Era U-2 Spy Planes Keep Watch on N. Korea," www.washingtontimes .com, March 1, 2012, http://www.washingtontimes.com/news/2012/mar/1/famed-cold-war-era -u-2-spy-planes-keep-watch-n-kor; Bill Gertz, "Chinese Jets Chase U.S. Surveillance Jet over Taiwan Strait," *Washington Times*, July 25, 2011, http://www.washingtontimes.com/news/2011 /jul/25/chinese-jets-chase-us-surveillance-jet-over-taiwan; "Satellite Imagery, U-2 Chart Japan's

Earthquake, Tsunami Devastation," *Defense Update*, March 14, 2011, http://defense-update.com
/20110314_japan_disaster.html; Pocock, *Dragon Lady Today*, 62.

65. Office of Air Combat Command History, *History of the Air Combat Command, 1 January
31–December 2011* (Langley Air Force Base, VA: Air Combat Command, 2012), 364–365; Office
of Air Combat Command History, *History of the Air Combat Command, 1 January–31 December
2012* (Langley Air Force Base, VA: Air Combat Command, 2013), 304.

66. Aaron Mehta, "HASC Markup Limits Air Force Options on A-10, U-2," www.defensenews
.com, May 5, 2014, http://archive.defensenews.com/article/20140505/DEFREG02/305050018/
HASC-Markup-Limits-Air-Force-Options-10-U-2; Brian Everstine, "US Air Combat Command
Chief Reluctantly Accepts Global Hawk over U-2," www.defensenews.com, September 21, 2014,
http://archive.defensenews.com/article/20140921/DEFREG02/309210019/US-Air-Combat
-Command-Chief-Reluctantly-Accepts-Global-Hawk-Over-U-2; Tim Starks, "Cold War spy plan
[sic] isn't ready to retire," *Stars and Stripes*, October 13, 2014, http://www.stripes.com/news/us/
cold-war-spy-plane-isn-t-ready-to-retire-1.308214; Amy Butler, "Three More Years," *AW&ST*, January 15–February 1, 2015, 32.

67. George A. Wilmoth, "Lockheed's Antisubmarine Warfare Aircraft: Watching the Threat,"
Defense Systems Review 3, no. 6 (1985): 18–25; Vice Admiral W. Mark Skinner, Principal Military
Deputy, Assistant Secretary of the Navy (Research, Development and Acquisition), *Statement Be-
fore the Airland Subcommittee, Senate Armed Services Committee on Department of the Navy's Avi-
ation Procurement Program*, April 24, 2013, 18; "Upgrades for P-3s to Begin in 1998," *AW&ST*,
March 31, 1997, 33; Robert Wall, "Navy to Link UAVs Manned Aircraft Units," *AW&ST*, April
29, 2002, 58–59; David A. Fulghum, "MMA = P8A," *AW&ST*, March 28, 2005, 36; David A.
Fulghum, "Air Patrols Watch for Fleeing Leaders," *AW&ST*, March 4, 2002, 62; Casey Coombs,
"Prying Eyes," *AW&ST*, September 9, 2013, 48–49; David A. Fulghum, "P-3 Tactical Value Increases with Age," *AW&ST*, March 4, 2002, 65; Robert Wall, "Patrol's Partner," *AW&ST*, April
30, 2007, 51–52; U.S. Navy, Fact File: "P-3C *Orion* Long Range ASW Aircraft," *America's Navy*,
February 18, 2009, http://www.navy.mil/navydata/fact_display.asp?cid=1100&tid=1400&ct=1.

68. Wall, "Patrol's Partner"; David A. Fulghum and Amy Butler, "Budget Changes," *AW&ST*,
September 21, 2009, 23–25; Keith Button, "Revealing Radar," *C4ISR Journal* (January–February
2009): 20–21; *P-3C Orion Weapon System Update* (Burbank, CA: Lockheed, n.d.), 18; David A.
Fulghum, "Navy Exploits P-3 in Overland Recce Role," *AW&ST*, March 4, 2002, 60–62.

69. U.S. Navy, Fact File: "P-8A Multi-Mission Maritime Aircraft (MMA)," *America's Navy*,
February 17, 2009, http://www.navy.mil/navydata/fact_display.asp?cid=1100&tid=1300&ct=1;
Department of Defense, *P-8A Poseidon Multi-Mission Maritime Aircraft (P-8A) as of FY 2015
President's Budget*, Selected Acquisition Report, April 16, 2014, 17; "Patrol Squadrons," www
.gonavy.jp/NavalSqn06.html (accessed October 5, 2014); Government Accountability Office,
GAO-14-340SP, *Defense Acquisitions: Assessments of Selected Weapon Programs*, March 2014, 110;
Amy Butler, "Maritime Patrol," *AW&ST*, March 24, 2014, 23; Andrew Orchard, "First P-8A
Poseidons Report for Duty," *America's Navy*, December 2, 2013, http://www.navy.mil/submit
/display.asp?story_id=78007; Craig Whitlock, "China, Russia Flex Muscles in Increasing Number of Close Calls with U.S. Aircraft," www.washingtonpost.com, October 4, 2014, http://www
.washingtonpost.com/world/national-security/china-russia-flex-muscles-in-increasing-number-of
-close-calls-with-us-aircraft/2014/10/04/a398731c-4b21-11e4-891d-713f052086a0_story.html.

70. U.S. Air Force, Fact Sheet, "MC-12," http://www.af.mil/AboutUs/FactSheets/Display/
tabid/224/Article/104497/mc-12.aspx (accessed May 16, 2013).

71. Ibid.; Ben Iannotta and Mike Hoffman, "Pentagon Tries to Get Liberty ISR Planes Back
on Track," *C4ISR Journal* (July 2009): 8.

72. "List of United States Air Force Reconnaissance Squadrons," Wikipedia, http://en
.wikipedia.org/wiki/List_of_United_States_Air_Force_reconnaissance_squadrons (accessed October 5, 2014); Jeff Schogol, "Time to Move Beyond MC-12, Official Says," www.armytimes.com,
June 11, 2012, http://archive.armytimes.com/article/20120611/NEWS/206110323/Time-move
-beyond-MC-12-official-says; Brian Everstine, "Last MC-12W Liberty Returns from Kandahar,

Bagram Unit," *Air Force Times*, September 28, 2014, http://archive.airforcetimes.com/article/20140928/NEWS/309280015/Last-MC-12W-Liberty-returns-from-Kandahar-Bagram-unit-remains; Brian Everstine, "Air Force's MC-12 Mission Ends in Afghanistan," *Air Force Times*, October 18, 2014, http://archive.airforcetimes.com/article/20141018/NEWS08/310180039/Air-Force-s-MC-12-mission-ends-Afghanistan; Arie Church, "Oklahoma Guard Slated for MC12," *AFA Daily Report* (via e-mail), February 18, 2015.

73. "Latest Army Spy Plane Readied in Secret Lab," www.defensenews.com, May 7, 2013, http://archive.defensenews.com/article/20130507/C4ISR02/305070028/Latest-Army-Spy-Plane-Readied-Secret-Lab; Michael Peck, "EMARSS Aircraft Begin Flight Tests," www.defensenews.com, August 19, 2013, http://archive.defensenews.com/article/20130819/C4ISRNET08/308190007/EMARSS-Aircraft-Begin-Flight-Tests; Amy Butler, "Intelligence Plans," *AW&ST*, November 11–18, 2013, 42.

74. David A. Fulghum, "CIA to Deploy UAVs in Albania," *AW&ST*, January 31, 1994, 20–22; "Gnats Weathered Out," *AW&ST*, February 14, 1994, 19; Frank Strickland, "The Early Evolution of the Predator Drone," *Studies in Intelligence* 57, no. 1 (Extracts, March 2013): 1–6. For a history of the origins and evolution of the Predator, see Richard Whittle, *Predator: The Secret Origins of the Drone Revolution* (New York: Henry Holt, 2014).

75. James Risen, "Eyes (Arms) in the Sky," *New York Times*, November 10, 2002, Section 4, 5; Karen DeYoung and Thomas E. Ricks, "Iraqis Down Reconnaissance Drone," *Washington Post*, December 24, 2002, A11; U.S. Air Force, Fact Sheet, "MQ-1B," http://www.af.mil/AboutUs/FactSheets/Display/tabid/224/Article/104469/mq-1b-predator.aspx (accessed December 16, 2010); Chitra Ragavan, "Clinton, Bush, and the Hunt for Bin Laden," *U.S. News*, September 29, 2006, http://www.usnews.com.

76. Kenneth Israel, *NMIA Defense Intelligence Status '96 Supporting the Warfighter*, 21; Defense Airborne Reconnaissance Office, *UAV Annual Report FY 1996*, November 6, 1996, 7, 9, 18, 21; "World News Roundup," *AW&ST*, June 15, 1998, 41.

77. U.S. Air Force, "MQ-1B"; Marc V. Schanz, "The Indispensable Weapon," *Air Force Magazine* (February 2010): 32–36; U.S. Army, *Employment of Group 3/4/5 Organic/Nonorganic UAS Tactical Pocket Guide*, February 2010, 101.

78. David Carbajal, "62nd ERS Assists Base Defense, Supports Ground Troops," U.S. Air Forces Central Command, December 23, 2011, http://www.afcent.af.mil/News/ArticleDisplay/tabid/136/Article/218893/62nd-ers-assists-base-defense-supports-ground-troops.aspx; Matthew Aid, "Drones Crucial for Base Defense in Afghanistan," MatthewAid.com, May 8, 2013, http://www.matthewaid.com/post/49928466478/drones-crucial-for-base-defense-in-afghanistan; "Predators Back in Libya," *AW&ST*, April 25–May 2, 2011, 14; Craig Whitlock, "U.S. Military Drone Surveillance Is Expanding to Hot Spots Beyond Declared Combat Zones," www.washingtonpost.com, July 20, 2013, http://www.washingtonpost.com/world/national-security/us-military-drone-surveillance-is-expanding-to-hot-spots-beyond-declared-combat-zones/2013/07/20/0a57fbda-ef1c-11e2-8163-2c7021381a75_story.html; Eric Schmitt and Scott Sayare, "U.S. Troops at Drone Base in West Africa," *New York Times*, February 23, 2013, A4, A6; David S. Cloud and Kathleen Hennessey, "U.S. Opens Drone Base in Niger," *Los Angeles Times*, February 23, 2013, AA1, AA4; Eric Schmitt, "U.S. Signs New Lease to Keep Strategic Military Installation in the Horn of Africa," *New York Times*, May 6, 2014, A10; Stephen Losey, "US Predator Drone Teams Deploy to Find Kidnapped Nigerian Girls," www.defensenews.com, May 21, 2014; Salmon Masood, "U.S. Leaves Drone Base on Orders from Pakistan," *New York Times*, December 12, 2011, A8; [author name deleted], *History of the Air Force Intelligence, Surveillance, and Reconnaissance Agency, 1 January–31 December 2012* (San Antonio, TX: Air Force Intelligence, Surveillance, and Reconnaissance Agency, 2014), 83; Office of Air Combat Command History, *History of Air Combat Command, 1 January–31 December 2012*, 304–306.

79. Government Accountability Office, GAO-14-340SP, *Defense Acquisitions: Assessments of Selected Weapon Programs*, 115–116.

80. David A. Fulghum, "Global Hawk UAVs to Remain Unarmed," *AW&ST*, April 15, 2002, 20–21; Israel, *NMIA Defense Intelligence Status '96 Supporting the Warfighter*, 21; Defense Airborne Reconnaissance Office, *UAV Annual Report FY 1996*, 13, 31; Michael A. Dornheim, "Global Hawk Begins Flight Test Program," *AW&ST*, March 9, 1998, 22–23; Defense Airborne Reconnaissance Office, *UAV Annual Report FY 1997*, 1997, 32; "First Global Hawk Squadron in Place," *C4ISR Journal* (January–February 2005): 10; "Global Hawk Camera Range Will Double," *C4ISR Journal* (January–February 2005): 6; U.S. Air Force, Fact Sheet, "Global Hawk," http://www.af .mil/information/factsheets (accessed December 16, 2010).

81. "UAVs to UAE," *AW&ST*, March 3, 2003, 61; Rowan Scarborough, "Hovering Spy Plane Helps Rout Iraqis," *AW&ST*, April 3, 2003, A1, A12; "Loss Leaders," *AW&ST*, April 7, 2003, 21; "Production Global Hawks Enter War on Terrorism," *Space News*, January 30, 2006, 8. On Global Hawk's contribution to Operation IRAQI FREEDOM, also see David A. Fulghum, "War from 60,000 Ft.," *AW&ST*, September 8, 2003, 54–57; Northrop Grumman, "Photo Release—Global Hawk Unmanned Aerial Vehicle Returns After More Than 4,800 Flight Hours in Fight Against Terrorism," Chron, February 21, 2006, http://www.chron.com/news/article/PZ-Photo-Release -Global-Hawk-Unmanned-Aerial-1510450.php.

82. Mark Corcoran, "Revealed: US Flew Spy Drone Missions from Australia," *ABC News* (Australia), September 3, 2012, http://www.abc.net.au/news/2012-09-03/revealed-us-flew -drone-missions-from-australia/4236306; "Global Hawk Drone Activities Affect Flight Activities in Sicily," MatthewAid.com, April 7, 2013, http://www.matthewaid.com/post/47361824772 /global-hawk-drone-activities-affect-flight; Jim Miklaszewski and Courtney Kube, "U.S. 'Global Hawk' Drone Joins Search for Kidnapped Nigerian Schoolgirls," *NBC News*, May 13, 2014, http://www.nbcnews.com/storyline/missing-nigeria-schoolgirls/u-s-global-hawk-drone-joins -search-kidnapped-nigerian-schoolgirls-n104696; Dave Majumdar, "U.S. Global Hawks Operate in U.K. and Japan," *USNI News*, May 30, 2014, http://news.usni.org/2014/05/30/u-s-global -hawks-operate-u-k-japan; Craig Whitlock and Anne Gearan, "Agreement Will Allow U.S. to Fly Long-Range Surveillance Drones from Base in Japan," www.washingtonpost.com, October 2, 2013, http://www.washingtonpost.com/world/agreement-will-allow-us-to-fly-long-range -surveillance-drones-from-base-in-japan/2013/10/03/aeba1ccc-2be8-11e3-83fa-b82b8431dc92_ story.html; "U.S. Spy Drones Deployed to Misawa in Aomori," *Asahi Shimbun*, May 24, 2014, http://ajw.asahi.com/article/behind_news/politics/AJ201405240053; Patrick S. Ciccarone, "RQ-4 Global Hawk Leaves Misawa, Flies South for Winter," Misawa Air Base, October 16, 2014, http://www.misawa.af.mil/news/story.asp?id=123428212; U.S. Central Command Public Affairs, "Hawk Soars Past 10,000 Flying Hours," March 10, 2015, http://www.acc.af.mil/news/story.asp ?id=123441354; Office of Air Combat Command History, *History of Air Combat Command, 1 January–31 December 2011*, 364–365.

83. Aaron Mehta, "USAF Looks to Global Hawk Upgrades," www.defensenews.com, March 7, 2015, http://www.defensenews.com/story/defense/air-space/isr/2015/03/07/global-hawk-looks -to-future-upgrades/24120821.

84. U.S. Air Force, Fact Sheet, "MQ-9 Reaper," August 18, 2010, http://www.af.mil/AboutUs /FactSheets/Display/tabid/224/Article/104470/mq-9-reaper.aspx (accessed October 6, 2014); Christian Davenport, "Did the Air Force Waste $8.8 Billion on Drones?," www.washingtonpost .com, October 2, 2014, http://www.washingtonpost.com/news/checkpoint/wp/2014/10/02/ did-the-air-force-waste-8-8-billion-on-drones; U.S. Air Force, Air Force Historical Research Agency, Fact Sheet, "17th Reconnaissance Squadron (ACC)," May 5, 2012, http://www.afhra .af.mil/factsheets/factsheet.asp?id=9846 (accessed October 10, 2014); Daniel Liddicoet, "9th Attack Squadron Stands Up at Holloman," Holloman Air Force Base, October 4, 2012, http://www .holloman.af.mil/news/story.asp?id=123321112; Department of Defense, *MQ-9 Reaper Unmanned Aircraft System (MQ-9 Reaper)*, Selected Acquisition Report, April 16, 2014, 21–22.

85. Julian E. Barnes, "Military Refines a 'Constant Stare Against Our Enemies,'" *Los Angeles Times*, November 2, 2009, A1, A14; Colin Clark, "Many-Headed Dragon Heads to Af-Pak," *DoD*

Buzz, December 16, 2009, http://www.dodbuzz.com/2009/12/16/many-headed-dragon-heads-to
-af-pak. As of March 2009, another nineteen were to be procured. See Government Accountabil-
ity Office, *Defense Acquisitions: Assessments of Selected Weapon Programs*, March 2009, 117; 53WG/
CC, Memorandum for: USAFWC/CC, ACC/AS, Subject: MQ-9 Gorgon Stare (GS) Fielding
Recommendation, December 30, 2010 (DRAFT); Ellen Nakashima, "New Drone Sensors Not
Working as Hoped," *Washington Post*, January 25, 2011, A2; Colin Clark, "AF: Some Gorgon
Stare Probs Fixed," *DoD Buzz*, January 25, 2011; Marina Malenic, "USAF Declares Gorgon Stare
Follow-On Operationally Deployable," *IHS Jane's 360*, July 2, 2014, http://www.janes.com/article
/40290/usaf-declares-gorgon-stare-follow-on-operationally-deployable.

86. Department of Defense, *MQ-9 Reaper Unmanned Aircraft System (MQ-9 Reaper)*, 5; Eric
Schmitt, "Drones in Niger Reflect New U.S. Approach in Terror Fight," www.nytimes.com,
July 10, 2013, http://www.nytimes.com/2013/07/11/world/africa/drones-in-niger-reflect-new-us
-approach-in-terror-fight.html?pagewanted=all&_r=0; Office of Air Combat Command History,
History of Air Combat Command 1 January–31 December 2011, 365; Office of Air Combat Com-
mand History, *History of Air Combat Command 1 January–31 December 2012*, 304–306.

87. U.S. Air Force, Fact Sheet, "RQ-170 Sentinel," http://www.af.mil/AboutUs/FactSheets/
Display/tabid/224/Article/104547/rq-170-sentinel.aspx (accessed December 16, 2010); David A.
Fulghum and Bill Sweetman, "Stealth over Afghanistan," *AW&ST*, December 14, 2009, 26–31;
"Introducing the RQ-170 Wraith," *War Is Boring*, https://medium.com/war-is-boring/introducing
-the-rq-170-wraith-d5f0a062d257 (accessed June 12, 2014); Bill Sweetman, "Big Wing," *AW&ST*,
August 29–September 5, 2011, 46–48; David Fulghum and Bill Sweetman, "New Details,"
AW&ST, January 2, 2012, 28–29.

88. "Introducing the RQ-170 Wraith"; Sweetman, "Big Wing"; Fulghum and Sweetman,
"New Details"; Greg Miller, "Stealth Drones Kept Watch over Bin Laden Home," *Washington
Post*, May 18, 2011, A1, A9; David Fulghum and Bill Sweetman, "Seen and Unseen," *AW&ST*, De-
cember 12, 2011, 18–21; Scott Shane and David E. Sanger, "Crash of Stealth C.I.A. Drone in Iran
Reveals Secret U.S. Surveillance Effort," *New York Times*, December 8, 2011, A6; Office of Air
Combat Command History, *History of Air Combat Command, 1 January–31 December 2011*, 319.

89. Julian E. Barnes, "U.S. Made Covert Plan to Retrieve Iran Drone," *Wall Street Journal*,
November 7, 2011, A15; Greg Miller, "Drone Lost in Iran Was Used in CIA Secret Missions,
Officials Say," *Washington Post*, December 6, 2011, A11; Shane and Sanger, "Crash of Stealth
C.I.A. Drone in Iran Reveals Secret U.S. Surveillance Effort"; Associated Press, "Iran Claims
Its Experts Almost Done Recovering Data from Captured U.S. Drone," December 12, 2011,
http://www.washingtonpost.com; "Lost U.S. Drone Was Monitoring Iranian Nuclear Facilities,
Sources Say," *Global Security Newswire*, December 16, 2011, http://www.nti.org/gsn/article/lost
-us-drone-was-monitoring-iranian-nuclear-facilities-sources-say; Robert Mackey and Rick Glad-
stone, "Iran Shows Video It Says Was Made by U.S. Drone," *New York Times*, February 8, 2013,
A10; Office of Air Combat Command History, *History of Air Combat Command, 1 January–31
December 2012*, 409, 545.

90. Amy Butler and Bill Sweetman, "Return of the Penetrator," *AW&ST*, December 9, 2013,
20–23; Amy Butler, "Black on Track," *AW&ST*, June 23, 2014, 22–23.

91. General Atomics, "Gray Eagle: Armed Persistence," 2012; "MQ-IC Gray Eagle ER/MP
Unmanned Aircraft System (UAS), United States of America," www.army-technology.com;
David Cenciotti, "The U.S. Army's New Drone Is a Hunter and a Killer," *War Is Boring*, May
28, 2014, https://medium.com/war-is-boring/the-u-s-armys-new-drone-is-a-hunter-and-a-killer
-d5ada386ad04; Department of Defense, *MQ-1C Gray Eagle Unmanned Aircraft System (MQ-
1C Gray Eagle) as of FY 2015 President's Budget*, Selected Acquisition Report, April 16, 2014,
5–6; Department of Defense, *MQ-4C Triton Unmanned Aircraft System (MQ-4C Triton) as of FY
2015 President's Budget*, Selected Acquisition Report, April 16, 2014, 5, 17; Julie Yazdan and Greg
Miller, Northrup Grumman, *Triton Program Overview: Avalon Air Show 2015*, 2015 Slide 18.

92. Paul Bennett, *Strategic Surveillance* (Cambridge, MA: Union of Concerned Scientists,
1979), 5.

93. Richard A. Scribner, Theodore J. Ralston, and William D. Mertz, *The Verification Challenge: Problems of Strategic Nuclear Arms Control Verification* (Boston: Birkhauser, 1985), 70; John F. Ebersole and James C. Wyant, "Real-Time Optical Subtraction on Photographic Imagery for Difference Detection," *Applied Optics* 15, no. 4 (1976): 871–876.

94. Scribner, Ralston, and Mertz, *The Verification Challenge*, 69.

95. Campbell, *Introduction to Remote Sensing*, 226; James Fusca, "Space Surveillance," *Space/Aeronautics* (June 1964): 92–103.

96. U.S. Congress, Senate Committee on Commerce, Science, and Transportation, *NASA Authorization for Fiscal Year 1978*, pt. 3 (Washington, DC: U.S. Government Printing Office, 1977), 1642–1643.

97. Whittle, *Predator*, 134.

98. William Matthews, "Firm Adapting Civilian Geospatial Tool for Intel Applications," *Space News*, May 4, 2009, 16.

99. Julian E. Barnes, "U.S. Military Borrows from NFL," *Los Angeles Times*, June 8, 2010, A1, A11. One system developed is the Multi-INT Analysis and Archive System. See Turner Brinton, "New Video Exploitation Tools Geared Toward Tactical Users," *Space News*, November 1, 2010, 12; Ted Girard, "Big Data and Virtualization: A Formidable Defense," www.defensesystems .com, May 5, 2015, http://defensesystems.com/articles/2015/03/05/comment-defense-big-data -and-virualization.aspx.

100. Walter Pincus, "DARPA Contract Description Hints at Advanced Video Spying," www .washingtonpost.com, October 20, 2008, http://www.washingtonpost.com/wp-dyn/content/ article/2008/10/19/AR2008101901572.html; Ben Iannotta, "Playing Catch-Up," *C4ISR Journal* (October 2009): 26, 28; Turner Brinton, "NGA Pushes Full-Motion Video Analysis," *Space News*, October 19, 2009, 12.

101. "From Video to Knowledge," *Science & Technology Review* (April/May 2011): 4–11; George I. Seffers, "Coping with the Big Data Quagmire," *Signal* (August 2013): 31–33.

102. *Report on the Pilot Study on National Intelligence Support to Field Commanders*, January 12, 1976, CREST. The study was prepared by an interagency working group.

103. James Bamford, "America's Supersecret Eyes in Space," *New York Times*, January 13, 1985, 39ff.; Paul Stares, *Space and National Security* (Washington, DC: Brookings Institution, 1987), 18; Scott F. Large, "Memorandum for: Honorable Daniel K. Inouye and the Honorable Thad Cochran, Subject: Declassification of the 'Fact of' National Reconnaissance Mission Ground Stations and Presence Overseas," September 24, 2008. It is notable that the uplinks for the NRO Global Broadcast System are located in Hawaii, Europe, and Virginia.

104. Dwayne Day, "Relay in the Sky: The Satellite Data System," *Journal of the British Interplanetary Society* 51, Supp. 1 (2006): 56–62; Bamford, "America's Supersecret Eyes in Space."

105. Day, "Relay in the Sky"; confidential interviews.

106. "USA 236—Satellite Information," http://www.heavens-above.com/satinfo.aspx?satid =38466&lat=0&lng=0&loc=Unspecified&alt=0&tz=UCT (accessed October 23, 2014).

107. Robert C. Toth, "Anaheim Firm May Have Sought Spy Satellite Data," *Los Angeles Times*, October 10, 1982, 1, 32; Warren Ferster, "NRO Studies Relay Satellites," *Space News*, September 1–7, 1997, 1, 19; National Space Science Data Center, "NASA's Tracking and Data Relay Satellites (TDRS)," http://nssdc.gsfc.nasa.gov (accessed September 15, 2006).

108. U.S. Air Force, "Air Force Distributed Common Ground System," Fact Sheet, August 31, 2009, http://www.af.mil/AboutUs/FactSheets/Display/tabid/224/Article/104525/air-force -distributed-common-ground-system.aspx (accessed December 9, 2010); Northrop Grumman, "Distributed Common Ground System—Army (DCGS-A)," www.es.northropgrumman.com (accessed December 9, 2010). On problems with the Army system, see Associated Press, "Inside Washington: Profiting from Failure," October 27, 2014 (via. www.mattheaid.com).

109. Craig Covault, "Info War Advanced by Navy GBS Satcom," *AW&ST*, March 23, 1988, 28; Jeremy Singer, "U.S. Air Force Pays Raytheon Millions to Fix GBS System," *Space News*, August 14, 2000, 6; Jeremy Singer, "U.S. Air Force Maps Out Plans for Lighter GBS Ground

Terminals," *Space News*, September 9, 2002, 22; Stew Magnuson, "Satellite Data Distribution Lagged, Improved in Afghanistan," *Space News*, September 2, 2002, 6.

110. U.S. Congress, House Committee on Appropriations, *Department of Defense Appropriations for 1992*, pt. 6 (Washington, DC: U.S. Government Printing Office, 1991), 470; Craig Covault, "NRO KH-11 Readied for Afghan Recon," *AW&ST*, October 8, 2001, 68–69; Jason Stahl, "Bringing National Space System Capabilities to the Fleet," *Domain* (Fall 2002): 17–18.

111. "AF Would Send Real-Time Recce Satellite Images to Tactical Planes," *Aerospace Daily*, January 8, 1993, 1; James R. Asker, "F-16, EA-6B to Fire Missiles Cued by Intelligence Satellites," *AW&ST*, April 19, 1993, 25; Ben Iannotta, "Space to Play Bosnian Role," *Space News*, May 10–16, 1993, 1, 2; Tony Capaccio, "Air Force Pushes 'In Your Face from Outer Space,'" *Defense Week*, July 12, 1993, 1, 8; David A. Fulghum, "Talon Lance Gives Aircrews Timely Intelligence from Space," *AW&ST*, August 23, 1993, 71; Captain Michelle Dietrich, "Talon Lance Supports Warfighters," *Guardian*, August 1993, 6–7; Colonel Jack Fry, Space Warfare Center, *AF TENCAP Programs— AF TENCAP Briefing to AFSAB New World Space Applications Panel*, March 15, 1995; William B. Scott, "USAF to Broadcast Mission Data to Cockpit," *AW&ST*, June 5, 1995, 23.

8

SIGNALS INTELLIGENCE AND CYBER COLLECTION

Signals intelligence (SIGINT) is defined by the Department of Defense (DOD) as "intelligence comprising, either individually or in combination, all communications intelligence, electronic intelligence, and foreign instrumentation signals, however transmitted."[1] It consists of three components: communications intelligence (COMINT), electronic intelligence (ELINT), and foreign instrumentation signals intelligence (FISINT).

COMINT is intelligence obtained through the interception, processing, and analysis of the electronic communications of foreign government or organizations. Those communications have traditionally, and often explicitly, excluded radio and television broadcasts; today they exclude postings on social media sites. The communications may take a variety of forms—voice (transmitted via telephone, standard or more advanced mobile phone, Blackberry device, satellite telephone, radio-telephone, walkie-talkie), the Internet, Morse code, or facsimile—and may be encrypted or transmitted in the clear.

ELINT collection operations gather the noncommunications signals from military and civilian hardware, excluding those from atomic detonations. The earliest of the ELINT targets were World War II air defense systems. The objective was to gather sufficient information to identify the location and operating characteristics of radars and then to circumvent and neutralize them during bombing raids (through direct attack or electronic countermeasures).

While logically a subcategory of ELINT, FISINT was decreed several years ago to be a component of the SIGINT enterprise coequal with COMINT and the other elements of ELINT. Foreign instrumentation signals are electromagnetic emissions associated with the testing and operation of aerospace, surface, and subsurface systems that have military or civilian applications. Such signals include but are not limited to those from telemetry, beaconing, electronic interrogation, tracking/fusing/aiming command systems, and video data links.[2]

A subcategory of FISINT is telemetry intelligence (TELINT). Telemetry is the set of signals by which a missile or missile component sends back data about its performance during a test flight. Intercepted telemetry can provide data used to estimate the number of warheads carried by a given missile, its payload and throw-weight, the probable size of its warheads, and the accuracy with which the warheads are guided from the missile's postboost vehicles to their targets.[3]

The ease with which communications or electronic signals can be intercepted and understood depends on three factors: the method of transmission, the frequencies employed, and the encipherment (or lack thereof) used to conceal the signals' meaning from unauthorized personnel. Changes in communications transmission technology resulted in the susceptibility of communications signals to interception and have led to the development of corresponding intercept technology. The use of high-frequency (HF) communications for long-distance strategic communications by the Soviet Union and other countries of interest led to U.S. deployment of antenna systems—such as the AN/FLR-9 "Elephant Cage" systems that made up the IRON HORSE network—at a multitude of sites in Europe and Asia where those signals would arrive after bouncing off the atmosphere. With the end of the Cold War and the change in communications technologies, the United States has shut down all but one of those systems.[4]

The advent of communications systems employing microwave signals—which, in contrast to HF communications, do not bounce off the atmosphere but leak out into space—necessitated other means of interception. Microwave signals can be intercepted by two means: (1) ground stations near the invisible line connecting two microwave towers, or (2) space collections systems if the area of transmission is within the footprint of the system. Similarly, space systems can intercept very-high-frequency (VHF) and ultra-high-frequency (UHF) communications that leak out into space.

Communications transmitted via satellite can be intercepted by focusing on the uplink or downlink. The use of satellite systems for both foreign internal and international communications led the United States and other nations to establish major programs for the interception of communications transmitted via satellite. By placing satellite dishes in the proper locations, technicians can intercept an enormous volume of traffic. Whereas ground station antennas can direct signals to a satellite with great accuracy, satellite antennas are smaller, and the signals they send to Earth are less narrowly focused, perhaps covering several thousand square miles.[5]

Communications or other signals transmitted via cable cannot be snatched out of the air and do not leak out into space. Interception of cable traffic has involved physically tapping into the cables or placing "induction" devices in the proximity of the cables and maintaining the equipment at the point of access. This option might be impossible in the case of hardened and protected internal landlines—the type that carry much high-priority secret command and control communications. Another possibility is gaining access to the cables when they transition from the ocean surface onto land, with the cooperation of the relevant communications company or country.

Radio is the most traditional means of transmitting signals, including communications, missile telemetry, and foreign instrumentation signals. The accessibility of radio signals to interception often depends on their transmission frequencies and their geographic location. Messages transmitted at lower frequencies (extremely low, very low, and low frequency and HF) travel for long distances since they bounce off the atmosphere and come down in locations far from the transmitting and intended receiving locations.

In contrast, data sent at higher frequencies will "leak" throughout the atmosphere and out into space. To intercept such signals, intercept stations must be within line of sight of the radio communications. The curvature of the Earth can therefore make monitoring from ground-based sites impossible. Several years ago, former Central Intelligence Agency (CIA) deputy director for intelligence Sayre Stevens wrote that the Soviet ballistic missile defense test center at Sary Shagan "lies deeply enough within the USSR to make it difficult to monitor from peripheral intelligence gathering sites along the border. . . . [F]light operations at Sary Shagan can be conducted well below the radio-horizon from such external monitoring locations."[6]

TARGETS

Targets can be categorized in a variety of ways. One category is communication links (whether individual links or categories of links) that are the focus of intercept or other collection operations, as noted above. Two others are the identities of the targets (e.g., foreign leaders) or specific activities that might involve individuals or organizations of interest (e.g., gaming, porn viewing).

COMINT targets are varied. One prominent target is foreign leadership. In September 1994, the United States intercepted communications from Haitian dictator Raul Cedras stating that he would determine his response to President Bill Clinton's demands based on the reaction of the American public to the Clinton's forthcoming speech on U.S. policy toward Haiti. One recent National Security Agency (NSA) document listed 122 foreign leaders considered targets for U.S. COMINT collection. Thus, the NSA targeted Russian president Dmitry Medvedev during a visit to Britain to participate in the G20 summit. Other leadership targets included the presidents of Mexico and Brazil. A special report on a Brazilian television program asserted, "Communications between [Brazilian President Dina] Roussef and her main advisors, as well as communications between advisors and others, were allegedly monitored by the United States." A more controversial target was German chancellor Angela Merkel's mobile phone—a continuation of the targeting of Gerhard Schroder's phone when he was German chancellor. NSA reportedly eavesdropped on the communications of Mahmoud Karzai, brother of Afghan president Hamid Karzai, as part of a corruption investigation.[7]

The most traditional COMINT target is diplomatic communications—those from each nation's capital to its diplomatic establishments around the world and those taking place within the establishments. The United States has intercepted and deciphered the diplomatic and intelligence communications of a variety of nations—for example, Iraq's communications to its embassy in Japan in the 1970s and Libya's communications to the East Berlin People's Bureau prior to the bombing of a West Berlin nightclub in 1985. Intercepted diplomatic communications in 1996 and thereafter raised questions about whether the People's Republic of China (PRC) had attempted to funnel money to American politicians for use in their campaigns. A January 1997 intercept of Israeli diplomatic communications led to a Federal Bureau of Investigation (FBI) inquiry into possible Israeli penetration of the U.S. government. The embassies and missions of European allies have not been exempt, as revealed by stories in the

Guardian and *Der Spiegel* in 2013. One document provided by Edward Snowden listed thirty-eight embassies and missions as targets, employing a variety of eavesdropping methods.[8]

In early 2003, as the UN Security Council debated whether to approve the use of military force against Iraq, the United States stepped up its effort at targeting the diplomatic communications of council members. An August 25, 2013, a *Der Spiegel* report asserted, based on Snowden-disclosed documents, that the NSA had monitored and succeeded in decrypting the United Nations' videoconferencing in 2012. According to the article, the decryption "dramatically increased the data from video conferences and the ability to decode the data traffic." As a result of this decryption success, the number of UN decrypted communications rose from 12 to 458 over the course of three weeks.[9]

The United States also targets communications between different components of a large number of governments and organizations. On some occasions both components are located within the country being monitored; on others at least one is located outside national boundaries. Frequently targeted communications include those between government and military officials or a ministry or agency and its subordinate units throughout the country and abroad; weapons production facilities and various military or government officials; military units, especially during exercises and operations, and higher authorities; and police and security forces and their headquarters.

The U.S. COMINT effort has targeted communications between the Chinese Ministry of Defense and subordinate military units, the Russian government and its military units, the Pakistani Atomic Energy Commission and Pakistani nuclear facilities, the Egyptian president and his subordinates (including when Egypt was holding the hijackers of the *Achille Lauro*), and Israeli officials in Tel Aviv and Israeli representatives in the West Bank. In recent years, the United States has intercepted and deciphered the communications of the Iranian intelligence service. It has also been intercepting communications from various components of the Syrian regime of Bashar al-Assad, which has yielded intelligence on both the regime as well as the Islamic State in Iraq and Syria (ISIS).[10]

In 1968, intercepted voice communications in the Beijing Military Region indicated a field exercise involving the 4th Armored Division. In 1980, U.S. intercepts of Soviet communications led to a fear that the Soviets were about to invade Iran. COMINT played a significant role in preparing a 1982 study on Indian heavy-water shortages. Intercepts allowed the United States to piece together the details concerning the sinking of a Soviet submarine in the North Pacific in 1983, and in 1988 intercepted Iraqi military communications led U.S. officials to conclude that Iraq had used chemical weapons in its war with Iran. After the Iraqi invasion of Kuwait in August 1990, COMINT and other intelligence reports indicated that some Saudi leaders were considering an attempt to pay off Saddam Hussein. In 1998, intercepts revealed that the Russian foreign intelligence service had facilitated the sale of Russian missile technology to Iran. The following year, COMINT showed that high-ranking Yugoslav officials had ordered an attack on the village of Racak in Kosovo, resulting in the massacre of forty-five unarmed Albanian civilians.[11]

The communications of terrorist groups, particularly al-Qaeda, have been an important target of U.S. COMINT efforts. By 2001, NSA was listening to unencrypted calls made by Osama bin Laden on his portable INMARSAT (International Maritime Satellite) phone. Among the intercepted conversations was a call between bin Laden and Taliban leader Mullah Mohammed Omar concerning the Taliban's ban on growing opium poppies. The intercept effort failed to provide warning of the September 11 attacks, but it did yield convincing evidence that al-Qaeda was involved in those attacks, as well as earlier ones in Nairobi, Kenya, and Dar es Salaam, Tanzania. In 2002 an intercepted satellite telephone conversation enabled the apprehension of Abu Musab al-Zarqawi's deputy.[12]

Intercepts, used to track the movement of and identify terrorist leaders, aided the U.S. targeted killing effort, including the killing of Hassan Ghul, a former black site resident, in 2012. Other intercept and cyber activities have aimed to identify online sexual activity, including visits to pornographic websites. Online gaming activities have also been monitored, due to NSA's belief that leaving gaming communities unmonitored is risky and that they represent a "target-rich" environment.[13]

As noted above, governmental communications do not exhaust the set of COMINT targets. The communications of political parties and corporations involved in the sale of technology related to advanced weapons development may also be targeted. In addition, the communications of terrorist groups are targeted, both to permit understanding of how the group functions and of the personalities of its leaders and to allow prediction of where and how it will attempt to strike next.

Another major set of COMINT targets is associated with economic activity (of both the legal and illegal variety), such as the communications of international banking firms and narcotics traffickers. In 1970 the predecessor of the Drug Enforcement Administration informed the NSA that it had "a requirement for any and all COMINT information which reflects illicit traffic in narcotics and dangerous drugs." Specific areas of interest included organizations and individuals engaged in the distribution of narcotics, cultivation and production centers, efforts to control the traffic in narcotics, and all violation of U.S. laws concerning narcotics.[14]

Chinese targets have included, among others, President Hu Jintao, the Chinese Trade Ministry, banks, and telecommunications companies. A special effort, codenamed SHOTGIANT, was made with regard to the Huawei telecommunications company. An NSA briefing slide explained that "many of our targets communicate over Huawei produced products," and there was a desire to "determine if Huawei is doing SIGINT for PRC." In addition, the presentation stated, "if we can determine the company's plans and intentions, we hope that this will lead us back to the plans and intentions of the PRC."[15]

In the early 1950s, the primary ELINT targets were Soviet bloc (including PRC) radars. Russian radars, such as the missile warning radar that became operational in the Leningrad region in February 2012 or the four Voronezh early warning radars that came online in 2014, remain a target. Monitoring Soviet/Russian radars also had an arms control verification aspect from the 1972 signing of the Anti-Ballistic Missile (ABM) Treaty until U.S. abrogation of the treaty, since the treaty restricted the use of radars in an "ABM mode." Today, Iranian, North Korean, and PRC radars are among the prime targets. The information desired is intended both to identify the existence and location of the radars and to provide technical intelligence on the capabilities of each radar regarding how it works, its capabilities, and its vulnerabilities. Specific

information desired includes signal parameter measurements (frequency, pulse repetition interval, main beam scan pattern, bandwidth, and pulse duration), antenna
pattern, and power.[16]

FISINT data may be desired with regard to spacecraft, missiles, or aircraft. With
regard to missiles it may concern structural stress, rocket motor thrust, fuel consump-
tion, guidance system performance, maneuvering, and the physical conditions of the
ambient environment. Links transmitting a variety of measurements concerning different types of events may be targeted: one-time events (e.g., the firing of explosive
bolts or the separation of reentry vehicles [RVs] from the postboost bus), discontinuous
events (e.g., adjustments to the guidance system during flight), and continuous events
(e.g., fuel flow, motor burn, and acceleration of the missile during the boost phase).*[17]

The U.S. SIGINT effort is massive and employs space and airborne collectors,
ground stations, covert listening posts, surface ships, and submarines for remote collection operations. Other aspects of today's NSA-CIA SIGINT effort, some of which
stray outside the formal definition, are clandestine SIGINT (ClanSIG) and computer
network exploitation, including placement of audio or other collection devices in fixed,
hidden locations (including within computers) and hacking into computer systems to
extract data residing on them.

SPACE COLLECTION

The United States operates signals satellites in three different types of orbit: low Earth,
geosynchronous, and highly elliptical ("Molniya"). In June 1960, the Navy orbited
the first electronic intelligence satellites, known as GRAB (for Galactic Radiation and
Background), whose primary targets were Soviet radar systems. A follow-up to GRAB,
designated POPPY, was first orbited in 1962. In February of that year, the Air Force
also began operating low-Earth orbiting "ferret" satellites designed to intercept signals
emitted by Soviet, Chinese, and other nations' air defense, ABM, and early-warning
radars. From the first launch to the one on July 16, 1971, sixteen of these satellites,
involving three generations, were launched, with inclinations ranging from 75 to 82
degrees.[18]

A second class of ferrets was put into operation beginning in August 1963. Whereas
each satellite in the first class had been launched as a primary payload, the satellites in
the second class were piggybacked on launch vehicles carrying imaging satellites. The
orbits of both classes evolved in a similar fashion, with initial orbits of approximately
180 × 250 miles giving way to near-circular orbits of around 300 miles. From 1972

---

*Which particular characteristic an intercepted reading refers to or the particular values
being used will not necessarily be evident, requiring further analysis to associate the values
with their meaning. A fuel tank reading may be given as "30," which may refer to a tank
that is either 30 percent full or 30 percent empty. The temperature in the rocket combustion
chamber can be measured from the temperature of another part known to have a specific
temperature relative to that in the chamber. See David S. Brandwein, "Telemetry Analysis,"
Studies in Intelligence (Fall 1964): 21–29; Farooq Hussain, *The Future of Arms Control*, pt. 4:
The Impact of Weapons Test Restrictions (London: International Institute of Strategic Studies,
1980), 46.

to 1988, all ferret satellites were launched as secondary payloads. One set of ferret satellites, designated 989, was launched along with KH-9 imagery satellites (which were launched from 1971 to 1984) as well as a class of SIGINT satellites designated JUMPSEAT (discussed below).[19]

On September 5, 1988, the first satellite of what was intended to be a new four-satellite constellation of ferrets was launched as the primary payload on a Titan II launched from Vandenberg Air Force Base (AFB). It was placed into a five-hundred-mile circular orbit with an 85-degree inclination. This launch was followed by similar Titan II launches on September 5, 1989, and April 25, 1992. However, in 1993, three Titan II boosters that had been designated for a "classified user" were assigned to the Strategic Defense Initiative Organization (now the Missile Defense Agency).[20]

That action reflected a decision, noted in a draft version of the Joint Chiefs of Staff (JCS) "Roles and Missions" report, that the missions being performed by two existing national satellite systems would be performed in the future by a single new system. That system would be a follow-up to the advanced version of the PARCAE ELINT ocean surveillance satellite. PARCAE (as well as the advanced PARCAE satellite constellation), first launched in 1976, and its associated ground sites had, for many years, the unclassified designation CLASSIC WIZARD (subsequently known as ICEbox, with "ICE" being an acronym for "Improved Collection Equipment").[21]

The CLASSIC WIZARD Global Surveillance System, as one Naval Security Group Command instruction referred to it, had its origins in U.S. Navy studies in 1968 investigating the feasibility of a dedicated ocean surveillance satellite system. In 1970 the Chief of Naval Operations ordered a study of overall ocean surveillance requirements. This project resulted in a five-volume *Naval Research Laboratory Ocean Surveillance Requirements Study*. In turn, the study produced Program 749, a study that focused on the development of high-resolution, phased-array radars that would allow all-weather ocean surveillance monitoring as well as detection of low-trajectory, sea-launched missiles.[22]

Despite the emphasis of these initial studies, the ocean surveillance satellite program that resulted, PARCAE, lacked radar capability. Rather, it was a passive interceptor, equipped with a passive infrared scanner and millimeter wave radiometers, as well as with radio-frequency antennas capable of monitoring radio communications and radar emissions from submarines and ships. It used passive interferometry techniques (the use of interference phenomena) to determine the location of ships; that is, the craft could compute a ship's position from data on radar or radio signals provided by several antennas.[23]

The PARCAE system consisted of a mother ship and three subsatellites tethered to the mother ship. PARCAE satellites were launched from Vandenberg AFB into a near-circular, 63-degree-inclined orbit with an altitude of approximately seven hundred miles. At that altitude, the spacecraft could receive signals from surface vessels more than 2,000 miles away. Given a displacement of approximately 1,866 miles between passes, PARCAE could provide overlapping coverage on successive passes.[24]

Eight operational clusters were put into orbit from 1976 to May 15, 1987. An increased rate in the 1980s led the Navy to request and receive funds for antenna upgrades at all CLASSIC WIZARD ground stations. Those stations, colocated with Navy Regional Reporting Centers, were situated in Diego Garcia, British Indian

Ocean Territory; Guam; Adak, Alaska; Winter Harbor, Maine; and Edzell, Scotland. Information received at the stations would be quickly transmitted to regional ocean surveillance centers and via satellite to a main downlink in the Washington, D.C., area. In recent years, all of the sites were closed, and Army and Air Force SIGINT personnel were colocated with Navy SIGINT personnel at other sites, further indicating that the system focused on more than naval targets. Army participation began in the mid-1980s under a program designated TRUE BLUE (which also involved Army participation at other sites). In 1995, Detachment 1 of the Air Intelligence Agency's 692nd Intelligence Group was established on Guam to participate in the CLASSIC WIZARD program, described in an Air Intelligence Agency publication as a "joint global surveillance reporting system."[25]

The first advanced PARCAE system was deployed during a June 1990 shuttle mission, launched from Cape Canaveral. The second was carried into orbit by a Titan IV, launched in November 1991 from Vandenberg AFB. In both cases, the satellites were deployed in orbits similar to those of the PARCAE satellites. However, it appears that there was no mother ship attached to the triplets. An August 1993 launch from Vandenberg produced an explosion shortly after takeoff that destroyed the booster and the spacecraft. A successful launch followed on May 12, 1996.[26]

Shortly after the 1993 explosion, it was reported that the National Reconnaissance Office (NRO) and the Navy planned to develop a new generation of spacecraft with improved detection capabilities. The new generation, code-named INTRUDER, is apparently even more of a dual system—employed against land- and sea-based targets—than the previous generation and apparently has some COMINT capability. The first launch on September 8, 2001, was followed by launches on December 2, 2003; February 3, 2005; June 15, 2007; and April 14, 2011. Unlike the previous generation of ELINT ocean surveillance satellites, the new generation has been launched into orbit on Atlas launch vehicles. And rather than using three objects in orbit, the new generation uses only a pair. As with earlier generations, the satellites orbit with a 63-degree inclination at about seven hundred miles above the Earth. Operational control of the satellites is the responsibility of the Programs Operations Coordination Group at NSA. However, all the original ground stations associated with CLASSIC WIZARD have now been closed. Apparently data are downlinked to two overseas sites, one at Misawa Air Base, Japan, and the other at Griesheim, Germany.[27]

Customers of CLASSIC WIZARD/ICEbox data could—and customers of INTRUDER data, such as commanders of U.S. fleets, presumably can—specify, through an automated process, particular data they require with respect to area, signals, and units of interest. Among the major targets of the new generation are thousands of civilian and merchant ships, particularly those suspected of transporting weapons or weapons-related material for terrorist groups and rogue regimes. According to one report, information from the satellites passed to the Spanish government allowed commandos to stop a North Korean ship carrying Scud missiles to Yemen.[28]

In the late 1960s and early 1970s, the NRO began orbiting the products of two geosynchronous satellite programs: CANYON and RHYOLITE (subsequently renamed AQUACADE). The first CANYON was launched in August 1968 from Cape Canaveral into orbit with a perigee of 19,641 miles, an apogee of 22,853 miles, and a 9.9-degree inclination. Controlled from a ground station at Bad Aibling, Germany, the satellite was America's first high-altitude SIGINT system and first dedicated COMINT satellite. Six more launches would follow, with the last in 1977.[29]

In 1970 the first of four RHYOLITE spacecraft were placed into orbit, although it was closer to achieving a pure geostationary orbit (0-degree inclination and 22,300 miles for both perigee and apogee) than CANYON. Rather than focusing on communications signals, RHYOLITE's primary function was intercepting telemetry from Soviet and Chinese offensive and defensive missile tests, antisatellite tests, and space launches. One satellite was apparently located somewhere above the Horn of Africa, at 69 degrees east, to gather telemetry signals transmitted from liquid-fueled intercontinental ballistic missiles (ICBMs) launched from Tyuratam in a northeasterly direction toward the Kamchatka Peninsula impact zone. Another station was over Borneo, at 115 degrees east, to monitor Soviet solid-fueled missiles, such as the SS-16 ICBM and SS-20 IRBM, launched from Pletsetsk.[30]

In addition to intercepting the telemetry signals from Soviet and Chinese missile tests, RHYOLITE satellites had a significant COMINT capability. The satellites apparently were used to intercept Soviet and Chinese telephone and radio communications across the UHF, VHF, and microwave frequency bands. Walkie-talkie communications generated by Soviet military exercises, which fell in the VHF/UHF range, were also regularly monitored by RHYOLITE satellites, which collectively covered virtually the entire world outside the Western Hemisphere and intercepted communications from China, Vietnam, Indonesia, Pakistan, and Lebanon.[31]

The RHYOLITE/AQUACADE satellites provided intelligence on Chinese development of ballistic missiles, cruise missiles, and surface-to-air missiles. A least one of the satellites detected the distress signal of Air Force Captain Scott O'Grady after he was shot down by Serbian forces during a mission over Bosnia. The satellites also collected intelligence related to the multiple conflicts with Afghanistan and Iraq related to Iraq's Global Positioning System (GPS) jamming systems, Afghan weapons systems, al-Qaeda leadership communications, and Scud missile radars.[32]

The CANYON and RHYOLITE/AQUACADE programs led eventually to follow-on programs originally code-named CHALET and MAGNUM, respectively. On June 10, 1978, the first CHALET satellite was placed into an orbit similar to those inhabited by the CANYON satellites. Subsequently, after disclosure of the program in the press in 1979, it was renamed VORTEX. In 1987, after another disclosure, its name was changed again, this time to MERCURY.[33]

CHALET's original mission was strictly COMINT. However, after the loss of ground stations in Iran and the discovery that information about RHYOLITE had been sold to the KGB, CHALET spacecraft were modified to allow them to intercept Soviet telemetry. The first modified CHALET was launched on October 1, 1979 (by which time it was known as VORTEX). Subsequent launches, not all successful, occurred on October 1, 1981; January 31, 1984; September 2, 1988; May 10, 1989; and September 4, 1989. The final MERCURY satellite was destroyed as a result of a 1998 launch failure.[34]

The primary targets of VORTEX, for most of the program's existence, were in the Soviet Union. In particular, they included the communications of Soviet missile and nuclear research, development, test, and evaluation sites, defense-related ministries, and defense industries. At the height of the VORTEX operations, there were at least three operating VORTEX satellites: one covering eastern Europe and the western USSR, another covering the central USSR, and the third covering the eastern portion of the USSR.[35]

Each also covered non-Soviet targets in its footprint, including Israel, Iran, and other Middle Eastern countries. Thus, the VORTEX ground station at Menwith Hill in the United Kingdom was heavily involved in supporting Operations DESERT SHIELD and DESERT STORM. In 1989 it received a Joint Meritorious Unit Award from Secretary of Defense Dick Cheney for "meritorious achievement from May 1987 to 1 September 1988," a period that matches U.S. naval operations in the Persian Gulf.[36]

On January 25, 1985, the first satellite developed under the MAGNUM program was launched from the space shuttle Discovery into a geosynchronous orbit. By the time of launch the program had been designated ORION. The second ORION spacecraft was placed into orbit on November 22, 1989, also from a space shuttle orbiter. The satellites were reported to weigh about 6,000 pounds and to have two huge parabolic antennas. One was intended to intercept communications and telemetry signals, the other to relay the intercepted material to Earth. The first ORION may have been stationed over Borneo, the second over the Horn of Africa.[37]

Another six to seven ORIONs have been orbited, from ORION 3 on May 14, 1995, to what was possibly ORION 9 on April 10, 2014, employing expendable launch vehicles. The ORION network has become the primary geosynchronous SIGINT constellation, although apparently two of the MERCURY follow-on systems were orbited in August 1994 and April 1996.[38]

Unlike the low-orbit and geosynchronous satellites, a third class of SIGINT satellites do not operate in geosynchronous orbit. The first generation of this class, code-named JUMPSEAT, was launched into a 63-degree, highly elliptical orbit (200 × 24,000 miles) from Vandenberg AFB. Apparently seven JUMPSEATs were launched, with the initial launch on March 20, 1971, and the final launch in 1987. The program's initial purpose was to monitor signals from the Soviet ABM test site at Sary Shagan as well as geolocation of radar systems. Subsequently, a COMINT mission was added, with targets in the northern Soviet Union. In its highly elliptical orbit, JUMPSEAT "hovered" over the Soviet Union for eight to nine hours at a time. When paired with 989 ferret satellites, the combination was first designated YIELD and then, from 1982, WILLOW.[39]

A more advanced version of JUMPSEAT, code-named TRUMPET, was launched on May 3, 1994. Another two launches followed on July 10, 1995, and November 8, 1997. The satellites weigh about 10,000 pounds. Like JUMPSEAT, TRUMPET operated in a highly inclined, elliptical orbit, but it had a more extensive mission. The program was eventually cancelled in favor of a less expensive alternative. That alternative program has involved at least three launches—one on June 27, 2006, when a Delta rocket launched from Vandenberg AFB in California placed the satellite at a 62.4-degree inclination in an orbit of 690 × 23,785 miles. It also carried an experimental sensor to be used in the Space-Based Infrared System (SBIRS). Subsequent launches also carrying SBIRS payloads took place on March 13, 2008, and December 12, 2014, both from Vandenberg AFB.[40]

SIGINT satellite operations are supported by several specialized ground stations located at Buckley AFB, Colorado; Menwith Hill, United Kingdom; and Pine Gap, Australia. The Buckley site serves as a ground station for perhaps four satellite programs: ORION, TRUMPET and its successor, INTRUDER, and possibly another (geosynchronous system). Although Buckley has been one of three ground stations associated with the ORION program, it is apparently the sole ground station for TRUMPET and its successor, whose orbit permits it to operate in view of the Buckley station when it is over the Northern Hemisphere. It is the most important of the two ground stations associated with another geosynchronous system, whose unclassified designation is RAMROD, "providing 75% of all information reported by the RAMROD system worldwide."[*41]

From 1972 to 1974, NSA began augmenting its listening post at Menwith Hill located eight miles west of Harrogate in Yorkshire. The station encompasses 562 acres and consists of a large array of satellite-tracking aerials. One objective was to make Menwith Hill the primary ground station for the forthcoming CHALET system. In addition, Menwith Hill serves as the ground station for the successor program to MERCURY.[42]

The Joint Defence Facility, Pine Gap, Australia, established to serve as the ground control station and downlink for the RHYOLITE satellite located over Borneo, was subsequently assigned the same mission for the ORION satellite over Borneo. It may have assumed a similar mission for one of the satellites associated with the RAMROD system. The facility consists of at least seven large radomes, a huge computer room, and about twenty other support buildings. The radomes (the first of which were built in 1968), which resemble gigantic golf balls with a slice off the bottom, are made of Perspex and mounted on a concrete structure. They were intended to protect the enclosed antennas against dust, wind, and rain and to hide some of their operational elements from Soviet reconnaissance satellites.[43]

The computer room is divided into three principal sections. The Station-Keeping Section is responsible for maintaining the satellites in geosynchronous orbit and for correctly aligning them toward targets of interest. The Signal Processing Office receives the signals transmitted from the satellite and coverts them into a form that the analysts in the Signals Analysis Section can use. In 1996 the U.S. and Australian governments announced plans to upgrade Pine Gap.[44]

Day-to-day tasking of the satellites is the responsibility of the Overhead Collection Management Center (OCMC), an NSA element at Fort Meade. The SIGINT Overhead Management System is a hardware and software tool that "provides the OCMC the capability to allocate SIGINT satellites against intelligence targets in

---

*SIGINT satellites are given unclassified designations (whose meaning is classified), all of which begin with an *R*. These unclassified designations have included REPTILE (POPPY), RAINFALL (RHYOLITE), RUNWAY (VORTEX/MERCURY), ROSTER (ORION), RUFFER, RANGER (INTRUDER), and RUTLEY (MERCURY follow-on). The designations allow reference to the satellites in unclassified publications or settings.

PHOTO 8.1   Inside the radomes at Buckley AFB, Colorado. *Photo credit:* USAF.

PHOTO 8.2   Joint Defence Space Facility, Pine Gap, Australia, the ground control station for RHYOLITE, ORION, and advanced ORION satellites. *Photo credit:* Desmond Ball.

accordance with priorities and guidance established by the [National SIGINT Collection Subcommittee]."[45]

AIRBORNE COLLECTION

Each of the three largest military services operates aircraft for the collection of signals intelligence. The 55th Wing of the 25th Air Force, headquartered at Offutt AFB, Nebraska, is responsible for the operations of the RC-135 fleet, which stands at twenty-one aircraft, seventeen of which are RC-135V/W Rivet Joint planes. These models have an overall length of 135 feet, a wingspan of 131 feet, and an overall height of 42 feet. At an operational altitude of 34,990 feet, they can fly at over 500 miles per hour. Their unrefueled range is 3,900 miles, but they can be refueled in the air, which they require after ten hours, and they can stay aloft for thirty hours. The plane's operational ceiling is 50,000 feet. It seats more than thirty individuals, including the cockpit crew, electronic warfare officers, intelligence operators, and in-flight maintenance technicians.[46]

The Rivet Joint aircraft fly missions, which have been designated BURNING WIND and MISTY WIND, and intercept both communications and electronic signals. One system carried by the plane is the Automatic Electronic Emitter Location System, which scans each side of the aircraft to identify a radar within seconds, although not with sufficient precision to permit targeting of smart weapons. The data can then be transmitted via a secure voice link—the Tactical Information Broadcast Service or the Tactical Digital Information Link. The Multiple Communications Emitter Location System carried on earlier versions has been replaced by plain blade antennas. The Rivet Joint aircraft operate from Offutt AFB, Souda Bay, Crete; Kadena Air Base, Okinawa, Japan; Prince Sultan Air Base, Al Kharj, Saudi Arabia (763rd Expeditionary Reconnaissance Squadron [ERS]), and Al Udeid Air Base, west of Doha, Qatar.[47]

With the end of the Cold War, the targets of the Rivet Joint fleet changed considerably. During 1995 and 1996, 79 percent of those missions were conducted in support of joint task force operations in the Middle East (Iraq) and Bosnia. On February 22, 1995, a Rivet Joint aircraft flew the program's thousandth mission in support of Operation SOUTHERN WATCH, the enforcement of UN sanctions against Iraq. In October 1996, a Rivet Joint from Mildenhall flew the thousandth Adriatic mission, four years after the beginning of those missions in support of Operation PROVIDE PROMISE. Another 19 percent targeted Cuba, the Mediterranean (particularly Libya), and the Pacific (including North Korea, China, and Vietnam). The remaining 2 percent of the flights involved training and exercises. RC-135s have "become a key tool in the electronic attack of enemy air defenses that rely on rapid exchanges of data about location of attacking enemy aircraft." Since 2000, Rivet Joint aircraft have flown missions in support of Operation IRAQI FREEDOM and Operation ENDURING FREEDOM (Afghanistan). According to a 2009 Air Force fact sheet, "RC-135s have maintained a constant presence in Southwest Asia since the early 1990s." In 2008 the 763rd ERS surpassed the 50,000 flight-hour mark during a mission over Afghanistan. Recent missions have involved Libya and Ukraine. In 2010, Rivet Joint planes flew missions over the Philippines to intercept communications of the Abu Sayyaf terrorist group. In 2011, Rivet Joint RC-135s, flying from Souda Bay, monitored Libyan air force and air defense communications. That year they flew eighty-three sorties in support of Operations ODYSSEY DAWN and UNIFIED PROTECTOR that sought to enforce a no-fly zone over Libya as well the arms embargo. In December 2014, the commander in chief of the Russian air force complained about the "almost daily" RC-135 flights in the Baltic region off the Russian coast, also asserting that there had been 140 RC-135 flights in 2014, compared to 22 in 2013.*48

Some of the those flights might be attributable to the two RC-135Us, which bear the designation Combat Sent; they fly at the same speed and operational altitude as the Rivet Joint planes but have a range of 4,000 nautical miles and a ceiling of over 35,000 feet. A crew consists of two pilots, one navigator, two airborne systems engineers, at least ten electronic warfare officers, and six or more mission area specialists. Like the Rivet Joint aircraft, the Combat Sents carry the Automatic Emitter Locating System. The primary sensor carried on the Combat Sent aircraft is the Precision Power Measurement System, which determines the absolute power, power pattern, and polarization of selected target emitters. In addition, a high-resolution camera and television and radar sensors are equipped with the COMPASS ERA system, which contains infrared thermal imaging, an interferometer-spectrometer, and spectral radiometer sensors. The objective of the Combat Sent missions is the location and identification of foreign military land, naval, and airborne radar signals. Specifically, the missions are intended to provide "signal parametrics used for the development of radar warning receivers, EW [electronic warfare] systems, threat system simulators, [and] mission planning." The signal parametrics include power, pulse, and polarization data. In October 2014, it was reported that the mission markings on an RC-135U indicated that it had been employed to monitor developments in the Ukrainian crisis.49

The final component of the RC-135 fleet is the RC-135S model, designated Cobra Ball, whose mission has been designated BURNING STAR. There are three such aircraft. The Cobra Ball aircraft had been based at Eielson AFB, Alaska, until late 1991 and often operated from Shemya, when the Cobra Ball mission was transferred to Offutt AFB.50

Cobra Ball missions, about one hundred per year in the mid-1990s, were directed at obtaining intelligence on the missile tests of Russia, China, India, and Israel. Thus, in January 1994, a Cobra Ball was deployed to the Bay of Bengal from its base on Diego Garcia to monitor an imminent Indian test. Aircraft stationed at Souda Bay can be employed to monitor Israeli and Iranian missile tests. In 1996, Cobra Ball aircraft monitored Chinese tests near Taiwan, Indian tests, and several Russian tests. In May 1997, a Cobra Ball monitored the test of a North Korean antiship missile. In early March 2003, North Korean fighter jets intercepted a Cobra Ball about 150 miles off

---

*The United Kingdom, which has purchased Rivet Joint aircraft, employed one in summer 2014 to fly over northern Iraq and monitor communications of the Islamic State in Iraq and Syria. See Hayden Smith and Joe Churcher, "Ministry of Defense Reveals It Has Deployed Spy Plane in Iraq to Boost Humanitarian Efforts as Conflict Intensifies," *Evening Standard*, August 16, 2014, http://www.standard.co.uk/news/world/ministry-of-defence-reveals-it-has -deployed-spy-plane-in-iraq-to-boost-humanitarian-efforts-as-conflict-intensifies-9673185 .html.

the North Korean coast and ordered it to land in North Korea, instructions the U.S. pilots ignored.[51]

Among the systems carried by the RC-135S aircraft is the Advanced Telemetry System (ATS), which automatically searches a portion of the frequency band and makes a digital record of all signals present.* The operator of the ATS system allocates collection resources to reentry vehicle links and records all telemetry detected.[52]

The Navy's counterpart SIGINT fleet is made up of EP-3E Airborne Reconnaissance Integrated Electronic System (ARIES) II aircraft. In 1999 the fleet of twelve was evenly divided between Fleet Air Reconnaissance Squadron One (VQ-1), the "World Watchers," located at Naval Air Station (NAS) Whidbey Island, Washington, and Fleet Air Reconnaissance Squadron Two (VQ-2), located at Rota, Spain. VQ-1's area of responsibility stretched from the west coast of the United States to the east coast of Africa and the Arabian Gulf. Its detachments were located at Bahrain, United Arab Emirates; Misawa, Japan; Kadena, Japan; and Osan, South Korea.[53]

In September 2005, VQ-2, its aircraft, and its 450 personnel were relocated from Rota, Spain, to NAS Whidbey Island, so that both were headquartered there. The move, the Navy stated, was "in keeping with the Navy's ongoing transformation of forces in Europe" and would give the squadrons the ability to "surge worldwide." Then, in May 2012, the Navy disestablished VQ-2 and transferred its personnel to VQ-1. As of 2012, the squadron's fleet comprised sixteen planes, although there were plans to reduce that number to twelve.[54]

The EP-3Es are 116-foot-long, four-engine turboprops that fly at altitudes just over 28,000 feet, at 466 miles per hour, for up to twelve hours, with a range of 2,738 miles. The plane is distinguished from the PC-3C by a flat circular radome under the fuselage, and it lacks the long, thin Magnetic Anomaly Detector boom at the tail. The planes are manned by a five-man flight crew, with another eighteen individuals working on various system operations. The plane's Story Book system is an integrated COMINT signal acquisition, data processing, and data fusion capability reported to provide tactical assessment and real-time transmission capability. Six operators operate the Story Classic system, which provides an upgraded search and acquisition capability for low-band signals. The Senior, Communication, and Tactical Evaluators have access at their workstations to data collected by the EP-3E as well as other U.S. intelligence assets (the latter through the Tactical Related Applications system, Tactical Digital Information Exchange System, Tactical Information Broadcast System, and other links), which allows them to integrate the data collected by the plane and other data to provide a comprehensive assessment of their target's activity and to disseminate their conclusions.[55]

VQ operations have included foreign surface and submarine activity as well as land-based radars and UHF/VHF communications. In 1996, VQ-1 flew 1,319 sorties, "both nationally and fleet-tasked SRO [Sensitive Reconnaissance Operations] and I&W missions, in support of DESERT STRIKE, SOUTHERN WATCH, VIGILANT WARRIOR, and VIGILANT SENTINEL." Its operating areas included the "Northern Arabian Sea, Gulf of Oman, Arabian Gulf, Overland Saudi Arabia, Sea

---

*The measurement and signature intelligence sensors on Cobra Ball are discussed in Chapter 9.

PHOTO 8.3   The COMBAT SENT version of the RC-135 collects the emanations of foreign radars. *Photo credit:* USAF.

PHOTO 8.4   RC-135V/W Rivet Joint aircraft. *Photo credit:* USAF.

of Japan, Sea of Okhotsk, Indian Ocean, South China Sea, East China Sea, Luzon Strait, Gulf of Thailand, Overland Korea, and the Western Pacific." As a result of the operations in those areas, VQ-1 "intercepted and processed 2,911 signals of tactical significance from target-country naval, airborne, and land-based emitters" and located seventy-two nonfriendly submarines. In 1997, VQ-2 EP-3Es from the squadron flew missions to monitor the crisis in Albania. Other missions at the time might have involved eavesdropping on military, government, and police communications in North Africa, primarily Algeria and Libya.[56]

In 2001, VQ-1 operated five EP-3Es (and three P-3s), whose area of operations included the Persian Gulf, South America, the Indian Ocean, Korea, Thailand, Afghanistan, Pakistan, the East China Sea, the Gulf of Thailand, Saudi Arabia, the South China Sea, and the Western Pacific. On April 1, 2001, an EP-3E, while conducting operations over international waters off the coast of Hainan Island, was disabled in a midair collision with a shadowing Chinese F-8 interceptor and forced to land on Hainan Island.[57]

Not long after the terrorist attacks of September 11, VQ-1 began operations in Southwest Asia in support of Operation ENDURING FREEDOM. It also conducted intercept operations in support of Operation SOUTHERN WATCH and Plan Colombia. According to its annual history, VQ-1 collected 6,113 signals of tactical significance in 2001. In 2005, VQ-1 detachments included those located at Manama, Bahrain, and Kadena Air Base, Japan. Subsequently, the Bahrain detachment was relocated to Qatar. In 2008, VQ-1 EP-3s participated in Operations IRAQI FREEDOM, NOMAD SHADOW (the European Command [EUCOM] counterterrorist effort involving Turkey and Iraq), WILLING SPIRIT (the recovery of three Americans held hostage by Colombia's Revolutionary Armed Forces), and INCA GOLD (a Southern Command [SOUTHCOM] counternarcotics operation).[58]

Between 2001 and 2005, the VQ-2 squadron flew missions in support of Operations ENDURING FREEDOM, JOINT FORGE (Yugoslavia), INCA GOLD, JOINT GUARDIAN (Adriatic Sea), NORTHERN WATCH (Iraq), SOUTHERN WATCH (Iraq), IRAQI FREEDOM, MOUNTAIN LION (Afghanistan), MOUNTAIN SWEEP (Afghanistan), DOLPHIN EAGLE (Latin America), CARIBBEAN SHIELD, ATLAS SHIELD (SOUTHCOM), and SECURE TOMORROW (EUCOM), as well as Maritime Intercept Operations and JCS Sensitive Reconnaissance Operations. In addition, VQ-2's 2001 operations in support of SOUTHCOM contributed to the seizure of 54.1 metric tons each of cocaine and marijuana.[59]

Plans to develop a successor to the EP-3E, designated the EP-X, were cancelled. The Navy instead planned to upgrade the EP-3Es to receive, by the end of 2015, with the Spiral 3, a SIGINT package that also provides the ability to disrupt enemy communications networks.[60]

In addition to their imagery capabilities, U-2 aircraft can be equipped with SIGINT sensors, and according to one U-2 expert, "Today, almost every operational U-2 mission carries a SIGINT system as well as an imagery system." In the past U-2 SIGINT systems included Senior Ruby—a near-real-time ELINT collection, processing, and reporting system that provided information (including type and location) on radar emitters within line of sight of the U-2—and Senior Spear, a near-real-time COMINT collection, processing, and reporting system that provided line-of-sight collection capability out to three hundred nautical miles from the aircraft. Current systems include the Remote Avionics System (RAS)–1R and the Advanced Signals Intelligence Payload (ASIP).[61]

The RAS-1R has two subsystems, one for COMINT and one for ELINT (which handles pulse, continuous wave, and special signals). Each subsystem can provide geolocation data. The ASIP has been available for U-2 missions since 2008. Its key attributes include "advanced algorithms for modern signal exploitation, including dense environments; large instantaneous bandwidth and simultaneity of signals; [and] onboard signals processing for more efficient utilization of the data link." In 2010 an overseas U-2 squadron replaced its RAS-1R system with the ASIP system.[62]

U-2 SIGINT missions have been flown from several bases against a variety of targets. From Patrick AFB, Florida, U-2s have flown collection missions against Cuba. The main targets are Cuban army, air force, and navy communications, with the intercepts being transmitted to Key West NAS, Florida. U-2s have flown from RAF Akrotiri (Operating Location OLIVE HARVEST) to intercept signals from Syria, Egypt, and Israel. The data are then uplinked to the Remote Operations Facility, Airborne. From Osan Air Base, South Korea, Senior Spear U-2s fly OLYMPIC GAME missions to intercept Chinese and North Korean communications, with the intercepted communications being downlinked to an Air Force intelligence unit at Osan.[63]

Two further airborne SIGINT systems are operated by the Army: the RC-12 Guardrail and the EO-5C (formerly RC-7B)/Airborne Reconnaissance Low–Multifunction (ARL-M). The RC-12s are two-engine turboprops that can fly as low as 20,000 feet or as high as 32,000 feet, at 130 knots, and operate for up to five hours. The planes have come in a variety of models—the RC-12H, RC-12K, RC-12N, RC-12P, and RC-12Q—and have carried remotely controlled, ground-based intercept and direction-finding systems to exploit HF, VHF, and UHF voice communications. They have also carried GPS receivers, permitting location of data to within sixty feet. An adjunct to the RC-12 is the Remote Relay System (RRS). Intercepted SIGINT data are downlinked to the RRS, where they can automatically be relayed by satellite to any location where the appropriate receiving antennas are set up. RC-12s have been deployed to military intelligence brigades in Korea, Germany, and Fort Bragg, North Carolina.[64]

In 2011 deployment began of upgraded versions of the RC-12, designated the RC-12X, possibly including the Advanced Signals Intelligence Payload. In addition, individual planes will be capable of geolocation of a target, reducing the time between detection and attack. According to a Northrop Grumman description, the RC-12X will be capable of "more modern diverse signals and prosecution of more high-value targets (HVTs) than any currently fielded system." The initial two RC-12Xs were deployed to the Middle East, with another ten to twelve (from the fleet of twenty-seven) to be upgraded between 2011 and 2012. The planes are expected to remain in service through 2025.[65]

The EO-5C/ARL-M, a four-engine turboprop, flies at altitudes between 6,000 and 20,000 feet at 220 knots and has a ten-hour endurance. The ARL-M is a modification of the Airborne Reconnaissance Low aircraft that were dedicated to either imagery or SIGINT missions exclusively. It carries HF, VHF, and UHF receivers and is capable of "interception and localization of radio frequency communications." It was originally designed to satisfy SOUTHCOM intelligence requirements, and its mission was to "provide low profile signals intelligence and imagery collection support for counter-narcotics." Of the Army's nine evolved ARL-Ms, three (or more) are assigned to Korea. In addition to SIGINT equipment, they carry a variety of imagery sensors (synthetic aperture radar, moving target indicator, infrared, and electro-optical). The planes' mission includes watching military and civilian movements near the Demilitarized Zone (DMZ) on the Korean Peninsula. An EO-5C was also spotted over Libya in late 2014, apparently monitoring developments at ISIS camps.[66]

In addition to the aerial SIGINT missions flown by NSA and the service cryptologic elements, other missions have been flown for more than two decades by the Army's Mission Support Activity (originally, the Intelligence Support Activity [ISA]). In the 1980s, Beechcraft and King Air aircraft were procured for ISA and equipped with a variety of communications intercept equipment, which was used to intercept communications involving the Sandinistas in Nicaragua as well as leftist Salvadoran and Honduran rebels. In the early 1990s, ISA airborne SIGINT missions helped in tracking Colombian drug lord Pablo Escobar, and in late 2001 they intercepted the communications of fleeing Taliban and al-Qaeda leaders.[67]

Unmanned aerial vehicles (UAVs) are also being employed for signals intelligence as well as imagery and measurement and signature intelligence. Along with imagery sensors, Global Hawk vehicles carry the Advanced Signals Intelligence Payload, which can collect communications and electronic signals as well as "special signals" and be employed for direction finding and geolocation. Scaled versions of the payload have also been developed for the MQ-1B Predator and MQ-9 Reaper.[68]

When it becomes operational the MQ-4C/Triton is expected to contain a SIGINT capability. The UAV's Electronic Support Measures system is expected to detect, identify, and geolocate radar signals. The Triton has been reported to be a possible successor to the EP-3E as the Navy's primary aerial SIGINT collector.[69]

GROUND-BASED REMOTE COLLECTION

Starting in the late 1940s, the United States began establishing ground stations from which to monitor the Soviet Union and Eastern Europe. The network changed composition over the years and grew to include stations targeting China, Vietnam, North Korea, the Middle East, Central America, and other areas. As the Cold War ended and the Soviet Union collapsed, and communications technologies changed, dramatic cutbacks were made in the overseas network operated by NSA and the service cryptological elements, particularly in Europe. As a result, major U.S. SIGINT facilities in Italy, Germany, the United Kingdom, and Turkey were closed or turned over to local governments.[70]

At the same time, NSA established three regional SIGINT operations centers, manned by personnel from each of the three major service cryptological elements and sometimes the Marine Corps Support Battalion, to receive data from manned and unmanned SIGINT sites in particular regions. The three regional centers are located in Texas, Hawaii, and Georgia. NSA/CSS Texas, located at Medina Annex, Lackland, Texas, focuses on Central and South America as well as the Caribbean. The units present at NSA/CSS Texas come from the Army Intelligence and Security Command (INSCOM), the 25th Air Force, the Navy, and Marine Corps Support Battalion, Company H. The unit is expected to add 1,000 personnel by 2016. NSA/CSS Hawaii, at Kunai, Hawaii, focuses on Asia and is also staffed by representatives from the Army,

Navy, and Air Force. The third regional SIGINT center, NSA/CSS Georgia at Fort Gordon, Georgia, focuses on Europe and the Middle East. In addition to representatives from the major services, it also relies on personnel from Marine Corps Support Battalion, Company D.[71]

Among the remaining stations in the SIGINT ground station network are those in Alaska, Japan, the United Kingdom, Germany, Thailand, and Korea. Shemya Island (also home of COBRA DANE radar), approximately four hundred miles across the Bering Sea from the Russian eastern seaboard, was for many years—and may still be—the home of the Anders Facility. Run by the Bendix Field Engineering Corporation (which became Allied Signal in 1992) for the NSA, the facility's Pusher antenna monitored Russian communications in the Far East.[72]

Joint Base Elmendorf-Richardson (JBER), located in Anchorage, is home to the sole remaining U.S.-operated AN/FLR-9 "Elephant Cage" antenna. The antenna consists of three circular arrays, each made up of antenna elements around a circular reflecting screen. In the middle of the triple array is a central building containing the electronic equipment used to form directional beams for monitoring and direction finding. The entire system is about nine hundred feet in diameter. The Air Force contingent has monitored Far Eastern military activity through voice, Morse, and printer intercepts and probably continues to do so.[73]

Three stations in Asia are unmanned—at Khon Kean, Thailand (code-named INDRA), Taegu, South Korea, and Taiwan—with the intercepted data being transmitted to NSA/CSS Hawaii. The Khon Kean facility was apparently set up in the fall of 1979 to correct a shortfall in intelligence during the China-Vietnam war earlier that year. The Taegu facility is equipped with a Pusher HF antenna and targeted against communications in China, North Korea, and Vietnam.[74]

Located at Pyong-Taek, South Korea, is the 719th Military Intelligence Battalion, a component of the 501st Military Intelligence Group. It has operated three detachments: Detachment J at Koryo-San Mountain on the island of Kangwna, Detachment K at Kain-San Mountain, six miles from the DMZ, and Detachment L on Yawol-San Mountain, within 1,500 meters of the DMZ. Collectively, the installations have a variety of North Korean COMINT and ELINT targets.[75]

Latin America, particularly Central America, became a target of increased importance during the Reagan administration. Although Central America is no longer a priority, Cuba is still a significant target. SIGINT sites in Florida used to include a Naval Security Group Activity at Homestead AFB, which monitored Cuban HF military communications. Although Homestead has closed, the antennas operated by the 749th Military Intelligence Company and the Navy SIGINT unit at Pensacola, Florida, still target Cuba and the Caribbean.[76]

There is also a collection of ground stations, operated by the United States and its UKUSA allies (see Chapter 13), dedicated to the interception of INTELSAT and other civilian communications satellites. The stations are part of the ECHELON program, a term that refers to the presence of computer software that allows the sorting of intercepts (particularly printed material such as faxes) by keyword. The software, or "dictionaries," allow intercepted traffic (particularly printed faxes) to be examined for keywords designated by the appropriate intelligence analysts in any UKUSA nation and the traffic containing them to be forwarded automatically to those analysts.[77]

This network has included stations at Sabana Seca, Puerto Rico (CORALINE); Alice Springs, Australia; Sugar Grove, Virginia (TIMBERLINE); and Yakima, Washington (JACKKNIFE), with all but the Alice Springs site seemingly having been closed down. A foreign satellite site is located in Thailand (LEMONWOOD). A latter addition to the ECHELON network is the satellite intercept equipment as Misawa Air Base. Previously, Misawa was the site of Project LADYLOVE, which involved the interception of communications transmitted via several Russian satellite systems, including the Molniya, Raduga, and Gorizont. By the mid-1990s, NSA was considering converting Misawa into an ECHELON site, which it did subsequently. In 2007, a new capability, code-named BOTANICREALITY, was installed at Misawa to intercept video signals from target satellites. During the final years of the Cold War, intercept equipment at Menwith Hill intercepted a variety of Russian satellite communications under Project MOONPENNY. Whether the satellite communications intercept equipment there is still targeting Russian satellites or has been retasked to focus on civilian communications satellites is not clear.[78]

Various naval units operated land-based SIGINT sensors that conducted HF direction-finding (HF/DF) monitoring of naval activity in pursuit of ocean surveillance and search-and-rescue operations. The stations generally used the AN/FRD-10 antenna array, with a nominal range of 3,000 nautical miles. Originally known as CLASSIC BULLSEYE, the system underwent a multiyear modernization program in the early 1990s, designated CLASSIC CENTERBOARD. The modification resulted in the renaming of the network as CROSSHAIR as well as the reduction of net control stations from three (Atlantic, Pacific, and Naval Forces Europe) to one, located at Northwest, Virginia.[79]

While the FRD/10 network has closed down, various collection sites apparently feed into the CROSSHAIR network, including mobile HF/DF systems in Turkey and Kuwait. In addition, HF intercept systems at Bad Aibling, Germany; Cyprus; Taiwan; and Taegu, South Korea, also feed into CROSSHAIR.[80]

EMBASSY AND CONSULAR INTERCEPT SITES

In addition to the ground-based listening posts such as those described above, which generally use large tracts of land, posts operated by the Special Collection Service (SCS) are located within and on top of U.S. embassies and consulates. Such listening posts allow the United States to target the internal military, political, police, and economic communications of the nation in which the embassy or consulate is located. The listening posts are designated Special Collection Elements.[81]

The embassy listening post in Moscow is the best known. In the late 1960s and early 1970s, this post intercepted the radio-telephone conversations of Soviet Politburo members, including General Secretary Leonid Brezhnev, President Nikolai Podgorny, and Premier Alexei Kosygin, as they drove around Moscow. Traffic from the interception operation was transmitted to a special CIA facility a few miles from the agency's Langley, Virginia, headquarters.[82]

Originally, the conversations simply needed to be translated, since no attempt had been made to scramble or encipher them. After a 1971 disclosure in the press concerning the operation, code-named BROADSIDE, the Soviets began encrypting their limousine telephone calls. Despite that effort, the United States managed to intercept and decode a conversation between General Secretary Brezhnev and Minister of Defense A. A. Grechko that took place shortly before the signing of the 1972 Strategic Arms Limitation Treaty (SALT I). Grechko assured Brezhnev that the heavy SS-19 missiles under construction would fit inside the launch tubes of lighter SS-11 missiles, making them permissible under the treaty.[83]

In general, however, the intelligence obtained, code-named GAMMA GUPY, was less than earthshaking. According to a former intelligence official involved in the operation, the CIA "didn't find out about, say, the invasion of Czechoslovakia. It was very gossipy—Brezhnev's health and maybe Podgorny's sex life." At the same time, the official said that the operation "gave us extremely valuable information on the personalities of top Soviet leaders."[84]

Undoubtedly, during the abortive coup of August 1991, the listening post was part of the effort to eavesdrop on the communications of those attempting to replace Gorbachev's government and those resisting the coup. Among the communications monitored by the United States were those from the Chairman of the KGB and the Minister of Defense, both coup plotters.[85]

Other covert listening posts are or have been located in the U.S. embassies in Beijing, Tel Aviv, Buenos Aires, Santiago, Tegucigalpa, Brasilia, and Karachi. The Tel Aviv outpost has been targeted on Israeli military and national police communications. Thus, the United States has closely followed police activities directed at the Palestinians. The presence of a U.S. eavesdropping site has not gone unnoticed by Israeli officials, as a large number of antennas are visible on the roof of the Tel Aviv embassy.[86]

In Tegucigalpa, the SCS monitored the communications of the police and military as well as some of the forces fighting the government. The Buenos Aires post was used to target the communications of the Argentine General Staff during the 1982 Falklands crisis; any information gleaned was quickly passed on to the British. The eavesdropping operation in the Karachi consulate yielded intelligence on drug trafficking, terrorist networks, and the Pakistani nuclear program. In 1996 an SCS unit in Nairobi began intercepting telephone and fax messages entering and leaving five telephone numbers in the city believed to belong to members of al-Qaeda.[87]

Today, two SCS sites, at Brasilia and New Delhi, are apparently being employed to target foreign satellites. SCS sites have also been instrumental in targeting the communications of foreign leaders, including German chancellor Angela Merkel and senior officials in the Italian government. The sites can intercept, in addition to foreign satellite signals, cellular signals, microwave and millimeter wave signals, and wireless networks.[88] Table 8.1 lists manned and unmanned SCS sites.

CLANDESTINE SIGINT

Clandestine SIGINT refers to the emplacement of listening devices and computer implants that serve as another means of gathering communications or transmitting data stored on computer networks. It also refers to the emplacement of sensors to intercept electronic signals, whether of communications or noncommunications.

The oldest of these devices are the traditional audio surveillance devices that might be placed in a phone, apartment, or office. In a 1961 memo, the President's Foreign Intelligence Advisory Board reported, "Audio surveillance techniques have potentialities

TABLE 8.1   Unmanned and Manned SCS Locations

Unmanned remote sites

Amarah, Iraq	Kabul Annex	Milan, Italy
Athens Annex, Greece	Kirkuk, Iraq	Moscow Annex, Russia
Basrah, Iraq	Lagos, Nigeria	Vienna Annex, Austria
Chiang Mai, Thailand	Monterrey, Mexico	
Hermasillo, Mexico	Merida, Venezuela	

Manned locations

Guatemala City, Guatemala	Tbilisi, Georgia	Riyadh, Saudi Arabia
Havana, Cuba	Vienna, Austria	Sana'a, Yemen
Managua, Nicaragua	Zagreb, Croatia	Sulaymariyah, Iraq
Mexico City, Mexico	Abu Dhabi, United Arab	Tehran in Exile
Panama City, Panama	Emirates	Tallil, Iraq
San José, Costa Rica	Algiers, Algeria	Islamabad, Pakistan
Tegucigalpa, Honduras	Amman, Jordan	Herat, Afghanistan
Brasilia, Brazil	Ankara, Turkey	Kabul, Afghanistan
Bogotá, Colombia	Baghdad, Iraq	Karachi, Pakistan
Caracas, Venezuela	Baghdad Annex, Iraq	Lahore, Pakistan
Quito, Ecuador	Beirut, Lebanon	New Delhi, India
Athens, Greece	Cairo, Egypt	Peshawar, Pakistan
Berlin, Germany	Damascus, Syria	Bangkok, Thailand
Budapest, Hungary	Istanbul, Turkey	Beijing, China
Frankfurt, Germany	Jeddah, Saudi Arabia	Chengdu, China
Geneva, Switzerland	Abuja, Nigeria	Hong Kong, China
Kiev, Ukraine	Addis Ababa, Ethiopia	Jakarta, Indonesia
Madrid, Spain	Lagos, Nigeria	Kuala Lumpur,
Moscow, Russia	Kinshasa, Democratic	Manila, Philippines
Paris, France	Republic of the Congo	Phnom Penh, Cambodia
Prague, Czech Republic	Lusaka, Zambia	Rangoon, Burma
Pristina, Kosovo	Khartoum, Sudan	Shanghai, China
Rome, Italy	Kuwait City, Kuwait	Taipei, Taiwan
Sarajevo, Bosnia and	Manama, Bahrain	
Herzegovina	Mosul, Iraq	

for providing a means of acquiring reliable, hard intelligence not otherwise obtained by our Government."[89]

Two prominent and older forms of audio surveillance technical collection are bugs and telephone taps. A bug, or audio device, that will transmit all conversations in a room to a monitoring site is planted by experts from of the Office of Technical Service of the Directorate of Science and Technology and officers from the Directorate of Operations. Planting such a device is a complex operation. According to an article in *Studies in Intelligence*, "The setting up of an audio installation must be the execution of a 'perfect crime.' It must be perfect not only in that you don't get caught, but also in that you give no inkling, from the interception of an operation until its termination sometimes five years later, that such an operation was even contemplated; any show of interest in your target would alert the opposition to lay on countermeasures."[90]

The operation involves surveillance of the site, acquisition of building and floor plans, and determination of the color of the interior furnishings and the texture of the walls. Activity in the room, as well as the movements of security patrols, is noted. When the information is acquired and processed, it is employed to determine the time of surreptitious entry and the materials needed to install the device in such a way as to minimize the probability of discovery.[91]

During the early 1970s, one target of CIA audio devices was South Vietnamese president Nguyen Van Thieu. Presents given to Thieu by the CIA—television sets and furniture—came equipped with audio devices, allowing the agency to monitor his personal conversations. The CIA also attempted to install devices in the office and living quarters of the South Vietnamese observer to the Paris Peace Talks. Another Asian ally that has been subjected to CIA and NSA technical penetration is South Korea. A substantial part of the evidence against Tongsun Park concerning his alleged attempts to bribe U.S. congressmen came from recordings of incriminating conversations inside the South Korean presidential mansion.[92]

During E. Howard Hunt's tenure in Mexico City, the CIA bugged or tapped several Iron Curtain embassies. During his tenure in Uruguay, the CIA station conducted technical penetrations of embassies and the living quarters of key personnel. During Philip Agee's time in Uruguay, seven telephone lines were monitored. Included were phones of the Soviet and Cuban embassies, consulates, and commercial offices.[93]

In 1982 or 1983, a unit of INSCOM—then known as the Quick Reaction Team (QRT) and subsequently as the Technical Analysis Unit—placed an electronic listening device in a Panamanian apartment belong to General Manuel Antonio Noriega. Paying bribes to the maids who cleaned the apartment and to the guards who protected it, a QRT member was able to place a listening device in Noriega's conference room. The six ninety-minute tapes that resulted did not produce any substantial intelligence information. QRT members also bugged the apartment of a Cuban diplomat in Panama. When the diplomat was away, agents slipped into his apartment and wired it with microtransmitters; again, the take was of little value.[94]

In 1983 the QRT targeted Soviet representatives on several occasions during their visit to the United States. Soviet officials who traveled to Lawrence Livermore National Laboratory had their rooms bugged by QRT agents. The bugging was repeated when the Soviets moved on to Denver. This time the results were more useful; sensitive discussions were recorded, yielding leads on possible Soviet agents in the United States.[95]

The CIA may have bugged the rooms of Iraqi and Iranian delegates to a November 1996 OPEC meeting in Vienna. Decorators found bugging devices in the walls of the hotel during a subsequent renovation. It was reported that the German Federal Intelligence Service, or Bundesnachrichtendienst, told its Austrian counterpart that the CIA had eavesdropped on the delegates. In 1997 a member of the U.S. embassy in Austria, presumably a CIA officer, left that country after being arrested for wiretapping the phone of a North Korean diplomat in Vienna.[96]

In early 2002, it was revealed that a joint FBI-NSA operation had attempted to place listening devices aboard a Boeing 767 300 ER aircraft that had been purchased for China's president and refitted at San Antonio International Airport. In October 2001, shortly before its initial voyage, Chinese military communication experts discovered at least twenty-seven listening devices aboard the plane.[97]

The collection activities of the NSA and the United Kingdom's Government Communications Headquarters (GCHQ) have included efforts to infect computers with malware for one of three purposes: computer network attack, computer network exploitation, and computer network defense. The operation's infrastructure includes NSA headquarters in Fort Meade, Maryland, and SIGINT bases in the United Kingdom (Menwith Hill Station) and Japan (Misawa Air Base). In addition, NSA, through its Tailored Access Operations unit, has been revealed to have intercepted computer servers during their shipment process in order to implant devices that would transmit data to NSA.[98]

The effort has involved development of a variety of malware tools. UNITEDRAKE can be employed with a variety of "plug-ins" that allow NSA to gain complete control of an infected computer. One of these plug-ins, CAPTIVATED AUDIENCE, can take over a computer's microphone and record conversations taking place near the device; another, GUMFISH, can secretly assume control of a computer's webcam and take photographs. A third, FOGGYBOTTOM, records Internet browsing history logs and gathers login details and passwords employed to access websites and e-mail accounts. Yet another, SAVAGERABBIT, exfiltrates data onto removable flash drives connected to an infected computer. HAMMERCHANT and HAMMERSTEIN, which NSA injects into network routes, enable the agency to intercept and conduct exploitation attacks against data that flows through a virtual private network, which employs encrypted "tunnels" to augment the security and privacy of an Internet session.[99]

There is also a class of techniques, code-named QUANTUM, for exploiting, attacking, or defending computers. Computer network exploitation methods include, QUANTUMINSERT, a "man-on-the-side technique" that briefly hijacks connections to a terrorist website and redirects the target to a server (designated FOXACID) operated by the agency's Tailored Access Operations unit. QUANTUMSKY, a computer network attack method instituted in 2004, can deny access to a webpage.[100]

Part of the effort involves capabilities code-named TURMOIL and TURBINE. The first refers to a set of sensors, including those at Misawa and Menwith Hill, that automatically identify data exfiltrated from infected computer systems and transmit it to NSA for analysis. In addition, the sensors can send alerts to NSA so that attacks can be initiated. Those alerts are received by TURBINE, an automated system designed to "allow the current implant network to scale to large size (millions of implants) by creating a system that does automated control implants by groups instead of individually."[101]

Table 8.2 illustrates the variety of diplomatic targets and ClanSIG techniques employed to gather data. It shows that a large number of embassies and UN missions are among the targets and that the collection techniques include use of computer implants (code-named HIGHLANDS), collection from computer screens (VAGRANT), imaging of the hard drive (LIFESAVER), and passive collection of emanations using an antenna (DROPMIRE).

TABLE 8.2   Clandestine SIGINT Against Diplomatic Targets

Suffix		Target/Country	Location	Coverterm	Mission
BE		Brazil/Emb	Washington, D.C.	KATEEL	LIFESAVER
SI		Brazil/Emb	Washington, D.C.	KATEEL	HIGHLANDS
HN		Brazil/UN	New York	POCOMOKE	VAGRANT
LJ		Brazil/UN	New York	POCOMOKE	LIFESAVER
YL	*	Bulgaria/Emb	Washington, D.C.	MERCED	HIGHLANDS
QX	*	Colombia/Trade Bureau	New York	BANISTER	LIFESAVER
SS		EU/UN	New York	PERDIDO	LIFESAVER
KD		EU/Emb	Washington, D.C.	MAGOTHY	HIGHLANDS
IO		EU/Emb	Washington, D.C.	MAGOTHY	MINERALIZ
XJ		EU/Emb	Washington, D.C.	MAGOTHY	DROPMIRE
VC		France/UN	New York	BLACKFOOT	VAGRANT
UC		France/Emb	Washington, D.C.	WABASH	HIGHLANDS
LO		France/Emb	Washington, D.C.	WABASH	PBX
NK	*	Georgia/Emb	Washington, D.C.	NAVARRO	HIGHLANDS
BY	*	Georgia/Emb	Washington, D.C.	NAVARRO	VAGRANT
HB		Greece/UN	New York	POWELL	LIFESAVER
CD		Greece/Emb	Washington, D.C.	KLONDIKE	HIGHLANDS
JN		Greece/Emb	Washington, D.C.	KLONDIKE	PBX
MO	*	India/UN	New York	NASHUA	HIGHLANDS
QL	*	India/UN	New York	NASHUA	MAGNETIC
ON	*	India/UN	New York	NASHUA	VAGRANT
IS	*	India/UN	New York	NASHUA	LIFESAVER
CQ	*	India/Emb	Washington, D.C.	OSAGE	HIGHLANDS
TQ	*	India/Emb	Washington, D.C.	OSAGE	VAGRANT
CU	*	India/EmbAnx	Washington, D.C.	OSWAYO	VAGRANT
SU	*	Italy/Emb	Washington, D.C.	BRUNEAU	LIFESAVER
IP	*	Japan/UN	New York	MULBERRY	MINERALIZ
BT	*	Japan/UN	New York	MULBERRY	MAGNETIC
RU	*	Japan/UN	New York	MULBERRY	VAGRANT

Suffix	Target/Country	Location	Coverterm	Mission
LM *	Mexico/UN	New York	ALAMITO	LIFESAVER
UX *	Slovakia/Emb	Washington, D.C.	FLEMING	HIGHLANDS
SA *	Slovakia/Emb	Washington, D.C.	FLEMING	VAGRANT
XR *	South Africa/UN & Consulate	New York	DOBIE	HIGHLANDS
YR *	South Korea/UN	New York	SULPHUR	VAGRANT
TZ *	Taiwan/TECO	New York	REQUETTE	VAGRANT
VN *	Venezuela/Emb	Washington, D.C.	YUKON	LIFESAVER
UR *	Venezuela/UN	New York	WESTPORT	LIFESAVER
OU *	Vietnam/UN	New York	NAVAJO	VAGRANT
GV *	Vietnam/Emb	Washington, D.C.	PANTHER	HIGHLANDS

Key:
HIGHLANDS: Collection from Implants
VAGRANT: Collection of Computer Screens
MAGNETIC: Sensor Collection of Magnetic Emanations
MINERALIZE: Collection from LAN Implant
OCEAN: Optical Collection System for Raster-Based Computer Screens
LIFESAVER: Imaging of the Hard Drive
GENIE: Multi-stage operation; jumping the airgap etc.
BLACKHEART: Collection from an FBI implant
PBX: Public Branch Exchange Switch
CRYPTO ENABLED: Collection derived from AO's efforts to enable crypto
DROPMIRE: passive collection of emanations using an antenna
CUSTOMS: Customs opportunities (not LIFESAVER)
DEWSWEEPER: USB (Universal Serial Bus) hardware host tap that provides COVER link over USB link into a target network. Operations w/RF relay subsystem to provide wireless Bridge into target network.
RADON: Bidirectional host tap that can inject Ethernet packets onto the same target. Allows bidirectional exploitation of Denied networks using standard on-net tools.

Source: Adapted from Glenn Greenwald, No Place to Hide: Edward Snowden, the NSA, and the U.S. Surveillance State (New York: Metropolitan Books, 2014), 145–147.

Another form of ClanSIG is the installation of emplaced SIGINT sensors. Unlike a bug in a room, phone, or computer, these systems are hidden near a target facility or in a location where they are well suited to intercept communications or other electronic signals. In 1965 the CIA planted a nuclear-powered device on the summit of Nanda Devi in Garhwal, India, intended to monitor Chinese missile tests from the Shuang-chenzi test center in north-central China. After it was swept away in an avalanche, a second device was placed, in 1967, on the summit of the neighboring 22,400-foot Nanda Kot.[102]

An even more daring operation conducted by the CIA, designated CK/TAW, involved the tapping of underground communications lines that linked the Krasnaya Pakhra Nuclear Weapons Research Institute in Tomsk, producing intelligence on Soviet particle beam and laser weapons research. CK/TAW ceased working around 1985 and may have been betrayed by Edward Lee Howard or Aldrich Ames, or both.[103] In another risky operation, in 1999 a team of CIA officers covertly entered southeastern Afghanistan to install a remote-controlled SIGINT collection system near al-Qaeda camps close to the town of Khost.[104]

RAMPART, MUSCULAR, AND PRISM

Part of NSA's collection effort, with the overall designation RAMPART, has been the tapping of cables, either with the cooperation of the cable owners, clandestinely, or through a Second or Third Party relationship. The RAMPART-A program, according to one account, is an "unconventional special access program leveraging Third Party partnerships"; it involves foreign partners providing access to fiber-optic cables and hosting U.S. equipment at "major congestion points around the world," allowing for the interception of e-mails, phone calls, and Internet chats. The code names and SIGINT addresses of the sites associated with the effort include AZUREPHOENIX (US-3127/VH), MOONLIGHT PATH (US-3145/KX), and FIREBIRD (US-3190/21). One account of the project quoted a 2010 document stating that most of the RAMPART-A efforts were conducted "under the cover of an overt comsat effort" and pointed to both Germany and Denmark as participants. Also associated with RAMPART-A was the WINDSTOP program, which involved provision of cable traffic by Second Parties to the UKUSA Agreement.[105]

An overview of where RAMPART-A fits into "Today's Cable Program" is the subject of a slide in an undated presentation produced by NSA's Special Source Operations unit. It describes "three access portfolios," one being "corporate," that is, access through cooperating telecommunications companies and Internet service providers, whether under court order or not. A second is designated "unilateral" and consists of five components, including MYSTIC, RAMPART-I/X, and RAMPART-T (ClanSIG).[106]

NSA's collection efforts have also involved "breaking into the main communications links that connect Yahoo! and Google data centers around the world." The *Washington Post* reported, based on a January 2013 document, that NSA was acquiring millions of records daily from Yahoo! and Google internal networks and that, in the previous thirty days, fields collectors had processed and relayed 181,280,466 new records, including metadata and content (text, video, and audio).[107]

The *Post* also reported that Google and Yahoo! "maintain fortress-like data centers across four continents and connect them with thousands of miles of fiber-optic cable"; the networks are referred to as clouds "because data moves seamlessly around them." According to one internal NSA document, tapping into the Google and Yahoo! clouds permits NSA to intercept communications in real-time and obtain "a retrospective look at target activity."[108]

The principal tool employed by NSA, in conjunction with the United Kingdom's GCHQ, to gather data from the data links is a project code-named MUSCULAR. According to the *Post*'s account, the GCHQ places all the intake into a "buffer" that can store three to five days of traffic before it is necessary to delete data to provide new storage space. From the buffer, tools constructed by NSA unpack and decode the special data formats that the two companies use inside their clouds. The data is then transmitted through a series of filters to select information desired by NSA and exclude the rest.[109]

Aside from breaking into Google and Yahoo! data centers, the NSA, under a program designated PRISM, obtains the traffic of at least nine Internet companies: Microsoft, Yahoo!, Google, Facebook, Paltalk, AOL, Skype, YouTube, and Apple. In general, material obtained from the servers includes e-mail, chat (video, voice), videos, photos, stored data, Voice over Internet Protocol, file transfers, video conferencing, notifications of target activity (including logins), and online social networking details.[110]

A variety of other PRISM documents described the program's growing access and offered measures of its value. Memos from 2013 indicated that Microsoft's Skydrive cloud service had become part of standard PRISM stored communications collection, as had Skype. Another described PRISM as "the most cited collection source in NSA 1st Party end-product reporting," that is, the reporting relying on U.S. interception activities. The same document noted that 1,477 product reports derived from the PRISM collection were cited as sources for articles that appeared in the *President's Daily Brief* (*PDB*)—and that number represented 18 percent of all SIGINT reports cited as sources in *PDB* articles, making PRISM the highest single NSA source.[111]

SURFACE SHIPS

The United States has employed surface ships for the collection of signals intelligence against both land- and sea-based targets. In the 1950s, destroyers and destroyer escorts were employed in intercept operations against land-based targets. In 1961 and 1965, respectively, two new types of ships were deployed: Auxiliary General Technical Research (AGTR) and Auxiliary General Environmental Research (AGER) ships. Transfer of the SIGINT mission to those ships was a response to fears among some Navy officials that stationing a destroyer off a foreign shore, especially that of a hostile nation, would be a provocation. However, the bombing of the AGTR USS *Liberty* by Israel during the 1967 Six-Day War and the seizure of the USS *Pueblo* by North Korea in 1969 led to eventual termination of the AGTR and AGER program.[112]

In the 1980s, the United States began employing Spruance-class destroyers and frigates to collect intelligence concerning Nicaragua and El Salvador. The 7,800-ton destroyer *Deyo* and its sister ship *Caron* were stationed in the Gulf of Fonseca. The ships could monitor suspected shipping, intercept communications, and probe the shore surveillance and defense capabilities of other nations. The ships were decommissioned in 2003 and 2001, respectively.[113]

A Ticonderoga-class cutter, the USS *Yorktown*, operated in the Black Sea, outfitted with electronic equipment that could monitor voice communications and radar signals. Such systems were used during a 1986 mission into the Black Sea to determine whether new radars had been deployed onshore and to check the readiness of Soviet forces. In a previous expedition, the *Yorktown*'s equipment was used in part to monitor aircraft movements within the Soviet Union.[114]

During the 1980s, two now retired Navy frigates, the *Blakely* and the *Julius A. Furei*, were used against targets in Nicaragua, El Salvador, and Honduras. The missions involved homing in on and recording voice and signal communications, locating transmitting stations, logging ships' movements, and studying their waterlines to help determine whether they were riding low in the water when entering port and high when exiting, indicating the unloading of cargo.[115]

Frigates were also employed for monitoring telemetry from missile tests. It was reported in 1979 that "American ships equipped with sensitive intelligence gear . . . patrol the North Atlantic, where they collect telemetry broadcast by the new Soviet submarine-launched missiles tested in the White Sea, northeast of Finland." Likewise, on the night of August 31, 1983, when the United States was expecting the Soviet Union to test an SS-X-24 missile, the frigate *Badger* was stationed in the Sea of Okhotsk.[116]

During the 1980s and early 1990s, the intercept equipment operated on Navy cruisers and destroyers was designated CLASSIC OUTBOARD. In the 1990s, the Navy began installing the COMBAT DF system on frigates and the newest cruisers and destroyers. COMBAT DF relies on a gigantic antenna built into the hull of a ship to intercept signals and determine the location of long-range, HF radios.[117]

A currently operational destroyer that carries an electronic warfare suite, the AN/SLQ-32 (V) (2), is the USS *Ross*, which was operating in the Black Sea in September 2014, along with a French signals intelligence ship. Also among the currently operating fleet is the USS *Vella Gulf*, which also carries an AN/SLQ-32 system. A number of Navy ships carry the Ship's Signal Exploitation Equipment system, whose latest version is Increment F. In October 2014, the producer, Boeing, delivered the Navy's order for the equipment, described as "a tactical cryptologic system which performs all signal processing functions necessary to acquire, identify, locate and analyze signals."[118]

UNDERWATER COLLECTION

The use of submarines for intelligence-gathering purposes had its genesis in the later years of the Eisenhower administration. Known by a variety of code names, the best known of which is HOLYSTONE, the program has been one of the most sensitive U.S. intelligence operations. HOLYSTONE began in 1959 and has involved the use of specially equipped electronic submarines to collect electronic communications and photographic intelligence. The primary target through 1991 was the Soviet Union, but at times countries such as Vietnam and China have been targets of operations, which have occasionally involved penetration of Soviet, Chinese, and Vietnamese three-mile territorial limits.[119]

It was reported in 1975 that each mission lasted about ninety days. Missions conducted through 1975 apparently provided vital information on the Soviet submarine fleet, including its configuration, capabilities, noise patterns, missiles, and missile-firing capabilities. One mission involved obtaining the "voice autographs" of Soviet submarines. Using detailed tape recordings of noise made by submarine engines and other equipment, naval intelligence analysts were able to develop a methodology for identifying individual Soviet submarines, even those tracked at long range under the ocean. The analysts could then follow the submarine from its initial operations to its decommissioning.[120]

HOLYSTONE operations also provided information about theater and strategic sea-based missiles. Some Soviet sea-based missiles were tested against inland targets to reduce U.S. monitoring. On occasion, HOLYSTONE submarines would penetrate close enough to Soviet territory to observe the missile launchings, providing information on the early stages of the flight. According to one government official, the most significant information provided by the missions was a readout of the computer calculations and signals put into effect by Soviet technicians before launching the missiles. Beyond that, the U.S. submarines provided intelligence by tracking the flights and eventual landings of the missiles and relaying continuous information on guidance and electronic systems.[121]

The submarines were also able to bring back valuable photographs, many of them taken through the submarine's periscope. In the mid-1960s, photographs were taken of the underside of an E-class submarine, apparently inside Vladivostok's harbor.[122]

More recent operations have employed, at various times, some of the thirty-eight nuclear-powered Sturgeon-class submarines, which have dimensions of 292 × 31.7 × 26 feet. With their 107-person complement (12 officers and 95 enlisted personnel), the ships can travel at speeds of more than thirty knots underwater and can reach a depth of 1,320 feet. Other operations have employed submarines from the more modern Los Angeles–class attack submarines. The subs measure 362 × 33 × 32.3 feet and can travel at thirty-two knots and carry 133 personnel.[123]

The special equipment on the HOLYSTONE missions included the WLR-6 Waterboy Signals Intelligence System. In the 1980s, the WLR-6 was replaced by a more advanced system known as SEA NYMPH, described in one document as an "advanced automatic, modular signals exploitation system designed for continuous acquisition, identification, recording, analysis and exploitation of electromagnetic signals." All the Sturgeon-class submarines carry a basic skeletal system that can be upgraded to full capacity when authorized.[124]

There is evidence that HOLYSTONE operations continued through the early 1990s. In February 1992, the USS *Baton Rouge*, a Los Angeles–class attack submarine, collided with a Russian submarine near the Kola Peninsula. It was reported that the *Baton Rouge* was on an intelligence-gathering mission targeting the Russian port of Murmansk. Another collision occurred on March 20, 1993, when the Sturgeon-class USS *Grayling* bumped into a Russian Delta-III-class ballistic missile submarine in the Barents Sea about one hundred miles north of Murmansk. During a summit with Russian president Boris Yeltsin the following month, President Clinton apologized for the incident. He also ordered a review of the submarine reconnaissance operations.[125]

Although such operations may have been curtailed temporarily with respect to Russia, they apparently did not cease altogether. In early December 1997, a Russian Typhoon submarine launched twenty ballistic missiles as part of the destruction routine under the 1991 Strategic Arms Reduction Treaty (START I). Subsequently, the Russians charged that a submerged Los Angeles–class submarine had monitored the event, although Navy officials indicated it was not an American sub (leaving open the possibility that it was British).[126]

In any case, there are other targets. The still operational Los Angeles–class subs USS *Topeka* and USS *Louisville* arrived in the Persian Gulf in November 1992 and January 1993, respectively. Their mission was to keep watch on Iran's new submarine fleet. When U.S. pilot Scott O'Grady was shot down over Bosnia in 1995, submarines intercepted communications among Bosnian Serbs hoping to capture him. That same year, a submarine assigned to counternarcotics work in the eastern Pacific intercepted transmissions from a suspicious trawler, helping the U.S. Coast Guard seize eleven tons of cocaine. In a more recent development, the USS *Virginia*, the first of a new class of attack submarines measuring 377 feet long, was sent to the Caribbean and South Atlantic in 2005 to intercept communications.[127]

As of 2009, a series of submarine reconnaissance missions, code-named AQUADOR, were conducted against a variety of targets. In some cases, the subs monitored Iranian naval activities in the Gulf of Hormuz, with the objective of protecting international shipping lanes. Other missions focused on monitoring foreign merchant shipping suspected of involvement in the transport of ballistic missile and nuclear weapons missile technology. An earlier mission in this class involved the tracking of North Korean ships that U.S. analysts believed were carrying ballistic missiles and support equipment to Syria and Iran.[128]

Other submarines have been employed as part of the SIGINT collection effort to place taps on undersea cables. In an operation designated IVY BELLS, the Navy placed induction devices on a Soviet military communications cable under the Sea of Okhotsk in the late 1970s and contemplated placing one on a similar cable under the Barents Sea. More recently, a new submarine, the USS *Jimmy Carter*, has been modified for use in operations to tap into fiber-optic cables. It replaces another submarine specially equipped for intelligence collection, the USS *Parche*. The USS *Jimmy Carter* is the third and last of the Seawolf class. This 18,130-ton, 453-foot-long submarine is capable of traveling at more than twenty-five knots per hour when submerged.[129]

Another submarine involved in current SIGINT operations is the USS *Annapolis*, which between March and September 2014 completed "four missions vital to national security" during its passing throught the European and Central Command areas of responsibility. It possesses the RADIANT GEMSTONE stystem, employed for target tracking and indications and warning capability. It has a role in computer network operations.[130]

Notes

1. DOD Instruction O-3115.07, "Signals Intelligence," September 15, 2008, 19.
2. U.S. Congress, House Permanent Select Committee on Intelligence, *Annual Report* (Washington, DC: U.S. Government Printing Office, 1978), 38.

3. John Prados, *The Soviet Estimate: U.S. Intelligence Analysis and Russian Military Strength* (New York: Dial, 1982), 203; Farooq Hussain, *The Future of Arms Control*, pt. 4: *The Impact of Weapons Test Restrictions* (London: International Institute of Strategic Studies, 1980), 44; Robert Kaiser, "Verification of SALT II: Art and Science," *Washington Post*, June 15, 1979, 1.

4. Armando R. Limon, "Misawa to Tear Down Massive 'Elephant Cage' Antennae," *Star and Stripes*, November 19, 2012, http://www.stripes.com/news/pacific/misawa-to-tear-down -massive-elephant-cage-antennae-1.197638; Andrew Tranatola, "This Electronic Stonehenge Once Divined the Secrets of Soviet Radio," *Gizmodo*, October 21, 2014, http://gizmodo.com/this -electronic-stonehenge-once-divined-the-secrets-of-1647210382.

5. Deborah Shapley, "Who's Listening? How NSA Tunes In on America's Overseas Calls and Messages," *Washington Post*, October 7, 1997, C1, C4.

6. Sayre Stevens, "The Soviet BMD Program," in *Ballistic Missile Defense*, ed. Aston B. Carter and David N. Schwartz (Washington, DC: Brookings Institution, 1984), 182–221, at 192; interview with Albert Wheelon, Montecito, CA, June 29, 2011.

7. George J. Church, "Destination Haiti," *Time*, September 26, 1994, 21–26; Spiegel Staff, "Embassy Espionage: The NSA's Secret Spy Hub in Berlin," *Spiegel Online*, October 27, 2013, http://www.spiegel.de/international/germany/cover-story-how-nsa-spied-on-merkel-cell-phone -from-berlin-embassy-a-930205.html; "Iraq War Critic: NSA Targeted Gerhard Schröder's Mobile Phone," *Spiegel Online*, February 5, 2014, http://www.spiegel.de/international/germany/nsa -reportedly-spied-on-former-chancellor-gerhard-schroeder-a-951628.html; Laura Poitras, Marcel Rosenbach, and Holger Stark, "'A' for Angela: GCHQ and NSA Targeted Private German Companies and Merkel," *Spiegel Online*, March 29, 2014, http://www.spiegel.de/international/germany/ gchq-and-nsa-targeted-private-german-companies-a-961444.html; Ewen MacAskill, Nick Davies, Nick Hopkins, Julian Borger, and James Ball, "NSA Targeted Dmitry Medvedev at London G20 Summit," *Guardian*, June 16, 2013, http://www.theguardian.com/world/2013/jun/16/nsa-dmitry -medvedev-g20-summit; Vincent Bevins and Tracy Wilkinson, "New Snowden Documents Allege U.S. Spying on Brazil, Mexico," *Los Angeles Times*, September 2, 2013, A4; James Risen, "Afghan Leader's Brother Is Subject of Wiretapping," *New York Times*, September 28, 2010, A12.

8. Ewen MacAskill and Julian Borger, "New NSA Leaks Show How US Is Bugging Its European Allies," www.theguardian.com, June 30, 2013, http://www.theguardian.com/world/2013/ jun/30/nsa-leaks-us-bugging-european-allies; Laura Poitras, Marcel Rosenbach, Fidelius Schmid, Holger Stark, and Jonathan Stock, "Cover Story: How the NSA Targets Germany and Europe," *Spiegel Online*, July 1, 2013, http://www.spiegel.de/international/world/secret-documents-nsa -targeted-germany-and-eu-buildings-a-908609.html; Glenn Greenwald, *No Place to Hide: Edward Snowden, the NSA, and the U.S. Surveillance State* (New York: Metropolitan Books, 2014), 146–147; Bill Gertz, "U.S. Intercepts from Libya Play Role in Berlin Bomb Trial," *Washington Times*, November 19, 1997, A13; Christopher Andrew, *For the President's Eyes Only: Secret Intelligence and the American Presidency from Washington to Bush* (New York: HarperCollins, 1995), 520; David Johnston, "U.S. Agency Secretly Monitored Chinese in '96 on Political Gifts," *New York Times*, March 13, 1997, A1, A25; Nora Boustany and Brian Duffy, "A Top U.S. Official May Have Given Sensitive Data to Israel," *Washington Post*, May 7, 1997, A1, A28; Russell Watson and John Barry, "Our Target Was Terror," *Newsweek*, August 31, 1998, 24–29; Matthew M. Aid, "The Time of Troubles: The US National Security Agency in the Twentieth-First Century," *Intelligence and National Security* 15, no. 3 (Autumn 2000): 1–32; Matthew M. Aid, "All Glory Is Fleeting: SIGINT and the Fight Against International Terrorism," *Intelligence and National Security* 18, no. 4 (Winter 2003): 72–120.

9. Scott Shane and Ariel Sabar, "Alleged NSA Memo Details U.S. Eavesdropping at U.N.," *Baltimore Sun*, March 24, 2003, http://www.baltimoresun.com/bal-te.md.nsa04mar04-story .html; Associated Press, "German Magazine: NSA Decrypted, Spied On, United Nations' Internal Video Conferencing System," August 25, 2013, http://www.washingtonpost.com.

10. James Risen and David Johnston, "Chalabi Reportedly Told Iran That U.S. Had Code," *New York Times*, June 2, 2004, A1, A11; Siobhan Gorman and Julian E. Barnes, "U.S Spying on Syria Yields Bonus: Intelligence on Islamic State," *Wall Street Journal*, November 1, 2014 (via www .matthewaid.com).

11. Christopher Andrew, *For the President's Eyes Only: Secret Intelligence and the American Presidency from Washington to Bush*, 520; David Johnston, "U.S. Agency Secretly Monitored Chinese in '96 on Political Gifts," *New York Times*, March 13, 1997, A1, A25; Nora Boustany and Brian Duffy, "A Top U.S. Official May Have Given Sensitive Data to Israel," *Washington Post*, May 7, 1997, A1, A28; Russell Watson and John Barry, "Our Target Was Terror," *Newsweek*, August 31, 1998, 24–29; Aid, "The Time of Troubles," 1–32; Aid, "All Glory Is Fleeting," 72–120; Defense Intelligence Agency, *Soviet and People's Republic of China Nuclear Weapons Employment Policy and Strategy*, March 1972, II-B-5; [deleted], "Indian Heavy Water Shortage" (from an undetermined National Security Agency publication), October 1982; George C. Wilson, "Soviet Nuclear Sub Reported Sunk," *Washington Post*, August 11, 1983, A9; David B. Ottaway, "Iraq Said to Have Expelled High-Level US Diplomat," *Washington Post*, November 17, 1988, A33; George J. Church, "Destination Haiti," *Time*, September 26, 1994, 21–26.

12. Aid, "All Glory Is Fleeting"; Patrick E. Tyler, "British Detail Bin Laden's Link to U.S. Attacks," *New York Times*, October 5, 2001, A1, B4; James Bamford, *Body of Secrets: Anatomy of the Ultra-Secret National Security Agency, from the Cold War Through the Dawn of a New Century* (New York: Doubleday, 2001), 410; Patrick E. Tyler, "Intelligence Break Led U.S. to Tie Envoy Killing to Iraq Qaeda Cell," *New York Times*, February 6, 2003, A1, A12; David Rose, "9/11: The Tapping Point," *Vanity Fair* (September 2011), http://www.vanityfair.com/news/2011/09/preventing -9-11-201109.

13. Greg Miller, Julie Tate, and Barton Gellman, "Documents Reveal NSA's Extensive Involvement in Targeted Killing Program," www.washingtonpost.com, October 16, 2013, http://www .washingtonpost.com/world/national-security/documents-reveal-nsas-extensive-involvement-in -targeted-killing-program/2013/10/16/29775278-3674-11e3-8a0e-4e2cf80831fc_story.html; Glenn Greenwald, Ryan Gallagher, and Ryan Grim, "Top Secret Document Reveals NSA Spied on Porn Habits as Part of Plan to Discredit 'Radicalizers,'" *Huffington Post*, November 26, 2013, http://www.huffingtonpost.com/2013/11/26/nsa-porn-muslims_n_4346128.html.

14. John F. Ingersoll, "Request for COMINT of Interest to Bureau of Narcotics and Dangerous Drugs," in U.S. Congress, Senate Select Committee to Study Governmental Operations with Respect to Intelligence Activities, *The National Security Agency and Fourth Amendment Rights* (Washington, DC: U.S. Government Printing Office, 1976), 152–155.

15. "Targeting Huawei: NSA Spied on Chinese Government and Networking Firm," *Spiegel Online*, March 22, 2014, http://www.spiegel.de/international/world/nsa-spied-on-chinese -government-and-networking-firm-huawei-a-960199.html; David E. Sanger and Nicole Perlroth, "U.S. Penetrated Chinese Servers It Saw as Spy Risk," *New York Times*, March 23, 2014, 1, 9.

16. "Russia to Switch On Advanced Long-Range Radar," *Global Security Newswire*, February 13, 2012, http://www.nti.org/gsn/article/russia-shortly-bring-online-advanced-radar; Mark Stokes, Project 2049 Institute, "China's Air Defense Identification System: The Role of PLA Surveillance," Futuregram 14-003, May 9, 2014, http://www.project2049.net/documents/Stokes_ China_Air_Defense_Identification_System_PLA_Air_Surveillance.pdf; Robert M. Clark, *The Technical Collection of Intelligence* (Washington, DC: CQ Press, 2011), 159; Max Metzger, "Four Long Range Russian Radar Installations Start Active Combat Duty," www.newsweek.com, January 15, 2015, http://www.newsweek.com/four-long-range-russian-radar-installations-start-active -combat-duty-299651.

17. David S. Brandwein, "Telemetry Analysis," *Studies in Intelligence* (Fall 1964): 21–29; Hussain, *The Future of Arms Control*, pt. 4, 46; Clark, *The Technical Collection of Intelligence*, 210–211.

18. Robert A. McDonald and Sharon K. Moreno, *Grab and Poppy: America's Early ELINT Satellites* (Chantilly, VA: National Reconnaissance Office, 2005); Dwayne Day, "Listening from Above: The First Signals Intelligence Satellite," *Spaceflight* 41, no. 8 (August 1999): 339–347; private information; Anthony Kenden, "U.S. Reconnaissance Satellite Programs," *Spaceflight* 20, no. 7 (1978): 243ff.; Philip Klass, *Secret Sentries in Space* (New York: Random House, 1971), 194.

19. Kenden, "U.S. Reconnaissance Satellite Programs"; Philip Klass, *Secret Sentries in Space*, 194.

20. "Refurbished Titan Missile Orbits Secret Payload," *Washington Post*, September 6, 1988, A2; William J. Broad, "Military Launches First New Rocket for Orbital Loads," *New York Times*, September 6, 1988, A1, B7; "New Military Satellites," *AW&ST*, May 25, 1992, 13; "Mission Control," *Military Space*, June 15, 1992, 1; John Lancaster, "The Shroud of Secrecy—Torn," *Washington Post*, June 5, 1992, A29; "Navy Uses Space to Spot Stealth Fighters," *Military Space*, April 23, 1980, 1

21. ITT Industries, *Authorized Federal Supply Schedule Price List Professional Engineering Services* (Arlington, VA: ITT Industries, n.d.), 20.

22. Naval Security Group, "Mission, Functions and Tasks of Naval Security Group Command Detachment (NAVSECGRU Det.) Potomac, Washington, D.C.," NAVSECGRU Instruction 5450.9A, February 7, 1994; Kenden, "U.S. Reconnaissance Satellite Programs"; Janko Jackson, "A Methodology for Ocean Surveillance Analysis," *Naval War College Review* 27, no. 2 (September–October 1974): 71–89; "Navy Plans Ocean Surveillance Satellites," *AW&ST*, August 30, 1971, 13; "Industry Observer," *AW&ST*, February 28, 1972, 9.

23. "Navy Ocean Surveillance Satellite Depicted," *AW&ST*, May 24, 1976, 22; "Expanded Ocean Surveillance Effort Set," *AW&ST*, June 10, 1978, 22–23; Mark Hewlish, "Satellites Show Their Warlike Face," *New Scientist*, October 1, 1981, 36–40.

24. "Expanded Ocean Surveillance Effort Set"; Hewlish, "Satellites Show Their Warlike Face." For further details on PARCAE, see Major A. Andronov, "Komischeskaya Sistema Radiotecknicheskoy Razvedki VMS Ssha 'Vayt Klaud,'" *Zarubezhnoye Voyennoye Obozreniyo (Foreign Military Review)* 7 (1993): 57–60.

25. Paul Stares, *Space and National Security* (Washington, DC: Brookings Institution, 1987), 188; U.S. Military Communications—Electronic Board, *Message Address Directory*, USMCEB Publication No. 6 (Washington, DC: U.S. Government Printing Office, July 25, 1986), 48; U.S. Army Intelligence and Security Command, "Analysis of Project TRUE BLUE—INFORMATION DF," May 28, 1986; Dan Marcella, "Det. 1 Builds upon Operational Missions," *Spokesman* (October 1995): 20.

26. "U.S. Defense and Intelligence Space Programs," *AW&ST*, March 19, 1990, 37; Edward H. Kolcum, "Second Titan 4 Carries Secret Surveillance Satellite into Orbit," *AW&ST*, June 18, 1990, 27; "Sky Peepers Learn Titan Secrets," *Space News*, January 13–26, 1992, 2; "Air Force Launches Second Titan 4 from Vandenberg," *AW&ST*, November 18, 1991, 20; Bruce Van Voorst, "Billion Dollar Blowup," *Time*, August 16, 1993, 41.

27. R. Jeffrey Smith and John Mintz, "Pentagon Plans Multibillion-Dollar Sea Spy Satellite System," *Washington Post*, August 7, 1993, A5; John R. Cushman Jr., "Pentagon Found to Have Ignored Congress in Buying Spy Satellite," *New York Times*, September 24, 1993, A14; Theresa Hitchens and Neil Munro, "Pentagon Review Might Terminate Nuclear Spy Plans," *Defense News*, October 18–24, 1993, 3; Ralph Vartabedian, "TRW Loses Key Military Jobs to Archrival," *Los Angeles Times*, July 26, 1994, A1, A6; John Mintz, "Martin Gets Big Contract for Satellites," *Washington Post*, July 26, 1994, D1, D5; "World News Roundup," *AW&ST*, September 17, 2001, 30; "In Orbit," *AW&ST*, December 8, 2003, 17; "World News Roundup," *AW&ST*, February 7, 2005, 20; Justin Ray, "Atlas 3B Launch Successful," www.spaceflightnow.com, February 3, 2005; Craig Covault, "Sea Recon Readied," *AW&ST*, December 3, 2003, 30–32; e-mail from Ted Molczan, Subject: Observation of Atlas 2AS Mission, September 10, 2001; Craig Covault, "Secret Maneuvers," *AW&ST*, July 23, 2007, 38–39; Aid, "Time of Troubles," 14–15.

28. Commander, U.S. Pacific Fleet, CINCPACFLT Instruction S3251.1D, "Classic Wizard Reporting System," September 27, 1991; "In Orbit"; Niles Latham, "Spy Satellites Set Up Commandos' Daring Sea Raid," *NY Post*, December 12, 2002, http://nypost.com/2002/12/12/spy-satellites-set-up-commandos-daring-sea-raid.

29. Christopher Anson Pike, "CANYON, RHYOLITE, and AQUACADE: U.S. Signals Intelligence Satellites in 1970s," *Spaceflight* 37, no. 1 (November 1995): 381–382; private information.

30. Philip Klass, "U.S. Monitoring Capability Impaired," *AW&ST*, May 14, 1979, 18; Victor Marchetti in *Allies* (a Grand Bay film directed by Marian Wilkinson and produced by Sylvia Le Clezio, Sydney 1983).

31. Robert Lindsey, *The Falcon and the Snowman: A True Story of Friendship and Espionage* (New York: Simon & Schuster, 1979), 111; Desmond Ball, *Pine Gap: Australia and the US Geostationary Signals Intelligence Satellite Program* (Sydney: Allen & Unwin, 1988), 14–15.

32. Desmond Ball, foreword to David Rosenberg, *Inside Pine Gap: The Spy Who Came in from the Desert* (Melbourne: Hardie Grant Books, 2011), vi- viii.

33. The initial planned follow-on to RHYOLITE, ARGUS, was cancelled in the late 1970s. Richard Burt, "U.S. Plans New Way to Check Soviet Missile Tests," *New York Times*, June 29, 1979, A3; William Burrows, *Deep Black: Space Espionage and National Security* (New York: Random House, 1986), 192.

34. Hussain, *The Future of Arms Control*, pt. 4, 42; Ball, *Pine Gap*, 14–15; "U.S. Spy Satellite Falls Short on Orbit and Expectations," *New York Times*, September 4, 1988, 22; Edward H. Kolcum, "Titan 34D Upper Stage Failure Sets Back Pentagon Intelligence Strategy," *AW&ST*, June 5, 1989, 32; "Last Titan 3 Rocket Lofts a Secret Military Satellite," *Washington Post*, September 5, 1989, A2; Edward H. Kolcum, "Last Titan 34D, Transtage Launches Classified Military Spacecraft," *AW&ST*, September 11, 1989, 41; Craig Covault and Joseph C. Anselmo, "Titan Explosion Destroys Secret 'Mercury' SIGINT," *AW&ST*, August 17, 1998, 28–30.

35. Private information.

36. Dick Cheney, Joint Meritorius Unit Award, June 23, 1989.

37. James Gerstenzang, "Shuttle Lifts Off with Spy Cargo," *Los Angeles Times*, January 25, 1985, 1, 11; "Final Launch Preparations Under Way for Signals Intelligence Satellite Mission," *AW&ST*, November 6, 1989, 24.

38. That ORION has become the primary geosynchronous SIGINT program is suggested by Office of the Director of National Intelligence, *FY 2013 Congressional Budget Justification*, vol. 1: *National Intelligence Program Summary*, 2012, 167.

39. Seymour Hersh, *"The Target Is Destroyed": What Really Happened in Flight 007 and What America Knew About It* (New York: Random House, 1986), 4; Burrows, *Deep Black*, 223; Philip J. Klass, "NSA 'Jumpseat' Program Winds Down as Soviets Shift to Newer Satellites," *AW&ST*, April 2, 1990, 46–47; Wheelon interview; private information.

40. James T. McKenna, "Titan 4/Centaur Orbits Classified Payload," *AW&ST*, May 9, 1994, 24; "Titan/Centaur Lofts Classified Payload," *AW&ST*, July 17, 1995, 29; Tom Bowman and Scott Shane, "Battling High-Tech Warriors," *Baltimore Sun*, December 15, 1995, 1, 15; "News Breaks," *AW&ST*, November 17, 1997, 27; private information; Michael Mecham, "A Re-creation," *AW&ST*, June 26, 2006, 43–44; Justin Ray, "New Era of Rocket Launches Begins at California Base," www.space.com, June 28, 2006, http://www.space.com/2549-era-rocket-launches-begins-california-base.html; Fitzgerald, "Observations on 'The Decline of the NRO'"; Steve Weber, "Third Straight Titan 4 Launch Success Buoys Martin," *Space News*, September 5–11, 1994, 3, 21; James T. McKenna, "Martin, USAF Speed Titan 4 Processing," *AW&ST*, September 12, 1994, 54–55; James T. McKenna, "Titan 4 Lofts Classified Payload," *AW&ST*, May 22, 1995, 62; "DOD Titan 4 Launched," *AW&ST*, April 29, 1996, 28; "Titan on Defense Mission," *AW&ST*, May 6, 1996, 16; Craig Covault, "Eavesdropping Satellite Parked over Crisis Zone," *AW&ST*, May 18, 1998, 30–31; "World News Roundup," *AW&ST*, September 15, 2003, 21; Craig Covault, "Launch Surge Begins for Secret NRO Missions," *AW&ST*, September 10, 2001, 43; National

Reconnaissance Office, "National Reconnaissance Office Accomplishes Third Successful Launch in 33 Days," October 12, 2001; Craig Covault, "Intel Operations Delayed as Iraq, Al Qaeda Looms," *AW&ST,* September 21, 2002, 34–35; "Atlas V Debuts at Vandenberg," *AW&ST,* March 17, 2008, 22.

41. Naval Security Group Activity Denver, *Annual Command History Report for 1996,* March 5, 1997, 4.

42. Ball, *Pine Gap,* 27–28; private information.

43. Desmond Ball, *A Suitable Piece of Real Estate: American Installations in Australia* (Sydney: Hale & Iremonger, 1980), 59.

44. Ball, *Pine Gap,* 67–80; Dan Greenglass, "Pine Gap Upgrades Aim to Enhance US Alliance," *Australian,* July 22, 1996, 5.

45. Aid, "The Time of Troubles," 1–32; National Reconnaissance Office, *FY 2006–2007 Congressional Budget Justification,* vol. 4: *National Reconnaissance Program,* February 2005, 200.

46. U.S. Air Force, Fact Sheet, "RC-135V/W Rivet Joint," March 2009, http://www.af.mil /information/factsheets.

47. "Specialized Equipment Key to Rivet Joint," *AW&ST,* June 24, 1996, 59; David A. Fulghum, "Rivet Joint Carves Out New Combat Roles," *AW&ST,* June 24, 1996, 52–53; "Rivet Joint Hits 6,000 Days Deployed in Southwest Asia," *Spokesman* (February 2007): 4; Jon Lake, "Elite ELINT," *Combat Aircraft* 9, no. 4 (August–September 2008): 38–47; David A. Fulghum, "Large, Diverse Crews Make RC-135 a Heavy Hitter," *AW&ST,* June 24, 1996, 61–62; Karina Jennings, "RJ Adriatic Operations," *Spokesman* (December 1996): 11–12; Air Combat Command ACCMD 23-108, "Reconnaissance Squadrons," June 25, 1993; Karina Jennings, "Vice Chief of Staff Visits Mildenhall, Flies Aboard RC-135 Rivet Joint," *Spokesman* (June 1996): 24–25; Matthew Aid, "Keeping the RC-135 RIVET JOINTS Flying in the Middle East," MatthewAid.com, February 6, 2013, http://www.matthewaid.com/post/42426600948/keeping-the-rc-135-rivet-joints -flying-in-the; "Diverse Missions, New Challenges: Boeing RC-135 RIVET JOINT," *Air International* (June 2011): 66–75; Christian Michael, "Maintainers Help Rivet Joint Fly, Intel Operate, Mission Succeed," U.S. Air Forces Central Command, February 6, 2013, http://www.afcent .af.mil/Units/379thAirExpeditionaryWing/News/Display/tabid/298/Article/350286/maintainers -help-rivet-joint-fly-intel-operate-mission-succeed.aspx; David Cenciotti, "You Don't Happen to See Many Close Up Footage of the RC-135 Rivet Joint Spyplane," *Aviationist,* July 24, 2014, http://theaviationist.com/2014/07/26/elusive-rc-135-video; Joseph Trevithick, "Pentagon Might Still Be Hunting Terrorists in the Philippines," *War Is Boring,* November 4, 2014, https://medium .com/war-is-boring/pentagon-might-still-be-hunting-terrorists-in-the-philippines-c5436e77f708.

48. Fulghum, "Large, Diverse Crews Make RC-135 a Heavy Hitter"; Michael Harris, "Rivet Joint Flies 700th Adriatic Mission," *Spokesman* (November 1995): 27; "RC-135 Takes to the Sky," *Spokesman* (April 1995): 7; Jennings, "RJ Adriatic Operations"; David A. Fulghum, "Storied Rivet Joint Adds New Missions," *AW&ST,* November 25, 2002, 54–55; U.S. Air Force, "RC-135 V/W Rivet Joint"; Tania Bryan, "RC-135 Surpasses 50,000 Flying-Hour Mark," U.S. Air Force, April 1, 2008, http://www.af.mil/News/ArticleDisplay/tabid/223/Article/124111/rc-135-surpasses-50000 -flying-hour-mark.aspx; Matthew A. Aid, *Intel Wars: The Secret History of the Fight Against Terror* (New York: Bloomsbury, 2012), 52, 195; Trevithick, "Pentagon Might Still Be Hunting Terrorists in the Philippines"; "Planes Flying Near Russian Border Almost Every Day: Russian Air Force," *Sputnik International,* December 16, 2014, http://sputniknews.com/russia/20141216/1015907245.html.

49. Defense Airborne Reconnaissance Office, *Manned Airborne Reconnaissance Division,* 1995, 19; Captain Paul Issler, "97th IS Participates in Recce Expo '96," *Spokesman* (September 1996): 15; U.S. Air Force, "RC-135U Combat Sent"; "'Soviet Mission Markings' on a U.S. RC-135U Spyplane Used to Monitor the Ukrainian Crisis," *Aviationist,* October 23, 2014, http://theaviationist .com/2014/10/23/combat-sent-mission-markings.

50. Martin Streetly, "U.S. Airborne ELINT Systems, Part 3: The Boeing RC-135 Family," *Jane's Defense Weekly,* March 16, 1985, 460–465; "6985th Deactivates," *Spokesman* (July 1992): 10.

51. Jeffrey Richelson, "Cold War Recon Planes Find New Missions," *Defense Week*, September 5, 1995, 6–7; "Recon Wing Famed for Skill, Endurance," *AW&ST*, August 14, 1997, 53; Bill Gertz, "N. Korea Fires New Cruise Missile," *Washington Times*, June 30, 1997, A1, A8; Eric Schmitt, "North Korea MIG's Intercept U.S. Jet on Spying Mission," *New York Times*, March 4, 2003, A1, A5; Eric Schmitt, "North Korean Fliers Said to Have Sought Hostages," *New York Times*, March 8, 2003, A1, A11; David A. Fulghum, "Risky Business," *AW&ST*, March 10, 2003, 38.

52. Defense Intelligence Agency, *Capabilities Handbook, Annex A, to the Department of Defense Plan for Intelligence Support to Operational Commanders*, March 1983, 220.

53. Fleet Air Reconnaissance Squadron One, *1994 VQ-1 Command History*, March 23, 1995, 2, 5; Fleet Air Reconnaissance Squadron One, *Command Composition and Organization*, 1996, 1; Major General Kenneth R. Israel, Director, DARO, *DARO: Supporting the Warfighter, NMIA Defense Intelligence Status '96*, November 19, 1996, 20; "VQ-1 Command History," www.nsawai .navy.mil/vq-1/history.htm (accessed March 1, 2006).

54. David A. Fulghum and Robert Wall, "Mixed Signals," *AW&ST*, April 10, 2006, 22–23; Keith Button, "As U.S. Navy Consolidates Spy Plane Units, Critics Say ISR Will Suffer," www.defensenews.com, November 6, 2012, http://archive.defensenews.com/article/20121106/ C4ISR01/311060007/As-U-S-Navy-Consolidates-Spy-Plane-Units-Critics-Say-ISR-Will-Suffer; Kathy Reid, "A Sad Day at NAS Whidbey as VQ-2 Disestablished," *Whidbey News-Times*, May 22, 2012, http://www.whidbeynewstimes.com/news/152689545.html; U.S. Navy, Fact File: "EP-3E (ARIS II) Signals Intelligence Reconnaissance Aircraft," February 17, 2009, http://www.navy.mil/ navydata/fact_display.asp?cid=1100&tid=1000&ct=1 (accessed September 6, 2014); Keith Button, "SIGINT Question Marks," www.defensenews.com, April 1, 2011, http://archive.defensenews .com/article/20110401/C4ISR02/104010304/SIGINT-question-marks.

55. Martin Streetly, "Secretive Orion: EP-3E ARIES II," *Air International* (September 2004): 31–38; "Flexibility, Endurance Are Valued EP-3 Assets," *AW&ST*, May 5, 1997, 50, 52; Defense Airborne Reconnaissance Office, *Manned Airborne Reconnaissance Division*, 11; Fleet Air Reconnaissance Squadron One, *Command Composition and Organization*, 1; Dick Van der Art, *Aerial Espionage: Secret Intelligence Flights by East and West* (New York: Arco/Prentice Hall, 1986), 53–54; private information; U.S. Navy, "EP-3E (ARIS II) Signals Intelligence Reconnaissance Aircraft."

56. Fleet Air Reconnaissance Squadron One, *Command Composition and Organization*, 4; "Flexibility, Endurance Are Valued as EP-3 Assets"; Fleet Air Reconnaissance Squadron Two, *Fleet Air Reconnaissance Squadron Two History*, n.d.

57. Fleet Air Reconnaissance Squadron One, *2001 Command Composition and Organization*, n.d., 2.

58. Ibid., 2–3; Fleet Air Reconnaissance Squadron Two, *Command Operations Report*, May 17, 2006; Fleet Air Reconnaissance Squadron One, *Command Operations Report*, 2009, 3, 6; U.S. Marine Corps, MARADMIN Notice 654/08, Subject: Expansion of the Area of Eligibility (AOE) for the Global War on Terrorism Expeditionary Medal (GWOTEM), November 20, 2008, http://www.marines.mil/News/Messages/MessagesDisplay/tabid/13286/Article/112945/ expansion-of-the-area-of-eligibility-aoe-for-the-global-war-on-terrorism-expedi.aspx; U.S. Southern Command, *U.S. Southern Command 2009 Posture Statement*, 2009, 26.

59. Fleet Air Reconnaissance Squadron Two, *Command History 2001*, n.d., 3, 7; DOD Highlights (Enclosure 5), 2; Fleet Air Reconnaissance Squadron Two, *Command History 2002*, June 8, 2004, 2, 6; Fleet Air Reconnaissance Squadron Two, *Command History 2004*, March 15, 2005, 2, 5–6; Fleet Air Reconnaissance Squadron Two, *Command Operations Report*, 1; Commander, Naval Forces Europe/Commander, U.S. 6th Fleet Public Affairs, "VQ-2 Scheduled for Homeport Change," June 8, 2005, http://www.navy.mil/submit/display.asp?story_id=18681; Commander, Naval Forces Europe/Commander U.S. 6th Fleet, "VQ-2 Scheduled for Homeport Change," EUCOM, June 15, 2005, http://www.eucom.mil/media-library/article/21594/VQ-2-Scheduled -Homeport-Change; Chief of Naval Operations, OPNAV Notice 3111, Subj: Relocation of Fleet

Air Reconnaissance Squadron Two (VQ-2), June 9, 2005; Fleet Air Reconnaissance Squadron Two, *Command History 2001*, 10.

60. Button, "SIGINT Question Marks."

61. Chris Pocock, *Dragon Lady Today: The Continuing Story of the U-2 Spyplane* (CreateSpace, 2014), 32–34; Chris Pocock, "U-2: The Second Generation," *World Airpower Journal* 28 (Spring 1997): 50–99; Defense Intelligence Agency, *Capabilities Handbook, Annex A, to the Department of Defense Plan for Intelligence Support to Operational Commanders*, 254–262; U.S. Air Force, Fact Sheet, "U-2S/TU-2S," http://www.af.mil/AboutUs/FactSheets/Display/tabid/224/Article/104560 /u-2stu-2s.aspx (accessed December 19, 2010); Jim Coulter, "Senior Spear Maintenance Facility," *Spokesman* (January 1992): 10.

62. Pocock, *Dragon Lady Today*, 32–33.

63. Private information.

64. Defense Airborne Reconnaissance Office, Manned Airborne Reconnaissance Division, 18; Israel, *DARO*, 20; private information; "News in Brief," *Jane's Defense Weekly*, July 22, 1989, 110; James W. Rawles, "Guardrail Common Sensor Comes on Line," *Defense Electronics*, October 1990, 33–41; Dennis Buley, *The US Army's Fleet of Special Electronic Mission Aircraft (SEMA)*, March 14, 1997, http://www.jncps.com/dbuley; Colonel Ronald W. Wilson, "Eyes in the Sky: Aerial Systems," *Military Intelligence* (July–September 1996): 16–18; William M. Arkin, Joshua M. Handler, Julia A. Morrisey, and Jacquelyn M. Walsh, *Encyclopedia of the U.S. Military* (New York: Harper & Row, 1990), 183.

65. John Reed, "First RC-12X SIGINT Spy Planes Making Their Way Downrange," *Defense Tech*, February 6, 2011, http://defensetech.org/2011/02/08/first-rc-12x-sigint-spy-planes-making -their-way-downrange; "The USA's RC-12X Guardrail SIGINT Modernization," *Defense Industry Daily*, March 7, 2013, http://www.defenseindustrydaily.com/up-to-462m-for-rc-12-guardrail -modernization-03756; Northrop Grumman, "RC-12X: The U.S. Army Premier State-of-the-Art Tactical Airborne SIGINT System," n.d.

66. Defense Airborne Reconnaissance Office, *Manned Airborne Reconnaissance Division*, 18; Israel, *DARO*, 20; Wilson, "Eyes in the Sky"; Stacey Evers, "U.S. Army Deploys Third Patrol Aircraft to Korea," *Jane's Defence Weekly*, August 20, 1987, 6; David A. Fulghum, "Army Spy Aircraft Watch North Korea," *AW&ST*, November 24, 1997, 58–59; David A. Fulghum, "Multisensor Observations Key to Army's RC-7," *AW&ST*, November 24, 1997, 60–61; Loren Thompson, Lexington Institute, *The Right Way to Modernize: The Army's Airborne Reconnaissance Low Planes*, October 2013, 1, 3, 5–6; David Cenciotti, "U.S. Army Mysterious Sensor Plane Spotted over Libya, Along with a US Navy Spyplane," *Aviationist*, December 5, 2014, http:theaviationist .com/2014/12/05/eo-5c-over-benghazi.

67. Jeffrey T. Richelson, "'Truth Conquers All Chains': The Army Intelligence Support Activity," *International Journal of Intelligence and Counterintelligence* 12, no. 2 (Summer 1999): 168–200; Mark Bowden, *Killing Pablo: The Hunt for the World's Greatest Outlaw* (New York: Atlantic Monthly Press, 2001), 204; Michael Smith, *The Killer Elite: The Inside Story of America's Most Secret Special Operations Team* (London: Weidenfeld and Nicolson, 2006), 224.

68. "Predator, Reaper to Get SigInt Sensors," *C4ISR Journal* (June 2008): 8; Government Accountability Office, GAO-10-388SP, *Defense Acquisitions: Assessments of Select Weapon Programs*, March 2010, 31–32; Northrop Grumman, "Global Hawk," http://www.northropgrumman.com /capabilities/globalhawk (accessed September 9, 2014); Northrop Grumman, "RQ-4 Block 30 Global Hawk," n.d.; Northrop Grumman, "Airborne SIGINT Payloads for Manned and Unmanned Aircraft from the Premier Developer—Northrop Grumman," n.d.

69. Michelle Connolly, "Northrop Grumman Unveils U.S. Navy's MQ-4C BAMS Triton," America's Navy, June 14, 2012, http://www.navy.mil/submit/display.asp?story_id=67815; "MQ-4C Triton Broad Area Maritime Surveillance (BAMS)," GlobalSecuritry.org, http://www .globalsecurity.org/military/library/budget/fy2012/dot-e/navy/2012mq4c_bams.pdf (accessed

September 9, 2014); "MQ-4C Triton Broad Area Maritime Surveillance," NavalDrones, http://www.navaldrones.com/BAMS.html (accessed September 9, 2014); Colin G. Larkins, Naval Postgraduate School, *The EP-3C VS the BAMS UAS: An Operating and Support Comparison*, September 2012, 2.

70. Susan Dowdee, "Farewell to the Last Outpost of Freedom," *INSCOM Journal* (April 1992): 10–11; "6917th Bids San Vito Arrivederci," *Spokesman* (July 1993): 14–15; T. K. Gilmore, "The 701st MI Brigade and Field Station Augsburg's Discontinuance and Farewell Ceremony," *INSCOM Journal* (March 1993): 8–9.

71. Naval Security Group, "Mission, Functions and Tasks of Naval Security Group Activity (NAVSECGRUACT), Medina, Texas," NAVSECGRU Instruction 5450.6A, April 8, 1996; Gabriel Marshall, "Medina Offers Multi-Service Intelligence," *Spokesman* (July 1995): 15; Richard J. Fisher, "GRSOC," *INSCOM Journal* (July–August 1996): 35–36; Naval Security Group, "Mission, Functions, and Tasks of Naval Security Group Activity (NAVSECGRU), Fort Gordon, Georgia," NAVSECGRU Instruction 5450.66, April 26, 1996; National Security Agency/ Central Security Service, *FY 2007 Military Construction Program: Fort Gordon, Georgia*, February 2006; National Security Agency/Central Security Service, *FY 2007 Military Construction Program: Naval Security Group Activity, Kunia, Wahiawa, Hawaii*, February 2006; U.S. Army Intelligence and Security Command, Fort Gordon, Georgia, "Vigilant Knights," June 20, 2006, http://wwwgordon.army.mil/513mi; Lynn Brezosky, "NSA Chief: 1,000 New Jobs Coming to N.S.A.," *San Antonio Express-News*, October 16, 2014, http://www.mysanantonio.com/business/local/article/Cyber-commander-says-1-000-new-jobs-coming-to-S-A-5827450.php.

72. Private information; Bendix Field Engineering Corporation, http://www.bfec.us (accessed December 18, 2010).

73. Duncan Campbell, *The Unsinkable Aircraft Carrier: American Military Power in Britain* (London: Michael Joseph, 1984), 155; "British MP Accuses U.S. of Electronic Spying," *New Scientist*, August 5, 1976, 268; Department of the Army, Field Manual 34-40-12, *Morse Code Intercept Operations*, August 26, 1991, 4-4; "Northern Lights of Freedom," *Insight* (Spring 1991): 16–18; U.S. Air Force, Fact Sheet, "JBER Chiefs Group Choice Award Winner of the Month—December 2013," Joint Base Elmendorf-Richardson, http://www.jber.af.mil/library/factsheets/factsheet .asp?id=21341; private information; Department of the Army, TM 32-5985-217-15, *Operator's, Organizational, Direct Support, General Support, and Depot Maintenance Manual for Antenna Group Countermeasures Receiving Set AN/FLR-9 (V7) (V8)*, June 1976, 1-1 to 1-2.

74. Private information; Brian Toohey and Marian Wilkinson, *The Book of Leaks: Exposés in Defense of the Public's Right to Know* (North Ryde, Australia: Angus & Robertson, 1987), 135.

75. U.S. Army Field Station Korea, *Fiscal Year 1986, Annual Historical Report*, 1987, 2; private information; History Office, INSCOM, *Annual Historical Review: U.S. Army Intelligence and Security Command, Fiscal Year 1988*, 1989, 105; Jason Merrell, "501st MI Soldiers Maintain Excellence," *INSCOM Journal* (Spring 2004): 14–16; 501st Military Intelligence Brigade, "719th Military Intelligence Battalion," http://8tharmykorea.army.mil/501MI/719.html.

76. Private information; History Office, U.S. Army Intelligence and Security Command, *Fiscal Year 1988*, 105; Naval Security Group, "Mission, Functions, and Tasks of Naval Security Group Activity (NAVSECGRUACT) Pensacola, Florida," Instruction 5450.58B, October 15, 1996.

77. Jeffrey Richelson, "Desperately Seeking Signals," *Bulletin of the Atomic Scientists* (March–April 2000): 47–51.

78. Hersh, *The Target Is Destroyed*, 49; U.S. Congress, House Committee on Appropriations, *Military Construction Appropriations for 1981*, pt. 2 (Washington, DC: U.S. Government Printing Office, 1980), 875; Richelson, "Desperately Seeking Signals"; David Morison, "Site Unseen," *National Journal*, June 4, 1998, 1468–1472; Duncan Campbell and Linda Melvern, "America's Big Ear on Europe," *New Statesman*, July 18, 1980, 10–14; "The National Security Agency in 2002," *Top Level Telecommunications*, July 3, 2014, http://electrospaces.blogspot.gr/2014/07/the-national

-security-agency-in-2002.html; "TEC Succesfully Installs BOTANICREALITY at LADYLOVE (USJ-799)," https://www.eff.org/files/2014/06/23/report_on_the_nsa-bnd_cooperation_known_as_joint_sigint_activity_jsa.pdf.

79. Naval Security Group, "Bullseye Concept of Operations," NSG Instruction C3270.2, June 30, 1989; Naval Security Group, "Mission Functions, and Tasks of U.S. Naval Security Group Activity (NAVSECGRUACT) Hanza, Japan," NAVSECGRU Instruction C5450.27D, September 5, 1995; private information.

80. Private information.

81. Tom Bowman and Scott Shane, "Espionage from the Front Lines," Baltimore Sun, December 8, 1995, 1A, 20A–21A.

82. Laurence Stern, "U.S. Tapped Top Russians' Car Phones," Washington Post, December 5, 1973, A1, A16; Ernest Volkman, "U.S. Spies Lend an Ear to the Soviets," Newsday, July 12, 1977, 7.

83. Stern, "U.S. Tapped Top Russians' Car Phones"; Volkman, "U.S. Spies Lend an Ear to the Soviets"; Bill Gertz, "CIA Upset Because Perle Detailed Eavesdropping," Washington Times, April 15, 1987, 2A; Michael Frost and Michael Gratton, Spyworld: Inside the Canadian and American Intelligence Establishments (Toronto: Doubleday Canada, 1994), 60.

84. Jack Anderson, "CIA Eavesdrops on Kremlin Chiefs," Washington Post, September 16, 1971, F7.

85. Seymour Hersh, "The Wild East," Atlantic Monthly (June 1994): 61–86. Possibly more on the operation is contained in the unredacted version of "Night of the Living Coup: The 18/19 August 1991 Coup in Moscow," Cryptologic Almanac 50th Anniversary Series, November–December 2002, https://www.nsa.gov/public_info/_files/crypto_almanac_50th/Night_of_the_Living_Coup.pdf.

86. Howard Kurtz, "Pollard: Top Israelis Back Spy Ring," Washington Post, February 28, 1987, A8.

87. Arthur Gavshon and Desmond Rice, The Sinking of the Belgrano (London: Seeker & Warburg, 1984), 205n5; Bowman and Shane, "Espionage from the Front Lines."

88. "The National Security Agency in 2002"; "Embassy Espionage: The NSA's Secret Spy Hub in Berlin"; Glenn Greenwald and Stefania Maurizi, "Revealed: How the NSA Targets Italy," L'Espresso, December 5, 2013, http://espresso.repubblica.it/inchieste/2013/12/05/news/revealed-how-the-nsa-targets-italy-1.144428.

89. President's Foreign Intelligence Advisory Board, "Intelligence Collection Through Audio Surveillance," att to: National Security Action Memorandum 170, "NSAM 170 Intelligence Collection through Audio Surveillance," July 6, 1962.

90. Alfred Hubest, "Audiosurveillance," Studies in Intelligence 4, no. 3 (Summer 1960): 39–46.

91. Victor Marchetti and John Marks, The CIA and the Cult of Intelligence (New York: Knopf, 1974), 189.

92. John Stockwell, In Search of Enemies: A CIA Story (New York: W. W. Norton, 1978), 107; Thomas Powers, The Man Who Kept the Secrets: Richard Helms and the CIA (New York: Knopf, 1979), 189; Steven Weissman and Herbert Krosney, The Islamic Bomb (New York: Berkley, 1981), 151.

93. E. Howard Hunt, Undercover: Memoirs of an American Secret Agent (New York: Berkley, 1974), 80, 126; Philip Agee, Inside the Company: A CIA Diary (New York: Stonehill, 1975), 346–347.

94. Steve Emerson, Secret Warriors: Inside the Covert Military Operations of the Reagan Era (New York: Putnam, 1988), 111.

95. Ibid., 116.

96. "Weekly Notes," Washington Times, April 16, 1997, A10; "Intelligence Monitor," Jane's Intelligence Review, July 1997, 336; Tim Weiner, "U.S. Diplomat Leaves Austria After Being Caught Wiretapping," New York Times, November 6, 1997, A10.

97. John Pomfret, "China Finds Bugs on Jet Equipped in U.S.," *Washington Post*, January 19, 2002, A1, A21; James Risen and Erich Lichtblau, "Spy Suspect May Have Told Chinese of Bugs, U.S. Says," *New York Times*, April 15, 2002, A12.

98. Ryan Gallagher and Glenn Greenwald, "How the NSA Plans to Infect 'Millions' of Computers with Malware," *Intercept*, March 12, 2014, https://firstlook.org/theintercept/2014/03/12/nsa-plans-infect-millions-computers-malware.

99. Ibid.

100. Ibid. Also see Nicholas Weaver, "A Close Look at the NSA's Most Powerful Internet Attack Tool," www.wired.com, March 13, 2014, http://www.wired.com/2014/03/quantum; Kevin Poulsen, "NSA Has Been Hijacking the Botnets Other Hackers," www.wired.com, March 12, 2014, http://www.wired.com/2014/03/nsa-botnet.

101. Gallagher and Greenwald, "How the NSA Plans to Infect 'Millions' of Computers with Malware." Also see David E. Sanger and Thom Shanker, "N.S.A. Devises Radio Pathway into Computers," *New York Times*, January 15, 2014, A1, A10.

102. Jeffrey T. Richelson, *The Wizards of Langley: Inside the CIA's Directorate of Science and Technology* (Boulder, CO: Westview, 2001), 93.

103. Robert Wallace and H. Keith Melton, *Spycraft: The Secret History of the CIA's Spytechs from Communism to al-Qaeda* (New York: Dutton, 2008), 138; Peter Earley, *Confessions of a Spy: The Real Story of Aldrich Ames* (New York: Putnam, 1997), 19, 117, 197.

104. Aid, "All Glory Is Fleeting"; Barton Gellman, "Broad Effort Launched After '98 Attacks," *Washington Post*, December 19, 2001, A1, A26.

105. Ryan Gallagher, "How Secret Partners Expand NSA's Surveillance Dragnet," *Intercept*, June 18, 2014, https://firstlook.org/theintercept/2014/06/18/nsa-surveillance-secret-cable-partners-revealed-rampart-a; National Security Agency, *RAMPART-A Project Overview*, October 1, 2010.

106. Special Source Operations, National Security Agency, *Special Source Operations: The Cryptologic Provider of Intelligence from Global High-Capacity Telecommunications System*, n.d.

107. Barton Gellman and Ashkan Soltani, "NSA Infiltrates Links to Yahoo, Google Data Centers Worldwide, Snowden Documents Say," www.washingtonpost.com, October 30, 2013, http://www.washingtonpost.com/world/national-security/nsa-infiltrates-links-to-yahoo-google-data-centers-worldwide-snowden-documents-say/2013/10/30/e51d661e-4166-11e3-8b74-d89d714ca4dd_story.html.

108. Ibid.

109. Ibid.

110. Special Source Operations, Signals Intelligence Directorate, National Security Agency, *PRISM/US-984XN Overview*, April 2013; Greenwald, *No Place to Hide*, 108, 110.

111. Greenwald, *No Place to Hide*, 108–116.

112. Julie Alger, National Security Agency, *A Review of the Technical Research Ship Program, 1961–1969*, 1970, http://www.governmentattic.org/5docs/ReviewTechResearchShipPgm_1961-1969u.pdf; Mitchell B. Lerner, *The Pueblo Incident: A Spy Ship and the Failure of American Foreign Policy* (Lawrence: University Press of Kansas, 2002); A. Jay Cristol, *The Liberty Incident: The 1967 Israeli Attack on the U.S. Navy Spy Ship* (Dulles, VA: Brassey's 2002).

113. Richard Halloran, "2 U.S. Ships Enter Soviet Waters Off Crimea to Gather Intelligence," *New York Times*, March 19, 1986, A1, A11; George C. Wilson, "Soviet Ships Shadowed U.S. Vessels' Transit," *Washington Post*, March 20, 1986, A33; Captain Richard Sharpe, ed., *Jane's Fighting Ships, 1994–1995* (Surrey, UK: Jane's Information Group Limited, 1994), 792.

114. Halloran, "2 U.S. Ships Enter Soviet Waters Off Crimea to Gather Intelligence"; Sharpe, ed., *Jane's Fighting Ships, 1994–1995*, 768.

115. George C. Wilson, "U.S. Detects Slowdown in Shipments of Weapons to El Salvador," *Washington Post*, April 29, 1983, A13.

116. Richard Burt, "Technology Is Essential to Arms Verification," *New York Times*, August 14, 1979, C1, C2; Murray Sayle, "KE 007: A Conspiracy of Circumstance," *New York Review of Books*, April 25, 1985, 44–54.

117. Robert Holzer and Neil Munro, "Navy Eyes Eavesdropping System," *Defense News*, November 25, 1991, 12.

118. Sam LaGrone, "Two NATO Ships Leave Black Sea," *USNI News*, September 12, 2014, http://news.usni.org/2014/09/12/two-nato-ships-leave-black-sea; "Boeing Delivers Maritime Signals Intelligence System Ahead of Schedule," Boeing, October 15, 2014, http://boeing.mediaroom .com/2014-10-15-Boeing-Delivers-Maritime-Signals-Intelligence-System-Ahead-of-Schedule.

119. Seymour Hersh, "Submarines of U.S. Stage Spy Missions Inside Soviet Waters," *New York Times*, May 25, 1975, 1, 42; Christopher Drew, Michael L. Millenson, and Robert Becker, "A Risky Game of Cloak-and-Dagger Under the Sea," *Chicago Tribune*, January 7, 1991, 1, 8–9; Sherry Sontag and Christopher Drew, with Annette Lawrence Drew, *Blind Man's Bluff: The Untold Story of American Submarine Espionage* (New York: Public Affairs, 1998), 83.

120. Ibid.

121. Ibid.

122. Ibid.

123. John E. Moore, ed., *Jane's Fighting Ships, 1983–1984* (London: Jane's Publishing, 1983), 639; Richard Sharpe, ed., *Jane's Fighting Ships, 1994–1995* (Surrey, UK: Jane's Information Group Limited, 1994), 774.

124. Private information.

125. "Pentagon Describes Damage to Sub After Arctic Collision," *New York Times*, February 28, 1992, A10; John H. Cushman Jr., "Two Subs Collide Off Russian Port," *New York Times*, February 19, 1992, A6; Bill Gertz, "Russian Sub's Sail Damaged in Collision," *Washington Times*, February 27, 1992, A4; John Lancaster, "U.S., Russian Subs Collide in Arctic," *Washington Post*, February 19, 1993, A1, A24; Bill Gertz, "Clinton Apologizes for Sub Collision," *Washington Times*, April 5, 1993, A7; Sharpe, *Jane's Fighting Ships, 1994–1995*, 773.

126. "Moscow Files Complaint with U.S. over Sub Incident," *Washington Post*, May 5, 1998, A16.

127. "Second U.S. Sub Monitors Iran's Fleet," *Washington Times*, February 12, 1993, A7; Sharpe, *Jane's Fighting Ships, 1994–1995*, 774; Richard J. Newman, "Breaking the Surface," *U.S. News and World Report*, April 6, 1998, 28–42; William Arkin, "Sub Spying in Latin America: An Incredible Story," *Washington Post, Early Warning*, January 31, 2006, https://www.mail-archive .com/medianews@twiar.org/msg08226.html; "Attack Subs—SSN," www.navy.mil (accessed December 18, 2010).

128. Aid, *Intel Wars*, 52.

129. Sontag and Drew, with Drew, *Blind Man's Bluff*, 158–163; "Jimmy Carter: Super Spy?," *Defense Tech*, February 21, 2005, http://defensetech.org/2005/02/21/jimmy-carter-super-spy (accessed February 27, 2011); Neil King Jr., "Spy Agency Taps into Underseas Cable," *ZDNet*, May 22, 2001, http://www.zdnet.com/article/spy-agency-taps-into-undersea-cable; "Navy Commission Super-Spy Submarine," *Washington Post*, February 20, 2005, A16.

130. Adam Weinstein and William M. Arkin, "Spying on the U.S. Submarine That Spies for the NSA and CIA," April 7, 2015, http://phasezero.gawker.com/spying-on-the-u-s-submarine-that -spies-for-the-nsa-and-1693109418.

9

MEASUREMENT AND SIGNATURE INTELLIGENCE

Imagery intelligence and signals intelligence (SIGINT) can trace their identities as collection disciplines back to at least the early twentieth century. The use of the term "measurement and signature intelligence" (MASINT) as a category encompassing a number of distinct collection activities is much more recent. It was coined in the mid-1970s, and the U.S. Intelligence Community first classified MASINT as a formal intelligence discipline in 1986, establishing an interagency committee to supervise MASINT activities.[1]

Measurement and signature intelligence is defined in the most recent Department of Defense (DOD) Instruction on the subject as "Information produced by quantitative and qualitative analysis of physical attributes of targets and events to characterize, locate, and identify them." It also states, "MASINT exploits a variety of phenomenologies to support signature development and analysis, to perform technical analysis and to detect, characterize, locate, and identify targets and events." In addition, the instruction states, "MASINT is derived from specialized, technically-derived measurements of physical phenomena intrinsic to an object or event and it includes the use of quantitative signatures to interpret the data."[2] Thus, MASINT includes all technical collection other than SIGINT and traditional imagery intelligence (which includes visible-light, radar, and infrared—but not multispectral, hyperspectral, or ultraspectral—imaging). Identification of MASINT's various components indicates its scope and diversity:

- Radar (line of sight, bistatic, over the horizon)
- Radio frequency (wideband electromagnetic pulse, unintentional radiation)
- Geophysical data (acoustic, seismic, magnetic)
- Nuclear radiation (X-ray, gamma ray, neutron)
- Materials (effluents, particulates, debris)
- Multispectral, hyperspectral, and ultraspectral imagery
- Biometrics (fingerprints, digital mug shots, speech recognition and voice prints, iris scans, DNA).[3]

It should not be surprising that, given the diversity of the phenomena monitored and the means employed to monitor them, MASINT can be used in pursuit of a large number of missions, both strategic and tactical. Thus, MASINT mission areas include support to military operations, defense acquisition and force modernization, arms control and treaty monitoring, proliferation, counterterrorism, environmental intelligence, and counternarcotics. Table 9.1 provides a more detailed breakdown.

Some MASINT missions are well known—for example, the detection of acoustic signals from submarines that allow their tracking and identification, the collection and analysis of seismic signals from nuclear detonations, and the use of radars to detect and monitor foreign missile tests. Other missions, particularly tactical applications, may be less appreciated. Thus, the collection of electro-optical spectral signatures from an aircraft's exhaust, the measurement of an aircraft's radar cross section, and the gathering of its acoustic signatures can be used to determine range, speed, acceleration, climb rate, stability, turn radius, tactics, and proficiency, all of which are useful in combat. Such data can be loaded into an air defense system to aid in targeting such aircraft. Hyperspectral data can be crucial in identifying the presence of improvised explosive devices (IEDs) in the vicinity of approaching military forces.[4]

It should be noted that MASINT's components lack the commonality of those of imagery and SIGINT. Visible-light, infrared, and radar imagery collection all produce an image from which intelligence is extracted. Similarly, SIGINT, in whatever form, involves the interception of a transmitted signal whose content is then mined for its intelligence value. There is no similar commonality between multispectral imagery and acoustic intelligence or between the employment of radar for monitoring foreign missiles and the detection of X-rays from nuclear detonations. In many ways, "MASINT" is more a description of the product, stemming from a particular type of analysis of the data produced by a variety of collection activities, than a coherent collection activity itself.

In addition, measurement of objects and identification of signatures form a large portion of the work done by those interpreting and analyzing traditional imagery and signals intelligence data. Such observations, although important with respect to issues of the scope and organization of the MASINT effort, can, to a large extent, be put aside in surveying the collection systems that produce the data that are turned into measurement and signature intelligence.[5]

MASINT collection systems, which operate across the electromagnetic spectrum, can be found in space, on aircraft, at ground stations, on surface ships, and below the ocean surface.

SPACE COLLECTION

The U.S. government operates several satellite systems that carry MASINT sensors. Those sensors fall into two categories: those that produce nonimaging infrared data and those that carry specialized nuclear detection sensors.* As is the case with many

---

*Nonimaging infrared sensors on satellites were originally described by the term Overhead Nonimaging Infrared, but that term has been replaced by Overhead Persistent Infrared. See Robert Clark, *The Technical Collection of Intelligence* (Washington, D.C.: CQ Press, 2010), 78–80; Government Accountability Office, GAO 14-287R, *Space Acquisitions: Assessment of Overhead Persistent Infrared Technology Report*, January 13, 2014.

TABLE 9.1   MASINT Mission Areas

Support to Military Operations
  Precision Guided Munitions Targeting
  Intelligence Preparation of the Battlefield
  Naval and Ground Combat
  Space Control
  Search and Rescue
  Non-Cooperative Target Identification
  Mission Planning
  Indications and Warning
  Tactical Warning/Attack Assessment
  Theater Missile Defense
  Scud Hunting
  Air Defense
  Strike Warfare
  Peacekeeping

Defense Acquisition/Force Modernization
  Signatures
  Threat Definition
  Countermeasures

Arms Control/Treaty Monitoring
  Missile
  Nuclear
  Chemical and Biological

Proliferation
  Missile
  Nuclear
  Chemical and Biological
  Advanced Conventional Weapons

Environment
  Natural Disasters
  Pollution
  Phenomena

Counterdrugs
  Production
  Transport
  Storage

Source: Adapted from John L. Morris, *MASINT: Progress and Impact, Brief to NMIA*, November 1996, slide 6.

other MASINT sensors, some of the space sensors produce MASINT as a by-product of a more fundamental mission or are specialized and carried as secondary payloads, often on satellites not operated by the National Reconnaissance Office (NRO) or any other component of the Intelligence Community.

Satellite systems that carry nonimaging infrared sensors include Defense Support Program (DSP), Space-Based Infrared System (SBIRS), and NRO highly elliptically orbiting SIGINT satellites. The DSP satellites constitute a legacy system and are in the processed of being replaced by the SBIRS satellites. In addition, a commercial satellite has carried a nonimaging infrared sensor for the Air Force.[6]

DSP satellites are also equipped with nuclear detonation (NUDET) detection sensors. In addition, the spacecraft of the Global Positioning System (GPS), the Defense Meteorological Satellite Program (DMSP), and the QUASAR programs may also carry NUDET sensors, although the sensors carried by different spacecraft may target very different nuclear detonation signatures (e.g., X-rays, optical gamma rays). Furthermore, several commercial satellites carry multispectral and hyperspectral imagery sensors.

The principal mission of the Defense Support Program satellites is to detect the launches of intercontinental ballistic missiles (ICBMs) and submarine-launched ballistic missiles (SLBMs), using an infrared sensor to monitor the missile's plume. In the 1970s, it was observed that DSP satellites could also detect the launches of intermediate-range ballistic missiles such as Scuds. The missiles might be launched as part of a research and development program or military exercise or during an actual military conflict. DSP collection has yielded data on the level of such activities and, in the case of war, specific targets. In addition, analysis of DSP infrared data allows determination of what type of fuel is being burned and identification of the spectral signatures associated with different missile systems. DSP satellites have also provided intelligence on terrestrial events that generate sufficient infrared radiation, such as explosions resulting from missile and bomb attacks, accidental massive explosions of ammunition dumps, certain industrial processes, and aircraft explosions and crashes.* Furthermore, DSP satellites have been used to monitor aircraft flying on afterburner, particularly Soviet Navy Backfires during the Cold War, an effort designated SLOW WALKER.[7]

DSP satellites have also provided intelligence on nuclear detonations. The infrared sensor is capable of detecting the heat generated by surface nuclear tests—and did so when France and China conducted aboveground tests in the 1970s. In addition, DSP satellites have carried several NUDET sensors. The Advanced Radiation Detection Capability (RADEC) I sensor package consists of bhangmeters, atmospheric fluorescence detectors, and an X-ray locator system. The bhangmeters are optical sensors whose

---

*Neither DSP or SBIRS satellites (discussed below) detected an explosion associated with the disappearance of Malaysian Airlines Flight MH370, but one or more did detect the SA-11 missile that shot down the airline's MH17 flight over the Ukraine. See Robert Windrem, "U.S. Spy Satellites Detected No Explosion as Flight 370 Vanished," *NBC News*, March 12, 2014, http://www.nbcnews.com/storyline/missing-jet/u-s-spy-satellites-detected -no-explosion-flight-370-vanished-n51061; Peter Baker, Michael R. Gordon, and Mark Mazzetti, "U.S. Sees Evidence of Russian Links to Jet's Downing," *New York Times*, July 19, 2014, A1, A9.

mission is to detect the bright flash that would result from the fireball of a nuclear explosion. The Advanced X-Ray Fluorescence Altimeter sensor records the bright pulse of visible (fluorescent) radiation resulting from the interaction of thermal X-rays from a high-altitude or exoatmospheric nuclear explosion with the low-density air in the upper portions of the Earth's atmosphere. The X-ray locator employs several detectors to measure the direction and arrival time of X-rays from near-Earth exoatmospheric nuclear detonations. The information provided by the most recent version of the locator, the Advanced Atmospheric Burst Locator, allows estimates of yield, location, burst height, number of detonations, and timing. The estimates have a smaller range of uncertainty than those produced by previous sensors, and the improved sensors can detect events below the threshold reached by earlier versions. The Advanced RADEC II package carries four sensors: the Advanced Neutron, Advanced Prompt Gamma, Advanced Delayed Gamma, and Advanced Directional X-Ray Spectrometer.[8]

The DSP program has involved several generations since the initial launch in November 1970. The DSP spacecraft currently in orbit, designated DSP-1, are thirty-three feet long and ten feet in diameter and weigh approximately 5,300 pounds. Detection is achieved by a twelve-foot-long Schmidt telescope that is thirty-nine inches in diameter. The telescope has a two-dimensional array of lead sulfide detectors at its focus to detect energy emitted by ballistic missile exhausts during the powered stages of their flights.[9]

The satellites were placed in geosynchronous orbit from Cape Canaveral, Florida. The three-satellite constellation with two on-orbit spares, standard in the late 1970s and into the 1980s, had become a four-satellite operational constellation by 1984, with Atlantic, European, Indian Ocean, and Pacific slots. In addition, one or two retired satellites could potentially be recalled to service if an operational satellite failed. As of late 2014 at least two DSP satellites appeared to be operational, including Flight 20 (launched on May 9, 2000, and occupying the Pacific station) and Flight 22 (launched February 14, 2004, and occupying the Eastern Hemisphere station). The final DSP launch, of DSP-23 on November 9, 2007, failed to produce an operational satellite.[10]

In 1995 the Defense Department and Air Force, after a number of stops and starts, decided on a follow-on program to the Defense Support Program: the Space-Based Infrared System. As with DSP, SBIRS is projected to consist of four satellites in geosynchronous orbit, as well as infrared sensors on two highly elliptical orbiting NRO SIGINT satellites. The first of the geosynchronous SBIRS spacecraft, GEO-1, was launched on May 7, 2011, from Cape Canaveral; GEO-2 was launched from there as well on March 19, 2013. The GEO spacecraft weigh approximately 5,600 pounds in orbit and, when deployed, have dimensions of 48.6 × 22.4 × 19.7 feet. GEO-1 was declared fully operational in May 2013, while GEO-2 achieved that status in November 2013. As of late 2014, they occupied slots over the Pacific and Europe, respectively. As noted above, three highly elliptical orbiting sensors were launched on NRO SIGINT satellites orbited on June 27, 2006, March 13, 2008, and December 12, 2014. The GEO-3 and GEO-4 are scheduled for launch in 2015 and 2016.[11]

SBIRS satellites have a scanning sensor and a staring sensor. The scanning sensor performs the strategic missile warning and global technical intelligence missions, as well as the initial phase of the strategic missile defense mission. The staring sensor performs the theater missile warning and defense missions as well as the battle space awareness missions and technical intelligence in specific areas. The SBIRS payloads in highly elliptical orbit weigh six hundred pounds and consist of a scanning sensor.[12]

The original ground segment for DSP included three dedicated ground stations, a main operating base for six Mobile Ground Terminals at Fort Greeley, Colorado, and a DSP multipurpose facility at Lowry Air Force Base (AFB), Colorado. The dedicated ground stations included the CONUS Ground Station at Buckley Air National Guard Base, Colorado; the Overseas Ground Station (also known as the Joint Defence Facility–Nurrungar) at Woomera Air Station, Australia; and the European Ground Station at Kapuan, Germany.[13]

In 1999 the manned sites at Nurrungar and Kapuan were closed and replaced by unmanned "bent pipes" at Pine Gap, Australia (Relay Ground Station–Pacific) and Menwith Hill, United Kingdom (Relay Ground Station–Europe), which simply receive the data from DSP satellites and relay them on to Buckley. The CONUS Ground Station at Buckley has been replaced by the SBIRS Mission Control Station (MCS), also at Buckley, operated by the 2nd Space Warning Squadron (SWS). It also receives data from all the remaining DSP satellites, either directly or via satellite and/or cable relay. Buckley also hosts Detachment 45 of the Air Force Technical Applications Center (AFTAC), with AFTAC personnel at Buckley being responsible for processing any NUDET data provided by DSP spacecraft. Ground control of the highly elliptical orbiting segment is handled by the 11th SWS at the MCS Back-Up at Schriever AFB, Colorado. Other elements of the DSP/SBIRS ground network include the Mobile Ground Stations, headquartered at Holloman AFB, New Mexico (to be replaced by the SBIRS Survivable Endurable Evolution), and Joint Tactical Ground Stations (JTAGs) in Europe and Asia. In 2013 it was reported that the JTAGs would be transitioned to process SBIRS data.[14]

The data received at Buckley can be relayed to a number of intelligence agencies or warning centers, including the Joint Space Operations Center at Colorado Springs, Colorado, the Defense Special Missile and Aerospace Center at Fort Meade, Maryland, the National Geospatial-Intelligence Agency, at Fort Belvoir, Virginia, and the National Air and Space Intelligence Center at Wright-Patterson AFB, Ohio. In 2012 the commander of the Air Force Space Command stated, "NASIC officials are analyzing the [staring sensor] data from the first SBIRS satellite every day." In 2013 Congress appropriated extra funds to facilitate exploitation of the product from the SBIRS staring sensors for technical intelligence and battle space awareness.[15]

The Global Positioning System is a constellation of satellites whose primary function is to provide navigation data to military and civilian users across the world. The GPS satellites are launched from Cape Canaveral and operate in circular orbits approximately 12,500 miles above the Earth with a 55-degree inclination. They circle the Earth every twelve hours. With proper equipment, users can employ GPS signals to calculate time, location, and velocity. The signals "are so accurate [that] time can be figured to within a millionth of a second, velocity within a fraction of a mile per hour and location to within 100 feet."[16]

Nominally, the GPS constellation is designed and operated as a twenty-four-satellite system, in six orbital planes, with at least four satellites per plane. However, as of early 2014 there were thirty-one satellites in orbit, partially due to the U.S. government

PHOTO 9.1   An artist's rendering of an SBIRS GEO spacecraft. *Photo credit:* Courtesy of Lockheed Martin Corporation.

commitment to a 95 percent probability of maintaining operational satellites and partially because several of the satellites had exceeded their expected lifetime.[17]

The GPS Master Control Station (MCS) is located at Schriever AFB, Colorado, with the Alternate MCS at Vandenberg AFB, California. The GPS ground segment includes six dedicated monitor stations, ten National Geospatial-Intelligence Agency monitoring stations, and four ground stations with uplink capabilities. The MCS operates the satellites and regularly updates the navigation messages on them.[18]

In addition to their primary function, the GPS satellites also provide a means to monitor nuclear detonations via the Nuclear Detonation (NUDET) Detection System (NDS) carried on board. The NDS package includes an X-ray detector (possibly combined with a Burst Detection Dosimeter), an electromagnetic pulse sensor, bhangemeters, and a data processing capability that can detect a nuclear weapons detonation "anywhere in the world at any time" and get its location down to less than one hundred feet. In addition to housing the Alternate MCS, Schriever AFB is also home to AFTAC Detachment 46, which provides support for GPS NUDET operations. NUDET data have reportedly been downlinked directly to ground stations at Diego Garcia, Kwajalein Atoll, Ascension Island, and Kaena Point, Hawaii.[19]

There have been seven launches of the most recent version of GPS, the Block IIF spacecraft, the most recent being in October 2012 and May 2013, then on February 20, May 17, August 1, and October 29, 2014. In March 2015, it was expected that four launches in the succeeding ten months would complete the deployment of Block IIF satellites, with the first Block III spacecraft not being placed in orbit until 2017. The NUDET detection equipment on the IIF satellites includes the V-sensor, a broadband very-high-frequency (VHF) receiver operating in the low to mid VHF frequency range, designed to detect and geolocate electromagnetic pulses from nuclear detonations on a continuous worldwide basis. The V-sensor is the size of a pack of cigarettes when stored but 6.5 feet long once deployed. Data collection from a V-sensor will be triggered when the amplitude of a detected signal exceeds a preset amplitude in a predetermined number of subbands distributed within the receiver bandwidth. The triggering technique, along with an associated digital signal analysis algorithm, allows the instrument to (1) trigger on and detect weak signals of interest in the presence of strong interfering man-made carriers, and (2) distinguish and discriminate between electromagnetic pulses and other man-made and naturally occurring events.[20]

In recent years, another possible means of employing the GPS system to detect even underground nuclear tests has been discovered. Scientists were able to determine that within minutes of North Korea's nuclear test in 2009, eleven GPS stations in nearby countries registered a change in ionospheric electron density. Examination of GPS data at the time of other tests produced similar results. A remaining question has been whether the ionospheric disturbances that result from nuclear tests can be distinguished from those generated by earthquakes and mining explosions.[21]

The United States has also employed at least two other satellite systems to carry NUDET sensors: the DMSP and SDS systems. DMSP satellites have hosted a variety of AFTAC sensors over the last several decades. The sensors have included the Single Side Band (SSB) Gamma Tracker (to track fallout and nuclear debris in the atmosphere), the SSB Gamma X-Ray Detector, and the SSB/A X-Ray Spectrometer (for the detection of X-rays and gamma rays emitted by bomb debris), as well as several that could monitor electromagnetic radiation. Usually, two DMSP satellites are in circular orbits of 450 nautical miles. DMSP ground stations are located at New Boston Air Force Station, New Hampshire; Thule Air Base (AB), Greenland; Fairbanks, Alaska; and Kaena Point, Hawaii. The stations transfer data to the Air Force Weather Agency at Offutt AFB, Nebraska.[22]

Prior to the placement of SBIRS sensors on the highly elliptical orbiting SIGINT satellites, such satellites, JUMPSEAT and TRUMPET, carried infrared sensors code-named HERITAGE. The sensors were designed to detect infrared emissions in a narrower time frame than those of DSP in order to permit detection of any quick-burning anti-ballistic missiles that the Soviet Union/Russia might develop. Those sensors, some of which may still be in orbit, provided additional nonimaging infrared intelligence to the Intelligence Community.[23]

The United States decided in the mid-1970s to employ NUDET detection sensors—bhangmeters at the least—on the Satellite Data System (now QUASAR) relay satellites, starting with the third spacecraft launched in August 1978. As noted in Chapter 7, the QUASAR program now involves launches in both geosynchronous and highly elliptical orbit. Whether the DMSP or SDS QUASAR systems still host

FIGURE 9.1   Sample Alert Report Text: Atmospheric

```
30                                         CENR 55-5    Attachment 12    28 May 1992


         Figure A12-1.  (U) Sample Alert Report Text:  Atmospheric
                        (This figure is classified SECRET)


  SUBJECT:  ALERT _____  (U)
  1. (S) DATA RECORDED BY THE US ATOMIC ENERGY DETECTION SYSTEM (USAEDS) INDICATE AN ATMOSPHERIC NUCLEAR

  EXPLOSION WITH A YIELD OF ABOUT _____ ( ____ ) KT

  OCCURRED AT _____    _____

  (____) DEGREES _____ ( ____ ) MINUTES NORTH,

  _____ ( ____ ) DEGREES

  _____ ( ____ ) MINUTES EAST, AT _____ COLON

  _____ ( _____ ) GMT ON _____ ( _____ ) _____ 19 ____ .

  2. (S) THE FOLLOWING SATELLITES/LOOK ANGLES (IN DEGREES) RECORDED THE EVENT:

  _____/_____

  _____/_____

  _____/_____

  3. (S) THE LOCATION WAS OBTAINED FROM COMBINED INPUTS FROM ████████████████████

  4. (S) SEISMIC DATA ARE/ARE NOT AVAILABLE FROM THIS EVENT.

  5. (S) THE PRELIMINARY ESTIMATE OF YIELD OF ABOUT _____ ( ___ ) KT, WITH AN UNCERTAINTY RANGE██

  OF _____ ( ___ ) TO _____ ( ___ ) KT, IS BASED ON██████████A YIELD ESTIMATE OF

  _____ ( ___ ) KT WAS OBTAINED FROM████

  6. (S) THE PRELIMINARY ESTIMATE OF HEIGHT OF BURST IS _____ ( ___ ) KILOMETERS.

  7. (S) THE EARLIEST THAT██████████████████

  ████████████████ ( _____ ) _____ 19 ____ .

  █████████████████████████

  8. (U) THE INFORMATION CONTAINED IN THIS DOCUMENT WILL BE SAFEGUARDED AS DIRECTED BY NATIONAL SECURITY DECISION

  MEMORANDUM NO. 50.

  DECL OADR.      OPR:  AFTAC/DOB     INITIALS: _____  DATE: _____
  ===============================================================================
```

.b.(1)

Source: AFTAC Regulation 55-5, "Alert Procedures," May 28 1992.

NUDET sensors is not clear, since a 2010 AFTAC instruction notes only two satellite systems as being part of the United States NUDET Detection System (USNDS): the DSP and GPS systems. Figure 9.1 shows a sample alert report for atmospheric tests detected by satellites.[24]

Digital Globe operates several commercial satellites that, unlike U.S. government satellites, produce multispectral or hyperspectral imagery. The Quickbird satellite, launched in October 2001, operates in a sun-synchronous 280-mile orbit and produces multispectral images with eight-foot resolution. GeoEye-1, acquired in the merger with Space Imaging and launched on September 6, 2008, orbits at 422 miles and returns multispectral images with a thirteen-foot resolution. The company's Worldview-2 satellite, launched in October 2009, operates in a 477-mile orbit and also produces multispectral images with a maximum resolution of six-feet. Worldview-3 orbits at 380 miles with eighth multispectral bands with four-foot resolution at nadir.[25]

AIRBORNE COLLECTION

Airborne MASINT systems are flown on Air Force and Navy aircraft that also serve as platforms for imagery and/or SIGINT sensors; among these systems are the RC-135S Cobra Ball, P-3C Orion, P-3C Iron Clad, P-8 Poseidon, and MQ-1 Predator. In addition a number of aircraft serve as platforms for sensors that can detect evidence of nuclear, chemical, or biological warfare activities.

Currently the Air Force inventory includes three Cobra Ball aircraft, operated by the 25th Air Force's 55th Wing, located at Offutt AFB, Nebraska. They are manned with aircrews from the 45th Reconnaissance Squadron and 97th Intelligence Squadron, also located at Offutt. At minimum, the crews consist of three electronic warfare officers, two airborne systems engineers, and two airborne mission specialists. The planes are 135 feet long and 42 feet high, fly at over 500 mph, and have an unrefueled range of 3,900 miles.[26]

In addition to the Advanced Telemetry System discussed in Chapter 8, Cobra Ball aircraft carry two Medium-Wave Infrared Arrays (MIRA), a Real-Time Optical System that records visible-light images using a combination of eight acquisition and five tracking sensors, and a Large Aperture Tracking System (LATS) with a twelve-inch focal length for small targets picked up the LATS. Each MIRA system comprises six infrared cameras, and each camera's field of view marginally overlaps those on either side to produce a panoramic picture of slightly less than 180 degrees. The original arrays were modified to permit detection of cooler targets. A Cobra Ball can locate a missile launch within one hundred yards, track missile flight at greater than 250 miles, and determine engine burnout and predict impact point within seconds.[27]

MASINT analysis of the data returned by Cobra Ball's infrared and optical sensors provides intelligence in a variety of areas. Analysis of the colors that appear around a reentry vehicle (RV) when heated by the friction of the Earth's atmosphere can reveal the materials that the vehicle is composed of and whether it has a hardened titanium warhead for penetrating deep targets. In addition, plotting the warhead's flight path can indicate its speed and whether it can maneuver to avoid defensive missiles. Stability and accuracy of the RV can be estimated by calculating the speed-to-rotation ratio. Tracking the debris that surrounds a reentry vehicle allows analysts to extrapolate the quality of workmanship. Missiles manufactured during the Soviet era were "sloppy and dirty," and the warheads operated with "lots of debris."[28]

Cobra Ball's more recent missions have included monitoring Iran's and North Korea's ballistic missile tests. In 2010 two of the three Cobra Ball's deployed thirty-four times, including to Kadena AB, Japan; Diego Garcia in the Indian Ocean; and Al Udeid AB, Qatar. Targets included eleven Russian, three Chinese, and two Syrian missile tests, as well as several Indian tests. In addition, the planes also gathered data on one Taiwanese and one Egyptian test. Missions from Qatar were directed against Pakistani missile tests on three occasions. A Cobra Ball plane may also be assigned missions outside the realm of foreign intelligence, such as tracking the path of the National Aeronautics and Space Administration's Compton Gamma Observatory when it reentered the atmosphere in the spring of 2002.[29]

Prior to its extensive use for overland imagery purposes, the PC-3C Orion, named after the Greek god of the hunt, was primarily an antisubmarine warfare aircraft. The

PHOTO 9.2 RC-135S Cobra Ball aircraft. *Photo credit:* USAF.

P-3C can carry up to eighty-four sonobuoys, expendable sonar systems that can be dropped into the water. Forty-eight are preset and loaded in external launch chutes prior to takeoff. The remaining thirty-six are carried internally, and their operating channels can be chosen during the mission. For many of the sonobuoys, it is possible to select the operating depth and length of transmission time. The acoustic operators on the PC-3C can monitor up to sixteen sonobuoys simultaneously. A sonar-type recorder stores all acoustic data for reference so that the missions can be reconstructed in detail.[30]

In addition to sonobuoys, there are several nonacoustic detection systems on the P-3C. Its Magnetic Anomaly Detector (MAD) is used in concert with the Submarine Anomaly Detector to determine whether known submarine magnetic profiles are present. To get a good MAD reading, the plane must fly two hundred to three hundred feet above the water. An airborne search radar, designated AN/APS-115, is used to detect radar returns from ships or submarines on the surface and pick out periscopes at the waterline.[31]

Five P-3C aircraft were specially configured for the collection, analysis, and recording of high-quality acoustic data on Soviet submarines, sonars, and underwater communications equipment. These aircraft, code-named BEARTRAP, have a 4,000 nautical-mile range, an operational altitude of 200 to 10,000 feet, and an endurance capability of twelve hours. Enhancements of BEARTRAP antisubmarine warfare capabilities during the 1994 fiscal year focused on the littoral/regional conflict environment.[32]

Another version of the P-3C, which has been designated Reef Point, Storm Jib, and, more recently, Iron Clad, is a four-engine turboprop that can fly at 28,000 feet at 250 knots for up to twelve hours (but is not refuelable in flight). It has been described as engaged in "all-weather, worldwide multisensor scientific and technical collection of naval and littoral targets" in support of joint task force, fleet, and maritime operations. In the past, the aircraft carried a wide variety of sensors. More recently, the planes' sensors have included the Directional Low-Frequency Analysis and Recording system, which relies on signals from sonobuoys to locate targets within 10 to 15 degrees of true target location, and the electro-optical Tactical Optical Surveillance System. The planes may also be equipped, under the Adaptive Spectral Reconnaissance Program, with hyperspectral sensors.[33]

For many years, the four Iron Clad aircraft were evenly split between Special Projects Patrol Squadron One (VPU-1) at Naval Air Station (NAS) Maine and VPU-2 at Marine Corps Air Facility Kaneohe Bay, Hawaii. In 2011 VPU-1 relocated to NAS Jacksonville. VPU-1 focused on the Atlantic and Mediterranean, while VPU-2 operated over the Pacific and Indian Ocean theaters. In 2012, VPU-1 was disestablished, with its aircraft and personnel transferred to VPU-2. In Desert Storm, Iron Clad aircraft were used to photograph Iraqi fortifications, gather data on Iraq's electronic order of battle, and hunt for mobile Scuds. They have also been used to monitor developments in the Spratly Islands, whose ownership has been disputed by China and the Philippines.[34]

As noted above, P-3Cs are in the process of being replaced by the P-8A Poseidon multimission aircraft. The P-8As MASINT sensors include an "active multi-static and passive acoustic sensor system" and a digital magnetic anomaly detector.[35]

At one time, aerial sampling was extensively employed to detect the atomic particles that an atmospheric nuclear explosion would emit or an underground test might "vent." Aircraft employed in aerial sampling operations included the U-2, the P-3, the WC-135, and the B-52. Today only WC-135s perform that mission.

The Air Force inventory includes two WC-135 Constant Phoenix aircraft, both located at Offutt AFB. Their European missions are designated CREEK PHOENIX and their Pacific missions DISTANT PHOENIX. The cockpit crew is drawn from the 45th Reconnaissance Squadron at Offutt, with special equipment operators assigned to AFTAC's Detachment 1, also at Offutt. The aircraft possess "external flow-through devices to collect particulates on filter paper and a compressor system for whole air samples collected in holding spheres." The aircraft are over 139 feet long, have a wingspan greater than 130 feet, and stand 42 feet high. They have a 4,000 nautical mile range and 40,000 foot ceiling.[36]

Aircraft from the 55th Weather Reconnaissance Squadron, then at McClellan AFB, were used to monitor nuclear fallout from the 1986 Chernobyl accident, designated SPECIAL EVENT 86-05. The planes, deployed to Royal Air Force Mildenhall, flew missions over Germany, Switzerland, Italy, and the Mediterranean. A May 21, 1992, Chinese nuclear test at Lop Nor produced a large cloud of radioactive gas that, by early June, had passed over the Sea of Japan. A WC-135 flew into the cloud to collect nuclear particles. A WC-135 was possibly also employed to monitor the effects of a plutonium leak from a nuclear plant in Siberia in July 1993. The WC-135 was deployed to Diego Garcia to conduct aerial sampling missions following the May 1998 Indian detonation of several nuclear devices. In October 2006, the WC-135 was ordered to fly from Kadena AB to gather air samples over the Sea of Japan after North Korea's announcement that it had conducted a nuclear test. One WC-135 was employed in March 2011 as part of the U.S. response following the earthquake and tsunami that struck Japan. During the early stages of the resulting Fukushima Daiichi nuclear power plant meltdown, that WC-135 flew nine missions and analyzed 660 samples, which were forwarded to Energy Department national laboratories for further analysis.

In February 2013, WC-135 aircraft were dispatched to try to gather debris from North Korea's third nuclear test.[37]

In 2011 the Raytheon Corporation delivered the first Airborne Cueing and Exploitation System Hyperspectral (ACES-HY), designated the AN-DGS-68, to the Air Force, reportedly intended for use on an MQ-1 Predator operating over Afghanistan. Its ability to collect data from the near-visible to the boundary of the mid-wave infrared spectrum would make it useful in penetrating camouflage in addition to "plumes" or aerosols from IED production facilities.[38]

GROUND COLLECTION

MASINT collection systems operated from the ground involve a variety of different targets and employ assorted sensor systems. In addition, MASINT ground sensors include those employed for strategic as well as tactical purposes. Key MASINT ground systems include radars for missile detection and tracking and seismic stations to detect nuclear detonations. In addition, the U.S. Army Intelligence and Security Command (INSCOM) has, for many years, operated a number of tactical MASINT collection systems. Further, clandestine MASINT operations include the emplacement of MASINT sensors at strategic locations and directed at specific targets.

For many years one or another Air Force component has operated the COBRA DANE phased-array radar in Shemya, Alaska. Before the collapse of the Soviet Union, the primary purpose of COBRA DANE was described as "acquir[ing] precise radar metric and signature data on developing Soviet ballistic missile weapon systems for weapon system characteristics determination. The Soviet developmental test to Kamchatka and the Pacific Ocean provide[s] the United States with primary source for collection of these data early in the Soviet developmental programs." In 1997 its primary mission was described as "the collection of precise exoatmospheric radar metric and signature data on Russian ballistic missiles." It was estimated to have a near 100 percent detection rate for Russian ICBMs. In November 2011, Director of National Intelligence James R. Clapper Jr. agreed to a proposal to terminate the COBRA DANE intelligence mission and transfer it to the Air Force Space Command, which would continue employing it for space surveillance and missile defense purposes. Its missile warning mission makes it part of the Integrated Tactical Warning and Attack Assessment network. COBRA DANE provides warning of all "Earth-impacting objects," including missiles targeted on the United States. Its secondary mission was space object tracking and identification—which is discussed in Chapter 10.[39]

Another radar employed to detect and track Soviet and Russian missiles was established on Mount Olympus on Cyprus in 1964. Designated COBRA SHOE, it was described in 1994 as a "ground-based HF over-the-horizon radar, providing range, range rate, and relative azimuth on target at Russian test ranges." It was apparently also employed to monitor Iraqi missile launches and presumably other missile launches emanating from Middle Eastern nations, including from Iran and Israel.[40]

The United States also operates a number of X-band radars to monitor missile launches in Asia and the Middle East, which can provide data for both intelligence and missile defense purposes. The radars weigh thirty-four tons, are about forty-three feet in length, and can distinguish different types of warheads from over 620 miles away. One radar is located at the Shariki Communications Site in Tsugaru, part of Japan's Aomori Prefecture. In December 2014, the Department of Defense announced deployment of a second X-band radar system at Kyogamisaki in central Japan. The system is to be employed to monitor North Korean missile launches. The United States also operates an X-band radar atop Mount Keren, in the southwest of Israel, pointed northeast toward Iran. The site is manned by about 100 U.S. military service personnel. By early 2012, the United States had also placed an X-band radar in southeastern Turkey.[41]

A second set of ground stations are those operated by the Air Force Technical Applications Center for the purposes of monitoring compliance with test ban treaties and the collection of nuclear intelligence. The Limited Test Ban Treaty prohibits atmospheric testing, the Threshold Test Ban Treaty limits testing to underground tests of not more than 150 kilotons, and the Comprehensive Test Ban Treaty (CTBT) prohibits testing of any kind.* According to a 1997 official history of AFTAC, the "only technique of the [US Atomic Energy Detection System that is] truly effective in the detection of underground nuclear detonations" is the seismic technique.[42]

Seismic detection relies on the fact that nuclear detonations, like earthquakes, generate waves that travel long distances by either passing through the Earth (body waves) or traveling along the Earth's surface (surface waves). Seismometers or seismic arrays at significant distances (over 1,240 miles) from the point of detonation can record teleseismic body and surface waves. When the waves arrive at the seismic station, seismometers record the resulting motion of the ground and generate a seismogram.[43]

Analysis of the data involves distinguishing between earthquakes (which occur when two bodies of rock slip past each other) and detonations (a point source), filtering out background and instrument noise, and converting the seismic signal into an estimate of explosive yield, when appropriate. The conversion requires not only application of a mathematical formula but also data concerning the geology of the test site, because a disturbance in a stable geological structure results in stronger body waves than a disturbance in a more molten geologic structure.[44]

At a distance of less than 625 miles from an event, explosions of greater than a few kilotons can be easily distinguished from earthquakes. At greater distances, such distinctions become far more difficult. Moreover, the actual recording of a seismic signal is disturbed by both instrumental and natural background noise, the latter setting a threshold of detectability. Such limitations place a premium on situating monitoring stations or equipment in suitable locations and on development of techniques to enhance the signal-to-noise ratio obtained at any location. The simplest form of Earth-based monitoring equipment is a seismometer, which basically consists of a magnet fixed to the ground and a spring-suspended mass with an electric coil. According to the Stockholm International Peace Research Institute (SIPRI), "When seismic waves move the ground and the magnet attached to it, they leave the mass with the coil relatively unaffected. The relative motion of the magnet and coil generates a current in the coil which is proportional to their relative velocity." One method of enhancing

---

*Although the U.S. Senate has not ratified the CTBT, the United States has not conducted any nuclear tests since signing the treaty in 1996. The other signatories have also refrained from testing.

the signal-to-noise ratio is to place several seismometers in an array. An array allows the recording of seismic waves at a number of seismometers, which increases the data sets available for analysis.[45]

As a result of bilateral arrangements with the host governments, to which AFTAC has turned over previously U.S.-run seismic stations, and in accordance with the provisions of the CTBT, AFTAC will have access to data from an increased number of sites. The CTBT establishes an International Monitoring System (IMS), consisting of nationally run sites relying on seismic and other techniques. Data from those sites—such as ARCESS in Norway and KEV in Finland—as well as any additional data provided are transmitted to an International Data Center (IDC) in Vienna, Austria. Under the provisions of the treaty, each state party will be able to receive all the data transmitted to the IDC.[46]

Even prior to the signing of the CTBT, AFTAC operations began to shift from a reliance on AFTAC-operated stations to a combination of AFTAC- and allied-government-operated stations. Most of the allied stations were either previously operated by AFTAC or established by AFTAC for the host government. The seismic arrays and seismometers operated by or for AFTAC are distributed throughout the world. Each detachment possesses broadband seismic detection capabilities and is responsible for detecting, recording, and analyzing all seismic activity that occurs in its area of responsibility twenty-four hours a day.[47]

AFTAC seismic detection is carried out by the AFTAC Distributed Subsurface Network (ADSN), which consists of six subsystems and support networks. The collection element of the ADSN is the Seismic Field Subsystem (SFS), which consists of equipment at Cambridge Bay, Canada (Equipment Location [EL] 079); Flin Flon, Canada (EL 244); Ramstein AB, Germany (Detachment 319); Yokota AB, Japan (Detachment 402); Chiang Mai, Thailand (Detachment 415, with OL-CW at Bangkok); Alice Springs, Australia (Detachment 421); Wonju Air Station, Korea (Detachment 452); Eielson AFB, Alaska (Detachment 460); and the southern U.S. stations in Lajitas, Shafter, and Marathon, Texas (ELs 190, 191, and 192, respectively).[48]

What used to be Detachment 313 at Sonseca, Spain, was turned over to the Spanish government in January 1996. Under the terms of a memorandum of understanding between AFTAC and the Spanish National Geographic Institute, AFTAC continues to receive data from the site, which includes two seismic arrays: a nineteen-instrument short-period array covering an area of about 125 square kilometers and a six-instrument long-period array covering an area of about 1,250 square kilometers. In addition, the Belbasi Seismic Research Station (Detachment 301) was turned over to the Turkish armed forces and the Kandili Seismic Center in 1999.[49]

Detachment 415 at Chiang Mai, Thailand, is actually operated by the Royal Thai Navy (RTN) Hydrographics Department as a result of a memorandum of agreement between the U.S. Air Force and the RTN. The detachment has an eighteen-instrument short-period array for detecting vertical Earth motion. A five-instrument long-period array is used to detect vertical and horizontal Earth motion.[50]

Detachment 460 (Eielson AFB) maintains forty-five seismic sites in seven arrays across Alaska, with the farthest located 2,000 miles away from Eielson. The geological data collected by the detachment form the largest joint data feed to the U.S. Atomic Energy Detection System. Detachment 452 (Wonju Air Station) is located fifty miles south of the Demilitarized Zone and operates the second-largest seismic array. The arrays are laid out over a six-hundred-square-mile area in north-central South Korea. A short-period array consisting of nineteen instruments detects vertical partial motion used for wave energy measurements. A long-period array consisting of six seismic instruments measures both vertical and horizontal Earth particle motions and provides data used for event discrimination and wave energy measurements. Both arrays contribute to the refinement of seismic magnitude calculations.[51]

Detachment 421 operates the installation at Alice Springs, Australia, code-named OAK TREE. The installation is officially known as the Joint Geological and Geophysical Research Station, although there is no Australian participation. An underground seismic array located about 1.5 miles northeast of the detachment consists of twenty-two detectors arranged in a circular pattern over an area of seven square miles. About thirteen of the seismometers are buried approximately two hundred feet in the ground and are designed to pick up the long-period waves that pass through the surface layer of Earth. The remaining seismometers are buried 1.1 miles deep and are tuned to detect the short-period waves that pass through the Earth's mantle and core. The seismometers are linked by cables to a central recording station where the signals are processed to provide an indication of the direction and speed at which they are traveling and the amplitude of the ground motion.[52]

AFTAC also obtains seismic data from stations it has set up in the Southern Hemisphere, but they are operated by foreign governments. This network—originally known as the Global Telemetered Seismic Network (GTSN) and subsequently as the Auxiliary Seismic Network—is now known as the AFTAC Southern Network (ASN). The GTSN became operational in January 1995, and the ASN now consists of four stations in South America (Brazil, Paraguay, Argentina, Bolivia), four in Africa (South Africa, Botswana, Central African Republic, Ivory Coast), and one in Antarctica, as well as an experimental station at the Albuquerque Seismic Laboratory for testing and debugging.[53]

Seismic signals, including those from ninety-four IMS stations, were among those that provided evidence of North Korea's nuclear test in February 2013 and showed that it was "approximately several kilotons," according to a press release from the Office of the Director of National Intelligence.[54] Figure 9.2 shows a sample alert report based on reporting from AFTAC seismic stations.

In addition to gathering seismic data, various AFTAC ground stations are part of a particulate sampling, or Ground Filter Unit (GFU), network, established to back up and augment aerial sampling operations. The GFU is an electrically powered, ground-based, air-filtering unit. The unit draws free air into a transition cone, which flows through a filter paper and is then emitted back into the atmosphere. The filter paper containing airborne particles from the atmosphere is then removed and forwarded for analysis and classification.[55]

AFTAC's Detachment 460 at Eielson AFB is part of the GFU network. It also operates the B/20-5, an automated cryogenic distillation device that employs very low temperatures to isolate rare elements (gases) contained in the atmosphere. The unit is designed to operate continuously over any preset sample run of twenty-four hours (or a multiple) for periods of up to seven days. Samples are collected in eight-hundred-cubic-centimeter metal containers for subsequent analysis.[56]

FIGURE 9.2   Sample Alert Report Text: CIS/PRC Underground Test Site Events

CENR 55-5   Attachment 12   28 May 1992   31

    Figure A12-2. (U) Sample Alert Report Text: CIS/PRC Underground Test Site Events
               (This figure is classified ~~SECRET~~)

SUBJECT: ALERT _____ (U)

1. _(S)_ DATA FROM _____ NORTH AMERICAN AND _____ OVERSEAS SEISMIC STATIONS OF THE US ATOMIC ENERGY DETECTION

SYSTEM (USAEDS) INDICATE AN UNDERGROUND EXPLOSION WITH A YIELD OF ABOUT _____ KT OCCURRED AT THE

_____ _____ _____ TEST SITE, _____ DEGREES _____ MINUTES NORTH

_____DEGREES _____ MINUTES EAST, AT _____ GMT ON _____ 19___. THE ERROR ELLIPSE

ASSOCIATED WITH THE ABOVE LOCATION HAS A ██

██████████████████████

2. _(S)_ DATA EVALUATED FROM _____ SATELLITES HAVING ███████████████████████████████████████

████████████ WITH THIS EVENT.

3. _(S)_ THE PRELIMINARY ESTIMATE OF YIELD OF ABOUT _____ KT, WITH AN UNCERTAINTY RANGE ████████ OF _____

TO _____ KT, IS BASED ON A SEISMIC MAGNITUDE (Mb) OF ABOUT _____ AND AN ASSUMPTION THE DETONATION OCCURRED

AT THE _____ TEST SITE, THE MAGNITUDE-YIELD FORMULA _____ WAS USED IN

DETERMINING THE YIELD.

4. _(S)_ SURFACE WAVE DATA _____

_____.

5. _(S)_ THE EARLIEST THAT ██

19___. AFTAC PLANS/DOES NOT PLAN TO CONDUCT ██

6. (U) THE INFORMATION CONTAINED IN THIS DOCUMENT WILL BE SAFEGUARDED AS DIRECTED BY NATIONAL SECURITY DECISION

MEMORANDUM NO. 50.

_____

_____

          COORD: _____

          DATE: _____

          CLASSIFIED BY: AFTAC GSSCG 20 DEC 90
          DECLASSIFY ON: OADR

Source: AFTAC Regulation 55-5, "Alert Procedures," May 28 1992.

    The prospect of monitoring CTBT compliance led to plans to deploy additional systems for NUDET detection monitoring. The IMS to be established in support of CTBT monitoring envisions 337 monitoring facilities, including seismological, radio-nuclide, hydroacoustic, and infrasound facilities. Of the planned eighty ground-based radionuclide collection sites around the world, the United States will be responsible for eleven. The key equipment at the radionuclide sites will be Radionuclide Aerosol Sampler/Analyzers, which push large volumes of air through six rolls of filter paper strips that, after a decay period, are mechanically passed through a gamma ray detector. The strips capture radioactive elements released into the atmosphere by a nuclear detonation even days afterward.[57]

Radars and seismic stations—whether operated by the United States or an ally or as part of the international system—are not dependent on operating in a covert manner. Another set of ground-based MASINT sensors are fixed or mobile clandestine MASINT sensors emplaced near a target to gather intelligence. One Central Intelligence Agency (CIA) project, code-named CKABSORB, involved secretly placing radiation detection devices with cargoes traveling on the trans-Siberian railroad in order to pick up the radiation emitted from missiles in the vicinity of the train tracks and thereby determine the number of warheads on each missile. A more recent CIA clandestine MASINT operation may have targeted the Iranian enrichment site at Fordo, where a monitoring device disguised as a rock was discovered (although it is possible that the operation was British or Israeli).[58]

SEABORNE COLLECTION

For over thirty years, a key seaborne collection asset was the COBRA JUDY system on the USNS *Observation Island*, a missile range instrumentation ship. The collection program was managed by AFTAC, although the ship was operated by contractor personnel (with one Air Force officer on board). The 564-foot ship carried a mechanically steered X-band radar and S-band phased-array radar. The S-band radar tracked missiles as they accelerated and informed the X-band radar where to look to focus on specific objects. On top of the superstructure, two thirty-two-foot-diameter geodesic radomes contained a complex of passive receiving antennas funded by the National Security Agency.[59]

The deployment of COBRA JUDY was intended to permit the monitoring of the final near-Earth trajectories of Soviet reentry vehicles during the portion of their flight not visible to COBRA DANE because of the Earth's line-of-sight constraints. In particular, the sensors provided information on the radar signatures of reentry vehicles and warheads. To enhance that capability, the X-band radar with dish antenna was added in 1985 to improve resolution and target separation, which may have resulted in the ability to distinguish between multiple warheads and penetration aides such as decoys and chaff. COBRA JUDY was also employed for missile warning. During Operation IRAQ FREEDOM in March 2003, the radar was used to detect launches of Iraqi Ababil-100 and Al Samoud missiles. It was also employed by the Missile Defense Agency during its antimissile tests over the Pacific.[60]

In 2014 COBRA JUDY and the USNS *Observation Island* were retired, as envisioned in the COBRA JUDY Replacement program. On November 1, 2011, the Air Force designated the replacement radar system (consisting of an X-band and S-band radar) as COBRA KING. The radar is installed on USNS *Howard O. Lorenzen* (T-AGM 25), a ship 534 feet long with an 89-foot beam and a speed of twenty knots. In an April 2013 test, the COBRA KING system acquired and tracked both stages of an Atlas V rocket launched from Cape Canaveral and "collected all associated data." In August 2014, AFTAC announced that the system had become operational. As with COBRA JUDY the ship carrying the radar is operated by the Military Sealift Command and manned by thirty civilian contractor personnel and one representative of the Air Force.[61]

PHOTO 9.3   USNS *Howard O. Lorenzen*, equipped with the Cobra King radar system. *Photo credit:* U.S. Coast Guard.

Another radar that resides on a missile range instrumentation ship is GRAY STAR, which has also been known as COBRA GEMINI. Located on the USNS *Invincible*—a 224-foot-long ship that can travel at eleven knots—GRAY STAR is a single-dish, dual-band X- and S-band radar system. Its principal mission is to support Defense Intelligence Agency MASINT requirements for ballistic missile data collection, and it has operated in the Indian Ocean and Arabian Sea. In late 2014 the ship was reported to be in the Persian Gulf and employed for monitoring Iranian missile tests.[62]

The Tactical Auxiliary Ocean Surveillance (T-AGOS) surface ships, operated by civilian contractors for the Military Sealift Command, deploy the Surveillance Towed-Array Sensor System (SURTASS) during missions to gather acoustic intelligence on foreign submarines from great distances. The T-AGOS ships include the USNS *Victorious* (T-AGOS 19), USNS *Able* (T-AGOS 20), USNS *Effective* (T-AGOS 21), USNS *Loyal* (T-AGOS 22), and USNS *Impeccable* (T-AGOS 23). These ships, which are 281.5 feet long and travel at three knots when towing the array, carry a crew of up to forty-five.[63]

The arrays gather acoustic intelligence—intelligence derived from the analysis of acoustic waves radiated either intentionally or unintentionally by a submarine into the surrounding ocean. This category of intelligence can be used to determine the "signature" of those vehicles in much the same manner as voice autographs of individuals can be developed. SURTASS operates in the low-frequency band and has both active and passive components. Its active component (SURTASS LFA) is a set of eighteen low-frequency acoustic transmitting source elements (called projectors) suspended by cable from underneath the T-AGOS ships. The passive component detects returning echoes from submerged objects, including submarines, employing hydrophones on a receiving array towed behind the ship.[64]

SURTASS was developed with the Soviet submarine threat in mind, but since the end of the Cold War, the focus has shifted "to include regional conflicts and the threat posed by diesel-electric submarines operating in littoral waters." Of particular interest are Chinese and North Korean submarines operating in Asian waters.[65]

While usually associated with ship-based collection, sea-based collection has also come to include fixed off-shore radar systems. The Sea-Based X-Band (SBX) radar—240 feet wide and 390 feet long—can be based on an oil-drilling platform. It "acquires, tracks and discriminates the flight characteristics of ballistic missiles" in support of intelligence and ballistic missile defense missions. The radar has been employed to monitor Russian ICBM and SLBM tests targeting the Klyuchi impact area on the Kamchatka Peninsula. It has also been deployed to the Pacific to monitor North Korean missile tests.[66]

UNDERSEA COLLECTION

Long before the mobile SURTASS sensors existed, the Navy had developed a fixed submarine detection and tracking system—a global network of large, fixed, sea-bottom hydrophones that passively listened for the sound generated by submarines. The primary targets in the 1950s and for decades after were Soviet submarines—both those able to launch ballistic missiles of various ranges and attack submarines employed in antisubmarine warfare—which represented a threat to the substantial underwater component of the United States' strategic nuclear arsenal.

The underwater arrays were known collectively as the Sound Surveillance System (SOSUS), although only about two-thirds of them were part of the SOSUS network proper. The other third are or were part of allied systems. In 1979 a U.S. admiral described SOSUS as the "backbone of our ASW [antisubmarine warfare] detection capability." Along with SURTASS, SOSUS is part of the Integrated Undersea Surveillance System (IUSS).[67] According to SIPRI,

> Each SOSUS installation consists of an array of hundreds of hydrophones laid out on the sea floor, or moored at depths most conducive to propagation, and connected by submarine cables for transmission of telemetry. In such an array a sound wave arriving from a distant submarine will be successively detected by different hydrophones according to their geometric relationship to the direction from which the wave arrives. The direction can be determined by noting the order in which the wave is detected at the different hydrophones. In practice, the sensitivity of the array is enhanced many times by adding the signals from several individual hydrophones after introducing appropriate time delays between them. The result is a listening "beam" that can be "steered" in various sectors of the ocean by varying the pattern of time delays. The distance from the array to the sound source can be calculated by measuring the divergence of the sound rays within the array or by triangulating from adjacent arrays.[68]

Two phenomena made it possible to deploy SOSUS. First, the decline in signal intensity is much less during propagation through the ocean than through the Earth, since the rate of absorption of sound energy in the ocean is very low. Second, the ocean has a layer of low-speed sound, called the Sound Fixing and Ranging channel, which acts like a "waveguide." Sound energy moves horizontally in this channel, rather than downward to the sea floor, where interaction with the bottom can cause significant attenuation. In addition, the waveguide effect limits the "geometrical spreading" of the sound wave. As a result, the effect of spreading increases only linearly with distance from the source, rather than as the square of the distance from the source (as occurs with seismic body waves).[69]

Development work on SOSUS began in the early 1950s, and by mid-1953 the Navy decided to install an array on the continental shelf of the U.S. East Coast. The array proved extremely effective in locating Soviet submarines during the Cuban missile crisis of October 1962. As a result, the United States decided to expand and upgrade the network. An array was established to cover the Greenland–Iceland–United Kingdom Gap, the portion of the Atlantic through which Soviet submarines stationed at the Polyarnyy submarine base in the northwestern Soviet Union had to pass in order to head toward the United States. An array strung between Andoya, Norway, and Bear Island, provided even earlier warning in this region.[70]

By the mid-1950s the Navy had also decided to establish arrays off the West Coast as well as Hawaii. Additional arrays had been established in the Pacific by the late 1960s. An upgraded array was deployed, extending from northern Alaska to the Baja Peninsula. Farther out in the Pacific, a 1,300-mile-long circular array, code-named SEA SPIDER, surrounds the Hawaiian Islands. Another array along the western side of the Kuril Islands allowed detection of Russian submarines exiting the naval base at Petropavlovsk or the Sea of Okhotsk.[71]

Other arrays included one built off the island of Santa Maria, off the west coast of Africa, employed to track Soviet submarines approaching the Strait of Gibraltar as well as those passing around the Cape of Good Hope. An array in the Bosporus Strait between Yugoslavia and Turkey detected submarines exiting the Black Sea port of Sevastopol. Arrays were also built near Taiwan and the Philippines and in the vicinity of Diego Garcia in the Indian Ocean. Other arrays were located off Turkey, Japan, Puerto Rico, Barbados, Canada, Italy, Denmark, Panama, and Guam.[72]

The hydrophones in the arrays were sealed in tanks, approximately twenty-four to a tank, and cables transmitted the data to facilities on shore. In previous decades the collected data were sent to a number of Naval Facilities (NAVFACs) and then on to Naval Regional Processing Centers (NRPCs) positioned around the world. Data are now transmitted to two Naval Ocean Processing Facilities (NOPFs). One is located at Whidbey Island and also receives data from SURTASS collection activities. The facility has approximately 325 enlisted personnel, 25 officers, a detachment of 30 Canadian Forces personnel, and 15 civilian employees. The other, located at Dam Neck, Virginia, has 222 enlisted men as well as 22 officers and 7 civilians from the U.S. Navy, the Royal Navy, and the Royal Air Force. The two facilities are responsible for centralized reporting, correlation, localization, and tracking of submarine targets. They provide analysis and processing of underwater signals and transmit data to naval forces around the clock.[73]

The Navy also operates Undersea Surveillance Detachments in Italy and Norway. The detachments provide support for the theater antisubmarine warfare commander. They are responsible for "detecting, classifying, tracking, and providing timely reporting of information on submarines," as well as "gathering long term oceano-graphic and undersea geological information."[74]

The data collected about each submarine detected—its sonar echo and the noises made by the engines, its cooling system, and the movement of its propeller—can be translated into a recognition signal. A distinctive pattern can be determined that indicates not only a particular type of submarine—an Alfa-class attack submarine instead of a Typhoon-class ballistic missile–carrying submarine, for example—but also the specific submarine. Thus, the data, when analyzed, operate much like fingerprints or voiceprints do in identifying individuals.

Gradually, a fundamental change in Soviet submarine capabilities reduced the value of SOSUS. The first three generations of Soviet sea-based ballistic missiles—the SS-N-4 Snark, the SS-N-5 Serb, and the SS-N-6 Sawfly—had ranges of between 350 and 1,600 nautical miles. Beginning in 1973—with the operation of the SS-N-8, which had a range of 4,200 nautical miles—Soviet subs did not have to exit Soviet home waters to hit targets in the United States. Soviet capability in this regard grew over the years, with the deployment of the SS-N-18 and SS-N-20, with ranges of 3,500 to 4,500 nautical miles. During the years preceding the Soviet collapse, Russian ballistic missile-equipped submarines conducted fewer operations off the Atlantic and Pacific coasts, reducing the value of the SOSUS arrays covering those areas. However, in the late 1990s, Russian subs were identified off each U.S. coast. And in August 2009 it was reported that a pair of nuclear-powered Russian attack submarines had been patrolling the eastern seaboard.[75]

As with DSP, SOSUS has been able to provide information about activities other than the primary strategic weapons systems it was created to monitor. One additional capability is the detection and tracking of surface ships. An even more surprising capability demonstrated by SOSUS is the tracking and identification of aircraft flying over the ocean. This capability was first discovered in 1965 and 1966, when the Norwegian SOSUS station detected Soviet Bear-D bombers flying over the Norwegian Sea.[76]

The same capabilities that made SOSUS such a valuable tool in monitoring Soviet submarine activity also enable it to detect nuclear and other detonations, whether conducted underwater or near the oceans. Thus, at one time AFTAC used nine hydroacoustic stations around the world to provide coverage of the North Pacific Ocean, the Atlantic Ocean, and the part of the Antarctic Ocean adjacent to the South Atlantic Ocean. Eight of the stations were collocated with SOSUS. AFTAC equipment was connected as near to the hydrophone cable short terminal as possible, bypassing all host electronics to the maximum extent. Digital data were then encrypted and transmitted over dedicated circuits via satellite links to the main Hydroacoustic Operations Center at AFTAC headquarters. Operated twenty-four hours a day, the hydroacoustic data center is tasked with identifying the source of each recorded wave. In any given year, it receives data on more than 650,000 events from both natural and man-made sources.[77]

In 1995 SOSUS arrays in the Pacific detected French nuclear tests conducted at Murorua Atoll; they also picked up what was probably the internal explosion that devastated the Russian nuclear submarine *Kursk* before it sank in August 2000.[78]

A more mobile form of underseas MASINT collection has involved collection systems designed to look like fish. In the 1990s, the CIA's Office of Advanced

Technologies developed "Charlie," a robotic catfish, "to study the feasibility of unmanned underwater vehicles . . . for intelligence collection purposes." Charlie's mission was to covertly collect water samples. In late 2014, it was reported that the Navy, under Project SILENT NEMO, was developing a vehicle code-named GHOSTSWIMMER—a five-foot, one-hundred-pound underwater vehicle that looked like a bluefin tuna (with the exception that it had a dorsal fin like a shark)—to covertly gather intelligence, which could include MASINT.[79]

Notes

1. INCA Project Office, Defense Intelligence Agency, *MASINT Handbook for the Warfighter*, November 1994, 8–8; U.S. Congress, House Permanent Select Committee on Intelligence, *IC 21: Intelligence Community in the 21st Century* (Washington, DC: U.S. Government Printing Office, 1996), 149.

2. Department of Defense Instruction 5105.28, "Measurement and Signature Intelligence (MASINT)," April 22, 2009, 13.

3. Department of Defense Instruction 5105.28, "Management of Measurement and Signature Intelligence (MASINT)," February 9, 1993, 2; John L. Morris, *MASINT: Progress and Impact, Brief to NMIA*, November 19, 1996, slide 1; Daniel B. Sibbet, "MASINT: Intelligence for the 1990s," *American Intelligence Journal* (Summer/Fall 1990): 23–26; Peter Bythrow, National MASINT Management Office, *National Consortium for MASINT Research*, September 15, 2009. Also see John Morris, "The Nature and Applications of Measurement and Signature Intelligence," *American Intelligence Journal* (Winter 1999–2000): 81–84; John Macartney, "John, How Should We Explain MASINT?," *Intelligencer* (Summer 2001): 28–34; "Biometrics: A New Intelligence Discipline," www.defensenews.com, May 12, 2013; Associated Press, "Millions of Voiceprints Quietly Being Harvested," www.theguardian.com, October 13, 2014, http://www.theguardian.com/technology/2014/oct/13/millions-of-voiceprints-quietly-being-harvested-as-latest-identification-tool.

4. Morris, *MASINT*, slide 8; Captain Chadwick T. Hawley, "MASINT: Supporting the Warfighter Today and Tomorrow!," *Communiqué* (May 1996): 14.

5. For a discussion of such issues, see U.S. Congress, House Permanent Select Committee on Intelligence, *IC 21: Intelligence Community in the 21st Century*, 144–175; Office of the Inspector General, Department of Defense, PO 97-031, *Evaluation Report on Measurement and Signature Intelligence*, June 30, 1997; Jeffrey T. Richelson, "MASINT: The New Kid in Town," *International Journal of Intelligence and Counterintelligence* 14, no. 2 (Summer 2001): 149–192.

6. Mike Gruss, "Air Force Draws from CHIRP Experiment in Developing 2 New Missile Warning Sensors," *Space News*, February 24, 2014, A1, A3; Dan Leone, "Missile Warning Sensor Not Among Early Hosted Payload Candidates," *Space News*, April 7, 2014, 6.

7. Jeffrey T. Richelson, *America's Space Sentinels: The History of the DSP and SBIRS Satellite Systems* (Lawrence: University Press of Kansas, 2012); David A. Fulghum, "Offensive Gathers Speed," *AW&ST*, March 24, 2003, 22–23; "Ship Blast Spotted," *AW&ST*, March 8, 2004, 19; U.S. Strategic Command, SD 523-2, *Theater Event Systems (TES) Architecture and Operations*, May 3, 2004, 6.

8. U.S. Congress, Senate Committee on Armed Services, *Department of Defense Authorization for Appropriations for FY 1986*, pt. 6 (Washington, DC: U.S. Government Printing Office, 1985), 3449; Science Applications International Corporation, *Fifty Year Commemorative History of Long Range Detection: The Creation, Development, and Operation of the United States Atomic Energy Detection System* (Patrick Air Force Base, FL: Air Force Technical Applications Center, 1997), 124–126; Air Force Technical Applications Center, Center Instruction 10-1201, *AFTAC Space-Based Nuclear Detonation Detection Operations*, January 14, 2010, 35–36, 42.

9. Richelson, *America's Space Sentinels*, 125, 130.

10. Ibid., 162, 290.

11. "Two Years Later, SBRIS Geo-1 Finally Declared Operational," *Space News*, June 10, 2013, 3; Stephen Clark, "Air Force Welcomes New Craft into Early Warning Network," www .spaceflightnow.com, November 26, 2013, http://spaceflightnow.com/news/n1311/26sbirs; U.S. Air Force, Fact Sheet, "Space Based Infrared Systems," March 2013; "Northrop Grumman Drops Off SBIRS Payload at Lockheed Martin," Satnews, October 7, 2014, http://www.satnews.com/ story.php?number=687275787.

12. U.S. Air Force, "Space Based Infrared System"; "2nd SBIRS Hosted Payload Ready to Gather Tech Intel," *Space News*, May 17, 2010, 8; Lockheed Martin, "SBIRS HEO: Space Based Infrared System, the Next Generation in Global, Persistent IR Surveillance," n.d. With regard to the future of SBRIS, see Mike Gruss, "Missile Warning Sats to Be Early Subject of USAF Reform Initiative," *Space News*, January 19, 2015, 10; Mike Gruss, "U.S. Air Force Planning New Missile Sensor Demonstration," *Space News*, February 16, 2015, A1; Mike Gruss, "Lockheed Martin Examines Cost-Cutting Options for SBIRS," *Space News*, December 8, 2014, 15; Mark Valerio, "Lockheed Still Exploring Options on SBIRS," *Space News*, December 15, 2014, 18.

13. Richelson, *America's Space Sentinels*, 148–152.

14. Ibid., 221, 224, 273; Desmond Ball, *A Base for Debate: The U.S. Satellite Ground Station at Nurrungar* (Sydney: Allen & Unwin Australia, 1987), 50; "Space Group Activates, Serves as Space-Based Missile Warning Focal Point," *Guardian*, July 1996, 23; Michael M. Jacobs and Ronald H. Herm, "Missile Warning: A National Priority from Strategic to Tactical: Past, Present, and Future," *High Frontier* 2, no. 1 (n.d.): 22–28; U.S. Strategic Command, "Theater Ballistic Missile Warning," http://www.stratcom.mil/fact_sheets (accessed January 29, 2014); U.S. Strategic Command, *Theater Event Systems (TES) Architecture and Operations*, 7; Rachel L. Griffith, "JTAGS Korea," *Army Space Journal* (Fall 2011): 46–47; Emily E. Amyotte, "SBIRS Constellation Forms Under One Roof," *Air Force Print News Today*, February 17, 2015, http://www.afspc .af.mil/news/story_print.asp?id=123439276.

15. Debra Werner, "Reputation on the Line," *C4ISR Journal* (April 1, 2011); Titus Ledbetter III, "Advanced SBIRS Sensor Capability Will Not Be Available Before 2016," *Space News*, March 26, 2012, 1, 4; Mike Gruss, "Funding Boost Accelerates Capability for SBIRS Sensor," *Space News*, September 8, 2014, 4.

16. U.S. Air Force, Fact Sheet, "Global Positioning System," September 15, 2010.

17. Ibid.; Government Accountability Office, GAO-10-636, *Global Positioning System: Challenges in Sustaining and Upgrading Persist*, September 2010, 6; "Third GPS-IIF Operational," *AW&ST*, December 10, 2012, 15.

18. Government Accountability Office, GAO-10-636, *Global Positioning System*, 6.

19. Ibid.; U.S. Congress, House Committee on Appropriations, *Department of Defense Appropriations for 1983*, pt. 5 (Washington, DC: U.S. Government Printing Office, 1982), 16; U.S. Congress, House Committee on Appropriations, *Department of Defense Appropriations for 1984*, pt. 8 (Washington, DC: U.S. Government Printing Office, 1983), 337; U.S. Congress, House Committee on Armed Services, *Department of Energy National Security and Military Applications of Nuclear Energy Authorization Act of 1984* (Washington, DC: U.S. Government Printing Office, 1983), 383–384; Paul Stares, *Space and National Security* (Washington, DC: Brookings Institution, 1987), 29; Charles A. Zraket, "Strategic Command, Control, Communications and Intelligence," *Science*, June 22, 1984, 1309; "Navstar Bloc 2 Satellites to Have Crosslinks, Radiation Hardening," *Defense Electronics* (July 1983): 16; Department of the Air Force, *Supporting Data for Fiscal Year 1985*, 1984, 394–395; AFSPC, "Global Positioning System and Nuclear Detonation (NUDET) Detection System (GPS/NDS) Mission Requirements and Doctrine (MRD)," AF-SPACECOM Regulation 55-29, September 1, 1989, 4, 6, 9; David A. Turner and Marcia Smith, Congressional Research Service, *GPS: Satellite Navigation and Positioning and the Navstar Global Positioning System*, 1994, 7; Air Force Technical Applications Center, CENI 38-101, *Organization*

and Functions Chartbook, June 2, 2003, 20; Air Force Technical Applications Center, Center Instruction 10-1201, *AFTAC Space-Based Nuclear Detonation Detection Operations,* 42.

20. Michael Mecham, "Finding the Pulse," *AW&ST,* February 6, 2012, 22; "ULA Delta IV Launches GPSIIF-3 from Cape Canaveral," www.nasaspaceflight.com, October 4, 2012, http://www.nasaspaceflight.com/2012/10/ula-delta-iv-launch-gpsiif-3-from-cape-canaveral; Justin Ray, "Atlas 5 Navigates Its Way to Successful GPS Launch," www.spaceflightnow.com, May 15, 2013, http://www.spaceflightnow.com/atlas/av039/#.VO89rEK3jwM; D. M. Suszcynsky, A. Jacobsen, J. Fitzgerald, C. Rhodes, and E. Tech, Los Alamos National Laboratory, LA-UR-00-4956, *Satellite-Based Global Lightning and Severe Storm Monitoring Using VHF,* 2000, 2–3; "Northrop Grumman Ships Nuclear Blast Sensors," *Space News,* November 20, 2006, 9; U.S. Congress, House of Representatives, *Enactment of Provisions of H.R. 5408, the Floyd D. Spence National Defense Authorization Act for Fiscal Year 2001* (Washington, DC: U.S. Government Printing Office, 2000), 715; Amy Butler, "Time for a Change," *AW&ST,* April 12, 2010, 44–47; National Nuclear Security Administration, "NNSA Launches New Detection Capability," May 28, 2010; Mike Gruss, "After Delays, GPS 2F-5 Launch on Delta 4 Goes Off Without a Hitch," *Space News,* February 24, 2014, 1, 4; "Mission Success for Delta IV Delivering Next GPS Satellite to Orbit," Spaceflight101.com, May 17, 2014, http://www.spaceflight101.com/delta-iv-gps-iif-6-launch.html; Mike Gruss, "GPS 2F-7 Launch Caps Air Force Use of C-Band Tracking Radar," *Space News,* August 11, 2014, 10; Justin Ray, "50th Atlas 5 Rocket Puts Up GPS Satellite," www.spaceflightnow.com, October 29, 2014, http://www.spaceflightnow.com/2014/10/29/50th-atlas-5-rocket-puts-up-new-gps-satellite; Justin Ray, "Preview: 10 Months, 4 Launches to Finish GPS Block 2F Deployment," www.spaceflightnow.com, March 22, 2015, http://spaceflightnow.com/2015/03/22/preview-10-months-4-launches-to-finish-gps-block-2f-deployment; Mike Gruss, "Launch of First GPS 3 Satellite Now Not Expected Until 2017," *Space News,* February 23, 2015, 10.

21. Tia Ghose, "GPS Satellites and Telescopes Can Detect Rogue Nuclear Tests," MSNBC.com, December 15, 2012, http://www.nbcnews.com/id/50091655/ns/technology_and_science-science/t/gps-satellites-telescopes-can-detect-rogue-nuclear-tests; Pam Frost Gorder, "GPS Stations Can Detect Clandestine Nuclear Tests," Research News, http://researchnews.osu.edu/archive/gpsnukes.htm (accessed June 8, 2011); Tracy Cozzens, "Detecting Nuclear Testing: Software Under Development by OSU Could Pinpoint Treaty Violations," *GPS World,* August 1, 2011, http://gpsworld.com/remote-sensingdetecting-nuclear-testing-11910; Jihye Park, Ralph R. B. von Frese, Dorota A. Grejner-Brzezinska, Yu Mortoni, and Luis R. Gaya-Pique, "Ionospheric Detection of 25 May 2009 North Korean Underground Nuclear Test," *Geophysical Research Letters* 38, no. 22 (November 2011): L22802.

22. Sylvia E. D. Ferry, *The Defense Meteorological Satellite System Sensors: An Historical Overview* (Los Angeles Air Force Base, CA: DMSS Program Office, 1989), 4–15; U.S. Air Force, Fact Sheet, "Defense Meteorological Satellite Program," March 1, 2004 (accessed February 1, 2014).

23. Richelson, *America's Space Sentinels,* 74.

24. Jeffrey T. Richelson, *Spying on the Bomb: American Nuclear Intelligence from Nazi Germany to Iran and North Korea* (New York: W. W. Norton, 2006), 287; Air Force Technical Applications Center, Center Instruction 10-1201, *AFTAC Space-Based Nuclear Detonation Detection Operations,* 5.

25. "Imagery Sources," www.geoeye.com (accessed November 22, 2010); Digital Globe data sheets: "GeoEye-1," "Quickbird," and "Worldview-2," https://www.digitalglobe.com/resources/product-data-sheets (all accessed February 1, 2014); "Worldview-3 Data Sheet," www.digitalglobe.com (accessed March 23, 2015).

26. U.S. Air Force, Fact Sheet, "RC-135S COBRA BALL," February 16, 2012.

27. David A. Fulghum, "Endurance, Standoff Range Remain Critical Attributes," *AW&ST,* August 4, 1977, 51–53.

28. David A. Fulghum, "Cobra Ball Revamped for Battlefield Missions," *AW&ST,* August 4, 1997, 51–53.

29. David A. Fulghum and John D. Morrocco, "First Arrow Battery Deployed Near Tel Aviv," *AW&ST,* April 10, 2000, 66–67; Robert Wall, "Compton Reentry Incident Free," *AW&ST,* June 12, 2000, 34; David Axe and Joe Trevithick, "The U.S. Air Force Even Spies on America's Friends and Allies," *War Is Boring,* January 23, 2014, https://medium.com/war-is-boring/bea6dd434d79.

30. Lori A. McClelland, "Versatile P-3C Orion Meeting Growing ASW Challenge," *Defense Electronics* (April 1985): 132–141; Miller, *An Illustrated Guide to Modern Sub Hunters,* 124; *P-3C Orion Weapon System Update* (Burbank, CA: Lockheed, n.d.), 17.

31. McClelland, "Versatile P-3C Orion Meeting Growing ASW Challenge"; Nicholas M. Horrock, "The Submarine Hunters," *Newsweek,* January 23, 1984, 38.

32. Private information; U.S. Congress, House Committee on Appropriations, *Department of Defense Appropriations for 1994,* pt. 1 (Washington, DC: U.S. Government Printing Office, 1993), 48.

33. Defense Airborne Reconnaissance Office, *Manned Airborne Reconnaissance Division,* 1995, 16; David A. Fulghum, "Navy Spying Masked by Patrol Aircraft," *AW&ST,* March 8, 1999, 32–33; "Lockheed Martin P-3B/C 'Iron Clad' Variants," *Jane's Aerospace,* April 2, 2001, http://www.janes.com.

34. Patrol Squadron Special Projects Unit Two, VPU-2, Inst. 5400.1H, "Squadron Organization and Regulations Manual (SORM)," February 7, 1995, 1-1; "Firms Specialize in Secret Aircraft," *AW&ST,* August 4, 1997, 50; "Special Projects Patrol Squadron One [VPU-1] 'Old Buzzards,'" GlobalSecuritry.org, http://www.globalsecurity.org/military/agency/navy/vpu-1.htm (accessed March 1, 2006); "Special Projects Patrol Squadron TWO [VPU-2], 'Wizards,'" GlobalSecuritry.org, http://www.globalsecurity.org/military/agency/navy/vpu-2.htm (accessed June 2, 2006); Tom Kaminski, "United States Navy: Airpower Update 2006," *Combat Aircraft* 7, no. 9 (November 2006): 26–53; "VPU-1 History," www.navypub.co/vpu1_history.html (accessed November 22, 2010); U.S. Navy Patrol Squadrons, "NAS Brunswick, Maine," www.vpnavy.com/nasbrunswick.html (accessed April 19, 2010); "U.S. Navy Touts Cost Savings from Intel Squadron Cuts," www.defensenews.com, July 17, 2012, http://archive.defensenews.com/article/20120717/C4ISR01/307170007/U-S-Navy-Touts-Cost-Savings-From-Intel-Squadron-Cuts; Fulghum, "Navy Spying Masked by Patrol Aircraft."

35. U.S. Navy, Fact File, "P-8A Multi-mission Maritime Aircraft (MMA)," February 17, 2009, http://www.navy.mil/navydata/fact_display.asp?cid=1100&tid=1300&ct=1; Department of Defense, *Selected Acquisition Report (SAR): P-8A Poseidon Multi-Mission Maritime Aircraft (P-8A),* December 31, 2012, 18.

36. U.S. Air Force, Fact Sheet, "WC-135 Constant Phoenix," May 27, 2005, http://www.af.mil/AboutUs/FactSheets/Display/tabid/224/Article/104494/wc-135-constant-phoenix.aspx (accessed February 3, 2014).

37. Jerry King, Chris Lucey, Mike Lyons, Grant Phifer, and Leslie Yokoyama-Peralta, 55th Weather Reconnaissance Squadron, *History of the 55th Weather Reconnaissance Squadron, 1 Jan to 30 June 1986,* n.d., 11; Bill Gertz, "Chinese Nuke Test Releases Gas Cloud," *Washington Times,* June 11, 1992, A5; James Rupert, "Plutonium Leak Reported at Russian Nuclear Plant," *Washington Post,* July 20, 1993, A14; William B. Scott, "Sampling Missions Unveiled Nuclear Weapon Secrets," *AW&ST,* November 3, 1997, 54–57; Science Applications International Corporation, *Fifty Year Commemorative History of Long Range Detection,* 66, 68; "USAF Aircraft Monitors Fallout of Nuclear Tests," *Jane's Defence Weekly,* May 20, 1998, 4; Associated Press, "N. Korea Air Sample Has No Radioactivity," www.nytimes.com, October 13, 2006; Craig A. Kibbe, Dale W. McGavran, and Tracey M. Paretlow, Air Combat Command, *History of the 55th Wing, 1 January 1997–30 June 1998,* Volume 1, 33; Mark Hosenball and Jack Kim, "Spy Agencies Scrounge for Details on North Korean Nuclear Test," Reuters, February 20, 2013, http://www.reuters.com

/article/2013/02/20/us-korea-north-nuclear-usa-idUSBRE91J1CY20130220; Susan A. Romano, Air Force Technical Applications Center Public Affairs, "Nuclear Treaty Monitoring Aircraft Visits Patrick AFB," U.S. Air Force, November 5, 2012, http://www.af.mil/News/ArticleDisplay/tabid/223/Article/110180/nuclear-treaty-monitoring-aircraft-visits-patrick-afb.aspx.

38. Amy Butler, "Eyes Wide Open," *AW&ST*, September 19, 2011, 36–37.

39. Michael E. del Papa, Electronic Systems Division, *Meeting the Challenge: ESD and the Cobra Dane Construction Effort on Shemya Island*, 1979, 1–2; AFSPACECOM Regulation 55-123, "Cobra Dane Tactical Requirements and Doctrine," December 15, 1992; Juan R. Jimenez, Dennis F. Casey, Gabriel G. Marshall, Sharon N. Wright-Davis, and Joyce M. Hons, *History of the Air Intelligence Agency, 1 January 1995–30 June 1996* (San Antonio, TX: Air Intelligence Agency History Office, December 15, 1997), 1:109; Air Force, Intelligence, Surveillance, and Reconnaissance Agency, *History of the Air Force, Intelligence, Surveillance and Reconnaissance Agency, 1 January–31 December 2012*, vol. 1: *Narrative and Appendices* (San Antonio, TX: Air Force Intelligence, Surveillance, and Reconnaissance Agency, 2014), 99–100.

40. Giorgos Georgi, "British Bases in Cyprus and Signals Intelligence," n.d., http//cryptome.org/2012/01/0060.pdf; INCA Project Office, Defense Intelligence Agency, *MASINT Handbook for the Warfighter*, 2–10, Glossary 2; D. B. Trizna and J. M. Hudnall, Naval Research Laboratory, NRL Memorandum Report 2701, *Radar Ionospheric Propagation Effects Determined from One-Way Path Tests*, January 1974, 1; Alon Ben David, "Quite Leap," *AW&ST*, July 29, 2013, 36–37.

41. Associated Press, "China Criticizes Japan for Military Radar Plans," Inquirer.net, September 23, 2013, http://newsinfo.inquirer.net/493447/china-criticizes-japan-for-military-radar-plans; Masaomi Ogawa, "U.S. to Deploy Mobile Radar in Kyoto Prefecture to Detect Missile Launches," *Asahi Shimbun*, August 2, 2013, http://ajw.asahi.com/article/behind_news/politics/AJ201308020043; Faith Aquino, "US Military to Set Up X-Band Radar in Kyoto to Monitor Missile Launches," *JPD*, August 2, 2013, http://japandailypress.com/us-military-to-set-up-x-band-radar-in-kyoto-to-monitor-missile-launches-0233282; Karl Vick and Aaron J. Klein, "How a U.S. Radar Station in the Negev Affects a Potential Israel-Iran Clash," *Time*, May 30, 2012, http://www.time.com; "U.S. Confirms Radar Site in Turkey Is Operational," *Global Security Newswire*, February 27, 2012, http://www.nti.org/gsn/article/us-confirms-radar-site-turkey-operational.

42. Science Applications International Corporation, *Fifty Year Commemorative History of Long Range Detection*, 71.

43. Ibid.

44. Ibid.

45. Henry R. Myers, "Extending the Nuclear Test Ban," *Scientific American*, January 1972, 13–23; Lynn R. Sykes and Jack F. Everden, "The Verification of a Comprehensive Nuclear Test Ban," in *SIPRI Yearbook 1978: World Armaments and Disarmament* (New York: Crane, Russak, 1978), 317–359, at 335, 340.

46. Paul G. Richards and Won Young-kim, "Testing the Nuclear Test Ban Treaty," *Nature*, October 23, 1997, 781–782.

47. 3400 Technical Training Wing, *Introduction to Detection Systems* (Lowry Air Force Base, CO: 3400 TTW, October 18, 1984), 17.

48. Air Force ISR Agency "Air Force Intelligence, Surveillance, and Reconnaissance Agency Organization Chart," October 2013; Scientific Applications International Corporation, *Fifty Year Commemorative History of Long Range Detection*, 77–78; Air Intelligence Agency, *Air Intelligence Agency Almanac*, August 1997, 36, 41; Amy Webb, "Changing Technologies, Times and Politics . . . ," *Spokesman* (April 1996): 20–21.

49. "Seismic Site Turned Over to Spanish Government," *Spokesman* (March 1996): 35; "Detachment 313–Sonseca, Spain," www.aftacgov; "Turkey Assumes Former US Seismic Facility," *Jane's Defence Weekly*, December 1, 1999, 5.

50. Air Force Technical Applications Center, CENI 38-101, *Organization and Functions Chartbook*, 20.

51. Ibid.; Air Intelligence Agency, *Air Intelligence Agency Almanac*, 37–38, 41.

52. Desmond Ball, *A Suitable Piece of Real Estate: American Installations in Australia* (Sydney, Australia: Hale & Iremonger, 1980), 84–85; Science Applications International Center, *Fifty Year Commemorative History of Long Range Detection*, 79–80; Amy Webb, "National Data Center Will Support Comprehensive Test Ban Treaty," *Spokesman* (October 1995): 26–27.

53. Science Applications International Center, *Fifty Year Commemorative History of Long Range Detection*, 79–80; Amy Webb, "National Data Center Will Support Comprehensive Test Ban Treaty," *Spokesman* (October 1995): 26–27.

54. David E. Sanger and Choe Sang-Hun, "Evidence Points to Nuclear Test by North Korea," *New York Times*, February 12, 2013, A1, A6; Office of the Director of National Intelligence, "Statement by the Office of the Director of National Intelligence on North Korea's Declared Nuclear Test on February 12, 2013," February 12, 2013; Joby Warrick, "Surveillance Network Built to Spot Secret Nuclear Tests Yields Surprise Scientific Boon," www.washingtonpost.com, January 1, 2014, http://www.washingtonpost.com/world/national-security/surveillance-network-built-to-spot-secret-nuclear-tests-yields-surprise-scientific-boon/2014/01/01/ea9c126e-6f3a-11e3-b405-7e360f7e9fd2_story.html.

55. Science Applications International Center, *Fifty Year Commemorative History of Long Range Detection*, 84–85; 3400 Technical Training Wing, *Introduction to Detection Systems*, 17.

56. Science Applications International Center, *Fifty Year Commemorative History of Long Range Detection*, 107–108; 3400 Technical Training Wing, *Introduction to Detection Systems*, 17.

57. "Test Ban Checking," *AW&ST*, May 4, 1998, 13; William B. Scott, "Debris Collection Reverts to Ground Sites," *AW&ST*, November 3, 1997, 57–59; Department of State, "CTBT: International Monitoring Station," July 24, 2013. Also, see Paul G. Richards and Won-Young Kim, "Monitoring for Nuclear Explosions," *Scientific American*, March 2009, 70–77.

58. Peter Earley, *Confessions of a Spy: The Real Story of Aldrich Ames* (New York: Putnam, 1997), 19, 117, 197; "Spy Rock Explodes near Secret Iranian Nuclear Compound—Report," http://rt.com/news/iran-spy-rock-nuclear-777.

59. "USNS Observation Island (T-AGM)," wwwmsc.navy.mil (accessed April 10, 2010); Ben Iannotta, "Cobra Judy," *C4ISR Journal* (May 2007): 32–33; [deleted], "The *Cobra Judy* Acquisition," *Cryptologic Quarterly* 1, no. 4 (Winter 1983): 78–84; Kenneth J. Stein, "Cobra Judy Phased Array Radar Tested," *AW&ST*, August 10, 1981, 70–73; "X-Band Expands Cobra Judy's Repertoire," *Defense Electronics*, January 1985, 43–44; Science Applications International Corporation, *Fifty Year Commemorative History of Long Range Detection*, 195.

60. Stein, "Cobra Judy Phased Array Radar Tested"; "X-Band Expands Cobra Judy's Repertoire"; Coalition Media Center, Qatar, *Media Briefing Support Imagery: Attack on Ababil 100 Surface to Surface Missile*, March 28, 2003; Iannotta, "Cobra Judy."

61. Department of Defense, *Selected Acquisition Report (SAR): COBRA JUDY Replacement*, December 31, 2011, 4–5; Raytheon, "Cobra Judy Replacement Radars Perform Exceptionally During First Live-Launch Test," April 2, 2013, http://investor.raytheon.com/phoenix.zhtml?c=84193&p=irol-newsArticle&ID=1802380; Military Sealift Command, "Ship Inventory—Missile Range Instrumentation Ships," www.msc.navy.mil (accessed February 7, 2014); Susan A. Romano, Office of Public Affairs, Air Force Technical Applications Center, "AFTAC's Maritime Radar Becomes Operational," August 7, 2014; "Military Range Instrumentation Ships," www.msc.navy.mil/inventory (accessed October 8, 2014).

62. "COBRA GEMINI," www.fas.org (accessed March 16, 2007); Air Force Technical Applications Center, CENI 38-101, *Organization and Functions Chartbook*, 8; Military Sealift Command, "Ship Inventory—Missile Range Instrumentation Ships"; Military Sealift Command, *2012 in Review*, 2013, 13; Military Sealift Command, *2013 in Review*, n.d., 13; David Axe, "The U.S. Air Force Has a Spy Ship—Yes, Ship—in the Persian Gulf," *War Is Boring*, December 30, 2014, https://medium.com/war-is-boring/the-u-s-air-force-has-a-spy-ship-yes-ship-in-the-persian-gulf-6ebb07cc6a33.

63. U.S. Navy, Fact File: "Ocean Surveillance Ships—T-AGOS," http://www.navy.mil/navydata/fact_display.asp?cid=4500&tid=600&ct=4 (accessed February 7, 2014).

64. Department of the Navy, *Record of Decision for Surveillance Towed Array Sensor System Low Frequency Active (SURTASS LFA) Sonar*, August 2012, 11–12.

65. Travis Graham, "SURTASS Ships Return from Deployment," May 6, 2005, http://www.northwestnavigator.com; General Accounting Office, GAO-02-692, *Defense Acquisitions: Testing Needed to Prove SURTASS/LFA Effectiveness in Littoral Waters*, June 2002, 1.

66. Missile Defense Agency, Fact Sheet, "Sea Based X-Band Radar," September 2013, http://www.mda.mil/global/documents/pdf/sbx.pdf; Luis Martinez, "U.S. Sea Radar Tracking N. Korean Threat," ABC News, April 11, 2013, http://abcnews.go.com/blogs/politics/2013/04/us-sea-radar-tracking-n-korean-threat; "Missile Surveillance Radar at Adak, Alaska," MatthewAid.com, February 9, 2013, http://www.matthewaid.com/post/42655116603/missile-surveillance-radar-at-adak-alaska.

67. U.S. Congress, Senate Committee on Armed Services, *Department of Defense Authorization for Appropriations for Fiscal Year 1980*, pt. 6 (Washington, DC: U.S. Government Printing Office, 1979), 2925; U.S. Navy, "Commander, Undersea Surveillance, IUSS Headquarters Staff," www.cus.navy.mil (accessed May 9, 2006).

68. Owen Wilkes, "Strategic Anti-submarine Warfare and Its Implications for a Counterforce First Strike," in *World Armaments and Disarmament, SIPRI Yearbook 1979* (London: Taylor & Francis, 1979), 430.

69. Science Applications International Corporation, *Fifty Year Commemorative History of Long Range Detection*, 113.

70. John Howard, "Fixed Sonar Systems: The History and Future of the Underwater Silent Sentinel," *Submarine Review* (April 2011): 1–12; Gary E. Weir, National Geospatial-Intelligence Agency, "American Sound Surveillance System: Using the Ocean to Hunt Soviet Submarines, 1950–1961," 2007; Edward C. Whitman, "SOSUS: The 'Secret Weapon of Undersea Warfare," *Undersea Warfare* 7, no. 2 (Winter 2005), http://www.chinfonavy.mil; Commander, Undersea Surveillance, "Origins of the Sound Surveillance System (SOSUS)," www.cus.navy.mil/sosus.htm (accessed May 9, 2006).

71. Defense Market Survey (DMS), "Sonar-Sub-Surface-Caesar," *DMS Market Intelligence Report* (Greenwich, CT: DMS, 1980), 1; Clyde Burleson, *The Jennifer Project* (Englewood Cliffs, NJ: Prentice Hall, 1977), 17–18, 24–25; Joel S. Wit, "Advances in Antisubmarine Warfare," *Scientific American* (February 1981): 36ff.; Silverstein, "CAESAR, SOSUS, and Submarines."

72. Howard B. Dratch, "High Stakes in the Azores," *Nation*, November 8, 1975, 455–456; "NATO Fixed Sonar Range Commissioned," *Armed Forces Journal International* (August 1972): 29; "Atlantic Islands: NATO Seeks Wider Facilities," *International Herald Tribune*, June 1981, 75; Richard Timsar, "Portugal Bargains for U.S. Military Aid with Strategic Mid-Atlantic Base," *Christian Science Monitor*, March 24, 1981, 9; Wit, "Advances in Antisubmarine Warfare."

73. "Naval Ocean Processing Facility, Whidbey Island—About NOPF," http://nopfwi.ahf.nmci.navy.mil (accessed February 7, 2014); "Naval Ocean Processing Facility, Whidbey Island—Canadian Detachment," http://nopfwi.ahf.nmci.navy.mil (accessed February 7, 2014); Commander, Undersea Surveillance, "Naval Ocean Processing Facility (NOPF) Dam Neck," www.public.navy.mil/subfor/cus/Pages/NOPFDN.aspx; "About NOPF Whidbey Island," www.naswi.navy.mil/nopf/ABOUT_NOPF.htm (accessed May 9, 2006); Commander, Undersea Surveillance, "Naval Ocean Processing Facility (NOPF) Whidbey Island, July 1987–Present," wwwcus.navy.mil/nopfwi.htm (accessed April 10, 2010); Commander, Undersea Surveillance, "Naval Ocean Processing Facility (NOPF) Dam Neck, September 1979–Present," www.cus.navy.mil/nopfdn.htm (accessed April 10, 2010).

74. U.S. Navy "Milpersman 1306-423, Assignment to Undersea Detachment Billets," December 7, 2012, http://www.public.navy.mil/bupers-npc/reference/milpersman/1000/1300Assignment/Documents/1306-423.pdf.

75. Robert P. Berman and John C. Baker, *Soviet Strategic Forces: Requirements and Responses* (Washington, DC: Brookings Institution, 1982), 106–107; Bill Gertz, "Russian Sub Stalks Three U.S. Carriers," *Washington Times*, November 23, 1997, A1, A5; Mark Mazzetti and Thom Shanker, "2 Russian Submarines Off East Coast of U.S. Evoke Echoes of Cold War," *New York Times*, August 5, 2009, A5.

76. Office of the Chief of Naval Operations, OPNAVINST C3501.204A, Subject: Projected Operational Environment (POE) and Required Operational Capabilities (ROC) Statements for the Integrated Undersea Surveillance System (IUSS), March 14, 1995; confidential interview.

77. Science Applications International Center, *Fifty Year Commemorative History of Long Range Detection*, 114; 3400 Technical Training Wing, *Introduction to Detection Systems*, 18.

78. William J. Broad "Anti-sub Seabed Grid Thrown Open to Research Uses," *New York Times*, July 2, 1996, C1, C7; Patrick E. Tyler and Steven Lee Myers, "Russian Admiral Acknowledges Explosion Inside Sub," *New York Times*, August 15, 2000, A6.

79. CIA, "Charlie: CIA's Robotic Fish," June 4, 2013, https://www.cia.gov/library/video-center/video-transcripts/charlie-cias-robotic-fish.html; Husna Haq, "U.S. Navy's Newest Spy? A Drone Fish Named Nemo," www.csmonitor.com, December 16, 2014, http://www.csmonitor.com/Technology/2014/1216/US-Navy-s-newest-spy-A-drone-fish-named-Nemo.

10

SPACE SURVEILLANCE

In addition to being concerned with events on Earth, the U.S. Intelligence Community is also concerned with events in outer space—in "space situational awareness." An accurate understanding of foreign space capabilities and activities is required for assessing the overall military and intelligence capabilities of foreign nations, selecting and implementing security measures, warning of actions (intentional or not) that threaten U.S. or other space systems (including manned vehicles), developing plans for the interception of communications or other signals transmitted through satellites, preparing and implementing plans to neutralize foreign space systems, and monitoring compliance with an assortment of treaties, including the Outer Space Treaty, which prohibits the deployment of nuclear weapons in space.[1]

Space surveillance operations involve detection, payload identification, cataloging, and tracking. Specific foreign space operations monitored by U.S. space surveillance assets include those that follow launch preparations: launch, deployment into orbit, mission, orbital parameters, maneuvering, deployment of subsatellites, breakup of satellites, and reentry of satellites or debris into Earth's atmosphere. Space surveillance systems are also used to determine the size, shape, and other characteristics of space systems.*[2]

During the Cold War, the driving force behind U.S. space surveillance activities was, of course, the Soviet Union. Of primary concern were Soviet reconnaissance, communications, navigation, meteorological, and other military support satellites. The capabilities and orbits of Soviet reconnaissance satellites had to be factored into plans to provide operational security to U.S. military forces and research and development efforts, including the activities of U.S. forces preparing for the April 1980 attempt to rescue American hostages in Iran as well as the highly classified aeronautical activities at Area 51 in Nevada. In addition, Soviet antisatellite testing was of significant concern to U.S. military officials. Even nonmilitary space activities, including lunar missions and space probes to Mars and Venus, were of interest to the Intelligence Community.[3]

---

*As a Strategic Command regulation notes, mission and payload assessment also relies on imagery, signals intelligence, human intelligence, and open source intelligence. See U.S Strategic Command, SCD 505-1, Volume 1, *Space Surveillance Operations—Basic Operations*, February 13, 2004, 42. Assessments may also rely on the analysis of recovered space debris.

In response to the threat from Soviet imagery satellites, the United States initiated the Satellite Reconnaissance Advanced Notice (SATRAN) program, also known by the nickname STRAY CAT, in 1966. The SATRAN program became part of the Satellite Reconnaissance Operations Security Program. The Navy established a complementary program: the Satellite Vulnerability Program.[4] By 1987, the Naval Space Surveillance System (NAVSPASUR) was providing four types of satellite vulnerability information to Navy units:

- Large Area Vulnerability Reports (LAVR) provided satellite vulnerability information to units in established operating areas.
- Satellite Vulnerability Reports (SVR) provided tailored vulnerability information to units in a transit status or operating outside established operating areas.
- Safe Window Intelligence (SWINT) Reports provided periods when the requesting units were not vulnerable to reconnaissance satellite coverage.
- One-line CHARLIE elements allowed units with the Reconnaissance Satellite Vulnerability Computer program to compute their own satellite vulnerability data.[5]

In 1988 the Naval Space Command instituted the CHAMBERED ROUND program for support to deployed elements of the fleet and Fleet Marine Force. Under CHAMBERED ROUND, the Naval Space Command provided naval forces with tactical assessments of hostile space capabilities and specific reactions to their operations. The support was tailored to a unit's specific equipment, geographic area of interest, and intentions during predeployment workups or while in transit to the theater of operations.[6]

Although the collapse of the Soviet Union resulted in a reduced Russian military space program, the remaining program is still of interest to the U.S. Intelligence Community and its space surveillance assets, such as those that tracked a Persona-class reconnaissance satellite after its launch in June 2013. Those same assets also tracked the Russian Lotus S SIGINT satellite launched in December 2014. Operational security measures to prevent Russian imaging satellites from viewing particularly sensitive activities continue. Likewise, data concerning Russian communications satellites are required to support U.S. communications intelligence activities.[7]

In the post–Cold War era the use of satellites for intelligence purposes has expanded significantly. China orbited its first photographic reconnaissance spacecraft in 1975 and now launches a wide variety of imagery spacecraft, including those employing electro-optical and synthetic aperture radar sensors. It also has deployed spacecraft with electronic intelligence, ocean surveillance, mapping, meteorological, and communications missions. Chinese space exploration activities have also included orbiting and then landing unmanned spacecraft on the moon.[8]

Since 1995, there has been an explosion of foreign nations—including France, Israel, Japan, Germany, Italy, India, and Iran—orbiting spacecraft with imagery intelligence capabilities. There has been an improvement in capabilities as well as an expansion in the type of sensors employed to produce imagery, with imaging radars being deployed as well as electro-optical sensors. In addition, the numbers and capabilities of commercial imagery systems with a resolution that can be readily exploited for intelligence purposes have also grown. Other nations also operate a variety of military

FIGURE 10.1   Number of Nations and Government Consortia Operating in Space

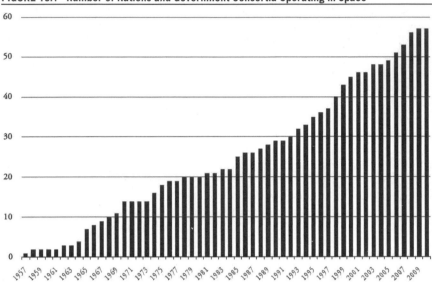

Source: National Air and Space Intelligence Center, via Department of Defense and Office of the Director of National Intelligence, National Security Space Strategy, Unclassified Summary, January 2011, 2.

and civil satellites with other missions, including communications, navigation, mete-orology, relay, and signals intelligence.[9] Figure 10.1 shows the growth in the number of organizations operating space systems.

Foreign space activities have on occasion threatened U.S. space assets. In 2006 China employed a laser to interfere with the operations of U.S. reconnaissance satel-lites. In the future, interference could be carried out by a Chinese antisatellite system. On January 11, 2007, China successfully tested such a system, designated SC-19 by U.S. intelligence, after two failed attempts. The test involved firing a missile from the Xichang launch site in Szechuan province. The target, a Chinese weather satellite, FY-1C, had been launched in 1999 into a sun-synchronous, five hundred-mile orbit. The satellite was destroyed when it was 715 miles from the launch site, resulting in two clusters of debris.[10]

Then, in August 2010 a Chinese satellite, SJ-12, launched in June, undertook a series of orbital maneuvers to approach an older Chinese satellite, SJ-06F, at a very slow speed. The two satellites may have actually come into contact as a result of a Chinese test of an orbital rendezvous capability. Developing a capability could be a prelude to constructing a space station, inspecting or servicing satellites, flying satel-lites in formation, or (at higher speed) developing an antisatellite capability. A test of an advanced antisatellite system may have occurred in May 2013. In January 2014, according to the State Department, China conducted a "nondestructive test" of an antisatellite weapon.[11]

In August 2006, due to concerns over threats to U.S. space systems, President George W. Bush signed a policy directive stating that the United States would "take those actions necessary to protect its space capabilities . . . and deny, if necessary, adversaries the use of space capabilities hostile to U.S. national interests." The succeeding directive, *National Space Policy of the United States of America*, signed by President Barack Obama in June 2010, similarly stated, "The United States will employ a variety of measures to help assure the use of space for all responsible parties, and consistent with the inherent right of self-defense, deter others from interference and attack, defend our space systems and contribute to the defense of allied space systems, and, if deterrence fails, defeat efforts to attack them." It also stated that the United States would "develop, maintain, and use space situation awareness (SSA) information from commercial, civil, and national security sources to detect, identify, and attribute actions in space that are contrary to responsible use and the long-term sustainability of the space environment."[12]

The focal point of the U.S. space surveillance effort is the Strategic Command's Joint Space Operations Center (JSpOC) at Vandenberg Air Force Base (AFB), California (formerly the Space Surveillance Center at Cheyenne Mountain AFB). The JSpOC maintains *The Space Catalogue*, a listing of orbiting objects, and regularly receives data from three types of sensors—dedicated, collateral, and contributing—that make up the Space Surveillance Network (SSN), which produces about 380,000 to 420,000 observations each day. In December 2012, JSpOC was tracking more than 22,000 objects in Earth orbit. Of those, about 1,100 were functioning payloads or satellites, while approximately 1,750 were rocket bodies. Over 19,000 of the objects, the remaining 87 percent of those tracked, were debris or inactive satellites.*[13]

DEDICATED SSN SENSORS

Dedicated SSN sensors are those whose primary mission is space surveillance. They account for approximately 70 percent of SSN detections of near-Earth objects and about 90 percent of SSN detections of deep-space objects.[14] They may rely on a variety of techniques, including optical and infrared detection, radars, "a fence" that detects objects passing through it, and radio frequency monitoring. The sensors are located in space and on the ground, with ground sensors in both the United States and foreign nations.

The United States operates three satellite systems with a primary mission of space surveillance. One, the Space-Based Surveillance System (SBSS), launched on September 25, 2010, from Vandenberg AFB; the 2,275-pound SBSS Pathfinder Block 10 satellite entered a 390-mile sun-synchronous orbit but only attained operational status in August 2012. The satellite, which has a seven-year design life, carries an 11.8-inch telescope and is able to image satellites in geosynchronous orbit as well as ones at lower altitude. The telescope is moveable rather than fixed and can operate twenty-four hours a day, seven days a week. In addition, it can reportedly detect objects that are half as dim as other systems and is able to rapidly move from one target to another and

---

*A breakdown along different lines appears in DOD and ODNI, *National Security Space Strategy, Unclassified Summary*, January 2011, 1. Of the 22,000 objects in the catalog approximately 7,000 are classified as unknown objects of unknown origin. Of the remaining 15,000, there are 10,500 items of debris, 1,500 rocket bodies, and 3,000 payloads.

to track a moving object, such as a satellite entering into orbit. The next generation SBSS is expected to begin development in 2016, with the first launch anticipated to come in 2020.[15]

Another, previously classified effort was revealed in early 2014: the Geosynchronous Space Situational Awareness Program (GSSAP). The first two satellites were launched into space on a Delta IV rocket from Cape Canaveral Air Force Station on July 28, 2014. In January 2015, they were going through the checkout phase, with initial operating capability still at least a couple of months away. They will drift above and below the geosynchronous belt. An Air Force fact sheet stated that the system "will have a clear, unobstructed and distinct vantage point for viewing resident space objects orbiting Earth in a near-geosynchronous orbit without the disruption of weather or atmosphere that can limit ground-based systems." The satellites are also expected to have the ability to do close-up inspections of foreign satellites. They will be controlled by the Air Force Space Command's (AFSPC) 50th Space Wing at Schriever AFB, Colorado, via the Air Force Satellite Control Network. Launch of a pair of replacement satellites on an Atlas rocket is scheduled for 2016.[16]

The Air Force Space Command also employs for space surveillance a satellite originally launched for the Missile Defense Agency on May 5, 2009. The Advanced Technology Risk Reduction (ATRR) satellite was launched from Vandenberg AFB and placed into a low-Earth (537 × 542 mile), sun-synchronous orbit, then turned over to AFSPC in 2011. An additional satellite to monitor spacecraft in geosynchronous orbit is planned for launch in 2017. Designated ORS-5, it is to be designed and built by the Massachusetts Institute of Technology's (MIT) Lincoln Laboratory under the supervision of the Air Force's Operationally Responsive Space Office at Kirtland AFB in New Mexico.[17]

Until the mid-1980s, the primary dedicated ground-based electro-optical sensors for space surveillance consisted of a series of Baker-Nunn cameras, which could detect a satellite illuminated by the sun while the Earth's surface was in twilight or darkness. Measurement of the satellite's position against a known star field produced precise locational data. Over the course of the program, Baker-Nunn cameras were located at nearly a dozen sites, although they were not all operational at the same time.[18]

The role of the Baker-Nunn cameras in the U.S. space surveillance network was assumed by the Ground-Based Electro-optical Deep Space Surveillance (GEODSS) program, operated by three detachments of the 21st Operations Group, a component of the Air Force Space Command's 21st Space Wing at Peterson AFB, Colorado: Detachment 1 (Socorro, New Mexico, specifically Stallion Station, White Sands Missile Range), Detachment 2 (Diego Garcia, British Indian Ocean Territory), and Detachment 3 (Maui, Hawaii). A site at ChoeJong San, South Korea, was closed in 1993 due to poor tracking conditions.[19]

The GEODSS sites employ three one-meter telescopes equipped with "a highly sensitive digital camera technology" designated Deep STARE (Surveillance Technology Advancement and Replacement for Ebsicons)—the replacements being charge-coupled devices). The telescopes, which can be used either separately or together, are capable of seeing objects 10,000 times dimmer than the human eye can detect.[20] According to an Air Force fact sheet, "The Deep STARE camera system is able to track multiple satellites in the field of view. The telescopes take rapid electronic snapshots of satellites in the night sky, showing up on the operator's console as tiny streaks. Computers then measure these streaks and use the data to compute the position of satellites in their orbits. Star images, which remain fixed, are used as reference or calibration points for each of the three telescopes. The resulting metric observation data is then sent instantaneously to the Joint Space Operations Center."[21]

The system provides the capability to optically track objects higher than 3,000 nautical miles out to geosynchronous orbit. More than 2,500 objects are in orbits from 6,200 to almost 28,000 miles above Earth. The ability of GEODSS to reach geosynchronous altitude was demonstrated in 1985, when a GEODSS site photographed a Navy Fleet Satellite Communications satellite. At geosynchronous altitude the GEODSS telescopes can detect a reflective object the size of a soccer ball. GEODSS is also able to search up to 17,400 square degrees per hour. Furthermore, some GEODSS installations are close enough together to provide overlapping coverage as a means of overcoming poor weather at an adjacent site.[22]

Like the Baker-Nunn system, GEODSS depends on the collection of light reflected by objects under investigation and is operational only at night during clear weather. Additionally, adverse atmospheric conditions limit sensitivity and resolution. Unlike the earlier system, however, GEODSS is able to provide real-time data with a computer-managed instant video display of surveillance data. Furthermore, the computer automatically filters stars from the night-sky backdrop and then uses its memory of known space objects to determine the existence of new or unknown objects, alerting the user when such objects are found.[23]

Prior to the closing of the GEODSS Korea station, the stations' areas of coverage were 165W–050W for Stallion Station; 010W–140E for Maui, Hawaii; 010E–130E for Diego Garcia; and 070E–178E for ChoeJong San. GEODSS sensors were responsible for over 65 percent of all deep-space object tracking and identification and provided almost worldwide coverage of the equator.*[24]

A second, longtime set of dedicated sensors, the Air Force Space Surveillance System (AFSSS), has been in mothball status since October 1, 2013. The system began operations in 1961 as NAVSPASUR. AFSSS consisted of the Alternate Space Control Center at Dahlgren, Virginia, and the Air Force Space Fence, which could detect and track satellites passing through an electronic fence consisting of a fan-shape radar beam with a 7,500-mile range, extending from San Diego, California, to Fort Stewart, Georgia. Since the beam could not be steered, detection resulted when a satellite passed through the beam and deflected its energy back to Earth, where it would be detected by several arrays of dipole antennas—inexpensive and unsophisticated antennas similar to a traditional television antenna.[25]

The central transmitter for the beam was located at Lake Kickapoo, Texas, and there were two smaller transmitting stations at Gila River, Arizona, and Jordan Lake,

---

*Beginning in late 1997, the Moron Optical Space Surveillance System (MOSS) at Moron, Spain—consisting of a twenty-two-inch telescope and the MOSS Space Operations Center (MOSC) van—operated in conjunction with GEODSS. It filled a gap in GEODSS's geosynchronous coverage. On March 31, 2013, the detachment closed. See Steve Brady, 21st Space Wing Public Affairs Office, "Wing closing one detachment," CSMNG.com, April 11, 2013, http://csmng.com/wp-files/space-observer-weekly-pdfs/spaceobserver_2013-04-11.pdf.

Alabama. The six receiver stations—San Diego, California; Elephant Butte, New Mexico; Red River, Arkansas; Silver Lake, Mississippi; Hawkinsville, Georgia; and Tattnall, Georgia—were all located, as were the transmitting stations, across the southern United States, along a great circle inclined at about 33 degrees to the equator. All satellites with an inclination greater than 33 degrees (about 80 percent of the current population) pass through this circle twice each day. The data obtained was transmitted to Dahlgren in real-time.[26]

Objects in low-inclination orbit (which includes geosynchronous satellites as well Israel's Offeq reconnaissance satellite) and very small objects were not routinely detectable with the fence. It did have a longitudinal width that stretched from Africa (less than 15 degrees west longitude) to beyond Hawaii (greater than 165 degrees west longitude) and was capable of detecting objects beyond 22,000 miles. As recently as 2012, the Space Fence was collecting over 5 million observations on space objects every month, most generated by satellites in near-Earth orbit. There are more than one hundred satellites that no sensor other than the fence would routinely observe, representing over 40 percent of the 12 million observations that the SSN gathered each month.*[27]

In early June 2014, the Air Force awarded a contract to Lockheed Martin to build a new Space Fence. One site, to be located at Kwajalein Atoll, is expected to be operational in 2018, while a second site, anticipated to be located in western Australia, is expected to enter service in 2022. Construction on the Kwajalein site began in February 2015. The maximum coverage area of the fence is projected to be 24,800 miles—in contrast to 13,640 miles for the AFSSS—and it will be able to detect an object the size of a softball at a distance of 1,200 miles. As a result, the system will have the ability to track more than 200,000 objects.[28]

As a means of mitigating the loss of information, a number of changes were made in the operations of other space tracking assets, including an AN/FPS-85 radar and a collateral sensor in North Dakota. The AN/FPS-85 phased-array radar is operated by the 20th Space Control Squadron (formerly the 20th Space Surveillance Squadron), whose headquarters are at Eglin AFB, Florida, although the radar itself is located near the city of Freeport, about thirty-five miles east of the base. The radar, which was constructed in 1967 and became operational in December 1968, is 143 feet high and 318 feet long and has separate transmitter and receiver arrays. Its principal axis is aligned due south across the Gulf of Mexico, and it is capable of receiving and transmitting over an arc extending 60 degrees on either side. Most satellites pass through its beam, which has a range of 2,500 miles, twice a day. The radar provides tracking information on space objects in low-Earth orbit and has had a limited deep-space capability since 1988. As a result of its low-Earth orbiting capability, it has given "theater warfighters advance knowledge of possible enemy intelligence-gathering satellites" and improved "their knowledge about what information those satellites could provide an adversary."[29]

The radar can track an object the size of a basketball at a distance of more than 22,000 miles. It can detect, track, and identify up to two hundred satellites simultaneously. In a given year it collects more than 16 million observations of satellites, which make up 30 percent of the SSN's total workload. It can also track space junk;

---

*Percentage figures for each SSN sensor will sum to far more than 100 percent since multiple sensors may detect the same satellite.

in the early 1970s, it located and tracked the glove lost by astronaut Ed White during a space walk.[30]

Another ground-based space surveillance system is a U.S. AN/FPS-129 radar with an eighty-nine-foot mechanical dish, operated as a joint program by the Air Force Space Command and the Norwegian Military Intelligence Service. Designated HAVE STARE when located at Vandenberg AFB, it was deployed in 1999 to Vardo, Norway, forty miles from the Russian border, and is now known by its Norwegian project name: GLOBUS II. According to an Air Force Space Command official, it "provides metric tracking and imagery of near-Earth and deep space satellites" and provides the only all-weather, around-the-clock, space tracking capability for the 0–90 degrees east region. The radar can also be employed for spectral data collection, such as reading the exhaust fumes of a jet engine to determine aircraft type. The radar's ability to obtain detailed imagery of Russian warheads and decoys, and its replacing another U.S. radar in Norway (CREEK CHART) that was used for that purpose, raised suspicions and concerns in Norway and Russia that its real purpose was to provide data to a U.S. national missile defense system—a charge denied by both the United States and Norway. During testing in 2001, it detected and imaged both a Russian Ono-satellite in Molniya orbit as well a Russian Kobalt reconnaissance satellite in low-earth orbit.[31]

Two additional dedicated sensors are scheduled for deployment in Australia. One, at a location to be determined, is the Space Surveillance Telescope (SST) developed by the Defense Advanced Research Projects Agency and tested at White Sands Missile Range, New Mexico. The telescope will be able to detect and track objects in geosynchronous as well as low-Earth orbit and to conduct faster, more accurate, and more sensitive searches than GEODSS. The second sensor is a C-band radar that was moved from Antigua to the Harold E. Holt Naval Communications Station at Exmouth in June 2014; it is expected to become operational around May 2016 (operated by the Royal Australian Air Force No. 1 Radar and Surveillance Unit), increasing coverage of the Southern Hemisphere. It will be operated by Australian personnel and able to track up to two hundred objects, including those too faint for other space surveillance systems to detect. In addition, it will be particularly well suited to track "high-interest" launches from Asia, such as China, as it will be located directly under the initial flight path of Chinese satellites.[32]

COLLATERAL SENSORS

Collateral sensors are designed primarily for missions such as missile warning or intelligence but are also employed for space surveillance. Such sensors account for approximately 25 percent of SSN detections of near-Earth objects and 5 percent of SSN detections of deep-space objects. Collateral sensors include the three Ballistic Missile Early Warning System (BMEWS) sites, the two remaining PAVE PAWS sites,* and

---

*PAVE had been reported to be an acronym for "Perimeter Acquisition Vehicle Entry," but a 2013 Air Force fact sheet stated only, "The acronym PAVE is a military program identification code." See U.S. Air Force, "PAVE PAWS Radar System," April 15, 2013, http://www.afspc.af.mil/library/factsheets/factsheet.asp?id=3656. The acronym is apparently formed from "Precision Avionics Vectoring Equipment."

collection systems at Cavalier Air Station, North Dakota; Kaena Point, Hawaii; and Ascension Island.[33]

The BMEWS is designed primarily to track missiles and to determine the number launched and their intended targets. The radars provide real-time information to the Ballistic Missile Defense System Command and Control, can track objects as small as four inches up to 3,000 miles above Earth, and provide 120-degree coverage from each face (for a total of 240-degree coverage). The system is dispersed across three sites: Clear Air Force Station, Alaska; Thule Air Base, Greenland; and Royal Air Force (RAF) Fylingdales, United Kingdom.[34]

The 12th Space Warning Squadron (SWS) at Thule (Site I), which operated an AN/FPS-120 phased-array radar, now operates an AN/FPS-132 Upgraded Early Warning Radar (UEWR) system as a result of upgrading the AN/FPS-123 operated at the site. An identical upgraded early-warning radar is also operated by the 13th SWS at Clear, Alaska (Site II), eighty-five miles southwest of Fairbanks. Its primary mission is to provide early warning of sea-launched and intercontinental missiles to the Northern Aerospace Defense Command (NORAD).[35]

BMEWS Site III at RAF Fylingdales, where the Air Force is represented by a liaison officer, is British operated. The UEWR at Fylingdales can track up to 55,000 objects in a day, many multiple times. Its primary mission is to provide warning of missile attacks against the United Kingdom and western Europe; it also helps provide coverage of Iranian launches. Its secondary mission is to provide warning of an intercontinental ballistic missile (ICBM) or submarine-launched ballistic missile (SLBM) attack against the continental United States. Space surveillance is its third function. In addition to the Air Force Space Command, the National Air and Space Intelligence Center receives its data. Another mission of the site is the Satellite Warning Service for the United Kingdom, which "gives U.K. forces warning of surveillance by satellites of potentially hostile or other nations," including both military and commercial intelligence gathering satellites.[36]

Two of the original four PAVE PAWS sites, those at El Dorado Air Station in Texas and at Robins AFB in Georgia, were placed in caretaker status, and the associated space warning squadrons were deactivated. The El Dorado radar was transferred to the Clear Air Force Station, where it replaced the mechanical radar previously operated by the Clear squadron. The remaining squadrons are located at Cape Cod Air Force Station (6th SWS) and Beale AFB (7th SWS), with the primary mission of detecting SLBMs.[37]

The Cape Cod warning squadron operates an AN/FPS-123, whose beams can sweep for 240 degrees and reach outward and upward for nearly 3,000 nautical miles. At its extreme range, it can detect an object the size of a small car, while it can detect smaller objects at closer range. On a typical day, the 6th SWS performs approximately 2,600 satellite tracks and about 9,100 observations. Modernization of the radar began in the 2013 fiscal year. The Beale squadron was upgraded in 2007 and operates an AN/FPS-132 radar, which has also been integrated into to the Ballistic Missile Defense System. It provides coverage of the Pacific region, including North Korean launches. The Cape Cod radar may be similarly upgraded.[38]

The Perimeter Acquisition Radar Characterization System (PARCS), operated by the 10th SWS at Cavalier Air Station, North Dakota, is a vestige of the U.S. antiballistic missile system dismantled in 1975. With a 3,100-mile range, the PARCS is a single-faced phased-array radar, designated AN/FPQ-16, that stands 121 feet high and can track hundreds of objects simultaneously. Its primary mission is to provide early warning of ICBM and SLBM attacks, but it also provides surveillance, tracking, reporting, and space object identification (SOI) of highly inclined and polar-orbiting objects. It is able to provide near-Earth metric and radar cross section measurements.[39]

The mission of the AN/FPQ-14 mechanical radar at Kaena Point, Hawaii, is to provide low-Earth satellite observation. The radar is tasked on a limited basis with supporting the space surveillance mission, primarily for high-priority objects requiring instantaneous observational data. The site is operated by civilians twenty-four hours a day, seven days a week. Kaena Point provides pointing data to the Air Force Maui Optical and Supercomputing Site (AMOS) (discussed below).[40]

On Ascension Island, located midway between the east coast of Brazil and the west coast of South Africa, are two radars. The primary radar is the AN/FPQ-15 tracker, which provides space and missile-launch support to the Eastern Space and Missile Center (ESMC), near-Earth satellite observations to the Joint Space Operations Center, and narrow-band SOI data to the Air Force Space Command intelligence components. The second radar is an AN/TPQ-18 tracker.[41]

CONTRIBUTING SSN SENSORS

Contributing sensors are those under contract or agreement to provide space surveillance data when requested by U.S. Air Force Space Command headquarters. They provide about 5 percent of near-Earth observations as well as 5 percent of deep-space observations. Contributing sensors include a phased-array radar on Shemya Island, the Maui Space Surveillance System (MSSS), the Reagan Test Site on Kwajalein Atoll, and the Lincoln Space Surveillance Complex.

The phased-array COBRA DANE (AN/FPS-108), as noted in Chapter 9, had, until 2012, an intelligence mission, which was its primary mission. At the same time, it also served as a contributing sensor for the space surveillance network—a mission that continues.

The COBRA DANE system consists of an AN/FPS-108 radar facility that measures 87 × 107 feet at its base; it rises approximately six stories, or 120 feet, and includes an attached one-story, 87-square-foot Precision Measurement Equipment Laboratory. This facility overlooks the Bering Sea from a 230-foot-high bluff in the northwestern section of Shemya.[42]

COBRA DANE is a phased-array radar. To observers relying on their eyes or using binoculars, a phased-array radar is simply a dormant structure, sort of an electronic pyramid. This contrasts sharply with the older, more traditional dish, "sweeping its beam of microwave radiation along the horizon for distant objects." COBRA DANE consists of 15,360 radiating elements that occupy ninety-five feet in diameter on the radar's face. Each element emits a signal that travels in all directions. When the signals are emitted at the same time, only targets in the immediate vicinity of the array's perpendicular axis are detectable. By successively delaying the signals by a fraction of a wavelength, however, one can "steer" the beam to objects away from the perpendicular axis.[43]

COBRA DANE, which achieved initial operating capability in July 1977, can detect (with a 99 percent probability) and track a basketball-sized object at a range of

2,000 miles with a 136-degree field of view, extending beyond the northern half of Sakhalin Island to just short of the easternmost tip of Russia near the Bering Strait. Its ability to provide information on the size and shape of the object, however, is available only over a 44-degree range centered on the upper portion of Kamchatka. In its space surveillance mode, it can track up to two hundred satellites.[44]

With its coverage extending northward over an arc from Kamchatka to the Bering Strait, COBRA DANE, which operates in the L-band, can be used for tracking satellites in polar and near-polar orbits out to 3,000 miles. By 2010 it had been upgraded to allow it to perform a missile defense mission (tracking ballistic missiles with sufficient accuracy to allow the launch of interceptors), as well as its traditional intelligence and space tracking missions. Tasking for COBRA DANE emanates both from the National Air and Space Intelligence Center (for SOI) and Joint Space Operations Center (for both metric and space object identification).[45]

The contributing sensors at Maui, Hawaii, form the MSSS. The Air Force Maui Optical and Supercomputing Site at Mount Haleakala, Maui, is a photometric and laser facility assigned to the Air Force Materiel Command's Phillips Laboratory. Its basic mission is to conduct research and development of new and evolving electro-optical sensors and to provide support to the Air Force Space Command. It has also provided support to the National Aeronautics and Space Administration and the Jet Propulsion Laboratory. AMOS experiments have included detection and tracking of orbital debris, observation of shuttle and satellite operations, and laser illumination of satellites.[46]

Mount Haleakala's location, 10,000 feet above sea level, places AMOS's equipment above much of the atmosphere and the interference associated with it. The equipment includes a 5.2.-foot Cassegrain telescope, a laser beam director, and an AMOS acquisition system. The space surveillance research and development work at AMOS includes metric, tracking, infrared space object identification, and compensated imaging.[47]

AMOS's laser was used to illuminate Soviet spacecraft at night for the purpose of telescope photography. It was also used to determine whether Soviet nuclear-powered radar ocean surveillance satellites were operating or properly shut down at the end of their missions. The visible-wavelength images of the satellites produced by AMOS were good enough to show a Soviet reactor glowing red-hot.[48]

AMOS's telescope has sufficiently high resolution to discern objects in a space shuttle's open payload bay. Such a capability could have been employed to obtain intelligence on Soviet shuttle missions, had the Soviet program reached operational status. Its telescope has allowed identification of objects as small as 3.1 inches in diameter in geosynchronous orbit. Another optical sensor, the AMOS Daylight Near-Infrared Imaging System, extends AMOS capability to twenty-four hours a day.[49]

Collocated with the GEODSS and AMOS systems is the Maui Optical Tracking Identification Facility (MOTIF), code-named TEAL BLUE. MOTIF consists of a forty-seven-inch telescope (along with a beam director/tracker) capable of both near-Earth and deep-space satellite tracking and object identification using visible-light and long-wave infrared imaging. One telescope is used primarily for infrared and light intensity measurements. The other is employed for low-light level tracking and imagery. For satellites orbiting at 3,000 miles or less, MOTIF's sensors can measure reflectivity and heat emissions and provide images. MOTIF has identified objects as small as eight centimeters in geosynchronous orbit.[50]

PHOTO 10.1   The TEAL BLUE space surveillance site in Hawaii. *Photo credit:* Robert Windrem.

In 1997 the Air Force Materiel Command's Phillips Laboratory began testing another sensor at the Maui complex: the Advanced Electro-optical System, which is
optimized for satellite tracking and SOI. With a primary mirror 3.64 meters wide,
it should have permitted detection and tracking of four-inch pieces of debris in low-
Earth orbit at a range of 186 miles. In 2012 the Air Force completed an upgrade of the
system, which is jointly operated by the Air Force Office of Scientific Research and
the National Science Foundation. In addition, the MSSS includes a small commercial
off-the-shelf-based autonomous telescope, designated RAVEN. It is employed by the
MSSS to perform the majority of its metric collection mission.[51]

Contributing sensors are also located at the Reagan Test Site on Roi-Namur Island and on the two largest islands of the hundred that make up the Kwajalein Atoll.
The Advanced Research Projects Agency (ARPA) Lincoln C-Band Observables Radar
(ALCOR), operated by the Army Space and Missile Defense Command, consists of a
forty-foot antenna and provides wideband radar imaging data for SOI on low-Earth
orbit satellites, as well as radar cross section measurements. Support to the SSN is on
a noninterference basis with support to the Kwajalein Missile Range.[52]

ALCOR observed China's first satellites, launched in 1970. The images of the
booster rocket body revealed the dimensions of the object, information of the great interest to the Defense Department because it provided insight into the size and payload
capacity of Chinese ICBMs. The following year, ALCOR imaged the Soviet Union's
SALYUT-1 space station.[53]

A second radar located on Roi-Namur, the ARPA Long-Range Tracking and Instrumentation Radar (ALTAIR), is also operated by the Army Space and Strategic
Defense Command. The ALTAIR is a 150-foot paraboloid antenna that provides
metric data on near-Earth and deep-space spacecraft. The radar operates in a space
surveillance mode for 128 hours per week. It has a capability against both near-Earth
and deep-space objects and can track one-third of the geosynchronous belt. Over 50

percent of the launches from Russia, China, and Japan pass through ALTAIR's coverage area on their way to achieve orbit.[54]

Also located on Roi-Namur are the Target Resolution and Discrimination Experiment (TRADEX) and Millimeter Wave (MMW) radars. Like ALTAIR, TRADEX is a low-frequency dish radar that can pick up incoming objects as soon as they come over Kwajalein's horizon at a distance of approximately 2,400 miles. It can track up to sixty-three objects simultaneously. Like ALCOR, MMW operates at high frequencies, allowing it to image objects in space. MMW, the highest-resolution imaging radar in the space surveillance network, can detect objects as small as five inches in low-Earth orbit and as small as sixteen feet at geosynchronous altitude, which makes it of significant value to the Intelligence Community.[55]

The Millstone, Haystack, and Haystack Auxiliary radars, located about half a mile apart at Westford, Massachusetts, are operated by MIT's Lincoln Laboratory and form the Lincoln Space Surveillance Complex. The Millstone Hill Radar is a deep-space, large-dish tracking radar capable of tracking one-square-meter targets at geosynchronous altitude. It was the first radar to detect the radar signals reflected off Sputnik I in 1957. The Haystack Ultra-Wideband Satellite Imaging Radar (HUSIR) is a high-quality imaging radar that can resolve objects as small as one foot in diameter in low-Earth orbit. It has been described in congressional hearings as providing "images of orbiting satellites that we can get from no other location." It is a "long-range, high-altitude capable radar which provides extremely good intelligence data and now has a real-time operational reporting capability." The National Air and Space Intelligence Center employs data from the radar to assess payload, mission, and status. The Haystack Auxiliary Radar was deployed so that space surveillance efforts would not suffer when the Haystack was operating in a radio-astronomy mode. According to one account, it can produce "finer and sharper images of satellites than the Haystack [radar]."[56] Figure 10.2 shows the distribution of ground-based sensors belonging to the SSN.

ADDITIONAL SPACE SURVEILLANCE CAPABILITIES

The Space Surveillance Network makes an average of 45,000 sightings of orbiting objects each day. Twenty percent of the objects and debris cannot be reliably tracked. More than 16,000 objects have been catalogued. A commander in chief of the (now disestablished) U.S. Space Command characterized the system as "predictive . . . rather than a constant surveillance system."

Continuity on deep-space objects is sometimes difficult to maintain because the radars are part-time contributors, and the optical and electro-optical sensors are restricted to nighttime operation during clear weather.[57] But the SSN also receives help from other systems.

The United States has for many years made use of National Reconnaissance Office systems to provide intelligence on foreign space activities. The possibility of employing U.S. imagery satellites to photograph Soviet satellites was achieved no later than 1965, with the KH-4 satellite. Over a decade later, the KH-11 satellites were used on occasion for "space-to-space" imagery operations.[58]

FIGURE 10.2 Distribution of Space Surveillance Network Sensors

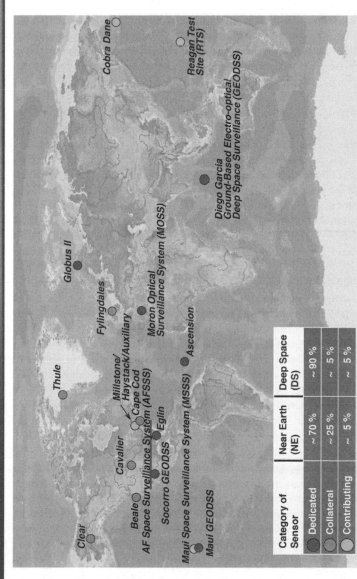

Space Surveillance Network (SSN)

Cobra Dane

Reagan Test
Site (RTS)

Diego Garcia
Ground-Based Electro-optical
Deep Space Surveillance (GEODSS)

Globus II

Thule

Fylingdales

Moron Optical
Surveillance System (MOSS)

Millstone/
Haystack/Auxiliary

Cape Cod

Ascension

Cavalier

AF Space Surveillance System (AFSSS)

Eglin

Beale

Socorro GEODSS

Maui Space Surveillance System (MSSS)

Maui GEODSS

Clear

Category of Sensor	Near Earth (NE)	Deep Space (DS)
Dedicated	~ 70 %	~ 90 %
Collateral	~ 25 %	~ 5 %
Contributing	~ 5 %	~ 5 %

Source: Paul W. Schumacher Jr., Air Force Research Laboratory, *The Future Satellite Catalog* [workshop on "Data Fusion of Rare and Anomalous Events," December 17–19, 2012, Dayton, Ohio, Slide 4].

More frequent contributors have been the Defense Support Program (DSP) satellites described in Chapter 9, which have proved useful in monitoring foreign satellites. The employment of DSP sensors to detect space objects, including satellites and their debris, is designated FAST WALKER. Most FAST WALKER detections have been routine observations of foreign spacecraft. The infrared readings obtained by DSP sensors, resulting from the reflection of sunlight off the spacecraft, have provided analysts at the Central Intelligence Agency, Defense Intelligence Agency, and the National Air and Space Intelligence Center with data on spacecraft signatures and movements. Such data have allowed analysts to estimate the path of a satellite and its mission.[59]

In addition, DSP sensors have provided data concerning the reentry of satellites and other man-made space platforms. In January 1978, DSP sensors detected the reentry of COSMOS 954, a Soviet ocean reconnaissance satellite with a nuclear reactor that the Soviets could not control. Unable to boost it into an orbit that would keep it in space, the Soviets could only watch as the satellite's orbit decayed to the point that reentry took place. At the Aerospace Corporation, the DSP track of the reentry was subjected to mathematical analysis and the impact point determined. In 1979 DSP sensors provided data on the reentry of Skylab, the 130,000-pound space station whose reentry threatened various populated areas.[60]

Among the satellite movements and debris that the DSP detected from the early 1970s to the early 1980s were those associated with the Soviet antisatellite program. From 1972 to 1982, the Soviets conducted sixteen antisatellite tests. After an intercept satellite was placed in orbit by an SL-11 booster, ground controllers would maneuver the satellite so that either one or two orbits would pass sufficiently near the target satellite to permit its own guidance system to take over. When in range, an explosive charge aboard the intercept vehicle was detonated, sending a cloud of shrapnel at high speed to destroy the target. The DSP's monitoring of the launch, satellite movement, and aftermath contributed to U.S. intelligence analysis of the Soviet program. In 1996 a DSP satellite detected the descent of a malfunctioning Chinese FSW-1 reconnaissance satellite back to Earth and into the Atlantic Ocean. A DSP satellite also detected the launch of the kill vehicle used in China's January 11, 2007, antisatellite test.[61]

In 2009 the Air Force launched two Space Tracking and Surveillance System (STSS) prototype satellites into an 840-mile circular orbit, with a 58-degree inclination, to test their capabilities with regard to missile detection and tracking. They may also be employed to contribute to the space surveillance mission.[62]

Even searchers for extraterrestrial intelligence and amateur astronomers have contributed to the space surveillance mission. In 2012 it was reported that the Air Force Space Command had enlisted help from the Search for Extraterrestrial Intelligence's (SETI) Allen Telescope Array, a forty-two-dish array that is part of the Hot Creek Radio Observatory located about 310 miles northeast of San Francisco. The dishes can provide data on low, medium, and geosynchronous orbiting satellites. In addition, the Defense Advanced Research Projects Agency (DARPA) SpaceView program, which is part of a larger DARPA program (OrbitalOutlook) that seeks the improved accuracy and timeliness of the SSN, enrolls amateur astronomers to help track orbital debris and detect possible satellite constellations.[63]

Notes

1. Gene H. McCall, Air Force Space Command, *Space Surveillance Requirements*, July 10, 1995, 7–8; General Accounting Office, GAO/NSIAD 98-42, *Space Surveillance: DOD and NASA Need Consolidated Requirements and a Coordinated Plan*, December 1997, 12; U.S. Air Force, Fact Sheet, "Space Situational Awareness Integration Office," October 12, 2006, http://www.afspc.af .mil/library/factsheets/factsheet.asp?id=3650; Peter B. de Selding, "U.S.-France Agree on Space Surveillance as Top Priority," *Space News*, July 5, 2004, 4; Jeremy Singer, "Surveillance Remains Most Pressing Space Control Need," *Space News*, October 11, 2004, A1–A2; Jeremy Singer, "Chilton Stresses Need for Space Situational Awareness," *Space News*, October 30, 2006, A2.

2. Government Accountability Office, GAO 11-545, *Space Acquisitions: Development and Oversight Challenges in Delivering Improved Space Situational Awareness Capabilities*, May 2011, 5; Air Force Space Command, *Space Surveillance Requirements*, 12–13.

3. See Michael R. Mantz, *The New Sword: A Theory of Space Combat Power* (Maxwell AFB, AL: Air University Press, 1995); Edna L. Jenkins and Paul W. Schumacher Jr., "Close Encounters Parallel Processing Improves Space Debris Tracking," *Space Tracks* (Summer 1997): 15–16; Paul W. Schumacher Jr., "Cataloging Space," *Space Tracks* (Fall 1997): 10–13; Nicholas L. Johnson, *Soviet Military Strategy in Space* (London: Jane's, 1987); Nicholas L. Johnson and David M. Rodvold, *Europe and Asia in Space, 1993–1994* (Colorado Springs, CO: Kaman Sciences Corp., n.d.); Jeffrey T. Richelson, ed., National Security Archive Electronic Briefing Book No. 501, *U.S. Intelligence and the Soviet Space Program: From Satellites to Space Probes*, February 4, 2015.

4. Aerospace Defense Command, *ADCOM Command & Control*, November 30, 1980, 8–12; USSPACECOM Regulation 200-1, "Satellite Reconnaissance Operations Security Support Program," August 18, 1989; U.S. Strategic Command, SCD 505-1, *Space Surveillance Operations– Basic Operations*, February 13, 2004, 1:7.

5. USSPACECOM Regulation 200-1, "Satellite Reconnaissance Operations Security Support Program"; Naval Education and Training Command, NAVEDTRA A 95-08-00-87, *Cryptologic Technician Training Services, Module 8, Fleet Operations—Electronic Warfare*, 1987.

6. Frank Murphy, "Chambered Round," *Space Tracks* (March–April 1991): 8–9.

7. Stephen Clark, "Russian Spy Payload in Orbit After Successful Soyuz Launch," *Spaceflight Now*, June 8, 2013, http://www.spaceflightnow.com/news/n1306/08soyuz/#.VO9EckK3jwM; "News Breaks," *AW&ST*, March 15, 1993, 23.

8. Office of the Secretary of Defense, *Annual Report to Congress: Military and Security Developments Involving the People's Republic of China*, 2013, 65; Ian Easton, Project 2049 Institute, *China's Revolving Reconnaissance-Strike Capabilities: Implications for the U.S.-Japan Alliance*, February 2014, 10; Stephen Clark, "China Successfully Lands Robotic Rover on the Moon," *Spaceflight Now*, December 14, 2013, http://spaceflightnow.com/china/change3/131214landing /#.VO9DHkK3jwM; Stephen Clark, "Chinese Surveillance Payload Put in Orbit by Long March 2C," *Spaceflight Now*, October 29, 2013, http://www.spaceflightnow.com/news/n1310 /29longmarch/#.VO9DXUK3jwM; Stephen Clark, "Chinese Surveillance Satellites Launched into Orbit," *Spaceflight Now*, August 12, 2014, http://www.spaceflightnow.com/news/n1408 /12longmarch/#.VO9DgkK3jwM.

9. Thomas G. Mahnken, "Why Third World Space Systems Matter," *Orbis* (Fall 1991): 563– 579; Theresa Hitchens, "European Eyes in the Sky," *Imaging Notes* (Fall 2006): 20–24; Jeffrey T. Richelson, "The Whole World Is Watching," *Bulletin of the Atomic Scientists* (January–February 2006): 26–35; Craig Covault, "India Readies Israeli Radar Spysat to Eye Pakistan," *Spaceflight Now*, April 18, 2009, http://spaceflightnow.com/news/n0904/17milsar; "Delta 2 Lofts Italy's Final Cosmo-Sky Med Satellite," *Space News*, November 11, 2010, 8; William J. Broad, "After Delay, Iranians Launch a Satellite," *New York Times*, June 16, 2011, A13; "India Launches Radar Imagery Craft on PSLV," *Space News*, April 30, 2012, 3.

10. Warren Ferster and Colin Clark, "NRO Confirms Chinese Laser Test Illuminated U.S. Spacecraft," *Space News*, October 2, 2006, 10; Vago Muradian, "Poke in the Eye," *C4ISR Journal* (November–December 2006): 48–49; William J. Broad and David E. Sanger, "Flexing Muscle, China Destroys Satellite in Test," *New York Times*, January 19, 2007, A1, A11; Colin Clark and Jeremy Singer, "China's ASAT Test Widely Criticized, U.S. Says No New Treaties Needed," *Space News*, January 22, 2007, 1, 4; Peter B. de Selding, "Debris from FY-1C Destruction Poses Long-Term Concern," *Space News*, January 29, 2007, 6; Michael R. Gordon and David S. Cloud, "U.S. Knew of China's Missile Test, but Kept Silent," *New York Times*, April 23, 2007, A1, A9.

11. "Data Point to Chinese Orbital Rendezvous," *Space News*, August 30, 2010, 3; Stephen Clark, "China Remains Silent on Satellite Rendezvous," *Spaceflight Now*, September 8, 2010, http://spaceflightnow.com/news/n1009/08china; Brian Weeden, "Dancing in the Dark: The Orbital Rendezvous of SJ-12 and SJ-06F," *Space Review*, August 30, 2010, http://www.thespacereview.com/article/1689/1; Yasmin Tadjdeh, "New Chinese Threats to U.S. Space Systems Worry Officials," *National Defense*, July 2014, http://www.nationaldefensemagazine.org/archive/2014/July/Pages/NewChineseThreatstoUSSpaceSystemsWorryOfficials.aspx; Brian Weeden, *Through a Glass, Darkly: Chinese, American, and Russian Anti-satellite Testing in Space*, Secure World Foundation, March 17, 2014, http://swfound.org/media/167224/Through_a_Glass_Darkly_March2014.pdf.

12. George W. Bush, *U.S. National Space Policy*, White House, August 31, 2006; Barack Obama, White House, *National Space Policy of the United States of America*, June 28, 2010, 3, 7; Micah Zenko, "Dangerous Space Incidents," Council on Foreign Relations, April 2014, http://www.cfr.org/space/dangerous-space-incidents/p32790.

13. AFSPACECOM Regulation 55-10, "2nd Space Wing (SWG) Satellite Operations," October 13, 1989, 6; Jess Hall, "Command Activities at 21st SPW at Peterson," *Space Trace* (June 1992): 4; General Accounting Office, *Space Surveillance*, 10; U.S. Air Force, "Media Advisory: Space Unit to Move from Cheyenne Mountain," Air Force Space Command, September 15, 2006, http://www.afspc.af.mil/news/story.asp?id=123027156; McCall, Air Force Space Command, *Space Surveillance*, 34; James Kitfield, "Crowed, Congested Space," *Air Force Magazine* (August 2010): 24–29; Amy Butler, "Collision Avoidance," *AW&ST*, July 6, 2009, 18–19; U.S. Air Force, Fact Sheet, "Joint Space Functional Component Command for Space," Vandenberg AFB, December 2012, http://www.vandenberg.af.mil/library/factsheets.

14. Paul W. Schumacher Jr., Air Force Research Laboratory, *The Future Satellite Catalog* (presentation to Workshop on Data Fusion for the Detection of Rare and Anomalous Events, Dayton Ohio, December 17–19, 2012), 4.

15. Justin Ray, "Space Surveillance Project Successfully Blasts Off," *Spaceflight Now*, September 26, 2010, http://www.spaceflightnow.com/minotaur/sbss; Government Accountability Office, GAO-09-326SP, *Defense Acquisitions: Assessments of Selected Weapons System*, March 2010, 125–126; "SBSS Satellite Begins Long-Delayed Mission," *Space News*, August 27, 2012, 9; Stephen Clark, "Space Tracking Satellite Launch Delayed Indefinitely," *Spaceflight Now*, October 5, 2009, http://www.spaceflightnow.com/news/n0910/05minotaur; Government Accountability Office, GAO-09-326SP, *Defense Acquisitions; Assessments of Selected Weapon Programs*, March 2009, 137–138; Jeremy Singer, "SBSS Facing Cost Growth, Launch Delay," *Space News*, June 11, 2007, 18; Amy Butler, "On Watch in Space," *AW&ST*, April 14, 2008, 32–33; "SBSS Follow-On Sat Could Launch by 2020," *Space News*, March 12, 2012, 14; Aaron Mehta, "USAF Focuses on Space Debris, Other Threats," www.defensenews.com, May 24, 2014, http://archive.defensenews.com/article/20140524/DEFREG/305240019/USAF-Focuses-Space-Debris-Other-Threats.

16. Mike Gruss, "With SBSS Follow-On in Limbo, U.S. Space Surveillance Gap Looms," *Space News*, February 24, 2014, A1; U.S. Air Force, Fact Sheet, "Geosynchronous Space

Situational Awareness Program (GSSSAP)," May 2014, http://www.afspc.af.mil/library/factsheets/factsheet.asp?id=21389; Mike Gruss, "Shelton Discloses Previously Classified Surveillance Satellite Effort," *Space News*, February 24, 2014, A3; Stephen Clark, "Air Force General Reveals New Space Surveillance Program," *Spaceflight Now*, February 25, 2014, http://spaceflightnow.com/news/n1402/25gssap/#.VO9FJ0K3jwM; Amy Butler, "Neighborhood Watch," *AW&ST*, March 3, 2014, 22–23; "Space Surveillance Craft Launched by Delta 4 Rocket," *Spaceflight Now*, July 28, 2014, http://spaceflightnow.com/delta/d368/#.VO9FPkK3jwM.

17. U.S. Air Force, Fact Sheet, "Missile Defense Systems Division," Los Angeles AFB, November 2010, http://www.losangeles.af.mil/library/factsheets/factsheet.asp?id=7175; "USA-205," Wikipedia, http://en.wikipedia.org/wiki/USA-205; Missile Defense Agency, "Missile Defense Agency Space Tracking and Surveillance System Advanced Technology Risk Reduction Satellite Transfers to Air Force Space Command," February 26, 2011, http://www.mda.mil.news/11news0004.html; Kevin Williams, Air Force Space Command Public Affairs, "1st Space Ops Assumes Space Surveillance Mission," June 10, 2014, http://www.af.mil/News/ArticleDisplay/tabid/223/Article/485411/1st-space-ops-assumes-space-surveillance-mission.aspx; Stephen Clark, "Air Force Satellite to Continue Tracking of Space Traffic," *Spaceflight Now*, September 3, 2014, http://spaceflightnow.com/news/n1409/03ors5/#.VO9FUkK3jwM; "STSS ATRR (USA-205)—Satellite Information," http://www.heavens-above.com/satinfo.aspx?satid=34903&lat=0&lng=0&loc=Unspecified&alt=0&tz=CET (accessed October 12, 2014).

18. USSPACECOM Regulation 55-6, "Space Surveillance Network Data User Support," April 15, 1991, 10; AFSPACECOM 002-88, "Statement of Operational Need (SON): Space Surveillance (S2)," August 7, 1989, A1-1; Curtis Peebles, *High Frontier: The U.S. Air Force and the Military Space Program* (Washington, DC: U.S. Government Printing Office, 1997), 39–41.

19. U.S. Air Force, Fact Sheet, "Ground-Based Electro-optical Deep Space Surveillance," March 2013, http://www.afspc.af.mil/library/factsheets/factsheet.asp?id=3653.

20. Ibid.; Air Force Space Command, *Space Surveillance Network (SSN) Site Information Handbook*, October 24, 2007, 121; Walter J. Facenda, David Ferris, C. Max Williams, and David Brisnehan, "Deep STARE Technical Advancements and Status," MITRE Corporation, 2003, https://www.mitre.org/sites/default/files/pdf/faccenda_deepstare.pdf.

21. U.S. Air Force, "Ground-Based Electro-optical Deep Space Surveillance."

22. Ibid.; David M. Russell, "NORAD Adds Radar, Optics to Increase Space Defense," *Defense Electronics* (July 1982): 82–86; William C. Jeas and Robert Anctil, "The Ground Based Electro-optical Deep Space Surveillance (GEODSS) System," *Military Electronics Countermeasures* (November 1981): 47–51; "GEODSS Photographs Orbiting Satellite," *AW&ST*, December 5, 1985, 146–147; Office of Technology Assessment, *Anti-satellite Weapons, Countermeasures and Arms Control* (Washington, DC: U.S. Government Printing Office, 1985), 55; USSPACECOM Regulation 55-12, "Space Surveillance Network (SSN)," June 1, 1992, 15.

23. "U.S. Upgrading Ground-Based Sensors," *AW&ST*, June 16, 1980; Russell, "NORAD Adds Radar, Optics to Increase Space Defense."

24. Michael Muolo, *Space Handbook: A Warfighter's Guide to Space* (Maxwell AFB, AL: Air University Press, 1993), 1: 98–99.

25. Roger Easton and Chester Kleczek, "Origins of Naval Space Surveillance," *Space Tracks* (May–June 1998): 14–16; Gary R. Wagner, "The Longest Watch," *Space Tracks* (January 2001): 12–14; "Air Force Activates Space Surveillance Detachment at Dahlgren," *Domain* (Winter 2005): 22; "U.S. Air Force Takes Over Fence Space-Surveillance Network," *Space News*, October 18, 2004, 11; U.S. Air Force, Fact Sheet, "20th Space Control Squadron, Detachment 1," Peterson AFB, August 16, 2012, http://www.peterson.af.mil/library/factsheets/factsheet.asp?id=4729; Air Force Space Command, *Space Surveillance Network (SSN) Site Information Handbook*, 143; Armed Forces News Service, "Air Force Space Command to Discontinue Space Surveillance System," U.S.

Air Force, August 13, 2013, http://www.af.mil/News/ArticleDisplay/tabid/223/Article/466832/air-force-space-command-to-discontinue-space-surveillance-system.aspx.

26. U.S. Air Force, "20th Space Control Squadron, Detachment 1"; Schumacher, "Cataloging Space"; United States Space Command Regulation 55-12, "Space Surveillance Network (SSN)," 15; T. S. Kelson, "Space Surveillance," *Satellite Times* (September–October 1997): 68–69.

27. Schumacher, "Cataloging Space"; "A Constant Vigil," *Space Tracks* (March–April 1998): 5; Brian Weeden, "Gambling with a Space Fence," *Space Review*, August 26, 2013, http://www.thespacereview.com/article/2357/1.

28. Mike Gruss, "As Space Fence Award Nears, Lockheed Offers Some Detail of Its Proposal," *Space News*, April 28, 2014, A1; Stephen Clark, "Lockheed Martin Wins Contract for Space Fence," *Spaceflight Now*, June 2, 2014, http://spaceflightnow.com/news/n1406/02spacefence/#.VO9FbEK3jwM; "U.S. Picks Kwajelin Atoll for First Space Radar," *Space News*, October 1, 2012, 10; Mike Gruss, "With Current System Slated for Closure, Air Force Defers Next-Gen Space Fence," *Space News*, August 26, 2013, 1, 4; Armed Forces News Service, "Air Force Space Command to Discontinue Space Surveillance System"; "U.S. Putting Space-Tracking Radar, Telescope in Australia," *Space News*, November 19, 2012, 9; "Lots of Space Surveillance," *AW&ST*, November 19, 2012, 18; Government Accountability Office, GAO-11-233SP, *Defense Acquisitions: Assessments of Major Weapon Programs*, March 2013, 121–122; Bradley Perrett, "Due South," *AW&ST*, March 25, 2013, 33.

29. Mike Gruss, "Space Fence Shutdown Expected to Weaken Orbit Surveillance Network," *Space News*, August 12, 2013, 1, 4; Mike Gruss, "So Far, Stopgap Space Fence Replacement 'Looks Pretty Good' Shelton Says," *Space News*, September 23, 2013, 6; U.S. Air Force, "20th Space Control Squadron, Detachment 1"; Mark Major, "Upgrading the Nation's Space Surveillance Radar," *Technology Today* (September 1994); Peebles, *High Frontier*, 40; Air Force Space Command, *Space Surveillance Network (SSN) Site Information Handbook*, 143; AFSPCMD 5-103, "Space Surveillance Squadrons (SPSS)," October 1, 1996; "AN/FPS-85," *Jane's Weapons Systems, 1982–1983* (London: Jane's Publishing, 1982), 505–506; John Hamre, Congressional Budget Office, *Strategic Command, Control, and Communications Alternate Approaches for Modernization*, 1981, 10; USSPACECOM Regulation 55-12, "Space Surveillance Network (SSN)," 15; Science Applications International Corporation, *OUSD(A) Defense Space Systems Study, Final Report* (Falls Chruch, VA: SAIC, 1989), B-68; Air University, *Air University Space Primer* (Maxwell AFB, AL: Air University, 2009), 252–253.

30. U.S. Air Force, "20th Space Control Squadron"; Major, "Upgrading the Nation's Largest Space Surveillance Radar."

31. Richard F. Colarco, L-3 Communications, "Space Surveillance Network Sensor Development, Modification, and Sustainment Program" (presentation to the 2009 AMOS Conference, Maui, Hawaii, September 1–4, 2009); Brian Orban, "Worldwide Support," *Guardian*, December 1995, 3–6; Gordon Van Vleet, "STAREway into Space," *Guardian*, October 1995, 14–15; Shepherd, Air Force Space Command, *Space Surveillance Network*, 4; Elizabeth Becker, "Russians Challenge U.S. over Radar in Norway," *New York Times*, February 22, 2000, A11; David Mulholland and Simon Saradzhyan, "Norwegian Radar Draws Russian Charge of Espionage," *Space News*, April 3, 2000, 8; Inge Sellevag, "Vardo Exposed," *Bulletin of the Atomic Scientists* (March–April 2000): 26–29; Theodore A. Postol, "Target Is Russia," *Bulletin of the Atomic Scientists* (March–April 2000): 30–35; Gerard O'Dwyer, "Role of Arctic Radar Site Stirs Controversy in Norway," *Space News*, October 24, 2005, 12; McCall, Air Force Space Command, *Space Surveillance*, 12; Air Force Space Command, *Space Surveillance Network (SSN) Site Information Handbook*, 100; 17th Test Squadron, U.S. Air Force, *GLOBUS II Force Development Evaluation (FDE) & Fix Verification Test, Final Report*, n.d., not paginated.

32. Turner Brinton, "DARPA Space Telescope Will Track Objects in Geostationary Orbit," *Space News*, May 2, 2011, 6; "Lots of Space Surveillance," 18; "U.S. Putting Space-Tracking Radar, Telescope in Australia," *Space News*, November 16, 2012, 9; Cheryl Pellerin, Armed Forces Press

Service, "U.S. to Locate Key Space Systems in Australia," November 12, 2012, http://www.defense.gov/news/newsarticle.aspx?id=118537; "US Moves Satellite Surveillance Out of Antigua," *Antigua Observer*, November 15, 2012, http://antiguaobserver.com/us-moves-satellite-surveillance-out-of-antigua; Travis Blake, Defense Advanced Research Projects Agency, *Space Domain Awareness* (briefing prepared for 2011 AMOS Conference, September 14, 2011); "U.S. Space Radar at Exmouth," *DMO Bulletin*, no. 1 (2015), http://www.defence.gov.au/dmo/NewsMedia/DMOBulletin/US-Space-Radar-at-Exmouth.

33. Schumacher, Air Force Research Laboratory, *The Future Satellite Catalog*, 3; USSPACECOM Regulation 55-12, "Space Surveillance Network"; Shepherd, Air Force Space Command, *Space Surveillance Network*, 6.

34. Amy Butler, "Discriminating Sensors," *AW&ST*, July 13, 2009, 26.

35. Butler, "Discriminating Sensors"; U.S. Air Force, Fact Sheet, "13th Space Warning Squadron," August 16, 2012, http://www.peterson.af.mil/library/factsheets/factsheet.asp?id=4714; Missile Defense Agency, Fact Sheet, "Upgraded Early Warning Radars (UEWR), AN/FPS-132," April 2013; Air Force Space Command, *Space Surveillance Network (SSN) Site Information Handbook*, 71.

36. U.S. Air Force, Fact Sheet, "RAF Fylingdales, U.K.," August 16, 2012, http://www.peterson.af.mil/library/factsheets/factsheet_print.asp?fsID=4719; Missile Defense Agency, Fact Sheet, "Upgraded Early Warning Radars (UEWR), AN/FPS-132," April 2013; Butler, "Discriminating Sensors"; Air Force Space Command, *Space Surveillance Network (SSN) Site Information Handbook*, 72.

37. U.S. Air Force, Fact Sheet, "PAVE PAWS Radar System," Air Force Space Command, April 15, 2013, http://www.afspc.af.mil/library/factsheets/factsheet.asp?id=3656; U.S. Air Force, Fact Sheet, "6th Space Warning Squadron," http://www.peterson.af.mil/library/factsheets/factsheet.asp?id=4702 (accessed February 17, 2014); U.S. Air Force, Fact Sheet, "7th Space Warning Squadron," Beale AFB, http://www.beale.af.mil/library/factsheets/factsheet.asp?id=3976 (accessed February 17, 2014).

38. U.S. Air Force, "6th Space Warning Squadron"; U.S. Air Force, "7th Space Warning Squadron"; Missile Defense Agency, "Upgraded Early Warning Radars (UEWR), AN/FPS-132"; Butler, "Discriminating Sensors"; Missile Defense Agency, "Upgraded Early Warning Radars, AN/FPS-132," July 2014, http://www.mda.mil/global/documents/pdf/uewr1.pdf.

39. U.S. Air Force, Fact Sheet, "10th Space Warning Squadron," April 18, 2013, http://www.peterson.af.mil/library/factsheets/factsheet.asp?id=4710; Air University, *Air University Space Primer*, 255; Government Accountability Office, GAO 11-545, *Space Acquisitions*, 38.

40. Science Applications International Corporation, *OUSD(A) Defense Space Systems Study, Final Report*, B-64, B-70.

41. Ibid., B-65; USSPACOM Regulation 55-12, "Space Surveillance Network (SSN)," 16; Air University, *Air University Space Primer*, 255–256.

42. Dr. Michael E. Papa, *Meeting the Challenge: ESD and the Cobra Dane Construction Effort on Shemya Island* (Bedford, MA: Electronic Systems Division, Air Force Systems Command, 1979), 2–3.

43. Eli Brookner, "Phased-Array Radars," *Scientific American*, April 1985, 94–102.

44. Shepherd, Air Force Space Command, *Space Surveillance Network*, 6; USSPACECOM Regulation 55-12, "Space Surveillance Network (SSN)," 17; Schumacher, *The Space Catalogue*, 4.

45. Paul Stares, *Space and National Security* (Washington, DC: Brookings Institution, 1985), 205; "The Arms Race in Space"; U.S. Air Force, "SAC Fact Sheet," August 1981; Missile Defense Agency, Fact Sheet, "COBRA DANE Upgrade," September 2013, http://www.mda.mil/global/documents/pdf/cobradane.pdf; Air Force Space Command, *Space Surveillance Network (SSN) Site Information Handbook*, 94.

46. Shepherd, Air Force Space Command, "Space Surveillance Network (SSN)," 6; Science Applications International Corporation, *OUSD(A) Defense Space Systems Study, Final Report*,

B-64; Vincent Kiernan, "Air Force Begins Upgrades to Satellite Scanning Telescope," *Space News*, July 23–29, 1990, 8; U.S. Air Force, Fact Sheet, "Air Force Maui Optical & Supercomputing Site (AMOS)," April 30, 2012, http://www.kirtland.af.mil/library/factsheets/factsheet.asp?id=16930.

47. Science Applications International Corporation, *OUSD(A) Defense Space Systems Study, Final Report*, B-64; Kiernan, "Air Force Begins Upgrades to Satellite Scanning Telescope."

48. Craig Covault, "Maui Optical Station Photographs External Tank Reentry Breakup," *AW&ST*, June 11, 1990, 52–53.

49. Ibid.; Bruce D. Nordwall, "Air Force Uses Options to Track Space Objects," *AW&ST*, August 16, 1993, 66–68; Bruce D. Nordwall, "Optics/Laser Research Seeks to Improve Images," *AW&ST*, August 16, 1993, 69.

50. Stares, *Space and National Security*, 204; John Piotrowski, "C3I for Space Control," *Signal*, June 1987, 25–33; Science Applications International Corporation, *OUSD(A) Defense Space Systems Study, Final Report*, B-72; Kiernan, "Air Force Begins Upgrades to Satellite Scanning Telescope"; Air University, *Air University Space Primer*, 253.

51. William B. Scott, "Satellite-Tracking Telescope Readied for USAF Service," *AW&ST*, July 21, 1997, 57; "Telescope That Tracks Satellites Is Unveiled," *Space News*, July 14–20, 1997, 22; Air Force Research Laboratory, "AFOSR and NSF Joint Initiatives for U.S. Civilian Research at the 3.67m Advanced Electro-optical System (AEOS) Telescope at the Air Force Maui Optical Station (AMOS) on Hawaii," September 15, 2006, http://www.afsor.af.mil; "Boeing Completes Update of U.S. Air Force Telescope," *Space News*, June 25, 2012, 3; U.S Strategic Command, SCD 505-1, *Space Surveillance Operations—Basic Operations*, 1:10.

52. Science Applications International Corporation, *OUSD(A) Defense Space Systems Study, Final Report*, B-62; USSPACECOM Regulation 55-12, "Space Surveillance Network (SSN)," 17; Stephen M. Hunt, "Space Surveillance Always Tracking at the U.S. Army Kwajelin Atoll's Reagan Test Site," *Army* 53, no. 12 (December 2003), accessed through www.findarticles.com; Government Accountability Office, GAO-11-545, *Space Acquisitions*, 39.

53. William W. Camp, Joseph T. Mayhan, and Robert O'Donnell, "Wideband Radar for Ballistic Missile Defense and Range-Doppler Imaging of Satellites," *Lincoln Laboratory Journal* 12, no. 2 (2000): 267–280.

54. Science Applications International Corporation, *OUSD(A) Defense Space Systems Study, Final Report*, B-63; USSPACECOM Regulation 55-12, "Space Surveillance Network (SSN)," 17; Air University, *Air University Space Primer*, 256; Hunt, "Space Surveillance Always Tracking at the U.S. Army Kwajelin Atoll's Reagan Test Site"; Government Accountability Office, GAO 11-545, *Space Acquisitions*, 39.

55. Tony Reichart, "Catch a Falling Missile," *Air & Space* (December 1997–January 1998): 26–37; Camp, Mayhan, and O'Donnell, "Wideband Radar for Ballistic Missile Defense and Range-Doppler Imaging of Satellites"; McCall, *Space Surveillance*, 24; U.S Strategic Command, SCD 505-1, *Space Surveillance Operations—Basic Operations*, 1:9.

56. Science Applications International Corporation, *OUSD(A) Defense Space Systems Study, Final Report*, B-71; USSPACECOM Regulation 55-12, "Space Surveillance Network (SSN)," 17; Air University, *Air University Space Primer*, 256; Melvin L. Stone and Gerald P. Banner, "Radars for the Detection and Tracking of Ballistic Missiles, Satellites, and Planets," *Lincoln Laboratory Journal* 12, no. 2 (2000): 217–243; Camp, Mayhan, and O'Donnell, "Wideband Radar for Ballistic Missile Defense and Range-Doppler Imaging of Satellites"; William P. Delaney and William W. Ward, "Radar Development at Lincoln Laboratory: An Overview of the First Fifty Years," *Lincoln Laboratory Journal* 12, no. 2 (2000): 147–166; Richard F. Colarco, "Space Surveillance Network Sensor Development, Modification, and Sustainment Programs," AMOS, http://www.amostech.com/technicalpapers/2009/space_situational_awareness/colarco.pdf; Air Force Space Command, *Space Surveillance Network (SSN) Site Information Handbook*, 105.

57. AFSPACECOM 002-08, "Statement of Operational Need (SON): Space Surveillance (S2)," 3; William J. Broad, "New Space Challenge: Monitoring Weapons," *New York Times*, December 8, 1987, C1, C6.

58. [Deleted], Chief, Systems Analysis Staff, "Memorandum for: Mr. William A. Tidwell, Subject: Use of KH-4 to Photograph Orbiting Satellites," October 1, 1965; private information.

59. AFSPACECOM Regulation 55-55, "Space Based Sensor (SBS) Large Processing Station (LPS) and European Ground Station (EGS) Tactical Requirements Doctrine (TRD)," September 30, 1992, 38; confidential interview; Jeffrey T. Richelson, *America's Space Sentinels: The History of the DSP and SBIRS Satellite Systems* (Lawrence: University Press of Kansas, 2012), 106–107; Richard P. Osedacz, *Orbit Determination of Sunlight Illuminated Objects Detected by Overhead Platforms* (master's thesis, Air Force Institute of Technology, 1989).

60. Gus W. Weiss, "The Life and Death of Cosmos 954," *Studies in Intelligence* (Spring 1978); Jack Manno, *Arming the Heavens: The Hidden Military Agenda for Space, 1945–1995* (New York: Dodd, Mead, 1984), 148; private information.

61. Stares, *Space and National Security*, 85–87; confidential interviews; Craig Covault, "Chinese Military Satellite Poses Falling-Debris Risk," *AW&ST*, March 18, 1996, 62; Covault, "Space Control."

62. Government Accountability Office, *Defense Acquisitions*, 143–144; Justin Ray, "Delta 2 Rocket Launches Missile Defense Satellites," *Spaceflight Now*, September 25, 2009, http://www.spaceflightnow.com/delta/d344; "STSS Eyed for Possible Space Surveillance Role," *Space News*, March 26, 2007, 3; John Watson and Keith P. Zondervan, "The Missile Defense Agency's Space Tracking and Surveillance System," *Crosslink* (Spring 2008): 15–19; Missile Defense Agency, Fact Sheet, *Space and Tracking Surveillance System*, September 2013.

63. Leonard David, "U.S. Air Force Enlists SETI Telescope Array to Track Space Junk," *Space News*, May 7, 2012, A4; Leonard David, "U.S. Military Enlists Amateur Astronomers to Bolster Space Surveillance Network," *Space News*, November 19, 2012, 11; SpaceView, "DARPA," www.spaceviewnetwork.com/partners/darpa (accessed March 1, 2014).

11

HUMAN INTELLIGENCE

During the Cold War, the increasing ability to collect information through technical means reduced the need to rely on human sources for many types of intelligence, such as the coordinates of missile silos, the location of bomber bases, and the technical characteristics of missile systems.* However, human intelligence (HUMINT) was not inconsequential then and is even more important today. HUMINT activity involves intelligence officers and their agents, attachés, diplomats, defectors and émigrés, detainees, travelers, and Defense Department personnel in contact with intelligence targets.

Much valuable information, particularly when contained in documents, is accessible only through human sources. Such sources can be used to fill often important gaps left by technical collection systems. Sometimes intelligence gaps are the result of the inherent limitations of technical collection systems. Proper security insulates discussions from interception or eavesdropping. Technical systems cannot photograph policy documents or weapon systems manuals locked in vaults or acquire weapons systems or their components. In addition, properly protected computers cannot be penetrated without human assistance.

Obtaining a comprehensive overview of a particular program—be it a nuclear, missile, or biological weapons program—can be difficult when relying solely on technical sources of information. It has been reported that in the experience of intelligence officials, a "program's workings become clear only when described by the participants."[1]

Certain stages of military research and development (R&D) are simply not available for technical monitoring. Once plans have reached the testing stage, a variety of U.S. technical collection systems can be employed. But when the weapon is being designed and its characteristics debated, technical collection can be of very limited utility, particularly if information security is stringent. It is desirable to know about the characteristics of weapon systems when they have reached the testing stage, but it is also important to collect information about any activity in design organizations.

---

*The United States did, in 1962, wonder about how well the Soviets might do in using human sources to determine the precise location of U.S. missile silos and conducted an experiment to try to determine the likelihood of success. See Walter W. Romig, "Spy Mission to Montana," *Studies in Intelligence* 13, no. 1 (Winter 1969): 77–84.

Even nations that purchase weapons from abroad may develop their own modified versions. Iraq modified the Scud missiles it purchased from the Soviet Union, and Pakistan developed its Prithvi missiles from weapons that originated in North Korea.

U.S. intelligence objectives go beyond the deployment and technical characteristics of foreign government weapons systems, however. The Intelligence Community wants to know the intentions and plans of foreign governments, both hostile and friendly, with respect to foreign, defense, and economic policy. An understanding of both the processes and the people can lead to more accurate estimates of future actions. Much data on such matters may be obtained through open sources or by technical means, particularly communications intelligence (COMINT), but there will likely be gaps that only human intelligence can fill.

Human intelligence plays a critical role in monitoring terrorist groups and their facilities. Although training facilities may be monitored by overhead imagery, the most essential data are the locations of leaders and other key personnel and their intentions and plans. Human intelligence, along with COMINT and intelligence from liaison arrangements, offers the best chance of gathering such data.

HUMINT is generally classified into two basic categories: clandestine and overt. Clandestine HUMINT involves either a secret relationship with a foreign source to provide classified data or a U.S. intelligence officer's direct access and secret collection of intelligence.* Overt HUMINT involves open collection activities conducted by Department of Defense (DOD) attachés and State Department Foreign Service officers, as well as the debriefing of émigrés, defectors, and travelers. The use of enhanced interrogation methods to extract intelligence from detainees suggests that a third category exists: coerced HUMINT.

Twelve 1994 intelligence reviews provided some—albeit not necessarily perfect—measure of the value of HUMINT at that time. Of the 376 specific intelligence issues, HUMINT was judged as making a "critical contribution" in 205. In regard to terrorism, HUMINT items represented 75 percent of the critical items. The figures for some other key issues were as follows: over 50 percent for narcotics, over 40 percent for nonproliferation, and over 33 percent for economics.[2]

During the 1991 Persian Gulf War, HUMINT was employed in real-time "to nominate, target, and destroy key Iraqi command, control, communications, and other military targets." HUMINT was used, in conjunction with imagery, not only to aid in the destruction of military facilities but to identify mosques and hospitals and to permit U.S. war planners to avoid targeting civilian facilities. One source provided information that, according to an Army intelligence history, "significantly contributed to the impact of the air campaign, which undoubtedly saved many American and coalition lives."[3]

---

*That contact with the source may be largely conducted in cyberspace, or that the source may be unaware to whom he is providing information is suggested by Department of Defense Instruction S-3325.10, Subject: Human Intelligence Activities in Cyberspace, June 6, 2013, which includes a section on "HUMINT Cyberspace Tradecraft" and defines "cyber persona" as "an identity used in cyberspace to obtain information or influence others, while dissociating the actor's true identity or affiliation."

OFFICERS AND DIPLOMATS

The intelligence officers of the Central Intelligence Agency's Directorate of Operations compose the core of U.S. human intelligence. These officers are U.S. citizens who generally operate under the cover of U.S. embassies and consulates, an approach that provides them with secure communications (within the embassy and to other locations), protected files, and diplomatic immunity.

Others have operated under "nonofficial cover" (NOC), as part of a Global Deployment Initiative. NOCs may operate as businessmen, sometimes under the cover of working at the overseas office of a U.S. firm. In 1995 it was reported that 110 CIA officers were serving as NOCs and that RJR Nabisco, General Electric, IBM, Bank of America, Pan Am, Rockwell International, and other major corporations allowed CIA officers to pose as overseas employees. In the aftermath of the September 11 attacks, the George W. Bush administration planned to expand overseas operations by 50 percent.[4]

Those overseas operations included CIA-created front companies with six to nine case officers plus support staff. Valerie Plame, an officer with the Counterproliferation Division, operated overseas while ostensibly employed by the CIA-created Brewster Jennings & Associates. Some front companies were created by the CIA to provide cover for officers seeking to recruit sources inside Iran's nuclear and missile procurement programs.[5]

In 2008 it was reported that the CIA had shut down all but two of as many as twelve front companies set up in Europe and elsewhere in the aftermath of the September 11 attacks. The agency apparently concluded that the companies were "ill conceived and poorly positioned" for collecting intelligence on terrorist groups and networks dealing in the proliferation of unconventional weapons. A 2013 report described the program as a "colossal flop," attributing problems to inexperience, bureaucratic hurdles, and a lack of language skills.[6]

CIA stations in foreign countries are headed by a Chief of Station (COS) and vary substantially in size, from just to a few officers to hundreds. In the 1980s the CIA station in the Philippines had over 150 personnel. The agency's Nairobi station grew significantly after the 1998 embassy attacks. The CIA stations in Afghanistan and Iraq grew to hundreds of personnel after 9/11 and the 2003 invasion, respectively. The COS and his or her officers operate under a variety of cover positions that vary from embassy to embassy, including political counselor, second secretary, and economic attaché.[7]

A second set of collectors draws from the Defense Department and military services. Reporting to the Defense Intelligence Agency (DIA) are officers operating from Defense Attaché Offices in U.S. embassies and clandestine collectors with the Defense Clandestine Service. In addition, the Army Intelligence and Security Command's Army Operations Group, the Naval Criminal Investigative Service, the 25th Air Force's Global Activities Squadron, the U.S. Special Operations Command's Mission Support Activity, and other units conduct human intelligence efforts.

The responsibilities of defense attachés include

- Identifying and gaining the cooperation of human sources believed to possess the ability to furnish intelligence information

- Identifying and capturing collection opportunities presented by trade fairs, military demonstrations, parades, symposia, convocations, conferences, meetings, and the like
- Traveling to identified geographic target areas to observe, photograph, and report information specifically needed by consumers/users
- Identifying, establishing contact with, and maintaining liaison with foreign military officers who by virtue of rank, position, or assignment can furnish potential intelligence information or are considered to be future leaders
- Gaining and maintaining area reality to observe and report political, sociological, psychological, and economic developments of potential value in gauging foreign governments and their military forces' intentions, plans, capabilities, and stability
- Identifying foreign military equipment and materiel and gaining access to assist in its acquisition and exploitation.[8]

Foreign Service officers stationed in U.S. embassies and consulates are also a source of HUMINT reporting. These officers include those with political, economic, or cultural assignments. According to the 1995 congressional testimony of Under Secretary of State Peter Tarnoff, "The Foreign Service is a primary collector and producer of diplomatic and overseas reporting." That reporting, according to Tarnoff, contributed significantly, particularly in the political and economic areas, to the data that go into national intelligence production.[9]

Drug Enforcement Administration (DEA) investigation officers (or their sources) may also provide human intelligence, the vast majority of which, as expected, relates to narcotics trafficking. Such intelligence is transmitted not only to the DEA but also to the CIA. In addition, some of DEA's reporting may be related to terrorist activities. In a 2008 audit, the Department of Justice's inspector general found that, among eighty-one cables sampled, three concerned terrorism. One of those concerned Stinger missiles and other heavy arms for sale via a terrorist group seeking to attack coalition forces in Afghanistan. The other two concerned Taliban drug trafficking to finance terrorist activities and the identification of a significant terrorist cell training and operations activity in a specific district of Afghanistan.[10]

Specific collection efforts of defense attachés have, on occasion, become a matter of public record as a result of confrontation with foreign authorities. In early 1987, Colonel Marc B. Powe, the attaché at the U.S. embassy in Baghdad, was given two weeks to leave Iraq after he was accused of spying on and photographing truckloads of tanks and other military equipment in Kuwait in early December. Powe, who also served as attaché to Kuwait, had discovered a convoy of Soviet military equipment in Kuwait en route to Baghdad, and Kuwaiti authorities spotted him photographing the convoy and taking notes.[11]

In early 1989, two U.S. attachés, Colonel Clifford Robert Ward and Major Robert Siegel, were apprehended near a Palestinian commando base, twenty-five miles outside Damascus. Taken into custody by armed guerillas of the Popular Front for the Liberation of Palestine–General Command (PFLP-GC), they were reported to have been carrying cameras, maps, binoculars, and telephoto lenses.[12]

Incidents involving attachés operating in China occurred in 1995 and 1996. Early in August 1995, two U.S. Air Force officers, Colonel Joseph Wei Chan and Captain Dwayne Howard Florenzie, were expelled from China after being detained on July 28 and accused of spying on activities in restricted military zones along the country's southeastern coast. The two attachés, who operated out of the U.S. Consulate General's office in Hong Kong, were charged with illicitly entering restricted areas and "illegally acquiring military intelligence by photographing and videotaping" the areas before being detained "on the spot" by Chinese soldiers.[13]

The attachés had entered China on July 23 on visas issued for the purpose of consulting with officials at the U.S. embassy in Beijing and the Consulate General in Guangzhou. According to a Defense Department spokesman, the attachés were riding bicycles and wearing civilian clothes, had photographic equipment stored away in their backpacks, and were "observing" and "carrying along with the normal business" of military attachés when they were picked up by the Chinese soldiers. But their actual objective was reported to be monitoring ongoing Chinese military exercises north of Taiwan. The officers were said to be looking for Chinese Su-27 warplanes that had been moved to an airfield up the coast from Canton and close to Taiwan.[14]

Then, on January 8, 1996, Air Force Colonel Bradley Gerdes, the assistant military attaché, and a Japanese military attaché were stopped near a military area on Hainan Island, off the southern tip of China, after allegedly sneaking into a military airport near the city of Zhanjiang, the headquarters of the South China Fleet. Chinese authorities confiscated film and videotapes, according to a Foreign Ministry spokesman. The attachés may have been checking unconfirmed rumors of a temporary deployment of Su-27 fighter-bombers around Hainan Island, which China first employed in an exercise off Taiwan in November 1995.[15]

Russia has also been the site of attaché operations that have aggravated security authorities. In 1999 the Federal Security Service objected to the actions of Assistant Army Attaché Lieutenant Colonel Pete Hoffman, who hired a local taxi to drive to the training facility of the 242nd Airborne Training Center at the village of Posyotok Svetlyl. In 2008 Russia expelled two military attachés who had made an uninvited visit that March to the Novosibirsk Aviation Production Association in Siberia, a factory involved in manufacturing Sukhoi-34 fighter-bombers.[16]

Foreign Service officers provided on-the-ground reporting of critical events in China during June 1989. On June 3, 1989, the day before the events in Tiananmen Square, a cable from the U.S. embassy in Beijing to the State Department reported, "Ten to fifteen thousand helmeted, armed troops moved into Beijing during the late afternoon/early evening hours of June 3," provided information on the location of troop trucks and troops' weapons, and confirmed that elite airborne troops were moving from the south. The cable also noted that the embassy had received reports of trucks being surrounded and stopped by city residents.[17]

More recently the Tokyo embassy reported on the views and claims of a member of the Japanese Diet concerning nuclear matters, based on statements the member had made to embassy personnel at an October 2008 dinner concerned with energy and economics matters. Among the assertions reported were that Japanese electric companies were concealing the safety problems associated with nuclear energy and that the Ministry of International Trade and Industry was covering up nuclear accidents.

In addition, the Diet member claimed that Japan had no permanent high-level waste storage capability and no solution to the problem of waste storage.[18]

AGENTS AND ASSETS

Normally, agents are foreign nationals recruited by U.S. intelligence officers to collect information in their home countries or in a third nation, or they are individuals who volunteer their services.* During the Cold War, despite the closed nature of Soviet society and the size and intensity of the KGB's counterintelligence operation, the CIA had a number of notable successes. The most notable involved Colonel Oleg Penkovskiy, a Soviet military intelligence (GRU) officer who, as was the case with many Soviet sources, volunteered his services. In 1961 and 1962, Penkovskiy passed great quantities of material to the CIA and the British Secret Intelligence Service, including information on Soviet strategic capabilities and nuclear targeting policy. He provided a copy of the official Soviet medium-range ballistic missile manual, which was of critical importance at the time of Cuban missile crisis.[19]

In subsequent years the CIA would have assets in the Soviet Foreign Ministry, Defense Ministry, General Staff, GRU, KGB, and at least one military research facility. Other Soviet nationals reported to the CIA while working at the United Nations or other international organizations. Included in the group was Adolf G. Tolkachev, an electronics expert at the Moscow Aviation Institute. Tolkachev was, according to a U.S. official, "one of our most lucrative agents," who "saved us billions of dollars in development costs" by telling the United States about the nature of Soviet military aviation efforts. Over the years, Tolkachev passed on information concerning Soviet research efforts in electronic guidance and countermeasures, advanced radar, and stealth technologies. As a result, the Air Force "completely reversed its direction on a multi-million dollar electronics package for one of its latest fighter aircraft." Betrayed by former CIA officer Edward Lee Howard, Tolkachev was arrested in 1985 and executed.[20]

Such operations generally did not cease with the end of the Cold War and the collapse of the Soviet Union. In September 1995, a worker at a Defense Ministry research institute in St. Petersburg was arrested on suspicion of providing the United States with secret information on Russia's new attack submarine. In 1997 a former Russian diplomat was convicted of having spied since his recruitment in 1976.[21]

More recently, a number of Russian courts have convicted Russian citizens of aiding the CIA. In February 2012, Lieutenant Colonel Vladimir V. Nesterets, launch director of the Plesetsk Missile Test Center, pled guilty to "delivering classified information about tests relating to Russia's newest strategic military rocket complexes to the C.I.A." That information included details of a new generation of Soviet intercontinental

---

*A notable exception was Robert Levinson, a former FBI agent recruited by analysts from the CIA Directorate of Intelligence to gather information, who subsequently disappeared in Iran. See Matt Apuzzo and Adam Goldman, "American Missing in Iran Since 2007 Was Working for the CIA," www.theguardian.com, December 12, 2013, http://www.theguardian.com/world/2013/dec/12/robert-levinson-iran-missing-cia-secret; Barry Meier, "A Vanished American and a C.I.A. Scandal," *New York Times*, December 14, 2013, A1, A8–A9.

ballistic missiles. That May, a Yekaterinburg court convicted Alexander Gniteyev of passing secrets about the Bulava, a new submarine-launched ballistic missile, to the United States. Also in May, Colonel Vladimir Lazar, a retired Russian military officer convicted of providing the CIA with 7,000 classified Russian military maps, was sentenced to twelve years in prison. In 2015, a Russian court handed down a fifteen-year sentence to a former police officer charged with selling the CIA classified information.[22]

U.S. intelligence personnel have sought information from assets or potential assets in Europe, Africa, the Middle East, Southwest Asia, and Latin America over the past several decades. In early 1997, the German government ordered a CIA officer expelled. According to one account, the officer had been accused of trying to recruit senior German officials to provide information on high-technology projects. According to another account the officer was gathering information about a third country, probably Iran, and was ordered to leave because the operation had not been cleared with the German government.[23]

More recent evidence suggests that CIA operations in Germany have also targeted German government employees. In July 2014, it was reported that in addition to the CIA's having recruited a member of the German foreign intelligence service (discussed in Chapter 15), the German Federal Prosecutor's Office was investigating an employee of the Defense Ministry's political department, which focused on international security policy, for having passed information to the United States. Another account claimed that the CIA had assets in a number of other German ministries, including the interior, economics, and development.[24]

In 1993 the CIA targeted Henri Plagnol, an advisor to Premier Edouard Balladur of France, although how successful they were has been a matter of dispute. At approximately the same time, the agency also approached Thierry Miléo, who handled cable and satellite issues for the Minister of Communications and attempted to purchase information about the French negotiating strategy on telecommunications. In another instance, an employee of French Telecom, the national telephone company, was asked to "sell documents and information on France's international structure and networks," according to the Directorate for Territorial Surveillance (DST), France's security service at the time. Both targets reported the overtures to the DST, which encouraged them to continue contacts with the CIA officers. Among those involved in the operation was one NOC who represented herself as an employee of a Texas foundation interested in world economics.[25]

Another European target has been the International Atomic Energy Agency (IAEA). According to one account, officers at the CIA's Vienna station "were expected to develop sources inside the IAEA to learn about its secret deliberations."[26]

Recent HUMINT operations in the Middle East have targeted Iraq, Iran, and Syria. In the aftermath of the 2003 U.S. invasion of Iraq, it was revealed that Naji Sabri, Saddam Hussein's last foreign minister, had been a CIA asset. Sabri first began his espionage career as a spy for France's Directorate General of External Security (DGSE), which turned him over to the CIA more than six months before the war to provide intelligence on Iraqi nuclear, biological, and chemical weapons programs. Reportedly, Sabri told the CIA that while Hussein hoped to reestablish a nuclear weapons program, it was not active, and although research was taking place, no biological weapons were being produced or stockpiled. With respect to chemical weapons, he allegedly stated that some existed but not under military control.[27]

Not long before the invasion of Iraq, the CIA's Iraq Operations Group recruited a network of more than eighty agents, designated DB/ROCKSTARS, "DB" being the CIA digraph for Iraq. Each was equipped with a satellite telephone to send intelligence to a communications station atop a mountain in northern Iraq. After one of the agents was captured and shown on Iraqi television along with his Thuraya telephone, thirty of the eighty-seven ROCKSTARS halted communications with the CIA.[28]

ROCKSTARS assets included agents in the Republican Guard, regular army, and security services. Intelligence obtained included the locations of surface-to-surface missiles and antiaircraft positions, which would then be confirmed by satellite imagery. A ROCKSTARS asset headed the security unit in the Iraqi port of Umm Qasr and provided information on the locations of mines and security forces that would make it easy for U.S. Marines to seize the port.[29]

Two days before the invasion was scheduled to begin, one of the agents reported a heightened level of activity at the Dora Farms compound outside Baghdad, which Saddam Hussein's wife used and Saddam had also used. The heightened activity included the stocking of food and supplies and the arrival of a significant security presence (follow-up satellite imagery would show thirty-six vehicles). One agent reported that seeing Saddam, who had left for a meeting but was to return to sleep. The information led President Bush to authorize an attack on the compound, employing cruise missiles and F-117 aircraft, in an effort to kill the Iraqi president. Saddam survived, apparently because he was not at the facility during the attack.[30]

In April 1989, a number of Iranian military officers were arrested and charged with spying for the United States. Before its detection, the network, coordinated from Frankfurt, apparently produced valuable military intelligence about Iranian operations in the Persian Gulf at a time when U.S. naval forces were confronting Iranian forces.[31]

In mid-2004, the CIA acquired, through an Iranian source, a laptop computer containing studies for essential features of a nuclear warhead, including a sphere of detonators to trigger a nuclear explosion. The documents also examined the question of how to position a heavy ball, presumably consisting of fissile material, inside the warhead so as to guarantee stability and accuracy as it descended toward its target. In addition, they specified an explosion about 2,000 feet above the target—the preferred altitude for a nuclear detonation.[32]

The documents on the computer also included sophisticated drawings of a 130-foot-deep underground shaft with remote-controlled sensors to measure pressure and heat—the type of shaft used for an underground nuclear test. A test control team was to be located six miles away. There were also designs, with the most recent dated February 2003, for a small-scale facility to produce UF4, uranium tetraflouride, or "green salt," an intermediate product in the transformation of uranium into gaseous form. Absent from the documents was evidence, in the form of construction orders or payment invoices, that the projects had gotten beyond the drawing-board stage.[33]

In April 2010, it was reported that turmoil in Iran had "prompted a growing number of the country's officials to defect or leak information to the West, creating a new flow of intelligence about [Iran's] nuclear programs." Several months later, in October,

Iranian officials stated that some personnel at the nation's nuclear facilities had passed secret information to the West in exchange for money.[34]

Sometime during the Bush administration the CIA operated an asset in Syria's military program to develop chemical and biological weapons, who provided information on the pathogens being used.[35]

CIA targets in Southwest Asia have included India, Afghanistan, and al-Qaeda. In India, in 1977, six individuals were charged with spying for the United States. They had access to information about India's main aircraft design and production center, plus drawings of Soviet-made guns, missiles, and radar. According to a former senior Indian government official, in the early 1990s a top Indian civil servant was providing information about India's nuclear program to the CIA. A former member of the nation's Research and Analysis Wing stated, "We know the Americans had somebody inside. They knew about plans to test nuclear weapons and stopped us in the early 1990s." In 2006 a former Indian intelligence official who worked for Microsoft was arrested, followed by the departure of a senior U.S. embassy official.[36]

The Federal Bureau of Investigation (FBI) was able to place a source in direct contact with Osama bin Laden in 1993 while the individual was in Yemen. The source also reported to the CIA. The FBI determined that bin Laden was looking to finance terrorist attacks in the United States. The *Washington Post* reported that the source's information had led to the neutralization of a plot directed against a Masonic lodge in Los Angeles. The source was killed by al-Qaeda operatives in Bosnia.[37]

For several years prior to the terrorist attacks of September 11, 2001, the CIA paid a team of about fifteen Afghans to regularly track bin Laden in Afghanistan—with mixed results. Approximately once a month, the team pinpointed bin Laden's presence in a specific facility—intelligence that was then confirmed by satellite imagery or communications intelligence. After 9/11, Afghan recruits used satellite telephones to provide the U.S. government with exact locations of several buildings housing Taliban fighters and weapons on the west end of Kandahar; that intelligence led to a bombing attack on October 5, 2001.[38]

A few days after the 9/11 attacks, a CIA-led team, code-named JAWBREAKER, was dispatched to Afghanistan to work with the Northern Alliance (NA) and provide intelligence in anticipation of the arrival of U.S. combat troops. Information sources for the team included Taliban soldiers co-opted by the Northern Alliance as well as civilians residing within NA territory who had friends or relatives on the Taliban side and were willing to risk passing through enemy lines to collect intelligence. From September 27 to October 26, 2001, the collection effort resulted in over four hundred intelligence reports, which allowed U.S. aircraft to attack Taliban and al-Qaeda positions "with great accuracy and a minimum of collateral damage."[39]

In 2008 it was reported that al-Qaeda had remained impervious to penetration, but eighteen months later U.S. and international officials were touting improved recruitment of spies within the terrorist organization. One former CIA official referred to "our penetration of al-Qaeda." Director of National Intelligence Dennis Blair told reporters that the primary means of determining which terrorist organizations pose a direct threat is "to penetrate them and learn whether they're talking about making attacks against the United States."[40]

One means of penetrating the terrorist organization, in the early years after 9/11, involved recruiting Guantánamo Bay detainees. A secret facility at Guantánamo Bay, code-named PENNY LANE, consisted of cottages where prisoners who had agreed to serve as CIA assets resided before "rejoining" al-Qaeda. Some of those individuals, who were paid from a CIA account designated PLEDGE, helped the CIA find and kill, via Predator strikes, several senior al-Qaeda officials.[41]

In early 2011, the CIA instructed Pakistani doctor Shakeel Afridi, who had been an asset for a year, to spearhead a vaccination drive focusing on the hepatitis B virus and women between fifteen and forty-five—an effort actually designed to gather DNA evidence from the Abbottabad compound suspected to house bin Laden and members of his family. One of the doctor's nurses managed to get inside the compound but was unable to get the samples required for a comparison with the DNA samples collected from other members of the bin Laden family.[42]

In Asia, China has been the most important HUMINT target. At least one penetration of the Chinese establishment has involved someone with access to information on Chinese nuclear relations with a variety of foreign nations. That source was able to gain intelligence on a number of sensitive issues in the 1980s, including China's nuclear exports to Argentina and South Africa, Chinese technicians assisting at a suspected Pakistani bomb development site, Chinese scientific delegations spending substantial time at a centrifuge plant in Kahuta where Pakistani scientists were attempting to enrich uranium, Pakistani scientists from a secret facility at Wah showing a nuclear weapons design to Chinese physicists in late 1982 or early 1983 to obtain an evaluation of the design, and the triggering mechanism for a bomb (which appeared very similar to one employed by China in its fourth nuclear test).[43]

In 1995, a man claiming to be a missile expert walked into the Taiwanese security services and delivered documents. Among them were a twenty-page 1988 memo prepared for China's First Ministry of Machine Building, which employed missile designers and builders, and a five-year strategic plan for China's future missile forces describing the characteristics of both Chinese and American weapons. Taiwan passed the information and walk-in to the CIA station in Taiwan.[44]

The walk-in made frequent trips back to China and ultimately returned with over seven hundred documents, totaling 13,000 pages. A CIA translation team was flown to Taiwan to begin working on them, while a CIA polygrapher tested the walk-in and found his answer to the question of whether he was working on behalf of a foreign intelligence agency to be deceptive. He was then flown back to the United States so that the CIA and FBI could try to determine whether the entire operation had been managed by China's intelligence services. Ultimately, he was deemed a likely double agent, although some of the information provided was judged valid.[45]

Information about the Taiwanese nuclear program was provided by a longtime agent, Colonel Chang Hsien-Yi, the Deputy Director of the Institute for Nuclear Energy Research. Chang had been recruited by the CIA when he was a military cadet and defected in 1987. The information he provided indicated that the Taiwanese were in the process of building a secret installation that could be used to produce plutonium. Construction of the installation would have violated Taiwanese commitments to the United States not to undertake nuclear weapons research. U.S. pressure forced the

Taiwanese to stop work on the secret installation and to shut down its largest civilian reactor, which the United States felt had military potential.[46]

Given the concern with transnational targets—including terrorist groups, drug and criminal cartels, and proliferation networks—the United States also seeks to recruit assets in such organizations. One such asset was Urs Tinner, whose father owned or was associated with a number of Swiss precision engineering firms and who had supplied Pakistan and A. Q. Khan starting in the mid-1970s. In 2000 Tinner was recruited by the CIA; he subsequently persuaded his father and brother to join him in working for the agency. They were able, for payments that may have totaled as much as $10 million, to provide the CIA with secret information concerning both the Iranian and Libyan nuclear programs.[47]

In 2002 Urs Tinner went to work for Scomi Precision Engineering (SCOPE), a Malaysian-based company established by associates of Khan, ostensibly to produce high-tech components for use in the oil industry. Tinner actually supervised production of centrifuge components, which were loaded on a ship, the BBC *China*, headed for Libya—information that he apparently gave to the CIA. Agents of the United States and other countries intercepted the ship, which led, in part, to Libya's ending its nuclear program and providing the United States with intelligence about its nuclear supplies.[48]

Overt and controlled (i.e., clandestine) sources for military intelligence organizations have also provided a variety of information. During the 1993 fiscal year, Army intelligence sources reported on mass murders and other atrocities committed by Bosnian Serbs against Bosnian Muslims, the rise of membership in neo-Nazi organizations in Germany, the activities of the Algerian Front Islamique de Salvation, a planned campaign of violence against U.S. interests and personnel by a member of the Panama National Police, Russian-directed energy programs, the status of Cuba's biological warfare program, the purchase of advanced tunnel-boring equipment by North Korea, and a planned coup d'état in Afghanistan supported by Russia.[49]

DEFECTORS AND ÉMIGRÉS

Defectors and émigrés also sometimes serve as valuable intelligence sources. During the Cold War, the United States established a coordinated Defector Program managed by the CIA-led Interagency Defector Committee (IDC).[50]

A defector may be able to resolve uncertainties concerning data acquired through technical collections systems. In one instance, a Soviet defector was asked to "look at an elaborate analysis of something U.S. cameras had detected by chance when there was an opening in the clouds that normally shrouded a particular region. Learned men had spent a good deal of time trying to figure out what it was and concluded that it was something quite sinister, an Air Force officer said. 'Viktor took one look at it and convincingly explained why what we thought was so ominous was in fact comically innocuous.'"[51]

During the 1980s, CIA sources included a defector from Nicaragua, Roger Miranda Bengoechea, a senior military officer and chief contact for all military advisers in Nicaragua, which probably gave him knowledge concerning the Cuban presence in that country. He had toured all Sandinista military bases the week prior to his defection. Miranda, who made frequent trips to Mexico for medical reasons, may have been passing information to the CIA before his defection. According to the Nicaraguan defense minister, Miranda had made copies of Air Force plans as well as documents concerning artillery brigades and other installations in Managua.[52]

Iraqi defectors provided U.S. intelligence agencies with information on Iraqi weapons of mass destruction (WMD) programs in the years between the 1991 Gulf War and the 2003 invasion of Iraq, although much of the information was fabricated. A senior Iraqi scientist, Khidhir Abdul Abas Hamza, who fled his country in 1994, provided the CIA with important details concerning the Iraqi nuclear program. Hamza, the highest-ranking scientist ever to defect from Baghdad, was able to provide information on the origins of the nuclear program, the role of foreign suppliers, the treatment of nuclear scientists in Iraq, and Iraqi success in perfecting methods of uranium enrichment.[53]

In October 1994, the Iraqi National Congress (INC) "provided a steady stream of low-ranking walk-ins from various Iraqi army and Republican Guard units who generally had interesting information," according to a Senate report. Then, in the summer of 1995, two of Saddam Hussein's sons-in-law defected to Jordan, where they were interrogated by U.S. officials. One defector was Lieutenant General Hussein Kamel Hassan, who headed the Industry Ministry and military industrialization program, which included the nuclear weapons and biological weapons program. The other, Lieutenant Colonel Saddam Kamel Hassan, headed the presidential security detail. (Not surprisingly, after they decided to return to Iraq, they were killed.)[54]

Among the best known of the Iraqi defectors, code-name CURVEBALL, resided in Germany under the care of that nation's Federal Intelligence Service, or Bundesnachrichtendienst (BND). CURVEBALL claimed to be a project manager "with intimate details of an Iraqi mobile BW program" who "was specifically involved in the design of mobile production facilities," according to a DIA memo. The CIA did not have direct access to CURVEBALL and did not even know his name, Ahmed Hassan Mohammed, until after the war, when the agency obtained access. The BND claimed, falsely as it would turn out, that CURVEBALL did not speak English and hated Americans. Analysts from the Weapons Intelligence, Nonproliferation, and Arms Control Center accepted his prewar assertions, believing his information too detailed to be fabricated.[55]

Although the Intelligence Community eventually concluded, after the war, that CURVEBALL was not who he had claimed to be and that his information had been fabricated, another Iraqi defector was deemed a fabricator as early as 2002. A former major in the Iraqi intelligence service, he was debriefed twice by DIA and claimed that Iraq had built mobile labs to test biological agents. By May 2002 DIA had posted a "fabrication notice" about the major on a classified computer network.[56]

At least three Iraqi defectors were introduced to the U.S. Intelligence Community through Ahmad Chalabi's Iraqi National Congress. One, who claimed to be a physicist working on isotope separation, was rejected outright after the initial contact. Another, Adnan Ihsan Saeed al-Haideri, met U.S. intelligence officers in Turkey, while a third, Mohammed Harith, met with U.S. intelligence officers in Amman. Harith claimed to have worked on the development of mobile biological weapons vans.[57]

Another "defector" from a Middle East nation who proved less than reliable was "Ahmad Behbahani," who appeared on *60 Minutes* in 2000, claiming that the bombing of Pan Am Flight 103 over Lockerbie, Scotland, in December 1988 was the result of a joint Iranian-Libyan operation. But the CIA and FBI concluded that the "defector" was not Ahmad Behbahani and that he had not directed foreign assassination and terrorism operations, as he had claimed.[58]

Today, the most valuable defectors come from China, North Korea, and Iran. In December 2000, Director Xu Junping of the American and Oceanic Office of the Foreign Affairs Bureau of the Ministry of National Defense, who had been a student at Harvard in 1999, defected during a visit to the United States where, according to one report, he had a mistress. A China expert at the RAND Corporation observed, "Someone at his level, especially operating in a political hothouse like Beijing, would have access to a wide range of formal and informal information, ranging from high-level gossip about the military and civilian leadership to the basic stuff of daily life in the PLA." He also added, "All of his information, high and low, would be extremely valuable to his current custodians . . . since our collective knowledge about even the most mundane aspects of PLA life are so limited."[59]

In 1997 two high-level North Korean officials defected. One was the country's chief ideologist, Hwang Jan Yop, who defected to South Korea. He reportedly told his South Korean, then American interrogators about North Korea's strategy for nuclear war, its nuclear and chemical weapons programs, and the identities of North Korean agents in South Korea. However, one Clinton administration official remarked that Hwang didn't have "as much knowledge as he hoped" and had "no direct knowledge of military matters." Some of his information was characterized as "old, dated, not true."[60]

A more useful defector was Chang Sung Kil, the North Korean ambassador to Egypt prior to his defection to the United States in 1997. It was believed that Chang could provide the CIA with a "wealth of information about his country's sensitive dealings with Middle East nations." Of particular interest were North Korean sales of Scud-B missiles to Egypt and sales of other arms to Iran and Syria. Some of that information may have been provided prior to his defection; it was reported that the CIA had recruited Chang well before his defection.[61]

Other North Korean defectors have included Ju-Hwal Choi, a former official of the Ministry of the People's Army, and Young-Hwan Ko, a former Ministry of Foreign Affairs official. They were able to tell a Senate committee (and presumably the CIA) about the production and employment of rockets by the 4th General Bureau, the production of chemical weapons by the 5th General Bureau, and North Korean missile exports. In late 2013, a high-ranking military officer, reported to have been a close associate of Kim Jong-un's recently executed uncle, reportedly defected.[62]

In 2004 it was reported that a stream of information concerning the Iranian nuclear program had come from defecting nuclear scientists (and possibly from some who remained behind). The defections, at least from 2004, were the objective of a CIA program designated BRAIN DRAIN, designed to lure scientists away from the Iranian nuclear program.[63]

In 2009 a scientist who had apparently been providing information to the CIA while in Iran defected while in Saudi Arabia. Shahram Amiri was a thirty-two-year-old radiation detection specialist who worked at Malek Ashtar University, an institution linked to the Revolutionary Guard and involved in nuclear weapons research. Amiri also worked at a number of Iranian nuclear facilities, possibly including the Lavizan facility in Tehran, which was demolished in 2003 and 2004 after atomic inspectors raised questions about its possession of highly enriched uranium. According to one report, he was also able to provide information on the Iranian projects to develop nuclear warheads that could fit on missiles.[64]

In 2010 Amiri released a video claiming, implausibly, that he had been kidnaped and drugged by the CIA—possibly due to some combination of homesickness and Iranian government threats to harm the family he left behind (whom the CIA reportedly failed to exfiltrate from Iran) if he didn't return home. Not long afterward, he returned to Tehran and the Iranian government subsequently claimed that he had served as a double agent. However, U.S. officials asserted that Amiri provided "significant, original information that's checked out." In 2011 it was reported that Iran had arrested Amiri.[65]

Other Iranian officials have also defected. One, Ali Reza Asgari, a former deputy defense minister who once commanded the Revolutionary Guards, disappeared in Turkey in February 2007, and the information he provided was "fully available" to U.S. intelligence, according to newspaper reports. According to one Iranian dissident, Asgari "had very precious intelligence about the Iranian nuclear program." According to one account, he told CIA debriefers when he arrived in the United States, "I brought my computer along, my entire life is there." The computer contained documents concerning Hezbollah, Lebanon, and Iran's uranium enrichment program.[66]

Another defector, Amir Farshad Ebrahimi, fled Iran in 2003 and wound up in Berlin, where he became, according to the *Los Angeles Times*, "a valuable asset for Western intelligence agencies and analysts seeking information on the Islamic Republic." In March 2007, it was reported that Iran had lost contact with Colonel Amir Muhammad Shirazi, an officer in the Quds unit of the Revolutionary Guards who was stationed in Iraq.[67]

In recent years, the United States has sought intelligence from both Iraqi and Iranian émigrés. In October 2002, the Defense Intelligence Agency assumed responsibility for the Intelligence Collection Program (ICP), previously administered by the State Department. The ICP placed primary emphasis on "debriefing Iraqi citizens worldwide who can establish and maintain a continuous flow of tactical and strategic information regarding Iraq, in general, and the Saddam Hussein regime in particular."[68]

Those Iraqi citizens were provided by the Iraqi National Congress, which had an interest in providing intelligence that would help justify a U.S. invasion of Iraq. The approximately twenty sources that DIA debriefed included fabricators, at least some of whose fabrications were known to the INC, as well as individuals who provided useful information. After the invasion, the DIA reported that the intelligence provided by these sources "covered a myriad of information and was not uniform in quality, accuracy, and utility. In some cases, [the ICP] provided solid intelligence leads, corroborated other information, and contributed to our knowledge base. In other cases, the information was of low or no value."[69]

Specifically, the INC sources provided intelligence "that identified sensitive site locations used by CENTCOM for coalition strikes," as well as information on forged travel documents of known terrorists and on violations of UN sanctions. In addition, an INC-provided source identified a senior member of al-Qaeda previously unknown to the U.S. Intelligence Community and provided a photograph to assist in his capture. Information obtained through the ICP also led to the arrest of two of the fifty-five Iraqi high-value targets sought after the defeat of Saddam's regime.[70]

The Iranian émigré community in Los Angeles has long been the target of the CIA's station in Los Angeles in its efforts to glean intelligence about Iran. For several years, the station has cultivated contacts with members of the community, seeking information from Iranians who have traveled to Iran or communicated with relatives in their native country.[71]

DETAINEES AND POWS

In past wars, prisoners of war (POWs) were a potential source of intelligence about an adversary's plans and capabilities. However, the Geneva Conventions provide extensive protections to such prisoners. A POW is required to provide only a very limited amount of information (name, rank, serial number), and signatories to the convention have clear obligations and limits concerning treatment of POWs.

However, the George W. Bush and Barack Obama administrations have considered those captured and detained as a result of the U.S. war on terror that followed the attacks on September 11 to be not prisoners of war but unlawful enemy combatants. The legal rationale lies in al-Qaeda members' targeting of civilians, not wearing uniforms, and not belonging to a conventional army. Taliban fighters were also judged not to be POWs because they did not serve under a "legitimate" government. Because al-Qaeda fighters were judged not to qualify legally as enemy combatants, the United States determined that it may not only ask those captured and detained for more information than a POW is obligated to provide but also subject those fighters to harsher interrogation methods to extract desired information.[72]

Those detained were held in a variety of installations around the world, operated by different agencies. At U.S. bases at Kandahar and Bagram in Afghanistan, the latter of which is still in operation, Army interrogators questioned detainees. At one time, Kandahar had a detainee population of over five hundred. Best known is the facility at Guantánamo Bay, Cuba—known first as Camp X-ray and then as Camp Delta. The newest detention facility there has been designated Camp VI. In June 2005, there were more than 500 detainees; as of November 2014 there were 148.[73]

Other detainees have reportedly been interrogated at the joint British-American base on Diego Garcia and at U.S. military bases in the northeastern United States. In addition, the CIA operated a number of black sites until September 2006, when the fourteen remaining prisoners from those sites were transferred to Guantánamo Bay. A year earlier, it had been reported that thirty-six detainees were being held at those facilities. In April 2007, the CIA transferred another al-Qaeda leader, held since the previous fall, to the Pentagon. Among the nations identified as hosts to CIA detention facilities were Afghanistan (one near Kabul, designated SALT PIT), Thailand (originally designated CAT'S EYE and located near the Udon Thani Royal Air Force Base), Romania (at Mikhail Kogalniceanu Airfield, code-named BRIGHT LIGHT or BRITE LITE, and closed in May 2006), Lithuania (closed in May 2006), Mauritania, and Poland (at the Kejkuty intelligence facility, code-named QUARTZ and emptied in September 2003). A site planned for Morocco, code-named BOMBAY, was never used. It has been reported that the CIA also has a secret prison in the basement of Somalia's National Security Agency, where suspected members of the al-Shahab terrorist group are held.[74]

Subsequent to the closure of the black sites, detainees have, in 2011 and 2013, been held on U.S. Navy ships (the USS *San Antonio* and the USS *Boxer*), which was one of the earliest options for housing detainees to be considered (along with some remote islands, such as the uninhabited islands dotting Zambia's Lake Kariba).[75]

Detainees were apprehended in a variety of ways. Some were swept up in conventional military operations. Others were captured in raids conducted by Special Forces personnel, such as Task Force Hatchet, a group of Rangers and special operations forces that conducted raids across Afghanistan in search of al-Qaeda and Taliban leadership figures. Still others were acquired via CIA operations, such as the joint CIA-Thai operation that resulted in the August 2003 capture of the operations chief of al-Qaeda's Indonesia affiliate, Jemaah Islamiyah (JI), or operations conducted by the CIA and Pakistani intelligence units. In addition, some suspects were arrested by foreign nations and turned over to United States.[76]

The individuals detained and interrogated varied greatly in terms of the threat they represented and their potential intelligence value. According to one former Army interrogator, al-Qaeda trained tens of thousands of fighters at its camps in Afghanistan: "There are hundreds of low-level Al Qaeda alumni who were all but anonymous. Some may be harmless, others not." Some were detained because of information, not always accurate, that indicated their involvement in terrorist operations—such as Mohamed Mansur Jabarah, a Canadian citizen, arrested for being part of a cell that intended to blow up the U.S., Israeli, British, and Australian embassies in Singapore. Others held at Guantánamo included a businessman who had lived in the United States between 1971 and 1987, charged with aiding an al-Qaeda operative planning to bomb American targets, and a man captured in Afghanistan and believed to be the twentieth hijacker.[77]

The presumed twentieth hijacker, Mohamed al-Kahtani, according to a Defense Department press release, clarified the relationship of Jose Padilla and shoe bomber Richard Reid with al-Qaeda, provided information on infiltration routes and methods used by al-Qaeda to slip past unprotected borders, explained how bin Laden evaded capture and provided information on his health, and provided detailed information on about thirty of bin Laden's bodyguards, being held at Guantánamo. In addition, he is reported to be one of two detainees (Hassan Ghul, interrogated at a black site in eastern Europe, being the other) who helped identify bin Laden's courier ("Abu Ahmed al-Kuwaiti," real name: Ibrahim Saeed Ahmed), key information in locating and killing bin Laden in May 2011.[78]

The detainees held at the CIA's black sites were considered "high-value targets," a term reflecting the fact not just senior al-Qaeda leaders could provide potentially valuable intelligence. Such intelligence might come from those responsible for logistics or involved in training fighters. In fact, fourteen high-value targets transferred to Guantánamo Bay in September 2006 included several key operatives, according to a summary by the Office of the Director of National Intelligence: 'Ali 'Abd al 'Aziz 'Ali (a "Pakistani-based al-Qaeda operative"), Ahmed Khalfan Ghailani (an al-Qaeda forger and travel facilitator),* Hambali (operation chief for the Indonesian Jemaah Islami-yah), Mustafa Ahmad al-Hawsawi (a financial facilitator), Mohammed Nazir bin Lep (one of Hambali's key lieutenants), Majid Khan (tasked by Khalid Sheikh Moham-med to conduct research on poisoning U.S. water reservoirs, among other projects), Abdal-Rahim Hussein Muhammed Abdu (al-Qaeda's operations chief in the Arabian Peninsula until his capture in 2002), Abu Faraj al-Libi (a communications conduit to bin Laden), Abu Zubaydah (originally believed to be a senior al-Qaeda operations official and then a facilitator), Ramzi bin al-Shibh (a "key facilitator" of the September 11 attacks), Zubair (a JI operational planner under Hambali), Walid bin 'Attash (an operational planner), Khalid Sheikh Mohammed, and Gouled Hassan Dourad ("head of the Mogadishu-based facilitation network of al-Ittihad al-Islami").[79]

Interrogators were allowed to use more than the standard array of psychological ploys in trying to extract intelligence from the detainees. The Army interrogation training manual in force until fall 2006 focused on sixteen basic alternatives, but it prohibited torture. However, the manual was not binding on those working at CIA; nor was it explicit as to what acts constituted torture. CIA enhanced interrogation techniques (EITs), authorized under the counterterrorist program designated GREY-STONE, included water boarding and water dousing (both meant to make prisoners feel like they are drowning), hard slapping, isolation, sleep deprivation, liquid diets, stress positions, and withholding of pain medication.[†80] Figure 11.1 provides additional details.

One detainee, held at Kandahar facility, provided, according to one of the interro-gators, "critical intelligence about the Hamburg al-Qaeda cell, betray[ed] many other enemy fighters, and expose[d] a never-before-understood connection between al-Qaeda and Islamic groups across North Africa." Another prisoner told of assignments involv-ing a planned poison attack on the U.S. embassy in Rome, which led to the arrests of eight Moroccans (who were eventually acquitted) and the discovery of 8.8 pounds of a cyanide-based compound, a tourist map with the U.S. embassy circled, and maps

---

*Ghailani was the first to be tried in a U.S. civilian court, where he faced charges of murder and conspiracy to use weapons of mass destruction, stemming from his role in the 1998 at-tacks on U.S. embassies in Tanzania and Kenya. Abu Zubaydah and Ramzi bin al-Shibh were two of four residents of the black sites who had been transported to Guantánamo in 2003 and then to a black site for fear that the Supreme Court might rule that they must have access to legal counsel. Ultimately, Ghailani, whose statements were withheld from the jury, was ac-quitted of all but one count, which was sufficient to result in a life sentence. See Tina Susman, "Trial Begins for Embassy Blast Suspect," *Los Angeles Times*, October 13, 2010, A8; Adam Goldman and Matt Apuzzo, "Guantanamo Prisoners Moved Earlier Than Disclosed," www.washingtonpost.com, August 7, 2010, http://www.washingtonpost.com/wp-dyn/content/article/2010/08/06/AR2010080605828.html; Benjamin Weiser, "Defendant's Statements Were Kept from Jury," *New York Times*, November 18, 2010, A26; Benjamin Weiser, "U.S. Jury Acquits Detainee of Most Charges," *New York Times*, November 18, 2010, A1, A26; Benjamin Weiser, "Ex-Detainee Gets Life Sentence in Embassy Blasts," www.nytimes.com, January 25, 2011, http://www.nytimes.com/2011/01/26/nyregion/26ghailani.html?_r=0.
†A number of books and articles, including by some individuals directly involved in the in-terrogation effort, have discussed the efficacy and morality of EITs (or at least the harshest of them). Those questions are discussed in Chapter 20.

FIGURE 11.1 Enhanced Interrogation Techniques

◆ The attention grasp consists of grasping the detainee with both hands, with one hand on each side of the collar opening, in a controlled and quick motion. In the same motion as the grasp, the detainee is drawn toward the interrogator.

◆ During the walling technique, the detainee is pulled forward and then quickly and firmly pushed into a flexible false wall so that his shoulder blades hit the wall. His head and neck are supported with a rolled towel to prevent whiplash.

◆ The facial hold is used to hold the detainee's head immobile. The interrogator places an open palm on either side of the detainee's face and the interrogator's fingertips are kept well away from the detainee's eyes.

◆ With the facial or insult slap, the fingers are slightly spread apart. The interrogator's hand makes contact with the area between the tip of the detainee's chin and the bottom of the corresponding earlobe.

◆ In cramped confinement, the detainee is placed in a confined space, typically a small or large box, which is usually dark. Confinement in the smaller space lasts no more than two hours and in the larger space it can last up to 18 hours.

◆ Insects placed in a confinement box involve placing a harmless insect in the box with the detainee.

◆ During wall standing, the detainee may stand about 4 to 5 feet from a wall with his feet spread approximately to his shoulder width. His arms are stretched out in front of him and his fingers rest on the wall to support all of his body weight. The detainee is not allowed to reposition his hands or feet.

◆ The application of stress positions may include having the detainee sit on the floor with his legs extended straight out in front of him with his arms raised above his head or kneeling on the floor while leaning back at a 45 degree angle.

◆ Sleep deprivation will not exceed 11 days at a time.

◆ The application of the waterboard technique involves binding the detainee to a bench with his feet elevated above his head. The detainee's head is immobilized and an interrogator places a cloth over the detainee's mouth and nose while pouring water onto the cloth in a controlled manner. Airflow is restricted for 20 to 40 seconds and the technique produces the sensation of drowning and suffocation.

Source: Inspector General, CIA, Special Review, 20073-7123-IG, *Counterterrorism Detention and Interrogation Activities (September 2001–October 2003)*, May 7, 2004, 15.

showing the location of underground utility lines near the embassy. Still another prisoner provided details about al-Qaeda's European recruitment and procurement activities, as well as information on bin Laden's security detachment and movements.[81]

Under guidelines from President Obama, the only techniques permitted, irrespective of the agency handling the interrogation, are those specified in the relevant Army field manual. In addition, he established a High-Value Detainee Interrogation Group (HVDIG) to conduct interrogations of such prisoners. The group consists of three to five mobile interrogation teams drawn primarily from the FBI, with some CIA and DOD participation. The National Security Council issued the group's charter, "Charter for Operations of Interagency High-Value Detainee Interrogation Group," on April 19, 2010.[82]

Among those interrogated before that change in guidelines was Abu Zubaydah. Shipped to CAT'S EYE after his capture in March 2001, he provided some information that proved to "be quite valuable," according to an American official. His disclosures led to the 2002 arrest of Jose Padilla, who was first charged with planning a dirty-bomb attack on an American city. He also confirmed Khalid Sheikh Mohammed's role as the mastermind of the September 11 attacks and provided information that led to the capture of 9/11 plotter Ramzi bin al-Shibh. A CIA assessment stated, "AZ has corroborated intelligence on key Al Qa'ida planners and facilitators." JI operations chief Hambali told CIA interrogators about al-Qaeda plans to attack two American-managed hotels in Bangkok as well as airlines using the international airport, information that led airlines using the airport to alter their schedules.[83]

According to a CIA assessment, Khalid Sheikh Mohammed, who was held in Poland and one of three individuals to be water-boarded, "shed light on the plots, capabilities, the identity and location of [al-Qaeda] operations, and affiliated terrorist organizations and networks." He also provided considerable detail on the "traits and profiles" that al-Qaeda sought in Western recruits after 9/11 and, according to the agency, provided insight into how al-Qaeda might conduct surveillance of potential targets in the United States. In addition, he provided information on his use of the JI network for Western operations, "setting off a chain of detentions and reporting that ultimately led to the capture not only of Hambali, but of his brother and a cell of JI operatives." He and other detainees also provided leads to an "elusive operative" who, prior to 9/11, had been tasked with casing financial buildings in major East Coast cities. In 2003 information from detainees led to the disruption of a plot to attack London's Heathrow Airport using hijacked commercial airliners.[84]

Information from either a defector or a detainee contributed to the U.S. ability, in June 2006, to kill Abu Musab al-Zarqawi, leader of al-Qaeda in Iraq. The individual revealed that Zarqawi often met with a religious adviser, Sheikh Abdel Rashid Rahman. As a result, Rahman's movements were monitored by human assets, electronic intelligence, and overhead surveillance—the first two methods were probably used by members of the Mission Support Activity operating as part of a Special Forces task force. Eventually, U.S. Special Forces located Zarqawi in an isolated house near the village of Habib, eight miles west of Baghdad. Zarqawi was killed when U.S. forces dropped a five-hundred-pound bomb on the house.[85]

In May 2010, Mullah Abdul Ghani Baradar, the highest-ranking Taliban leader in custody, was being detained in Pakistan, having been apprehended in January by Pakistani forces. He was providing CIA personnel with information on Mullah

Omar's strategy with respect to negotiations and explaining a new Taliban code of conduct intended to avoid civilian casualties. The following year, according to one account, after weeks in custody on the USS *Boxer*, Ahmed Abdulkadir Warsame "sang like a bird," telling interrogators of his meetings with Anwar al-Awlaki, who would be killed in a drone strike, and major weapons deals between al-Shahab and al-Qaeda in the Arabian Peninsula. He also provided intelligence on the structure and capabilities of both groups. According to one account, his revelations represented "an intelligence watershed." In October 2013 another al-Qaeda leader, Nazih Abdul-Hamed al-Ruqai (aka Abu Anas al-Libi), was captured in Libya and interrogated on the USS *San Antonio*.[86]

TRAVELERS AND DOD PERSONNEL

Travelers who are not intelligence officers may often be able to provide useful intelligence information. At one time, before the United States developed satellites to penetrate the Soviet interior and other denied areas, travelers played a more significant role in intelligence activities than they do today.[87]

During at least the 1980s, the United States Air Forces in Europe (USAFE) conducted a traveler collection program designated CREEK GRAB. The USAFE regulation on the program stated, "During peacetime, USAF military and DAF [Department of the Air Force] civilian personnel, other US employees, and contractors may occasionally have opportunities to acquire information of intelligence value either while performing their normal duties or by pure chance. . . . USAFE personnel must be able to respond effectively to unexpected opportunities for foreign intelligence collection in peacetime as well as wartime."[88]

Among those considered potential intelligence contributors, in addition to travelers, are amateur radio operators, people in contact with foreign friends and relatives, and individuals living adjacent to sites where foreign military aircraft have landed or crashed. The USAFE regulation also outlined procedures for photographing aircraft, specifying that photographs of the following items could be particularly useful: (1) cockpit interiors, (2) weapons systems controls, panel instruments, (3) seat(s), (4) weaponry, (5) electronic gear (avionics, radar, black boxes, etc.), (6) propulsion systems (air intake, variable geometry, fuel parts, and fuel tankages), and (7) documents and management records.[89]

CIA-trained military travelers have been used in Africa to provide political intelligence as well as information relevant to ensuring the security of U.S. forces employed in humanitarian and peacekeeping operations. Specific information provided by the travelers has included threats to U.S. military personnel, general security threats, and the status of airfields and ports. During political upheaval in one country, "the collectors provided extensive data on five neighboring countries, two of which were either considered or used as forward staging areas for US troops. The US military regularly relied on their detailed reporting on airports and air fields."[90]

The CIA's National Resources Division has sought to interview business people, tourists, and professionals, either because of specific contacts they may have during their foreign travels or because of the sites of their travel, such as Iran or China. The information sought may include the health and attitudes of a national leader, the military activities in a particular region, or developments in foreign science and technology.[91]

The CIA has also received intelligence from Americans invited to visit China, meet with Chinese nuclear scientists, and visit Chinese nuclear facilities. Those Americans included George Keyworth, shortly before he became President Ronald Reagan's scientific advisor in 1981, former Los Alamos chief Harold Agnew in 1989, and from 1990 to 1999, Danny Stillman, first in his capacity as chief of Los Alamos Laboratory's intelligence division and then as a private citizen.[92]

Sullivan's nine visits included tours of Chinese nuclear facilities, equipped with video recorders and cameras. Stops included the Southwest Institute of the Chinese Academy of Physics, from which he and his deputy brought back a brochure of pictures of the facility, which was often blanketed by cloud cover. Other facilities he visited were Fudan University and the Shanghai Institute of Nuclear Research, where scientists worked on neutron initiators and sources. He also toured the headquarters of the Chinese Academy of Engineering Physics, China's equivalent to the Los Alamos, Livermore, and Sandia labs. In addition, there were visits to the Northwest Institute of Nuclear Technology, which designed and produced diagnostic equipment to monitor nuclear tests, and the Lop Nor nuclear test site. Reports on what he saw on those visits and material he brought back were provided to the CIA, along with names of more than 2,000 Chinese scientists working at the nuclear weapons facilities.[93]

In 2001 and 2002, the CIA recruited about thirty Iraqis who were living in the United States and had relatives in Iraq; these individuals agreed to travel to their homeland in search of information about Iraqi WMD programs. One of those was Dr. Sawsan Alhaddad, of the Cleveland Clinic. In May 2002, she was asked to travel to Iraq to speak with her brother, Saad Tawfiq, an electrical engineer living in Baghdad, whom the CIA had identified as a key figure in the Iraqi nuclear weapons programs. She was given a set of questions to ask and trained in secret writing. Dr. Alhaddad's brother told her that although Saddam Hussein was certain to resume the nuclear weapons program if sanctions were lifted, there was no ongoing program at the time.[94]

U.S. defense intelligence officers and Special Forces have also made use of travelers to gather data. In 2009 General David Petraeus, then the commander of the Central Command, ordered an effort to employ troops, foreign businesspeople, academics, and others to gather intelligence on insurgents or terrorists and their locations. It has also been reported that around 2005, U.S. Special Forces were "taking advantage of the commercial traffic crossing Iraq's eastern border into Iran . . . paying agents to cross the border using phony cover-stories [including stories about plans to purchase truckloads of fruit or other merchandise] to collect intelligence about military installations."[95]

The contacts and activities of DOD personnel may also yield intelligence when those personnel are debriefed by intelligence analysts. An activity performed by DOD human intelligence personnel, and known as FORMICA (Foreign Military Intelligence Collection Activities), involves "the overt debriefing . . . of all DoD personnel who have access to information of potential foreign intelligence value."[96]

Notes

1. Judith Miller, "Baghdad Arrests a Germ Specialist," *New York Times*, March 24, 1998, A1, A11.

2. John I. Millis, "Our Spying Success Is No Secret," *Wall Street Journal*, October 12, 1994, A15.

3. U.S. Army, Office of the Deputy Chief of Staff for Intelligence, *Annual Historical Review, 1 October 1990 to 30 September 1991*, 1993, 4-10 to 4-12.

4. Robert Dreyfuss, "The CIA Crosses Over," *Mother Jones* (January–February 1995): 40ff.; Greg Miller, "CIA Spy Plan for Post 9/11 Era Crumbles," *Los Angeles Times*, February 17, 2008, A1, A27; Ken Dilanian, "Program 'Colossal Flop' for the CIA," *Los Angeles Times*, December 8, 2013, A1, A25.

5. Dreyfuss, "The CIA Crosses Over"; Miller, "CIA Spy Plan for Post 9/11 Era Crumbles"; Dilanian, "Program 'Colossal Flop' for the CIA."

6. Miller, "CIA Spy Plan for Post 9/11 Era Crumbles"; Dilanian, "Program 'Colossal Flop' for the CIA." Also see "Agencies Debate the Value of Being Out in the Cold," *Washington Post*, January 12, 1996, A18.

7. Mark Mazzetti, *The Way of the Knife: The CIA, a Secret Army, and a War at the Ends of the Earth* (New York: Penguin Press, 2013), 140; Philip Agee and Louis Wolf, eds., *Dirty Work: The CIA in Western Europe* (Secaucus, NJ: Lyle Stuart, 1978), 131–132.

8. Defense Intelligence Agency, *Capabilities Handbook, Annex A, to the Department of Defense Plan for Intelligence Support to Operational Commanders*, 1983, 352. Also see Robert Baldi, "Jack-of-All-Trades," *INSCOM Journal* (April–June 1999): 34–38.

9. Peter Tarnoff, "Intelligence Support of Foreign and National Security Policy in a Post–Cold War World" (presentation to the U.S. Congress, Senate Select Committee on Intelligence, September 20, 1995).

10. Department of Justice, Audit Report 08-23, *The Drug Enforcement Administration's Use of Intelligence Analysts*, May 2008, xvi.

11. Richard MacKenzie, "Gulf War Intrigue: The Tale of the Colonel's Camera," *Washington Times*, April 20, 1987, 9A.

12. Nora Boustany and Patrick E. Tyler, "Syria Suspects U.S. Attachés Meant to Aid Israel," *Washington Post*, March 13, 1989, A28.

13. Steven Mufson, "China Expels Two U.S. Attachés Accused of Spying," *Washington Post*, August 3, 1995, A1, A27.

14. Martin Sieff, "Two American Officers Ordered Out of China," *Washington Times*, August 4, 1995, A15; Linda Chong, "Expelled Americans Arrive in Hong Kong," *Washington Times*, August 5, 1995, A15.

15. Steven Mufson, "U.S. and Japanese Attaches Detained Twice, China Says," *Washington Post*, January 18, 1996, A19; Martin Sieff, "U.S. Military Aide to Be Sent Home from China," *Washington Times*, January 18, 1996, A13.

16. Bill Gertz and Rowan Scarborough, "Inside the Ring," *Washington Times*, August 13, 1999, A8; C. J. Chivers, "Factory Visit Tied to Ouster of Attachés from Russia," *New York Times*, May 14, 2008, A6.

17. U.S. Embassy, Beijing, to Sec State Wash DC, Subject: SITREP No. 28: Ten to Fifteen Thousand Armed Troops Stopped at City Perimeter by Human and Bus Barricades, June 3, 1989.

18. U.S. Embassy, Tokyo, to Sec State, Subject: MP Criticizes Japanese Nuclear Plans, October 27, 2008.

19. Jerrold S. Schechter and Peter S. Deriabin, *The Spy Who Saved the World: How a Soviet Colonel Changed the Course of the Cold War* (New York: Scribner's, 1992).

20. William Kucewicz, "KGB Defector Confirms Intelligence Fiasco," *Wall Street Journal*, October 17, 1985, 28; Barry G. Royden, "Tolkachev, a Worthy Successor to Penkovskiy," *Studies in Intelligence* 47, no. 3 (Fall 2003): 5–33; Joseph W. Wippl, "The CIA and Tolkachev vs. the KGB/SVR and Ames: A Comparison," *International Journal of Intelligence and Counterintelligence* 23, no. 4 (Winter 2010): 636–646.

21. "Russian Arrested as U.S. Spy," *Washington Post*, September 26, 1996, A22; "Russians Assail U.S. Spy 'Trick,'" *Washington Post*, November 5, 1996, A15; Gareth Jones, "Russian Sentenced in Spying," *Washington Times*, July 4, 1997, A9.

22. Michael Schwartz, "Russian Convicted of Passing Secrets to U.S.," *New York Times*, February 11, 2012, A8; Matthew Aid, "Dark Days for Russian Intelligence," MatthewAid.com, June 9, 2012, http://www.matthewaid.com/post/24759114372/dark-days-for-russian-intelligence; Peter Spinella, "Russian Ex-Cop Gets 15 Years for Treason in CIA Spy Rock Case," *Moscow Times*, March 5, 2015, http://www.themoscowtimes.com/news/article/russian-ex-cop-gets-15-year-sentence-in-cia-spy-rock-case/517083.html.

23. William Drozdiak, "Bonn Expels U.S. Officials for Spying," *Washington Post*, March 9, 1997, A1, A25; Walter Pincus, "Expelled CIA Agent Was Not Gathering Data on Germany, Sources Say," *Washington Post*, March 11, 1997, A11.

24. Matthias Gebauer, "Retaliation for Spying: Germany Asks CIA Official to Leave Country," *Spiegel Online*, July 10, 2014, http://www.spiegel.de/international/germany/germany-asks-top-cia-official-to-leave-country-a-980372.html; Alison Smale, "New Case of Spying Is Alleged by Germany," *New York Times*, July 10, 2014, A6; "More Than a Dozen US Spies Infiltrate German Ministries Says Bild," *Deutsche Welle*, July 13, 2014, http://www.dw.de/more-than-a-dozen-us-spies-infiltrate-german-ministries-says-bild/a-17782082.

25. William Drozdiak, "France Accuses Americans of Spying, Seeks Recall," *Washington Post*, February 23, 1995, A1, A20; Craig R. Whitney, "France Accuses 5 Americans of Spying: Asks They Leave," *New York Times*, February 23, 1995, A1, A12; Walter Pincus, "Agencies Debate Value of Being Out in the Cold," *Washington Post*, January 12, 1996, A18; Kim Willsher, "French Official Was CIA Contact," *Washington Times*, September 9, 2003, A15.

26. Mazzetti, *The Way of the Knife*, 155.

27. Walter Pincus, "Ex-Iraqi Official Unveiled as Spy," *Washington Post*, March 23, 2006.

28. Bob Woodward, *Plan of Attack* (New York: Simon & Schuster, 2004), 144, 335–337; James Risen, *State of War: The Secret History of the CIA and the Bush Administration* (New York: Free Press, 2006), 130–131.

29. Woodward, *Plan of Attack*, 352.

30. Ibid., 144, 374, 380–399; Risen, *State of War*, 130–131.

31. Youssef M. Ibrahim, "Tehran Is Said to Arrest Officers on Charges of Spying for U.S.," *New York Times*, April 22, 1989, 5; Stephen Engelberg and Bernard E. Trainor, "Iran Broke C.I.A. Spy Ring, U.S. Says," *New York Times*, August 8, 1989, A6.

32. William J. Broad and David E. Sanger, "Relying on Computer, U.S. Seeks to Prove Iran's Nuclear Aims," *New York Times*, November 13, 2005, 1, 2.

33. Ibid.

34. Joby Warrick and Greg Miller, "Iranian Technocrats, Disillusioned with Government, Offer Wealth of Intelligence to U.S.," www.washingtonpost.com, April 25, 2010, http://www.washingtonpost.com/wp-dyn/content/article/2010/04/24/AR2010042402710.html; Ali Akbar Dareimi, Associated Press, "Iran Acknowledges Espionage at Nuclear Facilities," *Huffington Post*, October 9, 2010, http://www.huffingtonpost.com/2010/10/09/iran-acknowledges-espiona_0_n_756850.html.

35. Adam Goldman, Associated Press, "U.S. Sees Israel, Tight Mideast Ally, as Spy Threat," *Huffington Post*, July 28, 2012, http://www.huffingtonpost.com/huff-wires/20120728/us-us-israel-spying.

36. Sanjoy Hazarika, "In Secret Trial, India Sentences 6 for Spying for U.S.," *New York Times*, October 30, 1986, A5; Randeep Ramesh, "Top Indian Civil Servant 'Was CIA Spy,'" *Guardian*, July 28, 2006.

37. Guy Taylor and John Solomon, "FBI and Human Source in Contact with Bin Laden As Far Back As 1993," www.washingtontimes.com, February 25, 2014, http://www.information clearinghouse.info/article37776.htm; United Press International, "Report: 1990s FBI/CIA Mole

Killed by al-Qaeda Operatives in Bosnia War," February 27, 2014, http://www.upi.com/Top_News/US/2014/02/27/Report-1990s-FBICIA-mole-killed-by-al-Qaida-operatives-in-Bosnia-War/11431393513729.

38. Bob Woodward, "CIA Paid Afghans to Track Bin Laden," *Washington Post*, December 23, 2001, A1, A12; Eric Slater, "These Spies Called the Shots in Strikes Against Taliban," www.latimes.com, February 14, 2002, http://articles.latimes.com/2002/feb/24/news/mn-29609.

39. Gary C. Schroen, *First In: An Insider's Account of How the CIA Spearheaded the War on Terror in Afghanistan* (New York: Ballantine Books, 2005), 111–112.

40. Craig Whitlock, "After a Decade at War with West, al-Qaeda Still Impervious to Spies," www.washingtonpost.com, March 20, 2008, http://www.washingtonpost.com/wp-dyn/content/article/2008/03/19/AR2008031903760.html; Karen DeYoung and Walter Pincus, "Success Against al-Qaeda Cited," www.washingtonpost.com, September 30, 2009, http://www.washingtonpost.com/wp-dyn/content/article/2009/09/29/AR2009092903699.html.

41. Associated Press, "CIA Turned Guantanamo Bay Inmates into Double Agents, Ex-Officials Claim," www.theguardian.com, November 26, 2013, http://www.theguardian.com/world/2013/nov/26/cia-guantanamo-bay-double-agents.

42. Alex Rodriguez, "CIA's Vaccine Ruse in Pakistan Carries Fallout," *Los Angeles Times*, October 8, 2011, A5; Mark Mazzett, "Vaccination Ruse Used in Pursuit of Bin Laden," *New York Times*, July 12, 2011, A8; Mazzetti, *The Way of the Knife*, 279.

43. Jack Anderson and Dale Van Atta, "Nuclear Exports to China?," *Washington Post*, November 3, 1985, C7; Patrick E. Tyler and Joanne Omang, "China-Iran Nuclear Link Is Reported," *Washington Post*, October 23, 1985, A1, A19; Joanne Omang, "Nuclear Pact with China Wins Senate Approval," *Washington Post*, November 22, 1985, A3; Patrick E. Tyler, "A Few Spoken Words Sealed China Atom Pact," *Washington Post*, January 15, 1986, A1, A20–A21.

44. Jeffrey T. Richelson, *Spying on the Bomb: American Nuclear Intelligence from Nazi Germany to Iran and North Korea* (New York: W. W. Norton, 2006), 417.

45. Ibid.; Walter Pincus and Vernon Loeb, "China Spy Probe Shifts to Missiles," *Washington Post*, October 19, 2000, A1, A18–A19.

46. Stephen Engelberg and Michael R. Gordon, "Taipei Halts Works on Secret Plant to Make Nuclear Bomb Ingredient," *New York Times*, March 23, 1988, A1, A15; Tim Weiner, "How a Spy Left Taiwan in the Cold," *New York Times*, December 28, 1997, A7.

47. Mark Hosenball and Christopher Dickey, "A Shadowy Nuclear Saga," *Newsweek*, October 30, 2006, 48; William J. Broad and David E. Sanger, "In Nuclear Net's Undoing, a Web of Shadowy Deals," *New York Times*, August 25, 2008, A1, A8; Gordon Corera, *Shopping for Bombs: Nuclear Proliferation, Global Insecurity, and the Rise and Fall of the A. Q. Khan Network* (New York: Oxford, 2006), 114; David Albright, *Peddling Peril: How the Secret Nuclear Trade Arms America's Enemies* (New York: Free Press, 2010), 208–212, 222–226.

48. Hosenball and Dickey, "A Shadowy Nuclear Saga."

49. Department of the Army, Office of the Deputy Chief of Staff for Intelligence, *Annual Historical Review, 1 October 1992 to 30 September 1993*, n.d., 4-32 to 4-42.

50. E. Howard Hunt, *Undercover: Memoirs of an American Secret Agent* (New York: Berkeley, 1974), 80.

51. John Barron, *MiG Pilot* (New York: Avon, 1981), 186.

52. Glenn Garvin and John McCaslin, "Key Nicaraguan Aide Dubs Military Defector U.S. Spy," *Washington Times*, November 4, 1987, A10.

53. Judith Miller and James Risen, "Defector Describes Iraq's Atom Bomb Push," *New York Times*, August 15, 1998, A1, A4; Judith Miller and James Risen, "C.I.A. Almost Bungles Intelligence Coup with Iraqi Refugee," *New York Times*, August 15, 1998, A4.

54. U.S. Congress, Senate Select Committee on Intelligence, *Report of the Senate Select Committee on Intelligence on the Use by the Intelligence Community of Information Provided by the Iraqi National Congress Together with Additional Views*, September 8, 2006, 8; Daniel Williams, "U.S.

Questions Top-Level Iraqis," *Washington Post*, August 12, 1995, A15; "Saddam's Sons-in-Law Talk to U.S. After Pair's Defection," *Washington Times*, August 12, 1995, A6; Kevin Fedavko, "Dead on Arrival," *Time*, March 4, 1996, 44; William J. Broad and Judith Miller, "Iraq's Deadliest Arms: Puzzles Breed Fears," *New York Times*, February 26, 1998, A1, A10–A11.

55. Bob Drogin and Greg Miller, "Iraqi Defector's Tales Bolstered U.S. Case for War," www.latimes.com, March 28, 2004, http://articles.latimes.com/2004/mar/28/world/fg-curveball28; Bob Drogin and John Goetz, "How U.S. Fell Under Spell of 'Curveball,'" www.latimes.com, November 20, 2005, http://minstrelboy.blogspot.gr/2005/11/how-us-fell-under-spell-of-curveball.html; Joby Warrick, "Warnings on WMD 'Fabricator' Were Ignored, Ex-CIA Aide Says," www.washingtonpost.com, June 25, 2006, http://www.washingtonpost.com/wp-dyn/content/article/2006/06/24/AR2006062401081.html; Tyler Drumheller, *On the Brink: An Insider's Account of How the White House Compromised American Intelligence* (New York: Carroll & Graf, 2006). The primary work on the CURVEBALL saga is Bob Drogin, *CURVEBALL: Spies, Lies, and the Con Man Who Caused a War* (New York: Random House, 2007). Also see John Goetz and Bob Drogin, "'Curveball' Lies Low and Denies It All," *Los Angeles Times*, June 18, 2008, A1, A4; Vice Admiral L. E. Jacoby, Info Memo, Subject: CURVEBALL Background, January 14, 2005.

56. Drogin and Miller, "Iraqi Defector's Tales Bolstered U.S. Case for War."

57. Bill Gertz, "Iraqi Groups Aided CIA Intelligence," *Washington Times*, June 12, 2003, A22.

58. "Defector Blames Iran for Pan Am Bombings," *Washington Post*, June 4, 2000, A10; John Lancaster, "Defector Ties Iran to Bombings," *Washington Post*, June 6, 2000, A2; Vernon Loeb, "Iranian Defector Claiming Terrorist Links Is Called an Impostor," *Washington Post*, June 11, 2000, A25; Bill Carter "'60 Minutes' Faces Doubts on Reported Terrorist Czar," *New York Times*, June 16, 2000, A18.

59. James Risen, "Defection of Senior Chinese Officer Is Confirmed," *New York Times*, March 24, 2001, A6; John Pomfret, "Senior Chinese Military Officer Defects to U.S.," *Washington Post*, March 13, 2001, A18; John Pomfret, "Defector Described as 'Walk-In,'" *Washington Post*, March 31, 2001, A14.

60. Kevin Sullivan, "Key Defector Warns Again of North Korean War Plans," *Washington Post*, July 10, 1997, A23; Nicholas D. Kristof, "North Korean Defector's 'Spy List' Proves a Hot Topic in Seoul," *New York Times*, September 5, 1997, A9; Kevin Sullivan, "N. Korea Defector Takes Questions, Raises Them," *Washington Post*, July 11, 1997, A27; Bill Gertz, "Hwang Says N. Korea Has Atomic Weapons," *Washington Times*, June 5, 1997, A12.

61. R. Jeffrey Smith, "North Korean May Bring Arms Data," *Washington Post*, August 27, 1997, A1, A24; Stephen Lee Myers, "Detecting Envoy from North Korea to Get U.S. Asylum," *New York Times*, August 21, 1997, A1, A9; Bill Gertz, "CIA Seeks Missile Data from Defector," *Washington Times*, August 27, 1997, A1, A10; "North Korean Defector Reportedly a CIA Agent," *Washington Times*, August 31, 1997, A2; Tony Emerson, "The CIA Lands a Big Fish," *Newsweek*, September 8, 1997, 54.

62. U.S. Congress, Senate Committee on Governmental Affairs, Report 105-50, *Compilation of Hearings on National Security Issues* (Washington, DC: U.S. Government Printing Office, 1998), 467–495; Jung-Yoon Choi, "North Korean Official Said to Seek Asylum in South," *Los Angeles Times*, December 20, 2013, A9.

63. Louis Charbonneau, "Iran Keeps Tabs on Nuclear Officials," *Washington Times*, April 29, 2004, A17; Siobhan Gorman and Farnaz Fassihi, "In Iran, a Defector Disappears Again," *Wall Street Journal*, July 16, 2010, A11.

64. Nazila Fathi, "Videos Deepen Mystery of Iranian Scientist," *New York Times*, June 9, 2010, A4; David E. Sanger, "Iranian's Saga Takes a U-turn Toward Bizarre," *New York Times*, July 14, 2010, A1, A10; David E. Sanger, "Going Home, but to What End?," *New York Times*, July 18, 2010, Section 4, 3.

65. Fathi, "Video Deepens Mystery of Iranian Scientist"; Siobhan Gorman, Farnaz Fassihi, and Jay Solomon, "As Iranian Scientist Surfaces, Intrigue Builds," *Wall Street Journal*, July 14,

2010, A9; Gorman and Fassihi, "In Iran, a Defector Disappears Again"; William Yong and Robert F. Worth, "Iran Now Says Nuclear Scientist Was Operating as Double Agent," *New York Times*, July 22, 2010, A4; Hugh Tomlinson, "Iran Jails Nuclear Scientist Shahram Amiri," www.theaustralian.com.au, March 31, 2011, http://www.theaustralian.com.au/news/world/iran-jails-nuclear-scientist-shahram-amiri/story-e6frg6so-1226030965754.

66. Dafna Linzer, "Former Iranian Defense Official Talks to Western Intelligence," www.washingtonpost.com, March 8, 2007, http://www.washingtonpost.com/wp-dyn/content/article/2007/03/07/AR2007030702241.html; Sebnem Arsu, "German Official Adds to Mystery of Iranian Missing in Turkey," *New York Times*, March 14, 2007, A11; Michael Young, "By Way of Defection," www.reason.com, March 15, 2007, http://reason.com/archives/2007/03/15/by-way-of-defection; Kai Bird, *The Good Spy: The Life and Death of Robert Ames* (New York: Crown, 2014), 346.

67. Borzou Daragahi, "Iranian Dissident's Case Throws Light on a Key Defection," *Los Angeles Times*, March 29, 2008, A8; Bird, *The Good Spy*, 345.

68. U.S. Congress, Senate Select Committee on Intelligence, *Report of the Select Committee on Intelligence on the Use by the Intelligence Community of Information Provided by the Iraqi National Congress Together with Additional Views*, 30–31.

69. Ibid.

70. Ibid., 142–143.

71. Greg Miller, "U.S. Lacks Reliable Data on Iran Arms," www.latimes.com, November 27, 2004, http://articles.latimes.com/2004/nov/27/world/fg-iranintel27.

72. Daniel Eisenberg and Timothy J. Burger, "What's Going on at Gitmo," *Time*, June 2, 2005, 30–31.

73. John Mintz, "Al Qaeda Interrogations Fall Short of the Mark," *Washington Post*, April 21, 2001, A1, A20; Chris Mackey and Greg Miller, *The Interrogators: Task Force 500 and America's Secret War Against Al Qaeda* (Boston: Back Bay Books, 2005), 149, 217: Eisneberg and Burger, "What's Going On at Gitmo?"; Karen McVeigh, "US Sends Two Guantánamo Bay Prison Detainees Home to Algeria," www.theguardian.com, August 29, 2013, http://www.theguardian.com/world/2013/aug/29/us-guantanamo-bay-detainees-algeria; Department of Defense, Press Release 559-14, "Guantanamo Bay Detainee Transferred to Kuwait; 148 Detainees Still at Guantanamo," November 5, 2014 (via www.matthewaid.com).

74. Simon Elegant, "The Terrorist Talks," *Time*, October 13, 2005, 46–47; William K. Rashbaum, "Captured Qaeda Member Gives Details on Group's Operations," *New York Times*, July 27, 2002, 8; Mackey and Miller, *The Interrogators*, 149; Glenn Kessler, "Rice to Go on Offensive over Secret Prisons," www.washingtonpost.com, December 3, 2005; "Poland Suppresses CIA Prison Report," www.abcnews.au, December 24, 2005; Craig Whitlock, "European Probe Finds Signs of CIA-Run Secret Prisons," www.washingtonpost.com, June 8, 2006, http://www.washingtonpost.com/wp-dyn/content/article/2006/06/07/AR2006060700505.html; "U.S. Use of Romanian Base Is Described," *Los Angeles Times*, November 22, 2005, A12; Douglas Jehl, "Report Warned on C.I.A.'s Tactics in Interrogation," *New York Times*, November 9, 2005, A1, A16; Ryan Lucas, Associated Press, "Polish Intelligence Base Focus of Probe," December 1, 2005, http://www.comcast.net; "Allegation of Secret CIA Prison," *Los Angeles Times*, November 6, 2009, A27; Mark Mazzetti and David S. Cloud, "CIA Held Qaeda Leader in Secret Prison for Months," *New York Times*, April 2, 2007, A7; Gordon Fairclough and Marcin Sobczyk, "Poland Probes Secret CIA Prison," *Wall Street Journal*, March 30, 2012, A9; Joanna Bernedt and Nicholas Kulish, "Polish Ex-Official Charged with Aiding C.I.A. on Secret Prisons, Report Says," *New York Times*, March 28, 2012, A9; Adam Goldman, Associated Press, "Inside Romania's Secret Prison," December 8, 2011, http://news.yahoo.com/ap-exclusive-inside-romanias-secret-cia-prison-050239912.html; Jeremy Scahill, "The CIA's Secret Sites in Somalia," www.thenation.com, July 12, 2011, http://www.thenation.com/article/161936/cias-secret-sites-somalia; Mazzetti, *The Way of the Knife*, 118; Garrett M. Graff, *The Threat Matrix: The FBI at War in the Age*

of Global Terror (Boston: Little, Brown, 2011), 361; Jeremy Scahill, *Dirty Wars: The World Is a Battlefield* (New York: Nation Books, 2013), 26; Associated Press, "Harry Potter Series Favorite at CIA Black Site," www.usatoday.com, July 11, 2013, http://www.usatoday.com/story/news /world/2013/07/11/harry-potter-series-cia/2509055. For an overall review of detention sites, see *The Report of the Constitution Project's Task Force on Detainee Treatment* (Washington, DC: Constitution Project, 2013), 163–202; Adam Goldman, "The Hidden History of the CIA's Prison in Poland," www.washingtonpost.com, June 23, 2014, http://www.washingtonpost.com/world /national security/the-hidden-history-of-the-cias-prison-in-poland/2014/01/23/b77f6ea2-7c6f -11e3-95c6-0a7aa80874bc_story.html.

75. "Is U.S. Using Warships as the New Floating Black Sites for Indefinite Detention? Terror Suspect Just Captured in Libya Is Being Interrogated at Sea Instead of Gitmo," www.dailymail .co.uk, October 9, 2013, http://www.dailymail.co.uk/news/article-2449907/Is-US-using-warships -black-site-interrogate-terrorists.html; Scahill, *Dirty Wars*, 26; Daniel Klaidman, *Kill or Capture: The War on Terror and the Soul of the Obama Presidency* (Boston: Houghton Mifflin Harcourt, 2012), 256; Bob Orr, "Libyan Terror Suspect Anas Al-Libi Being Interrogated at Sea," www.cbs .news, October 2, 2013, http://www.cbsnews.com/news/libyan-terror-suspect-anas-al-libi-being -interrogated-at-sea.

76. Mackey and Miller, *The Interrogators*, 151, 254; Deb Reichmann, Associated Press, "Bush Says Cooperation Thwarted 2002 Attack," February 9, 2006, http://www.comcast.net; Raymond Bonner, "Qaeda Operative Said to Give C.I.A. Inside Information," *New York Times*, September 20, 2003, A3; William K. Rashbaum, "Captured Qaeda Member Gives Details on Group's Operations," *New York Times*, July 27, 2002, A8.

77. Mackey and Miller, *The Interrogators*, xxvii; Rahbaum, "Captured Qaeda Member Gives Details on Group's Operations"; Carol J. Williams, "Detainee Refuses Surgery," *Los Angeles Times*, November 23, 2006; Adam Zagorin and Michael Duffy, "Inside the Interrogation of Detainee 063," *Time*, June 20, 2005, A8.

78. Office of the Assistant Secretary of Defense (Public Affairs), No. 592-05, "Guantanamo Provides Valuable Intelligence Information," June 12, 2005, http://www.defense.gov/releases/ release.aspx?releaseid=8583; Peter L. Bergen, *Manhunt: The Ten-Year Search for Bin Laden from 9/11 to Abbottabad* (New York: Crown, 2012), 97–98, 100–101.

79. Director of National Intelligence, "Biographies of High Value Detainees Transferred to the US Naval Base at Guantanamo Bay," September 6, 2006, http://www.dni.gov. Also, on Abu Zubaydah, see Central Intelligence Agency, "Psychological Assessment of Zain al-'Abedin al-Abideen Muhammad Hassan, a.k.a., Abu Zubaydah," January 31, 2003. For a decidedly different assessments of Zubaydah, see George J. Tenet with Bill Harlow, *At the Center of the Storm: My Years at the CIA* (New York: Harper Collins, 2007), 240–243; Ali H. Soufan, *The Black Banners: The Inside Story of 9/11 and the War Against al-Qaeda* (New York: W. W. Norton, 2011), 132.

80. Mackey and Miller, *The Interrogators*, xxviii; Dana Priest, "Covert CIA Program Withstands New Furor," www.washingtonpost.com, December 30, 2005, http://www.washingtonpost .com/wp-dyn/content/article/2005/12/29/AR2005122901585.html; Bergen, *Manhunt*, 59.

81. Mackey and Miller, *The Interrogators*, 13, 173, 253.

82. Barack Obama, The White House, "Ensuring Lawful Interrogations," January 22, 2009, http://www.whitehouse.gov/the_press_office/EnsuringLawfulInterrogations; Adam Entous, "Obama Starts Deploying Interrogation Teams," www.reuters.com, May 18, 2010, http://www .reuters.com/article/2010/05/19/us-usa-intelligence-idUSTRE64I0BZ20100519; Anne E. Kornblut, "New Unit to Question Key Terror Suspects," www.washingtonpost.com, August 24, 2009; Evan Perez and Siobhan Gorman, "Interrogation Team Is Still Months Away," *Wall Street Journal*, January 22, 2010, A5; DOD Directive 3115.13, "DoD Support to High-Value Interrogation Group," December 9, 2010, 3.

83. Curt Anderson, Associated Press, "Prosecutors Identify Al Qaeda Informant in Padilla Case," www.boston.com, November 18, 2006, http://www.boston.com/news/nation/articles/2006

/11/18/prosecutors_identify_al_qaeda_informant_in_padilla_case; Philip Shenon, "Officials Say Qaeda Suspect Has Given Useful Information," *New York Times*, April 26, 2002, A12; Bonner, "Qaeda Operative Said to Give C.I.A. Inside Information"; James Risen, "Traces of Terror: The Intelligence Reports; September 11 Suspect May Be Relative of '93 Plot Leader," www.nytimes.com, June 5, 2002, http://www.nytimes.com/2002/06/05/us/traces-terror-intelligence-reports-sept-11-suspect-may-be-relative-93-plot.html; Office of the Director of National Intelligence, "Summary of the High Value Terrorist Detainee Program," September 6, 2006, http://www.defense.gov/pdf/thehighvaluedetaineeprogram2.pdf; Mazzetti, *The Way of the Knife*, 118; Inspector General, Central Intelligence Agency, *The CIA Interrogation of Abu Zubaydah, March 2001–Jan. 2003*, 2007, 8.

84. Central Intelligence Agency, *Khalid Shayk Muhammed: Preeminent Source on al-Qaeda*, July 13, 2004, 1; Office of the Director of National Intelligence, "Summary of the High Value Terrorist Detainee Program," 3; Goldman, "The Hidden History of the CIA's Prison in Poland." For a different view from those of the CIA and ONDI, see Soufan, *The Black Banners*, 368.

85. Office of the Director of National Intelligence, "Summary of the High Value Terrorist Detainee Program," 4; Solomon Moore and Gregory Miller, "U.S. Tracks Aide to Zarqawi's Door; Bush Says War Is Far from Over," *Los Angeles Times*, June 9, 2006, A1, A24; Dexter Filkins, Mark Mazzetti, and Richard A. Oppel, "How Surveillance and Betrayal Led to a Hunt's End," *New York Times*, June 9, 2006, A1, A11; Ellen Knickmeyer, "Zarqawi's Hideout Was Secret till Last Minute," www.washingtonpost.com, June 11, 2006, http://www.washingtonpost.com/wp-dyn/content/article/2006/06/10/AR2006061000528.html; Mark Bowden, "The Ploy," *Atlantic* (May 2007): 54–68.

86. Eric Schmitt, "Questioning of Captured Taliban Leader Offers Insight into How the Group Works," *New York Times*, May 6, 2010, A13; Klaidman, *Kill or Capture*, 51; Spencer Ackerman, "U.S. Delays Prison for Somali Man as Officials Tell of 'Intelligence Watershed,'" www.theguardian.com, December 4, 2013, http://www.theguardian.com/world/2013/dec/04/somali-terrorism-intelligence-us-officials; Charlie Savage and Benjamin Weiser, "How the U.S. Is Interrogating a Qaeda Suspect," *New York Times*, October 8, 2013, A9.

87. See Jeffrey T. Richelson, *American Espionage and the Soviet Target* (New York: Morrow, 1987), 52–55.

88. United States Air Force Europe, USAFE Regulation 200-6, "CREEK GRAB," May 31, 1986, p. 2.

89. Ibid., 15.

90. The Central Intelligence Agency Lieutenant General Vernon A. Walters Award presented to the Operational Architect for a New Collection Capability, NMIA XXIV Anniversary and Awards Banquet, June 5, 1998, http://www.nmia.org/1998Awards/CIAAwards98.htm.

91. Victor Marchetti and John Marks, *The CIA and the Cult of Intelligence* (New York: Dell, 1980), 236–237.

92. Richelson, *Spying on the Bomb*, 408–409.

93. Ibid., 409.

94. Risen, *State of War*, 85–108.

95. Scahill, *Dirty Wars*, 283; Mazzetti, *The Way of the Knife*, 131.

96. Department of Defense Instruction S-5205.01, Subject: DoD Foreign Military Intelligence Collection (FORMICA), March 9, 2015.

12

OPEN SOURCES, SITE EXPLOITATION, AND FOREIGN MATERIEL ACQUISITION

Significant intelligence concerning foreign nations and domestic and foreign organizations can be obtained through means other than technical or human source collection. Open sources, seized documents and videos, and foreign materiel all have proven valuable sources of intelligence.

Open source acquisition involves procuring verbal, written, or electronically transmitted material that can be obtained legally. In addition to documents and videos available via the Internet or provided by a human source, others are obtained after U.S. or allied forces have taken control of a facility or site formerly operated by a foreign government or terrorist group. Foreign materiel, which includes weapons systems or their components, can be obtained by a variety of means: theft, defection, or covert purchase (by the U.S. government or a private organization operating on its behalf). Such materiel can be exploited to determine capabilities and develop countermeasures.

OPEN SOURCES

Open sources can be divided into six, at times overlapping, categories. One category is media, which includes print newspapers and magazines, radio, and television. A second is the Internet, which includes a wide variety of sources: online publications, blogs, discussion groups, citizen media (people taking pictures with their cell phones and posting them), YouTube, and social media sites such as Facebook, Twitter, and Paltalk. Such sources have proven useful in monitoring the June 2014 shoot-down of Malaysian Flight 17 over the Ukraine, rebellions in Syria, Egypt, and elsewhere, and the activities of the Islamic State in Iraq and Syria (ISIS). A former director of National Intelligence (DNI) Open Source Center (OSC) has noted that YouTube "carries some unique and honest-to-goodness intelligence."[1]

A 1995 Department of Defense report concluded that the Internet could provide useful intelligence information by providing reports on current events, "analytical assessments by politically astute observers on or near the scene of those events, many of whom offer unique insights," and information about the plans and operations of politically active groups. (The report also noted that "a great deal of message traffic on the Internet is idle chit-chat with no intelligence value" and that the accuracy of much information on the Internet is suspect, requiring validation. As a result, an alternative use of the Internet is to "cue higher confidence means of U.S. intelligence collection, by alerting us to potentially important factors and allowing us to orient and focus our collection more precisely."[2]

A third category is public government data, available in print or online, which includes government reports, budgets, hearings, telephone directories, press conferences, websites, and speeches. In addition, there are professional and academic publications (journals, conferences, symposia, academic papers, dissertations, and theses) and commercial data (commercial imagery, financial and industrial assessments, and databases, including Jane's, Lexis-Nexis, Factiva, Dialog, and Stratfor).* Finally, there is gray literature, defined in 1995 by the U.S. Interagency Gray Literature Working Group as "foreign or domestic open source material that is usually available through specialized channels and may not enter normal channels or systems of publication, distribution, bibliographic control, or acquisition by booksellers or subscription agents." Gray literature includes, but is not limited to, technical reports, preprints, patents, working papers, business documents, unpublished works, dissertations, and newsletters.[3]

Open sources, according to one account, can provide (1) early information on emerging crises and regional instability; (2) biographic details on key leaders, dissidents, and opposition leaders, as well as terrorists and criminals; (3) information on the security implications of geography, demographics, and national infrastructure; (4) indications of domestic and foreign policy changes; (5) information on the organization, equipment, and deployment of military forces; (6) insights into the security implications of nationality, ethnicity, and religion; (7) strategies underlying information-warfare approaches; and (8) insights about criminal organizations.[4]

In 1948 Director of Central Intelligence Roscoe Hillenkoeter wrote that "80 percent of intelligence is derived from such prosaic sources as foreign books, magazines, and radio broadcasts, and general information from people with a knowledge of affairs abroad." Far more recently, the former head of the Central Intelligence Agency's Bin Laden Unit commented, "Open source information contains 90% of what you need to know," the same figure given by a deputy director of national intelligence, while a former senior DNI staffer gave the figure at 95 percent.[†5]

---

*Although the U.S. government pays for a substantial amount of commercial imagery, other commercial imagery that appears on a variety of websites may supplement coverage—for example, imagery of an explosion at the Parchin Military Base in Iran. See Sean O'Connor and Jeremy Binnie, "Satellite Imagery Shows Parchin Explosion Aftermath," *IHS Jane's Defence Weekly*, October 8, 2014, http://www.janes.com/article/44257/satellite-imagery-shows-parchin-explosion-aftermath.

†It should be noted that not only will the percentage of information that can be obtained from open sources vary from issue to issue, but the intelligence available only from clandestine sources may be the most important in many cases. Extensive reporting on al-Qaeda based on open sources is unlikely to turn up explicit information on the next planned attack. For some of the debate on the value of open sources, see Hamilton Bean, "The Paradox of Open Source: An Interview with Douglas J. Naquin," *International Journal of Intelligence and Counterintelligence* 27, no. 1 (Winter 2014): 42–57; Arthur J. Hulnick, "The Downside of Open Source Intelligence," *International Journal of Intelligence and Counterintelligence* 15, no. 4

The Defense Intelligence Agency (DIA) and military service intelligence organizations acquire foreign science and technology publications and materials, publications concerning foreign weapon systems, training and doctrine manuals, military organization and planning documents, and maps and town plans. In 1992 a database of foreign scientific and technical information references and abstracts contained about 10 million records, of which approximately 6 million were unclassified. And as of late 1992, the CIA had identified about 8,000 commercial databases worldwide.[6]

In more open societies, a variety of data concerning political, military, and economic affairs is available through print and online versions of newspapers, magazines, trade journals, academic journals, and government publications. The published sources may yield intelligence concerning the internal disputes plaguing a European political party, French or Russian arms developments, Japanese defense and trade policy, or advances in computer or laser technologies.

Of course, in closed societies much less information is available; reporting on these societies' internal regimes and militaries is more restricted and subject to censorship or retribution from government organizations. Even in those societies, however, a significant amount of intelligence can be gleaned from legally obtainable documents, including newspapers, magazines, collected speeches, academic journals, and even official documents on military affairs. Further, a variety of social media outlets enable individuals to provide real-time information on current events, including demonstrations and civil wars.

Open sources proved useful in the 1991 Persian Gulf War and with regard to Kosovo. During Operation DESERT SHIELD, the CIA and other intelligence agencies found that the television appearances of Saddam Hussein and other Iraqi officials provided useful information. CIA doctors and psychologists examined interviews with Iraqi leaders to look for signs of stress and worry. DIA analysts studied TV reports, particularly those from Baghdad, that might show scenes of military vehicles in the background. They would freeze the frames and try to compare a vehicle's unit designation with the lists of Iraqi equipment in DIA computers to determine whether anything new had been added to the force.[7]

U.S. intelligence analysts also studied transcripts of radio broadcasts "by both sides [in the Yugoslav crisis] to gain insights into the intensity of the conflict." At the theater/tactical level, in support of U.S. forces in the region, the intelligence component of the Army's 1st Infantry Division, headquartered in Tuzla, monitored Serbian, Bosnian, and Croatian media. It produced the daily *Tuzla Night Owl*, whose approximately ten pages contained excerpts of media reports on political, economic, and military developments in the region, such as "Investigation of Black Marketing Denied," "Bosnians Have Chemical Weapons?," and "Milosevic Pressures RS Socialist Party."[8]

(Fall 2002): 565–579; Stephen C. Mercado, "Sailing the Sea of OSINT in the Information Age," *Studies in Intelligence* 48, no. 3 (2004): 45–55; Stephen C. Mercado, "Reexamining the Distinction Between Open Information and Secrets," *Studies in Intelligence* 49, no. 2 (2005); Robert W. Pringle, "The Limits of OSINT: Diagnosing the Soviet Media, 1985–1989," *International Journal of Intelligence and Counterintelligence* 16, no. 4 (Summer 2002): 280–289; Amy Sands, "Integrating Open Sources into Transnational Threat Assessments," in *Transforming U.S. Intelligence*, ed. Jennifer E. Sims and Burton Gerber (Washington, D.C.: Georgetown University Press, 2005), 63–78.

Today, open sources contribute to understanding the activities of terrorist groups as well as friendly and hostile nations, even intensely secretive nations. Although terrorist groups strive to maintain secrecy about their operations, location, and much of their personnel, they make public threats against those whose actions they seek to alter, actively recruit followers, and attempt to energize those who already subscribe to their doctrines. A significant part of their public face is presented through various elements of the Internet.

Monitoring of the numerous jihadist websites provides information about the messages being conveyed to those who access them, as well as about declarations from prominent terrorists. As of 2006, there were over 4,000 pro-al-Qaeda sites, chat rooms, and message boards, which recruit members, spread propaganda, and broadcast news. The online publication *Sada-al-Jihad* (*Echo of Jihad*) translated and posted a speech by Abu Musab al-Zarqawi and posted messages and images of violence.[9] In October 2010, the website of al-Qaeda in the Arabian Peninsula (AQAP) began to publish the magazine *Inspire*, containing articles on encryption, "Mujahedeen 101," and how to build a bomb in the kitchen. Its second issue, which ran to seventy-four pages, encouraged jihadists to engage in "lone-wolf" attacks with firearms, such as a shooting rampage at a crowded Washington, D.C., restaurant. The twelfth issue, published in March 2014, provided information to enable jihadists to build a car bomb without assistance. It also suggested looking "for a dense crowd" and specifically mentioned restaurants and bars in Arlington and Alexandria, Virginia, and Washington, D.C.'s M Street. The December 2014 issue of the magazine suggested targeting major American personalities as well as commercial airliners. Another terrorist magazine, *Azan: A Call to Jihad*, appeared in 2013. The first issue called on Muslims throughout the world to hack U.S. drones; it also contained a "wanted dead" poster of Barack Obama. That was followed in 2014 by the publication of *Dabiq*, the magazine of ISIS. Its first issue discussed ISIS's strategic direction, recruitment methods, political-military strategy, and tribal alliances.[10]

Other open source data on al-Qaeda and ISIS has come from videotapes, played by various television stations, particularly Al Jazeera, containing messages from Osama bin Laden, his deputy Ayman al-Zawahiri, and until his death in June 2006, Abu Musab al-Zarqawi, the leader of al-Qaeda in Iraq. Among the data analysts seek to extract are when and where the tapes were made, the health of the speaker, and indications of upcoming attacks, which might be suggested by code words, images, or particular phrases. In May 2006, it was reported that analyses of the tapes produced by three al-Qaeda leaders indicated differing motives and political interests within the organization's leadership, including the possible emergence of a rivalry between bin Laden and Zarqawi. In early October 2010, jihadist websites carried two audio recordings by bin Laden containing a wide range of comments on current events.*[11]

ISIS propaganda videos revealed that "a force characterized as poorly equipped and lightly trained [was] neither," with some scenes showing "an extremely capable

---

*As can be imagined, the propaganda output of terrorist groups, including al-Qaeda central, AQAP, Hezbollah, and others, is vast. The extent of open source information extends far beyond what can be examined here. Further information is available on the Jihadology website (http://www.jihadology.net) as well as the website of the SITE Intelligence Group (https://news.siteintelgroup.com).

fighting force, especially those depicting ISIS fighters attacking fixed positions." A video also showed ISIS fighters launching what appeared to be an SA-7 Man Portable Air-Defense System, as well as a wire-guided antitank missile. Analysts also watch beheading videos as part of an attempt to identify the terrorists involved—an effort that includes the use of biometric data.[12]

You Tube was employed extensively by the American-born, Yemen-based Anwar al-Awlaki who was subsequently killed in an American drone strike. Awlaki appeared on over seven hundred videos with 3.5 million views on the site. Quite likely, the CIA had copies of each appearance and examined them in an effort to determine his precise location and any shifts in his message. Even Twitter may provide intelligence on terrorist activities. The Twitter feed @alemarahweb posts links to the official website of the Islamic Emirate of Afghanistan (the Taliban), while @al nukhba post links to an Arabic-language website called Nukhba al-Ilam al-Jihadi (Jihad Media Elite), which features Arabic transcripts of audio and video messages from al-Qaeda and its affiliates in Yemen, North Africa, and Iraq.[13]

Among the studies produced from open sources is a September 2011 Open Source Center report titled *Special Report: Al-Qaeda*, which examines six "master narratives" of al-Qaeda in the Arabian Peninsula and al-Qaeda in the Islamic Lands of the Maghreb. Those narratives include the "war on Islam," "agents of the West," "The Nakba (Israel)," "violent Jihad," "Blood of the Martyrs," and "restoring the Caliphate." Sources cited in the report include books (*Knights Under the Prophet's Banner, The Call for Global Islamic Resistance*), Egyptian newspapers, videos, Islamic discussion forums, and a variety of jihadist websites.[14]

Chinese open sources can also be exploited to produce intelligence. A 2003 assessment of the utility of Chinese open sources in studying the People's Liberation Army examined research directories, encyclopedias and dictionaries, monographs and books, magazines and journals, and electronic databases. The author concluded, "Open source materials have proven useful in shedding light on the traditionally opaque issue of Chinese strategic doctrine," and "Chinese sources can provide broad insights into force planning debates and discussion within the PLA."[15]

Chinese journals exploited as sources of intelligence include *Knowledge of Ships* and *Journal of Shipbuilding*. *Knowledge of Ships* was judged, in the mid-1980s, to generally provide low-quality and unreliable naval information but on occasion to contain useful data. One article, "The Role of the Guided Missile Speedboat in Engagement," stated that the "planners" were considering assigning an antiaircraft mission to one or two of the six boats in a typical OSA or KOMAR squadron. *Journal of Shipbuilding* focused on research topics in marine engineering. According to one analyst, "The publication can be valuable in providing new information about marine engineering topics of interest in China, an appreciation of the foreign sources being exploited by the Chinese, and the results of their experiments in the field." This information, when combined with other intelligence, "offers a reasonably accurate assessment of where China stands in this area of technology." Also of interest to intelligence analysts was *Contemporary Military Affairs*, in which the Pacific and Indian Ocean theaters of operation received good coverage. A current publication undoubtedly of interest is *Aerospace Electronic Warfare*, whose first issue of 2013 contained over fifteen articles, including "Global Hawk and Thinking of Countermeasures Against It," "Location Model and Error

Analysis of Space Target Location by Early-Warning Satellite," and "Research on Clustering-Based Radar Signal Sorting."[16]

State media and websites also provide useful information to those tracking the PLA's organization, operations, and weapons. In the spring of 2011, a number of Chinese unmanned aerial vehicles were on display at an air show in Zhuhai while the Chinese state media posted photographs of China's first aircraft carrier on the Internet and then published close-up photos of the J-15 Flying Shark that will operate from the carrier. In 2013 the Chinese government also allowed publication of photos of its stealth fighter, the J-20 Annihilator, as well as the plane's weapons bay and the air-to-air missiles within the bay. In August 2014, a Chinese provincial government website provided information on the DF-41 multiple-warhead intercontinental ballistic missile (ICBM).[17]

Another website sure to be of interest is that of the Chinese Institute of Atomic Energy. In addition to providing access the institute's annual reports, the site contains links to topics such as research projects, papers, organization, leadership and personnel, patents, research and development results, and key laboratories.[18]

Chinese views on information warfare, the new military revolution, Taiwan, the future security environment, and high-technology warfare can also be judged, at least in part, through a review of a variety of published sources. Those sources have included *On Meeting the Challenge of the New Military Revolution*, *Latest Trends in China's Military Revolution*, *Logical Concepts of Information Warfare*, *Information Warfare and Training of Skilled Commanders*, and *Exploring Ways to Defeat the Enemy Through Information*. In 2010 it was reported that U.S. intelligence agencies had obtained a copy of a 2007 book, *Information Warfare Theory*, written by the president of the PLA Information Engineering University, which promised to "provide new insights into the Chinese military's information-warfare plans."[19]

Just as the number of publications in China has increased dramatically, so has the number of radio and television outlets. In late 1997, there were an estimated 700 broadcast TV stations, 3,000 cable stations, and 1,000 radio stations. During May 1989, U.S. monitoring of Chinese radio broadcasts provided important information on the support for student protesters in Beijing. The reports indicated that 40,000 students, teachers, and writers in Chengdu marched in support of democracy in mid-May. Guangdong provincial radio reported a march of 30,000 students. Altogether, radio reports indicated that there had been demonstrations of more than 10,000 people in at least nine other provinces.[20]

Video footage taken at the Dingxin missile test center and Yangliang flight test center, components of China's Flight Test Establishment, and posted on the Internet provided insight into the Chinese air force's air-to-air and air-to-surface missile programs. Imagery, which analysts with the National Air and Space Intelligence Center (NASIC) have undoubtedly studied, has included firings of China's PL-12 radar-guided air-to-air missile as well as variants of the KD-88 air-to-surface missile.[21]

Information on developments within the country, including military developments, can be found in the writings of Chinese bloggers. Their comments were considered of sufficient interest to be the focus of weekly reports by the CIA's Open Source Works. The issue of December 17, 2010, reported on bloggers' condemnation of "the sale of mentally retarded workers into slavery," their skepticism of draft reviews to laws on land seizures and forced relocations, their support of a provincial official sentenced to thirteen years in prison for accepting bribes, and their monitoring and commenting on the case of WikiLeaks founder Julian Assange.[22]

Reports by the DNI Open Source Center, the National Air and Space Intelligence Center, and the Army Intelligence and Security Command's (INSCOM) Asian Studies Detachment all illustrate the variety of open sources examined. An August 2011 OSC report, *China—Profile of MSS-Affiliated PRC Foreign Policy Think Tank CICIR*, provided an extensive treatment of China Institutes of Contemporary International Relations (CICIR) components, personnel, areas of focus, and publications. Information for the report came from the CICIR website, a journal (*Liowang*) published by Xinhua News Agency, a non-PRC monthly magazine (*Cheng-Ming*), an independent Hong Kong monthly (*Chien Shao*), CICIR publications (*Xiandai Guoji Guanxi* and *Contemporary International Relations*), and numerous other Chinese media sources.[23]

A November 2010 Open Source Works product, *China: Student Informant System to Expand, Limiting School Autonomy, Free Expression*, also relied on a multitude of open sources. Included were a February 2010 study published in *Education and Teaching Research* (a leading academic journal published at Chengdu University), an article in the *Southern Metropolis Daily* (a Guangzhou newspaper), online bulletin boards, a news item posted on China Shou-Bo Net (a comprehensive commercial education website), and the "The Work Regulations of Student Informants" from the Jilin University website.[24]

The National Air and Space Intelligence Center has prepared reports such as *Abstracts of Presentations Given at the 2007 Chinese Airship Research Association Conference* and *Chinese Airship Research Association*. Sources included abstracts of presentations given at the conference as well as the book *An Introduction to Airship Technology*. With respect to China, the Asian Studies Detachment of INSCOM's 501st Military Intelligence Brigade has produced reports, relying on open sources, concerning, inter alia, a variety of Chinese underground facilities, including a hangar for Chinese naval aviation fighters, submarine facilities, caves and underground facilities for the Second Artillery Engineer units, and an Army depot.[25]

During the Cold War, the prime focus of U.S. open source collection was the Soviet Union. The introduction of glasnost in 1985 and the Soviet Union's subsequent dissolution into the Russian Federation dramatically increased the availability of open source intelligence. The type of military intelligence obtainable from open sources was qualitatively different from that acquired under the Soviet regime. In August 1993, *Rossiyskaya Gazeta* reported on an air defense missile defense demonstration in Kapustin Yar. In December 1993, in an unprecedented public announcement, the government of Russia revealed that the first unit of its fourth-generation attack submarine, to be named the Severodvinsk, was laid down. The November 4, 1994, issue of *Nezavisimaya Gazeta* included an interview concerning the future of the Russian strategic forces with a Defense Ministry scientist. In early 1995, *Izvestia* contained "an unusually detailed description" of the silo-based Topol-M ICBM, including information on its accuracy as well as the time between launch command and the missile leaving its silo. In early 1997, a retired Russian colonel, in an article in the mass-circulation newspaper *Komsomolskaya Pravda*, wrote about the deterioration of the Russian command and control system, which echoed Defense Minister Igor Rodionov's comments in a letter to President Boris Yeltsin. The article was subsequently discussed in a CIA report outlining Rodionov's concerns about command and control. In late 2013, *RIA Novosti* reported that Russia planned to deploy more RS-24 mobile ICBMs and that a new class of ballistic submarines was not yet operational. A year later, TASS reported that the Russian strategic missile forces planned fourteen launches in 2015. And in February 2015, the *Moscow Times* carried an article on the construction of four Russian nuclear submarines, including two strategic missile subs.[26]

Russian concern with Iran's space program was the subject of a report by the CIA's Open Source Works, relying on information from interviews, press conferences, and comments on the Strana.ru online news agency. The DNI Open Source Center produced a 2010 report, relying on information from Russian and non-Russian Internet sites, ITAR-TASS, Interfax, and the *Moscow Times*, concerning growing Kremlin control of the Internet.[27]

Russian open sources have also provided information on military officers, including Alexander Shlyakhuturov, who served as head of the Defense Ministry's Chief Intelligence Directorate (GRU) from April 2009 to December 2011. The DNI's Open Source Center, relying on a variety of Russian sources, produced reports that covered Shlyakhturov's appointment as GRU chief, the reasons for his predecessor's replacement, personnel cuts, and the state of the organization.[28]

In January 1985, anticipating the launch of the first ARABSAT geosynchronous satellites, whose function would be to provide domestic and regional television coverage to the Arab world, the Foreign Broadcast Information Service had developed plans for monitoring the broadcasts. Monitoring of Arab television stations became a higher priority after the Cold War. One station, Al Mantar, according to a DNI Open Source Center analysis, "uses its newscasts, talk shows on political, social, and cultural issues, and education and religious programming to push Hezbollah's pro-Palestinian agenda and to educate its viewers in line with its Shiite principles." The analysis also notes, "Al-Mantar continues its negative treatment of the United States but has dropped the more incendiary anti-U.S. material seen in the past." The U.S. Central Command (CENTCOM) and other agencies operate a computer system that monitors newscasts of Al Jazeera and other Arabic television stations and translates them in real-time. In addition, the system flags passages and excerpts of potential interest to intelligence analysts.[29]

Even the controlled Iranian press may yield useful information on Iran's nuclear decision making and nuclear strategy. In late September 2005 the Iranian press published a speech, titled "Beyond the Challenges Facing Iran and the IAEA Concerning the Nuclear Dossier," given by Hassan Rohani, Iran's chief nuclear negotiator from October 2003 to August 2005 (who became Iran's president in August 2013), to the Supreme Cultural Revolution Council. According to a nongovernmental evaluation of the speech, it provided "an interesting analysis of Iran's domestic scene and of the decisonmaking process" and "reinforced the cynical view that Iran's main objective in negotiating is to gain time," as Rohani told the council that during negotiations with the EU-3 (France, Germany, and the United Kingdom), Iran agreed to suspend activities only in the areas where it was not experiencing technical problems and that Iran had completed the Isfahan Uranium Conversion Facility in the midst of the negotiations.[30]

Analysis of Iranian video revealed that Iran's claim to have successfully fired a submarine-launched missile might have been false and that the video itself might represent an attempt at deception. U.S. intelligence analysts discovered that the plume of smoke from the missile shown in the video was an exact match to that in a video of an earlier Chinese test. "It's an identical launch," according to a Pentagon official. "The plume, everything is the same."[31]

In 2006 the director of the Open Source Center commented, "A lot of blogs now have become very big on the Internet, and we're getting a lot of rich information on blogs that are telling us a lot about social perspectives and everything from what the general feeling is to . . . people putting information on there that doesn't exist anywhere else." At the time, Farsi was one of the top five languages employed by bloggers, and snapshots posted on Iranian blogs showed whether young women were following or defying the mullah's edicts on head coverings and skirt lengths—one indicator of the public's mood.[32]

Developments in the Syrian civil war have been another focus of open source collection. Dissidents produced and edited videos of the Syrian government's crackdown and posted them on a YouTube channel that carried video of attacks on Syrian military forces. Twitter was used to provide reports of Scud missile firings. Beginning in 2013, Syrian government officials, including President Bashar al-Assad, began opening accounts on Facebook, Twitter, YouTube, and Instagram.[33]

At least two reports concerning Syria were produced by the Open Source Center in May 2012. The first focused on the status of the uprising and relied on reports from the pan-Arab daily *Al-Sharq al-Awsat*, Beirut Now, Al Jazeera, and the Syrian government's SANA news agency. The second focused on promotion, via social media, of a Syrian jihadist group and its activities. The report discussed two Facebook pages and a Syria-focused jihadist blog, even noting the number of likes and views.[34] And a regular Open Source Works report on developments with regard to Pakistan's leadership was published in November 2010. Among the sources cited were Islamist daily newspapers (*Jasarat, Ausaf*), the *Daily Express, Daily Intekhab*, the English-language *Daily Times, Dawn, Azadi*, and an Urdu-language news talk program.[35]

Open sources are also employed to monitor developments in North Korea. The appearances of the late Kim Jong-il—and what those appearances revealed about his health—were of concern to the U.S. Intelligence Community. Thus, analysts were undoubtedly interested in North Korean television's showing of still pictures of Kim chatting with soldiers and watching a military training exercise a month after his absence from an important anniversary had inspired rumors of his having suffered a stroke. In 2010, photos from a North Korean gathering, which showed General Ri Yong Ho sitting between Kim Jong-il and his son, Kim Jong-un, suggested increased status for the general.[36]

North Korean media have also been examined for clues about developments, including shifts in the power structure under new leader Kim Jong-un. Video from early in Kim's tenure showed his subsequently executed uncle, Jang Song-taek, in a military uniform with a general's insignia, which hinted at "his emerging role as a go-between to the nation's powerful military." North Korean television reports from late 2011 "showed senior military leaders saluting young Mr. Kim," thus portraying him as the nation's "unchallenged ruler." In May 2014, the Korean Central News Agency revealed that Vice Marshal Choe Ryon-hae, considered the number two official in the government, had been removed from office. In 2014 Kim's absence from public appearances, as revealed on state television, undoubtedly triggered U.S. Intelligence Community attempts to determine the cause of his disappearances from public view.[37]

The health of Fidel Castro was also a topic of interest to U.S. leaders and medical intelligence analysts once it began to deteriorate in late 2006. Photos and video released by the Cuban government, in the face of reports of Castro's then temporarily relinquishing power for medical reasons, showed a bandage covering his neck and a bulge under his running suit. The former was believed to hide the location where he was receiving dialysis, while the latter was believed to conceal a colostomy bag.[38]

SITE EXPLOITATION

Important intelligence can also be obtained from document and media exploitation (DOMEX)—that is, exploitation of documents, videotapes, audiotapes, and digital video discs not intended for public release that are seized during or after military operations. The acquisition of such items may come from sensitive or tactical "site exploitation." It may also come from material recovered from soldiers or terrorists killed or captured during combat.[39]

Tactical site exploitation is "the action taken to ensure that documents, material, and personnel are identified, collected, protected, and evaluated in order to facilitate follow-on actions." Sensitive site exploitation—a sensitive site is "a geographically limited area with special diplomatic, informational, military or economic sensitivity to the U.S."—is a broader series of activities usually undertaken by joint agencies, "normally for the purpose of exploiting personnel, documents, electronic data, and material in regards to tactical, technical intelligence, evidence, and criminal exploitation."[40]

Examples of military operations that have produced significant document hauls include those in Grenada, Afghanistan, Iraq, Colombia, and Pakistan. On October 25, 1983, U.S. forces invaded the island of Grenada in response to the overthrow of the Marxist government of Maurice Bishop by a hard-line faction that executed him. The perceived importance of the documents seized resulted in President Ronald Reagan's signing National Security Decision Directive 112, "Processing and Disposition of Documents Acquired by U.S. Forces in Grenada," in November. The directive stated, "The documents acquired by U.S. forces in Grenada represent a unique resource, which is of significant value to U.S. national security interests. It is vital that this resource be protected and carefully utilized to obtain maximum benefit."[41]

The directive went on to specify subjects that it was hoped the documents could shed additional light on, many of which involved Cuban activities. A few months after the directive was issued, a secret memorandum noted that the Defense Intelligence Agency had received about 4,800 documents and that at least 3,000 additional documents were en route to DIA for processing. In addition, the memo noted, "Hundreds—if not thousands—more documents may still be identified for exploitation."[42]

Among the results of the exploitation process was a December 19, 1983, Interagency Intelligence Assessment *Grenada: A First Look at Mechanisms of Control and Foreign Involvement*, and an August 20, 1984, follow-up memorandum to holders of the assessment. The August 1984 study notes that the December 1983 assessment was based on 3,500 documents that had been processed at the time, while the new study relied on an additional 8,000 documents.[43]

The August 1984 assessment covered the New Jewel movement—specifically, the coup that overthrew Bishop—interworkings with the People's Revolutionary Government, political indoctrination, and relations with the Catholic Church. It also examined the Grenadian Revolutionary Armed Forces—their organization, armed strength, and weapons—as well as the Ministry of Interior. Significant attention was devoted to Cuba's influence in Grenada—Cuban military advisers and Cuba's use of Grenada and the Port Salines Airport. "Growing Soviet Influence" was the title of one section, while another examined Soviet-Cuban cooperation. In a final section titled "Dealing with Other Nations," the assessment focused on Vietnam and narcotics.[44]

Among the documents recovered in Afghanistan after the beginning of U.S. military operations in 2001 by the CIA and U.S. military forces were Arabic-language manuals that outlined the step-by-step construction of booby traps and improvised explosive devices. In another instance, they acquired a notebook with cell phone and fax numbers for Mullah Omar, Osama bin Laden, and senior al-Qaeda commanders. Also discovered, in December 2001, was a set of documents describing attempts by a Pakistani scientist to obtain anthrax spores and equipment needed to convert them into biological weapons. Audiotapes recovered in 2001 also provided a portrait of bin Laden's evolution "from Saudi militant to global threat" and opened "a window on the daily lives of men recruited for Jihad."[45]

In addition, a reporter who inadvertently purchased a computer that had belonged to the number two and number three al-Qaeda officials—Ayman al-Zawahiri and Mohammed Atef—turned it over to the CIA. Among the items discovered on the hard drive were statements describing the pursuit of biological weapons: "A germ attack is often detected days after it occurs, which raises the number of victims. . . . Defense against such weapons is very difficult. . . . I would like to emphasize what we previously discussed: that looking for a specialist is the fastest, safest, and cheapest way." Other correspondence on the computer revealed that al-Qaeda had hired an expert who built a rudimentary laboratory and established a charitable foundation as a front for the group's chemical weapons program.[46]

In addition to correspondence, the documents of the hard drive included "budgets, training manuals for recruits, and the scouting reports for international attacks"; they "shed light on everything from personnel matters and petty bureaucratic sniping to theological discussions and debates about the merits of suicide operations." The computer also contained "video files, photographs, scanned documents, and Web pages" that constituted the organization's Internet-based publicity and recruitment effort. Hundreds of pages of additional documents found in a house in Kabul, reportedly used by al-Qaeda, indicated that the group was interested in developing a nuclear weapon. Among those items was a twenty-five-page document containing information about nuclear weapons, including the design for a device.[47]

In late December 2003, U.S. forces from the 1st Battalion, 501st Brigade killed several insurgents during a firefight near Khost. Recovered materiel included ten documents, one film negative, a small amount of cash, and three types of medical capsules. The recovered documents revealed that the dead fighters were members of the Taliban, had entered Afghanistan from Miram Shah, Pakistan, and were probably planning to engage in propaganda operations and possibly an assassination or an attack. The next month, documents recovered from a sniper killed by U.S. Special Forces revealed phone numbers and instructions to contact certain individuals in Afghanistan and Pakistan, uncovering "a network that spanned from Pakistani areas within and east of the Federally Administered Tribal Area to locations in the Bermal Valley."[48]

In the aftermath of the 2003 invasion of Iraq, the United States acquired an enormous number of documents concerning Iraq's policymaking, military and intelligence apparatus, procurement activities concerning weapons of mass destruction (WMD) and other weapons, links to terrorist organizations, foreign relations, and financial affairs. Among the publicly released products of the review and analysis of the documents is the multivolume *Comprehensive Report of the Special Advisor to the DCI on Iraq's WMD* of September 2004. In addition, a five-volume study commissioned by the now defunct Joint Forces Command and performed under the auspices of the Institute for Defense Analyses, titled *Saddam and Terrorism: Emerging Insights from Captured Iraqi Documents*, has been released in redacted form. The study relied on 600,000 captured documents.[49]

Even though the Saddam Hussein regime has been removed as an adversary, examination of the captured documents and media yields not only a means of assessing the validity of past intelligence estimates and obtaining historical accuracy but also actionable information on government and private organizations that provide technology relevant to WMD procurement efforts, terrorist organizations, and hidden assets.

In January 2007, U.S. forces conducted two raids on Iranian targets in Iraq—the Iranian Liaison Office in Ibril and the Ibril airport—in response to Iranian arming, funding, and training of Iraqi military groups. In addition to detaining five Iranians, the forces confiscated "vast amounts of documents and computer data," which CENTCOM analysts in Washington undoubtedly scrutinized.[50]

In early 2008, "American investigative teams" were in Bogota, Colombia, and Washington, D.C., examining documents pulled from laptops and hard drives belonging to the Marxist Revolutionary Armed Forces of Colombia (FARC), which had been seized by the Colombian military. The documents apparently showed that the Venezuelan government had provided about $300 million to the FARC and offered to provide rockets to the rebels.[51]

In the May 2, 2011, raid on the compound in Abbottabad, Pakistan, where Osama bin Laden was living, members of the Naval Special Warfare Development Group (aka Seal Team 6) did more than kill the terrorist leader. A participant in the raid wrote, "The SEALs focused on grabbing all the electronic media—recorders, memory cards, thumb drives, and computers." What they seized was the equivalent of "a small college library" of material according to President Barack Obama's national security adviser. Included were ten hard drives, one hundred thumb drives, and a dozen cell phones, as well as DVDs, video tapes, paper files, and other material. An interagency task force established to review the material produced more than four hundred intelligence reports in a span of six weeks before being disbanded. Its findings also led to a small number of operations and arrests of individuals.[52]

Revelations from the materials included that bin Laden was exploring attacks on trains in the United States, possibly to be launched on the anniversary of 9/11, and was concerned with recruiting potential attackers who had legitimate passports and

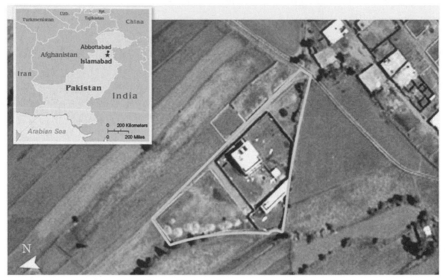

PHOTO 12.1   CIA aerial photo of Osama bin Laden's compound in Abbottabad, Pakistan. *Photo credit:* CIA.

other travel documents. He was also examining the possibility of attacks on President Obama and General David Petraeus. Communications between bin Laden and his deputy Ayman al-Zawahiri and between bin Laden and al-Qaeda operations chief Atiyah Abd al-Rahman were included in the recovered materials. The communications with al-Rahman demonstrated how he had become a central figure in the organization.[53]

The few documents released to the public also provided several insights into aspects of the state of of of al-Qaeda. A 2010 message from al-Rahman indicated his frustration with the CIA's drone attacks, noting that the attacks were killing al-Qaeda targets faster than they could be replaced. In addition, analysts discovered that bin Laden and his organization were facing significant financial limitations, which led the al-Qaeda chief to instruct a deputy to form a group to obtain funds via the kidnapping and ransom of diplomats. The documents also revealed bin Laden's fear of U.S. intelligence activities—including signals intelligence, imagery intelligence, and human intelligence—which manifested itself in the creation of a counterintelligence unit. In mid-2010 that unit's chief complained that the organization was losing the "espionage war" and couldn't function on its current budget; he also noted "ideas" to reduce the threat from human penetration and electronic eavesdropping.*[54]

In October 2014 a joint raid, conducted by Afghan intelligence personnel and U.S. Special Operations forces, captured a senior al-Qaeda official. They also seized a laptop computer and files providing details on the terrorist group's activities on both sides of

---

*The released documents, about two dozen, represented only a "thimble-full" of the 1.5 million captured. The extent to which reporting of the released documents produced an accurate view of the state of al-Qaeda has been challenged in Stephen F. Hayes and Thomas Jocelyn, "How America Was Misled on al Qaeda's Demise," *Wall Street Journal*, March 6, 2015, A13.

the Afghanistan-Pakistan border. According to Afghan and American officials, "The trove of intelligence has helped fuel a significant increase in night raids by American Special Operations forces and Afghan intelligence commandos," which targeted both al-Qaeda and Taliban operatives.[55]

ISIS activities were also a subject of document exploitation after the hideout of the head of the ISIS military council, near Mosul, was raided and 160 computer flash drives recovered. The information extracted from those flash drives included, according to one account, "names and noms de guerre of all foreign fighters, senior leaders and their code words, initials of sources inside ministries, and full accounts of the group's finances."[56]

FOREIGN MATERIEL ACQUISITION

Particularly valuable intelligence also comes from the acquisition of new or used foreign materiel, including weapons systems, communications equipment, and other devices of military significance. In many cases, information on small systems cannot be obtained by overhead imagery or signals intelligence. In any event, possession of the actual system adds significant new information to whatever is already known. The analysis of acquired systems, materiel exploitation, a function of all military scientific and technical intelligence units, allows scientists to determine not only the capabilities of the system but how such capabilities are achieved. Such knowledge can then be exploited to improve U.S. systems and to develop countermeasures.

According to Army Regulation 381-26, materiel exploitation involves
- The production of scientific and technical intelligence in support of force, combat, and material development
- The assessment of foreign technology, design features, and scientific developments for infusion into U.S. developmental efforts
- The support of U.S. systems and developmental/operational testing by providing adversary systems for use in evaluating U.S. systems capabilities
- The development of systems in support of simulations of foreign systems.[57]

The materiel acquisition effort spans the spectrum from small pieces of equipment to missiles and tanks. Thus, the 1993 report by the Armed Forces Medical Intelligence Center, the predecessor to the National Center for Medical Intelligence, details a number of its exploitation efforts involving foreign pharmaceutical products and medical devices. The report notes the utility of its exploitation efforts in producing a description of foreign medical industries, assessing antidotes and treatments for exposure to chemical agents, developing toxin detection technology and antiviral drugs, assessing the chemical warfare treatment capabilities of foreign nations, analyzing foreign biological warfare capabilities, and assessing the limitations of U.S. medical systems.[58]

The most significant ground forces equipment the CIA obtained during the Cold War was the T-72 tank. In 1981 the Army Intelligence Support Activity (ISA), in an operation code-named GRAND FALCON, attempted to obtain a T-72 and other equipment (including a MiG-25) from Iraq in exchange for U.S. 175-mm cannons. Ultimately, Iraqi officials vetoed the deal. A CIA attempt to acquire a T-72 from Romania also failed in 1981. Another unsuccessful ISA attempt to acquire a T-72 involved the attempted delivery of U.S.-made machine guns to Iran in October 1986 in exchange for a T-72 captured from Iraq. But, by March 1987, the CIA had acquired several T-72s.[59]

In the 1960s, the CIA conducted an operation in Indonesia designated HA/BRINK. In one phase of the operation, CIA assets entered a warehouse holding Soviet-made SAM-2 missiles, removed the guidance system from one of them, and took it with them—an acquisition that allowed the U.S. Air Force to equip B-52s with appropriate countermeasures. On other occasions, Soviet equipment was obtained from nominal Soviet allies, particularly Romania. During the final ten years of the Nicolae Ceauşescu regime, the CIA was able to buy advanced Soviet military technology through Ceauşescu's brothers, one of whom was the deputy defense minister. The equipment obtained from Romania included the latest version of the Shikla, one of the most effective Soviet antiaircraft systems; mobile rocket launchers modified and improved by the Romanian military; and radar systems used in identifying targets and directing the firing of various Soviet antiaircraft weapons.[60]

In the 1980s, the CIA acquired several advanced Soviet military helicopter gunships, specifically the Mi-24 HINDs, from Pakistan and Chad. The helicopters were obtained as a result of the defection of a Soviet pilot from Afghanistan and Chad's victory in a border war with Libya. As a result of acquiring the helicopters, the United States reportedly discovered how to penetrate the Mi-24's defense systems with Stinger surface-to-air missiles. In 1983 the Deputy Under Secretary of Defense had refused to sanction an operation to acquire an Mi-24 from Iraq in exchange for permission for Iraq to buy up to one hundred Hughes helicopters; he believed that the background of the Iraqi intermediary meant that "the potential for causing embarrassment to the U.S. Government is too great."[61]

The United States also engaged in a number of recovery efforts, both on land and under the sea. During the 1960s, Project MOON DUST focused on the "national-level coordination of information concerning the decay and deorbit of space debris [including rocket boosters], regardless of country of origin."* When sightings and/ or recovery were considered possible, attachés were notified to maintain watch and consider action for recovery. In 1970 the United States recovered a nuclear weapon from a Soviet aircraft that crashed into the Sea of Japan, in 1971 the Navy recovered electronic-eavesdropping equipment from a sunken trawler, and in 1972 a joint U.S.-British operation recovered electronic gear from a Soviet plane that had crashed earlier that year into the North Sea. In 1975, in Project AZORIAN, the CIA recovered a part of a Golf-II submarine that had sunk northwest of Hawaii.[62]

The repeated recovery of Soviet test warheads that landed in the Pacific Ocean was known as SAND DOLLAR. By international agreement, the Soviet Union was required to specify the impact areas for such tests. U.S. radars tracked the warheads to determine the precise impact points, probably aided by U.S. undersea detection systems, including the Sound Surveillance System. What appeared to be civilian drilling

---

*Recently, the United States had the opportunity to examine debris from a Soviet spy satellite that apparently broke up over Wyoming, South Dakota, and several other states. See Leonard David, "Space Sleuths Piece Together Fiery Fall of Russian Spy Satellite Debris," www.space .com, October 2, 2014, www.space.com/27318-russian-military-spy-satellite-fall.html.

PHOTO 12.2 T-72 tank. *Photo credit:* Sovfoto/UIG via Getty Images.

ships were sent to the Pacific test range after the tests had concluded to recover nose cones that had not self-destructed. Ships were guided to the proper locations by computers coordinated with U.S. satellites, and the objects were located by sonar and magnetometer devices. Scientists at the Air Force Foreign Technology Division then analyzed the design and construction of the retrieved nose cones.[63]

In 1983, during Operation BRIGHT STAR, personnel from INSCOM's 513th Military Intelligence Group were able to examine and evaluate Soviet and other foreign communications equipment that had been left behind in Somalia. The INSCOM personnel examined and repaired eighty-one pieces of Soviet and other foreign communications equipment.[64]

The end of the Cold War and collapse of the Soviet Union did not decrease the emphasis on acquiring Soviet- and Russian-produced weapons systems. In addition to providing intelligence about innovative aspects of current Russian weapons systems, acquisition operations provide a hedge against any future conflict. Of much greater importance, however, is the extent to which Soviet and Russian weapons systems are the foundation of other nations' military arsenals, and Russia continues to sell advanced weaponry. For example, in 1990, the Soviet Union exported a variety of high-tech aircraft: the Su-7, Su-24, MiG-21, MiG-23, MiG-29, Mi-17, and Mi-24. In 1998 significant portions of the Iraqi, Libyan, North Korean, and Syrian air forces consisted of Soviet aircraft.[65]

In March 1991, the United States recovered the nose section of a MiG-29 Fulcrum-A from Jalibah Air Base in Iraq. It provided analysts at the National Air and Space Intelligence Center with a SLOTBACK I radar and with the Fulcrum's infrared search-and-track system, a heat-seeking targeting device, both of which were subject to "much study." In April 1991, the Army received from Germany T-55 and T-72 tanks, assorted signals and communications equipment, small battlefield weapons, automatic rifles, and mortars—equipment inherited from the East German army. In late 1992, the CIA was reported to be involved in a program of buying high technology from former Soviet republics. In 1992 NASIC acquired an MiG-23 Flogger after it had been bought by a U.S. citizen from the Finnish company that Russia had sold it to, only to have it seized by the Bureau of Alcohol, Tobacco, and Firearms because the buyer brought the plane's 23-mm cannon into the country illegally. For over five years, it was housed at the center's Foreign Materiel Exploitation Facility.[66]

In October 1997, the United States signed an agreement with the Republic of Moldova to purchase twenty-one MiG-29 nuclear-capable fighters: one Fulcrum-B trainer, six Fulcrum-As, and fourteen advanced Fulcrum-Cs. Allegedly, the primary goal was to prevent their being sold to Iran, but acquisition also "represented something of an intelligence coup," since the planes were the first MiG-29s to be acquired by the United States. NASIC characterized the MiG-29 as "one of the leading threat aircraft in the world today." The planes were disassembled and flown to NASIC headquarters at Wright-Patterson Air Force Base, after which the center's materiel exploitation experts "began the highly complex task of studying the aircraft's capabilities and limitations." It was suggested that its nuclear wiring system and nuclear safeguards would be of particular interest to analysts at NASIC, since other versions obtained by the United States were not set up to deliver nuclear weapons.[67]

In 1999, under a program designated Project BAIL, the Defense Department purchased several Su-27 jet engines for testing and intelligence purposes. At that time, China was flying hundreds of Su-27 sorties over the Taiwan Strait. A large number of Third World nations possess Soviet-made tanks and surface-to-air missiles in addition to aircraft. In particular, Soviet-produced surface-to-air missiles form a significant part of the Syrian, Libyan, Iranian, Cuban, and North Korean arsenals.[68]

Russia has also sought to export its most modern surface-to-air missile systems, the S-300 PMU (designated the S-10 GRUMBLE by the United States) and S-300V (SA-12A/B GLADIATOR/GIANT). Not surprisingly, the United States acquired both systems. It also acquired, from Eastern European governments, thirty-one Scud-B missiles and four MAZ 543 transporter-erector-launchers, in a program designated WILLOW SAND. The missiles have been employed both in theater missile defense exercises and as subjects of intelligence exploitation by the DIA's Missile and Space Intelligence Center.[69]

Currently, the Department of Defense's Foreign Materiel Acquisition and Exploitation program seeks to "procure every Russian and Chinese plane any adversary may, one day, fly in combat. It means getting hold of surface-to-air missiles around the world to see how to evade them, every radar ever invented so that stealth technology can stay stealthy, and every Multiple Launch Rocket System to look into how barrages of rockets might be evaded." Private defense contractors handle a significant part of that effort. Targets of acquisition efforts have been two Russian systems: the Shkval torpedo and the Moskit, or 3M80, antiship missile (designated the SS-N-22 SUNBURN by NATO). The United States apparently did acquire a SA-15B radar.[70]

Notes

1. Julian E. Barnes, "Spies Plugging into Social-Media Networks," *Wall Street Journal*, August 7, 2014, A4; Kimberly Dozier, Associated Press, "CIA Tracks Revolt by Tweet, Facebook," *Newsvine*, November 4, 2011, http://www.newsvine.com/_news/2011/11/04/8628719-ap-exclusive-cia-tracks-revolt-by-tweet-facebook; Kirk A. Duncan, *Assessing the Use of Social Media in a Revolutionary Environment*, Naval Postgraduate School, June 2013, http://calhoun.nps.edu/bitstream/handle/10945/34660/13Jun_Duncan_Kirk.pdf, 78–79; Douglas Ernst, "U.S. Intelligence to ISIL: Please Keep Using Twitter, You Tube and Instagram," www.washingtontimes.com, July 16, 2014, http://www.washingtontimes.com/news/2014/jul/16/us-intelligence-isil-please-keep-using-twitter-you; "Remarks by Doug Naquin, Director, Open Source Center, CIRA Luncheon, 3 October 2007," *CIRA Newsletter* 33, no. 4 (Winter 2007): 3–9.

2. Charles Swett, Office of the Assistant Secretary of Defense for Special Operations and Low-Intensity Conflict, *Strategic Assessment: The Internet*, July 17, 1995, 25–26.

3. John F. Burns and Miguel Helft, "Under Pressure, You Tube Withdraws Muslim Cleric's Videos," *New York Times*, November 4, 2010, A13; Michael C. Taylor, "Open Source Intelligence Doctrine," *Military Intelligence* (October–December 2005): 12–14; Richard A. Best Jr. and Alfred Cumming, Congressional Research Service, *Open Source Intelligence (OSINT): Issues for Congress*, December 5, 2007, http://fas.org/sgp/crs/intel/RL34270.pdf, 6; "We've Launched," August 2000, http://graylit.osti.gov/whatsnew.html; "Gray Literature," www.cslubedu/library/sub/gray_literature; "Remarks by Doug Naquin, Director, Open Source Center, CIRA Luncheon, 3 October 2007"; North Atlantic Treaty Organization, *Open Source Intelligence Handbook*, November 2001, 7.

4. Graham H. Turbiville Jr., Lieutenant Colonel Karl E. Prinslow, and Lieutenant Colonel Robert E. Waller, "Assessing Emerging Threats Through Open Sources," *Military Review* (September–October 1999).

5. Roscoe H. Hillenkoeter, "Using the World's Information Sources," *Army Information Digest* (November 1948): 3–6; Hamilton Bean, "The DNI's Open Source Center: An Organizational Communication Perspective," *International Journal of Intelligence and Counterintelligence* 20, no. 2 (Summer 2007): 240–257.

6. A. Denis Clift, "Remarks by A. Denis Clift, Chief of Staff, Defense Intelligence Agency, to the First International Symposium on National Security and National Competitiveness: Open Source Solutions"; William O. Studeman, "Remarks by Admiral William O. Studeman, Deputy Director of Central Intelligence," to the First International Symposium on National Security and National Competitiveness: Open Sources Solutions, McLean, Virginia, December 1, 1992, 12.

7. "Live from Baghdad," *Newsweek*, September 24, 1990, 4.

8. Studeman, "Remarks by William O. Studeman," 5; 1st Infantry *Tuzla Night Owl*, November 30, 1997, 1.

9. Scott Shane, "The Struggle for Iraq: The Internet: The Grisly Jihadist Network That He Inspired Is Busy Promoting Zarqawi's Militant Views," www.nytimes.com, June 9, 2006, http://query.nytimes.com/gst/fullpage.html?res=9D01E7DF1231F93AA35755C0A9609C8B63; Arnaud be Borchgrave, Thomas Sanderson, and John MacGaffin, *Open Source Information: The Missing Dimension of Intelligence* (Washington, DC: Center for Strategic and International Studies, 2006), 3; Scott Shane, "Bin Laden, Resurfacing in Audio Recordings, Urges Aid for Pakistan Flood Victims," *New York Times,* October 3, 2010, 5.

10. Jeremy W. Peters, "Terrorists' Magazine, Now in English," *New York Times*, July 2, 2010, A8; Shaun Waterman, "In Online Journal, al Qaeda Pushes 'Lone-Wolf' attacks," www.washingtontimes.com, October 13, 2010, http://www.washingtontimes.com/news/2010/oct/13/online-journal-al-qaeda-pushes-lone-wolf-attacks; Greg Miller, "Al-Qaeda Affiliate Calls for

D.C. Strikes," www.washingtonpost.com, October 13, 2010, http://www.washingtonpost.com/
wp-dyn/content/article/2010/10/12/AR2010101206244.html; Judith Miller and David Samuels,
"A Glossy Approach to Soliciting Terrorism," *Wall Street Journal*, November 27–28, 2010, C3; Bob
Drogin, "It's Like the Vanity Fair of Al Qaeda," *Los Angeles Times*, November 27, 2010, A1, A19;
Thomas Jocelyn, "Al Qaeda in the Arabian Peninsula Releases 12th Issue of Inspire Magazine,"
www.longwarjournal.com, March 17, 2014, http://www.longwarjournal.org/archives/2014/03/al
_qaeda_in_the_arab.php; Jessica Chasmar, "'Azan—a Call to Jihad'—New Terrorist Magazine
Targets Obama," www.washingtontimes.com, May 8, 2013, http://www.washingtontimes.com/
news/2013/may/8/azan-call-jihad-new-terrorist-magazine-targets-oba; Michael S. Ryan, "Dabiq:
What Islamic State's New Magazine Tells Us About Their Strategic Direction, Recruitment Patterns and Guerilla Doctrine," Jamestown Foundation, August 1, 2014, http://www.jamestown
.org/programs/tm/single/?tx_ttnews%5Btt_news%5D=42702&cHash=0efbd71af77fb92c064b
9403dc8ea838#.VO-TIEK3jwM; Karen DeYoung, "New Issue of Jihadist Magazine Produced
by Al-Qaeda in Yemen Suggests Attacks on U.S.," www.washingtonpost.com, December 25,
2014, http://www.washingtonpost.com/world/national-security/new-issue-of-jihadist-magazine
-produced-by-al-qaeda-in-yemen-suggests-attacks-on-us/2014/12/24/06f03d9a-8b9c-11e4-8ff4
-fb93129c9c8b_story.html.

11. David Johnson and Mark Mazzetti, "Some See Hints of Disharmony in Qaeda Tapes," *New
York Times*, May 1, 2006, A1, A11; Shane, "Bin Laden, Resurfacing in Audio Recordings, Urges
Aid for Pakistan Flood Victims," 5.

12. Thomas Gibbons-Neff, "ISIS Propaganda Videos Show Their Weapons, Skills in Iraq,"
www.washingtonpost.com, June 18, 2014, http://www.washingtonpost.com/news/checkpoint/wp
/2014/06/18/isis-propaganda-videos-show-their-weapons-skills-in-iraq; Aki Pertiz, "I Watched
All the Terrorist Beheadings for the U.S. Government, and Here's What I Learned," www
.washingtonpost.com, July 2, 2011, http://www.washingtonpost.com/posteverything/wp/2014
/07/02/i-watched-all-the-terrorist-beheadings-for-the-u-s-government-and-heres-what-i-learned;
Patrick Tucker, "'Jihadi John' and the Future of the Biometrics Terror Hunt," *Defense One*, February 27, 2015, http://www.defenseone.com/technology/2015/02/jihadi-john-and-future-biometrics
-terror-hunt/106263.

13. Brian Bennett, "Terror Watch on You Tube," *Los Angeles Times*, December 13, 2010,
A1, A7; Shaun Waterman, "Terrorists Discover Uses for Twitter," www.washingtontimes.com,
April 28, 2011, http://www.washingtontimes.com/news/2011/apr/28/terrorists-discover-uses-for
-twitter. Also see Melonie K. Richey and Mathias Binz, "Open Source Collection Methods for
Identifying Radical Extremists Using Social Media," *International Journal of Intelligence and
Counterintelligence* 28, no. 2 (Summer 2014): 347–364.

14. Director of National Intelligence, Open Source Center, *Special Report: Al-Qaeda*, September 2011, 29–41.

15. Evan S. Medeiros, "Undressing the Dragon: Researching the PLA Through Open Source
Exploitation," in *A Poverty of Riches: New Challenges and Opportunities in PLA Research*, ed. James
C. Mulvernon and Andrew N. D. Yang (Santa Monica, CA: RAND, 2003), vi, 133, 137.

16. Carl B. Crawley, "On the Exploitation of Open Source Chinese Documents," *Naval Intelligence Quarterly* 2, no. 4 (1981): 7–9; "Aerospace Electronic Warfare, 2013 Issue 1," OriProbe,
http://www.oriprobe.com/journals/htdzdk/2013_1.html (accessed November 28, 2013); Bill
Gertz, "Inside the Ring: China Targets Global Hawk Drone," www.washingtontimes.com, December 11, 2013, http://www.washingtontimes.com/news/2013/dec/11/inside-the-ring-china
-targets-global-hawk-drone.

17. Michael Wines, "Chinese State Media, in a Show of Openness, Print Jet Photos," *New
York Times*, April 26, 2011, A4; Graham Warwick, "Unmanned Advance," *AW&ST*, April 25–
May 2, 2011, 62–63; Dan Lamothe, "Is This China's New Stealth Bomber?," www.foreignpolicy
.com, http://foreignpolicy.com/2013/12/30/is-this-chinas-new-stealth-bomber (accessed January
2, 2014); Bill Gertz, "Chinese Government Website Confirms New Multi-Warhead ICBM," www

.freebeacon.com, August 1, 2014, http://freebeacon.com/national-security/chinese-government -website-confirms-new-multi-warhead-icbm.

18. See the website of the China Institute of Atomic Energy (www.ciae.ac.cn).

19. M. Ehsan Ahrari, "Chinese Prove to Be Attentive Students of Information Warfare," *Jane's Intelligence Review* (October 1997): 469–473; Michael Pillsbury, *China Debates the Future Security Environment* (Washington, DC: NDU Press, 2000), esp. 325–354; Bill Gertz, "Inside the Ring," www.washingtontimes.com, June 2, 2010.

20. Todd Hazelbarth, *The Chinese Media: More Autonomous and Diverse Within Limits* (Washington, DC: CIA Center for the Study of Intelligence, September 1997), 1; Robert Pear, "Radio Broadcasts Report Protests Erupting All over China," *New York Times*, May 23, 1989, A14.

21. Douglas Barrie, "Chinese Rockets," *AW&ST*, May 7, 2007, 40–41.

22. Open Source Works, Central Intelligence Agency, CIA-DI-10-05359, *This Week in the Chinese Blogosphere Week, Ending 17 December 2010*, December 17, 2010.

23. Director of National Intelligence, Open Source Center, *China—Profile of MSS-Affiliated PRC Foreign Policy Think Tank CICIR*, August 25, 2011, http://fas.org/irp/dni/osc/cicir.pdf.

24. Open Source Works, Central Intelligence Agency, *China: Student Informant System to Expand, Limiting School Autonomy, Free Expression*, November 23, 2010, http://fas.org/irp/world/ china/docs/cia-sis.pdf.

25. National Air and Space Intelligence Center, NASIC-OS-0029-2009, *Abstracts of Presentations Given at the 2007 Chinese Airship Research Association Conference*, July 9, 2009; National Air and Space Intelligence Center, NASIC-OS-0018-2009, *Chinese Airship Research Association*, June 2, 2009; Asian Studies Detachment, "Underground Hangar for Chinese Naval Aviation 4th Division's Su-30MK2 Fighters," March 8, 2007; Asian Studies Detachment, "Chinese Navy 1st Nuclear Submarine Zhidui Base Has Underground Submarine Facilities," July 16, 2007; Asian Studies Detachment, "Caves and Underground Facilities Associated with China's Second Artillery Engineer Units," September 27, 2007; Asian Studies Detachment, "Chinese People's Liberation Army Underground Depot Facility in Guilin City, Guangxi Zhuangzu Autonomous Region," October 28, 2010.

26. Foreign Broadcast Information Service, FBIS-SOV-93-164, "Air Missile Defense Demonstration Observed," August 26, 1993, 33–34; Office of Naval Intelligence, *Office of Naval Intelligence Command History 1994*, 1995, 55; Foreign Broadcast Information Service, FBIS-SOV-94-215, "Top-Secret Scientist on Future of Strategic Rocket Forces," November 7, 1994, 34–35; "Topol-M Silo Based SS-25 Upgrade Said More Accurate Than MX," *Aerospace Daily*, January 24, 1995, 113; David Hoffman, "Cold War Doctrines Refuse to Die," *Washington Post*, March 15, 1998, A1, A24–A25; Bill Gertz, *Betrayal: How the Clinton Administration Undermined American Security* (Washington, DC: Regnery, 1999), 229–230; RIA Novosti, "Russia to Deploy More Yars Ballistic Missiles by Year-End," *Sputnik International*, November 6, 2013, http://sputniknews .com/military/20131106/184554661/Russia-to-Deploy-More-Yars-Ballistic-Missiles-by-Year-End .html; RIA Novosti, "Russian Navy's Newest Missile Subs Not Operational—Source," *Sputnik International*, November 1, 2013, http://sputniknews.com/military/20131101/184467946.html; TASS News Agency, "Russian Strategic Missile Forces Plan 14 Launches in 2105—Commander," December 16, 2014, http://tass.ru/en/russia/767147; Matthew Bodner, "Russian Shipbuilder Sets Post-Soviet Record by Building 4 Nuke Subs Simultaneously," *Moscow Times*, February 17, 2015, http://www.themoscowtimes.com/business/article/516108.html.

27. Open Source Works, Central Intelligence Agency, *Russia: Security Concerns About Iran's Space Program Growing*, November 16, 2010, http://fas.org/irp/cia/product/iran-space.pdf; Director of National Intelligence, Open Source Center, *Kremlin Allies Expanding Control of Runet Provokes Only Limited Opposition*, February 28, 2010, http://fas.org/irp/dni/osc/runet.pdf.

28. RIA Novosti, "Defense Ministry Confirms Spy Chief Retirement," (http//en.ria.ru/ military_news), *Sputnik International*, December 12, 2011, http://sputniknews.com/military /20111226/170500830.html; Open Source Center, Subject: Russia; Commentary on New GRU's

Chief Inability to Represent Spetznaz Interests, May 19, 2009; Open Source Center, Subject: New Head to Ensure Continuity in Russian Military Intelligence Say Experts, April 24, 2009; Open Source Center, Subject: Russia: Minister Serdyukov Hand-Picking Officials for Key MOD Posts, April 30, 2009.

29. [Deleted], Director, Foreign Broadcast Information Service, Memorandum for: Director, Near East/South Asia Analysis, Subject: ARABSAT, January 22, 1985, CIA Records Search Tool (CREST), National Archives and Records Administration, College Park; Director of National Intelligence, Open Source Center, "Al-Manar Promotes 'Resistance,' Tones Down Anti-U.S. Material," December 8, 2005, http://fas.org/irp/news/2005/12/osc120805.html; "Attitude Check," *C4ISR Journal* (November–December 2006): 50.

30. Chen Kane, "Nuclear Decision Making in Iran: A Rare Glimpse," *Middle East Brief 5* (May 2006), esp. 2–5.

31. Julian E. Barnes, "Video of Iranian Missile Test Is Fake, Pentagon Says," *Los Angeles Times*, September 10, 2006, A12.

32. Bill Gertz, "CIA Mines 'Rich' Content from Blogs," www.washingtontimes.com, April 19, 2006, http://www.washingtontimes.com/news/2006/apr/18/20060418-110124-3694r; Scott Shane, "A T-Shirt-and-Dagger Operation," *New York Times*, November 13, 2005, Section 4, 5.

33. Liam Stack, "Activists Using Video to Bear Witness in Syria," *New York Times*, June 19, 2011, 11; "Syria Opens New Front in Social Media War: Instagram," www.latimes.com, August 2, 2013, http://articles.latimes.com/2013/aug/02/world/la-fg-wn-syria-president-bashar-assad-instagram-20130801; Melik Kaylan, "Syria's YouTube War," *Wall Street Journal*, September 28–29, 2013, C13; Sonni Efron, "Meet the Hacktivist Who Wants to Warn Syrians About Incoming Missiles," www.theatlantic.com, July 2, 2013, http://www.theatlantic.com/international/archive/2013/07/meet-the-hacktivist-who-wants-to-warn-syrians-about-incoming-missiles/277461 (accessed July 3, 2013).

34. Director of National Intelligence, Open Source Center, "Syria—Status of Uprising, Regime Cohesion 18–24 May," May 24, 2012; Director of National Intelligence, Open Source Center, "Terrorism—Social Media Promote Jihadist Group, Attacks in Syria," May 14, 2012.

35. Open Source Works, Central Intelligence Agency, *Pakistan Leadership Watch: October 2010*, November 8, 2010.

36. Choe Sang-Hun, "North Korean TV Shows Photos of Elusive Leader," *New York Times*, October 12, 2008, 8; Evan Ramstad and Yoree Koh, "In North Korean Photos, a General Trend Emerges," *Wall Street Journal*, October 2–3, 2010, A8.

37. John M. Glionna, "Looking for Clues to the New Hierarchy in North Korea," *Los Angeles Times*, December 26, 2011, A4; Choe Sang-Hun, "North Korea Portrays Son as Firmly in Charge," *New York Times*, December 22, 2011, A6; Choe Sang-Hun, "Buzz over Who's Not in North Korea Picture(s)," *New York Times*, December 23, 2011, A1, A10; Choe Sang-Hun, "In Latest Government Shuffle, North Korean Leader Removes No. 2 Official from Top Posts," www.nytimes.com, May 2, 2014, http://www.nytimes.com/2014/05/03/world/asia/korean-official-loses-a-post.html; Choe Sang-Hun, "In Leader's Absence, Rumors of a Coup Fly in North Korea," *New York Times*, October 9, 2014, A6, A8; Guy Taylor, "Out or Gout? Suspicion Behind Missing North Korean Dictator," www.washingtontimes.com, October 9, 2014, http://www.washingtontimes.com/news/2014/oct/8/us-intel-kim-jong-un-still-in-charge-in-north-kore.

38. Katherine Shrader, Associated Press, "U.S.: Castro's Health Is Deteriorating," *Washington Post*, November 12, 2006, http://www.washingtonpost.com/wp-dyn/content/article/2006/11/12/AR2006111200169.html; Carmine Gentile, "Suspicions Growing That Castro Is Terminally Ill," www.washingtontimes.com, November 23, 2006, http://www.washingtontimes.com/news/2006/nov/22/20061122-100851-7045r; private information.

39. Joseph M. Cox, "DOMEX: The Birth of a New Intelligence Discipline," *Military Intelligence* (April–June 2010): 22–32; Vanessa Holden and Kerry Forester, "Building a Modular and Enduring Site Exploitation Capability," *Military Intelligence* (July–September 2013): 32–35.

40. U.S. Army, Center for Army Lessons Learned, Handbook 07-26, *Tactical Site Exploitation and Cache Search Operations*, May 2007, 3; U.S. Marine Corps, *Intelligence Exploitation of Enemy Material*, June 20, 2006, 6.

41. Ronald Reagan, National Security Decision Directive 112, "Processing and Disposition of Documents Acquired by U.S. Forces in Grenada," November 15, 1983.

42. John Horton, National Intelligence Officer for Latin America, Memorandum for: Director of Central Intelligence, Subject: Grenada Exploitation Status Report, January 10, 1984.

43. Director of Central Intelligence, Interagency Intelligence Assessment, *Grenada: A First Look at Mechanisms of Control and Foreign Involvement*, December 19, 1983; Director of Central Intelligence, *Grenada: A First Look at Mechanisms of Control and Foreign Involvement, Interagency Intelligence Assessment Memorandum to Holders of NIC M83-10021*, August 20, 1984, 1.

44. Director of Central Intelligence, *Grenada: A First Look at Mechanisms of Control and Foreign Involvement, Interagency Intelligence Assessment Memorandum to Holders of NIC M83-10021*, 3–14.

45. Gary Bernsten and Ralph Pezzullo, *Jawbreaker: The Attack on Bin Laden and Al Qaeda: A Personal Account by the CIA's Key Commander* (New York: Crown, 2005), 206–294, 303–304; Joby Warrick, "Suspect and a Setback in al-Qaeda Anthrax Case," www.washingtonpost .com, October 11, 2006, http://www.washingtonpost.com/wp-dyn/content/article/2006/10/30/ AR2006103001250.html; Neil MacFarguhar, "Tapes Offer a Look Beneath the Surface of bin Laden and Al Qaeda," *New York Times*, September 11, 2008, A14.

46. Alan Cullison, "Inside al-Qaeda's Hard Drive," www.theatlantic.com, September 1, 2004, http://www.theatlantic.com/magazine/archive/2004/09/inside-al-qaeda-s-hard-drive/303428.

47. Ibid.; Mike Boettacher and Ingrid Arnesen, "Al Qaeda Documents Outline Serious Weapons," www.cnn.com, January 25, 2002, http://edition.cnn.com/2002/US/01/24/inv.al.qaeda .documents.

48. Vernie Liebl, "Paper and COIN: Exploiting the Enemy's Documents," *Military Review* (September–October 2007): 133–137.

49. Central Intelligence Agency, "DCI Special Advisor Report on Iraq's WMD," https://www .cia.gov/library/reports/general-reports-1/iraq_wmd_2004, and Kevin M. Woods and James Lacey, Institute for Defense Analyses, Iraqi Perspectives Project: Saddam and Terrorism: Emerging Insights from Captured Iraqi Documents, http://fas.org/irp/eprint/iraqi/v1.pdf.

50. Robin Wright and Nancy Trejos, "U.S. Troops Raid 2 Iranian Targets in Iraq, Detain 5 People," www.washingtonpost.com, January 12, 2007, http://www.washingtonpost.com/wp-dyn /content/article/2007/01/11/AR2007011100427.html.

51. Alexei Barroneuvo, "U.S. Studies Rebels' Data for Chavez Link," *New York Times*, March 14, 2008, A8; José de Cordoba and Jay Solomon, "Chavez Aided Colombia Rebels, Captured Computer Files Show," *Wall Street Journal*, May 9, 2008, A1, A13; José de Cordoba and David Gauthier-Villars, "Interpol Says Colombia Didn't Alter Seized Files," *Wall Street Journal*, May 16, 2008, A5.

52. Peter Bergen, *Manhunt: The Ten-Year Search for Bin Laden from 9/11 to Abbottabad* (New York: Crown, 2012), 255–258; Siobhan Gorman, "Bin Laden Plotted New Attack," *Wall Street Journal*, July 15, 2011, A5; Greg Miller, "Bin Laden Files Show al-Qaeda Under Pressure," *Washington Post*, July 2, 2011, A1, A12; Mark Bowden, *The Finish: The Killing of Osama bin Laden* (New York: Atlantic Monthly Press, 2012), 232; Mark Owen with Kevin Maurer, *No Easy Day: The Autobiography of a Navy SEAL: The Firsthand Account of the Mission That Killed Osama bin Laden* (New York: Dutton, 2012), 247; Stephen F. Hayes, "Al Qaeda Wasn't 'on the Run,'" www .weeklystandard.com, September 15, 2014, http://www.weeklystandard.com/articles/al-qaeda -wasn-t-run_804366.html.

53. Gorman, "Bin Laden Plotted New Attack," A5; Daniel Dombey, "Bin Laden Sought to Target US President," www.ft.com, July 15, 2011, http://www.ft.com/intl/cms/s/0/73844eb2-af07 -11e0-bb89-00144feabdc0.html; Peter Finn and Jerry Markon, "Items Found at bin Laden Home Sharpen Focus of 9/11 Security," *Washington Post*, September 3, 2011, A3.

54. Miller, "Bin Laden Files Show al-Qaeda Under Pressure"; Liam Collins, "The Abbottabad Documents: Bin Ladin's Security Measures," *CTC Sentinel* 5, no. 5 (May 2012): 1–4.

55. Matthew Rosenberg and Eric Schmitt, "Data from Seized Computer Fuels a Surge in US Raids on Al Qaeda," www.nytimes.com, February 12, 2015, http://www.nytimes.com/2015/02/13/world/asia/data-from-seized-computer-fuels-a-surge-in-us-raids-on-al-qaeda.html?_r=0.

56. Martin Chukov, "How an Arrest in Iraq Revealed ISIS's $2bn Jihadist Network," www.theguardian.com, June 15, 2014, http://www.theguardian.com/world/2014/jun/15/iraq-isis-arrest-jihadists-wealth-power.

57. Department of the Army, AR 381-26, *Army Foreign Materiel Exploitation Program*, March 6, 1987, 3.

58. Armed Forces Medical Intelligence Center, *Foreign Medical Materiel Exploitation Annual Report*, December 1991.

59. Steven Emerson, *Secret Warriors: Inside the Covert Military Operations of the Reagan Era* (New York: Putnam, 1988), 185; Michael Wines and Richard E. Meyer, "North Apparently Tried a Swap for Soviet Tank," *Washington Post*, January 22, 1987, A37; Richard Halloran, "U.S. Has Acquired a T-72 Tank," *New York Times*, March 13, 1987, A12; Benjamin Weiser, "One That Got Away: Romanians Were Ready to Sell Soviet Tank," *Washington Post*, May 6, 1990, A30.

60. John Barron, *The KGB Today: The Hidden Hand* (New York: Reader's Digest, 1983), 233–234; *Statement of Facts, United States of America v. David Henry Barnett, K80-0390*, United States District Court, Maryland, 1980; Benjamin Weiser, "Ceausescu Family Sold Military Secrets to U.S.," *Washington Post*, May 6, 1990, A1, A30.

61. James Bruce, "CIA Acquires Soviet MI-24 and T-72," *Jane's Defence Weekly*, March 28, 1987, 535; James Brooke, "Chad Reaps a Windfall in War Booty," *New York Times*, August 17, 1987, A4; Brigadier General Harry E. Soyster, Acting ACS for Intelligence, Memorandum thru Director, Defense Intelligence Agency, for Deputy Under Secretary of Defense (Policy), Subject: Possible Acquisition Opportunity (U)—Action Memorandum, April 11, 1983; General Richard O. Stilwell (Ret.), Deputy Undersecretary of Defense (Policy), "Memorandum for the Assistant Chief of Staff for Intelligence, Department of the Army," [day and month illegible], 1983.

62. Air Force Office of the Assistant Chief of Staff, Intelligence, *History, Directorate of Collection, AFNIC, 1 July–31 December 1968*, n.d., 250–251; James David, "Was It Really Space Junk? U.S. Intelligence Interest in Space Debris That Returned to Earth," *Astropolitics* 3, no. 1 (Spring 2005): 43–65; [author name deleted], "Project AZORIAN: The Story of the Hughes Glomar Explorer," *Studies in Intelligence* 29, no. 3 (Fall 1985): 1–45; Norman Polmar and Michael White, *Project AZORIAN: The CIA and the Raising of the K-129* (Annapolis, MD: Naval Institute Press, 2010); David H. Sharp, *The CIA's Greatest Covert Operation: Inside the Daring Mission to Recover a Nuclear-Armed Soviet Sub* (Lawrence: University Press of Kansas, 2012); "The Great Submarine Snatch," *Time*, March 31, 1975, 20–27; William J. Broad, "Russia Says U.S. Got Sub's Atom Arms," *New York Times*, June 30, 1993, 4.

63. Roy Varner and Wayne Collier, *A Matter of Risk* (New York: Random House, 1977), 26; Willard Bascom, *The Crest of the Wave: Adventures in Oceanography* (New York: Harper & Row, 1988), 242–242; William J. Broad, *The Universe Below: Discovering the Secrets of the Deep Sea* (New York: Simon & Schuster, 1996), 69–70.

64. U.S. Army Intelligence and Security Command, *Annual Historical Review, FY 1983*, September 1984, 72.

65. *Statement of Rear Admiral Thomas A. Brooks, USN, Director of Naval Intelligence, Before the Seapower, Strategic, and Critical Materials Subcommittee of the House Armed Services Committee on Intelligence Issues*, March 7, 1991, 36; Paul Quinn-Judge, "CIA Buys Ex-Soviet Arms, US Aide Says," *Boston Globe*, November 15, 1992, 1, 14; Bill Gertz, "Soviets Flee with Secrets," *Washington Times*, January 1, 1991, A1, A6; "World Military Aircraft Inventory," *AW&ST*, January 12, 1998, 222–238.

66. National Air and Space Intelligence Center, "Have Nose," www.wpafb.af.mil/naic/havenose.html (accessed February 12, 2006); Rob Young, "NAIC Donates MiG-23 to AF Museum," *Spokesman* (September 1999): 4; Richard H. P. Sia, "U.S. Army Gets Soviet Weapons from Germany," *Philadelphia Inquirer*, May 5, 1991, 14E.

67. National Air and Space Intelligence Center, "MiG-29 Purchase," www.wpafb.af.mil/naic/mig29s.html (accessed February 12, 2006); National Air and Space Intelligence Center, "Blue 62," wwwwpafb.af.mil/blue62.html (accessed February 12, 2006); Steven Lee Myers," U.S. Is Buying MiGs So Rogue Nations Will Not Get Them," *New York Times*, November 5, 1997, A1, A6; David A. Fulghum, "Moldovan MiG-29s to Fly for USAF," *AW&ST*, November 10, 19997, 37–38; Brian Barr and Rob Young, "Russian Aircraft Cross Borders: Moldovan MiGs Call NAIC Home," *Spokesman* (January 1998): 4–5.

68. Bill Gertz and Rowan Scarborough, "Inside the Ring," *Washington Times*, September 3, 1999, A6; Quinn-Judge, "CIA Buys Ex-Soviet Arms, US Aide Says."

69. Nikolya Novichkov and Michael A. Dornheim, "Russian SA-12, SA-10 on World ATMB Market," *AW&ST*, March 3, 1997, 59; David Hughes, "U.S. Army to Assess Russian SA-10 SAM System," *AW&ST*, January 2, 1995, 60; Jeff Gerth, "In a Furtive, Frantic Market, America Buys Russian Arms," *New York Times*, December 24, 1994, 1, 7; Barbara Starr, "USA Fields 'Scuds' to Test Theater Missile Defense," *Jane's Defence Weekly*, May 7, 1997, 3.

70. Aram Roston, "Buying Un-American: Bribery Case Spotlights DoD's Covert Effort to Obtain Foreign Weapons," www.defensenews.com, March 1, 2013, http://archive.defensenews.com/article/20130301/C4ISR02/303010019/Buying-un-American-Bribery-Case-Spotlights-DoD-8217-s-Covert-Effort-Obtain-Foreign-Weapons; Viktor Baranets and Mikhail Timoshenko, "How Our Guns and Tanks Ended Up with the Yankees," *Komsomolskaya Pravda Online*, July 10, 2011.

13

COOPERATION WITH FOREIGN SERVICES

Despite its huge investments in technical and human intelligence (HUMINT), the United States relies on liaison and cooperative arrangements with foreign intelligence and security services for a significant portion of its intelligence. As then defense secretary Caspar Weinberger explained in 1985, "The United States has neither the opportunity nor the resources to unilaterally collect all the intelligence information we require. We compensate with a variety of intelligence sharing arrangements with other nations in the world."[1]

The United States can benefit in several ways from such cooperative relationships with foreign intelligence and security services. The ability to monitor events in a foreign country can be enhanced because an ally is particularly well situated, in terms of geography, to conduct a variety of technical collection operations against the target. The United States has often helped establish collection sites in exchange for access to the information collected. In the case of nations where the United States has no diplomatic representation, allied intelligence services can run agents on behalf of the United States. Allies can also provide additional manpower or sensors to collect or process intelligence. In addition, the commentary and analysis presented by allied analysts can improve understanding of foreign developments.[2]

Such arrangements also involve risks. The cooperating service may be penetrated by an adversary, who may gain new knowledge about U.S. collection activities and their products. In the 1970s, the product of the National Reconnaissance Office's CANYON COMINT satellite was provided to the United Kingdom in exchange for its provision of translators to process the vast quantity of intercepted material. One of those involved in the translation effort, Geoffrey Prime, also reported to the Soviet KGB. In 1999 Jean-Philippe Wispelaere, an imagery interpreter employed by the Australian Defence Intelligence Organisation, was charged with trying to sell U.S. satellite imagery to unspecified foreign governments. In 2012 Lieutenant Jeffrey Delisle, who worked at the Canadian Navy's Trinity intelligence center and had previously worked at the headquarters of Canadian defense intelligence in Ottawa, was revealed to have been providing top secret U.S. intelligence data to Russian intelligence since 2007. And a National Security Agency (NSA) information paper reported that intelligence data indicated a possible Iranian connection with the head of the Turkish National

Intelligence Organization's signals intelligence (SIGINT) directorate, which has a co-operative relationship (discussed below) with NSA.[*3]

Reliance on a liaison relationship may also allow the partner insights into the techniques employed against it, as illustrated by an article in an NSA journal that referred to Third Parties (to the UKUSA Agreement) as "allies and targets." A partner may also provide a skewed view of reality to the United States in an attempt to influence decisions in accord with its preferences. In addition, the presence of U.S. collection facilities in a country may tempt that nation to use those facilities as a means of blackmail or retaliation, as when Turkey shut down U.S. missile monitoring facilities in the mid-1970s during a dispute over arms sales. Finally, the cooperating nation may be cooperating to some extent but also providing data on U.S. operations to American targets—as the Pakistani Inter-Services Intelligence Directorate has been accused of doing.[4]

Some arrangements are long-standing and highly formalized and involve the most sensitive forms of intelligence collection. Others are less wide-ranging and reflect limited common interests between the United States and particular nations—or focus on a specific topic or target.[†] In addition, exchange arrangements may involve different components of the intelligence communities in the United States and other nations. Whereas some arrangements may involve links between the Central Intelligence Agency (CIA) and a nation's counterpart agency, others may involve cooperation between the National Security Agency, the National Geospatial-Intelligence Agency (NGA), the Defense Intelligence Agency (DIA), or a service intelligence component and its foreign counterparts.

Cooperation extends across virtually all intelligence disciplines and applications of interest to the United States: SIGINT, HUMINT, geospatial intelligence (GEOINT), measurement and signature intelligence (MASINT), space surveillance, open sources, counterterrorist operations, counternarcotics operations, and analysis and data exchange.[‡] In addition, the sum of intelligence cooperation between the United States and a foreign nation can be a catalyst for further cooperation and an important part of the overall relations between the United States and that country.

---

*The risk works in both directions, as exemplified by the disclosures about Australian, Canadian, and U.K. SIGINT activities that resulted from the Edward Snowden disclosures. See Reuters, "Australian Spy Bosses Brief Government on Possible Asian Fallout over Snowden: Report," June 25, 2013, http://www.reuters.com/article/2013/06/25/us-usa-security-australia-idUSBRE95O1IV20130625; Jim Bronskill, "NSA Leaks Prompted Major Canadian Review: Declassified Memo," *MacLeans*, January 17, 2014, http://www.macleans.ca/news/canada/nsa-leaks-prompted-major-canadian-eavesdropping-review-declassified-memo.

†Thus, in December 2014, the United States, Japan, and South Korea signed a trilateral agreement for the exchange of classified information concerning the North Korean nuclear and missile programs. See Martin Fackler, "Japan and South Korea Vow to Share Intelligence About North via the U.S.," *New York Times*, December 30, 2014, A7.

‡Exchanges may not be confined to a single discipline, as when the United States receives human intelligence and provides intelligence collected from technical systems in return. Or it may involve U.S. sharing of information to assist foreign military forces involved in counterterrorirst, counternarcotics, or other operations.

GEOSPATIAL INTELLIGENCE COOPERATION

For many years the United States' ability to produce overhead imagery of target areas and then geospatial intelligence was largely a product of its own resources—its constellation of imagery satellites—whose capabilities grew substantially over the years. Allies might receive U.S. satellite imagery product, such as Britain having access to CORONA imagery or Israel being granted access to KH-11 images. In recent years, however, U.S. allies such as Canada, Israel, Japan, France, Italy, and Germany have begun orbiting electro-optical and/or radar imagery reconnaissance spacecraft.[5]

Those nations' satellites can provide coverage of targets when U.S. spacecraft are not overhead and reduce the time between coverage of important targets. Such additional capabilities can complicate foreign denial and deception measures or provide more timely warning of an impending foreign military action. Whether Japan, Israel, and other allies have provided the United States with reconnaissance satellite imagery, either on an ad hoc basis or as part of an imagery sharing arrangement, is not publically known. But given U.S. provision of imagery to such nations in the past, it is highly probable that the United States receives some of the "take" from the imagery satellites of allies with respect to targets of mutual interest—of North Korea and China from Japan and of Syria and Iran from Israel.

Even nations without satellite imagery capabilities can contribute by supplying imagery interpreters to help process and interpret the vast volume of imagery produced by U.S. satellites and to provide specialized knowledge of their areas of the world. Thus, although only Canada and the United States, among the FIVE EYES nations (which also include Australia, New Zealand, and the United Kingdom), operate satellites with a reconnaissance capability, the geospatial intelligence organizations of each of those nations have become partners with the NGA. All five nations—members of the Allied System for Geospatial Intelligence—participate in quarterly video conferences on geospatial intelligence.[6]

In 1998 the imagery intelligence functions housed in the Australian Defence Intelligence Organisation were placed in the newly created Australian Imagery Organisation (AIO). AIO developed the ability to exploit digital imagery—the sort returned by U.S. electro-optical imagery satellites. In November 2000, after the completion of an Australian government study, AIO was merged with the other military units to form the Defence Imagery and Geospatial Organisation (DIGO).[7]

The cooperative arrangement between the NGA and DIGO includes NGA office space at DIGO headquarters. In a 2008 interview, the NGA director stated, "We have joint requirements in terms of topographic, aeronautical and also nautical information—which is very important in the Pacific because of the vast water areas that are involved. We are cooperating very closely with Australia on all of that because of the sheer amount of effort it takes to have the best geospatial data we can have for all of the Pacific region."[8] That year the United States and Australia also signed an agreement that provided for increased cooperation and intelligence exchange between NGA and DIGO with regard to intelligence derived from satellite and aerial surveillance. A cable from the U.S. embassy in Canberra characterized the agreement as intended "to take GEOINT co-operation to the same level that signals intelligence has reached between the two countries." Australian cooperation may also come to involve orbiting its own imagery satellite.[9]

NGA's Canadian partner is the Directorate of Geospatial Intelligence (DGI), which consists of components for mapping and charting, imagery interpretation, and meteorology. In 2006 the Canadian Forces Joint Imagery Centre (CFJIC), which would become part of the DGI, apparently provided assistance to NGA with respect to imagery interpretation with regard to Hurricane Katrina. Two CFJIC liaison officers were stationed at NGA headquarters by 2006.[10]

In the spring and early summer of 2008, Canada's geospatial intelligence directorate participated, along with NGA and the United Kingdom's geospatial intelligence unit, in Operation RAMPANT LION 2 in Afghanistan, producing geospatial intelligence that was employed in real-time to support Canadian and allied forces. After the January 2010 earthquake in Haiti, the Canadian Forces Mapping and Charting Establishment, at NGA's request, accelerated production of topographic maps of Haitian territory. Cooperation also includes the exchange of liaison officers at NGA and DGI headquarters.[11]

The New Zealand component of the geospatial intelligence alliance is GEOINT New Zealand, formed in July 2012 from the merger of the New Zealand Defence Force Geospatial Intelligence Organization and the GEOINT elements of the Government Communications Security Bureau. The United Kingdom, in July 2012, established the Defence Geospatial and Intelligence Fusion Centre. NGA provided assistance to U.K. geospatial efforts intended to help protect that summer's London Olympics. Products included a map depicting London's Olympic route network and venue access points at Olympic Park.[12]

In 1994 the Bundeswehr Geoinformation Office (BGIO) entered into a cooperative arrangement with the Defense Mapping Agency (DMA), exchanging topographic products, two years before DMA was absorbed by the National Imagery and Mapping Agency (NIMA). In 2000 the BGIO director decided that Germany should expand its role as a provider of international geospatial data, which required the office to build a new production facility in Euskirchen, Germany. With support from NIMA, BGIO established a test bed to develop and test digital production processes. In February 2001, NIMA and BGIO expanded their geospatial coproduction relationship.[13]

BGIO and NGA signed an agreement on September 15, 2004, that provided for "bilateral co-production and the exchange and release of geospatial data and information." As a consequence of the arrangement, BGIO "sends digital data to NGA for inclusion in the NGA's Geospatial Intelligence Feature Database (GIFD)." Reportedly the NGA and BGIO also "exchange topographic, aeronautic, and hydrographic data in hardcopy and digital formats," and BGIO is a partner in the twenty-eight-nation Multinational Geospatial Co-production Program "designed to coordinate high-resolution vector data production." In 2008 an NGA-BGIO liaison position was established at NGA's Reston, Virginia, facility. In 2009 NGA officials met with officials from the German Federal Intelligence Service, or Bundesnachrichtendienst (BND), to discuss Germany's plans for expansion of its satellite reconnaissance efforts.[14]

Well before Israel was able to provide the United States with satellite imagery of its own, it received such imagery from the United States, although at times Israel requested more than the United States was willing to provide—including dedicated satellites or ground stations that could access U.S. real-time satellite imagery. In 1976 the United States supplied Israel with both aerial and satellite imagery of Uganda's Entebbe International Airport to supplement the information obtained by Israeli agents in preparation for an Israeli hostage rescue mission.[15]

William J. Casey, during his first three years (1981–1984) as Director of Central Intelligence (DCI), provided Israel with access to satellite imagery and other reconnaissance data that had been denied under the administration of Jimmy Carter. The head of Israeli military intelligence (AMAN) from 1979 to 1983, Major General Yehoshua Saguy, said in early 1984 that the CIA was providing Israel with access to data from reconnaissance satellites and to "not only the information but the photos themselves." Carter's director of central intelligence, Admiral Stansfield Turner, had refused to provide the satellite imagery shared during George H. W. Bush's tenure as DCI in 1976 and 1977.[16]

After 1981, the satellite photos were often referred to inside the Israeli intelligence community as "Casey's gifts," and they were considered invaluable. After Israel used some of the photos to aid its aerial attack on Iraq's Osirak reactor in 1981, and a review determined that Israel had received imagery of targets in Libya, Pakistan, and other nations a considerable distance from Israel, Deputy DCI Bobby Ray Inman restricted Israel's access to photographs of targets within 250 miles of its borders.[17]

During Operations Desert Shield and Desert Storm, the U.S.-Israeli intelligence exchange included Israeli provision of data on Iraqi air defenses, while the United States granted Israel access to relevant U.S. satellite imagery. As it had in the past, Israel pressed for establishment of a ground station to allow real-time access to KH-11 imagery. Another aspect of U.S-Israeli cooperation with regard to overhead imagery also involved Iraq and the attempt to discover further details of Iraqi nuclear, chemical, and biological warfare activities. Israeli imagery interpreters analyzed overhead photography obtained by U.S. U-2 aircraft operating in support of the UN Special Commission in the light of intelligence in Israeli data bases about the targets.[18]

A possible step to expanded provision of satellite intelligence to Israel took place in July 2012, when President Barack Obama signed the United States–Israel Enhanced Security Cooperation Act. One provision directed that the United States "expand already-close intelligence cooperation, including satellite reconnaissance, with Israel."[19]

Another cooperative arrangement exists with South Korea, the result of a November 2010 agreement between NGA and two South Korean organizations, the Ministry of National Defense's Defense Intelligence Agency and the National Intelligence Service. It specifies that "GEOINT information and related materials exchanged or produced under this Agreement shall generally be unclassified" but allows for the exchange of classified information. The agreement also restricts the range of material exchanged to Korean Peninsula and contiguous border regions, unless modified by written agreement. An exception allows informal agreement to exchange GEOINT information and materials related to humanitarian assistance, disaster relief, and Republic of Korea defense, humanitarian, and peacekeeping activities. As one component of the cooperation, the NGA provides source packages to the Korean Army Geospatial Intelligence Agency, which produces updated maps and transmit the digital print files and attributed feature data back to NGA to print and include in the Geospatial Intelligence Feature Database.[20]

According to a 2004 report on Mexican intelligence, the nation's Center for Intelligence and National Security (Centro de Inteligencia y Seguridad Nacional) has liaison relationships with over forty intelligence services from twenty-eight nations. Of those, the CIA is the "foremost strategic partner" and, along with other U.S. intelligence organizations, provides "valuable information on drug cartels," which includes satellite intelligence related to drug production within Mexico. According to a 2010 fact sheet, the Office of the Director of National Intelligence "surged intelligence support to Mexico to help combat drug cartels and their impact on Mexican governance and U.S. border security."[21]

The United States provided satellite imagery to the board of the International Atomic Energy Agency (IAEA) to convince members that North Korea was violating its commitments under the Nuclear Nonproliferation Treaty by seeking to secretly store nuclear waste from its Yongbyon reactor—waste that would be reprocessed to extract plutonium for nuclear states. The IAEA Board of Governors met in Vienna in closed session. The governors examined a series of black-and-white images that showed a storage facility under construction as well as what appeared to be an older facility at Yongbyon being covered with dirt and later planted with trees and shrubs. The images were intended to provide convincing proof that North Korea had buried nuclear waste under a camouflage mound and constructed a new facility to serve as a decoy. The board approved a resolution demanding that North Korea permit inspections, "without delay," of waste storage sites.[22]

In November 1993 a team of IAEA inspectors conducted an examination of previously unchecked buildings at Iranian nuclear sites, looking for evidence of a clandestine nuclear weapons program. The targets of the unannounced inspection included sites that the U.S. Intelligence Community suspected might be involved in nuclear-related work—isolated and camouflaged buildings surrounded by tall wire fencing and tight security.[23]

SIGNALS INTELLIGENCE COOPERATION

The U.S.-British military alliance in World War II necessitated a high degree of cooperation with respect to intelligence activities. It was imperative for the United States and Britain, as the main Western combatants in the European and Pacific theaters, to establish a coordinated effort in the acquisition of intelligence. By far the most important aspect of that cooperation was in the area of signals intelligence. An apparently limited SIGINT cooperation agreement was reached in December 1940. A visit by four U.S. officers, including two members of the Army's Signals Intelligence Service, to the British Government Code and Cypher School (GC&CS) followed in January 1941. That June the United States and Britain agreed to exchange signals intelligence concerning Japan. Not until October 2, 1942, did they sign an agreement for extensive cooperation in the area of naval SIGINT. Then, on May 17, 1943, a new agreement, generally known as the British-U.S. Communications Intelligence Agreement (BRUSA), was reached and provided for extensive cooperation between the U.S. Army's SIGINT agency and the GC&CS. SIGINT cooperation also included Canada, Australia, and New Zealand.[24]

The intelligence relationships forged during World War II among Australia, Britain, Canada, New Zealand, and the United States did not end with the fighting. Rather, they became formalized and grew stronger. At about the time that World War II ended, the already ongoing cooperation between the United States and the

United Kingdom to target and exploit Soviet communications was assigned the code name BOURBON. On March 5, 1946, the United States and Britain signed an updated British-U.S. Communications Intelligence Agreement, which superseded the BOURBON effort. Both countries agreed to exchange the products of operations relating to collection of foreign communications traffic, acquisition of communications documents and equipment, traffic analysis, cryptanalysis, and procurement of information regarding communications organizations' practices, procedures, and equipment. The agreement stipulated that the exchange would be unrestricted except for specific exclusions at the request of either party.[25]

The agreement also specified the terms of any interaction with Third Parties, defined as all individuals or authorities other than those of the United States, the British Empire, and the British Dominions. Specifically, it was agreed that "each party will seek the agreement of the other to any action with third parties, and will take no such action until its advisability is agreed upon" and that "each party will ensure that the results of any action are made available to the other."[26]

In 1954, at the behest of the British, U.S. bilateral SIGINT relationships with Britain and Canada developed into the UKUSA Agreement, also known as the UKUSA Security Agreement or "Secret Treaty." The primary emphasis of the agreement was to provide a division of SIGINT collection responsibilities between the First Party (the United States) and the Second Parties (Australia, Britain, Canada, and New Zealand). The specific agencies now involved are the National Security Agency, the Australian Signals Directorate (ASD, formerly the Defence Signals Directorate), the British Government Communications Headquarters (GCHQ), the Canadian Communications Security Establishment (CSE), and the New Zealand Government Communications Security Bureau (GCSB).[27]

The original division of responsibilities predated not only the creation of the Internet but the advent of satellite communications and space SIGINT collection. The United States was responsible for SIGINT in Latin America, most of Asia, Russia, and northern China. Australia's area of responsibility included it neighbors (such as Indonesia), southern China, and the nations of Indochina. Britain's responsibility included Africa and Russia west of the Urals. The polar regions of Russia were the responsibility of Canada, and New Zealand's area of responsibility was the western Pacific. The SIGINT Combined Operating List specified tasking assignments.[28]

While many of aspects of the communications environment have changed over the last several decades, the key characteristics of the agreement(s) have remained. The UKUSA component of the FIVE EYES relationship is more than an agreement to coordinate separately conducted intelligence activities and share the intelligence collected. Rather, it is cemented by the presence of U.S. facilities on British, Canadian, and Australian territory; by joint (U.S.-U.K., Australian-U.S., and U.K.-Australian) operations within and outside UKUSA territory; by an assortment of bilateral meetings and multilateral conferences; and, in the case of Australia, by the presence of U.K. and U.S. staff at ASD facilities.[29]

In addition to dividing SIGINT collection responsibilities, the agreement addresses access to the collected intelligence and security arrangements for handling of data. Standardized code words, security agreements that all employees of the respective agencies must sign, and procedures for storing and disseminating code-word material are implemented under the terms of the agreement.[30]

PHOTO 13.1   Communications Security Establishment headquarters. *Photo credit:* C. W. Clark.

Thus, in 1967, the "COMINT Indoctrination" declaration, which all British-cleared personnel had to sign, included the statement "I declare that I fully understand the information relating to the manner and extent of the interception of communications of foreign powers by H.M. Government and *other cooperating governments*, and intelligence produced by such interception known as Communications Intelligence (COMINT) is information covered by Section 2 of the Official Secrets Act 1911 (as amended)" (emphasis added). The requirements for standardized code words (see Chapter 19), security arrangements, and procedures for the handling and dissemination of SIGINT material were detailed in a series of International Regulations on SIGINT (IRSIG) that was in its third edition in 1967.[31]

One of the best examples of UKUSA cooperation has been what was known as the ECHELON program. As noted in Chapter 8, despite press reports suggesting otherwise, ECHELON is not the overall UKUSA collection program but one limited to the interception of the traffic through selected civilian communication satellites, particularly the INTELSAT spacecraft in geosynchronous orbit. The computer dictionaries at each site search intercepted material for key words submitted by analysts from UKUSA partners, and intercepts that contain those key words are automatically forwarded to those analysts. In addition to the U.S. intercept facilities that are part of the ECHELON network, there are ECHELON stations operated by the ASD (at Geraldton, Australia, which targets communications concerning the North Korean military, Pakistani nuclear weapons technology, and Japanese trade ministry plans), the CSE (at Leitrim, which apparently targets Latin American communications), the GCHQ (at Morwenstow, near Bude, Cornwall), and the GCSB (at Waihopai, code-named IRONSAND).[32]

In addition to the ECHELON stations, each of the United States' UKUSA partners operates a number of other SIGINT sites that produce intelligence that will make its way to the other partners. Australian sites include those targeted on land-based as well as naval activity—the latter of which gets fed into the U.S. Ocean Surveillance Information System (OSIS).

Australian land-based SIGINT sites include intercept sites on the Cocos Islands; the Shoal Bay Receiving Station near Darwin, Riverina; satellite ground stations at HMAS Harman in Canberra; Morundah near Wagga in New South Wales (Riverina); Cabarlah near Toowoomba in Queensland; and Geraldton in Western Australia. Australian ocean-oriented stations are located at Pearce, Western Australia; Cabarlah, Queensland; and Shoal Bay, New Territories. The Cabarlah station on the east coast of Australia is operated by the ASD, and its main function is monitoring transmissions through the Southwest Pacific. The Pearce station has as its primary purpose the monitoring of naval and air traffic over the Indian Ocean. In the early 1980s, a Pusher antenna was installed for the purpose of intercepting, monitoring, direction finding (DF), and analyzing radio signals in a portion of the high-frequency band. The most important station for monitoring Southeast Asia is the ASD station at Darwin (Shoal Bay), which originally had a very limited DF capability. However, contracts signed in 1981 provided for the procurement of modern DF equipment to enable the station to "participate fully in the OSIS."[33]

Another aspect of Australian SIGINT activity is its use of embassies for eavesdropping operations, part of a FIVE EYES effort code-named STATEROOM. The effort targets radio, telecommunication, and Internet traffic. Specific embassy sites, not revealed in the Snowden-leaked documents but reported in the Australian press, include those in Jakarta, Bangkok, Hanoi, Beijing, and Dili. In addition, intercept facilities are also located at the High Commissions in Kuala Lumpur and Port Moresby and at other diplomatic posts.[34]

Canada's current sites include those at Canadian Forces Station Alert (which targets northern Russia, the site of Russian naval and missile testing activity), as well those at Masset, Queen Charlotte Islands, and Gander, Newfoundland, whose targets can be found in Latin America, the northern Atlantic, and the northern Pacific Ocean. Canadian stations at Halifax and a joint U.S-British station on Ascension Island (which monitors naval traffic in the South Atlantic) contribute to the monitoring of naval movements in the Atlantic Ocean.[35]

While aspects of the UKUSA network are multilateral in nature, the FIVE EYES relationship also includes various bilateral relationships and activities. Canada's SIGINT relationship with the United States is defined by the CANUS Agreement (as well as the UKUSA Agreement), which was initially drafted more than six decades ago. On September 15, 1950, Canada and the United States exchanged letters giving formal recognition to the Security Agreement Between Canada and the United States of America (which was followed exactly two months later by the Agreement for the Exchange of Information Between the U.S., U.K. and Canada).[36]

In one case, U.S.-Canadian cooperation in the SIGINT area resulted from a U.S. inability to process the data produced by the CANYON COMINT satellite. That program commenced operations with a launch in April 1968, followed by five additional successful launches through 1977. Despite initial difficulties, the satellite eventually produced such a heavy volume of intercepted communications that the United States recruited the CSE, along with GCHQ, to help in processing the take, thus granting Canada access to the intercepted communications.[37]

In the 1970s, U.S.-Canadian SIGINT cooperation led the Canadian SIGINT organization to conduct a feasibility study of embassy-based eavesdropping operations. The overall program, code-named PILGRIM, involved eavesdropping operations in India, China, Venezuela, Mexico, the Soviet Union, Romania, Morocco, Jamaica, and the Ivory Coast. More recently, Canada provided the United States with an intelligence assessment based on communications intelligence, "Afghanistan: Taliban Challenges, Regional Concerns," dated October 17, 1996.[38] A top secret April 2013 NSA assessment of the NSA-CSE relationship described the Canadian organization as a "highly valued second party partner" and the "basic tenet" of the relationship as "cooperation in all aspects of SIGINT except when considered prejudicial to the national interests of the parties." It went on to note that the relationship involved "exchange of liaison officers and integrees, joint projects, shared activities and a strong desire for closer collaboration in the area of cyber defense."[39]

The United Kingdom, as noted earlier, was also involved in processing the take from CANYON. A more recent component of the U.S.-U.K. bilateral SIGINT relationship involves space SIGINT. Britain's decision to cancel an indigenous SIGINT satellite program, code-named ZIRCON, was followed by a February 1987 decision to purchase a share in the ORION system at a cost of $750 million. ZIRCON had originally been conceived by GCHQ director Brian Tovey "to keep the special relationship sweet and to take his organization into space."[40]

One indicator of the U.S.-U.K. SIGINT relationship was the "visit précis" for the visit of GCHQ director Sir Iain Lobban to NSA from April 30 to May 1, 2013. It provided information about the extent of NSA sharing of PRISM data with GCHQ, demonstrating that, at the time, GCHQ wanted to gain "unsupervised access" to PRISM, in contrast to the restricted access it currently had—a proposal supported by NSA leadership. Agreement on a program, Triage 2.0, that involved supervised access was apparently near. A separate briefing slide and other documents indicated that GCHQ had expanded access to PRISM data during the 2012 London Olympics, an effort designated OLYMPIC OPTION.[41]

A 2013 NSA information paper on the agency's relationship with New Zealand noted that the GCSB gathered intelligence on China; on the diplomatic communications of Japan, North Korea, Vietnam, Paksitan, India, Iran, and countries of South America; and on French police and nuclear testing activities in New Caldeonia. The GCSB has also engaged in computer network exploitation and, according to a leaked document, has obtained a malware tool that allows the organization to extract data from computers and smart phones.[42]

An important adjunct for the United States to the Second Parties to the UKUSA Agreement are "Third Parties" to the treaty, foreign SIGINT agencies whose relations with NSA are governed by the terms of the UKUSA Agreement. In 2009 two NSA officials noted that among the benefits to the United States of Third Party relationships are "our partners' geography and access to high-priority target communications" as well as "their expertise on specific targets." In addition, the partners "know their regional 'hoods better than we do and they exponentially add to our foreign language capability."[43] A slide from a top secret NSA document titled "Approved SIGINT Partners," shown in Figure 13.1, identifies the nations that constitute third parties.

An NSA document explores the question of what the United States wants to achieve from its Third Party relationships and what Third Party agencies want from the United States. It explores four issues: (1) whether Third Party relationships are designed to

FIGURE 13.1   U.S. Third Party Allies

Algeria	Hungary	Poland
Austria	India	Romania
Belgium	Israel	Saudi Arabia
Croatia	Italy	Singapore
Czech Republic	Japan	Spain
Denmark	Jordan	Sweden
Ethiopia	Korea	Taiwan
Finland	Macedonia	Thailand
France	Netherlands	Tunisia
Germany	Norway	Turkey
Greece	Pakistan	United Arab Emirates

Source: Adapted from Glenn Greenwald, *No Place to Hide: Edward Snowden, the NSA, and the U.S. Surveillance State* [New York: Metropolitan Books, 2014], 123.

meet specific needs or have a longer-term focus, (2) what the NSA wants specifically from the relationships (e.g., access, expertise), (3) whether U.S. foreign intelligence relationships are affected by the state of relations with a country, (4) and what Third-Parties want from the United States. The article observed that, for the United States, "our partners' geography and access to high-priority target communications are a huge plus, as is their expertise on specific targets." It also stated that in the case of many foreign partners, "few senior officials outside of their defense intelligence apparatuses are witting to any SIGINT connection of the U.S./NSA."[44] Among the 2013–2014 revelations concerning U.S. SIGINT relationships were those with a number of Third-Parties: France, Germany, Israel, the Netherlands, Norway, Saudi Arabia, and Sweden.

An April 2013 NSA document titled "Visit Précis" focuses on the upcoming visit to the NSA by the technical director of the French foreign intelligence service, the Directorate General of External Security (DGSE), and the director of National Information Systems Security. The paper notes that the two French officials "will lead a technical discussion relating to the May 2102 cyberattacks against the French Presidential network." It also notes two "potential landmines": that helping determine the origins of the attack "may reveal a U.S. ally is responsible" and that "the French have not been forthcoming in sharing technical details of the cyberattacks."[45]

A 2013 NSA information paper traced the evolution of the NSA-BND relationship, discussed the information assurance and computer network defense relationship with Germany, noted three key issues, contained a short discussion section, provided several success stories, and noted "Problems/Challenges with the partner." The key issues section reported, "The BND has been working to influence the German Government to relax interpretation of the privacy laws over the long term to provide greater opportunity for intelligence sharing." Success stories included BND modernization of its foreign satellite collection effort as well as "sustained collection" against a number of targets, including the Ministries of Foreign Affairs of two nations (whose identities were redacted). It also noted that "the BND has been working to influence the German

Government to relax interpretation of the privacy laws over the long term to provide greater opportunity for intelligence sharing" and that NSA is provided access to communications intercepted by the BND-operated satellite communications intercept site at Bad Aibling.[46]

Revelations concerning NSA's gathering of Internet traffic (particularly e-mails) and phone calls raised the question of whether the German government was aware of the extent to which such collection targeted German citizens. Reports, particularly in *Der Spiegel*, asserted a number of areas of U.S. (NSA)–German (BND) cooperation. That cooperation reportedly included NSA assistance to the BND in analyzing Internet traffic from the Middle East and an NSA presence at the Bad Aibling listening post, which the United States had turned over to Germany and which the BND uses to monitor Thuraya satellite phones in remote regions of Pakistan and Afghanistan. One document is quoted as stating that BND intercepts from Afghanistan are shared with NSA "on a daily basis." It was also reported that both NSA and the BND were collecting hundreds of million pieces of information from the digital data hub located in Frankfurt.[47]

Among the documents concerning Germany's SIGINT capability were those showing that the Office for the Protection of the Constitution was equipped with the NSA-developed XKeyscore program intended to "expand their ability to support NSA as we jointly prosecute CT (counterterrorism) targets." Instruction in using the program was provided by the BND.[48]

Past examples of SIGINT sharing with Israel include U.S. provision of data from the RHYOLITE satellite during the 1973 Yom Kippur War. Then, during the 1985 hijacking of the *Achille Lauro*, Israel provided the United States with the location of the ship on several occasions, the location of the ship's hijackers when they were in Egypt, and the identification number and call sign of the plane carrying the hijackers seconds after it took off from Egypt. In 2004, the NSA "detected a suspiciously high number of telephone calls between Syria and North Korea, with a noticeably busy line of communication between the North Korean capital of Pyonyang and a place in the northern Syrian desert called Al-Kibar." The file compiled by NSA was sent to Israel, which, in September 2007, destroyed the reactor that was under construction at Al-Kibar.[49]

The U.S.-Israeli SIGINT relationship includes NSA provision to the Israeli SIGINT organization, Unit 8200 or the Israeli SIGINT National Unit (ISNU), of raw SIGINT data that has not been reviewed by U.S. authorities or had the identities of U.S. persons redacted. Although the NSA-ISNU agreement calls for Israel to apply the same "minimization" procedures NSA was required to apply with regard to U.S. persons, the memorandum stated it was "not intended to create any legally enforceable rights" or be "a legally binding instrument according to international law."[50]

According to an NSA history of the U.S.-Israeli SIGINT relationship, *The Guardian* newspaper reported, "Balancing the SIGINT exchange equally between US and Israeli needs has been a constant challenge. In the last decade it arguably tilted heavily in favor of Israeli security concerns. 9/11 came, and went, with NSA's only true Third Party CT relationship being driven almost totally by the needs of the partner. Nevertheless, the survival of the state of Israel is a paramount goal of US Middle East policy. There is no doubt that the NSA-ISNU relationship is built upon a solid foundation of trust and common purpose."[51]

An April 2013 information paper on the SIGINT relationship, most recently designated STONE RUBY, summarized key issues, what NSA provides to Israel's SIGINT unit and vice versa, success stories, and problems/challenges. It noted, "The largest single exchange between NSA and ISNU is on targets in the Middle East which constitute strategic threats to U.S. and Israeli interests." It reports that one benefit of the arrangement to the United States is "access to world-class Israeli cryptanalytic and SIGINT engineering expertise." In addition, "several recent and successful joint operations between NSA and ISNU have broadened both organizations' ability to target and exploit Iranian nuclear efforts." Also noted were concerns raised by Israel about NSA's "reluctance to share" technology "that is not directly related to a specific target" as well as "ISNU's perceived reduction in the amount and degree of cooperation in certain areas."[52]

One aspect of the NSA-Netherlands SIGINT relationship was Dutch provision to NSA of 1.8 million intercepted telephone calls and e-mails over a thirty-day period (December 2012–January 2013). The source of the intercepts was the National SIGINT Organization (NSO), a subsidiary of the Dutch Military Intelligence and Security Service (MIVD). An article on the relationship revealed that the NSA designator for NSO/MIVD is US-985Y. According to one commentator, the implication was that much of the interception reported as being carried out by NSA was actually carried out by cooperating SIGINT agencies.[53]

The existence of a U.S.-Norwegian SIGINT relationship goes back to at least the early 1960s and has involved U.S. funding for Norwegian ground and naval SIGINT assets for the purposes of monitoring Soviet missile and naval activity. According to a December 2013 report, Norwegian Intelligence Service SIGINT activities provide the United States with "access to Russian targets in the Kola Peninsula" and "SIGINT reports on Russian civilian targets of mutual targets, particularly Russian energy policy." Meanwhile, information provided by NSA to Norway includes data on Russian counterintelligence operations in Norway.[54]

Sweden, unlike its Norwegian neighbor, is not a member of NATO and during the Cold War maintained an official posture of neutrality, although there was little doubt that it leaned toward the West in security, including intelligence, matters. But according to a 2006 document cited by a Swedish newspaper, "The [SIGINT] relationship with Sweden is protected on the top-secret level because of the country's political neutrality."[55]

The relationship between the NSA and the Swedish Defense Radio Establishment, or Forsvarets Radioanstalt (FRA), was established in 1954 under the terms of the UKUSA Agreement and assigned GCHQ responsibility for exchange of communications intelligence, while NSA handled the exchange of electronic intelligence (ELINT). Then, in 2004, NSA and GCHQ, with the consent of the FRA, agreed that both would hold bilateral exchanges with FRA on both COMINT and ELINT.[56]

A 2013 NSA information paper described the FRA as "an extremely competent, technically innovative and trusted Third Party partner." It reported that the relationship "continues to grow" and noted that in 2011 the FRA provided NSA with "access to its cable collection," which provided "unique collection on high-priority Russian targets such as leadership, internal politics, and energy." Sweden, it also observed, provides NSA with "unique intelligence on Russia, the Baltic, Middle East, and CT," as well as "outstanding and unique input on ELINT signals."[57]

The paper was produced about a week in advance of the annual SWEDUSA Strategic Planning Conference. Subjects to be discussed included QUANTUM operations, cable access/reporting and analysis, cyber, counterterrorism, and Russia. It noted that NSA desired FRA's assistance with "high-priority CT Swedish language traffic that [NSA] is currently unable to fully analyze" and that "FRA's cable access has resulted in unique SIGINT reporting" on the Russian target.[58]

The SIGINT relationship with Saudi Arabia, specifically the Ministry of Defense's Radio Reconnaissance Department, since the Gulf War in 1991 was "very limited," according to a 2013 NSA assessment—but noted that on December 11, 2012, the Director of National Intelligence (DNI) approved expansion of NSA's Third Party SIGINT relationship with Saudi Arabia to include the Ministry of Interior's Technical Affairs Directorate. The paper also reports that NSA had been collaborating with the directorate since February 2011 on "a sensitive access initiative." It went on to state that Saudi Arabia had provided "unencrypted collection against the IRGC QODs Maritime Force targets of mutual interest."[59]

The U.S.-Turkish SIGINT relationship goes back to 1949, when the CIA and the Electronic and Technical Intelligence Directorate (ETID) of the Turkish National Intelligence Organization (MIT) reached a verbal agreement involving the CIA's provision of funding and equipment in exchange for raw COMINT traffic. In 1979 the program for support of ETID became the responsibility of the NSA. Another component of the U.S.-Turkish relationship was a 1962 agreement between NSA and the Turkish General Staff (which operates General Electronic Service as part of its Intelligence Directorate), which authorized the United States to operate SIGINT sites on Turkish territory.[60]

According to an NSA assessment of the relationship, the exchange of SIGINT relevant to counterterrorism was expanded in July 2002 to include "actionable intelligence." That exchange was expanded in 2007 to include actionable intelligence against the Kurdish People's Congress (KGK, formerly PKK) leadership in northern Iraq, including voice transcripts of KGK communications. Other counterterrorism SIGINT cooperation has involved the Marxist-Leninist Revolutionary People's Liberation Party (DHKP/C) as well as al-Qaeda and its affiliated groups. The United States also benefits from receiving real-time reporting from Turkey on military, air, naval, ground, and paramilitary targets in Russia, Georgia, and Ukraine.[61]

MEASUREMENT AND SIGNATURE INTELLIGENCE COOPERATION

MASINT cooperation between the United States and foreign nations goes back to before the term "MASINT" existed. The United States, Britain, and Australia cooperated in nuclear detection efforts, as illustrated by U.S.-built, British-operated facilities on Australian territory in the 1960s. U.S.-British cooperation was also apparently the subject of an understanding on test ban monitoring requirements that followed technical discussions in 1964. A draft agreement envisioned U.S. installation of equipment at U.K. stations and specified, "All data from UK operated stations will be promptly transmitted to the US (AFTAC) through a single communications link" and the United States "will similarly provide to the UK data recorded at US detection facilities."[62]

Canada has been a partner in the Sound Surveillance System (SOSUS), first becoming involved when one of its first naval facilities, at Shelburne, Nova Scotia, opened. In 1972 Canada expanded its role in SOSUS and sent a small detachment to work with U.S. personnel at the U.S. Naval Facility at Argentia, Newfoundland. By the early 1980s, it had expanded its capabilities, and Canadian participation had grown, with additional Canadian Forces personnel being assigned to the Naval Ocean Processing Facility at Dam Neck, Virginia; the Naval Facility at Bermuda; and Headquarters, Commander, Undersea Surveillance Pacific, Ford Island, Hawaii. A Canadian detachment was also formed at the Whidbey Island Naval Facility. In 1994 the Canadian Offshore Surveillance Center at Halifax, Nova Scotia, opened to process all acoustic information gathered in Argentia.[63]

MASINT cooperation also extends to space, specifically the Defense Support Program and Space-Based Infrared System, which involve ground relay sites in the United Kingdom and Australia. Australia is also a recipient of data produced by those systems. In September 2013, the U.S. Air Force announced that it had awarded a contract to Northrop Grumman to provide Australia with the Australian Mission Processor Phase 3, a system for processing the infrared data produced by the two systems.[64]

SPACE SURVEILLANCE COOPERATION

Despite its deployment of extensive space surveillance assets, the United States, as noted in Chapter 10, does not have the capability to continuously monitor foreign satellite operations. However, "for the longest time, the [U.S. Government] was one of the few organizations able to find and conduct space surveillance using optical telescope and various types of radar." In recent years, though, "the number of organizations who have developed or are developing space situational awareness (SSA) capabilities . . . has . . . increased."[65]

One significant impetus for the increased U.S. desire to access foreign space situational awareness data, in addition to availability, was the February 2009 collision, 490 miles above the Earth, of a Russian Comsos and an American Iridium satellite. Undoubtedly, China's increasingly active space program, including its antisatellite component, is another. Since 2010 the United States has signed agreements with five different nations—Australia, Italy, France, Japan, and Canada—for the exchange of space surveillance data.[66]

In November 2010, U.S. and Australian defense chiefs signed a one-page statement of principles for the "Australian–United States Space Situational Awareness Partnership." One provision of the statement included investigating "the potential for jointly establishing and operating space situational awareness facilities in Australia to support the United States space surveillance network and to support the development of Australia's space situational awareness . . . capability." In addition, the statement called for sharing of SSA data and required that the Australian government have "full knowledge" of "any activities being undertaken in, through or from Australian territory." The statement of principles produced the further agreement, in November 2012, to relocate a C-band space radar to Harold E. Holt Naval Communications Station in Exmouth in 2014. In November 2013, the United States and Australia agreed that a Defense Advanced Research Projects Agency space telescope would also move to Exmouth and become operational in 2016.[67]

The United States and France—specifically the Secretary of Defense and the French Minister of Defense—signed an agreement on space surveillance cooperation in February 2011. According to a French Defense Ministry official, the primary focus of the agreement was France's GRAVES (Grand Réseau Adapté à la Veille Spatiale) radar, which is capable of identifying large objects in low-Earth orbit up to approximately 620 miles.[68]

In May 2012, the U.S. Air Force and the Canadian Department of National Defence concluded a five-year agreement for sharing orbital surveillance data, with the expectation that a longer arrangement would follow. Among the Canadian assets expected to provide orbital data was the Sapphire space surveillance satellite, which was launched in February 2013 and became operational in January 2014, as well as a planned successor. The Sapphire operates in a circular 465-mile sun-synchronous orbit, and its electro-optical sensor is capable of providing information on objects between 3,720 and 24,800 miles above Earth. The data will, according to an Air Force spokesman, allow "for more timely, complete and accurate SSA." Prior to the launch, it was announced that the Sapphire ground element, the Satellite Sensor Systems Operations Centre, "will function as the interface between the Sapphire system and the U.S. Joint Space Operations Center."[69]

The United States and Canada signed a second space surveillance agreement on December 26, 2013. This time the signatories were the U.S. Department of Defense (DOD), Canadian Department of Defence, and Canadian Forces. That agreement concerned sharing of unclassified space surveillance information and contained the same language as agreements between the DOD and a number of Japanese organizations (Director of Cabinet Intelligence and Research Office; Ministry of Education, Culture, Sports, Science, and Technology; Ministry of Land, Infrastructure, Transport, and Tourism; Ministry of Defense; Japan Aerospace Exploration Agency), the Italian Defense General Staff, and the Commander of the French Joint Space Command. The agreements with Japan, Australia, and Italy were signed in March, April, and October 2013, respectively. The agreement with France was signed in January 2014.[70]

Article 5 of each of those five agreements specified that classified information would not be exchanged under the agreement, the primary purpose of which was collision avoidance. Space surveillance data exchanged concerned resolution of spacecraft anomalies, prediction of close approaches between space objects, deorbit and reentry support, disposal/end-of-life support, on-orbit information, and electromagnetic interference investigation.[71] On occasion, that information may inevitably involve the movements of satellites of intelligence interest because of fears that they might be involved in an antisatellite test or have an uncontrolled return to Earth and thus pose a risk to some country's inhabitants.

A further space-related agreement among the United States, Australia, and the United Kingdom was signed in May 2014. A senior U.S. Air Force official described it as providing the foundation for cooperation on space situational awareness for the years ahead. Specific details of the agreement are to be finalized in the next few years but will likely, according to the Air Force official, entail data sharing or access to each other's space surveillance assets. That agreement was followed by SSA agreements in October 2014 and January 2015 with the European Space Agency and in early January 2015 with the European Space Agency and Germany. Germany, whose Defense Staff has established a Space Surveillance Center, will provide data acquired by its Tir Tracking and Imaging Radar space surveillance facility near Bonn.[72]

HUMAN INTELLIGENCE COOPERATION

With respect to the U.S-British intelligence relationship, one observer has noted, "In contrast to SIGINT, HUMINT tends to be shared more narrowly and directly on more of a strict 'need-to-know' basis." The central component of the HUMINT relationship is the one between the CIA and Britain's Secret Intelligence Service, although there is also some exchange between the nations' defense HUMINT organizations (currently the U.S. Defense Clandestine Service and the U.K. Defence HUMINT Office).[73]

One area where British HUMINT has an advantage over that of the United States has been identified by former assistant director of central intelligence for analysis and production Mark Lowenthal, who remarked, "British HUMINT does not completely overlap that of the United States, with Britain having some advantages in Commonwealth countries." In addition, British HUMINT reportedly contributed to the effort to halt Libya's pursuit of weapons of mass destruction.[74]

The longest running aspect of the relationship between the German BND and U.S. intelligence agencies is the one that concerns human intelligence. In the aftermath of World War II the CIA helped establish the Gehlen Organization, run by Reinhard Gehlen, the former head of Hitler's Foreign Armies East, who reported to the CIA. With West Germany's transition from occupied country to independent state, the Gehlen Organization became the BND.[75]

In 2003, despite Germany's opposition to the U.S. invasion of Iraq, the BND allegedly provided intelligence to the United States in support of the military effort. According to one account, on April 7, 2003, German military intelligence operatives dispatched to Baghdad before the war drove by a chicken restaurant in the city's well-to-do Mansour district and noticed a convoy of armored vehicles similar to those used by Saddam Hussein. The information was passed from the BND to the Defense Intelligence Agency and served as the catalyst for a B-1 strike on the site, which occurred less than forty minutes later.* While the strike killed at least a dozen people, none of them was Saddam Hussein or his two sons, as had been hoped.[76]

German intelligence assistance, through intelligence officers in Baghdad, also involved the provision of coordinates of civilian sites, including hospitals, foreign embassies, and places of worship, so that they would not be hit in U.S. air attacks. The Germans also provided information on the possible location of a missing U.S. pilot.[77] Furthermore, according to an account in the *New York Times*, German intelligence personnel in Baghdad provided a copy of Saddam Hussein's plan for the defense of

---

*The German foreign minister denied this allegation. See Jeffrey Fleishman, "Official Denies Germany Aided U.S. in Iraq War," *Los Angeles Times*, January 21, 2006, A7.

Baghdad, which gave the United States "an extraordinary window into Iraq's top-level deliberations, including where and how Mr. Hussein planned to deploy his most loyal troops."* The plan had been unveiled at a December 18, 2002, strategy session that included Hussein and his commanders. In February 2003, a German intelligence officer serving as a representative to the Central Command provided the plan to a DIA official who worked there.[78]

The liaison officer provided twenty-five reports to the United States, which answered eighteen of the thirty-three specific requests for information made during the first few months of the Iraq War in what was "a systematic exchange" between U.S. intelligence officials and the Germans. Eight of the reports concerned the mood and provisioning of the residents of Baghdad, while another eight focused on the nature of the military and police presence in the city. Two reports provided coordinates of military forces.[79]

Officers from the Canadian Security Intelligence Service (CSIS) gathered intelligence on the ground in Afghanistan, playing "a crucial and long-standing role as interrogators of a vast swath of captured Taliban fighters," according to a Canadian press account. While the interrogations would focus primarily on threats to Canadian troops in Afghanistan, such information would also be of interest to the CIA and other intelligence organizations. The Canadian Minister of Defence acknowledged that both Afghan and NATO officials were kept informed.[80]

South Korea's National Intelligence Service turned over to the DIA data collected through interviews with around 9,000 North Korean defectors between 1997 and 2007. The information concerned the integrity of the North Korean regime, the possibility of its collapse, human rights abuses, reform programs, and how North Koreans obtain information about South Korean society.[81]

In July 2005, senior U.S. intelligence officials briefed the top echelon of the IAEA in Vienna on the contents provided by an Iranian source (discussed in Chapter 11). At the same time, the United States hoped to benefit from the IAEA's inspections in Iran throughout 2005 and 2006. In late 2005, Iran was not as forthcoming as the IAEA (and the U.S. government) had hoped it would be in responding to the agency's requests for information. However, during visits in October and November, inspectors examined buildings of interest at Parchin, where environmental samples were taken. The agency's inspectors reported that they "did not observe any unusual activities in the building visited." They also reported that the uranium hexafluoride (UF6) being produced at the uranium conversion facility at Esfahan "ha[d] remained under Agency containment and surveillance measures." In contrast to those items of information, another that the IAEA reported—that civil engineering and construction of the reactor at Arak was continuing—came directly from intelligence derived from U.S. satellite reconnaissance.[82]

At the end of January 2006, the IAEA had more to contribute, providing data that U.S. intelligence officials would have been more than a little pleased to have acquired through a spy. Iran showed the international agency more than sixty documents

---

*Germany also denied this assertion, which is based on a classified report by the Joint Forces Command. See Richard Bernstein and Judy Dempsey, "Germany Denies Giving U.S. Iraq's Plan to Defend Baghdad," *New York Times*, February 28, 2006, A9.

concerning uranium metal. Included was a fifteen-page document describing the procedures for the reduction of UF6 to metal in small quantities and the casting of enriched and depleted uranium metal into hemispheres, both of which relate to the production of nuclear weapon components. Iranian officials claimed that the documents, along with other material, had been provided by A. Q. Khan's network, at the network's own initiative. However, Iran did not permit the agency to make copies. Iran also provided documentation on some of its efforts to acquire dual-use technology, including laser equipment and electric-drive equipment.[83]

OPEN SOURCE INTELLIGENCE COOPERATION

The United States and Britain have, for over half a century, had a highly formalized arrangement dividing up, on a geographic basis, the responsibility for monitoring public radio and television broadcasts—mainly news and public affairs broadcasts. The specific organizations involved are British Broadcasting Corporation (BBC) Monitoring (a component of the BBC World Service) and the DNI's Open Source Center (OSC), formerly the Foreign Broadcast Information Service (FBIS). Together, these two organizations monitor most of the world's significant news reports and other broadcasts. Both BBC Monitoring and the OSC have a network of overseas stations that operate with varying degrees of secrecy to gather raw material.[84]

Post–World War II cooperation between the BBC Monitoring Service and the United States was formalized in 1947 as the result of an exchange of letters between the head of the Foreign Broadcast Information Branch of the CIA's Office of Operations and the head of BBC Monitoring. The basic provisions were noted in a 1950 document, the two-page "FBIS-BBC Reciprocal Agreement, Basic Provisions." The agreement divided the monitoring tasks among the small number of stations then operating, provided for FBIS personnel to be stationed at BBC headquarters to select material, and required FBIS to provide material to satisfy BBC requirements. It also provided for a joint FBIS-BBC Monitoring Coordination Committee.[85] The 1950 document also noted, "The organization of mutually complementary operations requires continuous consultation and cooperation between the services in respect to the location of monitoring stations, the allocation of monitoring coverage, the standardization of operational principles and procedures, their communications networks, and all other matters of mutual concern."[86]

The cooperation began as an openly acknowledged arrangement, which was clearly stated in the *BBC Annual Report for 1948–1949*: "There [is] close cooperation between the BBC's Monitoring Service and its American counterpart, the Foreign Broadcast Information Branch of the United States Central Intelligence Agency, and each of the two services maintain[s] liaison units at each other's stations for the purpose of a full exchange of information."[87]

The area of responsibility for the Monitoring Service, at least originally, was roughly equivalent to the GCHQ's area of responsibility for SIGINT collection: Europe, Africa, and western Russia. Thus, the Monitoring Service maintained a remotely controlled listening post on top of the British embassy in Vienna to monitor very-high-frequency radio and television broadcasts originating in Hungary and Czechoslovakia. It also maintained listening posts in Accra, Ghana, and Abidjan, Ivory Coast. In 1976 and 1977, the Monitoring Service turned over responsibility for monitoring Far East broadcasts to the FBIS. To compensate, it stepped up its reporting of events in Portugal and Spain to meet CIA requirements.[88]

From 1979 to 2009, according to the BBC's *Summary of World Broadcasts*, relatively large increases occurred in the coverage of Iran and Pakistan, while there was little change in coverage of the Middle Eastern nations. Meanwhile, coverage of Russia and China declined, with the decline in China coverage substantial.[89]

Also involved in open source cooperation with the United States and Britain is the Open Source Branch of the Australian Office of National Assessments. The United States also benefits from participation in the International Open Source Working Group, which includes representatives of the United States, Germany, Denmark, the Netherlands, the United Kingdom, Canada, Italy, Australia, Sweden, Israel, Australia, Norway, France, and Belgium. All those nations share open source intelligence (OSINT) via the opensource.gov portal, managed by the United States.[90]

COUNTERTERRORISM COOPERATION

In the aftermath of 9/11, the CIA established joint counterterrorism intelligence centers (CTICs) in about two dozen countries, adding to the two created in the 1990s to monitor and apprehend Islamic militants traveling from Saudi Arabia, Yemen, Egypt, and Chechnya to participate in the conflict in Bosnia and other parts of the former Yugoslavia. At those centers, U.S. and foreign intelligence officers have worked together to track and capture suspected terrorists and to destroy or penetrate their networks. The centers make decisions on a daily basis about "when and how to apprehend suspects, whether to whisk them off to other countries for interrogation and detention, and how to disrupt al-Qaeda's logistical and financial support." CTICs were established in Europe, the Middle East, and Asia. "CTICs were a step forward in codifying, organizing liaison relationships that elsewhere would be more ad hoc," according to a former counterterrorism official.[91]

One of the CTICs, known as Alliance Base, was located in Paris, with the French DGSE in the lead. The CIA was a key participant, and the center also had case officers from Canada, Australia, and Germany. The Paris center selected a case and choose a lead country for an operation; that country's service then directed the operation.[92]

It has been reported that in the aftermath of the terrorist attacks of 9/11, President Jacques Chirac ordered the French intelligence services to place no limits on the information concerning terrorism that it would share with U.S. intelligence services. The French also detained about sixty suspects between the end of 2001 and mid-2005. In addition, France permitted the United States to fly armed Predator drones from the French air base in Djibouti. In return, France was given access to detainees held at Guantánamo Bay, and French interrogators traveled there to gather evidence for use in French courts.[93]

Cooperation between the CIA and DGSE has included covert support to the Algerian and Moroccan governments to counter al-Qaeda in the Lands of the Islamic Maghreb (AQIM). The two organizations assisted the Algerian military security service in apprehending or killing a number of AQIM leaders. They also passed relevant information to the Moroccan foreign intelligence service, the General Directorate of

Studies and Documentation, and provided significant technical support to the nation's internal security service. That aid helped the Moroccan organizations capture several violent Muslim extremists opposed to the Moroccan regime.[94]

Jordan has been another key partner in counterterrorist operations—a result of a relationship that predated 9/11 for years. According to one report, "Jordan's General Intelligence Directorate, or GID, has surpassed Israel's Mossad as America's most effective counterterrorism agency in the Middle East." A former CIA operations officer explained, "They're going to get more information [from a terrorism suspect] because they're going to know his language, his culture, his associates and more about the network he belongs to." According to the same officer, the Jordanians were particularly valued for their skill in interrogating captives and recruiting assets due to their "expertise with radicalized militant groups and Shia/Sunni culture." CIA-GID cooperation has reportedly helped disrupt several terrorist plots, including the 2009 "millennium" plan to attack tourists at hotels and other sites. The GID has also been credited with helping the United States find and kill Abu Musab al-Zarqawi, the former leader of al-Qaeda in Iraq.[95]

Cooperation began several decades ago. In the 1980s, the two services conducted a joint campaign to subvert and cripple the Abu Nidal organization, then one of the world's most dangerous terrorist groups. The project involved creation of false foreign bank accounts that appeared to show Nidal's aides receiving mysterious payments from overseas sources. As a result, Nidal had many of them executed. In the summer of 2001, the Jordanians provided the United States with communications intercepts indicating an upcoming terrorist attack in the United States.[96]

The General Intelligence Directorate also cooperated with the United States by serving as a rendition partner, interrogating a number of individuals detained or apprehended by the CIA after they had been delivered to the GID. One example is Jamal Mari, a Yemeni citizen seized in Karachi by Pakistani security forces. After being held in a secret prison for several weeks, he was turned over to American intelligence officials, who believed that he was working for a charity group in Pakistan with ties to al-Qaeda. U.S. officials then transported him to Jordan, where he spent four months before being returned to U.S. custody, presumably after a number of interrogations.[97]

Also long-standing is U.S. financial support for the GID. According to one former U.S. intelligence official, "It is not a huge sum of money to us, but it's a significant amount of money for [the GID] and allows them to buy a lot of equipment, mostly technical stuff that they otherwise could not afford." That financial support probably extends to paying, at least in part, for the CIA-GID bilateral operations center established after the 9/11 attacks. According to a 2010 account, the relationship had progressed to the point that "the CIA liaison in Amman enjoys full, unescorted access to the GID's fortress-like headquarters"—although in 2015 the Obama administration turned down a Jordanian request for unarmed Predator drones.[98]

The United States, after 9/11, "funneled hundreds of millions of dollars" to the Pakistani Inter-Services Intelligence Directorate (ISI), contributing as much as a third of the organization's budget. The directorate also received payments for the capture or killing of militants as part of a CIA clandestine reward. It received $10 million for its role in the capture of Abu Zubaydah and $25 million for the capture of Khalid Sheikh Mohammed. In addition, ISI officers have been brought to the CIA training facility in North Carolina.[99]

In February 2010, the second in command of the Afghan Taliban, Mullah Abdul Ghani Baradar, was captured in Karachi in an ISI raid that was the result of intelligence provided by the United States and that had CIA assistance. U.S. intelligence agencies had been tracking Baradar's communication and activity closely since December and also received "an unexpected break."

By early 2011, it was being reported that CIA-ISI relations had "deteriorated sharply in recent months" and that the ISI was, generally, no longer providing the CIA with targeting information for drone strikes. The deterioration was attributed to Pakistani anger over U.S. comments questioning Pakistan's commitment to combating militants, concern that the CIA was establishing its own network to avoid reliance on the ISI, and irritation at the U.S. belief that the ISI had leaked the name of the agency's station chief, leading to his recall. The arrest of a CIA contractor for killing individuals who apparently attempted to rob him further exacerbated tensions.[100]

In April 2011, Pakistani officials visited Washington and asked the CIA to reduce drone missile strikes after a March 17 attack in North Waziristan that Pakistani officials claimed killed more than forty civilians, a claim disputed by U.S. officials. In addition they requested a significant reduction in CIA and Special Forces personnel totaling about 335 individuals. By May, the Pakistani government informed the United States that it was closing three intelligence fusions centers—two in Peshawar and one in Quetta—where the United States shared satellite imagery, target data, and other intelligence with Pakistani ground forces responsible for operations against the Taliban.[101]

The May 2, 2011, U.S. SEAL raid on Osama bin Laden's Abbottabad complex, resulting in his death, illustrated the U.S. lack of trust in Pakistan's reliability as a counterterrorist partner, further straining the relationship. In early June 2011 the Pakistani Foreign Ministry announced that the United States and Pakistan had agreed to resume joint intelligence operations against Islamic militants. But that same month, the *Washington Post* reported that "twice in recent weeks" the United States had provided Pakistan with overhead surveillance video and other information, as well as specific locations for insurgent bomb-making facilities, only to have the militants vacate the sites prior to the raids. In addition, the United States shared information about other sites, including weapons-storage facilities, which were also found empty.[102]

In September 2011, it was reported that Pakistan had arrested Younis Mauritani, suspected of planning attacks on American targets, and two other senior al-Qaeda operatives. The CIA provided technical assistance, possibly communications intelligence, to aid the ISI in the search. In August 2012, the new ISI chief, Lieutenant General Zahir ul-Islam, visited Washington and met with then CIA director David H. Petraeus. One report stated that the two "will seek to rebuild a counterterrorism relationship that has severely frayed." One senior administration official observed, "Petraeus will try to forge a relationship with him. . . . We've got business to do."[103]

In March 2011, the Federal Bureau of Investigation's (FBI) legal attaché in Moscow received a memorandum from the Russian Federal Security Service (FSB)—in Russian—regarding future Boston Marathon bomber Tamerlan Tsarnaev and his mother. In September the FSB provided the same information to the CIA. According to the FBI's translated version (which incorrectly spelled their last names as Tsarnayev and Tsarnayeva), the FSB described both as adherents of radical Islam and asserted that Tsarnaev was preparing to travel to Russia to join unnamed "bandit underground groups" in Dagestan and Chechnya. The memo also provided information on the duo's telephone numbers and e-mail addresses and requested that the FBI provide specific information about the pair. On March 9, 2011, the FBI Moscow legal attaché sent a letter to the FSB acknowledging receipt of the information and requesting that the FBI be kept informed.[104]

The letter, according to the House Homeland Security Committee, lacked "compelling derogatory information on exactly why [Tsarnaev] posed a threat," and the FBI-led Joint Terrorism Task Force found no link to terrorism. Subsequently, in August the legal attaché sent two letters to the FSB, the second of which provided information about Tsarnaev and his mother collected during the bureau's follow-up to the FSB's initial warning. Both letters requested that the Russian security service provide any additional information in its possession regarding Tsarnaev, but apparently there was no Russian reply. Reportedly, a second notice from Russian intelligence, sent after Tsarnaev visited Russia in 2012, claimed that he had met with a suspected militant during his six-month stay.[105]

A recent subject of U.S.-Russian intelligence cooperation has concerned the Islamic State in Iraq and Syria (ISIS). In October 2014, Secretary of State John Kerry announced that the United States and Russia had agreed to share more intelligence on the terrorist group. Kerry told reporters that, given that five hundred or more Islamic State volunteers had come from Russia, he had suggested that the two nations increase intelligence sharing on ISIS, and the Russian foreign minister had agreed.[106]

On two occasions in recent years, Saudi Arabia's General Intelligence provided the United States with information concerning planned terrorist actions directed against the United States. In early October 2010, Prince bin Nayef, Saudi Arabia's chief counterintelligence official, warned John Brennan, then President Obama's top counterterrorism adviser, that al-Qaeda in the Arabian Peninsula (AQAP) was planning an attack employing one or more aircraft. On October 28, Saudi intelligence informed the United States that bombs might be placed on cargo flights, which "prompted officials in the United States and several other countries to begin a frantic search." Two shipments from Yemen, with explosives packed into ink toner cartridges within Hewlett-Packard printers and addressed to synagogues in Chicago, were intercepted in Britain and Dubai.[107]

In 2012 a double agent working for Saudi intelligence was able to provide details of a new underwear bomb plot involving a more sophisticated device than the one that failed to detonate aboard a jetliner over Detroit in December 2009 and targeted against a U.S.-bound airliner. The Saudi double agent delivered both the device and "a trove of intelligence to U.S. and other authorities," which included information on AQAP leaders, locations, methods, and plans. The intelligence helped in tracking down and killing via a drone strike Fahd Mohammed Ahmad Quso, the operations chief of AQAP, who had been implicated in the 2000 USS *Cole* bombing in Yemen that killed seventeen U.S. sailors.[108]

The United States has reportedly also operated a counterterrorist center in Mogadishu, Somalia—referred to by the Somalis as the "Pink House"—run by the CIA and used by members of the Joint Special Operations Command. According to one account, "At the facility, the CIA ran a counterterrorism training program for Somali intelligence agents and operatives aimed at building an indigenous strike force capable of snatch operations and targeted 'combat operations' against al Shahab." In addition, the "CIA also utilized the secret prison buried in the basement of Somalia's National Security Agency headquarters, where prisoners suspected of being al-Shahab members or having links to the group were held."[109]

Joint counterterrorist activity has also involved providing CIA training to Sudan's National Intelligence and Security Service (NISS), supplying equipment such as computers, and conducting joint operations with the NISS. A former U.S. intelligence official has been quoted as describing the Sudan as "an exceptional partner in helping us against the terrorist target."[110]

Two MQ-9 Reaper drones are located at a base in Niamey, Niger, established in February 2013 and staffed by about 120 U.S. Air Force personnel. The drones provide live video and data from other sensors to American analysts working with French commanders, who reported that the aerial intelligence was crucial to their success in a four-month effort to drive jihadists from a vast desert refuge in northern Mali. The United States provided sensitive intelligence pinpointing militant targets to be attacked. The Reapers led to nearly sixty French airstrikes in one week alone. Possibly killed was Mokhtar Belmokhtar, mastermind of a January hostage raid on an Algerian natural gas plant that claimed that lives of at least thirty-eight employees, and Abou Zeid, commander of AQIM's Mali wing.[111]

In February 2013 it was reported that the U.S. ambassador to Algeria and senior counterterrorism officials had proposed sharing additional information with Algerian security forces "to help them kill or capture militants, both in Algeria and in areas just across their borders."[112]

COUNTERNARCTOTICS COOPERATION

In National Security Decision Directive 221, "Narcotics and National Security," President Ronald Reagan directed the Director of Central Intelligence to "enhance where appropriate, support of the drug enforcement effort targetted [sic] against international drug traffickers, particularly those with known or suspected ties or terrorist or insurgent groups." In addition, the directive instructed the DCI "to ensure that the intelligence community gives special emphasis to collecting, assessing, and disseminating foreign intelligence on all aspects of the international illicit drug trade."[113]

Mexico is among the nations with which the United States has had an extensive relationship concerning counternarcotics operations and intelligence. On October 19, 2009, DNI Dennis Blair met with Mexican defense secretary General Guillermo Galvan, who suggested that increased U.S. intelligence assistance could shorten the time required to transition from the use of military forces to civilian units for counternarcotics cooperation. Subsequently, Blair suggested that improving the intelligence capabilities of Mexico's deployed counternarcotic units would improve "the troops' ability to launch more rapid operations." Galvan responded that Mexico would "be willing to accept any training the [U.S. government could] offer."[114]

Since 2006 the United States had been funding the Mexico Technical Surveillance System, which allows the Mexican government to "intercept, analyze and use intercepted information from all types of communications systems operating in Mexico." The system is capable of real-time monitoring, pinpointing the location on a map of an intercepted call, and linking intercepted communications with "graphical display links between events." It can also store up to 25,000 hours of conversation.[115]

The U.S. provision of intelligence aided several Mexican counternarcotics operations in 2009 and 2010. A December 2009 operation that resulted in the death of one cartel leader, Arturo Beltran Leyva, was aided by U.S. intelligence on Leyva's whereabouts. U.S. intelligence also led Mexican marines to go after Gulf cartel boss Antonio Ezequiel Guilen, resulting in his death in November 2010.[116]

In 2011 it was reported that U.S. involvement in the Mexican government's operations against the country's drug cartels had expanded. After a surge in violence in 2010 in the vicinity of Monterrey, Mexican president Felipe Calderon requested further intelligence support. As a consequence, the United States established an intelligence facility on a northern Mexico military base (apparently Military Air Base 14 at Monterrey), which included representatives from the CIA, Drug Enforcement Administration, and Northern Command (NORTHCOM) and was modeled after fusion centers in Iraq and Afghanistan.[117]

U.S. assistance also involved a CIA-managed program, code-named SCENIC, that focused on training Mexican personnel in targeting and vetting potential assets for recruitment, as well preventing cartels from infiltrating Mexican counternarcotics efforts. Under Calderon's presidency the United States employed "high-flying spy planes" over Mexico for intelligence gathering. One aerial surveillance effort, with intelligence being provided to the Mexican government, includes a Northern Command program designated LOWRIDER, which began in 2011. It involves the use of two propeller planes that carry communications intelligence and imagery sensors whose intelligence is employed to determine the schedules and routines of high-level narcotics traffickers. Products from U.S. efforts have included cell phone geolocation and communications intercepts. A Northern Command spokesman, when asked about LOWRIDER, noted, "We work closely with the Mexican military and assist them wherever we can. . . . We have been involved in sharing equipment, information and other activities."[118]

The cooperative relationship was reported, in May 2013, to have deteriorated under Calderon's successor—American officials were asked to leave an intelligence fusion center in Monterey. In addition, the Mexican government intended to reduce the extensive contacts between U.S. and Mexican agencies, with all intelligence being funneled through the Ministry of the Interior.*[119]

ANALYSIS AND DATA EXCHANGE

The FIVE EYES nations are also involved in cooperative arrangements concerning defense intelligence analysis, holding periodic conferences on dealing with a wide range of scientific and defense intelligence matters. One analyst has observed, "The Five Eyes national assessment community is professionally tight, bound by gravities

---

*The United States also operates a U.S.-only Mexico Fusion Center (MFC) located within the U.S. embassy in Mexico City, with representatives from the NSA, DIA, NGA, and NORTHCOM. Will Wechsler, DASD (CN&GT), to Mike Vickers, ASD (SO/LIC & IC), Subject: CN & GT Support to Mexico Fusion Center, n.d.

of trust and confidence. Heads of national assessment meet at least annually and joint working groups are formed when needed to address relevant issues of mutual concern. Inter-agency is routine at working levels, where the default inclination is to consult widely before assessments are finalized."[120]

U.S. analysts have participated in the Annual Land Warfare Technical Intelligence Conference, the International Scientific Intelligence Exchange, the Quadripartite Intelligence Working Party on Chinese Guided Missiles, and the Tripartite Defense Intelligence Estimates Conference.[121]

In 1948 and 1950, the United States and Britain produced the Burns-Templer agreements, named for the chief negotiators, U.S. Assistant Secretary of Defense James Burns and Vice Chief of the Imperial Staff Gerald Templer. The most significant agreement, concluded in 1950, "allowed the two intelligence communities to pool their resources in 'a full and frank exchange' to the greatest practicable degree of all classified military information and intelligence." The 1950 agreements, which remain in force, led to sharing of information on Soviet guided missile technology as well as the sales of arms to the Eastern bloc.[122]

U.S.-Canadian joint estimates produced in the late 1950s focused on Soviet capabilities and likely actions in the event of a major Soviet attack on North America. Preparation of such estimates continued on a yearly basis, at least into the 1980s, under the title *Canadian–United States Intelligence Estimate of the Military Threat to North America*. More recently, it has been reported that the Privy Council Office's Intelligence Assessment Secretariat also cooperates with the Bureau of Intelligence and Research (INR), generally through the sharing of draft assessments and analysts. That link is supplemented by the relationship between INR and the Canadian Department of Foreign Affairs and International Trade Threat Assessment and Intelligence Services Division—via which the two units share diplomatic reporting and threat analysis.[123]

U.S., Canadian, and U.K. representatives regularly attended the Annual CANUKUS Maritime Intelligence Conference. Air force intelligence representatives from each nation also meet to examine topics such as surface-to-air missiles. In addition, U.S. and U.K. military intelligence representatives have participated in the U.S./U.K. Chemical Warfare Intelligence Conference and the U.S./U.K. Armor Conference (held at the CIA).[124]

The National Center for Medical Intelligence is involved in medical intelligence exchanges with Australia, Canada, and the United Kingdom through the Quadripartite Medical Intelligence Exchange, which maintains its own website. The National Center for Medical Intelligence is a member of the Quadripartite Medical Intelligence Committee. Other members include the Canadian and U.S. medical liaison officers and the Australian scientific attaché. In 1974 a senior U.S. intelligence official wrote, with respect to U.S. participation in the Quadripartite Medical Intelligence Exchange, "I believe that an objective study would show that the U.S. is ahead of the game, keeping [deleted] analysts informed of activities here allows them to channel their work into more productive areas. And, in spite of the small size of the [deleted] intelligence groups, they keep coming up with nuggets in the form of unique analysis which have been very helpful to us."[125]

Another example of cooperation in the analytical and data exchange area that involves the United States, Australia, Canada, and the United Kingdom is STONE

GHOST, a "database comprised of worldwide intelligence products, applications, databases and services." STONE GHOST's infrastructure comprises more than thirty-eight U.S. Intelligence Community servers and sites (including ones operated by the CIA, the Department of Homeland Security, and the combatant commands), as well as sites operated by the participating nations' military intelligence organizations. This database operates at the Top Secret/Special Intelligence level and is accessible to cleared individuals in the four countries.[126]

Notes

1. Declaration of the Secretary of Defense, Caspar Weinberger, *United States of America v. Jonathan Jay Pollard, Defendant*, United States District Court for the District of Columbia, Criminal No. 86-02070, 1986 (AER), 22; Acting Director, Special Activities, DR/CIA, "Memorandum for: Special Requirements Staff, DD/R, Subject: Accessibility of LANYARD Take to the British," January 31, 1963.

2. See Jeffrey T. Richelson, "The Calculus of Intelligence Cooperation," *International Journal of Intelligence and Counterintelligence* 4, no. 3 (Fall 1990): 307–324; H. Bradford Westerfield, "America and the World of Intelligence Liaison," *Intelligence and National Security* 11, no. 3 (July 1996): 523–560; Commission on the Roles and Capabilities of the United States Intelligence Community, *Preparing for the 21st Century: An Appraisal of U.S. Intelligence* (Washington, DC: U.S. Government Printing Office, 1996), 128; Stéphen Lefebvre, "The Difficulties and Dilemmas of International Intelligence Cooperation," *International Journal of Intelligence and Counterintelligence* 16, no. 4 (Winter 2003–2004): 527–542; Jennifer Sims, "Foreign Intelligence Liaison: Devils, Deals, and Details," *International Journal of Intelligence and Counterintelligence* 19, no. 2 (Summer 2006): 195–217; Don Munton and Karima Fredj, "Sharing Secrets: A Game Theoretic Analysis of International Intelligence Cooperation," *International Journal of Intelligence Cooperation* 26, no. 4 (Winter 2013): 666–692; [author name deleted], "Third Party Nations: Partners and Targets," *Cryptologic Quarterly* 7, no. 4 (Winter 1989): 15–22.

3. Richard J. Aldrich, *GCHQ: The Uncensored History of Britain's Most Secret Intelligence Agency* (London: Harper Press, 2010), 376; Robert Suro, "Australian Arrested on Spy Charge," *Washington Post*, May 18, 1999, A9; Jerry Sepper, "Court Jails Australian in Sale of U.S. Secrets," *Washington Times*, May 18, 1999, A1, A11; David Johnston, "U.S. Arrests an Australian in Spying Case," *New York Times*, May 18, 1999, A3; Alistair MacDonald and Siobhan Gorman, "Canadian Military Leak to Russia Riles Allies," *Washington Post*, March 28, 2012, A9; Tonda Charles and Bruce Campton-Smith, "Russia Used Canadian Spy to Obtain U.S. Secrets, Newly Released Documents Say," www.thestar.com, November 29, 2012, http://www.thestar.com/news/canada/2012/11/29/russia_used_canadian_spy_to_obtain_us_secrets_newly_released_documents_say.html; James Cox, *Canada and the Five Eyes Intelligence Community*, Canadian Defense and Foreign Affairs Institute, December 2012, https://d3n8a8pro7vhmx.cloudfront.net/cdfai/pages/95/attachments/original/1413683744/Canada_and_the_Five_Eyes_Intelligence_Community.pdf?1413683744; National Security Agency/Central Security Service, Information Paper, "Subject: NSA Intelligence Relationship with Turkey—Turkish National Intelligence Organization (MIT) and the Turkish SIGINT Intelligence Directorate (SIB)," April 15, 2013.

4. [Author name deleted], "Third Party Nations: Partners and Targets"; Richelson, "The Calculus of Intelligence Cooperation"; Sims, "Foreign Intelligence Liaison"; Mark Mazzetti, "When Spies Don't Play Well with Their Allies," *New York Times*, January 20, 2008, Section 4, 1, 6.

5. On the Israeli and Japanese programs, see E. L. Zorn, "Israel's Quest for Satellite Intelligence," *Studies in Intelligence* (Winter/Spring 2001): 33–38; William W. Radcliffe, "Origins and Current State of Japan's Reconnaissance Satellite Program," *Studies in Intelligence* 54, no. 3 (Extracts, September 2010): 9–21.

6. Lachlan Wilson, "Australia's GEOINT Relationships Prove Vital," *Pathfinder* 7, no. 2 (March–April 2009): 17–18; Joint Chiefs of Staff, Joint Publication 2-03, *Geospatial Intelligence Support to Joint Operations*, March 22, 2007, 11–10.

7. Philip Flood, *Report of the Inquiry into Australian Intelligence Agencies* (Canberra: Government of Australia, 2004), 139–146.

8. Joe Obermeier, "Motto Says Much About Australia's Challenge and Ours," *Pathfinder* 5, no. 1 (January–February 2007): 12–13; Wilson, "Australia's GEOINT Relationships Prove Vital."

9. Philip Dorling, "Australia and the US Agree on a Spy Satellite Deal," www.smh.com, February 7, 2011, http://www.smh.com.au/technology/technology-news/australia-and-the-us-agree-on-a-spy-satellite-deal-20110206-1aii0.html; U.S. Embassy, Canberra, to D, NEA/I, PM and EAP, Subject: AUSMIN 2008: Session IV: Alliance and Defense Partnership, February 23, 2008, https://wikileaks.org/cable/2008/02/08CANBERRA178.html.

10. Bachelor, "Canada Responds to Haiti Earthquake"; Williams, "Your Canadian Partner."

11. D. H. N. Thompson, "Meet Canada's Directorate of Geospatial Intelligence," *Pathfinder* 7, no. 2 (March–April 2009): 3–4; Ed Bachelor, "Canada Responds to Haiti Earthquake," *Pathfinder* 8, no. 6 (November–December 2010): 16; R. S. Williams, "Your Canadian Partner," *Pathfinder* 4, no. 1 (January–February 2008): 9.

12. New Zealand Defence Force, "Geospatial Intelligence," http://nzdf.mil.nz/about-us/jgsf (accessed March 31, 2004); Paul Hamer, "UK JARIC Transitions to Defence Geospatial and Intelligence Fusion Centre," *Pathfinder* 10, no. 6 (November–December 2012): 6; Kathi Ghannam, "Agency Uses New Technology to Support London Olympics," *Pathfinder* 10, no. 6 (November–December 2012): 12–14.

13. David Fontenot and Kevin Firmin, "Germany Expands Co-Production Capabilities," *Pathfinder* 4, no. 1 (January–February 2006): 30–31.

14. Ibid.; Heidi Whitesell, "NGA Welcomes New German Geospatial Liaison," *Pathfinder* 6, no. 2 (March–April 2008); Gregory Davis, "Leveraging NGA Co-production Agreements," *Pathfinder* 5, no. 1 (January–February 2007): 22; Joshua Keating, "Germany Planning Secret Satellite Recon," www.foreignpolicy.com, January 3, 2011, http://foreignpolicy.com/2011/01/03/germany-planning-secret-satellite-recon.

15. "How the Israelis Pulled It Off," *Newsweek*, July 19, 1976, 42–47.

16. Bob Woodward, "CIA Sought 3rd Country Contra Aid," *Washington Post*, May 19, 1984, A1, A13.

17. "Statement of Bobby Ray Inman on Withdrawing His Nomination," *New York Times*, January 19, 1994, A14; E. L. Zorn, "Israel's Quest for Satellite Intelligence," *Studies in Intelligence* (Winter/Spring 2001): 33–38.

18. Theodore Sanger, "A Not Very Hidden Agenda," *Newsweek*, September 10, 1990, 20; Gerald F. Seib and Bob Davis, "Fighting Flares Again at Saudi Town; Allied Planes Attack Big Iraqi Column," *Wall Street Journal*, February 1, 1991, A12; Martin Sieff, "Israelis Press U.S. for Direct Access to Intelligence Data," *Washington Times*, November 28, 1992, A7; Barton Gellman, "Israel Gave Key Help to U.N. Team in Iraq," *Washington Post*, September 29, 1998, A1, A12.

19. Barbara Opall-Rome, "Senate Weighs Bill Boosting U.S.-Israeli Military Ties, Satellite Intelligence Sharing," *Space News*, May 28, 2012, 17; White House, "President Obama Signs the United States–Israel Enhanced Security Cooperation Act of 2012," July 27, 2012, http://www.whitehouse.gov/photos-and-video/video/2012/07/27/president-obama-signs-us-israel-enhanced-security-cooperation-act; H.R. 4133, *United States–Israel Enhanced Security Cooperation Act*, May 10, 2012.

20. Letitia A. Long, Won-Dong Hwang, and Oj-Joong Nam, *Basic Exchange Agreement Between the National Geospatial-Intelligence Agency of the Department of Defense of the United States of America and the Korean Defense Intelligence Agency of the Ministry of National Defense and the Science and Technology Bureau of the National Intelligence Service of the Republic of Korea Concerning Geospatial Intelligence*, November 19, 2010.

21. Christophe Leroy, "Mexican Intelligence at a Crossroads," *SAIS Review* 14, no. 1 (Winter–Spring 2004): 107–129; American Embassy, Mexico to State Department, Subject: Weekly Narcotics Roundup, August 13–17, August 22, 1990, 1; Office of the Director of National Intelligence, "ODNI Fact Sheet," October 2010, http://www.dni.gov/files/documents/ODNI%20Fact%20Sheet_2011.pdf.

22. Joel S. Wit, Daniel B. Poneman, and Robert L. Gallucci, *Going Critical: The First North Korean Nuclear Crisis* (Washington, DC: Brookings Institution, 2004), 20; R. Jeffrey Smith, "North Korea and the Bomb: High Tech Hide-and-Seek," *Washington Post*, April 27, 1993, A1, A11.

23. Steve Coll, "Nuclear Inspectors Check Sites in Iran," *Washington Post*, November 20, 1993, A13, A16.

24. On the U.K.-U.S. World War II SIGINT alliance, see Bradley F. Smith, *The Ultra-Magic Deals* (Novato, CA: Presidio, 1993). On Canadian participation, see John Bryden, *Best Kept Secret: Canadian Secret Intelligence in the Second World War* (Toronto: Lester, 1993). On Australian New Zealand involvement, see Jeffrey T. Richelson and Desmond Ball, *The Ties That Bind: Intelligence Cooperation Among the UKUSA Countries* (Boston: Allen & Unwin, 1985), 3–4; Desmond Ball, "Allied Intelligence Cooperation Involving Australia During World War II," *Australian Outlook* 32, no. 4 (1978): 299–309; Nicky Hager, *The Origins of Signals Intelligence in New Zealand* (Auckland: Centre for Peace Studies, Auckland, August 1995), 2–16; Desmond Ball, Cliff Lord, and Meredith Thatcher, *Invaluable Service: The Secret History of New Zealand's Signals Intelligence During Two World Wars* (Auckland: New Zealand Resource Books, 2011).

25. State-Army-Navy Communications Intelligence Board and London Signals Intelligence Board (signatories), "British-U.S. Communications Intelligence Agreement," March 5, 1946, 3–4; Michael L. Peterson, "Before BOURBON: American and British COMINT Efforts Against Russia and the Soviet Union Before 1945," *Cryptologic Quarterly* 12, nos. 3–4 (Fall/Winter 1993): 1–20; "The Days of Bourbon," *Cryptologic Almanac 50th Anniversary Series*, January–February 2002, https://www.nsa.gov/public_info/_files/crypto_almanac_50th/Days_of_Bourbon.pdf.

26. State-Army-Navy Communications Intelligence Board and London Signals Intelligence Board (signatories), "British-U.S. Communications Intelligence Agreement," 4–5.

27. Ball, "Allied Intelligence Cooperation Involving Australia During World War II"; Duncan Campbell, "Threat of the Electronic Spies," *New Statesman*, February 2, 1979, 140–144; John Sawatsky, *Men in the Shadows: The RCMP Security Service* (New York: Doubleday, 1980), 9n; transcript of "The Fifth Estate—the Espionage Establishment," broadcast by the Canadian Broadcasting Company, 1974; Matthew Aid, *The Secret Sentry: The Untold History of the National Security Agency* (New York: Bloomsbury, 2009), 12–13; [deleted], "Six Decades of Second Party Relations," *Cryptologic Almanac 50th Anniversary Series*, January–February 2002, https://www.nsa.gov/public_info/_files/crypto_almanac_50th/six_decades_of_second_party_relations.pdf.

28. Private information; Seymour Hersh, *"The Target Is Destroyed": What Really Happened to Flight 007 and What America Knew About It* (New York: Random House, 1986), 48n.

29. Desmond Ball, *A Suitable Piece of Real Estate: American Installations in Australia* (Sydney: Hale & Iremonger, 1980), 40.

30. Campbell, "Threat of the Electronic Spies."

31. Richelson and Ball, *The Ties That Bind*, 148–149.

32. Nicky Hager, *Secret Power: New Zealand's Role in the International Spy Network* (Nelson, NZ: Craig Potter, 1996), 42–56; Jeffrey Richelson, "Desperately Seeking Signals," *Bulletin of the Atomic Scientists* 56, no. 2 (March–April 2000): 47–51.

33. Desmond Ball, "The U.S. Naval Ocean Surveillance Information System (NOSIS)—Australia's Role," *Pacific Defence Reporter* (June 1982): 40–49; "Britannia Scorns to Yield," *Newsweek*, April 19, 1982, 41–46; Philip Dorling, "Listening Post Revealed on Cocos Islands," *Sydney Morning Herald*, November 1, 2013, http://www.smh.com.au/federal-politics/political-news/listening-post-revealed-on-cocos-islands-20131031-2wlyz.html; Andrew Pearson, "Spy Games at Riverina's Secret Base," *Daily Advertiser*, November 15, 2013, http://www.dailyadvertiser.com.au/story

/1907150/spy-games-at-riverinas-secret-base; Ian McPhedran, "How We Spied on the Indonesians and How Expats Are Targeted Overseas," www.heraldsun.com, November 21, 2013, http://finance .clydeenterprise.com/news/google/how-we-spied-on-the-indonesians-and-how-expats-are-targeted -overseas-herald-sun/how-we-spied-on-the-indonesians-and-how-expats-are-targeted-overseas -herald-sun-12169112.htm.

34. Philip Dorling, "Exposed: Australia's Asia Spy Network," *Sydney Morning Herald* (www .smh.com), October 31, 2013, http://www.smh.com.au/federal-politics/political-news/exposed -australias-asia-spy-network-20131030-2whia.html.

35. Cox, *Canada and the Five Eyes Intelligence Community*, 6, 6n19, 20.

36. Institute for Policy Studies, *Canada-U.S. Arrangements in Regard to Defence, Defence Production, Defence Sharing*, 1985, 31.

37. Christopher Anson Pike, "CANYON, RHYOLITE, and AQUACADE: U.S. Signals Intelligence in the 1970s," *Spaceflight* 37, no. 11 (November 1995): 381–383; Mark Urban, *UK Eyes Alpha: Inside Story of British Intelligence* (London: Faber and Faber, 1996), 58; private information.

38. Mike Frost as told to Michel Gratton, *Spyworld: Inside the Canadian and American Intelligence Establishments* (Toronto: Doubleday Canada, 1994), 15, 274–275; Intelligence Advisory Committee, "Afghanistan: Taliban Challenges, Regional Concerns," October 17, 1996.

39. National Security Agency/Central Security Service, Information Paper, "Subject: NSA Intelligence Relationship with Canada's Communications Security Establishment Canada (CSEC)," April 3, 2013.

40. Urban, *UK Eyes Alpha*, 60–65; Duncan Campbell, "The Parliamentary Bypass Operation," *New Statesman*, January 13, 1987, 8–12; James Bamford, *Body of Secrets: Anatomy of the Ultra-Secret National Security Agency, from the Cold War Through the Dawn of a New Century* (New York: Doubleday, 2001), 400–401.

41. Ryan Gallagher, "British Spy Chiefs Secretly Begged to Play in NSA's Data Pools," *The Intercept* (https://firstlook.org/theintercept), April 30, 2014, https://firstlook.org/theintercept/2014 /04/30/gchq-prism-nsa-fisa-unsupervised-access-snowden/; National Security Agency, "Visit Précis, Sir Iain Lobban, KCMG, CB, Director, Government Communications Headquarters (GCHQ), 30 April 2013–1 May 2013," n.d.; Special Source Operations, NSA, "PRISM Operations Highlight," n.d.

42. National Security Agency/Central Security Service, Information Paper, Subject: NSA Intelligence Relationship with New Zealand, April 2013; Ryan Gallagaher, "New Zealand Targets Trade Partners, Hacks Computers in Spy Operations," *The Intercept*, March 10, 2015, https://firstlook.org/theintercept/2015/03/10/new-zealand-gcsb-spying-trade-partners-nsa.

43. *SIDToday* editor and [deleted], FAD's Deputy Assistant for SIGINT Operations, "What Are We After with Our Third Party Relationships?—and What Do They Want from US, Generally Speaking?," September 15, 2009. Also see Glenn Greenwald, "Foreign Officials in the Dark About Their Own Spy Agencies' Cooperation with NSA," *Intercept*, March 13, 2014, https://firstlook.org/theintercept/2014/03/13/nsa-elected-officials-foreign-countries-unaware -countries-cooperation-us.

44. *SIDToday* editor and [deleted], "What Are We After with Our Third Party Relationships?"; Glenn Greenwald, "Foreign Officials in the Dark About Their Own Spy Agencies' Cooperation with NSA."

45. National Security Agency, "Visit Précis—Bernard Barber, Technical Director, Directorate for External Security (DGSE), France; Patrick Pailloux, Director, National Information Systems Security (ANSSI), France, 12 April 2013," n.d.

46. "Spying Together: Germany's Deep Cooperation with the NSA," *Spiegel Online*, June 18, 2014, http://www.spiegel.de/international/germany/the-german-bnd-and-american-nsa -cooperate-more-closely-than-thought-a-975445.html; "NSA in Germany: Why We Are Posting Secret Documents," *Spiegel Online*, June 18, 2014, http://www.spiegel.de/international/germany/ why-spiegel-is-posting-leaked-nsa-documents-about-germany-a-975431.html; "Abbreviations Explained: How to Read the NSA Documents," *Spiegel Online*, June 18, 2014, http://www.spiegel

.de/international/world/glossary-of-nsa-abbreviations-a-975930.html; "New NSA Revelations: Inside Snowden's Germany File," *Spiegel Online*, June 18, 2014, http://www.spiegel.de/international /germany/new-snowden-revelations-on-nsa-spying-in-germany-a-975441.html; National Security Agency/Central Security Service, Information Paper Subject: NSA Intelligence Relationship with Germany—Bundesnachrichtendienst, January 17, 2013.

47. "Indispensible Exchange: Germany Cooperates Closely with NSA," *Spiegel Online*, July 8, 2013, http://www.spiegel.de/international/world/spiegel-reveals-cooperation-between-nsa-and -german-bnd-a-909954.html; Hubert Gude, Laura Poitras, and Marcel Rosenbach, "Mass Data: Transfers from Germany Aid US Surveillance," *Spiegel Online*, August 5, 2013, http://www.spiegel .de/international/world/german-intelligence-sends-massive-amounts-of-data-to-the-nsa-a-914821 .html.

48. "'Prolific Partner': German Intelligence Used NSA Spy Program," *Spiegel Online*, July 20, 2013, http://www.spiegel.de/international/germany/german-intelligence-agencies-used-nsa-spying -program-a-912173.html.

49. "How the Israelis Pulled It Off," *Newsweek*, July 19, 1976, 42–47; David Halevy and Neil C. Livingstone, "The Ollie We Knew," *Washingtonian*, July 1987, 77ff.; Eric Follath and Holger Stark, "How Israel Destroyed Syria's Al Kibar Nuclear Reactor," *Spiegel Online*, November 2, 2009, http://www.spiegel.de/international/world/the-story-of-operation-orchard-how-israel -destroyed-syria-s-al-kibar-nuclear-reactor-a-658663.html.

50. Commander, Israel SIGINT National Unit and Director, National Security Agency, "Memorandum of Understanding (MOU) Between the National Security Agency/Central Security Service (NSA/CSS) and the Israeli SIGINT National Unit (ISNU) Pertaining to the Protection of U.S. Persons," n.d.; Glenn Greenwald, Laura Poitras, and Ewen MacAskill, "NSA Shares Raw Intelligence Including Americans' Data with Israel," www.theguardian.com, September 11, 2013, http://www.theguardian.com/world/2013/sep/11/nsa-americans-personal-data-israel -documents. Also see Shane Harris, "Irony Alert: NSA Targets Israel—and Still Gives Your Data to Its Spies," www.foreignpolicy.com, September 11, 2013, http://foreignpolicy.com/2013/09/11/ irony-alert-nsa-targets-israel-and-still-gives-your-data-to-its-spies; Ken Dilanian, "Leaked Memo Details NSA Data Sharing with Israel," *Los Angeles Times*, September 12, 2013, A3.

51. Greenwald, Poitras, and MacAskill, "NSA Shares Raw Intelligence Including Americans' Data with Israel."

52. National Security Agency/Central Security Service, Subject: NSA Intelligence Relationship with Israel.

53. Steven Derix and Huib Modderkolk, "NSA hielp Nederland met onderzoek naar herkomst 1,8 miljoein," www.nrc.nl, February 8, 2014, http://www.nrc.nl/nieuws/2014/02/08/nsa-hielp -nederland-met-onderzoek-naar-herkomst-18-miljoen; "New Document Confirms Dutch Military Intelligence Service Gave NSA 1.8 Million Telephone Intercepts," www.MattheWaid.com, February 8, 2014, http://www.matthewaid.com/post/76006175914/new-document-confirms-dutch -military-intelligence.

54. See Jeffrey T. Richelson, *The Wizards of Langley: Inside the CIA's Directorate of Science and Technology* (Boulder, CO: Westview, 2001), 87–88; Arne Halvorsen, Anne Marte Blindheim, and Harald S. Klungtveit, "Norway's Secret Surveillance of Russian Politics for the NSA," December 17, 2013, http://www.dagbladet.no; Olav Riste, *The Norwegian Intelligence Service, 1945–1970* (London: Frank Cass, 1999), 146–163.

55. "Cold War Treaty Confirms Sweden Was Not Neutral," www.thelocal.se, December 9, 2013, http://www.thelocal.se/20131209/secret-cold-war-treaty-confirms-sweden-was-never -neutral.

56. National Security Agency/Central Security Service, Information Paper, "Subject: NSA Intelligence Relationship with Sweden," April 18, 2003.

57. Ibid.

58. National Security Agency/Central Security Service, Visit Précis: SWEDUSA 2013 Strategic Planning Conference (SPC), Mr. Ingvar Akesson, Director General, Forsvarets Radioanstalt (FRA), Sweden, April 24–26, 2013, n.d. On U.S. intelligence cooperation with Finland, including SIGINT cooperation, see Jukka Rislakki, "'Without Mercy'—U.S. Strategic Intelligence and Finland in the Cold War," *Journal of Military History* 79, no. 1 (January 2015): 127–149.

59. National Security Agency/Central Security Service, Information Paper, Subject: NSA Intelligence Relationship with Saudi Arabia, April 8, 2013; Glenn Greenwald and Murtaza Hussain, "The NSA's New Partner in Spying: Saudi Arabia's Brutal State Police," *Intercept*, July 25, 2014, https://firstlook.org/theintercept/2014/07/25/nsas-new-partner-spying-saudi-arabias-brutal -state-police/.

60. "NSA's Oldest Third Party SIGINT Partnership," *SIDToday*, October 7, 2005; National Security Agency/Central Security Service, Information Paper, Subject: NSA Intelligence Relationship with Turkey—Turkish National Intelligence Organization (MIT) and the Turkish SIGINT Intelligence Directorate (SIB), April 15, 2013.

61. National Security Agency/Central Security Service, Subject: NSA Intelligence Relationship with Turkey; Laura Poitras, Marcel Rosenbach, and Michael Sontheimer, "A Two-Faced Friendship: Turkey Is 'Partner and Target' for the NSA," *Spiegel Online*, August 31, 2014, http://www .spiegel.de/international/world/documents-show-nsa-and-gchq-spied-on-partner-turkey-a-989011 .html.

62. U.S. Arms Control and Disarmament Agency, "Subject: US-UK Cooperation in the Detection of Nuclear Explosions," September 22, 1964; Hugh W. Wolf, Office of the Assistant Secretary of Defense, to Mr. Arnold Freeman, Department of State, October 12, 1964 w/att: "Test Ban Monitoring Requirements-Understandings Reached in US/UK Technical Discussions of September 1964-Draft Agreement with Annex," n.d.; Department of State, "Subject: PROJECT CLEAR SKY—Proposed Take-Over by UK of US AEDS Station Perth," June 18, 1966.

63. Lieutenant Colonel Rodney R. Bickford, "Canadian Underseas Surveillance," *Proceedings* (March 1995): 70–71.

64. "Missile Warning Data System Ordered for Australia," www.spacenews.com, September 30, 2013, http://spacenews.com/37458missile-warning-data-system-ordered-for-australia.

65. Duane Bird, U.S. Strategic Command, "Sharing Space Situational Awareness Data" September 2010, prepared for the 2010 Advanced Maui Optical and Space Surveillance Technologies Conference, September 14–17, 2010, Maui, Hawaii).

66. Ibid.

67. Stephen Smith, Minister for Defense, and Robert M. Gates, Secretary of Defense, "Australian–United States Space Situational Awareness Partnership—Statement of Principles," undated, unsigned copy; Turner Brinton, "U.S., Australia Sign Agreement on Space Situational Awareness," *Space News*, November 15, 2010, 4; Department of Defense, Australia, "Minister for Defence—Australia and the United States Agreement on Defence Space Cooperation," November 22, 2013, http://www.minister.defence.gov.au/2013/11/22/minister-for-defence-australia-and-the -united-states-agreement-on-defence-space-cooperation; "U.S., Australia Sign Deal on Surveillance Telescope," *Space News*, December 9, 2013, 8. For a discussion of Australian space surveillance activities, see G. N. Newsam, Defense Science & Technology Organisation, Department of Defence, Australia, "Surveillance of Space in Australia" (presentation to the AMOS Maui Optical and Space Surveillance Technologies Conference, September 16–19, 2008, Maui, Hawaii).

68. Peter B. de Selding, "France, U.S. Sign Framework Agreement for Space Surveillance Cooperation," *Space News*, February 14, 2011, A2; *A GRAVES Sourcebook*, August 7, 2013, http://fas .org/spp/military/program/track/graves.pdf.

69. "U.S., Canada to Share Space Surveillance Data," *Space News*, May 28, 2012, 3; Gunter's Space Page, "Sapphire," http://space.skyrocket.de/doc_sdat/sapphire_end.htm (accessed March 29, 2014); Paul Maskell and Lorne Oram, "Sapphire: Canada's Answer to Space-Based Surveillance of Orbital Objects" (presentation to the AMOS Maui Optical and Space Surveillance

Technologies Conference, September 16–19, 2008, Maui, Hawaii); Robert Leitch and Ian Hemphill, "Sapphire: A Small Satellite System for the Surveillance of Space" (presentation to the 24th Annual AIAA/USU Conference on Small Satellites, August 2010); "Canada's Sapphire Satellite Begins Tracking Operations," *Space News*, February 3, 2014, 3; David Pugliese, "Canada Eyes 'Son of Sapphire' as a Way to Keep Helping U.S. Watch over Space," www.spacenews.com, July 24, 2014, http://spacenews.com/41374military-space-quarterly-canada-eyes-son-of-sapphire -as-a-way-to-keep; Alan Scott, John Hackett, and Kam Man, "On-Orbit Results for Canada's Sapphire Optical Payload" (presentation to the AMOS Maui Optical and Space Surveillance Technologies Conference, September 9–12, 2014, Maui, Hawaii).

70. "U.S., Canadian Governments Sign SSA Data-Sharing Accord," *Space News*, January 13, 2014, 3; e-mail, Kendall Cooper, USSTRATCOM, to Jeffrey Richelson, March 3, 2014; "U.S., Japan Sign Pact on Space Situational Awareness," *Space News*, March 18, 2013, 9; U.S. Strategic Command, Public Affairs Office, "U.S., Italy Come Together on Space Situational Awareness," October 2013; Donna Miles, American Forces Press Service, "U.S.-Australia Agreement Promotes Space Situational Awareness," DOD, April 24, 2013, http://www.defense.gov/news/newsarticle .aspx?id=119865; "Stratcom Signs SSA Data Sharing Accord with France," *Space News*, February 3, 2014, 9; U.S. Strategic Command, Public Affairs Office, "USSTRATCOM Signs Fifth Data Sharing Agreement," January 27, 2014, http://www.stratcom.mil/news/2014/464/USSTRATCOM_ Signs_Fifth_Data_Sharing_Agreement.

71. U.S. Strategic Command, "Agreement for Sharing Space Situational Awareness Services and Information Between the Department of Defense of the United States of America and the Department(s) of [Name of Department(s)] of [Name of Country]," n.d. This document constitutes the boilerplate portion of each agreement, prior to inclusion of the specific names of foreign institutions, individuals, and dates.

72. Mike Gruss, "U.S., Australia, U.K. and Canada Sign Space Situational Awareness Accord," *Space News*, May 26, 2014, 8; "U.S. and Germany Sign Space Surveillance Pact," *Space News*, February 2, 2015, 3; "U.S. Strategic Command, ESA Sign Data-Sharing Agreement," *Space News*, November 10, 2014, 11; U.S. Strategic Command Public Affairs, "USTRATCOM, Germany Make Arrangement to Share Space Services, Data," www.stratcom.mil, January 28, 2015, http://www.stratcom.mil/news/2015/534/USSTRATCOM_Germany_make_arrangement_to_ share_space_services_data.

73. Adam D. M. Svendsen, *Intelligence Cooperation and the War on Terror: Anglo-American Security Relations after 9/11* (London: Routledge, 2010), 15.

74. Ibid., 16.

75. See Jeffrey T. Richelson, *A Century of Spies: Intelligence in the Twentieth Century* (New York: Oxford University Press, 1995), 232–236; James H. Critchfield, *Partners at the Creation: The Man Behind Postwar Germany's Defense and Intelligence Establishments* (Annapolis, MD: Naval Institute Press, 2003); Mary Ellen Reese, *General Reinhard Gehlen: The CIA Connection* (Fairfax, VA: George Mason University Press, 1990). For a multitude of declassified documents on the early years of the CIA-BND relationship, see Kevin C. Ruffner's two-volume documentary history, *Forging an Intelligence Partnership: CIA and the Origins of the BND, 1945–1949: A Documentary History* (Washington, DC: Central Intelligence Agency, 1999), and another multipart (and undated) CIA product, *Forging an Intelligence Partnership: CIA and the Origins of the BND, 1945–1956.*

76. Bob Drogin, "German Spies Aided in U.S. Attempt to Kill Hussein in Aerial Attack," *Los Angeles Times*, January 12, 2006, A3.

77. Richard Bernstein, "Germans Ask How Agents Helped U.S.," *New York Times*, January 21, 2006, A6; Michael R. Gordon, "German Intelligence Gave U.S. Iraqi Defense Plan, Report Says," *New York Times*, February 27, 2006, A1, A9.

78. Gordon, "German Intelligence Gave U.S. Iraqi Defense Plan, Report Says."

79. Richard Bernstein and Michael R. Gordon, "Berlin File Says German's Spies Aided U.S. in Iraq," *New York Times*, March 2, 2006, A1, A12.

80. Canadian Press, "CSIS Played Critical Role in Afghan Prisoner Interrogations: Documents, Sources," *CP24*, March 8, 2010, http://www.cp24.com/csis-played-critical-role-in-afghan-prisoner-interrogations-documents-sources-1.490047.

81. "South Korean Intelligence Gave U.S. Its Entire Database on North Korean Defectors, Wikileaks," MatthewAid.com, July 13, 2013, http://www.matthewaid.com/post/55366313765/south-korean-intelligence-gave-u-s-its-entire.

82. Mohamed El Baradei, Director General, International Atomic Energy Agency, "Implementation of the NPT Safeguards Agreement in the Islamic Republic of Iran," November 18, 2005, 4–5; Alissa J. Rubin, "Iran Still Not Opening Up to the IAEA," *Los Angeles Times*, November 19, 2005, A3; Nazila Fathi, "Iran Parliament Votes to Close Atomic Sites to U.N. Monitors," *New York Times*, November 21, 2005, A10.

83. Deputy Director General for Safeguards, IAEA, "Developments in the Implementation of the NPT Safeguards Agreement in the Islamic Republic of Iran and Agency Verification of Iran's Suspension of Enrichment-Related and Reprocessing Activities," January 31, 2006, 2–3.

84. Duncan Campbell and Clive Thomas, "BBC's Trade Secrets," *New Statesman*, July 4, 1980, 13–14; Svendsen, *Intelligence Cooperation and the War on Terror*, 19.

85. Louise D. Davison, "Historical Note on the 'Agreement' Between the Foreign Broadcast Information Service (CIG/CIA) and the British Broadcasting Corporation Monitoring Service, 1947," August 23, 1971; "FBIS-BBC Reciprocal Arrangement, Basic Provisions," 1950.

86. "FBIS-BBC Reciprocal Arrangement, Basic Provisions."

87. Campbell and Thomas, "BBC's Trade Secrets."

88. Ibid.

89. Kalev Leetatu, "The Scope of FBIS and BBC Open Source Media Coverage, 1979–2008," *Studies in Intelligence* 54, no. 1 (Extracts, March 2010): 17–37, at 33.

90. Svendsen, *Intelligence Cooperation and the War on Terror*, 19–20.

91. Dana Priest, "Foreign Network at Front of CIA's Terror Fight," *Washington Post*, November 18, 2005, A1, A12.

92. Dana Priest, "Help from France Key in Covert Operations," *Washington Post*, July 3, 2005, A1, A16.

93. Ibid.

94. Matthew M. Aid, *Intel Wars: The Secret History of the Fight Against Terror* (New York: Bloomsbury, 2012), 135–136.

95. Dana Priest and William M. Arkin, *Top Secret America: The Rise of the New American Security State* (Boston: Little, Brown, 2011), 31; Ken Silverstein, "U.S., Jordan Forge Closer Ties in Covert War on Terrorism," *Los Angeles Times*, November 11, 2005, A1, A10–A11; Joby Warrick, "Jordan Emerges as Key CIA Counterterrorism Ally," www.washingtonpost.com, January 4, 2010, http://www.washingtonpost.com/wp-dyn/content/article/2010/01/03/AR2010010302063.html; Shane Harris, "The Mouse That Roars," www.foreignpolicy.com, September 12, 2014, http://foreignpolicy.com/2014/09/12/the-mouse-that-roars.

96. Silverstein, "U.S., Jordan Forge Closer Ties in Covert War on Terrorism"; Warrick, "Jordan Emerges as Key CIA Counterterrorism Ally."

97. Silverstein, "U.S., Jordan Forge Closer Ties in Covert War on Terrorism"; Craig Whitlock, "Jordan's Spy Agency: Holding Cell for the CIA," www.washingtonpost.com, December 1, 2007, http://www.washingtonpost.com/wp-dyn/content/article/2007/11/30/AR2007113002484.html.

98. Silverstein, "U.S., Jordan Forge Closer Ties in Covert War on Terrorism"; Warrick, "Jordan Emerges as Key CIA Counterterrorism Ally"; Rowan Scaborough, "Obama Denied Request from Jordan for Predator Drones in Islamic State Fight," www.washingtontimes.com, February 6, 2015, http://www.washingtontimes.com/news/2015/feb/5/obama-denied-request-jordan-predator-drones-islami.

99. Karen De Young, "U.S., Pakistan Bolster Joint Efforts, Treading Delicately," www.washingtonpost.com, April 29, 2010, http://www.washingtonpost.com/wp-dyn/content/article/2010/04/28/AR2010042805580.html; Karin Brulliard and Karen De Young, "U.S., Pakistan

Chiefs of Intelligence Meet," www.washingtonpost.com, September 30, 2010, http://www
.washingtonpost.com/wp-dyn/content/article/2010/09/29/AR2010092907108.html.

100. Greg Miller and Alex Rodriguez, "U.S. Told Pakistan Where to Look," *Los Angeles Times*, February 17, 2010, A1, A8; Adam Entous, Julian E. Barnes, and Tom Wright, "Spy Feud Hampers Antiterror Efforts," *Wall Street Journal*, February 18, 2011, A1, A8; Alex Rodriguez and Ken Dilanian, "CIA's Ties to Pakistan Are Fraying," *Los Angeles Times*, February 26, 2011, A3; June Perlez, "Pakistani Spy Agency Demands That C.I.A. Account for Contractors," *New York Times*, February 26, 2011, A4.

101. Alex Rodriguez, "U.S. and Pakistan Work to Fix Ties," *Los Angeles Times*, April 13, 2011, A4, A5; Jane Perlez and Ismail Khan, "Pakistan Pushes for Drastic Cuts in C.I.A. Activity," *New York Times*, April 12, 2011, A1, A10; David S. Cloud, "Pakistan Rolls Back U.S. Military Support," *Los Angeles Times*, May 27, 2011, A1, A8.

102. Paul S. Richter, David S. Cloud, and Alex Rodriguez, "Angry Pakistan Rejects Appeal from U.S.," *Los Angeles Times*, May 28, 2011, A1, A8; Zeeshan Haider, "Pakistan, U.S. Agree to Resume Joint Intel Ops: Foreign Ministry," Reuters, June 3, 2011, http://www.reuters.com/article/2011/06/03/us-pakistan-usa-idUSTRE75210920110603; Griffe Witte and Karen De Young, "Thwarted Raids Add to Tension with Pakistan," *Washington Post*, June 11, 2011, A1, A8.

103. Declan Walsh, "Pakistan's New Spy Chief Visits Washington at a Time of Frayed Relations," *New York Times*, August 1, 2012, A9; Alex Rodriguez, "Pakistan Captures Al Qaeda Leader," *Los Angeles Times*, September 6, 2011, A5.

104. Statement of the Inspectors General of the Intelligence Community, Central Intelligence Agency, Department of Justice, and Department of Homeland Security, *Unclassified Summary of Information Handling and Sharing Prior to the April 15, 2013 Boston Marathon Bombings*, Director of National Intelligence, April 10, 2014, 1, 7–8, http://www.dni.gov/index.php/newsroom/reports-and-publications/204-reports-publications-2014/1042-unclassified-summary-of-information-handling-and-sharing-prior-to-the-april-15,-2013-boston-marathon-bombings.

105. Ibid., 1, 10–11; U.S. Congress, House Committee on Homeland Security, *The Road to Boston: Counterterrorism Challenges and Lessons from the Marathon Bombings*, March 2014, 11; Michael S. Schmidt and Eric Schmitt, "Russia Didn't Share Details on Boston Suspect, Report Says," *New York Times*, April 10, 2014, A1, A12; Scott Shane, "Phone Calls Discussing Jihad Prompted Russian Warning on Tsarnaev," *New York Times*, April 28, 2013, 18; Pervaiz Shallwani, Alan Cullison, and Evan Perez, "U.S. Is Probing Suspect's Alleged Links to Militants," *Wall Street Journal*, April 23, 2013, A6.

106. Michael R. Gordon, "U.S. and Russia Agree to Share More Intelligence on Islamic State," *New York Times*, October 15, 2014, A14.

107. Eric Schmitt and Scott Shane, "U.S. Received Early Warning on Qaeda Plot," *New York Times*, November 6, 2010, A1, A8; Robert F. Worth and Eric Schmitt, "Long-Running Antiterrorism Work with Saudis Led to Airline Plot's Failure," *New York Times*, May 10, 2012, A9.

108. Adam Goldman, Associated Press, "US: CIA Thwarts New Al-Qaida Underwear Bomb Plot," Yahoo! News, May 7, 2013, http://news.yahoo.com/us-cia-thwarts-al-qaida-underwear-bomb-plot-200836835.html; Siobhan Gorman, Laura Mecker, and Evan Peres, "Jetliner Bomb Plot Is Foiled," *Wall Street Journal*, May 8, 2012, A1, A10; Ken Dilanian and Brian Bennett, "Double Agent Snagged Al Qaeda Bomb," *Los Angeles Times*, May 9, 2012, A1, A4; Scott Shane and Eric Schmitt, "Airline Plotter a Double Agent, U.S. Officials Say," *New York Times*, May 9, 2012, A1, A6.

109. Jeremy Scahill, *Dirty Wars: The World Is a Battlefield* (New York: Nation Books, 2013), 470–473.

110. Jeff Stein, "CIA Training Sudan's Spies as Obama Officials Fight over Policy," *Spy Talk*, August 30, 2010, http://voices.washingtonpost.com/spy-talk/2010/08/cia_training_sudans_spies_as_o.html (accessed September 3, 2010).

111. Eric Schmitt, "Drones in Niger Reflect New U.S. Tack on Terrorism," *New York Times*, July 11, 2013, A3; Adam Entous, David Gauthier-Villars, and Drew Hinshaw, "U.S. Boosts War Role in Africa," *Wall Street Journal*, March 4, 2013, A1, A8.

112. Michael R. Gordon and Eric Schmitt, "U.S. Officials Propose Sharing Surveillance Data with Algerians," *New York Times*, February 27, 2013, A10.

113. Ronald Reagan, National Security Decision Directive 221, "Narcotics and National Security," April 8, 1986.

114. Amembassy Mexico, To Sec State Wash DC, Subject: Director of National Intelligence Dennis Blair's Meeting with General Galvan, October 19, October 26, 2009.

115. Robert Beckhusen, "U.S. Looks to Re-up Its Mexican Surveillance System," www.wired .com, May 1, 2013, http://www.wired.com/2013/05/mexico-surveillance-system.

116. Nick Miroff and William Booth, "Mexico's Marines Team with U.S. DEA," www .washingtonpost.com, December 4, 2010, http://www.washingtonpost.com/wp-dyn/content/article/2010/12/03/AR2010120307106.html.

117. Ginger Thompson, "U.S. Widens Its Role in Battle Against Mexico's Drug Cartels," *New York Times*, August 7, 2011, 1, 8.

118. William La Jeunesse, "Covert U.S. Operation Sends Manned Aircraft to Help Mexican Police," www.foxnews.com, August 28, 2013, http://www.foxnews.com/politics/2013/08/28/covert-us-operation-sends-manned-aircraft-to-help-mexican-police; Aram Roston, "Exclusive: Inside the Pentagon's Top Secret Spy Plane Operation Against Mexican Drug Cartels," www.vocativ .com (accessed April 13, 2014); Dana Priest, "U.S. Role at a Crossroads in Mexico's Intelligence War on Cartels," www.washingtonpost.com, April 27, 2013.

119. Randal C. Archibold, Damien Cave, and Ginger Thompson, "New Friction as Mexico Curbs U.S. Cooperation in Drug War," *New York Times*, May 1, 2013, A1, A3.

120. Cox, *Canada and the Five Eyes Intelligence Community*, 8.

121. Joint Intelligence Organisation, *Fourth Annual Report, 1974* (Canberra: JIO, 1974), F1–F2; Department of the Army, Office of the Deputy Chief of Staff for Intelligence, *Annual Historical Review, 1 October 1993 to 30 September 1994*, n.d., 6–11.

122. Michael B. Petersen, "60 Years of a 'SPECIAL RELATIONSHIP,'" *Communiqué* (January–February 2010): 15–16.

123. Canadian-U.S. Joint Intelligence Committee, *Soviet Capabilities and Probable Course of Action Against North America in a Major War Commencing During the Period 1 January 1958 to 31 December 1958*, March 1, 1957, Declassified Documents Reference Service, 1981-169A; U.S. Congress, Senate Select Committee on Armed Services, *Department of Defense Authorization for Appropriations for Fiscal Year 1984*, pt. 5 (Washington, DC: U.S. Government Printing Office, 1983), 2708; Cox, *Canada and the Five Eyes Intelligence Community*, 8.

124. Navy Field Operational Office, *Command History for CY 1981*, April 15, 1982, 5; Assistant Chief of Staff for Intelligence, Air Force, *History of the Assistant Chief of Staff, Intelligence, Hq. United States Air Force, 1 July 1974–31 December 1974*, n.d., 9; Department of the Army, Office of the Assistant Chief of Staff, Intelligence, *Annual Historical Review, 1 October 1985–30 September 1986*, n.d., 4–5.

125. Armed Forces Medical Intelligence Center, *Organization and Functions of the Armed Forces Medical Intelligence Center*, April 1986, viii; Lynn A. McNamara, "AFMIC Responds to Tsunami Disaster," *Communiqué* 17, no. 1 (January 2005): 10–11; David S. Brandwein, "Confessions of a Former USIB Committee Chairman," *Studies in Intelligence* 18, no. 2 (Summer 1974): 43–50.

126. Elizabeth K. King, "Analysts and Collectors: TAKE NOTE!," *Communiqué* (March–April 2006): 30–31.

14

ANALYSIS

The vast quantity of data collected by U.S. and allied intelligence agencies requires an assortment of special techniques and analysts to produce the large variety of analytical documents made available to U.S. policymakers, military personnel, and individuals responsible for implementing policy.

ANALYSTS

The Central Intelligence Agency distinguishes several different types of foreign intelligence analysts, most tied to specific subject matter: political, leadership, medical/psychological, economic, military, weapons systems, foreign media, terrorism, crime and narcotics, and foreign intelligence activities. Political analysts evaluate "the goals and motivations of foreign governments and entities" and examine "their culture, values, society and ideologies; their resources and capabilities; their political and decision making processes; the strengths and weaknesses of their strategies for achieving their goal; and the implication of all of the above for US interests."[1]

Leadership analysts "produce assessments of foreign leaders and other key decision makers in the political, economic, military, science and technology, social and cultural fields." Medical and health analysts are "physicians who analyze and assess global health issues, such as disease outbreaks, and who follow the health of foreign leaders." Also contributing to the analyses of foreign leaders are psychological/psychiatric analysts, "who research, analyze, and write assessments of foreign leaders, societal impacts of disease and disaster, and decisionmaking groups." They also assess the psychological and social factors that influence world events.[2]

Economic analysts interpret economic trends and developments as well as "assess foreign economic policies and foreign financial issues—explicit as well as illicit—that affect US security interests." The illicit financial activities and networks examined include those of terrorist and criminal organizations, those involved in weapons proliferation, money launderers, and corrupt governments and companies.[3]

Military analysts evaluate weapons systems, military resources, and the intentions and war-fighting capabilities of foreign governments as well as of terrorist and insurgent groups. They also examine peacekeeping activities, civil-military relations, denial and deception, regional security arrangements, arms control, and nonproliferation regimes. Science, technology, and weapons analysts examine foreign weapons development, proliferation, weapons of mass destruction (WMD), information warfare, and emerging technologies.[4]

Foreign media analysts "review and assess foreign open media sources, including Internet sites, newspapers, press agencies, television, radio, and specialized publications," which allows them to "identify trends and patterns." A growing component of foreign media analysis looks at social media sites, including Twitter, Facebook, Reddit, and others.[5]

Counterterrorism analysts "monitor and assess the leadership, motivations, plans and intentions of foreign terrorist groups and their state and non-state sponsors." Crime and counternarcotics analysts "follow international narcotics trafficking and organized crime groups to detect emerging trends and patterns." Counterintelligence threat analysts "identify, monitor and analyze the efforts of foreign intelligence entities against US persons, activities and interests, including the threats posed by emerging technologies to US operations and interests."[6]

ANALYTICAL TECHNIQUES

In the past, finished intelligence reports were largely, although not exclusively, based on the judgments reached by analysts after reviewing the data, whether technical data about an intercontinental ballistic missile or comments by foreign political figures. Other studies might have examined data using either basic statistical analysis (e.g., the number or severity of terrorist incidents) or, less frequently, Bayesian analysis (in which new evidence or observations are used to revise an estimate that a hypothesis is true).[7]

Today's analytical products reflect the increasing use of a number of new analytical techniques, particularly with respect to the structure and activities of terrorist groups. These techniques include clustering (to exploit the most useful data sets first), link analysis (to establish relationships between a known problem and unknown actors), time series analysis (to identify time trends), visualization (to see complex data in new forms), and automated database population (to eliminate the need to maintain databases). Thus, among the classes of analysts identified by the CIA is the "targeting analyst," who uses "network analysis techniques and specialized tools to identify and detail key threats to the U.S."[8]

The best-known new techniques are data mining and social-network analysis. Data mining involves the use of algorithms to discover previously undetected but valid patterns and relationships in large data sets. One of the best-known data-mining efforts was ABLE DANGER, initiated in late 1999 by the U.S. Special Operations Command to uncover terrorists and their activities. In addition, after 9/11 the National Security Agency (NSA) initiated new data-mining projects. Social-network analysis, also used in support of counterterrorism, employs mathematics, anthropology, psychology, and sociology to uncover social networks—that is, sets of actors and the relationships that define them.[9]

Social-network analysis was used to aid in the December 2003 capture of Saddam Hussein, according to a U.S. Army field manual. New items of information "led to coalition forces identifying and locating more of the key players in the insurgent network," including not only highly visible ones but also "lesser ones who sustained and supported the insurgency." The result was the production of detailed diagrams showing the structure of the former Iraqi dictator's personal security apparatus and the relationships among the individuals identified.[10]

During the summer of 2003, intelligence analysts from the 4th Infantry Division constructed link diagrams "showing everyone related to Hussein by blood or tribe." The diagrams "led counterinsurgents to the lower-level, but nonetheless highly trusted, relatives and clan members harboring Hussein and helping him move around the countryside." Later in the year, operations produced new intelligence about Hussein's whereabouts, which led commanders to design "a series of raids to capture key individuals and leaders of the former regime who could lead counterinsurgents to him."[11]

Among the more recent innovations is the establishment of collaborative analysis. The first of these efforts, Intellipedia, has been an attempt to create an Intelligence Community (IC) Wikipedia with three levels of classification: TOP SECRET/SI/ NOFORN (Top Secret/Special Intelligence/Not Releasable to Foreign Nationals) SECRET/NOFORN, and Controlled Unclassified. Its genesis was a 2004 paper by a CIA employee titled "The Wiki and the Blog: Toward an Adaptive Intelligence Community." Policymakers can participate in Intellipedia, and by September 2008, it had more than 40,000 registered users and 349,000 active pages.[12]

A more restrictive workspace for analysts only is A-Space. The goal is "to create a common collaborative workspace where IC analysts in diverse locations can work together, in a new simultaneous fashion, on common projects." It allows posting of "emerging insights" during the course of research so that other analysts can see and comment on the work in progress. As of September 2008, A-Space was open to 9,000 analysts.[13]

The Office of the Director of National Intelligence (ODNI) reported that following the 2008 Mumbai terrorist attacks, an ad hoc group of analysts convened on the sites to "post video, photos, and satellite imagery, and discuss the events as they were unfolding in real-time." In addition, "analysts used intelligence that had been posted and discussed on A-Space in the previous months to identify an al-Qaida-affiliated extremist group as the perpetrator of the attacks."[14]

CURRENT INTELLIGENCE

Current intelligence is pertinent to a topic of immediate interest, such as military movements in Beijing during early June 1989, terrorist attacks in Israel, London, or Madrid, a military conflict between Israel and Hamas, movements of Russian troops toward the border with Ukraine, or the latest movements of the Islamic State's armed forces. Such intelligence is generally transmitted without the opportunity for the extensive evaluation possible with other types of reports; it is also more likely to be based on one or two sources than an all-source product.

A variety of products, whose sensitivity and consumers vary, fall into the current intelligence category. The most restrictive and sensitive of those products is the *President's*

Daily Brief (*PDB*), "a compilation of current intelligence items of high significance to national policy concerns prepared six days a week." The *PDB*, which began as the *President's Intelligence Checklist* during the administration of John F. Kennedy and took its present name in December 1964, is tailored to meet the daily intelligence requirements as defined by the president. According to a former CIA deputy director for intelligence, "one of the earliest changes in the new administration is usually the format of the *President's Daily Brief*." Because it contains information from the most sensitive U.S. sources—on average, about 60 percent of the items covered in the *PDB* do not appear in the press even in unclassified form—it has been the most restricted of current intelligence products, at times being distributed only to the president, vice president, the Secretaries of State and Defense, the National Security Advisor, the Chairman of the Joint Chiefs of Staff, and possibly a few other key officials.[15]

According to a former CIA official, the *PDB* "is a powerful tool for focusing the attention of the President on potential crisis areas and for alerting him to situations that may require rapid policy adjustment." It has also been described as being "designed to give policy officials an understanding about what happened in the world during the past 24 hours, and what is likely to happen during the next 24 hours."[16]

The size, organization, and medium employed to deliver the *PDB* may change from president to president. Under Gerald Ford, the brief was rather lengthy, but it was reduced to a maximum of about fifteen pages under Jimmy Carter, although Director of Central Intelligence (DCI) Stansfield Turner occasionally appended longer "trend pieces." During the Clinton administration it was nine to twelve pages long and printed with four-color graphics, while during the George W. Bush administration it apparently consisted of six to eight relatively short (one- to two-page) articles or briefs covering a wide variety of topics. Appended to the *PDB* is the *National Terrorism Brief*, prepared by the National Counterterrorism Center.[17]

An article in the December 4, 1998, *PDB* was titled "Bin Laden Preparing to Hijack US Aircraft and Other Attacks." According to the item, motivation for the hijacking plans was "to obtain the release of Shayk 'Umar 'Abd al-Rhamn, Ramzi Yousef, and Muhammad Sadiq 'Awada," The August 6, 2001, *PDB* carried an article titled "Bin Ladin Determined to Strike in US." It began by noting, "Clandestine, foreign government and media reports indicate Bin Ladin since 1997 has wanted to conduct terrorist attacks in the U.S." It also stated, "Al-Qa'ida members—including some who are US citizens—have resided in or traveled to the US for years, and the group apparently maintains a support structure that could aid attacks."[18] Figure 14.1 shows the entire August 6, 2001, *PDB*.

A key subject in the September 21, 2001, *PDB* concerned whether there was an Iraqi connection with the terrorist attacks of ten days earlier. One long piece involved the implications of the capture of Abu Zubaydah. The May 26, 2009, *PDB* contained an article titled "North American al Qaeda Trainees May Influence Targets and Tactics in the United States and Canada." During 2013 and 2014, the *PDB* contained a number of articles on the threat posed by the Islamic State in Iraq and Syria (ISIS) terrorist group.[19]

After 9/11 the *PDB* was, according to one study, "elevated . . . to unprecedented levels of importance," with President Bush spending as much as an hour on the *PDB*

FIGURE 14.1 Excerpt from the *President's Daily Brief*, August 6, 2001

Bin Ladin Determined To Strike in US

Clandestine, foreign government, and media reports indicate Bin Ladin since 1997 has wanted to conduct terrorist attacks in the US. Bin Ladin implied in US television interviews in 1997 and 1998 that his followers would follow the example of World Trade Center bomber Ramzi Yousef and "bring the fighting to America."

After US missile strikes on his base in Afghanistan in 1998, Bin Ladin told followers he wanted to retaliate in Washington, according to a ▆▆▆▆▆▆▆▆ service.

An Egyptian Islamic Jihad (EIJ) operative told an ▆▆▆▆ service at the same time that Bin Ladin was planning to exploit the operative's access to the US to mount a terrorist strike.

The millennium plotting in Canada in 1999 may have been part of Bin Ladin's first serious attempt to implement a terrorist strike in the US. Convicted plotter Ahmed Ressam has told the FBI that he conceived the idea to attack Los Angeles International Airport himself, but that Bin Ladin lieutenant Abu Zubaydah encouraged him and helped facilitate the operation. Ressam also said that in 1998 Abu Zubaydah was planning his own US attack.

Ressam says Bin Ladin was aware of the Los Angeles operation.

Although Bin Ladin has not succeeded, his attacks against the US Embassies in Kenya and Tanzania in 1998 demonstrate that he prepares operations years in advance and is not deterred by setbacks. Bin Ladin associates surveilled our Embassies in Nairobi and Dar es Salaam as early as 1993, and some members of the Nairobi cell planning the bombings were arrested and deported in 1997.

Al-Qa'ida members—including some who are US citizens—have resided in or traveled to the US for years, and the group apparently maintains a support structure that could aid attacks. Two al-Qa'ida members found guilty in the conspiracy to bomb our Embassies in East Africa were US citizens, and a senior EIJ member lived in California in the mid-1990s.

A clandestine source said in 1998 that a Bin Ladin cell in New York was recruiting Muslim-American youth for attacks.

We have not been able to corroborate some of the more sensational threat reporting, such as that from a ▆▆▆▆▆▆▆▆ service in 1998 saying that Bin Ladin wanted to hijack a US aircraft to gain the release of "Blind Shaykh" 'Umar 'Abd al-Rahman and other US-held extremists.

(continues)

For the President Only
6 August 2001

Declassified and Approved
for Release, 10 April 2004

— Nevertheless, FBI information since that time indicates patterns of suspicious activity in this country consistent with preparations for hijackings or other types of attacks, including recent surveillance of federal buildings in New York.

The FBI is conducting approximately 70 full field investigations throughout the US that it considers Bin Ladin–related. CIA and the FBI are investigating a call to our Embassy in the UAE in May saying that a group of Bin Ladin supporters was in the US planning attacks with explosives.

Declassified and Approved
for Release, 10 April 2004

briefing.* The CIA noted, "It has become common for the President and his senior advisors who also receive PDB materials to ask follow-up questions." Members of the analytic briefing team returned after the briefings and tasked Intelligence Community personnel to provide answers to the questions raised. The answers were contained in the *Presidential Daily Brief Memorandum*. In addition, analysts began presenting verbal "deep dives" into an issue of particular concern to the president. The former deputy director for analysis estimated that President Bush had received almost one hundred deep dives, involving over two hundred analysts, by September 2008. Initially the responsibility of the DCI, the briefing became the responsibility of the Director of National Intelligence (DNI) after that position was established.[20]

Under President Barack Obama, the *PDB* has been delivered on a tablet rather than on paper and on at least one occasion by a Defense Intelligence Agency (DIA) analyst.[†] Currently, *PDB* articles have no fixed length, but items longer than two pages are rare and come with a two- to three-sentence summary at the beginning.[21]

The second regular current intelligence publication is the *Worldwide Intelligence Review* (*WIRe*), previously known as the *Senior Executive Intelligence Brief* (*SEIB*) and, for decades before that, as the *National Intelligence Daily*. The daily *SEIB* contained six to eight relatively short articles or briefs on a variety of subjects, similar to the *PDB*. It was prepared by the CIA but was coordinated with other Intelligence Community production organizations. Although the brief had no classification limits, it excluded some of the more sensitive information contained in the *PDB*, since it was distributed to several hundred policymakers in the executive branch. Dissenting views were noted either in the text of the article or in a separate paragraph.[22]

SEIB articles included "Saudi Terrorist Threat Growing" (February 6, 2001); "Terrorism: Terrorist Groups Said Cooperating on US Hostage Plot" (May 23, 2001); "Terrorism: Bin Ladin Planning High-Profile Attacks" (June 30, 2001); "Terrorism:

---

*The study also concluded that there was an overemphasis on the *PDB*, which had a variety of negative effects on the overall analytic effort, including skewing incentives with respect to topic selection, use of hyperbolic language, an excessive attachment to classified sources, and tailoring of subject matter to presidential policy preferences. See Kenneth Lieberthal, *The U.S. Intelligence Community and Foreign Policy: Getting Analysis Right* (Washington, D.C.: Brookings Institution, 2009), 11–12.

†The possibility of an alternative to paper production of the *PDB* was raised as early as the Richard Nixon administration. It was widely believed that Nixon did not read the *PDB*, relying instead on a package produced by the National Security Council staff in the White Situation Room. A memo to National Security Advisor Henry Kissinger raised the possibility of developing a TV-like device that would be a "reading program," continuously available to the President, that would allow him to pick the subjects he wished to read about, begin reading at a summary level, select areas to read about in more detail, and stop reading and move on to another subject. See A. W. Marshall, Memorandum for Henry A. Kissinger, Subject: Transmittal of Memorandum on President's Reading Package, March 18, 1970; A. W. Marshall, Memorandum for Henry A. Kissinger, Subject: Evaluation of the Process Leading to the President's Morning Intelligence Reading Package, March 18, 1970; Charles Joyce, Memorandum for Andrew Marshall, Subject: Possible Technical Improvements in Handling the President's Daily Brief, February 6, 1970; Charles Joyce, Memorandum for Andrew Marshall, Subject: Description of Proposed On-Line Briefing Capability, February 13, 1970.

Bin Ladin Plans Delayed but Not Abandoned" (July 13, 2001); "Iraqi: Nuclear Related Procurement Efforts" (October 18, 2001); "Lebanon: Many Suspects in Assassination" (January 26, 2002); "FARC-AUC Conflict Intensifying" (May 18, 2002); "Iraq: Terrorists Are Threat to US Forces at War's Outset" (March 21, 2003); and "Iraq: Russian, French Oil Companies Want Post-War Role" (March 21, 2003).[23]

The *WIRe*, prepared by the CIA in consultation with the DIA, NSA, and Bureau of Intelligence and Research (INR), is the agency's "daily (except Sundays) corporate intelligence publication, intended for customers below the PDB level—from Cabinet Deputy Secretaries and Under Secretaries to working-level officials, members of the military, and IC analysts." *WIRe* articles have included "Libya: Attack on British Diplomatic Convoy Underscores Risks to Western Interests" (June 11, 2012); "Libya: Recent Attacks Highlight Persistent Threats in Eastern Libya" (August 1, 2012); "Libya: Struggling to Create Effective Domestic Security System" (August 29, 2012); and "Libya: Update on Planning and Capability for Benghazi Attacks" (March 29, 2013).[24]

Additional CIA current intelligence products include the *Senior Executive Article*, published in the same format as the *WIRe* but "sent to a limited list of officials due to source sensitivity or high level interest," and the *Economic Intelligence Brief*, which discusses "key economics-related developments and trends." Two further CIA current intelligence products are the Situation Report (SITREP) and the Spot Commentary (SPOTCOM). The SITREP may include multiple items and provides "recent intelligence and analysis of ongoing high-importance events or situations," while the SPOTCOM is produced for *PDB* recipients "following a significant event (such as coup or natural disaster)."[25]

A current intelligence website, created by the Office of the Director of National Intelligence, is Intelligence Today. According to one account, a twenty-two-person staff examines reports from twenty-nine agencies and sixty-three analytic websites on classified networks and "select[s] the best information, and package[s] it by originality, topic, and region, producing a daily publication that [is] dozens of screens long." The website has a feedback mechanism that "allows policymakers to submit comments, ask questions, and solicit additional information on a specific intelligence product."[26]

The State Department's INR produces the Secretary's Morning Summary seven days a week. It includes approximately a dozen brief reports with commentary and three or four longer articles, all related to policy issues. A supplementary *Weekend Edition* covers selected issues in detail. Topics have included "China's Forecast: Cloudy with Summer Storm Possible" (February 9–10, 1991) and "China's Defense Conversion: Lessons for the USSR?" (June 29–30, 1991). In addition to receiving limited dissemination within the State Department, the Morning Summary goes to the White House, National Security Council, and key ambassadors.[27]

The Defense Department's (DOD) premier current intelligence product is the *Defense Intelligence Digest* (*DID*), formerly the *Military Intelligence Digest* (*MID*). Produced in magazine format and published Monday through Friday, it focuses on the events of the previous day or two or on issues expected to arise over the following few days. A joint publication of the DIA, the military service intelligence organizations, and the unified commands, it contains items likely to be of interest to national-level policymakers on military or military-related topics. General areas covered include regional security, nuclear security, proliferation, strategy, and resources. The January 24, 1997, issue carried a report on a Russian program code-named FOLIANT, which concerned the production of a highly lethal nerve gas agent. The February 2, 1998, issue carried an article titled "Iraq: Unmanned Aerial Vehicle Program." An April 7, 2009, issue listed reports of former Guantánamo Bay detainees allegedly involved in terrorism. Articles appearing in 2012 *DID* issues included one that discussed the founding of Ansar al-Sharia.[28]

Two additional Defense Department current intelligence products are the *NMJIC Executive Highlights* (*EH*) and the *Defense Intelligence Terrorism Summary* (*DITSUM*). The *EH*, published Monday through Friday, is based on data from the DIA and the NSA and contains articles on crisis or near-crisis situations. The September 7, 2000, issue carried an article on Russian testing activities at Novaya Zemlya, while the February 12, 2002, edition included an article titled "Niamey Signed an Agreement to Sell 500 Tons of Uranium a Year to Baghdad." It is intended to keep the Secretary of Defense, the Chairman of the Joint Chiefs of Staff, and other key decision makers informed of developments that might require immediate action by the United States.[29]

The *DITSUM* is a compilation of information and analysis concerning terrorism threats and developments that could affect DOD personnel, facilities, and interests. *DITSUM* articles include brief notes on terrorism, regional terrorism developments, and in-depth special analyses. It also contains a monthly terrorism review by combatant commands. A 2002 issue contained a discussion of chemical and biological weapons training in Iraq. The *DITSUM* is distributed Monday through Friday in the Washington, D.C., area in hard copy and via e-mail to military commands outside the area.[30]

Two specialist current intelligence products are the *National SIGINT File* (which replaced the *SIGINT Digest* in October 1997) and the *World Imagery Report*. The former, distributed in hard copy on weekdays in the Washington, D.C., area and electronically to customers in the field, contains the most significant daily signals intelligence. The *World Imagery Report* is a video-format compilation of current intelligence items derived from imagery collection.[31]

Other current intelligence may also be conveyed by video rather than paper or electronic formats. By the early 1990s the DIA was distributing finished intelligence via television through the Defense Intelligence Network (DIN), formally known as the Joint Worldwide Intelligence Communications System. For approximately twelve hours a day, five days a week, the DIN broadcast top secret reports to defense intelligence and operations officers at the Pentagon and nineteen other military commands in the United States.[32]

In addition to having anchors who reported finished intelligence, the DIN showed satellite reconnaissance photos, reported communication intercepts, and carried reports from defense attachés overseas. Reporting began at 6:15 a.m., with a thirty-minute "Global Update." At 6:45 the head of the DIA J2 conducted a forty-five-minute interview show featuring visiting briefers who gave classified reports on developing events. "Global Update" resumed at 8:00 a.m. and continued at the top of each hour, updated as required and interspersed with special features. In addition, regular features included "Regional Intelligence Review" and "Military Trends and Capabilities."[33]

WARNING INTELLIGENCE

Warning intelligence products "identify and focus on developments that could have sudden and deleterious effects on U.S. security or policy." Among the national-level products that have been dedicated specifically to warning is the *Strategic Warning Committee's Watchlist*, a weekly report that tracked and assigned probabilities to potential threats to U.S. security or policy interests within the following six months. The September 15, 2000, issue contained an item on Colombia, which discussed threat from "rising insurgent violence and a weak economy." The Strategic Warning Committee also produced the *Strategic Warning Committee's Atrocities Watchlist*. Another warning intelligence product has been the *Warning Memorandum*, which served as a special warning notice. It focused on "a potential development of particularly high significance to U.S. interests."[34]

The Defense Intelligence Agency issues a number of regular and special warning reports designed to guide U.S. commands around the world. The *Weekly Intelligence Forecast* and *Weekly Warning Report* include assessments from the various commands. In addition, the *Quarterly Warning Forecast* reviews a wide range of potential events that could affect U.S. security interests. The DIA and the commands also publish two ad hoc products as issues arise: the *Warning Report*, an assessment of a specific warning issue considered to require the immediate, specific attention of senior U.S. officials within the Washington, D.C., area, and the *Watch Condition Change*, a notification of a change in the threat level presented by a specific warning problem.[35]

Defense warning system forecasts make up a set of DIA periodicals that "provide evaluation of critical threat issues that could reach crisis proportions in the period covered." The *Weekly Warning Forecast* covers the following two-week period, whereas the *Quarterly Warning Forecast* focuses on the coming year. The forecasts were distributed in hard copy to members of the Defense Warning System and other decision makers in the Washington, D.C., area and in message form to other recipients.[36]

ESTIMATES

The best-known estimative intelligence products are the National Intelligence Estimates (NIEs), which attempt to project existing military, political, and economic trends into the future and to estimate for policymakers the likely implications of such trends. In 1980 the House Committee on Foreign Affairs described the NIE as "a thorough assessment of a situation in the foreign environment which is relevant to the formulation of foreign, economic, and national security policy, and which projects probable future courses of action and developments." A Congressional Research Service (CRS) report explained that NIEs "represent the highest and most formal level of strategic analysis by the U.S. Intelligence Community." They are not predictions of the future, however, but judgments as to the likely course of events.[37]

Another CRS memorandum explained that NIEs "represent the coordinated judgments of the Intelligence Community, and thus represent the most authoritative assessment of the [Director of National Intelligence] with respect to a particular national security issue." In addition, the author noted, "Coordination of NIEs involves not only trying to resolve any interagency differences but also assigning confidence levels to the key judgments and rigorously evaluating the sources for them."[38]

Based on inputs from the Intelligence Community, NIEs are produced by the National Intelligence Council and intended for a variety of customers, from the president and National Security Council to other senior policymakers to analysts.[39] NIEs produced between 2000 and 2006 concerning Iraq, weapons of mass destruction, or terrorism included *Worldwide Biological Warfare Programs: Trends and Prospects Update* (December 2000), *Iraq's Continuing Programs for Weapons of Mass Destruction* (October 2002), *Nontraditional Threats to the U.S. Homeland Through 2007* (November 2002), *Foreign Missile Developments and Ballistic Missile Threat Through 2003* (February 2003), and *Trends in Global Terrorism: Implications for the United States* (April 2006).[40]

NIEs published in 2007 included *The Terrorist Threat to the US Homeland*; *Prospects for Iraq's Stability: Some Security Progress but Political Reconciliation Elusive*; and *Iran: Nuclear Intentions and Capabilities*. The first of those estimates stated, "The US Homeland will face a persistent and evolving terrorist threat over the next three years," and the "main threat comes from Islamic terrorist groups and cells, especially al-Qa'ida." In addition, the NIE stated, "We assess that al-Qa'ida will continue to try to acquire and employ chemical, biological, radiological, and nuclear material in attacks." The national estimate on prospects for Iraqi stability stated, "We assess, to the extent that Coalition forces continue to conduct robust counterinsurgency operations and mentor and support the Iraqi Security Forces (ISF), that Iraq's security will continue to improve modestly during the next six to 12 months but that levels of insurgent and sectarian violence will remain high. And the Iraqi Government will continue to struggle to achieve national-level political reconciliation and improved governance."[41]

The November 2007 NIE on Iranian nuclear capabilities proved controversial. In addition to its substance, the estimate contained an explanation of estimative language and the relationship of the terms used (from "remote" to "almost certainly"). It also contained the judgment (with high confidence) that in the fall of 2003, Iran had halted its nuclear weapons program—wherein the term "nuclear weapons program" was defined to mean nuclear weapon design, weaponization work, covert uranium conversion, and enrichment-related work.[42]

In June 2010, the Intelligence Community completed a National Intelligence Estimate on monitoring the latest Strategic Arms Reduction Treaty. Late that year, NIEs were completed on the situations in Afghanistan and Pakistan. The essence of the estimates asserted, according to media reports, that Pakistan's government was unwilling to halt its covert support for members of the Afghan Taliban who were attacking U.S. troops and that such support would make it difficult for American strategy in Afghanistan to succeed. In early 2011 an updated NIE on the Iranian nuclear program reportedly concluded that there was a split among Iran's rulers over whether to continue the pursuit of nuclear weapons.[43]

A more recent NIE is *The Global Cyber Threat to the US Information Infrastructure*, which stated, "We assess with high confidence that the increasing role of international companies and foreign individuals in US information technology supply chains and services will increase the potential for persistent, stealthy subversions." Other recent NIEs have included one on space vulnerabilities that focused on foreign laser threats to U.S. imagery and signals intelligence satellites and another about the situation in Afghanistan.[44]

NIEs are distilled into a separate President's Summary, which is distributed to the highest levels of the foreign policymaking community. Other national estimative products include Special Estimates (formerly Special National Intelligence Estimates), "short, tightly focused papers . . . designed to provide consumers with policy-relevant analysis needed under a short deadline," and Update Memoranda, which update a previous NIE "when new evidence, analysis, or perspective is available." In addition, NIE Memoranda are mini-NIEs, longer than Special Estimates but shorter than NIEs. A 1994 Special Estimate focused on Russian government failures to halt the spread of Russian arms and weapons technology.[45]

A shorter estimative product is the Intelligence Community Brief, a quickly prepared six-page paper focusing on a particular issue. It is produced under the auspices of a National Intelligence Officer, who is expected either to resolve any disagreements or to note those that remain unresolved. Briefs have included *The BW Threat to the Global and US Agricultural Sectors* (March 2001), *Smallpox: How Extensive a Threat?* (December 2001), and *Iraq: Unusual Logistical Activities in Preparation for an Anticipated US-Led Campaign* (May 2002).[46]

Beginning in late 1969 or early 1970, DIA produced Defense Intelligence Estimates (DIEs) and Special Defense Intelligence Estimates (SDIEs), which often covered topics similar to those examined by NIEs and SNIEs but also tended to deal in depth with military issues treated only briefly in NIEs and SNIEs. In the late 1980s, the DIEs and SDIEs were replaced by Defense Intelligence Assessments, which are intended to respond to "broad consumer interest by presenting comprehensive analysis on a policy-relevant event, situation, issue, or development in 5 to 25 pages." The assessments are targeted at planning and policy staff at various levels.[47]

Defense Intelligence Assessments concerning Iraq or al-Qaeda have included *Usama Bin Laden/Al-Qaida Information Operations* (September 1999), *Iraq's Nuclear, Biological, and Chemical Weapons and Missile Programs: Progress, Prospects, and Political Vulnerabilities* (May 2000), *Iraq's Weapons of Mass Destruction and Theater Ballistic Missile Programs: Post 11 September* (January 2002), and *Iraq's Reemerging Nuclear Program* (September 22, 2002). A Defense Intelligence Assessment produced by the DIA's National Center for Medical Intelligence (NCMI) is *Worldwide: New 2009-H1N1 Influenza Virus Poses Potential Threat to U.S. Forces* (May 1, 2009).[48] The assessment on Iraq's reemerging nuclear weapons program, approximately twenty pages in length, contained sections on the lack of inspections as a catalyst, activities at a variety of locations, acquisition and processing of uranium, facilities for uranium enrichment, the design and fabrication of nuclear weapons and components (with subsections on neutron generators and integration of a warhead with a missile delivery system), possible assistance from foreign nations (including Pakistan), and the timeline for completion of a nuclear weapon.[49]

Another DIA estimative product is the Defense Intelligence Report (DIR), "a concise report that addresses a topic of interest to senior policymakers and commanders." A January 2010 report, prepared by the NCMI, was titled *Haiti: Health Risks and Health System Impacts Associated with Large-Scale Earthquake*. A June 2012 DIR was titled *Libya: Terrorists Now Targeting U.S. and Western Interests*.[50]

Estimative intelligence produced by the State Department's Bureau of Intelligence and Research is sometimes contained in the bureau's Intelligence Research Report series but is mainly found in memoranda circulated within the department. The Drug Enforcement Administration (DEA) also produces an estimative product, the annual Narcotics Intelligence Estimate, a compendium of worldwide production, smuggling, and trafficking trends and projections.[51]

In January 2008, the U.S. Coast Guard's Intelligence Coordination Center produced a sixty-three-page estimate, titled *National Maritime Terrorism Threat Assessment*, containing sections on alternative analysis, analytic assumptions, four varieties of threats (international terrorists, domestic extremists, lone offenders, and insider saboteurs), and the outlook for the future.[52]

REPORTS AND STUDIES

The Intelligence Community also produces a variety of reports and studies whose main focus is the analysis of political, economic, military, or social matters. Intelligence Community analytical products include Intelligence Community Assessments (ICAs), which are twenty- to thirty-page research papers that provide a "detailed logic trail on key national security issues," and Sense of Community Memos, one-page memos that evaluate current or day-to-day events.[53]

ICAs published since 1998 include *The Foreign Biological and Weapons Threat to the United States* (July 1998), *Iraq: Steadily Pursuing WMD Capabilities* (December 2000), *Regional Consequences of Regime Change in Iraq* (January 2003), *Principal Challenges in Post Saddam Iraq* (January 2003), and *Global Water Security* (February 2012). Sense of Community Memos include *Iraq: Saddam's Next Moves* (March 4, 1999) and *Niger: No Recent Uranium Sales to Iraq* (August 5, 2003).[54]

Among the interagency products generated since 1995 are a CIA-DIA Joint Intelligence Memorandum, *Chinese Nuclear Testing: Racing Against a Comprehensive Test Ban* (October 5, 1994); an October 19, 1995, report by the DCI Interagency Balkan Task Force, *Croatia: Tomislav Mercep's Role in Atrocities*, prepared by analysts from CIA, DIA, and NSA; and a February 1999 study, *Iraq: WMD and Delivery Capabilities After Operation Desert Fox*, produced by CIA, National Imagery and Mapping Agency (NIMA), DIA, and Central Command (CENTCOM) analysts. A joint CIA-FBI May 2003 product is *Al-Qa'ida Remains Intent on Defeating US Immigration Inspections*.[55]

The Joint Atomic Energy Intelligence Committee produced *Iran's Nuclear Program: Building a Weapons Capability* (February 1993), *Iraq's Nuclear Weapons Program: Elements of Reconstitution* (September 1994), *Reconstitution of Iraq's Nuclear Weapons Program: An Update* (October 1997), and *Reconstitution of Iraq's Nuclear Weapons Program: Post Desert Fox* (June 1999).[56]

A 2005 examination of Intelligence Community analytical products identified four types of analytical products. These include the twenty-five-page Intelligence Assessments (IA), which are the primary form of in-depth research and can focus on larger analytic questions or include great detail on a narrower, complex issue. In addition, there is the Strategic Perspective Series (SPS), which focuses on a key strategic issue and often cuts across analytic disciplines or regions, for instance, addressing Muslims in the European Union or China's global strategic ambitions. Serial Fliers (SFs) are short, concise memorandum-style products, generally a few pages in length, on a single topic of current relevance. There are also research projects or papers, which are the primary means employed to explore new analytic research areas and may culminate in an IA, SPS, or SF.[57]

CIA products include the Intelligence Assessment (IA), the Intelligence Memorandum (IM), and the Intelligence Note (IN). The IA is five pages or longer (with no upper limit), with a key findings section of one-page and optional appendices. The IM is a two- to five-page product, with a short summary paragraph, while the IN is a memo written in response to policymaker questions.[58] CIA reports and studies since 2000 have included *Colombia: Burgeoning Coca Industry in Norte de Santander* (August 17, 2000), *Afghanistan: An Incubator for International Terrorism* (March 27, 2001), *Pursuing the Bin Laden Financial Target* (April 2001), *Identifying al-Qa'ida's Donors and Fundraisers: A Status Report* (February 27, 2002), *Iraq and al-Qa'ida Interpreting a Murky Relationship* (June 21, 2002), *Iraq: Expanding WMD Capabilities Pose Growing Threat* (August 1, 2002), *Iraq's Hunt for Aluminum Tubes: Evidence of a Renewed Uranium Enrichment Program* (September 2002), *Saddam's Timeline for Using WMD* (October 2002), *Al-Qa'ida in Sudan, 1992–1996: Old School Ties Lead Down Dangerous Paths* (March 10, 2003), *Afghanistan Camps Central to 11 September Plot: Can Al-Qa'ida Train on the Run?* (June 20, 2003), *Misreading Intentions: Iraq's Reaction to Inspections Created Picture of Deception* (January 5, 2005), and *Libya: Al-Qa'ida Establishing Sanctuary* (July 6, 2012).[59]

A more recently established type of CIA report, the Red Cell Special Memorandum, is produced by the CIA's Red Cell, which is responsible for taking an "out-of-the-box" approach to provoke thought and offer alternative viewpoints. A February 5, 2010, report, "What If Foreigners See the United States as an 'Exporter of Terrorism?,'" focused on the implications of U.S.-born individuals' engaging in terrorism against non-U.S. targets. Another Red Cell Special Memorandum from March 2010 was titled "Afghanistan: Sustaining Western European Support for the NATO-led Mission—Why Counting on Apathy Might Not Be Enough."[60]

DIA produces the Defense Analysis Report–Terrorism series, which includes updates on the participation of former detainees at Guantánamo Bay in terrorist activities subsequent to their release. A January 2009 report noted that of "the 531 Guantanamo Bay (GTMO) detainees transferred from Department of Defense custody, 18 are confirmed and 43 are suspected to be subsequently reengaging in terrorist activities." A more recent report focused on the status of the North Korean nuclear weapons program, particularly whether it was capable of placing a nuclear warhead on a ballistic missile.[61]

DIA centers also produce reports and studies devoted to specific topics: missile and space intelligence, medical intelligence, and underground facilities. Products of the missile and space intelligence center have included *Egypt: ATGM System Inventory and Acquisitions* (September 23, 2013), *Mistral System Description* (September 24, 2013), *FN-6 Propulsion* (September 4, 2013), *SA-14 System Description* (October 1, 2013), *CH-LS-13 Laser Weapon System Summary* (October 7, 2013), *SA-16 SAM Summary* (October 9, 2013), and *CSA-3a (HN-5) SAM Summary* (October 21, 2013).[62]

Analytical studies by the State Department's INR were for many years published under three titles: Current Analyses, Assessments and Research, and Policy

Assessments. Those studies analyzed recent or ongoing events, assessed prospects and implications for the following six months, analyzed the context or results of past policies, or assessed policy options. The distinct series were subsequently merged into a single Intelligence Research Report series, although INR has since produced products labeled as "Assessments" or "Briefs."[63] INR products since 1998 have included *Bin Ladin's Jihad: Political Context* (August 28, 1998), *Afghanistan: Taliban External Ambitions* (October 28, 1998), *Iceland: Old Friend on Base, Not on Whales, Climate* (August 6, 2001), *Niger: Sale of Uranium to Iraq Is Unlikely* (March 1, 2002), and *Poland: Facing Fallout from Secret Detention Center* (December 16, 2005).[64]

Department of Energy intelligence products include the department's Technical Intelligence Notes, such as *Iraq: High Strength Aluminum Tube Procurement* (April 11, 2001), *Iraq's Gas Centrifuge Program: Is Reconstitution Underway?* (August 17, 2001), *Iraq: Seeking Additional Aluminum Tubes* (December 2001), and *Iraq: Gas Centrifuge Program Recounted* (November 8, 2002). Products produced by Z Division have included *Challenges of Advanced Nuclear Weapon Development in India* (November 1998) and *Challenges of Advanced Nuclear Weapon Development in Pakistan* (May 1999).[65]

The military service intelligence organizations also produce their own reports and studies, sometimes in response to DIA tasking as part of the Defense Intelligence Production Program. National Ground Intelligence Center (NGIC) products concerning Iraq have included *Iraq: Specialty Aluminum Tubes Are an Exercise in Deception* (November 25, 2002), *Iraq: Current Chemical Warfare Capabilities* (October 23, 2001), and *Complex Environments: Battle of Fallujah I, April 2004* (n.d.). Other products, NGIC Assessments, have included *China: Medical Research on Bio-effects of Electromagnetic Pulse and High-Power Microwave Radiation* (August 17, 2005), *Foreign Ground Forces Exercise and Training Assessment (EXTRA): China (Guanghzou Military Region)—January 2003 to December 2004* (September 12, 2005), and *China: Z-10 Attack Helicopter Program—2007 Update* (May 21, 2008).[66]

The Office of Naval Intelligence (ONI) has produced *Chinese Space-Based Remote Sensing Programs and Ground Processing Capabilities* (September 1994), *Worldwide Threat to U.S. Navy and Marine Forces [deleted], Volume II: Country Study—China* (December 1993), and *Chinese Exercise Strait 961: 8–25 March 1996* (May 1996). In 1995 it produced Special Intelligence Studies titled *Algeria*; *Air Defenses: Iraqi Threat to Naval Forces—95*; *Cuban Helicopter Operations, Training, and Tactics*; and *Maritime Surveillance Capabilities—Iran*.[67] In the last several years, ONI has produced a number of large unclassified studies, including *China's Navy 2007: The People Liberation Army's Navy—a Modern Navy with Chinese Characteristics* (August 2009) and *Iran's Naval Forces: From Guerilla Warfare to a Modern Naval Strategy* (Fall 2009).

The National Air and Space Intelligence Center (NASIC) periodically produces the unclassified *Ballistic and Cruise Missile Threat*. A 2001 study was *China: Country Force Assessment—Air Force*, while a 2002 product was the SECRET *Foreign MRBM/IRBM/ICBM C3 Capabilities—China*. A January 2005 SECRET NASIC Analysis Report was "The Future of China's F-11 FLANKER Program." Among its 2009 and 2010 products are the open source studies *Chinese Airship Research Association* (June 2, 2009) and *Current and Potential Applications of Chinese Aerostats (Airships)* (March 23, 2010).[68]

Unclassified DEA intelligence reports have included *China: Country Brief* (February 2004), *Heroin Trafficking in Russia's Troubled East* (October 2003), *The Drug*

Trade in the Caribbean: A Threat Assessment (September 2003), *Changing Dynamics of Cocaine Production in the Andean Region* (June 2002), *Russian Organized Crime Groups* (January 2002), and *Heroin Signature Program—2011*.[69]

Reports produced by unified command intelligence organizations include "Libya: Extremism in Libya Past, Present, Future" (September 5, 2012) and "Venezuela (VEN): The Bad Things Chavez Does . . . " (August 15, 2003), produced by the Africa Command and Southern Command intelligence organizations, respectively.[70]

LEADERSHIP PROFILES

Both the CIA and DIA devote extensive effort to preparing biographic sketches of key civilian and military officials, respectively. The sketches serve as both reference and analytical documents, providing basic information on the individual, as well as exploring his or her motivations and attempting to provide explanations for past and likely future actions. A CIA Leadership Profile is often prepared for a particular meeting.[71]

Before the demise of the Soviet Union, the CIA produced *Biographic Handbooks* that provided biographies of key Soviet officials who made and implemented policy, as well as of many individuals in lesser positions. Thus, the April 1977 *Biographic Handbook, USSR Supplement IV,* includes profiles on twenty-one officials, including the chief editor of *Pravda*, the Minister of Construction, and the chairman of the board for the State Bank.[72] A few years earlier in 1974, the CIA prepared a nine-page Biographic Report on Yitzhak Rabin, who served as Israeli prime minister on a number of occasions, including in the 1990s. The report contained seven sections: "Prime Minister," "The Sons of the Founding Generation," "Military Hawk/Political Dove," "The General as Ambassador," "Exodus Hero," "Strong Belief and Extreme Caution," and "A Fighting Family."[73]

In January 1991, the CIA produced the *Political and Personality Handbook of Iraq*, which examined Saddam Hussein's Iraq (especially the structure of the government, the Ba'ath Party, and the security services), Saddam's inner and outer circles, and key military commanders. Twelve years later, DIA prepared *Iraqi Key Regime Personalities*, containing brief biographies of high-value targets the United States wanted to capture. The entry for Amir-Hamudi Hasan al-Sadi, Saddam's science advisor, stated that Saddam "has knowledge of Iraq's WMD programs and personnel . . . [ellipsis in original] oversaw interaction of the National Monitoring Directorate (NMD) with UN inspections . . . holds doctorate from University of London in chemical engineering."[74]

In 1996 the CIA prepared a profile, a little over two pages long, titled "Usama Bin Ladin: Islamic Extremist Financier," that examined his background, his actions in response to the Soviet invasion of Afghanistan, his stay in Sudan, and his support of Islamic jihadist training and operations.[75]

The DIA prepares military leadership profiles (formerly known as biographic sketches) of foreign military officers, even junior officers. The agency prepared its first sketch of Andres Rodriguez no later than April 1966, at which time he was commander of the 1st Cavalry Division of the Paraguayan Army. In February 1989, he led the coup that deposed longtime Paraguayan dictator Alfredo Stroessner.[76] Each sketch usually runs several single-spaced pages and provides information on the subject's position, significance, politics, personality, personal life, and professional career. An October

2003 military leadership profile of General Cao Gangchuan notes his positions, including as Minister of National Defense and Vice Chairman of the Central Military Commission. It notes, "Cao is primarily concerned with military, not political, matters and likely adhere to the party line on a range of issues." It also states, "Cao emphasizes applying Jiang Zemin's 'three represents' by highlighting science and technology to 'realize new development of weaponry.'" The sketch is reproduced in Figure 14.2.

Sketches of Iraqi military officials completed prior to the Persian Gulf War include those of Lieutenant General Husayn Rahsid Mohammad Hasan (December 18, 1990), chief of the General Staff at the time, and Lieutenant General Ayyad Futayih Khalifa Al Rawi (October 18, 1990), commander of the Iraqi Republican Guard forces.[77]

REFERENCE DOCUMENTS AND DATABASES

The DIA also produces or delegates production of the Defense Intelligence Reference Document (DIRD) series. A DIRD can be a onetime or recurring (often encyclopedic) study on military forces and force capabilities, infrastructure, facilities, systems, and equipment, or associated topics for military planning and operations. It may consist of foldout wall charts intended as reference aids or be a more typical book-length publication.[78]

A May 1995 DIRD, prepared by the National Ground Intelligence Center, is *Nonlethal Technologies—Worldwide*. The eighty-one-page document covers a variety of nonlethal technologies, including chemical, biotechnical, acoustic, electromagnetic, kinetic, and informational. The section on electromagnetic efforts examined laser weapons in the United Kingdom, France, China, Israel, and other countries. More recent NGIC-produced DIRDs include *Assessment of Chinese Radiofrequency Weapon Capabilities* (April 2001) and *Chinese Ground Propulsion Technology* (July 2002). The former DIRD includes sections on research into high-power radio frequency (RF) susceptibility and propagation as well as on evidence for RF weapon development programs and postulated Chinese RF weapons. The later DIRD contains an overview of Chinese engines as well as sections on military ground propulsion, engine subsystems, and engine specifications and parameters.[79] A 1996 DIRD prepared by the Office of Naval Intelligence is *Foreign Oceanographic Research and Development with Naval Implications—China*. DIRDs prepared by the National Air and Space Intelligence Center include *Iraq L-29 UAV Conversion* (December 30, 1999) and *Foreign Weaponized Unmanned Aerial Vehicles* (December 2001). The latter contains sections on electronic warfare systems, unmanned attack drone systems, unmanned combat aerial vehicles, and advanced concepts.[80]

The Marine Corps Intelligence Activity is responsible for producing another kind of reference document: the *Country Handbook*. Each handbook is intended to provide, for each nation, information on "its geography, history, government, military forces, and communications and transportation networks." Its purpose is to "familiarize military personnel with local customs and area knowledge." Handbooks, which can reach about three hundred pages, include those prepared for Afghanistan, Kuwait, Malaysia, Vietnam, Botswana, China, Norway, Peru, and a multitude of other nations.[81]

One database is the Terrorist Identities Datamart Environment (TIDE), a collection of data about individuals whom the Intelligence Community believes pose a

FIGURE 14.2 Military Leadership Profile of General Cao Gangchuan

CHINA
General *CAO* Gangchuan
October 2003

Military
Leadership
Profile

UNCLASSIFIED

(U) Photo date: 2002

(U) *NAME:* General *Cao* Gangchuan (pronounced "tsaow") (STC 2580/0474/1557), People's Liberation Army (PLA).

(U) *POSITION:* Minister of National Defense and State Councilor since March 2003; Vice Chairman, Central Military Commission (CMC), since November 2002; member, Central Committee, Chinese Communist Party (CCP) Congress, since September 1997.

(S//NF) *SIGNIFICANCE:* Gen Cao succeeded Chi Haotian as Vice Chairman of the Central Military Commission (CMC), the PLA's senior military policy-making body, at the 16th Party Congress in November 2002 and as Minister of National Defense and State Councilor at the National People's Congress (NPC) in March 2003. Gen Cao is the second-most senior military officer in the PLA.

(S//NF) Before November 2002, Cao was Director of the General Armament Department (GAD).

(b)(1)

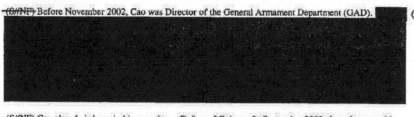

(S//NF) Cao already is busy in his capacity as Defense Minister. In September 2003 alone, he met with defense representatives from at least ten countries.

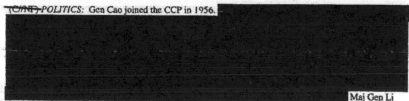

(C//NF) *POLITICS:* Gen Cao joined the CCP in 1956.

Maj Gen Li Andong, who was Cao's former personal assistant when Cao was GAD director, frequently travels with Cao and is generally considered to be his protégé.

(continues)

424

FIGURE 14.2 (Continued)

SECRET//NOFORN//X1

(C//NF) Cao is primarily concerned with military, not political, matters and likely will adhere to the party line on a range of issues. In late 1999, he reportedly began a stern lecture on the "evils" of Falungong at a GAD-sponsored meeting by comparing PLA deployment times with those of the Falungong (probably referring to the April 1999 demonstration in Beijing). Noting that Falungong moves 10,000 people more rapidly than the PLA does, Cao reportedly stated, "I think they are political, don't you?" Cao emphasizes applying Jiang Zemin's "three represents" by highlighting science and technology to "realize new development of weaponry" and high-technology acquisitions to support the PLA's modernization and participation in a high-technology war.

(C//NF)   (b)(1)

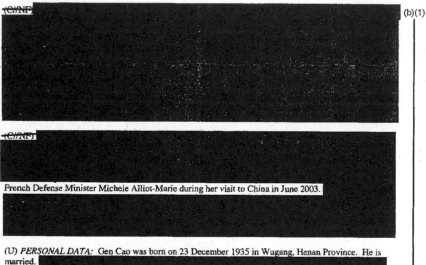

(C//NF)

French Defense Minister Michele Alliot-Marie during her visit to China in June 2003.

(U) *PERSONAL DATA:* Gen Cao was born on 23 December 1935 in Wugang, Henan Province. He is married.

(U) *CAREER:* Gen Cao began his military career when he entered the Third Artillery Ordnance School in Nanjing in 1954, after which he became a teacher at the First Artillery Technical School. In 1956, he enrolled at the Dalian Russian Language Special School. In 1957, he went to the Soviet Union to study artillery, graduating from the prestigious Soviet Advanced Military Engineering School in 1963.

(S) Upon returning to China, Cao was assigned to the General Logistics Department (GLD), serving first in the Ordnance Department (1963-1969) and later in the Equipment Department (1969-1975). In April 1975, when the Equipment Department was transferred from the GLD to the General Staff Department (GSD), Cao was assigned as a staff officer with and later deputy director of the Comprehensive Planning Section of the GSD Equipment Department.
Official biographies and state news accounts report that he served in the GSD Equipment Department

SECRET//NOFORN//X1

continuously from 1975 until 1989.

(S) In late 1979, Cao was noted as serving in the GSD Equipment Department, where he remained until 1989, when he was the senior Deputy Director. He was named a major general when PLA ranks were restored in July 1988. In 1989, he became Director of the GSD Military Affairs Department

In November 1992, Cao was named Deputy Chief of the General Staff. He was promoted to lieutenant general in 1993 and became the senior Deputy Chief of the General Staff in August 1995. In November 1996, he was named director of the Commission of Science, Technology, and Industry for National Defense (COSTIND),

(S//NF) In April 1998, Cao was named director of the newly created GAD, which was formed to centralize PLA weapons development and procurement.

In October 1998, commensurate with his position as head of one of the PLA general departments, Cao was named a member of the CMC. As GAD Director, Gen Cao exercised central oversight of the PLA acquisition system and research and development (R&D)

During China's launch of its first man in space on the Shenzhou 5 in October 2003, Cao communicated with the astronaut live on television,

(S)

He has visited Russia and other former Soviet republics several times.

Cao visited the United Kingdom and Israel in June 2000—

Cao visited the Ukraine in April 2001. He traveled to Italy, France, and South Africa in June 2002.

(U) Questions and comments may be addressed to

threat to the United States. It serves as a database from which watch lists are generated and distributed to airlines, law enforcement, border posts, and U.S. consulates. At its inception in 2003, there were fewer than 100,000 listed individuals; that number had grown to about 435,000 by 2007. By the end of 2013, over 1 million identities appeared in the TIDE. A somewhat smaller database is the Terrorist Screening Database, "the U.S. government's consolidated watchlist." As of mid-2014, there were 680,000 names in the database.[82]

A DNI-sponsored project is the Library of National Intelligence, which aims to "create an authoritative repository for all disseminated intelligence products," making it a database of intelligence reports. As of September 2008, it included 750,000 products, with 20,000 being added each week.[83]

Databases also include signature libraries or manuals. Among the material compromised by Jonathan Jay Pollard was the *RASIN* (*Radio Signal Notation*) manual, which "lists the physical parameters of every known signal . . . and links all the known communications links then used by the Soviet Union." Other libraries contain chemical signatures, which allow analysts to identify the laboratory or plant that produces a specific chemical, as well as nuclear material signatures and foreign instrumentation signals.[84]

The utility of databases or data repositories is significantly augmented by the development of search tools that allow analysts to quickly sort through the massive data gathered by U.S. collection efforts. One DNI project has been the Knowledge Discovery and Dissemination Program, which aims "to enable an analyst to utilize large complex and varied data sets that he has not seen before to produce actionable intelligence." Another DNI project is the Automated Low-Level Analysts and Description of Diverse Intelligence (ALADDIN) Video Program, which seeks "to enable an analyst to query large video data sets to quickly and reliably locate those video clips that show a specific type of event."[85]

An NSA-developed search engine, ICREACH, has been accessible to more than 1,000 intelligence analysts at twenty-three U.S. government agencies. It was constructed to share more than 850 billion records concerning phone calls, e-mails, cell phone locations, and Internet chats. Work on ICREACH goes back to at least 2007, with the CIA, FBI, DEA, and DIA as core members of the effort. The CIA turned to Amazon Web Services to develop a cloud computing capability for the agency. It was reported in July 2014 that the entire Intelligence Community would use this cloud.[86]

DOMESTIC INTELLIGENCE ANALYSIS

A number of organizations produce domestic intelligence on their own: the FBI, Department of Homeland Security (DHS), and Northern Command. In other instances, domestic intelligence results from collaboration between one or more organizations.

FBI finished intelligence products include Intelligence Assessments ("intended to convey analytic conclusions about an issue or threat based on a comprehensive analysis of all available information"), Intelligence Bulletins (which are more limited in focus and depth than the assessment and highlight new developments or trends), and Intelligence Studies (which "are comprehensive analytical works intended to convey conclusions about issues or threats" based on comprehensive analysis of all available information. The difference between assessments and studies is that the former are "tailored to the needs of intelligence consumers" and intended to be "timely, and forward-looking." Two further FBI intelligence products are Intelligence Memoranda (IMs) and Special Threat Event Assessments (SETAs). IMs are products for senior management officials, with condensed reporting and analysis. SETAs are intended to inform law enforcement and security planners of a potential threat to an event, its venue, or its participants.[87]

An April 15, 2004, SECRET/NOFORN FBI product was *The Terrorist Threat to the US Homeland: An FBI Assessment.* The key issue was the risk of another attack on the United States by foreign or domestic terrorists. Among the specific topics examined were the threats posed by al-Qaeda, other Sunni extremists, other Islamic extremist groups, domestic terrorism, and Islamic terrorist trends.[88]

Another FBI assessment, produced in September 2007, was *A Threat Assessment for Domestic Terrorism, 2005–2006.* The thirty-two-page report covered the activities of anarchist extremists, animal rights extremists and ecoterrorists, antiabortion extremists, black separatist extremists, militias/sovereign citizen extremists, and white supremacist extremists. Among its conclusions was that "animal rights extremists/ecoterrorists committed the overwhelming majority of criminal incidents during 2005 and 2006."[89]

Other FBI intelligence assessments have included *Tactics Used by Eco-terrorists to Detect and Thwart Law Enforcement Operations* (April 15, 2004), *White Supremacist Infiltration of Law Enforcement* (October 17, 2006), *State of the Domestic White Nationalist Extremist Movement in the United States* (December 13, 2006), *White Supremacy: Contexts and Constraints for Suicide Terrorism* (April 20, 2007), and *White Supremacist Recruitment of Military Personnel Since 9/11* (July 7, 2008). An FBI Intelligence Bulletin, produced in October 2006, is *Ghost Skins: The Fascist Path of Stealth* (October 17, 2006).[90]

The Department of Homeland Security's Office of Intelligence & Analysis produces several different intelligence products. *Homeland Intelligence Today* is an unclassified daily product delivered to the secretary, DHS operational component leadership, and other federal organizations with "homeland-relevant analysis and reporting." The Intelligence Assessment, which can range from unclassified to top secret, "provides strategic analysis on a variety of topics that impact homeland security" and may be devoted to a single or multiple topics. A Homeland Security Note, which also may vary from unclassified to top secret, provides information on a recent or current event or development, while a HSIN SLIC (Homeland Security Information Network State and Local Community of Interest) Information Warning, an HSIN SLIC Information Notification, or an HSIN SLIC Information Alert provides information on "rapidly developing situations or events that may have homeland implications. HSIN SLIC documents are unclassified."[91]

The Roll Call Release is produced for frontline law enforcement officers to "highlight emergent terrorist or criminal techniques or tactics they may encounter in the field," while the Fire Line is a "sister product to the *Roll Call Release* and is intended for fire, rescue, and emergency management personnel to assist in planning, response, and mitigation." The Reference Aid "provides an informational overview of an issue, development, key figure, or lasting trend." The first two products come only in unclassified form, while a reference aid may range from unclassified to top secret.[92]

Intelligence Assessments include *Leftwing Extremists Likely to Increase Use of Cyber Attacks over the Coming Decade* (January 26, 2009), *Threats to College Sports and Entertaining Venues and Surrounding Areas* (January 26, 2009), *Rightwing Extremism: Current Economic and Political Climate Fueling Resurgence in Radicalization and Recruitment* (April 7, 2009), *Mexico: Sonora-Based Threats to U.S. Border Security* (August 26, 2010), *Domestic Violent Extremists Pose Increasing Threat to Government Officials and Law Enforcement* (July 22, 2014), *Potential Tactics and Targets in ISIL-Linked Western Attacks* (October 17, 2014), and *Sovereign Citizen Extremist Ideology Will Drive Violence at Home, During Travel, and at Government Facilities* (February 5, 2015).[93]

Also among the assessments is the SECRET/NOFORN *Homeland Security Threat Assessment: Evaluating Threats, 2009–2014.* Topics covered in the assessment are chemical, biological, radiological, and nuclear threats; cyber and explosive threats to critical infrastructure; threats to health security; international and domestic terrorism; illicit travel and migration; and illicit border activity. Among the specifics examined are an anthrax attack on a major urban center, an influenza pandemic, a cyber attack on the nation's electric grid system, and a state failure that leads to the movement of nuclear weapons.[94]

Homeland Security Notes have included *2009 Fourth of July Security Awareness* (June 30, 2009), *Internet Sites Allow Detailed Surveillance and Pre-attack Planning* (August 12, 2010), *Insider Threat to Utilities* (July 18, 2011), and *Self-Identified Anarchist Extremists Target Urban "Gentrification" Sites with Arson* (July 23, 2013). An HSIN SLIC Initial Notification is *India: HUJI Claims Responsibility for India High Court Bombing* (September 7, 2011).[95]

Roll Call Release products have included *Incendiary Devices: Potential Terrorist Attack Method* (April 18, 2010), *Suspicious Activity Reporting (SAR): Observation/Surveillance* (October 15, 2012), *Improvised Explosive Device Concealed in Human Remains* (May 24, 2013), and *Attacks in Russia Highlight Terrorists' Continued Interest in Targeting Individuals Using Mass Transit* (January 9, 2014). Fire Line products have included *Cyanide: Awareness of Potential Threat* (October 31, 2012) and *Terrorist Tradecraft—Impersonation: Use of Stolen, Cloned, or Repurposed Vehicles* (January 18, 2013). Two reference aids are *National Socialist Movement* (September 26, 2008) and *Violent Extremist Profile: Walter Edmund Bond* (October 24, 2013). The reference aid covering Bond, who was sentenced to twelve years in prison for arson attacks directed against three businesses he claimed were involved in the exploitation of animals, discusses his personal background, grievances, and ideological influences.[96]

Additional DHS Office of Intelligence & Analysis products include the *Homeland Security Monitor* (a collection of articles on a theme or topic), the Homeland Information Note (a nonanalytic product concerning upcoming events and issues), *Daily Intelligence Highlights* (which provides operational and intelligence information to federal, state, and local officials and focuses on "perceived threats in light or actual or potential vulnerabilities"), and the *Snapshot* (which provides the tactics, techniques, and procedures of an emerging event). Three of the four products are produced only at the unclassified level, while *Highlights* may be top secret.[97]

The Northern Command intelligence center also produces intelligence products relevant to homeland security, including special events assessments such as the SECRET/NOFORN *2009 United States Presidential Inauguration, Washington D.C.*

15–24 January 2009 and *Space Shuttle Launch Baseline Assessment*. The later examined "the static vulnerabilities and general threats associated with space shuttle launch operations in [the 2009 fiscal year]."⁹⁸

A joint product involving DHS is the *Joint Intelligence Bulletin*, produced with the FBI "in response to significant or emerging threats or developments"; it can be either unclassified or secret. Bulletin topics since May 2011 have included al-Qaeda's interest in targeting trains, the potential for lone wolves to conduct retaliatory attacks after the death of Osama bin Laden, the threat to aviation posed by al-Qaeda, the potential for events in Afghanistan to incite violence in the United States, indicators in light of the Boston Marathon bombings, and the impact of the ISIS (ISIL) social message on Western youth.⁹⁹

Another set of joint products are those prepared by DHS, the FBI, and a variety of federal, regional, state, and local entities. Those products have included threat assessments for the 2009 inauguration of Barack Obama, the 2009 and 2011 Super Bowls, and the 2011 Major League Baseball All-Star Game—all designated Unclassified/For Official Use Only. The inaugural assessment—prepared in concert with the National Counterterrorism Center, National Geospatial-Intelligence Agency, Northern Command, and several regional fusion centers, as well as the Capitol Police—examined international and domestic terrorism threats, the criminal threat environment, the foreign intelligence and cyber threat environments, the WMD threat environment, threats to facilities, the transportation threat environment, and other scenarios of concern.¹⁰⁰

The joint assessment for the 2011 Major League Baseball All-Star Game, played on July 12 at Chase Field in Phoenix, was prepared by the FBI, DHS, Phoenix Police Department, Arizona Counterterrorism Information Center, and Maricopa County Sheriff's Office. It examined possible threats from international terrorism, domestic terrorism, lone wolves, and foreign intelligence services; criminal threat trends; the criminal, cyber, and transportation threat environments; and intelligence gaps. The common element in each case was the lack of any credible threat information.¹⁰¹

Notes

1. Central Intelligence Agency, "Political Analyst," www.cia.gov/careers (accessed October 19, 2010).

2. "Leadership Analyst," and "Psychological/Psychiatric Analyst," at www.cia.gov/careers (accessed October 19, 2010); Central Intelligence Agency, "Analytical Positions," https://www.cia.gov/careers/opportunities/analytical (accessed August 28, 2014).

3. "Economic Analyst," www.cia.gov/careers (accessed October 19, 2010); Central Intelligence Agency, "Analytical Positions."

4. "Military Analyst" and "Science, Technology, and Weapons Analyst," both at www.cia.gov/careers (accessed October 19, 2010); Central Intelligence Agency, "Analytical Positions."

5. "Open Source Officer (Foreign Media Analyst)," www.cia.gov/careers (accessed October 19, 2010).

6. "Counterterrorism Analyst," and "Counterintelligence Threat Analyst," both at www.cia.gov/careers (accessed October 19, 2010); Central Intelligence Agency, "Analytical Positions."

7. Sharon Bertsch McGrayne, *The Theory That Would Not Die: How Bayes' Rule Cracked the Enigma Code, Hunted Down Russian Submarines & Emerged Triumphant from Two Centuries of Controversy* (New Haven, CT: Yale University Press, 2011).

8. Address by John C. Gannon Chairman, National Intelligence Council to the Washington College of Law at American University, Washington, D.C., October 6, 2000, https://www.cia.gov /news-information/speeches-testimony/2000/gannon_speech_10062000.html; "Targeting Analyst," www.cia.gov/careers (accessed October 19, 2010).

9. See Jeffrey W. Seifter, Congressional Research Service, *Data Mining: An Overview*, December 16, 2004, http://fas.org/irp/crs/RL31798.pdf; Mary DeRosa, *Data Mining and Data Analysis for Counterterrorism* (Washington, DC: Center for Strategic and International Studies, 2004); Office of the Director of National Intelligence, *2009 Data Mining Report or the Period February 1, 2009 Through December 31, 2009*, n.d.; Inspector General, Department of Defense, *Alleged Misconduct by Senior DOD Officials Concerning the ABLE DANGER Program and Lieutenant Colonel Anthony A. Shaffer, U.S. Army Reserve*, September 18, 2006; Anthony A. Shaffer, *Operation Dark Heart: Spycraft and Special Ops on the Frontlines of Afghanistan—and the Path to Victory* (New York: St. Martin's, 2010); Stuart Koschade, "A Social Network Analysis of Jeremiah Islamiyah: The Applications to Counterterrorism and Intelligence," *Studies in Conflict & Terrorism* 29 (2006): 559–575; Patrick Radden Keefe, "Can Network Theory Thwart Terrorists?," *New York Times Magazine*, March 12, 2006, 16, 18; Nancy K. Hayden et al., *Dynamic Social Network Analysis: Present Roots and Future Fruits* (Washington DC: Defense Threat Reduction Agency, 2009).

10. Department of the Army, *Counterinsurgency*, FM 3-24, December 2006, B-14.

11. Ibid.

12. Kenneth Lieberthal, *The U.S. Intelligence Community and Foreign Policy: Getting Analysis Right* (Washington, DC: Brookings Institution, 2009), 4; Steve Vogel, "For Intelligence Officers, a Wiki Way to Connect the Dots," www.washingtonpost.com, August 27, 2009, http://www .washingtonpost.com/wp-dyn/content/article/2009/08/26/AR2009082603606.html.

13. Lieberthal, *The U.S. Intelligence Community and Foreign Policy*, 4.

14. Office of the Director of National Intelligence, "ODNI Fact Sheet," October 2010, http://www.dni.gov/files/documents/ODNI%20Fact%20Sheet_2011.pdf.

15. Central Intelligence Agency, *A Consumer's Guide to Intelligence*, July 1995, 30; Walter Pincus, "PDB, the Only News Not Fit for Anyone Else to Read," *Washington Post*, August 27, 1994, A7; Cord Meyer, *Facing Reality: From World Federalism to the CIA* (New York: Harper & Row, 1980), 352; Zbigniew Brzezinski, *Power and Principle: Memoirs of the National Security Advisor, 1977–1981* (New York: Farrar, Straus & Giroux, 1983), 224; Alfred Cumming, Congressional Research Service, Memorandum to Sen. Dianne Feinstein, Subject: Congress as a Consumer of Intelligence Information, December 14, 2005, 5; Russell Jack Smith, *The Unknown CIA: My Three Decades with the Agency* (New York: Berkeley, 1992), 173–174; William Newton, "The President's Daily Brief," *Studies in Intelligence* 26, no. 4 (Winter 1982): 57–66; Lieberthal, *The U.S. Intelligence Community and Foreign Policy*, 9; Helgerson, *Getting to Know the President*, xii.

16. Meyer, *Facing Reality*, 352; Loch K. Johnson, "Glimpses into the Gems of American Intelligence: The *President's Daily Brief* and the National Intelligence Estimate," *Intelligence and National Security* 23, no. 3 (June 2008): 333–370, at 333.

17. Loch K. Johnson, "Making the Intelligence 'Cycle' Work," *International Journal of Intelligence and Counterintelligence* 1, no. 4 (Winter 1986–1987): 1–23; Pincus, "PDB, the Only News Not Fit for Anyone Else to Read"; Cumming, Congressional Research Service, "Memorandum to Sen. Dianne Feinstein"; Richard J. Kerr and Peter Dixon Davis, "Ronald Reagan and the President's Daily Brief," *Studies in Intelligence* (Winter 1998–1999): 51–56; Johnson, "Glimpses into the Gems of American Intelligence," 337; George Tenet with Bill Harlow, *At the Center of the Storm: My Years at the CIA* (New York: HarperCollins, 2007), 31.

18. Central Intelligence Agency, "Bin Ladin Preparing to Hijack US Aircraft and Other Attacks," December 4, 1998; Central Intelligence Agency, "Bin Ladin Determined to Strike in US," *President's Daily Brief*, August 6, 2001; Thomas S. Blanton ed., National Security Archive Electronic Briefing Book No. 116, *The President's Daily Brief*, April 12, 2004, Section 1, http://www2 .gwu.edu/~nsarchiv/NSAEBB/NSAEBB116.

19. Murray Waas, "Key Bush Intelligence Briefing Kept from Panel," www.nationaljournal.com, November 22, 2005, http://www.nationaljournal.com/whitehouse/key-bush-intelligence-briefing -kept-from-hill-panel-20051122; Bob Woodward, *Obama's Wars* (New York: Simon & Schuster, 2010), 120–121; Philip Mudd, *Take Down: Inside the Hunt for Al Qaeda* (Philadelphia: University of Pennsylvania Press, 2013), 58–59; Guy Benson, "Report: Obama Briefed on ISIS Threat for More Than a Year," http://townhall.com, September 2, 2014, http://townhall.com/tipsheet/guybenson /2014/09/02/report-obama-briefed-on-isis-threat-for-more-than-a-year-n1886225.

20. Cumming, Congressional Research Service, Memorandum to Sen. Dianne Feinstein, Subject: Congress as a Consumer of Intelligence Information; U.S. District Court for the District of Columbia, *United States of America v. I. Lewis Libby*, March 3, 2006, *Government's Response to Court Orders of February 23 and February 27, 2006*, 6; Lieberthal, *The U.S. Intelligence Community and Foreign Policy*, 10–11.

21. Christina A. Cawley, "Breaking Through the Barrier: DIA's First PDB Briefer," *Communiqué* (Summer 2012): 26–27; Amber Corrin, "Technology's Evolving Role in White House Intelligence," www.c4isrnet.com, April 18, 2014, http://archive.c4isrnet.com/article/20140417/ C4ISRNET04/304170003/Technology-s-evolving-role-White-House-intelligence; Central Intelligence Agency, "DI Written Products," n.d.

22. Central Intelligence Agency, *A Consumer's Guide to Intelligence*, 30; Meyer, *Facing Reality*, 353–354; Cumming, Congressional Research Service, Memorandum to Sen. Dianne Feinstein, Subject: Congress as a Consumer of Intelligence Information, 11; Central Intelligence Agency, "DI Written Products."

23. U.S. Congress, Select Committee on Intelligence, *Report on U.S. Intelligence Community's Prewar Intelligence Assessments on Iraq*, July 7, 2004, 36; "Saudi Terrorist Threat Growing," *Senior Executive Intelligence Brief*, February 6, 2001; "Terrorism: Bin Ladin Planning High-Profile Attacks," *Senior Executive Intelligence Brief*, June 30, 2001; "Terrorism: Bin Ladin Plans Delayed but Not Abandoned," *Senior Executive Intelligence Brief*, July 13, 2001; "Terrorism: Terrorist Groups Said Cooperating on US Hostage Plot," May 23, 2001, in National Security Archive Electronic Briefing Book No. 381, *The Central Intelligence Agency's 9/11 File*, ed. Barbara Elias-Sanborn, June 19, 2012, http://www2.gwu.edu/~nsarchiv/NSAEBB/NSAEBB381; others are available at the CIA's Electronic Reading Room (www.foia.cia.gov).

24. Central Intelligence Agency, "DI Written Products"; U.S. Congress, Senate Select Committee on Intelligence, *Review of the Terrorist Attacks on U.S. Facilities in Benghazi, Libya, September 11–12, 2012 Together with Additional Views*, January 15, 2014, 13n52–54, 25n97.

25. Central Intelligence Agency, "DI Written Products."

26. Dana Priest and William M. Arkin, *Top Secret America: The Rise of the New American Security State* (Boston: Little, Brown, 2011), 81; Office of the Director of National Intelligence, "ODNI Fact Sheet."

27. Central Intelligence Agency, *A Consumer's Guide to Intelligence*, 30.

28. Susan McFarland and Mike Zwicke, "MID: Providing Insights for Policymakers and Warfighters," *Communiqué* (September 1996): 12–13; Bill Gertz, "Russia Dodges Chemical Arms Ban," *Washington Times*, February 4, 1997, A1, A20; Bill Gertz, "Hidden Iraqi Scuds Threaten Israel, Gulf Countries," *Washington Times*, February 11, 1998, A1, A12; Cumming, Congressional Research Service, Memorandum to Sen. Dianne Feinstein, Subject: Congress as a Consumer of Intelligence Information, 11; U.S. Congress, Select Committee on Intelligence, *Report on U.S. Intelligence Community's Prewar Intelligence Assessments on Iraq*, 233, 396; Defense Intelligence Agency, "Unsubstantiated Cases," *Defense Intelligence Digest*, April 9, 2009, http://www.dia.mil/public_ affairs/foia; U.S. Congress, Senate Select Committee on Intelligence, *Review of the Terrorist Attacks on U.S. Facilities in Benghazi, Libya, September 11–12, 2012 Together with Additional Views*, 10.

29. Central Intelligence Agency, *A Consumer's Guide to Intelligence*, 31; NMJIC Executive Highlights No. 170-00, September 7, 2000; U.S. Congress, Select Committee on Intelligence, *Report on U.S. Intelligence Community's Prewar Intelligence Assessments on Iraq*, 38.

30. Central Intelligence Agency, *A Consumer's Guide to Intelligence*, 31; letter, Kathleen P. Turner, Defense Intelligence Agency, to Hon. John Rockefeller IV, October 26, 2005.

31. Central Intelligence Agency, *A Consumer's Guide to Intelligence*, 31; James Bamford, *Body of Secrets: Anatomy of the Ultra-Secret National Security Agency, from the Cold War Through the Dawn of a New-Century* (New York: Doubleday, 2001), 515.

32. George Lardner Jr. and Walter Pincus, "On This Network, All the News Is Top Secret," *Washington Post*, March 3, 1992, A1, A9.

33. Ibid.

34. Central Intelligence Agency, *A Consumer's Guide to Intelligence*, 36; U.S. Congress, Select Committee on Intelligence, *Report on U.S. Intelligence Community's Prewar Intelligence Assessments on Iraq*, 397; DCI Strategic Warning Committee, *The DCI Strategic Warning Committee's Watchlist*, September 15, 2000, 10.

35. Central Intelligence Agency, *A Consumer's Guide to Intelligence*, 36–37.

36. Ibid., 37.

37. U.S. Congress, House Committee on Foreign Affairs, *The Role of Intelligence in the Foreign Policy Process* (Washington, DC: U.S. Government Printing Office, 1980), 235; Richard A. Best Jr., Congressional Research Service, *Intelligence Estimates: How Useful to Congress?*, November 21, 2006, http://fas.org/sgp/crs/intel/RL33733.pdf, 1.

38. Cumming, Congressional Research Service, Memorandum to Sen. Dianne Feinstein, Subject: Congress as a Consumer of Intelligence Information, 10. For more on NIEs (past and present), see Johnson, "Glimpses into the Gems of American Intelligence"; Lieberthal, *The U.S. Intelligence Community and Foreign Policy*, 12–15.

39. Central Intelligence Agency, *A Consumer's Guide to Intelligence*, 35. On recent developments concerning the NIEs, see Kristan J. Wheaton, "The Revolution Begins on Page Five: The Changing Nature of NIEs," *International Journal of Intelligence and Counterintelligence* 25, no. 2 (Summer 2012): 330–349.

40. U.S. Congress, Select Committee on Intelligence, *Report on U.S. Intelligence Community's Prewar Intelligence Assessments on Iraq*, 227; Commission on the Intelligence Capabilities of the United States Regarding Weapons of Mass Destruction, *Report to the President of the United States* (Washington, DC: U.S. Government Printing Office, 2005), 197n3, 215n239, 238n631; National Intelligence Council, *Declassified Key Judgments of the National Intelligence Estimate "Trends in Global Terrorism: Implications for the United States,"* April 2006, http://www.dni.gov.

41. National Intelligence Council, *The Terrorist Threat to the US Homeland*, Key Judgments, July 2007; National Intelligence Council, *Prospects for Iraq's Stability: Some Security Progress but Political Reconciliation Elusive*, Key Judgments, August 2007.

42. National Intelligence Council, *Iran: Nuclear Intentions and Capabilities*, Key Judgments, November 2007. For more on this NIE, see David Sanger, *The Inheritance: The World Obama Confronts and the Challenges to American Power* (New York: Harmony Books, 2009), 3–13, 17–20; Richard A. Best Jr., Congressional Research Service, *Intelligence Estimates*, 10–12.

43. U.S. Congress, Senate Select Committee on Intelligence, *Report of the Select Committee United States Senate Covering the Period January 3, 2009 to January 4, 2011* (Washington, DC: U.S. Government Printing Office, 2011), 11; Elisabeth Bumiller, "Intelligence Reports Offer Dim View of Afghan War," *New York Times*, December 15, 2010, A1, A12; Ken Dilanian and David S. Cloud, "Grim Reports Cast Doubt on War Progress," *Los Angeles Times*, December 15, 2010, A1, A8; Adam Entous, "U.S. Spies: Iran Split on Nuclear Program," *Wall Street Journal*, February 17, 2011, A1, A14; Greg Miller and Joby Warrick, "U.S. Report Finds Debate in Iran on Building Nuclear Bomb," www.washingtonpost.com, February 19, 2011, http://www.washingtonpost.com /wp-dyn/content/article/2011/02/18/AR2011021805632.html.

44. William M. Arkin, "#learnedtoday," December 13, 2013, https://twitter.com; Ken Dilanian and David S. Cloud, "Intelligence Study Glum on Afghan War," *Los Angeles Times*, January 12, 2012, A1, A5.

45. Central Intelligence Agency, *A Consumer's Guide to Intelligence*, 35; Bill Gertz, "Yeltsin Can't Curtail Arms Spread," *Washington Times*, September 27, 1994, A3.

46. Cumming, Congressional Research Service, Memorandum to Sen. Dianne Feinstein, Subject: Congress as a Consumer of Intelligence Information, 10; U.S. Congress, Select Committee on Intelligence, *Report on U.S. Intelligence Community's Prewar Intelligence Assessments on Iraq*, 145; National Intelligence Council, *Iraq: Unusual Logistical Activities in Preparation for an Anticipated US-Led Campaign*, May 2, 2002.

47. Harold P. Ford, *Estimative Intelligence: The Purposes and Problems of National Intelligence Estimating* (Washington, DC: Defense Intelligence College, 1989), 136; Central Intelligence Agency, *A Consumer's Guide to Intelligence*, 31.

48. Defense Intelligence Agency, *Usama Bin Ladin/Al-Qaida Information Operations*, September 1999; U.S. Congress, Senate Select Committee on Intelligence, *Report on the U.S. Intelligence Community's Prewar Intelligence Assessments on Iraq*, 185, 232; Commission on the Intelligence Capabilities of the United States Regarding Weapons of Mass Destruction, *Report to the President of the United States*, 41; National Center for Medical Intelligence, DI-1812-1544-09, *Worldwide: New 2009-H1N1 Influenza Virus Poses Potential Threat to U.S. Forces*, May 1, 2009.

49. Defense Intelligence Agency, Defense Intelligence Assessment, *Iraq's Reemerging Nuclear Weapon Program*, September 2002, iii.

50. Central Intelligence Agency, *A Consumer's Guide to Intelligence*, 35; Defense Intelligence Agency, *Haiti: Health Risks and Health System Impacts Associated with Large-Scale Earthquake*, January 14, 2010; U.S. Congress, Senate Select Committee on Intelligence, *Review of the Terrorist Attacks on U.S. Facilities in Benghazi, Libya, September 11–12, 2012 Together with Additional Views*, 10n41.

51. Central Intelligence Agency, *A Consumer's Guide to Intelligence*, 35; U.S. Congress, House Committee on Appropriations, *Department of Commerce, Justice, and State, the Judiciary and Related Agencies Appropriations for FY 1986*, pt. 7 (Washington, DC: U.S. Government Printing Office, 1985), 492.

52. U.S. Coast Guard Intelligence Coordination Center, *National Maritime Terrorism Threat Assessment*, January 7, 2008, 7.

53. Cumming, Congressional Research Service, Memorandum to Sen. Dianne Feinstein, Subject: Congress as a Consumer of Intelligence Information, 10.

54. U.S. Congress, Senate Select Committee on Intelligence, *Report on the U.S. Intelligence Community's Prewar Intelligence Assessments on Iraq*, 75, 215, 386, 390; Commission on the Intelligence Capabilities of the United States Regarding Weapons of Mass Destruction, *Report to the President of the United States*, 198n23, 200n41, 247n834; National Intelligence Council, *Global Water Security*, Intelligence Community Assessment, February 2, 2012, http://fas.org/irp/nic/water.pdf.

55. Central Intelligence Agency and Defense Intelligence Agency, *Chinese Nuclear Testing: Racing Against a Comprehensive Test Ban*, October 5, 1994; DCI Interagency Balkan Task Force, *Croatia: Tomislav Mercep's Role in Atrocities*, October 19, 1995, http://www.foia.cia.gov/sites/default/files/document_conversions/89801/DOC_0001063835.pdf; Central Intelligence Agency and Federal Bureau of Investigation, *Al-Qa'ida Remains Intent on Defeating US Immigration Inspections*, May 20, 2003.

56. Joint Atomic Energy Intelligence Committee, *Iran's Nuclear Program: Building a Weapon's Capability*, February 1993; Commission on the Intelligence Capabilities of the United States Regarding Weapons of Mass Destruction, *Report to the President of the United States*, 198n14, n. 18n22.

57. Cumming, Congressional Research Service, Memorandum to Sen. Dianne Feinstein, Subject: Congress as a Consumer of Intelligence Information, 11.

58. Central Intelligence Agency, "DI Written Products."

59. Central Intelligence Agency, *Terrorist: Recruiting and Operating Behind Bars*, August 20, 2002, http://fas.org/irp/cia/product/ctc082002.pdf; Central Intelligence Agency, *Colombia:*

Burgeoning Coca Industry in Norte de Santander, August 17, 2000; U.S. Congress, Senate Select Committee on Intelligence, *Report on the U.S. Intelligence Community's Prewar Intelligence Assessments on Iraq*, 186; Commission on the Intelligence Capabilities of the United States Regarding Weapons of Mass Destruction, *Report to the President of the United States*, 198n23; 200n41, 247n834; U.S. Congress, Senate Select Committee on Intelligence, *Review of the Terrorist Attacks on U.S. Facilities in Benghazi, Libya, September 11–12, 2012 Together with Additional Views*, 10; Central Intelligence Agency, *Afghanistan: An Incubator for International Terrorism*, March 27, 2001; Central Intelligence Agency, *Pursuing the Bin Ladin Financial Target*, April 2001; Central Intelligence Agency, *Identifying al-Qa'ida's Donors and Fundraisers: A Status Report*, February 27, 2002; Central Intelligence Agency, *Al-Qa'ida in Sudan, 1992–1996: Old School Ties Lead Down Dangerous Paths*, March 10, 2003; Central Intelligence Agency, *Afghanistan Camps Central to 11 September Plot: Can al-Qa'ida Train on the Run?*, June 20, 2003; Central Intelligence Agency, *Misreading Intentions: Iraq's Reaction to Inspections Created Picture of Deception*, January 5, 2006.

60. CIA Red Cell, "What If Foreigners See the United States as an 'Exporter of Terrorism?," February 5, 2010; CIA Red Cell, "Afghanistan: Sustaining Western European Support for the NATO-led Mission—Why Counting on Apathy Might Not Be Enough," March 11, 2010.

61. Defense Intelligence Agency, *Terrorism: Former Guantanamo Bay Detainee Terrorism Trends*, Defense Analysis Report—Terrorism, January 7, 2009, http://www.defense.gov/news/returntothefightfactsheet2.pdf; Ken Dilanian, "Intelligence Agencies Split on N. Korea," *Los Angeles Times*, April 13, 2013, A3; Thom Shanker, David E. Sanger, and Eric Schmitt, "Pentagon Finds Nuclear Strides by North Korea," *New York Times*, April 12, 2013, A1, A10.

62. Title pages obtained from DIA in response to a FOIA request.

63. Central Intelligence Agency, *A Consumer's Guide to Intelligence*, v.

64. Bureau of Intelligence and Research, *Bin Ladin's Jihad: Political Context*, August 28, 1998; Bureau of Intelligence and Research, *Afghanistan: Taleban External Ambitions*, October 28, 1998; Bureau of Intelligence and Research, *Iceland: Old Friend on Base, Not on Whales, Climate*, August 6, 2001; Bureau of Intelligence and Research, *Niger: Sale of Uranium to Iraq Is Unlikely*, March 1, 2002; Bureau of Intelligence and Research, *Poland: Facing Fallout from Secret Detention Center*, December 16, 2005.

65. U.S. Congress, Senate Select Committee on Intelligence, *Report on the U.S. Intelligence Community's Prewar Intelligence Assessments on Iraq*, 48; Commission on the Intelligence Capabilities of the United States Regarding Weapons of Mass Destruction, *Report to the President of the United States*, 199n32, 199n35, 209n160; William Burr and Jeffrey T. Richelson, eds., National Security Archive Electronic Briefing Book No. 451, *Proliferation Watch: U.S. Intelligence Assessments of Potential Nuclear Powers, 1977–2001*, December 16, 2013, http://www2.gwu.edu/~nsarchiv/nukevault/ebb451.

66. Commission on the Intelligence Capabilities of the United States Regarding Weapons of Mass Destruction, *Report to the President of the United States*, 210n111, 245n82; National Ground Intelligence Center, *Complex Environments: Battle of Fallujah I, April 2004*, n.d.; NGIC assessments were obtained by the National Security Archive under the FOIA.

67. Documents obtained under the FOIA; Office of Naval Intelligence, *Office of Naval Intelligence Command History 1995*, 1996, 54–55.

68. National Air and Space Intelligence Center, NASIC-OS-0037 2010, *Current and Potential Applications of Chinese Aerostats (Airships)*, March 23, 2010; National Air Intelligence Center, *China: Country Force Assessment—Air Force*, 2001; National Air Intelligence Center, *Foreign MRBM/IRBM/ICBM C3 Capabilities—China*, April 2002; National Air and Space Intelligence Center, NASIC Analysis Report, *The Future of China's F-11 FLANKER Program*, January 6, 2005.

69. Drug Enforcement Administration, "Intelligence Reports," www.justice.gov/dea/pubs/intel.htm (accessed October 27, 2010); Drug Enforcement Administration, *Heroin Signature Program—2011*, February 2013.

70. U.S. Congress, Senate Select Committee on Intelligence, *Review of the Terrorist Attacks on U.S. Facilities in Benghazi, Libya, September 11–12, 2012 Together with Additional Views*, 11; U.S. Southern Command, Joint Intelligence Center, "Venezuela (VEN): The Bad Things Chavez Does," August 15, 2003.

71. Cumming, Congressional Research Service, Memorandum to Sen. Dianne Feinstein, Subject: Congress as a Consumer of Intelligence Information, 11; Central Intelligence Agency, "DI Written Products."

72. Central Intelligence Agency, *Biographic Handbook, USSR Supplement IV*, April 1977.

73. Central Intelligence Agency, *Biographic Handbook: Yitzhak RABIN, Prime Minister of Israel*, June 1974.

74. Jeffrey T. Richelson, ed., National Security Archive Electronic Briefing Book No. 167, *Saddam's Iron Grip*, October 18, 2005, Document 6, http://www2.gwu.edu/~nsarchiv/NSAEBB/NSAEBB167/06.pdf; Defense Intelligence Agency, *Iraqi Key Regime Personalities*, 2003, 63.

75. Central Intelligence Agency, *Usama bin Ladin: Islamic Extremist Financier*, 1996.

76. Defense Intelligence Agency, "Biographic Sketch: Andres Rodriguez," April 1966.

77. Sketches and profiles released under the FOIA.

78. Central Intelligence Agency, *A Consumer's Guide to Intelligence*, 32.

79. National Ground Intelligence Center, *Nonlethal Technologies—Worldwide*, May 1995, vii–ix; National Ground Intelligence Center, NGIC-1867-0285-01, *Assessment of Chinese Radiofrequency Weapon Capabilities*, April 2001, v; National Ground Intelligence Center, NGIC-1841-0178-02, *Chinese Ground Propulsion Technology*, July 2002, v.

80. ONI, *Foreign Oceanographic Research and Development with Naval Implications*, 1996; National Air Intelligence Center, NAIC-1361-2253-00, *Iraq L-29 UAV Conversion*, December 30, 1999; National Air Intelligence Center, *Foreign Weaponized Unmanned Aerial Vehicles*, December 2001, v–vii.

81. The handbooks can be found at www.publicintelligence.net.

82. Karen DeYoung, "Terror Database Has Quadrupled in Four Years," www.washingtonpost.com, March 25, 2007, http://www.washingtonpost.com/wp-dyn/content/article/2007/03/24/AR2007032400944.html; Government Accountability Office, GAO-12-476, *Terror Watchlist: Routinely Assessing Impacts of Agency Actions Since the December 25, 2009, Attempted Attack Could Help Inform Future Efforts*, May 2012, 6; Jeremy Scahill and Ryan Devereaux, "Barack Obama's Secret Terrorist—Tracking System, by the Numbers," *Intercept*, August 5, 2014, https://firstlook.org/theintercept/2014/08/05/watch-commander; National Counterterrorism Center, *Directorate of Terrorist Identities (DTI) Strategic Accomplishments 2013*, 2014, 2.

83. Lieberthal, *The U.S. Intelligence Community and Foreign Policy*, 4.

84. M. E. "Spike" Bowman, "The Drumbeats for Clemency for Jonathan Jay Pollard Reverberate Again," *Intelligencer* (Winter/Spring 2011): 31–34; Robert Clark, *The Technical Collection of Intelligence* (Washington, DC: CQ Press, 2010), 242, 244, 276; Foreign Denial and Deception Analysis Committee, *The Jonathan Jay Pollard Espionage Case: A Damage Assessment*, October 30, 1987, 19, 38, in National Security Archive Electronic Briefing Book No. 407, *The Jonathan Jay Pollard Spy Case: The CIA's 1987 Damage Assessment Declassified*, ed. Jeffrey T. Richelson, January 9, 2013.

85. Office of the Director of National Intelligence, *2012 Data Mining Report for the Period January 1, 2012 through December 31, 2012*, n.d., 5–6.

86. Ryan Gallagher, "The Surveillance Engine: How the NSA Built Its Own Secret Google," *Intercept*, August 25, 2014, https://firstlook.org/theintercept/2014/08/25/icreach-nsa-cia-secret-google-crisscross-proton; Frank Konke, "How the CIA Partnered with Amazon and Changed Intelligence," *Defense One*, July 11, 2014, http://www.defenseone.com/technology/2014/07/how-cia-partnered-amazon-and-changed-intelligence/88555 (accessed July 11, 2014); Henry Kenyon, "Intelligence Agencies Move Towards Single-Cloud," *Breaking Defense*, December 17, 2012, http://breakingdefense.com/2012/12/intelligence-agencies-move-towards-single-super-cloud.

87. Federal Bureau of Investigation, *FBI Information Sharing Report 2011*, 2011, Appendix B.

88. Federal Bureau of Investigation, *The Terrorist Threat to the US Homeland: An FBI Assessment*, April 15, 2004.

89. Federal Bureau of Investigation, *A Threat Assessment for Domestic Terrorism, 2005–2006*, September 18, 2007, 3 and passim.

90. Documents obtained via FOIA requests or from www.publicintelligence.net.

91. Government Accountability Office, GAO-14-397, *DHS Intelligence Analysis: Additional Actions Needed to Address Analytic Priorities and Workforce Challenges*, June 2014, 38; Department of Homeland Security, *2012 Intelligence Enterprise Product Line Brochure*, 2012, 6–7.

92. Government Accountability Office, GAO-14-397, *DHS Intelligence Analysis*, 38; Department of Homeland Security, *2012 Intelligence Enterprise Product Line Brochure*, 6.

93. *Leftwing Extremists Likely to Increase Use of Cyber Attacks over the Coming Decade*, January 26, 2009, http://fas.org/irp/eprint/leftwing.pdf; *Rightwing Extremism: Current Economic and Political Climate Fueling Resurgence in Radicalization and Recruitment*, April 7, 2009, http://fas .org/irp/eprint/rightwing.pdf; *Homeland Security Threat Assessment: Evaluating Threats, 2008– 2013*, 2009, https://info.publicintelligence.net/DHS-Threats2008-2013.pdf; *Threats to College Sports and Entertaining Venues and Surrounding Areas*, January 26, 2009, https://publicintelligence .net/ufouo-threats-to-college-sports-and-entertainment-venues-and-surrounding-areas; *Mexico: Sonora-Based Threats to U.S. Border Security*, August 26, 2010, https://publicintelligence.net /ufouoles-lulzsec-release-dhs-mexico-sonora-based-threats-to-u-s-border-security; *Domestic Violent Extremists Pose Increasing Threat to Government Officials and Law Enforcement*, July 22, 2014, https://publicintelligence.net/dhs-domestic-violent-extremists; *Potential Tactics and Targets in ISIL-Linked Western Attacks*, October 17, 2014, https://publicintelligence.net/dhs-isil-attack -tactics; *Sovereign Citizen Extremist Ideology Will Drive Violence at Home, During Travel, and at Government Facilities*, February 5, 2015, http://fas.org/irp/eprint/sovereign.pdf.

94. Office of Intelligence and Analysis, Department of Homeland Security, *Homeland Security Threat Assessment: Evaluating Threats, 2009–2014*, 2009, 2, 10–11, 13, 17.

95. *2009 Fourth of July Security Awareness*, June 30, 2009; *Internet Sites Allow Detailed Surveillance and Pre-attack Planning*, August 12, 2010, https://publicintelligence.net/ufouo-internet-sites -allow-detailed-surveillance-and-pre-attack-planning; *Insider Threat to Utilities*, July 18, 2011, https://info.publicintelligence.net/DHS-InsiderThreat.pdf; *Self-Identified Anarchist Extremists Target Urban "Gentrification" Sites with Arson*, July 23, 2013, https://publicintelligence.net/dhs -anarchist-gentrification-arson; *India: HUJI Claims Responsibility for India High Court Bombing*, September 7, 2011, https://publicintelligence.net/ufouo-dhs-huji-claims-responsibility-for-india -high-court-bombing.

96. Office of Intelligence and Analysis, Department of Homeland Security, *Incendiary Devices: Potential Terrorist Attack Method*, April 18, 2010; Office of Intelligence and Analysis, Department of Homeland Security, *Suspicious Activity Reporting (SAR): Observation/Surveillance*, October 15, 2012, https://publicintelligence.net/dhs-fbi-observation; Office of Intelligence and Analysis, Department of Homeland Security, *Improvised Explosive Device Concealed in Human Remains*, May 24, 2013, https://publicintelligence.net/dhs-fbi-dead-body-bombs; Office of Intelligence and Analysis, Department of Homeland Security, *Attacks in Russia Highlight Terrorists' Continued Interest in Targeting Individuals Using Mass Transit*, January 9, 2014, https://publicintelligence.net/ dhs-fbi-nctc-mass-transit-attacks; Office of Intelligence and Analysis, Department of Homeland Security, *Cyanide: Awareness of Potential Threat*, October 31, 2012, https://publicintelligence.net /dhs-fbi-cyanide-awareness; Office of Intelligence and Analysis, Department of Homeland Security, *Terrorist Tradecraft—Impersonation: Use of Stolen, Cloned, or Repurposed Vehicles*, January 18, 2013, https://publicintelligence.net/dhs-fbi-cloned-vehicles; Office of Intelligence and Analysis, Department of Homeland Security, *National Socialist Movement Reference Aid*, September 26, 2008, https://publicintelligence.net/ufouo-lulzsec-release-dhs-national-socialist-movement -reference-aid; Office of Intelligence and Analysis, Department of Homeland Security, *Violent*

Extremist Profile: Walter Edmund Bond, October 24, 2013, https://publicintelligence.net/dhs -walter-bond.

97. Department of Homeland Security, *2012 Intelligence Enterprise Product Line Brochure*, 6–7.

98. Northern Command, *2009 United States Presidential Inauguration, Washington D.C. 15–24 January 2009*, December 19, 2009; Northern Command, *Space Shuttle Launch Baseline Assessment*, January 9, 2009.

99. DHS, *2012 Intelligence Enterprise Product Line Brochure*, 6; *Early 2010 Al-Qaʻida Interest in Targeting Trains on 11 September 2011*, May 5, 2011, https://info.publicintelligence.net/DHS-FBI -911Trains.pdf; *Potential for Unaffiliated Individuals to Conduct Retaliatory Attacks in the Homeland Following the Death of Usama Bin Ladin*, May 9, 2011, https://publicintelligence.net/ufouo -dhs-fbi-potential-for-retaliatory-attacks-following-the-death-of-osama-bin-laden; *Al Qaʻida and the Threat to General Aviation*, September 2, 2011, https://publicintelligence.net/ufouo-dhs-fbi -al-qaeda-and-the-threat-to-general-aviation; *Recent Events in Afghanistan Could Incite Homegrown Violent Extremist in the United States*, March 14, 2012, https://publicintelligence.net/ufouo -dhs-fbi-intelligence-bulletin-on-homegrown-extremist-retaliation-for-afghan-massacre; *Indicators and Protective Measures in Light of Boston Marathon Explosions*, April 16, 2013, https://public intelligence.net/dhs-fbi-boston-marathon-indicators.

100. Department of Homeland Security, Washington Regional Threat and Analysis Center, U.S. Capitol Police, Maryland Coordination and Analysis Center, Federal Bureau of Investigation, National Counterterrorism Center Virginia Fusion Center, National Geospatial-Intelligence Agency, and the U.S. Northern Command, *56th Presidential Inauguration: Joint Threat Assessment*, January 7, 2009, 2–7.

101. Federal Bureau of Investigation, Phoenix Police Department, Arizona Counter Terrorism Information Center, Department of Homeland Security, and Maricopa County Sheriff's Office, *82nd Major League Baseball All-Star Game: Joint Special Event Threat Assessment*, June 17, 2011.

15

COUNTERINTELLIGENCE

Foreign intelligence operations may attempt to acquire U.S. national security secrets; manipulate and distort the facts and reality presented to U.S. policymakers by manipulating the intelligence collected or through covert influence operations; detect, disrupt, and counter U.S. national security operations (including clandestine collection and special operations); and obtain critical technologies and other information to enhance their military capabilities or for economic gain.[1]

Counterintelligence (CI) is defined by Executive Order 12333, as amended in 2008, as "information gathered and activities conducted to identify, deceive, exploit, disrupt or protect against espionage, other intelligence activities, sabotage or assassinations conducted for or on behalf of foreign powers, organizations or persons, or their agents or other international terrorist organizations or activities."[2] Under this definition one can identify six components of counterintelligence activity:

- *Investigation* aimed at detecting U.S. citizens or others who operate on behalf of foreign national or terrorist intelligence organizations
- *Collection* of information, employing open and clandestine sources, on foreign (including terrorist) intelligence and security services and their activities
- *Evaluation* of defectors and prospective agents
- *Research, analysis, and production* concerning the structure, personnel, and operations of foreign intelligence and security services
- *Disruption and neutralization* of intelligence and security services or activities hostile to the United States
- *Support*, via provision of functional services, to other intelligence or operational activities.[3]

These activities serve to fulfill the objectives stated in *The National Counterintelligence Strategy of the United States*, the most recent version of which was issued in 2009:

- Secure the nation against foreign espionage and electronic penetration
- Protect the integrity of the U.S. intelligence system
- Support national policy and decisions
- Protect U.S. economic advantage, trade secrets, and know-how
- Support U.S. armed forces.[4]

THE FOREIGN INTELLIGENCE THREAT

Foreign intelligence and security services and their activities—those of friendly as well as hostile governments—are the focus of collection and analysis by a variety of U.S. intelligence and security organizations, including, but not limited to, the Central Intelligence Agency (CIA), the National Security Agency (NSA), the Federal Bureau of Investigation (FBI), the Defense Intelligence Agency (DIA), the Defense Security Service (DSS), the Army Counterintelligence Center, the Army Intelligence and Security Command's 902nd Military Intelligence Group, the Naval Criminal Investigative Service, and the Air Force Office of Special Investigations. Thus, the counterintelligence community is partially a subset of the U.S. Intelligence Community but also has members from outside the community.

Some nations that are allies of the United States employ their intelligence services to engage in activities inimical to U.S. economic interests, such as industrial espionage. The French Directorate General of External Security penetrated several U.S. companies, including IBM, Texas Instruments, and Bell Textron. A French government document, apparently obtained by the CIA, indicated a broad effort to obtain information about the work of U.S. aerospace companies. Other allies, including Germany, Israel, Japan, and South Korea, have also been involved in economic/industrial espionage. Targets of such collection activities, according to a 2013 report by the Defense Security Service, included information systems, electronics, lasers, optics, sensors, and aeronautic systems technologies.[5]

Of course, the intelligence communities of several nations have also been involved in operations inimical to U.S. national security. The Russian, Israeli, South Korean, Cuban, and Chinese intelligence services have received intelligence from within the CIA, FBI, DIA, Office of Naval Intelligence (ONI), State Department Bureau of Intelligence and Research (INR), and other national security institutions, as indicated by the cases of Aldrich Ames (CIA), Harold Nicholson (CIA), Larry Wu-Tai Chin (CIA), Robert Hanssen (FBI), Earl Pitts (FBI), Richard Miller (FBI), Ana Bellen Montes (DIA), Walter Kendall Myers (INR), Jonathan Jay Pollard (Naval Investigative Service), John Walker (U.S. Navy), James Wilbur Fondren Jr. (Pacific Command), Benjamin Bishop (Pacific Command contractor), and Peter Lee (Los Alamos National Laboratory).[6]

An attempted Chinese penetration of the CIA took place between 2005 and 2010. Glenn Duffie Shriver was indicted in the Eastern District of Virginia in 2010 and charged with making false statements to the CIA in a 2007 employment application and 2010 interview. He would admit to being recruited by three People's Republic of China (PRC) intelligence offices while living in Shanghai in 2004 and given the option of attempting to join the Foreign Service or the CIA. He also acknowledged that he had lied when he claimed that he had not had any contact with or received money from any foreign government or intelligence service. The indictment charged that he had met with PRC intelligence officers on several occasions and received $70,000 from them.[7]

Collectively, Ames, Nicholson, Pitts, and Hanssen were able to provide information about the identities of Soviets/Russians giving intelligence to the CIA, about technical surveillance operations, and about the identities of CIA personnel. Pollard provided an enormous number of documents, including more than 800 classified Top Secret documents, to Israel's Scientific Liaison Bureau, along with 1,500 intelligence summaries he stole on his own initiative. The documents provided information on Palestine Liberation Organization (PLO) headquarters in Tunisia, specific capabilities of Tunisian and Libyan air defense systems, Iraqi and Syrian chemical warfare production capabilities (including detailed satellite imagery), Soviet arms shipments to Syria and other Arab states, naval forces, port facilities, the MiG-29 fighter, and Pakistan's nuclear program. Also included was an assessment of Israeli military capabilities. Montes provided information on highly sensitive U.S. intelligence operations directed against Cuba. Chin, who worked for the CIA's Foreign Broadcast Information Service (FBIS), "reviewed, translated and analyzed classified documents from covert and overt human and technical collection sources," while Lee examined the feasibility of detecting submerged submarines via radar imagery. Both provided intelligence on their activities to Chinese intelligence.[8]

The Russian Foreign Intelligence Service (SVR) also operated a group of eleven illegals in the United States, some of whom arrived in the 1990s and were not arrested until June 2010, although the FBI was aware of their activities for a decade. The illegals' objectives were to become "Americanized," recruit sources who could penetrate U.S. policymaking institutions, and collect information that could be transmitted back to the SVR. That those arrested were charged with money laundering or acting as agents of a foreign power (or both), rather than espionage, reflects their apparent lack of success in actually acquiring secrets. They would soon be swapped for four Russians. A twelfth suspect would be detained and deported.[9]

Another Russian ring of eleven was indicted in 2012, charged with acting as unregistered foreign agents and accused of smuggling U.S. microchips out of the country. Then, in January 2015, a trio of Russians were charged, in New York, with being undeclared agents of the economic intelligence component of the SVR—although two possessed diplomatic immunity. Evgeny Buryakov, who operated under nonofficial cover, as an employee of the Manhattan office of a Russian bank, was alleged in the indictment to be interested in "destabilization of the markets" and automated trading alogirithms.[10]

A 1999 report by the CIA's Counterintelligence Center stated that Russian intelligence was sabotaging international peacekeeping operations in the Balkans. In addition, it was reported that the SVR had spied on personnel of the UN Special Commission responsible for investigating Iraq's compliance with its pledge to eliminate its capacity for producing weapons of mass destruction (WMD) and that the SVR may have passed on some of the information collected to Iraq. Subsequent to the March 2003 invasion of Iraq, a Joint Forces Command study stated that the SVR had passed information, sometimes inaccurate, about U.S. war plans and troop movements. In addition, the Russian Federal Security Service (FSB) has recruited Russian scientists from technological institutes and weapons factories to train Iranian scientists in missile development.[11]

For years, the Soviet Union, and later Russia, maintained a communications intelligence (COMINT) facility at Lourdes, Cuba, which was a significant target for U.S. counterintelligence. The facility, one of the world's largest intercept facilities, was capable of intercepting a wide range of communications within the United States and between the United States and Europe. The Russian president denied reports that Russia was going to reopen the facility, although Russian electronic intelligence ships do operate near U.S. facilities, such as the Kings Bay submarine base in Georgia.[12]

Today, there is a Chinese signals intelligence (SIGINT) facility in Cuba, which undoubtedly targets some of the same communications links that the Lourdes facility intercepted. These SIGINT facilities and the activities of a number of other, sometimes allied countries, including efforts related to economic and industrial espionage, are targets for U.S. counterintelligence collection. For example, France has systematically monitored the telephone conversations and cable traffic of many businesses based in the United States. Other nations, in pursuit of economic, business, and industrial intelligence, also operate SIGINT ground stations that intercept U.S. government and commercial communications.[13]

In recent years, the intelligence services of nations such as Iran, Pakistan, and Syria have been of even greater concern than in the past. According to testimony by then Director of Central Intelligence (DCI) John Deutch, Iranian agents contacted officials at nuclear facilities in Kazakhstan on several occasions, attempting to acquire nuclear-related materials. In 1992 Iran unsuccessfully approached the Ulba Metallurgical Plant to obtain enriched uranium. The following year, three Iranians believed to have connections to Iran's intelligence service were arrested in Turkey while seeking to acquire nuclear material from smugglers from the former Soviet Union.[14]

In 1996 the CIA reported that in 1995 there had been "several instances of suspected Iranian surveillance of US persons and facilities abroad." The report went on to state, "These incidents involved brazen techniques, especially the frequent use of easily traced diplomatic vehicles. The surveillance probably was a matter of intimidation rather than planning for terrorist attacks, but the information collected could facilitate future planning for terrorist operations."[15]

The following year it was reported that Iranian agents in Bosnia were engaged in extensive operations and had infiltrated the U.S. program to train the Bosnian army. In addition, for several years the Iranian Ministry of Intelligence and Security left a trail of dead bodies across Europe and the Middle East, the result of a campaign to assassinate Iranian dissidents. The campaign was orchestrated by a Committee for Special Operations, which included the country's spiritual leader, president, foreign minister, and high security officials.[16]

In 2011 it was reported that Iran had plotted to murder Saudi Arabia's ambassador to the United States (an effort code-named CHEVROLET) and that there were also plans to bomb the Israeli and Saudi embassies in Washington, D.C., and Buenos Aires, Argentina—plans that allegedly involved the deputy commander of the Qods Force. The following year, it was reported that Iran had targeted members of the U.S. embassy in Azerbaijan for assassination by Iran.[17]

Pakistan's Inter-Services Intelligence Directorate (ISI) is also of concern to the United States. Even when it was thought that the higher levels of ISI might be committed to operations against the Taliban, there was still concern about the loyalties of those at lower levels. Subsequently, it was reported that the organization's "S Wing," responsible for operations against India and Afghanistan, operated with a certain degree of autonomy. And leaked documents suggested that Pakistan was permitting ISI representatives "to meet directly with the Taliban in secret strategy sessions to organize networks of militant groups that fight against American soldiers in Afghanistan, and even hatch plots to assassinate Afghan leaders." Closer to home, by mid-2011 the ISI had spent $4 million over two decades in a covert effort to influence U.S. policy concerning Indian control of Kashmir. The campaign included contributions to congressional and presidential candidates.[18]

The detection of Osama bin Laden in Pakistan raised the question of who, if anyone, in the ISI was aware of his presence. According to one account, "The ISI actually ran a special desk assigned to handle the al Qaeda leader. It was operated independently, headed by an officer who made his own decisions." The same account also asserted that CIA concern that ISI would warn bin Laden of the May 2011 raid was one reason the agency decided not inform the Pakistani intelligence service in advance.[19]

Pakistani operations in the United States also included intelligence collection and intimidation. Mohammed Tasleem, an attaché with the Pakistani consulate in New York, was named in 2011 as a clandestine ISI operative. It was reported that he had been posing as an FBI agent in order to extract information from Pakistanis living in the United States, as well as making threats to deter open opposition to Pakistan's government.[20]

Another individual, Mohammad Ana Soueid, of Fairfax, Virginia, was indicted in 2011 and charged with working for the Syrian Military Intelligence and General Intelligence directorates. Soueid was alleged to have been responsible for the production of "audio and video recordings of anti–Government of Syria and anti–President al-Assad protests in the United States," as well recordings of conversations with individual protestors. He was also charged with collecting names, phone numbers, and e-mail addresses.[21]

The intelligence organizations and activities of terrorist/insurgent organizations—human, open source, and technical—particularly of al-Qaeda, the Taliban, and Hezbollah also concern U.S. counterintelligence organizations. In 2007 a CIA officer pled guilty to charges of illegally seeking to extract from government computers classified information on Hezbollah (although she was not charged with passing the information to that organization). More dramatically and tragically, an apparently valuable source with access to al-Qaeda killed four CIA officers, three agency contractors, and a Jordanian intelligence officer at the CIA's base in Khost province when he blew himself up in an operation apparently orchestrated by al-Qaeda.[22]

Beyond employing human sources, foreign intelligence services—including China, Iran, Russia, and Israel, among others—conduct computer network exploitation operations. In 2009 it was reported that "computer spies have broken into the Pentagon's $300 billion Joint Strike Fighter project." The penetration resulted in the siphoning off of several terabytes of data concerning design and electronic systems. The penetration, according to one report, appeared to have started no later than 2007. In its 2013 report, the Defense Security Service noted that the top technologies targeted by foreign entities were information systems, electronics, lasers, optics, sensors, and aeronautic systems technologies and that suspicious network activity was a significant method by which data acquisition attempts were made.[23]

As with human counterintelligence, there are a number of different agencies involved in counterintelligence operations in cyberspace, a sufficient number to require the Department of Defense (DOD) to delineate responsibilities among multiple entities (within and outside the Intelligence Community) and have deconfliction procedures. Those entities include the NSA and DOD components with counterintelligence components, a category that includes the National Reconnaissance Office, National Geospatial-Intelligence Agency, DIA, and military services.[24]

INVESTIGATIONS

Counterintelligence investigations are defined as "formal investigative activities undertaken to determine whether a particular person is acting for or on behalf of, or an event is related to, a foreign power engaged in spying or committing espionage, sabotage, treason, sedition, subversion, assassinations, or international terrorist activities, and to determine actions required to neutralize such acts."[25] They may be triggered by a variety of factors. Human sources may be arrested or disappear, technical or human operations may be shut down by a foreign security service, or a previously reliable source may begin to provide apparently deceptive material. In addition, suspicious travel or unexplained income may raise concerns about an individual's possible involvement with a foreign intelligence service.

Warning of a compromise may also come from a defector. In August 1985, the CIA station in Rome informed headquarters in Langley that defector Vitaly Yurchenko knew of a "U.S. volunteer to KGB, code-named Mr. Robert," who identified Adolf Tolkachev as a CIA asset and also "compromised a CIA technical operation in Moscow and one other technical operation CIA was running against USSR." Information provided by Yurchenko about "Mr. Robert"—particularly that he was a former CIA officer who had been fired for "unsuitability and polygraph problems in 1983–84"— soon led to the identification of Edward Lee Howard, who escaped to the Soviet Union and eventually died in Russia.[26]

The same cable reported that Yurchenko had revealed that the KGB had recruited an NSA employee "who provided details on sensitive NSA maritime operations against Soviet North Sea submarine fleet"—information that led to the indictment and conviction of Ronald Pelton. Or, as in the case of the DIA counterintelligence analyst who first questioned the loyalty of Ana Belen Montes in 1996, suspicion may be the result "not [of] a single incident or observation but from an accumulation of small incidents and observations that troubled him in the aggregate." Then, by the late 1990s, "the U.S. Intelligence Community had . . . reason to believe . . . that a Cuban spy might be operating among us, perhaps in the very heart of the nation's capital."[27]

If it is not possible to precisely identify the source of a compromise, an investigation will seek to identify individuals with access to the information compromised (whether the identities of sources or the details of ongoing technical operations), gather data on their foreign travel or local movements, look for changes in their finances, explore their possible vulnerabilities, and then move on to monitoring or entrapping primary suspects. It may also be necessary to explore the possibility that a foreign source is seeking to provide deceptive information about the reason for a series of intelligence loses—as the KGB did with respect to the Ames compromises, using an individual the CIA designated GTPROLOGUE.[28]

Thus, the investigation that ultimately led to the 1994 arrest of Aldrich Ames for having compromised almost a dozen CIA human sources (often leading to their execution) as well as technical collection operations involved both a specific focus on Ames and a more general examination of possible suspects. Suspicions about Ames, as with Montes, initially stemmed from a colleague's hunch—although unlike in the Montes situation, the colleague became concerned due to a sudden and dramatic change in Ames's lifestyle after he returned to Washington following an overseas assignment. That change included purchase of a house for over $500,000 and plans for extensive remodeling.[29]

The investigation of Ames involved exploring the possible sources of his affluence, including his wife; it looked at whether there was a mortgage on the house, performed a credit check, conducted a polygraph, and ultimately did a search of the home. The broader investigation identified six potential suspects and selected a group to focus on based on the rankings produced by having each member of the ten-man investigative team order the suspects from most to least likely, then assigning six points to a suspect every time he or she was listed first, down to one point for each time the suspect was listed last. A ranking was then produced based on the sum of points for each suspect. Ames finished first with twenty-one points, but the team decided to focus on all suspects who finished with fifteen points or more.* The subsequent investigation took a number of avenues, including reviewing files on the cases compromised, producing a list of all CIA employees who resigned, retired, or died in 1985 and 1986, interviewing CIA personnel stationed in Moscow, looking for travel that might have involved contact with KGB officers, reviewing previous CIA-FBI reporting of possible penetrations, and redebriefing defectors and in-place sources. Ames's position as prime suspect was considerably strengthened when the team found that significant bank deposits followed his authorized meetings with a KGB officer.[30]

COLLECTION

Information desired about foreign intelligence and security services, which may ultimately be used to neutralize any hostile intelligence activities directed against the United States, includes data on their facilities, leadership, personnel at headquarters and in the field, means of communication, methods of operation, and areas of interest. This intelligence may come from a variety of sources.[31]

Open sources concerning friendly and hostile services may include official government documents (e.g., telephone directories, brochures, yearly reports, parliamentary hearings, and reports of commissions of inquiry), websites, books and articles

---

*The ranking system employed is known as the Borda count, named for the eighteenth-century French aristocrat who proposed it as an election method. The rule has been the subject of detailed research in the field of social choice theory. See Donald G. Saari, "Which Is Better: The Condorcet or Borda Winner?," *Social Choice and Welfare* 26, no. 1 (January 2006): 107–129; Jeffrey Richelson, "A Comparative Analysis of Social Choice Functions," *Behavioral Science* 20, no. 5 (September 1975): 331–337.

(including those written by former officers of a service of interest), and newspapers. Examples of such sources include Russian newspaper articles on that nation's reconnaissance satellites; a book written by a former member of Israel's Mossad; investigative books on the German Federal Intelligence Service, or Bundesnachrichtendienst (BND), or on the Russian Federal Security Service; and official websites of a large number of foreign intelligence services.[32]

One undoubtedly unexpected example of open source information on China's intelligence activities was a video of an address by Major General Jin Yinan of the People's Liberation Army (PLA), intended as an internal talk, in which the general discussed Chinese officials who had spied for the United States, Britain, and other nations. The talk, which lasted for hours, appeared on at least two Chinese websites before government censors removed it. They took that action too late to prevent its becoming available on YouTube.[33]

A report on the Iranian Ministry of Intelligence and Security (MOIS) produced by the Library of Congress's Federal Research Division (FRD) illustrates the extent to which more conventional opens sources can be mined to produce a detailed profile of the intelligence and service apparatus of a hostile, closed society. Employing English- and Farsi-language sources (including newspapers, blogs, radio, and television from within and outside Iran) the FRD produced a report that examined, inter alia, MOIS's historical background, organization, principal leaders, headquarters, command and control, membership and recruitment, operations and tactics, intelligence capabilities, principal areas of operation, finances, foreign affiliations and support, and use of communications media.[34]

Iranian media also provided information about the claims of the defense minister about a new armed reconnaissance drone. The Islamic Republic News Agency reported that, according to the minister, the Fotros drone had a range of 1,250 miles (allowing it to cover much of the Middle East) and could be equipped with air-to-surface missiles. A Chinese drone was the subject of an annotated video that appeared on the Internet and showed satellite uplink equipment and a synthetic aperture radar.[35]

Two reports by private organizations have illustrated the ability to mine open sources for information on foreign computer network exploitation organizations and activities in recent years. One report, produced by the Project 2049 Institute, examined the role of several PRC organizations—including the Third Department of the PLA General Staff Department, its Second Bureau, and its Beijing North Computing Center—in cyber operations. The other, produced by the Mandiant cybersecurity firm, also examined the activities of the Third Department's Second Bureau.[36]

Information about friendly services may also come from liaison and training arrangements. In 1978 a member of the U.S. Military Liaison Office at the U.S. embassy in Rome obtained from several sources inside the Italian government information on the effectiveness, or lack thereof, of the newly established Italian intelligence and security services, then the Military Security and Information Service (SISMI) and the Democratic Security and Information Service (SISDE). He was able to prepare a 4,000-word report for the DIA asserting that the resources devoted to SISDE's anti-terrorist activities were making effective counterespionage impossible, that the SISDE commander was not qualified for his job, and that both the SISDE and the SISMI were performing poorly.[37]

A November 2009 cable from the U.S. embassy in Mexico, based on an embassy officer's reporting, focused on Mexico's intelligence apparatus. It began by stating, "President Calderon's security strategy lacks an effective intelligence apparatus to produce high quality information and targeted operations." It went on to discuss the Mexican government's intelligence strategy, the organizations involved in managing or conducting intelligence activities, challenges, and "taking steps to get smart," then concluded with a comments section that observed, "Mexico is a long way off from developing a self-sufficient and expert intelligence apparatus."[38]

Liaison with allied services also provides information about the activities of hostile services, such as when the French Directorate for Territorial Surveillance (DST) provided the CIA with information from its agent in Directorate T of the KGB, Vladimir Vetrov, code-named FAREWELL. Beginning in 1981, FAREWELL provided the DST with more than 4,000 documents on Soviet scientific and technical espionage, including information on the Soviet Union's plans to steal Western technological secrets and on internal assessments of its covert technology acquisition activities. Specifically, FAREWELL provided (1) a complete, detailed list of all Soviet organizations involved in scientific and technical intelligence; (2) reports on Soviet plans, accomplishments, and annual savings in all branches of the military industry due to illegal acquisition of foreign technology; (3) a list of all KGB officers throughout the world involved in scientific and technical espionage; and (4) the identities of the principal agents recruited by the officers of "Line X" in ten Western nations, including the United States, West Germany, and France. French president François Mitterrand informed President Ronald Reagan about FAREWELL in 1981 and gave him sample material from Vetrov. Several weeks later, the head of the DST, Marcel Chalet, visited Vice President George H. W. Bush in Washington, D.C., to discuss FAREWELL.[39]

Several types of human sources may provide useful information. The first is the agent who holds an official position within a hostile service. The type is either a mole (someone recruited prior to entry into the service) or a "defector in place" (someone who agrees to provide information after having attained an intelligence or security position, such as FAREWELL). An individual may agree to provide information for ideological or financial reasons or as a result of coercion or blackmail, possibly based on evidence of sexual or financial misbehavior.

The United States had some significant successes during the Cold War in penetrating the Soviet military service, the Chief Intelligence Directorate (GRU) of the Soviet General Staff. GRU Colonel Oleg Penkovskiy (discussed in Chapter 11) provided counterintelligence as well as positive intelligence information. The CIA also began receiving information in the early 1960s from GRU officer Dmitri Polyakov, who reached the rank of major general; he was eventually betrayed by Aldrich Ames and executed in 1988. In November 2002, a Russian military court convicted Colonel Alexander Sypachev, identified as a Russian intelligence officer, of espionage. He had been accused of preparing a two-page report about Russian intelligence personnel for U.S. contacts.[40]

Two apparent recruitment attempts in 2013 illustrated current U.S. interest in recruiting Russian intelligence officers. That January, embassy employee Benjamin Dillon was arrested while attempting to recruit a Russian counterintelligence (FSB) officer. Then, in May, Ryan C. Fogle, listed as the third secretary of the embassy's political department, was detained in the midst of a recruitment attempt, also apparently an FSB counterterrorism official. Russia claimed Fogle was carrying technical equipment as well as a letter offering $100,000 initially and $1 million per year for continuing cooperation.[41]

One indication of possible CIA success in penetrating the PRC Ministry of State Security (MSS) entailed reports, in June 2012, that the Chinese government had detained an MSS employee under suspicion that he had been passing information to the United States. The employee was reported to be the thirty-eight-year old secretary of MSS vice minister Qiu Jin. One account stated he had been recruited and trained by the CIA after getting caught in a honey trap operation.[47]

The CIA also apparently penetrated the India's Research and Analysis Wing (RAW), the country's principal foreign intelligence agency. In 1987 a senior RAW official, K. V. Unnikrishnan, was reportedly stationed in Madras, where he was responsible for coordinating Tamil Tiger insurgency activities. Unnikrishnan was reportedly blackmailed with compromising photographs of himself and a "stewardess." A more recent case involved Rabinder Singh, a RAW officer who reportedly disappeared in 2004 before being arrested for providing information to the CIA.[43]

The penetration of the Cuban General Directorate of Intelligence (DGI)—now the Directorate of Intelligence—reportedly allowed the FBI to dismantle three major Cuban spy operations in the United States, including Ana Belenn Montes, Walter Myers, and the "Cuban Five." Rolando Sarraff Trujillo, a cryptographer with the Cuban service, provided information that would permit U.S. intelligence agencies to decipher messages sent from Cuban intelligence to assets in the United States. Arrested in 1995, he would be exchanged in 2014 for the three members of the Cuban Five who were in prison at that time.[44]

Probably the CIA's most controversial possible penetration of a foreign intelligence organization was revealed in 2014, when it was reported that it had a clandestine relationship with a member of the German BND. Reports stated that he had worked in the mailroom of the BND Areas of Operation/Foreign Relations Department and had provided over two hundred documents, including at least one on the Bundestag's probe of NSA surveillance activities, for which he had been paid $34,000.[45]

The second type of human source is the defector. Defectors provide information concerning various aspects of an intelligence or security service's structure, operations, and leadership. The CIA certainly reaped an intelligence bonanza when Major Hunter Bolanos of the Nicaraguan Directorate General of State Security (DGSE) defected in 1983. For almost the entire period from January 1980 to May 7, 1983, Bolanos had special responsibility for surveillance of U.S. embassy and CIA activities in Nicaragua. He provided information on the structure of the DGSE, the number of Nicaraguans in the directorate, the number of foreign advisors to the DGSE broken down by nation, and the Soviet provision of sophisticated eavesdropping devices.[46]

Similarly, senior intelligence officers who have defected from Cuba and China have provided the United States with new information on intelligence and counterintelligence operations in those nations. In June 1987, Major Florentino Apillaga Lombard defected to the United States from the Cuban DGI and proceeded to inform CIA officials that the great majority of CIA "assets" in Cuba were actually double agents working for the Cuban government. In 1986 Yu Zhensan, former head of the

Foreign Affairs Bureau of the PRC's Ministry of State Security, defected and provided the United States with extensive information about Chinese intelligence operations abroad, including the names of Chinese agents and of suspected agents from other nations operating in China. Before defecting, he apparently provided the United States with information leading to the arrest of FBIS employee and long-term Chinese mole Larry Wu-Tai Chin.[47]

During the Cold War, the United States benefitted from information provided by a substantial number of KGB and GRU defectors. As a result, the CIA was able to develop a detailed, albeit incomplete, picture of the structures and activities of those organizations. As noted above, before his redefection, KGB official Vitaly Yurchenko provided the CIA with information concerning several Soviet penetrations of the U.S. Intelligence Community—information that led to the discovery that former CIA officer Edward Lee Howard and former NSA employee Ronald Pelton had been providing information to the Soviet Union. He also stated that Pelton and naval spy John Walker were the KGB's most prized assets in the United States.[48]

In June 1986, it was reported that KGB head of operations in North Africa and PLO liaison Oleg Agraniants had defected to the United States. Agraniants, who may have been working for the CIA for the three years prior to his defection, apparently supplied the names of KGB agents in Tunisia, Algeria, Morocco, and Libya.[49]

The changing domestic situation in the Soviet Union during the Mikhail Gorbachev era and the subsequent collapse of the Soviet Union led to the defection of numerous KGB officers. In 1990 Igor Cherpinski, reportedly the KGB's station chief in Belgium, defected. In 1991 Sergei Illarionov, a KGB colonel based in Genoa, defected and helped Western security services identify the KGB's European networks. A defecting SVR officer, code-named AVENGER, led the CIA to another Soviet intelligence officer who provided information on Robert Hanssen. In 2000 or early 2001, Sergei Tretykov, a senior aide to the Russian ambassador and an SVR officer, defected.[50]

The breakup of a network of eleven Russian agents in June 2010 was apparently the result of information provided by the deputy chief of the American division (5th Department) of the SVR's Directorate S, responsible for the running of illegal agents (those not operating under diplomatic cover). The source was originally identified as a Colonel Shcherbakov. Subsequently, however, it was reported that the information was provided, prior to his defection, by Colonel Aleksandr Poteyev—with Shcherbakov having defected earlier. The eleven agents were arrested and traded for prisoners being held in Russia. Poteyev was convicted, in absentia, by the Moscow Military District Court in June 2011.[51]

A third type of source on foreign counterintelligence services and activities is surveillance by CIA and other intelligence personnel. In 1999 it was reported that a major CIA operation in Germany involved monitoring of Iranian intelligence personnel in Frankfurt, which was believed to serve as their base of operations in Europe.[52]

Documents from the intelligence services of a collapsed or deposed regime may provide valuable information about the regime's intelligence operations and covert procurement activities or about similar operations and activities of the regime's allies. The CIA apparently acquired the archives of the East German Ministry of State Security (MfS), better known as the STASI, from a Russian source for between $1 million and $1.5 million, which allowed the agency to identify thousands of East German agents around the world, agents who might have transformed from East German spies into spies for another hostile government.[53]

In the wake of the fall of Saddam Hussein's government, the CIA seized a large set of files from the newly defunct Iraqi Intelligence Service. That seizure, according to a report in late 2003, "spurr[ed] U.S. investigations of weapons procurement networks and agents of influence who took money from the government of Saddam Hussein." The records, which would stretch ninety-four miles if laid out from end to end, contained the names of virtually every Iraqi intelligence officer and all of their agents. In 2003 the CIA was also busy examining files of the Special Security Organization.[54]

Beyond human sources and documents, technical collection also provides data of value for counterintelligence. Intercepted communications from within a country or its embassies overseas can reveal the activities of either the internal security or the foreign intelligence services. For example, the U.S.-British interception of Soviet communications traffic in the 1940s paid off significantly in the late 1940s, 1950s, and beyond when the traffic was partially decrypted under the VENONA program. From the 1960s until the collapse of the East German regime, the targets of the U.S. Army Field Station Berlin included the communications of the MfS. Today, it is highly likely that the communications of a number of domestic security services are targets of Special Collection Service outposts at U.S. embassies. In addition, intercepts of signals from foreign reconnaissance satellites can provide information about the targets imaged by those satellites.[55]

Along with traditional intelligence, computer network exploitation operations might have been employed to gather information on the structure, communications, and activities of foreign intelligence services. Even if the computers belonging to the foreign intelligence service target are not connected to the Internet, the NSA and CIA have been able to gather information from computers around the world—via either assets who can download information from those computers or bugs emplaced in those computers.

Satellite imagery is decidedly less useful than human sources, open sources, or COMINT in providing information about most activities of foreign intelligence services. It can, however, provide information on the precise location and layout of intelligence and security service complexes, which may prove particularly useful if a direct attack on such facilities is authorized. For example, reconnaissance flights in support of UN inspectors provided information on the regional centers of the Iraqi Special Security Organization. And in periods before and after the March 2003 invasion of Iraq, U.S. reconnaissance satellites photographed the headquarters of the Special Security Organization as well as the Iraqi Intelligence Service, producing pre- and poststrike imagery.[56]

In addition, satellite imagery can provide information on the presence and capabilities of SIGINT facilities and ground stations, be they Chinese facilities in the 1960s, KGB and GRU COMINT collection stations in 1981 and 1983, or Soviet/ Russian GRU LOW EAR intercept dishes. A 1981 report produced by the National Photographic Interpretation Center (NPIC), *Soviet Krug Facilities*, focused on thirty-one Soviet sites involved in collecting high-frequency signals; most were apparently still active in May 2012. A 1983 report on KGB COMINT collection stations, also produced by NPIC, described the results of the interpretation of satellite imagery from eleven stations. The latter report provided data on each site's designation, location, antennas, and buildings. It also noted new construction since the previous report as well as ongoing construction. Almost thirty years after the report, most of the stations were in operation, as indicated by commercial satellite imagery. Other commercial satellite imagery from 2013, undoubtedly matched by classified satellite imagery, provides details of a Chinese satellite communications (SATCOM) intercept site near Changji.[57]

EVALUATION OF DEFECTORS AND AGENTS

The evaluation and debriefing of defectors are additional responsibilities of a counterintelligence organization.[58] The United States has provided political asylum to officials from the Soviet Union and Russia, China, Nicaragua, Cuba, and a number of eastern European nations. Since 2005 it appears that a number of Iranian officials (Ali Reza Asgari, Colonel Amir Muhammad Shirazi) have defected and provided information to Western intelligence agencies, as noted in Chapter 11.

Debriefers seek information on the personnel, policies, structure, capabilities, and activities of whichever government component employed the defector, especially if it was a hostile intelligence service, as well as information about the defector's activities outside that component. In addition to eliciting information, debriefers seek to determine the reliability of the information offered.

When dealing with defectors, debriefers must determine where the defectors' knowledge begins and ends. Exaggeration or fabrication in the face of depleted information is one possibility. Complicating debriefers' task is the fact that many defectors hold back valid information as insurance for continued protection.[59]

According to a former CIA officer, one defector, Sergei Papushin, a KGB officer who defected in late 1989, "had been fully debriefed by the CIA and FBI, and it had become obvious that his knowledge of KGB counterintelligence operations against the United States was limited. . . . [H]e didn't have much for us." Frustrated at being largely ignored by both the FBI and CIA, "he did something he knew was guaranteed to once again grab attention"—he claimed that there was a mole in the CIA. "As he was questioned further," however, "it became apparent that he was scrambling with a fabricated story. Nothing he told his debriefers checked out."[60]

The inability to determine conclusively the bona fides of defectors can paralyze intelligence collection operations in one or more nations, create unwarranted suspicions about and damage to the careers of valuable intelligence officers, result in failure to fully exploit valuable information, or lead to reliance on false information in making policy or conducting military operations. The 1962 defection of KGB officer Anatoli Golitsin to the CIA in Helsinki, Finland, combined with the suspicions of CIA counterintelligence chief James Angleton, produced a mole hunt that ruined the careers of several CIA officers, led to unjustified suspicion of other KGB defectors, and helped immobilize CIA clandestine collection operations in the Soviet Union throughout much of the 1960s.[61]

In the case of Vitaly Yurchenko, the CIA's counterintelligence officials and analysts faced the task of assessing whether he was a legitimate defector who subsequently changed his mind or a plant who had intended to redefect from the very beginning. From August 1975 until August 1980, Yurchenko was the security officer at the Soviet embassy in Washington, D.C., where he was responsible for the security of Soviet facilities and citizens in that city, for protecting classified information, and for handling foreign visitors. In September 1980, he became chief of Department K of the First Chief Directorate, a position he retained until March 1985. His responsibilities included, but were not limited to, investigating suspected incidents of espionage involving KGB personnel and information leaks concerning the directorate. From April to July 1985, he was deputy chief of the First Department, which carried out operations against the United States and Canada.[62]

Three months after his defection Yurchenko appeared at a press conference at the Soviet embassy in Washington, claiming to have been kidnaped, drugged, and kept in isolation at a CIA safe house in Fredericksburg, Virginia. According to Yurchenko, he owed his "escape" to a "momentary lapse" by his captors. (In fact, he had walked out of a Georgetown restaurant unopposed by his CIA escort.) Two days later, after a visit from U.S. officials to determine whether he was acting of his own free will, Yurchenko flew back to the Moscow, where he held a two-hour press conference at which he and other Soviet officials accused the United States of "state terrorism." Subsequent reports that he had been executed were proved incorrect when he was spotted walking on a Moscow street.[63]

Following Yurchenko's defection, U.S. officials speculated about the reasons for his actions. If Yurchenko was a plant who had planned to redefect from the beginning, KGB motives could have been to gather information on CIA treatment and debriefing of defectors or to embarrass the CIA and discourage the agency from accepting defectors. Among those suggesting that Yurchenko was a plant were President Ronald Reagan, Senator Patrick Leahy (then Vice Chairman of the Senate Select Committee on Intelligence), and other officials who considered Yurchenko's information to be largely "historical."[64]

Others suggested that Yurchenko had been a legitimate defector who had changed his mind. Reasons given for his about-face included his rejection by the wife of a Soviet official stationed in Canada (whom he visited almost immediately after his arrival in the United States), the great publicity generated by his defection, a general homesickness for "Mother Russia" often experienced by Soviet defectors, and a specific longing to be reunited with his family, especially his sixteen-year-old son. Among those doubting a staged defection was then FBI chief William H. Webster, who said that Yurchenko had provided the United States with valuable information on the roles of Edward Lee Howard and Ronald Pelton.[65]

In early 1993, DCI Robert Gates stated that the CIA had concluded that Yurchenko was a bona fide defector. According to Gates, "My view, and I think the view of virtually everybody in this building, is that Yurchenko was genuine. He provided too much specific information, including in the counterintelligence arena, that has been useful, for him, in my judgment, to have been a plant."[66]

In more recent years, cases from China, Iraq, and Iran have demonstrated the need to properly assess the claims and loyalties of defectors and professed assets as to both the validity of their information and their stability. In 1995 the United States received documents delivered by a walk-in claiming to be a missile expert to the Taiwanese security services. Among the documents he provided were a twenty-page 1988 memo prepared for China's First Ministry of Machine Building, which employed missile

PHOTO 15.1   Vitaly Yurchenko. *Photo credit:* © Bettmann/CORBIS.

PHOTO 15.2   Aldrich Ames. *Photo credit:* © Reuters/CORBIS.

designers and builders, and a five-year strategic plan for China's future missile forces describing the characteristics of both Chinese and American weapons. Taiwan passed the information and walk-in to the CIA station in Taiwan.[67]

The walk-in made frequent trips back to China and returned with more documents—over seven hundred, totaling 13,000 pages. A CIA translation team was flown to Taiwan to begin working on them, while a CIA polygrapher tested the walk-in and found his answer to the question of whether he was working on behalf of a foreign intelligence agency to be deceptive. He was then flown back to the United States so that the CIA and FBI could try to determine whether the entire operation had been managed by China's intelligence services. Ultimately, it was concluded that he was likely a double agent—although some of the information provided was judged to be valid.[68]

In 2001 the DIA debriefed a number of defectors who claimed to have information about Saddam Hussein's WMD efforts. One told his debriefers about an alleged "substitute sites" program, involving the use of government company buildings, private villas, and underground wells to conceal storage and production facilities. Another defector, introduced to Western intelligence by the Iraqi National Congress (INC), reported on what he claimed were Iraq's WMD efforts as well as on its support of foreign terrorist groups. The CIA would determine that he had embellished and exaggerated his access.[69]

In the period leading up to the U.S. invasion of Iraq in 2003, the INC introduced additional defectors to U.S. intelligence representatives. In one of its reports on U.S. intelligence and the war, the Senate Select Committee on Intelligence noted that the INC-provided individuals debriefed by DIA included both fabricators and individuals who provided useful information. The report also stated that after the invasion DIA reported that intelligence provided by the INC sources "covered a myriad of information and was not uniform in quality, accuracy, and utility. In some cases, [the INC's

Intelligence Collection Program] provided solid intelligence leads, corroborated other information, and contributed to our knowledge base. In other cases the information was of little or no value."[70]

Among the most prominent defectors associated with the 2003 war and U.S. claims concerning Iraqi WMD activities was known by the code name CURVEBALL. CURVEBALL, who had defected to the Germans and was in custody of the BND, claimed that Iraq was operating mobile biological weapons laboratories. That appeared to confirm other information, and the claim became a key element in Secretary of State Colin Powell's February 5, 2003, presentation to the United Nations. Assessment of CURVEBALL was hindered, rather dramatically, by the BND's refusal to grant the CIA access to him, claiming falsely (as would later be discovered) that CURVEBALL did not speak English and did not like Americans.[71]

In a case reminiscent of Yurchenko's, Iranian nuclear scientist Shahram Amiri (discussed in greater detail in Chapter 11) apparently defected in 2009, then redefected in 2010 after providing the CIA with information on Iranian nuclear activities. Like Yurchenko, Amiri claimed CIA mistreatment and coercion, leaving the agency to assess the original intent of his defection and the reliability of the information he provided.[72]

The most dramatic and tragic example of the consequences of failing to detect a would-be agent's true intentions involved Human Khalil Abu-Mulal Balawi. On December 30, 2009, Balawi, a Jordanian doctor allegedly turned by the Jordanian General Intelligence Directorate who provided "independently verified" information and whom CIA believed could provide access to top al-Qaeda's officials (including Ayman al-Zawahiri), blew himself up at the CIA's Khost outpost (Forward Operating Post Chapman) in Afghanistan. In a prerecorded suicide video, he claimed to have provided U.S. and Jordanian intelligence secrets to "fellow militants." The explosion killed Balawi and eight others, including two contractors, base chief Jennifer Matthews, analyst Elizabeth Hanson, three other CIA employees, and a Jordanian intelligence officer. Balawi, a review group concluded, "was not fully vetted and . . . sufficient security precautions were not taken." One result of the review was the creation of an integrated counterintelligence vetting cell within the Counterterrorism Center to focus on high-risk/high-gain assets and to evaluate potential threats.[73]

RESEARCH, ANALYSIS, AND PRODUCTION

It is fundamental to both intelligence and counterintelligence missions to have individuals able to decipher, understand, and report on the personalities, structure, facilities, tradecraft, and past and current operations of other nations' intelligence and security services. Only with such knowledge can positive intelligence collection operations be planned and conducted effectively. Likewise, only with such knowledge can effective penetration, disruption, and neutralization activities be carried out.

One significant output of research on foreign intelligence services conducted within the U.S. Intelligence Community is contained in reports prepared by the CIA's Counterintelligence Center (CIC), the successor to the agency's Counterintelligence Staff. The CIC prepares reports on intelligence communities of interest, both hostile and friendly. Some of the reports detail the origins of the intelligence services, their structures, functions, modes of operation, and arrangements for control by a higher authority. Thus, for example, the forty-seven-page study *Israel: Foreign Intelligence and Security Services*, published in March 1977, focused its first section on the background and development of the Israeli services, objectives, and structure; the relationship between the government and the services; and professional standards. The second, third, and fourth sections focused on the three major Israeli intelligence and security units: the Mossad, the General Security Service (Shin Bet), and the Intelligence Branch (AMAN), respectively. In each case, the report examined the service's functions, organization, administrative practice (including training), and methods of operation. Additionally, liaison with other Israeli and foreign services was considered. The three penultimate sections examined the Foreign Ministry's Research and Political Planning Center, the National Police, and key officials, while the final section commented on principal sources.[74]

A more recent, and more limited, counterintelligence product concerning Israel is the CIA's July 25, 2006, *Assessment of the Counterintelligence Environment in Israel.* That report presumably discussed topics such as Israel's human and technical surveillance and counterintelligence efforts that sought to limit the CIA's ability to gather intelligence about political and military developments.[75]

In 1985 the CIA's Counterintelligence Staff produced a twenty-four-page study titled *Iraq: Foreign Intelligence and Security Services.* The study examined the background and development of the services in general and included a section on key personalities as well as individual chapters on the Iraqi Intelligence Service, the Directorate of Military Intelligence, and the Directorate General of Security, with the functions, organization, and administrative practices of each service explored.[76] Figure 15.1 shows the study's table of contents.

The 2003 invasion of Iraq and the removal of the Saddam Hussein regime required updated reports, despite the U.S. presence. In June 2006, Secretary of Defense Donald Rumsfeld informed Under Secretary Stephen Cambone, "I have no visibility on Iraqi intelligence"; he went on to state, "We need to do a study on it. I'm afraid we are going to find out either nothing has been done, or we are uncomfortable with things that have been done." Less than a week later, in a memo to commander of the U.S. Central Command (CENTCOM) General John Abizaid, Rumsfeld wrote, "I have no visibility into the intelligence capabilities of either the Afghan government or the Iraqi government," and "I would appreciate an update."[77]

A 1984 study titled *Soviet Intelligence: KGB and GRU* discussed the background and development of the Soviet services, their national intelligence objectives and organizational structures, their relationship to the Communist Party and government, and their internal security and counterintelligence operations.[78]

In at least some respects, Russia's intelligence and security structure differs significantly from that of the Soviet Union. Today, there are three key services: the Foreign Intelligence Service (SVR), the Federal Security Service (FSB), and the Chief Intelligence Directorate (GRU) of the General Staff.[79] Any present studies of the Russian security services probably examine their Soviet heritage, the transition from the Soviet structure to the early post-Soviet structure and, then, to today's structure (a transition that involved the creation, abolition, merging, and renaming of key institutions), and their present organization, size, targets, and key personalities.

FIGURE 15.1 Table of Contents: Iraq: Foreign Intelligence and Security Services

SECRET

TABLE OF CONTENTS

FIGURES

SECRET

(REVERSE BLANK) iii

Such studies are likely to be far more detailed examinations of the questions that appeared in the unclassified September 1992 CIA study *The Russian Security Services: Sorting Out the Pieces*. This seven-page study contains a diagram of the evolution of the Soviet services (except the GRU) between August 1991 and September 1992, a brief description of the organization at the time of publication, and short biographies of service heads.[80]

Counterintelligence studies are also prepared by the Defense Intelligence Agency and military service intelligence and security components. The DIA prepared a November 15, 1978, intelligence appraisal titled *Italy: Reorganization of the Intelligence and Security Services*, which discussed the background and structure of Italy's services, key personalities, intelligence reforms, and outlook for the future. During 1998 and 1999, DIA produced a multitude of "Foreign Intelligence Threat Assessment" documents—including those for Israel, Japan, the Koreas, Algeria, Burma, Cuba, Mexico, Saudi Arabia, Kenya, and Egypt. Studies prepared by the Army Intelligence and Threat Center, absorbed into the National Ground Intelligence Center in 1995, included *Italy: A Counterintelligence Assessment* (April 1984), which reviewed the country's security and intelligence organizations as well as various threats, including terrorism, wartime sabotage, and espionage; *The DST: An Organization in Flux* (September 1986); *France: A Counterintelligence Assessment* (June 1981); *GRU Activity in the Washington, D.C. Area* (April 1983); and *The Cuban Intelligence Threat in Panama* (May 1978).[81]

Among the products of the Army Counterintelligence Center are its 2006 study *Iraqi Insurgent and Militia Group Intelligence Capabilities to Counter US Counter–Improvised Explosive Device Systems* and its 2007 product, *Multidiscipline Counterintelligence Threat Assessment for the Counter Radio Control Improvised Explosive Device Electronic Warfare (CREW-2) Program*. But perhaps its best-known product, given the unwanted publicity it received, is its 2008 report titled *Wikileaks.org: An Online Reference to Foreign Intelligence Services, Insurgents, or Terrorist Groups*.[82] The report's key judgments included the observation that WikiLeaks represented "a potential force protection, counterintelligence, [operations security, and information security] threat to the Army" and that "recent unauthorized release" of classified Defense Department information provided intelligence services, foreign terrorist groups, insurgents, and other foreign adversaries with "potentially actionable information for targeting US forces." The report also suggested, "The identification, exposure, termination of employment of or legal actions against current or former insiders, leakers, or whistleblowers could damage or destroy this center of gravity and deter others from using Wikileaks.org to make such information public."[83]

The Defense Security Service also produces a number of finished intelligence products. Beginning in 2011 the DSS began publishing a classified monthly report, *The Crimson Shield*, "which documents significant counterintelligence, intelligence, and security-related issues relevant to the cleared contractor community." The service also produces a quarterly open source publication, *Scarlet Sentinel*, as well as the classified report *Targeting U.S. Technologies: A Trend Analysis of Cyber Reporting from Defense Industry*. In addition, it publishes an unclassified annual report titled *Targeting U.S. Technologies: A Trend Analysis Reporting from Defense Industry*.[84]

DISRUPTION AND NEUTRALIZATION

The neutralization of foreign intelligence services' activities can be accomplished by various means. Penetration of a hostile service can be used to gather information as well as to damage the service's operations. In 1980 the Polish civilian intelligence and security service, the Służba Bezpieczeństwa (SB), began receiving classified information from James D. Harper, a Silicon Valley engineer. Harper, through his wife, who was employed by a Southern California defense contractor, obtained copies of well over one hundred pounds of classified reports, which he sold to the SB for more than $250,000. Most were Confidential or Secret documents pertaining to missile and ballistic missile defense programs, including the 1978 *Minuteman Defense Study (Final Report)*, the 1981 *Report on the Task Force on U.S. Ballistic Missile Defense*, and a 1978 Martin-Marietta Corporation study titled *Endoatmospheric Nonnuclear Kill Technology Requirements and Definition Study*. The CIA discovered Harper's activities via its penetration of the SB. When arrested, Harper was preparing to deliver an additional 150 to 200 pounds of documents.[85]

A second means of neutralizing a hostile intelligence service is by passing information to a third country that will lead that country to take action against the officers and agents of the hostile service. In many cases, the CIA passes such information on as a natural result of its liaison with a friendly security service, such as when it provided the British Security Service with information on East German intelligence operations in the United Kingdom. At the time of his defection, GRU officer Sergei Bokhane, code-named GTBLIZZARD, who had been stationed in Greece, provided information on at least three Greeks involved in spying for the Soviet Union. Included was Michael Megalokonomos, who, when apprehended, was in possession of a code book, a microfilm reading device, a radio capable of picking up special frequencies, and instructions on how to work a radio transmitter. Also named by Bokhane was Nikos Pipitsoulis, who sold an electrical device to Soviet officials for $43,000. In addition, a lieutenant commander working in the data processing unit at Greek defense headquarters was involved in passing information to the Soviet Union. The information provided to the CIA by Bokhane was passed on to Greek security authorities, leading to the arrest of the three agents.[86]

On other occasions the recipient of the information may be a hostile nation. In the spring of 1983, when the Iranian Communist (Tudeh) Party had been closed down, the CIA provided a list of Soviet agents and collaborators operating in Iran to the regime of Ayatollah Ruhollah Khomeini and its security service. As a result, eighteen Soviet diplomats were expelled, two hundred suspects were executed, and Tudeh Party leaders were imprisoned.[87]

Another method of neutralization entails running double agents. One CIA double agent operation that backfired involved Captain Nikolai Federovich Artamonov, the youngest commanding officer of a destroyer in Soviet naval history, who defected in Sweden in 1959. Artamonov was subsequently recruited by the Office of Naval Intelligence to come to the United States. In his debriefing, he provided the ONI with information on the Soviet use of trawlers for intelligence collection, Soviet nuclear strategy, and Soviet destroyer tactics against submarines. Subsequently, he was given a new name, Nicholas Shadrin, and a position as a translator in the Naval Science and Technical Intelligence Center. In 1966 Shadrin went to work for the Defense Intelligence Agency and was also approached by a Soviet intelligence officer who tried to recruit him. Shadrin reported the offer to the FBI, which persuaded him, despite his initial reluctance, to become a double agent, to "accept" the Soviet offer, and to feed the KGB CIA-doctored information.[88]

After several years of pretending to work for the KGB, Shadrin began to make trips abroad to meet his controller. He never returned from a December 20, 1975, meeting in Vienna. According to temporary defector Vitaly Yurchenko, Shadrin was fatally chloroformed, by accident, while struggling in the backseat of a sedan with Soviet agents trying to spirit him out of Vienna.[89]

The military also runs offensive counterintelligence operations (OFCO), which are conducted "against a target having suspected or known affiliation with foreign intelligence and security services, international terrorism, or other foreign persons or organizations, to counter terrorism, espionage, or other clandestine intelligence activities that threaten the security of the [Defense] Department or the United States." Such operations can be either CI controlled source or double agent operations. According to a 1982 Army regulation, such double agent operations "may require engagement in unorthodox operations and activities." These unorthodox activities may be at variance with recognized standards or methods normally associated with the military service. They are "undertaken only when authorized by the commander of a counterintelligence unit or higher authority." More recently, in 2008, a Department of Defense instruction directed that a "Joint Counterintelligence Unit (JCIU), formed under the authority of a Secretary of Defense–approved order, shall have the authority to conduct OFCO." The unit is to focus on "combatant command strategic and operational CI missions within an area of conflict."[90]

Double agent operations often are initiated after a member of the U.S. armed forces reports an approach by a foreign intelligence officer. In 1984 there were 481 incidents of soldiers being approached by people suspected of being Soviet bloc intelligence officers or sympathizers.[91] Under the direction of counterintelligence authorities, the service personnel maintain contact with the foreign intelligence officers, providing a combination of low-grade factual and false, but apparently valuable, information supplied by the military services. Such operations yield information on the intelligence targets of hostile services, allow identification of the intelligence officers and agents of hostile services, tie up hostile service resources, and permit the transmission of disinformation concerning the plans and capabilities of U.S. military forces.[92]

One operation involved Chief Warrant Officer Janos Szmolka, who had left Hungary to become a U.S. citizen and eventually joined the U.S. Army. Stationed in West Germany, he went on authorized leaves to Budapest to visit his mother in 1978 and 1979. On this third trip he was approached by a man described as a Hungarian intelligence officer, who offered to ensure better living conditions for Szmolka's family in exchange for information.[93]

Szmolka returned to West Germany and reported the offer to his superiors. For the next four years, under the direction of Army counterintelligence officers, he was in contact with Hungarian agents in Europe and the United States. In 1980, under normal rotation procedures, he was transferred to the United States, and in 1982, when the Army desired to uncover the Hungarian intelligence network in the United States, Szmolka was instructed to inform the Hungarians, through coded letters, that he had valuable information to turn over. On April 17, 1982, he went to the Confederate monument in Augusta, Georgia, near his post at Fort Gordon, to meet a Hungarian agent. Federal agents arrested Otto A. Gilbert, an expatriate Hungarian and naturalized U.S. citizen, and charged him with espionage. Gilbert received a reduced sentence in exchange for information about Hungarian intelligence.[94]

Attempts to recruit foreign intelligence officers may either lead to actual recruitments or at least because of uncertainty and suspicion within the targeted services. A joint CIA-FBI operation code-named COURTSHIP aimed at recruiting KGB and GRU officers during the latter part of the Cold War. Candidates were identified through a review of available information about different Soviet intelligence officers and consultation with psychologists. One product of the program was the FBI's recruitment of KGB officer Valery Martynov, code-named GTGENTILE by the CIA and PIMENTA by the FBI, whose activity was compromised by both Aldrich Ames and Robert Hanssen.[95]

During George J. Tenet's tenure at the CIA, the agency conducted a disruption campaign against Iran's Ministry of Intelligence and Security. Agency officers approached ministry officers—on the streets or wherever they had the opportunity—and asked if they would be willing to work for the CIA or sell information. Those approaches "undoubtedly ruined some careers," according to Tenet, as well as occasionally producing actual intelligence dividends.[96]

Disruption and neutralization may target not only foreign intelligence collection operations but also foreign service acquisition technology operations, which, in turn, may be conducted on behalf of either the civilian or the military sector. The information provided by FAREWELL allowed the CIA to devise an operation that led the KGB's "Line X" representatives to acquire altered, defective products, including contrived computer chips and flawed turbines, as well as misinformation about stealth aircraft and space defense.[97]

CI FUNCTIONAL SERVICES

Counterintelligence functional services include technical surveillance countermeasures, polygraphs and credibility assessments, behavioral sciences, and cyber services. Technical surveillance countermeasures are technical measures designed to "detect, neutralize, and/or exploit a wide variety of hostile and foreign penetration technologies that are used to obtain unauthorized access to classified and sensitive information."[98] Included are traditional measures to detect bugged offices as well as measures to determine if computers have been compromised.

The polygraph and credibility assessment category includes the longtime practice of requiring some Intelligence Community employees to take "lie detector" tests in the expectation of either deterring certain behavior, detecting deception, or encouraging admissions of possible compromising behavior. Credibility assessment techniques include "existing as well as potential techniques and procedures to assess truthfulness."[99]

Behavioral sciences include studies of both the motivations for spying and the behavior of those involved in espionage. One item, published in the January 1993 issue of *Counterintelligence Trends*, produced by the CIA Counterintelligence Center, was "Why People Spy: A Project Slammer Report." The article reports on the results of interviews with twenty-five convicted U.S. spies, exploring their motivations for espionage. According to the article, anger and revenge were the most frequently cited motivation for spying.[100]

Cyber services include digital forensics—investigations to determine the digital fingerprints left by successful or unsuccessful computer intrusions. Cyber vulnerability assessments, as the name suggests, explore ways in which computers may be vulnerable to exploitation or disruption.[101]

Notes

1. Office of the National Counterintelligence Executive, *The National Counterintelligence Strategy of the United States*, March 2005, 1.

2. "NCIS CI & Insider Threat Awareness and Reporting Brief," http://www.ncis.navy.mil/CoreMissions/CI/Pages/default.aspx (accessed November 20, 2013).

3. Mark L. Reagan, *Introduction to US Counterintelligence: CI 101-A Primer*, July 1, 2005, 29.

4. Office of the National Counterintelligence Executive, *The National Counterintelligence Strategy of the United States*, 2009, 1–5.

5. Jay Peterzell, "When 'Friends' Become Moles," *Time*, May 28, 1990, 50; "Parlez-Vous Espionage?," *Newsweek*, September 23, 1991, 40; Douglas Jehl, "U.S. Expanding Its Effort to Halt Spying by Allies," *New York Times*, April 30, 1993, A1, A10; R. Jeffrey Smith, "U.S. to Protest Industrial Spying by Allies," *Washington Post*, April 30, 1993, A39; John J. Fialka, *War by Other Means: Economic Espionage in America* (New York: W. W. Norton, 1997); Peter Schweitzer, *Friendly Spies: How America's Allies Are Using Economic Espionage to Steal Our Secrets* (New York: Atlantic Monthly Press, 1993); General Accounting Office, GAO/NSIAD 96-64, *Weaknesses in U.S. Security Arrangements with Foreign-Owned Defense Contractors*, 1996, 22–26; Defense Security Service, *Targeting U.S. Technologies: A Trend Analysis of Cleared Industry Reporting*, 2013, 8–10.

6. Evan Perez, "Spy for Cuba, Unrepentant Gets Life," *Wall Street Journal*, July 17–18, 2010, A3; Department of Justice, "Recent Espionage-Related Prosecutions Involving China," n.d., 1; Associated Press, "Hawaii: Tropical Paradise and Spying Destination: Sun, Surf and Spies: Military Secrets Case a Reminder That Hawaii Is a Major Espionage Target," MatthewAid.com, April 3, 2013, http://www.matthewaid.com/post/47023719306/hawaii-tropical-paradise-and-spying-destination; *United States of America v. BENJAMIN PIERCE BISHOP, Criminal Complaint, Case No. 13-0207 RLP*, United States District Court for the District of Hawaii, March 14, 2013.

7. Department of Justice, "Recent Espionage-Related Prosecutions Involving China," 1; Federal Bureau of Investigation, "Michigan Man Sentenced 48 Months for Attempting to Spy for the People's Republic of China," www.fbi.gov, January 21, 2011, http://www.fbi.gov/washingtondc/press-releases/2011/wfo012111.htm.

8. David Wise, *Nightmover: How Aldrich Ames Sold the CIA to the KGB for $4.6 Million* (New York: HarperCollins, 1995); David Wise, *Spy: The Inside Story of How the FBI's Robert Hanssen Betrayed America* (New York: Random House, 2002); Nicholas Eftimiades, *Chinese Intelligence Operations* (Annapolis, MD: Naval Institute Press, 1994), 21–37; "Physicist Admits to Spying for China," *Washington Times*, December 10, 1997, A9; *United States of America v. Larry Wu-Tai Chin aka Chin Wu-Tai in the United States District Court for the Eastern District of Virginia, Alexandria Division*, Criminal No. 85-00263-A, January 2, 1986, 2–3; National Counterintelligence Executive, *A Counterintelligence Reader*, vol. 4: *American Revolution into the New Millennium*, n.d., 434–439, http://fas.org/irp/ops/ci/docs/ci4/ch4.pdf; Director of Central Intelligence, Foreign Denial and Deception Committee, *The Jonathan Jay Pollard Espionage Case: A Damage Assessment*,

October 30, 1987, 45; David Wise, *Tiger Trap: America's Secret Spy War with China* (Boston: Houghton Mifflin Harcourt, 2011), 202–213, 151–166, 278n241; Jim Popkin, "Ana Montes Did Much Harm Spying for Cuba. Chances Are, You Haven't Hear of Her," www.washingtonpost .com, April 18, 2013, http://www.washingtonpost.com/sf/feature/wp/2013/04/18/ana-montes-did -much-harm-spying-for-cuba-chances-are-you-havent-heard-of-her; Brian Latell, *Castro's Secrets: The CIA and Cuba's Intelligence Machine* (New York: Palgrave Macmillan, 2012), 240–244.

9. Stéphane Lefebvre and Holly Porteous, "The Russian 10 . . . 11: An Inconsequential Adventure?," *International Journal of Intelligence and Counterintelligence* 24, no. 3 (Fall 2011): 447–466; *United States of America v. Defendant #1 a/k/a "Christopher R. Metsos,"* . . . *Defendant #8 a/k/a Vicky Pelaez*, Sealed Complaint, June 25, 2010, 2; *United States of America v. Anna Chapman and Mikhail Semnko*, Sealed Complaint, June 27, 2010, 1; Peter Baker and Benjamin Weiser, "10 Plead Guilty in Spy Ring Case as Swap Unfolds," *New York Times*, July 9, 2010, A1, A3; Devlin Barrett and Cassell Bryan-Low, "Twelfth Suspect in Russian Spy-Ring Case Is Deported," *Wall Street Journal*, July 14, 2010, A6; Andrew E. Kramer, "F.B.I. Says Russians Smuggled Out U.S. Microchips," *New York Times*, October 5, 2012, A10. Claims that the ring was a significant threat can be found in Ken Dilanian, "Spy Ring Was Genuine Threat, FBI Says," *Los Angeles Times*, November 1, 2011, A8; Bill Gertz, "FBI Says Russian Spies Got Close to Cabinet," www.washingtontimes .com, October 31, 2011, http://www.washingtontimes.com/news/2011/oct/31/fbi-says-russian -spies-got-close-to-cabinet/?page=all.

10. Terence McCoy, "This Alleged Russian Spy Ring Was Interested in Some Very Dangerous Things," www.washingtonpost.com, January 27, 2015, http://www.washingtonpost.com /news/morning-mix/wp/2015/01/27/this-alleged-russian-spy-ring-was-interested-in-some-very -dangerous-things; Benjmain Weiser, "3 Men Are Charged with Serving as Secret Agents for Russia in New York," *New York Times*, January 27, 2015, A16; Gregory Monaghan, Sealed Complaint, *United States of America v. Evgeny Buryakov a/k/a "Zhenya," Igor Sporyshev, and Victor Podobnyy, Defendants*, United States Southern District of New York, January 23, 2015, 1, 4, 15.

11. R. Jeffrey Smith, "Did Russia Sell Iraq Germ Warfare Equipment?," *Washington Post*, February 12, 1998, A1, A35; Peter Spiegel and Greg Miller, "Russians Told Iraqi Regime of U.S. Troop Movements," *Los Angeles Times*, March 25, 2006, A1, A7; Thom Shanker, "U.S. Inquiry Finds Russians Passed Spy Data to Iraq in '03," *New York Times*, March 25, 2006, A7; Mark Kramer, "Did Russia Help Saddam During the War?," www.washingtonpost.com, April 2, 2006; Kim Murphy, "Russia Denies Slipping U.S. War Plans to Iraq," *Los Angeles Times*, March 26, 2006, A32; Daniel Williams, "Russian Spy Agency Linked to Iran," *Washington Post*, March 23, 1998, A14; Bill Gertz, "U.S. Official Claims Russia Cutting Aid to Iran on Missiles," *Washington Times*, March 11, 1998, A5; Bill Gertz, "Russia Spies Active in the Balkans, CIA Says," *Washington Times*, March 23, 1999, A14; Kevin M. Woods with Michael R. Pease, Mark E. Stout, Williamson Murray, and James G. Lacey, Joint Forces Command, *Iraqi Perspective Project: A View of Operation Iraqi Freedom from Saddam's Senior Leadership*, 2006, 138–139, 144–145.

12. Juan O. Tamayo, "Soviets Spied on Gulf War Plans from Cuba, Defector Says," *Miami Herald*, April 3, 1998, 21A; William Rosenau, "A Deafening Silence: US Government Policy and the Sigint Facility at Lourdes," *Intelligence and National Security* 9, no. 4 (October 1994): 723–734; Andrew E. Kramer, "Russia Plans to Reopen Post in Cuba for Spying," *New York Times*, July 17, 2014, A8; Juan A. Tamayo, "Putin Denies Reports That Russia Plans to Reopen Spy Base in Cuba," www.washingtonpost.com, July 17, 2014, http://www.washingtonpost.com/ world/national-security/putin-denies-reports-that-russia-plans-to-reopen-spy-base-in-cuba/2014 /07/17/d8f6a288-0e20-11e4-8341-b8072b1e7348_story.html; Bill Gertz, "Pentagon: Russian Spy Ship, Tug Operating Near U.S.," *Washington Free Beacon*, April 25, 2014, http://freebeacon.com/ national-security/pentagon-russian-spy-ship-tug-operating-near-u-s.

13. National Counterintelligence Executive, *A Counterintelligence Reader*, 4: 202–203; Interagency OPSEC Support Staff, *Intelligence Threat Handbook*, n.d., 18–50.

14. John Deutch, "The Threat of Nuclear Diversion," Statement for the Record to the Permanent Subcommittee on Investigations of the Senate Committee on Governmental Affairs, March 20, 1996, 4.

15. Central Intelligence Agency, "Iranian Surveillance of US Persons and Facilities in 1995," FOIA Electronic Reading Room, January 1996, http://www.foia.cia.gov/sites/default/files/document_conversions/89801/DOC_0000676450.pdf.

16. Mike O'Connor, "Spies for Iranians Are Said to Gain a Hold in Bosnia," *New York Times*, November 28, 1997, A1, A8; Alan Cowell, "Berlin Court Says Top Iran Leaders Ordered Killings," *New York Times*, April 11, 1997, A1, A10; Carl Anthony Wege, "Iranian Intelligence Organizations," *International Journal of Intelligence and Counterintelligence* 10, no. 3 (Fall 1997): 287–298; Department of State, *Patterns of Global Terrorism, 1997*, 1998, 31.

17. Charlie Savage and Scott Shane, "Iranians Accused of Plot to Kill Saudis," *New York Times*, October 12, 2011, A1, A7; Siobhan Gorman, Devlin Barrett, and Stephanie Simon, "Accusations Against Iran Fleshed Out," *Wall Street Journal*, October 13, 2011, A5; Neil MacFarquhar, "Odd Twist for Elite Unit Guiding Iran's Proxy Wars," *New York Times*, October 12, 2011, A7; Joby Warrick, "U.S. Officials Among the Targets of Iran-Linked Assassination Plots," May 27, 2012, http://www.washingtonpost.com, http://www.washingtonpost.com/world/national-security/us-officials-among-the-targets-of-iran-linked-assassination-plots/2012/05/27/gJQAHlAOvU_story.html.

18. Mark Mazzetti, Jane Perlez, Eric Schmitt, and Andrew W. Lehren, "Pakistan Spy Unit Aiding Insurgents, Reports Suggest," *New York Times*, July 26, 2010, A1, A12; Julian E. Barnes, Matthew Rosenberg, and Habib Kahn Totakhill, "Pakistan Urges on Taliban," *Wall Street Journal*, October 7, 2010, A1, A14; Charlie Savage and Eric Schmitt, "F.B.I. Points to Pakistani Military in Long Plot to Tilt U.S. Policy," *New York Times*, July 20, 2011, A1, A6; Department of Justice, Office of Public Affairs, "Two Charged with Conspiring to Act as Unregistered Agents of Pakistani Government," July 10, 2011, http://www.fbi.gov/washingtondc/press-releases/2011/two-charged-with-conspiring-to-act-as-unregistered-agents-of-pakistani-government; *United States of America v. Syed Ghulam Nabi Fai and Zaheer Ahmad*, Case No. 1:11 MJ 558, United States District Court for the Eastern District of Virginia, July 18, 2011.

19. Carlotta Gall, *The Wrong Enemy: America in Afghanistan, 2001–2014* (Boston: Houghton Mifflin, 2014), 248–249.

20. Mark Mazzetti, Eric Schmitt, and Charlie Savage, "Pakistan Spies on Its Diaspora, Spreading Fear," *New York Times*, July 24, 2011, 1, 11.

21. Charlie Savage and J. David Goodman, "Syrian-American Is Arrested on Charges of Spying for Damascus," *New York Times*, October 13, 2011, A10; *United States of America v. Mohammad Anas Haitham Soueid (a/k/a "Alex Soueid," a/k/a "Anas Alswaid")*, Criminal No. 1:11cr494, United States District Court for the Eastern District of Virginia, Alexandria Division, October 2011, 3, 4, 6.

22. Ben Brandt, "The Taliban's Conduct of Intelligence and Counterintelligence," *CTC Sentinel* 4, no. 6 (June 2011): 19–23; Philip Shenon, "C.I.A. Officer Admits Guilt in Seeking Hezbollah Files," *New York Times*, November 14, 2007, A17; Department of Justice, "Former Employee of CIA and FBI Pleads Guilty to Conspiracy, Unauthorized Computer Access and Naturalization Fraud," November 13, 2007; Sheryl Gay Stolberg and Mark Mazzetti, "Suicide Bombing Puts a Rare Face on C.I.A.'s Work," *New York Times*, January 7, 2010, A1, A18; Robert Baer, "A Dagger to the CIA," www.gq.com, April 2010, http://www.gq.com/news-politics/politics/201004/dagger-to-the-cia; Stephen Farrell, "Video Bolsters Pakistani Link to C.I.A. Deaths," *New York Times*, January 10, 2010, 1, 10; "CIA Blast Blamed on Double Agent," *Wall Street Journal*, January 5, 2010, A1, A10; Mark Magnier, "CIA Spy Said He Gave Secrets to Militants," *Los Angeles Times*, January 10, 2010, A24; Joby Warrick, *The Triple Agent: The al-Qaeda Mole Who Infiltrated the CIA* (New York: Doubleday, 2011). Also see Michael J. Sulick, "Counterintelligence in the War Against Terrorism," *Studies in Intelligence* 48, no. 4 (2004): 25, http://www2.gwu.edu/~nsarchiv/NSAEBB/NSAEBB431.

23. Siobhan Gorman, August Cole, and Yochi Dreazen, "Computer Spies Breach Fighter-Jet Project," *Wall Street Journal*, April 21, 2009, A1, A12; Defense Security Service, *Targeting U.S. Technologies: A Trend Analysis of Cleared Industry Reporting*, 2013, 8–10; Danny Yadron, James T. Areddy, and Paul Mozur, "China Hacking Deep, Diverse," *Wall Street Journal*, May 30, 2014, A1, A8.

24. Inspector General, Department of the Air Force, General Counsel, Department of the Navy, Subject: Deconfliction of DOD Counterintelligence (CI) Cyber Operations with the Intelligence Community (IC), February 3, 2007; DOD Instruction S-5240.23, Subject: Counterintelligence (CI) Activities in Cyberspace, December 13, 2010.

25. Department of Defense Instruction 5240.04, Subject: Counterintelligence (CI) Investigations, February 2, 2009 (Incorporating Change 1, Effective October 15, 2013).

26. David Wise, *The Spy Who Got Away: The Inside Story of Edward Lee Howard, the CIA Agent Who Betrayed His Country's Secrets and Escaped to Moscow* (New York: Random House, 1988); Milt Bearden and James Risen, *The Main Enemy: The Inside Story of the CIA's Final Showdown with the KGB* (New York: Random House, 2003), 77–78.

27. Bearden and Risen, *The Main Enemy*, 77–78; Scott W. Carmichael, *True Believer: Inside the Investigation and Capture of Ana Montes, Cuba's Master Spy* (Annapolis, MD: Naval Institute Press, 2007), 3, 29.

28. Sandra Grimes and Jeanne Vertefeuille, *Circle of Treason: A CIA Account of Traitor Aldrich Ames and the Men He Betrayed* (Annapolis, MD: Naval Institute Press, 2012), 19.

29. Ibid., 120–121; John Deutch, Director of Central Intelligence, *Statement of the Director of Central Intelligence on the Clandestine Services and the Damage Caused by Aldrich Ames*, December 7, 1995, 6–8.

30. Grimes and Vertefeuille, *Circle of Treason*, 122–143.

31. Department of the Army, AR 381-47, *U.S. Army Counterintelligence Operations*, June 15, 1982, 2.

32. "Russian Newspaper Says Spy Satellite Was Expensive Test Dummy," *Aerospace Daily*, June 11, 1997, 399; Erich Schmidt-Eenboom, *Schnüffer ohne Nase: Der BND—Die Unheimliche Macht im Staate* (Dusseldorf: ECON Verlag, 1993); Andrei Soldatov and Irina Borogan, *The New Nobility: The Restoration of Russia's Security Service and the Enduring Legacy of the KGB* (New York: Public Affairs, 2010); Victor Ostrovsky and Claire Hoy, *By Way of Deception: The Making and Unmaking of a Mossad Officer* (New York: St. Martin's Press, 1990); Security Intelligence Review Commission, *Bridging the Gap: Recalibrating the Machinery of Security Intelligence and Intelligence Review, Annual Report 2012–2013*, September 2013.

33. David Wise, "China's Spilled Secrets," *Los Angeles Times*, September 6, 2011, A13.

34. Federal Research Division, Library of Congress, *Iran's Ministry of Intelligence and Security: A Profile*, December 2012.

35. Associated Press, "Iran Unveils Its New Fotros Unmanned Reconnaissance Drone," MatthewAid.com, November 18, 2013, http://www.matthewaid.com/post/67358058942/iran-unveils-its-new-fotros-unmanned; Gerry Doyle, "New Chinese Drone Unveiled in Video," *Sinosphere*, November 6, 2013, http://sinosphere.blogs.nytimes.com/2013/11/06/new-chinese-drone-unveiled-in-video.

36. Marc A. Stokes and L. C. Russell Hsiao, Project 2049 Institute, *Countering Chinese Cyber Operations: Opportunities and Challenges for U.S. Interests*, October 29, 2012; Mandiant Corporation, *APT 1: Exposing One of China's Cyber Espionage Units*, February 2013.

37. Dominic Perrone, "I&SS, Status of SISDE/SISMI Anti-terrorist Orientation," *Covert Action Information Bulletin* (April–May 1979): 6–9.

38. Amembassy Mexico, To: RUEHC/Sec State WashDC, Subject: Mexico: More Interagency Cooperation Needed on Intelligence Issues, November 10, 2009, http://wikileaks.org/cable/2009/11/09MEXICO3195.html.

39. Thierry Wolton, *Le KGB en France* (Paris: Bernard Grasser, 1986), 248–249.

40. Grimes and Vertefeuille, *Circle of Treason*; "Russian Convicted of Spying," *Washington Post*, November 12, 2002, A21.

41. Sergei L. Loiki, "Spy Case Is 2nd This Year, Russia Says," *Los Angeles Times*, May 16, 2013, A3; Gregory L. White, Paul Sonne, and Siobhan Gorman, "Russia Expels American on Spy Allegations," *Wall Street Journal*, May 15, 2013, A8; Khristina Narizhnaya and Sergei L. Loiko, "Russian Officials Allege Spying by U.S. Diplomat," *Los Angeles Times*, May 5, 2013, A3; David M. Herszenhorn and Ellen Barry, "From Russia, with Wig: U.S. Spy Suspect Ejected," *New York Times*, May 15, 2013, A1, A13.

42. Edward Wong, "China Is Said to Have Intelligence Official Suspected of Spying for U.S.," *New York Times*, June 2, 2012, A9; Barbara Demick, "China Is Said to Arrest Alleged U.S. Spy," *Los Angeles Times*, June 2, 2012, AA1, AA5.

43. Iderjit Badhwar, "Spy-Catching," *India Today*, September 20, 1987, 33; Yatish Yadav, "Former Spy Reveals Secrets of Research and Analysis Wing," *New Indian Express*, April 6, 2014, http://www.newindianexpress.com/nation/Former-Spy-Reveals-Secrets-of-Research-and-Analysis -Wing/2014/04/06/article2151632.ece.

44. Adam Goldman and Missy Ryan, "Spy Helped Unmask 3 Cuban Spy Networks, U.S. Officials Say," www.washingtonpost.com, December 18, 2014, http://www.washingtonpost.com /world/national-security/spy-helped-unmask-3-cuban-spy-networks-us-officials-say/2014/12/18/ b8d01242-86f1-11e4-b9b7-b8632ae73d25_story.html; Office of the Director of National Intelligence, "Statement on the Release of a Cuban Individual," December 17, 2014; Carol J. Williams, "Spy Released in Cuba Deal 'Did Heroic Work,'" *Los Angeles Times*, December 19, 2014, A7; Felicia Schwartz, "U.S. Spy in Havana Exposed American Moles," *Wall Street Journal*, December 19, 2014, A11.

45. Eli Lake, "One Big Reason the CIA Spied on Germany: Worries About Russian Moles in Berlin," *Daily Beast*, July 12, 2014, http://www.thedailybeast.com/articles/2014/07/12/ one-big-reason-the-cia-spied-on-germany-worries-about-russian-moles-in-berlin.html; Anton Troianovski, "New U.S. Spying Allegations Rock Germany," *Wall Street Journal*, July 5–6, 2014, A5; Philip Oltermann, "Germany Arrests BND Member on Suspicion of Spying For US," www .theguardian.com, July 4, 2014, http://www.theguardian.com/world/2014/jul/04/germany-arrest -bnd-spying-allegations-double-agent-us; "Germany Prepares Further Spying Clampdown," *Spiegel Online*, July 14, 2014.

46. Don Oberdorfer and Joanne Omang, "Nicaraguan Bares Plan to Discredit Foes," *Washington Post*, June 19, 1983, 1, 4.

47. Jack Anderson and Dale Van Atta, "Cuban Defector Impeaches CIA Spies," *Washington Post*, March 21, 1988, B15; Jack Anderson and Dale Van Atta, "CIA Recruits Were Castro's Agent," *Washington Post*, March 23, 1988, D11; Jack Anderson and Dale Van Atta, "CIA, Cubans in Looking-Glass War," *Washington Post*, March 25, 1988, E5; "Chinese Official Said Exposer of CIA Turncoat," *Washington Post*, September 5, 1986, A18; Michael Wines, "Spy Reportedly Unmasked by China Defector," *Los Angeles Times*, September 5, 1986, 1, 12; Daniel Southerland, "China Silent on Reported Defection of Intelligence Official," *Washington Post*, September 4, 1986, A30.

48. "Did Yurchenko Fool the CIA?," *Newsweek*, November 18, 1995, 34–39.

49. "High-Ranking KGB Agent Defects," *Washington Post*, June 20, 1986, A5.

50. "Defection of KGB Agent Causes Stir," *Washington Times*, June 6, 1990, A11; Bill Gertz, "CIA Learning from KGB Defector," *Washington Times*, March 5, 1992, A3; Mike Mattson, "A Counterintelligence Cold Case File: The Fourth Mole," *Intelligencer* (Winter/Spring 2009): 39–50, at 43; James Risen, "Defection of Senior Chinese Officer Is Confirmed," *New York Times*, March 24, 2001, A6.

51. Clifford J. Levy, "Defector Aided in Thwarting Russian Spies, Article Says," *New York Times*, November 12, 2010, A6; Sergei L. Loiko, "Russia Spy Saga Has New Twist: An Alleged Defector," *Los Angeles Times*, November 12, 2010, A3; Sergei L. Loiko, "Ex-Spymaster Convicted in Russian Court," *Los Angeles Times*, June 28, 2011, A4; Gregory L. White, "Russia Convicts Former Spy Official for Exposing Agents in U.S. Ring," *Wall Street Journal*, June 28, 2011, A11; Adam Rawnsley, "Did One of These Russian Colonels Sell Out the Sexy Spy?," www.wired.com,

November 19, 2010, http://www.wired.com/2010/11/did-one-of-these-russian-colonels-sell-out -the-sexy-spy.

52. William Drozdiak, "Germans Force U.S. to Recall 3 CIA Agents in Spy Case," *Washington Post*, September 30, 1999, A17, A20.

53. William Drozdiak, "The Cold War in Cold Storage," *Washington Post*, March 8, 1999, A17.

54. Steve Coll, "Seized Intelligence Files Spur U.S. Investigations," *Washington Post*, November 3, 2003, A15.

55. Robert Louis Benson and Michael Warner, eds., *VENONA: Soviet Espionage and the American Response, 1939–1957* (Washington, DC: National Security Agency/Central Intelligence Agency, 1996); Markus Wolf with Ann McElvoy, *Man Without a Face: The Autobiography of Communism's Greatest Spymaster* (New York: Times Books, 1997), 294; private information. Also see "SIGINT Support to Counterintelligence: The National Cryptologic Museum Library Collection," *Link* (May 2012): 2–7.

56. Barton Gellman, "Raids May Strike at Power Structure," *Washington Post*, February 17, 1998, A1, A9; Jeffrey T. Richelson, ed., National Security Archive Electronic Briefing Book No. 88, *Eyes on Saddam*, April 30, 2003, http://www2.gwu.edu/~nsarchiv/NSAEBB/NSAEBB88.

57. Central Intelligence Agency, CIA/PIR-1017/65, *Tung-Ching-Shan Electronic Intercept Site, China*, June 1965; National Photographic Interpretation Center, Z-12101/83, *KGB COMINT Collection Stations, USSR*, October 1983; Jeffrey T. Richelson, *America's Secret Eyes in Space: The U.S. KEYHOLE Spy Satellite Program* (New York: Harper & Row, 1990), 245; Matthew Aid, "More on Soviet SIGINT Sites," May 25, 2012, http://www.matthewaid.com/post/23730253552 /more-on-soviet-sigint-sites; Matthew Aid, "Most Soviet-Era KGB Listening Posts Still Operating and Listening to the West," July 2, 2013, http://www.matthewaid.com/post/54433673869/ most-soviet-era-kgb-listening-posts-still; Matthew Aid, "New Chinese SATCOM Intercept Site Discovered Near Changji," July 22, 2013, http://www.matthewaid.com/post/56159743665/new -chinese-satcom-intercept-site-discovered-near.

58. For a Cold War overview, see Stanley B. Farndon, "The Interrogation of Defectors," *Studies in Intelligence* 4, no. 3 (Summer 1960): 9–30. Also see Joseph Weisberg, "With Spies Like These," *Washington Post*, December 15, 2007, A21.

59. Ralph Blumenthal, "Moscow Moves Rapidly in Defections to the U.S.," *New York Times*, November 7, 1985, A12.

60. Bearden with Risen, *The Main Enemy*, 449–450.

61. See David Wise, *Molehunt: The Search for Traitors That Shattered the CIA* (New York: Random House, 1992); Tom Mangold, *Cold Warrior: James Jesus Angleton: The CIA's Master Spy Hunter* (New York: Simon & Schuster, 1991); [deleted], "James J. Angleton, Anatoliy Golitsyn, and the 'Monster Plot': Their Impact on CIA Personnel and Operations," *Studies in Intelligence* 55, no. 4 (December 2011), http://www2.gwu.edu/~nsarchiv/NSAEBB/NSAEBB431.

62. Central Intelligence Agency, "Vitaly Sergeyevich Yurchenko," November 8, 1985, 1–3.

63. "Did Yurchenko Fool the CIA?"; Celestine Bohlen, "Yurchenko Regales Moscow Audience," *Washington Post*, November 15, 1985, A33; "How Yurchenko Bade the C.I.A. Adieu," *New York Times*, November 7, 1985, A12; Stephen Engelberg, "U.S. Is Convinced That K.G.B. Agent Wants to Go Home," *New York Times*, November 6, 1985, A1, A12.

64. "Did Yurchenko Fool the CIA?"; Stephen Engelberg, "President Sees a Soviet 'Ploy' in 3 Defections," *New York Times*, November 7, 1985, A1, A12; Stephen Engelberg, "Washington Ponders Yurchenko: A Troubled Spy or Actor," *New York Times*, November 10, 1985, 20; Bob Woodward, "CIA Takes Serious Look at Theory That Yurchenko Was Double Agent," *Washington Post*, November 20, 1985, A35; Stephen Engelberg, "U.S. Aides Split on Yurchenko's Authenticity," *New York Times,* November 8, 1985, A10.

65. John Mintz, "FBI Chief Doubts Defection of Yurchenko Was Staged," *Washington Post*, December 2, 1985, A1, A14; Joel Brinkley, "Publicity Said to Have Upset Defector," *New York Times*, November 14, 1985, A12; Christopher Wren, "K.G.B. Man Reportedly Met with Envoy's

Wife," *New York Times*, November 9, 1985, 4; Arkady N. Shevchenko, "A Lesson of the Yurchenko Affair," *New York Times*, November 12, 1985, 35; Dale Russakof, "In Yurchenko Case, Truth Remains a Covert Factor," *Washington Post*, November 10, 1985, A1, A40–A41.

66. "Gates Calls '85 Defector Bona Fide," *Washington Post*, January 16, 1993, A7.

67. Richelson, *Spying on the Bomb*, 417.

68. Ibid.; Walter Pincus and Vernon Loeb, "China Spy Probe Shifts to Missiles," *Washington Post*, October 19, 2000, A1, A18–A19.

69. Jeffrey T. Richelson, *Spying on the Bomb: American Nuclear Intelligence from Nazi Germany to Iran and North Korea* (New York: W. W. Norton, 2006), 470–471.

70. U.S. Congress, Senate Select Committee on Intelligence, *Report of the Select Committee on Intelligence on the Use by the Intelligence Community of Information Provided by the Iraqi National Congress Together with Additional Views*, September 8, 2006, 30–31, 93.

71. Bob Drogin, *CURVEBALL: Spies, Lies, and the Con Man Who Caused a War* (New York: Random House, 2007), 112–114.

72. Siobhan Gorman, Farnaz Fassihi, and Jay Solomon, "As Iranian Surfaces, Intrigue Builds," *Wall Street Journal*, July 14, 2010, A9.

73. Central Intelligence Agency, "Message from the Director: Lessons from Khowst," October 20, 2010; Magnier, "CIA Spy Said He Gave Secrets to Militants" ; Ken Dilanian, "Failures Allowed Attack on CIA," *Los Angeles Times*, October 20, 2010, A1, A5; Mark Mazzetti, "Officer Failed to Warn C.I.A. Before Attack," *New York Times*, October 20, 2010, A1, A12; Stolberg and Mazzetti, "Suicide Bombing Puts a Rare Face on C.I.A.'s Work"; Stephen Farrell, "Video Bolsters Pakistani Taliban Link to C.I.A. Deaths," *New York Times*, January 10, 2010, 1, 10; Reuel Marc Gerecht, "The Meaning of al Qaeda's Double Agent," *Wall Street Journal*, January 8, 2010, A17; Baer, "A Dagger to the CIA." Also see Warrick, *The Triple Agent*.

74. Central Intelligence Agency, *Israel: Foreign Intelligence and Security Services*, March 1979, http://www2.gwu.edu/~nsarchiv/NSAEBB/NSAEBB407/docs/EBB-PollardDoc1.pdf.

75. Army Counterintelligence Center, *Wikileaks.org: An Online Reference to Foreign Intelligence Services, Insurgents, or Terrorist Groups*, March 18, 2008, 27.

76. Central Intelligence Agency, *Iraq: Foreign Intelligence and Security Services*, August 1985, iii. The study, in redacted, released form can be found as document 5 at Richelson, ed., National Security Archive Electronic Briefing Book No. 167, *Saddam's Iron Grip*.

77. Donald Rumsfeld, "To: Eric Edelman, Steve Cambone, Subject: Iraqi Intelligence," June 14, 2006, http://library.rumsfeld.com/doclib/sp/3879/2006-06-14%20to%20Eric%20Edelman %20et%20al%20re%20Iraqi%20Intelligence.pdf; Donald Rumsfeld, "To: Gen. John Abizaid, Subject: Intelligence Capabilities in Iraq and Afghanistan," June 20, 2006, http://library.rumsfeld .com/doclib/sp/3892/2006-06-20%20to%20GEN%20John%20Abizaid%20re%20Intelligence %20Capabilities%20in%20Iraq%20and%20Afghanistan.pdf.

78. Central Intelligence Agency, *Soviet Intelligence: KGB and GRU*, 1984.

79. See Amy Knight, *Spies Without Cloaks: The KGB's Successors* (Princeton, NJ: Princeton University Press, 1996); J. Michael Waller, *Secret Empire: The KGB in Russia Today* (Boulder, CO: Westview Press, 1994); Soldatov and Borogan, *The New Nobility*.

80. Central Intelligence Agency, *The Russian Security Services: Sorting Out the Pieces*, September 1992.

81. Documents obtained under the FOIA; Dennis F. Casey, Juan R. Jimenez, Gabriel G. Marshall, and Sharon N. Wright-Davis, *History of the Air Intelligence Agency, 1 July 1996–31 December 1997* (San Antonio, TX: Air Intelligence Agency, 2001), 1: 111–113.

82. Army Counterintelligence Center, *Wikileaks.org*. References to the first two reports mentioned are on 28.

83. Ibid., 3.

84. Defense Security Service, "Counterintelligence," http://www.dss.mil/ci/index.html (accessed July 25, 2013).

85. "Partners in Espionage," *Security Awareness Bulletin*, August 1984, 1–8; Linda Melvern, David Hedbitch, and Nick Anning, *Techno-Bandits: How the Soviets Are Stealing America's High-Tech Future* (Boston: Houghton, Mifflin, 1984), 242; *Affidavit of Allen M. Power, Federal Bureau of Investigation, Submitted to State and Northern District of California, City and County of San Francisco*, October 16, 1983, 1–2; "For Love of Money and Adventure," *Time*, October 31, 1983, 39–40; Howard Kurtz, "California Man Charged with Spying," *Washington Post*, October 18, 1983, A1, A4; David Wise, "How Our Spy Spied Their Spy," *Los Angeles Times*, October 23, 1983, 1, 6.

86. "Greece Charges Three as Spies After U.S. Tip," *Washington Post*, September 17, 1985, A29; Mattson, "A Counterintelligence Cold Case File," 45.

87. Bob Woodward and Dan Morgan, "Soviet Threat Toward Iran Overstated, Casey Concluded," *Washington Post*, January 13, 1987, A1, A8.

88. Henry Hurt, *Shadrin: The Spy Who Never Came Back* (New York: McGraw-Hill, 1981), 52–82, 140–151.

89. Ibid., 206; Patrick E. Tyler, "Missing U.S. Agent Dead," *Washington Post*, October 30, 1985, A9.

90. Department of Defense Instruction S-5240.17, Subject: Counterintelligence Collection, January 12, 2009; Department of Defense Instruction S-5240.09, Subject: Offensive Counterintelligence Operations (OFCO), October 29, 2008, 2, 24, 26; Department of the Army, AR 381-47, *U.S. Army Offensive Counterintelligence Operations*, 1982, 7.

91. Richard Halloran, "Overtures to Soldiers to Spy for Soviet Bloc Said to Rise," *New York Times*, June 29, 1985, A1, B5.

92. "Former Counterspy for Army Is Indicted on Subversion Charges," *New York Times*, April 10, 1984, A20.

93. Ibid.

94. Ibid.

95. Ronald Kessler, *Inside the CIA: Revealing the Secrets of the World's Most Powerful Spy Agency* (New York: Pocket Books, 1992), 20–21; Mike Mattson, "A Counterintelligence Cold Case File," *Intelligencer* (Winter/Spring 2009): 39–50.

96. George Tenet with Bill Harlow, *At the Center of the Storm: My Years at the CIA* (New York: HarperCollins, 2007), 124.

97. Gus Weiss, "The Farewell Dossier," *Studies in Intelligence* 39, no. 5 (1996): 121–126.

98. Reagan, *Introduction to US Counterintelligence*., 29; Department of Defense Instruction 5240.05, Subject: Technical Surveillance Countermeasures (TSCM) Program, February 22, 2006.

99. Department of Defense Directive 5210.48, Subject: Polygraph and Credibility Assessment Program, January 25, 2007 (Incorporating Change 2, Effective November 15, 2013).

100. DCI Counterintelligence Center, "Why People Spy: A Project Slammer Report," *Counterintelligence Trends*, January 1993, 9ff.

101. Reagan, *Introduction to US Counterintelligence*, 29.

16

COVERT ACTION

Traditionally, covert action involved activities designed to influence foreign governments, events, organizations, or persons in support of U.S. foreign policy in such a way that the involvement of the U.S. government was not apparent. During the Ronald Reagan and George H. W. Bush administrations, the practice of "overt-covert action" emerged, the clearest examples being the attempt to overthrow the Sandinista government and support for the Afghan resistance. In the George W. Bush and Barack Obama administrations, targeted killing, an activity traditionally considered covert, if conducted at all, was conducted openly.

During the Cold War, U.S. covert actions included (1) political advice and counsel; (2) subsidies to individuals; (3) financial support and technical assistance to political parties or groups; (4) support to private organizations, including labor unions and business firms; (5) covert propaganda; (6) training of individuals; (7) economic operations; (8) paramilitary or political action operations designed to overthrow or support a regime; and up until the mid-1960s (9) attempted assassination.[1] Many of those activities, such as paramilitary or political action operations, were highly visible and designed to achieve a specific objective—the overthrow of a regime or the defeat of an insurgent force. Many behind-the-scenes political and propaganda activities have also been intended to achieve a specific objective, such as the electoral defeat of a political candidate or party.

Other low-visibility operations involving propaganda or aid to individuals or organizations have focused more on enhancing long-term U.S. objectives and countering similar Soviet activities rather than achieving a specific near-term objective. Furthermore, a high-visibility operation might be conducted without expectation of "success." When the United States began aiding the Afghan rebels, after the 1979 Soviet invasion, there was no expectation of actually inducing Soviet withdrawal; the intention was simply to drain Soviet resources and keep international attention on the Soviet role in Afghanistan.

Thus, beginning in 1946 and extending for various periods, the United States, principally through the Central Intelligence Agency (CIA), engaged in a wide variety of covert action operations. These included support to political parties and labor unions in France and Italy; support to resistance groups in the Soviet Union; masterminding the overthrow of Guatemalan and Iranian governments; a full-scale covert action campaign (including an attempted assassination) directed against the Cuban regime of Fidel Castro; political action in an attempt to prevent Salvador Allende from becoming president of Chile and then to remove him once he attained that position; propaganda operations directed against the Soviet SS-20 deployment in Europe and against the Sandinista regime in Nicaragua; paramilitary operations in Afghanistan and Nicaragua; and political support for operations in El Salvador and Panama.[2]

The years between the end of the Cold War and the terrorist attacks of September 11, 2001, represent the first era of post–Cold War covert action. The Soviet collapse meant the end of that worldwide ideological conflict that had led to covert support of publications in Western Europe and elsewhere that advanced Western democratic values and sought to undermine the propaganda of the Soviet Union and other Marxist regimes. In contrast, no similar ideological conflict was being waged between the United States and its allies on one side and Iraq, North Korea, and Libya on the other.

In addition, formerly covert activities, such as support of political parties or broadcasting, are now often conducted overtly. Thus, the National Endowment for Democracy (NED) provided support to Nicaraguan political parties that ran against the Sandinistas in the 1990 election. A September 22, 1989, National Security Directive declared, "The Department of State shall undertake a vigorous *overt* program to support a free and fair election process. Every effort will be made, consistent with U.S. law, to assist the democratic opposition to compete effectively with the Sandinista regime." Further, the directive specified, "There shall be no *covert* assistance to political or other groups in Nicaragua in the upcoming election campaign."[3]

In 1995 the Agency for International Development (AID) began providing funds, which totaled $26 million by May 1998, to Indonesian human rights and free speech groups, including the Indonesian Legal Aid Society headed by a leading figure in the Indonesian democracy movement. Altogether, AID provided funds to thirty nongovernmental organizations in Indonesia. Prior to the 2000 Serbian election, AID and the NED provided support to student groups, labor unions, independent media outlets, and Serbian heavy metal bands that participated in street concerts as part of a voter registration drive. Likewise, some of the broadcast operations, such as Radio Free Asia and Radio Farda (approved by Congress in 1997), are openly acknowledged and funded rather than being conducted as covert operations.[4]

The emergence of a number of rogue states that the Soviet Union might previously have restrained also had an impact on U.S. policy. Although undermining these states politically was one objective of U.S. covert action policy, an equally or more critical concern was impeding the acquisition of technologies that would facilitate the production of weapons of mass destruction (WMD) and potentially destroying the facilities used to produce such weapons.

During this period, there were three major transnational targets: proliferation of weapons of mass destruction, terrorism, and international narcotics trafficking. Proliferation could involve the acquisition of technologies and information from Europe, their transportation (by physical or electronic means) to the acquiring nation, and, finally, their exploitation to produce weapons of mass destruction. Likewise, terrorism could be planned in Lebanon or Afghanistan, funded through Switzerland, and carried out in London, Paris, New York, or Africa. Ultimately, narcotics trafficking involved leadership, production facilities, transportation, transit points, and delivery to a variety of nations. In each case, operations could be directed toward a number of points, and a number of techniques could be employed in an attempt to disrupt or neutralize such activities.

There were other important aspects of the first era of post–Cold War covert action. The greater prevalence of underground targets, designed to avoid overhead surveillance and to protect the facility from attack, added a new dimension to any paramilitary operation seeking to destroy such targets. Such targets might include command and control facilities, missile factories, aircraft shelters, submarine bases, and nuclear sites.[5]

In addition, new means became available for covert operators to employ. Among the most important of the new technologies was cyber warfare, which can be used to deprive hostile parties of the financial resources needed to perform terrorist acts or acquire WMD technologies, or they can be used to damage facilities themselves. According to one account, during the Bill Clinton administration, the CIA had been ordered to "diddle with" Serbian strongman Slobodan Milošević's bank accounts. In 1997 the Secretary of Defense authorized the National Security Agency (NSA) to engage in computer network attack operations. More recently, in 2003, "Pentagon planners . . . devised strategies for possible cyber-attack to disrupt the financial infrastructure of the Iraqi state," although those strategies were never implemented.[6]

The changes in both targets and the techniques employed meant that covert action operations were now planned and carried out not only by the CIA but also by other organizations. The NSA and the military service signals intelligence organizations assumed cyber warfare operations responsibilities. In addition, the U.S. Special Operations Command and its subsidiary organizations (discussed in Chapter 6) now play a significant role in the operations designed to neutralize WMD or narcotics production facilities.

After the 1998 attacks on U.S. embassies in Africa, the CIA was authorized to use covert means to disrupt and preempt terrorist operations planned abroad by al-Qaeda. President Clinton signed three Memoranda of Notification, which first authorized the killing of Osama bin Laden, then expanded the authorization to several senior al-Qaeda officials, and finally authorized the shooting down of private civilian aircraft on which they flew.[7]

The 9/11 attacks ushered in a new era of covert action. Almost all aspects of the first post–Cold War era of covert action mentioned above still pertain. But the United States now finds itself facing a new worldwide conflict driven by ideology—with this era's opposing ideology being militant Islam or Islamic totalitarianism. If that was not apparent immediately after the September 11 attacks, it has become more so in subsequent years and has been dramatically reemphasized by the rise of the Islamic State in Iraq and Syria (ISIS).*

---

*As numerous analyses have noted, militant Islam is not a centrally directed movement, and it has become even less so since the onset of military actions against the Taliban and al-Qaeda. Militant Islam includes al-Qaeda-affiliated and al-Qaeda-inspired organizations, as well as the too-radical-for-al-Qaeda ISIS. But there is an adherence to a common ideology and a desire, rather than a plan, to establish a caliphate through terrorism and intimidation and, along the way, to force significant changes in Western behavior, including that of cartoonists and satirists.

The attacks also led to a far more widespread use of prisoner renditions and unapologetic willingness to engage in targeted killings of Taliban and al-Qaeda leaders. President George W. Bush signed a Presidential Finding calling for the destruction of bin Laden and his organization and for doing "whatever necessary" to achieve the result. Al-Qaeda's communications, security apparatus, and infrastructure were among the specific elements to be destroyed. Furthermore, the Bush administration concluded, based on two classified memoranda (one written in 1998 and the other after the 9/11 attacks), that executive orders banning assassination did not prevent singling out individuals to be killed if those individuals were engaged in an ongoing terrorist war against the United States.* As a result, the United States has developed an extensive network of drone bases from which to conduct intelligence/strike operations employing Predator and Reaper unmanned vehicles. Bases are or have been located in Afghanistan, Djibouti, Qatar (Al Udeid Air Base), Ethiopia, the Seychelles, and Pakistan.[8]

In December 2009, the Director of the CIA presented President-elect Obama with a list of fourteen covert action operations in progress, including the following:

- Conduct secret, lethal counterterrorism operations in more than sixty nations
- Stop or delay Iran's development of nuclear weapons
- Deter North Korea from adding to its nuclear weapons arsenal
- Engage in counterproliferation operations to prevent select nations from developing weapons of mass destruction
- Conduct lethal and other operations in support of the U.S. forces in Afghanistan or independently
- Run a variety of lethal operations in Iraq
- Aid secret efforts to halt genocide in the Darfur region of Sudan
- Provide Turkey with intelligence and other support to prevent the Kurdish Worker's Party (PKK) in northern Iraq from establishing a separatist enclave within Turkey
- Counter narcotics production and trafficking
- Perform propaganda operations
- Conduct rendition, detention, and interrogations operations.[9]

In addition to such operations conducted by the CIA, a set of operations was ordered on September 30, 2010, when CENTCOM commander General David H. Petraeus signed the Joint Unconventional Warfare Execute Order. Reportedly, the order's goals were to create networks that could "penetrate, disrupt, defeat or destroy" al-Qaeda and other militant groups as well as "prepare the environment" for future attacks by U.S. or local military forces.[10]

---

*The issue of the utility of targeted killings of high-value targets is discussed in Andrew Cockburn, *Kill Chain: The Rise of the High-Tech Assassins* (New York: Henry Holt, 2015); Directorate of Intelligence, CIA, *Making High-Value Targeting Operations an Effective Counterinsurgency Tool*, July 7, 2009; Bryan C. Price, "Targeting Top Terrorists: How Leadership Decapitation Contributes to Counterterrorism," *International Security* 36, no. 4 (Spring 2012): 9–46; Patrick B. Johnston, "Does Decapitation Work? Assessing the Effectiveness of Leadership Targeting in Counterinsurgency Campaigns," *International Security* 36, no. 4 (Spring 2012): 47–79.

PHOTO 16.1 The Predator MQ-1B can carry imagery sensors for intelligence and target location, as well as two Hellfire missiles. *Photo credit:* USAF.

PHOTO 16.2 MQ-9 Reaper drone. *Photo credit:* USAF.

AFGHANISTAN

In 1998 the CIA began deploying officers to northern Afghanistan to convince Ahmad Shah Massoud, the leader of the Northern Alliance (NA), to marshal his forces to capture and possibly kill Osama bin Laden, offering him a large amount of money. The effort to recruit Massoud followed the unsuccessful attempt to kill bin Laden with a cruise missile attack on a site where he was scheduled to meet with two to three hundred members of al-Qaeda. In 1999 members of the Special Activities Division (SA) secretly entered Afghanistan, at least once, to prepare a desert airstrip to extract bin Laden, should he be captured, or to evacuate U.S. tribal allies should they be cornered.[11]

In the aftermath of 9/11, President Bush decided to seek to destroy not only al-Qaeda but the Taliban regime that had given bin Laden and his organization a home after their expulsion from Sudan. The CIA's Counterterrorism Center (CTC) conceived a plan that involved sending teams of CTC, Special Activities, and Special Forces personnel to various parts of Afghanistan to work with the Northern Alliance and other Afghan opposition groups. The teams were to be headed by a Farsi- or Dari-speaking officer, with a deputy from the SA.[12]

By the evening of September 26, the first JAWBREAKER team, also designated the Northern Alliance Liaison Team, had arrived in the Panjshir Valley in northeastern Afghanistan. Part of the team's mission was to provide intelligence to U.S. forces, as well as to assist Northern Alliance, including COMINT collection, efforts. But it also had a covert action mission: to convince the Northern Alliance to accept U.S. military forces into the area and to provide the NA with financial support.[13]

The first JAWBREAKER team provided General Mohammad Fahim Khan, the overall leader of the Northern Alliance, with $1 million to assist in preparing his forces for upcoming battles. The team also gave $500,000 to the head of the NA intelligence organization and, in mid-October, provided an additional $1.7 million to General Fahim and Dr. Abdullah Abdullah, the NA's foreign minister. Of that sum, $750,000 was to help Fahim bring his forces to full combat readiness, while another $250,000 was to be used to purchase humanitarian supplies for the civilian population living near the battlefields. A further $250,000 was intended for General Osad Atta, a senior Northern Alliance commander. The remaining $450,000 was for the daily operation of the NA's intelligence organization and for possible bribes to persuade Taliban commanders to defect to the Northern Alliance.[14]

In early October 2001, a CIA-led team in southern Afghanistan, the ECHO Team, met with Hamid Karzai, then a popular tribal leader who had been forced out of Afghanistan and was organizing resistance to the Taliban from Pakistan. Karzai had been the first Pashtun leader to offer to cooperate with the United States in establishing a military resistance in the southern part of the country. In their discussions, the ECHO Team and Karzai prepared the foundation of support for his return and arranged airdrops of weapons and ammunition for his supporters.[15]

The CIA would supply the Taliban's opposition in the south, including Karzai's forces and those led by the former governor of Kandahar, with AK-47 assault rifles from agency holdings and with other light weaponry. In addition, it provided uniforms and food. The CIA made contact with other tribal leaders, offering weapons, money, and other benefits to induce them to join the opposition to the Taliban. CIA representatives also used money and threats in an effort to get dissident Taliban commanders to switch sides.[16]

Afghanistan has also been the site of both failed and successful attempts at targeted killing. In May 2002, former Afghan prime minister Gulbuddin Hekmaytar, the leader of a hardline Islamic group, was the target of, or one of a group that was the target of, a Hellfire missile fired from a Predator. Hekmaytar had been planning to attack Karzai's government and possibly Karzai himself. The missile missed Hekmaytar but killed some of his followers. An administration official stated that the missile was aimed at a group of people from his organization, not solely Hekmaytar, who "sadly" survived.[17]

The United States conducted well over two hundred drone strikes in Afghanistan each year in 2009 and 2010 and almost three hundred in 2011. In 2012 the number of strikes had risen to 506. In July 2012, a strike killed three Taliban leaders when it destroyed the SUV they were in, along with the civilians who were unwillingly giving them a ride. Another, in Marawara district of Kunar province in September 2012, killed two Taliban commanders who "littered the area with roadside bombs and threatened to kill Afghans who worked for the U.S. military."[18]

In addition to launching Predator strikes on targets, U.S. and Afghani forces pursued and attempted to kill Taliban insurgents on the ground. In early 2010, it was reported that "small teams of Army commandos, Navy Seals, and Central Intelligence Agency operatives ha[d] intensified the pace of what the military often calls 'kill-capture missions'—hunting down just one or two insurgents at a time." A little over a year later, according to another account, the U.S. strike teams had grown from four in 2009 to twenty in 2011, with 10 to 200 men in each. Between April 24, 2010, and April 15, 2011, U.S. Special Forces had conducted 11,500 operations in Afghanistan, killed or captured 1,500 insurgent leaders, captured 8,000 insurgents, and killed another 3,200.[19]

In addition, the CIA trained and deployed, in response to authorization from President George W. Bush, a 3,000-member paramilitary force, consisting mostly of Afghans and known as Counterterrorism Pursuit Teams. One of those is apparently the Paktita Defense Force, described as "one of six C.I.A.-trained Afghan militias that serve as a special operations force against insurgents throughout Afghanistan." The team's primary function is to kill or capture Taliban insurgents, although it has also conducted pacification operations as well as cross-border operations into Pakistan.[20]

Another, the Khost Protection Force, has been described as a "C.I.A.-trained paramilitary unit that has carried out operations along the border with Pakistan for more than a decade." In an October 2014 operation, force members descended on a compound believed to house suicide bombers, killing three people. At that time, such units were scheduled to be turned over to the Afghan National Directorate of Security in 2015.[21]

GREYSTONE

On September 17, 2001, President Bush authorized a global counterterrorist effort, which consisted of dozens of component programs. This effort, known as

GREYSTONE (GST), included efforts to capture and hold suspected al-Qaeda officials, maintenance of secret prisons ("black sites"), and use of enhanced interrogation techniques (the latter two were discussed in Chapter 11). Other GST components involved improving the CIA's ability to sort through international financial data and to monitor the communications of suspects globally. The authorization also permitted creation of paramilitary units to hunt and kill designated targets anywhere in the world.[22]

The acquisition of suspected al-Qaeda personnel has been accomplished through a variety of means: abductions by CIA officers, arrests by foreign governments and transfer to U.S. custody, and raids, sometimes conducted in concert with or by foreign intelligence services or special forces in Pakistan, Afghanistan, and other nations. For example, in March 2002, Pakistani special forces took al-Qaeda official Abu Zubaydah into custody and turned him over to the United States, and a joint U.S.-Pakistani operation resulted in the arrest of chief 9/11 planner Khalid Sheikh Mohammed. Most controversial has been the practice of rendition, the holding and interrogation of terrorism suspects in other nations without due process.*[23]

In November 2001, Muhammad Saad Iqbal Madni was arrested by Indonesia's State Intelligence Agency after it was informed by the CIA that he was an al-Qaeda operative who had worked with shoe bomber Richard Reid. Madni was then sent to Egypt for interrogation. In 2002, in a case of mistaken identity, the CIA arranged for Khalid el-Masri, a German citizen with Lebanese parents, to be detained during a visit to Macedonia and sent to Afghanistan for interrogation. In February 2003, the CIA snatched a radical Muslim cleric, Hassan Mustafa Osama Nasr, also known as Abu Omar, off the street in Milan, Italy.[24]

In October 2001, Jamil Qasim Saeed Mohammed, a Yemeni student of microbiology wanted in connection with the attack on the USS *Cole*, was transported from Pakistan to Jordan on a U.S.-registered Gulfstream jet. The rendition followed his being surrendered to U.S. authorities in Karachi by Pakistan's Inter-Services Intelligence Directorate (ISI). The Gulfstream was one of twenty-six planes owned by the CIA, ten of which had been acquired after 2001. The planes are owned by shell companies with no employees and operated by actual companies controlled by or tied to the CIA.

---

*At least one terrorism rendition took place prior to the 9/11 attacks. CIA officers worked with the Albanian security service to seize five Egyptian members of Islamic Jihad suspected of planning to bomb the U.S. embassy in Albania's capital, Tirana. The five were soon flown to Egypt, where two were executed. See Andrew Higgins and Christopher Cooper, "A CIA-Backed Team Used Brutal Means to Crack Terror Cell," *Wall Street Journal*, November 20, 2001, A1, A10. On earlier renditions to the United States, see Daniel Benjamin and Steven Simon, *The Age of Sacred Terror* (New York: Random House, 2002), 251–252. According to those authors a rendition qualifies as an "extraordinary rendition" only if an individual is removed from the country without the approval of the host government. See Daniel Benjamin and Steven Simon, *The Next Attack: The Failure of the War on Terror and a Strategy for Getting It Right* (New York: Owl, 2006), 256. In contrast, former CIA counsel John Rizzo describes "extraordinary rendition" as a "term that has become a permanent part of the post-9/11 lexicon" that he never heard of previously; he characterizes it as a "pejorative redundancy." See John Rizzo, *Company Man: Thirty Years of Controversy and Crisis in the CIA* (New York: Scribner, 2014), 260.

In addition to two different types of Gulfstream jets, the fleet included a Boeing Business Jet, a DC-3, a Hercules transport, a de Havilland Twin Otter, a Learjet 35, and a Beech Super King 200. A report to the European Parliament in spring 2006 estimated that this CIA fleet had made 1,000 flights.[25]

In December 2011, a hearing in a federal court resulted in the disclosure that Mohamed Ibrahim Ahmed, an Eritrean citizen, had been questioned in a Nigerian jail by American intelligence personnel without being informed of his Miranda rights. A subsequent rendition involved three men arrested as they attempted to pass through Djibouti. The men, two Swedes and one resident of the United Kingdom, were accused of supporting the al-Shahab Islamist militia. Eventually, they would be taken into custody by the Federal Bureau of Investigation (FBI) and transported to the United States for trial.[26]

Probably the best-known rendition, since it landed numerous CIA officers in trouble with the Italian legal system, occurred in February 2003. A team of agency officers kidnapped radical imam Abu Omar, who had been under surveillance by the Milan police, and shipped him off to Egypt, where he was interrogated and eventually released.[27]

About seventy others arrested or captured under the GREYSTONE program were transferred to the custody of foreign governments. Afghanistan, Algeria, Pakistan, Uzbekistan, Morocco, Egypt, and Jordan are among those that have received individuals rendered by the United States for interrogation.[28]

IRAN

The covert operation directed by President Reagan's National Security Council (NSC) that ended in the highly publicized Iran-Contra affair was only one of a number of covert operations targeted against Iran. CIA operations during the Reagan and Bush years were designed to aid Iranian paramilitary and political exile groups, counter Soviet influence in Iran, and give the United States a role of its own in the event that the Khomeini regime collapsed. The initial goal was to knit together a coalition of exile groups and their supporters still in Iran so that, if the opportunity arose, they could be a significant factor in shaping the future of the country.[29]

The covert action included providing several million dollars to units composed largely of Iranian exiles in eastern Turkey. The larger of the paramilitary groups had 6,000 to 8,000 men under the command of former rear admiral Ahmad Madani, the commander of the Iranian navy under the Shah, who was court-martialed for "being against the government" and became the first defense minister in the Khomeini regime. The second unit, which consisted of fewer than 2,000 men, was commanded by General Bahram Aryana, chief of staff of the Iranian army under the Shah. The paramilitary groups were intended to perform two functions: in the event of a Soviet invasion of Iran, they could harass the flanks of the Soviet armed forces, and in the event of a civil war or domestic upheaval, they could enter Iran to protect and bolster any centrist forces. The CIA was also reported to be financing Iranian exile groups said to be situated principally in France and Egypt. Support was made available to groups both on the left (up to but not including Abolhassan Bani-Sadr) and the right (up to but not including the monarchist factions).[30]

The CIA established and financed a radio station in Egypt to broadcast anti-Khomeini information. In 1987 regular features included reports on long food lines, pockets of opposition and small uprisings against the clergy and Revolutionary Guards, torture and killings by the government, and gains made by Iranian Communists and agents of the Soviet Union. In September 1986, the CIA provided a miniaturized suitcase television transmitter for a clandestine broadcast to Iran by the Shah's son. The broadcast disrupted two channels of Iranian television for eleven minutes at 9 p.m. on September 5.[31]

In addition, the CIA secretly provided Iraq with detailed intelligence to assist with Iraqi bombing raids on Iran's oil terminals and power plants. In 1984, when some feared that Iran might overrun Iraq, the United States began supplying intelligence that reportedly enabled Iraq to calibrate mustard gas attacks on Iranian ground troops. In early 1985, Iraq began receiving regular satellite information from Washington, particularly after Iraqi bombing raids. It is not clear whether the Iraqis were receiving actual photos or information derived from the photos at that point. In any case, in August 1986, the CIA established a top secret Washington-Baghdad link to provide the Iraqis with better and more timely satellite intelligence. The Iraqis would thus receive information from satellite images "several hours" after a bombing raid in order to assess damage and plan the next attack. By December 1986, the Iraqis were receiving selected portions of the actual photos taken by KH-11 and SR-71 overhead platforms. According to one account, some of the information and imagery provided was incomplete or had been doctored, with the size of Soviet troop strength on the Iranian border being inflated, in order to advance the administration's goals.[32]

A more recent objective of U.S. covert action programs with respect to Iran has been to retard Iran's progress toward development of nuclear weapons. One operation revolved around the Tinners' sale to Iran of allegedly high-quality vacuum pumps needed so that the centrifuges employed in uranium enrichment can operate inside a vacuum seal (see Chapter 11). The pumps, though produced in Germany, were first purchased by the Oak Ridge and Los Alamos laboratories and altered so that they would break down under operational conditions. In 2010 a study estimated that Iranian centrifuges were operating at only 20 percent efficiency. An International Atomic Energy Agency (IAEA) report indicated that there were 3,936 uranium enrichment centrifuges operating at the Natanz site, while 4,592 were not operating. Also a victim of sabotage was a power supply purchased from Turkey. In 2006, after the Iranians installed the power supply at their Natanz facility, it failed, causing fifty centrifuges to explode.[33]

Another operation had as its objective provisions to Iran of deceptive material about a nuclear weapons component—the TBA-480 Fireset that was employed in the Soviet nuclear weapons programs to trigger a nuclear detonation. The CIA's Counterproliferation Division raised the possibility, in September 1996, of locating a Russian émigré asset with a nuclear weapons background, particularly in the electronics/firing set area, who would be recruited to offer "help" to the Iranian nuclear weapons program. That November, the CIA approached a candidate to serve as the conduit to Iran. The individual, who had worked at the Arzamas-16 design bureau, agreed and was code-named MERLIN.[34]

The CIA intended to provide the Iranians with flawed but promising information about the triggering mechanism that would induce them to waste time and money in pursuit of development. The flawed plans were produced with assistance of nuclear weapons experts at one or more of the Department of Energy national laboratories. One memo noted that in the opinion of one lab's personnel, "it would take a long time to realize that the more advanced design won't work on a simple weapon"—reference to the fact that the device the Iranian's would be attempting to produce was suitable for advanced Soviet-era weapons but not for an Iranian "starter" bomb.[35]

Over the next several years a number of Iranian individuals and institutions were identified as targets for the deception pitch and various methods of approach, including written communications from the Russian émigré offering information to assist the Iranian nuclear program. Ultimately, in March 2000, MERLIN delivered a package with schematics, drawings, and a letter to the Iranian mission to the International Atomic Energy Agency in Vienna. According to the CIA, the contents were taken "seriously" by the Iranians, who "couriered them back to Iran rather than rejecting them at the outset." The declassified record includes a March 2003 CIA memo titled "Surveilling the Iranians in City A for a Classified Program No. 1 Approach." However, subsequent to MERLIN's appearance at the Iranian mission to the IAEA, there was no response from Iran to MERLIN.*[36]

In 2009 President Bush authorized covert efforts to undermine electrical systems, computer systems, and other networks associated with Iran's nuclear program. One consequence was the U.S.-Israeli effort, part of the U.S. computer network attack program designated OLYMPIC GAMES, that produced the Stuxnet computer worm. It was developed with the specific objective of changing the rotor speed of Iranian centrifuges, first increasing and then lowering it, with the apparent intention of causing extensive vibrations or distortions that would destroy the centrifuges. The worm, which targeted Siemens software systems and took over industrial control systems, has also affected facilities in India, Indonesia, and the United States, although 60 percent of the computers infected were in Iran.[37]

Other covert operations have been proposed or authorized with regard to Iran's activities within in Iraq. In 2011 it was reported that military commanders and intelligence officials were pushing for greater authority to conduct covert operations designed to block Iranian influence in Iraq. Possible operations would be intended to increase interdiction efforts at the Iraq-Iran border and devote greater effort to halting Iranian arms smuggling operations.[38]

In 2011 and 2012, the White House approved the employment of the CIA to train Iraq's Counterterrorism Service (CTS), a mission that had been the responsibility of the U.S. military. The CTS consists of elite units that used to belong to the Iraqi Ministry of Defense and Ministry of the Interior. The decision to use the CIA was a consequence of the withdrawal of U.S. military forces from Iraq and would allow "the U.S. to covertly help Iraq build up the effectiveness of its counterterrorism operations." According to one official, "This relationship is focused on supporting the Iraqis to deal with terrorist threats within their borders, and not about ramping up unilateral operations" by the CIA or U.S. military.[39]

---

*A version of the operation was disclosed in James Risen, *State of War: The Secret History of the CIA and the Bush Administration* (New York: Free Press, 2006).

LIBYA

In addition to authorizing an NSC disinformation operation, Ronald Reagan authorized a CIA covert operation to undermine the Libyan regime of Mu'ammar Qaddafi. The plan involved CIA assistance to other countries in North Africa and the Middle East that opposed Qaddafi. Authorized in a fall 1985 Presidential Finding, the program's first objective was to disrupt, preempt, and frustrate Qaddafi's subversive and terrorist plans. Beyond that, the CIA hoped to lure him into some foreign adventure or terrorist exploit that would give a growing number of Qaddafi opponents in the Libyan military a chance to seize power or justify a military response by Algeria or Egypt. Another CIA operation, code-named TULIP, involved support for anti-Qaddafi exile movements, including the National Front for the Salvation of Libya, and for the efforts of other countries such as Egypt.[40]

In 1988 the CIA began an operation to destabilize Qaddafi's regime using U.S-trained Libyan commandos. The program, which began in the final months of the Reagan administration, provided military aid and training to six hundred former Libyan soldiers at a base outside the Chadian capital of N'Djamena. The Libyan force consisted of solders captured in 1988 border fighting between Libya and Chad. The commandos never actually launched a serious military operation. After Chad's government fell in December 1990, the force was moved to Zaire and then to Kenya. The commandos were disarmed before leaving Chad and subsequently permanently disbanded.[41]

U.S. relations with Libya improved significantly after Qaddafi's decision to terminate his nuclear weapons program in 2003, but in the face of his 2011 crackdown on rebel groups, the CIA was authorized to aid those groups. As a result, the agency inserted officers into parts of Libya where they provided intelligence to U.S. military and coalition forces conducting airstrikes and made contact with the rebel groups.[42]

PAKISTAN

In 1999 the CIA trained and equipped approximately sixty special forces personnel from Pakistan's ISI tasked with apprehending and killing Osama bin Laden. The operation was arranged with the Clinton administration by Pakistani prime minister Nawaz Sharif and his intelligence chief, in exchange for economic benefits. The plan was canceled later that year when Sharif was overthrown by a military coup, and his successor, General Pervez Musharraf, refused to continue the operation. Communications intercepts also indicated that the training effort had been compromised.[43]

More recent covert actions in Pakistan have involved targeted killings of al-Qaeda leadership employing Hellfire-armed Predators. An apparent Predator attack killed a former Taliban commander, Nek Mohammed, along with five others, in South Waziristan in June 2004. On May 10, 2005, Haithem al-Yemeni, a potential successor to Abu Faraj al-Libi, who had been captured a week earlier, was killed in Pakistan by a Hellfire missile. In December 2005, a Hellfire was used to kill Hamza Rabia, identified by American officials as al-Qaeda's chief of international operations, at a safe house located in Asorai in western Pakistan.[44]

In January 2006, based on intelligence suggesting that Ayman al-Zawahiri, bin Laden's deputy, was visiting a home in a village in the northwestern region of Pakistan, the CIA attempted to kill Zawahiri with a Hellfire missile. The attack on the target within the village of Damadola occurred at 12:30 a.m. on January 13. However, Zawahiri had left the village two hours earlier. Local officials claimed that eighteen civilians had been killed in the attack, as had at least eleven militants, including seven Arab fighters and four Pakistani militants from Punjab province. In addition, according to Pakistani officials, although Zawahiri was not among the dead, two and possibly three senior al-Qaeda members and Zawahiri's son-in-law appeared to be among those killed. One of those (Midhat Mursi al-Sayid Umar, also known as Abu Khabab al-Masri) was an expert on explosives and poisons and was on the United States' "most wanted" list. He had operated an al-Qaeda camp in eastern Afghanistan and prepared a training manual with recipes for crude chemical and biological weapons. Another of the believed dead, Abu Ubayda al-Misri, was chief of insurgency operations in the southern Afghanistan province of Kunar. Zawahiri's son-in-law was in charge of al-Qaeda propaganda in the region.[45]

Starting in 2008, drone strikes against al-Qaeda and Taliban officials and training facilities in Pakistan were stepped up and became a common occurrence. From 2004 to 2007 there were four strikes. Then in 2008, there were thirty-four. By the end of 2009 there had been ninety-nine strikes inside Pakistan, employing both Predator and Reaper drones. In 2010 there had been seventy-four additional strikes by the end of September. In mid-December 2010, it was reported that there had been over one hundred Predator strikes that year. The expansion in the number of strikes followed a 2008 policy change in which individuals could be targeted not only when identified as approved targets but also as a result of a "pattern of life analysis."[46]

The attacks have killed a number of senior al-Qaeda and Taliban officials. In early 2009, it was reported that the attacks had killed nine of al-Qaeda's twenty leaders. The strikes have continued a particularly successful campaign to kill or capture a succession of al-Qaeda operations chiefs (other than the ones who were captured). Sheikh Sa'id al-Masri was killed in May 2010; he was a key al-Qaeda official believed to have been behind the attempt of Najibullah Zazi to blow up the New York subway and to have provided funds to three of the September 11 hijackers. Intelligence concerning a terrorist plot aimed at Europe led the United States to further increase the pace of drone strikes in Pakistan's tribal regions in October 2010. The strikes succeeded in killing several terrorists with German citizenship. Of particular interest with respect to the European plot were three German bombers, one of whom, Imram al-Amani, was killed in an early October attack. The 117 drone strikes in Pakistan in 2010 killed 581 individuals identified as militants.[47]

Assorted militant commanders were killed in 2011 in drone strikes. Then, in June 2011, Ilyas Kashmiri—a former member of the Pakistani Special Services Group, reported leader of a unit called the 313 Brigade, and a member of the Harkat-ul-Jehad-e-Islami who had been brought under the leadership of al-Qaeda—was killed by a strike in South Waziristan. In August, Atiyah Abd al-Rahman, al-Qaeda's top operational planner, was killed by a drone strike. In September, Abu Hafs al-Shariri, described as a "top Qaeda operative responsible for plotting terrorist attacks inside Pakistan," was killed in a similar manner. His death was followed in October by the drone strike that killed Janbaz Zadran, a high-level leader of the Haqqani network, in North Waziristan.[48]

After a suspension of drone strikes beginning in mid-November 2011 and extending into early 2012—due to Pakistan's reaction to several incidents, including a mistaken attack that killed twenty-four Pakistani soldiers—the strikes resumed in mid-January. A drone strike killed four suspected militants in northwestern Pakistan, under a mile from Miram Shah, a major site of Islamist militant groups. A top Pakistani Taliban commander, Bandar Mansoor, was also killed by a drone strike in February. Three Haqqani network fighters were killed via drone in April, and the more important Abu Yahya al-Libi was killed by the same method in June. One account reported that he was "considered to be the No. 2 leader of al Qaeda" and "was seen as al Qaeda's most versatile leader."[49]

In early 2013, Mualvi Nazir and five others were killed in a drone attack on his vehicle in the Angoor Adda area of Pakistan. Nazir had been leader of the Ahmadzai Wazir tribe, and his fighters regularly participated in attacks on U.S. forces across the Afghan border. In September and October 2014, a series of CIA drone strikes killed eleven suspected militants in various areas of Pakistan.[50] Table 16.1 summarizes notable deaths due to the drone campaign.

SOMALIA

CIA covert action in Somalia in 2005 and the first part of 2006 had several aims, including neutralizing a small number of al-Qaeda members believed to be hiding in the country. The CIA operation, run from the agency's station in Nairobi, Kenya, involved channeling hundreds of thousands of dollars to secular warlords within Somalia, with the objective of killing or capturing the suspected al-Qaeda members. The operation occasionally involved Nairobi-based CIA officers arriving at warlord-controlled airstrips in Mogadishu, carrying large amounts of money to be dispensed to the Somali warlords.[51]

The plan to enlist the warlords in this effort was largely due to apprehension about deploying large numbers of American personnel in Somalia; the 1994 attempt to capture warlord Mohammed Farah Aidid had resulted in the deaths of eighteen American Special Forces personnel and the withdrawal of U.S. personnel from the country. Since November 2002, however, U.S. representatives had had success in their contacts with Somali clansmen, who provided intelligence about suspected al-Qaeda members in Somalia. As a result, Suleiman Abdalla Salim Hemed, a suspected al-Qaeda operative, was turned over to U.S. officials in April 2003. However, the plan failed to achieve further results, and Islamic militias took control of the country in early June 2006. That control was short-lived; it was terminated by invading Ethiopian troops, covertly supported by the U.S. military, that December.[52]

In early January 2007, an AC-130 gunship was used to launch an attack on al-Qaeda members in southern Somalia. Among the targets of the attack was Abu Talha al-Sudani, described as an explosives expert with a close relationship with bin Laden and, more recently, as a close associate of Gouled Hassan Dourad, head of a Mogadishu-based network that supported al-Qaeda. Some had also named Sudani as the financier for the individuals believed responsible for the 1998 bombings of the U.S. embassies in Kenya and Tanzania.[53]

TABLE 16.1   Notable Deaths Due to Drone Campaign Attacks in Pakistan

Name	Position
Saad bin Laden	Son of Osama bin Laden
Khalid Habib	Deputy to Sheikh Sa'id al-Masri, al-Qaeda's No. 3
Rashid Rauf	Mastermind of the 2006 transatlantic airliner plot
Abu Khabab al-Masri	Leader of al-Qaeda's chemical and biological weapons effort
Usama al-Kini	Planner of September 2008 attack on Marriott in Islamabad
Sheikh Ahmed Salim Swedan	Usama al-Kini's lieutenant; on FBI's terrorist most-wanted list
Abu Sulaiman al-Jaziri	Senior external operations planner and facilitator for al-Qaeda
Abu Jihad al-Masri	Senior operational planner and propagandist for al-Qaeda
Abdullah Azzam	Senior aide to Sheikh Sa'id al-Masri
Najmiddin Kamolitdinovich Jalolov	Leader of the Islamic Jihad Union
Saleh al-Somali	Member of al-Qaeda's inner circle
Mohammed Haqqani	Brother of Sirajuddin Haqqani, leader of Haqqani network, with close ties to the Taliban and al-Qaeda
Hussein Yemeni	Al-Qaeda bomb expert
Mohammed Qari Zafar	Taliban commander
Sheikh Mansoor	Egyptian Canadian al-Qaeda leader
Mahmud Mahdi Zeidan	Jordanian Taliban commander
Sheikh Sa'id al-Masri	Al-Qaeda operations chief (2007–2010)
Ilyas Kashmiri	Leader of the 313 Brigade
Bandar Mansoor	Pakistani Taliban commander
Atiyah Abd al-Rahman	Al-Qaeda operational planner
Janbaz Zadran	Haqqani network member

Sources: Jay Solomon, Siobhan Gorman, and Matthew Rosenberg, "U.S. Plans New Drone Attacks in Pakistan," *Wall Street Journal*, March 26, 2009, A1, A18; Jonathan Karl and Matthew Cole, "CIA Kept bin Laden Son's Death Secret for Months," *ABC News*, July 23, 2009, http://abcnews.go.com/Blotter/story?id=8156930; Siobhan Gorman and Peter Spiegel, "Drone Attacks Target Pakistan Militants," *Wall Street Journal*, September 17, 2009, A8; Mark Mazzetti and Souad Mekhennet, "Qaeda Planner in Pakistan Killed by Drone," *New York Times*, December 12, 2009, A8; Zahid Hussain, "Another Militant Is Killed by Drone," *Wall Street Journal*, February 20–21, 2010, A6; David S. Cloud, "Suspect in CIA Attack Slain," *Los Angeles Times*, March 18 2010, AA1, AA6; David S. Cloud, "CIA Drones Have Broader List of Targets," *Los Angeles Times*, May 6, 2010, A1, A6; Siobhan Gorman, "Al Qaeda Is Again Forced to Fill Risky No. 3 Post," *Wall Street Journal*, June 2, 2010, A12; Carlotta Gall, "Militant Commander in Pakistan Is Reported Killed by U.S. Drone Strike," *New York Times*, June 5, 2011, 1, 8; Brian Bennett, "U.S. Certain of Key al-Qaeda Planner's Death," *Los Angeles Times*, July 8, 2011, AA2; Mark Mazzetti, "C.I.A. Kills Top Qaeda Operative in a Drone Strike," *New York Times*, September 16, 2011, A8; Scott Shane, "Drone Strike in Pakistan Kills Haqqani Commander," *New York Times*, October 14, 2011, A8.

Subsequent to 2010, U.S. covert action operations with respect to Somalia have included both support to local groups as well as drone strikes. Other actions have included several covert programs to provide aid to local Somali security forces involved in combating al-Shahab, according to a 2012 report from the UN Somalia Eritrea Monitoring Group. One project involved CIA officers assisting the government of Puntland, a semiautonomous area not recognized by the United Nations, with U.S. Special Forces fighting in concert with Puntland soldiers. The media adviser to Puntland's president said that the CIA was providing nonlethal aid to the Puntland Intelligence Agency. The United States also had been providing aid to the Somali National Security Agency, which operates an "Alpha Group" unit that was being employed as a proxy for U.S. intelligence operations in government-controlled territory.[54]

In late June 2011, a drone strike launched by Joint Special Operations Command (JSOC) personnel targeted several Somalis belonging to the al-Shahab group, representing the first attack in Somalia since 2009. In January 2012, another strike ended the life of Bilal al-Barjawi, a senior foreign commander who had been fighting with al-Shahab. Then, in September 2013, Ahmed Godane, al-Shahab's cofounder and commander, was killed by a drone strike. Drone strikes in December 2014 and February and March 2015 killed the group's intelligence chief, its chief of external operations, and a senior official who had helped plan the group's attack on a Nairobi shopping mall in 2013.[55]

SYRIA

U.S. covert action in Syria has included a CIA–Special Operations forces helicopter assault in October 2008. The assault involved crossing the Iraqi border into eastern Syria to kill Abu Ghadiya, a logistical planner for al-Qaeda, allegedly involved in smuggling weapons, money, and foreign fighters from Syria into Iraq during the insurgency in that country.[56]

More recently, CIA covert action operations have sought to provide assistance, in a variety of ways, to resistance forces opposed by the government of Bashar al-Assad. By mid-2012, CIA officers were operating in southern Turkey to help allies decide which Syrian opposition forces would receive arms, including automatic rifles, rocket-propelled grenades, ammunition, and some antitank weapons. In addition, the CIA provided selected intelligence to some opposition groups and used its assets to work with opposition units.[57]

In 2013 the CIA was reported to have increased its contingency planning in the face of increased turmoil in Syria, which included gathering intelligence on Islamic extremists for possible drone attacks. In addition, the CIA was feeding intelligence to selected opposition fighters to employ against government forces. According to Syrian opposition commanders, the CIA was working with the British, French, and Jordanian intelligence services to train rebels in the use of assorted weapons at a base in Jordan. The agency was also helping Arab governments shop for weapons to provide the Syrian opposition, which would then be airlifted to the rebels.[58]

In the summer of 2014, with ISIS advancing across Syria, the CIA was accelerating, in conjunction with European and Arab allies, the supply of arms, ammunition, and money across the Turkish and Jordanian borders to selected rebel groups in northern

Syria. The joint organization assisting the rebels, led by the CIA, was designated the Military Operations Command, and the arms it was providing were mostly light arms rather than antitank missiles that the Free Syrian Army could employ in defense of their positions. According to one opposition official, "They've been giving us enough weapons to stay alive for three years, but never to progress." In the fall, it was reported that one problem facing the United States and CIA was that "the U.S. finds itself without a credible partner on the ground in Syria as it bombs [ISIS]."[59]

Reports in late 2014 and early 2015 depicted the limited CIA effort as being ineffective—with "CIA-backed factions . . . routed by Jabhat al-Nusra, al-Qaeda's primary affiliate in Syria." In addition, "entire CIA-backed rebel units, including fighters numbering in the 'low hundreds' who went through the training program, have changed sides by joining forces with Islamist brigades, quit the fight or gone missing." It was also reported that the CIA had ceased offering assistance to "all but a few trusted commanders in Syria."[60]

YEMEN

On November 2, 2002, a Hellfire missile launched from a Predator struck a car carrying six men through the desert. The attack took place one hundred miles east of Sanaa, the capital of Yemen, after the Predator detected the vehicle as it moved along a highway toward the city of Marib. All six men were killed, including the target of the attack, Qaed Salim Sinan al-Harethi. Harethi, believed to be a leader of al-Qaeda in Yemen, was suspected of involvement in the bombing of the Navy destroyer USS *Cole* in October 2000. The men, including one who was a U.S. citizen, were al-Qaeda operatives, according to U.S. officials. According to another account, four were members of the Aden-Ayben Islamic Army, a terrorist sect with ties to al-Qaeda. The U.S. citizen had recruited Muslims to attend al-Qaeda training camps, according to the FBI.[61]

In late 2009 and the first half of 2010, the U.S. military, with CIA drones tied up in attacks on Pakistani targets, conducted a number of strikes designed to eliminate members of al-Qaeda in the Arabian Peninsula (AQAP), which was responsible for the failed bombing of a U.S.-bound aircraft on Christmas Day, 2009. A December 17, 2009, cruise missile attack was believed to have hit an al-Qaeda training facility in Abyan province. A week later, on December 24, a cruise missile attack killed five al-Qaeda members, although it missed the primary targets, the AQAP leader and deputy chief. A March attack killed Jamil al-Anbari, an al-Qaeda operative, in Mudiyah, while a May 25 attack in Marib province, targeting what was believed to be a group of al-Qaeda members, killed the province's deputy governor. In the midst of the December 2009 and spring 2010 attacks, the Yemeni government, possibly with intelligence and other assistance from the United States, conducted an airstrike that killed at least five senior AQAP members, including the group's military commander.[62]

In August 2010, it was reported that the CIA and U.S. special operations forces had positioned drones and surveillance equipment in Yemen and other nations with the intention of stepping up operations against AQAP. In November of the same year, it was reported that "U.S. officials said . . . Predators have been patrolling the skies over Yemen for several months in search of leaders and operatives of . . . AQAP," but as a result of the cruise missile strikes earlier in the year, the AQAP leaders "went to ground."[63]

Not until 2011 did the first drone strike in Yemen since 2002 take place. A JSOC drone killed two al-Qaeda operatives in the Arabian Peninsula in the Yemeni governorate of Shabwa. That strike was followed by an unsuccessful drone attack targeting Anwar al-Awlaki, an American-born cleric believed to be involved in directing terrorist attacks in the United States. He is linked to the shootings at Fort Hood, Texas, the Christmas 2009 plot to blow up a U.S.-bound passenger plane, and a plot to blow up cargo planes. The Treasury Department had made Awlaki a "Specially Designated Global Terrorist" in July 2010. A month after that attempt, it was reported that the CIA would be joining JSOC in conducting drone operations in Yemen—a sign of plans to significantly expand the effort to eliminate members of the AQAP.[64]

In mid-July U.S. drones and fighter jets attacked suspected al-Qaeda-affiliated militants, killing eight who had been sleeping in a police station they had seized. Then, in September, in what was described as the first CIA drone strike since 2002, the agency succeeded in killing Awlaki, and along with him, Samir Khan, editor of *Inspire* and author of some of its articles, such as "How to Make a Bomb in the Kitchen of Your Mom" and "What to Expect in Jihad." Awlaki's death was considered significant enough to prompt a statement from President Obama, who called it a "major blow" to the AQAP.[65]

Awlaki's death in 2011 was followed by further drone strikes in 2012. In March 2012, a JSOC-commanded drone was used to track and kill a mid-level al-Qaeda commander along with twenty-two other suspected militants, apparently recruits undergoing training. Another victim, Fahd al-Quso, who had been tied to a plot to smuggle explosive-laden underwear onto a flight into the United States, was killed by a strike in May. A CIA strike in January 2015 killed individuals described as al-Qaeda operatives, while Harith al-Nadhari, a senior al-Qaeda leader, was hit while riding in a car in southern Yemen in early February 2015.[66]

Notes

1. "The Bissell Philosophy," appendix to Victor Marchetti and John Marks, *The CIA and the Cult of Intelligence* (New York: Knopf, 1974), 387; U.S. Congress, Senate Select Committee to Study Governmental Operations with Respect to Intelligence Activities, *Alleged Assassination Plots Involving Foreign Leaders* (Washington, DC: U.S. Government Printing Office, 1976). On the results of arming rebel groups, see Mark Mazzetti, "C.I.A. Study Says Arming Rebels Seldom Works," *New York Times*, October 15, 2014, A1, A3; Christopher Dickey, "The CIA's Wrong: Arming Rebels Works," *Daily Beast*, October 19, 2014,http://www.thedailybeast.com/articles/2014/10/19/the-cia-s-wrong-arming-rebels-works.html.

2. For histories of U.S. covert action, see William J. Daugherty, *Executive Secrets: Covert Action and the Presidency* (Lexington: University Press of Kentucky, 2004); John Prados, *Safe for Democracy: The Secret Wars of the CIA* (Chicago: Ivan R. Dee, 2006); Gregory F. Treverton, *Covert Action: The Limits of Intervention in the Postwar World* (New York: Basic Books, 1987).

3. George Bush, National Security Directive 25, "U.S. Policy Toward the February 1990 Nicaraguan Election," September 22, 1989. It should be noted that a secret annex to NSD-25, "[Deleted] NSD-25 on U.S. Policy Toward the February 1990 Nicaraguan Election," was issued on the same day as NSD-25.

4. Tim Weiner, "U.S. Has Spent $26 Million Since '95 on Suharto Opposition," *New York Times*, May 20, 1998, A11; John Lancaster, "U.S. Funds Help Milosevic's Foes in Election Fight," *Washington Post*, September 19, 2000, A1, A8; U.S. Congress, Senate Committee on Foreign

Relations, *Broadcasting to China: Applying the Lessons from European Freedom Radios* (Washington, DC: U.S. Government Printing Office, 1992); U.S. Congress, Senate Committee on Foreign Relations, *The Radio Free China Act S. 2985* (Washington, DC: U.S. Government Printing Office, 1992); Kennon H. Nakamura and Susan B. Epstein, "Pleased Yet Wary, U.S. Offers Gestures of Support for Iran," *New York Times*, March 26, 1998, A1, A10; Elaine Sciolino, "White House Agrees to Radio Broadcasts to Iran," *New York Times*, April 15, 1998, A3.

5. See Jeffrey T. Richelson, ed., National Security Archive Briefing Book No. 439, *Underground Facilities: Intelligence and Targeting Issues*, September 23, 2013, http://www2.gwu.edu/~nsarchiv/NSAEBB/NSAEBB372.

6. Walter Pincus, "CIA Turns to Boutique Operations, Covert Action Against Terrorism, Drugs, Arms," *Washington Post*, September 14, 1997, A6; Craig Covault, "Cyber Threat Challenges Intelligence Capability," *AW&ST*, February 10, 1997, 20–21.

7. Bob Woodward and Vernon Loeb, "CIA's Covert War on Bin Laden," *Washington Post*, September 14, 2001, A1, A14; Barton Gellman, "Broad Effort Launched After '98 Attacks," *Washington Post*, December 19, 2001, A1, A26; William B. Black, "Thinking Out Loud About Cyberspace," *Cryptolog* 23, no. 1 (Spring 1997): 1–4; Gregory L. Vistica, "Cyberwar and Sabotage," *Newsweek*, May 31, 1999, 36; Juan C. Zarate, *Treasury's War: The Unleashing of a New Era of Financial Warfare* (New York: Public Affairs, 2013).

8. Bob Woodward, "CIA Told to Do 'Whatever Necessary' to Kill Bin Laden," *Washington Post*, October 21, 2001, A1, A22; Barton Gellman, "CIA Weighs 'Targeted Killing' Missions," *Washington Post*, October 28, 2001, A1, A19; Philip Ewing, "U.S. Builds Secret Drone Base for Yemen Attacks," *DoD Buzz*, June 15, 2011, http://www.dodbuzz.com/2011/06/15/u-s-builds-secret-drone-base-for-yemen-attacks; Sharon Weinberger, "Droning On," *AW&ST*, December 3, 2012, DT7–DT9; Greg Miller, "Under Obama, a Drone Network," *Washington Post*, December 28, 2011, A1, A6; Craig Whitlock and Greg Miller, "U.S. Creating a Ring of Secret Drone Bases," *Washington Post*, September 21, 2011, A1, A12.

9. Bob Woodward, *Obama's Wars* (New York: Simon & Schuster, 2010), 52–53.

10. Mark Mazzetti, "U.S. Said to Order an Expanded Use of Secret Action," *New York Times*, May 25, 2010, A1, A12.

11. James Risen, "U.S. Pursued Secret Efforts to Catch or Kill bin Laden," *New York Times*, September 10, 2001, A1, B3; Gellman, "Broad Effort Launched After '98 Attacks."

12. Gary Bernsten and Ralph Pezzullo, *Jawbreaker: The Attack on bin Laden and Al Qaeda: A Personal Account by the CIA's Key Field Commander* (New York: Crown, 2005), 74.

13. Gary C. Schroen, *First In: An Insider's Account of How the CIA Spearheaded the War on Terror in Afghanistan* (New York: Ballantine, 2005), 22, 38, 75, 78.

14. Ibid., 96, 101, 195.

15. Ibid., 274.

16. David S. Cloud, "CIA Supplies Anti-Taliban Forces in South," *Wall Street Journal*, December 7, 2001, 4; Alan Sipress and Walter Pincus, "U.S. Making Covert Drive for Pashtun Support," *Washington Post*, November 4, 2001, A18; Alan Sipress and Vernon Loeb, "CIA's Stealth War Centers on Eroding Taliban Loyalty and Aiding Opposition," *Washington Post*, October 10, 2001, A1, A16.

17. "CIA Effort to Kill Ex-Warlord Fails," *Washington Times*, May 10 2002, A8; Walter Pincus and Thomas E. Ricks, "CIA Fails in Bid to Kill Afghan Rebel with a Missile," *Washington Post*, May 10, 2002, A24–A25. Also see Alex S. Wilner, "Targeted Killings in Afghanistan: Measuring Coercion and Deterrence in Counterterrorism and Counterinsurgency," *Studies in Conflict & Terrorism* 33, no. 4 (April 2010): 307–329.

18. Shashank Bengali and David S. Cloud, "U.S. Drone Use in Afghanistan Is Up Sharply," *Los Angeles Times*, February 22, 2013, A1, A8–A9.

19. Michael M. Phillips, "U.S. Steps Up Missions Targeting Taliban Leaders," *Wall Street Journal*, February 2, 2010, A1, A10; Julian E. Barnes, "U.S. Secretly Adds Strike Teams," *Washington Post*, May 6, 2011, A6.

20. Woodward, *Obama's Wars*, 8, 367; Mark Mazzetti and Dexter Filkins, "U.S. Commanders Push to Expand Raids in Pakistan," *New York Times*, December 21, 2010, A1, A12.

21. Declan Walsh, "Car Bomb Kills 8 Afghans from Unit Linked to C.I.A.," *New York Times*, October 16, 2014, A11.

22. Dana Priest, "Covert CIA Program Withstands New Furor," www.washingtonpost.com, December 30, 2005, http://www.washingtonpost.com/wp-dyn/content/article/2005/12/29/AR2005122901585.html; Dana Priest and Willam M. Arkin, *Top Secret America: The Rise of the New American Security State* (Boson: Little, Brown, 2011), 19–20.

23. Dana Priest, "CIA Holds Terror Suspects in Secret Prisons," www.washingtonpost.com, November 2, 2005.

24. Rajiv Chandrasekaran and Peter Finn, "U.S. Behind Secret Transfer of Terror Suspects," *Washington Post*, March 11, 2002, A1, A15; Don Van Natta Jr., "German Looking into Complicity in Seizure by U.S.," *New York Times*, February 21, 2006, A1, A8; Dana Priest, "Italy Knew About Plan to Grab Suspect," *Washington Post*, June 30, 2004, A1, A18; Steve Hendricks, *A Kidnaping in Milan: The CIA on Trial* (New York: W. W. Norton, 2010).

25. Chandrasekaran and Finn, "U.S. Behind Secret Transfer of Terror Suspects"; Scott Shane, "C.I.A. Expanding Terror Battle Under Guise of Charter Flights," *New York Times*, May 31, 2005, A1, A10; Dan Bilefsky, "European Inquiry Flew 1,000 Flights in Secret," *New York Times*, April 27, 2006, A12; Stephen Gray, *Ghost Plane: The True Story of the CIA Torture Program* (New York: St. Martin's Press, 2006), 45, 62, 79, 105, 190, 248.

26. Craig Whitlock, "Renditions Continue Under Obama, Despite Due-Process Concerns," www.washingtonpost.com, January 1, 2013, http://www.washingtonpost.com/world/national-security/renditions-continue-under-obama-despite-due-process-concerns/2013/01/01/4e593aa0-5102-11e2-984e-f1de82a7c98a_story.html.

27. Steve Hendricks, *A Kidnaping in Milan: The CIA on Trial* (New York: W. W. Norton, 2010).

28. Priest, "CIA Holds Terror Suspects in Secret Prisons"; Craig Whitlock, "European Probe Finds Signs of CIA-Run Secret Prisons," www.washingtonpost.com, June 8, 2006, http://www.washingtonpost.com/wp-dyn/content/article/2006/06/07/AR2006060700505.html.

29. Malcolm Byrne, *Iran-Contra: Reagan's Scandal and the Unchecked Abuse of Presidential Power* (Lawrence: University Press of Kansas 2014); Leslie H. Gelb, "U.S. Said to Aid Iranian Exiles in Combat and Political Units," *New York Times*, March 7, 1982, 1, 12.

30. Gelb, "U.S. Said to Aid Iranian Exiles in Combat and Political Units."

31. Ibid.; Bob Woodward, "CIA Curried Favor with Khomeini Exiles," *Washington Post*, November 19, 1986, A1, A28.

32. Bob Woodward, "CIA Aiding Iraq in Gulf War," *Washington Post*, December 15, 1986, A1, A18–A19; Stephen Engelberg, "Iran and Iraq Got 'Doctored' Data, U.S. Officials Say," *New York Times*, January 12, 1987, A1, A16.

33. Eli Lake, "Operation Sabotage," *New Republic*, July 22, 2010, 16–17; William J. Broad and David E. Sanger, "In Nuclear Net's Undoing, a Web of Shadowy Deals," *New York Times*, August 25, 2008, A1, A8; "Covert Action Suspected in Iranian Nuclear Troubles," *Global Security Newswire*, July 23, 2010, http://www.nti.org/gsn/article/covert-action-suspected-in-iranian-nuclear-troubles.

34. From: [Deleted], To: CIA Office #16, Subject: Query Regarding [Deleted] Asset Possibilities, September 23, 1996; From: [N/A], To: Priority Langley, Subject: APP Request for Operational Use of MERLIN (M), Against Iranian Nuclear Target, January 6, 1997.

35. From: [Deleted], To: CIA Office #1, CIA Office #2, CIA Office #3, Subject: Merlin (M) Evaluation, C/O Change Planning, May 28, 1997.

36. Walter Pincus, "Twisted View of CIA's Operation Merlin," www.washingtonpost.com, January 26, 2015, http://www.washingtonpost.com/world/national-security/twisted-view-of-cias-operation-merlin/2015/01/26/dc107fd6-a3e7-11e4-9f89-561284a573f8_story.html; From: [Deleted], To: Priority CIA Office #2, et al., Subject: Iranians Take the Initial Bait, May 5, 2000.

37. David E. Sanger, "Iran Fights Malware Attacking Computers," *New York Times*, September 26, 2010, 4, 9; Robert McMillan, "Was Stuxnet Built to Attack Iran's Nuclear Program?," www .pcworld.com, September 21, 2010, http://www.pcworld.com/article/205827/was_stuxnet_built _to_attack_irans_nuclear_program.html (accessed September 21, 2010); "Iran Nuclear Agency Is Working to Defeat a Computer Worm," *Los Angeles Times*, September 26, 2010, A4; Siobhan Gorman, "Computer Worm Hits Plant in Iran," *Wall Street Journal*, September 27, 2010, A12; Paul A. Kerr, John Rollins, and Catherine A. Theohary, Congressional Research Service, *The Stuxnet Computer Worm: Harbinger of an Emerging Warfare Capability*, December 9, 2010, http://fas.org /sgp/crs/natsec/R41524.pdf; David A. Albright, Paul Brannan, and Christina Walrond, Institute for Science and International Security, *Skynet Malware and Natanz: Update of ISIS December 22, 2010 Report*, February 15, 2010; William J. Broad, "Worm in Iran Was Perfect for Sabotaging Nuclear Centrifuges," *New York Times*, November 19, 2010, A1, A4; Joby Warrick, "Iran's Natanz Nuclear Facility Recovered Quickly from Stuxnet Cyberattack," www.washingtonpost.com, February 16, 2011; David E. Sanger, *Confront and Conceal: Obama's Secret Wars and Surprising Use of American Power* (New York: Crown, 2012), 188–225; Ralph Langner, Langner Group, *To Kill a Centrifuge: A Technical Analysis of What Stuxnet's Creators Tried to Achieve*, November 2013.

38. Julian E. Barnes, Adam Entous, and Siobhan Gorman, "U.S. Eyes Covert Plan to Counter Iran in Iraq," *Wall Street Journal*, September 6, 2011, A1, A12.

39. Adam Entous, Julian E. Barnes, and Siobhan Gorman, "CIA Ramps Up Role in Iraq," *Washington Post*, March 12, 2013, A1, A10.

40. Bob Woodward, "CIA Anti-Qaddafi Plan Backed," *Washington Post*, November 3, 1985, A1, A19; Bob Woodward, *VEIL: The Secret Wars of the CIA, 1981–1987* (New York: Simon & Schuster, 1987), 411.

41. Clifford Krauss, "Failed Anti-Qaddafi Efforts Leaves U.S. Picking Up the Pieces," *New York Times*, March 12, 1991, A15; "Have Rebels, Will Travel," *Newsweek*, March 26, 1991, 43.

42. Adam Entous, "CIA Operatives Are Aiding Rebels," *Wall Street Journal*, March 31, 2011, A11; Mark Mazzetti and Eric Schmitt, "C.I.A. Spies Aiding Airstrikes and Assessing Qaddafi's Foes," *New York Times*, March 31, 2011, A1, A8; Ken Dilanian, "CIA Officers Working with Libya Rebels," *Los Angeles Times*, March 31, 2011, AA1, AA2.

43. Bob Woodward and Thomas E. Ricks, "CIA Trained Pakistan to Nab Terrorist but Military Coup Put an End to 1999 Plot," *Washington Post*, October 3, 2001, A1, A18; Gelman, "Broad Effort Launched After '98 Attacks."

44. "Airstrike by U.S. Draws Protests from Pakistanis," *New York Times*, January 15, 2006, 1, 4; Josh Meyer, "CIA Expands Use of Drones in Terror War," *Los Angeles Times*, January 29, 2006, A1, A28–A29.

45. "Airstrike by U.S. Draws Protests from Pakistanis"; Carlotta Gall and Ismail Khan, "American Strike in January Missed Al Qaeda No. 2 by a Few Hours," *New York Times*, November 10, 2006, A10; Carlotta Gall, Douglas Jehl, and Ismail Khan, "Strike Aimed at Qaeda Figure Stirs More Pakistani Protests," *New York Times*, January 16, 2005, A3; Carlotta Gall and Douglas Jehl, "U.S. Raid Killed Qaeda Leaders, Pakistanis Say," *New York Times*, January 19, 2006, A1, A8.

46. Peter Bergen and Katherine Tiedeman, "Revenge of the Drones, Appendix 1," New America Foundation, October 19, 2009, http://www.newamerica.net/files/appendix1.pdf, 1; Greg Miller and Julian E. Barnes, "Drone Plan Opens New Front," *Los Angeles Times*, December 14, 2009, A1, A24; Bill Roggio and Alexander Mayer, "Analysis: US Air Campaign In Pakistan Heats Up," *Long War Journal*, January 5, 2010, http://www.longwarjournal.org/archives/2010/01/analysis _us_air_camp.php; Scott Shane and Eric Schmitt, "C.I.A. Deaths Prompt Surge in Drone War," *New York Times*, January 23, 2010, A1, A3; David S. Cloud, "CIA Drones Have Broader List of Targets," *Los Angeles Times*, May 6, 2010, A1, A6: Mark Mazzetti, "C.I.A. Intensifies Drone Campaign," *New York Times*, September 28, 2010, A1, A12; Helene Cooper and David E. Sanger, "U.S. Will Widen War on Militants Inside Pakistan," *New York Times*, December 17, 2010, A1, A14.

47. Mark Mazzetti and David E. Sanger, "Obama Expands Missile Strikes Inside Pakistan," *New York Times*, February 21, 2009, A1, A6; David E. Sanger and Eric Schmitt, "U.S. Weighs

Taliban Strike in Pakistan," *New York Times*, March 18, 2009, A1, A8; Siobhan Gorman, "Qaeda Aide Believed Dead," *Wall Street Journal*, June 1, 2010, A11; David S. Cloud, "Al Qaeda's No. 3 Man Likely Dead," *Los Angeles Times*, June 1, 2010, AA1, AA6; Siobhan Gorman, "Al Qaeda Is Again Forced to Fill Risky No. 3 Post," *Wall Street Journal*, June 2, 2010, A12. For a skeptical account of the effectiveness of drone strikes, see Greg Miller, "Increased U.S. Drone Strikes in Pakistan Killing Few High-Value Militants," www.washingtonpost.com, February 20, 2011, http://www.washingtonpost.com/wp-dyn/content/article/2011/02/20/AR2011022002975.html. It has also been reported that the CIA may be decreasing the number of drone strikes to reduce civilian casualties. See Ken Dilanian, "CIA May Be Tempering Its Drone Use," *Los Angeles Times*, February 22, 2011, A9; Tom Wright and David Crawford, "Drone Strike Killed European Plotters," *Wall Street Journal*, October 9–10, 2010, A10; Mark Mazzetti and Souad Mekhennet, "Drones Kill Militants from West in Pakistan," *New York Times*, October 5, 2010, A6. For an assessment of the drone war in Pakistan, see Brian Gyn Williams, "The CIA's Covert Predator Drone War in Pakistan, 2004–2010: The History of an Assassination Campaign," *Studies in Conflict & Terrorism* 33, no. 10 (October 2010): 871–892; Miller, "Increased U.S. Drone Strikes in Pakistan Killing Few High-Value Militants"; Eric Schmitt, "Americans Launch Drone Missile Attacks," *New York Times*, April 14, 2011, A9.

48. Carlotta Gall, "Militant Commander in Pakistan Is Reported Killed by U.S. Drone Strike," *New York Times*, June 5, 2011, 1, 8; Brian Bennett, "U.S. Certain of Key al-Qaeda Planner's Death," *Los Angeles Times*, July 8, 2011, AA2; Mark Mazzetti, "C.I.A. Kills Top Qaeda Operative in a Drone Strike," *New York Times*, September 16, 2011, A8; Scott Shane, "Drone Strike in Pakistan Kills Haqqani Commander," *New York Times*, October 14, 2011, A8.

49. Ken Dilanian, "CIA Cuts Off Drone Strikes in Pakistan," *Los Angeles Times*, December 24, 2011, A1, A4; Alex Rodriguez and Zulfiqar Ali, "U.S. Resumes Drone Campaign in Pakistan, Killing 4 in Airstrike," *Los Angeles Times*, January 12, 2012, A4; Alex Rodriguez, "Strike Kills Pakistan Taliban and Al Qaeda Figure," *Los Angeles Times*, February 10, 2012, A9; Declan Walsh, "3 Are Killed by U.S. Drones in Pakistan," *New York Times*, April 30, 2012, A4; Siobhan Gorman, "CIA Kills al Qaeda's No. 2," *Wall Street Journal*, June 6, 2012, A9.

50. Tom Wright, "Drone Kills Pakistani Militant Leader," *Wall Street Journal*, January 4, 2013, A7; Salmoon Masood and Ismail Khan, "Drone Kills a Pakistani Militant Behind Attacks on U.S. Forces," *New York Times*, January 4, 2013, A4; Reuters, "Drone Strike Kills Suspected Militants in Pakistan, Officials Say," September 24, 2014, http://uk.reuters.com/article/2014/09/24/uk-pakistan-drones-idUKKCN0HJ0RI20140924; Associated Press, "Officials: US Drone Kills 4 Militants in Pakistan," *Lubbock Avalanche-Journal*, September 28, 2014, http://lubbockonline.com/filed-online/2014-09-28/officials-us-drone-kills-4-militants-pakistan; Reuters, "Drone Strikes Kills Two Suspected Militants in Northwestern Pakistan," October 8, 2014, http://ca.reuters.com/article/topNews/idCAKCN0HX20K20141008.

51. Mark Mazzetti, "Efforts by C.I.A. Fail in Somalia, Officials Charge," *New York Times*, June 8, 2006, A1, A10.

52. Ibid.; Karen DeYoung, "U.S. Sees Growing Threats in Somalia," www.washingtonpost.com, December 18, 2006, http://www.washingtonpost.com/wp-dyn/content/article/2006/12/17/AR2006121701184.html; Stephanie McCrummen, "In Somalia, Confusion Remains in Command," www.washingtonpost.com, January 6, 2007, http://www.washingtonpost.com/wp-dyn/content/article/2007/01/05/AR2007010500504.html; Jeffrey Gettleman, "U.S. Aiding Somalia in Its Plan to Retake Its Capital," www.nytimes.com, March 5, 2010, http://www.nytimes.com/2010/03/06/world/africa/06somalia.html; Mark Mazzetti and Eric Schmitt, "U.S. Expands Its Drone War into Somalia," *New York Times*, July 2, 2011, A1, A3.

53. Karen DeYoung, "U.S. Strike in Somalia Targets al-Qaeda Figure," www.washingtonpost.com, January 9, 2007, http://www.washingtonpost.com/wp-dyn/content/article/2007/01/08/AR2007010801635.html.

54. Eli Lake, "Obama's Not-So-Secret Terror War," *Daily Beast*, July 24, 2012, http://www.thedailybeast.com/articles/2012/07/24/obama-s-not-so-secret-terror-war.html.

55. Mazzetti and Schmitt, "U.S. Expands Its Drone War into Somalia"; Mohammed Ibrahim, "U.S. Drone Strike Kills Foreign Commander," *New York Times*, January 23, 2012, A4; Helene Cooper, Eric Schmitt, and Jeffrey Gettleman, "Strikes Killed Militant Chief, in Somalia, U.S. Reports," *New York Times*, September 6, 2014, A4; Eric Schmitt, "Drone Strike in Somalia Is Said to Kill Shahab Leader," www.nytimes.com, December 30, 2014, http://www.nytimes.com/2014/12/31/world/africa/drone-strike-is-said-to-kill-shabab-leader.html; Hedi Vogt, "Somalia Confirms U.S. Strike Killed Insurgent," *Wall Street Journal*, February 7–8, 2015, A6; Robyn Dixon and W. J. Hennigan, "Shahab Leader Is Reported Killed by U.S. Drone Strike," *Los Angeles Times*, March 14, 2015, A3.

56. Ken Dilanian and Brian Bennett, "CIA Sizes Up Syria Radicals for Drone Hits," *Los Angeles Times*, March 16, 2013, A1, A6.

57. Eric Schmitt, "C.I.A. Said to Aid in Steering Arms to Syrian Rebels," *New York Times*, June 21, 2012, A1, A12; Adam Entous, Julian E. Barnes, and Nour Malas, "U.S. Mounts Quiet Effort to Weaken Assad's Rule," *Wall Street Journal*, July 23, 2012, A1, A7.

58. Dilanian and Bennett, "CIA Sizes Up Syria Radicals for Drone Hits"; Adam Entous, Siobhan Gorman, and Nour Malas, "CIA Expands Role in Syria Fight," *Wall Street Journal*, March 23–24, 2013, A1, A6; C. J. Chivers and Eric Schmitt, "Airlift to Rebels in Syria Expands with C.I.A.'s Help," *New York Times*, March 25, 2013, A1, A10; Mazzetti, "C.I.A Study Says Arming Rebels Seldom Works."

59. Liz Sly, "New U.S. Help Arrives for Syrian Rebels as Government Extremists Gain," www.washingtonpost.com, July 27, 2014, http://www.washingtonpost.com/world/new-us-help-arrives-for-syrian-rebels-as-government-extremists-gain/2014/07/27/d4805a82-43b3-4583-85b5-f51efd6940a4_story.html; Maria Abi-Habib, "While Strikes Hit, Rebels Await Other Help," *Wall Street Journal*, September 27–28, 2014, A8; Ken Dilanian and Zeina Karam, Associated Press, "US Still Searching for Credible Allies in Syria," *Huffington Post*, October 16, 2014, http://www.huffingtonpost.com/2014/10/16/us-islamic-state-syria-alllies_n_5999254.html.

60. Adam Entous, "Covert CIA Mission to Arm Syrian Rebels Goes Awry," *Wall Street Journal*, January 27, 2015, A1, A8.

61. Walter Pincus, "U.S. Strikes Kill Six in al-Qaeda," *Washington Post*, November 5, 2002, A1, A22; David Johnston and David E. Sanger, "Fatal Strike in Yemen Was Based on Rules Set Out by Bush," *New York Times*, November 6, 2002, A14; Dana Priest, "CIA Killed U.S. Citizen in Yemen Missile Strike," *Washington Post*, November 8, 2002, A1, A22; "They Didn't Know What Hit Them," *Time*, November 18, 2002, 58–59; Seymour M. Hersh, "Manhunt," *New Yorker*, December 23 and December 30, 2002, 66–74.

62. Scott Shane, Mark Mazzetti, and Robert F. Worth, "A Secret Assault on Terror Widens on Two Continents," *New York Times*, August 15, 2010, 1, 10–11; Robert F. Worth, "Senior Members of Al Qaeda in Yemen Killed in Strike, Officials Say," *New York Times*, January 16, 2010, A4; Adam Entous and Siobhan Gorman, "U.S. Eyes Expanded Strikes in Yemen," *Wall Street Journal*, August 25, 2010, A1, A9.

63. Entous and Gorman, "U.S. Eyes Expanded Strikes in Yemen"; Greg Miller, Greg Jaffe, and Karen DeYoung, "U.S. Drones on Hunt in Yemen," www.washingtonpost.com, November 7, 2010, http://www.washingtonpost.com/wp-dyn/content/article/2010/11/06/AR2010110604516.html.

64. Jeb Boone and Greg Miller, "U.S. Conducts First Drone Strike in Yemen Since '02," *Washington Post*, May 6, 2011, A13; Margaret Coker, Adam Entous, and Julian E. Barnes, "Drone Targets Yemeni Cleric," *Wall Street Journal*, May 7–8, 2011, A1, A7; Greg Miller, "CIA Will Direct Yemen Drones," *Washington Post*, June 14, 2011, A1, 12; Mark Mazzetti, "U.S. Is Intensifying a Secret Campaign of Yemen Airstrikes," *New York Times*, June 9, 2011, A5; Siobhan Gorman and Adam Entous, "CIA Plans Yemen Drone Strikes," *Washington Post*, June 14, 2011, A8; Jeremy Scahill, *Dirty Wars: The World Is a Battlefield* (New York: Nation Books, 2013), 369.

65. Nasser Arrabyee and Mark Mazzetti, "U.S. Strikes in Yemen Said to Kill 8 Militants," *New York Times*, July 15, 2011, A9; Mark Mazzetti, Eric Schmitt, and Robert F. Worth, "C.I.A. Strike

Kills U.S.-Born Militant in a Car in Yemen," *New York Times*, October 1, 2011, A1, A8; David Zucchino, "Radical Blogger Was 'Al Qaeda to the Core,'" *Los Angeles Times*, October 1, 2011, A6; Hakim Almasmari, Margaret Coker, and Siobhan Gorman, "Drone Kills Top Al Qaeda Figure," *Wall Street Journal*, October 1–2, 2011, A1, A8.

66. Ken Dilanian and David S. Cloud, "Yemen Sees Rise in U.S. Strikes," *Los Angeles Times*, April 2, 2012, A1, A4; Greg Miller, "U.S. Drone Targets in Yemen Raise Questions," www .washingtonpost.com, June 2, 2012, http://www.washingtonpost.com/world/national-security/ us-drone-targets-in-yemen-raise-questions/2012/06/02/gJQAP0jz9U_story.html; Helene Cooper and Mona El-Naggar, "U.S. Drone Kills 3 Qaeda Operatives in Yemen, Continuing Policy on Strikes," *New York Times*, January 23, 2015, A8; Shuaib Almosawa and Rod Nordland, "Drone Strike in Yemen Said to Kill Senior Qacda Figure," *New York Times*, February 6, 2015, A6.

17

MANAGING NATIONAL INTELLIGENCE

World War II was the first time that the United States operated a national intelligence agency, the Office of Strategic Services. Before that time, although the intelligence activities of the War and Navy departments had national implications, they were managed on a departmental basis and guided by departmental requirements.

With the postwar creation of the position of Director of Central Intelligence (DCI), as well as the establishment of the National Security Council (NSC) and the Central Intelligence Agency (CIA), intelligence was formally considered to be a national as well as a departmental activity. The president issued executive orders to guide intelligence activities and approved sensitive collection and covert action operations. The NSC issued its own directives to guide intelligence activities. The DCI was given the charter of leading, if not commanding, the Intelligence Community (IC) on behalf of the president and the nation.

In performing that job, the DCI built up an apparatus, consisting of staffs, councils, and committees, and was empowered to issue directives covering the full range of intelligence activities, which applied not only to the CIA but to other elements of the Intelligence Community. He also had organizations with national missions placed directly under him, such as the National Intelligence Council (NIC) and, more recently, the Terrorist Threat Integration Center and the National Counterterrorism Center. He also had considerable say in, but not direct control over, the activities of other organizations, such as the National Reconnaissance Office (NRO) and the National Security Agency (NSA).

Then, as result of 9/11 attacks and the report of the commission appointed to investigate them, the position of DCI was abolished. The new Director of National Intelligence (DNI) has greater powers than the DCI had and is not tied to the job of managing the CIA. Some of the DCI's apparatus was transferred to the nation's new intelligence director, while other parts were eliminated. What did not change was the continued involvement of the president and the NSC in directing national intelligence activities.

THE PRESIDENT, THE NATIONAL SECURITY COUNCIL, AND THE PRESIDENT'S INTELLIGENCE ADVISORY BOARD

Direction of the national intelligence effort begins with the president and the National Security Council, as manifested by the issuance of executive orders and directives as well as by the decisions of NSC groups that review intelligence activities.

The most visible documents issued by the president concerning intelligence activities are unclassified executive orders. Such orders were issued in the Ford, Carter, Reagan, and George W. Bush administrations. The Bush order is an extensive amendment of Reagan's Executive Order 12333, "United States Intelligence Activities," of December 4, 1981. The amendments consume eighteen single-spaced pages in the *Federal Register*.[1]

The Bush order deleted the entire first paragraph of Reagan's order, substituting new text. Part 1 designates the DNI as the head of the Intelligence Community and principal intelligence advisor to the president and the NSC. It also sets forth the obligations and responsibilities of the DNI, including establishing objectives and priorities for the Intelligence Community, formulating policies with respect to intelligence and counterintelligence arrangements with foreign governments, and ensuring the development of programs to protect intelligence sources and methods from unauthorized disclosures. In addition, it permits the DNI to establish Functional and Missions Managers and designates the directors of the NSA, CIA, and National Geospatial-Intelligence Agency (NGA) as the functional managers for their respective disciplines.[2] The order specifies that the DNI "shall oversee and direct the establishment of the National Intelligence Program [NIP] budget," while heads of Intelligence Community elements are directed to "provide all programmatic and budgetary information necessary to support the Director in developing the National Intelligence Program."[3]

The revised first part also specifies IC elements and the responsibilities of the elements' directors, as well as those executive branch departments that contain intelligence elements. The CIA is directed, under the guidance of the DNI, "to coordinate the implementation of intelligence and counterintelligence relationships between the elements of the Intelligence Community and the intelligence and security services of foreign governments or international organizations." The order further specifies that the Department of State shall "collect (overtly or through publicly available sources) information relevant to the United States' foreign policy and national security concerns," while the Department of Energy shall "provide expert scientific, technical, analytic, and research capabilities to other agencies within the Intelligence Community."[4]

Presidents also issue presidential decision and study directives, which are frequently classified. In the Reagan administration, those directives were known as National Security Decision Directives (NSDDs) and National Security Study Directives (NSSDs). National Security Directives (NSDs) and National Security Reviews (NSRs) took their place in the George H. W. Bush administration and, in turn, were replaced by the Presidential Decision Directives (PDDs) and Presidential Review Directives (PRDs) in the Clinton administration. When George W. Bush assumed the presidency, he replaced the PDDs and PRDs with a single series—the National Security Presidential Directives (NSPDs).[5] President Barack Obama reestablished the two-directives system, with Presidential Policy Directives (PPDs) and Presidential Study Directives (PSDs).

Although the product of a specific administration, each directive generally remains in force until either cancelled or replaced by a subsequent administration. At least nine Reagan administration NSDDs concerned intelligence matters. NSDD-22 of January 29, 1982, concerned the "Designation of Intelligence Officials Authorized to Request FBI Collection of Foreign Intelligence," while NSDD-42 of July 4, 1982, "National Space Policy," focused, in part, on space reconnaissance. NSDD-84 of March 11, 1983, "Safeguarding National Security Information," specified new security review requirements for individuals permitted access to code word information. NSDD-159 of January 18, 1985, specified "Covert Action Policy Approval and Coordination Procedures," while "Counterintelligence/Countermeasure Implementation Task Force" was the title of NSDD-196 of November 1, 1985. "Transfer of National Intelligence Collection Tasking Authority" was the title of NSDD-204 of December 24, 1985.[6]

National Security Directives, from the George H. W. Bush administration, concerning intelligence matters included a February 1989 NSD on "National Space Policy"; an August 1990 NSD on covert action directed against Iraq; the October 5, 1990, NSD-47 on "Counterintelligence and Security Countermeasures"; the October 21, 1991, NSD-63 on "Single Scope Background Investigations"; and NSD-67 of March 30, 1992, on "Intelligence Capabilities, 1992–2005." Two Clinton Presidential Decision Directives that dealt directly with intelligence are PDD-24 on "U.S. Counterintelligence Effectiveness," which was the product of an interagency review mandated by PRD-44, and PDD-35, which established intelligence priorities, designating five different tiers, from crisis coverage down to no coverage.[7]

There are also only two known National Security Presidential Directives from the George W. Bush administration: NSPD-5 of May 9, 2001, which mandated a comprehensive review of U.S. intelligence, and NSPD-26 of February 2003, which focused on intelligence priorities. The result of NSPD-5 was a ten-page, single-spaced report by an external panel chaired by former national security advisor Brent Scowcroft, with three basic sections: "An Imperative for Change," "Actions Required by the Administration," and "A Time for Action."[8]

President Obama has employed directives more sparingly than any of his predecessors, but at least three have concerned intelligence, in whole or in part: PPD-19 of October 10, 2012, the unclassified "Protecting Whistleblowers with Access to Classified Information"; PPD-20 of October 16, 2012, the top secret "U.S. Cyber Operations Policy"; and PPD-28 of January 17, 2014, the unclassified "Signals Intelligence [SIGINT] Activities." The latter formed part of the administration's response to the Edward Snowden revelations.[9]

More detailed and systematic guidance across much of the spectrum of intelligence activities was provided from the beginning of the post–World War II era in the form of National Security Council Intelligence Directives (NSCIDs), which were revised periodically up through February 17, 1972, when the most recent versions of all eight current NSCIDs were reissued. A project to produce an omnibus NSCID in the late 1970s was never completed. Consideration was given in the 1980s to further updating

TABLE 17.1   NSCIDs Issued on February 17, 1972

Number	Title
1	Basic Duties and Responsibilities
2	Coordination of Overt Activities
3	Coordination of Intelligence Production
4	The Defector Program
5	U.S. Espionage and Counterintelligence Activities Abroad
6	Signals Intelligence
7	Critical Intelligence Communications
8	Photographic Interpretation

the directives, but it was decided to issue new guidance through the DCI directives derived from the NSCIDs, which have never been rescinded.*[10] Table 17.1 lists the numbers and names of the NSCIDs.

NSCID No. 1, "Basic Duties and Responsibilities," was first issued in 1947. The 1972 version assigned four major responsibilities to the head of the Intelligence Community:

- Planning, reviewing, and evaluating all intelligence activities and allocation of all intelligence resources
- Producing national intelligence required by the president and national consumers
- Chairing and staffing all intelligence advisory boards
- Establishing and reconciling intelligence requirements and priorities with budgetary constraints.[11]

NSCID No. 1 also (1) instructs the DCI to prepare and submit to the Office of Management and Budget (OMB) a consolidated budget, (2) authorizes the issuance of DCI directives as a means of implementing the NSCIDs, and (3) instructs the DCI to protect sources and methods.[12]

NSCID No. 2 makes the DCI responsible for planning how to use the overt collection and reporting capabilities of the various government departments and makes the CIA responsible for conducting, as a service of common concern, radio broadcast monitoring. The Department of State is charged with overt collection of political, sociological, economic, scientific, and technical information; militarily pertinent scientific and technical intelligence; and economic intelligence.[13]

NSCID No. 3 makes the Department of State responsible for the production of political and sociological intelligence on all countries and economic intelligence on the countries of the "Free World." It makes the Department of Defense (DOD) responsible for the production of military intelligence and scientific and technical intelligence

---

*With the replacement of the DCI by the DNI as head of the Intelligence Community, the authorities conferred by the NSCIDs on the DCI transferred to the DNI. The DCI directives (discussed in more detail below) issued prior to the creation of the DNI remain in force—unless rescinded or replaced by DNI Intelligence Community Directives.

pertinent to the missions of DOD components. The CIA is assigned responsibility for economic and scientific and technical intelligence, plus "any other intelligence required by the CIA." In practice, this clause has meant that the CIA is heavily involved in the production of political and military intelligence, especially strategic intelligence. In addition, atomic energy intelligence is decreed to be the responsibility of all Intelligence Community agencies.[14]

NSCID No. 4, titled "The Defector Program," presumably concerns the inducement of defections and the responsibilities of the CIA and other agencies in the program. NSCID No. 5, "U.S. Espionage and Counterintelligence Activities Abroad," authorizes the DCI to "establish the procedures necessary to achieve such direction and coordination, including the assessment of risk incident upon such operations as compared to the value of the activity, and to ensure that sensitive operations are reviewed pursuant to applicable direction."[15]

NSCID No. 6, "Signals Intelligence," has served as NSA's charter. The February 1972 version defines the nature of SIGINT activities and directs the Director of NSA (DIRNSA) to produce intelligence "in accordance with objectives, requirements and priorities established by the Director of Central Intelligence and the United States Intelligence Board." It further authorizes the DIRNSA "to issue direct to any operating elements engaged in SIGINT operations such instructions and assignments as are required. All instructions issued by the Director under the authority provided in this paragraph shall be mandatory, subject only to appeal to the Secretary of Defense."[16]

NSCID No. 7 established the Critical Intelligence Communications (CRITIC) system, which governs procedures and criteria for the transmission of particularly important intelligence to top officials, including the president, within the shortest possible period. The information may concern an imminent coup (such as the overthrow of Salvador Allende in 1973), the assassination of a world leader, or the shooting down of a civilian airliner (the KAL 007 incident in 1983). The information may be acquired via SIGINT, human intelligence (HUMINT), or imagery intelligence (IMINT). NSA's goal is to have a CRITIC message on the president's desk within ten minutes of the event. NSCID No. 8, "Photographic Interpretation," continued the National Photographic Interpretation Center (NPIC), subsequently absorbed by the NGA, as a service of common concern to be provided by the DCI. It also specified that the DCI was to select the Director of NPIC with the concurrence of the Secretary of Defense.[17]

An additional mechanism for presidential oversight and direction of intelligence activities is the President's Intelligence Advisory Board, a successor to the President's Board of Consultants on Foreign Intelligence Activities, established in 1956, and its successor, the President's Foreign Intelligence Advisory Board. In 2008 President George Bush, with Executive Order 13462, retitled the board to reflect that national intelligence involves both foreign and domestic intelligence. The order specified that the President's Intelligence Advisory Board should "assess the quality, quantity, and adequacy of intelligence collection, of analysis and estimates, and of counterintelligence and other intelligence activities." It also established an Intelligence Oversight Board, which is responsible for informing the president of intelligence activities that it believes "may be unlawful or contrary to Executive Order or presidential directives." President Obama further amended the directive in minor ways in November 2009.[18]

DIRECTOR OF NATIONAL INTELLIGENCE AND DEPUTIES

Ever since the Central Intelligence Agency was established in July 1947, there has been controversy and conflict over its role in managing agencies other than the CIA, both because existing agencies and their departments sought to protect their bureaucratic turf and because it was feared that increased authority for the DCI could result in a reduction in the responsiveness of military organizations to the requirements of the military.

Notable milestones over the years have included DCI Walter Bedell Smith's successful fight to establish that the Intelligence Advisory Committee, consisting of the chiefs of the nation's intelligence agencies, existed to provide him with advice rather than to serve as a board of directors. Allen Dulles, DCI from 1953 to 1961, fought and won a number of battles to prevent the Defense Department from gaining control of key institutions and programs for the collection and analysis of intelligence. His successor, John McCone, became embroiled in bitter battles between the CIA's Directorate of Science and Technology and the leadership of the National Reconnaissance Office over control of satellite reconnaissance programs. During his tenure as DCI, Richard Helms (1966–1973) complained that while he was ostensibly responsible for the activities of the entire Intelligence Community, he controlled only 15 percent of its resources, with almost all of the remaining 85 percent in the hands of the Secretary of Defense.

Over the years, presidents took a number of actions to enhance the authority of the DCI, some of which followed one or more of the multitude of studies undertaken to examine the workings of the Intelligence Community. Investigations into IC performance have been conducted since at least 1949 by private citizens or government officials appointed by the DCI, by interagency groups, by the Office of Management and Budget, by internal CIA panels, and by congressional committees and other entities. Often the options considered have included some far more radical than the administration of the time was willing to adopt. Among the more radical proposals was the creation of an intelligence czar, a Director of National Intelligence, who would replace the DCI as the president's primary intelligence advisor and be responsible for the entire Intelligence Community's activities.

As a result of the events of September 11, 2001, the Congressional Joint Inquiry and the National Commission on Terrorist Attacks upon the United States examined the issue of intelligence organization and recommended the creation of a Director of National Intelligence, with two main areas of responsibility: (1) overseeing national intelligence centers on specific subjects of interest across the U.S. government, and (2) managing the National Intelligence Program and overseeing its contributing agencies.[19]

Indeed, creation of a DNI was one of the commission's principal recommendations. The Bush administration eventually supported the proposal, but opposition from the Pentagon and the chairman of the House Armed Services Committee blocked passage of legislation creating a DNI. With a compromise reached on December 6, 2004, the road was finally cleared to establish a Director of National Intelligence.

The 2004 Intelligence Reform and Terrorism Prevention Act (IRTPA) did not give the DNI complete power over the NRO, NSA, or NGA, which remained located within the Department of Defense, although it confirmed the increased authority that

President Bush gave the DCI in August 2004 and further increased his authority with regard to those other organizations in several areas. Under the act, the Director of Management and Budget, under the exclusive direction of the DNI, is to apportion, or direct, how congressionally appropriated funds are to flow from the Treasury Department to each of the cabinet-level agencies containing Intelligence Commuity elements. Thus, the DNI is in a better position to control the pace of spending and can withhold funds until recipients comply with DNI spending priorities. The DNI also has the authority to allocate appropriations directly at the subcabinet agency and department level, giving him or her an additional opportunity to control spending. The IRTPA also requires the DNI to inform Congress if a departmental comptroller refuses to act in accordance with a DNI spending directive. The DCI had neither authority.[20]

The DNI is also charged with the responsibility to "develop and determine" the National Intelligence Program budget, ensure its effective execution, and monitor its implementation. In addition, the DNI is permitted, with OMB approval, to unilaterally transfer funds up to $150 million from one agency or program to another, provided that the sum is less than 5 percent of the affected agency's or department's budget. DCIs could make such a transfer only with the concurrence of the agency or department head, which could take several months to negotiate.[21]

The DNI is also able to transfer IC personnel for up to two years, without the concurrence of the agency or department head—a concurrence that DCIs were required to obtain. If the DNI establishes any new national intelligence centers in addition to the two that already exist (he has the authority to create another four), the director has the authority to transfer up to one hundred personnel to staff the new center.[22]

With regard to appointments, agency or department heads having jurisdiction over the appointment must seek the DNI's concurrence, without which the position cannot be filled. The DNI also has approval authority over major acquisitions. Although the DCI had significant impact on a number of acquisition decisions in the past, primarily concerning satellite reconnaissance systems, he had no statutory authority. The DNI, as a result of the legislation, serves as the executive milestone decision authority on major acquisitions. His power is limited to the extent that acquisitions concern Defense Department programs. In that case, he shares power with the Secretary of Defense. If they cannot reach agreement, it is up to the president to resolve the dispute.[23]

The IRTPA enhanced the DNI's tasking authority over that possessed by the DCIs by stating that the DNI shall "manage and direct the tasking of, collection, analysis, production, and dissemination of national intelligence . . . by approving requirements and resolving conflicts." In 2010 the DNI reached agreement with the Secretary of Defense such that the entire National Intelligence Program would be under the purview of the DNI by 2013. However, congressional action has blocked implementation of that agreement.[24]

In October 2010, President Obama signed legislation (the FY 2010 Intelligence Authorization Act), which further enhanced the DNI's authorities. It requires the DNI to assess personnel levels of all intelligence agencies and forward the results to Congress and to conduct initial vulnerability assessments of each major system, and it gives him authority to assess critical cost growth in major systems. The DNI was also given authority to undertake accountability reviews of elements of the Intelligence Community.[25]

Subordinate to the DNI are approximately 1,500 individuals: deputy directors, assistant deputy directors, mission managers and their staffs, a counterintelligence

FIGURE 17.1   Organizational Chart of the Office of the Director of National Intelligence

LEADERSHIP

Director (DNI)

Principal Deputy Director (PDDNI)
Chief Management Officer (CMO)

CORE MISSION

Deputy DNI for Intelligence Integration (DDNI/II)
Assistant Deputy DNI for Intelligence Integration (ADDNI/II)

Mission Integration Division (MID)	Cyber Threat Intelligence Integration Center
National Intelligence Council (NIC)	National Counterterrorism Center (NCTC)
National Intelligence Management Council (NIMC)	National Counterproliferation Center (NCPC)
	Counterintelligence and Security Center

ENABLERS

Acquisition, Technology & Facilities (AT&F)	Information Sharing Environment (ISE)
Chief Financial Officer (CFO)	Partner Engagement (PE)
Chief Human Capital Officer (CHCO)	Policy & Strategy (P&S)
IC Chief Information Officer (IC CIO)	Systems & Resource Analyses (SRA)

OVERSIGHT

Civil Liberties and Privacy Office (CLPO)	Office of the General Counsel (OGC)
IC Equal Employment Opportunity & Diversity (IC EEOD)	Office of Legislative Affairs (OLA)
IC Inspector General (IC IG)	Public Affairs Office

Source: ODNI.

organization, and two national centers created by the IRTPA.[26] Figure 17.1 shows the organization chart for the Office of the Director of National Intelligence (ODNI). Key deputies to the DNI include the Principal Deputy Director of National Intelligence and the Deputy Director of National Intelligence for Intelligence Integration (DDII), a position that absorbed the responsibilities of the Assistant DNIs for Collection and for Analysis. The DDII's responsibility is to help produce "a fully integrated Intelligence Community." Reporting to the DDII are the National Intelligence Management Council and the National Intelligence Managers, the National Intelligence Council, the President's Daily Briefing Staff, and the Mission Integration Division.[27]

COMMITTEES, BOARDS, AND COUNCILS

The DNI has a variety of Intelligence Community committees, boards, and councils to provide advice and council—some on overall IC issues, others with specific areas of responsibility.* Some are legacies of the DCI era; others are more recent.

---

*The DNI also has a number of external boards and committees that provide advice: Director of National Intelligence Senior Advisory Group, National Counterterrorism Center Director's Advisory Board, National Counterproliferation Center Senior Counterproliferation Partners Advisory Board, Homeland Security and Law Enforcement Partners Board, Advanced Technology Board, Financial Sector Advisory Board, and Review Group on Intelligence and Communications Technologies. See Office of the Director of National Intelligence, untitled report, 2013.

The Executive Committee (EXCOM) is a senior advisory group, consisting of "the DNI and Directors of the 16 IC elements," that "advises and supports the DNI, conducts in-depth discussions on critical issues such as intelligence support to Afghanistan and Pakistan and terrorist finance, and enables proper resource allocation," according to a DNI fact sheet.[28]

The National Intelligence Board is the successor to the National Foreign Intelligence Board and the United States Intelligence Board. Its functions include advising the DNI on a variety of issues, including the production, review, and coordination of national intelligence; interagency exchanges of national intelligence data; the sharing of IC products with foreign governments; the protection of intelligence sources and methods; and activities of common concern and other matters that the DNI may refer to it. Its membership includes the DNI as chairman; the Principal Deputy DNI; the Chairman of the National Intelligence Council; the Deputy DNI for Intelligence Integration; the Directors of the Defense Intelligence Agency (DIA), Bureau of Intelligence and Research (INR), CIA, NGA, and NSA; the National Counterintelligence Executive; the FBI's National Security Branch; the assistant secretaries for intelligence analysis of the Departments of the Treasury and Homeland Security; the director of the Energy Department Office of Intelligence and Counterintelligence; and the Under Secretary of Defense for Intelligence.[29]

The Joint Intelligence Community Council (JICC) includes the DNI as chair, the Secretaries of State, Treasury, Defense, Energy, and Homeland Security, the U.S. Attorney General, and others that the president may designate. It assists the DNI in developing and implementing a joint unified national intelligence effort by advising the DNI on requirements, developing budgets, managing finances, monitoring and evaluating the performance of the Intelligence Community, and ensuring timely execution of DNI programs, policies, and directives.[30]

The National Counterintelligence Policy Board, established in May 1994 by PDD-24, consists of senior executive representatives from the DNI, the CIA, and the Departments of Defense, State, Justice (including the FBI), Homeland Security, and Energy. The board considers, develops, and recommends counterintelligence policy and planning directives to the president's National Security Advisor. Subordinate to the policy board is the National Counterintelligence Operations Board.[31]

Current DNI committees include the Document and Media Exploitation (DOMEX) Committee, the Foreign Language Executive Committee, the National Integrated Technical Surveillance Countermeasures (TSCM) Committee (NITC), the Foreign Denial and Deception Committee, and the National Intelligence Science and Technology (S&T) Committee.

The DOMEX Committee is established by Intelligence Community Directive (ICD) 302 to advise the Assistant Deputy DNI for Open Sources on the "execution of responsibilities and development of guidance" to IC document and media exploitation activities. The committee members include representatives to the National Media Exploitation Center, DIA, CIA, FBI, Defense Cyber Crime Center, U.S. Army, NSA, Department of Homeland Security, Drug Enforcement Administration, and others as determined by the Assistant Deputy DNI.[32]

The National Integrated TSCM Committee (NITC), chartered by the DCI via Intelligence Community Directive 702, is responsible for providing "policy, strategic, and procedural guidance on all TSCM [Technical Surveillance Countermeasures] matters involving the [Intelligence Community]." It is chaired by the Assistant Deputy Director of National Intelligence for Security, with the National Counterintelligence Executive serving as vice chairman. The NITC chairman is responsible for reporting to the DNI annually on Intelligence Community compliance with the directive.[33]

The DCI Foreign Language Committee has been reestablished as the DNI's IC Foreign Language Executive Committee to serve as the senior advisory body to the Assistant Director of National Intelligence for Human Capital in matters related to the community's foreign-language capabilities. It is chaired by the Intelligence Community's Senior Language Authority.[34]

The Foreign Denial and Deception Committee, chaired by the National Intelligence Officer for Science and Technology, advises and assists the DNI on foreign activities that thwart U.S. intelligence through denial and deception. It is also responsible for promoting the effective use of IC resources to counter foreign denial and deception and serves as one of four DNI production committees.[35]

INTELLIGENCE COMMUNITY DIRECTIVES

While NSC intelligence directives, first issued in 1947, were intended to provide broad policy guidance to the Intelligence Community, there was a need for more detailed guidance on the multiple issues associated with each NSCID. The main mechanism for providing that guidance was the Director of Central Intelligence Directive (DCID)—with each taking the form "DCID x/y," where x represented the NSCID that the DCID pertained to and y represented the number in that particular series of DCIDs.

When Jimmy Carter's executive order on intelligence activities covered issues not addressed in the NSCIDs, there was internal discussion of the need to revise them. A similar discussion followed Ronald Reagan's Executive Order 12333. Instead, the decision was made to issue DCIDs regardless of any nonmatching aspects of the NSCIDs and an executive order. In effect the DCIDs were decoupled from the NSCIDs that had originally served as the basis for their promulgation.[36]

Following the creation of the Office of the Director of National Intelligence, the DNI created three new series of documents: Intelligence Community Policy Memoranda (ICPMs), Intelligence Community Policy Guidance (ICPG), and Intelligence Community Directives. The ICPMs are issued to provide policy direction to the Intelligence Community prior to the issuance of an ICD on the same subject. Over time ICDs have replaced ICPMs issued in the early years of the ODNI. An ICPG is subsidiary to an ICD and provides more detailed implementation information. The ICPMs and ICDs, with the exception of some early ICDs, are divided into nine series covering the following topics:

- 100: Enterprise management
- 200: Intelligence analysis
- 300: Intelligence collection
- 400: Customer outcomes
- 500: Information management
- 600: Human capital

- 700: Security and counterintelligence
- 800: Science and technology
- 900: Mission management

ICD 204, issued in September 2007, rescinded DCID 2/3 and established roles and responsibilities for the National Intelligence Priorities Framework (NIPF). It declares the NIPF to be "the DNI's sole mechanism for establishing national intelligence priorities." It also defines the NIPF as consisting of intelligence topics approved by the president, a process for assigning priorities to countries and nonstate actors relevant to the approved intelligence topics, and a matrix showing those priorities.[37]

ICD 402, dated December 23, 2009, and classified SECRET/NOFORN (Not Releasable to Foreign Nationals), concerns the responsibilities of DNI representatives. The main body of the directive concerns DNI representatives overseas and specifies that the DNI "determines the need for DNI representatives in organizations or locations based upon dynamic IC mission and customer requirements." It engendered a losing conflict with the CIA over the issue of who would appoint the chief U.S. intelligence representative at U.S. embassies. An annex concerned an eighteen-month pilot program involving DNI representatives in the United States. It specified that representatives were to be located at FBI field offices in Chicago, Los Angeles, New York, and Washington, D.C., and charged with a variety of functions, including facilitating and monitoring "the implementation of DNI directives, policies, and procedures."[38]

ICD 902, "Global Maritime and Air Intelligence Integration," was issued in January 2009 to "provide policy and direction to the Intelligence Community (IC) elements for integrating activities and information sharing to improve, develop, and enhance maritime and air domain intelligence to effectively identify and respond to national security threats." It specifies, "A national intelligence center for the integration of strategic maritime information will be established at the National Maritime Intelligence Center."[39] Table 17.2 lists the set of current directives that have been identified.

NATIONAL INTELLIGENCE PROGRAM

Until 2005, the allocation of resources for national intelligence activities was governed by the National Foreign Intelligence Program (NFIP). The nonmilitary components of the NFIP were the Central Intelligence Agency Program, the State Department Intelligence Program, the Community Management Staff, and the intelligence elements of the FBI and the Departments of Energy and the Treasury. There were five DOD components: the Consolidated Cryptologic Program (CCP), the General Defense Intelligence Program (GDIP), Navy Special Reconnaissance Activities, the National Reconnaissance Program (NRP), and the Defense Foreign Counterintelligence Program.[40]

The CCP, managed by NSA, included all SIGINT resources in the NFIP. The GDIP included all non-SIGINT, nonreconnaissance programs. Specifically, the GDIP included eight activities: general military intelligence production, imagery collection and processing, HUMINT, nuclear monitoring, research and development, procurement, field support, and scientific and technical intelligence production. The CCP and

GDIP, when combined, formed the Consolidated Defense Intelligence Program. The Navy Special Activities program allocated attack submarines (SSNs) and other craft for sensitive reconnaissance missions. The NRP specified the spending, procurement, and operational activities of the NRO.[41]

One component of the Intelligence Reform and Terrorism Prevention Act of 2004 was the redesignation of the NFIP as the National Intelligence Program, a change that highlighted the DNI's role in domestic intelligence. Today, the National Intelligence Program includes the Central Intelligence Agency Program, the Community Management Account, Department of Energy Program, Department of Homeland Security Program, Department of Justice Programs, Department of State Program, and the Department of Treasury Program. Additionally, it includes five Department of Defense programs: the Consolidated Cryptologic Program (CCP), the General Defense Intelligence Program (GDIP), the National Geospatial-Intelligence Program (NGP), the National Reconnaissance Program (NRP), and the Specialized Reconnaissance Program (SRP).[42]

Table 17.3 provides data on the budget amount associated with the various components of the National Intelligence Program. Figure 17.2 shows the percentage of each program as part of the total fiscal year 2013 budget request, while Figures 17.3(a) and (b) show the various activity percentages that constitute the fiscal year 2013 requests for the CCP and NRP, respectively.

NATIONAL INTELLIGENCE MANAGEMENT COUNCIL

The National Intelligence Management Council is the headquarters of the National Intelligence Managers, positions first established in 2005. The mission managers are "the DNI's principal advisors for community oversight and coordination of their respective mission area." They are responsible for integrating the Intelligence Community's collection and analytic efforts for their designated region, country, functional issue, or topic and with maintaining awareness of IC activities and understanding "the range of customer requirements." They also maintain "senior-level contacts within the intelligence, policymaking, and warfighting communities to ensure that the full range of informational needs related to their mission are met."[43]

Originally, mission managers were established for Iran, North Korea, Venezuela, and Cuba. Today, there are fifteen mission managers, including those for counterproliferation, cyber threat finance, military, science and technology, economics, counterterrorism, and counterintelligence. The National Intelligence Officers (discussed below) for Economics, Military Issues, and Science & Technology also serve as mission managers. Other mission managers are responsible for the Western Hemisphere, Near East, Europe and Eurasia, Africa, Iran, South Asia, and East Asia. Among their functions, the NIMs develop Unifying Intelligence Strategies "to align the IC's efforts in their country, region, or issue mission area."[44]

The Mission Integration Division "works to leverage Intelligence Community analytic, collection and other capabilities to advance the priorities of the NIMs and develops "integrated efforts to address NIM mission and enterprise challenges, tackle identified intelligence gaps, and assess community progress against IC priorities."[45]

TABLE 17.2   Intelligence Community Directives

ICD #	Title	Date
101	Intelligence Community Policy System	June 12, 2009
102	Process for Developing Interpretative Principles and Proposing Amendments to Attorney General Guidelines Governing the Collection, Retention, and Dissemination of Information Regarding U.S. Persons	November 17, 2009
103	Intelligence Enterprise Exercise Program	July 14, 2008
104	National Intelligence Program (NIP) Budget Formulation and Justification, Execution, and Performance Evaluation	April 30, 2013
107	Civil Liberties and Privacy	August 31, 2012
108	Intelligence Community History Programs	August 29, 2007
109	Independent Cost Estimates	April 26, 2010
110	Intelligence Community Equal Employment Opportunity and Diversity	December 31, 2012
111	Accountability Reviews	August 4, 2011
112	Congressional Notification	November 16, 2011
113	Functional Managers	May 19, 2009
114	Comptroller General Access to Intelligence Community Information	June 30, 2011
115	Intelligence Community Capability Requirements Process	December 31, 2012
116	Intelligence Planning, Programming, Budgeting and Evaluation System	September 14, 2011
117	Outside Employment	June 9, 2013
118	Intelligence Community Continuity Program	November 12, 2013
119	Media Contacts	March 20, 2014
120	Intelligence Community Whistleblower Protection	March 20, 2014
203	Analytic Standards	June 21, 2007
204	Roles and Responsibilities of the National Intelligence Priorities Framework	September 13, 2007
205	Analytic Outreach	N/A
206	Sourcing Requirements for Disseminated Analytic Products	October 17, 2007
207	National Intelligence Council	June 9, 2008
208	Write for Maximum Utility	December 17, 2008
209	Tearline Line Production and Dissemination	September 6, 2012
300	Management, Integration, and Oversight of Intelligence Collection and Covert Action	October 3, 2006
302	Document and Media Exploitation	July 6, 2007
304	Human Intelligence	July 9, 2009
402	Director of National Intelligence Representatives	December 23, 2009
403	Foreign Disclosure and Release of Classified National Intelligence	N/A
404	Executive Branch Intelligence Customers	July 22, 2013
500	DNI Chief Information Officer	August 7, 2008
501	Discovery and Dissemination or Retrieval of Information Within the Intelligence Community	January 21, 2009
502	Integrated Defense of the Intelligence Community Information Environment	March 11, 2011

ICD #	Title	Date
503	Intelligence Community Information Technology Systems Security: Risk Management, Certification and Accreditation	September 15, 2008
602	Human Capital—Intelligence Community Critical Pay Positions	August 16, 2006
610	Competency Directories for the Intelligence Community Workforce	October 4, 2010
612	Intelligence Community Core Contract Personnel	October 30, 2009
623	Appointment of Highly Qualified Experts	October 16, 2008
630	Intelligence Community Foreign Language Capability	May 14, 2012
650	National Intelligence Civilian Compensation Program: Guiding Principles and Framework	April 28, 2008
651	Performance Management System Requirements for the Intelligence Community Civilian Workforce	April 4, 2012
652	Occupational Structure for the Intelligence Community Civilian Workforce	April 28, 2008
653	Pay-Setting and Administration Policies for the Intelligence Community Civilian Workforce	May 14, 2008
654	Performance-Based Pay for the Intelligence Community Civilian Workforce	April 28, 2008
655	National Intelligence Awards Program	February 9, 2012
656	Performance Management System Requirements for Intelligence Community Senior Civilian Officers	April 4, 2012
660	Intelligence Community Civilian Joint Duty Program	February 11, 2013
700	Protection of National Intelligence	June 7, 2012
701	Security Policy Directive for Unauthorized Disclosures of Classified Information	N/A
702	Technical Surveillance Countermeasures	February 18, 2008
703	Protection of Classified National Intelligence, Including Sensitive Compartmented Information	
704	Personnel Security Standards and Procedures Governing Eligibility for Access to Sensitive Compartmented Information and Other Controlled Access Program Information	October 1, 2008
705	Sensitive Compartmented Information Facilities	May 26, 2010
707	Center for Security Evaluation	October 17, 2008
709	Reciprocity for Intelligence Community Employee Mobility	June 10, 2009
710	Classification Management and Control Markings System	June 21, 2013
731	Supply Chain Risk Management	December 7, 2013
732	Damage Assessments	N/A
750	Counterintelligence Programs	N/A
801	Acquisition	August 16, 2009
900	Integrated Mission Management	Not Available
902	Global Maritime and Air Intelligence Integration	January 14 2009

Sources: ODNI, "Intelligence Community Directives," http://www.dni.gov/index.php/intelligence-community/ic-policies-reporg/irp/dni/icd; Office of the Director of National Intelligence, "Instrument: ICD—Intelligence Community Directives (62)" n.d.

TABLE 17.3   Budget for NIP Programs

Program	FY 2011 Actual	FY 2012 Appropriated	FY 2013 Base	FY 2013 OCO	FY 2013 Request	FY 2012–FY 2013 Change (Funds / Percent)	FY 2013–FY 2017 Total*
CCP	10,737,163	10,514,035	10,036,851	730,914	10,767,765	253,730 / 2	50,652,537
CIAP	14,652,379	15,332,901	12,037,708	2,672,317	14,710,025	−622,876 / −4	64,567,982
CIARDS	292,000	513,700	514,000	—	514,000	300 / —	2,570,000
CMA	2,063,394	1,870,255	1,676,387	—	1,676,387	−193,868 / −10	10,274,665
DHS	275,136	307,359	284,332	—	284,332	−23,027 / −7	1,462,089
DOD-FCIP	517,720	505,895	456,475	72,485	528,960	23,065 / 5	2,487,905
DOJ	2,978,329	3,010,795	3,019,958	—	3,019,958	−9,163 / —	15,596,944
Energy	163,700	186,699	188,619	—	188,619	1,920 / 1	943,095
GDIP	4,767,009	4,815,583	3,655,662	774,480	4,430,142	−385,441 / −8	19,901,677
NGP	5,227,945	5,041,569	4,339,195	539,735	4,878,930	−162,639 / −3	22,786,959
NRP	11,401,745	10,411,335	10,268,773	53,150	10,321,923	−89,412 / −1	54,842,860
SRP	1,466,792	1,267,751	1,099,820	33,784	1,133,604	−134,147 / −11	6,010,922
State	68,773	68,203	72,655	—	72,655	4,452 / 7	377,056
Treasury	27,422	27,123	27,297	—	27,297	174 / 1	138,274
NIP Total	54,639,507	53,873,203	47,677,732	4,876,865	52,554,597	−1,318,606 / −2	252,612,965

*FY 2013–2017 total includes the OCO Request for FY 2013 only.

Source: ODNI, *FY 2013 Congressional Budget Justification*, vol. 1, *National Intelligence Program Summary*, February 2012, http://fas.org/irp/budget/nip-fy2013.pdf. OCO: Overseas Contingency Operations.

FIGURE 17.2   FY 2013 Request by Program

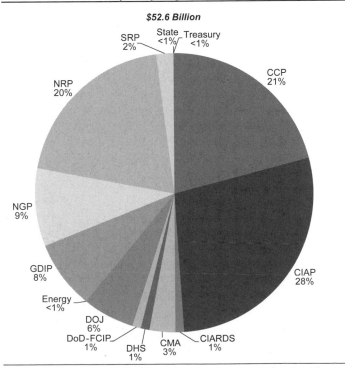

Source: ODNI, *FY 2013 Congressional Budget Justification*, vol. 1: *National Intelligence Program Summary*, February 2012.

FIGURE 17.3a Consolidated Cryptologic Program

Fiscal Year 2013 Funding by Budget Category

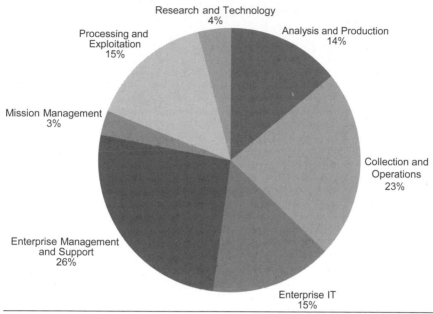

Source: ODNI, *FY 2013 Congressional Budget Justification*, vol. 1: *National Intelligence Program Summary*, February 2012.

FIGURE 17.3b National Reconnaissance Program

Fiscal Year 2013 Funding by Budget Category

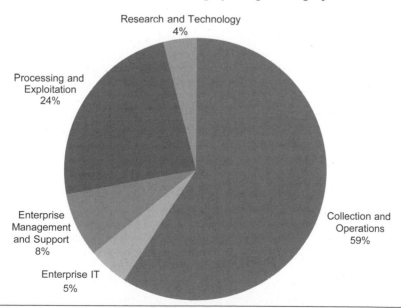

Source: ODNI, *FY 2013 Congressional Budget Justification*, vol. 1: *National Intelligence Program Summary*, February 2012.

NATIONAL INTELLIGENCE COUNCIL

The National Intelligence Council was the DCI's principal vehicle for producing National Intelligence Estimates, Special Estimates, and Interagency Intelligence Memoranda; it now performs its mission on behalf of the DNI. Its origins go back to 1950, when an Office of National Estimates (ONE) was established within the CIA. The office, tasked with drafting national estimates, consisted of the Board of National Estimates (BNE) and its staff. The board consisted of seven to twelve senior officials with expertise in particular areas who were initially drawn from academia and subsequently the CIA.[46]

The ONE suffered a decline in prestige and influence during the Richard Nixon administration for a variety of reasons, including Henry Kissinger's unhappiness with its product. In June 1973, the BNE chairman was forced to retire. DCI William Colby decided not to replace him and abolished the ONE.[47] Colby gave two reasons for his decision:

> One, I had some concern with the tendency to compromise differences and put out a document which was less sharp than perhaps was needed in certain situations. Second, I believed that I needed the advantage of some individuals who could specialize in some of the major problems not just as estimative problems but as broad intelligence problems. They could sit in my chair, so to speak, and look at the full range of an intelligence problem: Are we collecting enough? Are we processing the raw data properly? Are we spending too much money on it? Are we organized right to do the job?[48]

Colby created the National Intelligence Officer (NIO) system, whereby specific individuals were held solely responsible for producing a particular estimate. In a 1987 memo, "The Integrity and Objectivity of National Foreign Estimates," then deputy director for intelligence Richard J. Kerr observed,

> The role of the National Intelligence Officer, in our judgment, is critical. An impartial estimative process requires the full expression of views by participating agencies and the clear identification for our consumers of areas of agreement and, often most importantly, disagreement. In order to fight what is often an unhealthy desire to reach consensus, the NIO must, above all, see himself as a manager of the process, the one who ensures that the tough questions are addressed, that consensus views represent real agreement, and not papered-over differences, and that minority views are fully expressed. It has been our experience that when the NIO subordinates this responsibility to the advocacy of a particular analytic line that the integrity of the estimative process suffers.[49]

Initially, NIOs were purposely not given a staff but were expected to draw on the resources of the CIA, DIA, INR, and other analytical units to produce the required estimates. On January 1, 1980, with the establishment of the National Intelligence Council, the NIOs were given not only a collective identity but also an Analytic Staff.[50]

The NIOs serve as "the analytic arm" of the National Intelligence Manager teams. Their core missions are to

- Promote "exemplary" use of analytic tradecraft and standards, including alternative analysis, new analytic tools and techniques, and wider collaboration within the Intelligence Community
- Provide senior policymakers with the Intelligence Community's coordinated views, including NIEs
- Prepare IC principals and represent the community at meetings of NSC principals and deputies
- Identify and employ non U.S. government experts in academia and the private sector to expand the community's knowledge and perspectives.[51]

The three top officials of the NIC are the chairman, vice chairman, and Director of the Analysis and Production Staff. There are fifteen NIOs. Nine are responsible for specific nations or regions: Africa, East Africa, Europe, Iran, the Near East, North Korea, Russia-Eurasia, South Asia, and the Western Hemisphere. The remaining six focus on specific subject areas: Cyber Issues, Economics, Military Issues, Science & Technology, Transnational Threats, and WMD & Proliferation. That lineup represents four changes from the NIO lineup of late 2010, when there were thirteen NIOs.[52]

One change was the elimination of one position: the NIO for Warning. Two positions were established to focus on specific countries of concern: Iran and North Korea. The final change was the creation of the NIO for Cyber Issues in 2011. The duties of the NIO for North Korea include, but are not limited to, overseeing Intelligence Community–wide production and coordination of analytic assessments on North Korea, briefing senior Intelligence Community members, policymakers, and military decision makers on the Intelligence Community's assessment of North Korea, and reviewing and presiding over research and production plans on North Korea.[53]

The NIO for Cyber Issues serves as the Director of National Intelligence's "analytic manager for cyber issues." He or she is responsible for orchestrating and directing "Community-wide mid- and long-term strategic analysis support" and "advance[ing] the cyber mission, which includes cybersecurity, cyber operations, and broader goals." The NIO is responsible for overseeing "IC-wide production and coordination of National Intelligence Estimates (NIE) and other community papers . . . concerning cyber issues for the President, DNI, and other senior policy makers."[54]

When Robert Gates transferred the NIC out of the Directorate of Intelligence, he also transferred three DCI interagency intelligence production committees to the NIC: the Joint Atomic Energy Intelligence Committee (JAEIC), the Weapons and Space Systems Intelligence Committee (WSSIC), and the Scientific and Technical Intelligence Committee (STIC).[55]

The JAEIC was created "to foster, develop and maintain a coordinated community approach to the problems in the field of atomic energy intelligence, to promote interagency liaison, and to give added impetus and community support to the efforts of individual agencies." Its specific responsibilities include assessing the adequacy of the U.S. nuclear intelligence program and its ability to effectively monitor compliance with various nuclear testing treaties; evaluating the methodology used in estimating the yield of foreign nuclear detonations; assessing major developments in foreign nuclear weapons power; considering the possible impact of nuclear energy programs on proliferation in nations not yet possessing nuclear weapons; providing national decision makers with advice on the possible authorization of U.S. foreign sales in the nuclear energy area; and providing warning of a country's obtaining nuclear weapons.[56]

Its products have included a 1976 assessment, "The Soviet Atomic Energy Program," a 1989 assessment of Iraq's ability to build an atomic weapon, and a 1992 study, "Geology of the Qinggir Underground Nuclear Test Site." It may also commission work, such as tasking a national laboratory intelligence unit to produce a study on the state of nuclear materials security in Russia. JAEIC components have included a Nuclear Test Intelligence Subcommittee and a Nuclear Weapons Logistics Working Group.[57]

The failure to convene a second meeting of the JAEIC in 2002 to examine the Intelligence Community's varied views about the implications of Iraq's purchase of aluminum tubes became a subject of controversy. An August 2002 meeting was to be followed by a meeting later in the month, but this was cancelled, as was a scheduled September meeting.[58]

The Weapons and Space Systems Intelligence Committee was created in 1956 as the Guided Missile Intelligence Committee, which subsequently became the Guided Missile and Astronautics Intelligence Committee. In addition to coordinating the guided missile and astronautics intelligence activities of the Intelligence Community during the Cold War, the WSSIC performed technical studies on Soviet missiles as inputs to the NIEs. These papers were coordinated in the same manner as NIEs but were directed at informing the Intelligence Community. The WSSIC also assigned designators and code names for such systems.[59]

The WSSIC's Biological and Chemical Warfare Working Group reviewed all available intelligence concerning the suspected biological warfare incident at Sverdlovsk in 1979. It concluded that there was a high probability that the Soviets maintained an active biological warfare program. Earlier committee products concerned Soviet tank developments, the air defense capabilities of Soviet nuclear-equipped surface-to-air missiles, and estimates of Soviet intercontinental ballistic missile silo hardness. In 1997 the committee produced a report concluding that Chinese-supplied M-11s in Pakistan should be considered operational.[60]

The Scientific and Technical Intelligence Committee is responsible for "advising and assisting the [DNI] with respect to the production, coordination, and evaluation of intelligence on foreign scientific and technical developments that could affect U.S. national security." STIC products have included "Soviet R&D Related to Particle Beam Weapons" (October 1976), "Collection Guide: Chinese Students and Visitors from Important Institutes Seeking Critical Technologies" (1986), and "A Preliminary Assessment of Soviet Kinetic Energy Weapons Technology" (1986). In the 1991 fiscal year, its Collection Subcommittee examined "existing and planned approaches to S&T intelligence collection, identified gaps, and provided a forum for discussion of S&T collection issues."[61]

The National Intelligence Production Board, formerly known as the Intelligence Producers Council, operates under the NIC, is chaired by the Chairman of the NIC, and is composed of senior Intelligence Community production managers, including the chairmen of the DNI production committees. In addition to advising the DNI on production matters, it "oversees several Community programs that focus on minimizing unnecessary duplication of effort and maximizing efforts to meet consumer needs."[62]

NATIONAL COUNTERTERRORISM CENTER

In his January 2003 State of the Union address, President Bush announced plans to establish a Terrorist Threat Integration Center (TTIC) outside the CIA organizational structure but reporting to the Director of Central Intelligence. Director of Central Intelligence Directive 2/4 followed, formally establishing the center and specifying its missions. On May 1, 2003, the center opened with fifty officers from the Departments of State, Defense, Justice, and Homeland Security and from the Intelligence Community. It was expected to have several hundred officers by the time it moved into a new facility in May 2004, with the FBI Counterterrorism Division and CIA Counterterrorism Center relocating to that facility at the same time.[63]

The center was assigned four key missions: providing terrorist threat assessments to U.S. national leaders, ensuring information sharing across agency lines, integrating domestic and foreign intelligence related to terrorist threats, and optimizing the use of terrorist-threat-related information, expertise, and capabilities to conduct threat analysis and guide collection strategies. By December 2003, it was producing a daily terrorist threat matrix, a daily terrorist threat report for the executive branch, a daily terrorist situation report, spot commentaries, threat warnings, IC assessments, and special analysis reports.[64]

One impetus for the president's actions was a 2002 report from a review panel headed by former national security advisor Brent Scowcroft, established pursuant to Bush's National Security Presidential Directive 5. The report had recommended, "The President should establish a single National Counterterrorism Center for the federal government reporting to the DCI and building upon and expanding the membership of the current Counterterrorist Center at the CIA." The report also delineated a number of responsibilities for the proposed center, including collecting, analyzing, and disseminating "all terrorism-related foreign intelligence, whether gathered domestically or abroad." Its director, operating under the DCI's authorities, "would establish requirements and priorities for the collection of foreign intelligence whether collected domestically or abroad."[65]

While President Bush's action gave the center a different name, it would not be long before the TTIC took on the name recommended by the Scowcroft panel. A major recommendation of the National Commission on Terrorist Attacks upon the United States in its July 2004 report was the creation of a National Counterterrorism Center (NCTC), to be built on the foundation of the TTIC. As envisioned by the commission, it would be a center for not only joint intelligence but also joint operational planning, staffed by personnel from the CIA, FBI, and other agencies.[66]

With respect to intelligence, the NCTC "should lead strategic analysis, pooling all-source intelligence, foreign and domestic, about transnational terrorist organizations with global reach," the commission wrote. The center, the commission believed, should develop net assessments, comparing terrorist capabilities with U.S. defenses and countermeasures and providing warning and task collection assets both within and outside the United States.[67]

The commission recommended that the NCTC's operational planning functions should include assigning operational responsibilities to agencies such as the State Department, CIA, FBI, Defense Department, combatant commands, and Department of Homeland Security. While the NCTC would not direct the actual execution of operations, it would track their implementation by the operational agencies. It would also "look across the foreign-domestic divide and across agency boundaries, updating plans to follow through on cases."[68]

In response to the commission's recommendation, President Bush issued an executive order in late August 2004 establishing a National Counterterrorism Center, under the supervision of the Director of Central Intelligence. Consistent with the commission's recommendations, the order assigned NCTC responsibility for being the U.S. government's primary organization for analyzing and integrating all intelligence possessed by the government pertaining to terrorism and counterterrorism, with the exception of "purely domestic counterterrorism information." And, as the commission recommended, the NCTC was assigned the mission of "strategic operational planning for counterterrorism activities." It was also assigned the recommended missions of information sharing and serving as a central bank of knowledge.[69]

Two months later, Congress passed the Intelligence Reform and Terrorism Prevention Act, which, in effect, transferred the NCTC from the former Office of the Director of Central Intelligence to the Office of the Director of National Intelligence. The primary NCTC missions in the legislation were essentially identical to those outlined in the executive order. However, with respect to the planning of counterterrorist operations, the NCTC reports to the president, whereas it reports to the DNI with respect to center budget and programs and the activities of the Directorate of Intelligence.[70]

As shown in Figure 17.4, the NCTC's two key officials are its director and principal deputy director, and it consists of three directorates, in addition to the Directorate of Intelligence and the Office of National Intelligence Management.

Among the director's functions is the periodic presentation of classified and unclassified assessments of the terrorist threat, such as the director's September 2011 presentation to the Senate Committee on Homeland Security and Governmental Affairs, "Ten Years After 9/11: Are We Safer?" It covered the evolving terrorist threat, the evolution of al-Qaeda's regional affiliates, homegrown violent extremist activity, state sponsors of terrorism, and the NCTC's role, activities, and challenges.[71]

The Directorate of Intelligence "leads the production and integration of counterterrorism analysis for the U.S. Government." It produces assessments of issues such as terrorist safe havens, state sponsors of terrorism, worldwide counterterrorism cooperation, and regional terrorism and groups—assessments coordinated throughout the Intelligence Community.[72]

One component of the intelligence directorate is apparently the center's Pursuit Group, established in January 2010 to develop tactical leads and pursue terrorism threats. It focuses exclusively on information that could lead to the discovery of threats against the United States or its interests abroad. Pursuit Group analysts pursue "nonobvious and unresolved connections, identifying unknown, known or suspected terrorists, and [focus] on seemingly unimportant details that could yield relevant

FIGURE 17.4   National Counterterrorism Center Organization Chart

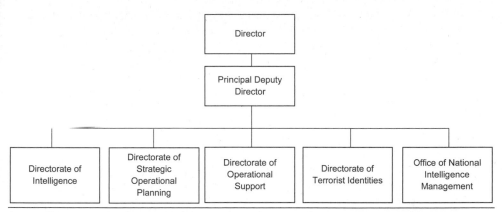

Sources: ODNI, *U.S. National Intelligence: An Overview*, 2013; Matthew G. Olsen, Director, NCTC, "Ten Years After 9/11: Are We Safer?" [hearing before the Senate Committee on Homeland Security and Governmental Affairs, September 13, 2011].

information." Additional Directorate of Intelligence components include, or have included, the Radical and Extremist Messages, the Weapons, Tactics, and Targets, and the al-Qaeda and Sunni Extremism groups—all of which include analysts from several IC organizations.[73]

The Directorate of Strategic Operational Planning is responsible for directing U.S. government planning efforts "to focus all elements of national power against the terrorist threat." According to the NCTC director in 2011, the directorate "integrates all phases of the planning cycle—developing a plan, monitoring its implementation, and assessing its effectiveness and resource allocations—and creates communities of interest to coordinate and integrate implementation."[74] The Directorate of Operational Support "provides the common intelligence picture for the counterterrorism community with 24 hours a day/7 days a week situational awareness; terrorist threat reporting; management and incident information tracking; and support for worldwide, national, and international special events."[75]

The Directorate of Terrorist Identities (DTI), formerly the Directorate of Information Sharing and Knowledge Development, maintains a consolidated repository of information on international terrorist identities and is responsible for ensuring "that appropriate Federal agencies can access the information they need through the Terrorist Identities Datamart Environment (TIDE)." A May 2012 NCTC policy document, "Information Sharing Rules of the Road," provides guidance by which "NCTC personnel will share information with counterterrorism community partners."[76]

A DTI document describing strategic accomplishments in 2013 identified as two successes the achievement of 1 million people in TIDE and the expansion of the Kingfisher terrorist screening tool, which "correlates large data sets to help enhance existing terrorist identity information." It also named DTI provision of support to the Boston Marathon bombing investigation, production of biometric analysis reports, and generation of a TIDE classification guide as among its accomplishments.[77]

The Office of National Intelligence Management, formerly the Directorate of Mission Management, is charged with providing strategic management of all national intelligence relating to the Intelligence Community's counterterrorism mission to establish analytic and collection priorities, with advancing analytic tradecraft and training, and with leading strategic planning, evaluation, and budgeting.[78]

Among the NCTC's interagency activities is its participation, along with the FBI and Department of Homeland Security, on the Joint Counterterrorism Assessment Team (JCAT). The JCAT was established in April 2013 as the successor to the Interagency Threat Assessment Coordination Group, which had been formed in 2007. The JCAT is responsible for producing federal coordinated intelligence on "significant international terrorism events that have the potential to impact local or regional public safety conditions" in the United States.[79]

NATIONAL COUNTERPROLIFERATION CENTER

The National Commission on Terrorist Attacks upon the United States suggested the possibility of establishing a center focusing on WMD proliferation under a Director of National Intelligence. In its March 2005 report, the Commission on the Intelligence Capabilities of the United States Regarding Weapons of Mass Destruction explicitly recommended that the president "establish a National Counter Proliferation Center (NCPC) that is relatively small (i.e. fewer than 100 people) and that manages and coordinates analysis and collection on nuclear, biological, and chemical weapons across the Intelligence Community."[80]

Even before that report was issued, a provision of the Intelligence Reform and Terrorism Prevention Act of 2004 specified that no later than eighteen months after the enactment of the legislation, the president was required to establish a National Counterproliferation Center. Its responsibilities would include serving as the primary organization for analyzing and integrating all intelligence possessed or acquired by the United States pertaining to proliferation, ensuring that agencies had full access to all-source intelligence needed to support their counterproliferation activities, coordinating the counterproliferation plans and activities of various departments and agencies, and conducting strategic operational counterproliferation planning for U.S. government agencies. The legislation did provide a provision that the president could waive any of the requirements of the section if he or she determined that the provisions would not materially improve U.S. counterproliferation capabilities. On August 8, 2005, in compliance with the IRTPA, DNI John Negroponte appointed Kenneth C. Brill as the Counterproliferation Mission Manager as well as director of the future NCPC, making him the principal advisor to the DNI on issues and matters related to the proliferation of WMD.[81]

Because President Bush waived some of the new requirements, the new center was not the precise counterpart to the NCTC that the intelligence reform act envisioned. Thus, it did not replace the CIA's Weapons Intelligence, Nonproliferation, and Arms Control Center. Rather, the new center was made responsible for coordinating strategic planning within the Intelligence Community to enhance intelligence support to U.S. efforts to halt proliferation of WMD, associated delivery systems, and materials and technology. The center is chartered to "work with the Intelligence Community

FIGURE 17.5   Organization of the National Counterproliferation Center

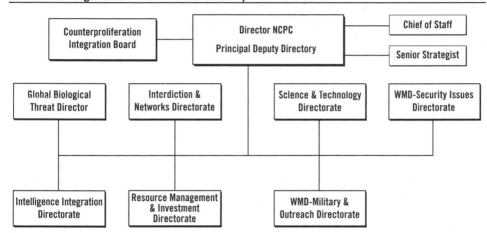

to identify critical intelligence gaps or shortfalls in collection, analysis or exploitation, and develop solutions to ameliorate or close [such] gaps." It is also responsible for working with the Intelligence Community to identify long-term ("over-the-horizon") proliferation threats and requirements and to develop strategies "to ensure the IC is positioned to address these threats and issues."[82] The NCPC also maintains contact with organizations within and outside the Intelligence Community that might help identify new methods or technologies that can improve the community's capabilities to detect and prevent future proliferation threats. This includes contacts with the Intelligence Community, other government agencies, the policy community, and experts in the private sector and academia.[83] Figure 17.5 shows the organization chart of the NCPC.

NATIONAL COUNTERINTELLIGENCE AND SECURITY CENTER

The National Counterintelligence and Security Center (NCSC) was established on December 1, 2014, as the successor to the National Counterintelligence Executive (NCIX), which was established in 1995. The 2002 Counterintelligence Enhancement Act designated the NCIX as head of the Office of the National Counterintelligence Executive (ONCIX) and made him or her "responsible for counterintelligence and security for the United States Government." The 2004 Intelligence Reform and Terrorism Prevention Act made the NCIX and ONCIX part of the Office of the Director of National Intelligence.[84]

The NCSC is responsible for producing the National Threat Identification and Prioritization Assessment (NTIPA), other analytical counterintelligence products, and the National Counterintelligence Strategy of the United States, as well as for setting priorities for collection, investigations, and operations. It is also responsible for oversight of counterintelligence program budgets and evaluations and developing counterintelligence awareness, outreach, and training standards policies. In addition,

FIGURE 17.6   Organization of the Office of the National Counterintelligence Executive

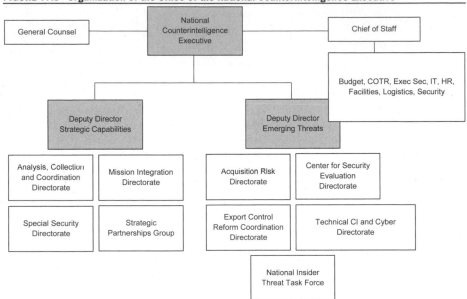

Source: NCIX.

it is responsible for conducting damage assessments, such as the one conducted with regard to Ana Belen Montes, a DIA employee who provided sensitive intelligence to the Cuban intelligence service.[85]

In 2010 the NCIX absorbed the DNI's Special Security Center, which became the ONCIX Special Security Directorate (SSD), and the Center for Security Evaluation (CSE). SSD focused on tasks ranging from management and oversight of the Intelligence Community's classification marking systems to serving as the DNI's point of contact for Security Executive Agent authorities. CSE coordinates security issues between the Intelligence Community and the Department of State.[86] Figure 17.6 shows the organization of the NCIX before it became the NCSC.

CYBER THREAT INTELLIGENCE INTEGRATION CENTER

On February 28, 2015, President Obama directed, by memorandum, that the Director of National Intelligence establish a Cyber Threat Intelligence Integration Center (CTIIC). Creation of such an agency had been proposed by the staff of the White House cybersecurity coordinator but was initially opposed by some agencies. One catalyst of the presidential decision was the lack of any agency to integrate analysis with regard to the intrusion into Sony Pictures computers the previous November.[87]

The memorandum delineated five responsibilities for the new organization, the first of which is to "provide integrated all-source analysis of intelligence related to foreign cyber threats or related to cyber incidents affecting U.S. national interests." The center was also instructed to provide support to a number of cyber organizations—including the National Cybersecurity and Communications Integration Center, the National Cyber Investigative Task Force, and the U.S. Cyber Command.[88]

In addition, CTIC is to oversee the "development and implementation of intelligence sharing capabilities . . . to enhance shared situational awareness of intelligence related to foreign cyber threats or related to cyber incidents affecting U.S. national interests." It is also responsible for ensuring that indicators of hostile cyber activity and, "as appropriate," related threat reporting in intelligence channels be downgraded to the lowest possible classification possible for distribution within the U.S. government and to U.S. private-sector organizations. Finally, CTIC is to "facilitate and support interagency efforts to develop and implement coordinated plans to counter foreign cyber threats to U.S. national interests." It is expected that the center will begin with a staff of about fifty and a budget of $35 million.[89]

Notes

1. George W. Bush, "Further Amendments to Executive Order 12333, United States Intelligence Activities," Executive Order 13470, July 30, 2008, *Federal Register*, 73, no. 150 (August 4, 2008): 45325–45342.

2. Ibid., 45325–45328.

3. Ibid., 45326, 45331.

4. Ibid., 45333–45337. On the process of amending the Executive Order 12333, see Stephen B. Slick, "The 2008 Amendments to Executive Order 12333, United States Intelligence Activities," *Studies in Intelligence* 58, no. 2 (Extracts, June 2014): 1–18.

5. Two compilations of declassified National Security Directives are National Security Archive, *Presidential Directives on National Security from Truman to Clinton* (Alexandria, VA: Chadwyck-Healey, 1994), and National Security Archive, *Presidential Directives on National Security from Truman to Bush* (Alexandria, VA: Chadwyck-Healey, 2002). Listings of and access to directives can also be found on the website of the Federation of American Scientists (www.fas.org).

6. On NSDD-42, see U.S. Congress, House Committee on Science and Technology, *National Space Policy* (Washington, DC: U.S. Government Printing Office, 1982), 13. NSDDs 22, 42, 84, 196, and 204 were obtained, in whole or part, under the FOIA, by the National Security Archive. NSDD-159 was released during the Iran-Contra hearings.

7. Elaine Sciolino, "Pakistan Keeping Afghan Aid Role," *New York Times*, February 26, 1989, 15; "Saudi Help for the CIA," *Newsweek*, September 10, 1990, 6; Bill Gertz, "Despite Thaw in Cold War, Bush Heats Up Counterspy Operations," *Washington Times*, October 24, 1990, A1, A6; Edward D. Shaefer Jr., Director, Office of Naval Intelligence, *Strategic Planning for the Office of Naval Intelligence: Vision and Direction for the Future*, 1992, 10; George H. W. Bush, National Security Directive 67, "Intelligence Capabilities, 1992–2005," March 30, 1992; National Security Council, "U.S. Counterintelligence Effectiveness," May 1994; William J. Clinton, "Remarks at the Central Intelligence Agency in Langley, Virginia, July 14, 1995," American Presidency Project, http://www.presidency.ucsb.edu/ws/index.php?pid=51616&st=langley&st1=; Defense Science Board, *Defense Mapping for Future Operations* (Washington, DC: Office of the Undersecretary of Defense for Acquisition and Technology, 1995), E-9.

8. George J. Tenet, Memorandum for: Assistant to the President for National Security Affairs, Subject: Comments on Draft National Security Presidential Directive on Intelligence, April 9, 2001; George J. Tenet, Memorandum, Subject: National Security Presidential Directive 5 (NSPD-5), April 4, 2002; NSPD-5 External Panel, Memorandum for: The Director of Central Intelligence, Subject: Finding and Recommendations, n.d.

9. The directives are available at the Federation of American Scientists (www.fas.org).

10. Douglas F. Garthoff, *Directors of Central Intelligence as Leaders of the U.S. Intelligence Community, 1946–2005* (Washington, DC: Center for the Study of Intelligence, 2005), 158n.

11. NSCID No. 1, "Basic Duties and Responsibilities," February 17, 1972, Declassified Documents Reference System (DDRS) 1976-167G.

12. Ibid.

13. NSCID No. 2, "Coordination of Overt Collection Activities," February 17, 1972, DDRS 1976-253D.

14. NSCID No. 3, "Coordination of Intelligence Production," February 17, 1972, DDRS 1976-253E.

15. U.S. Congress, House Permanent Select Committee on Intelligence, *Annual Report* (Washington, DC: U.S. Government Printing Office, 1978), 70; NSCID No. 5, "U.S. Espionage and Counterintelligence Activities Abroad," February 17, 1972, DDRS 1976-253F.

16. Department of Justice, *Report on Inquiry into CIA-Related Electronic Surveillance Activities*, 1976, 77–78.

17. National Security Agency/Central Security Service, *NSA/CSS Manual 22-1*, 1986, 1; Department of Defense Directive S-5100.9, "Implementation of National Security Council Intelligence Directive No. 7," March 19, 1960; James Bamford, *The Puzzle Palace: A Report on NSA, America's Most Secret Agency* (Boston: Houghton Mifflin, 1982), 104; Seymour M. Hersh, *"The Target Is Destroyed": What Really Happened to Flight 007 and What America Knew About It* (New York: Random House, 1986), 53; Jack Devine with Vernon Loeb, *Good Hunting: An American Spymaster's Story* (New York: Farrar, Straus & Giroux, 2014), 43–44; NSCID No. 8, "Photographic Interpretation," February 17, 1972, DDRS 1976-253G.

18. Phillip K. Edwards, "The President's Board: 1956–60," *Studies in Intelligence* 13, no. 2 (Summer 1969): 113–128; White House, "The President's Intelligence Advisory Board—History," http://www.whitehouse.gov/administration/eop/piab; George W. Bush, "Executive Order 13462—President's Intelligence Advisory Board and Intelligence Oversight Board," *Federal Register* 73, no. 43 (March 4, 2008): 11805–11809; Barack Obama, "Amending Executive Order 13462," *Federal Register* 74, no. 2 (November 2, 2009), 56521–56522. For a history of the board, see Kenneth Michael Absher, Michael C. Desch, and Roman Popadiuk, *Privileged and Confidential: The Secret History of the President's Intelligence Advisory Board* (Lexington, KY: University Press of Kentucky, 2012).

19. National Commission on Terrorist Attacks upon the United States, *The 9/11 Commission Report: Final Report of the National Commission on Terrorist Attacks upon the United States* (New York: W. W. Norton, 2004), 411.

20. Richard A. Best Jr., Alfred Cumming, and Todd Masse, Congressional Research Service, *Director of National Intelligence Statutory Authorities: Status and Proposals*, April 11, 2005, http://fas.org/sgp/crs/intel/RS22112.pdf, 3.

21. Ibid., 4.

22. Ibid.

23. Ibid., 4–5.

24. Ibid., 5; Ellen Nakashima, "Control of Intelligence Budget Will Shift," www.washingtonpost.com, November 3, 2010, http://www.washingtonpost.com/wp-dyn/content/article/2010/11/02/AR2010110207136.html.

25. Richard A. Best Jr., Congressional Research Service, *Director of National Intelligence Statutory Authorities: Status and Proposals,* December 16, 2011, http://fas.org/sgp/crs/intel/RL34231.pdf, 5. On the passage of the IRTPA and the transition from DCI to Director of National Intelligence, see Michael Allen, *Blinking Red: Crisis and Compromise in American Intelligence After 9/11* (Washington, DC: Potomac Books, 2013); Richard A. Best Jr., "Leadership of the U.S. Intelligence Community: From DCI to DNI," *International Journal of Intelligence and Counterintelligence* 27, no. 2 (Summer 2014): 253–333; Jeffrey T. Richelson, ed., National Security Archive Electronic Briefing Book No. 144, *From Director of Central Intelligence to Director of National Intelligence*, August 12, 2005, http://www2.gwu.edu/~nsarchiv/NSAEBB/NSAEBB144.

For the ODNI's assessment of its accomplishments, see Office of the Director of National Intelligence, "ODNI Fact Sheet," October 2010, http://www.dni.gov/files/documents/ODNI%20Fact%20Sheet_2011.pdf.

26. David E. Kaplan and Kevin Whitelaw, "Playing Defense," *U.S. News & World Report*, November 13, 2006, 43–53; "Getting Smarter About Intelligence," *C4ISR Journal* (March 2007): 45–46.

27. Director of National Intelligence, "Intelligence Integration—Who We Are," http://www.dni.gov/index.php/about/organization/intelligence-integration-who-we-are (accessed August 6, 2014); Office of the Director of National Intelligence, Public Affairs Office, "Intelligence Integrator: Strategically Aligning the IC to the Nation's Highest Priorities: Interview with Robert Cardillo, Deputy Director of National Intelligence for Intelligence Integration," July–August 2012.

28. Office of the Director of National Intelligence, "ODNI Fact Sheet," October 2010, 5.

29. Intelligence Community Directive 202, "National Intelligence Board," July 16, 2007.

30. Office of the Director of Central Intelligence ICD-1, "Policy Directive for Community Leadership," May 1, 2006, 45–46.

31. "National Counterintelligence Policy Board," wwwdni.gov/ncix (accessed January 2, 2007).

32. Intelligence Community Directive 302, "Document and Media Exploitation," July 6, 2007.

33. Intelligence Community Directive 702, "Technical Surveillance Countermeasures," February 18, 2008.

34. Intelligence Community Directive 630, "Intelligence Community Foreign Language Capability," May 14, 2012.

35. Office of the Director of National Intelligence, *National Intelligence Program: FY 2013 Congressional Budget Justification*, vol. 12: *Community Management Account*, February 2012, 142.

36. "Old" DCID categories were "Production of Sources and Methods" (1), "Selected Services of Common Concern" (2), "DCI Advisory Bodies" (3), "Espionage, Counterintelligence, and Foreign Liaison Activities" (5), "Warning, Critical Communications, and Emergency Planning" (6), and "Other DCI Policies and Procedures" (7). The newer categories were "Management" (1), "Analysis and Production" (2), "Collection" (3), "Program and Budget" (4), "Relationships" (5), "Security" (6), and "Other" (7). See Director of Central Intelligence, "Index of Director of Central Intelligence Directives," n.d.

37. Intelligence Community Directive 204, "Roles and Responsibilities for the National Intelligence Priorities Framework," September 13, 2007.

38. Intelligence Community Directive 402, "Director of National Intelligence Representatives," December 23, 2009. With regard to the Director of National Intelligence–Central Intelligence Agency conflict, see Allen, *Blinking Red*, 163.

39. Intelligence Community Directive 902, "Global Maritime and Air Intelligence Integration," January 14, 2009.

40. Caspar Weinberger, *FY 1983 Report of the Secretary of Defense, Caspar Weinberger*, III-88; Department of Defense, Inspector General, *Defense Intelligence Agency Inspection Report 91-INS-06*, 1991, 14.

41. DOD, "Memorandum for Correspondents No. 264-M," September 18, 1992.

42. U.S. Congress, Senate Committee on Governmental Affairs, *Summary of Intelligence Reform and Terrorism Prevention Act of 2004*, December 6, 2004; Intelligence Community Directive 104, "National Intelligence Program (NIP) Budget Formulation and Justification, Execution and Program Evaluation," April 30, 2013.

43. Ibid.; Office of the Director of National Intelligence, "Intelligence Community Policy Memorandum Number 2005-100-2, Subject: Director of National Intelligence Mission Managers," November 15, 2005; Office of the Director of National Intelligence, "Offices of the National Intelligence Managers—Records Control Schedule," May 24, 2013.

44. Office of the Director of National Intelligence, *Leading Intelligence Integration*, n.d., unpaginated; Office of the Director of National Intelligence, "National Intelligence Council

Organization Chart," 2014; Office of the Director of National Intelligence, Public Affairs Office, "Intelligence Integrator: Strategically Aligning the IC to the Nation's Highest Priorities: Interview with Robert Cardillo, Deputy Director of National Intelligence for Intelligence Integration," July–August 2012: Office of the Director of National Intelligence, "Mission Managers," n.d.

45. Director of National Intelligence, "Intelligence Integration—Who We Are."

46. Lawrence Freedman, *U.S. Intelligence and the Soviet Strategic Threat* (Princeton, NJ: Princeton University Press, 1986), 321; Richard A. Best Jr., Congressional Research Service, *The National Intelligence Council: Issues and Options for Congress*, January 10, 2011, http://fas.org/sgp/crs/intel/R40505.pdf, 3–4.

47. Freedman, *U.S. Intelligence and the Soviet Strategic Threat*, 54.

48. Ibid. Also see William E. Colby, *Honorable Men: My Life in the CIA* (New York: Simon and Schuster, 1978), 351–353.

49. Richard J. Kerr, Deputy Director for Intelligence, Memorandum for Chairman, National Intelligence Council, Subject: The Integrity and Objectivity of National Foreign Intelligence Estimates, May 12, 1987, 1. The memo is reprinted in U.S. Congress, Senate Select Committee on Intelligence, *Nomination of Robert M. Gates* (Washington, DC: U.S. Government Printing Office, 1992), 2: 106–108.

50. U.S. Congress, House Select Committee on Intelligence, *U.S. Intelligence Agencies and Activities: Fiscal Costs and Procedures*, pt. 1 (Washington, DC: U.S. Government Printing Office, 1975), 389; U.S. Congress, House Committee on Foreign Affairs, *The Role of Intelligence in the Foreign Policy Process* (Washington, DC: U.S. Government Printing Office, 1980), 135.

51. Office of the Director of National Intelligence, "National Intelligence Council: What We Do," http://www.dni.gov/index.php/about/organization/national-intelligence-council-what-we-do (accessed August 4, 2014).

52. Office of the Director of National Intelligence, "National Intelligence Council Organization Chart."

53. James R. Clapper, "Memorandum, Subject: National Intelligence Council (NIC) Appointments," May 25, 2011; Office of the Director of National Intelligence, "ODNI Vacancy Notices—National Intelligence Officer, Cyber," n.d.; Office of the Director of National Intelligence, "Job Title: National Intelligence Officer, North Korea—AB091-SNIS Tier 2P," www.usajobs.gov (accessed October 19, 2013).

54. Office of the Director of National Intelligence, "ODNI Vacancy Notices—National Intelligence Officer, Cyber," n.d.

55. U.S. Congress, Senate Select Committee on Intelligence and House Permanent Select Committee on Intelligence, *S. 2198 and S. 421 to Reorganize the United States Intelligence Community* (Washington, DC: U.S. Government Printing Office, 1993), 15.

56. DCID 3/3, "Production of Atomic Energy Intelligence," April 23, 1965, DDRS 1980-131G. The JAEIC's role in evaluating the U.S. capability to monitor compliance with the Threshold Test Ban Treaty is mentioned in Attachment to Memorandum, Hosley G. Handyside, Deputy Assistant Secretary, International Nuclear and Technical Programs, Department of Energy for Leslie H. Brown, Senior Deputy Assistant Secretary for Oceans and International, Environmental and Scientific Affairs, Department of State, "Response to Congressional Questions on Nuclear Explosives," March 7, 1980.

57. U.S. Congress, House Committee on Energy and Commerce, *Nuclear Nonproliferation: Failed Efforts to Curtail Iraq's Nuclear Weapons Programs* (Washington, DC: U.S. Government Printing Office, 1992), 20; William J. Broad, "Warning on Iraq and Bomb Bid Silenced in '89," *New York Times*, April 20, 1992, A1, A5; Director of Central Intelligence, NIE 11–3/8–76, *Soviet Forces for International Conflict Through the Mid-1980s*, vol. 1: *Key Judgments and Summary*, 1976, iii; Air Force Intelligence Agency, *History of the Air Force Intelligence Agency, 18 April 1987–31 December 1989*, vol. 1: *Narrative and Appendices*, 1990; Air University, *China: Military Capabilities*, Special Bibliography Series, Special Bibliography No. 207, Supplement No. 5 (Maxwell AFB, AL:

Air University, February 1993), 14; Andrew and Leslie Cockburn, *One Point Safe* (New York: Anchor Books, 1997), 188; R. Jeffrey Smith, "U.S. Officials Acted Hastily in Nuclear Test Accusation," *Washington Post*, October 20, 1997, A1, A6–A7.

58. Jeffrey T. Richelson, *Spying on the Bomb: American Nuclear Intelligence from Nazi Germany to Iran and North Korea* (New York: W. W. Norton, 2006), 480.

59. DCID 3/4, "Production of Guided Missile and Astronautics Intelligence," April 23, 1965, DDRS 1980-132A; John Prados, *The Soviet Estimate: U.S. Intelligence Analysis and Russian Military Strength* (New York: Dial, 1982), 59–61; U.S. Congress, House Committee on Appropriations, *Department of Defense Appropriations for 1978*, pt. 1 (Washington, DC: U.S. Government Printing Office, 1977), 224.

60. Department of the Army, Office of the Assistant Chief of Staff for Intelligence, *Annual Historical Review, 1 July 1975–30 September 1976*, n.d., 39–40; Director of Central Intelligence, NIE 11-3/8-76, *Soviet Strategic Forces for International Conflict Through the Mid-1980s*, Vol. 1: *Key Judgments and Summary*, iii; Andrew Koch, "Pakistan Persists with Nuclear Procurement," *Jane's Intelligence Review* (March 1997): 131–133.

61. Central Intelligence Agency, *A Consumer's Guide to Intelligence*, July 1995, 57; Department of the Army, Office of the Deputy Chief of Staff for Intelligence, *Annual Historical Review, 1 October 1990 to 30 September 1991*, n.d., 4–30.

62. Central Intelligence Agency, *A Consumer's Guide to Intelligence*, 43; National Intelligence Council, *A Guide to the National Intelligence Council*, 41.

63. Director of Central Intelligence, "Terrorist Threat Integration Center Begins Operations," May 1, 2003, https://www.cia.gov/news-information/press-releases-statements/press-release-archive-2003/pr05012003.html; John O. Brennan, "Responses from John O. Brennan to Post-Hearing Questions," December 4, 2003, 8.

64. White House, Fact Sheet, "Strengthening Intelligence to Better Protect America," January 28, 2003, http://www.whitehouse.gov, John O. Brennan, "Responses from John O. Brennan to Post-Hearing Questions."

65. NSPD-5 External Panel, Memorandum for: the Director of Central Intelligence, Subject: Findings and Recommendations, n.d. att to: George J. Tenet, Memorandum Subject: National Security Presidential Directive 5 (NSPD-5), April 4, 2002.

66. *The 9/11 Commission Report*, 403.

67. Ibid., 404.

68. Ibid.

69. George W. Bush, The White House, "Executive Order: National Counterterrorism Center," August 27, 2004, http://georgewbush-whitehouse.archives.gov/news/releases/2004/08/20040827-5.html.

70. Todd M. Masse, Congressional Research Service, *The National Counterterrorism Center: Implementation Challenges and Issues for Congress*, March 24, 2005, http://fas.org/sgp/crs/intel/RL32816.pdf, summary and 6. With regard to the battles and rivalries involved in the creation and operation of the TTIC and NCTC, see Philip Mudd, *Take Down: Inside the Hunt for Al Qaeda* (Philadelphia: University of Pennsylvania Press, 2013), 144–147, 168–169; Michael Allen, *Blinking Red*, 87–91, 152–153, 167–168, 175, 177.

71. Matthew G. Olsen, Director, National Counterterrorism Center, "Ten Years After 9/11: Are We Safer?" (hearing before the Senate Committee on Homeland Security and Governmental Affairs, Washington, DC, September 13, 2011).

72. Office of the Director of National Intelligence, *U.S. National Intelligence*, 10; Olsen, Director, National Counterterrorism Center, "Ten Years After 9/11: Are We Safer?," 7.

73. Olsen, Director, National Counterterrorism Center, "Ten Years After 9/11: Are We Safer?," 9; Bridget Rose Nolan, *Information Sharing and Collaboration in the United States Intelligence Community: An Ethnographic Study of the National Counterterrorism Center* (PhD diss., University of Pennsylvania, 2013), 20.

74. Office of the Director of National Intelligence, *U.S. National Intelligence*, 10; Olsen, Director, National Counterterrorism Center, "Ten Years After 9/11: Are We Safer?," 8.

75. Office of the Director of National Intelligence, *U.S. National Intelligence*, 10.

76. Office of the Director of National Intelligence, *U.S. National Intelligence*, 10; Andrew M. Liepman, Principal Deputy Director, National Counterterrorism Center, NCTC Policy Number 1, "Information Sharing Rules of the Road," May 14, 2012.

77. National Counterterrorism Center, *Directorate of Terrorist Identities (DTI) Strategic Accomplishments 2013*, n.d., 1–3; Jeremy Scahill and Ryan Devereaux, "Barack Obama's Secret Terrorist-Tracking System, by the Numbers," *Intercept*, August 5, 2014, https://firstlook.org/theintercept /2014/08/05/watch-commander.

78. Office of the Director of National Intelligence, *U.S. National Intelligence*, 10.

79. Matthew G. Olsen, Director, National Counterterrorism Center, "The Homeland Threat Landscape and U.S. Response" (hearing before the Senate Committee on Homeland Security and Governmental Affairs, Washington, DC, November 14, 2013), 7.

80. *The 9/11 Commission Report*, 413; Commission on the Intelligence Capabilities of the United States Regarding Weapons of Mass Destruction, *Report to the President of the United States* (Washington, DC: U.S. Government Printing Office, 2005), 567.

81. U.S. Congress, House of Representatives, *Intelligence Reform and Terrorism Prevention Act of 2004 Conference Report*, December 7, 2004, 40–41; "National Counterterrorism Center— Ambassador Kenneth Brill," www.dni.gov (accessed December 30, 2006).

82. Office of the Director of National Intelligence, News Release No. 9-05, "ODNI Announces Establishment of National Counterproliferation Center (NCPC)," December 21, 2005, http://www.dni.gov; National Counterproliferation Center: Office of the Director of National Intelligence (www.counterwmd.gov, accessed August 5, 2014); Kathleen Turner, Director of Legislative Affairs, Office of the Director of National Intelligence, Memorandum, Subject: Congressional Notification: Progress Made in Strengthening Intelligence Community Efforts Against Weapons of Mass Destruction 2006–2008, June 6, 2009.

83. National Counterproliferation Center, Office of the Director of National Intelligence.

84. "NCIX: National Counterintelligence Executive," www.dni.gov/ncix (accessed January 2, 2007); Office of the Director of National Intelligence, ODNI News Release No. 26-14, "DNI Appoints New National Counterintelligence Executive," June 12, 2014; Office of the Director of National Intelligence, ODNI News Release No. 46-14, "DNI Clapper Establishes the National Counterintelligence and Security Center," December 1, 2014.

85. Office of the Director of National Intelligence, ODNI News Release No. 26-14, "DNI Appoints New National Counterintelligence Executive"; "NCSC Mission," www.ncix.gov/about /index.php (accessed December 4, 2014).

86. "Merger of the SCC and CSE into ONCIX," http://www.ncix.gov/about/ssc-cse-merger -with-ncix.php (accessed August 6, 2014).

87. Barack Obama, Memorandum, "Establishment of the Cyber Threat Intelligence Integration Center," February 25, 2015, *Federal Register* 80, no. 41 (March 3, 2015): 11317–11318; Ellen Nakashima, "New Agency to Sniff Out Threats in Cyberspace," www.washingtonpost.com, February 10, 2015, http://www.washingtonpost.com/world/national-security/white-house-to -create-national-center-to-counter-cyberspace-intrusions/2015/02/09/a312201e-afd0-11e4-827f -93f454140e2b_story.html; Brian Bennett, "U.S. Agency to Combat Cyberthreats," *Los Angeles Times*, February 11, 2015, C1, C5.

88. Barack Obama, Memorandum, "Establishment of the Cyber Threat Intelligence Integration Center."

89. Ibid.; Nakashima, "New Agency to Sniff Out Threats in Cyberspace."

18

MANAGING DEFENSE INTELLIGENCE

During the years that the Director of Central Intelligence (DCI) served as the president's chief intelligence advisor and head of the Intelligence Community, that community included national agencies located within the Department of Defense (DOD): the National Security Agency (NSA), the National Reconnaissance Office (NRO), and after October 1, 1996, the National Imagery and Mapping Agency (NIMA)/National Geospatial-Intelligence Agency (NGA). Although after 1977 the DCI had authority to approve their budgets, the Secretary of Defense and those officials he designated to handle intelligence matters were responsible for day-to-day management.

Over the years, the secretary and his key aides handled management of the national intelligence agencies within the Defense Department and other defense intelligence agencies, particularly the Defense Intelligence Agency (DIA). During the 1970s there was an Assistant Secretary of Defense for Intelligence, while more recently an under secretary was responsible for intelligence along with command, control, communications, and computers. In 2001 Secretary of Defense Donald H. Rumsfeld proposed the creation of an Under Secretary of Defense for Intelligence (USD [I]), which was then established by Congress.[1]

Other means by which the Defense Department and its military services manage intelligence activity include the Military Intelligence Program, a variety of boards and committees, the Joint Chiefs of Staff (JCS) Reconnaissance Operations Division (ROD), Defense Intelligence Officers, and Directives, Instructions, and Regulations.

THE USD (I)

Within a very short time of assuming the position of Secretary of Defense, Donald Rumsfeld concluded that he needed an official directly below him in the chain of command whose sole responsibility would be managing the department's intelligence activities. One catalyst for Rumsfeld's conclusion was an April 2001 meeting, held to discuss the intelligence lost after the crash landing of an EP-3 in China and attended by officials from eleven different military intelligence units. A second catalyst was the long-standing reluctance of the DCI to deal with lower-level subordinates of the Secretary of Defense in settling budget issues. A third issue, for some, was the belief that assigning intelligence and C3 responsibilities to the same assistant secretary meant that the more expensive C3 systems "dominated the Assistant Secretary's time and attention."[2]

In August 2002, Rumsfeld stated that he wanted a single "more senior person overseeing those aspects of intelligence that are in the Department of Defense." A former senior Pentagon official in the Bill Clinton administration said at the time that "it would be a step forward" if a new under secretary "serve[d] as an action officer for the department's intelligence budget," since trying to work out different budget issues took "a huge piece of the secretary's time."[3]

John McCone, during his tenure as DCI (1961–1965), believed that he could better carry out his responsibilities if there was a single Defense Department official supervising the department's intelligence operations. In the spring of 2002, Rumsfeld was able to persuade DCI George J. Tenet of the desirability of an arrangement whereby he and other senior Central Intelligence Agency (CIA) officials would have a single point of contact on intelligence policy and resource matters. However, Rumsfeld's proposal was greeted with some concern: some feared that such an official, with unitary focus on intelligence and his day-to-day authority over the national intelligence agencies in DOD, would become a serious competitor to the DCI. There was also resistance "from some defense intelligence leaders . . . who . . . feared that they would lose some authority and autonomy."[4]

Despite such concerns, Congress quickly approved the creation of the position via the National Defense Authorization Act of 2003, and in March 2003 the Senate confirmed Rumsfeld's nominee, Stephen Cambone. The office's responsibilities were first outlined in a memo, "Implementation Guidance on Restructuring Defense Intelligence and Related Matters," which also specified an initial personnel strength of 114 employees. That memo was superseded on November 23, 2005, by DOD Directive 5143.01, "Under Secretary of Defense for Intelligence (USD [I])," signed by Rumsfeld but coordinated with the Director of National Intelligence (DNI). An updated directive was issued in October 2014.[5]

The twenty-one-page directive, significantly longer than its predecessor, specifies that the under secretary serves as the principal staff assistant and advisor to the Secretary and Deputy Secretary of Defense with regard to intelligence, counterintelligence, security, sensitive activities, and other intelligence-related matters. It assigns the under secretary responsibility, on behalf of the secretary, for oversight of the DIA, NGA, NRO, NSA, and Defense Security Service. Also reflected in the directive is the May 2007 agreement between the Secretary of Defense and the DNI that the USD (I) should also be designated as the Director of Defense Intelligence (DDI) within the DNI's office. In his role as DDI, he is responsible for overseeing the development of DOD's national intelligence requirements, "facilitating alignment, coordination, and deconfliction between National and Defense Intelligence Activities," and providing advice and assistance to the DNI by "synchronizing and integrating DOD intelligence functions with other components of the Intelligence Community."[6] The directive also specifies that under secretary's responsibilities (including providing oversight and direction) with respect to defense intelligence analysis, defense HUMINT, technical collection (geospatial, SIGINT, MASINT, biometrics enabled, and forensics enabled), open source intelligence, Defense counterintelligence, Defense security programs, operational support, international intelligence engagement, the DOD Foreign Materiel Program, intelligence information sharing, and Defense Intelligence Enterprise mission support.[7]

The USD (I)'s office originally consisted, in addition to the under secretary and principal deputy under secretary, of four deputy under secretaries—for intelligence and war-fighting support, preparation and warning, counterintelligence and security, and policy, resources, and requirements. In June 2008 the office was restructured based on four core functions—joint force operations, technical intelligence, programs and resources, and HUMINT and counterintelligence—a restructuring dictated in a memo by then USD (I) James R. Clapper Jr. In addition, early that year Secretary of Defense Robert Gates established an Intelligence, Surveillance, and Reconnaissance (ISR) Task Force to "rectify major shortfalls in support to ongoing military and counterterrorism operations," according to USD (I) Michael Vickers. In 2010 Gates made the task force part of the USD (I)'s responsibilities.[8] Further reorganizations took place in 2010 and in late 2013 and early 2014.

The 2014 reorganization followed an internal review, guidance from Secretary of Defense Chuck Hagel, and congressional direction (involving a reduction in deputy under secretary of defense positions). As reflected in Figure 18.1, subordinate to the under secretary are four defense intelligence directors. The ISR task force established by Robert Gates became the ISR Operations component under the Director of Defense Intelligence for Warfighter Support.

The organization chart also reflects the merger of counterintelligence and security functions under the Director of Defense Intelligence (Intelligence & Security), who is also responsible for supervising HUMINT, sensitive activities, and defense analysis. The replacement of the Technical Collection & Analysis component by the Technical Collection & Special Programs Directorate was intended to strengthen oversight of the NSA, NGA, and DIA science and technology directorate.[*9]

MILITARY INTELLIGENCE PROGRAM

The Joint Military Intelligence Program (JMIP) was established in 1995 to "improve the effectiveness of DOD intelligence activities when those activities involve resources from more than one DOD Component; when users of the intelligence data are from more than one DOD component; and/or when centralized planning, management, coordination or oversight will contribute to the effectiveness of the effort."[10]

There were three major programs aggregations within the JMIP: the Defense Cryptologic Program, the Defense Imagery and Mapping Program, and the Defense

---

*For assessments of the office's performance see, Center for Strategic & International Studies, *Transitioning Defense Organizational Initiatives: An Assessment of Key 2001–2008 Defense Reforms*, December 2008, 21–25; Janet A. McDonnell, "The Office of the Under Secretary of Defense for Intelligence: The First 10 Years," *Studies in Intelligence* 58, 1 (Extracts, March 2014), 9–16; Cheryl Pellerin, Armed Forces Press Service, "Defense Intelligence Office Marks 10 Years of Progress," www.defense.gov, December 4, 2012; "Perspective of the Under Secretary of Defense for Intelligence," *Studies in Intelligence* 47, 4 (2003): 19–25.

FIGURE 18.1   Organization of the Office of the Under Secretary of Defense for Intelligence

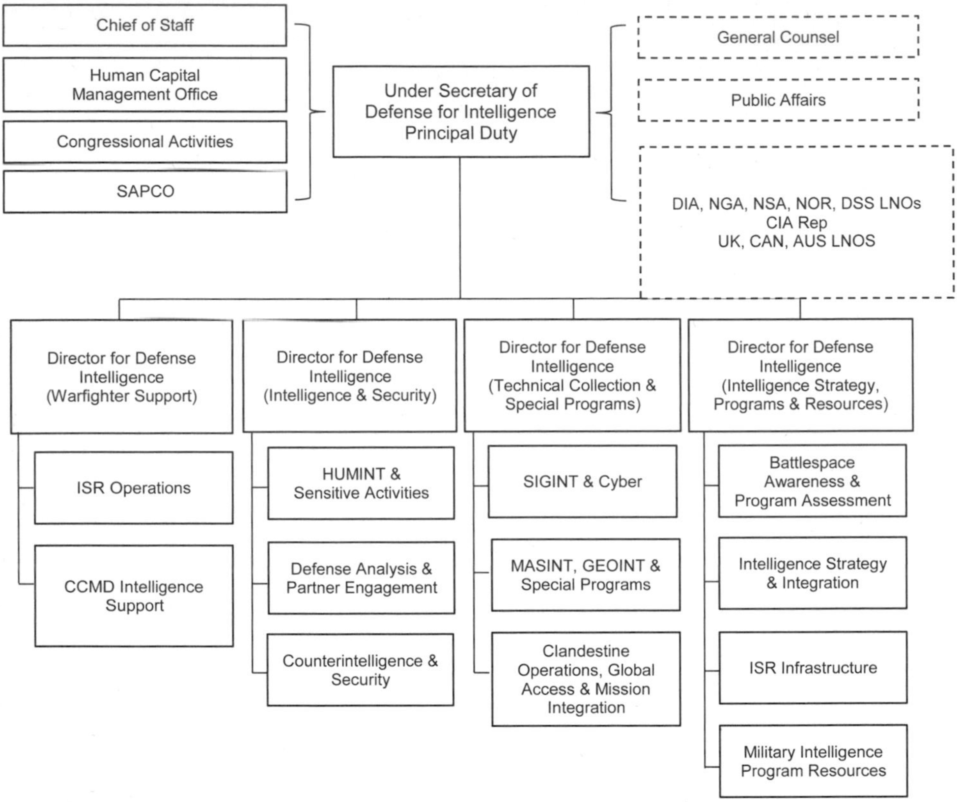

Source: DOD.

General Intelligence and Applications Program (DGIAP). Each comprised resources previously funded within the Tactical Intelligence and Related Activities (TIARA) program. The DGIAP consisted of the Defense Airborne Reconnaissance Program, the Defense Intelligence Counterdrug Program, the Defense Intelligence Agency's Tactical Program, the Defense Space Reconnaissance Program, and the Defense Intelligence Special Technologies Program.[11]

Creation of the JMIP stripped the TIARA program of two of its three elements—the Defense Space Reconnaissance Program (previously known as the Defense Reconnaissance Support Program) and the Tactical Cryptologic Program—leaving only the Reconnaissance, Surveillance, and Target Acquisition component. On September 1, 2005, the Department of Defense, through a memorandum signed by the Acting Secretary of Defense, "Establishment of the Military Intelligence Program," combined the JMIP and TIARA to form the Military Intelligence Program (MIP).[12] Figure 18.2 shows the contents of the MIP for fiscal year 2013 as listed in the table of contents of that year's *Congressional Justification Book.*[13]

FIGURE 18.2 Military Intelligence Program Elements

Multi-Component

- Advanced Technology and Sensors
- Aerial Common Sensor
- Counterintelligence Support to Force Protection
- Counterintelligence Technical Services
- Critical Infrastructure Protection
- Distributed Common Ground/Surface Systems
- Integrated Broadcast Service
- Intelligence Continuity and Enablers
- Intelligence Management (OSD)
- Intelligence Support to Information Operations
- Intelligence Support to the COCOMs
- Intelligence Support to the Common Operational Picture
- Joint Technology Center/Systems Integration Laboratory
- MQ-1 Medium Altitude Endurance Unmanned Aircraft System
- RC-135
- Research and Technology Protection
- RQ-4 Unmanned Aircraft System
- U-2

ARMY

- Airborne Reconnaissance–Low
- All Source Analysis System
- Army Tactical Unmanned Aircraft Systems
- Biometrics Enabled Intelligence
- Counterintelligence and Human Intelligence Automated Reporting and Collections Systems
- Future Combat Systems
- GUARDRAIL Common Sensor
- HUMINT Training JCOE
- Intelligence Force Structure
- Joint Tactical Ground Station
- Mapping and Geodesy
- Operational Human Intelligence (HUMINT)
- Project Foundry
- Prophet
- Tactical Exploitation of National Capabilities and Program Support
- TROJAN

NAVY

- Broad Area Maritime Surveillance
- COBRA JUDY Replacement
- Digital Photo Lab
- EP-3E Replacement
- EP-3E/ARIES II
- Global Command and Control System-Maritime Afloat (Intelligence Applications)
- Marine Corps Tactical Unmanned Aircraft System
- MQ-8 Unmanned Aircraft System
- Small Tactical Unmanned Aircraft System/Tier II UAS
- Special Project Aircraft
- Submarine Support Equipment Program
- Surveillance Towed Array Sensor System
- Tactical Control System
- Trusted Information System
- Unmanned Aircraft System Concept of Operations

USAF

- Airborne SIGINT Enterprise
- Combatant Commanders' Intelligence Capabilities and Applications
- General Intelligence Skill Training
- MC-12W Project Liberty
- Nuclear Detonation Detection System
- Space Based Infrared System High
- Space Intelligence Systems Activities

USMC

- Communication Emitter Sensing and Attacking System
- Intelligence Analysis System
- Intelligence Broadcast Receiver
- Intelligence Communications Network
- Marine Corps Operational Intelligence Support
- Radio Reconnaissance Equipment Program
- Tactical Exploitation Group
- Tactical Exploitation of National Capabilities
- Tactical Intelligence Support
- Tactical Remote Sensor System
- Team Portable Collection System-Multi-Platform Capable
- Technical Control and Analysis Center
- Technical Surveillance Countermeasures
- Topographic Production Capability
- USMC Unmanned Aircraft System Family of Systems
- Wide Field of View Persistent Surveillance

DIA

- Analysis Enabling
- Counterintelligence Analysis and Integration
- Enterprise Management Operations & Support
- MASINT Enabling

NGA

- Deployed Operations
- GeoScout Block II
- Intelligence Support to the COCOMs
- Purchases (Commercial Remote Sensing)
- Commercial Imagery Integration into Ground Infrastructure

NSA

- Airborne Cryptologic Capabilities
- Cryptologic Capabilities Research & Systems Engineering
- Electronic Intelligence Programs
- Ground Cryptologic Capabilities
- Maritime Cryptologic Capabilities
- Rapid Technology Insertion
- Real-Time Architecture Development.
- Technical Response to Cryptologic Operations

OSD

- Advanced Sensors Application Program
- Foreign Materiel Acquisition and Exploitation
- International Intelligence Technology Assessment, Advancement and Integration

SOCOM

- Counterproliferation Analysis and Planning System
- Global Sensor Network
- Intelligence Staff Support.
- Joint Threat Warning System
- Sensitive Site Exploitation
- Special Operations Forces Organic Intelligence, Surveillance and Reconnaissance
- Special Operations Joint Interagency Collaboration Center.
- Special Operations Tactical Video System

THE MILITARY INTELLIGENCE BOARD AND
DEFENSE INTELLIGENCE SPACE THREAT COMMITTEE

The Military Intelligence Board (MIB), chaired by the Director of DIA, was established on August 15, 1961, to assist in the development of the DIA activation plan and in the selection of personnel. The MIB met on an irregular basis during its first thirty years and persisted as a mechanism for coordinating defense positions on DOD intelligence issues among the Director of DIA, the Joint Staff Director for Intelligence, and the service intelligence chiefs. During Operations DESERT SHIELD and DESERT STORM, the DIA director restructured the board as an advisory and decision making body chaired by himself, with significant new members, including the Director of NSA.[14]

MIB members, in addition to the DIA director, include the Deputy Director of DIA, the Directors of NSA and NGA, and the service intelligence chiefs. It meets approximately once a week. In addition, three groups are associated with the MIB although not subordinate to it: the Council of Defense Intelligence Producers, the Military Target Intelligence Committee, and the Council on Functional Management.[15]

The MIB coordinates intelligence support to military operations and provides a forum for discussion and development of a coordinated military intelligence position on issues going before the MIB. It also provides oversight and direction to the defense intelligence functional managers for collection, production, and infrastructure. It has considered topics such as Korea, Iraq, and intelligence support to the NIMA Implementation Plan, the Quadrennial Defense Review, the National Intelligence Estimates, the European Command, and Operations DESERT STORM, JOINT ENDEAVOR, and ENDURING FREEDOM.[16]

In 1994, former DIA director James R. Clapper Jr. stated, "MIB proved its worth during the Gulf War when it played a critical role in fostering greater cooperation within the military intelligence community. Since that time MIB has met virtually every week and provided a forum for senior community leaders to oversee program development, review integrated programs and budgets, resolve programmatic issues of mutual concern, and deal with substantive intelligence matters."[17]

The board has no executive authority. Its recommendations and the actions of its chairman are not permitted to alter the missions, responsibilities, functions, authorities, and resources assigned to any Defense Department component by the Secretary of Defense. The Deputy Secretary of Defense, the Chairman of the Joint Chiefs of Staff, and the Under Secretary of Defense may convene and preside over special meetings of the MIB.[18]

A more specialized committee is the Defense Intelligence Space Threat Committee (DISTC), chaired by a representative of the National Air and Space Intelligence Center. It was established "to oversee and coordinate a wide variety of complex space/counterspace analytical activities." That committee was established at a time that space/counterspace intelligence requirements were being reevaluated, reprioritized, and rewritten "to more clearly focus the intelligence community."[19]

DEFENSE WARNING COUNCIL

The Defense Department warning mission, specified in DOD Directive 3115.16, "The Defense Warning Network," of December 5, 2013, is to identify and warn of potential threats from adversaries, political and economic instability, failed or failing states, and other emerging challenges that could affect the United States. One objective is to provide warning of actions that would require or trigger the employment of U.S. and allied forces, as well as developments that could influence the development of policies, plans, or capabilities. A second is to "identify and convey threats, vulnerabilities, and address potential opportunities associated with U.S. interests, objectives . . . and ongoing operations or activities." In addition, warning is intended to "inform debates and decisions by intelligence and operational consumers within DoD."[20]

The directive defines the Defense Warning Network (DWN) as "a collaborative and integrated network made up of DoD organizations, that provides senior decision makers warning on emerging and enduring warning threats to U.S. and allied interests." It is intended to provide warning to DOD leaders "in enough time and with sufficient information to allow DoD leaders to proactively confront emerging challenges, leverage opportunities, avoid or mitigate the impact of surprise, and produce strategic outcomes favorable to the United States."[21]

Supervision of the network is the responsibility of the Defense Warning Council (DWC), "the primary forum for coordinating activities and reaching consensus on issues related to the DWN, such as issuing warning about particular situations, new order of battle information, or recommendations to inform senior DoD leadership." It is chaired by the Chairman of the Joint Chiefs of Staff. Its other voting members include the USD (I), the Directors of the NSA, NGA, and DIA, the secretaries of the military departments, and the combatant commanders.[22]

DEFENSE OPEN SOURCE COUNCIL

The Defense Open Source Council is "the primary mechanism for DoD OSINT [open source intelligence]." It is chaired by a senior executive designated by the Director of the DIA. Other members include a representative appointed by the USD (I) as well as representatives from the NSA and NGA, the secretaries of the military departments, the commanders of the combatant commands, the Under Secretary of Defense for Acquisition, Technology, and Logistics, and the Assistant Secretary of Defense for Networks and Information Integration.[23] The council's responsibilities include coordinating activities and resolving conflicts across DOD open source intelligence programs and activities, coordinating recommendations and activities with the National Open Source Committee, setting priorities for DOD open source requirements, and establishing "a strategy to guide the full range of DoD OSINT efforts." It is authorized to establish working groups to "facilitate the coordination or execution of specific programs." The council is also responsible for advising and reporting to the USD (I) on OSINT issues and recommending initiatives "to improve the effectiveness and efficiency of the DoD OSINT programs, activities, and systems."[24]

JCS RECONNAISSANCE OPERATIONS DIVISION

Reconnaissance conducted by satellite is relatively nonintrusive because it does not require actual violation of a target nation's airspace. Further, with the exception of Russia and China, no nation possesses the means to destroy U.S. satellites. And even during the Cold War, the likely costs to the Soviet Union of interfering in an obvious way with such satellites were likely to far outweigh the potential benefits.

When airborne overflights on air, sea, or submarine missions close to a nation's borders are involved, the potential for an international incident is much greater. Early Cold War aircraft reconnaissance missions directed at the Soviet Union involved this risk because they approached or penetrated the margins of Soviet and Eastern European territory to collect several varieties of intelligence, including the signatures and operating frequencies of air defense systems.[25]

Over the years, incidents involving air and sea missions have occurred. In 1962, during the Cuban missile crisis, one U-2 strayed into Soviet territory, and another was shot down during a flight over Cuba. In 1967 the Israeli air force bombed the USS *Liberty* while it was collecting signals intelligence in the midst of the Six-Day War. In 1968 North Korea seized the USS *Pueblo* during a SIGINT mission off the North Korean coast, and in 1969, North Korean forces shot down an EC-121 SIGINT aircraft as it patrolled the same coast.[26] The North Koreans also made hundreds of attempts to shoot down overflying SR-71s and, as noted previously, in 2003 attempted to force an RC-135 to land in North Korea. Also noted in Chapters 7 and 8 were a number of encounters with Chinese fighters, including the collision between an EP-3 and a Chinese fighter that forced the U.S. plane to make an emergency landing on Hainan Island, a 2011 U-2 encounter in the Taiwan Strait, and a 2014 incident in which a J-11 flew within ninety feet of a P-8 off Hainan Island. In addition, several incidents have involved U.S. submarines conducting HOLYSTONE-type missions, including collisions with Soviet/Russian submarines.*[27]

Management of such sensitive missions reflects many considerations. Many of the missions are proposed and conducted in support of the unified military commands. Others are clearly designed to provide national intelligence. In either case, such missions could cause an international incident and thus require national-level approval and close monitoring.

Missions originating from the unified commands go through a chain of supervisory offices and divisions, beginning with the command's joint reconnaissance center. Until the mid-1990s, a national Joint Reconnaissance Center (JRC) operated as part of the J3 (Operations Directorate) of the Joint Chiefs of Staff and colocated with the National Joint Military Intelligence Center. The JRC was established on October 24, 1960, as the result of the May 1, 1960, loss of a U-2 over the Soviet Union and the July 1, 1960, loss of an RB-47 over the Barents Sea and President Dwight D. Eisenhower's desire to avoid a repetition. Until the mid-1990s, it operated as part of the Operations Directorate (J3) of the Joint Chiefs of Staff and was colocated with the National Joint Military Intelligence Center.[28] The JRC acted as an initial approval authority for reconnaissance plans developed by unified and component commands. It also developed a Joint Reconnaissance Schedule "several inches thick and filled with hundreds of pages of highly technical data and maps" that monitored the progress of the missions and provided the National Military Command Center with real-time information regarding the status and disposition of forces, mission activity, and other reconnaissance-related

---

*As noted in Chapter 2, management of submarine reconnaissance missions is the responsibility of the National Underwater Reconnaissance Office.

FIGURE 18.3   SR-71 Mission Request

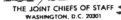
THE JOINT CHIEFS OF STAFF
WASHINGTON, D.C. 20301

3 November 1980

THE JOINT STAFF

MEMORANDUM FOR DIRECTOR, JOINT RECONNAISSANCE CENTER

Subject: SR 71 Mission Request

1. (U)(TS) Request consideration be given to conducting several
SR 71 surveillance missions of the Persian Gulf during the
next 3-6 weeks.

2. (U)(TS) Purpose of mission is to determine locations of
major oil rig concentrations and typical flow pattern of Gulf
shipping to assist in selection of low level air penetration
routes.

3. (U)(TS) Recognize that missions could raise Soviet/Iran/ME
speculation; however, given irregular scheduling, direct
association with any US military planning will probably be
low. On the other hand, periodic SR 71 missions would
provide "reason" for increased tanker support in the area
prior to the execution of any US military contingency
action.

JAMES B. VAUGHT
Major General, USA

CLASSIFIED BY JCS, J-3
DECLASSIFY ON 3 NOV 2000

information.[29] Figure 18.3 shows a 1980 request related to planning for a possible
second mission to rescue U.S. hostages in Iran.

The JRC performed several functions:

- Receiving, reviewing, evaluating, and submitting for approval to the JCS the
  reconnaissance plans, programs, and schedules originated by the commanders of
  the unified commands, the military services, and other governmental agencies
- Preparing the planning guidance for the execution of reconnaissance operations
  of special significance or sensitivity
- Reviewing intelligence support plans and preparing policy guidance, planning,
  analysis, and review of reconnaissance-related activities that supported trans-
  and postnuclear attack operations
- Monitoring the missions approved by the JRC and ensuring that all incidents
  were brought to the attention of appropriate authorities

FIGURE 18.4   Organization of the Joint Chiefs of Staff Reconnaissance Operations Division

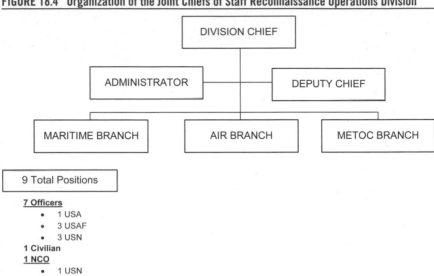

```
                         ┌─────────────────┐
                         │  DIVISION CHIEF  │
                         └─────────────────┘
                                  │
        ┌──────────────────┐      │      ┌──────────────────┐
        │  ADMINISTRATOR   │──────┴──────│   DEPUTY CHIEF    │
        └──────────────────┘             └──────────────────┘
                                  │
   ┌──────────────────┐  ┌──────────────────┐  ┌──────────────────┐
   │  MARITIME BRANCH  │  │    AIR BRANCH    │  │   METOC BRANCH   │
   └──────────────────┘  └──────────────────┘  └──────────────────┘
```

┌─────────────────────────┐
│   9 Total Positions   │
└─────────────────────────┘

7 Officers
  • 1 USA
  • 3 USAF
  • 3 USN
1 Civilian
1 NCO
  • 1 USN

Source: DOD.

• Displaying, on a current basis, all peacetime military reconnaissance and some other sensitive operations.[30]

These functions are now performed by the Reconnaissance Operations Division of the J3 Directorate, as the JRC has been retitled.[31] As indicated in Figure 18.4, the ROD consists of the Maritime, Air, and Meteorology and Oceanographic (METOC) branches.

DEFENSE INTELLIGENCE OFFICERS

In 1974, as part of a reorganization, DIA director Lieutenant General Daniel O. Graham established a group of Defense Intelligence Officers (DIOs), as a counterpart to the National Intelligence Officer system established in 1973 by DCI William Colby. The DIOs were to serve as the "DIA Director's senior staff representatives on major intelligence matters." By 2003, "the role of the DIOs had diminished in the face of DIA's transformation in the wake of the Sept. 11 attacks and the wars in Afghanistan and Iraq." DIA Director Lowell Jacoby dissolved the DIO apparatus and transferred its responsibilities to the Directorate for Analysis.[32]

In July 2008, DIA Director Michael Maples reestablished the DIOs. In 2012 the DIA's deputy director specified three major functions for the officers. They would serve as DIA's principal intelligence advisors for their areas of responsibility by providing all-source analysis for their area of responsibility, understanding of collection and collection gaps, and "an appreciation of the resources at hand." In addition, the DIOs represent defense intelligence to "a wide variety of outside customers" in Congress and the executive branch. They also serve as counterparts to the DNI's National Intelligence Managers.[33]

As of spring 2012, there were eight DIOs whose areas of responsibility were Latin America, Europe and NATO, South Asia, Eurasia, East Asia, the Middle East and North Africa, Africa, and Cyber. Their previous positions included DIA, combatant commands, and other parts of the Intelligence Community.[34]

DOD AND SERVICE DIRECTIVES AND INSTRUCTIONS

The most important departmental regulations on intelligence matters are the DoD Directives, Instructions, and Directive-Type Memoranda (DTMs), which concern intelligence policies, procedures, and responsibilities with regard to activities (e.g., human intelligence) and specific organizations (e.g., the National Security Agency). DOD Directive C-5230.23 of November 18, 1983, "Intelligence Disclosure Policy," specifies the functions of various DOD officials in the disclosure process. Thus, the Director of DIA was directed to "coordinate within and for the Department of Defense, proposed disclosures of classified U.S. intelligence to senior foreign officials," and the Deputy Under Secretary for Policy was to "resolve conflicts among DOD components relating to disclosure of classified U.S. intelligence to senior foreign officials"—a responsibility that has undoubtedly been transferred to the USD (I).[35]

Other DOD directives, instructions, and DTMs concerning foreign intelligence policy and activities include "DoD Intelligence Activities" (Directive 5240.1, August 27, 2007); "DoD Guidance for Reporting Questionable Intelligence Activities and Significant or Highly Sensitive Matters" (DTM 08-052, June 17, 2009); "Oversight, Coordination, Assessment and Reporting of DoD Intelligence and Intelligence-Related Sensitive Activities" (Instruction O-5100.94, September 27, 2011); "Signals Intelligence" (Directive O-3115.07, September 15, 2008); "Measurement and Signature Intelligence (MASINT)" (Instruction 5105.58, April 22, 2009); "Military Intelligence Program" (Directive 5205.12, November 14, 2008); "Open Source Intelligence" (Instruction 3115.12, August 24, 2010); "Civil Aviation Intelligence" (Instruction 3115.14, July 29, 2011); "Geospatial Intelligence" (Instruction 3115.15, December 6, 2011); "Defense Biometric Enabled Intelligence (BEI) and Forensic Enabled Intelligence (FEI)" (Instruction O-3300.04, May 25, 2012); "DoD Foreign Military Intelligence Collection Activities (FORMICA)" (Instruction C-5205.01, January 22, 2009); "Foreign Materiel Program (FMP)" (Directive S-3325.01, December 30, 2011); "Transfer of National Intelligence Collection Authority" (Directive S-3325.02, March 16, 2009); and "DoD Document and Media Exploitation (DOMEX)" (Directive 3300.03, January 1, 2011).[36]

Directives, instructions, and DTMs with regard to human intelligence include "Defense Cover Program (DCP) Guidance" (DTM 08-050, March 31, 2009); "Management and Execution of Defense Human Intelligence (HUMINT)" (Directive S-5200.37, February 9, 2009); "Guidance for the Conduct of DoD Human Source Validation" (Instruction S-3325.07, June 22, 2009); "Defense Human Intelligence (HUMINT) and Related Intelligence Activities" (Instruction S-5200.42, December 8, 2009); "Intelligence Commercial Activities (ICAs)" (Instruction S-5240.12, April 21, 2010); "DoD Support to the High-Value Detainee Interrogation Group (HIG)" (Directive 3115.13, December 9, 2010); "DoD Intelligence Interrogations, Detainee Debriefings, and Tactical Questioning" (Directive 3115.09, October 11, 2012);

"Oversight, Management, and Execution of Defense Clandestine Source Operations" (Directive S-3325.09, January 9, 2013); "Human Intelligence (HUMINT) Activities in Cyberspace" (Directive S-3325.10, June 6, 2013); and "DoD Cover and Cover Support Activities" (Directive S-5105.61, July 15, 2014).*[37]

Other directives or instructions concern counterintelligence activities. These include "Counterintelligence" (Directive O-5240.02, December 20, 2007); "Offensive Counterintelligence Operations" (Instruction 5240.09, October 29, 2008); "Counterintelligence Investigations" (Instruction 5240.04, February 2, 2009); "Counterintelligence (CI) Inquiries" (Instruction O-5240.21, May 14, 2009); "Counterintelligence Support to Force Protection" (Instruction 5240.22, September 24, 2009); "Counterintelligence (CI) Analysis and Production" (Instruction 5240.18, November 17, 2009); "Counterintelligence (CI) Activities in Cyberspace" (Instruction S-5240.23, December 13, 2010); "Counterintelligence Awareness and Reporting (CIAR)" (Directive 5240.06, May 17, 2011); "Counterintelligence (CI) in the Combatant Commands and Other DoD Components" (Instruction 5240.10, October 5, 2011); "DOD Counterintelligence Functional Services" (Instruction 5240.16, August 27, 2012); "Counterintelligence Support to the Defense Critical Infrastructure Program" (Instruction 5240.19, January 31, 2014); and "Counterintelligence Collection Activities" (Instruction S-5240.17, March 14, 2014).[38]

Still other DOD directives or instructions specify the missions and functions of the Principal Deputy Under Secretary of Defense for Intelligence (Directive 5143.02, August 18, 2010), the National Reconnaissance Office (Directive 5105.23, June 28, 2011), the National Security Agency (Directive 5100.20, January 26, 2010), the Defense Intelligence Agency (Directive 5105.21, March 18, 2008), the National Geospatial-Intelligence Agency (Directive 5105.60, July 29, 2009), the National Center for Medical Intelligence (Instruction 6240.1, March 20, 2009), and the Defense Special Missile and Aerospace Center (Instruction 5100.43, September 24, 2008).[39]

The services also promulgate regulations covering intelligence matters. Army Regulations (AR) governing intelligence activities include "U.S. Army Intelligence Activities" (AR 381-10, May 3, 2007); "Technical Counterintelligence" (AR 381-14, September 30, 2002); "The Army Counterintelligence Program" (AR 381-20, May 26, 2010); "Army Foreign Materiel Exploitation Program" (AR 381-26, May 27, 1991); "Offensive Counterintelligence Operations" (AR 381-47, September 27, 2013); "Army Human Intelligence Collection Programs" (AR 381-100, May 15, 1988); and "U.S. Army Cover Program" (AR 381-102, December 29, 2000).[40]

Air Force Instructions concerning intelligence include "Sensitive Reconnaissance Programs" (10-1103, April 29, 1994); "Oversight of Intelligence Activities" (14-04, April 23, 2012); "International Intelligence Agreements" (14-102, April 29, 2013); "Intelligence Support to the Acquisition Life Cycle" (14-111, May 18, 2012); "Intelligence Support to Force Protection" (14-119, May 4, 2012); "Air Force Open Source

---

*Some of the human intelligence and many of the counterintelligence directives were modified in 2013, with no change to their official date of issuance, to reflect changes in the organization of the Office of the Under Secretary of Defense for Intelligence and the disestablishment of the Defense Counterintelligence and HUMINT Center.

Intelligence (OSINT)" (14-130, May 18, 2012); "Control, Protection, and Dissemination of Sensitive Compartmented Information" (14-302, January 18, 1997); "RC 135 Unit Intelligence Procedures" (14-2RC 135, Vol. 3, September 4, 2013); "Human Intelligence (HUMINT)" (14-127, November 7, 2011); and "Geospatial Intelligence (GEOINT)" (14-132, August 10, 2012).[41]

Notes

1. Initially, Rumsfeld envisioned the Pentagon's intelligence chief as an assistant secretary but then concluded that an under secretary would be more effective. See Bradley Graham, *By His Own Rules: The Ambition, Successes, and Ultimate Failures of Donald Rumsfeld* (New York: Public Affairs, 2009), 367.

2. James Risen and Thom Shanker, "Rumsfeld Moves to Strengthen His Grip on Military Intelligence," *New York Times*, August 3, 2002, A1, A8; Walter Pincus, "Pentagon May Get New Intelligence Chief," *Washington Post*, August 19, 2002, A11; Center for Strategic & International Studies, *Transitioning Defense Organizational Initiatives: An Assessment of Key 2001–2008 Defense Reforms*, December 2008, http://csis.org/files/media/csis/pubs/081209_hicks_transdeforg_web.pdf, 21.

3. Pincus, "Pentagon May Get New Intelligence Chief."

4. Douglas E. Garthoff, *Directors of Central Intelligence as Leaders of the U.S. Intelligence Community, 1946–2005* (Washington, DC: Center for the Study of Intelligence, 2005), 48; Graham, *By His Own Rules*, 366–367; Risen and Shanker, "Rumsfeld Moves to Strengthen His Grip on Military Intelligence"; Janet A. McDonnell, "The Office of the Under Secretary of Defense for Intelligence: The First 10 Years," *Studies in Intelligence* 58, no. 1 (Extracts, March 2014): 9–16.

5. Margan A. Carlstrom, "OUSD (I) Charts Its Course," *Communiqué* (May–June 2006): 12–14; Paul Wolfowitz, Memorandum, Subject: Implementation Guidance on Restructuring Defense Intelligence—and Related Matters, May 8, 2003; Donald H. Rumsfeld, Department of Defense Directive 5143.01, "Under Secretary of Defense for Intelligence (USD [I])," November 23, 2005; Chuck Hagel, Department of Defense Directive 5143.01, "Under Secretary of Defense for Intelligence (USD [I])," October 24, 2014.

6. Chuck Hagel, Department of Defense Directive 5143.01, "Under Secretary of Defense for Intelligence (USD [I])"; Office of the Director of National Intelligence, ODNI News Release No. 16-07, "Under Secretary of Defense for Intelligence to Be Dual-Hatted as Director of Defense Intelligence," May 24, 2007; Senate Armed Services Committee, *Advance Questions for Michael Vickers, Nominee for the Position of Under Secretary of Defense for Intelligence*, February 15, 2011, https://www.fas.org/irp/congress/2011_hr/021511vickers-q.pdf, 19; J. Michael McConnell, Director of National Intelligence, and Robert M. Gates, Secretary of Defense (signatories), "Memorandum of Agreement Between the Secretary of Defense and the Director of National Intelligence," May 21, 2007.

7. Chuck Hagel, Department of Defense Directive 5143.01, "Under Secretary of Defense for Intelligence (USD [I])."

8. James R. Clapper Jr., Memorandum, Subject: Reorganization of the Office of the Under Secretary of Defense for Intelligence, June 18, 2008; Senate Armed Services Committee, *Advance Questions for Michael Vickers*, 18; McDonnell, "The Office of the Under Secretary of Defense for Intelligence: The First 10 Years."

9. Claudette Roulo, Armed Forces Press Service, "Intel Office Realignment Addresses Future Challenges," DOD, December 17, 2013; Zachary Fryer-Biggs, "DoD Intel Office Shuffled Ahead of Cuts," www.defensenews.com, December 28, 2013, http://archive.defensenews.com/article/20131217/DEFREG02/312170017/DoD-Intel-Office-Shuffled-Ahead-Cuts.

10. DOD Directive 5205.9, "Joint Military Intelligence Program," April 7, 1995.

11. Ibid.; U.S. Congress, House of Representatives, Report 105-508, *Intelligence Authorization Act for Fiscal Year 1999* (Washington, DC: U.S. Government Printing Office, 1998), 7.

12. Rumsfeld, DOD Directive 5143.01, "Under Secretary of Defense for Intelligence (USD [I])"; Office of the Director of National Intelligence, *Report on the Progress of Director of National Intelligence in Implementing the "Intelligence Reform and Terrorism Prevention Act of 2004,"* May 2006, 6; U.S. Congress, House of Representatives, Report 109–411, *Intelligence Authorization Act for Fiscal Year 2007* (Washington, DC: U.S. Government Printing Office, 2006), 15.

13. Department of Defense, *FY 2010 Budget Congressional Justification Book, Military Intelligence Program*, vol. 1: *Summary*, 2009, 46–48.

14. Lieutenant Colonel Steve Palm, "DOD's Military Intelligence Board," *Communiqué* (April–May 1997): 13; "Military Intelligence Board," www.dia.mil/history (accessed September 10, 2010).

15. Palm, "DOD's Military Intelligence Board."

16. Ibid.

17. James R. Clapper Jr., "Challenging Joint Military Intelligence," *Joint Forces Quarterly* (Spring 1994): 92–99.

18. DOD Directive 5105.21, "Defense Intelligence Agency (DIA)," February 18, 1997, 2–3.

19. U.S. Congress, House Committee on Armed Services, HASC No 110–126, *Hearing on National Defense Authorization Act for Fiscal Year 2009 and Oversight of Previously Authorized Programs, March 5, 2008* (Washington, DC: U.S. Government Printing Office, 2009), 95.

20. Department of Defense Directive 3115.16, Subject: The Defense Warning Network, December 5, 2013.

21. Ibid.

22. Ibid.

23. Department of Defense Instruction 3115.12, "Open Source Intelligence (OSINT)," August 24, 2010.

24. Ibid.

25. See Jeffrey T. Richelson, *American Espionage and the Soviet Target* (New York: Morrow, 1987), 120–126.

26. Chris Pocock, *Dragon Lady: The History of the U-2 Spyplane* (Shrewsbury, UK: Airlife Publishing, 1989), 75–89; A. Jay Cristol, *The Liberty Incident: The 1967 Israeli Attack on the U.S. Navy Spy Ship* (Dulles, VA: Brassey's, 2002); Jack Cheevers, *Act of War: Lyndon Johnson, North Korea, and the Capture of the Spy Ship Pueblo* (New York: NAL Caliber, 2013).

27. James Bamford, *The Puzzle Palace: A Report on NSA, America's Most Secret Agency* (Boston: Houghton-Mifflin, 1982), 184–185, 216–231; U.S. Congress, House Committee on Armed Services, *Inquiry into U.S.S. Pueblo and EC-121 Plane Incidents* (Washington, DC: U.S. Government Printing Office, 1969); "Radar Detector Aboard SR-71 Alerted Plane to Missile Attack," *New York Times*, August 29, 1983, 3; Bill Gertz, "Chinese Jets Chase U.S. Surveillance Jet over Taiwan Strait," www.washingtontimes.com, July 25, 2011, http://www.washingtontimes.com/news/2011/jul/25/chinese-jets-chase-us-surveillance-jet-over-taiwan; Wendell Minnick, "China Incident with US P-8 Sparks Debate on Pacific Posture," *Defense News*, August 31, 2014, http://archive.defensenews.com/article/20140831/DEFREG03/308310014/China-Incident-US-P-8-Sparks-Debate-Pacific-Posture.

28. U.S. Congress, House Committee on Appropriations, *Department of Defense Appropriations for 1994*, pt. 1 (Washington, DC: U.S. Government Printing Office, 1993), 37; Colonel Thomas G. Shepherd, chief, Reconnaissance Programs Division, J-3, Memorandum for the Record, "Conversation Between Colonel Earnest R. Harden (USAF Ret.) and Colonel Thomas G. Shepherd, OJCS/JRC, 11 August 1977," August 12, 1977; L. L. Lemnitzer, Chairman, Joint Chiefs of Staff, JCSM-451-60, Memorandum for the Secretary of Defense, Subject: Establishment of a Joint Reconnaissance Center, October 10, 1960.

29. Victor Marchetti and John D. Marks, *The CIA and the Cult of Intelligence* (New York: Knopf, 1974), 332.

30. Joint Chiefs of Staff, JCS Publication 4, *Organization and Functions of the Joint Chiefs of Staff* (Washington, DC: U.S. Government Printing Office, 1985), III-3-28 to III-3-29.

31. Charles P. Wilson, *Strategic Reconnaissance in the Middle East* (Washington, DC: Washington Institute for Near East Policy, 1997), 13–14; Chairman of the Joint Chiefs of Staff Instruction, CJCSI 3141.01D, "Management and Review of Campaign and Contingency Plans," April 24, 2008, B-2.

32. DIA Office of Historical Research, *A History of the Defense Intelligence Agency* (Washington, DC: DIA, 2007), 23; Michael Petersen, "Defense Intelligence Officers and the March of HISTORY," *Communiqué* (Spring 2012): 22–24; DIA Public Affairs, "DIA Director Appoints First Defense Intelligence Officers," DIA, December 2, 2014, http://www.dia.mil/News/Articles/ArticleView/tabid/11448/Article/567037/dia-director-appoints-first-defense-intelligence-officers.aspx.

33. Petersen, "Defense Intelligence Officers and the March of HISTORY"; Agency Communications and Branding Division, CP, "Deputy Director Sheed Revitalizes the Defense Intelligence Officers," *Communiqué* (Spring 2012): 20–22.

34. "DIO Areas of Responsibility," *Communiqué* (Spring 2012): 18–19.

35. Department of Defense Directive C-5230.23, "Intelligence Disclosure Policy," November 18, 1983.

36. Titles and unclassified directives/instructions are available at "DoD Issuances" (www.dtic.mil/whs/directives).

37. Ibid.

38. Ibid.

39. Ibid.

40. Titles and unclassified regulations are available at the Army Publishing Directorate (www.apd.army.mil).

41. Titles and unclassified instructions are available at Air Force E-Publishing (www.e-publishing.af.mil).

19

MANAGING INTELLIGENCE COLLECTION, COVERT ACTION, AND INFORMATION ACCESS

Management of four different types of intelligence collection—satellite imagery, SIGINT, MASINT, and HUMINT—reflects both the commonality and diversity of the operations and collection systems employed by the Intelligence Community. Imagery is collected largely by satellites and aircraft, while SIGINT and MASINT rely, in addition to space and aerial systems, on ground- and sea-based as well as undersea platforms. And human intelligence is quite a different method of collection.

Managing covert action is yet another aspect of the management task. Inadequate management can result not only in an inefficient use of resources but in serious international consequences—as President John F. Kennedy discovered after the failure of the April 1961 Bay of Pigs operation. A further management task is controlling access to information about intelligence collection and covert action operations.

MANAGING SATELLITE IMAGING

For many years, the job of translating general imagery collection priorities into the targeting of systems against installations or activities was the responsibility of the Committee on Imagery Requirements and Exploitation (COMIREX), established on July 1, 1967, by Director of Central Intelligence Directive (DCID) 1/13. It replaced the Committee on Overhead Reconnaissance (COMOR), whose responsibilities included coordination of collection requirements for the development and operation of all imaging satellites. As these programs grew, the number of photographs increased substantially, resulting in serious duplication of imagery exploitation activities. One solution involved replacing COMOR with COMIREX, whose membership consisted of representatives from all United States Intelligence Board/National Foreign Intelligence Board agencies, plus the intelligence chiefs of the Army, Navy, and Air Force. The committee was staffed by personnel from the Central Intelligence Agency (CIA) and the Defense Intelligence Agency (DIA).[1]

Former chairman (1969–1979) Roland Inlow summarized the committee's functions: "COMIREX performs the interagency coordination and management functions needed to direct photographic satellite reconnaissance, including the process of deciding what targets should be photographed and what agencies should get which photos to analyze. It also evaluates the needs for, and the results from, photographic reconnaissance, and oversees security controls that are designed to protect photography and information derived from photography from unauthorized disclosure."[2]

COMIREX dealt with three basic questions with regard to the establishment of targets and priorities:

1. What installations/areas/activities were to be imaged?
2. What systems were to be targeted on specific installations/areas/activities?
3. What was to be the frequency of coverage?

When the United States operated a single type of imaging satellite system (the KH-11) from 1985 through 1988, COMIREX's decision with regard to the second question was simple, but as different variants of the KH-11s, the ONYX and MISTY satellites, joined the constellations, the decisions became more complicated. Two factors have complicated these issues even further: the advent of high-resolution commercial imagery and the proliferation of imagery satellites operated by allied nations.

In any case, there are always significant areas of contention among consumers over priorities and targeting. In addition, decisions concerning items 1 and 2 must take into account a multitude of technical questions, including the angle and altitude at which the imagery is to be obtained.

Conflicts over satellite imagery targeting priorities occur for a variety of reasons. Current intelligence requirements may conflict with long-term requirements—as when coverage of the Iran-Iraq battlefield during the 1980–1988 war meant bypassing some opportunities for monitoring the Iraqi nuclear program. Strategic and tactical intelligence requirements may also conflict. Day-to-day coverage, revealing movements of troops or weapons and small changes in capabilities, may be of interest to military commanders; at the national level, in the absence of a crisis, such information is of little interest. COMIREX served to prioritize the claims of the CIA, the DIA, the military services, and other consumers with the objective of distributing a strictly limited resource in such a way as to satisfy, at least minimally, the legitimate requests of several competing bureaucracies.

In the area of imagery exploitation, COMIREX allocated interpretation tasks among the National Photographic Interpretation Center (NPIC), the CIA's Office of Imagery Analysis, the imagery exploitation components of the DIA, the military service intelligence organizations, and the combatant commands. COMIREX's National Tasking Plan for Imagery Processing and Exploitation spelled out the basic division of labor.[3] With NGA's absorption (when it was the National Imagery and Mapping Agency [NIMA]) of NPIC, the CIA's Office of Imagery Analysis, and the DIA's imagery exploitation component, the National Geospatial-Intelligence Agency (NGA) now decides which interpretation tasks to perform itself and which to assign to military service intelligence organizations.

Following its creation after the 1991 Gulf War, the Central Imagery Office (CIO) assumed responsibility for tasking satellites and exploitation components. According to DCID 2/9 of June 1, 1992, "Management of National Imagery Intelligence," the CIO was to "perform those Intelligence Community responsibilities previously vested in COMIREX." Tasking was to be performed by a central imagery tasking authority "in accordance with intelligence requirements established by the DCI in peacetime and the Secretary of Defense in wartime." The CIO was also to produce the National Tasking Policy for Imagery Exploitation to allocate interpretation tasks among the different agencies.[4]

NIMA's Central Imagery Tasking Office was the successor to the CIO. Today, NGA's Source Operations & Management Directorate, specifically its Source Operations Group, is responsible for taking requests for satellite imagery coverage from organizations both within and outside the Intelligence Community. The directorate then produces the tasking for the National Reconnaissance Office's (NRO) imagery satellites as well as commercial imagery satellites whose product is available to the U.S. government.[5]

Among the innovations in imagery tasking during the 1970s was the COMIREX Automated Management System (CAMS), which employed operations research procedures to take the requirements from different customers and create a tasking plan to optimize satellite operations in pursuit of those requirements and established priorities. In 1996 NIMA established the Requirements Management System to replace CAMS. As of 1998, the system could be accessed from over eighty locations around the world.[6]

MANAGING SIGINT

Management of the U.S. SIGINT effort is vested in the Director of NSA by National Security Council Intelligence Directive (NSCID) No. 6. The most recent version of that directive, promulgated on February 17, 1972, is still in force.[7] In addition to defining the components of SIGINT, the directive states,

> The Secretary of Defense is designated as Executive Agent of the Government for the conduct of SIGINT activities in accordance with the provisions of this directive and for the direction, supervision, funding, maintenance and operation of the National Security Agency (NSA). The Director of the National Security Agency shall report to the Secretary of Defense, the Director of Central Intelligence (DCI), and the Joint Chiefs of Staff. The Secretary of Defense may delegate, in whole or part, authority over the Director of the National Security Agency within the Office of the Secretary of Defense.
>
> It shall be the duty of the Director of the National Security Agency to provide for the SIGINT mission of the United States, to establish an effective unified organization and control of all SIGINT collection and processing activities of the United States, and to produce SIGINT in accordance with the objectives, requirements and priorities established by the Director of Central Intelligence Board.
>
> No other organizations shall engage in SIGINT activities except as provided in this directive. Except as provided in paragraphs 5 and 6 of this directive (re unique responsibilities of CIA and FBI) the Director of the National Security Agency shall exercise full control over all SIGINT collection and processing activities. . . . The Director of the National Security Agency is authorized to issue direct to any

operating elements engaged in SIGINT operations such instructions and assignments as are required. All instructions issued by the Director under the authority provided in this paragraph shall be mandatory, subject only to appeal to the Secretary of Defense. . . .

The Armed Forces and other departments and agencies often require timely and effective SIGINT. The Director of the National Security Agency shall provide such SIGINT. . . .

The intelligence components of the individual departments and agencies may continue to conduct direct liaison with the National Security Agency in the interpretation and amplification of requirements and priorities established by the Director of Central Intelligence. (emphasis in original)[8]

Based on NSCID No. 6 and other guidance documents, SIGINT is also managed in accord with a Department of Defense (DOD) instruction on signals intelligence. Consistent with NSCID No. 6, the instruction designates the Under Secretary of Defense for Intelligence (USD [I]) as the Secretary of Defense's executive agent for SIGINT and the senior Defense Department official for coordinating SIGINT responsibilities with the Director of National Intelligence. In addition, it assigns the USD (I) "responsibility for exercising authority, direction, and control over" the Director of NSA. Among the under secretary's additional SIGINT responsibilities is development of a SIGINT Roadmap "for the future with NSA/CSS and other DoD Components involved in SIGINT activities."*[9]

One means of managing the SIGINT system is through the U.S. Signals Intelligence Directives (USSIDs) issued by the Director of NSA. At one time, the numbering scheme for the directives was keyed to the different types of subject matter they covered: policy (1–99), collection (100–199), processing (200–299), analysis and reporting (300–399), standards (400–499), administration (500–599), training (600–699), automatic data processing (700–799), and tasking (1000–). Table 19.1 lists USSIDs from prior to 1990.

Current USSIDs are designated by subject abbreviation, including "SP" for "SIGINT Policy" and "FA" for "Foreign Affairs." Such USSIDs include USSID SP0018, "Legal Compliance and U.S. Persons Minimization Procedures" (January 25, 2011); USSID SP0018J, "Procedures for Monitoring Radio Communications of Suspected International Narcotics Traffickers" (April 24, 1986); and USSID SP0019, "NSA/CSS Signals Intelligence Directorate—Oversight and Compliance" (November 13, 2012). The first specifies and promulgates U.S. SIGINT System minimization policy and procedures "required to protect the privacy rights of U.S. persons." The second "regulates certain COMINT activities of the United States Signals Intelligence System which are directed against radio communications of suspected international narcotics traffickers." The third "outlines the oversight and compliance policy and procedures governing Signals Intelligence (SIGINT) activities by elements of the United States SIGINT System (USSS) operating under the Director, National Security Agency."[10]

---

*The instruction also specifies the SIGINT responsibilities of the NRO and DIA directors, the Chairman of the Joint Chiefs of Staff, the commanders of the combatant command commanders, and a number of other DOD and military service officials.

TABLE 19.1   U.S. Signals Intelligence Directives

Number	Title/Subject	Date
3	SIGINT Security	August 1972
4	SIGINT Support to Military Commanders	July 1, 1974
18	Legal Compliance and Minimization Procedures	July 27, 1993
40	ELINT Operating Policy	October 1970
52	SIGINT Support to Electronic Warfare Operations	n.a.
56	Exercise SIGINT	n.a.
58	SIGINT Support to MIJI	n.a.
101	COMINT Collection Instructions	Dec. 1, 1989
110	Collection Management Procedures	Dec. 18, 1987
150	SIGINT Numerical Tasking Register	Feb. 1, 1985
240	ELINT Processing, Analysis, and Reporting	n.a.
300	SIGINT Reporting	n.a.
301	Handling of Critical (CRITIC) Information	Nov. 25, 1987
302	SIGINT Alert Systems	n.a.
316	Non-Codeword Reporting System	June 19, 1987
319	Tactical Reporting	n.a.
325	AIRBOAT Procedures	n.a.
326	Electronic Warfare Mutual Support Procedures	n.a.
341	Technical ELINT Product Reporting	n.a.
369	Time-Sensitive SIGINT Reporting	n.a.
402	Equipment and Manning Standards for SIGINT Positions	Sept. 8, 1986
404TM	Technical Extracts from Traffic Analysis (TEXTA)	Dec. 14, 1988
505	Directory of SIGINT Organizations	n.a.
550	Technical SIGINT Support Policies, Procedures, and Responsibilities	n.a.
601	Technical Support for Cryptologic Training	n.a.
602	Specialized Operational Training	n.a.
701	Sanitizing and Declassifying ADP Storage Devices	Sept. 30, 1976
702	Automatic Data Processing Systems Security	Sept. 1980
1045	SIGINT Tasking for USM-45, Misawa	Jan. 16, 1980
1600	SIGINT Tasking for US Army Tactical SIGINT Units	June 7, 1989

Sources: U.S. Congress, House Permanent Select Committee on Intelligence, *Annual Report* (Washington, D.C.: U.S. GPO, 1978), 70, 72; Working Group on Computer Security, *Computer and Telecommunications Security* (Washington, D.C.: National Communication Security Committee, July 1981), 110, 157; Defense Intelligence College, *Instructional Management Plan: Advanced Methods of Intelligence Collection*, March 1984; Department of the Army, AR 350-3, "Tactical Intelligence Readiness Training (REDTRAIN)," November 20 1984, 7; Department of the Army, *FM 34-1, Intelligence and Electronic Warfare operations*, July 1987, Ref. 2; Department of the Army, *FM 34-40-12, Morse Code Intercept Operations (U)*, August 26, 1991, ref. 3; U.S. European Command, ED 40-6, Operations and Administration of JIC, April 25, 1989; private information.

Additional USSIDs include USSID AP2231, "SIGINT Targeting of Maritime Vessels" (December 19, 2008); USSID FA6001, "Second Party SIGINT Relationships" (August 22, 2012); USSID FA6101, "Third Party SIGINT Relationships" (October 31, 2007); USSID CR610, "SIGINT Production and Raw SIGINT Access" (August 25, 2005); USSID SP0009, "Host Nation Collection" (October 28, 2011); USSID DA3110, "Collection Management Procedures"; and USSID DA3620, "Collected Signals Data Format."[11]

Although the Secretary of Defense is the executive agent, the USD (I) is designated to serve in that capacity on his behalf, and the Director of NSA is the program manager of U.S. SIGINT activities, requirements, and priorities are set by the Executive Committee and the National SIGINT Committee. The committee is the successor to a series of predecessors. As of 1950, prior to the creation of the NSA, the work was divided between the Armed Forces Security Agency Council's Intelligence Requirements Committee (AFSAC/IRC) and the U.S. Communications Intelligence Board's Intelligence Committee (USIB/IC). The AFSAC/IRC was primarily responsible for targeting and setting priorities for intercepts of military traffic; the latter was primarily concerned with nonmilitary traffic.[12]

Following the creation of the NSA, NSCID No. 9 of December 9, 1952, reconstituted the USCIB to operate under the Special Committee of the National Security Council (NSC) for COMINT, which consisted of the Secretaries of State and Defense and the Attorney General, assisted by the DCI. In 1958, when the USCIB and the Intelligence Advisory Committee were merged into the U.S. Intelligence Board (USIB), two committees were created: the COMINT Committee and the Electronic Intelligence (ELINT) Committee (by means of DCID 6/1 and DCID 6/2, respectively, both issued on October 21, 1958). DCID 6/1 of May 31, 1962, merged the ELINT and COMINT committees to form the SIGINT Committee.[13]

The responsibilities of the National SIGINT Committee (as it is now known) are extensive, as indicated by DCID 6/1 of May 12, 1982, reprinted in Figure 19.1. They include developing specifications for SIGINT collection requirements, monitoring the responsiveness of U.S. and cooperating foreign SIGINT agencies, and developing policies for the conduct of SIGINT liaison and the security of SIGINT-obtained information. In the 1993 fiscal year, key SIGINT Committee activities included development of a new architecture for SIGINT satellites, review and approval of selected allied relationships, review of foreign military sales requests, and several special evaluations.[14]

Prior to the Middle East war in 1973, the USIB SIGINT Committee recommended that the Middle East be a priority target for intelligence collection if hostilities erupted. The NSA was asked to evaluate the intelligence collected and to determine appropriate targets. On the outbreak of war, the NSA implemented these policies under the SIGINT Committee's guidance. The committee discussed and approved the DIA's recommendation to change the primary target of one collector. In addition to validating requirements and tasking collection assets, the SIGINT Committee examines the relationships between U.S. SIGINT agencies and foreign agencies. Thus, in 1972 the committee developed a new set of objectives regarding SIGINT relations with Japan.[15]

The SIGINT Committee operated for many years with two permanent subcommittees: the SIGINT Requirements Validation and Evaluation Subcommittee (SIRVES) and the SIGINT Overhead Reconnaissance Subcommittee (SORS). SIRVES was established in the 1970s as a successor to the Evaluation Subcommittee to, among other

SECRET
NOFORN

DIRECTOR OF CENTRAL INTELLIGENCE DIRECTIVE[1]
SIGINT Committee
(Effective 12 May 1982)

Pursuant to the provisions of Section 102, the National Security Act of 1947, and Executive Order 12333, there is established a Signals Intelligence (SIGINT) Committee.

1. Mission

The mission of the SIGINT Committee is to advise and assist the Director of Central Intelligence (DCI) and the Director, National Security Agency (DIRNSA) in the discharge of their duties and responsibilities with respect to Signals Intelligence as specified in Executive Order 12333, to monitor and assist in coordinating within the Intelligence Community the accomplishment of objectives established by the DCI, and to promote the effective use of Intelligence Community SIGINT resources.

2. Functions:

Under the general guidance of the Deputy Director of Central Intelligence, the SIGINT Committee shall:

a. advise the DCI on the establishment of SIGINT requirements, priorities, and objectives;

b. develop statements, based on the DCI's objectives and priorities, of collection and exploitation requirements for COMINT, ELINT, foreign instrumentation signals, nonimagery infrared, coherent light, and nonnuclear electromagnetic pulse (EMP) sources. (These statements will provide guidance for resource programming, mission planning, and reporting. Each statement should take into account practical limitations, costs, and risk factors.)

c. monitor and evaluate the responsiveness of present and programmed United States and cooperating foreign SIGINT resources to United States needs for intelligence information;

d. monitor the impact on SIGINT programs of information needs levied by intelligence comsumers;

e. advise and make recommendations on the dissemination and sanitization of SIGINT or information derived therefrom and the release of disclosure of SIGINT or derived information to foreign governments or international organizations in which the United States Government participates;

f. develop and recommend to the DCI policies, directives, and guidance for the conduct of SIGINT arrangements with foreign governments;

g. assess and report to the DCI on the potential impact on current and future United States SIGINT capabilities of providing cryptographic assistance to foreign governments; and

---

[1]This directive supersedes DCID No. 6/1, 18 May 1976.

SECRET

Classified by: DCI
Declassify on: OADR

(continues)

h. review, develop, and recommend to the DCI policies for the protection, through classification and compartmentation, of COMINT, ELINT, and other SIGINT or of information about them or derived from them and procedures enabling United States Government entities outside of the Intelligence Community to receive and use SIGINT.

3. Intelligence Community Responsibilities

Upon request of the Committee Chairman, Intelligence Community elements shall provide information pertinent to the Committee's mission and functions within DCI-approved security safeguards.

4. Composition and Organization

The Committee Chairman will be appointed by the Director of Central Intelligence.

The members of the committee will be representatives designated by Intelligence Community principals.

The Chairman will establish subcommittees or task forces as required.

With the approval of the DCI, the Committee Chairman may invite representatives of relevant United States Government entities to participate as appropriate.

The Committee will be supported by an Executive Secretariat.

William J. Casey
Director of Central Intelligence

things, oversee the National SIGINT Requirements System (discussed in more detail below). SIRVES restructured the key SIGINT requirements covering the former Soviet Union and Eastern Europe. SORS was established in the 1960s with the arrival of satellite SIGINT collection. It was "responsible for receipt, approval, and subsequent generation of intelligence guidance in response to tasks to be levied on national resources" and "continually monitor[ed] requirements and provid[ed] collection and processing guidance for both long- and short-term needs."[16]

In the mid-1990s, two new groups were established: the Weapons and Space Systems Advisory Group (WSSAG) and the National Emitter Intelligence Subcommittee (NEIS). The WSSAG was created to "coordinate SIGINT on foreign weapons and space systems," whereas the NEIS is concerned with SIGINT production on foreign radars and other noncommunication signals. The committee may also employ working groups and task forces on a short-term basis, such as the Third Party Ad Hoc Working Group of 1972.[17]

In March 2004, the DCI signed a new charter for the National SIGINT Committee. As a result, SIRVES became the National SIGINT Analysis and Production Subcommittee, while SORS became the National SIGINT Collection Subcommittee, which is responsible for providing a perspective on the relative merits of SIGINT collection assets. In addition, the two groups established in the 1990s were merged into the National Emitter, Weapons, and Space Subcommittee.[18]

As noted above, a National SIGINT Requirements System was established in 1975, after USIB approval. Under this system, a formal community review and approval procedure must be conducted for each requirement before it can be validated and placed on the National SIGINT Requirements List (NSRL). Today, the NSRL is the basic guidance document for the NSA and specifies SIGINT targets according to well-defined priorities, including cross-references to DNI (e.g., National Intelligence Priorities Framework) and other national requirements documents. The system does not, however, prevent the Director of NSA from determining which specific signals to intercept in fulfillment of requirements. Nor does it prevent the Secretaries of State and Defense or military commanders from directly tasking NSA in a crisis and then informing the DNI and SIGINT Committee afterward.[19]

MANAGING HUMINT

Throughout the Cold War and beyond, the fundamental guidance for U.S. human intelligence activities—clandestine as well as overt—was contained in NSCID No. 5, "U.S. Espionage and Counterintelligence Abroad," of February 17, 1972 (still the current version), and the DCIDs derived from it.*

---

*Another aspect of human intelligence, defectors, was the subject of NSCID No. 4, "The Defector Program," of February 17, 1972. Among the DCIDs issued under its authority were DCID 4/1, "The Interagency Defector Committee," and DCID 4/2, "The Defector Program Abroad." See DCID 4/2 "The Defector Program Abroad," June 26, 1959, in *Documents from the US Espionage Den (53): The U.S.S.R., the Aggressive East*, section 4 (Tehran: Muslim Students Following the Line of the Iman, n.d.), 4–11; U.S. Congress, House Permanent Select Committee on Intelligence, *Annual Report*, 70.

The DCIDs governing aspects of the HUMINT effort—including DCID 5/1, "Espionage and Counterintelligence Activities Abroad" (December 19, 1984) and DCID 3/2, "Coordination of Overt Collection Abroad" (November 26, 2001)—were rescinded in part and in whole, respectively, by Intelligence Community Directive (ICD) 304, originally issued in March 2008 and amended in July 2009. The current version of ICD 304 "delineates the role and responsibilities of the DNI, the National HUMINT Manager (NHM), and those principal agencies or departments that conduct HUMINT activities [including counterintelligence activities using human sources]," especially the Central Intelligence Agency, the Federal Bureau of Investigation, and the Department of Defense.[20]

The directive delegated to the Deputy Director of National Intelligence (DDNI) for Collection (whose responsibilities have been assumed by the DDNI for Intelligence Integration) the DNI's authorities and responsibilities with regard to establishing objectives, priorities, and guidance for national HUMINT activities, resolving conflicts in collection requirements, and evaluating the effectiveness of national HUMINT activities. In addition, the directive assigned the DDNI for Collection responsibility, in conjunction with other officials, for advising the DNI HUMINT resource allocation in the National Intelligence Program and Military Intelligence Program.[21]

The directive also designates the Director of the Central Intelligence Agency as National HUMINT Manager (NHM)—a position that the director delegated to the Director of Operations. The NHM's responsibilities include production of an integrated national HUMINT plan containing goals and performance objectives, integrating national HUMINT collection capabilities into the National Intelligence Coordination Center, and creating and implementing command standards for HUMINT activities, including source validation, training, collection requirements, evaluation, reporting, and cover support.[22]

Additional NHM responsibilities include developing and implementing procedures to deconflict HUMINT operations and activities conducted by Intelligence Community organizations or funded by the National Intelligence Program, as well as negotiating written agreements with other U.S. government "entities engaged in collection activities involving clandestine methods, or that collect intelligence through HUMINT or counterintelligence activities," such as the June 2005 "Memorandum of Understanding Concerning Overseas and Domestic Activities of the Central Intelligence Agency and Federal Bureau of Investigation."[23]

Several initiatives were launched in the 1990s and post-9/11 to improve coordination of clandestine collection. In 1992 a National HUMINT Requirements Tasking Center (NHRTC) was established within the CIA's Directorate of Operations (DO) to allocate tasks among the collection agencies. At the time, DCI Robert Gates described the center as "an integrated interagency mechanism for tasking human intelligence requirements to that part of the community that has the best chance of acquiring the information at least cost and risk."[24] The center, which consists of representatives from the DIA, the State Department, and the CIA, has a staff of about twelve drawn from the military and three CIA directorates (Intelligence, Operations, and Science and Technology). It has three key areas of responsibility:

- Identifying information needs from policymakers, the military, science and technology centers, law enforcement, and analysts

- Establishing collection priorities for collection and reporting
- Tasking requirements to the most suitable collector and accessing its capability to respond to these requirements.[25]

In accordance with NHRTC guidance, a 1993 State Department cable requested information from various embassies about "host government laws and policies regarding encryption." The information was expected to be a "key input" to a National Security Council study concerning U.S. policy on commercial encryption. Key topics included reaction to the "Clipper Chip" proposal, general policy on public encryption, and economic and trade issues.[26]

The principal products of the center are the National HUMINT Collection Directives (NHCDs), which define the requirements for HUMINT collection and tasking. They attempt to focus on the succeeding two-year period, although many are periodically updated. As of late 1997, there were more than one hundred current NHCDs on countries and transnational issues. Issues covered in the directives included support to military operations, weapons of mass destruction, advanced conventional weapons, and counterterrorism.[27]

A number of directives became publically available in 2010 due to Wikileaks, including those focusing on the United Nations, Bulgaria, Paraguay, Palestinian issues, Romania, and the African Sahel region. The directive concerning the United Nations requested from State Department officers detailed biographic information about foreign nations' UN representatives and specified a number of priority issues regarding the United Nations, including near-term concerns such as Iran and North Korea, continuing issues such as UN Security Council reform and the Middle East peace process, and UN General Assembly tactics and voting blocs.[28]

The NHCD on Palestinian issues requested information on the Palestinian-Israeli peace process, Palestinian leadership and governance, Palestinian internal security and control, and terrorism and Islamic activism. In addition, the directive requested information on Palestinian social development and infrastructure; the plans, policies, and actions of the Israeli government; and telecommunications systems.[29]

If the subject of an NHCD requires more detailed treatment, which may occur with technical subjects such as proliferation, Intelligence Community analysts write a Collection Support Brief (CSB), which is appended to the directive.[30]

NHRTC guidance is binding on the clandestine and overt HUMINT collections components of the Directorate of Operations and Defense Clandestine Service. It is advisory with respect to collection elements outside the Intelligence Community, such as the Foreign Commercial Service of the Department of Commerce and Department of State embassy reporting. Thus, State Department officers ignored portions of the United Nations NHCD requesting them to gather personal and technical information, including cell phone and frequent-flier numbers, about other nations' diplomats.[31]

As noted in Chapter 2, the NHRTC and the Community HUMINT Coordination Center are managed by the Deputy Director of the NCS for Community HUMINT. The coordination center is responsible for deconfliction and coordination of the HUMINT activities of the Directorate of Operations, DIA, FBI, military service counterintelligence components, and unified commands.[32]

MANAGING COVERT ACTION

To initiate a covert action, a Presidential Finding is required by the Hughes-Ryan Amendment to the Foreign Assistance Act of 1961. Under that and subsequent legislation, the finding must state that the president has determined that the "operation in a foreign country . . . is important to the national security of the United States" and then describe the scope (the country or countries that are the target) of the operation and what the operation entails. Findings must also specify each U.S. government entity that will participate in any significant way in the program's implementation and whether any third party will participate in the program in a significant way; findings may not authorize violation of the Constitution or any U.S. statute. Since 1991, under Title V of the National Security Act, Presidential Findings must be in writing and may not confer retroactive authorization for covert activities—except in emergencies, when oral findings may be used for up to twenty-four hours.[33] Figure 19.2 shows one of the findings signed in support of the attempt to establish contact with Iranian "moderates."

Findings are initially prepared within the CIA's Directorate of Operations, either as a result of a DO initiative or in response to requests from the CIA director, who in turn may be responding to a DNI or presidential request. In 1986 an article in the CIA's *Studies in Intelligence* reported that before a proposed finding left the Directorate of Operations, it was reviewed by the Covert Action Planning Group (CAPG), composed of the directorate's Associate Deputy Director, senior staff chiefs, and those individuals who had a substantive responsibility for the finding and its eventual implementation. If approved by the CAPG, the finding was sent to the top echelon of CIA management for review and recommendations, then to the Director of the CIA, and finally to the DCI.[34]

During the Reagan administration, if the DCI approved the proposed finding, it would go to the Planning and Coordination Group (PCG) of the NSC, which consisted of senior representatives of the State Department, Defense Department, and NSC. If the PCG supported the finding, it sent a favorable recommendation to the National Security Planning Group (NSPG). NSPG approval then resulted in a Presidential Finding. National Security Decision Directive (NSDD) 159, "Covert Action Policy Approval and Coordination Procedures," of January 18, 1985, specified that all intelligence findings be written and circulated among the eight members of the NSPG before being put into effect.[35]

George W. Bush's first National Security Presidential Directive, signed on February 13, 2001, "Organization of the National Security Council System," continued the existence of the NSC Principals Committee from the Bill Clinton administration (which continued it from the preceding administration) as "the interagency forum for consideration of policy issues affecting national security," including covert action. The regular membership consisted of the Secretaries of State, Defense, and the Treasury, the president's Chief of Staff, and the Assistant to the President for National Security Affairs, who served as the chair.[36]

Presidential Policy Directive 1, "Organization of the National Security Council System," of February 13, 2009, directed the Principals Committee to "continue to be the senior interagency forum for consideration of policy issues affecting national

FIGURE 19.2 Presidential Finding on Iran

Finding Pursuant to Section 662 of
The Foreign Assistance Act of 1961
As Amended, Concerning Operations
Undertaken by the Central Intelligence
Agency in Foreign Countries, Other Than
Those Intended Solely for the Purpose
of Intelligence Collection

I hereby find that the following operation in a foreign country (including all support necessary to such operation) is important to the national security of the United States, and due to its extreme sensitivity and security risks, I determine it is essential to limit prior notice, and direct the Director of Central Intelligence to refrain from reporting this Finding to the Congress as provided in Section 501 of the National Security Act of 1947, as amended, until I otherwise direct.

SCOPE	DESCRIPTION
Iran	Assist selected friendly foreign liaison services, third countries and third parties which have established relationships with Iranian elements, groups, and individuals sympathetic to U.S. Government interests and which do not conduct or support terrorist actions directed against U.S. persons, property or interests, for the purpose of: (1) establishing a more moderate government in Iran, (2) obtaining from them significant intelligence not otherwise obtainable, to determine the current Iranian Government's intentions with respect to its neighbors and with respect to terrorist acts, and (3) furthering the release of the American hostages held in Beirut and preventing additional terrorist acts by these groups. Provide funds, intelligence, counter-intelligence, training, guidance and communications and other necessary assistance to these elements, groups, individuals, liaison services and third countries in support of these activities.

The USG will act to facilitate efforts by third parties and third countries to establish contact with moderate elements within and outside the Government of Iran by providing these elements with arms, equipment and related materiel in order to enhance the credibility of these elements in their effort to achieve a more pro-U.S. government in Iran by demonstrating their ability to obtain requisite resources to defend their country against Iraq and intervention by the Soviet Union. This support will be discontinued if the U.S. Government learns that these elements have abandoned their goals of moderating their government and appropriated the material for purposes other than that provided by this finding.

The White House
Washington, D.C.
Date January 17, 1986

security." The directive also stipulated that the committee would be chaired by the National Security Adviser, while its other members would include the Secretaries of State, Defense, Energy, Homeland Security, and the Treasury, the Attorney General, the Director of the Office of Management and Budget, the U.S. Representative to the United Nations, the president's Chief of Staff, the Director of National Intelligence, and the Chairman of the Joint Chiefs of Staff.[37]

MANAGING INFORMATION ACCESS

The basic means of managing or controlling access to intelligence information is the classification system, which defines different levels of sensitivity and restricts access to those who have been cleared at that level and have a "need to know." Classification and dissemination are the results of guidance issued in the form of executive orders, NSCIDs, DCIDs, ICDs, and guidances from the heads of agencies, such as the NRO, NSA, and Office of Naval Intelligence.

The best-known classifications are those used to restrict access to a wide range of national security information: Confidential, Secret, and Top Secret. Confidential information, as defined in the most recent (2009) "Classified National Security Information" executive order, is "information, the unauthorized disclosure of which reasonably could be expected to cause damage to the national security that the original classification authority is able to identify or describe." Secret information differs from Confidential information in that the expected damage would be "serious." In the case of Top Secret information, the damage would be "exceptionally grave."[38]

In theory at least, access for an individual with clearances at a certain level is further restricted to the information the individual needs to know in order to perform his or her job (although what an individual needs to know is subject to different interpretations). In some cases, the need-to-know principle is implemented by compartmentalization. Thus, the Army Intelligence and Security Command's offensive counterintelligence programs have been designated by a special code word used to restrict access to information about those operations. Similar operations conducted by the Air Force Office of Special Investigation have been designated SEVEN DOORS.[39]

In addition to specifying the traditional three classifications, the executive order on national security information allows the Director of National Intelligence to continue the long-standing practice of establishing Special Access Programs with respect to intelligence sources, methods, and activities. The executive order directs that the number of programs be kept "at an absolute minimum" and specifies that such programs can be created only if "the vulnerability of, or threat to, specific information is exceptional" and "the normal criteria for determining eligibility for access applicable to information classified at the same level are not deemed sufficient to protect the information from unauthorized disclosure."[40]

Information covered by Intelligence Community special access programs has been known as Sensitive Compartmented Information (SCI). A 1984 report by the National Foreign Intelligence Board's Security Committee (SECOM) described SCI as

> data about sophisticated technical systems for collecting intelligence and information collected by those systems. The characteristics of the systems that necessitated

the development of SCI programs are (a) that compared to conventional intelligence activities employing human sources, many more people must know sensitive information in order to develop, build and operate the systems and to analyze the material they collect; (b) that they generally produce large quantities of accurate, detailed intelligence, which is needed and relied upon by senior planners and policymakers, and which, by its nature, is extremely fragile, in that it reveals the characteristics of the systems that collect it; and (c) that they are extremely vulnerable to adversary countermeasures, i.e. denial and deception.[41]

The systems that generate SCI, as described by the SECOM in 1984, include overhead imaging, SIGINT and MASINT systems, submarines involved in Special Navy reconnaissance activities, and other systems involved in the interception of foreign signals. In addition, as noted by the committee, the information about many of the systems that produce SCI falls into the SCI category.

The first public hint of the existence of such a category occurred during the Senate hearing on the Gulf of Tonkin Resolution in 1964, when Senate Foreign Relations Committee Chairman William J. Fulbright inquired into the source of a report that North Vietnamese patrol boats were about to attack the USS *Turner Joy* on the night of August 4, 1964. Fulbright, Secretary of Defense Robert McNamara, and Senators Frank Lausche and Albert Gore Sr. engaged in the following colloquy:

McNamara: We have some problems because the [committee] staff has not been cleared for certain intelligence.

Lausche: I do not understand that. The members of the staff are not cleared?

Fulbright: All of those who have worked on this matter, but he is talking of a special classification of intelligence communications . . .

Gore: Mr. Chairman, could we know what particular classification that is? I had not heard of this super classification.

McNamara: Clearance is *above Top Secret* for the particular information on the situation. (emphasis added).[42]

The "above Top Secret" category dealt with communications intelligence rather than intelligence communications, and McNamara revealed that it was called Special Intelligence (SI). The institutionalization of that category can be traced to the successful interception and decryption of Axis signals during World War II by the United States and United Kingdom. Intelligence from decrypted Japanese diplomatic messages was designated MAGIC, and access to such intelligence was highly restricted to a "Top List" of officials. The decryption of Japanese military communications produced several categories: DEXTER (the highest-level intercepts), CORRAL (less sensitive intercepts), and RABID (intelligence from traffic analysis).[43]

The British also instituted a code word system to protect the fact that they were decrypting German and Italian communications. After going through a number of code names, they settled on two: ULTRA and PINUP. With the signing of the British-U.S. Communications Intelligence Agreement in May 1943, which standardized signals intelligence procedures between the United States and Britain, ULTRA was made a prefix to each of the military-related classifications, resulting in the double U.S. code words ULTRA DEXTER, ULTRA CORRAL, and ULTRA RABID.[44]

For many years, Special Intelligence contained three primary compartments indicating different levels of sensitivity—UMBRA, SPOKE, and MORAY—whose sensitivity was indicated by the prefixes attached to each code word: TOP SECRET for UMBRA and SECRET for SPOKE and MORAY. UMBRA, beginning in 1968, became the successor to the post–World War II SI code words (always five-letters in length), including CREAM, EIDER, DINAR, and TRINE. While the UMBRA category might involve intelligence derived from the intercept of Soviet or Chinese communications, the less sensitive SPOKE compartment would cover data derived from, inter alia, the intercept of Palestine Liberation Organization communications.[45]

In 1998 the Director of Central Intelligence decided that the code words UMBRA, SPOKE, and MORAY should no longer be classified, although the information they protected should be. Then, as a result of a decision by the National SIGINT Committee in May 1999, those code words were eliminated altogether. Information that used to be classified as TOP SECRET UMBRA would become TOP SECRET COMINT, while SECRET SPOKE or SECRET MORAY items would become SECRET COMINT.*[46]

Currently, Special Intelligence is one of six SCI Control Systems that appear in the DNI's December 2013 *Intelligence Community Markings System: Register and Manual* and whose purpose is "to protect technical and intelligence information derived from the monitoring of foreign communications signals by other than the intended recipients." The SI control system, according to the manual, "protects SI-derived information and information relating to SI activities, capabilities, techniques, process and procedures." The manual also notes that the previously used COMINT title as a substitute for Special Intelligence, present in many of the documents leaked by Edward Snowden, "is longer valid."[47]

Within SI is the GAMMA compartment, which may itself have subcompartments. GAMMA, which apparently came into use between 1956 and 1957, has been employed for particularly sensitive COMINT. That sensitivity can result "when the dissemination of the information could reveal an unusually sensitive method or location" or "an unusually sophisticated SIGINT technique." Alternatively, the sensitivity might be the result of "security provisos, when a providing Agency (other than NSA) determines that restricted protection is necessary to protect a sensitive means of collection or when the existence or contents of the report could reveal the means of collection." The final two catalysts for COMINT to be placed in the GAMMA compartment are identified as "sensitive substantive content" and "a sensitive target."[48]

Until 1969, GAMMA was employed exclusively for intelligence derived from intercepts of Soviet communications. But that year, NSA received instructions to use the same methods and procedures to monitor of U.S. antiwar leaders. At one point, there were at least twenty GAMMA subcompartments, including GILT, GOAT, GANT,

---

*For reasons not yet explained, the UMBRA code word has reappeared in at least one Snowden-leaked document produced by NSA's Counter–Improvised Explosive Device Analysis Integration Cell–Muhammad Tahir Shahzad AKA Abu Hamza, January 22, 2011. The document is classified TOP SECRET//COMINT//UMBRA//ORCON//REL USA, FVEY. See Top Level Communications, "NSA Still Uses the UMBRA Compartment for Highly Sensitive Intercepts," July 8, 2014, http://electrospaces.blogspot.com. That article also points out that the term "SPOKE" appears in a 2009 U.K. Government Communications Headquarters document.

GUPY, GABE, GULT, GYRO, and GOUT, with each code name referring to a specific operation or method. As noted in Chapter 8, GAMMA GUPY referred to the interception of radiotelephone conversations conducted by Soviet leaders as they rode around Moscow in their limousines. GAMMA GOUT referred to the material obtained by interception of Soviet-Vietnamese government communications.*[49]

In addition to GAMMA two other SIGINT designations survived the May 1999 National SIGINT Committee eliminations: Very Restricted Knowledge (VRK) and Exceptionally Controlled Information (ECI). The VRK designation was established in November 1974 by the Director of NSA "to limit access to uniquely sensitive SIGINT activities and programs." ECI has been described in a DOD document as a subcompartment of COMINT and in an NRO document as "an NSA administrative flag." At least one compartment has been used to protect information about companies cooperating with NSA surveillance programs such as PRISM. Another compartment, REDHARVEST, protects information concerning foreign partners involved in the RAMPART-A cable tapping effort. The WHIPGENIE ECI compartment protects information pertaining to the relationship between NSA's Special Source Operations unit and corporate partners.[50]

Table 19.2 lists ECI compartments as of September 2013. Included among those compartments is RAGTIME. Thus, the collection of phone and Internet data authorized by President Bush shortly after 9/11 was first assigned the code word STARBUST, which was soon replaced by STELLARWIND. Subsequently designated RAGTIME, the program contains four components: RAGTIME-A (U.S. interception of all foreign-to-foreign counterterrorism related data), RAGTIME-B (foreign government data that passes through the United States), RAGTIME-C (whose target is counterproliferation data), and RAGTIME-P. The "P" stands for the PATRIOT Act and involves interception with one end of the call or the e-mail within the United States.[51]

An additional set of code words attached to SIGINT documents indicate that the SIGINT was obtained from Third Party intercepts. DRUID has been used to identify a Third Party intercept, while code words employed to identify specific parties have included JAEGER (Austria), ISHTAR (Japan), SETTEE (South Korea), DYNAMO (Denmark), RICHTER (Germany), and DIKTER (Norway), as well as SEABOOT, KEYRUT, and FRONTO.[52]

A second long-existing SCI control system is TALENT-KEYHOLE (TK), which is "designed to protect information and activities related to space-based collection of imagery, signals, measurement and signature intelligence, certain products, processing, and exploitation techniques, and the design, acquisition and operation of reconnaissance satellites." The system began as the TALENT Control System (TCS) to protect the product of the U-2 missions over the Soviet Union that began in 1956 and was expanded in 1960 to also cover the product from U.S. photographic reconnaissance satellites.[53]

---

*At one time, there was a complementary UMBRA compartment, code-named DELTA, for intercepts relating to Soviet military operations, such as the location of Soviet submarines or aircraft operations. Subcompartments included DACE, DICE, and DENT. See Bob Woodward, "Messages of Activists Intercepted," *Washington Post*, October 13, 1975, 1, 14.

In the years since its creation, the TK control system has changed in two ways. For many years it operated with three key four-letter compartments: RUFF, ZARF, and CHESS. RUFF pertained to information produced by imaging satellites (with the exception of the ARGON/KH-5 mapping satellite, whose product was designated DAFF). ZARF indicated satellite-collected ELINT, while CHESS was employed to designate certain aerial imagery (such as that produced by SR-71 and U-2 aircraft). Thus, the 1986 final report of the DCI Mobile Missile Task Force Intelligence Requirements and Analysis Working Group was classified TOP SECRET RUFF ZARF UMBRA. In May 1999, ZARF was abolished as a code word, apparently followed by RUFF and CHESS in succeeding years.[54]

The second change was the extension of the control systems to cover information about the satellites producing the data, which from 1961 to 2005 had been the purpose of the BYEMAN Control System. During the first three decades of that system, each satellite program was represented by a specific code word (a practice still in existence), with clearances being granted on a system-by-system basis. As a result of the 1993 BYEMAN Compartmentation Restructure Study, a single major compartment was established with access to specific programs on a need-to-know basis. Then, in early 2005, the Director of the NRO informed the DCI that he would like to see the BYEMAN system retired because "it has become an impediment to . . . initiatives to encourage greater sharing of the NRO's capabilities and resources." That request was approved, along with the NRO director's plan to "transfer virtually all BYEMAN information into the Talent-Keyhole (TK) system where it will be available to TK-briefed personnel with a need-to-know."[55] Code words associated with current and past overhead systems are given in Tables 19.3 and 19.4.

Also approved was the NRO director's plan to establish the RESERVE Control System to "protect a very small body of information related to research and development of breakthrough technologies and specific vulnerabilities in order to glean the maximum lead-time for development and acquisition." RESERVE compartment information would be converted to TK "at the earliest reasonable time to facilitate interagency collaboration and product utility."[56] Three further SCI control systems appear in the December 2013 manual: KLONDIKE Control System (KCS), ENDSEAL (EL), and HCS. KLONDIKE (KDK), first established on an interim basis in February 2007 and originally known as ALCHEMY, is "designed to protect sensitive Geospatial Intelligence." There are three KLONDIKE compartments—BLUEFISH, IDITAROD, and KANDIK—all of which may have subcompartments. The manual does not indicate different levels of sensitivity among the compartments or what particular aspects of geospatial intelligence they cover.[57] Another SCI system noted in the manual indicates that the 1984 SECOM explanation of SCI is somewhat dated, for HCS is an abbreviation for HUMINT Control System, described as a system "that comprises two compartments, Operations [O] and Product [P], and is intended to provide enhanced protection to exceptionally fragile clandestine HUMINT sources, methods, and activities based on assessed value, critical nature, and vulnerability of the information." The manual also specifies, "IC clandestine collector organizations may elect to use HCS to protect their most sensitive HUMINT information upon the approval of the Director of the National Clandestine Service."[58]

TABLE 19.2   Exceptionally Controlled Information (ECI) Compartments and Classification Levels

(U) ECI Coverterm	(U) Trigraph	(U) Protected Information	(U) Overlapping Programs
(U//FOUO) ABEYANT	(U) N/A	(TS/SI) Protects information related to sensitive SIGINT Enabling relationships.	(S) Encompasses four ECIs: APERIODIC, AUNTIE, AMBULANT, and FIRSTDOWN
(U//FOUO) AMBULANT	(U//FOUO) AMB	(TS/SI) Protects information related to sensitive SIGINT Enabling relationships.	(S) Under ABEYANT program
(U//FOUO) APERIODIC	(U//FOUO) APR	(TS/SI) Protects information related to sensitive SIGINT Enabling relationships.	(S) Under ABEYANT program
(U//FOUO) AUNTIE	(U//FOUO) APR	(TS/SI) Protects information related to sensitive SIGINT Enabling relationships.	(S) Under ABEYANT program
(U/IFOUO) BOATMEN	(U//FOUO) BTM	(TS/ISI//NF) Feasibility study for special exfiltration initiatives between NSA and a Third Party.	(U) N/A
(U//FOUO) BOXWOOD	(U//FOUO) BXD	(TS//SI/NF) Protects a sensitive sole source of lucrative communications intelligence emanating from a target.	(U) N/A
(U//FOUO) BULLET	(U//FOUO) BLT	(TS/SI/NF) Protects NSA's potential assistance in reconstituting a Third Party's SIGINT collection capability.	(U) N/A
(U//FOUO) CHILLY	(U//FOUO) CHI	(TS/ISI//NF) Protects details of NSA association with and active participation in planning and execution of sensitive Integrated Joint Special Technical Operations (IJSTO) offensive Information Warfare (IW) strategies.	(TS/ISI//NF) IJSTO is the US Government process for the planning, deployment and employment of Special Access Program (SAP) weapons
(U//FOUO) CLERIC	(U//FOUO) CLC	(TS/SI) Protects policy exchanges between NSA and GCHQ related to Special Source activities.	(U) N/A
(U//FOUO) CONQUERER	(U//FOUO) CON	(TS/SI//NF) Protects fact of joint NSA/CIA clandestine Radio Frequency operations.	(S) CIA's KLAMATH (KLM) Control Channel
(U//FOUO) DECKSTOP	(U//FOUO) DKP	(TS/SI//NF) Protects information that would reveal clandestine SIGINT sources of collection against a high-priority target's internal domestic communications.	(U) N/A
(U//FOUO) DICHOTOMY	(U//FOUO) DCH	(TS/SI) Protects raw traffic and signals reporting information gained from especially sensitive (perishable) and clandestine sources.	(U) Disestablished on 1 Oct 03.
(U//FOUO) DILEMMA	(U//FOUO) DLM	(TS/SI) Summary description: A dormant ECI. A failed attempt to convince an IC partner to remove the "Fact Of" a particular collection capability from their tightly controlled channel and placed in this ECI.	(TS//ISI) Relates to a US Military unacknowledged SAP and Control System referred to at NSA as RAMPART M.

(U) ECI Coverterm	(U) Trigraph	(U) Protected Information	(U) Overlapping Programs
(U//FOUO) DOMINATE	(U//FOUO) DOM	(TS//SI//NF) Protects sensitive sources and methods used to determine the frequencies targeted by a target COMINT collection system.	(C) All intelligence derived under this program is handled via FLEXURE reporting channels.
(U//FOUO) ENSIGN	(U//FOUO) ENS	(TS//SI//NF) Protects potential NSA partnership with a Third Party in clandestine SIGINT activity in a specific location.	(TS//SI//NF) STAIRWELL also covers NSA partnership with this Third Party in unconventional SIGINT initiatives.
(U//FOUO) ESCAPEE	(U//FOUO) ESCP	(TS//SI//NF) U.S. component to ECI STATEROOM.	(U//FOUO) STATEROOM
(U//FOUO) EVADEYIELD	(U//FOUO) EVY	(TS//SI//NF) Protects NSA's capability to exploit voice or telephonic conversations from an extremely sensitive source.	(U) N/A
(U//FOUO) FIRSTDOWN	(U//FOUO) FRS	(TS//SI) Protects information related to sensitive SIGINT Enabling relationships.	(S) Under ABEYANT program
(U//FOUO) FLEXURE	(U//FOUO) FLX	(S) Protects military and civilian assets from detection by an adversary.	(S) Works with data collected by DOMINATE
(U//FOUO) FORBIDDEN	(U//FOUO) FBD	(TS//SI//NF) Protects information pertaining to joint operations conducted by NSA, GCHQ, CSE, CIA, and FBI against foreign intelligence agents.	(U) N/A
(U//FOUO) FORBORNE	(U//FOUO) FBR	(C//REL TO USA, CAN, AND GBR) Protects the fact that the National Security Agency, GCHQ, and CSE can exploit ciphers used by hostile intelligence services.	(U) N/A
(U//FOUO) GRAYSCALE	(U//FOUO) GRL	(TS//SI//REL TO USA, AUS, CAN, GBR, AND NZL) Protects information that could allow Second-Party-partner-assisted network infiltration operations to be detected and recognized.	(U) N/A
(U//FOUO) HELLFIRE	(U//FOUO) HLF	(TS//SI//NF) Protects activities of non-INFOSEC elements of NSA providing INFOSEC assistance to another nonhostile government.	(U) N/A
(U//FOUO) HISTORY	(U//FOUO) HST	(TS//SI//NF) Protects NSA and certain commercial cryptologic equipment manufacturer relationships.	(U) N/A
(U//FOUO) INVEIGH	(U//FOUO) INV	(S//SI) Protects vendor access to various diplomatic targets within the United States.	(U) N/A

(*continues*)

TABLE 19.2   (Continued)

(U) ECI Coverterm	(U) Trigraph	(U) Protected Information	(U) Overlapping Programs
(U//FOUO) INVENT	(U//FOUO) IVT	(TS//SI//NF) Protects NSA partnership with a Third Party in special SIGINT collection efforts in a specific location.	(TS//SI//NF) ENSIGN covers clandestine SIGINT activity with this Third Party as INVENT. STAIRWELL covers unconventional SIGINT activity with this Third Party.
(U//FOUO) LYSERGIC	(U//FOUO) LSG	(TS//SI) Protects NSA's efforts to select and prosecute foreign deployed telecommunications cables as SIGINT targets.	(S) CIA's KLAMATH (KLM) Control System.
(U//FOUO) MISCHIEF	(U//FOUO) MSF	(TS//SI) The highest level of access protecting sources, targets, sites, and unique collection techniques of the BLARNEY program.	(U//FOUO) RAGTIME
(U//FOUO) OPALESCE	(U//FOUO) OPS	(S//SI//REL TO USA, AUS, CAN, GBR AND NZL) Protects Close Access SIGINT collection operations, which require a specialized sensor, positioned in close physical proximity to the target device or facility.	(U) N/A
(U//FOUO) PAWLEYS	(U//FOUO) PAW	(TS//SI) Protects and covers clandestine access to cryptographic information and material. It protects the operational details, as well as any materials, technical information and SIGINT capabilities.	(S) CIA is the primary partner organization, which includes the FBI and DIA/DHS through TAREX. Also includes 2nd Party counterpart organizations.
(U//FOUO) PENDLETON	(U//FOUO) PEN	(TS//SI//REL TO USA, AUS, CAN, GBR, NZL) Protects NSA's investment in manpower and resources to acquire our current bottom line capabilities to exploit SIGINT targets by attacking public key cryptography as well as investment in technology.	(U) N/A
(U//FOUO) PIEDMONT	(U//FOUO) PIE	(TS//SI//REL TO USA, AUS, CAN, GBR, NZL) Provides protection to NSA's bottom line capabilities to exploit SIGINT targets by attacking the hard mathematical problems underlying public key cryptography as well as any future technologies as may be developed.	(U) N/A
(U//FOUO) PITCHFORD	(U//FOUO) PIT	(TS//SI) Details of certain cryptographies in which materials have been derived from a sensitive source or method.	(U) N/A
(U//FOUO) RAGTIME	(U//FOUO) RGT	(TS//SI) The second level of access protecting the identity of targets/target locations and cooperative relationships within the BLARNEY program. See MISCHIEF entry.	(U) N/A

(U) ECI Coverterm	(U) Trigraph	(U) Protected Information	(U) Overlapping Programs
(U//FOUO) REFRACTOR	(U//FOUO) RFR	(TS//SI//NF) Protects engineering and operational processes associated with tailoring U.S. Information Assurance equipment for release to and use by foreign countries.	(U) N/A
(U//FOUO) RUBIOUS	(U//FOUO) RBI	(TS//SI//NF) Protects information that could allow otherwise unilateral U.S. network infiltration operations to be detected and recognized.	(U) N/A
(U//FOUO) STAIRWELL	(U//FOUO) STRW	(TS//SI//NF) Protects NSA partnership with a Third Party in unconventional SIGINT activity.	(U//FOUO) ENSIGN and INVENT
(U//FOUO) STATEROOM	(U//FOUO) STRM	(S//SI) Restricts access to information about personnel involved in covert collection, processing, and reporting of SIGINT from diplomatic missions abroad. This activity is conducted by USA, AUS, CAN, GBR, and NZL.	(S) U.S.-only version is ESCAPEE
(U//FOUO) STEREO	(U//FOUO) SRO	(TS//SI) The same level of access as ECI RAGTIME though used to identify those individuals who require special handling/ data sanitization training.	(U) N/A
(U//FOUO) STRESSFUL	(U//FOUO) SRF	(TS//SI//NF) Protects exploitation of specific communications associated with individuals and organizations involved in money laundering in support of narcotics traffickers and organized crime targets of interest.	(U) N/A
(U//FOUO) TAXONOMY	(U//FOUO) TXM	(TS//SI) Protects policy exchanges between NSA and CSE related to Special Source activities.	(U) N/A
(U//FOUO) VISITOR	(U//FOUO) VSR	(TS//SI) The lowest level of access protecting the fact of the BLARNEY program and that it is governed by the Foreign Intelligence Surveillance Act.	(U) N/A
(U//FOUO) WASHBURN	(U//FOUO) WSB	(TS//SI) Covers CLANSIG effort with CIA to exploit a SIGINT source in a Middle Eastern location then in the research and analysis phase. ECI created for use solely with GCHQ to shield GCHQ from CIA's NOFORN Control Channel.	(S) CIA's KLAMATH (KLM) Control System.

Source: "National Security Agency/Central Security Service Exceptionally Controlled Information (ECI), as of September 12, 2003," Electronic Frontier Foundation, https://www.eff.org/files/2014/10/13/20141010-intercept-exceptionally_controlled_information_listing.pdf.

TABLE 19.3 Overhead Imagery System Code Words

Code Word	Mission	Initial Operation
AQUATONE/CHALICE/IDEALIST	Imagery	1956
CORONA	Search	1960
ARGON	Mapping	1961
GAMBIT	Close look	1963
LANYARD	Close look	1963
QUILL	Radar imagery	1964
OXCART	Aerial Imagery	1968
EARNING	Aerial Imagery	1968
HEXAGON	Search	1971
KENNAN/CRYSTAL	Real-time EOI	1976
ENHANCED CRYSTAL	Real-time EOI	2001
INDIGO LACROSSE ONYX	Radar imagery	1988
TOPAZ	Radar imagery	2010

TABLE 19.4 SIGINT Satellite Code Words

Code Word	Mission	Initial Operation
DYNO	ELINT	1960
POPPY	ELINT	1962
CANYON	COMINT	1968
RHYOLITE/AQUACADE	TELINT/COMINT	1970
JUMPSEAT	COMINT	1971
PARCAE	ELINT	1977
CHALET/VORTEX/MERCURY	COMINT/TELINT	1975
MAGNUM/ORION	TELINT/COMINT	1985
TRUMPET	COMINT/ELINT	1993
INTRUDER	ELINT/COMINT	2001
NEMESIS	SIGINT	?
RAVEN	SIGINT	?

The ENDSEAL Control System, which dates back to 1962, is described in the December 2013 manual only in terms of a system to protect information contained in its two compartments, as "a sensitive compartmented information (SCI) control system designed to protect access levels established for personnel whose duties require only overview knowledge, aperiodic access, or administrative handling of ECRU and NONBOOK material." Both compartments are "used for products intended for dissemination to IC consumers."[59] However, the SIGINT-related nature of relevant guidance documents, the requirement that ENDSEAL only be used in conjunction with the TOP SECRET and SI designations, and the existence of a memorandum of understanding between the NSA and the Chief of Naval Operations (the declassified version of which includes a partially redacted title) together suggest that this control system probably concerns SIGINT and submarine activity—either information acquired by U.S. SIGINT and other technical collection operations or SIGINT and other technical information concerning foreign submarine movements.[60]

Other SCI control systems may be considered too sensitive for inclusion in the unclassified manual. Thus, even in the TOP SECRET/CODEWORD fiscal year 2013 budget request, there is an entry that refers only to "Specialized Reconnaissance Programs," which, especially given its link to the Navy, is an even more euphemistic reference to what used to be called Special Navy activities. At one time there were two systems (or designations) associated with such activities: the Special Navy Control Program (SNCP), which covered use of submarines for intelligence collection, including within Soviet territorial waters, and MEDITATE, which covered data related to IVY BELLS–type operations. Subsequently, the terms "Naval Activities Support Program" and "DNI's Special Access Program" appear to have replaced SNCP and MEDITATE, respectively.[61]

A number of other code words, including PANGRAM and VERDANT, have apparently been associated with Navy programs. Three that were associated without doubt were AZORIAN, MATADOR, and JENNIFER. The first designated the project to recover a K-129 Soviet nuclear-missile-carrying submarine that sank in the Pacific in 1968. The second designated the never-launched second effort to recover the pieces left behind by the first effort. The last was the code word for the control system employed to control information concerning AZORIAN.[62]

Other code words have been associated with covert action or counterterrorist activities. One pre-9/11 code word, SPECTRE,* concerned intelligence relating to terrorist activities. Two code words for the control of covert action program information were VEIL (during the 1980s) and PEARL. An order classified TOP SECRET PEARL authorized the CIA to operate "freely and fully" in Afghanistan in the aftermath of the terrorist attacks of September 11, 2001. Code words associated with the targeted killings of al-Qaeda members include SYLVAN and MAGNOLIA.[63]

The code word GREYSTONE (GST) covered the variety of CIA rendition, interrogation, and counterterrorism programs. It had over a dozen subcompartments, each assigned a number (e.g., GST-001). Among the GREYSTONE compartments were

---

*This spelling suggests strongly that SPECTRE was based on the fictional organization that first appeared in the James Bond novel *Thunderball* (1961); the Special Executive for Counterespionage, Terrorism, Revenge, and Extortion.

those for the CIA black sites and the logistics involved (including the airplanes) for transporting their prisoners.[64]

Along with code words indicating compartments for SCI, there are designators used as dissemination controls for intelligence information. Some designators stipulate "Dissemination and Extraction of Information Controlled by Originator" (ORCON) or that information is not releasable to foreign nationals (NOFORN). A 1995 DCID explained that NOFORN might be used on intelligence whose release to foreign governments or nationals "could jeopardize intelligence sources or methods [or] would not be in the best interest of the United States." When one NOFORN document, the 1977 CIA study *Foreign Intelligence and Security Services: Israel*, became public after its seizure from the U.S. embassy in Tehran, it caused acute embarrassment to both the Israeli and U.S. governments because it alleged that Israeli intelligence had blackmailed, bugged, wiretapped, and attempted to bribe U.S. government employees in an effort to gain sensitive information. An Israeli spokesman denounced the allegations as "ridiculous."[65]

Other dissemination controls indicate the eligibility of a particular country (designated by a trigraph), set of countries, or organization to receive certain items of intelligence. Thus, Top Secret Special Intelligence releasable only to Canada and the United Kingdom would be designated TOP SECRET//SI//REL TO CAN GBR. If such intelligence were releasable to all of the FIVE EYES nations, it would be designated TOP SECRET//SI//REL TO FVEY. Thus, an NSA Special Source Operations slide, "PRISM (US-984XN) Based Reporting: January–May 2012," is classified TOP SECRET//SI//ORCON/NOFORN, while the USSID SP0018 on compliance with minimization procedures is SECRET//SI/REL TO FVEY.[66]

Access to intelligence information also involves policies concerning personnel as well as physical security, particularly with regard to SCI. Traditionally, a more stringent background investigation was required to gain access to top secret information. The logic was that whereas denial of top secret clearance required the presence of a well-defined character or personality defect that posed a threat to national security, "no risk is tolerable where SCI is involved and individuals who have been granted Top Secret clearances may be denied approval for access to SCI." National Security Directive 63, of October 21, 1991, established the practice of single-scope background investigations, which allow the same minimum standards for top secret and SCI background investigations. The directive does not prohibit more stringent requirements for access to SCI, however. Thus, an SCI screening interview might delve into an individual's family, financial, sexual, drug, criminal, political, travel, mental health, and physical histories.[67]

Several ICDs and derived documents deal with personnel and physical security with respect to SCI. ICD 703, "Protection of Classified National Intelligence, Including Sensitive Compartmented Information," stipulates policy for protection from unauthorized disclosure of classified national intelligence, including SCI. It also specifies steps for implementation of the policy and defines the roles and responsibilities of Intelligence Community officials.[68]

ICD 704, of October 1, 2008, "Personnel Security Standards and Procedures Governing Eligibility for Access to Sensitive Compartmented Information and Other Controlled Access Program Information," provides the DNI's guidance on the subject. It delegates to the heads of Intelligence Community elements the authority to grant access to SCI in accordance with the directive, which states general policy, personnel security standards, exceptions to those standards, and the responsibilities of assorted officials. An Intelligence Community Policy Guidance document issued on October 2 of the same year concerns denial or revocation of access to SCI and includes a specification of the documents and information that an individual will be supplied if access is denied or revoked.[69]

ICD 705, issued in May 2010, focuses on the facilities that house SCI. It states DNI policy with regard to the facilities, including that "all SCI must be processed, stored, used or discussed and that "all SCIFs shall be accredited prior to being used for the processing, storage, use, or discussion of SCI." More detailed guidance is supplied in Intelligence Community Standard (ICS) 705-1, "Physical and Technical Security Standards for Sensitive Compartmented Information Facilities," and ICS 705-2, "Standards for the Accreditation of and Reciprocal Use of Sensitive Compartmented Information," both issued in September 2010.[70] Standard 705-1 covers authority, purpose, applicability, reciprocal use, risk, management, SCIF planning and design, physical and technical security standards, waivers, operations and management, and roles and responsibilities. The section on technical security standards covers perimeter security, access control systems, intrusion detection, unclassified telecommunications systems, and portable electronic devices.[71]

Notes

1. DCID 1/13, "Coordination of Collection and Exploitation of Imagery Intelligence," February 2, 1973, Declassified Document Reference System (DDRS) 1980-132D; DCID 1/13, "Committee on Imagery Requirements and Exploitation," July 1, 1967, DDRS 1980-132B; U.S. Congress, Senate Select Committee to Study Governmental Operations with Respect to Intelligence Activities, *Final Report, Book I: Foreign and Military Intelligence* (Washington, DC: U.S. Government Printing Office, 1976), 85.

2. Roland S. Inlow, "An Appraisal of the Morison Espionage Trial," *First Principles* 11, no. 4 (May 1986): 1–5.

3. CINCPACFLT Instruction S3822.1E, Subject: PACOM Imagery Reconnaissance Procedures and Responsibilities, July 5, 1983, 1; HQ EUCOM Directive No. 40-4, "Exploitation and Dissemination of of Time-Sensitive Imagery," November 4, 1983, 1.

4. DCID 2/9, "Management of National Imagery Intelligence," June 1, 1992.

5. Jeffrey T. Richelson, *America's Secret Eyes in Space: The U.S. KEYHOLE Spy Satellite Program* (New York: Harper & Row, 1990), 252–256. On the directorate's other functions, see Gene Reich, "Source Directorate Expands," *Pathfinder* (May–June 2006): 9–10.

6. Walter Pincus, "Space Imagery Overhaul Aims at Better Data and Easier Access," *Washington Post*, January 20, 1998, A7.

7. National Security Agency, *NSA Transition Briefing Book*, 1980, unpaginated; National Security Agency/Central Security Service, *NSA/CSS Manual 22-1*, 1986, 1; Department of Defense Instruction O-3115.07, Subject: Signals Intelligence (SIGINT), September 15, 2008, 5; U.S. Signals Intelligence Directive SP0019, "NSA/CSS Signals Intelligence Directorate–Oversight and Compliance Policy," November 13, 2012.

8. Department of Justice, *Report on CIA-Related Electronic Surveillance Activities*, 1976, 77–79.

9. Department of Defense Instruction O-3115.07, Subject: Signals Intelligence (SIGINT).

10. USSID SP0018, "Legal Compliance and U.S. Persons Minimization Procedures," January 25, 2011; USSID SP0018J, "Procedures for Monitoring Radio Communications of Suspected

International Narcotics Traffickers," April 24, 1986; USSID SP0019, "NSA/CSS Signals Intelligence Directorate–Oversight and Compliance."

11. USSID SP0019, "NSA/CSS Signals Intelligence Directorate—Oversight and Compliance"; Signals Intelligence Directorate, SID Management Directive Number 422, "United States SIGINT System Mission Delegation," April 30, 2007; USSID CR610, "SIGINT Production and Raw SIGINT Access," August 25, 2005.

12. George A. Brownell, *The Origins and Development of the National Security Agency* (Laguna Hills, CA: Aegean Park Press, 1981), 5.

13. James Bamford, *The Puzzle Palace: A Report on NSA, America's Most Secret Agency* (Boston: Houghton Mifflin, 1982), 50; Department of Justice, *Report on CIA-Related Electronic Surveillance Activities*, 91; DCID 6/1, "Communications Intelligence Committee," October 21, 1958, DDRS 1980-130C; DCID 6/2, "Electronic Intelligence Committee," October 21, 1958, DDRS 1980-130D; DCID 6/1, "SIGINT Committee," May 1, 1962, DDRS 1980-131D.

14. Department of the Army, Office of the Deputy Chief of Staff for Intelligence, *Annual Historical Review, 1 October 1992 to 30 September 1993*, n.d., 4–4.

15. U.S. Congress, Senate Select Committee to Study Governmental Operations with Respect to Intelligence Activities, *Final Report, Book I: Foreign and Military Intelligence*, 85; Naval Intelligence Command, *Naval Intelligence Command (NAVINTCOM) History for CY-1972*, August 1, 1973, 20.

16. Department of the Army, Office of the Assistant Chief of Staff for Intelligence, *Annual Historical Review, 1 October 1984–30 September 1985*, 2–30; Department of the Army, Office of the Deputy Chief of Staff for Intelligence, *Annual Historical Review, 1 October 1990–30 September 1991*, 4–34; Lois G. Brown, "National SIGINT Committee," *NSA Newsletter* (February 1997): 2; Theresa M. Atwell, *Overhead SIGINT: The Process, the Challenge, the Quality* (Washington, DC: Joint Military Intelligence College, August 1995), 23–25.

17. Brown, "National SIGINT Committee"; Naval Intelligence Command, *Naval Intelligence Command (NAVINTCOM) History for CY-1972*, 19.

18. Michael V. Hayden, Director, DIRgram-417, "Evolving Role of the National SIGINT Committee," April 18, 2005.

19. U.S. Congress, Senate Select Committee to Study Governmental Activities with Respect to Intelligence Activities, *Final Report, Book I: Foreign and Military Intelligence*, 85–86; U.S. Congress, House Permanent Select Committee on Intelligence, *Annual Report* (Washington, DC: U.S. Government Printing Office, 1978), 55; Stephen J. Flanagan, "The Coordination of National Intelligence," in *Public Policy and Political Institutions: United States Defense and Foreign Policy—Policy Coordination and Integration*, ed. Duncan Clarke (Greenwich, CT: JAI, 1985), 177.

20. ICD 304, "Human Intelligence," March 6, 2008 (amended July 9, 2009), 1, 2.

21. Ibid., 3.

22. Ibid., 4.

23. Ibid., 3.

24. Remarks by Robert M. Gates, Director of Central Intelligence, to Association of Former Intelligence Officers, Boston, Massachusetts, November 14, 1992, 5.

25. Teresa M. Jones, "The National HUMINT Requirements Tasking Center," *Communiqué* (October–November 1997): 11–12.

26. Department of State, Subject: (U) Encryption Technologies, July 2, 1993.

27. Jones, "The National HUMINT Requirements Tasking Center."

28. State Department, "Reporting and Collection Needs: The United Nations," *New York Times*, July 31, 2009, http://www.nytimes.com/interactive/2010/11/28/world/20101128-cables-viewer.html#report/spy-09STATE80163.

29. State Department, "Reporting and Collection Needs: Palestinian Issues," October 31, 2008, http://www.wikileaks.org/cable/2008/10/08STATE116392.html.

30. Jones, "The National HUMINT Requirements Tasking Center."

31. U.S. Congress, House Permanent Select Committee, *IC 21: Intelligence Community in the 21st Century* (Washington, DC: U.S. Government Printing Office, 1996), 194n; Ken Dilanian, "Data-Seeking Cables Ignored, Officials Say," *Los Angeles Times*, December 3, 2010, A8; Mark Mazzetti, "Blurring Line Between Spy and Diplomat," *New York Times*, November 29, 2010, A1, A11.

32. Office of the Director of National Intelligence, ODNI Press Release No. 3–05, "Establishment of National Clandestine Service (NCS)," October 13, 2005; information provided by the CIA Public Affairs Office.

33. U.S. Congress, Senate Select Committee on Intelligence, *U.S. Actions Regarding Iranian and Other Arms Transfers to the Bosnian Army, 1994–1995*, 3; U.S. Congress, House Select Committee to Investigate Covert Arms Transactions with Iran and Senate Select Committee on Secret Military Assistance to Iran and the Nicaraguan Opposition, *Report of the Congressional Committees Investigating the Iran-Contra Affair with Supplemental, Minority, and Additional Views* (Washington, DC: U.S. Government Printing Office, 1987), 376–377; Caspar Weinberger, Memorandum to the Secretary of the Army, Subject: DOD Support to [CIA Special] Activities, June 13, 1983, 1; U.S. Congress, Senate Select Committee on Intelligence, *U.S. Actions Regarding Iranian and Other Arms Transfers to the Bosnian Army, 1994–1995*, 1996, 3.

34. William G. Hinsleigh, "Covert Action: An Update," *Studies in Intelligence* (Spring 1986).

35. Ibid.; NSDD 159, "Covert Action Approval and Coordination Procedures," January 18, 1985; NSDD 266, "Implementation of the Recommendations of the President's Special Review Board," March 31, 1987, 7.

36. George W. Bush, National Security Presidential Directive 1 (NSPD-1), "Organization of the National Security Council System," February 13, 2001.

37. Barack Obama, Presidential Policy Directive 1, Subject: Organization of the National Security Council, February 13, 2009. The size and composition of the committee suggest that some smaller subcommittee would actually be responsible for covert action issues.

38. Barack Obama, "Executive Order 13526 of December 29, 2009, Classified National Security Information," *Federal Register* 75, no. 2 (January 5, 2010): 707–731, at 707–708.

39. *Documents from the U.S. Espionage Den (52): The U.S.S.R., the Aggressive East* (Tehran: Muslim Students Following the Line of the Imam, n.d.), 46–94; Army Regulation 381-47, "U.S. Army Offensive Counterintelligence Operations," May 15, 1982, B-1.

40. Barack Obama, "Executive Order 13526."

41. Security Committee, National Foreign Intelligence Board, "Sensitive Compartmented Information: Characteristics and Requirements," June 1984, 1.

42. Quoted in David Wise, *The Politics of Lying: Governmental Deception, Secrecy, and Power* (New York: Viking, 1973), 86.

43. Ronald Lewin, *The American Magic: Codes, Ciphers and the Defeat of Japan* (New York: Farrar, Straus & Giroux, 1982), 17; Anthony Cave Brown, *The Last Hero* (New York: Times Books, 1982), 183; Bamford, *The Puzzle Palace*, 314.

44. Bamford, *The Puzzle Palace*, 314; Nigel West, *MI6: British Secret Intelligence Service Operations, 1909–1945* (London: Weidenfeld and Nicolson, 1983), 163; Cave Brown, *The Last Hero*, 182; David Martin, *Wilderness of Mirrors* (New York: Harper & Row, 1980), 15.

45. Wise, *The Politics of Lying*, 83; Jack Anderson, "Syrians Strive to Oust Arafat as PLO Chief," *Washington Post*, November 10, 1982, D22; Bob Woodward, "ACDA Aide Faulted on Security," *Washington Post*, November 4, 1986, A1, A16; National Intelligence Council, *National Intelligence Daily (Cable)*, December 13, 1983; David Easter, "Code Words, Euphemisms and What They Can Tell Us About Cold War Anglo-American Communications Intelligence," *Intelligence and National Security* 27, no. 6 (December 2012): 875–895, at 883–884; "Classification: A Bigger Picture," *Cryptolog* 4, no. 10 (October 1977): 13–14.

46. "Director of Central Intelligence Declassification Decisions," May 18, 1998; SSO, USAF, Subject: Elimination of COMINT and TK Codewords, October 22, 1999; SSO, DIA, Subject: Implementation Guidance for Elimination of Codewords, October 22, 1999.

47. Special Security Directorate, Office of the National Counterintelligence Executive, Director of National Intelligence, *Intelligence Community Markings System: Register and Manual*, December 31, 2013, 91.

48. Easter, "Code Words, Euphemisms and What They Can Tell Us About Cold War Anglo-American Communications Intelligence," 886; "Indoctrination for Sensitive Series COMINT," January 29, 2009, Enclosure 14, Prosecution Motion, *United States of America v. Manning, Bradley E.*, June 22, 2012; Richard D. Sylvester, "The Mysteries of GAMMA," *Cryptolog* 17, no. 1 (1990): 21.

49. Special Security Directorate, Office of the National Counterintelligence Executive, Director of National Intelligence, *Intelligence Community Markings System: Register and Manual*, 91; Bob Woodward, "Messages of Activists Intercepted," *Washington Post*, October 13, 1975, 1, 14; Seymour Hersh, *The Price of Power: Kissinger in the Nixon White House* (New York: Summit, 1983), 183.

50. Inspector General, Department of Defense, IR-96-03, *Final Report on the Verification Inspection of the National Security Agency*, February 13, 1996, 13; SSO DIA, Subject: Implementation Guidance for Elimination of Codewords; Office of the Under Secretary of Defense for Intelligence, *Classification and Control Markings Implementation Manual*, April 1, 2008, 15; National Reconnaissance Office, *National Reconnaissance Office: Review and Redaction Guide for Automatic Declassification of 25-Year Old Information, Version 1*, 2006, 119; National Security Agency, *RAMPART-A Project Overview*, October 10, 2010; "The US Classification System," *Top Level Telecommunications*, September 13, 2013, http://electrospaces.blogspot.gr/2013/09/the-us-classification-system.html; National Security Agency/Central Security Service, *Classification Guide for ECI WHIPGENIE*, May 21, 2004.

51. Office of the Inspector General, National Security Agency/Central Security Service, *ST-09-0002 Working Draft*, March 24, 2009, 12; Marc Ambinder and D. B. Grady, *Deep State: Inside the Government Secrecy Industry* (New York: Wiley, 2013), 246–247.

52. Seymour Hersh, *"The Target Is Destroyed": What Really Happened to Flight 007 and What America Knew About It* (New York: Random House, 1986), 4; private information.

53. Special Security Directorate, Office of the National Counterintelligence Executive, Director of National Intelligence, *Intelligence Community Markings System: Register and Manual*, 99; Dwight D. Eisenhower, Memorandum for the Secretary of State et al., August 26, 1960, in *CORONA: America's First Satellite Program*, ed. Kevin Ruffner (Washington, DC: CIA, 1995), 75.

54. James Ott, "Espionage Trial Highlights CIA Problems," *AW&ST*, November 27, 1978, 21–22; Gregory A. Fossedal, "U.S. Said to Be Unable to Verify Missile Ban," *Washington Times*, November 18, 1987, A6; Dale Van Atta, "The Death of the State Secret," *New Republic*, February 18, 1985, 20–23; SSO, USAF, Subject: Elimination of COMINT and TK Codewords; SSO, DIA, Subject: Implementation Guidance for Elimination of Codewords; "Classification: A Bigger Picture."

55. Admiral David Jeremiah et al., *Report to the Director of the National Reconnaissance Office: Defining the Future of the NRO for the 21st Century*, August 26, 1996, 171; Peter B. Teets, Memorandum for the Director of Central Intelligence, Subject: Retirement of the BYEMAN Control System, January 4, 2005.

56. Teets, Memorandum for the Director of Central Intelligence, Subject: Retirement of the BYEMAN Control System.

57. Special Security Directorate, Office of the National Counterintelligence Executive, Director of National Intelligence, *Intelligence Community Markings System: Register and Manual*, 73–86; Donald M. Kerr, Principal Deputy Director of National Intelligence, Memorandum for: Vice Admiral Robert B. Murrett, Subject: Establishment of KLONDIKE Control System, December 14, 2007.

58. Special Security Directorate, Office of the National Counterintelligence Executive, Director of National Intelligence, *Intelligence Community Markings System: Register and Manual*, 63–72.

59. Ibid., 57–62; "Memorandum of Understanding Between the National Security Agency/Central Security Service and the Chief of Naval Operations Governing Definitions, Access, and

Dissemination Control Policies for [Deleted] Under the Protection of the ENDSEAL Program," December 23, 2004.

60. Special Security Directorate, Office of the National Counterintelligence Executive, Director of National Intelligence, *Intelligence Community Markings System: Register and Manual*, 57–62; "Memorandum of Understanding Between the National Security Agency/Central Security Service and the Chief of Naval Operations Governing Definitions, Access, and Dissemination Control Policies for [Deleted] Under the Protection of the ENDSEAL Program."

61. Director of National Intelligence, *FY 2013 Congressional Budget Justification*, vol. 1: *National Intelligence Program Summary*, February 2012, 2, 135; Headquarters U.S. Air Force, Assistant Chief of Staff, Intelligence, INOI 205-4, "Designation of Special Security Officer (SSO), TK Control Officer (TCO), Gamma Control Officer (GCO), and Bravo Control Officer (BCO)," March 15, 1985, 2; private information.

62. Norman Polmar and Michael White, *Project AZORIAN: The CIA and the Raising of the K-129* (Annapolis, MD: Naval Institute Press, 2010), 59, 63; David H. Sharp, *The CIA's Greatest Covert Operation: Inside the Daring Mission to Recover a Nuclear-Armed Soviet Sub* (Lawrence: University Press of Kansas, 2012), ix, 42–47.

63. Bob Woodward, *Bush at War* (New York: Simon & Schuster, 2002), 101; Bob Woodward, *Obama's Wars* (New York: Simon & Schuster, 2010), 6.

64. Ambinder and Grady, *Deep State*, 166–167; Dana Priest and William M. Arkin, *Top Secret America: The Rise of the New American Security State* (Boston: Little, Brown, 2011), 19–20, 32.

65. Office of the Under Secretary of Defense for Intelligence, *Department of Defense Classification and Control Markings Implementation Manual*, 33; Director of Central Intelligence Directive 1/7, "Security Controls on the Dissemination of Intelligence Information," April 12, 1995, 3; Scott Armstrong, "Israelis Have Spied on U.S. Secret Papers Show," *Washington Post*, February 1, 1982, A1, A18; "Israel Calls Report on CIA Findings Ridiculous," *Washington Post*, February 3, 1982, 10.

66. Stephen A. Cambone, Memorandum, Subject: Security Classification Marking Instructions, September 27, 2004, with att: "Security Classification Marking Instructions."

67. National Foreign Intelligence Board Security Committee, "Sensitive Compartmented Information," 3; George Bush, National Security Directive 67, "Single Scope Background Investigations," October 21, 1991; U.S. Strategic Command, USSTRATCOM Administrative Instruction 321-28, *Sensitive Compartmented Information (SCI) Personnel Security Operating Policy and Procedures*, June 30, 1992, 25–27.

68. Intelligence Community Directive 703, "Protection of Classified National Intelligence, Including Sensitive Compartmented Information," June 21, 2013.

69. Intelligence Community Directive 704, "Personnel Security Standards and Procedures Governing Eligibility for Access to Sensitive Compartmented Information and Other Controlled Access Program Information," October 1, 2008; Intelligence Community Policy Guidance 704.3, "Denial or Revocation of Access to Sensitive Compartmented Information, Other Controlled Access Program Information, and Appeals Processes," October 2, 2008.

70. Intelligence Community Directive 705, "Sensitive Compartmented Information Facilities," May 26, 2010; Intelligence Community Standard Number 705–1, "Physical and Technical Security Standards for Sensitive Compartmented Information Facilities," September 17, 2010; Intelligence Community Standard Number 705–2, "Standards for the Accreditation and Reciprocal Use of the Sensitive Compartmented Information," September 17, 2010.

71. Intelligence Community Standard Number 705-1, "Physical and Technical Security Standards for Sensitive Compartmented Information Facilities."

20

ISSUES

Several U.S. Intelligence Community activities—particularly those of the Central Intelligence Agency (CIA), Federal Bureau of Investigation (FBI), and National Security Agency (NSA)—have been the focus of intense controversy in recent years, especially due to the revelations that resulted from Edward Snowden's provision of documents to journalists. One of those controversies involves the scope of U.S. intelligence activities, both in terms of targets and collection methods. Another has to do with the methods used by the CIA to combat al-Qaeda and associated groups—including targeted killings, renditions, and enhanced interrogation techniques (EITs)—and the legal justifications employed. The battle between the CIA and the Senate Select Committee on Intelligence over release of the committee's report on CIA rendition, detention, and interrogation techniques has been a recent focal point for the controversy.

NSA and FBI collection activities that have gathered data on U.S. persons—including their telephone and Internet use—have also been the subject of intense debate. The extent of those collection activities and the interrelated question of their constitutionality have been the subject of investigation and commentary. A related issue, raised by the Snowden disclosures, is the nature of congressional intelligence oversight—specifically the extent to which members of oversight committees are willing or able to provide critical review of Intelligence Community activities.

Both the Snowden case and the Barack Obama administration's unprecedented legal actions and investigations concerning leakers and journalists represent the latest installment in the battle between the government and the media concerning the unauthorized disclosure of national security secrets. Not unrelated is the issue of transparency—the extent to which an administration or Intelligence Community is willing to disclose information relevant to public understanding of intelligence—either through proactive disclosure or in response to Freedom of Information Act (FOIA) requests.

It is also important to consider the possibility that a better understanding of issues with regard to Intelligence Community activities may be gained by considering that some problems, including actions that limit privacy and undercut civil liberties, as well as a resistance to transparency, are not unique to national security or intelligence organizations. Indeed, they are not unique to the federal government.

SPYING ALL OVER THE WORLD

That the United States, specifically the Special Collection Service, had been eaves-dropping on the mobile phone calls of German chancellor Angela Merkel was un-doubtedly one of the most controversial revelations due to Edward Snowden. That the United States also targeted the communications of over 122 other foreign leaders was also a cause of controversy—how much depended on the identity of the targets and their inclination to express objections to the practice.

Many of the objections, particularly from Germany, stemmed from the premise that allies shouldn't spy on allies. The history of intelligence suggests, however, that not only is spying on allies (at least, most allies) not unprecedented—it is common practice. The United States and Israel, while strategic allies, have been engaged in decades-long intelligence collection efforts directed against each other. The Jonathan Jay Pollard case is the best-known component of the Israeli effort, but other aspects of that effort, including the collection of scientific and technical intelligence, have often been reported. In early 2015, there were allegations that Israel had conducted commu-nications intelligence and human intelligence (HUMINT) operations targeted on the U.S-Iranian nuclear talks. The United States, for its part, has used spy satellites and spy planes to photograph Israeli military and nuclear facilities and signals intelligence (SIGINT) satellites and Special Collection Service sites to intercept Israeli commu-nications. The presence of "Special Arabic" (aka Hebrew) translators at the Menwith Hill Station reflects targeting of Israeli communications employing overhead SIGINT assets. In Washington, D.C., the FBI has wiretapped the Israeli embassy. The CIA also received information from at least one human source in the Israeli Defense Forces during the 1980s.[1]

The reality is that for all but the closest allies, U.S. security interests may require collection against targets, government or private, located in an allied nation. Obtain-ing the cooperation necessary from the ally may be impossible for a variety of reasons, such as legal constraints on its security and legal apparatus, capability and/or resource constraints, political constraints, or a conflict of interest. In the case of Germany, the intelligence services are not permitted to share information with the United States that might be employed for drone strikes.[2] In addition, there may be concerns that an ally is unable to live up to military commitments or to protect sensitive information shared with it or that it is planning to initiate military action.

Beyond legal constraints, Germany provides a number of examples that illustrate a case for the United States occasionally conducting unilateral intelligence operations against German targets. Two words, "Hamburg Cell," provide a reminder that some of the key participants in the 9/11 attack on the United States planned the assault while living in a German city. A few years later, as the 2003 invasion of Iraq approached, the German Federal Intelligence Service (BND) deceived the CIA about the Iraqi defector code-named CURVEBALL, whose statements seemed to confirm U.S. claims of Iraqi biological weapons activities. The deception involved false claims by the BND that the defector hated Americans and could not speak English. In addition, a number of German corporations have been willing to sell to Iran and Iraq advanced technologies that would assist those nations in attaining weapons of mass destruction, particularly nuclear weapons. And at least one German firm has been reported to have "done over a billion dollars of business for Iranian companies associated with Iran's conventional military and ballistic missile procurement programs, including companies blacklisted by the U.S., the United Nations, and the European Union." German companies may have also provided assistance to the Syrian chemical weapons program.[3]

But that doesn't necessarily imply that every intelligence technique is acceptable or advisable with regard to every possible target in Germany or the other nations that fall outside the FIVE EYES (United Kingdom, Australia, Canada, and New Zealand) alliance. Any particular country contains a multitude of potential target types: leadership, military communications links, terrorist cells, and corporations specializing in certain technologies. And within each category are the specific potential targets. At the same time, a multitude of classes of intelligence techniques can be used to gather intelligence: imagery, SIGINT, measurement and signature intelligence, and human intelligence. And those classes contain a significant number of different techniques. SIGINT can involve remote interception from space, from an embassy-based listening post, or from an audio device placed in a residence (including a bedroom). HUMINT might be obtained from a junior member of a ministry or a member of a prime minister's staff.

The potential choices can be represented by a huge matrix of techniques down the side and countries and targets across the top. For each resulting cell, there is a yes or no choice to be made. In many cases, when dealing with an ally, a no decision may be the most appropriate—as when the choice concerns monitoring the cell phone of the chancellor of a close ally. But that doesn't imply that a yes decision would not be appropriate for another target in the chancellor's country, such as the chief executive officer of a firm doing business with Iran. Likewise, it might make sense to operate a human source in an ally's defense forces, whereas running an agent inside the prime minister's office might be considered a step too far.

FIGHTING TERROR

Even more controversial than U.S. spying on allies are some of the activities associated with the war on terror that has been waged since the attacks of September 11, 2001—particularly the use of EITs, some of which have been labeled, including by President Obama, as torture. In addition, several aspects of the use of drones to conduct targeted killings have produced vociferous objections.

Waterboarding has been used in trying to extract information from three al-Qaeda officials, including Khalid Sheikh Mohammed, the mastermind of 9/11, and facilitator Abu Zubaydah. Former CIA director Leon Panetta, as well as CIA officials with direct knowledge of the use of EITs, including Jose Rodriguez, have asserted that they elicited valuable information concerning al-Qaeda activities. Rodriguez has charged, "Almost every critic who dismisses the results of the EIT program is someone who did not then and does not now have access to the full output of the interrogation from the detainees."[4]

Critics of the practice have included former CIA officers, FBI agents, authors, and activists, who have objected on the grounds of morality as well as effectiveness. Former FBI agent Ali Soufan, who was involved in some interrogations, has claimed that approved interrogation techniques and even more severe ones will not get the desired results because "terrorists are trained to resist torture . . . the sort of torture they would expect if caught by dictatorships," including "being attacked by dogs, being sodomized, and having family members raped in front of them." Thus, according to Soufan, "sleep deprivation and nudity would be unlikely to work on a regular terrorist, let alone someone of Abu Zubaydah's stature and experience." The author of a book on the FBI's response to terror has dismissed the whole notion of a ticking-time-bomb scenario—often a justification in television shows or movies for the use of torture— claiming that "it had never happened in history."*⁵

It may be impossible to reconcile alternative versions of the extent to which water-boarding or other harsh techniques have produced valuable intelligence, particularly given the destruction of tapes of the persuasion efforts by CIA officials. And it is certainly clear that some detainees are eager to talk and others are more likely to respond to a kinder, gentler approach.⁶ It might also be argued that in dealing with a large population of detainees in one place, avoiding harsh tactics may produce "better" results overall (measured by some combination of quantity, quality, and timeliness).

Yet, many of the critics seem to demonstrate such an intense ideological commitment to the belief that torture never works and is always wrong as to suggest that they may be unwilling to credit any success to enhanced interrogation methods.† Indeed, the presumptions that the Senate Select Committee on Intelligence's (SSCI) much awaited and highly controversial report on CIA detention and interrogation report is actual proof that the CIA's enhanced interrogation program did not produce actionable intelligence—and that the objections of the CIA and several former CIA directors and others involved in the program yielded valuable intelligence and that the report is fatally flawed due to bias (including that of SSCI chairman Dianne Feinstein) can simply be dismissed are far from obvious.⁷

One indication of bias is the extent to which there was an uncritical willingness to accept the anticipated conclusions of the SSCI report—even before publication of the report, and certainly before the report could be subject to critical analysis. Some of the very same individuals who weren't willing to accept (with good reason) Senator Feinstein's reassurance concerning the utility of the NSA's bulk collection program had no problem uncritically embracing her and her staff's claims concerning the CIA interrogation program.

Further supporting suspicion of a severe lack of objectivity are some implausible claims by some critical of the use of EITs. One such implausible notion is the claim

---

*The television show *24* is the best-known example. Another is the 2010 film *Unthinkable*, starring Samuel L. Jackson and centering on a former member of the U.S. Special Forces who claims to have obtained four nuclear devices and threatens their detonation within days unless the president announces the withdrawal of U.S. forces from the Middle East. The most recent controversy concerning the efficacy of EITs concerns the depiction of their use in *Zero Dark Thirty* (2012) to help locate Osama bin Laden's compound.

†Actually, one might suggest that there are four pillars to the belief system—that torture is always wrong, that it never works, that if it does work one should pretend that it doesn't, and that no film director should win a significant award for directing a film that suggests torture might work. See Jennifer Marsico, "The Snubbing of Bigelow," www.nationalreview.com, January 29, 2013, http://www.nationalreview.com/article/339026/snubbing-bigelow-jennifer -marsico; "Zero Dark Feinstein," *Wall Street Journal*, December 27, 2012, A12.

that a terrorist will be immune to certain techniques if he or she knows of them or of possible worse techniques. There is a difference between being informed about what could happen and experiencing it. And one could make a more plausible argument that knowing about interrogators' psychological ploys would render terrorists less vulnerable to them. Equally implausible is the claim that there are no ticking-time-bomb situations. Every plot with a beginning, middle, and end on this planet (as opposed to a science fiction scenario in which the plot is prepared in an alternative universe) represents such a situation in one sense or another—whether it involves flying hijacked aircraft into buildings or bombs detonating in London or Madrid.

Nor is it plausible that information obtained by such techniques would be completely unreliable. Much information can potentially be verified, such as where a terrorist is hiding, where improvised explosive devices are being made, when and where someone is crossing a border, and the target of the next attack. The assertion that terrorists are immune to EITs or worse techniques and those techniques won't yield reliable information only indicates that the critics who make that argument are starting from a revulsion or professional opposition to the technique and accepting any claims that support their perspective without critical analysis.

Drone strikes have also been another source of controversy with regard to the loss of innocent life, standards for striking at a particular moment, and targeting American citizens. Numerous reports indicate a discrepancy between U.S. claims concerning civilian deaths and those made by outside groups—claims that may be impossible to settle given the U.S. desire to minimize both civilian deaths and estimates of those deaths and for groups on the receiving end of drone strikes to maximize estimated casualties. But as the number of strikes increases and the target set expands, there will certainly be more civilian deaths than otherwise.[8]

The issue of targeting Americans is particularly thorny and provides an example of another attempt by government lawyers to twist language to make policy seem to conform to law. A number of critics have questioned the authority of the president to approve targeted killing of American citizens like Anwar al-Awlaki, objecting that such actions violate the due process requirement of the Constitution. Taking the easy way out, the administration has claimed that those due process requirements are met by presidential consideration of the merits of killing such an individual, even though no judicial process is involved.[9]

An alternative response would be to argue that an individual who joins a terrorist group at war with the United States, who moves to a locale where he or she cannot be easily extradited or captured (that is, without a significant risk to the lives of U.S. personnel or the potential to escape custody), and engages in operational activities in support of that terrorist group forfeits any claim to due process. A hypothetical parallel might be an American nuclear scientist who moved to Germany in 1941 and went to work in the German nuclear weapons program. Would it be any more or less acceptable to arrange for his death than for the death of a current-day American who becomes involved in operational activities for al-Qaeda?

Another objection that has more merit is concern over the definition of "imminent" in administration legal documents concerning drone strikes. The documents manage to conflate imminent threat with existing threat—that is, any al-Qaeda or other designated terrorist official is at any time an imminent threat. Such a definition of "imminent" creates problems as to when a drone strike may be justified and when it is not. An al-Qaeda official in a crowd of innocent people and about, intelligence suggests, to call a phone number that will trigger a terrorist attack can be considered an imminent threat, and thus a certain loss of innocent life could be justified. But without intelligence suggesting he is about to make such a call, there is an argument for delaying the strike. There is no certainty that delaying it will cost innocent lives, but launching a strike most definitely will.[10]

BULK COLLECTION

The revelation in December 2005 that the United States was engaging in warrantless wiretapping of those suspected of terrorist connections produced criticism that the administration was flouting the legislation that created the Foreign Intelligence Surveillance Court as well as Fourth Amendment constitutional protections. But according to reports the targets of such operations were hundreds of people at any one time. In contrast, the bulk collection program first revealed in June 2013 potentially targeted every single individual who made a phone call to any person for any reason. And if the program did not wind up gathering calling data for every individual for every call, it involved gathering data on tens of millions of phone calls.[11]

At least three aspects of the effort, in addition to the deception about the existence and nature of the program, are disturbing. One is the attempted reassurance that the program did not involve actually listening to phone calls, which missed the point—purposely it seemed—that analyzing calling data (metadata) could reveal more than just listening to an occasional phone call. As a variety of individuals have pointed out, calling data allows identification of the individuals or organizations called, how often, when, and the length of the conversation. The data can reveal medical issues, intimate personal relationships, psychological issues, and political activities. The collection of such information represents an invasion of privacy, even if it were to sit unexamined.[12]

In addition, the effort relies on a Supreme Court decision, in some key ways not truly relevant to claims that bulk collection is legitimate, and pleading its relevance to a secret court with no opportunity for opposing views to be presented. The case in question, the 1979 *Smith v. Maryland* case, involved the Baltimore police having identified a suspect in a theft and a victim who reported that she had been receiving calls from an individual who claimed to be the culprit. Based on that information the police requested that the relevant phone company provide data on the suspect's phone calls. The phone company did so, and this led to confirmation that the suspect had been calling the victim. Application for a warrant to search his apartment followed and was granted, leading to his conviction. The Supreme Court, by a 5–3 vote, rejected the defendant's appeal that the pen register placed on his phone was an unconstitutional search, on the grounds that he had no expectation of privacy with regard to the calling data because it was freely made available to a third party (the phone company).[13]

But an honest appraisal of the case and its relevance to the desire to obtain calling records en masse would certainly note a significant disparity. The Baltimore Police Department was not claiming that in order to deal with an ongoing threat of crime, it should be given access to the calling data of every individual in Baltimore for the next three months, with the likelihood of follow-up requests. Had it done so, the request would likely have been denied quickly and decisively.

Further, the third-party doctrine is flawed in an obvious way. Provision of information to a third party does not, as noted by Potter Stewart in his *Smith v. Maryland* dissent, equate to an expectation that it may be turned over to others whenever the holder wishes. One can ask how customers of a variety of enterprises would react if their transactional data were made freely available to any outsiders interested in it. Imagine if a phone company allowed anyone (whether for a fee or for free) to enter a phone number in the database and receive the calling data associated with that number, or if a credit card company allowed searches of all the purchases by any of its cardholders. Some very angry customers would object that their privacy had been grossly violated because they believed that those enterprises were obliged to treat the information about their personal activities as confidential or at least to limit what information they provided and to whom.*

SECRECY, TRANSPARENCY, AND LEAKS

In the prolonged history of the confrontation between the media and the executive branch over unauthorized disclosures (i.e., leaks), the Obama administration represents one of the most significant eras—although some actions by executive branch agencies are products not of the administration in which they occurred but of their internal cultures and policies.[14]

Still, the Obama administration has prosecuted and jailed more leakers than all previous post–World War II administrations combined. And its Justice Department tried, backing off in the face of public opposition, to authorize agencies to replace the "Glomar" response to FOIA requests—a refusal to confirm or deny the existence of requested records—with a lie stating that no records exist. It has also, on several occasions, embraced the State Sercrets privilege, which generally permits the executive branch to refuse to disclose secret documents or information to any citizen in court.[15]

The administration also faced disclosures due to Bradley (now Chelsea) Manning, whom they successfully prosecuted, and Edward Snowden, who has eluded the grasp of the assorted government agencies that would like to apprehend him. In both cases, the usual claims of immense damage followed, although it is not clear that significant damage—in terms of actual harm to the nation—has resulted or ever will. Such an outcome would not be unprecedented, as past claims of damage from either authorized or unauthorized disclosures have often been made too casually and with too little (or even no) evidence, even by those who should know better. One of many examples is the 2000 report of the National Commission for the Review of the National Reconnaissance Office (NRO), which portrayed a golden age of secrecy about NRO operations prior to its 1992 declassification, despite the fact that espionage cases involving the existence and capabilities of key NRO systems—including the RHYOLITE SIGINT and KH-11 imagery satellites—took place well before 1992. More recently,

---

*NSA had considered ending the bulk collection program because "some officials believed the cost outweighed the meager counterterrorism benefits." See Ken Dilanian, Associated Press, "AP Exclusive: Before Leak, NSA Mulled Ending Phone Program," www.washingtonpost .com, March 29, 2015, http://www.washingtonpost.com/politics/federal_government/ap -exclusive-before-leak-nsa-mulled-ending-phone-program/2015/03/29/8e038c6e-d60c-11e4 -bf0b-f648b95a6488_story.html.

claims during the Bush administration that the *New York Times* disclosure about wireless wiretapping would tell terrorists something they didn't already know—that their communications might be monitored—ignored overwhelming evidence that terrorists were already well aware of the possibility.[16]

At the same time, the potential value of disclosure is often ignored. Leaks about the lack of evidence concerning the Gulf of Tonkin incident could possibly have deprived Lyndon Johnson of the freedom to escalate the level of U.S. efforts in Vietnam and the number of draftees sent there. And it is unequivocally clear that without the Snowden disclosures, there would have been no declassification of documents by the NSA and Office of the Director of National Intelligence, no review groups chartered and no report, no reports by the Privacy and Civil Liberties Oversight Board on the contested programs, and certainly no reforms or legislative proposals to curb those activities.*

There has clearly been a retreat on the part of many (but certainly not all) elements of the Intelligence Community concerning the provision of information—either through proactive disclosures or in responses to FOIA and Mandatory Declassification Review requests. It has retreated not only from the policies of the Clinton administration but even from those of the Reagan and George W. Bush administrations.

One notable change is that while the Bush administration disclosed the existence and key judgments of several National Intelligence Estimates, including those on Iraq, Afghanistan, and terrorism, the Obama administration has released no information on such estimates. In addition to the lack of discretionary releases, there do not seem to have been any releases of national estimates in response to FOIA requests. In response to a request for "any 2009–2012 NIE's or IIM's [Interagency Intelligence Memoranda] with the words 'Cyber,' 'Cyberwar,' or 'Cyberwarfare' in the title," the Office of the Director of National Intelligence responded that responsive documents were located but "must be withheld in their entirety."[17]

And in recent years, the informative website for the National Intelligence Council simply disappeared. The Defense Intelligence Agency (DIA), which in the early 1980s would promptly release its organization and functions manual in response to a FOIA request now posts a chart for the entire organization on its website but will release no further information about any component—FOIA requests for such information are denied in their entirety. DIA's secrecy was further exacerbated when recent director Michael Flynn, who spoke of the need for transparency in his departing remarks, ordered the agency to stop producing its unclassified in-house journal, *Communiqué*, which provided valuable information on DIA organization and operations and

---

*Snowden and journalist Glenn Greenwald, one of the primary conveyors of Snowden's disclosures, have been criticized not only by many establishment and conservative commentators but by assorted members of the Left, in some cases because of perceived libertarian "antistate" sympathies as well as the extent of the disclosures—which go beyond purely domestic collection. While it is impossible to be confident that no damage will result as the result of the disclosures, the simple distinction between foreign and domestic ignores the extent to which foreign intelligence activities can produce intelligence on U.S. citizens. It also seems to be based on the assumption that there should be no concern for the privacy of foreign nationals—that the United States need not have any ethical standards for SIGINT collection outside the United States. To hold such a position and object to activities such as bulk collection would seem to be somewhat hypocritical.

was easily obtainable via the Freedom of Information Act. The National Geospatial-Intelligence Agency has adopted a similar approach with regard to information about its organizational structure. In each case the agency has relied on congressional authorization to arbitrarily withhold organizational information, proving that some agencies will abuse any available exemptions and that congressional action can hinder rather than advance transparency. The U.S. Special Operations Command, without such congressional authority, has simply resorted to claiming inappropriate FOIA exemptions to forestall release of its rather unremarkable organizational chart—most recently asserting that because it contained the names of representatives from organizations such as the NRO, the chart could not be released, as if the command has never heard of the requirement to release segregable information or lacks any means of blacking out the names.[18]

The CIA has often adopted the tactic of implausibly claiming that requested documents are exempt in entirety—that is, not a single sentence can be released. It usually asserts that the entire document is exempt because the information is classified and reveals data about sources and methods. In recent years it has claimed that the charter of the now defunct Center for Climate Change and National Security, as well as all reports over five pages in length produced by the center, were exempt in entirety. The agency also claimed that numerous articles from its *Studies in Intelligence* journal were exempt in their entirety—including those on the founding of the Office of Special Operations (established in the late 1940s), national intelligence support to the Transportation Command, and the origins of nuclear intelligence. Such claims were clearly absurd and conclusively shown to be so when the CIA released those articles as a result of an unrelated lawsuit—and significant portions were clearly unclassified and marked as such. It was not the first example of the CIA's having two standards for disclosure: what it can get away with in response to a FOIA request, and what it can get away with when coming in front of a judge. Similarly, the Department of Justice denied in its entirety a request for a report by its Inspector General concerning FBI activities under Section 702 of the Foreign Intelligence Surveillance Act Amendments of 2008—but managed to release substantial portions of the 284-page document when faced with legal action by the *New York Times*.[19]

The solution to this lack of transparency, and at times duplicity, is partially an administration firmly committed to transparency—both internally and externally. But agencies resistant to disclosure can ignore or undermine broad directives in favor of transparency or a presumption for disclosure. Thus, it may be necessary, in some instances, to prohibit agencies from classifying or refusing to disclose certain information without a special waiver. In addition, the review of secrecy decisions and FOIA responses needs to be part of the mandate of adequately staffed offices of inspector generals who are firmly in support of disclosure and empowered to ensure good faith behavior and compliance.

CONGRESSIONAL OVERSIGHT

A number of events over the last several years have highlighted the utility and limitations of the oversight conducted by the House Permanent Select Committee on Intelligence (HPSCI) and the Senate Select Committee on Intelligence (SSCI), particularly with regard to informing the public about the organizations that receive tens of billions of dollars of taxpayer funds.

In the aftermath of the 2003 war with Iraq, the Senate Select Committee on Intelligence produced a series of detailed reports on the U.S. intelligence activities related to the decision to invade. More recently, the committees have held hearings and released reports on events such as Benghazi, the Boston Marathon bombings, and, as noted above, the massive executive summary of the committee's report on the CIA's rendition, detention, and interrogation program. The committees have also reacted to the Snowden disclosures with statements and hearings. As a result, they have provided some useful knowledge to the public to judge the wisdom and effectiveness of some Intelligence Community activities.[20]

But, as a whole, today's congressional oversight represents a pale legacy when compared to the early days of those committees, first established as temporary bodies in response to charges of improper CIA domestic activities. The Church and Pike committees conducted probing public hearings about Intelligence Community activities and brought new information into public view. Today, however, members of the committees are more likely to engage in unqualified defenses of Intelligence Community activities rather than critical examination. For example, HPSCI chairman Mike Rogers first suggested, without evidence, that Edward Snowden was working for Russian intelligence and later stated that Snowden should be charged with murder. He also asserted that NSA's bulk collection program did not violate the privacy of U.S. citizens as long as they did not know it was taking place. Similarly, his Senate counterpart denounced Snowden and made unsupported and false claims about the utility of the bulk collection program. As Representative Rush Holt (D-NJ) and Steven Aftergood, director of the Federation of American Scientists Project on Government Secrecy, wrote with regard to the House oversight committee, "That's the extent of the HPSCI's outrage: It is furious not at the NSA's abuses but rather at the disclosures of abuses."[21]

The committees also have a poor record in advancing transparency and declassification and seem to have no real interest in pushing agencies to be more transparent or more responsive with regard to FOIA requests or proactive disclosure. Nor have they been transparent about the oversight process: the SSCI blocked a former staffer from talking to the press about the process. Rather, they have served as enablers of secrecy, more interested in leak investigations and passing legislation that makes it easier to withhold data from the public. (A notable exception, although now two decades old, is the SSCI's push in 1991 to have the "fact of" the existence of the National Reconnaissance Office declassified.)[22]

Committee rules make it virtually impossible to alert the public, in any detail, to problems—whether they concern the amount of funds being spent on a program or possible threats to privacy and civil liberties. When the cost of a third MISTY stealth satellite had reached around $10 billion, some concerned members of the SSCI could only complain about an overly costly "major acquisition program." Even when Senators Ron Wyden (D-OR) and Mark Udall (D-CO) were disturbed by the nature of the executive branch's interpretation of Section 215 of the PATRIOT Act and the resulting bulk collection program, they could only offer vague warnings, such as the one that appeared in the August 2011 SSCI report on the Intelligence Authorization

Act for fiscal year 2012. They wrote, "The executive branch's decision to conceal the US government's official understanding of what this law means is unacceptable, and untenable in the long run."[23] But only as a result of the Edward Snowden leaks was the government's understanding exposed—with significant consequences. It is also notable that so few members of either committee have issued even vague complaints about such matters. In effect, they seem to represent another layer of executive branch review rather than protection for their constituents' civil liberties, privacy interests, and tax dollars.

A GOVERNMENT-WIDE PROBLEM

Hostility to privacy and civil liberties as well as transparency is not limited to the intelligence and national security components of the federal government—or to the federal government as a whole. Whether at the federal, state, or local level, one can expect government, liberal or conservative, to side with those wanting more data collection about citizens and more authority to act without court approval.

Among the more notable Supreme Court cases in recent years was *United States v. Jones*, which involved law enforcement installation, without a warrant, of a GPS tracker on the car of a suspected drug dealer while the car was on the suspect's property. The Supreme Court ruled, in January 2012, that such an action constituted a search under the Fourth Amendment, and an appeals court later found that such a search required a warrant. In an earlier case (*Kyllo v. United States*), a federal agent provided local police with a thermal imagery device that was employed to determine if high heat levels could be detected coming from the home of a suspected marijuana grower. The court, ruling 5–4 that such an action constituted a search under the Fourth Amendment, overturned the resulting conviction.[24]

Mass collection of data on citizens' activities is not just conducted by the FBI and NSA. In 1970, with President Richard Nixon's signing of the Bank Secrecy Act, all U.S. financial institutions were compelled to create a Currency Transaction Report, which reported the name, address, bank account data, and Social Security number for each customer that executed a cash transaction exceeding $10,000. In 2013 it was reported that the Consumer Financial Protection Bureau (CFPB) was demanding records from banks and purchasing information about at least 10 million consumers, an activity that resulted in its being compared to the NSA. Data collected included information on credit cards, mortgages, and financial products such as debt cancellation and checking account overdrafts. It was also reported that "such records are usually demanded by the CFPB during the routine inspection of U.S. banks, forcing them to comply with the request or face possible legal sanctions." In remarks similar to those of defenders of the FBI/NSA bulk collection program, the bureau's director stated, "The notion that we're tracking individual consumers or invading their privacy is quite wrong."[25]

In 2014 the Supreme Court adjudicated a case (*Riley v. California*) in which the state of California (with a liberal governor and even more liberal attorney general) argued that the police had the right to search the cell phones of anyone they arrested without any approval from a judge. The Supreme Court's 9–0 decision unequivocally rejected California's specious claims and arguments, informing the state's law enforcement agencies that if they wanted to examine the contents of a cell phone, they would just have to go to the trouble of obtaining a search warrant. Then, in late September 2014, the governor of California vetoed a bill that would have required police to obtain a warrant to conduct surveillance via drone, arguing that the exceptions in the law for emergency use were too narrow.[26]

Surveillance or intrusive demands for information on behalf of city governments can also be a problem for residents or businesses. Initiatives in Los Angeles, Oakland, and New York have sought to dramatically broaden the use of surveillance and data collection technologies in support of law enforcement in both low- and high-crime areas. Included among those technologies acquired by the Los Angeles Police Department are closed-circuit television, facial recognition software, license plate readers mounted on police cars or rooftops, and cameras that when attached to civilian airplanes can capture 10,000 times the area of a police helicopter. The New York Police Department "has a big data system that links 3,000 surveillance cameras with license plate readers, radiation sensors, criminal databases and terror suspect lists."[27]

Operators of motels and hotels in Los Angeles have faced a city ordinance that required them to turn over guest records without a warrant. The ordinance also required operators to record a guest's name and address; the make and license number of a guest's vehicle; the date and time of a guest's arrival; the scheduled date of departure; the guest's room number, rate, and method of payment; and the name of the employee who registered the guest. Failure to comply could results in a six-month jail sentence and a $1,000 fine. In late 2013, the Ninth Circuit Court of Appeals, in a 7–4 vote, ruled that the ordinance violated the Constitution—because it violated the rights of the operators, not the guests. In October 2014, the Supreme Court agreed to hear an appeal from the city of Los Angeles.[28]

It is also important to recognize that a preference for secrecy and opaqueness within government institutions at all levels may have nothing to do with national security issues. Such disclosures can reveal failures, misconduct, waste, or simply activities that officials would prefer not to have discussed publicly. Thus, the Obama administration has been reluctant to part with information on subjects such as the Troubled Assets Relief Program, the Solyndra debacle, and the Fast and Furious episode. Its Environmental Protection Agency has proved reluctant to release scientific studies that allegedly support its decision making. Agencies also seek to silence whistleblowers and those who would provide an alternative viewpoint to that of a given agency's "corporate communications" office. In 2006 an air marshal was fired after informing reporters of plans to cut security on longer flights—a revelation that spurred congressional action to forestall the cuts.* In 2011, when a senior scientist warned of design flaws at the Hanford facility to treat radioactive waste, he was assigned to work in a basement room that lacked furniture or a telephone. In 2014 the Customs and Border Protection agency instructed an agent who had spoken to the media to "immediately cease and desist."[29]

---

*In January 2015, the Supreme Court ruled in favor of the air marshal, stating that he was covered by a federal law that protected whistle-blowers. Adam Liptak, "Justices Rule Dismissal of Air Marshal Unlawful," *New York Times*, January 22, 2015, A15.

There has been a lack of transparency not only with regard to the public but even with regard to the executive branch's own watchdogs. As a result, in early August 2014 the chairmen and ranking members of the House Committee on Oversight and Government Reform and the House Homeland Security and Governmental Affairs from forty-seven inspectors general. They were writing "regarding the serious limitations on access to records that have recently impeded the work of Inspectors General at the Peace Corps, the Environmental Protection Agency, and the Department of Justice."[30]

State governments can also be less than forthcoming. It took a lawsuit to pry loose records of the Nevada Division of Insurance concerning the criminal histories of Obamacare navigators. In October 2014, the president of New York Public Radio complained that New Jersey governor Chris Christie's Inauguration Day pledge that "a new era of accountability and transparency is here" promised a change that never arrived, and records requests for information on taxpayer spending on the governor's out-of-state travel produced "a document so heavily redacted as to be all but meaningless." State universities can also be culprits. According to one account, "The University of Michigan Board of Regents routinely conducts its affairs behind closed doors, away from public scrutiny."[31]

At the local level, reporters covering northern Virginia police departments have found information routinely released by other departments, including incident reports, unavailable to them. One former police officer described a "striking lack of transparency" among the departments, while another account noted a police reporter's claim that the "default position of the Fairfax County Police Department is to decline all requests for information." And across the country, police have asserted "privacy rights" when placing people under arrest, seeking to prevent those acts from being photographed.[32]

Other examples of resistance to disclosure at the local level occurred in California in 2010. Information leaked to the press revealed a "series of administrative lapses that contributed to the deaths of children in the care of Los Angeles County," including a social worker's leaving an eleven-year-old at home alone after being told the boy was considering suicide. The response of the Los Angeles County Board of Supervisors was to order an investigation—into the leaks. The director of the Department of Children and Family Services complained that the leaks had created a morale issue for her colleagues. And in late 2011, planning officials of the city of Anaheim, following a Public Records Act request for communications between council members and the planning department, reportedly warned employees to purge computer files that might reflect poorly on the staff, officials, and developers.[33]

Across the country, the very liberal New York City administration has come under attack for failing to deliver on its promises of transparency. In late 2013, the New York Police Department ordered the city's seventy-seven precincts to stop providing information to the media on crimes occurring in their neighborhoods. According to a 2013 report by the Office of the New York City Public Advocate, a third of the FOIA requests received by the city were ignored. In addition, the city rejected a request for documentation on its accept-or-reject criteria.[34]

Such examples represent only the tip of the iceberg and suggest that we should at least consider with skepticism claims that intelligence and security agencies should be immune from transparency or respect for privacy instead of assuming such claims to be justified by the special requirements or conditions of intelligence and security activities.

Notes

1. Scott Shane, "Leak Offers Look at Efforts by U.S. to Spy on Israel," *New York Times*, July 6, 2011, A1, A6; Jeff Stein, "Spy vs. Spy: Espionage and the U.S.-Israel Rift," www.newsweek.com, March 25, 2015, http://www.newsweek.com/israel-spying-iran-nuclear-talks-barack-obama-benjamin-netanyahu-white-house-316623; Adam Entous, "Israel Spied on Iran Talks," *Wall Street Journal*, March 24, 2015, A1, A8.

2. Jochen Bittner, "Spies Unlike Us," *New York Times*, July 14, 2014, A17.

3. William E. Burrows and Robert Windrem, *Critical Mass: The Dangerous Race for Superweapons in a Fragmenting World* (New York: Simon & Schuster, 1994), 208–232; James Kirchick, "Why We Need to Spy on the Germans," *Daily Beast*, July 9, 2014, http://www.thedailybeast.com/articles/2014/07/09/why-we-need-to-spy-on-the-germans.html; Peter Fritsch and David Crawford, "Small Bank in Germany Tied to Iran Nuclear Effort," *Wall Street Journal*, July 9, 2010, A1, A14; Gunther Latsch, Fidelius Schmid, and Klaus Wiegrefe, "Did German Companies Aid Syrian Chemical Weapons Program?" *Spiegel Online*, January 23, 2015, http://www.spiegel.de/international/germany/german-companies-suspected-of-aiding-syrian-chemical-weapons-program-a-1014722.html.

4. Jose A. Rodriguez Jr., with Bill Harlow, *Hard Measures: How Aggressive CIA Actions After 9/11 Saved American Lives* (New York: Threshold, 2012)

5. Ali Soufan, *The Black Banners: The Inside Story of 9/11 and the War Against al-Qaeda* (New York: W. W. Norton, 2011), 398; Glenn L. Carle, *The Interrogator: An Education* (New York: Nation Books, 2011); Garrett M. Graff, *The Threat Matrix: The FBI at War in the Age of Global Terror* (Boston: Little, Brown, 2011), 378.

6. See Soufan, *The Black Banners*, for a discussion of this thesis. Also, Benjamin Weiser, "Some Captured Terrorists Talk Willingly and Proudly, Investigators Say," *New York Times*, October 14, 2014, A19.

7. U.S. Congress, Senate Select Committee on Intelligence, S. Report 113-288, *Committee Study of the Central Intelligence Agency's Detention and Interrogation Program Together with Foreword by Chairman Feinstein and Additional and Minority Views* (Washington, D.C.: Government Printing Office, 2014); John McLaughlin, "Senate Interrogation Report Distorts the CIA's Success at Foiling Terrorist Plots," www.washingtonpost.com, December 9, 2014, http://www.washingtonpost.com/opinions/senate-interrogation-report-distorts-the-cias-success-foiling-terrorist-plots/2014/12/09/de5b72ca-7e1f-11e4-9f38-95a187e4c1f7_story.html; Central Intelligence Agency, *CIA Comments on the Senate Select Committee on Intelligence Report on the Rendition, Detention, and Interrogation Program*, June 27, 2013, http://www.cia.gov; John O. Brennan, "The Senate Select Committee on Intelligence Study on the Former Detention and Interrogation Program: A Response," *Intelligencer* 21, no. 1 (Winter 2014–2015): 7–10.

8. Mark Landler, "Civilian Deaths Due to Drones Are Not Many, Obama Says," *New York Times*, January 31, 2012, A6; Richard Whittle, *Predator: The Secret Origins of the Drone Revolution* (New York: Henry Holt, 2014), 302–303.

9. Jacob Sullum, "Executive Kill Switch," *Reason*, January 2012, 10.

10. Department of Justice, White Paper, *Lawfulness of a Lethal Operation Directed Against a U.S. Citizen Who Is a Senior Operational Leader of al-Qa'ida or an Associated Force*, November 8, 2011; Jacob Sullum, "5 Disturbing Aspects of the DOJ White Paper on the President's License to Kill," www.reason.com, February 4, 2013, http://reason.com/blog/2013/02/04/the-fine-print-in-the-presidents-license.

11. Ellen Nakashima, "NSA Is Collecting Less Than 30 Percent of U.S. Call Data, Officials Say," www.washingtonpost.com, February 7, 2014, http://www.washingtonpost.com/world /national-security/nsa-is-collecting-less-than-30-percent-of-us-call-data-officials-say/2014/02/07 /234a0e9e-8fad-11e3-b46a-5a3d0d2130da_story.html.

12. Jonathan Mayer and Patrick Mutchler, "Metaphone: The Sensitivity of Telephone Metadata," Web Policy, March 12, 2014, http://webpolicy.org/2014/03/12/metaphone-the-senstivity -of-telephone-metadata.

13. U.S. Supreme Court, *Smith v. Maryland*, 442 U.S. 735, June 28, 1979, http://laws.findlaw .com/us/442/735.html.

14. The subject can be treated only briefly here. For more extensive examinations of the issues involved and contrasting views, see Gabriel Schoenfeld, *Necessary Secrets: National Security, the Media, and the Rule of Law* (New York: W. W. Norton, 2010); Jeffrey T. Richelson, "Intelligence Secrets and Unauthorized Disclosures: Confronting Some Fundamental Issues," *International Journal of Intelligence and Counterintelligence* 25, no. 4 (Winter 2012–2013): 639–677.

15. Charlie Savage, "Court Dismisses a Case Asserting Torture by C.I.A.," *New York Times*, September 9, 2010, A1, A3; Adam Liptak, "State Secrets Block Resolution of Contractors' Suit, Justices Say," *New York Times*, May 24, 2011, A17.

16. Richelson, "Intelligence Secrets and Unauthorized Disclosures"; National Commission for the Review of the National Reconnaissance Office, *The NRO at the Crossroads*, November 1, 2000, iv, 37–38; Jeffrey T. Richelson, "Back to Black," *Bulletin of the Atomic Scientists* (May–June 2001): 22–24, 74–75.

17. Jennifer Hudson, Director, Information Management Division, Office of the Director of National Intelligence, to Jeffrey T. Richelson, October 31, 2014.

18. James C. Boisselle, Deputy Chief of Staff, United States Special Operations Command, to Jeffrey T. Richelson, May 29, 2014.

19. See Jeffrey T. Richelson, ed., National Security Archive Electronic Briefing Book 493, *Studies in Intelligence: New Articles from the CIA's In-House Journal*, November 20, 2014, http://www2 .gwu.edu/~nsarchiv/NSAEBB/NSAEBB493; Office of the Inspector General, Department of Justice, *A Review of the Federal Bureau of Investigation's Activities Under Section 702 of the Foreign Intelligence Surveillance Act Amendments Act of 2008*, September 2012; Preet Bharara, United States Attorney Southern District of New York, To: David McCraw and Jeremy Kutner, Legal Department, The New York Times Company, January 9, 2015.

20. U.S. Congress, Senate Select Committee on Intelligence, *Report on the U.S. Intelligence Community's Prewar Intelligence Assessments on Iraq*, July 7, 2004; U.S. Congress, Senate Select Committee on Intelligence, *Review of Terrorist Attacks on U.S. Facilities in Benghazi, Libya, September 11–12, 2012, Together with Additional Views*, January 15, 2014; U.S. Congress, House Permanent Select Committee on Intelligence, *Investigative Report on the Terrorist Attacks on the U.S. Facilities in Benghazi, Libya, September 11–12, 2012*, November 21, 2014; U.S. Congress, House Committee on Homeland Security, *The Road to Boston: Counterterrorism Challenges and Lessons from the Boston Marathon Bombings*, March 2014.

21. Scott Shackford, "NSA Groupie Rep. Mike Rogers Wants Edward Snowden Charged with Murder," www.reason.com, October 22, 2014, http://reason.com/blog/2014/10/22/nsa -groupie-rep-mike-rogers-wants-edward; Representative Rush Holt and Steven Aftergood, "The House Committee on Intelligence Needs Oversight of Its Own," www.msnbc.com, May 30, 2014, http://www.msnbc.com/msnbc/who-watches-the-watchmen. Also see Darren Samuelsohn, "Hill Draws Criticism over NSA Oversight," *Politico*, March 2, 2014, http://www.politico .com/story/2014/03/hill-draws-criticism-over-nsa-oversight-104151.html; Yochai Benkler, "How The NSA and FBI Foil Weak Oversight," www.theguardian.com, October 16, 2013, http://www .theguardian.com/commentisfree/2013/oct/16/nsa-fbi-endrun-weak-oversight.

22. Brian Beutler, "Senate Intel Committee Blocks Former Staffer from Talking to the Press about Oversight Process," TPM.com, June 18, 2013, http://talkingpointsmemo.com/dc/senate-intel-committee-blocks-former-staffer-from-talking-to-press-about-oversight-process.

23. "Additional Views of Senators Wyden and Udall," in U.S. Congress, Senate Select Committee on Intelligence, Report 112-43, *Intelligence Authorization Act for Fiscal Year 2012*, August 1, 2011, 29–33.

24. Maryclaire Dale, Associated Press, "U.S. Appeals Court: Warrants Needed for GPS Tracking," Yahoo! News, November 3, 2013, http://news.yahoo.com/us-appeals-court-warrants-needed-gps-tracking-180615376.html.

25. Matt Welch, "Kiss Your Financial Privacy Goodbye," *Reason*, December 2014, 2; Carter Dougherty, "U.S. Amasses Data on 10 Million Consumers as Banks Object," Bloomberg, April 17, 2013, http://www.bloomberg.com/news/articles/2013-04-17/u-s-amasses-data-on-10-million-consumers-as-banks-object; Brendan Bordelon, "Consumer Financial Protection Bureau Compared to NSA," www.dailycaller.com, June 26, 2013, http://dailycaller.com/2013/06/26/consumer-financial-protection-bureau-compared-to-nsa.

26. Damon Root, "Supreme Court Announces Major Victory for Cellphone Privacy," www.reason.com, June 25, 2014, http://reason.com/blog/2014/06/25/supreme-court-announces-major-victory-fo; Zusha Elinson, "Bill Requiring Warrant for Drones Vetoed in California," *Wall Street Journal*, September 30, 2014, A6.

27. Darwin Bond-Graham and Ali Winston, "Forget the NSA: Local Government Is Surveilling Millions of Innocent L.A. Residents," *LA Weekly*, February 28–March 6, 2014, 10–11; Somini Sengupta, "Privacy Fears as Surveillance Grows in Cities," *New York Times*, October 14, 2013, A1, A16; Ed Krayewski, "L.A. Sheriff's Didn't Disclose Massive Surveillance Program, Because People Wouldn't Like It," www.reason.com, April 18, 2014, http://reason.com/blog/2014/04/18/la-sheriffs-department-didnt-disclose-ma.

28. Scott Shackford, "LA Motel Owners Fight Police Demands to Fork Over Guest Info," www.reason.com, July 1, 2013, http://reason.com/blog/2013/07/01/la-motel-owners-fight-police-demands-to; Joe Palazzolo, "Hotels' Privacy Rights Backed by Appeals Court," *Wall Street Journal*, December 26, 2013, A5; David G. Savage, "Supreme Court to Hear Hotel-Police Privacy Dispute," *Los Angeles Times*, October 21, 2014, AA1, AA7.

29. Gene Healy, "Obama's Solyndra Silence," *Reason*, November 8, 2011, http://reason.com/archives/2011/11/08/obamas-solyndra-silence; Dan Weinel, "Ex-Air Marshal Wins Whistle-Blower Case," *Los Angeles Times*, May 26, 2013, A18; Ryan Lovelace, "Border Patrol Agent Disciplined After Speaking with the Press," www.nationalreview.com, September 2, 2014, http://www.nationalreview.com/article/386804/border-patrol-agent-disciplined-after-speaking-press-ryan-lovelace; Lamar Smith, "What Is the EPA Hiding from the Public?," *Wall Street Journal*, June 24, 2014, A15.

30. Letter, Michael G. Carroll, Acting Inspector General, Agency for International Development, et al., to Darrell Issa, Thomas R. Carper, Elijah Cummings, and Tom Coburn, August 5, 2014.

31. Jillian Kay Melchior, "NR Wins Release of Nev. Obamacare Records," www.nationalreviewcom, February 7, 2014, http://www.nationalreview.com/article/370607/nr-wins-release-nev-obamacare-records-jillian-kay-melchior; Laura R. Walker, "The Secrets of New Jersey," *New York Times*, October 27, 2014, A25; Robby Soave, "The *Free Press* Is Suing Umich for Routinely Violating Open Meetings Law," www.reason.com, July 14, 2014, http://reason.com/blog/2014/07/14/the-free-press-is-suing-umich-for-routin.

32. Radley Balko, "Police Blackout," *Reason* (July 2010): 50–51; Radley Balko, "There's No Transparency and I Find That Inexcusable," www.reason.com, June 14, 2010, http://reason.com/archives/2010/06/14/theres-no-transparency-and-i-f; Radley Balko, "The War on Cameras," *Reason* (January 2011): 22–33.

33. Rong-Gong Lin II, "Aid in Leaks Probe Ordered," *Los Angeles Times*, August 18, 2010, AA1, AA5; "Leaks Don't Kill Kids," *Los Angeles Times*, August 21, 2010, A18; Jeff Gottlieb, "Anaheim Staffers Are Told to Delete E-mails," *Los Angeles Times*, December 6, 2012, AA1, AA2.

34. Murray Weiss, "NYPD Orders Precincts to Deny Journalists Access to Crime Reports," www.dnainfo.com, December 6, 2013, http://www.dnainfo.com/new-york/20131206/civic-center/nypd-orders-precincts-deny-journalists-access-crime-reports; Alyssa Hertig, "NYPD Claims Secrecy for Its Freedom of Information Request Criteria," www.reason.com, March 18, 2014, http://reason.com/blog/2014/03/18/nypd-shields-its-freedom.

ACRONYMS AND ABBREVIATIONS

ABM	Anti-Ballistic Missile
ACS	Assistant Chief of Staff
AEC	Atomic Energy Commission
AEDS	Atomic Energy Detection System
AFB	Air Force Base
AFIAA	Air Force Intelligence Analysis Agency
AFIC	Air Force Intelligence Command
AFIS	Air Force Intelligence Service
AFISA	Air Force Intelligence Support Agency
AFISRA	Air Force Intelligence, Surveillance, and Reconnaissance Agency
AFMIC	Armed Forces Medical Intelligence Center
AFOSI	Air Force Office of Special Investigations
AFRICOM	Africa Command
AFSA	Armed Forces Security Agency
AFSG	Air Force Security Group
AFSPC	Air Force Space Command
AFSS	Air Force Security Service
AFSSS	Air Force Space Surveillance System
AFTAC	Air Force Technical Applications Center
AIA	Air Intelligence Agency
AISR	Aerial Intelligence, Surveillance, and Reconnaissance
ALCOR	ARPA Lincoln C-Band Observables Radar
ALTAIR	ARPA Long-Range Tracking and Instrumentation Radar
AMOS	Air Force Maui Optical and Supercomputing Site
AOG	Army Operational Group
AOMC	Army Ordnance Missile Command
AQAP	Al-Qaeda in the Arabian Peninsula
AQIM	Al-Qaeda in the Lands of the Islamic Maghreb
ARIES	Airborne Reconnaissance Integrated Electronic System
ARPA	Advanced Research Projects Agency
ASARS-IIA	Advanced Synthetic Aperture Radar System IIA
ASD	Assistant Secretary of Defense; Australian Signals Directorate

ASIP	Advanced Signals Intelligence Payload
ASN	AFTAC Southern Network
ATRR	Advanced Technology Risk Reduction
ATS	Advanced Telemetry System
AW&ST	*Aviation Week & Space Technology*
BBC	British Broadcasting Corporation
BGIO	Bundeswehr Geoinformation Office (Germany)
BMEWS	Ballistic Missile Early Warning System
BND	Bundesnachrichtendienst (Federal Intelligence Service, Germany)
BNE	Board of National Estimates
BRUSA	British-U.S. Communications Intelligence Agreement
C3I	Command, Control, Communications, and Intelligence
C4ISR	Command, Control, Communications, Computers, Intelligence, Surveillance, and Reconnaissance
CAMS	COMIREX Automated Management System
CBP	Customs and Border Protection
CCP	Consolidated Cryptologic Program
CENTCOM	Central Command
CFJIC	Canadian Forces Joint Imagery Centre
CGCIS	Coast Guard Counterintelligence Service
CGICC	Coast Guard Intelligence Coordination Center
CI	Counterintelligence
CIA	Central Intelligence Agency
CIC	Counterintelligence Center
CIG	Central Intelligence Group
CINC	Commander in Chief
CIO	Central Imagery Office
ClanSIG	Clandestine SIGINT
CMO	Central MASINT Office
CNC	Crime and Narcotics Center
COMINT	Communications Intelligence
COMIREX	Committee on Imagery Requirements and Exploitation
COS	Chief of Station
CPC	Counterproliferation Center
CPD	Counterproliferation Division
CRITIC	Critical Intelligence Communications
CRS	Congressional Research Service
CSE	Center for Security Evaluation
CSEC	Communications Security Establishment Canada
CSIS	Canadian Security Intelligence Service
CSS	Central Security Service
CTBT	Comprehensive Test Ban Treaty
CTIC	Counterterrorism Intelligence Center
CTC	Counterterrorism Center

DARPA	Defense Advanced Research Projects Agency
DCCC	Defense Collection Coordination Center
DCGS	Distributed Common Ground System
DCI	Director of Central Intelligence
D/CIA	Director, Central Intelligence Agency
DCID	Director of Central Intelligence Directive
DCS	Defense Clandestine Service
DDI	Director of Defense Intelligence
DDMS	Deputy Director for Military Support
DDNS	Deputy Director for National Support
DEA	Drug Enforcement Administration
DEFSMAC	Defense Special Missile and Aerospace Center
DGI	Directorate of Geospatial Intelligence
DGIAP	Defense General Intelligence, and Applications Program
DGSE	Directorate General of External Security (France)
DHS	Defense HUMINT Service;
	Department of Homeland Security
DI	Directorate of Intelligence
DIA	Defense Intelligence Agency
DID	*Defense Intelligence Digest*
DIE	Defense Intelligence Estimate
DIGO	Defence Imagery and Geospatial Organisation (Australia)
DIN	Defense Intelligence Network
DIO	Defense Intelligence Officer
DIR	Defense Intelligence Report
DIRD	Defense Intelligence Reference Document
DIRNSA	Director of NSA
DITSUM	*Defense Intelligence Terrorism Summary*
DMA	Defense Mapping Agency
DMSP	Defense Meteorological Satellite Program
DNI	Director of National Intelligence
DOD	Department of Defense
DOE	Department of Energy
DOMEX	Document and Media Exploitation
DS&T	Directorate of Science and Technology
DSP	Defense Support Program
DSS	Defense Security Service
DST	Directorate for Territorial Surveillance (France)
DTI	Directorate of Terrorist Identities
DTM	Directive-Type Memorandum
ECI	Exceptionally Controlled Information
ECS	Enhanced CRYSTAL System
EECS	Evolved Enhanced CRYSTAL System
EH	*Executive Highlights*

EIT	Enhanced Interrogation Technique
ELINT	Electronic Intelligence
EMARSS	Enhanced Medium Altitude Reconnaissance and Surveillance System
EPA	Environmental Protection Agency
EPIC	El Paso Intelligence Center
ESC	Economic Security Center
ESMC	Eastern Space and Missile Center
EUCOM	European Command
EXCOM	Executive Committee
FARC	Revolutionary Armed Forces of Colombia
FBI	Federal Bureau of Investigation
FBIS	Foreign Broadcast Information Service
FCIP	Foreign Counterintelligence Program
FEMA	Federal Emergency Management Agency
FICPAC	Fleet Intelligence Center, Pacific
FIE	Field Intelligence Elements
FIGs	Field Intelligence Groups
FINCEN	Financial Crimes Enforcement Network
FISINT	Foreign Instrumentation Signals Intelligence
FOIA	Freedom of Information Act
FOSIC	Fleet Ocean Surveillance Information Center
FOUO	For Official Use Only
FRA	Forsvarets Radioanstalt (National Defence Radio Establishment, Sweden)
FRD	Federal Research Division
FSB	Federal Security Service (Russia)
FTAC	Farragut Technical Analysis Center
FTD	Foreign Technology Division
FVEY	FIVE EYES
GAO	Government Accountability Office
GCHQ	Government Communications Headquarters (United Kingdom)
GCSB	Government Communications Security Bureau (New Zealand)
GDIP	General Defense Intelligence Program
GEODSS	Ground-Based Electro-optical Deep Space Surveillance
GEOINT	Geospatial Intelligence
GFU	Ground Filter Unit
GID	General Intelligence Directorate (Jordan)
GPS	Global Positioning System
GRU	Chief Intelligence Directorate, General Staff (Russia)
GSSAP	Geosynchronous Space Situational Awareness Program
GST	GREYSTONE
GTSN	Global Telemetered Seismic Network
HAX	Haystack Auxiliary

HPSCI	House Permanent Select Committee on Intelligence
HSE	HUMINT Support Elements
HSIC	Homeland Security Intelligence Council
HUMINT	Human Intelligence
HUSIR	Haystack Ultra-Wideband Satellite Imaging Radar
HVDIG	High-Value Detainee Interrogation Group
I&W	Indications and Warning
IA	Information Assurance;
	Intelligence Assessment
IAD	Information Assurance Directorate
IAEA	International Atomic Energy Agency
IC	Intelligence Community
ICA	Intelligence Community Assessment
ICBM	Intercontinental Ballistic Missile
ICD	Intelligence Community Directive
ICE	Improved Collection Equipment
ICP	Intelligence Collection Program
IDC	Interagency Defector Committee
IED	Improvised Explosive Device
IMINT	Imagery Intelligence
IMS	International Monitoring System
INC	Iraqi National Congress
INR	Bureau of Intelligence and Research
INF	Intermediate Nuclear Forces
INSCOM	Army Intelligence and Security Command
IOB	Intelligence Oversight Board
IOC	Information Operations Center
IOD	Information Operations Directorate
IPAC	Intelligence Center, Pacific
IRTPA	Intelligence Reform and Terrorism Prevention Act
ISI	Inter-Services Intelligence Directorate (Pakistan)
ISIL	Islamic State in Iraq and the Levant
ISIS	Islamic State in Iraq and Syria
ISNU	Israeli SIGINT National Unit
ISA	Intelligence Support Activity
IUSS	Integrated Undersea Surveillance System
JAC	Joint Analysis Center
JAEIC	Joint Atomic Energy Intelligence Committee
JBER	Joint Base Elmendorf-Richardson
JCAT	Joint Counterterrorism Assessment Team
JCS	Joint Chiefs of Staff
JFCC	Joint Forces Combatant Command
JI	Jemaah Islamiyah
JIB	Joint Intelligence Brigade

JICC	Joint Intelligence Community Council
JICCENT	Joint Intelligence Center, Central
JICPAC	Joint Intelligence Center, Pacific
JICSOC	Joint Intelligence Center Special Operations Command
JIOC	Joint Intelligence Operations Center
JIOCEUR	Joint Intelligence Operations Center–Europe
JIOC-TRANS	Joint Intelligence Operations Center–Transportation
JITF-CT	Joint Intelligence Task Force–Combating Terrorism
JMIS	Joint Intelligence Centers/Joint Analysis Center Military Intelligence Program Implementation Study
JSOC	Joint Special Operations Command
JSTARS	Joint Surveillance Target Attack Radar System
JTAC	Joint Terrorism Analysis Center
JTAGs	Joint Tactical Ground Stations
LATS	Large-Aperture Tracking System
LEGAT	Legal Attaché
LLNL	Lawrence Livermore National Laboratory
MAD	Magnetic Anomaly Detector
MASINT	Measurement and Signature Intelligence
MCIA	Marine Corps Intelligence Activity
MCS	Mission Control Station
METOC	Meteorology and Oceanographic
MI	Military Intelligence
MIB	Military Intelligence Board
MID	*Military Intelligence Digest*
MIIA	Medical Intelligence and Information Agency
MIP	Military Intelligence Program
MIRA	Medium-Wave Infrared Arrays
MIT	Turkish National Intelligence Organization
MOCC	MASINT Operations Coordination Center
MOIS	Ministry of Intelligence and Security (Iran)
MOTIF	Maui Optical Tracking Identification Facility
MRBM	Medium-Range Ballistic Missile
MSIC	Missile and Space Intelligence Center
MSS	Ministry of State Security
MSSS	Maui Space Surveillance System
MTI	Moving Target Indicator
NAIC	National Air Intelligence Center
NAS	Naval Air Station
NASA	National Aeronautics and Space Administration
NASIC	National Air and Space Intelligence Center
NAVMIC	Naval Maritime Intelligence Center
NAVSPASUR	Naval Space Surveillance System
NCIS	Naval Criminal Investigative Service

NCIX	National Counterintelligence Executive
NCMI	National Center for Medical Intelligence
NCPC	National Counterproliferation Center
NCS	National Clandestine Service
NCTC	National Counterterrorism Center
NDS	Nuclear Detonation Detection System
NETWARCOM	Naval Network Warfare Command
NGIC	National Ground Intelligence Center
NHCD	National HUMINT Collection Directive
NHM	National HUMINT Manager
NHRTC	National HUMINT Requirements Tasking Center
NGA	National Geospatial-Intelligence Agency
NIA	National Intelligence Authority;
	National Imagery Agency;
	Naval Intelligence Activity
NIC	National Intelligence Council;
	Naval Intelligence Command
NIE	National Intelligence Estimate
NIM	National Intelligence Manager
NIMA	National Imagery and Mapping Agency
NIO	National Intelligence Officer
NIP	National Intelligence Program
NIPF	National Intelligence Priorities Framework
NISS	National Intelligence and Security Service (Sudan)
NITC	National Integrated TSCM Committee
NJIOC	National Joint Intelligence Operations Center
NMEC	National Media Exploitation Center
NNSA	National Nuclear Security Administration
NOC	Nonofficial Cover
NOFORN	Not Releasable to Foreign Nationals
NOIC	Navy Operational Intelligence Center
NORAD	Northern Aerospace Defense Command
NORTHCOM	Northern Command
NPC	Nonproliferation Center
NPIC	National Photographic Interpretation Center
NRO	National Reconnaissance Office
NRP	National Reconnaissance Program
NSA	National Security Agency
NSC	National Security Council
NSCID	National Security Council Intelligence Directive
NSD	National Security Directive
NSDD	National Security Decision Directive
NSGC	Naval Security Group Command
NSO	Nevada Site Office

NSOC	National Security Operations Center
NSPD	National Security Presidential Directives
NSR	National Security Review
NSRL	National SIGINT Requirements List
NTIC	Naval Technical Intelligence Center
NTOC	NSA/CSS Threat Operations Center
NTS	Nevada Test Site
NUDET	Nuclear Detonation
NURO	National Underwater Reconnaissance Office
OACSMI	Office of the Assistant Chief of Staff for Missile Intelligence
OD&E	Office of Development and Engineering
ODNI	Office of the Director of National Intelligence
OEL	Office of Electronic Intelligence
OFAC	Office of Foreign Assets Control
OFCO	Offensive Counterintelligence Operations
OTFI	Office of Terrorism and Financial Intelligence
OIA	Office of Intelligence & Analysis
OIG	Office of the Inspector General
OIS	Office of Intelligence Support
OMB	Office of Management and Budget
ONCIX	Office of the National Counterintelligence Executive
ONE	Office of National Estimates
ONI	Office of Naval Intelligence
ONSI	Office of National Security Intelligence
ORAG	Overhead Reconnaissance Advisory Group
ORCON	Originator Controlled
OSA	Office of Special Activities
OSC	Open Source Center
OSINT	Open Source Intelligence
OSIS	Ocean Surveillance Information System
OSO	Office of SIGINT Operations
OSS	Office of Strategic Services
OTFI	Office of Terrorism and Financial Intelligence
OTI	Office of Transnational Issues
OTC	Office of Technical Collection
OTR	Office of Technical Readiness
OTS	Office of Technical Service
PACFAST	Pacific Forward Area Support Team
PACOM	Pacific Command
PARCS	Perimeter Acquisition Radar Characterization System
PAVE	Precision Avionics Vectoring Equipment
PDB	*President's Daily Brief*
PFLP	Popular Front for the Liberation of Palestine
PLO	Palestine Liberation Organization

QRT	Quick Reaction Team
R&D	Research and Development
RAS	Remote Avionics System
RAW	Research and Analysis Wing (India)
S&T	Science and Technology
SA	Special Activities Division
SABER	Surface Analysis Branch for Evaluation and Reporting
SAIC	Science Applications International Corporation
SATRAN	Satellite Reconnaissance Advanced Notice
SBIRS	Space-Based Infrared System
SBSS	Space-Based Surveillance System
SBX	Sea-Based X-Band
SCI	Sensitive Compartmented Information
SCE	Special Collection Element
SCOPE	Scomi Precision Engineering
SCS	Special Collection Service
SDIE	Special Defense Intelligence Estimate
SDS	Satellite Data System
SECOM	Security Committee
SEIB	*Senior Executive Intelligence Brief*
SI	Special Intelligence
SIGDEV	SIGINT Development
SIGINT	Signals Intelligence
SIPRI	Stockholm Peace Research Institute
SIRVES	SIGINT Requirements Validation and Evaluation Subcommittee
SIS	Special Intelligence Service
SISDE	Democratic Security and Information Service (Italy)
SISMI	Military Security and Information Service (Italy)
SITREP	Situation Report
SLBM	Submarine-Launched Ballistic Missile
SNIE	Special National Intelligence Estimate
SOD	Special Operations Division
SOI	Space Object Identification
SOLO	Special Operations Liaison Officer
SORS	SIGINT Overhead Reconnaissance Subcommittee
SOSUS	Sound Surveillance System
SOUTHCOM	Southern Command
SPACECOM	U.S. Space Command
SPEAR	Strike Projection Evaluation and Anti-Air Warfare Research Division
SSA	Space Situational Awareness
SSCI	Senate Select Committee on Intelligence
SSD	Special Security Directorate
SSN	Space Surveillance Network

SST	Strategic Support Teams
STARE	Surveillance Technology Advanced and Replacement for Ebiscons
START	Strategic Arms Reduction Treaty
STIC	Scientific and Technical Intelligence Committee
STRATCOM	Strategic Command
STSS	Space Tracking and Surveillance System
SURTASS	Surveillance Towed-Array Sensor System
SWIFT	Society for Worldwide Interbank Financial Transactions
SWINT	Safe Window Intelligence
SWORD	Submarine Warfare Operations Research Division
SWS	Space Warning Squadron
SYERS	SENIOR YEAR Electro-optical Reconnaissance System
TCS	TALENT Control System
TELINT	Telemetry Intelligence
TIARA	Tactical Intelligence and Related Activities
TID	Technical Intelligence Division
TIDE	Terrorist Identities Datamart Environment
TIO	Technical Intelligence Officer
TK	TALENT-KEYHOLE
TRANSCOM	Transportation Command
TSCM	Technical Surveillance Countermeasures
TTIC	Terrorist Threat Integration Center
TTR	Tonopah Test Range
UAV	Unmanned Aerial Vehicle
UCP	Unified Command Plan
UEWR	Upgraded Early Warning Radar
UFAC	Underground Facility Analysis Center
USAF	U.S. Air Force
USAFE	United States Air Forces in Europe
USCYBERCOM	U.S. Cyber Command
USD (I)	Under Secretary of Defense for Intelligence
USIB	United States Intelligence Board
USSOCOM	U.S. Special Operations Command
UTC	Unified Transportation Command
VRK	Very Restricted Knowledge
WINPAC	Weapons Intelligence, Nonproliferation, and Arms Control Center
WIRe	World Intelligence Review
WMD	Weapons of Mass Destruction
WSSAG	Weapons and Space Systems Advisory Group
WSSIC	Weapons and Space Systems Intelligence Committee

INDEX